THE ENCYCLOPAEDIA OF SIKHISM

THE ENCYCLOPAEDIA OF SIKHISM

Volume I
A—D

HARBANS SINGH
Editor-in-Chief

PUNJABI UNIVERSITY, PATIALA
1995

ISBN 81-7380-100-2

First Edition : 1992
Second Edition : 1995
Third Edition : 1998
Pric
C

Published by Dr Ranbir Singh, Registrar,
Punjabi University, Patiala, and printed at
Ram Printograph (India), Delhi.

To the memory of my wife
KAILASH KAUR

FOREWORD TO THE SECOND EDITION

Encyclopaedias are not easy to make. They are generally a long time in preparation. This is a fact commonly known. That they vanish into thin air as quickly as did this first volume of the Sikh Encyclopaedia was nowhere within our calculations. Maybe, we had erred when putting down our initial arithmetic on paper. This was the first publication of its kind under Sikh auspices. So it may not be allowed to lapse. It must be kept alive. Hence, this hurried reprint. The volume presents Sikh life and letters on a wide spectrum. All entries, over 800 of them, have been very carefully chosen, covering major aspects of Sikh life and culture. There are detailed, well-researched essays in it on Sikh philosophy, history and scriptural texts. Also, on important Sikh shrines and locales. And, on important names. Professor Harbans Singh has laboured hard and created a work of high literary excellence. The writing aims at clarity, shunning all artifice and rhetoric. Easy intelligibility has been the principal focus. The work will be as useful to the lay reader as to the specialist. Its direct style of writing, its precision of language, and its well-attuned and orchestrated phrase are notable inputs of this composition. The venture seems to have been under the protection of some good angel. Five years ago, the Editor-in-Chief was felled by a stroke. He has been able to carry on despite the severe disability.

JOGINDER SINGH PUAR
Vice-Chancellor

Punjabi University
Patiala
January 13, 1995

FOREWORD

The Punjabi University rejoices today that it has been able to keep its tryst with the scholarly community. Some years ago it promised to produce a major reference work — an Encyclopaedia of Sikh faith. Happily, the first volume in a four-part series is being released today. "Talent alone cannot make a writer. There must be a man behind the book." To this affirmation of R.L. Emerson may be added the words that creating a work like an Encyclopaedia is more a matter of faith, of sustained labour and indefatigable search for accuracy. I personally felt very happy when Professor Harbans Singh opted to put himself behind the task, for I have had great confidence in his moral strength and intellectual abilities. By his lifelong devotion to Sikh learning, by his analytical acumen, and by his unmatched powers of concentration, he has been able to accomplish the task with outstanding success. Professor Harbans Singh has been known as a most distinguished scholar writing in English. The present work is a tribute to his spirit of dedication, immaculate scholarship and mastery of the English idiom.

Encyclopaedias encapsulate accurate information in a given area of knowledge and have become indispensable in an age in which the volume and rapidity of social change are making inaccessible much that lies outside one's immediate domain of concentration. At a time when Sikhism is attracting world-wide notice, a reference work embracing all essential facets of this vibrant faith is a singular contribution to the world of knowledge.

In the recent decades, Sikhism has experienced a very vital impulse to education and culture. The efflorescence of schools, colleges and universities is witness to this phenomenon. And then the mass of seminar deposits, learned works and other literature pouring forth from them. The latest is this Encyclopaedia of Sikhism which I have pleasure in issuing on behalf of the Punjabi University, Patiala. Sikhism already possesses that monumental work, *Gurushabad Ratanakar Mahan Kosh,* the creation of an individual, the celebrated Bhai Kahn Singh, of Nabha. I have often wondered at the spaciousness of the Bhai Sahib's genius. How he conceived the enterprise and how he accomplished the task which more aptly belonged to learned bodies and universities. That work is happily in Punjabi. This publication, an offering from the Punjabi University, especially focusing on Sikh religion, will appear in a Punjabi version as well.

One of my predecessors in the line of vice-chancellors, in whose time the work was initiated, entrusted it to Professor Harbans Singh. Professor Harbans Singh took it over willingly and has worked on it with a rare single-mindedness. I have had chances of seeing as part of official routine his files heavily worked over by him. I have also read some of the entries beyond the requirements of official duty. I can testify to the fact that each entry has been rethought and rewritten, partly or wholly, and has in the process gained a new clarity and authenticity. Overall, the entries read very lucidly and definitively explaining themselves as they go along. The emphasis is on information rather than on erudition. I admire Professor Harbans Singh's industry and diligence and his search for the exactness of idea and expression. His economy of phrase and a finely attuned verbal sense lend the text readability.

On behalf of the Punjabi University I am releasing this publication in the hope that it will prove useful to the cognoscente and the layman alike, and help elucidate several of the issues in Sikh theology and doctrine. I must also take this opportunity to thank scholars from within the University as well as from the outside who have contributed to the Encyclopaedia. To this, I add my personal gratitude and tribute to Professor Harbans Singh.

H.K. MANMOHAN SINGH
Vice-Chancellor

Punjabi University
Patiala
31 December 1992

PREFACE

"Encyclopaedias do not grow on trees," I had read somewhere as I was browsing among materials in the library. My object was to delve deeper into the mystique of the *genre* preparatory to drawing up my own plan of work on an Encyclopaedia of Sikhism I had been assigned to by the Syndicate of the Punjabi University. But I was not daunted by the dictum. I let it pass up. However, the admonishment it contained was not entirely lost upon me. I knew it would by no means be an easy task. It would be hard, arduous labour all the way up, demanding unceasing search and toil. I was not totally unaware of it, nor unprepared for it.

The Sikh Encyclopaedia was the brainchild of Professor Kirpāl Siṅgh Nāraṅg who was then the vice-chancellor of the Punjabi University. He had worked overtime to draw up for the University an elaborate programme in honour of the 300th anniversary of the birth of Gurū Gobind Siṅgh, the tenth Gurū or prophet-mentor of the Sikhs, which came off in 1966-67. The celebrations bequeathed to Paṭiālā two permanent monuments; one, Gurū Gobind Siṅgh Bhavan, an intriguing, modern-looking structure, planted as if it were in the heart of the University campus and, second, a department of Religion, embracing the study of five world traditions – Hinduism, Buddhism, Christianity, Islam and Sikhism, with the sixth, Jainism, diving in from the side a little later. Prior to putting down his plans on paper the vice-chancellor had taken a special trip out to Harvard University to seek the advice of the famous Professor Wilfred Cantwell Smith, Director, Center for the Study of World Religions. The department at Paṭiālā was going to be the first academic set-up of its kind in India where Religion in the academe had been considered a highly combustible substance and where everyone seemed to have a hush-hush attitude towards it. Professor Kirpāl Siṅgh Nāraṅg, with the weight of his argument and with a dash of prescience had his way. He linked up the academic programme with the Gurū Gobind Siṅgh celebrations and made it look generally as acceptable as the latter. When working out the courses of study and syllabi for the various traditions it soon became obvious that Sikhism among them was the least well-served by existing literary and historical materials. The suggestion emerged that the creation of a comprehensive reference work would be the first thing to do. The vice-chancellor promptly spelt out the title – the Encyclopaedia of Sikhism – and simultaneously nominated the chairman of the Gurū Gobind Siṅgh Department of Religious Studies to take charge of the matter.

How simplistic were the notions I had been nurturing in my mind began soon to dawn upon me. Also readily began to show up the shortcomings in the scheme I had devised. I had planned that, since it would not be practicable to collect under one roof specialists in different fields, most of the articles of the Encyclopaedia would be written by "outside" experts and that we would have a small editorial unit at the University to shepherd the manuscripts, fact-check them, and revise them to ensure some kind of a literary discipline and symmetry. It seems I was not above exaggerating my own editorial experience and capacities. Three or four of the scholars whose names were on the top of my list were too busy and were chary of putting anything additional on their plate. They declined our invitations. This in fact turned out to be the principal pitfall. The number of contributors we could call upon fell dismally short of our needs. Scholars with experience of research in Sikh studies and of specialized writing were few and far between. Our choice was thus severely limited. In some cases our invitations for articles got accumulated in a few pairs of hands and our files were soon bursting at the seams with copies of reminders we had had to send out chasing after our contributors. We had to wait for long periods of time before securing manuscripts from them.

Still we had no choice except to adhere to the plan we had originally prepared.

Then we had no precedents to go by. On Sikh doctrine no concisely argued work existed. Even historical fact was far from well sifted. To this may be added the paucity of reliable and firm documentation. Authorities of whatever vintage hopelessly contradicted one another. This, despite the fact that most of the Sikh enterprise had occurred within the full view of history ! It seems the focus has been woefully warped at some point. Efforts at rectification have remained tentative. It is not easy to restate and repack the entire range of information and knowledge of a people. An attempt has been made here precisely to define the ideas and terms of Sikhism. The writing is intended to be simple and tight, shunning the purple and the loose alike. The aim throughout has been clarity and precision.

Bypassing Amritsar, religious headquarters of Sikhism, as well as Anandpur Sāhib, the birthplace of the Khālsā, Paṭiālā became the focus of the world-wide Gurū Gobind Siṅgh celebrations in 1966-67. It is not on record if any other anniversary on the Sikh calendar had been observed with similar zeal and eclat. M.A. Macauliffe (1841-1913), British historian of the Sikhs, did draw their attention to the 200th birth anniversary of the Khālsā, due in 1899, but the event did not draw much popular attention. However, the tercentenary of Gurū Gobind Siṅgh's birth, 67 years later, was an event celebrated round the globe with unprecedented fervour. Festive and academic programmes to mark the occasion were set up in many parts of the world. The largest share of the responsibility was claimed by Paṭiālā where Gurū Gobind Siṅgh Foundation was formed to direct and guide the celebrations.

The chief minister of the Punjab, Rām Kishan, called on 8 August 1965, a convention representative of the religious, literary and lay elements in the life of the country. This gathering was the precursor of the permanent body called the Gurū Gobind Siṅgh Foundation. Mahārājā Yādavinder Siṅgh (1913-1974) of Paṭiālā was chosen to be the president of the Foundation and a sum of Rs 12 lakhs was set apart for the celebrations by the State government in its annual budget which amount was, happily through an oversight, most unusual for a financial set-up anywhere in the world, repeated in the following year's budget. The Foundation was thus born with a "silver spoon" in its mouth.

The next meeting of the Foundation took place in the chandeliered hall of the palace of the Mahārājā of Paṭiālā, with a large portrait of Mahārājā Ālā Siṅgh, 18th century Sikh hero and founder of the Paṭiālā dynasty, overlooking the assembly from one side and the Hungarian painter August Schoeftt's famous canvas depicting Mahārājā Raṇjīt Siṅgh's court with a replica in gold of the Amritsar Golden Temple underneath it, from the other. Past and present thus converged at the time of that small Sikh assembly on 30 November 1965, refracting history into the current moment. Chaṇḍīgaṛh, the State capital, was named the headquarters of the

Foundation with Giānī Zail Siṅgh as the general secretary. One of the several committees appointed was charged with planning and bringing out literature appropriate to the occasion. From the offices of the Foundation soon began to flow a steady stream of literature comprising a commemoration volume, illustrated books for young readers, annotated editions of Gurū Gobind Siṅgh's works, and a biography of Gurū Gobind Siṅgh in English which was simultaneously translated into all major Indian languages such as Saṅskrit, Hindī, Punjabi, Beṅgālī, Assamese, Marāṭhī, Gujarātī, Oṛiyā, Sindhī, Tamil, Telugū, Malayālam, Kannaḍa, Kashmīrī and Maithilī.

In this spontaneous enthusiasm for anniversary celebration is reflected the Sikhs' response to the historical memory of the Gurūs and to the important events of their history. Visible here is also their deep commitment to their faith, their joyous and urgent participation in their historical tradition, their cohesion and their love of the spectacular.

The burgeoning of interest in the study of Sikhism brought to light the grave paucity of materials on Sikhism, highlighting at the same time the need for serious academic research and study. The present publication aims at supplying the gap. The purpose of the undertaking was to prepare in English and Punjabi a general reference work about Sikh religion. The work was to be comprehensive in scope and was to cover topics such as Sikh theology, philosophy, history, ethics, literature, art, ceremonies, customs, personalities, shrines, sects, etc. The details of the scheme were worked out under the aegis of an advisory committee consisting of leading scholars of the day – Dr Bhāī Jodh Siṅgh, Dr Gaṇḍā Siṅgh, Professor Gurbachan Siṅgh Tālib, Dr Faujā Siṅgh, Dr Tāran Siṅgh and Professor Gulwant Siṅgh. The staff originally provided consisted of the Editor (Professor Harbaṅs Siṅgh), two Assistant Editors (Dr Harkīrat Siṅgh and Professor Harminder Siṅgh Kohlī; the former was on his retirement replaced by Dr Jodh Siṅgh), two Senior Research Fellows (Sardār Siṅgh Bhāṭīā and G.S. Nayyar), one Research Associate (Dharam Siṅgh), two Research Assistants (Gurnek Siṅgh and Major Gurmukh Siṅgh), and Research Scholar (Giānī Gurcharan Siṅgh). Some initial exploration was made by Himat Siṅgh.

The first task was to compile a list of subject-titles to be included in the Encyclopaedia. To this end, the staff, in the first instance, rummaged through libraries – on the campus, the University Library, Bhāī Mohan Siṅgh Vaid collection and Bhāī Kāhn Siṅgh collection, and off the campus, the Motībāgh Palace library, and the State Archives, and compiled a list of likely topics. A list of nearly 4,000 titles thus emerged. At the same time a roster of likely authors was prepared. This comprised lists in Punjabi and in English. Those who did not write in English were free to write in Punjabi. We had their work translated into English.

Having to work on a long-term project has its own hazards. I passed through several health crises. At one point, I was incapacitated following an eye-surgery, but was, thanks to the skill and devoted care of the surgeon, Dr Robert M. Johnston, Leesburg, U.S.A., rescued from a hopeless situation recovering the full use of the eye. In 1989 I was felled by a stroke which led to serious physical decrepity but, fortunately, left my mental faculties generally intact. This was all the Gurū's own mercy and I was able to continue my work on the Encyclopaedia. A tragedy hit me on the eve of the release of this volume. My beloved wife, Kailāsh Kaur, who had waited for a long time for the consummation of my life's work and who had nursed me most lovingly throughout this period, passed away suddenly on 12 November 1992, leaving me utterly forlorn and shaken.

I must record here my gratitude to the Punjabi University for providing me with the necessary facilities and help. Successive vice-chancellors after Professor Kirpāl Siṅgh Nāraṅg, namely, Mrs Inderjīt Kaur Sandhū, Dr Amrīk Siṅgh, Dr S.S. Johl, Dr Bhagat Siṅgh and Dr H.K. Manmohan Siṅgh nursed the project with all their heart, and treated me personally with much courtesy and affection. Dr H.K. Manmohan Siṅgh has especially been alive to its scholarly needs and I am very happy that the first volume is being issued during his time. The first thing the newly arrived Pro-Vice-Chancellor, Dr J.S. Puār, did upon stepping on the campus was graciously to call upon the ailing editor-in-chief. On that occasion and subsequently he had many a positive word to say about the Encyclopaedia project. I need scarcely say how delighted I am to see the Encyclopaedia in print. I trust it will fulfil the hopes with which it was launched and help fertilize Sikh learning. I feel especially gratified fulfilling the promise I made to the academic fraternity several years ago. To my colleagues I render my heart-felt, affectionate thanks for the solid manner in which they stood by me, through thick and thin. Dr Hazārā Siṅgh, Head, Publication Bureau, who has earned wide acclaim for himself in this part of the country by his contribution to the art of printing, had reserved his special love for this publication. I must thank him for the attention and care he gave it. I must not omit the name of Santosh Kumār, my P.A., who very cheerfully gave this work many of his Sundays and holidays especially after I had been struck down and spent many a long hour when taking down notes trying to come to terms with my speech somewhat lisped by the malady. I thank him and all the rest of my colleagues for bearing with me so sportingly.

A-1, Punjabi University
Patiala
12 December 1992

HARBANS SINGH
Editor-in-Chief

TRANSCRIPTION/PRONUNCIATION KEY FOR NON-ENGLISH WORDS/PHRASES

Certain names and terms have been used in the text in their original Punjabi form. In order to facilitate their correct pronunciation, the following key has been used while transcribing the original into the Roman script:

Punjabi phonemes (Gurmukhī script) Letter/Vowel symbol		Hindi/Sanskrit phonemes (Devanāgarī script) Letter/Vowel symbol		Urdu/Persian Arabic phonemes (Persian script) Letter/Vowel symbol	Roman script equivalents
ਅ		अ		اَ ـَ	a
ਆ	ਾ	आ	ा	آ	ā
ਇ	ਿ	इ	ि	اِ ـِ	i
ਈ	ੀ	ई	ी	اِی ـِی	ī
ਉ	ੁ	उ	ु	اُ ـُ	u
ਊ	ੂ	ऊ	ू	اُو ـُو	ū
ਏ	ੇ	ए	े	اے ـے	e
ਐ	ੈ	ऐ	ै	اَے ـَے	ai
ਓ	ੋ	ओ	ो	او ـو	o
ਔ	ੌ	औ	ौ	اَو ـَو	au
ਸ		स		ث، س، ص	s
ਹ		ह		ح، ھ، ہ	h
ਕ		क		ک	k
ਖ		ख		کھ	kh
ਗ		ग		گ	g
ਘ		घ		گھ	gh
ਙ		ङ		-	ṅ
ਚ		च		چ	ch or c (1)
ਛ		छ		چھ	chh or ch (1)
ਜ		ज		ج	j
ਝ		झ		جھ	jh
ਞ		ञ		-	ñ
ਟ		ट		ٹ	ṭ
ਠ		ठ		ٹھ	ṭh
ਡ		ड		ڈ	ḍ
ਢ		ढ		ڈھ	ḍh
ਣ		ण		-	ṇ

TRANSCRIPTION/PRONUNCIATION KEY

Punjabi phonemes (Gurmukhī script) Letter/Vowel symbol	Hindi/Sanskrit phonemes (Devanāgarī script) Letter/Vowel symbol	Urdu/Persian Arabic phonemes (Persian script) Letter/Vowel symbol	Roman script equivalents
ਤ	त	ت، ط	t
ਥ	थ	تھ	th
ਦ	द	د	d
ਧ	ध	دھ	dh
ਨ	न	ن	n
ਪ	प	پ	p
ਫ	फ	پھ	ph
ਬ	ब	ب	b
ਭ	भ	بھ	bh
ਮ	म	م	m
ਯ	य	ی	y
ਰ	र	ر	r
ਲ	ल	ل	l
ਵ	व	و	v, w (2)
ੜ	ड़	ڑ	ṛ (3)
ੜ੍ਹ	ढ़	ڑھ	ṛh
ਸ਼	श	ش	sh, ś
ਖ਼		خ	kh
ਗ਼		غ	gh
ਜ਼		ذ، ز، ض، ظ	z
ਫ਼		ف	f
	ऋ		ṛ (4)
	ष		ṣ (4)
	क्ष		kṣ
	त्र		tr
	ज्ञ		jñ, gi, gy (5)
		ع	' followed by vowel symbol
		ق	q

Nasalization

(i) ṅ preceding ਸ, ਹ, ਕ, ਖ, ਗ, ਘ, ਙ, ਯ, ਰ, ਲ, ਵ, ਸ਼

(ii) ñ preceding ਚ, ਛ, ਜ, ਝ, ਞ

(iii) ṇ preceding ਟ, ਠ, ਡ, ਢ, ਣ

(iv) n preceding ਤ, ਥ, ਦ, ਧ, ਨ

(v) m preceding ਪ, ਫ, ਬ, ਭ, ਮ

(1) Normally ch represents the sound ਚ, च or چ and chh has been used for the heavier phoneme ਛ, छ or چھ but in exceptional cases while transliterating Sanskrit terms or texts, c and ch have been used for the two sounds, respectively.

(2) Normally v has been used to represent Punjabi ਵ or Hindi व and w to represent و of Persian script in words of Persio-Arabic origin such as *kotwāl, fatwā,* etc. There are, however, exceptions, as in the case of *dīvān* (religious assembly or congregation) and *dīwān* (title or institutional designation), or Goindvāl (place name in India) and Gujrāṅwālā or Peshāwar (place names in Pakistan). W has also been used in certain personal names where the individuals concerned are known to have used it when spelling their own names. For instance, Balwant Siṅgh, Jawāharlāl, Tiwāṇā, etc.

(3) In spelling some place names, ḍ has been used for ੜ to follow prevalent usage, e.g. Nāndeḍ and Jinvāḍā. There may be found some other instances where current usage has been preserved, as in Scindīā, Gwālīor, Lucknow or Phagwāṛā.

(4) Use of ṛ and ṣ has been made sparingly in Sanskrit names and texts only. At other places ri and sh has been used to transliterate ऋ and ष, respectively. Examples are (Lord) Kṛṣṇa and (Gurū Har) Krishan.

(5) jñ for ञ is used only in spelling ज्ञान (*jñān*) and its derivatives in Sanskrit or classical context. Elsewhere gy or gi has been used as in Gyān or, more often, Giān.

USE OF ITALICS AND DIACRITICS

All non-English words, phrases and texts are printed in italics with diacritical marks as indicated in the transcription key. There is, however, an exception. Under 'Bibliography' diacritics are used only where works cited are in Indian languages or in Persian. In the case of works in English or other European languages, diacritics have not been used even for the names of the authors though they be Indian. Italics and diacritics have also not been used in names of countries and of languages.

DATES

Dates are generally given in the Christian era. Where, however, Bikramī or Hijrī dates are cited in the original sources, they have also been made use of along with corresponding Christian era dates.

ABBREVIATIONS

AD	Anno Domini (Christian era)
AH	Hijrī era
b.	born in
BC	Before Christ
Bk	Bikramī era
c.	circa
d.	died in
e.g.	for example
f./ff.	folio/folios
GG	Srī Gurū Granth Sāhib
i.e.	that is
km	kilometre (s)
lit.	literally
MS./MSS.	manuscript/manuscripts
p./pp.	page/pages
Skt.	Sanskrit

CONTRIBUTORS

A.C.B.	A.C. Banerjee
Aj.S.	Ajmer Siṅgh
Aj.S.L.	Ajmer Siṅgh, Lohgaṛh
B.J.H.	B.J. Hasrat
B.S.	Bhagat Siṅgh
B.S.D.	Balbīr Siṅgh Dil
B.S.N.	B.S. Nijjar
B.S.V.	Balbīr Siṅgh Viyogī
Bb.S.N.	Balbīr Siṅgh Nandā
Bh.K.S.	Bhāī Kirpāl Siṅgh
Bh.S.	Bhāg Siṅgh
C.H.L.	C.H. Loehlin
C.O.M.	Clarence O. McMullen
D.K.B.	Dilip K. Biswās
D.K.G.	Dharmendra Kumār Gupta
D.P.A.	Dharam Pāl Āshṭā
D.S.	Dharam Siṅgh
D.S.B.	Dīwān Siṅgh Bhallā
D.S.M.	Darshan Siṅgh Maiṇī
E.C.B.	Emily C. Brown
F.S.	Faujā Siṅgh
F.S.A.	F.S. Aijāzuddīn
G.A.H.	Gerald A. Heeger
G.B.S.	Giānī Balwant Siṅgh
G.G.S.	Giānī Garjā Siṅgh
G.K.	Gunindar Kaur
G.N.R.	G.N. Rājgurū
G.R.T.	G.R. Thursby
G.S.	Gaṇḍā Siṅgh
G.S.Ch.	G.S. Chhābṛā
G.S.D.	Gurdev Siṅgh Deol
G.S.G.	Gurcharan Siṅgh Giānī
G.S.M.	Gurbachan Siṅgh Māṅgaṭ
G.S.N.	G.S. Nayyar
G.S.P.	Gurdiāl Siṅgh Phul
G.S.R.	Gurdīp Siṅgh Randhāwā
G.S.T.	Gurbachan Siṅgh Tālib
G.S.Z.	Gurcharan Siṅgh, Zīrā
Gb. S.	Gurbax Siṅgh
Gbh. S.	Gurbhagat Siṅgh
Gch. S.	Gurcharan Siṅgh
Gd. S.	Gurdarshan Siṅgh
Gl. S.	Gulcharan Siṅgh
Gm. S.	Gurmukh Siṅgh
Gn. S.	Gurnek Siṅgh
Gr. S.	Gurdev Siṅgh
H.B.	Himādrī Banerjee
H.D.	Hameed ud-Dīn
H.R.G.	Harī Rām Gupta
Hch. S.	Harcharan Siṅgh
Hk.S.	Harkīrat Siṅgh

CONTRIBUTORS

Hn. S.	Harnām Siṅgh
Hr.B.	Hardev Bāhrī
Hr.S.	Harī Siṅgh
I.C.	Ian Copland
I.J.K.	Ian J. Kerr
J.B.S.	Jaṅg Bahādur Siṅgh
J.C.B.W.	John C.B. Webster
J.K.	Jitinder Kaur
J.M.L.	J.M. Lafont
J.P.	Jeffrey Perrill
J.P.S.U.	J.P.S. Uberoi
J.R.G.	Jatī Rām Gupta
J.S.A.	Jagjīt Siṅgh Anand
J.S.J.	Jaswant Siṅgh Jas
J.S.K.	J.S. Khurāṇā
J.S.N.	Jaswant Siṅgh Nekī
J.S.S.	Jīt Siṅgh Sītal
Jg.S.	Jagjīt Siṅgh
Jn.S.	Janak Siṅgh
K.A.N.	K.A.Nizāmī
K.J.S.	K.Jagjīt Siṅgh
K.L.T.	K.L. Ṭuṭejā
K.M.	Kamlesh Mohan
K.S.	Khushwant Siṅgh
K.S.D.	Kuldīp Siṅgh Dhīr
K.S.T.	K.S. Thāpar
K.S.Tl.	K.S. Talwāṛ
K.W.J.	Kenneth W. Jones
Kr.S.	Kirpāl Siṅgh
L.C.	Lachman Chellārām
L.M.J.	L.M. Joshī
M.A.S.	Mahārājā Amarinder Siṅgh of Paṭiālā
M.G.S.	Major Gurmukh Siṅgh
M.K.	Madanjīt Kaur
M.L.A.	M.L.Āhlūwālīā
M.R.A.	Mulk Rāj Anand
M.S.G.	Mohinder Siṅgh Gill
M.S.N.	Mān Siṅgh Niraṅkārī
Mb.S.	Mubārak Siṅgh
Md.A.	Mohammad Aslam
Mm. S.	Manmohan Sehgal
N.Q.K.	Noel Q. King
N.S.A.	Nirvair Siṅgh Arshī
Nz.S.	Nazer Siṅgh
P.M.W.	P.M. Wylam
P.S.	Piār Siṅgh
P.S.G.	Pratāp Siṅgh Giānī
P.S.J.	Parkāsh Siṅgh Jammū
P.S.P.	Piārā Siṅgh Padam
P.S.S.	Piārā Siṅgh Sambhī
Pd.S.	Parduman Siṅgh
Pk.S.	Parkāsh Siṅgh

CONTRIBUTORS

R.K.	Rachhpāl Kaur
R.S.J.	Rattan Siṅgh Jaggī
R.S.,Q.E.	Rājinder Siṅgh,Qaumī Ektā
Rj.S.	Rājinder Siṅgh
S.H.A.	Syed Hasan Askarī
S.L.	Spencer Lavan
S.M.	Swarnjīt Mehtā
S.P.S.	S.P. Siṅgh
S.R.S.	Srī Rām Sharmā
S.S.A.	Shamsher Siṅgh Ashok
S.S. Am.	Sarmukh Siṅgh Amole
S.S.B.	S.S. Bhāṭīā
S.S.Bl.	S.S.Bal
S.S.D.	Surjīt Siṅgh Dulāī
S.S.G.	Surjīt Siṅgh Gāndhī
S.S.J.	Sohan Siṅgh Josh
S.S.V.B.	S.S. Vañjārā Bedī
S.S.W.	Suraiṇ Siṅgh Wilkhū
Sb.S.S.	Sāhib Siṅgh Seṭhī
Sd.S.	Sudarshan Siṅgh
T.H.	Ṭeenā Hazoorīā
T.S.	Tāran Siṅgh
T.S.B.	Trilochan Siṅgh Bedī
T.S.R.	T.S.Rājū
W.H.M.	W.H. Mcleod
W.S.	Wazīr Siṅgh
Wm.S.	Waryām Siṅgh
Y.F.	Yohanan Friedmann
Z.S.	Zail Siṅgh

A

ABBOTT, SIR JAMES (1807-1896), British Resident's assistant at Lahore, capital of the Sikh kingdom, after the first Anglo - Sikh war (1845 - 46), was born on 12 March 1807, the son of Henry Alexius Abbott. Passing out of the military college of the East India Company at Addiscombe, England, Abbott received commission as a second-lieutenant in the Bengal artillery in 1823. In November 1830, he joined the army of the Indus, under Sir John Keane, for the invasion of Afghanistan. In 1842, he was appointed assistant to the British Resident at Indore. In 1846, Abbott was designated commissioner for settlement of the Punjab boundaries. He became Resident's assistant at Hazārā in 1848. From Hazārā, he sent reports to the British Resident at Lahore accusing Chatar Siṅgh Aṭārīvālā, the governor of Hazārā, of high treason and describing him as the leader of a conspiracy for a general uprising of the Sikhs against the British.

A minor disaffection in August 1848 in a Sikh brigade stationed at Hazārā so excited Abbott that, without any authority, he took upon himself to suppress what he described as "the national rising of the Sikhs." He incited the Hazārā chiefs and the armed Muslim peasantry to destroy the Sikh brigade. He then raised Muslim levies and marched on Hazārā to expel Chatar Siṅgh, the governor. Abbott's mercenary force surrounded the town. Commodore Canora, the Armenian artillery commander of the fortress, whom Abbott had won over, refused to move his batteries at Chatar Siṅgh's orders. At the orders of the Sikh governor, Canora was overpowered and killed. Abbott now demanded retribution, but Sir Frederick Currie, the Resident at Lahore, did not approve of the assumption of civil and military authority by his subordinate. Abbott, however, ignored the protestations from the Lahore residency and set up a *jihād,* crusade, against the Sikhs. His acts provoked the Hazārā revolt which culminated in the second Anglo-Sikh war.

James Abbott wrote *The Narrative: An Account of Personal Services at Hazara,* an English manuscript referred to by Captain L. J. Trotter in his *The Life of John Nicholson — Soldier and Administrator.* The chronicle gives details from Abbott's point of view of Chatar Siṅgh Aṭārīvālā's revolt against the British at Hazārā and at Lahore.

James Abbott who retired as a general died on 6 October 1896.

BIBLIOGRAPHY

1. Hasrat, B. J., ed. and annot., *The Punjab Papers.* Hoshiarpur, 1970
2. Khushwant Singh, *A History of the Sikhs.* Princeton, 1963, 1966
3. Buckland, C.E., *Dictionary of Indian Biography.* London, 1906

B. J. H.

ABCHAL NAGAR, more correctly spelt Abichalnagar (*abichal,* lit. firmly fixed, unshakably rooted), i.e. City Everlasting, is the name Sikh tradition has given Nānded, a district town in Mahārāshṭra. The place is sacred to Gurū Gobind Siṅgh, who passed away here on 7 October 1708. The shrine honouring his memory is treated as a *ta<u>kh</u>t*, seat constituting decisive religious authority for the Sikhs, and is named Ta<u>kh</u>t Sachkhaṇḍ Srī Hazūr Sāhib, Abchalnagar.

The name was probably suggested by a Scriptural line *abichal nagaru gobind gurū kā nāmu japat sukhu pāiā rām* (rooted steadfast stands the City of the Master-Lord where solace is attained by repeating the Name (GG, 783), usually interpreted as referring to the City of Amritsar founded by Gurū Rām Dās, Nānak IV.

BIBLIOGRAPHY

1. Tārā Siṅgh, *Srī Gur Tīrath Saṅgrahi*. Amritsar, n. d.
2. Ṭhākar Siṅgh, Giānī, *Srī Gurduāre Darshan*. Amritsar, 1923
3. Randhir, G. S., *Sikh Shrines in India*. Delhi, 1990

M. G. S.

'ABDULLĀ, BHĀĪ, Abdul according to some Sikh chroniclers, was a Muslim minstrel who recited heroic balladry at Sikh congregations in the time of Gurū Hargobind (1595 - 1644). Abdul was born in the village of Sursiṅgh, now in Amritsar district of the Punjab. He first came to Amritsar in1606 at the time of the installation ceremony for Gurū Hargobind at the Akāl Ta<u>kh</u>t. According to *Gurbilās Chhevīṅ Pātshāhī*, he and his companion, Bhāī Natthā, sang the stanza on the occasion:

> The Throne everlasting
> Has by the Holy Gurū's presence become haloed,
> Indescribable is its splendour,
> How may I sing its glory!
> Seeing the Gurū,
> Both the sun and the moon were shamed.
> So sat on the throne the Holy Gurū to the remembrance of the Lord God attached.
> Abdul and Natthā have composed verse to sing his praise.

Both Abdul and Natthā remained at Amritsar thereafter and recited poetry extolling chivalrous deeds of past heroes.

As Bābā Gurdittā, Gurū Hargobind's eldest son, got married, he was taken round by the Gurū to Akāl Ta<u>kh</u>t and Harimandar Sāhib to make obeisance. The Gurū then invited Abdul to recite a panegyric.

Abdul and Natthā, as reports *Gurbilās Chhevīṅ Pātshāhī*, accompanied Gurū Hargobind when he left Amritsar for Kīratpur in the Śivālik hills. As his time came, Gurū Hargobind asked them to return to their native Sursiṅgh.

BIBLIOGRAPHY

1. *Gurbilās Chhevīṅ Pātshāhī*. Patiala, 1970
2. Macauliffe, Max Arthur, *The Sikh Religion*. Oxford, 1909
3. Gupta, Hari Ram, *History of the Sikhs*, vol. I. Delhi, 1973

B. S.

'ABDULLĀ, <u>KH</u>WĀJĀ, a native of Manī Mājrā, near present-day Chaṇḍīgaṛh, was the keeper of the jail at Chāndnī Chowk *kotwālī* in Delhi, where Gurū Teg<u>h</u> Bahādur, Nānak IX, was detained under imperial warrant. He was a pious man and truly reverenced the holy detenu. He tried to mitigate the rigour of his incarceration as far as his official position permitted. After Gurū Teg<u>h</u> Bahādur's execution (1675), he resigned his post and went to live at Anandpur, where he served Gurū Gobind Siṅgh, Nānak X, as a physician. His son, <u>Gh</u>ulām 'Abbās, served under Nawāb Kapūr Siṅgh as a physician during *misl* times.

BIBLIOGRAPHY

1. Giān Siṅgh, Giānī, *Twārī<u>kh</u> Gurū <u>Kh</u>ālsā* [Reprint]. Patiala, 1970
2. Trilochan Singh, *Guru Tegh Bahadur: Prophet and Martyr*. Delhi, 1967

A.C.B.

'ABDUL RASŪL KASHMĪRĪ, a native of Srīnagar who was in trade at Amritsar as a shawl merchant, was for a time a close confidant of Mahārājā Duleep Siṅgh, the last Sikh king of the Punjab deposed by the British in 1849. Kashmīrī acted as the deposed Mahārājā's liaison man with governments of Turkey and Egypt. In 1860, 'Abdul Rasūl moved from India to Egypt, and thence to London where he joined the Nile expeditionary force as an interpreter. Owing to his secret connection with the Mahdī, he was discharged from the service. He was again in England to seek redress when he met the deposed Mahārājā Duleep Siṅgh who employed him to further his cause. When Duleep Siṅgh returned from Aden to Europe he sent for 'Abdul Rasūl from London to Paris and through him met Assud Pāshā, the Turkish ambassador in Paris. 'Abdul Rasūl travelled to Constantinople with a view to contacting the Caliph. Through his good offices Duleep Siṅgh seems to have befriended Patrick Casey, an Irishman, whose passport he used when travelling from Paris to Russia. Summoned by the Mahārājā, 'Abdul Rasūl also arrived in Moscow and campaigned to rally the local Muslims to his cause. Early in 1890, Duleep Siṅgh sent him to India. He was arrested on board the ship and upon landing in Bombay despatched to Asīrgaṛh Fort for detention. A few months later, he was released and provided passage to go to London. In March 1892, 'Abdul Rasūl sued Mahārājā Duleep Siṅgh in a Paris court seeking a life pension for the services he had rendered him.

BIBLIOGRAPHY

Ganda Singh, ed., *History of the Freedom Movement in the Punjab*, vol. III (Maharaja Duleep Singh Correspondence). Patiala, 1977

K. S. T.

'ABD US-SAMAD KHĀN (d. 1737), governor of Lahore from 1713 to 1726, a descendant of the Naqashbandī saint 'Abdullā Ahrār, a great-grandson of Khwājā Bākī of Baghdād, was born at Āgrā when his father, Khwājā 'Abd ul-Karīm Ansārī, had come out with his family from Samarkand on a tour of India during the reign of Emperor Auraṅgzīb. When Samad Khān was two years old, his parents returned to Samarkand where he passed the early years of his life and where he attained the office of Shaikh ul-Islām. Soon thereafter he came to India obtaining appointment at the court of Auraṅgzīb. He served for many years in the Deccan without attracting much notice. However, when Farrukh-Sīyar came to the throne of Delhi, he appointed 'Abd us-Samad Khān governor of Lahore in February 1713 charging him with the annihilation of the Sikh leader, Bandā Siṅgh Bahādur, who had raised a revolt in the Punjab. 'Abd us-Samad Khān's son, Zakarīyā Khān, was sent to Jammū as *faujdār* to render assistance to his father. 'Abd us-Samad Khān's troops succeeded in driving Bandā Siṅgh and his Sikhs out of their strongholds in the plains—Saḍhaurā and Lohgaṛh—into the hills. As Bandā Siṅgh descended from his mountain retreat in February 1715, Samad Khān assembled an army of Mughals, Paṭhāns, Bundelā Rājpūts and the Rājpūts of Kaṭoch and Jasroṭā and moved northwards to attack Bandā Siṅgh. According to *Akhbār-i-Darbār-i-Mu'allā*, 'Abd us-Samad Khān marched from Lahore at the head of twelve thousand *sowārs* and an equal number of foot-soldiers, besides a big *topkhānā* (artillery), and closed in upon Bandā Siṅgh as he was putting up his defence fortifications in a village, near Baṭālā. Artillery firing forced Bandā Siṅgh to come into the open field. He made a determined stand and fought fiercely, but overwhelmed by a force vastly superior in strength and resources, he escaped northwards and took shelter in the *havelī* or fortress of one Dunī Chand at the village of Gurdās-Naṅgal, about 6 km to the west of Gurdāspur. 'Abd us-Samad Khān threw such a tight cordon around the *havelī* that "not a blade of grass or a grain of corn could find its way in." For eight months the garrison resisted the siege under gruesome conditions. The royal troops at last broke through and captured Bandā Siṅgh and his famishing Sikhs (17 December 1715). Under the orders of Samad Khān over two hundred of the prisoners were executed. The rest, including Bandā Siṅgh and his family, were put in chains and taken to Lahore, thence to Delhi. In 1726, Samad Khān was transferred to Multān, his son, Zakarīyā Khān, replacing him as governor of Lahore.

'Abd us-Samad Khān died on 26 July 1737. For more than two decades he had enjoyed the confidence of the Delhi emperors and received from them titles such as Daler Jaṅg (Brave in Battle) and Saif ud-Daulā (Sword of the State), with a rank of seven thousand.

BIBLIOGRAPHY

1. Irvine, W., *Later Mughals.* London, 1922
2. Nijjar, B.S., *Panjab under the Later Mughals.* Jalandhar, 1972
3. Giān Siṅgh, Giānī, *Twārīkh Gurū Khālsā* [Reprint]. Patiala, 1970
4. Bhagat Singh, trans. and ed., *Akhbār-i-Darbār-i-Mu'allā.* Patiala, 1984
5. Harbans Singh, *The Heritage of the Sikhs.* Delhi, 1987

B. S.

ABUL FAZL (1551-1602), principal secretary-cum-minister to Akbar, the Mughal emperor. He was an accomplished man of learning and was the author of two celebrated works, *Ā'īn-i-Akbarī* and *Akbar-nāmā,* the former being a description of Akbar's administrative system and the latter a chronicle of the events of his reign. Like his father, Shaikh Mubārak, and brother, Faizī, Abul Fazl had Sūfī leanings, and all three of them were a major influence in moulding the religious policy of the emperor. Born at Akbarābād on 14 January 1551, Abul Fazl took up service at the royal court in 1574, and through his uncommon wisdom and learning soon rose to become Akbar's most trusted adviser. He accompanied the emperor on his visit to Goindvāl on 24 November 1598 to see Gurū Arjan. The meeting is recorded in Abul Fazl's *Akbar-nāmā.* Abul Fazl was assassinated by Bīr Siṅgh Bundelā on 12 August 1602 at the behest of Prince Salīm, later Emperor Jahāṅgīr, who harboured a dislike for him for being his father's favourite.

BIBLIOGRAPHY

1. Smith, Vincent A., *The Oxford History of India.* Oxford, 1958
2. Mujeeb, M., *The Indian Muslims.* London, 1967
3. Giān Siṅgh, Giānī, *Twārīkh Gurū Khālsā.* Patiala, 1970

B.S.D.

ACHAL SĀHIB, GURDWĀRĀ, sacred to Gurū Nānak, is located on the boundary of Sālho and Chāhal villages along the Jalandhar-Baṭālā road, 6 km south of Baṭālā (31°-49'N, 75°-12'E) in Gurdāspur district of the Punjab. The low mound on which the Gurdwārā is situated, in close proximity of the ancient Hindu temple dedicated to Kārtikeya, son of Lord Śiva, is popularly known as Achal Vaṭālā. The Achal temple had since old times been a place of pilgrimage visited by *sādhūs* from distant parts, especially during the annual fair held on the occasion of Śivarātri festival. Sujān Rāi Bhaṇḍārī, *Khulāsat ut-Twārīkh,* writing at the end of the seventeenth century, gives a graphic account of this fair. Gurū Nānak came here at the time of one such fair from Kartārpur, an habitation he had founded on the bank of the River Rāvī. In the words of the *Miharbān Janam Sākhī,* "As the Gurū entered Achal, the name Nānak spread everywhere among the crowds. Everyone began to say that Nānak, the renowned saint, had come. Nānak whose *śabdas* or hymns the world recited was himself there. Whoever was in Achal rushed to see him. Neither a *yogī* was left nor a *sannyāsī*; neither a householder was left nor a recluse. Not a soul remained behind; whosoever there was thronged to the spot saying, 'Nānak hath come, Nānak hath come.'" Gurū Nānak held a long discourse with the Nāth-yogīs led by Bhaṅgar Nāth, who, according to Bhāī Gurdās, *Vārāṅ*, I.40, began by questioning him, "Why hast thou soured the milk by adding vinegar to it? Whoever obtained butter by churning sour milk? Why, casting off the vestment of an Udāsī, hast thou again adopted the life of a householder?" "Bhaṅgar Nāth," replied the Gurū, "it is thou that hast been perversely instructed. Thou didst not cleanse the vessel well, so the butter turned rancid. Abandoning home-life thou turnest an anchorite, and yet thou goest to beg at the doors of the householders. Thou wouldst have nothing to live by if they gave thee nought." The Nāths then tried to overawe Gurū Nānak with a display of their magical powers, and challenged him to show them a miracle. But the Gurū condemned their wizardry and said, "The magic of the Siddhas is vain and futile. I rely on nothing except the holy fellowship and the Word. Besides the True Name, I possess no other miracle." "By the Gurū's Word," says Bhāī Gurdās, "contentment came to the Siddhas."

A memorial platform was raised on the site where Gurū Nānak had halted. A small *gurdwārā* was raised during the eighteenth century and was attended by a line of *mahants*. According to revenue records, the Gurdwārā was owned by one Maṅgal Siṅgh in 1892. His son, Sundar Siṅgh, succeeded him in 1904. Sundar Siṅgh's son, Sūrat Siṅgh, was the *mahant* or custodian when, around 1923, a *jathā* from the nearby village of Jaito Sarjā, under the leadership of Jathedār Kesar Siṅgh occupied the Gurdwārā and seven acres of land attached to it. Sūrat Siṅgh had offered no resistance. Subsequent to the passing of the Sikh Gurdwaras Act, 1925, the management was officially handed over to the Shiromaṇī Gurdwārā Parbandhak Committee on 28 April 1926. The foundation of the present building was laid on 17 October 1935. The complex, completed in 1946, consists of an 8-metre square sanctum within a high-ceilinged hall, with a gallery all around at mid-height and a pinnacled lotus dome on top. There are square domed kiosks at the corners of the hall roof and solid lotus blossoms-in-leaves on the wall-tops. Rooms for pilgrims and the Gurū kā Laṅgar are across a brick-paved courtyard close by.

The Gurdwārā is affiliated to the Shiromaṇī Gurdwārā Parbandhak Committee, but the administration has been temporarily handed over to the successors of Sant Gurmukh Siṅgh. In addition to morning and evening services, largely-attended congregations take place on every *amāvas*, the last day of the dark half of the month. The biggest function of the year is the annual fair which now takes place from the ninth to the eleventh day after the Dīvālī festival. The fair, although a continuation of the time-honoured pilgrimage to the Hindu temple and tank, has in recent decades become more local in its appeal and increasingly Sikh in religious character and attendance.

BIBLIOGRAPHY

1. Ṭhākar Siṅgh, Giānī, *Srī Gurduāre Darshan*. Amritsar, 1923
2. Tārā Siṅgh, *Srī Gur Tīrath Saṅgrahi*. Amritsar, n. d.
3. Randhir, G.S., *Sikh Shrines in India*. Delhi, 1990

J. C. B. W.

ACHCHHAR SIṄGH, JATHEDĀR (1892-1976), a Gurdwārā officiant and Akālī politician who twice held office as Jathedār (provost) of Srī Akāl Ta<u>kh</u>t at Amritsar, was born on 18 January 1892 in a farming family of modest means at Ghaṇīeṅke, a village in Lahore district. The youngest son of Hukam Siṅgh and Gaṅgī, he learnt to read Gurmukhī letters and to recite the Scripture at the village *gurdwārā*. At the age of 15, he migrated to Burma, where he learnt Burmese and Urdu. As he grew up, Achchhar Siṅgh enlisted in the Burmese military police. During World War I (1914-18), Burmese military police was converted into a regular army battalion and drafted to Mesopotamia (now Iraq). Achchhar Siṅgh served there for about three years. At the end of the war in 1918, his unit was stationed at Ṭoṅk, in the North-West Frontier Province, until its departure back to Burma in 1920. In 1919, Achchhar Siṅgh married Mahindar Kaur of Īchogil, a village in his native district of Lahore. He was promoted *havildār*, or sergeant, in 1920. The news of the Nankāṇā Sāhib massacre on 20 February 1921 came as a great shock to him. He resigned from the army and, returning to the Punjab, he made a visit to Nankāṇā Sāhib to pay homage to the memory of the martyrs. He joined the Central Mājhā K͟hālsā Dīwān and plunged into the agitation for the reform of *gurdwārā* management. As the Akālī campaign at Jaito started, the Shiromaṇī Gurdwārā Parbandhak Committee and the Shiromaṇī Akālī Dal were outlawed on 12 October 1923, and arrests began to be made all over the Punjab. Among those held were two successive *jathedārs* of the Akāl Tak͟ht—Tejā Siṅgh Akarpurī and Ūdham Siṅgh Nāgoke. Upon the latter's arrest, Achchhar Siṅgh was, on 10 February 1924, appointed to the high religious office. He, too, was taken into custody on 7 May 1924, was tried and sentenced to one and a half year in jail. Upon his release from the Central Jail at Mīāṅwālī at the end of 1925, he resumed his office in Amritsar which he retained until Tejā Siṅgh Akarpurī was set free in September 1926.

Amar Siṅgh, editor of the *Sher-i-Punjab*, who had been a co-prisoner in Mīāṅwālī jail and who was now president of the Lahore *gurdwārā* committee, persuaded Jathedār Achchhar Siṅgh to take over as *granthī* at Gurdwārā Ḍehrā Sāhib in Lahore. For 14 years he served in this position. In 1940, he moved to Amritsar as a *granthī* at the Harimandar, and continued there until his resignation in 1962. From 1955 to 1962, he was also Jathedār of the Akāl Tak͟ht. During the Punjabi Sūbā agitation, he was arrested from the premises of the Darbār Sāhib on 4 July 1955, but was released two days later. He headed the Pañj Piāre named to judge if Master Tārā Siṅgh had not violated the vow undertaken at the Akāl Tak͟ht before starting his fast-unto-death for the realization of the Sikh political objective of a Punjabi-speaking state. The Pañj Piāre made a close investigation of the circumstances leading to the abandonment of the fast and on 29 November 1961 pronounced Master Tārā Siṅgh guilty of having perjured his pledge and blemished thereby the Sikh tradition of religious steadfastness and sacrifice. They had no comments to make on Sant Fateh Siṅgh's fast which, they said, had been given up under the orders of the Pañj Piāre and the *saṅgat* in general. He was, however, laid under expiation for having acquiesced in Master Tārā Siṅgh breaking his fast. Master Tārā Siṅgh was awarded a severer penance.

As the Shiromaṇī Akālī Dal split into two groups, one led by Sant Fateh Siṅgh and the other by Master Tārā Siṅgh, Jathedār Achchhar Siṅgh resigned the office of head of the Akāl Tak͟ht to join the latter. He was elected president of this party in November 1962. In his address at the 15th All-India Akālī Conference held under his chairmanship at Karnāl on 7 December 1963, he pleaded for unity between the two Akālī factions.

Jathedār Achchhar Siṅgh died in the civil hospital at Amritsar on 6 August 1976 after a protracted illness.

BIBLIOGRAPHY

1. Sahni, Ruchi Ram, *Struggle for Reform in Sikh Shrines*. Ed. Ganda Singh. Amritsar, n.d.
2. Gulati, Kailash Chander, *The Akalis: Past and Present*. Delhi, 1974

3. Sukhdiāl Siṅgh, *Srī Akāl Takht Sāhib*. Patiala, 1984

P. S. G.

ADALĪ, BHĀĪ, of Chohlā village in present-day Amritsar district of the Punjab, was a devoted Sikh contemporary of Gurū Rām Dās and Gurū Arjan. It was, as says Bhāī Santokh Siṅgh, *Srī Gur Pratāp Sūraj Granth*, under his influence that Bhāī Bidhī Chand gave up banditry and came to receive instruction at the hands of Gurū Arjan.

Gn. S.

ĀDAM, BHĀĪ, also mentioned as Uddam in some chronicles, was, according to Giānī Giān Siṅgh, *Twārīkh Gurū Khālsā*, a Siddhū Jaṭṭ of Brāṛ clan living at Viñjhū, a village near Baṭhiṇḍā (30°-14'N, 74°-58'E). He had no male child and, advancing in years, he along with his wife came to Amritsar to devote himself to serving Gurū Rām Dās. Besides partaking of the holy *saṅgat* morning and evening, he daily brought two loads of firewood from the jungle, one of which he contributed to the Gurū kā Laṅgar, selling part of the second to buy food for himself and storing the remainder. Once on an extremely cold night a large number of Sikhs arrived to visit the Gurū. As they stood shivering in the open, Bhāī Ādam fetched his stock of firewood and lit bonfires for them. Gurū Rām Dās was highly pleased and bade him ask for a boon. Ādam shyly said that he had everything he wanted except a son. The Gurū gave him his blessing. It was, as goes the tradition, by the Gurū's blessing that Bhāī Bhagatū was born to the couple.

BIBLIOGRAPHY

1. Macauliffe, Max Arthur, *The Sikh Religion*. Oxford, 1909
2. Vīr Siṅgh, Bhāī, *Srī Ashṭ Gur Chamatkār*. Amritsar, 1952
3. Giān Siṅgh, Giānī, *Twārīkh Gurū Khālsā*. Patiala, 1970

Gr. S.

AḌḌAṆ SHĀH, BHĀĪ (1688-1757), third in succession to Bhāī Kanhaiyā, founder of the Sevāpanthī sect, was born in 1688 in the village of Laū in Jhaṅg district, now in Pakistan. His parents were of a devout temperament and he inherited from them a deeply religious bent of mind. He learnt Gurmukhī and got training in the exegesis of Sikh scriptural texts from Bhāī Gurdās Dakkhaṇī, a leading Sikh of Gurū Tegh Bahādur's time. He also remained in the company of Bhāī Sevā Rām, a disciple of and successor to Bhāī Kanhaiyā, for a long time and ultimately succeeded him as chief of the Sevāpanthī sect. Aḍḍaṇ Shāh laid down the sect's code of conduct and prescribed for it a distinctive apparel. He also pioneered the study of comparative religious thought at his *ḍerā* or monastery where nearly 250 saints were always in residence. Besides Sikh scriptures, other important books studied at the *ḍerā* included *Kīmīya-i-Sa'ādat, Masnavī,* and *Yoga Vasiṣṭa.* These classics were translated into Punjabi. *Pāras Bhāg,* a translation of *Kīmīya-i-Sa'ādat* still ranks as a classic of Punjabi prose. The *parchī* literature issuing from this school bears testimony to the literary taste and moral precept of Bhāī Aḍḍaṇ Shāh.

Bhāī Aḍḍaṇ Shāh was an eloquent speaker. His speeches were recorded by Bhāī Sahaj Rām, another disciple of Bhāī Sevā Rām, which are now available under the titles *Sākhīāṅ Bhāī Aḍḍaṇ Shāh, Sukhan Fakīrāṅ De* and *Bachan Gobind Lokāṅ De.*

Bhāī Aḍḍaṇ Shāh spent his last years in Jammū area where he died on 17 Baisākh *sudī* 8, 1814 Bk/26 April 1757.

BIBLIOGRAPHY

1. Gurmukh Siṅgh, *Sevāpanthīāṅ dī Pañjābī Sāhit nūṅ Deṇ*. Patiala, 1986
2. Lāl Chand, *Srī Sant Mālā*. Patiala, 1955

Gm. S.

ADHARKĀ, according to *Bhāī Bālā Janam Sākhī*, visited Gurū Nānak in the train of his master, Sālas Rāi, the jeweller. Both master and servant turned disciples and set up a Sikh *saṅgat,* fellowship or centre, in their native town, Bishambharpur.

BIBLIOGRAPHY

1. Kohlī, Surindar Siṅgh, ed., *Janam Sākhī Bhāī Bālā.* Chandigarh, 1975
2. Giān Siṅgh, Giānī, *Twārīkh Gurū Khālsā.* Patiala, 1970
3. Harbans Singh, *Guru Nanak and Origins of the Sikh Faith.* Bombay, 1969

Gn. S.

ĀDI GRANTH. See SRĪ GURŪ GRANTH SĀHIB

ĀDĪNĀ BEG KHĀN (d. 1758), governor of the Punjab for a few months in AD 1758, was, according to *Ahwāl-i-Dīnā Beg Khān*, an unpublished Persian manuscript, the son of Channū, of the Arāīṅ agriculturalist caste, mostly settled in Doābā region of the Punjab. He was born at the village of Sharakpur, near Lahore, now in Sheikhūpurā district of Pakistan. Ādīnā Beg was brought up in Mughal homes, for the most part in Jalālābād, Khānpur and Bajvāṛā in the Jalandhar Doāb. Starting his career as a soldier, he rose to be collector of revenue of the village of Kaṅg in the Lohīāṅ area, near Sultānpur Lodhī. He obtained half a dozen villages in Kaṅg area on lease and within an year the entire Kaṅg region. After some time Nawāb Zakarīyā Khān, the governor of Lahore, appointed him chief (*hākam*) of Sultānpur Lodhī. When after Nādir Shāh's invasion (1739) Sikhs started gaining power, Zakarīyā Khān made Ādīnā Beg Khān *nāzim* (administrator) of the Jalandhar Doāb to suppress them. Shrewd as he was, he tried to strengthen his own position by encouraging Sikhs instead of repressing them. Under pressure from Zakarīyā Khān, he however had to expel them from his dominion. For nonpayment of government dues he was taken into custody under the orders of the governor of Lahore and subjected to torture. On being set free after an year, he was appointed deputy *nāzim* under Shāh Nawāz Khān. After Zakarīyā Khān's death on 1 July 1745, his sons, Yāhīyā Khān and Shāh Nawāz Khān contested succession. Ādīnā Beg maintained good relations with both. Shāh Nawāz Khān having captured Lahore appointed Ādīnā Beg chief of Jalandhar Doāb. Meanwhile, Nādir Shāh died on 19 June 1747 and Ahmad Shāh Durrānī became ruler of Kābul and Qandahār. Shāh Nawāz following Ādīnā Beg's advice invited the Durrānī king to march towards the Punjab, warning at the same time the government at Delhi about the Durrānī's invasion. As Ahmad Shāh advanced into the country, Shāh Nawāz fled towards Delhi. Mu'īn ul-Mulk (Mīr Mannū), son of Qamar ud-Dīn, the chief *wazīr* of the Delhi king, succeeded in checking the invader at Mānūpur, near Sirhind. Ādīnā Beg joined hands with Mū'īn ul-Mulk and was wounded in the battle. Mū'īn ul-Mulk became governor of Lahore, with Kauṛā Mall as his *dīwān* and Ādīnā Beg as *faujdār* of the Jalandhar Doāb as before. Sikhs again started plundering the country. Ahmad Shāh Durrānī launched upon his third incursion into the Punjab (December 1751), this time forcing Mu'īn ul-Mulk to surrender. Mu'īn remained governor, now on the Durrānī's behalf. He and Ādīnā Beg directed their energies towards quelling the Sikhs. On the festival of Holā Mohallā in March 1753, Ādīnā Beg fell upon Sikh pilgrims at Anandpur killing a large number of them. The Sikhs retaliated by plundering villages in the Jalandhar and Bārī Doābs. Ādīnā Beg was as quick in coming to terms as he was in opening hostilities. He assigned some of the revenue of his territory to the Sikhs and admitted several of them, including Jassā Siṅgh Rāmgaṛhīā, into his army.

Mu'īn ul-Mulk died on 3 November 1753, and during the time of his widow, Murād Begam (Mughlānī Begam), Ādīnā Beg assumed independent authority in the Doāb, extending his influence up to Sirhind (March 1755). The Emperor of Delhi bestowed on him the title of Zafar Jaṅg Khān. The ruler of Kāṅgṛā accepted his overlordship. In May 1756, he was appointed governor of Lahore and Multān by the Mughal government of Delhi on payment of an annual tribute of thirty lakh of rupees. Ahmad Shāh Durrānī came to Mughlānī Begam's help and Ādīnā Beg took refuge in the Śivālik hills. The Afghāns reappointed him *faujdār* of the Jalandhar Doāb. During Taimūr Shāh's governorship (1757-58), Ādīnā Beg began to look around for allies with a view to expelling the Afghāns. The Sikhs and Ādīnā Beg's troops joined hands and defeated the Afghāns at Māhalpur, in Hoshiārpur district. Ādīnā Beg expressed his gratitude to the Sikhs by presenting a sum of a thousand rupees as homage to the Gurū Granth Sāhib and a lakh and a quarter as protection money for the Jalandhar Doāb. Keeping up appearances with the Sikh *sardārs,* he wished to weaken their power and invited to this end Marāṭhās who had taken Delhi to come to the Punjab, offering them one lakh of rupees a day on march. He also persuaded Sikhs to help the Marāṭhās against the Afghāns. The Marāṭhās led by Raghunāth Rāo and accompanied by the forces of the Sikhs and those of Ādīnā Beg entered Lahore in April 1758. Ādīnā Beg got the *sūbahdārī* of the Punjab at 75 lakh of rupees a year to be paid to the Marāṭhās. The Punjab had now three masters: the Mughals, the Afghāns and the Marāṭhās, but in reality only two—Ādīnā Beg and the Sikhs. Ādīnā Beg brooked no rivals, and resumed his campaign against the Sikhs, increasing his armed strength and hiring a thousand woodcutters to clear up the forests in which the Sikhs were wont to seek shelter in times of stress. He laid siege to the Sikh fort of Rām Rauṇī at Amritsar. Before the Sikhs rallied to confront him, Ādīnā Beg succumbed to an attack of colic at Baṭālā on 10 September 1758. His dead body was buried, honouring his will, at Khānpur, 2 km northwest of Hoshiārpur.

BIBLIOGRAPHY

1. Gupta, Hari Ram, *History of the Sikhs,* vol. II. Delhi, 1978
2. Gandhi, Surjit Singh, *Struggle of the Sikhs for Sovereignty.* Delhi, 1980
3. Bhagat Singh, *Sikh Polity.* Delhi, 1978

B. S.

ĀDI SĀKHĪĀṄ *(ādi* = first; *sākhīāṅ,* plural of *sākhī* = anecdotes, stories, discourses, parables) is one of the early compilations but not the first of the extant *janam sākhī* traditions to evolve. The manuscript, dated 1758 Bk/ AD 1701, and copied by Shambhū Nāth Brāhmaṇ was first located by Dr Mohan Siṅgh Dīwānā. While teaching at Pañjāb University, Lahore, prior to the partition of India in 1947, Mohan Siṅgh Dīwānā discovered in the University's library a *janam sākhī* manuscript which differed from other extant *janam sākhīs* and bore an earlier date. Dr Dīwānā believed it to be a version of the earliest of all *janam sākhī* traditions and bestowed on it the name *Ādi Sākhīāṅ.* Since then four more copies of the manuscript have been located on the Indian side of the border by Professor Piār Siṅgh who published in 1969 a text based on the manuscript held in the library of Motībāgh Palace, Paṭiālā, and supplemented by the manuscript in the Sikh Reference Library, Amritsar. This text was issued under the title *Shambhū Nāth Vālī Janam Patrī Bābe Nānak Jī Kī Prasidh Nāṅ Ādi Sākhīāṅ.*

The fact that the two earliest of the dated manuscripts were both completed in AD 1701 obviously implies that it is a work of the seventeenth century. It is, however, most unlikely that the tradition in its extant form would have evolved earlier than the mid-seventeenth century. This conclusion is indicated by such marks of maturity as a multiplicity of sources and a coherent ordering of its various anecdotes. Two principal sources were evidently used by the first compiler of the *Ādi Sākhīāṅ*. One of these provides a link with the *Purātan* tradition, particularly with the manuscript available in the Languages Department, Paṭiālā. The other appears to have been a manuscript, no longer extant, which was later to be used by the compiler of the *B40 Janam-sākhī*. Four anecdotes have also been taken from the *Miharbān* source (*sākhīs* 26, 27, 28a and 28b), thus introducing the *goṣṭī* form into the *janam sākhī*. Essentially, however, the *Ādi Sākhīāṅ* is a collection of narrative *sākhīs* and it seems clear that its first recension was exclusively narrative in content. The *goṣṭs* (discourses) borrowed from the *Miharbān* tradition appear to be a later supplement to an original compilation. Although the *Ādī Sākhīāṅ* shares an important source with the *Purātan* tradition it lacks the characteristic *Purātan* division of Gurū Nānak's travels into four separate journeys known as four *Udāsīs*. Almost all the travel anecdotes utilized by the *Ādi Sākhīāṅ* compiler are drawn from his second major source, i.e. the manuscript shared with the *B40* compiler, and most of them are presented as a single journey (*sākhīs* 8-16). The only exception to this pattern is the story of Gurū Nānak's visit to Rājā Śivanābh (*sākhī* 21B). This also derives from his second source, but appears in the *Ādi Sākhīāṅ* chronology as an isolated journey, solely concerned with Rājā Śivanābh. In addition to these two journeys beyond the Punjab, the manuscript also incorporates *sākhīs* describing Gurū Nanāk's visit to Pāk Paṭṭan, Saidpur, and Achal (*sākhīs* 17, 18, 19 and 23). Towards its conclusion (*sākhīs*, 29-30) an element of confusion becomes evident and the identity of the sources used for this portion is unclear. The compiler's usual care is relaxed, possibly because of a hasty concern to terminate the work or perhaps because the concluding portion is the work of a later, less competent contributor. The result is a somewhat garbled account of the death of Gurū Nānak. It is, however, an interesting account in that it draws heavily on the *Miharbān* tradition which was also used in the later stages of the *Bālā Janam Sākhī* development.

BIBLIOGRAPHY

1. Kirpāl Siṅgh, *Janam Sākhī Prampara*. Patiala, 1969
2. Piār Siṅgh, ed., *Shambhū Nāth Vālī Janam Patrī Bābe Nānak Jī Kī Prasidh Nāṅ Ādi Sākhīāṅ*. Patiala, 1969
3. McLeod, W. H., *Early Sikh Tradition*. Oxford, 1980

W. H. M.

ĀḌIT, a professional soldier of Soinī clan, came to take refuge at the feet of Gurū Arjan. He supplicated the Gurū thus: "We soldiers bear arms and live by fighting. How shall we be saved?" The Gurū, according to Bhāī Manī Siṅgh, *Sikhāṅ dī Bhagat Mālā*, said: "Remember God even when fighting. Fight only in a righteous cause. Protect the weak and the oppressed. Be true to the salt; be loyal to your Master. Thus will you obtain victory; thus will you glorify your countenance." Āḍit bowed at the Gurū's feet and became a disciple.

T. S.

ADVENTURES OF AN OFFICER IN THE PUNJAUB (2 vols.) by Major H. M. L. Lawrence, under the pseudonym of Bẹllasis, published in AD 1846 by Henry Colburn, London, and reprinted in 1970 by the Languages Department, Punjab, Paṭiālā. The book which is a rambling account, half fact half fiction, of the author's adventures, provides information about the rise of the Sikhs and about the person and government of Mahārājā Raṇjīt Siṅgh. This is "a dose of history, which the reader may read or not, as he pleases" (p. 236), mixed with scandal and bazaar gossip.

Colonel Bellasis, a soldier of fortune, enters the Punjab with a small suite, arrives at Lahore and meets the leading courtiers of Mahārājā Raṇjīt Siṅgh, including the Faqīr brothers, 'Azīz ud-Dīn and Nūr ud-Dīn. He was introduced to the court by the latter. The Mahārājā gave him appointment as *sūbahdār* of Kāṅgṛā. In his book, the author describes some of the men around the Mahārājā. For instance, Dhiān Siṅgh: " a fine-looking man, of a noble presence, polite and affable, of winning manners and modest speech" (p. 35). Khushāl Siṅgh: "a coarse, vulgar-looking man... was once sent to assist Kunwar Sher Singh, the Maharajah's son, in the government of Kashmir, and to recover its ruined finances... recovered some rents, screwed a few lakhs and turned a season of dearth into one of most frightful famine..." (p. 38). Khaṛak Siṅgh: "the eldest [of the three princes] is an imbecile, and affects the *religieux*" (p. 53). Avitabile: " a wild bull in a net," he "acts as a savage among savage men" (p. 43). The author draws numerous pen-portraits of the Mahārājā as well: "Of mean appearance, one-eyed, and small of stature...Wholly illiterate but gifted with great natural intelligence, and a wonderfully quick apprehension and retentive memory, he manages, better than those more learned, to transact the current business of the kingdom" (p. 29).

Referring to the revenue and the judicial administration of the kingdom, the author observes that the whole country was farmed out, two-fifths of the produce being taken by the State. The revenue-farmer was also judge, magistrate and often customs-master, within his area of jurisdiction. Adālat, court, was another rich source of revenue, fine being the punishment awarded in almost every case (p. 51). Customs brought a revenue of 24, 00, 000 rupees to the treasury, Amritsar alone yielding 9, 00, 000.

B. J. H.

AFGHĀN- SIKH RELATIONS spanning the years 1748 to 1849 go back to the first invasion of India by Ahmad Shāh Durrānī, although he must have heard of the Sikhs when in 1739 he accompanied Nādir Shāh, the Iranian invader, as a young staff officer. Having occupied Lahore after a minor engagement fought on 11 January 1748 during his first invasion of India, Ahmad Shāh advanced towards Sirhind to meet a Mughal army which he was informed was advancing from Delhi to oppose him. On the way he had two slight skirmishes at Sarāi Nūr Dīn and at the Vairovāl ferry, both in present-day Amritsar district, with a Sikh *jathā* or fighting band under Jassā Siṅgh Āhlūvālīā. While lying in wait at Sirhind between 2 and 11 March 1748 for a Mughal force, Ālā Siṅgh, leader of the Mālvā Sikhs, cut off his supplies of food and fodder. Ahmad Shāh, defeated in the battle of Mānūpur fought on 11 March, retraced his steps homewards. Sikhs harassed the retreating invader between the Sutlej and the Chenāb, Chaṛhat Siṅgh Sukkarchakkīā following him even up to the Indus, relieving him of a number of weapons, horses and camels.

Ahmad Shāh's subsequent invasions in a way helped the Sikhs to increase and consolidate their power. Anticipating a second invasion towards the close of 1748, the new Mughal governor of the Punjab, Mīr Mu'īn ul-Mulk (Mīr Mannū, in shortened form in Sikh chronicles), tried to conciliate Sikhs through his minister, Dīwān Kauṛā Mall, and granted them one-fourth of the revenue of the *parganah* of Paṭṭī, but the truce did not last long and during the second Durrānī invasion (December 1749-February 1750), the Sikhs made bold to enter and plunder Lahore itself. During Ahmad Shāh's next invasion (December 1751-March 1752), Kauṛā Mall again enlisted the help of several thousand Sikh warriors under the command of Saṅgat Siṅgh and Sukkhā Siṅgh of Māṛī Kambo. The latter was killed in a sudden skirmish with the invaders. As a result of this invasion the provinces of Lahore and Multān were annexed to the Afghān empire, although Mīr Mannū remained governor of these provinces on Ahmad Shāh Durrānī's behalf. This meant that Sikhs had now to contend with Afghāns as well as with Mughals.

The disorder which overtook the Punjab following the death of Mīr Mannū in November 1753 opened the way for them to establish their sway over vast tracts in the form of *rākhī* (*q.v.*) system under which local populations sought their protection on payment of a portion of their land revenue. During his fourth invasion (November 1756-April 1757), the Afghān invader had reached as far as the Mughal capital, Delhi. The Sikhs preyed upon him during his onward march and, when his son Prince Taimūr was transporting the plundered wealth of Delhi to Lahore, Ālā Siṅgh in concert with other Sikh *sardārs* barred his path at Sanaur, near Paṭiālā, and robbed him of his treasures, and again attacked and plundered him at Mālerkoṭlā. Prince Taimūr gave vent to his chagrin by destroying Sikh shrines at Kartārpur, 15 km northwest of Jalandhar, and subjecting its residents to indiscriminate massacre and plunder. Ahmad Shāh, during his brief stay at Lahore, sent out troops who sacked Amritsar and desecrated the sacred pool, besides killing a large number of Sikhs. He left his son Taimūr and his general Jahān Khān in charge of the Punjab and himself retired to Afghanistan. The two deputies were expelled from Punjab by Sikhs in 1758 with the help of the Marāṭhās and of Ādīnā Beg Khān, who was rewarded with the governorship of the province.

During Ahmad Shāh's fifth invasion (October 1759-May 1761), while the Marāṭhās retired from the Punjab without resistance, the Sikhs gave a battle to the invader in the neighbourhood of Lahore in which the Afghān lost as many as 2,000 men, with their general Jahān Khān wounded. The Marāṭhā's dream of supremacy in north India was shattered in the third battle of Pānīpat (14 January 1761). The Sikhs on the other hand were emboldened to raid Lahore in November 1760. They stayed there for eleven days and the Afghān deputy appeased them with a present of Rs 30,000 for sacramental *kaṛāhprasād*. They harassed the Afghān chief of Chahār Mahāl and sacked Jalandhar, Sirhind and Mālerkoṭlā. In November 1761, they captured Lahore and struck their own coin. Ahmad Shāh, on hearing of these developments, hurried to the relief of his deputies. Sikhs retreated as he marched upon them, but were overtaken near Kup and Rahīṛā villages, near Mālerkoṭlā, on the morning of 5 February 1762. About 25,000 Sikhs were killed in the day-long battle known in Sikh annals as Vaḍḍā Ghallūghārā or the great holocaust. On his return he blew up the holy Harimandar at Amritsar with gunpowder. The Sikhs retaliated with attacks on Sirhind in May 1762. They freely roamed around Lahore during July-August 1762 and celebrated Dīvālī at Amritsar in defiance of the Shāh who was still present in the Punjab.

After the departure of the Durrānī in December 1762, Sikhs sacked the Afghān principality of Kasūr in May 1763, overran Jalandhar Doāb during June, defeated in November near Wazīrābād an expeditionary force sent by Ahmad Shāh and invested Mālerkoṭlā, killing its Afghān chief, Bhīkhan Khān (December 1763). They followed these successes with the reduction of Moriṇḍā and Sirhind in January 1764. Zain Khān, the *faujdār* or governor of Sirhind, was killed, and the territories of Sirhind *sarkār* or district were appropriated by various Sikh *misls* or chiefships. The Dal Khālsā Jīo, as the confederated Sikh force was called, then fell upon the territories of Najīb ud-Daulah, a powerful Ruhīlā Afghān chief and Ahmad Shāh Durrānī's regent in India. Ransacking Sahāraṇpur on 20 February 1764, they pushed on seizing Shāmlī, Kāndhlā, Muzaffarnagar, Morādābād, Najībābād and several other towns. Najīb ud-Daulah, unable to meet the Sikhs in battle, paid them Rs 11,00,000, inducing them to return to Punjab by the end of February 1764. While the Buḍḍhā Dal, a division of the Dal Khālsā under Jassā Siṅgh Āhlūvālīā, was thus engaged in the Gangetic Doāb, its younger counterpart, the Taruṇā Dal, was active in the central and western Punjab. Lahore was attacked in February 1764 and its governor, Kābulī Mall, saved it from plunder only by paying a large sum to the Sikhs, by accepting a nominee of Harī Siṅgh of the Bhaṅgī *misl* as a resident at his court and allowing an agent of Sobhā Siṅgh of the Kanhaiyā *misl* to receive customs duty on all goods coming from the side of Multān. During April-June 1764, the Bhaṅgī and Nakaī *sardārs* captured the Lammā country lying between Lahore and Multān, and Charhat Siṅgh Sukkarchakkīā took Rohtās in the north. Ahmad Shāh Durrānī came out again, in December 1764, but harassed by Sikhs, he was forced to return homewards without reaching Delhi. On his way back, realizing the futility of appointing his own governors in the Punjab, he recognized Ālā Siṅgh of Paṭiālā as the ruling chief in Sirhind territory and bestowed upon him the title of Rājā, with *tabl-o-'alam* (drum and banner). He, however, sent back Kābulī Mall to resume governorship of Lahore, but before the latter could reach the city, the Sikhs had occupied it (17 April 1765). Ahmad Shāh made yet another (his last) bid to regain Punjab and Delhi during the winter of 1766-67, but failed. He died at Qandahār on 23 October 1772.

Ahmad Shāh's son and successor, Taimūr Shāh (1746-93), attempted five successive incursions, but could not reach Lahore. His successor, Shāh Zamān, also made several attempts to regain a foothold in India and did enter Lahore twice (January 1797; December 1798) but was forced to evacuate it within a few weeks on each occasion.

Raṇjīt Siṅgh, the chief of the Sukkarchakkīā *misl* of the Dal Khālsā was destined finally to clear Punjab of the Afghāns. He became master of Lahore on 7 July 1799. The provinces of Kashmīr and Multān were still ruled by Afghān satraps and Peshāwar across the Indus was directly under Kābul which, however, was weakened by internal dissensions. Shāh Zamān, was deposed and blinded in 1800 and the throne was seized by his brother, Mahmūd Shāh, with the help of a Bārakzaī chief, Fateh Khān who emerged as the king-maker. In 1803, Fateh Khān discarded Mahmūd in favour of Shujā' ul-Mulk, better known as Shāh Shujā', another brother of Shāh Zamān, but in 1809 Mahmūd was reinstated and Shāh Shujā' shifted to Peshāwar. The latter met Mahārājā Raṇjīt Siṅgh at Khushāb in 1810 in the hope of obtaining Sikh help. He tried to recover his kingdom with the help of 'Atā Muhammad Khān, governor of Kashmīr, who had not accepted the authority of Wazīr Fateh Khān and had been ruling the province independently since 1809. The attempt failed and ended in Shāh Shujā' taken captive in Kashmīr and his family including the ill-fated Shāh Zamān seeking refuge in Lahore. Wafā Begam, the senior wife of Shāh Shujā', approached Raṇjīt Siṅgh through his trusted courtiers, Dīwān Mohkam Chand and Faqīr 'Azīz ud-Dīn to have her husband rescued from Kashmīr. Wazīr Fateh Khān also solicited the Mahārājā's aid in the reduction of Kashmīr promising him one-third of the spoils. The joint expedition launched in 1812 was not a complete success. Fateh Khān refused to part with the promised share of the booty, but the Sikh general Mohkam Chand succeeded in bringing Shāh Shujā' to Lahore and Raṇjīt Siṅgh acquired the coveted diamond, Koh-i-Nūr. Kashmīr too was conquered and annexed to the Sikh kingdom in 1819.

Multān which had been retaken from the Sikhs by Taimūr Shāh in 1780 had been placed under his nephew Nawāb Muzaffar Khān. Repeated expeditions sent by Raṇjīt Siṅgh against him (in 1802, 1805, 1807, 1810, 1812 and 1815) had proved abortive. Multān ultimately fell to the Sikhs in June 1818. On 19 November of that year, Mahārājā Raṇjīt

Siṅgh entered Peshāwar, the eastern citadel of the rulers of Kābul. With the conquest of Ḍerā Ghāzī Khān in 1820 and Ḍerā Ismā'īl Khān in 1821, the frontiers of the Sikh kingdom had been pushed far to the west of the River Indus. The Paṭhāns (Afghāns) of this frontier region, however, had not fully accepted Sikh authority. In 1826, they under the leadership of Sayyid Ahmad, a Wahābī fanatic, rose in *jihād* or holy war against the Sikhs. The campaign, a prolonged one, came to an end with the death of the Sayyid in May 1831. In 1835, Dost Muhammad Khān, the youngest and the most energetic of the Bārakzaī brothers, who had supplanted the Durrānī dynasty and become Amīr (lord, chief or king) of Kābul in 1825, advanced up to Khaibar Pass threatening to recover Peshāwar. In 1836 Harī Siṅgh Nalvā, the Sikh general who along with Prince Nau Nihāl Siṅgh was guarding that frontier, built a chain of forts including one at Jamrūd at the eastern end of the Khaibar Pass to defend it. Dost Muhammad erected a fort at 'Alī Masjid at the other end. In the beginning of 1837, as Prince Nau Nihāl Siṅgh returned to Lahore to get married and the Mahārājā and his court got busy with preparations for the wedding, Dost Muhammad Khān sent a 25,000-strong force, including a large number of local irregulars and equipped with 18 heavy guns, to invest Jamrūd. The Sikh garrison there had only 600 men and a few light artillery pieces. The Afghāns besieged the fort and cut off its water supply while a detachment was sent to the neighbouring Sikh fort of Shabqadar to prevent any help from that direction. Mahā Siṅgh, the garrison commander of Jamrūd, kept the invaders at bay for four days and managed meanwhile to send a desperate appeal for help to Harī Siṅgh Nalvā at Peshāwar. Nalvā rose from his sickbed and rushed to Jamrūd. In the final battle fought on 30 April 1837, the Afghāns were driven away, but Harī Siṅgh Nalvā was mortally wounded. In 1838, the Sikh monarch became a party to the Tripartite Treaty as a result of which Shāh Shujā' was reinstalled on the throne of Kābul in August 1839 with British help. Dost Muhammad Khān was exiled to Calcutta in November 1839, but was restored to his former position after the murder of Shāh Shujā' in April 1842. He thereafter maintained cordial relations with the Lahore Darbār. The second Anglo-Sikh war reawakened Dost Muhammad's ambition to seize Peshāwar and the trans-Indus territories, although overtly he sympathized with the Sikhs and even hired out an irregular Afghān contingent of 1500 horse to Chatar Siṅgh, leader of Sikh resistance against the British.

BIBLIOGRAPHY

1. Shahamat Ali, *The Sikhs and Afghans*. Patiala, 1970
2. Harlan, Josiah, *A Memoir of India and Afghanistan*. London, 1842
3. Burnes, Alexander, *Cabool*. *London, 1843*
4. Ganda Singh, *Ahmad Shah Durrani*. Bombay, 1959
5. Sūrī, Sohan Lāl, *'Umdāt-ut-Twārīkh*. Lahore, 1885-89

B.J.H.

AGAMPUR or AGAMPURĀ, lit. city unapproachable or inaccessible (Skt. *agamya* plus *pur* or *purā*). The word appears in one of the hymns of Gurū Nānak in Āsā measure where it is used to signify God's abode or the ultimate state or stage of spiritual enlightenment and bliss. Another term used synonymously in the same hymn is *nijaghar*, lit. one's own real home signifying the ultimate sphere of *jīvātmā*. The relevant stanza first raises the question: "Tell me how the city unapproachable is reached," followed by the answer, "By discarding such measures as *japu* (mechanical repetition of God's name), *tapu* (bodily mortification) and *haṭh nigrahi* (forced control of the senses)." Realizing the Gurū's Word in practice is prescibed as the right path to *agampur* (GG, 436).

BIBLIOGRAPHY

Shabdārth Srī Gurū Granth Sāhib Jī. Amritsar, 1959

M. G. S.

AGAUL, village 10 km from Nābhā (30°-22'N, 76°-9'E) in Paṭiālā district, has a historical shrine called Gurdwārā Srī Gurū Tegh Bahādur Sāhib. In the course of a journey through this area, Gurū Tegh Bahādur came and sat here under a *pīpal* tree on the bank of a pond. The old *pīpal* tree is not there now, but the pond, called Rām Talāī and believed to possess medicinal properties for curing skin diseases, has since been lined and converted into a small *sarovar*, holy tank. Construction of the Gurdwārā was commenced in 1919 and completed on 1 Chet 1992 Bk/14 March 1935. The building comprises a square *dīvān* hall, which is an extension of the sanctum where the Gurū Granth Sāhib is installed. The Gurdwārā is managed by a village committee. There is a lithographed copy of the Gurū Granth Sāhib preserved in the Gurdwārā, printed in Nānak Shāhī Sammat 424 (AD 1893). It has 2134 pages and the volume ends with the *Rāgamālā* with which composition copies of the holy Scripture as a rule conclude.

BIBLIOGRAPHY

Faujā Siṅgh, *Gurū Teg Bahādur, Yātrā Asthān, Pramprāvāṅ te Yād Chinn*. Patiala, 1976

M. G. S.

AGHAṚ SIṄGH (d. 1764) was, according to Giānī Giān Siṅgh, *Panth Prakāsh*, one of the seven sons of Bhāī Nagāhīā, a Dullaṭ Jaṭṭ of Laungovāl, in present-day Saṅgrūr district of the Punjab. He received *amrit*, the Khālsā rites of initiation, from his uncle Bhāī Manī Siṅgh, then high priest of the Harimandar at Amritsar. He, along with his brother Tharāj Siṅgh, fought against the Mughals in Amritsar and avenged the execution of Bhāī Manī Siṅgh by slaying his tormentors. He also confronted and killed Mīr Momin Khān of Kasūr who, after the death in November 1753 of Mīr Mannū, the governor of the Punjab, had launched a renewed campaign of persecution against the Sikhs.

Aghaṛ Siṅgh died in January 1764 at Sirhind fighting against the provincial governor, Zain Khān.

BIBLIOGRAPHY

Giān Siṅgh, Giānī, *Panth Prakāsh*. Patiala, 1970

P. S.

AGHORĪ or AGHORPANTHĪ, one of the several Kāpālika sects, connected with the Tāntrik cult of Śaivism, notorious for its cannibalism and other abominable practices. *Aghora* literally means "not terrible," "not evil," otherwise, "pleasant" or "handsome," and is one of the euphemistic titles of the Hindu god, Śiva. *Aughaṛ* or *Aughaḍa* is another cognate word which stands for a follower of the Aghorpanth. Besides , there is also a Vaiṣṇava sect of Aghorīs of modern origin, said to have been founded by Bābā Kinārāma (1684-1787) who himself was a disciple of Bābā Kālārāma Aghorī of Vārāṇasī.

With no independent canonical text or organized church of their own, the Aghorīs derive their ideas and beliefs from those of Kāpālikas who are also known as Vāmāchārī Śaivites. Their chosen deity is Śiva or Aghora whose blessings they seek by following a degenerate and crude form of yoga. They practise a kind of divination by the examination of a child cut out of a pregnant woman at full time. They offer human sacrifices, generally, of volunteering victims who, immediately after they volunteer, become sacred and they are provided whatever they desire. On the appointed day and at a special ceremony, the volunteering victim is decapitated or slain by having a dagger struck in his throat. His blood and flesh are then consumed by the Aghorīs present.

The Aghorīs worship Aghorīśvara as the one Supreme Reality. Ethically, they believe that everything is good for a good person. Distinction between the pure and the impure is irrelevant from their standpoint. Their way of life is absolutely unconventional and the people in general feel much impressed and scared by their occult powers, their practice of human sacrifices, austerities, disregard for fame and wealth, indifference to cleanliness of food and their fearful dress. Living almost naked, they besmear their bodies with the ashes taken from funeral pyres. They wear the rosary made up of Rudrākṣa beads and a necklace made of the bones of a snake and the tusks of a wild boar. Some members of this sect wear necklaces made of human teeth. They invariably carry a skull in hand. They eat flesh from human corpses and animal carcasses except those of horses. They are even said to eat their own excretions. Sexual act with a woman is considered a symbolic way of union with the goddess. Their rituals are generally performed at cemeteries.

In the nineteenth and the beginning of the twentieth century, strict measures were adopted by the government to curb the Aghorīs and their practices which led to the gradual decline in their number. Only a very small number of Aghorīs exist today and they are generally confined to concentrations in Bengal, Bihār and Eastern U.P.

In the *Bālā Janam Sākhī*, the story is related of Gurū Nānak's encounter with a demon called Kauḍā. From the story it appears that Kauḍā was a Kāpālika Aghorī. Once travelling through Central India, Gurū Nānak, accompanied by Mardānā, passed through the tribal areas ministering to communities primitive in their ways. In this country, Mardānā once wandered out in search of food and was seized by a marauding giant. His name, as mentioned in *Bālā Janam Sākhī*, was Kauḍā. He was the leader of a clan of cannibals and always kept an oil-cauldron sizzling for man or beast that might fall into his hands. Mardānā would have met the fate of Kauḍa's many other luckless victims but for the Gurū's timely appearance. The Gurū uttered the greeting, "Sat Kartār—the Creator is the eternal truth." The ring of his words startled Kauḍā. When he turned to look towards the Gurū, his heart was touched as never before. He had not known such benignity and tenderness, nor such calm and tranquillity. He released Mardānā and fell at the Gurū's feet. He was, says *Bālā Janam Sākhī*, converted and charged with the rescuing of his companions. It is stated that Gurū Nānak and Mardānā stayed with Kauḍā for seven days.

Kāmākhyā (Assam), Vārāṇasī, Ujjain, Girnār and Mount Ābū were some of the well-known centres of Aghorī ascetics.

Bābā Kinārāma, a latter-day leader of the sect, was a Vaiṣṇava devotee whose teachings, like those of the medieval *sants*, are a mixture of Vaiṣṇava *bhaktī* and Siddha culture. He wrote *Rāmagītā*, *Rāmacapeṭā*, *Rāmarasāla*, *Gītāvalī* and *Vivekasāra*. A versified translation of the *Yogavasiṣṭha* is also attributed to him. Most of these texts expound Vaiṣṇavite piety of the *sant* variety. In the *Gītāvalī*, he stresses the soteriological importance of *satyaśabda* (the divine/true word) which incidentally is a point of convergence with Sikhism. *Vivekasāra*, his most important work, discusses the theological and moral ideas of the sect, such as creation of the world, self-introspection, meditation, *sahaja-samādhi*, *satsaṅg* and the ecstatic or mystical experience born of supreme devotion and *sādhanā*.

The term *aghorī* or *ghorī* has passed into popular Punjabi usage standing for one who is indolent of habit and indifferent in matters of personal hygiene and cleanliness.

BIBLIOGRAPHY

1. Crooke, W., "Aghoris", in *The Encyclopaedia of Religion and Ethics*, vol. I. Ed. James Hastings. Edinburgh, 1964
2. Eliade, Mircea, *Yoga, Immortality and Freedom*.

Princeton, 1969
3. Chaturvedī, Parśūrām, *Uttarī Bhārat kī Sant Prampra.* Allahabad, 1963
4. Kohlī, Surindar Siṅgh, ed., *Janam Sākhī Bhāī Bālā.* Chandigarh, 1975

L. M. J.

AGNEW, PATRICK ALEXANDER VANS (1822-1848), a civil servant under the East India Company. He was the son of Lt-Col Patrick Vans Agnew, an East India Company director. Agnew joined the Bengal civil service in March 1841. In 1842, he became assistant to the commissioner of Delhi division. In December 1845, he was appointed assistant to Major George Broadfoot, the superintendent of the cis-Sutlej states. He was present at the battle of Sabhrāoṅ in 1846. In April 1848, he was sent by the British resident at Lahore, the capital of the Sikh kingdom of the Punjab, to Multān to take over the government of that province from Dīwān Mūl Rāj who had resigned. He was accompanied by Lt William Anderson, of the Bengal army, the new governor-designate Kāhn Siṅgh, and an escort of Sikh troops from Lahore. The party reached Multān on 17 April 1848. Dīwān Mūl Rāj called on them the following day, but a dispute arose as Agnew demanded that accounts for the preceding six years be produced. On 19 April, the two English officers were taken round the fort and the various establishments. As they were returning to their camp both Agnew and Anderson were attacked and wounded by a retainer of Dīwān Mūl Rāj . Soon afterwards, Mūl Rāj's troops rose in arms and took him prisoner, thus preventing him from visiting the wounded officers in the British camp at the Īdgāh.

The Multān troops called a council of war on 20 April and issued proclamations in the name of Mūl Rāj, inviting the people to rise against the British. The same day, the Sikh escort from Lahore rebelled. Kāhn Siṅgh made terms for himself. In the evening both Agnew and Anderson were killed at the Īdgāh.

BIBLIOGRAPHY

1. Bal, S. S., *British Policy Towards the Panjab, 1844-49.* Calcutta, 1971
2. Kohli, Sita Ram, *Trial of Diwan Mul Raj.* Patiala, 1971
3. Edwardes, Herbert, *A Year on the Punjab Frontier in 1848-49.* London, 1851

H. R. G.

ĀGRĀ (27°-10'N, 78° E), became the seat of a Sikh *saṅgat* following a visit by Gurū Nānak during the first of his four long preaching journeys. Later, Gurū Rām Dās, in his early career as Bhāī Jeṭhā, was in Āgrā when he attended Akbar's court on behalf of Gurū Amar Dās, Nānak III. Gurū Tegh Bahādur, Nānak IX, passed through the city on his way to the eastern parts in 1665-66. Gurū Gobind Siṅgh, the last of the Gurūs, also visited Āgrā when he met Emperor Bahādur Shāh in 1707-08.

GURDWĀRĀ MĀĪ THĀN, marking Gurū Tegh Bahādur's second visit to Āgrā, is the only historical Sikh shrine in the city. It is said that Māī Jassī, an old lady who was a devout follower of the Sikh faith, had got a length of linen prepared from yarn spun with her own hands and had ever longed for an opportunity to present it to the Gurū in her own home. Gurū Tegh Bahādur did visit Māī Jassī's house in the heart of Āgrā and received the offering. He was pleased with her devotion and, as a parting boon, pronounced the blessing that her name would live forever. Māī Jassī's house is now a *gurdwārā.* It is known by the name of Māī Thān. By this name is also known the *mahallā* in which it is situated.

Gurdwārā Māī Thān, in a narrow lane, has a spacious square *dīvān* hall, with the Gurū Granth Sāhib seated in the centre on a canopied throne of white marble. In a room above the entrance gate, a museum has been established with pictures depicting scenes from Sikh history, especially martyrdoms. The Gurdwārā, registered as the Srī Gurū Siṅgh Sabhā, is managed by Srī Gurū Tegh Bahādur Central Board, Āgrā.

BIBLIOGRAPHY

1. Tārā Siṅgh, *Srī Gur Tīrath Saṅgrahi*. Amritsar, n.d.
2. Ṭhākar Siṅgh, Giānī, *Srī Gurduāre Darshan*. Amritsar, 1923

M.G.S.

ĀGYĀ KAUR, BĪBĪ (d. 1918), wife of Bhāī Takht Siṅgh and his helpmate in promoting women's education among Sikhs to which cause he was passionately devoted, was the daughter of Sardār Ṭek Siṅgh of the village of Sultānpur, near Rahīm Yār Khān railway station in the princely state of Bahāwalpur. She had been a resident student at the Sikh girls school, at Fīrozpur, founded in 1892 and nurtured by Bhāī Takht Siṅgh. Āgyā Kaur had studied at the Mahāvidyālā up to the high school level. Bhāī Takht Siṅgh's first wife Harnām Kaur who was a co-builder of the school died in 1906. He approached Āgyā Kaur's father to ask for her hand to be his ally in the enterprise he had launched upon. The nuptials took place at Sultānpur on 17 September 1910. On 16-17 February 1911, Bībī (lady) Āgyā Kaur left with her husband on a tour of some South Asian countries to raise funds for the school. At Sikh gatherings and at *dīvāns* at the *gurdwārās*, she recited holy hymns, *kīrtan*, and made fervent appeals for donations, for their nascent school. Returning to Punjab on 3 March 1912, she resumed her duties at the Mahāvidyālā as a teacher and as a matron of the hostel. She was taken ill with influenza during the epidemic of 1918, aggravated in her case by an attack of pneumonia. She died on 27 October 1918. She left behind four children, one of her daughters rising to the position of Director of Public Instruction in Punjab.

BIBLIOGRAPHY

1. *Pañjābī Bhaiṇ*. Firozpur, September 1910 and December 1918
2. *Silver Jubilee Book*. Amritsar, 1935

D.S.B.

ĀGYĀ RĀM, BHĀĪ (Bhāī Āgyā Siṅgh, according to Sukhā Siṅgh, *Gurbilās Dasvīṅ Pātshāhī)*, a Sikh of Delhi, who accompanied Bhāī Jaitā, Bhāī Nānū and Bhāī Ūdā to carry from Chāndnī Chowk in Delhi to the Dilvālī Mahallā the severed head of Gurū Tegh Bahādur who was executed there on 11 November 1675. Bhāī Jaitā and Bhāī Gurbakhsh were among the eye-witnesses to this gruesome happening. According to *Gurū kīāṅ Sākhīāṅ*, they returned to their homes muttering: "Glory be unto the Gurū; glory unto his Sikhs." As the sad word spread, Sikhs poured one by one into Dilvālī Mahallā and congregated in the house of Bhāī Nānū. There they sat far into the evening listening to the woeful narration and making plans to rescue the body. Lakkhī Dās Lubāṇa's caravan of bullock-carts had arrived on that day from Nārnaul. Bhāī Āgyā Rām, along with Bhāī Jaitā, Bhāī Nānū and Bhāī Ūdā, hid himself in the wagons near the Fort and reached the *kotwālī*, in Chāndnī Chowk. According to tradition, the severed head was kept for the night in Bhāī Jaitā's house in Dilvālī Mahallā from where he carried his sacred charge to Anandpur where Gurū Gobind Siṅgh, the spiritual successor to Gurū Tegh Bahādur, then lived and where the obsequies were performed, with dignity and reverence, on 16 November 1675.

BIBLIOGRAPHY

1. Padam, Piārā Siṅgh, and Giānī Garjā Siṅgh, eds., *Gurū kīāṅ Sākhīāṅ*. Patiala, 1986
2. Trilochan Singh, *Guru Tegh Bahadur: Prophet and Martyr*. Delhi, 1967
3. Harbans Singh, *Guru Tegh Bahadur*. Delhi, 1982

G. S. G.

AHAṄKĀR (*haṅkār* as it is commonly pronounced in Punjabi) is a compound of Sanskrit *aham* ('I') and *kār* ('maker') and means I-maker, i.e. what individuates the person as 'I'. It stands for egotism, egoism, self-conceit, self-centredness, vanity or simply pride. Other synonyms used in the sacred texts of the Sikhs are *mān, abhimān, garab, gumān, ahaṅg, ahammeu, ahambudh, haumai* and *khudī*. Pride is regarded as an undesirable trait in all ethical systems; it is counted among the seven deadly sins in the religious literature of the West. Sikhism considers it not as a metaphysical myth as is done in Sāṅkhya and Buddhism but as one of the five common human weaknesses or evils. *Ahaṅkār* is vanity, elation or exultation arising from an exaggerated view of one's own merit. The merit may consist in real or presumed intellect, scholarship, physical strength or beauty, worldly rank and possessions or even spiritual accomplishments. Whatever the source, *ahaṅkār* is counted a frailty. Says Gurū Amar Dās, "it is a deadly disease and the cause of the unending cycle of birth, death and rebirth" (GG, 592). Again, "Pelf is like poison, for it engenders arrogance. None sunk in arrogance wins approval" (GG, 666). In another hymn, Gurū Amar Dās declares: "Egoity is the adversary of *nām* (absorption in God's Name); the two cannot abide together" (GG, 560). Gurū Arjan thus addresses *ahaṅkār* personified: " O thou, the cause of birth and death: O thou, the soul of sin: Thou forsakest friends and sowest enmities: Thou spreadest the net of illusion far and wide"(GG, 1358). Even virtues and pieties are rendered sterile if accompanied by *ahaṅkār*, as says Gurū Tegh Bahādur, Nānak IX: " Pilgrimages, fasting and charities if they lead to *gumān* (pride) go waste like the bath by an elephant (who after bathing besmears his body with dirt)" (GG, 1428).

Remedies suggested in Sikhism are humility and *sevā* (self-abnegating deeds of voluntary service). The two are complementary virtues. For Gurū Arjan humility is a weapon against not only *ahaṅkār* but all *vikārs* or evil tendencies. Says he, "Humility is my mace, being the dust of the feet of all, my dagger. These weapons vanquish all vices" (GG, 628). *Sevā* is a highly prized virtue in Sikhism. To quote Gurū Arjan again: "I feel blest rendering service to God's servants by drawing water for them (from the well), by swinging the fan over their heads (in holy congregation) and by grinding corn (for their meals). State, territory and mundane offices are of little value" (GG, 811). Another remedy is to be aware of the insignificance and transience of man in the context of cosmic vastness. Kabīr wonders at the vanity of men who pride themselves upon trifles. "Even kings mightier than Rāvaṇa," he says, "perished in a twinkle"(GG, 1251). Judicious self-respect and a sense of honour should not however be mistaken for pride. Humility does not rule out the former. Says Gurū Nanak: "If one loseth one's honour, all that he eats is unclean" (GG, 142).

BIBLIOGRAPHY

1. Kāhn Siṅgh, Bhāī, *Gurmat Sudhākar*. Patiala, 1970
2. ———, *Gurmat Prabhākar*. Patiala, 1970
3. Jodh Siṅgh, Bhāī, *Gurmati Nirṇaya*. Lahore, 1932
4. Caveeshar, Sardūl Siṅgh, *Sikh Dharam Darshan*. Patiala, 1969
5. Sher Singh, *Philosophy of Sikhism*. Delhi, n.d.
6. Taran Singh, ed., *Teachings of Guru Nanak Dev*. Patiala, 1977
7. Nripinder Singh, *The Sikh Moral Tradition*. Delhi, 1990

L. M. J.

AHIMSĀ. The term *ahimsā* is formed by adding the negative prefix *a* to the word *himsā* which is derived from the Sanskrit root *haṅ*, i.e. 'to kill', 'to harm', or 'to injure', and means not-killing, not-harming, not-injuring. The commonly used English equivalent 'non-violence' is inadequate as it seems to give a false impression that *ahimsā* is just a negative virtue. *Ahimsā* is not mere abstention from the use of force, not just abstention from killing and injuring; it also implies the positive virtues of compassion and benevolence because not-killing and not-injuring a living being implicitly amounts to protecting and preserving it and treating it with mercy. The commandment not to kill and not to offend any living being arises from a feeling of compassion and from a sense of respect for every sentient being. The injunction that one is defiled and becomes sinful by killing and harming a living being is a kind of warning to those who are heedless of the principle of compassion. It thus strengthens the doctrine of compassion and reinstates the sentiment of respect for life. The injunction that the practice of *ahimsā* is meritorious is likewise a kind of promise of reward to those who are compassionate and sensitive to all forms of sentient existence. *Ahimsā* may embrace a variety of motivation — compassion for living beings, earning religious merit, achieving self-purification and dread for the sinful consequences of violence and cruelty. For all these motives there is scriptural authority in India.

In addition to the word *ahimsā*, we have at least three others yielding the same sense. In Emperor Ashoka's Rock Edict No. 4 we have *avihimsā* and *anārambha,* while in the old Pālī canonical texts we have the phrase *pāṇātipāta veramaṇi.* The word *avihimsā* is another form of the word *ahimsā*, non-killing, not-injuring, inoffensiveness, harmlessness, kindness, compassion, benevolence, and love. The word *anārambha* (or *anālambha*) means not-slaughtering (living beings in sacrificial rituals). The pharse *pāṇātipāta veramaṇi* (Skt. *prāṇātipāta viratah)* means abstaining from destroying a living being.

It is now generally admitted that the principle of *ahimsā* originated outside the fold of the Vedic tradition. The non-Vedic ascetic sages, known as *munis* and *śramaṇas,* were perhaps the first teachers of the doctrines of *ahimsā* and *karuṇā* or compassion. However, its clear mention and its exposition as an important element in religious life are found only in the later Vedic age which is also the age of the earliest historical *śramaṇas* such as Pārśvanātha, Kapilamuni, Kaśyapa Buddha, Vardhamāna Mahāvīra, and Śākyamuni Buddha. Pārśvanātha (*circa* 750 BC) is known to have taught the fourfold moral restraint (*caturyāma*) which included the practice of *ahimsā*.

On the other hand, however, the ancient Brāhmaṇical literature gave only partial sanction to the practice of *ahimsā* and continued to respect the custom of slaughtering animals in sacrificial rituals. It shows that originally it was a principle peculiar to the Śramaṇic tradition. The slaughter of animals was, of course, prescribed by the rite, but the practical object of this slaughter was to admit animal flesh for food.

Sikhism accepts *ahimsā* as a positive value, and there are numerous hymns in the Gurū Granth Sāhib, the Sikh Scripture, advising man to cultivate the ethical values of *dayā* (compassion) and *prem* (love). It, however, does not accept *ahimsā* as a mere absence of *himsā* or violence. Love, justice, equality, self-respect and righteousness are some of the overriding social values to guarantee which even *himsā* would be permissible.

Sikhs' social and ethical values are all derived from their metaphysical doctrine. Sikhism believes in the unicity of God, who in His manifest form pervades the entire creation. Thus, all the created beings in this phenomenal world are His manifestation and intrinsically one with Him. This idea of inherent unity of being with the Supreme Being debars man from using *himsā* or violence against another being because that would amount to hurting the Divine. This ontological doctrine of divine unity is in Sikhism the basis of all positive values of *ahimsā* such as social equality, love, compassion, charity and philanthropy. Gurū Arjan, in one of his hymns, adjures man "not to injure anyone so that thou mayst go to thy true home with honour." Mercy or compassion towards living beings is said to be equivalent in merit earned by pilgrimage to sixty-eight holy spots. This religious value attached to the practice of mercy affirms the principle of *ahimsā*. Gurū Tegh Bahādur, Nānak IX, also says that one of the marks of a wise man is that he does not terrorize others nor does he allow himself to be terrorized by others.

The Sikh tradition is also replete with instances of sacrifices made for the sake of justice, righteousness and human freedom. Gurū Arjan and Gurū Tegh Bahādur laid down their lives to vindicate the right to freedom and religious belief. The creation of the Khālsā Panth by Gurū Gobind Siṅgh, Nānak X, and the use of sword as sanctioned by him were also to vindicate the same values. The positive values of *ahimsā* like compassion, love, universal brotherhood, freedom and self-respect must prevail. However, if these are violated, man must resist. When all peaceful methods for such resistance are exhausted, the use of sword, so says Gurū Gobind Siṅgh, is lawful (*Zafarnāmah,* verse 22). The use of sword, however, is not for any personal gain or advancement; it has to be for the general good. Thus was the doctrine of *ahimsā* reinterpreted. The Gurūs affirmed their faith in its positive values, but if *himsā* became necessary to resist and defeat the forces violating these values, it was not considered antagonistic to *ahimsā*.

BIBLIOGRAPHY

1. Davids, T. W. Rhys, "Ahimsā" in *Encyclopaedia of Religion and Ethics*. Ed. James Hastings. Edinburgh, 1964
2. Jack, Homer A. , ed., *Religion for Peace*. Delhi, 1973
3. Harbans Singh, *Peace Imperatives in Sikhism*. Patiala, 1991

L. M. J.

ĀHLŪVĀLĪĀ MISL. *See* MISLS

AHMADĪYAH MOVEMENT, started in the late nineteenth century as a reforming and rejuvenating current in Islam, originated in Qādīāṅ in Gurdāspur district of the Punjab. In the 1880's, Mirzā Ghulām Ahmad, son of the chief land-owning family of Qādīāṅ, after he had received revelations and preached a renewal of Islamic faith, began to draw followers. Although he had been educated traditionally by tutors in *Qur'ān* and *hadīth*, Ahmad had been sent to Siālkoṭ by his father to serve his apprenticeship as a law clerk and to train for the legal profession. Unsuccessful in his work and while becoming increasingly religious, Ahmad came in contact with Christian missionaries and became convinced that they posed a threat to Islam. Following the advent of the Ārya Samāj in the Punjab in 1877, Ghulām Ahmad also realized the threat posed by renascent militant Hinduism.

Spurred by a commitment to Islam reinforced by revelatory experiences, and aware of the growing threat posed by Christianity and Hinduism, Mirzā Ghulām Ahmad, in 1880, at the age of 40, began to publish a four-volume work, *Barāhīn-i-Ahmadīyah,* in which he attempted to refute the claims of several Hindu reform movements that they were superior to Islam. In 1889, he permitted his followers to make *bay'at* or confirm their allegiance to him. This *bay'at* was not the kind made by Sūfīs in joining a *tarīqah* or order but rather more of the traditional Islamic commitment made to a *khalīfah*.

In 1891, Ghulām Ahmad claimed to be the *masīh maw'ūd* (Promised Messiah) and *mahdī* of the Muslims. While the former claim was sufficient to bring the wrath of Muslim *'ulamā* or religious scholars down on him, the latter claim was explicitly offensive to most Muslims. The *mahdī*, usually understood by Muslims to be Jesus Christ, is the figure who will come at the end of time to establish the kingdom of God on earth.

Ahmad's claim to be the *mahdī* stemmed from his theory that he was the successor to Jesus. This involved an elaborate explanation proving that Jesus was not in heaven, as taught by Islam, but that on being taken off the cross, Jesus had been treated with a miraculous ointment and cured of his wounds. He had then escaped, wandering eastward, coming finally to Kashmīr. There he ministered to the lost tribes of Israel, until his death at the age of 120. Ghulām Ahmad demonstrated in his book, *Masīh Hindustān Meṅ*, that he had located Jesus' grave on Khān Yār Street in Srīnagar.

By proving that Jesus had died a natural death, Ghulām Ahmad believed he had proved his claims to be *mahdī* and promised Messiah of the Muslims. Through his writings in Urdu and Arabic as well as through his preaching in the Punjabi language, Ahmad won some thousands of followers during his lifetime. In 1891, the first Ahmadīyah *jalsah* or annual community gathering was held at Qādīāṅ. This meeting has been held annually during the last week of December ever since, though since partition it is also held in the new international headquarters at Rabwāh near Chiniot, West Punjab, Pakistan.

While Ahmad's forthright stand against Hindus and Christians at first won him the admiration of certain Islamic sects, his claims to a kind of prophethood and his call for *jihād* by missionary effort rather than by militant activity brought on him the wrath of both Shīah and Sunnī religious leaders. His right to prophecy was also challenged in court. He had also prophesied that the wrath of God would fall upon his enemies. When Paṇḍit Lekh Rām, the militant Ārya Samājist, was murdered by a Lahore Muslim in 1897, two years before the awful death predicted for him by Ghulām Ahmad, communal controversy in Lahore reached an unprecedented level for those times.

Mirzā Ghulām Ahmad's first interaction with the Sikh community occurred in 1895 at the height of his controversy with the Ārya Samāj. After studying Swāmī Dayānand's *Satyārth Prakāsh* (The Light of Truth), in which the Swāmī had attacked every other religion including the Sikh, Ahmad, though he had not heard of any Sikh responses to these attacks, decided to take up "the cudgels against Dayanand to protect the honour of Nanak," according to Ahmad's biographer, Abdur Rahmān Dard. It was thus that Ahmad began a work in Urdu on the life of Gurū Nānak, which not only sought to answer Dayānand's charges against Sikhism but also attempted to separate legend from known facts about Gurū Nānak. Ahmad's ultimate aim in this study was to win over the Sikhs to Islam and to convince the Sikhs that he was the promised Messiah by proving that Gurū Nānak had been a Muslim.

Sikh scholars answered the claims of Mirzā Ghulām Ahmad and refuted his arguments about Gurū Nānak. *Bhārat Sudhār*, an Ārya Samāj journal published at Lahore, sought a rapprochement with the Sikhs by attacking Ahmad.

Since the partition of the Punjab, the principal seat of the Ahmadīyah movement has moved to Rabwāh, Pakistan, with only a token staff remaining to care for the original shrines and buildings of Qādīāṅ, now situated a few miles on the Indian side of the border. In Pakistan the Ahmadīyahs have since been declared a heretic, non-Muslim sect.

BIBLIOGRAPHY

1. Lavan, Spencer, *Ahmadiyah Movement.* Amritsar, 1976
2. Abbott, Freeland, *Islam and Pakistan.* New York, 1968

S. L.

AHMAD SHĀH DURRĀNĪ (1722-1772), the first of the Saddozaī rulers of Afghanistan and founder of the Durrānī empire, belonged to the Saddozaī section of the Popalzaī clan of the Abdālī tribe of Afghāns.

In the 18th century the Abdālīs were to be found chiefly around Herāt. Under their leader Zamān Khān, father of Ahmad Khān, they resisted Persian attempts to take Herāt until, in 1728, they were forced to submit to Nādir Shāh. Recognizing the fighting qualities of the Abdālīs, Nādir Shāh enlisted them in his army. Ahmad Khān Abdālī distinguished himself in Nādir's service and quickly rose from the position of a personal attendant to the command of Nādir's Abdālī contingent in which capacity he accompanied the Persian conqueror on his Indian expedition in 1739. In June 1747, Nādir Shāh was assassinated by Qizilbāshī conspirators at Kuchān in Khurasān. This prompted Ahmad Khān and the Afghān soldiery to set out for Qandahār. On the way they elected Ahmad Khān as their leader, hailing him as Ahmad Shāh. Ahmad Shāh assumed the title of Durr-i-Durrān (Pearl of Pearls) after which the Abdālī tribe were known as Durrānīs. He was crowned at Qandahār where coins were struck in his name. With Qandahār as his base, he easily extended his control over Ghaznī, Kābul and Peshāwar. As for himself, he, as heir to Nādir Shāh's eastern dominions, laid claim to the provinces which Nādir had wrested from the Mughal emperor. He invaded India nine times between 1747 and 1769. He set out from Peshāwar on his first Indian expedition in December 1747. By January 1748, Lahore and Sirhind had been captured. Eventually Mughal forces were sent from Delhi to resist his advance. Lacking artillery and vastly outnumbered, he was defeated at Mānūpur in March 1748 by Mu'īn-ul-Mulk, the son of the Wazīr Qamar ud-Dīn who had been killed in a preliminary skirmish. Ahmad Shāh retreated to Afghanistan and Mu'īn ul-Mulk was appointed governor of the Punjab. Before Mu'īn ul-Mulk could consolidate his position, Ahmad Shāh, in December 1749, again crossed the Indus. Receiving no reinforcements from Delhi, Mu'īn ul-Mulk was forced to make terms with him. In accordance with instructions from Delhi, Ahmad Shāh was promised the revenues of the Chahār Mahāl (Gujrāt, Aurangābād, Siālkoṭ and Pasrūr) which had been granted by the Mughal emperor Muhammad Shāh to Nādir Shāh in 1739. The non-payment of the revenues of the Chahār Mahāl was the reason for his third Indian expedition of 1751-52. Lahore was besieged for four months and the surrounding country devastated. Mu'īn ul-Mulk was defeated in March 1752, but was reinstated by Ahmad Shāh to whom the emperor formally ceded the two *sūbahs* of Lahore and Multān . During this expedition Kashmīr was annexed to the Durrānī empire. By April 1752 Ahmad Shāh was back in Afghanistan. Mu'īn ul-Mulk found the Punjab a troublesome charge and his death in November 1753 only served to intensify the anarchy. All power was for a time in the hands of his widow, Mughlānī Begam, whose profligacy signalled many a rebellion. The Mughal Wazīr Imād ul-Mulk took advantage of this anarchy to recover the Punjab for the empire and entrusted its administration to Ādīnā Beg. Ahmad Shāh immediately set out to recover his lost province. He reached Lahore towards the end of December 1756, and, after an unopposed march, entered Delhi on 28 January 1757. The city was plundered and the defenceless inhabitants massacred. A similar fate befell the inhabitants of Mathurā, Vrindāvan and Āgrā. Towards the end of March 1757, an outbreak of cholera amongst his troops forced Ahmad Shāh to leave India. The territory of Sirhind was annexed to the Afghān empire. Najīb ud-Daulā, the Ruhīlā leader who had supported him, was left in charge of Delhi and his own son, Taimūr, appointed viceroy of the Punjab. He had no sooner left India than the Sikhs, together with Ādīnā Beg, rose in revolt against Taimūr. Early in 1758 Ādīnā Beg invited Marāṭhās to expel the Afghāns from the Punjab. This was accomplished by the Marāṭhās who actually crossed the Indus and held Peshāwar for a few months. These events brought Ahmad Shāh to India once again (1759-61). The Marāṭhās rapidly evacuated the Punjab before the Afghān advance and retreated towards Delhi. They were routed with enormous losses at Pānīpat on 14 January 1761.

After Pānīpat the main factor to reckon with was the growing power of the Sikhs who had constantly been assailing Ahmad Shāh's lines of communication. It was against them that the Afghān invader's sixth expedition (1762) was specifically directed. News had reached him in Afghanistan of the defeat, after his withdrawal from the country, of his general, Nūr ud-Dīn Bāmezaī, at the hands of the Sikhs who were fast spreading themselves out over the Punjab and had declared their leader, Jassā Siṅgh Āhlūvālīā, king of Lahore (1761). To rid his Indian dominions of them once for all, he set out from Qandahār. Marching with alacrity, he overtook the Sikhs as they were withdrawing into the Mālvā after crossing the Sutlej. The moving caravan comprised a substantial portion of the total Sikh population and contained, besides active fighters, a large body of old men, women and children who were being escorted to the safety of the interior of the country. Surprised by Ahmad Shāh, the Sikhs threw a cordon round those who needed protection, and prepared for the battle. Continuing their march in this form, they fought the invaders and their Indian allies desperately. Ahmad Shāh succeeded, in the end, in breaking through the ring and glutted his spite by carrying out a full-scale butchery. Near the village of Kup, near Mālerkoṭlā, nearly 25, 000 Sikhs were killed in a single day's battle (5 February 1762), known in Sikh history as Vaḍḍā Ghallūghārā, the Great Killing. But the Sikhs were by no means crushed. Within four months of the Great Carnage, the Sikhs had inflicted a severe defeat on the Afghān governor of Sirhind. Four months later they were celebrating Dīvālī in the Harimandar (Amritsar) which the Shāh had blown up by gunpowder in April 1762, and were fighting with him again a pitched battle forcing him to withdraw from Amritsar under cover of darkness (17 October). Ahmad Shāh left Lahore for Afghanistan on 12 December 1762.

Ahmad Shāh planned another crusade against the Sikhs and he invited this time his Balūch ally, Amīr Nasīr Khān , to join him in the adventure. He started from Afghanistan in October 1764 and reaching Lahore attacked Amritsar on 1 December 1764. A small batch of thirty Sikhs, in the words of Qāzī Nūr Muhammad, the author of the *Jaṅgnāmah*, who happened to be in the imperial train accompanying the Balūch division, "grappled with the *ghāzīs*, spilt their blood and sacrificed their own lives for their Gurū." Ahmad Shāh came down to Sirhind without encountering anywhere the main body of the Khālsā. This time he went no farther than Sirhind. As he was marching homewards through the Jalandhar Doāb, Sikh *sardārs*, including Jassā Siṅgh Āhlūvālīā, Jassā Siṅgh Rāmgaṛhīā, Chaṛhat Siṅgh Sukkarchakkīā, Jhaṇḍā Siṅgh Bhaṅgī and Jai Siṅgh Kanhaiyā, kept a close trail constantly raiding the imperial caravan. Their depredations caused great annoyance to the Shāh who lost much of his baggage to the Sikhs. The floods in the River Chenāb took a further toll of his men and property, and he returned to Afghanistan mauled and considerably shaken.

The fear of his Indian empire falling to the Sikhs continued to obsess the Shāh's mind and he led out yet another punitive campaign against them towards the close of 1766. This was his eighth invasion into India. The Sikhs had recourse to their old game of hide-and-seek. Vacating Lahore which they had wrested from Afghān nominees, Kābulī Mall and his nephew Amīr Siṅgh, they faced squarely the Afghān general, Jahān Khān at

Amritsar, forcing him to retreat, with 6,000 of the Durrānī soldiers killed. Ahmad Shāh offered the governorship of Lahore to Sikh *sardār*, Lahiṇā Siṅgh Bhaṅgī, but the latter declined the proposal. Jassā Siṅgh Āhlūvālīā, with an army of 30,000 Sikhs, roamed about the neighbourhood of the Afghān camp plundering it to his heart's content. Never before had Ahmad Shāh felt so helpless. The outcome of the unequal, but bitter, contest now lay clearly in favour of the Sikhs. The Shāh had realized that his Indian dominions were at the mercy of the Sikhs and he bowed to the inevitable. His own soldiers were getting restive and the summer heat of the Punjab was becoming unbearable. He, at last, decided to return home, but took a different route this time to avoid molestation by the Sikhs. As soon as Ahmad Shāh retired, Sikhs reoccupied their territories.

The Shāh led out his last expedition in the beginning of 1769. He crossed the Indus and the Jehlum and reached as far as the right bank of the Chenāb and fixed his camp at Jukālīāṅ to the northwest of Gujrāt. By this time the Sikhs had established themselves more firmly in the country. Moreover, dissensions broke out among the Shāh's followers and he was compelled to return to Afghanistan.

On Ahmad Shāh's death in 1772 of the cancerous wound said to have been caused on his nose by a flying piece of brick when the Harimandar Sāhib was destroyed with gunpowder, his empire roughly extended from the Oxus to the Indus and from Tibet to Khurāsān. It embraced Kashmīr, Peshāwar, Multān, Sindh, Balūchistān, Khurāsān, Herāt, Qandahār, Kābul and Balkh.

BIBLIOGRAPHY

1. Ganda Singh, *Ahmad Shah Durrani*. Bombay, 1959
2. Gupta, Hari Ram, *History of the Sikhs*, vol. II. Delhi, 1978
3. Sarkar, Jadunath, *Fall of the Mughal Empire*, vol. II. Delhi, 1971
4. Khushwant Singh, *A History of the Sikhs*, vol. I. Princeton, 1963

B. J. H.

AHMAD, SHAIKH (1564-1624), celebrated Muslim thinker and theologian of the Naqshbandī Sūfī order, was born on 26 May 1564 at Sirhind in present-day Paṭiālā district of the Punjab. He received his early education at the hands of his father, Shaikh 'Abd al-Ahad, and later studied at Siālkoṭ, now in Pakistan. About the year AD 1599, he met Khwājā Muhammad al-Bākī bi-Allah, who initiated him into the Naqshbandī order. Shaikh Ahmad soon became a leading figure in that school and wrote numerous letters and treatises on many fine points of the Sūfī doctrine such as the concepts of prophecy (*nubuwwah*) and sainthood (*walāyah*) and the relationship between *sharī'ah*, i.e. religious law, and *tarīqah*, the mystic path. He disapproved of Emperor Akbar's liberal approach to religion and wanted the rulers to reimpose *jizyah*, a special poll tax on Hindus, not only to suppress them but also to humiliate them. Basic to his philosophy was the idea that the State should be controlled by *sharī'ah*, the Islamic law, which was not to be modified to suit changing circumstances. He was also against the pantheistic and liberal views of other Sūfī sects. He thus antagonized not only the Hindus but also an influential section of the Muslims. Emperor Jahāṅgīr, in order to placate the public sentiment, imprisoned him in 1619 in the Gwālīor Fort. He was, however, released after a year. The next four years Shaikh Ahmad spent at the imperial court. He died on 30 November 1624 at Sirhind where his tomb still stands and attracts pilgrims from all over India and abroad.

Shaikh Ahmad Sirhindī, the most prominent figure of the Naqshbandī order in India, has been given the honorific title of *Mujaddid-i-Alf-i-Sānī*, the renewer of the second millennium (of Islamic era). The collection of his letters entitled *Maktūbāt-i-Imām-i-Rabbānī* (lit. epistles of the divine prelate) has been hailed as a landmark in the development of Muslim religious thought in India. His works and interpretations had a deep influence on Emperor Auraṅgzīb and his State policy. One who derived the most satisfaction from the execution of Gurū Arjan under Emperor Jahāṅgīr's orders in 1606 was Shaikh Ahmad Sirhindī. In his letter as quoted at No. 193, in his *Maktūbāt*, he gave expression to his sense of jubilation over "the execution of the accursed *kāfir* of Goindvāl."

BIBLIOGRAPHY

1. Abbott, Freeland, *Islam and Pakistan*. New York, 1968
2. Friedmann, Yohanan, *Shaykh Ahmad Sirhindi*. London, 1971
3. Gupta, Hari Ram, *History of the Sikhs*, vol. I. Delhi, 1973
4. Harbans Singh, *The Heritage of the Sikhs*. Delhi, 1983

Y. F.

AHMAD YĀR KHĀN ṬIWĀṆĀ (d. 1829), second son of Khān Muhammad Khān, the Ṭiwāṇā chief of Miṭṭhā Ṭiwāṇā, in Shāhpur district, measured swords with Sikhs more than once during Mahārājā Raṇjīt Siṅgh's time. Ahmad Yār Khān revolted against his father and, having succeeded in attracting most of the tribe to his side, compelled him to surrender the chiefship to him. In 1817, Mahārājā Raṇjīt Siṅgh despatched troops under the command of Misr Dīvān Chand against theṬiwāṇā chief at Nūrpur Ṭiwāṇā. The fort was conquered and Ahmad Yār Khān ran away to Jhaṇḍāvālā, situated in the Mankerā territory. On the withdrawal of the Sikh army, with some troops having been left behind under Jasvant Siṅgh Mokal in Nūrpur for guarding the fort, Ahmad Yār Khān came back and recovered control of the country, but he had to withdraw for the second time and again run back to Jaṇḍiālā. The Nawāb of Mankerā gave him no quarter, turned him out from there and imprisoned his sons. He then yielded to the authority of the Mahārājā who granted him a *jāgīr* worth Rs 10,000, subject to the service of sixty horse. In 1821, Mahārājā Raṇjīt Siṅgh left on a campaign against Hāfiz Ahmad Khān, the Nawāb of Mankerā, when Ahmad Yār Khān readily took the opportunity to join him in the enterprise just to settle some old scores with the Nawāb. The assistance rendered by Ahmad Yār Khān and his tribe, the Ṭiwāṇās, during this campaign was of crucial importance. The Mahārājā was especially struck with the handsome and manly bearing of his men and their bold riding, and insisted upon a troop of Ṭiwāṇā horse returning with him to Lahore. Ahmad Yār Khān died in 1829.

BIBLIOGRAPHY

Sūrī, Sohan Lāl, *'Umdāt-ut-Twārīkh*. Lahore, 1885-89

G. S. N.

ĀHRAURĀ, a small town in Mirzāpur district of Uttar Pradesh, 40 km south of Vārāṇasī (25°-20'N, 82°-58'E), has a Sikh shrine called Gurdwārā Bāgh Shrī Gurū Tegh Bahādur Jī Kā. Gurū Tegh Bahādur visited Āhraurā in 1666 in the course of his journey in the eastern parts. It is said that he told a devotee, Bhāī Sādhojī, to plant a tree. This was the beginning of a garden which still exists. From this garden (*bāgh*), the Gurdwārā derives its name. A closet called Nivās Sthān marks the room in which Gurū Tegh Bahādur is said to have stayed. The shrine is registered as Shrī Gurū Siṅgh Sabhā and is managed by a local committee. There is a handwritten copy of the Gurū Granth Sāhib, transcribed in 1799 Bk/AD 1742, kept in the private house of the *granthī*. A small slip, supposed to contain Gurū Tegh Bahādur's autograph, is pasted on it. Another handwritten *pothī* with a similar autograph, is in the possession of another individual, Hīrā

Siṅgh. He has even built a *gurdwārā* named Gurdwārā Gurū Gobind Siṅgh Jī Daskhatī Sāhib in honour of the *pothī*, but keeps the volume in his house and displays it in the Gurdwārā only on special occasions.

BIBLIOGRAPHY

Faujā Siṅgh, *Gurū Teg Bahādur, Yatrā Asthān, Prampravāṅ te Yād Chinn.* Patiala, 1976

M. G. S.

AHWĀL-I-DĪNĀ BEG KHĀN, Persian manuscript of unknown authorship, gives biographical details about Ādīnā Beg Khān, *faujdār* of Jalandhar. The manuscript forms part of the collection of Persian Manuscripts, Sir H. Elliot's Papers, Additional MS. 30780 (ff. 215-292), Extracts relating to India, vol. VIII. 1 , preserved in British Library, London. Copies of the manuscript are also held by Pañjāb University Library, Lahore, Sikh Historical Research Department, Khālsā College, Amritsar, and Dr Gaṇḍā Siṅgh Collection at Punjabi University, Paṭiālā (25 pages in neat and clear handwriting). The last-named collection also holds an English translation of the manuscript.

According to the author, Dīnā (Ādīnā) Beg Khān was born in a poor Arāīṅ, vegetable-growing, family in Sharakpur Paṭṭī village, near Lahore. He started his career as a sepoy exercising jurisdiction over a few villages in Lohīāṅ area near Sultānpur Lodhī for revenue collection. He, through his own prudence and astuteness and by the help of his patron, Lālā Srī Nivās Dhīr, a wealthy merchant of Sultānpur, rose, not without undergoing several ups and downs, to be the virtual ruler of the Jalandhar region. Shrewd in diplomacy and statecraft, he developed as it suited his interests friendly relations with Mughal governors, Afghān invaders, Sikh chiefs and the Marāṭhās. He married only towards the close of his career, but divorced his bride as soon as he learnt that she came of a high Sayyid caste. Thus he died childless and his territories and treasure were upon his death usurped by local chieftains.

M. G. S.

AHWĀL-I-FIRQAH-I-SIKKHĀṄ, variously titled as *Twārīkh-i-Sikkhāṅ, Kitāb-i-Tarīkh-i-Sikkhāṅ* and *Guzārish-i-Ahwāl-i-Sikkhāṅ*, by Munshī Khushwaqt Rāi, is a history in Persian of the Sikhs from their origin to AD 1811. Khushwaqt Rāi was an official newswriter of the East India Company accredited to the Sikh city of Amritsar. It was written at the request of Çol (afterwards General Sir) David Ochterlony, British political agent at Ludhiāṇā on the Anglo-Sikh frontier. Opinion also exists that it was written at the suggestion of Charles Theophilus Metcalfe. Henry Prinsep and Capt Murray based their accounts of the Sikhs on this manuscript. The British Library preserves a manuscript (No. Or. 187) under the title *Kitāb-i-Tārikh-i-Sikkhāṅ* (in the Preface it is designated *Guzārish-i-Ahwāl-i-Sikkhāṅ*). The name of the author is not mentioned. Copies of the manuscript are also preserved at Punjab State Archives, Paṭiālā, and at Khālsā College, Amritsar. The manuscript (No. M/800) entitled *Twārikh-i-Ahwāl-i-Sikkhāṅ* at the Punjab State Archives has 194 folios. The account begins with the birth of Gurū Nānak in 1469, followed by lives of the succeeding Gurūs, of the career and exploits of Bandā Siṅgh, the chiefs of the Āhlūvālīā, Phūlkīāṅ and Kanhaiyā *misls*, the hill chiefs of Kāṅgṛā or the Kaṭoch dynasty, and of the Sukkarchakkīā *misl*. Events of the reign of Mahārājā Raṇjīt Siṅgh up to 1811 such as Holkar's arrival in the Punjab in 1805 and the conquests of Paṭhānkoṭ and Ḍaskā are described in some precise detail. The account closes with the arrival in 1811 of the Afghān embassy for a meeting with Raṇjīt Siṅgh. Khushwaqt Rāi's work furnishes considerable information on the early history of the Sikhs though it is not exempt from inaccuracies or personal prejudices. The account of Sikhs' rise to power is however factual and straightforward.

The manuscript remains unpublished. An Urdu translation, the only one known to exist, was discovered by Dr Gaṇḍā Siṅgh in the armoury from under the debris after an accidental gunpowder explosion in Qilā Mubārak at Paṭiālā on 1 May 1950. The first 16 pages of the manuscript were missing. A Punjabi translation of the manuscript made by Milkhī Rām Kishan is preserved at the Department of Punjab Historical Studies, Punjabi University, Paṭiālā. The manuscript awaits publication.

Gb. S.

ĀĪ PANTH, one of the twelve sects of *yogīs*, whose adherents worship Āī Bhavāṇī, a tribal female deity, believed to be an extension of Śakti. Śiva in the form of *ardhanārīśvara* is said to have two forms represented by his own halves. His right side is the male whose followers are called *dakṣināchārīs*, whereas his left portion represents the female known as Śakti, the basic power also called Ambā, Durgā, Kālī or Bhavānī. Worshippers of the female aspect of Śiva are called *vāmamārgīs*, known for their peculiar beliefs and customs. They accept no taboos in the matter of food and accord religious sanction to sexual freedom. They practise austerities; for a living they would go begging from house to house. Their living style (*jugat*) consists in smearing their bodies with ashes (*bibhūt*), wearing heavy rings (*mundā* or *mundrā*) in their split ears and covering their bodies with a loose shroud (*khinthā*). When they go out begging, they carry a begging bowl in one hand and a club *(ḍaṇḍā)* or fire-tongs in the other.

In course of time, many sects based on this *śakti* principle appeared throughout the length and breadth of the Indian subcontinent. Āī Panth is one of them and the Mahar tribals once found almost exclusively along the River Sutlej, opposite Fāzilkā, especially in the Montgomery, Multān and Bahāwalpur area, worshipped this female spirit and kept her image in their homes. Gurū Nānak during his preaching journeys came across several varieties of *yogīs* at places like Gorakh Haṭaṛī, Achal Vaṭālā, Sumer Mountain and Gorakhmatā, now known as Nānak Matā. There are extensive references in the Gurū Granth Sāhib which testify to these meetings. In the *Japu* (stanza 28) Gurū Nānak exhorts an anonymous *yogī* beloning to the Āī Panth to cultivate control over the mind which was more important than all bodily exercises and discipline. Says Gurū Nānak: "Make contentment thy earrings, modesty thy begging bowl and wallet and the Lord's meditation thy ashes. Let the thought of death be thy patched coat, chastity like that of a virgin's body thy life's deportment, and faith in God thy staff. The realization of brotherhood with all is the real creed of the Āī Panth. "O Yogī, deem the conquering of the self as the conquest of the world" (GG, 6).

BIBLIOGRAPHY

1. Bhattacharyya, N. N., *Indian Mother Goddess*. Calcutta, 1971
2. ———, *History of the Tantric Religion*. Delhi, 1982
3. Chakravarti, Chintaharan, *Tantras: Studies on Their Religion and Literature*. Calcutta, 1972
4. Rose, H.A. , *A Glossary of the Tribes and Castes of the Punjab and North-West Frontier Province* [Reprint]. Patiala, 1970

Jd. S.

AJAB, BHĀĪ, a Jaṭṭ of Saṅghā clan who lived in the village of Ḍarauḷī, now called Ḍarauḷī Bhāī, in Farīdkoṭ district of the Punjab. He, like his brothers Umar Shāh and Ajāib, forsook his faith in Sultān Sakhī Sarwar, became a Sikh and rendered devoted service at the time of the construction of the Harimandar at Amritsar. The three brothers were appointed *masands,* or parish leaders, in the areas of Mogā, Zīrā and Dharamkoṭ. They often used to quote Gurū Arjan's line:

" If God so wills, He may keep one alive even after breath had departed the body." They were especially gratified once to have the line expounded by the Gurū himself.

BIBLIOGRAPHY

1. Macauliffe, M.A., *The Sikh Religion*. Oxford, 1909
2. Giān Siṅgh, Giānī, *Twārīkh Gurū Khālsā* [Reprint]. Patiala, 1970

T. S.

AJAB SIṄGH (d. 1705), son of Bhāī Manī Rām, a Rājpūt Sikh of 'Alīpur in Multān district, now in Pakistan, came to Anandpur with his father and four brothers, and received the rites of initiation at the inauguration of the Khālsā by Gurū Gobind Siṅgh on the Baisākhī day of 1699. He remained in Gurū Gobind Siṅgh's retinue until his death in the battle of Chamkaur on 7 December 1705.

BIBLIOGRAPHY

1. Padam, Piārā Siṅgh, and Giānī Garjā Siṅgh, eds. , *Gurū kīāṅ Sākhīāṅ*. Patiala, 1986
2. Harbans Singh, *Guru Tegh Bahadur*. Delhi, 1982

M. G. S.

AJĀIB, BHĀĪ , a Saṅghā Jaṭṭ who embraced the Sikh faith in the time of Gurū Arjan. He belonged to the village of Ḍaraulī Bhāī, in present-day Farīdkoṭ district. Two of his brothers, Umar Shāh and Ajab, were the Gurū's *masands* or vicars. Bhāī Ajāib took part in *sevā*, voluntary labour of hands, at the time of digging of the Amritsar pool and construction of the Harimandar.

See AJAB, BHĀĪ

BIBLIOGRAPHY

1. Macauliffe, Max Arthur, *The Sikh Religion*. Oxford, 1909
2. Giān Siṅgh, Giānī, *Twārīkh Gurū Khālsā* [Reprint]. Patiala, 1970

T. S

AJĀIB SIṄGH (d. 1705), one of the martyrs of Chamkaur, was the son of Bhāī Manī Rām, a Rājpūt Sikh of the time of Gurū Tegh Bahādur and Gurū Gobind Siṅgh. Manī Rām had presented five of his sons including Ajāib Siṅgh to Gurū Gobind Siṅgh at Anandpur where they took *amrit* or baptism of the double-edged sword on the historic day of the birth of the Khālsā on 30 March 1699. Ajāib Siṅgh thereafter remained in attendance upon the Gurū. He fell fighting at Chamkaur on 7 December 1705.

BIBLIOGRAPHY

1. Padam, Piārā Siṅgh, and Giānī Garjā Siṅgh, eds. , *Gurū kīāṅ Sākhīāṅ*. Patiala, 1986
2. Kuir Singh, *Gurbilās Pātshāhī 10*. Patiala, 1968

M. G. S.

AJĀT SĀGAR, by Surjan Dās Ajāt, is the religious book of the Ajātpanthī sect of the Udāsīs. Written in AD 1851, the only known manuscript of the work was available in the Sikh Reference Library, Amritsar, until it perished during the Blue Star action in the holy premises in 1984. The author Surjan Dās (father: Bāgh Siṅgh, mother: Gulāb Devī), a disciple of Sant Ṭahil Dās who was in the Bhagat Bhagvānīe sect of the Udāsīs, established his *gaddī* at Ajnevāl, in Gujrāṅwālā district, now in Pakistan. Surjan Dās preached the ideal of a casteless (*a* = without; *jāt* = caste) society and thus came to be called Ajāt and his followers Ajātpanthī. Another of his works was *Surjan Bodh* which is held in the Pañjāb University Library, Chaṇḍīgaṛh, under MS. No. 111. The poetry of Surjan Dās is uneven, though he tries to keep close to the *gurbāṇī* idiom. Transience of the world, man's forgetfulness of God and the importance of *nām* are the principal themes of *Ajāt Sāgar*. Gurū Nānak has been depicted in this work as "the destroyer of evil."

BIBLIOGRAPHY

Randhīr Siṅgh, Bhāī, *Udāsī Sikhāṅ dī Vithiā*. Chandigarh, 1972

D. S.

AJĪT SIṄGH (1881-1947), patriot and revolutionary, was born in February 1881 at Khaṭkaṛ Kalāṅ, in Jalandhar district of the Punjab, the son of Arjan Siṅgh and Jai Kaur. He had his early education in his village and then at Sāīṅ Dāss Anglo-Sanskrit High School, Jalandhar, and D.A.-V. College, Lahore. He later joined the Bareilly College to study law, but left without completing the course owing to ill health. He became a *munshī* or teacher of Oriental languages, establishing himself at Lahore. In 1903, he was married to Harnām Kaur, daugher of Dhanpat Rāi, a pleader of Kasūr.

Ajīt Siṅgh came into the political arena in the agrarian agitation in the Punjab in 1906-07. The passing of the Punjab Land Colonization Bill (1906) and enhancement in the rates of land revenue and irrigation tax had created widespread discontent in the rural areas. The Colonization Bill aimed at stopping further fragmentation of land holdings in the Chenāb Colony—mostly inhabited by Sikh ex-soldiers—by introducing the law of primogeniture. This, and some other clauses of the Bill, caused great resentment among the cultivators, who regarded it as unjustified interference with their traditional rights insofar as they related to the division of property. Popular feelings were further aroused by the prosecution, in 1907, of the editor of the *Punjabee*, an English-language bi-weekly of anti-government views.

In this climate of social unrest and of anti-British sentiment, Ajīt Siṅgh supported the setting up in 1907 of a revolutionary organization, Bhārat Mātā Society, with headquarters at Lahore. A large number of protest meetings and demonstrations against the Colonization Bill were held not only in villages but also in important cities such as Rāwalpiṇḍī, Gujrāṅwālā, Multān, Lahore and Amritsar. Many of these were addressed by Ajīt Siṅgh who had become a violent critic of the government. Besides referring to the immediate problems the peasantry faced, he exhorted the people to strive for the freedom of the country and end foreign rule. On the recommendation of the Punjab Government, the Government of India deported Ajīt Siṅgh to Mandalay on 2 June 1907.

Upon his release in November 1907, Ajīt Siṅgh returned to the Punjab amid much popular acclaim. He did not wait long to resume his anti-British activities. He launched a newspaper, the *Peshwā*, with Sūfī Ambā Prasād as its editor. He also brought out a series of tracts and pamphlets, such as *Bāg͟hī Masīhā, Muhibbān-i-Watan, Bandar Bāṇṭ* and *Uṅgalī Pakaṛte Pañjā Pakaṛā,* attacking British rule in India. Fearing prosecution for an article in the *Peshwā*, Ajīt Siṅgh, along with Zīā ul-Haq, escaped to Persia in 1909. There he continued to work for India's freedom and succeeded in building up a small revolutionary centre at Shīrāz. In May 1910, he and his associates started, in Persian, a revolutionary journal, the *Hayāt*. In September 1910, he shifted to Bushire, with a view to establishing contact with his comrades in India through Indian traders and seamen. His activities alarmed the British government. Considering further residence in Iran unsafe, Ajīt Siṅgh proceeded to Turkey via Russia where he met Mustafā Kamāl Pāshā, Turkish general and statesman. From Turkey he went to Paris and met Indian revolutionaries. Later he shifted to Switzerland where he made the acquaintance of Lālā Har Dayāl and revolutionaries from other parts of the world—South America, Germany, Italy, Poland, Russia, Egypt and Morocco. Here he also met the Italian leader and future dictator, Mussolini and the famous Russian revolutionist, Trotsky. Towards the end of 1913, he shifted to France which he left soon after the outbreak of World War I, to go to Brazil where he remained from 1914 to 1932. From Brazil it was easier for him to be in touch with the leaders of the G͟hadr Party in the United States. He also formed a society of Indians settled in Brazil to make them aware of their duty towards their mother country and also to raise funds to support India's struggle for freedom. From 1932 to 1938, Ajīt Siṅgh worked in France, Switzerland and Germany. He renewed his contacts with the Indian revolutionaries working in Europe. He also met Subhās Chandra Bose. He wanted to return to India where, he thought, he could work more effectively for the cause dear to his heart. But the government, viewing him as a "dangerous agitator" and an "undesirable foreigner" (he having secured Brazilian citizenship), did not allow his entry into the country.

On the eve of World War II, Ajīt Siṅgh shifted to Italy where, in order to intensify his activities and mobilize Italian public and government support in favour of India, he formed Friends of India Society. During his stay in Italy he formed a revolutionary army of the Indian prisoners of war. His passionate speeches in Hindustānī from Rome Radio and his own example of sacrifice and suffering for the country made a deep impact on the Indian soldiers. After the fall of Italy, Ajīt Siṅgh was imprisoned and kept in an Italian jail and later, when Germans surrendered, he was shifted to a jail in Germany. Hard life in military camps told upon his health. After the formation of the Interim government in the country under Jawāharlāl Nehrū, Ajīt Siṅgh returned to India via London. On 8 March 1847, he reached Karāchī and then came to Delhi where the great wanderer was given a warm welcome by his countrymen. In Delhi, he was the guest of Jawāharlāl Nehrū, and he participated in the Asian Relations Conference which was then in session in Delhi.

Ajīt Singh died at Dalhousie on 15 August 1947—the day India became an independent nation.

BIBLIOGRAPHY

1. Ganda Singh, ed., *History of the Freedom Movement in the Panjab*, vol. IV *(Deportation of Lala Lajpat Rai and Sardar Ajit Singh)*. Patiala, 1978
2. Pardaman Singh and Joginder Singh Dhanki, ed., *Buried Alive*. Chandigarh, 1984
3. Mohan, Kamlesh, *Militant Nationalism in the Punjab 1919-1935*. Delhi, 1985
4. Puri, Harish K., *Ghadar Movement*. Amritsar, 1983
5. Deol, Gurdev Siṅgh, *Shahīd Ajīt Siṅgh*. Patiala, 1973
6. Jagjīt Siṅgh, *G͟hadar Pārṭī Lahir*. Delhi, 1979

Pd. S.

AJĪT SIṄGH PĀLIT (d. 1725), adopted son of Mātā Sundarī, the mother of Sāhibzādā Ajīt Siṅgh . Little is known about the family he came of except that Mātā Sundarī took him over from a goldsmith of Delhi and adopted him because of his striking resemblance with her son, Ajīt Siṅgh, who had met a martyr's death at Chamkaur. She treated him with great affection and got him married to a girl from Burhānpur. Emperor Bahādur Shāh, considering Ajīt Siṅgh to be Gurū Gobind Singh's heir, ordered, on 30 October 1708, the bestowal of a *k͟hill'at* upon him as a mark of condolence for the Gurū's death. When Bahādur Shāh came to the Punjab in 1710 personally to handle the situation created by the exploits of Bandā Siṅgh, he ordered Rājā Chhatrasāl Bundelā to bring Ajīt Siṅgh to his court. Ajīt Siṅgh appeared in the imperial court on 26 September 1710 and was given a robe of honour, but on 27 December 1710 the emperor placed him under the surveillance of one Kār-talab K͟hān. On 1 June 1711, he was transferred to the camp of Sarbarāh K͟hān. On 30 December 1711, Bahādur Shāh assigned to him the *jāgīr* of Gurū Chakk (Amritsar). His purpose in honouring Ajīt Siṅgh as Gurū Gobind Siṅgh's successor was to use him as a counterweight against Bandā Siṅgh Bahādur, who was then leading a general uprising of the Sikhs. Suspecting his Hindu officers to be in sympathy with the Sikhs, Bahādur Shāh had issued a proclamation, early in September 1710, to "all Hindus employed in imperial offices to shave off their beards." On 10 December 1710 was issued a special order to all *faujdārs* around Shāhjahānābād "to kill the worshippers of Nānak wherever found." Ajīt Siṅgh, however, revelled in royal patronage. Back in Delhi after Bahādur Shāh's death in 1712, he continued to live in style as a courtier and grew arrogant and haughty even towards Mātā Sundarī. Once as she reproached him for his pretensions and for his desire to wear Gurū Gobind Siṅgh's weapons, he threatened to attack her. Mātā Sundarī disowned him, and he started living in a separate house. On receiving a complaint one day that Ajīt Siṅgh and his followers had mocked an assembly of Muslims at prayer, the emperor ordered him to present himself at court with hair shaven or face severe punishment. Ajīt Siṅgh cut off his hair and abjectly begged the emperor's pardon. This deprived him of whatever respect he commanded among the Sikhs of Delhi. Mātā Sundarī left Delhi and went to live at Mathurā with Ajīt Siṅgh's wife, Tārā Bāī, and his son, Haṭhī Siṅgh. Ajīt Siṅgh kept up the pretence of being a *gurū*. Once, in his haughtiness, he caused a Muslim mendicant to be beaten to death by his followers. Under the orders of Emperor Muhammad Shāh, he was sentenced to death by torture. Dragged behind an elephant in the streets of Delhi, he met with a painful end. This was on 18 January 1725. His dead body was cremated in Sabzī Maṇḍī area, where a shrine was raised in his memory. His son, Haṭhī Siṅgh, as he grew up, also belied the expectations of Mātā Sundarī, who came back to Delhi. Haṭhī Siṅgh, a pretender to gurūship like his father, went to live at Burhānpur after the sack of Mathurā by Ahmad Shāh Durrānī in 1757. He died there, issueless, in 1783.

BIBLIOGRAPHY

1. Padam, Piārā Siṅgh and Giānī Garjā Siṅgh, eds., *Gurū kīāṅ Sākhīāṅ*. Patiala, 1986
2. Chhibbar, Kesar Siṅgh, *Baṅsāvalīnāmā Dasāṅ Pātshāhīāṅ Kā*. Chandigarh, 1972
3. Sainãpati, Kavī, *Srī Gur Sobhā*. Patiala, 1980

S. S. A.

AJĪT SIṄGH, RĀJĀ, ruler of Lāḍvā, was born the son of Gurdit Siṅgh who had acquired territory around Thānesar after the conquest by Sikhs in 1764 of the Mug͟hal province of Sirhind. Gurdit Siṅgh, who belonged to the same clan as Raṇjīt Siṅgh, originally came from the village of Veīṅ Poīṅ, about 15 km south of Amritsar, and was a member of the Karoṛsiṅghīā *misl* or confederacy. In addition to his other acquisitions, Gurdit Siṅgh received in *jāgīr* from Mahārājā Raṇjīt Siṅgh the village of Baddovāl, near Ludhiāṇā. After Gurdit Siṅgh's death, Ajīt Siṅgh succeeded him as ruler of the Lāḍvā state. Ajīt Siṅgh, like his father, continued to be an ally of Raṇjīt Siṅgh in his campaigns of conquest and received favours from him. He built a bridge over the River Sarasvatī at Thānesar, and received the title of *Rājā* from Lord Auckland, the British governor-general of India. In the first Anglo-Sikh war, Ajīt Siṅgh fought on the side of the Sikhs against the British. He along with Raṇjodh Siṅgh Majīṭhīā crossed the Sutlej at Phillaur with a force of 8,000 men and 70 guns. In rapid marches Ajīt Siṅgh and Raṇjodh Siṅgh seized the forts of Fatehgaṛh, Dharamkoṭ, and Baddovāl, and stole into Ludhiāṇā cantonment, setting many of the barracks on fire. In the action fought on 21 January 1846 at Baddovāl, Sir Henry Smith's column was attacked and more than 200 of his men were slain. But Ajīt Siṅgh suffered a defeat in the action fought in 'Alīwāl after a week (28 January) and fled the battlefield. Ajīt Siṅgh's estates were confiscated by the British in 1846 and he was arrested and detained at Allāhābād. He, however, contrived to escape after killing his keeper and after long wanderings is supposed to have died in Kashmīr.

BIBLIOGRAPHY

1. Sūrī, Sohan Lāl, *'Umdāt-ut-Twārīk͟h*. Lahore, 1885-89

2. Griffin, Lepel, *The Rajas of the Punjab* [Reprint]. Delhi, 1971
3. Harbans Singh, *The Heritage of the Sikhs*. Delhi, 1983

S. S. B.

AJĪT SIṄGH, SĀHIBZĀDĀ (1687-1705), the eldest son of Gurū Gobind Siṅgh, was born to Mātā Sundarī at Pāoṇṭā on 26 January 1687. The following year, Gurū Gobind Siṅgh returned with the family to Anandpur where Ajīt Siṅgh was brought up in the approved Sikh style. He was taught the religious texts, philosophy and history, and had training in the manly arts such as riding, swordsmanship and archery. He grew up into a handsome young man, strong, intelligent and a natural leader of men. Soon after the creation of the Khālsā on 30 March 1699, he had his first test of skill. A Sikh *saṅgat* coming from Poṭhohār, northwest Punjab, was attacked and looted on the way by the Raṅghaṛs of Nūh, a short distance from Anandpur across the River Sutlej. Gurū Gobind Siṅgh sent Sāhibzādā Ajīt Siṅgh, barely 12 years of age then, to that village. Ajīt Siṅgh at the head of 100 Sikhs reached there on 23 May 1699, punished the Raṅghaṛs and recovered the looted property. A harder task was entrusted to him the following year when the hill chiefs supported by imperial troops attacked Anandpur. Sāhibzādā Ajīt Siṅgh was made responsible for the defence of Tārāgaṛh Fort which became the first target of attack. This, according to the *Bhaṭṭ Vahīs,* happened on 29 August 1700. Ajīt Siṅgh, assisted by Bhāī Ude Siṅgh, a seasoned soldier, repulsed the attack. He also fought valiantly in the battles of Nirmohgaṛh in October 1700. On 15 March 1701, a *saṅgat,* column of Sikh devotees, coming from Daṛap area (present Siālkoṭ district) was waylaid by Gujjars and Raṅghaṛs. Sāhibzādā Ajīt Siṅgh led a successful expedition against them. As instructed by Gurū Gobind Siṅgh, he took out (7 March 1703) 100 horsemen to Bassī, near Hoshiārpur, and rescued a young Brāhmaṇ bride forcibly taken away by the local Paṭhān chieftain. In the prolonged siege of Anandpur in 1705, Sāhibzādā Ajīt Siṅgh again displayed his qualities of courage and steadfastness. When, at last, Anandpur was vacated on the night of 5-6 December 1705, he was given command of the rearguard. As the besiegers, violating their solemn promises for a safe conduct to the evacuees, attacked the column, he stoutly engaged them on a hill-feature called Shāhī Ṭibbī until relieved by Bhāī Ude Siṅgh. Ajīt Siṅgh crossed the Sarsā, then in spate, along with his father, his younger brother, Jujhār Siṅgh, and some fifty Sikhs. Further reduced in numbers by casualties at the hands of a pursuing troop from Ropaṛ, the column reached Chamkaur in the evening of 6 December 1705, and took up position in a *gaṛhī,* high-walled fortified house. The host, since swelled by reinforcements from Mālerkoṭlā and Sirhind and from among the local Raṅghaṛs and Gujjars, soon caught up with them and threw a tight ring around Chamkaur. An unequal but grim battle commenced with the sunrise on 7 December 1705—in the words of Gurū Gobind Siṅgh's *Zafarnāmah,* a mere forty defying a million. The besieged, after they had exhausted the meagre stock of ammunition and arrows, made sallies in batches of five each to engage the encircling host with sword and spear. Sāhibzādā Ajīt Siṅgh led one of the sallies and laid down his life fighting in the thick of the battle. Gurdwārā Qatalgaṛh now marks the spot where he fell, followed by Sāhibzādā Jujhār Siṅgh, who led the next sally. An annual fair is held in commemoration of their martyrdoms on the 8th of the Bikramī month of Poh (December-January). The martyrdom of two of the sons of Gurū Gobind Siṅgh in the battle of Chamkaur is substantiated by a contemporary record in the form of an official letter preserved in a MS., *Ahkām-i-*

Ālamgīrī by Emperor Auraṅgzīb's official letter writer, Mirzā 'Ināyat Ullah Khān Ismī (1653-1725). The relevant extract from the MS., translated into English, reads:

> Received the letter containing miscellaneous matters including the arrival of Gobind, the worshipper of Nānak, to a place 12 *kos* from Sirhind; the despatch of a force of 700 with artillery and other material; his being besieged and vanquished in the *havelī* [i.e. large walled house] of a *zamīndār* of village Chamkaur and the killing of his two sons and other companions; and the capture of his mother and another son....

BIBLIOGRAPHY

1. Chhibbar, Kesar Siṅgh, *Baṅsāvalīnāmā Dasāṅ Pātshāhīāṅ Kā*. Chandigarh, 1972
2. Padam, Piārā Siṅgh, *Chār Sāhibzāde*. Patiala, 1967
3. Kuir Siṅgh, *Gurbilās Pātshāhī 10*. Patiala, 1968
4. Harbans Singh, *Guru Gobind Singh*. Chandigarh, 1966
5. Macauliffe, M.A., *The Sikh Religion*. Oxford, 1909

S. S. A.

AJĪT SIṄGH SANDHĀṄVĀLĪĀ (d. 1843), son of Basāvā Siṅgh Sandhāṅvālīā, was a leading actor in the gruesome drama of intrigue and murder enacted in the Sikh kingdom following the passing away of Mahārājā Raṇjīt Siṅgh. One of the younger generation of the Sandhāṅvālīās, he outstripped his uncles, Atar Siṅgh Sandhāṅvālīā and Lahiṇā Siṅgh Sandhāṅvālīā, in political ambition and conspiracy. In 1840, on his return from the expedition against the Rājā of Maṇḍī, he joined his uncles in supporting Rāṇī Chand Kaur's claim against Sher Siṅgh. Fearful of the Ḍogrā minister, Dhiān Siṅgh, who had supported Mahārājā Sher Siṅgh against Rāṇī Chand Kaur, Ajīt Siṅgh fled Lahore in January 1841 clandestinely, along with his jewellery, and arrived in Ludhiāṇā to seek the help and protection of the British political agent. Meanwhile, his uncle Atar Siṅgh also left Lahore and joined him in Ludhiāṇā. At this, Sher Siṅgh besieged the Sandhāṅvālīā fortress at Rājā Sāṅsī and ordered that both Lahiṇā Siṅgh Sandhāṅvālīā and his son, Kehar Siṅgh Sandhāṅvālīā, be detained in Koṭ Kāṅgṛā.

The Sandhāṅvālīā refugees in the British territory now came out openly against Mahārājā Sher Siṅgh. They wrote letters inciting the officers of the Khālsā army to rise against him. Ajīt Siṅgh took the journey to Calcutta to plead with the British governor-general the cause of Rāṇī Chand Kaur. Eventually, obtaining Mahārājā Sher Siṅgh's pardon through the good offices of the British, Atar Siṅgh and Ajīt Siṅgh returned to Lahore in May 1843. The unsuspecting Mahārājā released Lahiṇā Siṅgh Sandhāṅvālīā and Kehar Siṅgh Sandhāṅvālīā as well and restored all the confiscated Sandhāṅvālīā fiefs. Ajīt Siṅgh and other Sandhāṅvālīā *sardārs*, however, nursed feelings of malice in secret and waited for their opportunity to strike. On 15 September 1843, as Mahārājā Sher Siṅgh was inspecting troops in the Bārādarī of Shāh Bilāval, Ajīt Siṅgh shot him dead with an English rifle which he cunningly pretended to present to the Mahārājā for inspection. As the Mahārājā fell, Ajīt Siṅgh drew his sword and severed his head. The senior Sandhāṅvālīā Lahiṇā Siṅgh murdered, in a garden close by, the Mahārajā's minor son, Kanvar Partāp Siṅgh. Later, inside the Lahore Fort, while apportioning the office of prime minister among themselves, Ajīt Siṅgh killed Dhiān Siṅgh on the spot. Hīrā Siṅgh, son of Dhiān Siṅgh, and his uncle, Suchet Siṅgh, aroused a section of the army, and with General Avitabile's crack battalions, they besieged the Fort on 16 September 1843, and in the resultant action both Ajīt Siṅgh and Lahiṇā Siṅgh were slain. Their heads were cut off and bodies quartered and hung on the different gates of the city. At Rājā Sāṅsī the Sandhāṅvālīā fort was razed to the ground, and the houses of all Sandhāṅvālīā chiefs were destroyed. It was then ordered that henceforth all Sandhāṅvālīā lands be ploughed with asses instead of oxen. The only Sandhāṅvālīā chief to escape retribution was Atar Siṅgh who fled from Ūnā to the British territory.

BIBLIOGRAPHY

1. Sūrī, Sohan Lāl, *'Umdāt-ut-Twārīkh*. Lahore, 1885-89
2. Griffin, Lepel and C.F. Massy, *Chiefs and Families of Note in the Punjab*. Lahore, 1909
3. Chopra, Barkat Rai, *Kingdom of the Punjab*. Hoshiarpur, 1969
4. Chopra, Gulshan Lall, *The Panjab as a Sovereign State*. Hoshiarpur, 1960
5. Harbans Singh, *The Heritage of the Sikhs*. Delhi, 1983

B. J. H.

AJITTĀ, BHĀĪ, a Randhāvā Jaṭṭ, whose name occurs in Bhāī Gurdās's roster of prominent Sikhs of Gurū Nānak, *Vārāṅ*, XI. 14, was a resident of the village of Pakkhoke Randhāve, close to the present town of Ḍerā Bābā Nānak in Gurdāspur district of the Punjab. It was at Pakkhoke Randhāve that Gurū Nānak's wife and children stayed with his parents-in-law after he had left home to go out to preach his word. Ajittā first met Gurū Nānak as he arrived in his village at the conclusion of his long travels and sat near the well owned by him. Ajittā was instantly converted and sought instruction from the Gurū. Bhāī Manī Siṅgh, *Sikhāṅ dī Bhagat Mālā*, records the discourse that took place between them.

BIBLIOGRAPHY

1. Manī Siṅgh, Bhāī, *Sikhāṅ dī Bhagat Mālā*. Amritsar, 1955
2. Giān Siṅgh, Giānī, *Twārīkh Gurū Khālsā* [Reprint]. Patiala, 1970
3. Bhallā, Sarūp Dās, *Mahimā Prakāsh*. Patiala, 1971
4. Harbans Singh, *Guru Nanak and Origins of the Sikh Faith*. Bombay, 1969

Gn. S.

AJMER CHAND, ruler of Kahlūr (Bilāspur), one of the princely states in the Śivāliks. He succeeded his father, Rājā Bhīm Chand, who had retired in his favour. Bhīm Chand had led battles against Gurū Gobind Siṅgh, and his son, Ajmer Chand, continued the hostility. He formed a league of the hill chieftains and solicited help from Emperor Auraṅgzīb in order to evict Gurū Gobind Siṅgh from Anandpur which fell within his territory. Their attacks upon Anandpur in 1700 and 1703 proved abortive, but Gurū Gobind Siṅgh had to evacuate the citadel in 1705 under pressure of a prolonged siege. Ajmer Chand joined the imperial troops in their pursuit of the Gurū up to Chamkaur.

Ajmer Chand died in 1738.

BIBLIOGRAPHY

1. Kuir Siṅgh, *Gurbilās Pātshāhī 10*. Patiala, 1968
2. Hutchinson, J., and J. Ph. Vogel, *History of the Punjab Hill States*. Lahore, 1933
3. Harbans Singh, *Guru Gobind Singh*. Chandigarh, 1966
4. Macauliffe, Max Arthur, *The Sikh Religion*. Oxford, 1909

K. S. T.

AJMER SIṄGH was the name given a seventeenth-century Muslim recluse of Chhatteāṇā, a village in present-day Farīdkoṭ district of the Punjab, as he received the initiatory rites of the Khālsā. His original name was Ibrāhīm, popularly shortened to Brahmī or Bahmī. According to an old chronicle, *Mālvā Desh Raṭan dī Sākhī Pothī*, Ibrāhīm had himself dug a grave, duly lined with brick and mortar into which he intended to descend, through a hole he had kept for the purpose, when his time came. But when he met Gurū Gobind Siṅgh, who had come to Chhatteāṇā after the battle of Muktsar (1705), he was so deeply moved that he requested to be admitted to the Khālsā fold. The Gurū, says Bhāī Santokh Siṅgh, *Srī Gur Pratāp Sūraj Granth*, observed, "Being a

Muslim desiring with conviction to join the Khālsā Panth, you are setting a good example. Among the Khālsā it is only proper that every one, high or low, take the *pāhul* (baptism of the double-edged sword)." Ibrāhīm received the *pāhul* at the hands of Bhāī Mān Siṅgh, and the Gurū gave him his new name, Ajmer Siṅgh. Ajmer Siṅgh diligently learnt the Sikh prayers which he regularly recited morning and evening.

BIBLIOGRAPHY

1. *Mālvā Desh Raṭan dī Sākhī Pothī*. Amritsar, 1968
2. Santokh Siṅgh, Bhāī, *Srī Gur Pratāp Sūraj Granth*. Amritsar, 1927-35
3. Giān Siṅgh, *Giānī, Twārīkh Gurū Khālsā* [Reprint]. Patiala, 1970

P. S. P.

AJṚĀṆĀ KALĀṄ, village in Kurukshetra district of Haryāṇā, 12 km southwest of Shāhābād (30°-10'N, 76°-53'E), is sacred to Gurū Tegh Bahādur who stopped here in 1670 while on his way from Delhi to join his family at Lakhnaur. A Mañjī Sāhib established to commemorate the visit of the Gurū exists on the southern side of the village. It consists of a small octagonal domed structure, built on a wider base. The Gurdwārā is administered privately by a Sikh family of the village. A civil suit for the control of the shrine is going on between this family and the Shiromaṇī Gurdwārā Parbandhak Committee as represented by the Gurdwārā Committee of Shāhābād.

BIBLIOGRAPHY

Faujā Siṅgh, *Gurū Teg Bahādur, Yātrā Asthān, Pramprāvāṅ te Yād Chinn*. Patiala, 1976

M. G. S.

AJUDHIĀ PARSHĀD, DĪWĀN (1799-1870), soldier and civil administrator in Sikh times, was the adopted son of Dīwān Gaṅgā Rām. Mahārājā Raṇjīt Siṅgh first employed Ajudhiā Parshād in 1819 to serve in the military office in Kashmīr. Three years later, he was recalled to Lahore and appointed paymaster of the special brigade (Fauj-i-Khās), organized by Generals Allard and Ventura. After the death in 1826 of Dīwān Gaṅgā Rām, Ajudhiā Parshād received the title of Dīwān and was assigned to a variety of duties. As a protocol officer, he received in 1831 Alexander Burnes at Multān. In 1839, he accompanied the army of the Indus under Sir John Keane. Later, in 1840, he took charge of the Fauj-i-Khās and in 1843, he became its permanent commander. At the end of the Anglo-Sikh war in February 1846, when the Sikh army crossed the Sutlej to wage war with the British, he resigned. However, after the treaty of 16 March 1846, he was assigned, along with Captain Abbott to demarcating the boundary between Kashmīr and the Punjab. The British government granted him an annual pension of 7, 500 rupees. From April 1849 to September 1851, he remained on duty with the deposed young prince, Duleep Siṅgh.

Dīwān Ajudhiā Parshād has chronicled in Persian prose the events of the first Anglo-Sikh war (1845-46). The narrative, an eyewitness account of the battles of Pherūshahr and Sabhrāoṅ, has been translated into English by V.S. Sūrī and published under the title *Waqāi-Jaṅg-i-Sikhāṅ*.

Ajudhiā Parshād died in 1870.

BIBLIOGRAPHY

1. Sūrī, Sohan Lāl, *'Umdāt-ut-Twārīkh*. Lahore, 1885-89
2. Griffin, Lepel, and C.F. Massy, *Chiefs and Families of Note in the Punjab*. Lahore, 1909
3. Gupta, Hari Ram, *Punjab on the Eve of the First Sikh War*. Chandigarh, 1956
4. Sūrī, V. S., ed., *Waqāi-Jaṅg-i-Sikhāṅ*. Chandigarh, 1975

H. R. G.

AKĀL, lit. timeless, immortal, non-temporal, is a term integral to Sikh tradition and philosophy. It is extensively used in the *Dasam Granth* hymns by Gurū Gobind Siṅgh, who titled one of his poetic compositions *Akāl Ustati,* i.e. In Praise (*ustati*) of the Timeless One (*akāl*). However, the concept of Akāl is not peculiar to the *Dasam Granth.* It goes back to the very origins of the Sikh faith. Guru Nānak used the term in the Mūl Mantra, the fundamental creedal statement in the *Japu,* the first composition in the Gurū Granth Sāhib. The term also occurs in Gurū Rām Dās, Nānak IV, who uses it in conjunction with *mūrat* in Sirī Rāga *chhants* (GG, 78) and in conjunction with *purakh* in Gauṛī Pūrabī Karhale (GG, 235).The term occurs more frequently in Gurū Arjan's *bāṇī* (e.g. GG, 99, 609, 916, 1079 and 1082). We encounter the use of the term *akāl* in Kabīr as well.

It may be noted that the term *akāl* has been used in Gurbāṇī in two forms : (a) as a qualifier or adjective, and (b) as a substantive. In the expression *akāl mūrati,* the first part is often treated as a qualifier, even though some interpreters take the two words as independent units, viz. *akāl* and *mūrati.* In the Mārū Rāga Kāl and Akāl have been clearly used as substantives by Gurū Arjan and Kabīr. Gurū Gobind Siṅgh more often than not treats the expression as a noun. *Akāl Ustati* is the praise of Akāl and "Hail, O Akāl, Hail, O Kirpāl!" of *Jāpu* also takes the related expressions as substantives. The meaning of Akāl in this context is 'timeless', 'non-temporal', 'deathless', 'not governed by temporal process', or 'not subject to birth, decay and death'. This appears to be negative coining in each case. But the intent is affirmative. Akāl as deathless or non-temporal implies everlasting reality, eternal being, or Transcendent Spirit; it further implies Eternity, Being, or Essence. The linguistic form may be negative, but the semantic implication is unmistakably affirmative.

Gurū Gobind Siṅgh, in his *Jāpu* in the *Dasam Granth,* has designated the Supreme Reality Akāl. It is the same Reality that was given the epithet of *sati* in the Gurū Granth Sāhib. 'Sati' is the primordial name of the Eternal Being (GG, 1083) . All the names that we utter in respect of God are functional or attributive names. The basic reality is nameless, in Gurū Gobind Siṅgh's terminology *anāma.* But even the Nameless can serve as a name. When we say Brahman is featureless, 'featurelessness' becomes its feature. Niraṅkār (Formless) is a name, and so are other epithets so coined. To signify what they regard as the Eternal Spirit, beyond the pale of time, temporality or cosmic processes, the Gurūs have chosen the terms *sati* and *akāl. Vāhigurū* is a positive *saguṇa* substitute for the negative *nirguṇa* term Akāl.

Gurū Gobind Siṅgh's *bāṇī* is a repository of concepts and terms, especially of the epithets relating to 'time'. Besides Kāl and Akāl, he uses Mahā Kāl (macro-time) and Sarb-Kāl (all-time) to indicate a Being above and beyond the eventful times of the universe. For him, Kāl itself is a dimension of Akāl, the only difference being the process that characterizes temporal events, and the eternality of Akāl. Every occurrence or event has a beginning and an end, each event is a link in the on-going process of Time. The cosmic drama or the wondrous show of the world is all a creation of Time. The power of Time controls worldly events; the only entity independent of time is Time itself, and that is Akāl, the Timeless One. That is how God is both Time and Timeless in Gurū Gobind Siṅgh's *bāṇī.* The temporal aspect of Time is the immanent aspect, the presence of Spiritual Essence in each worldly occurrence. It is the 'personality' of the Supreme, the *chit* or consciousness of *sat-chit-anand.* The other, transcendent aspect, is the Eternal, the Beyond, the Inexpressible, the Fathomless, Nirguṇa Brahman, assigned the name Akāl, the Timeless One or the One-beyond-Time.

Akāl is not a fixed, unmoving substance,

but the dynamic spiritual principle of the entire cosmic existence. The phenomenal world emanates from Spirit, and the Spirit permeates the world. Akāl in Sikh *weltanschauung* is not mere consciousness, blank and void, but is the Creative Spirit, as the expression Kartā Purakh implies. In other words, creativity is the core of Akāl. And it is creativity that is manifest in the dimension of Kāl. Acting through Time, the Timeless One creates worlds and beings of the worlds. It is through creativity that the Timeless One transforms itself from *nirguṇ* to *sarguṇ*, from the *aphur* state into *saphur* state, from the pre-creation *sunn*, or dormant essence, into cosmic existence.

The creativity of Akāl is not confined to the timeless and temporal aspects of the Supreme. Through its *sarguṇ* facet the *nirguṇ* assumes the character of the Divine, of the gracious God, the loving Lord or Prabhu of the devotees. From 'It' the Ultimate becomes 'He', the person with whom communication is sought and established. From 'Akāl', He becomes 'Srī-Akāl'. The Sikh slogan and popular form of greeting *Sati Srī Akāl* sums up the concept that the timeless Being is the singular Eternal Reality. The phrase combines the concepts of Sati and Akāl, implying that the Eternal and the Timeless are one; Sati itself is the Everlasting Lord-beyond-Time. Thus, the creative essence turns the metaphysical Being into active principle of the world, into conscious Power involved in the cosmic process, into Hero or Master of the world, cherishing His creation with benign joy. Being the beneficent Lord, He lends some of His creativity to the created beings. Humanity draws its creativity and creative energy from the Divine reservoir of creativity.

Valour and heroism are pronounced characteristics of the Sikh tradition. The Akāl of Gurū Gobind Siṅgh is All Steel (*Sarb-Loh*), symbolically applauding valour. Gurū Nānak had applied the epithet of Jodhā-Mahābalī-Sūrmā to the valiant in *Japu*, 27 (GG, 6). Gurū Gobind Siṅgh, Nānak X, expresses His creativities with terms such as Sarb-Kāl (*Jāpu*, 19, 20), Sarb-Dayāl (*Jāpu*, 19, 23, 28), Sarb-Pāl (*Jāpu*, 28, 45). He calls Him Glorious and great, Super-form, Yogī of yogīs, Moon of moons, Melody of melodies, Rhythm of the dance, Liquidity of waters, Movement of the winds. He is Akāl as well as Kripāl, the Compassionate Lord. In fact, the whole composition of *Jāpu*, with its wide range of attributive names for the Timeless Being focusses on the Akāl-Kripāl unipolarity. The Impersonal appears through all persons, the Timeless encompasses all temporal beings emanating from His Essence. He transcends the human world, yet He is full of compassion for all. His timeless essence permeates the temporal existence.

The concept of Akāl, central to Gurū Gobind Siṅgh's *Jāpu* has percolated to the social, political and cultural aspects of Sikh life. Inspired by its theme, they call the Gurūs' *bāṇī*, *Akālī-Bāṇī*. The political wing of the community is known as Akālī Dal. The slogan *Sati Srī Akāl* has become a form of greeting for the Punjabis in general. The process had been initiated much earlier, half a century before the advent of Gurū Gobind Siṅgh on the scene. The Sixth Gurū, Gurū Hargobind, had already identified the throne built at Amritsar as Akāl Ta<u>kh</u>t—the Throne of the Timeless One.

BIBLIOGRAPHY

1. Kapur Singh, *Pārāśaraprasna* [Reprint]. Amritsar, 1989
2. Gopal Singh, *Thus Spake the Tenth Master*. Patiala, 1978
3. Talib, Gurbachan Singh, *Selections from the Holy Granth*. Delhi, 1982
4. Jodh Siṅgh, Bhāī, *Gurmati Nirṇaya*. Lahore, 1945

W. S.

ĀKAL, BHĀĪ, a carpenter resident of Vaḍḍā

Ghar in present-day Farīdkoṭ district of the Punjab and, according to *Gurbilās Chhevīṅ Pātshāhī*, maternal grandfather of the celebrated Bhāī Rūp Chand, became a devotee of Gurū Rām Dās. He also served Gurū Arjan and Gurū Hargobind. He was a man of devotion and piety.

BIBLIOGRAPHY

Gurbilās Chhevīṅ Pātshāhī. Patiala, 1970

M. G. S.

AKĀL BUṄGĀ, lit. the abode of the Timeless One, is the building that houses the Akāl Takht in the precincts of the Darbār Sāhib at Amritsar. The term is also used sometimes synonymously with Akāl Takht. Strictly speaking, while Akāl Takht is the institution possessing and exercising the highest religious authority for Sikhs, Akāl Buṅgā is the historical Gurdwārā where Akāl Takht is located.

See AKĀL TAKHT and AMRITSAR

BIBLIOGRAPHY

1. Giān Siṅgh, Giānī, *Twārīkh Srī Amritsar*. Amritsar, 1977
2. Sukhdiāl Siṅgh, *Akāl Takht Sāhib*. Patiala, 1984
3. *Gurbilās Chhevīṅ Pātshāhī*. Patiala, 1970
4. Dilgeer, Harjinder Siṅgh, *The Akal Takht*. Jalandhar, 1980

M.G.S.

AKĀLĪ, a term now appropriated by members of the dominant Sikh political party, the Shiromaṇī Akālī Dal, founded in 1920, and groups splitting from it from time to time, was earlier used for Nihaṅgs (*q.v.*), an order of armed religious zealots among the baptized Sikhs. The word Nihaṅg is from the Persian *nihaṅg* meaning crocodile, alligator, shark or water dragon, and signifies qualities of ferocity and fearlessness. The term Akālī is originally from Akāl, the Timeless One. Gurū Nānak (1469-1539) described God as Akāl Mūrati, the Eternal Form. Gurū Hargobind (1595-1644), who adopted a royal style, named his seat at Amritsar Akāl Takht, the Everlasting Throne. It was, however, Gurū Gobind Siṅgh who popularized the term Akāl as an attributive name of God. A set of his hymns is entitled *Akāl Ustati* (God's Praises). When he instituted, in 1699, the Khālsā, a body of warriors initiated through baptism of the double-edged sword, he gave them the war-cry "Sat Srī Akāl !" (theTrue, the Radiant, the Timeless One). It was probably from this war-cry that the Siṅghs or initiated Sikhs, variously called Bhujaṅgīs and Nihaṅgs, came also to be known as Akālīs. Although the Nihaṅgs trace their origin from Sāhibzādā Fateh Siṅgh, the youngest son of Gurū Gobind Siṅgh or from Bhāī Mān Siṅgh, a Sikh of the Tenth Gurū, the earliest use of Akālī as a title appears with the name of Naiṇā Siṅgh, an eighteenth-century Nihaṅg warrior and a junior leader in the Shahīd *misl*. Akālī Naiṇā Siṅgh is credited with introducing the tall pyramidal turban common among the Nihaṅgs to this day. Akālīs became prominent as an organized force under Akālī Phūlā Siṅgh (d. 1823), one time ward and disciple of Naiṇā Siṅgh. Phūlā Siṅgh's Akālīs formed the crack brigade in Mahārājā Raṇjīt Siṅgh's army as well as the custodians of the nation's conscience and morals. After the occupation of the Punjab by the British in 1849, Akālī regiments were disbanded and, military service being their only career, their numbers dwindled rapidly. In the 1892 census only 1,376 persons were returned as "Sikh Akalis or Nihangs," and in 1901 this number further came down to a bare 431, besides 136 who registered themselves as Akālīs by caste. Of these 457 were males and 110 females. During the Gurdwārā reform movement (1920-25), the term Akālī came to be associated with the reformers who organized themselves into a political body, the Shiromaṇī Akālī Dal. Even the reform movement itself was referred to as the Akālī movement. A rival body set up in mid-

1930's also named itself the Central Akālī Dal. The Nihaṅgs are no longer called Akālīs. The last prominent Nihaṅg known as an Akālī was Akālī Kaur Siṅgh (1886-1953).

BIBLIOGRAPHY

1. Gulati, Kailash Chander, *The Akalis: Past and Present.* Delhi, 1974
2. Harbans Singh, *The Heritage of the Sikhs.* Delhi, 1983
3. Cunningham, J.D., *A History of the Sikhs.* London , 1849

M. G. S.

AKĀLĪ, THE, a Punjabi daily newspaper which became the central organ of the Shiromaṇī Akālī Dal, then engaged in a fierce struggle for the reformation of the management of the Sikh *gurdwāras* and a vehicle for the expression of nationalist political opinion in the Punjab in the wake of the massacre of Jalliāṅvālā Bāgh in Amritsar (1919), followed by the annual session of the Indian National Congress. The first issue of the paper was brought out from Lahore on 21 May 1920 to honour the anniversary of the martyrdom of the Fifth Gurū of the Sikhs, Gurū Arjan. The paper was the brain-child of Master Sundar Siṅgh of Lyallpur who had fanatically pleaded the need for a periodical in Punjabi dedicated to the patriotic cause. Borrowing the paltry sum of Rs 500 from a friend, he launched the newspaper under the masthead "Akālī." He had the support of Sardār Harchand Siṅgh of Lyallpur, Tejā Siṅgh Samundarī, Master Tārā Siṅgh, Professor Nirañjan Siṅgh, Sardūl Siṅgh Caveeshar and Bhāī Dalīp Siṅgh who later fell a martyr at Nankāṇā Sāhib in the massacre of Akālī agitators in 1921. Sundar Siṅgh persuaded Giānī Hīrā Siṅgh Dard to take over as editor of the *Akālī*. Three months later Maṅgal Siṅgh, a University graduate, then serving as a *tahsīldār* in the revenue department of the government, resigned his post to join hands with Giānī Hīrā Siṅgh.

They between them made the *Akālī* very popular—Hīrā Siṅgh by his resounding patriotic verse and Maṅgal Siṅgh by his enlightened and penetrating comment. A series of incidents such as the Nankāṇā massacre, Gurū kā Bāgh brutality and the deposition by the British of the Sikh ruler of the princely state of Nābhā further radicalized Sikh opinion. The *Akālī* came into conflict with the government on several occasions and suffered forfeiture and suppression. Once it had to seek asylum under a baker's roof from where it was published clandestinely every morning. Passing through many vicissitudes and changing its name several times, it has survived to this day. In October 1922, it was merged with the *Pradesī Khālsā*, a daily run by Master Tārā Siṅgh at Amritsar. The *Pradesī Khālsā* was launched with funds provided by Sikhs settled in foreign countries, hence the name *Pradesī* (foreign). The *Akālī* merging with this paper shifted to Amritsar and assumed the new name *Akālī te Pradesī*. For a time, the *Akālī* was published from Amritsar in Urdu, Persian script, simultaneously with the *Akālī te Pradesī* (Punjabi). The *Akālī te Pradesī* too went through a succession of suspensions and prosecutions by government. Yet it kept re-emerging every time with renewed vigour and with a sharper militant message. In 1930 when it was banned under the Press Act, it was registered under the new name, *Akālī Patrikā*. It continued publication under this name from Lahore until 1939 when it reverted to the old name *Akālī*. After the partition of the Punjab in 1947, it shifted back to Amritsar. These days it is being published from Jalandhar under the name of *Akālī Patrikā*.

BIBLIOGRAPHY

1. Sūbā Siṅgh, *Pañjābī Pattarkārī dā Itihās.* Chandigarh, 1978
2. Nirañjan Siṅgh, *Jīvan Vikās.* Delhi, 1970
3. Harbans Singh, *Aspects of Punjabi Literature.*

Firozpur, 1961
4. Barrier, N. Gerald, *The Sikhs and Their Literature*. Delhi, 1970

S. S. B.

AKĀLIĀṄ DĪ CHHĀUṆĪ, also called Chhāuṇī Nihaṅgāṅ, situated outside Ghī Maṇḍī Sherāṅvālā Gate, Amritsar, was the seat of the Sikh warrior and hero, Akālī Phūlā Siṅgh (d. 1823). The present six-storeyed *burj* (tower) was built by the Nihaṅgs, a warrior sect of the Sikhs, in the early twentieth century with public donations. The ground floor of the tower consists of a big hall with four doors. The upper storeys have windows opening on all sides. The dome at the top is built of concrete. The central hall has a marble floor. A small shrine dedicated to Gurū Hargobind stands in the precincts of the Chhāuṇī. It commemorates the *akhāṛā* (wrestling-pit) where Sikhs in the time of Gurū Hargobind practised physical feats. Adjoining the shrine is an old well said to have been got dug by Gurū Hargobind.

Gn. S.

AKĀLĪ DAL, CENTRAL, a political organization of the Sikhs set up in March 1934 as a parallel body to the Shiromaṇī Akālī Dal. The latter was formed on 14 December 1920 to assist the Shiromaṇī Gurdwārā Parbandhak Committee in its campaign for the reformation of the management of the Sikh places of worship and, under pressure of the agitation it had launched, the Punjab Legislative Council passed on 7 July 1925 the Sikh Gurdwaras Act, providing for a Central Board elected by the Sikhs to take over control of the shrines. On 9 July 1925, the Governor of the Punjab announced that such of the Akālī prisoners as accepted the provisions of the Act and were willing to work by them would be freed. Some of the agitation leaders gave the required assurance and were released, but 15 of them, including Master Tārā Siṅgh and Tejā Siṅgh Samundarī, refused and preferred to stay back in jail. This split the Akālīs. Those released tried to capture the Central Board through the first elections under the Sikh Gurdwaras Act held in June 1926, but could win only 26 out of a total of 120 seats, 85 going to the Shiromaṇī Akālī Dal represented by those still under detention. Government withdrew the ban on the Akālīs on 27 September 1926 and the remaining batch of leaders was released from custody. At the first meeting of the Central Board held on 2 October 1926, Sardār Khaṛak Siṅgh (stilll in jail convicted in connection with the Gurū kā Bāgh agitation) and Master Tārā Siṅgh were unanimously elected president and vice-president, respectively. The Board, renamed at that first meeting Shiromaṇī Gurdwārā Parbandhak Committee, assumed charge of Gurdwārā management on 27 November 1926.

The Shiromaṇī Akālī Dal functioned as a well-knit party for the next three years under the leadership of Bābā Khaṛak Siṅgh, but fissures began to appear in the wake of elections to the Shiromaṇī Gurdwārā Parbandhak Committee in 1930. Bābā Khaṛak Siṅgh not only resigned the presidentship of the Shiromaṇī Akālī Dal, but also left the party along with Sardār Bahādur Mehtāb Siṅgh, Jathedār Kartār Siṅgh Jhabbar and Harbaṅs Siṅgh Sīstānī. Master Tārā Siṅgh took over as president of the Shiromaṇī Akālī Dal and remained at the helm of Sikh affairs for the next three decades. The question of constitutional reforms in the country under discussion at the time prompted the two groups to sink their differences for a while. But the next Gurdwārā elections coming off in February 1933 brought the differences to the surface again. At the Sikh National Conference convened at Lahore on 24-25 March 1934, Bābā Khaṛak Siṅgh presiding, the formation of a separate party—at first called Sikh National League and then renamed Central Akālī

Dal—was announced. The Conference, while rejecting the Communal Award as injurious to the Sikhs and to the cause of intercommunal harmony in the country, demanded 30 per cent representation for the Sikhs in the Punjab legislature. It exhorted the Sikhs to be ready to make all possible sacrifices for the achievement of their political objective and declared that the party would enlist one lakh volunteers for this purpose. Bābā Kharak Siṅgh became president of the Central Akālī Dal, with Amar Siṅgh, editor of the *Sher-i-Punjab*, as working president and Giānī Sher Siṅgh and Harbaṅs Siṅgh Sīstānī as vice-presidents. Among the members of the executive committee were Jaswant Siṅgh Jhabāl, Master Motā Siṅgh Anandpurī, Gopal Siṅgh Sāgarī and Jaṅg Bahādur Siṅgh.

The Central Akālī Dal's major concerns were safeguarding the religious entity of the Sikhs and ensuring a political status for them in the national setup. With the Shiromaṇī Akālī Dal it remained in constant conflict, especially because of the latter's alignment with the Indian National Congress. In the Shiromaṇī Gurdwārā Parbandhak Committee, it formed a strong opposition block led by men of the stature of Giānī Sher Siṅgh and Amar Siṅgh of the *Sher-i-Punjab*. It controlled under the provisions of the Gurdwaras Act some of the important Sikh shrines such as those at Amritsar (the Golden Temple), Nankāṇā Sāhib and Muktsar. In the 1936-37 general elections under the Government of India Act of 1935, Central Akālī Dal supported the newly formed Khālsā National Party which had the upper hand as against the Shiromaṇī Akālī Dal. But gradually the influence of the Central Akālī Dal waned. It convened All-India Akhaṇḍ Hindustān Conference at Lahore on 6 June 1943 to protest against the Muslim League's demand for Pakistan and the Āzād Punjab scheme sponsored by the Shiromaṇī Akālī Dal. It held an Anti-Āzād Punjab Conference at Pañjā Sāhib on 16 August 1943 and another Akhaṇḍ Hindustān Conference at Chakvāl on 15 September 1943. One of its last political acts was the submission of a memorandum to the British Cabinet Mission in 1946. The demands set forth in the Memorandum included grant of complete independence to a united India with a strong Centre and without the right for the provinces to secede; the establishment of a special court to guarantee and safeguard the rights of the minorities; special representation for the Sikhs in the Constituent Assembly and in the Central legislature; representation for the Sikhs in the Punjab legislature on an equal footing with the Hindus and Muslims; joint electorates, with reservation of seats for the minorities; guarantee for the protection of the religious and cultural interests of the Sikhs and of their share in the armed forces of the country.

The All-India Sikh League, controlled by the Central Akālī Dal, passed a resolution in its Lahore session on 4 June 1946 asking the British Government "to fix a date for the immediate withdrawal of British forces of occupation; to wipe out the undemocratic feudal and semi-feudal system of Indian states and the privileged position of the Princes; to limit the over-riding powers of the Viceroy only to foreign policy during the period of the Interim National Government; to purge the Cabinet Mission's proposal of the communal virus being injected through the system of provincial grouping and representation on communal basis; and to take immediate steps for the liquidation of the Indian debt through the transfer of British vested interests in finance and industry..." It further demanded that the Interim National Government be composed of elected members of the Central legislature and that complete sovereignty be granted to the Constituent Assembly without reservation and limitations.

No efforts were made to revive the Central Akālī Dal in Independent India. One of its principal architects, Sardār Amar Siṅgh of the *Sher-i-Punjab*, died on 9 July 1948. Bābā Khaṛak Siṅgh spent last sixteen years of his life in political retirement in Delhi.

BIBLIOGRAPHY

1. Sarhadi, Ajit Singh, *Punjabi Suba*. Delhi, 1970
2. Mohinder Singh, *The Akali Movement*. Delhi, 1978
3. Tuteja, K. L. , *Sikh Politics*. Kurukshetra, 1984
4. Josh, Sohan Siṅgh, *Akālī Morchiāṅ dā Itihās*. Delhi, 1972
5. Dilgeer, Harjinder Siṅgh, *Shiromaṇī Akālī Dal*. Jalandhar, 1978

J. B. S.

AKĀLĪ DAL KHARĀ SAUDĀ BĀR, an organization of Akālī reformers working for the liberation of Sikh shrines from the control of conservative Udāsī priests or *mahants*. The organization was originally called Khālsā Dīwān Kharā Saudā Bār set up in 1912 and comprised volunteers mostly from a cluster of villages inhabited by Virk Jaṭṭ Sikhs in the Lower Chenāb Canal Colony in Sheikhūpurā district, now in Pakistan. Canal colonies in West Punjab were usually called *bārs*, lit. semi-forests, which these areas really were before the introduction of canal irrigation. The name Kharā Saudā came from the historical Gurdwārā Sachchā Saudā, also called Kharā Saudā, near Chūhaṛkāṇā town around which the Virk villages were situated. The Dīwān was in the beginning purely reformist in its aim, and was engaged in the spread of Sikh religion and education. But with the heightening up of the political tempo after the implementation of Rowlatt Acts and particularly after the Jalliāṅvālā Bāgh tragedy in April 1919, the Dīwān became active politically, too, and came to be called Akālī Dal Kharā Saudā Bār. The reorganization took place at a convention held at Gurdwārā Mahārāṇī Nakaiṇ at Sheikhūpurā on 24 December 1920 when Akālī Jathā Kharā Saudā Bār was set up with Kartār Siṅgh Jhabbar as its Jathedār. Among other top-ranking leaders were Tejā Siṅgh Chūhaṛkāṇa and Maṅgal Siṅgh Serokā. The Dal played a leading part in the liberation of several historical *gurdwārās*, most notable among them being Bābe dī Ber at Siālkoṭ, Pañjā Sāhib at Hasan Abdāl, Janam Asthān at Nankāṇā Sāhib, and Gurdwārā Sachchā Saudā, Chūhaṛkāṇā, where the Dal had its headquarters. The Dal was ultimately amalgamated with the Shiromaṇī Akālī Dal *(q.v.)*.

Akālī Dal Kharā Saudā Bār worked in close co-operation with the Akālī Jathā of Bhāī Lachhmaṇ Siṅgh of Dhārovālī, one of the Nankāṇā Sāhib martyrs. According to the C.I.D. report of 22 February 1922, the "combined membership of these two *jathās* of the Sheikhūpurā district is about 2, 200."

BIBLIOGRAPHY

1. Naraiṇ Siṅgh, *Akālī Morche te Jhabbar*. Delhi 1967
2. Pratāp Siṅgh, Giānī, *Gurdwārā Sudhār arthāt Akālī Lahir*. Amritsar, 1975
3. Josh, Sohan Siṅgh, *Akālī Morchiāṅ dā Itihās*. Delhi, 1972

M. G. S.

AKĀLĪ DAL, SHIROMAṆĪ (*shiromaṇī* = exalted, foremost in rank; *dal* = corps, of *akālī* volunteers who had shed fear of death), the premier political party of the modern period of Sikhism seeking to protect the political rights of the Sikhs, to represent them in the public bodies and legislative councils being set up by the British in India and to preserve and advance their religious heritage, came into existence during the Gurdwārā reform movement, also known as the Akālī movement, of the early 1920's. Need for reform in the conditions prevalent in their places of worship had been brought home to Sikhs by the Siṅgh Sabhā upsurge in the last quarter of the nineteenth century. It had been increasingly felt that the purity of Sikh precept and practice could not be recovered unless there was a change in the structure of *gurdwārā* management which had been in the hands of clergy who had come into control of the Sikh holy places since the times Sikhs had been driven by Mug͟hal repression to seek safety in remote hills and deserts. A kind of professional coenobitism, contrary to the character of Sikhism, had since developed. Most of the clergy had reverted to Brāhmaṇical ritualism rejected by the Gurūs, and had become neglectful of their religious office. They had converted ecclesiastical assets into private properties, and their lives were not free from the taint of licentiousness and luxury. Even before the beginning of the Gurdwārā reform movement, sporadic voices had been raised against this retrogression and maladministration of these places of worship. Organized platforms to pursue reform had developed in the form of regional K͟hālsā *dīwāns.* For example, a K͟hālsā Dīwān had been set up in the Mājhā area in 1904, though it was soon afterwards merged with the Chief K͟hālsā Dīwān, successor to the Lahore and Amritsar *dīwāns* of the earlier phase of the Siṅgh Sabhā movement. But the Gurdwārā reform meant a confrontation with the *mahants* or the installed clergy who had the support of the government, and the Chief K͟hālsā Dīwān avoided, as a matter of policy, to antagonize the government. The Mājhā Dīwān was therefore revived in 1918 as Central Mājhā K͟hālsā Dīwān. It was becoming clear that the reformers would settle for nothing less than a complete restructuring of the maṇagement of the *gurdwārās* and ousting of the *mahants* through negotiations, legal action, or failing both, forcible eviction. All the different strategies were pressed into service at Gurdwārā Bābe dī Ber at Siālkoṭ with dramatic success. Srī Akāl Tak͟ht or Tak͟ht Akāl Buṅgā was vacated by the clergy under fear of force and/or losing caste by association with the "low-caste."

With the establishment in November 1920 of Shiromaṇī Gurdwārā Parbandhak Committee *(q.v.)*, the need arose for developing a system to co-ordinate the work of regional *jathās*, structured groups or bands of men and women. There were at least ten such *jathās* espousing *gurdwārā* reform in different regions of the Punjab. According to a contemporary press report, Master Motā Siṅgh was the first to suggest the formation of a Gurdwārā Sevak Dal of 500 Sikh volunteers, including 100 paid whole-timers, all ready for action at the call of the Shiromaṇī Gurdwārā Parbandhak Committee. At about the same time, Jathedār Kartār Siṅgh Jhabbar, who had liberated Gurdwārā Pañjā Sāhib, Hasan Abdāl, on 18 November 1920, had suggested in a report from there that a *jathā* of 200 Siṅghs be got up to be despatched wherever action was. These proposals were discussed at a meeting of leading activists in front of the Akāl Tak͟ht on 14 December 1920. It was decided to form a central *dal,* corps or contingent, of which Sarmukh Siṅgh Jhabāl was designated the first *jathedār* (president). This date (14 December 1920) is generally accepted to be the date of the formation of the Shiromaṇī Akālī Dal, although the title *shiromaṇī* was added only through a resolution passed by the Dal on 29 March 1922. A confidential memorandum (22 February 1922) of the Punjab police dealing with the activities of the Akālī Dal and Shiromaṇī Gurdwārā Parbandhak Committee during 1920-22 does not contain this appellation for the Dal, but refers to it as the "Central Akālī Dal" to stress its linking role for the various confederated *jathās.* According to this report, "the present strength of the Akālī Dal, including the figures for the Native States, is at least 25,000 and may be greatly in excess of that estimate." In some contemporary government documents, the Dal is also referred to as Akālī Fauj (army) which "functioned on military lines, marched in fours, wore badges, carried flags and organised camps."

The Shiromaṇi Akālī Dal was meant to function under the overall control of the Shiromaṇī Gurdwārā Parbandhak Committee making available to it volunteers when required. But initially the *jathās* tended to operate independently. Yet there was significant closeness between the two and, at times, overlapping of leadership and action. Amar Siṅgh Jhabāl, prominent in the Akālī hierarchy, continued to be the head of the Gurū Rām Dās Jathā, and Tejā Siṅgh Bhuchchar, the first *Jathedār* of Srī Akāl Ta<u>kh</u>t, continued to head his Gaṛgajj Akālī Dal and was at the same time one of the 5-member presidium of the Shiromaṇī Panth Milauṇī Jathā of the Central Mājhā <u>Kh</u>ālsā Dīwān. As the Akālī movement gathered momentum, unleashing a political storm in the Punjab with successive *morchās* or agitations such as those erupting over the issue of the keys of the Golden Temple treasury, and Gurū kā Bā<u>gh</u>, Jaito and at Bhāī Pherū— resulted in the complete integration of the regional *jathās* into the Shiromaṇī Akālī Dal. This also brought added power and prestige to the Shiromaṇī Gurdwārā Parbandhak Committee, bequeathing to it fuller control over the Dal, although the latter did maintain its separate identity, the two working on more or less similar lines for the achievement of a common goal. The apex leadership of both organizations was a common homogeneous group. The membership base of the Shiromaṇī Akālī Dal lay primarily in the rural Punjab. Akālī leaders preached the need and importance of *gurdwārā* reform in the villages or at gatherings held on religious festivals, and exhorted Sikhs to receive the rites of <u>Kh</u>ālsā baptism and join the ranks of the Akālī Dal to liberate their religious shrines from the control of an effete and corrupt clergy. Volunteers of a locality formed local Akālī *jathās* which were consolidated into district Akālī *jathās* affiliated to the Shiromaṇī Akālī Dal at the summit. The composition of the Shiromaṇī Gurdwārā Parbandhak Committee before the passing of the Sikh Gurdwaras Act, 1925, was also analogous, and headquarters of both organizations were located in the Golden Temple complex at Amritsar. Both the bodies were together declared unlawful by a government order issued on 12 October 1923, and the ban on both was simultaneously lifted on 13 September 1926.

The Akālī movement ended with the enactment of the Sikh Gurdwaras Act, 1925, and the lifting of the ban on the two Sikh organizations. The right of the Sikhs to possess and manage their *gurdwārās* and properties attached to them had been recognized. This right was to be exercised through a central board, subsequently redesignated the Shiromaṇī Gurdwārā Parbandhak Committee, a statutory body formed through an electoral process based on universal adult franchise of the Sikh Panth. The Shiromaṇī Akālī Dal thereafter became an independent political party which instead of functioning under the Shiromaṇī Gurdwārā Parbandhak Committee sought to control it through the electoral process. Differences among the Akālī leaders had already cropped up on the question of implementing the Gurdwaras Act. The Government had stipulated that only those detenues would be released from jail who gave an undertaking in writing that they accepted and were ready to implement the Act. While one group headed by Sardār Bahādur Mehtāb Siṅgh obtained their release by giving the required undertaking, the other group refused to accept the offer of a conditional release. The first election to the Central Board (Shiromaṇī Gurdwārā Parbandhak Committee) held on 18 June 1926 was fought mainly between the Mehtāb Siṅgh group and the faction led by those who had declined to accept the condition laid down by government and were still behind the bars. The result went clearly in favour of the latter, who rightfully claimed to be the Shiromaṇī Akālī Dal. This faction won 85 seats against 26 by the Sardār Bahādur group, 5 by the government sponsored Sudhār Committee and 4 by independents. Since then the Shiromaṇī Akālī Dal's control over the Shiromaṇī Gurdwārā Parbandhak Committee has been complete and continuous.

Thus gaining supremacy in Sikh affairs, the Shiromaṇī Akālī Dal extended the scope of its activity to the national arena. It fully supported the Indian National Congress during the Bārdolī *satyāgraha* (agitation) and the campaign for the boycott of the Simon Commission in 1928. But the report of the Motīlāl Nehrū Committee, a joint body representing the Indian National Congress, the Muslim League and the Sikhs to draft a constitution for free India, came as a sore disappointment to the Sikhs because it had defaulted in proposing any measures to protect their minority rights. Towards the end of December 1929, the Shiromaṇī Akālī Dal and its sister organization, the Central Sikh League, convened an Akālī conference at Lahore to coincide with the 44th annual session of the Congress Party. Presiding over the conference, Bābā Khaṛak Siṅgh reiterated Sikhs' determination not to let any single community establish its political hegemony in the Punjab. The Akālī Conference, and even more dramatically the huge Sikh procession which preceded it, made a tremendous impact. The Congress not only rejected the Nehrū Report but also assured the Sikhs that no political arrangement which did not give them full satisfaction would be accepted by the party.

The Shiromaṇī Akālī Dal, since its victory at the first Gurdwārā elections in 1926 had functioned as a well-knit party under the leadership of Bābā Khaṛak Siṅgh and Master Tārā Siṅgh, but rifts began to show up in the wake of the next elections which took place in 1930. Bābā Khaṛak Siṅgh not only resigned the presidentship of the Shiromaṇī Akālī Dal but also quit the party to form a rival body, the Central Akālī Dal. Master Tārā Siṅgh secured the presidentship of the Dal and remained at the helm of Sikh politics for the next three decades. The question of constitutional reforms under discussion at the time prompted the two groups to sink their differences, and act by mutual counsel. Their agreed standpoint in respect of the Round Table Conferences and the Communal Award was based on a charter of 17 demands adopted at the annual session of the Central Sikh League held on 8 April 1931 under the presidentship of Master Tārā Siṅgh. In this charter, the Sikhs expressed their opposition to communal representation and favoured joint electorates, adding the rider that if it was finally decided to resort to reservation of seats on communal basis they would demand a 30 per cent share of the assembly seats in the Punjab and five per cent in the Central legislature. Other demands included a one-third share in provincial services and the public service commission; maintenance of the then existing Sikh percentage in the army; Sikh representation in the Central cabinet and the central public service commission; recognition of Punjabi as the official language in Punjab; and protection of Sikh minorities outside the Punjab on a par with protection provided for other minorities. At the national level, the Sikhs wanted the government to be secular; and the Centre to have residuary powers including powers needed for the protection of minorities.

The dissident group of Bābā Khaṛak Siṅgh, the Central Akālī Dal, could never supplant the Shiromaṇī Akālī Dal as a representative of the Sikh mainstream, and became extinct after Independence (1947). Even before 1947, it was the Shiromaṇī Akālī Dal which had campaigned for Sikh rights and dignity at Ḍaskā (1931), Koṭ Bhāī Thān Siṅgh (1935-37) and Shahīd Gañj, Lahore (1935-40).

The Shiromaṇī Akālī Dal fought the first elections, under the Government of India Act, 1935, and on the basis of Communal Award, held in Punjab on 4 January 1937, in collaboration with the Indian National Congress. Out of the 29 Sikh seats, the Akālī Dal carried 10 seats (out of 14 contested) and the Congress won five. Opposing them was the Khālsā National Party aligned with the Chief Khālsā Dīwān and the Unionist Party. While the Unionist Party with 96 out of a total of 175 seats formed the ministry, the Akālīs joined hands with the Congress to form the Opposition. With the outbreak of the Second World War in September 1939, a rift occurred between the Congress and the Akālīs. While the former boycotted the assemblies, the Akālīs, although they were at one with the Congress in their demand for the declaration of war aims and the way these aims were to be applied to India, pressed the Government for the protection of their minority interests. Their representative, Baldev Siṅgh, joined the Unionist ministry in the Punjab as a result of a pact made with the premier, Sir Sikandar Hayāt Khān. Although known in history as the Sikandar-Baldev Siṅgh Pact signed on 15 June 1942, it essentially marked rapproachement between the Unionist leader and the Shiromaṇī Akālī Dal which had spearheaded a very active campaign against his government in the Punjab.

The Pakistan Resolution passed by Indian Muslim League at Lahore in 1940, demanding a separate country comprising Muslim majority provinces, posed a serious threat to the Sikhs. In Pakistan as envisaged by the Muslim League, Sikhs would be reduced to a permanent minority, hence to a subordinate position. The Shiromaṇī Akālī Dal opposed tooth and nail any scheme for the partition of the country. It successively rejected the Cripps' proposal (1942), Rājā Formula (1944) and the Cabinet Mission Plan (1946). But the existing demographic realities were against the Sikhs. Nowhere in the Punjab did they have a sizeable tract with a Sikh majority of population. To counter the League demand for Pakistan, the Shiromaṇī Akālī Dal put forward the Āzād Punjab scheme proposing the carving out of the Punjab of a new province, roughly between Delhi and the River Chenāb, where none of the three communities—Muslims, Hindus and Sikhs—would command an absolute majority. But the proposal did not gather sufficient support. Even the Central Akālī Dal led by Bābā Khaṛak Siṅgh, set itself up against it. The Shiromaṇī Akālī Dal, under the prevailing circumstances cast its lot with the Indian National Congress trusting to it the protection of Sikhs' minority rights. In a public statement made on 4 April 1946, Jawāharlāl Nehrū said, "redistribution of provincial boundaries was essential and inevitable. I stand for semi-autonomous units as well.... I should like them [the Sikhs] to have a semi-autonomous unit within the province so that they may experience the glow of freedom." The working committee of the Shiromaṇī Akālī Dal adopted on 17 March 1948 a resolution advising its representatives in the provincial assemblies as well as at the Centre formally to join the Congress party. Minority grievances, however, kept accumulating. Sikh members of the East Punjab Assembly, including a minister in the Congress government, complained of increasing communal tension and discrimination against their community in recruitment to governement services. The major irritant was the language question. After Independence, the Sikhs expected Punjabi, mother tongue of all Punjabis, to replace Urdu as the official language and medium of education in schools. Even a resolution of the Central Government published in the Gazette of India dated 14 August 1948 declaring that "the principle that a child should be instructed in the early stage of his education through the medium of his mother tongue has been accepted by the government" did not induce the Congress government of East Punjab to declare Punjabi as the medium of instruction. On the contrary, the majority Hindu community went so far as to disclaim

Punjabi as their mother tongue. At the Centre too the Constituent Assembly rescinded its own resolution of August 1947 and declared on 26 May 1949 that "statutory reservation of seats for religious minorities should be abolished." The leaders of the Shiromaṇī Akālī Dal finally veered round to the view that, in the absence of constitutional guarantees to safeguard rights of the minorities, the only way out for the Sikhs was to strive for an area where they would be numerous enough to protect and develop their language and culture. They therefore decided to press for the formation of a linguistic state coterminous with Punjabi language. Master Tārā Siṅgh reactivated the Shiromaṇī Akālī Dal and launched the campaign which came to be known as the Punjabi Sūbā movement. In a signed article published in the Punjabi monthly *Sant Sipāhī*, December 1949, he said that "whatever the name that might be given it, the Sikhs wanted an area where they were free from the domination of the majority community—an area within the Indian constitution but having internal autonomy as did Kashmir."

Two successive half-way measures, Sachar Formula and the Regional Formula, devised by Congress and Sikh leaders by mutual counsel, failed to resolve the linguistic and political issue. The Akālī leader, Master Tārā Siṅgh, once again gave the call for a Punjabi Sūbā in October 1958. The Sikh masses responded enthusiastically. The government once again initiated negotiations which culminated in what is known as the Nehrū-Tārā Siṅgh Pact of April 1959. The truce did not last long. Call for a fresh *morchā* issued from the Shiromaṇī Akālī Dal on 22 May 1960. The campaign meandering through many a vicissitude continued until the emergence on 1 November 1966 of a Punjabi-speaking state. But before this consummation was reached, the Shiromaṇī Akālī Dal had been riven into two, one section led by Master Tārā Siṅgh and the other by his lately arisen, but infinitely stronger rival, Sant Fateh Siṅgh.

Shadow of this division and of certain unresolved issues such as the non-transfer to it of the state capital, Chaṇḍīgaṛh, certain Punjabi-speaking areas still remaining outside of it and maldistribution of water resources, continued to bedevil electoral politics in the new Punjab. In the first election to the state legislature in the new Punjab (1967), the Shiromaṇī Akālī Dal carried 26 seats in a house of 104, and its leader, Gurnām Siṅgh, a retired judge of the Punjab High Court, formed on 28 March 1967 a ministry with the support of some other small groups, including Jana Saṅgh, Communists and independents. But the ministry fell soon afterwards owing to internal dissensions. On 26 May 1967, two Akālīs, Harcharan Siṅgh Huḍiārā and Lachhmaṇ Siṅgh Gill sided with the Congress during voting on a no-confidence motion against the ministry. The ministry survived the motion but Huḍiārā on the same day announced the formation of a separate Akālī Dal. On 22 November, Lachhmaṇ Siṅgh Gill with 19 other M.L.A.s openly rebelled against the Shiromaṇī Akālī Dal legislative party, reducing the joint front led by Gurnām Siṅgh into a minority. Lachhmaṇ Siṅgh Gill then formed, with the support of Congress party, a new ministry which fell on 21 August 1968 when the Congress group withdrew its support. The crisis led to the dissolution of the state legislature and the state was placed under President's, i.e. Central Government, rule necessitating a mid-term poll. The two factions of the Shiromaṇī Akālī Dal became one again and registered a resounding victory at the hustings, emerging as the largest single party with 43 seats against Congress 38, Jana Saṅgh 8, Communists 5, and others 11. Gurnām Siṅgh again formed a ministry in coalition with the Jana Saṅgh, the Communists supporting from outside. This ministry was brought down on 25 March 1970 by internal party dissent. A young Akālī leader, Parkāsh Siṅgh Bādal, then formed the government (27 March 1970) supplanting Gurnām Siṅgh as Chief Minister. This Akālī government too had a short tenure. In the fresh Punjab Assembly elections which took place in March 1972, the Shiromaṇī Akālī Dal could muster a bare 24 seats out of a total of 117, making way for the Congress party to form its government. This led to self-retrospection on the part of the Shiromaṇī Akālī Dal.

The Working Committee of the Dal at its meeting held at Anandpur Sāhib, in the Śivālik hills on 16-17 October 1973 adopted a statement of aims and objectives. This statement, known as the Anandpur Sāhib Resolution (*q.v.*), has, since then, been the cornerstone of Akālī politics and strategy.

The Shiromaṇī Akālī Dal enjoyed another brief spell of power in the Punjab when at the elections in the wake of Rājīv-Lauṅgovāl accord, settlement between Rājīv Gāndhī, then Prime Minister of India, and Sant Harchand Siṅgh Lauṅgovāl, the Akālī leader, signed on 25 July 1985, it won an overwhelming majority of seats in the state legislature and formed its government led by Surjīt Siṅgh Barnālā. Owing however to internal party pressures and the non-implementation by the Government of India of the Rājīv-Lauṅgovāl accord, this ministry also proved brittle. In the crisis which overtook the state after its dismissal by the Government of India, the Shiromaṇī Akālī Dal gradually became split into several factions—Akālī Dal (Bādal) led by a former chief minister of the Punjab, Parkāsh Siṅgh Bādal, Akālī Dal (Lauṅgovāl) led by Surjīt Siṅgh Barnālā, also a former chief minister of the Punjab, and Akālī Dal (Mān), led by a new entrant into politics, Simranjīt Siṅgh Mān, formerly, a high-ranking member of the Indian Police Service.

BIBLIOGRAPHY

1. Dilgeer, Harjinder Siṅgh, *Shiromaṇī Akālī Dal,* Jalandhar, n.d.
2. Pratāp Siṅgh, Giānī, *Gurdwārā Sudhār arthāt Akālī Lahir.* Amritsar, 1975
3. Ashok, Shamsher Siṅgh, *Pañjāb dīāṅ Lahirāṅ.* Patiala. 1974
4. Naraiṇ Siṅgh, *Akālī Morche te Jhabbar.* Delhi, 1967
5. Tuteja, K.L., *Sikh Politics.* Kurukshetra, 1984
6. Gulati, Kailash Chander, *The Akalis: Past and Present.* Delhi, 1974
7. Nayar, Baldev Raj, *Minority Politics in the Punjab.* Princeton, 1966
8. Sahni, Ruchi Ram, *Struggle for Reform in Sikh Shrines.* Ed. Ganda Singh. Amritsar, n.d.
9. Nijjar, B.S., *History of the Babbar Akalis.* Jalandhar, 1987
10. Sarhadi, Ajit Singh, *Punjabi Suba.* Delhi, 1970
11. Brass, Paul, R., *Language, Religion and Politics in North India.* Delhi, 1975
12. Mohinder Singh, *The Akali Movement.* Delhi, 1978
13. Teja Singh, *Gurdwara Reform Movement and the Sikh Awakening.* Jalandhar, 1922
14. Nayar, Kuldip, and Khushwant Singh, *Tragedy of Punjab.* Delhi, 1984

M.G.S.

AKĀLĪ MOVEMENT, variously known as Gurdwārā Reform Movement or Gurdwārā Agitation is how Sikhs' long-drawn campaign in the early twenties of the twentieth century for the liberation of their *gurdwārās* or holy shrines is described. The campaign which elicited enthusiastic support, especially, from the rural masses, took the form of a peaceful agitation—marches, *dīvāns* or religious gatherings, and demonstrations—for Sikhs to assert their right to manage their places of worship. This led to a series of critical episodes in which their powers of suffering were severely tested by government suppression. In the event, Akālīs, as the protesters were known, succeeded in their object and the control of the *gurdwārās* was vested through legislation in a representative committee of the Sikhs. The State, under Mahārājā Raṇjīt Siṅgh (1780-1839), had forborne from interfering with the management of Sikh shrines. It endowed the more prominent among them with land grants and other gifts but let the control remain in the hands of sectaries such as Udāsīs, or hereditary officiants, who had assumed charge of them generally since the days when Sikhs under pressure of Mughal persecution had been forced to seek safety in remote hills and deserts. A kind of professional coenobitism, contrary to Sikh religious structure, had developed over the generations. Some of its sinister aspects became apparent soon after the fall of the Sikh kingdom. Most of the clergy had become neglectful of their religious office. They had diverted ecclesiastical assests, including eleemosynary lands, to their own enrichment, and their lives were not free from the taint of licentiousness and luxury. The simple form of Sikh service had been supplanted in the shrines by extravagant ceremonial. This was repugnant to Sikhs freshly affranchised by the preachings of the Siṅgh Sabhā. The puritan reaction through which they had passed led them to revolt against the retrogression and maladministration of their holy places.

Their central shrine, the Golden Temple at Amritsar, was controlled by the British Deputy Commissioner through a Sikh manager whom he appointed. There were idols installed within the temple precincts. Paṇḍits and astrologers sat on the premises plying their trade unchecked. Pilgrims from the backward classes were not allowed inside the Harimandar before 9 o'clock in the morning. This was a travesty of Sikhism which permitted neither caste nor image worship. Vaguely, the feeling had been prevalent among the Sikhs since almost the advent of the British that the administration of the Harimandar at Amritsar was far from satisfactory. The religious ritual practised ran counter in many details to the teachings of the Gurūs. One audible voice of protest was that of Ṭhākur Siṅgh Sandhāṅvālīā, who was a member of the Srī Darbār Sāhib Committee in the seventies of the last century. The Khālsā Dīwān, Lahore, at its session (6-8 April 1907), proposed that the manager of the Golden Temple appointed by the government be removed and a committee of Sikh chiefs appointed in his place. Likewise, the Khālsā Dīwān, Mājhā, meeting at Tarn Tāran on 9-10 April 1907, had recorded its concern about the management of the shrine.

On 12 October 1920, a meeting of Sikh backward castes, sponsored by teachers and students of the Khālsā College was held in Jalliāṅvālā Bāgh at Amritsar. The following morning some of them were taken to Harimandar, but the priests refused to accept *kaṛāhprasād* they had brought as offering and to say the *ardās* on their behalf. Their supporters protested. A compromise was at last reached and it was decided that the Gurū's word be sought. The Gurū Granth Sāhib was, as is the custom, opened at random and the first verse on the page to be read was:

nirguṇiā no āpe bakhsi lai bhāī
satigur kī sevā lāi

He receives into grace (even) those without merit,
And puts them in the path of holy service.

(GG, 638)

The Gurū's verdict was clearly in favour of those whom the *pujārīs* or temple functionaries had refused to accept as full members of the community. This was a triumph for reformist Sikhs. The *kaṛāhprasād* of the Mazhabī (religious, devout) Sikhs, reformers' description of "low-caste" Sikhs, was accepted. The devotees then marched towards Takht Akāl Buṅgā in front of the Harimandar. The priests deserted the Takht and the visiting pilgrims appointed a representative committee of twenty-five for its management. This was the beginning of the movement for the liberation of the *gurdwārās*. The Akālīs set afoot operations for retrieving their holy places from the control of the *mahants* or clergy-cum-hereditary custodians. With a view to establishing a central committee of administration, a representative assembly of Sikhs from all walks of life was called by the new Jathedār, provost or chief, of Ta<u>kh</u>t Akāl Buṅgā on 15 November 1920. Two days before the proposed conference, the government set up its own committee consisting of thirty-six Sikhs to manage the Golden Temple. This committee was nominated by the Lt-Governor of the Punjab at the instance of Mahārājā Bhūpinder Siṅgh of Paṭiālā, who had been approached by Bhāī Jodh Siṅgh and a few of his faculty colleagues at <u>Kh</u>ālsā College, Amritsar, to intervene between the government and the Sikhs. The Sikhs held their scheduled meeting on 15 November and formed a committee of 175, including the thirty-six official nominees, designating it Shiromaṇī Gurdwārā Parbandhak Committee. The first session of the Committee was held at the Akāl Ta<u>kh</u>t on 12 December 1920. Sundar Siṅgh Majīṭhīā, Harbaṅs Siṅgh of Aṭārī and Bhāī Jodh Siṅgh were elected president, vice-president and secretary, respectively. The more radical elements organized a semi-military corps of volunteers known as the Akālī Dal (Army of Immortals). The Akālī Dal was to raise and train men for 'action' to take over *gurdwārās* from the recalcitrant *mahants.* This also signalled the appearance of a Gurmukhī newspaper, also called *Akālī.*

The formation of the Shiromaṇī Gurdwārā Parbandhak Committee and the Shiromaṇī Akālī Dal speeded up the movement for the reformation of Sikh religious institutions and endowments. Under pressure of Sikh opinion, backed frequently by demonstration of strength, the *mahants* began yielding possession of *gurdwārā* properties to elected committees and agreed to become paid *granthīs,* custodians of the scripture or scripture-readers. Several *gurdwārās* had thus come under the reformists' control even before the Shiromaṇī Committee and the Akālī Dal had been established. However, the transition was not so smooth where the priests were strongly entrenched or where the government actively helped them to resist mass pressure. At Tarn Tāran, near Amritsar, a batch of *gurdwārā* functionaries attacked an unwary delegation of reformers who had been invited to the shrine for negotiations. One of them, Hazārā Siṅgh of Alādīnpur, a descendant of Baghel Siṅgh, one of the *misl* chiefs, fell a victim to priestly violence on 20 January 1921. He died the following day and became the first martyr in the cause of *gurdwārā* reform. Another Akālī, Hukam Siṅgh of Vasāū Koṭ , succumbed to his injuries on 4 February 1921.

Nankāṇā Sāhib, the birthplace of Gurū Nānak, was the scene of violence on a much larger scale. The custodian, Naraiṇ Dās, the wealthiest of *mahants,* had a most unsavoury reputation, and his stewardship of the Nankāṇā Sāhib shrines had started many a scandal. On the morning of 20 February 1921, as a *jathā* or band of 150 Akālīs came to the Gurdwārā, the private army of Naraiṇ Dās fell upon them, raining bullets all around. The *jathā* leader, Bhāī Lachhmaṇ Siṅgh, of Dhārovāl, was struck down sitting in attendance of the Gurū Granth Sāhib. Bhāī Dalīp Siṅgh, a much-respected Sikh leader who was well known to the *mahant* and who came to intercede with him to stop the carnage, was killed with a shot from his pistol. Many of the *jathā* fell in the indiscriminate firing by the *mahant's* men. The news of the massacre caused widespread gloom. Among those who came to Nankāṇā to express their sense of shock were Sir Edward Maclagan, the British Lt-Governor of the Punjab. Mahātmā Gāndhī came accompanied by Muslim leaders, Shaukat 'Alī and Muhammad 'Alī. Naraiṇ Dās and some of his accomplices were arrested and the possession of the shrine was made over by government to a committee of seven Sikhs headed by Harbaṅs Siṅgh of Aṭārī, vice-president of the Shiromaṇī Gurdwārā Parbandhak Committee.

Another crisis arose as the Punjab Government seized on 7 November 1921 the keys of the Golden Temple treasury. The Shiromaṇī Gurdwārā Parbandhak Committee lodged a strong protest and called upon the Sikhs the world over to convene meetings to condemn the government action. Further means of recording resentment included a decision for Sikhs to observe a *haṛtāl,* i.e. to strike work, on the day the Prince of Wales, who was coming out on a tour, landed on Indian shores. They were also forbidden to participate in any function connected with the Prince's visit. To fill the British jails, volunteers, draped in black and singing hymns from Scripture, marched forth in batches. Ex-servicemen threw up their pensions and joined Akālī ranks. Under pressure of the growing agitation, the government gave way, and on 19 January 1922 a court official surrendered the bunch of keys, wrapped in a piece of red cloth, to Kharak Siṅgh, president of the Shiromaṇī Gurdwārā Parbandhak Committee. Mahātmā Gāndhī sent a wire saying, "First decisive battle for India's freedom won."

Gurū kā Bāgh (Garden of the Gurū), 20 km north of Amritsar, a small shrine commemorating Gurū Arjan's visit, witnessed a *morchā* most typical of the series in the Akālī movement. On 9 August 1922, the police arrested on charges of trespass five Sikhs who had gone to gather firewood from the Gurdwārā's land for *Gurū kā Laṅgar,* the community kitchen. The following day, the arrested Sikhs were summarily tried and sentenced to six months' rigorous imprisonment. Undeterred, the Sikhs continued coming in batches every day to hew wood from the site and courting arrest and prosecution. After 30 August, police adopted a sterner policy to terrorize the volunteers. Those who came to cut firewood from Gurū kā Bāgh were beaten up in a merciless manner until they to a man lay senseless on the ground. The Sikhs suffered all this stoically and went day by day in larger numbers to submit themselves to the beating. A committee appointed by the Indian National Congress to visit Amritsar, lauded the Akālīs and censured the police for atrocities committed by it. Rev C. F. Andrews, a Christian missionary, came on 12 September 1922, and was deeply moved by the noble "Christ-like" behaviour of the Akālī passive resisters. At his instance, Sir Edward Maclagan, the Lt-Governor of the Punjab, arrived at Gurū kā Bāgh (13 September) and ordered the beatings to be stopped. Four days later the police retired from the scene. By then 5, 605 Akālīs had been arrested, with 936 hospitalized. The Akālīs got possession of Gurdwārā Gurū kā Bāgh along with the disputed land.

Gurū kā Bāgh excited religious fervour to a degree unapproached during the 70 years of British rule. The judicial trials of the volunteers were followed with close interest and, when those convicted were being removed to jails to serve their sentences, mammoth crowds greeted them *en route.* On 30 October 1922, many men and women laid themselves on the rail track at Pañjā Sāhib in an attempt to stop a train to offer refreshments to Akālī prisoners being escorted to Naushehrā jail. Two Sikhs, Partāp Siṅgh and Karam Siṅgh, were crushed to death before the engine driver could pull up.

Not all Sikhs accepted the cult of non-violence to which the Shiromaṇī Committee had committed itself. The Nankāṇā massacre and the behaviour of the police at Gurū kā Bāgh induced some to organize an underground terrorist movement. These terrorists, who called themselves Babar (Lion) Akālīs, were largely drawn from the Ghadr party and army soldiers on leave. Babar violence was, however, of short duration. By the summer of 1923, most of the Babars had been apprehended. The trial conducted in camera began inside Lahore Central Jail on

15 August 1923 and was presided over by an English judge. Of the 91 accused, two died in jail during trial, 34 were acquitted, six including Jathedār Kishan Siṅgh Gaṛgajj, were awarded death penalty, while the remaining 49 were sentenced to varying terms of imprisonment.

Another Akālī *morchā* was precipitated by police interrupting an *akhaṇḍ pāṭh*, i.e. continuous recital of the Gurū Granth Sāhib, at Gurdwārā Gaṅgsar at Jaito, in the Princely state of Nābhā, to demonstrate Sikhs' solidarity with the cause of Mahārājā Ripudaman Siṅgh, the ruler of the state, who had been deposed by the British. Batches of passive resisters began arriving every day at Jaito to assert their right to freedom of worship. The Shiromaṇī Committee and the Akālī Dal were declared illegal bodies by government and more prominent of the leaders were arrested. They were charged with conspiracy to wage war against the King and taken to Lahore Fort for trial. The agitation continued and the size of the *jathās* going to Jaito was in fact increased from 25 each to a hundred, and then from one hundred to five hundred. One such *jathā* was fired upon on 21 February 1924 by the state police resulting in a number of casualities.

With the arrival in May 1924 of Sir Malcolm Hailey as Governor of the Punjab, the government began to relent. Negotiations were opened with the Akālī leaders imprisoned in Lahore Fort. A bill accommodating their demands was moved in the Punjab Legislative Council and passed into law in 1925, under the title the Sikh Gurdwaras Act, 1925. As this legislation was put on the statute book, almost all historical shrines, numbering 241 as listed in Schedule I of the Act, were declared as Sikh *gurdwārās* and they were to be under the administrative control of the Central Board, later renamed the Shiromaṇī Gurdwārā Parbandhak Committee. Procedure was also laid down in section 7 of the Act for the transfer of any other *gurdwārā* not listed in Schedules I and II to the administrative control of the Central Board. With the passage of this Act, the Akālī agitation ceased.

In the Akālī agitation for *gurdwārā* reform, nearly forty thousand went to jail. Four hundred lost their lives while two thousand suffered injuries. Sums to the tune of sixteen lakhs of rupees were paid by way of fines and forfeitures and about seven hundred Sikh government functionaries in the villages were deprived of their positions. In addition to this, a ban was placed on civil and military recruitment of Sikhs which, however, was subsequently withdrawn.

BIBLIOGRAPHY

1. Ganda Singh, *Some Confidential Papers of the Akali Movement*. Amritsar, 1965
2. Mohinder Singh, *The Akali Movement*. Delhi, 1978
3. Teja Singh, *Gurdwara Reform and the Sikh Awakening*. Jalandhar, 1922
4. Sahni, Ruchi Ram, *Struggle for Reform in Sikh Shrines*, Ed. Ganda Singh. Amritsar, n.d.
5. Gulati, Kailash Chander, *The Akalis : Past and Present*. Delhi, 1974
6. Harbans Singh, *The Heritage of the Sikhs*. Delhi, 1983
7. Pratāp Siṅgh, Giānī, *Gurdwārā Sudhār arthāt Akālī Lahir*. Amritsar, 1975
8. Dilgeer, Harjinder Siṅgh, *Shiromaṇī Akali Dal*. Jalandhar, n.d.
9. Josh, Sohan Siṅgh, *Akālī Morchiāṅ dā Itihās*. Delhi, 1972
10. Jagjīt Siṅgh, *Siṅgh Sabhā Lahir*. Ludhiana, 1974
11. Ashok, Shamsher Siṅgh, *Shiromaṇī Gurdwārā Prabandhak Committee dā Pañjāh Sālā Itihās*. Amritsar, 1982

S. S. B.

AKĀLĪ SAHĀYAK BUREAU, lit. a bureau to help (*sahāyak*, from Skt. *sahāya*, one who lends one company or support) the Akālīs, then engaged in a bitter struggle for the reformation of the management of their places of worship, was a small office set up at

Amritsar in 1923 by the Indian National Congress to assist the Akālīs with their public relations work. This Akālī struggle, aiming at ousting the priestly order who had come into control of Sikh shrines introducing therein conservative rituals and forms of worship rejected in Sikhism, came into conflict with the British authority who buttressed the entrenched clergy, and ran a course parallel to the Congress movement for the nation's freedom. The Akālīs' heroic deeds of sacrifice and disciplined suffering won them appreciation of Congress hierarchy as well as of the people in common. When under pressure mounted by the Akālīs, the British district magistrate of Amritsar was forced to return to the Golden Temple authorities keys of the *toshā<u>kh</u>ānā*, the Temple treasury, seized from them, the Congress applauded the incident as a victory for the nationalist cause. Mahātmā Gāndhī in fact sent a wire to Sardār Kharak Siṅgh, president of the Shiromaṇī Gurdwārā Parbandhak Committee which read as follows: "First decisive battle for India's freedom won congratulations—M. K. Gandhi."

The wholesale massacre of Akālī reformists (20 February 1921) at Nankāṇā Sāhib, birthplace of Gurū Nānak, shook the entire nation and Congress leaders such as Mahātmā Gāndhī, Shaukat 'Alī and Muhammad 'Alī travelled to Nankāṇā Sāhib to pay homage to the martyrs. The patient suffering of Akālī volunteers in the Gurū kā Bā<u>gh</u> campaign (1922) when they faced police brutalities calmly and stoically won them countrywide sympathy and admiration and the British scholar and missionary, C. F. Andrews, wrote a very touching account of the trial the Akālīs went through day after day.

At a special meeting held on 17 September 1922, the Working Committee of the Indian National Congress adopted a resolution condemning the police high-handedness. It also appointed a sub-committee to conduct enquiry into the Gurū kā Bā<u>gh</u> affair. When the Shiromaṇī Gurdwārā Parbandhak Committee and the Shiromaṇī Akālī Dal which were directing and guiding the Akālī campaigns (*morchās*) were banned by the British government in India, the Indian National Congress at a meeting in December 1923 declared the outlawing of the Shiromaṇi Gurdwārā Parbandhak Committee and the Shiromaṇī Akālī Dal as "a direct challenge to the right of the free association of all Indians and a blow aimed at all movements for freedom."

The Akālī and Congress movements had thus become intervolved and both served to feed the nationalist sentiment in the country. The Akālī Sahāyak Bureau was designed to serve as a vehicle for publicizing Akālī activity and to serve as a link between the Congress and the Akālīs. A. T. Giḍwānī, Principal of Gujarāt Vidyāpīṭh, was placed in charge of the Bureau. After Giḍwānī's arrest by the British, Mr Shuklā of the United Provinces took over charge, but he was soon replaced by K. M. Panikkar who had returned from Oxford with a first class degree in history—the first Indian ever to achieve the distinction, and who had left his academic position as head of the Department of History at Alīgaṛh Muslim University to take to politics and journalism. Panikkar was for this position the personal choice of Mahātmā Gāndhī who, though impressed by the successes Akālīs achieved through their adherence to passive resistance, was not clear about their ultimate objective. This was especially so in the case of Jaito Morchā. Panikkar sent reports which only deepened Mahātmā Gāndhī's sense of ambivalence. Panikkar warned Gāndhī about the organization of Akālī *jathās* which roamed the countryside as a strong force and which for Panikkar were reminiscent of Sikh *jathās* or bands of the second half of the eighteenth century and which were, according to him, tamed by Mahārājā Raṇjīt Siṅgh, only to re-emerge after his death. He stressed that these *jathās* with their military structure and discipline and their spirit of militancy constituted a menace to other communities in the Punjab. Having served for a while in the Sikh state of Paṭiālā and edited Sikhs' English newspaper, *The Hindustan Times,* he was fairly well aquainted with the Sikhs.

After the Sikh Gurdwaras Act was placed on the statute book in 1925, the Akālī agitation ceased. And so the Akālī Sahāyak Bureau became redundant.

BIBLIOGRAPHY

1. Josh, Sohan Siṅgh, *Akālī Morchiāṅ dā Itihās.* Delhi, 1972 –
2. Pratāp Siṅgh, Giānī, *Gurdwārā Sudhār arthāt Akālī Lahir.* Amritsar, 1975
3. Mohinder Singh, *The Akali Movement.* Delhi, 1978
4. Amrik Singh, ed. , *Punjab in Indian Politics.* Delhi, 1985
5. Kapur, Rajiv A. , *Sikh Separatism: The Politics of Faith.* London, 1986
6. Panikkar, K.M., *An Autobiography.* Oxford (Delhi), 1979

M. G. S.

AKĀLĪ TE PRADESĪ . *See AKĀLĪ,* THE

AKĀL MŪRATI, a composite term comprising *akāl* (non-temporal) and *mūrati* (image or form), occurring in the Mūl-Mantra, the root formula or fundamental creed of the Sikh faith as recorded at the beginning of the *Japu,* composition with which the Gurū Granth Sāhib opens, literally means 'timeless image'. Elsewhere, in the compositions of Gurū Rām Dās (GG, 78), and Gurū Arjan (GG, 99, 609, 916 and 1082), the expression Akāl Mūrati reinforces the original meaning of Divine Reality that is beyond the process of time, and yet permeates the cosmic forms. The non-temporal Being transcends the space-time framework and, as such, is Formless. However, in its manifest aspect, the same Being assumes the cosmic Form. The Sikh vision of God combines the Formless and its expression in natural forms, the transcendent and the immanent, the essence (spirit) and existence (creation).

The expression 'Akāl Mūrati' lends itself to interpretation in two ways. The exegetes, who treat it as one term, take *akāl* in the adjectival form that qualifies the substantive *mūrati,* the whole expression implying Everlasting Form equivalent to the Supreme Being. Those approaching the pair *akāl* and *mūrati* severally, treat both the units independently, each expressing an attribute of the Divine Reality, believed to transcend time and space, yet manifest in spacio-temporal forms. But, despite the divergence of approach, both interpretations agree in substance, i.e. the featureless eternal Reality assumes features and modes of empirical existence. To put it differently, 'Akāl Mūrati' presents a synthesis of *nirguṇ* and *saguṇ* facets of the Absolute-God of Gurū Nānak's vision. It however does not embrace the notion of incarnation. Non-incarnation is a basic theological postulate of Sikhism.

See AKĀL

BIBLIOGRAPHY

1. Talib, Gurbachan Singh, *Japuji—The Immortal Sikh Prayer-chant.* Delhi, 1977
2. Trilochan Singh, "Theological Concepts of Sikhism," in *Sikhism.* Patiala, 1969
3. Sher Singh, *The Philosophy of Sikhism.* Lahore, 1944
4. Jodh Siṅgh, *Gurmati Nirṇaya.* Ludhiana, 1932

W.S.

AKĀL-PURAKH stands in Sikh religious literature for the Divine Being, i.e. God. Like Akāl Mūrati, it is composed of two units, viz. *akāl* (non-temporal) and *purakh* (person). The latter figures in Mūl-Mantra, the preamble to Gurū Nānak's *Japu,* in conjunction with *Kartā* (Creator), the whole expression implying the Creator Divine Person. In the Sikh tradition, the expression Akāl-Purakh has gained common currency like the terms

Vāhigurū and Satinām, equivalently used.

'Purakh' as a linguistic symbol derives from the Sanskrit *puruṣa* (man), invariably employed in the masculine gender. In the Vedic literature, the term also stands for the world, indicating the entirety of universal existence. In the Indian systems of Sāṅkhya and Yoga, Puruṣa, as one of the two cardinal metaphysical principles, stands for spirituality or simply consciousness, which exerts influence on Prakriti (Nature) that is physical in its make-up. The core of *puruṣa*, therefore, is consciousness, denoted by *chit* in the Sat-Chit-Anand conception of the Absolute. This connotation of the term invests 'Purakh' with spirituality, signifying the Divine Person. In conjunction with *akāl*, the expression as a whole means the Everlasting Divine Person (God), in the Sikh tradition and literature.

'Akāl-Purakhu' as a single composite term appears only once in the Gurū Granth Sāhib (GG, 1038). We also come across the term in Gurū Rām Dās, Gauṛī-Pūrabī, Karhale (GG, 235), but in the inverse form as Purakhu-Akāli. However, the *Dasam Granth* compositions of Gurū Gobind Siṅgh often employ Akāl-Purakh as a substitute for God, the Eternal Being. Akāl being a cardinal and central concept in Sikhism, its use alongside of *Purakh*, accords it a distinct theological status.

See AKĀL

BIBLIOGRAPHY

1. Talib, Gurbachan Singh, *Japuji—The Immortal Prayer-chant.* Delhi, 1977
2. Trilochan Singh, "Theological Concepts of Sikhism" in *Sikhism.* Patiala, 1969
3. Sher Singh, *The Philosophy of Sikhism.* Lahore, 1944
4. Nripinder Singh, *The Sikh Moral Tradition.* Delhi, 1990
5. Jodh Siṅgh, Bhāī, *Gurmati Nirṇaya.* Ludhiana, 1932
6. Tārā Siṅgh Narotam, *Vāhigurū Sabdārth.* Patiala, 1862
7. Sādhū Siṅgh, *Gurū Sikhyā Prabhākar.* Lucknow, 1893

W.S.

AKĀL TAKHT is the primary seat of Sikh religious authority and central altar for Sikh political assembly. Through *hukamnāmās*, edicts or writs, it may issue decretals providing guidance or clarification on any point of Sikh doctrine or practice referred to it, may lay under penance personages charged with violation of religious discipline or with activity prejudicial to Sikh interests or solidarity and may place on record its appreciation of outstanding services rendered or sacrifices made by individuals espousing the cause of Sikhism or of the Sikhs. The edifice stands in the Darbār Sāhib precincts in Amritsar facing Harimandar, now famous as the Golden Temple. The word *akāl*, a negative of *kāl* (time), is the equivalent of timeless, beyond time, everlasting, and *takht*, in Persian, that of royal throne or chair of state. Akāl Takht would thus mean "timeless or everlasting throne" or "throne of the Timeless One, i.e. God." In the Sikh system, God is postulated as Formless (Niraṅkār), yet to proclaim His sovereignty over His creation, He is sometimes referred to as *sultān, pātsāh, sāchā sāh*, or the True King; His seat is referred to as *sachchā takht*, the True Throne, sitting on which He dispenses *sachchā niāo*, true justice (GG, 84, 1087). It also became common for Sikhs, at least by the time of Gurū Arjan (1563-1606), to refer to the Gurū as *sachchā pātshāh* and to his *gaddī* or spiritual seat as *takht* and the congregation he led as *darbār* or court. Panegyrizing the Gurūs, the bards Balvaṇḍ, Nalya and Mathurā, in their verses included in the Gurū Granth Sāhib, use the word *takht* in this very sense. Formally to proclaim Sikh faith's common concern for the spiritual and the worldly, synthesis of *mīrī* and *pīrī*, Gurū Hargobind (1595-1644), son and successor of Gurū Arjan, adopted royal style. For the ceremonies of succession, he had a platform constructed opposite the Harimandar, naming it Akāl Takht. According to *Gurbilās Chhevīṅ Pātshāhī*, a detailed versified and, going by the year of composition recorded in the text/colophon, the oldest account of Gurū Hargobind's life, the structure was raised on Hāṛ *vadī* 5, 1663 Bk/15 June 1606. The Gurū laid the cornerstone and Bhāī Buḍḍhā and Bhāī Gurdās completed the construction, no third person being allowed to lend a helping hand. Gurū Hargobind used the takht for the accession ceremonies which, according to the source quoted, took place on 26 Hāṛ *sudī* 10, 1663 Bk/24 June 1606. From here he conducted the secular affairs of the community. From here he is said to have issued the first *hukamnāmā (q.v.)* to far-flung *saṅgats* or Sikh centres announcing the creation of Akāl Takht and asking them to include in their offerings thenceforth gifts of weapons and horses. Bhāī Gurdās was named officiant in charge of the Akāl Takht. A building subsequently raised over the Takht was called Akāl Buṅgā (house) so that the Takht is now officially known as Takht Srī Akāl Buṅgā although its popular name Akāl Takht is more in common use.

The Sikhs recognize four other holy places as *takhts*, namely Takht Srī Kesgaṛh Sāhib, Anandpur; Takht Srī Harimandar Sāhib, Paṭnā; Takht Sachkhaṇḍ Hazūr Sāhib, Abchalnagar, Nānḍeḍ; and Takht Srī Ḍamdamā Sāhib, Talvaṇḍī Sābo. All four are connected with the life of Gurū Gobind Siṅgh (1666-1708). All five Takhts are equally venerated, but the Akāl Takht at Amritsar enjoys a special status. Historically, this is the oldest of the *takhts* and along with Harimandar, across the yard, constitutes the capital of Sikhism. Meetings of the Sarbatt Khālsā or general assembly representative of the entire Panth are traditionally summoned at Akāl Takht and it is only there that cases connected with serious religious offences committed by prominent Sikhs are heard and decided. *Hukamnāmās* or decrees issued by the Akāl Takht are universally applicable to all Sikhs and all institutions.

After Gurū Hargobind's migration to Kīratpur early in 1635, the shrines at Amritsar, including the Akāl Takht, fell into the hands of the descendants of Prithī Chand, elder brother of Gurū Arjan, his grandson, Harijī (d. 1696), remaining in charge for over fifty-five years. Soon after the creation of the Khālsā in March 1699, Gurū Gobind Siṅgh sent Bhāī Manī Siṅgh to Amritsar to assume control of the Harimandar and the Akāl Takht and manage these on behalf of the Khālsā Panth. During the troublous period following the martyrdom of Bandā Siṅgh in 1716, the sacred *sarovar*, or holy tank, at Amritsar, the Harimandar and the Akāl Takht continued to be a source of inspiration and spiritual rejuvenation for the Sikhs. Whenever circumstances permitted, and usually on Baisākhī and Dīvālī, their scattered bands defying all hazards converged upon Akāl Takht to hold *sarbatt khālsā* assemblies and discuss matters of policy and strategy. For instance, through a *gurmatā* (Gurū's counsel) the *sarbatt khālsā* at the Akāl Takht resolved on 14 October 1745 to reorganize their scattered fighting force into 25 *jathās* or bands of about 100 warriors each. By another *gurmatā* on Baisākhī, 29 March 1748, the *sarbatt khālsā* meeting, again, at Akāl Takht, formed the Dal Khālsā or the army of the Khālsā consisting of 11 *misls* or divisions. On Dīvālī, 7 November 1760, the *sarbatt khālsā* resolved to attack and occupy Lahore (till then Sikhs had not occupied any terrritory, their only possession being the small fortress of Rām Rauṇī or Rāmgaṛh they had built at Amritsar in 1746). Akāl Takht was again the venue of the *sarbatt khālsā* on Baisākhī day, 10 April 1763, when by a *gurmatā* it was decided to go out to the help of a Brāhmaṇ who had brought the complaint that his wife had been forcibly abducted by the Afghān chief of Kasūr.

Even after the Punjab had been parcelled out into several Sikh independencies or *misls*,

Amritsar remained the common capital where all *sardārs* or chiefs had built their *buṅgās* and stationed their *vakīls* or agents. But as the need for a common strategy and action decreased and rivalries among the *misl* chiefs raised their head, *sarbatt khālsā* and correspondingly the Akāl Takht lost their political pre-eminence. Mahārājā Raṇjīt Siṅgh felt little need for *sarbatt khālsā* assemblies after 1805 when it was summoned to consider the question whether or not the fugitive Marāṭhā prince Jasvant Rāo Holkar be assisted against the British. The religious authority of the Akāl Takht , however, remained intact and the State never challenged it in any manner. There are in fact instances of the State showing subservience as in the case of Mahārājā Raṇjīt Siṅgh himself responding to the summons from the Akāl Takht and accepting for a moral misdemeanour penalty imposed by its custodian, Akālī Phūlā Siṅgh, who had fought as a loyal soldier in several of the Mahārājā's military campaigns. In spite of its supremacy in the matter of enforcing religious discipline, Akāl Takht discharges no divine dispensation. It remits no sins, nor does it invoke God's wrath upon anyone.

On several occasions during the eighteenth century, Akāl Takht shared with the Harimandar desecration and destruction at the hands of Mughal satraps and Afghān invaders. Ahmad Shāh Durrānī, who had razed the Harimandar in 1762, again attacked Amritsar in December 1764. On this occasion a small band of 30 Sikhs under their leader, Nihaṅg Gurbakhsh Siṅgh stationed there to serve and protect the Akāl Takht, came out to dare the invading horde and fell fighting to the last man. Ahmad Shāh had the Akāl Buṅga completely demolished. Sikhs, however, continued to hold the *sarbatt khālsā* in front of the ruins and decided at one such gathering on Baisākhī, 10 April 1765, to rebuild the Akāl Buṅgā as well as the Harimandar. Funds for this purpose had already been set apart from the pillage of Sirhind in January 1764. The work was entrusted to Bhāī Des Rāj, who was also furnished with Gurū kī Mohar or the Gurū's seal to enable him to raise more funds. The construction of the ground floor of the Akāl Buṅgā was completed by 1774. The rest of the five-storeyed domed edifice was completed during the reign of Mahārājā Raṇjīt Siṅgh. The gilded dome atop the building was built by Harī Siṅgh Nalvā at his own expense. The facade of the first four storeys including the basement (originally ground floor but rendered partly below ground level because of the raising of the level of the circumambulatory terrace in front) had a semi-circular orientation. The ground floor was a large hall with an attached pillared marble portico. The facades of the next two floors had projected eaves supported on decorative brackets. The facade of the third floor, a large hall with galleries on the sides, had cusped arched openings, nine in number. The exterior of the fourth floor, covering the central hall of the lower floor, was decorated with projected ornamental eaves and a domed kiosk at each corner. The Gurū Granth Sāhib was seated on the first floor, where the *jathedār* of the Akāl Takht also took his seat. The second floor was used for important meetings and also for *amrit prachār*, administration of the initiation of the Khālsā. The hall on the third floor was used especially for the meetings of the Shiromaṇī Gurdwārā Parbandhak Committee until a separate office block, called Tejā Siṅgh Samundarī Hall, was constructed for the purpose during the 1930's.

The beautiful and sacred edifice was destroyed in the army action, called Operation Blue Star, in early June 1984. The Government of India got the building reconstructed in order to assuage the injured feelings of the Sikhs, but this was not acceptable to them. The reconstructed building was demolished in early 1986 to be replaced by one raised through *kār-sevā*, voluntary free service of the Panth and by money accruing from voluntary donations.

After the death of Gurū Gobind Siṅgh with whom ceased the line of living Gurūs, *hukamnāmās* were issued in the name of the Khālsā Panth from the different *takhts*, especially Akāl Takht at Amritsar. Any Sikh transgressing the religious code could be summoned, asked to explain his conduct and punished. Disobedience amounted to social ostracism of an individual or the group concerned. Mahārājā Raṇjīt Siṅgh, 19th-century ruler of the Punjab, was summoned by Akālī Phūla Siṅgh, the then *jathedār* of Akāl Takht, for violating established norms of Sikh behaviour and laid under expiation. Among instances from recent history a striking one is that of Tejā Siṅgh of Bhasauṛ who was censured for the liberties he was taking with the Sikh canon. A *hukamnāmā* issued from the Akāl Takht on 26 Sāvaṇ 1985 Bk/9 August 1928 read:

> The Pañch Khālsā Dīwān (Pañch Khaṇḍ), Bhasauṛ, has published books called Gurmukhī courses in which the *bāṇī* of Srī Gurū Granth Sāhib has been garbled and its order changed.
> Changes have been made in *gurmantra*, the *ardās* and the ceremonies for administering *amrit*. These are anti-Sikh proceedings. Hence Bābū Tejā Siṅgh and Bībī Nirañjan Kaur [his wife] are hereby excommunicated from the Panth. Other members of the Pañch Khālsā Dīwān are debarred from having *ardās* offered on their behalf at Srī Akāl Takht Sāhib or at any other Gurdwārā. No Sikh should purchase Gurmukhī courses published by the Pañch Khālsā Dīwān, nor keep them in his possession. The Pañch Khālsā Dīwān or whoever else has copies of these should send them to Srī Akāl Takht Sāhib.

An example of an individual penalized for disobeying the Akāl Takht edict was that of Bhāī Santā Siṅgh, the Nihaṅg, who for the charge brought against him was excommunicated from the Panth (*Hukamnāmā*, 8 Sāvaṇ 515 Nānak Shāhī/22 July 1984). *Hukamnāmās* have also been issued to settle points of religious and political disputation; also for commending the services to the Panth of individuals and for adding passages to Sikh *ardās*, the daily prayer of supplication, as a particular historical situation might demand. On 26 Jeṭh 1984 Bk/8 June 1927, the Akāl Takht eulogized in a *hukamnāmā* Bhāī Sāhib Sardār Kharak Siṅgh for his qualities of determination and steadfastness and for his sacrifices in the cause of the Panth; likewise, on 30 Bhādoṅ 1988 Bk/15 September 1931, Bhāī Sāhib Raṇdhīr Siṅgh was honoured for his outstanding services to the Panth. On 20 Asūj 1970 Bk/4 October 1913, Takht Sachkhaṇḍ Srī Hazūr Sāhib promulgated a *hukamnāmā* fixing the length of *kirpān* or sword a Sikh will carry slung from across his shoulder at a minimum of one foot. On 12 Māgh 483 Nānak Shāhī/25 January 1952, Akāl Takht enjoined upon the "entire Khalsā and all Gurdwārā ministers" to add these lines to the *ardās* :

> O Timeless Lord, the Benevolent One, ever the succourer of Thy Panth, we pray grant the Khālsājī the privilege of unhindered access to and control and maintenance of Srī Nankāṇā Sāhib and other holy shrines and sites from which the Panth has been parted [after the partition of the Punjab in 1947].

Such writs promulgated under the seal of a Takht carry sanction for the entire Sikh people.

BIBLIOGRAPHY

1. Gordon, John J. H. , *The Sikhs*. Patiala, 1970
2. Dilgeer, Harjinder Singh, *The Akal Takht*. Jalandhar, 1980
3. Kapur Singh, "Akal Takht," in *The Sikh Sansar*. June 1976

4. Harbans Singh, *The Heritage of the Sikhs*. Delhi, 1983
5. Sukhdiāl Siṅgh, *Akāl Takht Sāhib*. Patiala, 1984
6. Giān Siṅgh, Giānī, *Twārīkh Gurū Khālsā* [Reprint]. Patiala, 1970
7. *Gurbilās Chhevīṅ Pātshāhī*. Patiala, 1970
8. Gaṇḍā Siṅgh, *Hukamnāme*. Patiala, 1967
9. Ashok, Shamsher Siṅgh, *Nīsāṇ te Hukamnāme*. Amritsar, 1967

M.G.S.

AKĀL USTATI (In Praise of the Timeless Being) is a poetical composition by Gurū Gobind Siṅgh in the *Dasam Granth*. This is the only major composition in the Tenth Master's Book which is without a title. The title by which it is known is made up of its first word, *Akāl* (The Timeless One), and its last word, *Ustati* (praise). In the beginning is the note: *utār khāse daskhat kā Pātshāhī 10* (a copy of the Tenth Gurū's own handwriting). After four lines comes the next note: *āgai likhārī ke daskhat* (henceforth is the scribe's writing). This shows that in the original text the first four lines were written in the Gurū's own hand. The *bāṇī* comprises 271 verses excluding the first four lines. Twelve different metrical measures have been used. The language of *Akāl Ustati* is Braj Bhāṣā written in Gurmukhī characters. The dates given for its composition are1684 for the opening section, and 1691 for the remainder. Its final compilation came much later, about 1735, when Bhāī Manī Siṅgh prepared the first copy of the *Dasam Granth*.

The main theme of the poem is praise of the Timeless Eternal Being. In the opening invocation, God is addressed as Timeless Being, All-steel, "the personification and source of chivalry." He also is the Transcendent "Being, distinct from all the world"(verse 9). Ten *savaiyyās* follow. These four-line verses warn that religious books and rites, rigorous asceticism or worldly pomp and power, are useless without the love and favour of God (verses 21-30). The great God Hari is described at length in transcendent terms as the Omnipotent Creator and Sustainer of the universe. Austere ascetic feats, ceremonies, pilgrimages are performed by devotees everywhere, but the conclusion is:

> Know that all such things are vain,
> And that all such devotion is fruitless,
> Without the support of the One Name,
> Deem all religious ceremonies as superstition . (verses 31-50)

Then God's omnipresence is sung, " Thou art in the earth, Thou art in the firmament,'' ending in a burst of devotional fervour when "*Tū hī! Tū hī!* (Thou alone art)'' is repeated 16 times (verses 69-70). In the midst of another long portrayal of true and false conception of God, the unity of mankind before the Creator is thus emphasized:

> He is in the temple as He is in the mosque;
> He is in the Hindu worship as He is in the Muslim prayer
> Men are one though they appear different...
> The Hindus and the Muslims are all one,
> Have each the habits of different environments,
> But all men have the same eyes, the same body...
> Thus the Abhekh of the Hindus and the Allah of the Muslims are one,
> The Qura'n and the Purāṇas praise the same Lord.
> They are all of one form,
> The One Lord made them all. (verse 86)

About a third of the poem is a satire on false methods of worship; but it is satire with the kindly purpose of showing that true praise is an inner state consisting of heartfelt devotion to the One Supreme Creator. Satire, then, is the means to carry out the divinely given mission. Then God is again described mostly in negative terms (verses 91-200) and is to be found, not by austerities, but by worship of Him as the Treasury of Grace (verse 59), for God is Love, Holiness, Virtue, and Omnipotence (verse 172). A series of questions and riddles much in the nature of a religious catechism follow (verses 201-10).

The final section is a veritable paean of praise. People the world over are included, as the Gurū mentions, among the seekers after God, the people of Arabia and of France, the Qandahārīs, the Qureshīs, the Westerners, the Marāṭhās, the Bihārīs, the Oriyās, the Beṅgālīs, the English, the residents of Delhi, the Gurkhās, the Chinese, Manchurians, Tibetans, the Easterners of Kāmrūp and Kumāūṅ—all these were blessed as they sang the praises of the One Lord (verses 254-71).

In Oriental imagery His praise is likened to milk, buttermilk, moonlight on the Yamunā, crystal mirrors, swans, cranes, the Ganges, until finally:

> His splendour appeareth everywhere,
> He is the treasury of favour,
> His light dazzleth, His glory is perfect.
> The sky and the earth repeat His Name.
> (verse 271)

The Gurū commences his great work on praise with an invocation to the All-Steel, i.e. God. He ends with the hope of human brotherhood as men throughout the world seek the One God and sing His praises.

The *Ustati* overflows with many of the oft-quoted verses and stanzas of Gurū Gobind Siṅgh. It presents a mixture of devotional lyrics and philosophical reflections. It is composed in a style which is a blend of grandeur and beauty. Diction and style of Gurū Gobind Siṅgh are unique: no resemblance of these is available in Hindi or Punjabi literature. The main source of his vocabulary, in this text, is Sanskrit, though in some of his other compositions the Gurū has made free use of Perso-Arabic words. He uses Sanskrit words in their *tadbhav* form and has experimented with formation of new words and compounds. *Akāl Ustati,* like the *Jāpu,* is a treasury of adjectival vocabulary.

Many of these adjectives are of fresh coinage. A rich variety of poetic metres has been used. Some of the metres like *kabitt, savaiyyā* and *dīrgh narāj* are characterized by lengthy verse-forms, while some others like *tomar* and *pādharī* by short ones consisting of no more than two or three words.

BIBLIOGRAPHY

1. Loehlin, C.H., *The Granth of Guru Gobind Singh and the Khalsa Brotherhood.* Lucknow, 1971
2. Ashta, Dharam Pal, *The Poetry of the Dasam Granth.* Delhi, 1959
3. Padam, Piārā Siṅgh, *Dasam Granth Darshan.* Patiala, 1968
4. Jaggī, Rattan Siṅgh, *Dasam Granth Parichaya.* Delhi, 1990

C.H.L.

ĀKAṚ, a village in the interior of Paṭiālā district, possesses a historical shrine called Gurdwārā Nim Sāhib. The Gurdwārā commemorates the visit of Gurū Tegh Bahādur who, during one of his journeys through the Mālvā territory, put up here near a *nim* (*margosa*) tree, which still exists. The leaves of one of the boughs of this tree which leans over the shrine are tasteless while those on the rest of the tree possess their natural bitter taste. The miracle is attributed to Gurū Tegh Bahādur, who is said to have pulled off a twig from this branch and used it to cleanse his teeth. The one-room Mañjī Sāhib was replaced in 1924 by a larger building. The present complex, completed in 1972, consists of a spacious hall, with a verandah in front. The sanctum marking the original site of the Mañjī Sāhib is in the middle of this hall with a domed room over it on the first floor. The shrine is managed by a local committee.

BIBLIOGRAPHY

1. Ṭhākar Siṅgh, Giānī, *Srī Gurduāre Darshan.* Amritsar, 1923

2. Tārā Singh, *Srī Gur Tīrath Sangrahi.* Amritsar, n.d.

M.G.S.

AKBAR, JALĀL UD-DĪN MUHAMMAD (1542-1605), third in the line of Mughal emperors of India, was born on 23 November 1542 at Amarkoṭ, in Sindh, while his father, Humāyūṅ, was escaping to Persia after he had been ousted by Sher Khān Sūr. Akbar was crowned king at Kalānaur, in the Punjab, on 14 February 1556. At that time, the only territory he claimed was a small part of the Punjab, Delhi and Āgrā having been taken by Hemū. He was then fourteen years old, but he proved himself a great general and conqueror. Upon his death in 1605, he left to his son and successor, Jahāṅgīr, a stable kingdom comprising the whole of Upper India, Kābul, Kashmīr, Bihār, Bengal, Oṛīssā and a great part of the Deccan.

Great soldier as he was, it is as an administrator that he gained the highest fame. His revenue reforms and his liberal religious policy won him popular acclaim. He abolished *jizyah*, capitation tax on non-Muslims, and the pilgrimage tax Hindus had to pay. He curbed the power of the *'ulamā*. Although illiterate himself, he was genuinely interested in the study of comparative religion and built an *'ibādat-khānā* (house of worship) where learned men of all religions assembled to discourse on theological issues. These discussions convinced Akbar that there were good and positive elements in all religions and prompted him to promulgate a new eclectic faith called Dīn-i-Ilāhī (Divine Faith), which he vainly hoped would prove acceptable to all of his subjects.

The Sikh chronicles refer to Akbar's amicable relations with Gurū Amar Dās, Nānak III. They also allude to Akbar's visit to Goindvāl where he had to eat in the Sikh community refectory like any other pilgrim before he could see the Gurū. As the *Mahimā Prakāsh* records, the Emperor refused to step on the silks spread out for him by his servants when going to call on Gurū Amar Dās. He turned aside the lining with his own hands and walked to the Gurū's place barefoot. As recorded in Abul Fazl's *Akbar-nāmā*, a contemporary source, Akbar also visited Gurū Arjan at Goindvāl on 24 November 1598. At the Gurū's instance, he remitted the annual revenue of the peasants of the district, who had been hit hard by the failure of the monsoon. According to another account, complaints were made to Akbar that the Holy Book of the Sikhs, Granth Sāhib, contained references derogatory to Islam and other religions. Akbar, who was then encamped at Baṭālā in the Punjab, sent for Gurū Arjan. The Gurū despatched Bhāī Buḍḍhā and Bhāī Gurdās with the Holy Volume. The book was opened at random and read from a spot pointed out by Akbar. The hymn was in praise of God. So were the others read out subsequently. Akbar was highly pleased and made an offering of fifty-one gold *mohars* to the Granth Sāhib. He presented Bhāī Buḍḍhā and Bhāī Gurdās with robes of honour and gave a third one for the Gurū.

Akbar died at Āgrā on 16 October 1605 and was succeeded by his son, Jahāṅgīr.

BIBLIOGRAPHY

1. Bhallā, Sarūp Dās, *Mahimā Prakāsh*, part II. Patiala, 1971
2. Smith, Vincent A. , *Akbar.* Delhi, 1962
3. Beveridge, A.H., trans., *The Akbar Nama.* Delhi, 1989
4. Macauliffe, Max Arthur, *The Sikh Religion.* Oxford, 1909

S.R.S.

AKBAR KHĀN, MUHAMMAD (d. 1848), son of Dost Muhammad Khān, the ruler of Afghanistan. He was a fiery young man of great dash and daring. Like his father, he was keen to regain the Afghān possessions in India – Multān, Kashmīr, Attock and Peshāwar. In 1837, Dost Muhammad Khān declared a holy war against the Sikhs and attacked the fortress of Jamrūd at the entrance to the Khaibar Pass. An attack led by

Akbar K͟hān was repulsed, though the valiant Sikh general, Harī Siṅgh Nalvā, was killed in the action. After the assassination of Mahārājā Sher Siṅgh in September 1843, Akbar K͟hān's ambition to recover Peshāwar was revived. Early in 1844 he set up his camp at Jalālābād and began to make preparations for an attack on Peshāwar, but failed to take possession of the city. He died in 1848.

BIBLIOGRAPHY

1. Sūrī, Sohan Lāl, *'Umdāt-ut-Twārīk͟h*. Lahore, 1885-89.
2. Gupta, Hari Ram, *Panjab on the Eve of First Sikh War*. Chandigarh, 1975
3. Hasrat, Bikrama Jit, *Life and Times of Ṛanjit Singh*. Hoshiarpur, 1977

S.S.B.

AKBARPUR KHUḌĀL, village 6 km northeast of Bareṭā (29°-52'N, 75°-42'E), in Mānsā district of the Punjab, is sacred to Gurū Gobind Siṅgh, who came here in November 1706 to rescue a Sikh from captivity. According to Giānī Giān Siṅgh, *Twārīk͟h Gurū K͟hālsā*, Gulāb Siṅgh, a goldsmith of Akbarpur Khuḍāl, had been imprisoned by the village chief in a basement of his house on a false charge. The news of the Sikh in distress reached Gurū Gobind Siṅgh while he was at Sirsā, 80 km away, as the crow flies, already on his way to the South. But he turned his footsteps immediately with five of his Sikhs and, reaching Khuḍāl by a forced march, rescued Gulāb Siṅgh and instructed the chief, Nabī Bak͟hsh, in the path of virtue and justice. Gurū Gobind Siṅgh then returned to Sirsā. A *gurdwārā* was later established outside the village. The Mahārājā of Paṭiālā endowed it with 50 acres of land. The house of the chief inside the village was acquired after Independence, and Gurdwārā Bhorā Sāhib Pātshāhī 10 was constructed on the site in February 1951 by a Sikh landlord of the area, Harchand Siṅgh Jejī, who also made an endowment. The Gurdwārā, handed over to the Shiromaṇī Gurdwārā Parbandhak Committee in 1977, has a domed sanctum, within a hall, on the first floor. The *bhorā* or underground cell, in which Gulāb Siṅgh is believed to have been kept, is a small square cellar in the basement.

M.G.S.

AKHAṆḌ PĀṬH (*akhaṇḍ* = uninterrupted, without break; *pāṭh* = reading) is non-stop, continuous recital of the Gurū Granth Sāhib from beginning to end. Such a recital must be completed within 48 hours. The entire Holy Volume, 1430 large pages, is read through in a continuous ceremony. This reading must go on day and night, without a moment's intermission. The relay of reciters who take turns at saying Scripture must ensure that no break occurs. As they change places at given intervals, one picks the line from his predecessor's lips and continues. When and how the custom of reciting the canon in its entirety in one continuous service began is not known. Conjecture traces it to the turbulent days of the eighteenth century when persecution had scattered the Sikhs to far-off places. In those exilic, uncertain times, the practice of accomplishing a reading of the Holy Book by a continuous recital is believed to have originated.

Important days on the Sikh calendar are marked by *akhaṇḍ pāṭhs* in *gurdwārās*. Celebrations and ceremonies in Sikh families centre upon *akhaṇḍ pāṭhs*. The homes are filled with holiness for those two days and nights as the Gurū Granth Sāhib, installed with ceremony in a room, especially cleaned out for the occasion, is being recited. Apart from lending the air sanctity, such readings make available to listeners the entire text. The listeners come as they wish and depart at their will. Thus they keep picking up snatches of the *bāṇī* from different portions at different times. Without such ceremonial recitals, the Gurū Granth Sāhib, large in volume, would remain generally inaccessible to the laity except *for baṇīs* which are recited by the Sikhs as part of their daily devotions. In bereavement, families derive comfort from these *pāṭhs.* Obsequies in fact conclude with a completed reading of the Gurū Granth Sāhib. At such *pāṭhs,* the Holy Book is generally recited or intoned, not merely read. This brings out tellingly the poetic quality of the *bāṇī* and its power to move or grip the listener. But it must be listened to in silence, sitting on the floor in front of the Holy Book in a reverent posture. The start of the *akhaṇḍ pāṭh* is preceded by a short service at which holy hymns may be recited, followed by an *ardās* offered for the successful conclusion of the *pāṭh* and distribution ~~of~~ *kaṛāhprasād* or Sikh sacrament. A similar service marks the conclusion. *Ardās* and *kaṛāhprasād* are also offered as the reading reaches midway.

BIBLIOGRAPHY

1. Harbans Singh, *Berkeley Lectures on Sikhism.* Delhi, 1983
2. *Sikh Rahit Maryādā.* Amritsar, 1975

T.S.

AKHĀṚĀ, from Sanskrit *akṣpālā* or *akṣvālā* meaning stage or theatre or arena, is in common use a sectarian monastery, seminary or seat of Hindu anchorites such as Sannyāsīs and Bairāgīs and Sikh ascetics, Udāsīs and Nirmalās. Located at prominent places of pilgrimage, they provide facilities for board and lodging to inmates as well as to travellers. They also serve as centres of study and training for neophytes. Whereas Sannyāsī and Bairāgī *akhāṛās* had existed at various places since ancient times, it was Mahant Prītam Dās Nirbān (1753-1831), an Udāsī saint, who first conceived the idea of establishing separate *akhāṛās* for Udāsīs. During his travels in South India, he persuaded Nānak Chand, uncle of Dīwān Chandū Lāl of Hyderābād state, to make a donation of money for this purpose. This led to the setting up of the Pañchāitī Central Akhāṛā of Udāsīs in 1779 at Prayāg (Allāhābād), with branches at several other pilgrimage centres. Two years later, Mahant Prītam Dās founded Nirbān Akhāṛā, popularly called Saṅgalvālā Akhāṛā, at Amritsar, of which he himself was the head. Some other Udāsī saints also set up their own *akhāṛās* around the Darbār Sāhib complex at Amritsar. Many of them were taken over by the Shiromaṇī Gurdwārā Parbandhak Committee as the agitation for Gurdwārā reform got under way during the 1920's. The latest one was Brahm Būṭā Akhāṛā acquired towards the end of the 1980's. Saṅgat Sāhib (Bhāī Pherū) branch of Udāsī Sikhs had established a separate central institution at Kankhal, near Haridvār, in 1839. It was named Srī Guru Nayā Akhāṛā Udāsīn, but is popularly known as Udāsīāṅ dā Chhoṭā Akhāṛā.

Nirmalā Sikhs also established their own central *akhāṛā* in 1862 at Paṭiālā with funds provided by the rulers of Phūlkīāṅ states of Paṭiālā, Nābhā and Jīnd (*See* NIRMAL PAÑCHĀITĪ AKHĀṚĀ). Named Dharam Dhujā Akhāṛā Gurū Gobind Siṅgh, it is still in existence with branches at several towns throughout north India including those at Haridvār, Kankhal, Allāhābād, Ujjain, Nāsik and Kurukshetra. The central (Pañchāitī) Akhāṛā of Nirmalā Sikhs is now located at Kankhal.

M.G.S.

AKHBĀRĀT-I-ḌEOṚHĪ-I-MAHĀRĀJĀ RAṆJĪT SIṄGH BAHĀDUR, a Persian manuscript written in *nasta' līq,* mixed with *shikastā,* preserved in the National Archives of India at New Delhi. This is a copy of the *roznāmachā,* i.e. a day-to-day account, of the proceedings of the court of Mahārājā Raṇjīt Siṅgh covering the period from January to December 1825. Written in black ink on Siālkoṭ paper, it comprises 677 folios. The name of the author/copyist does not figure anywhere in the manuscript.

To refer to the contents: *Nazrānā* is collected at Amritsar (fol. 1). Allard, the Frenchman, collects Rs 40,000 from *ta'alluqā* Mansovāl and is ordered by Mahārājā Raṇjīt Siṅgh to retain the amount as *amānat* (fol. 1). Shortage of grass at Amritsar (fol. 250). Bullocks of the *topkhānā* (arsenal) arrive at Amritsar from Lahore and are sent to Haryāṇā Bhūmākā for grazing (fol. 1). Madsūdan Paṇḍit will procure articles to be given in charity on the *amāvas* (the last day of the dark half of the lunar month) day (fol. 1). A *harkārā* sent by the newswriters of Shāhjahānābād (Delhi) comes with news from that part. The *harkārā* is paid Rs 10 as *in'ām* (fol. 1). The *qanūngos* of *ta'alluqā* Mansovāl present Rs 30,000 to the Mahārājā and are paid Rs 200 by way of expense (fol. 1). Letters are issued to the *kārdārs* of Nūrpur, Paṭhānkoṭ, Sujānpur and Hājīpur to come with their account books (fol. 1). A *harkārā* brings an *'arzī* from Nawāb Shāh Nawāz Khān of Mankerā touching on events in that part. Rs 20 paid to the *harkārā* (fol. 1). Bābā Malak Dās and Mīhāṅ Siṅgh, the Nānakputras, request for the lease of *ta'alluqā* Mansovāl. They are told that Mansovāl will be farmed out to them after Barkhānī Khān *kārdār* has cleared his accounts (fols. 1-2). Hakīm Imām ud-Dīn, *qil'ādār* of Gobindgaṛh, is directed to sell the old grain and buy new instead (fol. 2). Shiv Dayāl, grandson of the late Rāmānand Sāhū, is summoned and asked to disclose the entire assets, in cash and kind, of Harsukh Dās (fol. 2). Chet Siṅgh, *thāṇedār* of *qilā* Jalandhar reports that the fort is in a dilapidated condition. He is ordered to execute necessary repairs after getting some money from Chaṛhat Siṅgh, *kārdār* of the place (fol. 2).The Mahārājā weighs himself against *ghī, shakaratarī, til, māsh* on the *amāvas* day and gives these and Rs 2,000 in cash, two pairs of gold bracelets, two cows and several robes to the Brāhmaṇs in charity. Afterwards, the Mahārājā makes an offering of Rs 5,000 and a tray of sacrament (*patāshe*) to the Gurū Granth Sāhib at the Harimandar at Amritsar (fol. 2). Nau Nihāl Siṅgh, son of Khaṛak Siṅgh, is summoned and seated in the lap by the Mahārājā. The Mahārājā talks to him for a while in a kind and sweet tone and gives him a pair of gold bracelets (fol. 3). The Mahārājā pays Rs 100 to the *chobedār* who leaves for Peshāwar to escort William Moorcroft to Lahore (fol. 4). The Mahārājā holds court at the Rām Bāgh *bārādarī* in Amritsar when officers such as Hakīm 'Azīz ud-dīn, Imām ud-dīn, Bhavānī Dās, Munshī Shiv Dayāl, Sarb Dayāl, Sardhā Rām, Dīwān Motī Rām, Sukh Dayāl, Jīvan Mall, Misr Dīvān Chand, Budh Siṅgh Sandhāṅvālīā, and Khushāl Siṅgh Jamādār are present (fol. 5). A courtier informs the Mahārājā about the intentions of the British government to lead expeditions against the rulers of Pegu (in Burma) and Assam to subdue them (fol. 5). The Mahārājā sends a *shuqqā*, or a royal order, to Bāj Siṅgh, *nāzim* of Multān, to maintain friendly relations with the local people and send the Bhaṅgī *top* (cannon) to him (fol. 6). Dharam Chand, a confidant of Nau Nihāl Siṅgh, son of Khaṛak Siṅgh, informs the Mahārājā that the *sālgirah* (birth anniversary) of the Sarkār's (Raṇjīt Siṅgh) grandson falls the next day (22 February 1825) and says that it will be appropriate for him to participate in the celebration. The Mahārājā expresses his inability to join owing to certain reasons and pays Rs 1,100 to meet the expenses (fol. 6). Sardār Himmat Siṅgh states that a slip in Gurmukhī relating to the release of Sardārnī Sadā Kaur was placed before the Gurū Granth Sāhib in the Harimandar at Amritsar. Nothing is known about the outcome. The Mahārājā replies that there was an indication that she should not be released (fol. 6). The Mahārājā crosses the Rāvī in the company of 150 riders and amuses himself with hunting. Mīāṅ Dhiān Siṅgh hunts two deer and three hogs. The Mahārājā hunts several hogs, deer and hare (fol. 7). A pair of *harkārās* brings news about Peshāwar. They are paid Rs 20 (fol. 9). The

Mahārājā listens to songs and music of the dancing girls who are paid Rs 1,000 for dresses (fol. 11). Gulāb Siṅgh Kabbā tells the Mahārājā that horsemen under him have requested for Holī payments. They are paid Rs 100 for wine, Rs 300 for payment to the dancing girls and Rs 50 for sweets (fol. 16). The *lāṅgarīs* (cooks) of the camp report famine of fuel and state that fuel is not available in Lahore at the rate of even one rupee per maund (fol. 16). The courtiers are provided with gold syringes. The trays of *gulāl* are asked for. Gulāl is thrown on the courtiers (fol. 16). Hakīm 'Azīz ud-dīn informs the Mahārājā that 'Imām ud-dīn, *qil'ādār-i-Gobindgaṛh*, has bought 500 maunds of *sikkā* (lead) from Amritsar. The Mahārājā orders for the purchase of 2,000 maunds of *sikkā* more for manufacturing cannons (fol. 23). Bābū Bāj Siṅgh, *qil'ādār* of Multān, offers 3 horses, 2 dromedaries and 2 *ashrafīs* and tells the Mahārājā that Jawāhar Mall, *kārdār* of Multān, had killed an innocent *zamīndār* and that such a person should not be appointed *sūbahdār* of any province. The Mahārājā on hearing it sends a *parwānā* with a k̲h̲ill'at and a pair of gold bracelets to Hazārī Madan Siṅgh appointing him *sūbahdār* of Multān, instructing him to rule with justice (fols. 23-24). Misr Belī Rām tells the Mahārājā that Misr Raliā Rām and Narsiṅgh Dās had been in his confinement for the last two or three days and asks what he should do further. The Mahārājā asks him to collect the arrears of revenue from them and the acceptance of the lease for the next year (fol. 489). The Mahārājā goes for a morning walk (fol. 489). The *qil'ādār* of Hājīpur presents a *nazr* of two rupees and requests payment of salary to troops under him (fol. 489). A sum of Rs 2,000 is sent to Srī Javālāmukhī on account of *pūjā* (fol. 489). A letter is sent to Nawāb Sādiq Muhammad K̲h̲ān of Bahāwalpur, with instructions to transmit all the arrears of revenue as early as possible failing which an army would be sent against him (fol. 489). Kauṛā Mall Sāhū is sent for and *pashmīnā* worth Rs 10,000 is sold to him (fol. 489). *Shuqqā* is addressed to Hazārī Madan Siṅgh, *sūbahdār* of Multān, with directions to execute repairs of the fort there (fol. 489). An *'arzī,* along with two *bahaṅgīs* of apples sent by Chūnī Lāl, *nāzim* of Kashmīr, is presented to the Mahārājā who gives Rs 10 to the bearers of the *bahaṅgīs* by way of *in'ām* and sends a *k̲h̲ill'at* of seven pieces and a pair of gold bracelets for the *nāzim* (fol. 490). Rām Ratan Sāhū of Qasbā Jalandhar is summoned by the Mahārājā who fixes upon him the lease money of one lakh and five thousand rupees per year in respect of Jalandhar and honours him with a turban and *dopaṭṭā-i-banārasī* on the occasion (fol. 490). The *zamīndārs* of Koṭ Kamāliā present one rupee each to the Mahārājā and then apprise him of the atrocities perpetrated on the subjects by the *'āmil* of the said place. The Mahārājā offers to them the lease of the *qasbā* but they express their inability to accept it (fol. 491). A *parwānā* is sent to the Rājā of Chambā to send two *bahaṅgīs* of preserves of green myrobalan to the Mahārājā (fol. 492). A letter is received from Sardār Fateh Siṅgh Āhlūvāliā to the effect that fever has broken out at Kapūrthalā (fol. 492). Kidār Nāth, a jeweller of Shāhjahānabād sells two bracelets made of emeralds to the Mahārājā for Rs 5, 000 (fol. 492). The *vakīl* of Sardārnī Sadā Kaur communicates her message to the Mahārājā saying, "I have grown old in the jail I am assigned to by the Mahārājā. I am ready to hand over the entire property to the Mahārājā. I request to be set free so that I may pass the remaining days of my life in worship and prayer to God." The Mahārājā gives no reply (fol. 493). The Mahārājā distributes fifty rupees among the Akālīs (fol. 484). Sundar Siṅgh Darog̲h̲ā-i-'Adālat is adjured by the Mahārājā to do justice and refrain from acts of high-handedness (fol. 586). Qāzī Badr ud-Dīn, *vakīl* of Sardār Yār Muhammad K̲h̲ān, informs the

Mahārājā about the death of William Moorcroft (fol. 593). Dīwān Motī Rām reports high prices of grain in Mankerā (fol. 616). Ganesh Datt, *kochwān*, is ordered to have a new *bugghī* made. He tells the Mahārājā that a *bugghī* could not be made locally; it could be had from Calcutta (fol. 616).

J.R.G.

AKHBĀRĀT-I-SIṄGHĀṄ, also known as *Twārīkh-i-Sikkhāṅ*, is a diary of the day-to-day events of the period from 1895 Bk/AD 1839 to 1903 Bk/AD 1847, based on official reports which General Avitabile (*q.v.*), military governor of Peshāwar during Sikh times, received from various districts under his jurisdiction. It is written in Khatt-i-Shikastā, also called Khatt-i-Dīwānī; the name of the compiler is not known. The only known manuscript is available, in three volumes, at the Pañjāb University Library, Lahore, under MS. No. PE III, 30.

Volume I, comprising 250 folios, covers the period from 12 Chet 1895 Bk to 3 Jeṭh, 1896/23 March 1839-May 1839 and contains news from Peshāwar. It starts with a meeting at Peshāwar between General Avitabile and Colonel Wade, the British political agent on the Anglo-Sikh frontier. Details of the effusive welcome given the latter are recorded, but nothing of what transpired between the two. There is also a report on the meeting between Colonel Wade and General Ventura (*q.v.*) on 10 Baisākh, 1896 Bk/21 April 1839. In the month of Baisākh Samvat 1896, Prince Nau Nihāl Siṅgh visited Peshāwar where special arrangements were made for his stay. Every morning after listening to *pāṭh* (reading of texts) from the Gurū Granth Sāhib, the prince held his *darbār*. Details are given of the income from revenue deposited in the treasury by the local landlords; also, of the expenditure of the army. It is recorded that the Sikh army officers stationed at Peshāwar were fully aware of the political situation in Afghanistan and that the Lahore Darbār received through them regular reports on the events in that country. Another report tells of Prince Nau Nihāl Siṅgh's visit to Peshāwar in Baisākh 1896/April-May 1839. The Prince held a *darbār* at which he gave audience to the Peshāwar Bārakzaīs—Pīr Muhammad Khān and Sultān Muhammad Khān. Those in attendance on the prince included Atar Siṅgh Sandhāṅvālīā, General Ventura, Lahiṇā Siṅgh Majīṭhīā, Fateh Siṅgh and Shaikh Ghulām Mohi ud-Dīn. The Prince fell ill at Peshāwar and was treated by Hakīm Aizād Bakhsh. Volume II, comprising 226 folios, covers the period from 2 Bhādoṅ 1898 Bk to 29 Māgh 1898 Bk/15 August 1841—9 February 1842. It describes in general activities of Avitabile on the northwest frontier. It begins with the General holding a *darbār* or court at which *kārdārs*, i.e. revenue officials and heads of the various departments, present reports of the conditions prevailing in the areas under their jurisdiction. The General checked the record of the income from revenue and the expenditure on the army. Reports from Bannū and Kohāṭ were presented and instructions by the General were issued on the spot. He was also informed that on his way from Peshāwar to Kohāṭ, Dr James, another of the European employees of Mahārājā Raṇjīt Siṅgh, was robbed by the Afrīdīs. Volume III, comprising 192 folios and covering the period from 16 Bhādoṅ 1903 Bk to 8 Phāgun 1903 Bk/29 August 1846-17 February 1847, contains reports from Bannū, Ḍerā Ismā'īl Khān, Īsā Khel, Mūsā Khel, Kulāchī and Ṭoṅk. The principal character of this volume is Dīwān Daulat Rām, who regularly held court and conducted official business. News on trade and commerce is also given. The author relies for his news on official reports which the military governor of Peshāwar received from various districts and this makes the work authentic and reliable. Though the style resembles that of *'Umdāt-*

ut-Twārīkh, the author is definitely a different person.

Md.A

AKHBĀR DARBĀR LAHORE, an unpublished collection of 92 letters, reports, notes and summaries of events connected with the second Anglo-Sikh war, 1848-49. The manuscript, in Persian, is preserved in Dr Gaṇḍā Siṅgh Collection at Punjabi University, Paṭiālā. The entire manuscript comprises 382 pages. These documents are communications written by or summaries of those received or procured by newswriters employed by the British and stationed at Lahore. The earliest of these is dated 23 August 1848 and the last 25 January 1849. A number of them are undated, too, but they relate to this very period. Several of those initiating from Lahore are by "Lālā Harsaran Dās, Akhbārnawīs, Darbār Lahore." Other places from which these papers originated include Multān, Fīrozpur, Bahāwalpur and Rāmnagar. A 4-page "Persian translation of a letter in English" gives an eye-witness account of the battle fought at Rāmnagar on 22 November 1848.

M.G.S.

AKHBĀR-I-DARBĀR-I-MAHĀRĀJĀ RAṆJĪT SIṄGH, also called *Akhbār-i-Ḍeoṛhī Sardār Raṇjīt Siṅgh Bahādur,* is a set of Persian manuscripts comprising 193 loose sheets of unequal size and containing, as the title indicates, news of the court of Mahārājā Raṇjīt Siṅgh (1780-1839). These sheets are believed to be newsletters sent from the Punjab for the Peshwā Daftar at Poonā (now Puṇe). The collection was first discovered in 1932-33 by Dr Muhammad Nāzim, an officer of the Archaeological Survey of India, in the Alienation Branch of the Divisional Commissioner's office at Poonā. The material was translated into English and published by Punjab Government Records Office in 1935 as Monograph No. 17, *Events at the Court of Ranjit Singh, 1810-1817.* The Languages Department, Punjab, brought out a reprint in 1970. Some of the original manuscripts are preserved in the Punjab State Archives at Paṭiālā under catalogue Nos. M-412 (I, II), M-419 (I, II) and M-352 (I, II). The newsletters, covering the period from 1 November 1810 to 2 September 1817 with one letter, dated 10 June 1822, are written in Persian *shikastā* or running hand. Each letter has a heading giving the title (usually, *Akhbār-i-Ḍeoṛhī Sardār Raṇjīt Siṅgh Bahādur*), the day of the week, the date in Hijrī era, and the place from which the letter was sent. The newswriter remains anonymous. He also remains impersonal in that he relates bare facts without comment or opinion. Most of the letters were written from the Fort of Lahore where the Mahārājā held his court, while there are some written from widely disparate places such as Fort of Gobindgaṛh (Amritsar), Gujrāt, Aṭṭock, Wazīrābād, Rājaurī, Siālkoṭ, Fatehgaṛh and Rāwalpiṇḍī. Ten letters relating to the period 1810-12 end with the sentence, "*Zabānī Khush-hāl Siṅgh Khabardār nawishtah shud*— this has been written on the basis of verbal information supplied by Khushāl Siṅgh, the informant," while three letters of the year 1817 end with the word, *arzī* followed by a seal which reads "'Azīm Ullah 1236 A. H.'' The latter remains unidentified, but the former has been conjectured to be Khushāl Siṅgh Jamādar, the *ḍeoṛhīdār,* or chamberlain, under Mahārājā Raṇjīt Siṅgh.

These letters, rich in variety and detail, provide intimate glimpses into the life of Raṇjīt Siṅgh, his daily routine, personal habits, character and pastimes. To refer to the newsletter, dated 9 June 1813, the Mahārājā rose early in the morning and came to the *dīwān khānā,* where the *sardārs* presented themselves and made obeisance. Here he received reports from different parts of the kingdom. Expeditiously disposing of State business, he would inspect troops mounted on a horse or an elephant. Thereafter, he returned to the *zanānā,* took meals and rested in the afternoon. In the late afternoon, he would come to the Saman Burj and transact business for four hours.

The letters contain valuable information about Ranjīt Siṅgh's financial, military and judicial administration during the earlier period of his reign. For example, the extent to which the Mahārājā had succeeded in training and reorganizing his forces on Western model, even before the advent of European officers, is revealed through his consistent endeavours in this behalf and through the names of battalion and higher commanders mentioned. The instructions issued to his *'adālatīs* or justices indicate his concern for impartiality in the administration of justice. The frequent mention of *joṛīs,* lit. pairs, who bring news from distant districts, even from foreign courts and offices, reveals the elaborate system of speedy and efficient intelligence-gathering which then existed.

B.S.

AKHBĀR-I-DARBĀR-I-MU'ALLĀ, in Persian, News of the Exalted (Imperial Mughal) Court (*darbār*), was not, as the title suggests, exclusively news of the royal court. They were, broadly speaking, court bulletins which included, besides provincial newsletters and reports of generals and governors, orders, activities and observations of the emperors, appointments, promotions, transfers, dismissals and references to other matters of State. The Mughal emperors had an elaborate system for the collection of news from all parts of the country through a network of officials, newswriters called *akhbār-nawīs, waqā'i-nawīs* or *waqā'i-nigār,* who regularly sent their news-sheets or reports to the imperial capital, where a regular department existed for the compilation of day-to-day news of the kingdom for presentation to the emperor for his information or orders. Copies of these bulletins were kept by feudatory chiefs, officers and governors through their *vakīls* or agents stationed at the capital. There is an invaluable stock of such news bulletins, in Persian, at Jaipur, now partly transferred to Bīkāner, in Rājasthān, covering the period from 1650 to 1730 with some gaps. Especially noteworthy is news from the Punjab from 1708 to 1716 when it faced a strong armed uprising led by the Sikh warrior Bandā Siṅgh Bahādur. The late Dr Gaṇḍā Siṅgh scrutinized these papers from September 1944 to January 1945 and prepared a manuscript, comprising extracts of reports pertaining to the Punjab, with special reference to the Sikhs. This manuscript, *Akhbār-i-Darbār-i-Mu'allā,* is now preserved in the Punjabi University Library, to which the learned historian had donated his entire collection of books, manuscripts and papers. The *Akhbār* manuscript comprises 220 foolscap pages and embraces events from the ninth year of Auraṅgzīb's reign to the seventh of Farrukh-Sīyar's, i.e. from 1667 to 1719. In the news of Auraṅgzīb's reign there are wide gaps, yet the manuscript provides interesting and authentic details about the Sikh movement from 1708 to 1716, and about the efforts made by the imperial government to suppress it. Although a contemporary record, the contents of the *Akhbār* have to be used with caution because at places the newswriters have been victims of grave misunderstanding or prejudice. For example, Bandā Siṅgh has been referred to variously as Gurū, Gobind, Gurū Gobind and Gurū Gobind Siṅgh. Similarly, Ajīt Siṅgh of the *Akhbār* was the adopted son of Mātā Sundarī, widow of Gurū Gobind Siṅgh, and not Sāhibzādā Ajīt Siṅgh, the real son of the Gurū.

As revealed by the *Akhbār,* the Sikh movement under Bandā Siṅgh had a strong base in the villages. As soon as he started his operations in the Punjab, the peasants promptly rallied round him and accepted him as their overlord. During the entire period of their struggle against the Mughals, Bandā Siṅgh and his Sikhs could move almost unchecked in the eastern part of the Punjab. The *zamīndārs* of the Punjab, mainly of the northeastern districts of Bārī Doāb, supplied arms and horses to Bandā Siṅgh and many of the hill chiefs of the Śivālik ranges provided him shelter. However, this does not mean that there was no opposition from any of the *zamīndārs*. Besides the Muslim *zamīndārs*, many Hindu chiefs also sided with the Mughals mainly with a view to escaping harassment at the hands of the government. For instance, in the early stages, Bhūp Parkāsh, son of Harī Parkāsh, ruler of Nāhan, supported the cause of Bandā Siṅgh. According to the *Akhbār*, Bhūp Parkāsh was called to Delhi and imprisoned. In order to prove her loyalty to the Emperor, Bhūp Parkāsh's mother captured many Sikhs and sent them to Delhi for execution or imprisonment. The *zamīndārs* of Kumāoṅ and Sirmūr, too, were hostile to Bandā Siṅgh.

According to the entry, dated 10 December 1710, the Emperor asked Bakhshī ul-Mumālik Mahābat Khān that under his name orders should be issued to the *faujdārs* around Shāhjahānābād that wherever Nānak worshippers be found they should be executed. This order was repeated by Emperor Farrukh-Sīyar in almost the same words. There are news items in the *Akhbār-i-Darbār-i-Mu'allā* about the help rendered to Bandā Siṅgh by the *banjārās*, grain carriers, who moved about in all parts of the country plying their trade. It is recorded in the *Akhbār* that on 11 October 1711, forty *banjārās*, who were Nānak-worshippers, were brought to Delhi and on their refusing to accept Islam were executed under the orders of the Emperor. In a newsletter of 28 October 1711, it was reported to the Emperor that the Hindu *faqīrs, yogīs, sannyāsīs* and *bairāgīs* conveyed the news of the Imperial court to Bandā Siṅgh. A newsletter of 29 May 1711 shows that the Mughal Emperor Bahādur Shāh had issued an edict ordering the *mutasaddīs* (accountants) to realize *jizyah* from the Nānak-worshippers at a double rate. A newsletter of 9 November 1713 records that Emperor Farrukh-Sīyar ordered that the *kotwāl* of Delhi should announce it with the beat of drum that the Hindus should not ride palanquins and horses of Iraqi and Arab breed. None of the Hindus should play or celebrate *holī*.

Despite the ruthlessly repressive measures adopted by the government, Bandā Siṅgh did not resile from his liberal principles. The newsletter of 28 April 1711 records Bandā Siṅgh's promise and proclamation: "I do not oppress the Muslims.'' For every Muslim who approached him, he fixed a daily allowance and wage and took good care of him. Another newsletter, dated 21 April 1711, records that Bandā Siṅgh permitted Muslims to recite *khutbā* and *namāz*. 5,000 Muslims had gathered around him.

From the news it is evident how seriously the Mughal authority took Bandā Siṅgh's revolt and how thorough were the operations launched against the Sikhs. Commanders and officers of very high rank were deputed by the Emperor to fight against them with all the resources at their command. According to newsletter, dated 20 October 1710, Fīroz Khān Mewātī chopped off 300 heads of the rebel Sikhs and made a gift of these to the Emperor. According to the newsletter of 6 December 1710, Amīn Khān Bahādur wrote to the Emperor that he had killed one thousand Sikhs at Sirhind. He sent 500 heads of the Sikhs to the Emperor who ordered them to be publicly displayed. According to the newsletter of 29 November 1713, 'Abd us-Samad Khān carried 900 heads of Nānak-worshippers to Delhi. The heads were exhibited in the Chāndnī Chowk Bāzār.

BIBLIOGRAPHY

Bhagat Singh, trans. and ed., *Akhbār-i-Darbār-i-Mu'allā*. Patiala, 1984

B.S.

AKHBĀR LUDHIĀṆĀ, a weekly newspaper in Persian sponsored by the British North-West Frontier Agency at Ludhiāṇā in November 1834. The paper, a four-page sheet initially, but doubling its size within two years, started printing at the American Missionary Press, Ludhiāṇā, shifting to the Pashaurī Mall Press, Ludhiāṇā, in June 1841. Three years later it ceased publication. It had a small circulation mainly determined by the requirements of the East India Company's government. The name of the editor or subscription rates were nowhere mentioned.

The *Akhbār* carried news furnished by English newsprinters from various parts of the Punjab. The main focus was Lahore, the Sikh capital, and news from Lahore was for several years the front-page caption in the paper, the day-to-day happenings at the court of Raṇjīt Siṅgh, the royal decrees to civil and military officers and visits of the *vakīls* or representatives of independent and feudatory states constituting the staple news taking up nearly half the space. Interesting incidental information is thus provided concerning the character of the Mahārājā and his administration such as his generous treatment of his soldiers (the paper in its issue No. 99, 19 November 1836, records how, on Suchet Siṅgh Ḍogrā's report that a platoon had returned after arduous duty in Bannū, the Mahārājā immediately sanctioned two months' leave of absence for them to visit their families), the severity with which he dealt with the law-breakers and miscreants (issue No. 114, 4 March 1837, records the decree issued by the Mahārājā for taking severe action against the Afrīdī *zamīndārs* for their unlawful activities), the hospitality shown by his government to foreign travellers and dignitaries (No. 106, 7 January 1837), and the realization of revenue from the turbulent tribes of trans-Indus region (No. 115, 19 December 1836). There are references to the condition of the peasantry, law and order situation, mode of collection of revenue, celebration of festival occasions, and to the feudal demesnes of the Sikh nobility resumable after the death of the occupant or sometimes even before (No. 109, 3 December 1836).

Besides news of the Lahore Darbār, the *Akhbār* reported an occasional item from Ludhiāṇā, though nothing about the activities of the English political agencies at Ludhiāṇā or Ambālā. In fact, it shunned all news relating to the East India Company and published only such reports as had nothing to do with the policy of the British in India. News about disputes and disturbances in Mahārājā Raṇjīt Siṅgh's territories, about court intrigues, murders of princes and *sardārs* and of the power of the Sikh army after the Mahārājā's death, received prominent display. At times important happenings at far-off places such as Calcutta, Leh, Hyderābād, Multān, Bahāwalpur, Balūchistān, Qandahār, Bukhārā and Khaibar, were also reported. News of local as well as of general public interest was featured sometimes; for instance, the opening of an English-medium school at Ludhiāṇā in 1834 (No. 111, 11 February 1837), and *habs-i-dam* (control of breath) performed by a *sādhū*, named Dharam Dās, by remaining alive for 40 days buried underground (No. 112, 11 February 1837).

The style of writing, unlike that of the Persian chronicles generally, was exempt from verbosity. The language used was simple and easily intelligible. The editor apparently had a good command of Persian and he made the maximum use of the space by his economy and precision of phrase. He dispensed with the elaborate forms of honorifics usually surrounding the names of chiefs and grandees.

B.S.

ĀKIL DĀS, an eighteenth-century head of the Handālī sect of Jaṇḍiālā in Amritsar district of the Punjab, also known as Haribhagat

Nirañjaṇīā, was an inveterate enemy of the Sikhs. Giānī Giān Siṅgh, *Shamsher Khālsā*, describes him as "Ākul Dās who basked in the name of Haribhagat.'' He was a State informer and revelled in spying on the Sikhs. He had had many of them arrested and executed. Most prominent among his victims were Bhāī Tārū Siṅgh and Bhāī Matāb Siṅgh Mīrāṅkoṭīā. On his information, Ādīnā Beg Khān, governor of the Punjab, in 1758, despatched him along with Dīwān Hīrā Mall against Sikhs, reportedly assembled in the neighbourhood of Adīnānagar, in present-day Gurdāspur district. In the fierce battle that took place near Qādīāṅ, Dīwān Hīrā Mall was killed but Ākil Dās escaped. At the open assembly at Amritsar on the occasion of Dīvālī, in October 1761, the Sarbatt Khālsā adopted a *gurmatā* or resolution to the effect that they must punish Ākil Dās for his Sikh-baiting. Information leaked out to Ākil Dās who forthwith despatched messengers to Ahmad Shāh Durrānī seeking his help and protection in consideration of his previous services. Sikhs besieged Jaṇḍiālā in January 1762 and would have captured the town but the wily Handālī suspended shanks of beef from the fort walls. This was a ruse he tried to exploit the religious scruples of the besiegers and make them retire from the scene. They did lift the siege and dispersed towards Sirhind.

Ākil Dās had figured prominently in the episode of the martyrdom of Bhāī Tārū Siṅgh in 1745. To quote Ratan Siṅgh Bhaṅgū, *Prāchīn Panth Prakāsh*, "Once the governor of Lahore asked his men, 'From where do the Sikhs obtain their nourishment? I have debarred them from all occupations. They realize no taxes. They do not farm, nor are they allowed to do business or join public employment. I have stopped all offerings to their places of worship. No provisions or supplies are accessible to them. Why do they not die of sheer starvation? My troops bar their way. They search for them and they kill them where they see them. I have burnt down entire villages with Sikh populations. I have destroyed their remotest kin. I have ferreted them out of the holes and slaughtered them. The Mughals are hawks; the Sikhs are like quail. Vast numbers of them have been ensnared and killed. No one can live without food. I know not how the Sikhs survive without it?'

"Haribhagat Nirañjaṇīā, who was a sworn foe of the Sikhs answered, 'There are Sikhs in this world who would not eat until they have fed their brethren. They may themselves go without clothes and food, but cannot bear their comrades' distress. They will pass the cold season by fireside and send them their own clothes. Some will sweat to grind corn and have it sent to them. They will do the roughest chores to earn a small wage for their sake. They migrate to distant places to eke out money for their brothers in exile.'

"The Nawāb shook his head in despair, 'They are unyielding people indeed. Their annihilation is beyond our power. God alone will destroy them.' Haribhagat Nirañjaṇīā spoke again. 'In the village of Pūhlā, in Mājhā, lives one, Tārū Siṅgh. He tills his land and pays the revenue to the official. He eats but little and sends what he saves to his brothers in the forest. He has his mother and a sister who both toil and grind to make a living. They eat sparingly and they wear the coarsest homespun. Whatever they save, they pass on to the Sikhs. Besides the Sikhs, they own none other. They recite the hymns of their Gurūs. Death they do not dread. They visit not the Gaṅgā or the Yamunā. They bathe in the tank constructed by their own Gurū.' ''

An officer was immediately sent with soldiers to apprehend Tārū Siṅgh. Tārū Siṅgh was captured and brought to Lahore. He was thrown into jail where he was given many tortures. But, says the *Prāchīn Panth Prakāsh*, "as the Turks tormented Tārū Siṅgh, ruddier became his cheeks with joy. As he was starved of food and drink, contentment reigned on his face. He was rejoiced to comply with the Gurū's will."

Eventually, Tārū Siṅgh was presented before the Nawāb. He greeted him with the Sikh salutation, *Vāhigurū jī kā Khālsā, Vāhigurū jī kī Fateh,* defiantly uttered. The Nawāb felt startled "as if some one had slit his finger and sprinkled salt on it.''

Tārū Siṅgh spoke out, "If we till your lands, we pay the revenue. If we engage in commerce, we pay taxes. What is left after our payments to you is for our bellies. What we save from our mouths, we give our brethren. We take nothing from you. Why do you then punish us?" The Nawāb was in a rage and pronounced, "If you become a Mussalmān, then alone will I remit your life.''

"How do I fear for my life? Why must I become a Mussalmān? Don't Mussalmāns die? Why should I abandon my faith? May my faith endure until my last hair, the last hair on my head—until my last breath,'' said Tārū Siṅgh.

The Nawāb tried to tempt him with offers of lands and wealth. When he found Tārū Siṅgh inflexible, he decided to have his scalp scraped from his head. The barbers came with sharp lancets and slowly ripped Bhāī Tārū Siṅgh's skull. He rejoiced that the hair of his head was still intact.

BIBLIOGRAPHY

1. Bhaṅgū, Ratan Siṅgh, *Prāchīn Paṅth Prakāsh* [Reprint]. Amritsar, 1962
2. Giān Siṅgh, Giānī, *Shamsher Khālsā* [Reprint]. Patiala, 1970
3. Gupta, Hari Ram, *History of the Sikhs*, vol II. Delhi, 1978
4. Harbans Singh, *The Heritage of the Sikhs*. Delhi, 1983

M.G.S.

AKOĪ, village 4 km north of Saṅgrūr (30°-14'N, 75°-50'E) in the Punjab, has an old historical shrine in memory of Gurū Hargobind, who is believed to have visited it during his travels through the Mālvā region in 1616. Here he was served with devotion by one Bhāī Māṇak Chand. After the Gurū's departure he constructed a memorial on the spot where the Gurū had stayed, on the northern edge of the village and where Gurdwārā Sāhib Pātshāhī Chheviṅ was later established. According to local tradition, Gurū Nānak had also visited Akoī. The building constructed by Sardār Dīvān Siṅgh of Baḍrukkhāṅ still survives. It consists of a small room for the Gurū Granth Sāhib, in a long and narrow hall, with a vaulted roof. A new hall, including the sanctum was constructed adjacent to the old building in 1979. A new complex comprising the Gurū kā Laṅgar and lodgings for pilgrims has also been added. The Gurdwārā owns 50 acres of land in three of the surrounding villages and is managed by a local committee under the auspices of the Shiromaṇī Gurdwārā Parbandhak Committee.

BIBLIOGRAPHY

1. Tārā Siṅgh, *Srī Gur Tīrath Saṅgrahi*. Amritsar, n.d.
2. Ṭhākar Siṅgh, Giānī, *Srī Gurduāre Darshan*. Amritsar, 1923

Jg.S.

ĀKUL, BHĀĪ, a resident of Sultānpur Lodhī in present-day Kapūrthalā district of the Punjab, embraced the Sikh faith in the time of Gurū Amar Dās. Bhāī Gurdās in his *Vārāṅ* praises his sincerity and devotion to the Gurū. Once Bhāī Ākul, along with several others from his village, waited on Gurū Arjan and begged to be instructed in how *sattvika guṇas*, or qualities of purity and goodness, might be cultivated. The Gurū explained that virtuous living was essential to spiritual well-being. He further said that simplicity, cleanliness, readiness to serve others, association with the virtuous and concentration on the Divine Name aided in moral refinement. Ākul and his companions returned to their village enlightened. The Gurū, according to Bhāī

Manī Siṅgh, *Sikhāṅ dī Bhagat Mālā,* ramarked, "Sultānpur is my devotees' citadel."

BIBLIOGRAPHY

Manī Siṅgh, Bhāī, *Sikhāṅ dī Bhagat Mālā*. Amritsar, 1955

T. S.

ALĀHṆĪĀṄ, Gurū Nānak's composition in measure Vaḍahaṅs in the Gurū Granth Sāhib. *Alāhṇī,* generally used in its plural form *alāhṇīāṅ*, is a dirge wailingly sung in chorus by women mourning the death of a relation. Etymologically, the word means an utterance in praise (of the departed person). The sorrowful singing of *alāhṇīāṅ* is part of the mourning custom of *siāpā*. The women assemble at the house of the dead person and cry aloud beating their breasts while standing, or sit together and bewail. They weep bitterly and sing *alāhṇīāṅ* in most pathetic tones. The village barbress (*naiṇ*) or *mirāsaṇ* starts the *alāhṇī* by singing aloud the first line of the dirge eulogizing the dead person, followed by the group in chorus. The *siāpā* goes on continually for a number of days until the last ceremonies are held; and the relatives of the deceased keep coming from far and near, the women joining in the heart-rending wail from day to day.

Alāhṇī is also a poetic form in Punjabi in the style of this mourning song. The strain may alter with the subject. Gurū Nānak employed this mode in his *bāṇī*, as he adopted several other popular and folk forms. Five of his *śabdas* (hymns) included in the Gurū Granth Sahib in Rāga Vaḍahaṅs (pp. 578 to 582) are entitled *Alāhṇīāṅ*. In these hymns, the sovereignty of God's Will is proclaimed. By implication, the customs of *siāpā* and *alāhṇīāṅ* are deprecated. One must not give way to idle wailing, but learn to accept what has been ordained by the Almighty. The reality of death is brought home to man. "As man hath come into this world, so must he depart." The recitation of *Alāhṇīāṅ* brings solace to the grief-afflicted soul and leads it to seek shelter in God. Surrender to His Will is the burden of this verse. "None ever die with the dead," says Gurū Nānak. "Blessed is he who praises the Lord's merits and weeps in fear of Him. They who bewail by remembering Him are through the ages acknowledged wise."

Death is inevitable. But death is for the *manmukh*, one who is ruled by his own ego, one who has turned away from God. Death is not for the *gurmukh* who is turned towards God. By *nām simran*, i.e. constant remembrance of the Name of God, one discards the fear of death. This is the way to achieving the state of fearlessness, the state of liberation and everlastingness. He is truly triumphant in the world who absorbs himself in *nām* and is firm in his faith, who performs his worldly duty and yet remains unattached, always ready to leave the world without sorrow. One, who submits to the Will of the Lord and leads a pious life, lives in peace and tranquillity and dreads not the call of death. Death for such virtuous persons is a victory. All have to reach the same destination, says Gurū Nānak. Instead of crying and wailing at the death of a relation, men should sit together and sing the praise of God.

The poetic metre used in *Alāhṇīāṅ* corresponds with the tune in which this folk form is cast. It is a kind of *duvaiyā chhand*, in which last line of each *śabda* echoes the burden of the in the first part of *Alāhṇīāṅ*. The language is Sādh Bhākhā with a strong flavour of Lahndī dialect. Alliteration has been used and new compounds formed to make the lines musical. Some of the verses convey the eternal truths in such homely yet terse language that they have become part of Punjabi speech. For instance: "*jehā likhiā tehā pāiā*"— as is it foreordained for one, so does one receive, and "*ko marai na moiā nāle*"— none ever die with the dead.

BIBLIOGRAPHY

1. Kohli, Surindar Singh, *A Critical Study of Adi Granth*. Delhi, 1961
2. Tāran Siṅgh, *Srī Gurū Granth Sāhib Jī dā Sāhitak Itihās*. Amritsar, n.d.

Hch.S.

ĀLAM CHAND was a *masand* or parish leader at Lahore in Gurū Arjan's time. He was known for his pious and honest ways. He brought to the Gurū regularly offerings collected from the Lahore *saṅgat*. His favourite maxim, tells Bhāī Manī Siṅgh in the *Sikhāṅ dī Bhagat Mālā*, was that the use for oneself even of a *kauḍī*, i.e. the smallest coin, out of the offerings was injurious to one's body as well as to one's soul.

BIBLIOGRAPHY

1. Manī Siṅgh, Bhāī, *Sikhān dī Bhagat Mālā*. Amritsar, 1955
2. Santokh Siṅgh, Bhāī, *Srī Gur Pratāp Sūraj Granth*. Amritsar, 1926-37

T.S.

ĀLAM CHAND HĀṆḌĀ, a Sikh of Gurū Arjan's time. As says Bhāī Manī Siṅgh, *Sikhāṅ dī Bhagat Mālā*, Ālam Chand, along with Bhāī Murārī Anand, Bhāī Kaliāṇā, Bhāī Nānoṅ, Bhāī Laṭkan of Bindrāo clan, and Bhāī Saisārū Talvāṛ, once came to the Gurū and spoke with folded hands, "O support of the supportless, show us the way to liberation." The Gurū said, "Practise the *śabda*, or the sacred word, and serve others." Ālam Chand said, "Lord, our minds are humble as long as we are listening to the sacred hymns, but they go wayward the moment we leave the *saṅgat*." Gurū Arjān explained: "Constant practice is the remedy. Pride results from ignorance accumulated through several births. Presevere, therefore; and you will gain humility." Ālam Chand and his companions bowed their head in reverence.

BIBLIOGRAPHY

1. Manī Siṅgh, Bhāī, *Sikhāṅ dī Bhagat Mālā*. Amritsar, 1955
2. Santokh Siṅgh, Bhāī, *Srī Gur Pratāp Sūraj Granth*. Amritsar, 1926-37

T.S.

'ĀLAMGĪR, a village in Ludhiāṇā district, 13 km to the southwest of the city (30°-54'N, 75°-52'E), is famed for its Gurdwārā Mañjī Sāhib Pātshāhī 10. Gurū Gobind Siṅgh made a halt in the village as he was travelling after the battle of Chamkaur in December 1705. Here the Gurū discarded the palanquin which he had used for part of the journey, and took a horse presented by an old disciple, Bhāī Naudhā. A Mañjī Sāhib was later constructed on the site. At present, the *gurdwārā* compound covers over three acres of land. A four-storeyed gateway topped over by a small lotus dome opens on a vast paved courtyard across which is the central building—a *dīvān* hall, with a verandah all around. The *prakāsh asthān* adjoining the hall has a basement marking the original site of the Mañjī Sāhib. Above the *prakāsh asthān* there is a 3-storeyed domed tower with domed turrets at the corners. For larger gatherings on festivals, a vast shelter of reinforced concrete was built in 1969 in honour of the 500th anniversary of the birth of Gurū Nānak. The dining hall can accommodate 2,000 persons at a time. There are several blocks of residential rooms for staff and pilgrims. A legend has grown around the 63-metre square *sarovar*, the holy tank, called Tīr Sar. It is said that the Gurū shot down a huge python occupying the only well in the vicinity. But the monster bled so profusely that it made the water of the well unfit for drinking. There being no other source of water near by, the Gurū shot another arrow into the ground and caused clean water to spring forth. The pool so formed came to be named after the arrow (*tīr*). People still believe that the water of this pool cures diseases. A three-day fair is held at 'Ālamgīr from 14-16 Poh (December-end) every year.

The management of Gurdwārā Mañjī Sāhib is in the hands of a local committee under the control of the Shiromaṇī Gurdwārā Parbandhak Committee.

BIBLIOGRAPHY

1. Tārā Siṅgh, *Srī Gur Tīrath Saṅgrahi*. Amritsar, n.d.
2. Ṭhākar Siṅgh, Giānī, *Srī Gurduāre Darshan*. Amritsar, 1923
3. Randhir, G.S., *Sikh Shrines in India*. Delhi, 1990

Jg.S.

'ĀLAM KHĀN, son of Nihaṅg Khān of Koṭla Nihaṅg Khān and son-in-law of Rāi Kalhā, the chief of Rāikoṭ, was a devotee of Gurū Gobind Siṅgh. According to Sarūp Siṅgh Kaushish, *Gurū kīāṅ Sākhīāṅ*, he was with Rāi Kalhā when he met Gurū Gobind Siṅgh passing through Rāikoṭ after having left Chamkaur on 8 December 1705.

Also, *see* NIHAṄG KHĀN

BIBLIOGRAPHY

1. Padam, Piārā Siṅgh, and Giānī Garjā Siṅgh, eds. , *Gurū kīāṅ Sākhīāṅ*. Patiala, 1986
2. Anand, Balwant Singh, *Guru Tegh Bahadur*. Delhi, 1979

Gn.S.

'ĀLAMPUR, village 11 km southwest of Dasūyā (31°-49'N, 75°-39'E) in Hoshiārpur district of the Punjab, is sacred to Gurū Hargobind (1595-1644), who stayed here for several days during an hunting expedition. The place where he pitched his tents (*tambū*, in Punjabi) came to be treated as holy. The shrine subsequently established here was called Gurdwārā Tambū Sāhib Pātshāhī Chhevīṅ. Situated on a low mound about 250 metres south of the village, it was endowed during Sikh rule with a land grant of 75 acres. Its present building constructed by the local *saṅgat* in 1983 is a small rectangular hall with the sanctum at one end. The Gurdwārā is affiliated to Nirmal Akhāṛā and is managed by Nirmalā priests.

Jg. S.

ĀLAM SIṄGH NACHNĀ (d. 1705), a warrior in the retinue of Gurū Gobind Siṅgh, was the son of Bhāī Durgū, a Rājpūt Sikh of Siālkoṭ. He earned the popular epithet Nachnā (lit. dancer) because of his uncommon agility. Sarūp Dās Bhallā, *Mahimā Prakāsh*, describes him as one of Gurū Gobind Siṅgh's constant companions. Possessing pluck as well as skill, he once killed a tiger single-handed. On another occasion when during the chase Gurū Gobind Siṅgh was suddenly attacked by two hill chiefs, Balīā Chand and Ālam Chand, with a force far outnumbering his own, Ālam Siṅgh Nachnā showed exemplary courage. In a face-to-face encounter with Ālam Chand, he slashed the latter's sword arm. He took part in almost all the battles fought around Anandpur. As Gurū Gobind Siṅgh himself testifies in his *Bachitra Nāṭak*, when Khānzādā, the son of Dilāwar Khān, Sūbahdār of Lahore, tried to storm Anandpur at night, it was Ālam Siṅgh's vigilance which alerted the Sikhs and forced the Khānzādā to retire without attempting the assault. During the final siege of Anandpur, Ālam Siṅgh was given the command of a 500 strong garrison in Agampur Fort; on the evacuation of the town, he along with Bhāī Dayā Siṅgh and Bhāī Ude Siṅgh led the vanguard. At Chamkaur on 7 December 1705, Ālam Siṅgh Nachnā joined the sally made by Sāhibzādā Ajīt Siṅgh and fell fighting the besieging host.

BIBLIOGRAPHY

1. Bhallā, Sarūp Dās, *Mahimā Prakāsh*. Patiala, 1971
2. Kuir Siṅgh, *Gurbilās Pātshāhī 10*. Patiala, 1968
3. Macauliffe, Max Arthur, *The Sikh Religion*. Oxford, 1909
4. Harbans Singh, *Guru Gobind Singh*. Chandigarh, 1966

P.S.P.

ĀLĀ SIṄGH, BĀBĀ (1691-1765), Sikh *misl*

leader who became the first ruling chief of Paṭiālā, was born in 1691 at Phūl, in present-day Baṭhiṇḍā district of the Punjab, the third son of Bhāī Rām Siṅgh. His grandfather, Bābā Phūl, had been as a small boy blessed by Gurū Hargobind, Nānak VI. Ālā Siṅgh's father and his uncle, Tilok Siṅgh, had both received the rites of initiation at the hands of Gurū Gobind Siṅgh who conferred on their family the panegyric,"Your house is mine own."

Ālā Siṅgh was married at an early age to Fateh Kaur, popularly known as Māī Fatto, daughter of Chaudharī Kālā of Khānā, a *zamīndār* of the village Kāleke, now in Saṅgrūr district of the Punjab, and had three sons, Bhūmīā Siṅgh, Sardūl Siṅgh and Lāl Siṅgh, all of whom died in his lifetime, and a daughter, Bībī Pardhān.

Ālā Siṅgh's career of conquest began soon after the execution of Bandā Siṅgh Bahādur in 1716 when central Punjab lay in utter confusion. Ālā Siṅgh was living at Phūl about 40 km from Baṭhiṇḍā. He gathered around him a band of dashing and daring young men. In 1722, he set up his headquarters at Barnālā, 32 km farther east, and his territory comprised 30-odd villages. At Barnālā, Ālā Siṅgh defeated in 1731 Rāi Kalhā of Rāikoṭ, an influential chief with a large force at his command. Aided by roving bands of the Dal Khālsā, he ransacked and annexed several villages belonging to the Bhaṭṭīs. He also founded several new villages such as Chhājalī, Dirbā, Lauṅgovāl and Sheroṅ. For a period Ālā Siṅgh remained in the custody of 'Alī Muhammad Khān Ruhīlā, Mughal governor of Sirhind from 1745-48, and was released only when the latter fled his capital at the approach in February 1748 of the Afghān invader Ahmad Shāh Durrānī. In the battle fought on 11 March 1748, near Mānūpur, 15 km northwest of Sirhind, between the Mughals and Ahmad Shāh Durrānī, Ālā Siṅgh sided with the former. He cut off Durrānī's supplies and captured his camels and horses. In 1749, Ālā Siṅgh defeated and repulsed Farīd Khān, a Rājpūt chieftain, who had sought the help of the imperial governor of Sirhind and stopped the construction by him of a fort at Bhavānīgaṛh. Three years later, Ālā Siṅgh, captured the district of Sanaur, called *chaurāsī*, lit. eighty-four, from the number of the villages it comprised. One of these where he built a fort in 1763 and which was thenceforth his permanent seat, became famous as Paṭiālā. At the end of 1760, Ālā Siṅgh possessed 726 villages including many towns. On the eve of the battle of Pānīpat (1761) when the Marāṭhās' camp was blockaded by Ahmad Shāh Durrānī, Ālā Siṅgh helped them with foodgrain and other provisions. In the Vaḍḍā Ghallūghārā or Great Carnage of February 1762, Ālā Siṅgh remained neutral. Ahmad Shāh punished him with the devastation of the town of Barnālā. Ālā Siṅgh, who presented himself in the Shāh's camp, was ordered to shave off his head and beard. This he declined to do and offered instead to pay a sum of one and a quarter lakh of rupees. The Shāh accepted the money but had him taken to Lahore where he secured his freedom by paying another five lakh of rupees.

Ālā Siṅgh took the *pāhul* in 1732 at the hands of Nawāb Kapūr Siṅgh, leader of the Dal Khālsā. He was an ally of Jassā Siṅgh Āhlūvālīā in the attack on Sirhind in 1764. Later he purchased this town from Bhāī Buḍḍhā Siṅgh to whom it had been assigned by the Khālsā. On 29 March 1761, Ahmad Shāh Durrānī had already recognized by a written decree the sovereignty of Ālā Siṅgh over the territories held by him. At the time of his seventh invasion of India, he confirmed him in the government of Sirhind (1765) and granted him the title of Rājā, with the robes of honour as well as with a drum and a banner as insignia of royalty.

Ālā Siṅgh died on 7 August 1765 at Paṭiālā and was cremated in the Fort, now inside the city.

BIBLIOGRAPHY

1. Kirpal Singh, *Life of Maharaja Ala Singh and His Times*. Amritsar, 1954
2. Griffin, Lepel, *The Rajas of the Punjab* [Reprint]. Delhi, 1977
3. Latif, Syad Muhammad, *History of the Panjab*. Delhi, 1964

B.S.

ALEXANDER alias MUHAMMAD SADĪQ, a European of unknown nationality, who drifted to Lahore in 1841 from Kābul, where he had served in Shāh Shujā's army, and had adopted the Muslim faith. He joined the Khālsā army as a battalion commander serving under John Holmes.

BIBLIOGRAPHY

Grey, C., *European Adventures of Northern India, 1785-1849* [Reprint]. Patiala, 1970

Gl.S.

ALIF KHĀN, who is mentioned in Gurū Gobind Siṅgh's *Bachitra Nāṭak*, was an officer in the Mughal army of Auraṅgzīb. In 1691, he was despatched by Mīāṅ Khān, the viceroy of Jammū, to Kāṅgṛā for collecting arrears of tribute from the hill chiefs. Rājā Kirpāl Chand Kaṭoch of Kāṅgṛā and Rājā Dyāl of Bijhaṛvāl submitted to Alif Khān, but not Rājā Bhīm Chand of Kahlūr. Bhīm Chand enlisted the support of several of the chieftains against Alif Khān. He also requested Gurū Gobind Siṅgh for help. The combined force reached Nadauṇ, on the bank of the River Beās, 32 km southeast of Kāṅgṛā. Kirpāl Chand Kaṭoch and Rājā Dyāl sided with the Mughal general. The battle in which Gurū Gobind Siṅgh himself took part was fought on 20 March 1691. Gurū Gobind Siṅgh described the action in his *Bachitra Nāṭak* in vivid and rousing verse. Alif Khān fled in utter disarray "without being able to fold up his camp."

BIBLIOGRAPHY

1. *Bachitra Nāṭak*.
2. Kuir Siṅgh, *Gurbilās Pātshāhī 10*. Patiala, 1968
3. Giān Siṅgh, Giānī, *Twārīkh Gurū Khālsā* [Reprint]. Patiala, 1970
4. Macauliffe, Max Arthur, *The Sikh Religion*, Oxford, 1909
5. Harbans Singh, *Guru Gobind Singh*. Chandigarh, 1966

B.S.

'ĀLIM, a Muslim poet, enjoyed the patronage of Gurū Gobind Siṅgh. Formerly in the employ of Prince Mu'azzam (later Emperor Bahādur Shāh), he probably came to Gurū Gobind Siṅgh sometime during the period 1687-94 when the prince, having fallen from the favour of his father, Auraṅgzīb, was under internment. Only a single stanza of 'Ālam in Hindi, in Gurmukhī script, survives in which he celebrates the bounty of his master, Gurū Gobind Siṅgh.

BIBLIOGRAPHY

Padam, Piārā Siṅgh, *Gurū Gobind Siṅgh Jī de Darbārī Ratan*. Patiala, 1976

P.S.P.

'ALĪ SHER, village 18 km north of Mānsā (29°-59'N, 75°-23'E) in Baṭhiṇḍā district of the Punjab, was visited by Gurū Tegh Bahādur during his travels in the Mālvā region. Arriving from Pandher, he sat outside the village. The *pañchāyat*, or village elders, of Pandher, who had shown little attention to him in their own village, on realizing their error came to 'Alī Sher to ask for pardon. They brought with them offerings of *guṛ* (jaggery) and money. On the way they met a person who was returning after seeing the Gurū. They asked his advice as to what offerings they might present to the Gurū to have their lapse condoned. He replied, "None. The Gurū is compassionate. He overlooks the faults of others." The residents of Pandher distributed amongst themselves the *guṛ* and money they had brought, and went to the Gurū empty-handed. The Gurū instructed them in the path of virtue and honest living.

The shrine established in memory of Gurū Tegh Bahādur was developed into a proper *gurdwārā* during the nineteenth century and was endowed by the rulers of Paṭiālā in whose territory 'Alī Sher lay. The Gurdwārā now owns 12 acres of land and is administered by the Shiromaṇī Gurdwārā Parbandhak Committee.

BIBLIOGRAPHY

1. Ṭhākar Siṅgh, Giānī, *Srī Gurdūare Darshan*. Amritsar, 1923
2. Tārā Singh, *Srī Gur Tīrath Saṅgrahi*. Amritsar, n.d.
3. *Mālvā Desh Raṭan dī Sākhī Pothī*. Amritsar, 1968
4. Harbans Singh, *Guru Tegh Bahadur*. Delhi, 1982

Jg.S.

ĀLĪ SIṄGH (d. 1716), a native of the village of Salaūdī, near Sirhind, was in the service of Wazīr Khān, the Mughal *faujdār* of Sirhind. According to Ratan Siṅgh Bhaṅgū, *Prāchīn Panth Prakāsh*, Wazīr Khān, on learning of Bandā Siṅgh's advance from the South towards the Punjab under the orders of Gurū Gobind Siṅgh, called Ālī Siṅgh to his presence and taunted him with the remark that another Gurū of theirs had appeared and that he should join him and bring him to Sirhind to be despatched after the previous Gurū's sons. Ālī Siṅgh took his comment as an insult. Wazīr Khān put him into prison from where he escaped and joined Bandā Siṅgh's ranks. Ālī Siṅgh took part in battles fought at Samāṇā and Saḍhaurā. In the battle of Sirhind fought on 12 May 1710 at the nearby village of Chappar Chiṛī, he was one of the commanders of the Mālvā Sikhs. After the sack of Sirhind, he was appointed deputy-governor of the town under Bāj Siṅgh. Ālī Siṅgh was captured in Lohgaṛh in 1710, while defending the fortress against the Mughal onslaught and after several years of imprisonment, was put to death in Delhi in June 1716 with Bandā Siṅgh Bahādur and his men seized in Gurdās-Naṅgal.

BIBLIOGRAPHY

1. Bhaṅgū, Ratan Siṅgh, *Prāchīn Panth Prakāsh* [Reprint]. Amritsar, 1962
2. Gaṇḍā Siṅgh, *Bandā Siṅgh Bahādur*. Amritsar, 1964

G.S.D.

ALLĀHĀBĀD (25°-28'N, 81°-50'E), Prayāg before the reign of Emperor Akbar, was visited by Gurū Nānak in the course of his first preaching journey to the east in the first quarter of the sixteenth century. In 1666, Gurū Tegh Bahādur visited the town and stayed in the house of a devotee in Mohallā Aihīyāpur. Gurdwārā Tap Asthān (Pakkī Saṅgat) Srī Gurū Tegh Bahādur Jī Pātshāhī 9 marks the place where Gurū Tegh Bahādur had put up. It became a centre for the congregation of Sikh devotees and was called Pakkī Saṅgat (Permanent Congregation). Later it came to be served by Nirmalā priests who still administer it. Mahant Prītam Siṅgh (d. 1972) rebuilt the shrine in 1965. A domed two-storeyed gateway leads to the *dīvān* hall where the Gurū Granth Sāhib is seated in a marble *pālakī*. One of the side rooms has a large portrait of Gurū Tegh Bahādur placed on a square platfrom. This is meant to mark the apartment used by the Gurū as a bedroom at the time of his visit.

BIBLIOGRAPHY

1. Ṭhākar Siṅgh, Giānī, *Srī* Gurduāre Darshan. Amritsar, 1923
2. Tārā Siṅgh, *Srī Gur Tīrath Saṅgrahi*. Amritsar, n.d.
3. Randhir, G.S., *Sikh Shrines in India*. Delhi, 1990

M.G.S.

ALLĀHDĀD KHĀN (d. 1843) was the last ruler of Khaṭṭekhēl family of Ṭoṅk, situated in Bannū district, on the northwest frontier. When Mahārājā Raṇjīt Siṅgh conquered this region in 1821, Allāhdād Khān became a tributary of the Sikh government. As the tribute had fallen in arrears, an expedition was sent against Ṭoṅk in 1836. Allāhdād Khān fled, but he continued his intrigues against the Sikhs. In 1843, Fateh Khān Ṭiwāṇā, who was sent to curb his revolt, proposed that Allāhdād Khān be appointed governor of Ṭoṅk to secure peace in the territory. The proposal was still under consideration of the Lahore Darbār when Allāhdād Khān died.

BIBLIOGRAPHY

1. Griffin, Lepel, *The Punjab Chiefs*. Lahore, 1890
2. Gupta, Hari Ram, *Punjab on the Eve of First Sikh War*. Chandigarh, 1956

H.R.G.

ALLARD, ACHILLE, a young Muslim boy whose parents had been killed in one of the battles of Multān, and who was saved by Mahārājā Raṇjīt Siṅgh, had been born at Sayyidpur in the then province of Multān. General Allard noticed his intelligence and asked the Mahārājā's permission to adopt him. Jacquemont saw him in Lahore, and Honigberger performed upon him a delicate surgical intervention. In 1834, he was christianized and rebaptized Achille by his adopted family. In October 1834, he accompanied General Allard to Paris. He was educated at the Ecole Speciale de Commerce in Paris at the expense of the French government. When General Allard had left for Lahore in June 1836, a regular correspondence went on between Achille and his foster-father through Feuillet de Conches, Head of the Protocole at the Ministry of Foreign Affairs (Paris). In 1840, Achille decided to go back to Lahore with Benjamin Allard in order to settle the succession of General Allard. He fell sick and died at Lahore in 1841 or 1842.

BIBLIOGRAPHY

1. Lafont, Jean-Marie, "Bannou Pan Dei Allard and the Family of General Allard," *Journal of Sikh Studies*, vol. 2. Amritsar, 1978
2. Honigberger, John Martin, *Thirty-five Years in the East*. Calcutta, 1852

J.M.L.

ALLARD, BANNOU PĀN DEĪ (1814-1884), born of Rājā Meṅgā Rām of Chambā and Bannī Pañje Deī at Chambā on 25 January 1814, married Jean Francois Allard, one of Mahārājā Raṇjīt Siṅgh's French generals, in March 1826, and bore him seven children, two of whom died in infancy and are buried in Lahore along with their father. Allard and his wife also adopted a little orphan, Achille. In 1834, Bannou Pān Deī, her children and two of her female attendants accompanied Allard to France. The reason given to Mahārājā Raṇjīt Siṅgh for the journey was that the children needed a Christian education. However, in a newspaper interview in France, Allard spoke of another reason. His wife being much younger than him and belonging to a strict Hindu family, he feared she would be obliged to commit *satī* if he died in the Punjab.

In July 1835 Bannou Pān Deī settled down in Saint-Tropez and remarried Allard in a French civil ceremony. Since she was a Hindu, they could not be married in a church. The children were legitimatized, and Allard made arrangements for their education between December 1835 and April 1836. He then left France for the Punjab, never to see his family again.

There are several descriptions in contemporary French press of Bannou Pān Deī Allard, her guests at Saint-Tropez (Garcin de Tassy, Mme de Salle, an Indian prince), her travels and her connections with the high society of her time. In 1841 after the demise of her husband at Peshāwar, she decided to convert to Christianity (Roman Catholic) and was baptized in the church of Saint-Tropez, the King and the Queen of France having accepted to be her godfather and godmother. The ceremony took place in grand style, and General Ventura, who had just arrived in Marseilles for one of his trips to Europe, attended on her and assisted her in receiving the guests at her residence in Saint-Tropez.

On 25 July 1845 Madam Allard lost her younger daughter, Felicie (born at Calcutta, 2 February 1835) and she got a special permission to bury her in her garden, according to the Punjabi custom. She had purchased a new estate in Saint-Tropez along the sea, where she lived among her souvenirs and paintings. These paintings, in the possession of the Allard family for five generations, were stolen in 1979. In her bedroom, she got reproduced on a larger scale the painting of the Allard family showing their seven children all sitting in their garden at Anārkalī. This included the two deceased children, whereas the original, signed Paris 1836, represented the five living children. Her faithful maid, Darana, also shown in the paintings, died in 1861. Her children married into good families. The tradition is still alive in Saint-Tropez that she never accepted the death of her husband in Peshāwar in 1839, and every evening she walked to the seaside to wait for him. In 1853, the fortune of the Allard family was estimated at 462,000 Francs (Rs 184,800) of which 134,000F belonged to Bannou Pān Deī and 82,000F to each of the four children. She died at Saint-Tropez on 13 January 1884, and is buried in the Allard family tomb in the 'Cimetiere Marin' of Saint-Tropez.

BIBLIOGRAPHY

1. Lafont, Jean-Marie, "Banno Pan Dei Allard and the Family of General Allard," in *Journal of Sikh Studies*, vol. 2. Amritsar, 1978
2. *La Présence francaise dans le Royaume Sikh du Penjab, 1822-1849.* Paris, 1992

J.M.L.

ALLARD, BENJAMIN (1796-1877), step-brother of General Allard, born at Saint-Tropez in 1796, was sent to Lahore in 1829 in order to replace his brother as the military adviser of Mahārājā Raṇjīt Siṅgh, but the two brothers failed to win the confidence of the Mahārājā, who would not release General Allard from his duties. Benjamin then acted as his brother's deputy for various commercial missions between Lahore and Calcutta, along with Falcon and Meifredy. In 1830 he returned to Saint-Tropez to manage the General's financial investments in France. From 1835 onwards he looked after Bannou Pān Deī and her children in Saint-Tropez, and in 1840 he returned to Lahore with Achille Allard in order to collect the General's inheritance. Nothing is known about him after his return to Saint-Tropez, except that he died there on 6 February 1877.

J. M.L.

ALLARD, JEAN FRANCOIS (1785-1839), Chevalier of the Legion of Honour, an order instituted in 1802 by Napoleon I, was born at Saint-Tropez, France, on 8 March 1785. In 1803, he joined the French army and served in it fighting in the Imperial Cavalry in far-flung fields in Italy, Spain and Portugal until its final defeat at the hands of the allies in 1815 when the Imperial Guard, in which he had been serving as a lieutenant since 1810, was disbanded. Allard returned to Saint-Tropez on *demi-solde* (half-pay), but as soon as he learnt of Napolean's escape and landing at Golfe Juan in March 1815, he joined the latter who promoted him Captain on 28 April 1815 and appointed him aide-de-camp to Marechal Brune in Provence and was therefore not present at Waterloo where Napolean was finally defeated. In 1818 he left for the Middle East on four months' leave but never re-joined service and was therefore dismissed from the army on 31 August 1819 for long absence without leave. He served at Tabriz in Iran from February 1820 to September 1821. By that time the British government agreed to pay a huge war contribution to Iran on condition that all French officers in the service of Persia be dismissed and sent back to Europe. However, Allard and Ventura escaped in disguise towards Kābul and on to India. In March 1822, Allard arrived at Lahore in company with Ventura, and secured employment at the court of Mahārājā Raṇjīt Siṅgh only after the Mahārājā had ensured that they were French officers of Napolean and not British spies. He was entrusted with the task of reorganizing the Mahārājā's cavalry on European lines. On 22 May 1822 Allard and Ventura took command of Shaikh Basāwan's Palṭan Khās and later Palṭan Devā Siṅgh (1822), and the Gurkhā Palṭan (1823). These formed the infantry of the Fauj-i-Khās. The cavalry (*Fransīsī Sowār*) was originally formed by two regiments raised by Allard on 16 July 1822—*Rajman* (Regiment) *Khās Lāṅsīā* (Lancers) and *Rajman Daragun* (Dragoon). In place of the traditional *ghoṛchaṛās,* who protested against the new drills, fresh recruitments were made. Allard raised another regiment of Dragoons in 1823. By 1825, the Fauj-i-Khās (infantry, cavalry and artillery) was 5000-6000 strong. The training was based on a French pamphlet Allard had brought with him. All the words of command were in French. Allard commanded the whole force, and took orders only from the Mahārājā. Ventura, under Allard's orders, was in charge of infantry. The uniform of the Fauj-i-Khās was inspired by the uniform of Napolean's Grande Armee; the standards of the regiments were the tricolour French flag inscribed with the motto *Vāhigurū Jī Kī Fateh,* and each regiment had the Imperial Eagles. Sikh cavalry, under Allard, had achieved a very high level of efficiency. His Cuirassiers, a "turbaned edition" of the steel-clad horsemen of the Garde Imperiale, were the most noble-looking troops on parade. The men and horses were well picked, their accoutrements were of the finest quality and the regularity and the order in which they manoeuvred could scarcely be matched by the East India Company's cavalry across the border. Besides the European form of drill, Allard introduced the use of carbine among the Sikh troops.

Allard's work won high appreciation from the Mahārājā and he came to occupy position of pre-eminence at the Sikh court. In addition to a salary of Rs 30,000 a year, he was granted numerous *jāgīrs* enabling him to live in style at Lahore. He was a man of high character and amiable disposition and all foreign travellers passing through Lahore spoke very highly of him. Raṇjīt Siṅgh considered Allard to be more a political and military adviser than as a commander in the field, although on extremely critical occasions he took command of the military forces in operation, as he did in 1825 in Peshāwar and Ḍerājāt for pacifying the Muslim tribes along the Indus; in 1827 and 1830 for quelling the *jihād* of Sayyid Ahmad Barelavī; and in 1837 in the attack on Jamrūd after the death of Sardār Harī Siṅgh Nalvā. From 1824 onwards, Allard was also responsible for the security of the Anglo-Sikh border along the Sutlej, from the Himalayas down to Harī kā Pattan.

The French naturalist Jacquemont, who visited Lahore in 1831, calls him the Suleman Bey of Raṇjīt Siṅgh. Allard often acted as host to the European visitors to the Mahārājā's court. On ceremonial occasions, he was chosen for special duties. He, for instance, escorted Mahārājā Raṇjīt Siṅgh at the time of his visit to Ropaṛ in October 1831 for a meeting with the Governor-General, Lord William Bentinck. Allard also occasionally informed the Mahārājā about Russian affairs as they were reported in the French newspapers or in the Russian Gazette (published in French).

In 1834, Allard along with his wife, Bannou Pān Deī, daughter of the chief of Chambā, whom he had married in 1826 at Lahore, and children proceeded to France on two years' leave of absence at the expiry of which he returned to the Punjab via Calcutta in early 1837, bringing for Raṇjīt Siṅgh gifts and a letter of greetings from Louis Philippe, the King of France.

Allard took part in almost all the major expeditions of Mahārājā Raṇjīt Siṅgh. In 1838, he was sent to Peshāwar to help General Avitabile in the administration of the province. On 23 January 1839, he died at Peshāwar, having suffered for some time from a diseased heart. His body was, as he had wished, brought to Lahore and buried with full military honours between the tombs of his two daughters in Kuṛī Bāgh on 19 February.

BIBLIOGRAPHY

1. Lafont, Jean-Marie, *La Présence francaise dans le Royaume Sikh du Penjab, 1822-1849.* Paris, 1992
2. Bopearachchi, Osmund, *Monnaies greco-bactriennes et indo-grecques. Catalogue raisonné* . Paris, 1991
3. Grey, C., *European Adventurers of Northern India, 1785-1849* [Reprint]. Patiala, 1970

J. M. L.

ALLĀYĀR, a wealthy Muslim horse-dealer of Delhi, who turned a preacher of Sikhism, first came to Gurū Amar Dās at Goindvāl escorted by Bhāī Pāro, a prominent Sikh of Ḍallā, a village in present-day Kapūrthalā district of the Punjab. It is said that returning from Kābul once with 500 newly purchased horses, he was held up near Goindvāl owing to the River Beās being in spate. He had not been there long before he saw someone tearing across the swollen river on horseback from the opposite bank. This was Bhāī Pāro coming to make his daily obeisance to Gurū Amar Dās. Allāyār was still wondering at the man's daring when Bhāī Pāro was again seen emerging from Goindvāl and preparing to plunge into the river on his way back. Allāyār beckoned him to come near him and asked him what made him run such a great risk. Bhāī Pāro replied that he had his Gurū's protection and felt no risk of any kind. The intrigued merchant begged him to take him to the Gurū who inspired such faith and confidence in the heart of his disciple. He was led into the Gurū's presence and was converted at first sight. Gurū Amar Dās remarked to him: "It is difficult to become a *yār* (friend) of Allāh (God), but I shall make God thy Master and thee His servant." Allāyār became a disciple. He left his trade to his son, and devoted himself whole-heartedly to the Gurū's service. Gurū Amar Dās appointed him head of a *mañji* or diocese to preach the word of Gurū Nānak. In later life, Allāyār came to reside near his friend Bhāī Pāro, at village Ḍallā, where a shrine in honour of his memory still exists.

BIBLIOGRAPHY

1. Santokh Siṅgh, Bhāī, *Srī Gur Pratāp Sūraj Granth.* Amritsar, 1926-37
2. Giān Siṅgh, Giānī, *Twārīkh Gurū Khālsā [Reprint].* Patiala, 1970

B. S. D.

ALL-PARTIES CONFERENCES (more aptly, ALL-PARTY CONFERENCES), a series of conventions which took place in 1928 bringing together representatives of various political parties and communities in India with a view to working out a mutually agreed formula for the country's constitutional advance in response to the invitation of the British government.

On 7 July 1925, Lord Birkenhead, the Secretary of State for India, had, in a speech in the House of Lords, said: "Let them [the Indians] produce a constitution which carries behind it a fair measure of general agreement among the great people of India. Such a contribution to our problems would nowhere be resented. It would, on the contrary, be most carefully examined by the Government of India, by myself, and I am sure, by the commission, whenever that body may be assembled." He repeated the statement at the time of the constitution, on 8 November 1927, of the Statutory Commission, better known as Simon Commission. The Indian National Congress at its annual session at Madrās in December 1927 authorized its Working Committee to confer with other parties and draft a Svarāj (self-government) constitution for India which should be placed before the All-Parties Conference to be held during early 1928. A large number of political parties and social organizations were invited to take part in the Conference which held its first meeting at Delhi on 12 February 1928. The Central Sikh League received the invitation as representative of the Sikhs. The League nominated Bābā Khaṛak Siṅgh, Sardār Bahādur Mehtāb Siṅgh, Master Tārā Siṅgh, Giānī Sher Siṅgh, Amar Siṅgh Jhabāl and Sardār Maṅgal Siṅgh to take part in the Conference.

Sharp differences on vital questions arose between the Muslim League on the one hand and the Hindu Mahā Sabhā and the Sikhs on the other during the first session of the All-Parties Conference held at Delhi on 12 February 1928 under the presidentship of Dr M.A. Ansārī. At the next session held on 19 May 1928, the Conference appointed a committee of ten members headed by Paṇḍit Motīlāl Nehrū to lay down broad principles which should serve as the basis for the new scheme. Maṅgal Siṅgh represented the Sikhs on the committee. The committee presented on 10 August 1928 a unanimous report known as the Nehrū Committee Report which was placed for review before the All-Parties Conference at Lucknow on 28-31 August 1928. The Report suggested Dominion Status for India; federal system of government with a strong centre; responsible executive; bicameral legislature at the Centre and unicameral ones in the provinces; adult franchise and joint electorates with reservation of seats proportionate to population for the Muslims in provinces where they were in a minority and for non-Muslims in the North-West Frontier Province. There were no provisions made specifically for the Sikhs. The recommendations of the Nehrū Committee, as adopted at the All-Parties Conference at Lucknow, were to be placed before an All-Parties Convention which met at Calcutta in December 1928.

Maṅgal Siṅgh, the sole Sikh member of the Nehrū Committee, had signed the Report and put the seal of Sikhs' assent on its recommendations. Some other Sikh Congress leaders such as Sardūl Siṅgh Caveeshar and Amar Siṅgh Jhabāl supported the stand taken by Maṅgal Siṅgh, but Master Tārā Siṅgh, Giānī Sher Siṅgh and some other Akālī leaders were strongly opposed. They argued that their demand had been complete abolition of communal representation not only in the Punjab but all over the country. If communal representation was to be given to any minority community in any other province, the same concession should have been given the Sikh minority in the Punjab as well. The Report was considered at the annual session of the Central Sikh League at Gujrāṅwālā on 22 October 1928. Giving his presidential address extempore, Bābā Khaṛak Siṅgh said that the Report had sinned against the self-respect and dignity of India by limiting the national objective to Dominion Status. This meant that the people would have to fight twice over—first, to win Dominion Status and then, Svarāj or complete independence. The second point of Bābā Khaṛak Siṅgh's criticism was that the Nehrū Report had laid the foundation of communalism by accepting separate electorates. Giānī Sher Siṅgh sponsored the main resolution castigating the Report for acquiescing in the principle of communal representation. The resolution advocated a system of joint electorates with plural constituencies, adding that, if community-wise representation became inevitable, Sikhs should have at least 30 per cent of the seats in the Punjab legislature and the same proportion of representation from the Punjab in the Central legislature. Among other speakers were Sant Siṅgh of Lyallpur, Amar Siṅgh Jhabāl and Būṭā Siṅgh, Advocate. Maṅgal Siṅgh, who was a signatory to the Nehrū Report, told the conference that he had urged upon the committee that either communal representation be discarded altogether or that Sikhs' share be fixed at 30 per cent. Master Tārā Siṅgh said that the Sikhs wanted neither British *rāj* nor Muslim. He declared that, while working with the Congress, he would not flinch from laying down his life to secure the Sikhs their rights. The original resolution, disapproving of the Nehrū Report and its goal of Dominion Status and demanding 30 per cent seats for the Sikhs in case separate electorates were adopted, was carried by a large majority.

At the All-Parties Convention held at Calcutta commencing from 22 December 1928, Sikhs were represented by 30 delegates of the Central Sikh League, besides 8 members of the Nāmdhārī sect. Sardār Bahādur Mehtāb Siṅgh, speaking on behalf of the Sikh League on 29 December 1928, opposed the provision for reservation of seats in any province, adding that if the principle was to be accepted in the case of one community it should apply to others as well. At the following session (30 December), an amendment was moved on behalf of the Sikh League to the effect that communalism should not be made the basis of future policy in India in any shape or form and that the Nehrū Report be amended accordingly, but it was ruled out of order by the President, Dr M.A. Ansārī. Harnām Siṅgh read out a long prepared statement on behalf of the Sikh League, stressing the historical, economic and political importance of the Sikhs in the Punjab, and how they had been ignored in the Nehrū scheme. The Sikhs, he said, were prepared to make all sacrifices in the interest of the nation, provided communalism was completely expunged from the Indian body politic, but the communal principle was on the contrary the basis of the Nehrū Report. He declared that his party did not support the Report and would take no further part in the proceedings of the Convention. The delegates representing the Sikh League walked out of the Convention. Mahātmā Gāndhī while moving for adjournment of the Convention *sine die* remarked that personally he felt that justice had not been done to the Sikhs.

The disappointment of the Sikhs with Nehrū Committee Report and the All-Parties Conference drove even some progressive and nationalist sections of the community away from the Indian National Congress. The Sikh leaders planned a strategy which forced the Congress leadership not only to shelve the Nehrū Committee Report for good, but also to come to terms with the Sikhs who held a conference at Lahore at the end of December 1929 to coincide with the 44th annual session of the Congress to be held there under the presidentship of Paṇḍit Jawāharlāl Nehrū. Bābā Khaṛak Siṅgh, who presided over the Sikh conference, reiterated the Sikhs' determination not to let any single community establish its hegemony in Punjab. A resolution passed by the conference demanded that, if communal representation was to continue, the Sikhs should get 30 per cent share of the assembly seats in Punjab, with adequate provisions for the protection of their rights in other provinces.

The Sikh conference, and even more dramatically the mammoth Sikh march that preceded it, made a tremendous impact. Congress leaders led by Mahātmā Gāndhī came to meet Bābā Khaṛak Siṅgh and his colleagues and gave them the assurance that no political arrangement which did not give full satisfaction to the Sikhs would be accepted by the Indian National Congress.

BIBLIOGRAPHY

1. Majumdar, R. C., ed., *The History and Culture of Indian People*, vol. V. Bombay, 1957
2. Harbans Singh, *The Heritage of the Sikhs*. Delhi, 1983
3. Khushwant Singh, *A History of the Sikhs*, vol. 2. Princeton, 1966
4. Gopal Singh, *A History of the Sikh People (1469-1978)*. Delhi, 1979

K. S. T.

ALMAST, BHĀĪ (1553-1643), Sikh preacher and head of a *dhūāṅ* or branch of the Udāsī sect, was born in a Gauṛ Brāhmaṇ family of

Srīnagar (Kashmīr) on 26 August 1553. He was the son of Bhāī Hardatt and Māī Prabhā, and was the elder brother of Bālū Hasnā, another equally prominent preacher of the sect. Almast's original name was Ālū; he came to be called Almast (lit. intoxicated, in a state of ecstasy, indifferent) because of his mystical proclivities and indifference towards worldly affairs. He was also called Kambalīā or Godaṛīā because he would normally be dressed only in a ragged blanket (*kambal*, in Punjabi) or *godaṛī*, a light quilt or padded sheet. Young Ālū was hardly past his adolescence when he left home in quest of spiritual knowledge. In 1574, he came to Ḍerā Bābā Nānak where he fell under the spell of Bābā Srī Chand, the elder son of Gurū Nānak and founder of the Udāsī sect. He served at the *dehurā* or mausoleum of Gurū Nānak, and for his livelihood tended a flock of goats. It was here that he began to be called Almast. Bābā Gurdittā (1613-38), the eldest son of Gurū Hargobind, who had succeeded Bābā Srī Chand as head of the Udāsī sect, deputed Bhāī Almast to preach the message of Gurū Nānak in the eastern provinces. He first went to Purī in Oṛissā where he established a shrine to commemorate Gurū Nānak's visit to the Jagannāth temple. The shrine, known as Gurdwārā Maṅgū Maṭh, is still in existence.

In 1633, Bhāī Almast went to Nānak Matā, formerly known as Gorakh Matā, where Gurū Nānak had a discourse with the Nāth yogīs under an old *pīpal* tree, and where a shrine dedicated to him had later been established. The place had been reoccupied by the yogīs who had razed the Sikh shrine and burnt down the *pīpal* tree. Almast applied for help to Gurū Hargobind who reached Nānak Matā in June 1634, chastised the Nāth intruders and restored the Sikh shrine. According to local tradition, he even miraculously rejuvenated the burnt *pīpal* tree. Bhāī Almast spent the remaining period of his life at Nānak Matā from where he sent out his eight principal disciples to preach in various districts of eastern India. These disciples established Sikh shrines at places visited by Gurū Nānak during his first *udāsī* or absence from home on a preaching journey.

BIBLIOGRAPHY

1. Randhīr Siṅgh, Bhāī, *Udāsī Sikhāṅ dī Vithiā*. Chandigarh, 1972
2. Prītam Siṅgh, ed., *Nirmal Sampradāi*. Amritsar, 1981

P.S.P.

ALO HARAKH, village in Saṅgrūr district, has a historical shrine called Gurdwārā Sāhib Ālo Harakh Pātshāhī Naumī. A low-domed Mañji Sāhib, under an old banyan tree marks the site where Gurū Tegh Bahādur once sat arriving from the neighbouring village of Guṇīke. The congregation hall has a vaulting ceiling with a domed sanctum inside. Both the hall and the Mañji Sāhib were constructed in 1909.

The Gurdwārā is administered by the Shiromaṇī Gurdwārā Parbandhak Committee through a local committee. Large congregations are held on full-moon day and on major anniversaries on the Sikh calendar.

M.G.S.

ĀLSŪN, an obscure village in Himāchal Pradesh, is alluded to in Gurū Gobind Siṅgh's *Bachitra Nāṭak*, canto IX, verse 24, as the site of a brief skirmish when the Gurū was on his way back to Anandpur after the battle of Nadauṇ (March 1690). According to Sikh chroniclers, the Rājpūts of Ālsūn were the subjects of Rājā Bhīm Chand of Kahlūr and were therefore inimical towards Gurū Gobind Siṅgh. They did not welcome the Gurū and his Sikhs and were chastised by Dīwān Nand Chand under orders from the Gurū.

The village of Ālsūn is no longer extant. A modern researcher, Nariñjan Siṅgh Sāthī, has identified the site as present-day village of Samālṛā, in Baṅgāṇā sub-division of Ūnā district, on the basis of local tradition. It is six kilometres from Baṅgāṇā on the road to Ūnā.

BIBLIOGRAPHY

1. *Bachitra Nāṭak.*
2. Kāhn Siṅgh, Bhāī, *Gurushabad Ratnākar Mahān Kosh.* Patiala, 1974

M.G.S.

ALVARINE, an Italian (Irishman, according to C. Grey's *European Adventurers of Northern India),* who joined service under the Sikh Darbār in 1841. He died at Lahore soon afterwards.

BIBLIOGRAPHY

Grey, C., *European Adventurers of Northern India* [Reprint]. Patiala, 1970

Gl.S.

AMAR DĀS, GURŪ (1479-1574), the third of the ten Gurūs of the Sikh faith, was born into a Bhallā Khatrī family on Baisākh *sudī* 14, 1536 Bk, corresponding to 5 May 1479, at Bāsarke, a village in present-day Amritsar district of the Punjab. His father's name was Tej Bhān and mother's Bakht Kaur; the latter has also been called by chroniclers variously as Lachchhamī, Bhūp Kaur and Rūp Kaur. He was married on 11 Māgh 1559 Bk to Mansā Devī, daughter of Devī Chand, a Bahil Khatrī, of the village of Sankhatrā, in Siālkoṭ district, and had four children—two sons, Mohrī and Mohan, and two daughters, Dānī and Bhānī.

Amar Dās had a deeply religious bent of mind. As he grew in years, he was drawn towards the Vaiṣṇava faith and made regular pilgrimages to Haridvār. Chroniclers record twenty such trips. Amar Dās might have continued the series, but for certain happenings in the course of the twentieth journey which radically changed the course of his life. On the return journey this time, he fell in with a *sādhū* who chided him for not owning a *gurū* or spiritual preceptor. Amar Dās vowed that he must have one and his pledge was soon redeemed when he was escorted in 1597 Bk/AD 1540 by Bībī Amaro, a daughter-in-law of the family, to the presence of her father, Gurū Aṅgad, at Khaḍūr, not far from his native place. He immediately became a disciple and spent twelve years serving Gurū Aṅgad with single-minded devotion. He rose three hours before daybreak to fetch water from the river for the Gurū's bath. During the day he worked in the community kitchen, helping with cooking and serving meals and with cleansing the utensils. When free from these tasks, he went out to collect firewood from the nearby forest for Gurū kā Laṅgar. His mornings and evenings were spent in prayer and meditation.

Several anecdotes showing Amar Dās's total dedication to his preceptor have come down the generations. The most crucial one relates how on one stormy night, he, braving fierce wind, rain and lightning, brought water from the River Beās for the Gurū. Passing through a weaver's colony just outside Khaḍūr, he stumbled against a peg and fell down sustaining injuries, but did not let the water-pitcher slip from his head. One of the weaver-women, disturbed in her sleep, disparagingly called him 'Amarū Nithāvāṅ' (Amarū the homeless). As the incident was reported to Gurū Aṅgad, he praised Amar Dās's devotion and described him as "the home of the homeless," adding that he was "the honour of the unhonoured, the strength of the weak, the support of the supportless, the shelter of the unsheltered, the protector of the unprotected, the restorer of what is lost, the emancipator of the captive." This also decided Gurū Aṅgad's mind on the issue of the selection of a successor. The choice inevitably fell on Amar Dās. Gurū Aṅgad paid obeisance to him by making the customary offerings of a coconut and five pice. He had the revered Bhāī Buḍḍhā apply the *tilak* or mark of investiture to his forehead, thus installing him as the future Gurū. Soon afterwards, on the fourth day of the light half of the month of

Chet in Bikramī year 1609 (29 March 1552), Gurū Aṅgad passed away.

Gurū Amar Dās made Goindvāl his headquarters. He was one of the builders of the town and had constructed there a house for his family as well. Goindvāl lay on the main road connecting Delhi and Lahore, at the head of one of the most important ferries on the River Beās. From there Gurū Amar Dās continued preaching the word of Gurū Nānak Dev. In his hands the Sikh faith was further consolidated. He created a well-knit ecclesiastical system and set up twenty-two *mañjīs* (dioceses or preaching districts), covering different parts of India. Each was placed under the charge of a pious Sikh, who, besides disseminating the Gurū's message, looked after the *saṅgat* within his jurisdiction and transmitted the disciples' offerings to Goindvāl. Gurū Amar Dās appointed the opening days of the months of Baisākh and Māgh as well as the Dīvālī for the Sikhs to forgather at Goindvāl where he also had a *bāolī*, well with steps descending to water level, built and which in due course became a pilgrim centre. A new centre was planned for where Amritsar was later founded by his successor, Gurū Rām Dās. He laid down for Sikhs simple ceremonies and rites for birth, marriage and death. The Gurū's advice, according to Sarūp Dās Bhallā, *Mahimā Prakāsh*, to his Sikhs as to how they must conduct themselves in their daily life was: "He who firmly grasps the Gurū's word is my beloved Sikh. He should rise a watch before dawn, make his ablutions and sit in seclusion. The Gurū's image he should implant in his heart, and contemplate on *gurbāṇī*. He should keep his mind and consciousness firmly in control. He should never utter a falsehood, nor indulge in slander. He should make an honest living and be prepared always to serve holy men. He must not covet another's woman or wealth. He should not eat unless hungry, nor sleep unless tired. He who breaks this principle falls a victim to sloth. His span is shortened and he lives in suffering. My Sikh should shun those who feign as women to worship the Lord. He should seek instead the company of pious men. Thus will he shed ignorance. Thus will he adhere to holy devotion."

From Goindvāl, Gurū Amar Dās made a few short trips in the area around to propagate Gurū Nānak's teaching. According to the *Mahimā Prakāsh*, "The Gurū went to all the places of pilgrimage and made them holy. He conferred favour on his Sikhs by letting them have a sight of him. He planted the seed of God's love in their hearts. He spread light in the world and ejected darkness." Liberation of the people was also cited by Gurū Rām Dās, Nānak IV, as the purpose of pilgrimage undertaken by his predecessor. According to his hymns in the Gurū Granth Sāhib, Gurū Amar Dās visited Kurukshetra at the time of *abhijit nakṣatra*. This, by astronomical calculations made by a modern scholar, fell on 14 January 1553. This is the one date authentically abstracted from the Gurū Granth Sāhib, which otherwise scarcely contains passages alluding to any historical events and this date is also one of the fewest so precisely known about the life of Gurū Amar Dās.

Gurū kā Laṅgar became still more renowned in Gurū Amar Dās's time. The Gurū expected every visitor to partake of food in it before seeing him. By this he meant to minimize the distinctions of caste and rank. Emperor Akbar, who once visited him at Goindvāl, is said to have eaten in the refectory like any other pilgrim. The food in the *laṅgar* was usually of a rich Punjabi variety. Gurū Amar Dās himself, however, lived on coarse bread earned by his own labour. Whatever was received in the kitchen during the day was used by night and nothing was saved for the morrow.

Gurū Amar Dās gave special attention to the amelioration of the position of women. The removal of the disadvantages to which they had been subject became an urgent concern. He assigned women to the responsibility of supervising the communities of disciples in certain sectors. The customs of *purdah* and *satī* were discouraged.

The *bāṇī*, the Gurū's revealed word, continued to be a precious endowment. Gurū Amar Dās collected the compositions of his predecessors and of some of the *bhaktas* of that time. When he had recorded these in *pothīs*—two of them preserved in the descendant families to this day—an important step towards the codification of the canon had been taken.

Like his predecessors, Gurū Amar Dās wrote verse in Punjabi. His compositions which express deep spiritual experience are preserved in the Gurū Granth Sāhib. They are in number next only to those of Gurū Nānak and Gurū Arjan, Nānak V. Gurū Amar Dās composed poetry in seventeen different musical measures or *rāgas,* namely Sirī, Mājh, Gauṛī, Āsā, Gūjarī, Vaḍahaṅs, Soraṭh, Dhanāsarī, Sūhī, Bilāval, Rāmkalī, Mārū, Bhairau, Basant, Sāraṅg, Malār, and Prabhātī. In terms of poetic forms, he composed *padās* (quartets), *chhants* (lyrics), *aṣṭpadīs* (octets), *ślokas* (couplets) and *vārs* (ballads). Best known among his compositions is the *Anandu*. Gurū Amar Dās's poetry is simple in style, free from linguistic or structural intricacies. Metaphors and figures of speech are homely, and images and similes are taken from everyday life or from the popular Pauranic tradition. The general tenor is philosophical and didactic.

Before his death on Bhādoṅ *sudī* 15, 1631 Bk/1 September 1574, Gurū Amar Dās chose Bhāī Jeṭhā, his son-in-law, as his spiritual successor. Bhāī Jeṭhā became Gurū Rām Dās, the Fourth Gurū of the Sikhs.

BIBLIOGRAPHY

1. Bhallā, Sarūp Dās, *Mahimā Prakāsh. Patiala, 1971*
2. Giān Siṅgh, Giānī, *Panth Prakāsh* [Reprint]. Patiala, 1970
3. Satibīr Siṅgh, *Parbatu Merāṇ*. Jalandhar, 1983
4. Macauliffe, Max Arthur, *The Sikh Religion*. Oxford, 1909
5. Jodh Singh, *Life of Guru Amar Das*. Amritsar, 1949
6. Ranjit Singh, *Guru Amar Das Ji*. Amritsar, 1980
7. Fauja Singh and Rattan Singh Jaggi, eds., *Perspectives on Guru Amar Das*. Patiala, 1982

P.S.P.

AMARGAṚH, village 3 km east of Goniāṇā Maṇḍī (30°-18'N, 74°-54'E) in Baṭhiṇḍā district of the Punjab, has an old shrine, Gurdwārā Vidyāsar Pātshāhī Satvīṅ, dedicated to Gurū Har Raī (1630-61) who, according to local tradition, visited the site during his stay at Bhokhaṛī, since renamed Har Rāipur. Amargaṛh was then called Jhabluṭṭī. The shrine was looked after by a line of Udāsī priests until the early 20th century. The present building of the Gurdwārā, constructed in 1912, comprises a *dīvān* hall with a verandah on three sides. The Gurdwārā is managed by a committee of the local *saṅgat*.

Jg.S.

AMAR KATHĀ, of unknown authorship, comprises a mixture of diverse hagiographic traditions bearing on the life of Gurū Nānak. The work remains unpublished, but several manuscripts are known to exist: for instance, two of them, dated AD 1818 and 1872, respectively, are preserved in the Gurū Nānak Dev University Library at Amritsar, one, dated 1877, in the Punjabi University Museum, Paṭiālā, one, dated 1870, at the Pañjābī Sāhitya Akademi, Ludhiāṇā, and one, dated 1825, in the Sikh Reference Library until it perished in the Army attack in 1984. Compiled probably towards the end of the eighteenth century, *Amar Kathā* draws upon all the prevalent *janam sākhī* cycles such as *Purātan*, *Miharbān* and *Bālā* along with the interpolations introduced by the Handālīās (*q.v.*). This miscellany narrates Gurū Nānak's life in terms of the usual legend, myth and miracle. It begins with the customary invocatory passages seeking immortality for the reader as well as for the listener. These are followed by the first cluster of about seven (in some manuscripts split into twelve) *sākhīs*. Opening with an account of the genesis of the Universe, this section tells us how Nirañjan Niraṅkār, the Immaculate Formless One, ramained in a nebulous state for full 144 aeons; how He, then, created by His will *māyā*, followed by the creation of various gods and goddesses. It was through gods Viṣṇu, Brahmā and Śiva that human beings were created. Then Niraṅkār ordained Bābā Nānak (who is none other than Niraṅkār's manifest facet) to retrieve the four Vedas for the benefit of mankind. Here follows the account of the four aeons detailing their salient features and enlisting the incarnations of Niraṅkār each aeon had witnessed. This section ends with Gurū Nānak's advent in the dark age, to show mankind the way to liberation.

The following section on Janampatrī is extension of the *Bālā* tradition. The date of the Gurū's birth given here is the full-moon day of the month of *kārtik* in 1526 Bk/AD 1469—an example of the compiler following the *Bālā* tradition which has been used as the broad framework into which anecdotes and accounts picked from other current sources have been fitted. Then there are *sākhīs* reiterating the significance of surrender to the Gurū's will and of the company of the holy in realizing the Supreme Being. A few of the *sākhīs* attempt to explain some of the sayings of Gurū Nānak. Some are purely folkloristic in character containing fragments from old ballads sung by minstrels to extol Gurū Nānak. Since most of the *sākhīs* comprising this work have been lifted from different traditions, the change in idiom and style becomes apparent with change in the source from where a particular *sākhī* is picked.

P.S.

AMARNĀMĀ, a Persian work comprising 146 verses composed in AD 1708 by Bhāī Natth Mall, a *ḍhāḍī* or balladeer who lived from the time of Gurū Hargobind to that of Gurū Gobind Siṅgh, Nānak X. The manuscript of the work in Gurmukhī script obtained from Bhāī Fattā, ninth in descent from Bhāī Natth Mall, through Giānī Gurdit Siṅgh, then editor of the Punjabi daily, the *Prakāsh*, Paṭiālā, was edited by Dr Gaṇḍā Siṅgh and published by Sikh History Society, Amritsar/ Paṭiālā in 1953.

The *Amarnāmā* opens with the words "*ath Amarnāmā taṭ Godāvarī Srī Mukhvāk Pātshāhī 10*" (This *Amarnāmā* was written on the bank of the River Godāvarī by the Tenth Lord, Gurū Gobind Siṅgh) and ends with the words "*iti Srī Amarnāmā Mukhvāk Pātshāhī Dasam sati sampūran*" (Thus this *Amarnāmā* of the Tenth Master was completed). In spite of these statements and in spite of the fact that the author at places uses the first person and directs the Sikhs, as Gurū, to follow certain rules of conduct, the work clearly is not the composition of Gurū Gobind Siṅgh but that of a poet who, with a view to imparting authenticity to it, attributed it to the Gurū. It seems that Natth Mall and his son had accompanied Gurū Gobind Siṅgh to the Deccan and entertained Sikhs at the afternoon assemblies reciting heroic poetry. From events narrated in the *Amarnāmā* it can easily be surmised that the author was an eye-witness to most of them.

The *Amarnāmā* is not a work of any high literary merit. The author, a Punjabi, possessed very little knowledge of Persian and his verse is desultory. However, it is historically very valuable, not only because it is a composition coming from one of Gurū Gobind Siṅgh's contemporaries and his companions but also because the author had personal knowledge of the events described in it. The work briefly refers to Gurū Gobind Siṅgh's meeting with Bandā on 3 September 1708, on the occasion of the solar eclipse, the fighting between the Sikhs and Bandā's men, the lodging of complaints by Hindus against the Gurū before Emperor Bahādur Shāh, Bhāī Nand Lāl's presence in the Emperor's camp at Nāndeḍ, the Gurū's generous and lavish distribution of charity among the needy, and the despatch of Bandā Siṅgh with five Sikhs to the Punjab. Among Gurū Gobind Siṅgh's precepts recorded in the text, primacy attaches to Sikhs receiving the rites of *amrit*, i.e. baptism of the double edged sword, disregarding Brāhmaṇical counsel (127-28). They must at all stages of their life, in childhood and in youth and before the end comes, seek to remain baptized (142-44). Animals must not be slaughtered in the Muslim way of *halāl* (132). As Sikhs engage in amusement and festivity, they must in the afternoon listen to bards reciting ballads (135).

B.S.

AMAR NĀTH, DĪWĀN (1822-1867), *ba<u>kh</u>shī* or paymaster of the irregular forces of the Sikh army who distinguished himself also as a historian, was born in 1822 the son of Rājā Dīnā Nāth, finance minister of Mahārājā Raṇjīt Siṅgh. During the prime ministership of Hīrā Siṅgh, Amar Nāth was assigned to the task of settling the accounts of government studs and stables. The town duties of Lahore and Amritsar were also leased out through him. Hīrā Siṅgh reposed great trust in Amar Nāth who became an intermediary between him and his uncle, Rājā Gūlāb Siṅgh, when the two had fallen out. Owing to strained relations with his father, Amar Nāth had to quit his government post during the first Anglo-Sikh war. But, being a man of letters, he continued enjoying an annual pension of 1,200 rupees, which was raised to 4,000 rupees after the death of his father in 1857. Besides some poetry, Amar Nāth wrote the *Zafar Nāmah-i-Raṇjīt Siṅgh*, a chronicle, in Persian, of the reign of Mahārājā Raṇjīt Siṅgh up to 1835-36. The work was edited by Sītā Rām Kohlī and published in 1928.

Amar Nāth died in 1867, his elder son, Dīwān Rām Nāth, succeeding him in his *jāgīr*.

BIBLIOGRAPHY

1. Sūrī, Sohan Lāl, *'Umdāt-ut-Twārī<u>kh</u>*. Lahore, 1885-89
2. Griffin, Lepel, *Ranjit Singh*. Delhi, 1957
3. Gupta, Hari Ram, *Panjab on the Eve of First Sikh War*. Chandigarh, 1956
4. Khushwant Singh, *Ranjit Singh: Maharajah of the Punjab*. Bombay, 1962

G.S.Ch.

AMARO, BĪBĪ, elder daughter of Gurū Aṅgad and Mātā Khīvī, is especially remembered in the Sikh tradition for introducing (Gurū) Amar Dās to Gurū Aṅgad whose disciple, and eventually successor in the holy office, he became. She was born in *c*. 1526 at Khaḍūr Sāhib, in present-day Amritsar district of the Punjab, and was married to a nephew of Amar Dās at Bāsarke, now called Bāsarke Gillāṅ, 11 km southwest of Amritsar. She was known for her piety and had memorized several of Gurū Nānak's hymns which she recited every morning, amid her household chores. Once Amar Dās happened to listen to a hymn from Bībī Amaro's lips, and felt deeply moved. He desired to see the living successor of Gurū Nānak, who had uttered poetry of such vivid spiritual insight. Bībī Amaro escorted him to Gurū Aṅgad's presence which he left never again. Bībī Amaro died at Bāsarke where a shrine built in her honour still exists.

BIBLIOGRAPHY

1. Bhallā, Sarūp Dās, *Mahimā Prakāsh*. Patiala, 1971
2. Satibīr Siṅgh, *Parbatu Merāṇu*. Jalandhar, 1983
3. Ranjīt Singh, *Guru Amar Das Jī*. Amritsar, 1980

M.G.S.

AMAR PAD or *amarāpad*, also called *parampada* (highest step), *turiāpada* or *turiāvasthā*, is the stage of deathlessness or immortality.

In the Gurū Granth Sāhib the term has been used for the highest stage of spiritual enlightenment which is also the highest state of self-realization, equivalent of God-realization. This is the stage of ultimate release.

See MUKTI and JĪVAN-MUKT

M.G.S.

AMAR SIDDHŪ, village 13 km southeast of Lahore along the Lahore-Kasūr road, is sacred to Gurū Hargobind (1595-1644), who once visited here travelling from Gurū Māṅgaṭ close to Lahore. Gurdwārā Pātshāhi VI, established to commemorate the visit, was outside the village to the east of it. The building, constructed by Rāi Bahādur Sir Gaṅgā Rām in 1922, was a domed structure in the middle of a small garden. The Gurdwārā was affiliated to the Shiromaṇī Gurdwārā Parbandhak Committee and was administered by the local managing committee of Lahore city. The shrine was abandoned at the time of mass migrations caused by the partition of the Punjab in 1947.

M.G.S.

AMAR SIṄGH (1888-1948), of the *Sher-i-Punjab*, journalist, scholar and a prominent figure in Sikh politics, was born on 27 May 1888 at Piṇḍī Gheb in Attock district of the Punjab, now in Pakistan. His grandfather, Gauhar Siṅgh, had held a civil appointment under Mahārājā Raṇjīt Siṅgh. He spent his childhood and received education in Urdu and Persian in Jammū and Kashmīr where his father, Gulāb Siṅgh, was an employee of the ruler, Mahārājā Pratāp Siṅgh. After his father's death, the family settled in Rāwalpiṇḍī where Amar Siṅgh ran a shop for some time before he adopted journalism as his profession. He launched the *Lyall Gazette*, a weekly in Urdu, under the patronage of the Chief K͟hālsā Dīwān whose point of view on political, religious and social issues he supported and discussed in his writings. He gradually turned away from the moderate policies of the Dīwān, and identified himself with the more radical politics of Bābā Khaṛak Siṅgh. In 1921, he renamed his paper *Sher-i-Punjab* ("Lion of the Punjab") which title became an epithet popularly added to his name. The paper still continues to be issued under this name, since the partition of the Punjab, from Delhi.

Besides journalism, Amar Siṅgh was active in civic and political affairs. He was a member of the municipal committee, Lahore, for 16 years. He was virtually a permanent president of Siṅgh Sabhā, Lahore, and of the managing board of the local historical Sikh shrines. In 1921, he was made a member of the Shiromaṇi Gurdwārā Parbandhak Committee and, during the Jaito *morchā* or agitation, he was arrested (7 January 1924) and sentenced to two years' rigorous imprisonment. He was elected to the Shiromaṇī Gurdwārā Parbandhak Committee under the Sikh Gurdwaras Act in 1926 and 1930. During subsequent elections in 1933, 1936 and 1939 (the last in the series till after Independence), he came in as a co-opted member. When in 1934 Bābā Khaṛak Siṅgh dissociated himself from the Shiromaṇi Akālī Dal and set up his own Central Akālī Dal, Amar Siṅgh was chosen to be the senior vice-president of the new party. In 1947, Amar Siṅgh migrated to Delhi. He died at Kasaulī on 9 July 1948.

Amar Siṅgh wielded a powerful pen. He was an acknowledged master of Urdu prose, and he employed the talent to devastating effect in political and religious polemics. His humorous column Argaṛā, written under a pseudonym, "Risāldār Major," mixing anecdote, wit and satire, was very popular in contemporary Urdu journalism. Amar Siṅgh also composed verse in Punjabi, Urdu and Persian. He translated Omar K͟hayām's *Rubāiyāt* into Punjabi verse. He also wrote two novels and several short stories in Urdu. He was as accomplished a speaker as he was a writer, and frequently addressed Sikh assemblies on religious and political issues.

BIBLIOGRAPHY

Harbans Singh, *The Heritage of the Sikhs.* Delhi, 1983

J.B.S

AMAR SIṄGH (1888-1962), who came into prominence in the Gurdwārā reform movement, was the eldest of the three sons of Gopāl Siṅgh of the village of Jhabāl, in Amritsar district of the Punjab. His great-grandfather, Gulāb Siṅgh, had served in the army of Mahārājā Ranjit Siṅgh and his grandfather, Harbhagat Siṅgh, had been an aide-de-camp to Kaṅvar Nau Nihāl Siṅgh. Born in 1888, Amar Siṅgh was educated at the village school and at Khālsā Collegiate School, Amritsar. After passing the matricualtion examination, he joined the police department and became a sub-inspector. Once as he saw police officials snatch away *kirpāns* from some Sikhs, he protested and told the superintendent of police that dispossessing a Sikh of his *kirpān* meant violating his religious freedom. Demolition by the British of a portion of the outer wall of Gurdwārā Rikābgañj in Delhi, ban on the wearing of *kirpāns* by Sikhs and incidents such as the Budge Budge firing led Amar Siṅgh to resign his appointment in the police. He got started on a political career by organizing and addressing, in association with Dān Siṅgh Vachhoā, a series of public meetings in his own village and in the neighbourhood. He defied orders of the deputy commissioner of Amritsar banning the meeting to be convened at Mañjī Sāhib, close to the Golden Temple, to protest against a robe of honour having been conferred by the manager of the Darbār Sāhib on General Dyer, who had ordered the firing in Jalliāṅvālā Bāgh. The meeting did take place and resolutions castigating the deputy commissioner as well as the manager were adopted.

Following a public appeal by Sardūl Siṅgh Caveeshar for volunteers for a Shahīdī Jathā or martyrs' band to march to Delhi on 1 December 1920 to rebuild the Gurdwārā Rikābgañj boundary wall demolished by the British, Amar Siṅgh and his brother, Jaswant Siṅgh, made a hurricane tour of the Punjab addressing meetings and enlisting names. At one such meeting during the Amāvas fair at Tarn Tāran under the auspices of the Central Mājhā Khālsā Dīwān complaints were received about the mismanagement of Gurdwārā Bābe dī Ber at Siālkoṭ. Amar Siṅgh was deputed to visit the shrine and make a report. He was joined there by his brother, Jaswant Siṅgh, and by Tejā Singh of Bhuchchar and Kartār Siṅgh of Jhabbar with their bands of volunteers. The government yielded to public pressure and the management of the *gurdwārā* was handed over to a committee of selected Sikhs on 6 October 1920. Henceforth the Jhabāl brothers were recognized as a force in Sikh affairs. When the control of the Akāl Takht was taken over by the Sikhs and Shiromaṇī Gurdwārā Parbandhak Committee formed on 16 November 1920, both of them and their third brother, Sarmukh Siṅgh, were included in it as members. Amar Siṅgh was nominated a member of the provisional commitee to manage the Tarn Tāran Gurdwārā after it had been taken over from the priests by the reformists. He took a leading part in assuming possession of *gurdwārās* at Oṭhīāṅ, Tejā Kalāṅ, Chomālā Sāhib, Pañjā Sāhib, Peshāwar, Ramdās and Jhabāl. For a public speech he delivered after the Nankāṇā Sāhib tragedy, he was arrested and imprisoned for six months.

Amar Siṅgh presided over the third annual session of the Sikh League held at Lyallpur in 1922. He participated in the non-cooperation movement launched by the Indian National Congress as well as in the Akālī *morchās* for the reformation of the *gurdwārās.* On 16 July 1922, he was elected vice-president of the Shiromaṇī Gurdwārā

Parbandhak Committee. He suffered imprisonment again for making seditious speeches at the time of the *morchā* for securing release from the British of the keys of the Golden Temple *toshā<u>kh</u>ānā*. After the Sikh Gurdwaras Act was passed, Amar Siṅgh drifted more towards the Congress and remained for some time president of the Punjab Provincial Congress Committee. He died on 28 March 1962 at the village of Dayāl Bhaṛaṅg, in Ajnālā *tahsīl* of Amritsar district, where he had been allotted lands after the partition of the Punjab (1947).

BIBLIOGRAPHY

1. Pratāp Siṅgh, Giānī, *Gurdwārā Sudhār arthāt Akālī Lahir*. Amritsar, 1975
2. Josh, Sohan Siṅgh, *Akālī Morchiāṅ dā Itīhās*. Delhi, 1972
3. Harbans Singh, *The Heritage of the Sikhs*. Delhi, 1983
4. Ganda Singh, ed., *Some Confidential Papers of the Akali Movement*. Amritsar, 1965
5. Sahni, Ruchi Ram, *Struggle for Reform in Sikh Shrines*. Ed. Ganda Singh. Amritsar, n.d.

Jg.S.

AMAR SIṄGH MAJĪṬHĪĀ, soldier and administrator in Sikh times, called Amar Siṅgh Kalāṅ (senior) to distinguish him from his namesake Amar Siṅgh <u>Kh</u>urd (junior) who was also from the village of Majīṭhā, was the son of Dargāhā Siṅgh Majīṭhīā. He took part in many an early campaign under Mahārājā Raṇjīt Siṅgh. When Dīwān Rām Diāl was killed in Hazārā in 1820, Amar Siṅgh was appointed governor of that country. While engaged in curbing the activities of the turbulent and unruly Af<u>gh</u>ān tribes, he was killed treacherously in an ambush. Amar Siṅgh was a fine bowman and the local tribesmen still point to a large tree pierced through and through by an arrow which, they say, came from the bow of Amar Siṅgh.

BIBLIOGRAPHY

1. Sūrī, Sohan Lāl, *'Umdāt-ut-Twārī<u>kh</u>*. Lahore, 1885-89
2. Griffin Lepel, and C.F. Massy, *Chiefs and Families of Note in the Punjab*. Lahore, 1909

B.J.H.

AMAR SIṄGH MAJĪṬHĪĀ (d. 1848), known as Amar Siṅgh <u>Kh</u>urd (junior) to distinguish him from his namesake Amar Siṅgh Kalāṅ (senior) who was also from the village of Majīṭhā, son of Māhṇā Siṅgh (d. 1802), was a *jāgīrdār* and military commander under Mahārājā Raṇjīt Siṅgh. He was placed in the Ḍerā <u>Kh</u>ās, a regiment of irregular cavalry composed of the sons of the Sikh nobility. The young Amar Siṅgh distinguished himself in the siege of Multān in 1818 and in the Kashmīr campaign the following year. In 1834, he accompanied the army under Prince Nau Nihāl Siṅgh and General Harī Siṅgh Nalvā to Peshāwar when the province was formally annexed to the Sikh kingdom. He was employed on outpost duty in this campaign and he had many a fierce encounter with the Af<u>gh</u>āns. At Shabqadar, he was wounded by a musket-ball in a night attack made by the Af<u>gh</u>āns in force, but he rallied his men and drove them back. He fought with distinction in the battle of Jamrūd (30 April 1837). Being a celebrated marksman, he was chosen in 1846 to instruct the young Mahārājā Duleep Siṅgh in shooting. In the year following, he left the Punjab on a pilgrimage to Haridvār, and died there in 1848.

BIBLIOGRAPHY

1. Sūrī, Sohan Lāl, *'Umdāt-ut-Twārī<u>kh</u>*. Lahore, 1885-89
2. Griffin, Lepel, and C.F. Massy, *Chiefs and Families of Note in the Punjab*. Lahore, 1909
3. Bhagat Singh, *Maharaja Ranjit Singh and His Times*. Delhi, 1990

S.S.B.

AMAR SIṄGH MĀN (d. 1805), landowner in Amritsar district who left his village about the year 1759, adopted the Sikh faith and joined the Kanhaiyā Misl. He overran and took possession of a large part of Gurdāspur district, including Sukālgaṛh and Dharamkoṭ. He built a fort at Sukālgaṛh which he made his main residence. After a lifelong fighting career, he died quietly in his bed in the year 1805.

BIBLIOGRAPHY

Griffin, Lepel, and C.F. Massy, *Chiefs and Families of Note in the Punjab*. Lahore, 1909

G.S.N.

AMAR SIṄGH, RĀJĀ (1748-1782), of Paṭiālā, was born on 6 June 1748, the son of Sardūl Siṅgh and Rāṇī Hukmāṅ. In 1765, he succeeded his grandfather, Ālā Siṅgh, who had no son living at the time of his death. His succession to the throne of Paṭiālā was challenged by his step-brother, Himmat Siṅgh, who seized a major portion of the town of Paṭiālā and the neighbouring area. Amar Siṅgh secured the eviction of Himmat Siṅgh through the help of the chiefs of Jīnd, Nābhā and Kaithal. In 1766, he captured Pāyal and Īsṛū from the Koṭlā Afg͟hāns with the help of trans-Sutlej Sikhs under Jassā Siṅgh Āhlūvālīā, from whom he had received the rites of K͟hālsā baptism. Pāyal was annexed to Paṭiālā state, while Īsṛū was given to Jassā Siṅgh Āhlūvālīā.

Ahmad Shāh Durrānī's invasion of the country in 1767 proved very beneficial to the rising power of Amar Siṅgh, who sent his *vakīls* to the Shāh with presents. The Shāh summoned Amar Siṅgh and granted him the *sūbahdārī* (governorship) of Sirhind with the title of Rājā-i-Rājgān. He was also given a flag and a drum as insignia of absolute authority. He paid a lakh of rupees to the Shāh to secure the release of several thousand Hindus taken captive in the vicinity of Mathurā and Sahāranpur. He issued coins in the name of Ahmad Shāh.

In 1768, Amar Siṅgh marched against, G͟harīb Dās of Manī Mājrā who, after the death of Ālā Siṅgh, had captured the fort and district of Piñjore. Amar Siṅgh, helped by the hill rulers of Hiṇḍūr, Kahlūr and Nāhan, defeated G͟harīb Dās and captured the Piñjore fort. G͟harīb Dās was, however, not fully reduced to submission. Rājā Amar Siṅgh marched against him again in 1778. G͟harīb Dās paid a large sum of money to the Paṭiālā chief and retained control of his territory.

Amar Siṅgh next attacked the fort of Koṭ Kapūrā, killing Jodh Siṅgh, the local chief, in the battle. In 1771, he occupied the district of Baṭhiṇḍā subduing Sukhchain Siṅgh to whom the Fort of Gobindgaṛh, commanding the town, belonged. Three years later, he reduced Saifābād, a strong fort 7 km to the northeast of Paṭiālā. In 1774, he occupied the Bhaṭṭī country lying south of Paṭiālā. Fatehābād, Sirsā and the fort of Rāṇīā now passed into his hands. In 1777, he again overran Farīdkoṭ and Koṭ Kapūrā but did not attempt to annex them. In 1779, he frustrated the designs of Abdul 'Ahad K͟hān against Sikh territories in the Mālvā. He received help from Jassā Siṅgh Āhlūvālīā, Jassā Siṅgh Rāmgaṛhīā, Tārā Siṅgh G͟haibā and Jodh Siṅgh, of Wazīrābād, and repulsed the Mug͟hal expedition at the village of Ghuṛām. By his extensive conquests and by the shrewd political alliances he made with the rulers of Nāhan and Bīkāner and with the Misldār *sardārs*, Amar Siṅgh had made Paṭiālā the most powerful state between the Yamunā and the Sutlej.

Rājā Amar Siṅgh died at Paṭiālā on 5 February 1782 in the prime of his youth.

BIBLIOGRAPHY

1. Griffin, Lepel, *The Rajas of the Punjab*. Delhi, 1977
2. Kirpal Singh, *Maharaja Ala Singh of Patiala and His Times*. Amritsar, 1954

Kr.S.

AMAR SIṄGH THĀPĀ, Nepalese general, was the son of Bhīm Sen Thāpā, the prime minister of Nepal. In 1794, he conquered

Kumāoṅ and began extending Gurkhā dominions westwards. He subdued the Gaṛhvāl state lying between the Gaṅga and the Yamunā. In 1805 he crossed the River Yamunā and overran most of the Shimlā hill states lying between the Yamunā and the Sutlej. The Rājā of Bilāspur solicited Amar Siṅgh's help against Saṅsār Chand, establishing his authority over the Kāṅgṛā hills. On hearing the news of Amar Siṅgh's advance, Saṅsār Chand raised the siege of Bilāspur and retired. Amar Siṅgh crossed the rivers Sutlej and Beās unopposed and defeated Saṅsār Chand at Mahal Morīāṅ in May 1806. He then laid siege to the Kāṅgṛā Fort. The Rājā sought the help of Mahārājā Raṇjīt Siṅgh who drove away the Gurkhās but himself occupied the Fort. Amar Siṅgh established himself at Arkī, near Shimlā, and made overtures to the British soliciting their support against Raṇjīt Siṅgh. They rejected the proposal. During the Gurkhā war of 1814-16, Amar Siṅgh in vain asked for Raṇjīt Siṅgh's help against the British. There being no response from the Mahārājā, Amar Siṅgh surrendered to the British who allowed him to retire unmolested to Nepal.

BIBLIOGRAPHY

1. Sūrī, Sohan Lāl, *'Umdāt-ut-Twārī<u>kh</u>*. Lahore, 1885-89
2. Griffin, Lepel, *Ranjit Singh*. Delhi, 1957
3. Harbans Singh, *The Heritage of the Sikhs*. Delhi, 1983

H.R.G.

AMAR SIṄGH WĀSŪ (1884-1932), Akālī activist and journalist, was born Gaṅga Rām at the village of Wāsū, in Gujrāt district, now in Pakistan, in 1884, the son of Ladhā Mall and Lachhmī Devī. Under the influence of the Siṅgh Sabhā movement, the family went through the Sikh initiatory rites, Gaṅgā Rām becoming Amar Siṅgh <u>Kh</u>ālsā and his father Rām Siṅgh. Amar Siṅgh matriculated from the Mission High School, Gujrāṅwālā, and joined in 1902 the <u>Kh</u>ālsā College at Amritsar, passing the intermediate examination of the Pañjāb University, Lahore, in 1904. In 1906, he went to the United States to train as a journalist, returning to India in 1908. He had vowed not to take up government service under the British. In partnership with the historian Karam Siṅgh, he set up an Āyurvedic pharmacy—the Sannyāsī Āshram—at Sargodhā in 1908. While at Sargodhā, Amar Siṅgh married Rām Kaur, daughter of Bhāī Naraiṇ Siṅgh, of Ghaṛūāṅ, a village in Paṭiālā district. It was an intercaste marriage encouraged by Siṅgh Sabhā enthusiasts but opposed by the orthodox. When Bhāī Jodh Siṅgh, theologian and educationist, formed in 1909 a group of Jīvan Sevaks or those dedicating their lives to the service of the Sikh community, Amar Siṅgh was amongst the few who volunteered to join the new society and work for it on a small fixed honorarium for twenty years. In 1920, Amar Siṅgh, now known as Amar Siṅgh Wāsū after the name of his village, became editor of the English weekly, the *Khalsa Advocate*, started by the Chief <u>Kh</u>ālsā Dīwān. When this paper closed down, he took over as assistant secretary of the Chief <u>Kh</u>ālsā Dīwān. As the reformist Sikhs assumed charge of the Nankāṇā shrines after the massacre of 1921, Amar Siṅgh was appointed to administer them. At the time of Gurū kā Ba<u>gh</u> *morchā*, he was shifted to Amritsar. From 1927-30 he remained a member of the Shiromaṇī Gurdwārā Parbandhak Committee.

Amar Siṅgh died at Sargodhā on 27 June 1932 after a prolonged illness.

BIBLIOGRAPHY

1. Ashok, Shamsher Siṅgh, *Shiromaṇī Gurdwārā Prabandhak Committee dā Pañjāh Sālā Itihās*. Amritsar, 1982
2. Sahni, Ruchi Ram, *Struggle for Reform in Sikh Shrines*. Amritsar, n.d.

S.S.Am.

AMARŪ, BHĀĪ, a devoted Sikh of the time

of Gurū Amar Dās. He lived at the village of Ḍallā, in present-day Kapūrthalā district of the Punjab, and was initiated a Sikh at the hands of Gurū Amar Dās.

See RĀMŪ BHĀĪ

BIBLIOGRAPHY

1. Manī Siṅgh, Bhāī, *Sikhāṅ dī Bhagat Mālā*. Amritsar, 1955
2. Santokh Siṅgh, Bhāī, *Srī Gur Pratāp Sūraj Granth*. Amritsar, 1926-37

B.S.D.

AMĀVAS (AMĀVASYĀ), *massiā* in Punjabi, lit. a combination of *amā*, i.e. together, and *vasyā*, i.e. stationing, signifying coming of the sun and the moon together in one line, is the last day of the dark half of the lunar month when the moon remains entirely hidden from our view. The twenty-eight *nakṣatras*, considered to be the wives of the moon, are the lunar mansions or stations through which the moon passes as does the sun through the twelve signs of the zodiac. The life of an individual is believed to be deeply influenced by the *nakṣatra* through which the moon passed at the time of his birth. Thus, different days such as *pañchamī* (fifth), *ekādaśī* (eleventh), *pūranmāshī* (the fifteenth day when the moon is full) and *amāvas* assumed a special significance in the Hindu tradition. Certain religious performances and observances came to be associated with these days. In Sikh Scripture, the Gurū Granth Sāhib, occur three compositions under the title *Thitī* or *Thitīṅ* with couplets to match the lunar days. The burden of these compositions is that no single day is more auspicious than the others. That day alone is auspicious and well spent which is spent in meditating on the Divine Name and in doing good deeds. Although there is no ritualistic or formal observance prescribed in Sikh system for Amāvas, the day is marked by special congregations in *gurdwārās*. Devotees gather for ablutions in *sarovars*, the holy tanks. The shrines at Tarn Tāran and Muktsar especially attract on the occasion pilgrims from long distances.

T.S.

AMBĀLĀ (30° -23'N, 76°- 47'E), a city in Haryāṇā, has several historical shrines sacred to the Gurūs.

GURDWĀRĀ BĀDSHĀHĪ BĀG͟H, situated near the district courts, occupies the site which used to be a halting place for the Mug͟hal emperors when travelling from Delhi to the Punjab or Kashmīr. Gurū Gobind Siṅgh came here at the end of 1670 or in early 1671 during one of his excursions from Lakhnaur. Then only a small child, he had greatly impressed Pīr Nūr Dīn (or Mīr Dīn), custodian of the nearby Muslim shrine. According to local tradition, the young Gurū miraculously made ordinary sparrows fight against the arrogant Pīr's hawk which, badly mauled, fell down dead near Labbhū kā Tālāb in another part of the city. The Pīr, now humbled, made obeisance to the Gurū, and built a platform in his honour. Later during the last quarter of the eighteenth century, Mehar Siṅgh of Nishānāṅvālī *misl* raised a small *gurdwārā* which, however, was blown off during a British attack on the rebel forces in 1857. The land thereafter passed into private possession. The owner, having become aware of the sanctity of the place, built a room on the old foundations, but it was in a state of neglect when the Shiromaṇī Gurdwārā Parbandhak Committee took it over in 1926. Five years later, through the initiative of Sant Gurmukh Siṅgh of Paṭiālā, the Sikhs erected a more befitting building and laid out a garden around it. The present complex was raised by Nirmalā saints after the partition of 1947. The management again passed to the Shiromaṇī Gurdwārā Parbandhak Committee and the Nirmalās shifted to an *āshram* near by.

The Gurdwārā is entered through a high gate in a wall with ramparts giving it the appearance of a fortress. The rectangular *dīvān* hall has a vaulted ceiling. The sanctum within the hall marks the site of the old shrine.

GURDWĀRĀ GOBINDPURĀ PĀTSHĀHĪ DASVĪṄ, located along the Jain College Road, close to an old tank called Labbhū kā Tālāb is sacred to Gurū Gobind Siṅgh. According to local tradition, Gurū Gobind Siṅgh, during his visit to Ambālā in 1670-71, in order to humble the pride of an arrogant Muslim divine, Pīr Nūr Dīn , miraculously made sparrows kill the Pīr's hawk. The hawk, chased by the sparrows, fell down dead near Labhū kā Tālāb. It was a Muslim locality. Pīr Sayyid Shāh, another Muslim divine, witnessed the miracle from here, and sought from the young Gurū the favour of a spring of sweet water as the wells in the area were brackish. The well dug at the Gurū's instance still exists in the backyard of the *gurdwārā*. The present building, however, was constructed only after 1947. It consists of a single flat-roofed hall, which includes a square sanctum, marking the site of the original shrine.

GURDWĀRĀ MAÑJĪ SĀHIB (BĀOLĪ SĀHIB) is the premier *gurdwārā* of the city. Gurū Hargobind, while on his way to Delhi to meet Emperor Jahāṅgīr, stayed here for a night. The place, then a small village called Khurrampur, suffered from a chronic scarcity of water. The Gurū asked his followers to construct a *bāolī,* or a well with steps reaching down to water level. The *bāolī* was ready by the time he returned and broke journey here again for an overnight halt. Gurū Gobind Siṅgh is also said to have visited the place travelling towards Kurukshetra in 1702. According to local tradition, Bandā Siṅgh Bahādur also halted here before advancing upon Chhat-Banūṛ and Sirhind in 1710. On the establishment of Sikh power in the Punjab during the second half of the eighteenth century, Ambālā and its surrounding territory fell to the share of the Nishānāṇvālī Misl. Mehar Siṅgh of this *misl* or chiefship got the *bāolī* restored and had a room built on the site of the old Mañjī Sāhib. Khurrampur village was subsequently destroyed by floods in the river Ṭāṅgrī, and the shrine remained in a state of neglect until Mahārājā Hīrā Siṅgh (1843-1911) of Nābhā rebuilt it at the beginning of the twentieth century. Following the partition of the Punjab in 1947, the Sikh population increased with migrations from West Punjab. The cornerstone of a new building was laid on 12 May 1951. The main building consists of an imposing three-storeyed gateway, flanked by octagonal domed towers and a spacious rectangular hall. Within the hall is the sanctum marking the site of the original Mañjī Sāhib. The *bāolī* is at the farthest end of the hall. A local committee manages the shrine subject to the overall control of the Shiromaṇī Gurdwārā Parbandhak Committee. A girls school, named in honour of Gurū Hargobind, functions on the premises of the Gurdwārā. The most important festival of the year is the birth anniversary of Gurū Hargobind which comes off in the month of June.

GURDWĀRĀ SATSAṄG SĀHIB honours the memory of Gurū Tegh Bahādur and Gurū Gobind Siṅgh. Gurū Gobind Siṅgh (1666-1708), once on his way from Anandpur to Kurukshetra, halted here under a tree near the potters' huts. An old man, Mehar Dhūmīāṅ, urged the Gurū to shift away from the tree which, he said, was haunted. He described an old incident saying that one evening an unidentified traveller had stopped there with his load of a covered basket and had asked him (Dhūmīāṅ) if there was a Sikh house in the vicinity. Dhumīāṅ had directed the wayfarer towards the locality where the shrine of Twakkal Shāh stood, but, to his horror, he observed bloodstains on the branch-leaves where the stranger had hung his basket. From the circumstances narrated Gurū Gobind Siṅgh could make out that the stranger was no other than Bhāī Jaitā, carrying to Anandpur the head of Gurū Tegh Bahādur. A platform was raised on the site. Gurū Gobind Siṅgh prolonged his stay holding holy assemblies or *satsaṅg* for the Sikhs. The shrine came to be known as Gurdwārā Satsaṅg. For a long time this sacred spot remained part of the private house of its priests. It was only in 1934 that a committee was formed. A new building was raised in 1935. In recent years another hall has been added, enclosing the older double-storeyed domed structure.

GURDWĀRĀ SĪS GAÑJ, about 300 metres from Gurdwārā Mañjī Sāhib, is sacred to Gurū Tegh Bahādur. After the Gurū had been executed publically in Delhi on 11 November 1675 under the orders of Emperor Auraṅgzīb, one of his Sikhs, Bhāī Jaitā carried off his severed head to Anandpur, while his body was cremated by Bhāī Lakkhī Shāh in Delhi. Bhāī Jaitā travelling incognito with the Gurū's head *(sīs)* stayed in a Sikh's house in Ambālā, the site of the present Gurdwārā Sīs Gañj. Local devotees raised a platform to mark the spot. In 1913, when the Sikh Educational Conference met for its sixth annual session at Ambālā, the site sprang into limelight. The custodians of the adjoining Muslim shrine of Twakkal Shāh objected to the Sikhs' visiting the place in large numbers. A civil suit followed which, however, went in the Sikhs' favour . In 1925, the control was entrusted to the newly constituted Shiromaṇī Gurdwārā Parbandhak Committee. The new building, completed in 1969, consists of a double-storeyed domed gateway and a small *dīvān* hall.

BIBLIOGRAPHY

1. Tārā Siṅgh, *Srī Gur Tīrath Saṅgrahi*. Amritsar, n.d.
2. Ṭhākar Siṅgh, Giānī, *Srī Gurduāre Darshan*. Amritsar, 1923
3. Randhir, G.S., *Sikh Shrines in India*. Delhi, 1990

M.G.S.

AMĪĀ, BHĀĪ (d. 1635), a devoted Sikh of the time of Gurū Hargobind. He was one of the five disciples sent to supervise the inhabitation of the village of Ruhelā, renamed after Gurū Hargobind. Bhāī Amīā took part in the battle of Amritsar (1634). According to *Gurbilās Chhevīṅ Pātshāhī*, he commanded, jointly with Bhāī Miharā, a contingent of 500 Sikhs in the battle of Kartārpur fought in April 1635. He was killed in action and Gurū Hargobind had the cremation rites performed, before leaving for Kīratpur the following day.

BIBLIOGRAPHY

1. Giān Siṅgh, Giānī, *Twārīkh Gurū Khālsā*. Patiala, 1970
2. *Gurbilās Chhevīṅ Pātshāhī*. Patiala, 1970

B.S.

AMĪR CHAND, son of Misr Rām Kumār of the village of Ḍalvāl, in Jehlum district, joined service in Mahārājā Raṇjīt Siṅgh's *toshākhānā* or treasury in 1830, soon becoming superintendent of Belā Toshākhānā, i.e. the treasury for charitable purposes. In June 1832, he was appointed to collect arrears of land revenue from the *zamīndārs* of Jalandhar and Rāhoṅ and was assigned to Kashmīr on similar duty in 1838. In 1839, he accompanied Kaṅvar Nau Nihāl Siṅgh to Peshāwar as custodian of the treasury. After Mahārājā Raṇjīt Siṅgh's death, Amīr Chand was sent to Haridvār to trace and recover the treasure of Jamādar Khushāl Siṅgh's son, Kishan Siṅgh, who had it secretly transferred to the British territory. He also served as agent of the Lahore Darbār at Ludhiāṇā, and as governor of Gujrāt and Piṇḍ Dādan Khān. After the first Anglo-Sikh war (1845-46), John Lawrence, the British Resident at Lahore, dismissed him from service for defalcation of funds and his *jāgīrs* were confiscated.

BIBLIOGRAPHY

1. Sūrī, Sohan Lāl, *'Umdāt-ut-Twārīkh*. Lahore, 1885-89
2. Griffin, Lepel, and C.F. Massy, *Chiefs and Families of Note in the Punjab*. Lahore, 1909
3. Gupta, Hari Ram, *Punjab of the Eve of First Sikh War*. Chandigarh, 1956
4. Khushwant Singh, *Ranjit Singh: Maharajah of the Punjab*. Bombay, 1962

H.R.G.

AMĪR SIṄGH, an Akālī or Nihaṅg who was a veteran soldier, joined the band of Bhāī Mahārāj Siṅgh, leading a popular rebellion against the British in 1848-49. When the British deputy commissioner of Jalandhar, Vansittart, raided Mahārāj Siṅgh's camp near Shām Chaurāsī on the night of 28-29 December 1849, Amīr Siṅgh attacked him with an axe but was himself wounded by a pistol shot fired by Vansittart. He died three days later.

BIBLIOGRAPHY

Ahluwalia, M.L., *Bhai Maharaj Singh*. Patiala, 1972

M.L.A.

AMĪR SIṄGH, GIĀNĪ (1870-1954), a widely revered Sikh schoolman, was born in 1870 at the village of Dargāhī Shāh in Jhaṅg district, now in Pakistan. His parents, Prem Siṅgh and Ṭhākarī Devī, a religious-minded couple of modest means, admitted him at the age of 15 to Mahant Jawāhar Siṅgh Sevāpanthī's *ḍerā* or monastery, in Sattovālī Galī in Amritsar, to learn Sikh sacred music and scriptures. After the death, in 1888, of Mahant Jawāhar Siṅgh, Amīr Siṅgh had his further education and religious training under Mahant Uttam Siṅgh, the new head of the *ḍerā*, and later from Giānī Bhagvān Siṅgh and Giānī Bakhshīsh Siṅgh, both noted men of letters of their time. Soon Giānī Amīr Siṅgh's scholarship came to be acknowledged. Mahant Uttam Siṅgh, head of the *ḍerā*, chose him his successor during his own lifetime. For over 60 years, Giānī Amīr Siṅgh taught Sikh scriptural texts to hundreds of scholars at his *ḍerā* in Sattovālī Galī, which became a well-known school of Sikh learning. In expounding the holy Gurū Granth Sāhib and other texts such as the *Dasam Granth* and *Srī Gur Pratāp Sūraj Granth*, he had few rivals.

Giānī Amīr Siṅgh, who remained celibate all his life, dressed himself in a white toga. In 1945, he was chosen president of the Rāgamālā Maṇḍan Committee formed to counteract the movement for the expunction from the Gurū Granth Sāhib of the last composition, *Rāgamālā*, recounting in verse some of the *rāgas* or musical measures employed in the Holy Book.

Giānī Amīr Siṅgh died at Amritsar on 17 October 1954 at the ripe age of 84 and was succeeded by Sant Kirpāl Siṅgh as head of the *ḍerā*.

BIBLIOGRAPHY

1. Gurmukh Siṅgh, *Sevāpanthīāṅ dī Pañjābī Sāhit nūṅ Deṇ*. Patiala, 1986
2. Lāl Chand, Bhāī, *Srī Sant Ratan Mālā*. Patiala, 1954

S.S.Am.

AMĪR SIṄGH SANDHĀṄVĀLĪĀ (d. 1827), a collateral of Mahārājā Raṇjīt Siṅgh, was born the son of Dīdār Siṅgh Sandhāṅvālīā. In 1784, he, upon the death of his father, succeeded to the family estates which he considerably enlarged. As Mahāṅ Siṅgh and Raṇjīt Siṅgh rose to power, he seized several villages in the neighbourhood of Rājā Sāṅsī. In 1803, however, Amīr Siṅgh fell into disgrace at the Sikh court. The story is that one morning as Raṇjīt Siṅgh came out of the Samman Burj and was preparing to mount his horse, Amīr Siṅgh was seen to unsling his gun, prime it and blow the match. The bystanders accused him of seeking the life of his chief, and Raṇjīt Siṅgh, who believed the charge, dismissed him from court. He took refuge with Bābā Sāhib Siṅgh Bedī of Ūnā at whose intercession the Mahārājā again took him into his favour, and placed him specially under the protection and in the force of Atar Siṅgh Kāliāṅvālā. Amīr Siṅgh accompanied the Mahārājā in the Kasūr campaign of 1807, and in the expedition against the Muhammadan tribes between the Chenāb and the Indus in 1810. In 1809, when on the death of Rājā Jai Siṅgh of Jammū, Raṇjīt Siṅgh seized that country, he made over the territory to Amīr Siṅgh. In 1821, Amīr Siṅgh received Shakargaṛh in *jāgīr*.

Amīr Siṅgh died in 1827. His *jāgīrs* amounting to upwards of rupees six lakhs annually were continued to his sons, Atar Siṅgh, Lahiṇā Siṅgh and Basāvā Siṅgh.

BIBLIOGRAPHY

1. Sūrī, Sohan Lāl, *'Umdāt-ut-Twārīkh*. Lahore, 1885-89
2. Griffin, Lepel, and C.F. Massy, *Chiefs and Families of Note in the Punjab*. Lahore, 1909

S.S.B.

AMĪR UL-IMLĀ, also known as *MUNTAKHAB UL-HAQĀ'IQ*, a collection of miscellaneous letters, in Persian script, mostly of Sikh chiefs of the Punjab addressed to one another on subjects relating to private and public affairs. Compiled by Amīr Chand in A.H. 1209 (AD1794-95), the manuscript comprises 127 folios and 247 letters and is preserved in the Oriental section of the British Library, London. On folio 125 of the manuscript is recorded a note referring to one Imānullah as its owner, implying that this is perhaps not the original copy prepared by Amīr Chand. However, no other copy, except a photostat of the British Museum manuscript secured by Dr Gaṇḍā Siṅgh for his personal use, is known to exist. The colophon inscribed on this copy indicates that it was Dalpat Rāi, son of Khushiābī Mall Sahgal, of Jaṇḍiālā Sher Khān, who originally collected these letters for compilation, but death prevented him from accomplishing the work which was then completed by his brother, Amīr Chand.

The collection contains correspondence of chiefs such as Mahārājā Raṇjīt Siṅgh, the Afghān Amīr Taimūr Shāh, Karam Siṅgh Bhaṅgī, Jai Siṅgh Kanhaiyā, Jodh Siṅgh, Sāhib Siṅgh of Paṭiālā, Fateh Siṅgh Āhlūvālīā, Jhaṇḍā Siṅgh Bhaṅgī, Rāṇī Sadā Kaur and some of the Marāṭhā rulers.

The contents of these letters cover a wide range of subjects such as the collection of revenue, formation of coalitions against aggressors, conquests, marriages and deaths in the families and the need for good neighbourly relations. In most of the letters the smaller rulers give vent to their sense of insecurity and apprehension at the expansionist policy of Mahārājā Raṇjīt Siṅgh who, they said, was vanquishing smaller kingdoms in the name of the unification of the scattered, broken and divided Punjab. A very important letter in this collection is from Mahārājā Raṇjīt Siṅgh addressed to the Emperor of Britain (ff. 20-21). The letter, besides commending the British Indian government for their equal treatment of all their subjects irrespective of their religious faith, attests to Mahārājā Raṇjīt Siṅgh's own conviction that the sovereignty was conferred upon the Khālsā by Gurū Gobind Siṅgh and that they still ruled in the name of their Gurū, declaring that he wielded power in the name of the Khālsā.

Ratan Siṅgh Bhaṅgī is critical of the aggressive designs of Raṇjīt Siṅgh who, he says, "inspired by his high position, army, artillery and treasury, wishes to place the whole of the Punjab under his own control." He writes to Muhammad Khān (ff. 39-40) about Raṇjīt Siṅgh's conquest of the area of the Syāls and his "impious designs" to establish his sovereignty over others. Similarly, there is a letter (ff. 23-24) by the Sūbahdār of Multān addressed to Taimūr Shāh requesting him to use his good offices with Raṇjīt Siṅgh so as to check his inroads into their territory.

There are several letters from Raṇjīt Siṅgh addressed to various *sardārs* informing them of the action he took against the unruly people (f. 83) such as despatching an army to subdue a rebel, K͟hān Beg Ṭiwāṇā, who was formerly his subordinate (ff. 71-72). A letter from Dal Siṅgh and Jodh Siṅgh addressed to Jai Siṅgh records the date (4 Baisākh/April; Wednesday) (*chār gharī rāt gae*, i.e. before midnight) and the time of the death of Mahāṅ Siṅgh Sukkarchakkīā (f.10). In all these letters, the Sikh chiefs address each other Siṅgh Sāhib, Bhāī Sāhib, or K͟hālsā Jīo.

B.S.

AMRĪK SIṄGH, a Jambar Jaṭṭ of Maghiāṇā in Lahore district, was a devoted Sikh of the time of Gurū Gobind Siṅgh. Bhāī Santokh Siṅgh, *Srī Gur Pratāp Sūraj Granth*, lists him among those who received baptismal rites on the day the K͟hālsā was initiated (30 March 1699). Amrīk Siṅgh, according to Bhāī Santokh Siṅgh again, took part in Gurū Gobind Siṅgh's first battle at Anandpur in 1700

BIBLIOGRAPHY

Santokh Siṅgh, Bhāī, *Srī Gur Pratāp Sūraj Granth*. Amritsar, 1926-37

Gn.S.

AMRĪK SIṄGH, BHĀĪ. *See* SRĪ DARBĀR SĀHIB

AMRIT, derived from Sanskrit *amṛta*, defined variously as not dead, immortal, imperishable; beautiful, beloved; world of immortality, heaven; immortality, eternity; final emancipation; nectar, ambrosia; nectar-like food; antidote against poison; or anything sweet, commonly means a liquid or drink by consuming which one attains everlasting life or immortality. It is in this sense that the word was first used in the Vedic hymns. According to Hindu mythology, *amrit* was extracted by the gods by churning the ocean with the assistance of the demons and it was by drinking it that the gods became immortal. A similar concept of an immortalizing drink also exists in Greek and Semitic mythologies wherein it is variously called ambrosia, nectar or *āb-i-hayāt*. In the Sikh tradition, *amrit* is not some magical potion that would confer upon the consumer an unending span of life or bring about automatic release from the cycle of birth, death and rebirth. The term is however retained figuratively to signify what leads to such release. In this sense, *amrit* is not something external to man "but is within him and is received by God's grace" (GG, 1056, 1238). In the holy hymns, *amrit* is repeatedly equated with *nām*, the Name, or *Śabda*, the Word (e.g. GG, 729, 644, 538, 394). It is *amrit* of the True Name which when imbibed quenches and satiates all appetites (GG, 594).

Amrit is also used in *gurbāṇī* in the adjectival sense of sweet, delicious, good, sweet-sounding, etc. in phrases such as *amritu bhojanu nāmu hari* — God's Name is delicious food (GG, 556), *amrit kathā* — dulcet discourse (GG, 255), *amrit drisṭi*— immortalizing glance (GG, 191), *amritā pria bachan tuhāre* — sweet are Thy words, O Dear One (GG, 534). Gurū Amar Dās in an *asṭpadī* (eight-stanza hymn) in Mājh measure describes different characteristics of *amrit* such as eradicator of egoity, producer of *amrit* effect, a means to *liv* (concentration,) and giver of happiness (GG, 118-19).

This *amrit* of God's Name is realized from within the self and can be realized at any hour of day or night, but the best time conducive to realization is the last quarter of night or the early morning to which Gurū Nānak refers as *amrit velā* when the devotee may contemplate the greatness of God (GG, 2). Gurū Aṅgad says that during early morning, the last quarter of night, the awakened ones develop a fondness for cultivating the True Name (GG, 146). Historically, *amrit* in the Sikh tradition refers to the baptismal water Gurū Gobind Siṅgh, Nānak X, consecrated for the initiatory rites promulgated in supersession of *charan-amrit* at the time of the creation of the Khālsā brotherhood. This is called *Khaṇḍe dā Amrit* or nectar touched with the double-edged sword.

See PĀHUL

BIBLIOGRAPHY

1. *Sikh Rahit Maryādā*. Amritsar, 1975
2. Kapur Singh, *Pārāśarapraśna*. Amritsar, 1989
3. Cole, W. Owen, and Piara Singh Sambhi, *The Sikhs: Their Religious Beliefs and Practices*. Delhi, 1978
4. Sher Singh, ed., *Thoughts on Symbols in Sikhism*. Lahore, 1927
5. Harbans Singh, *The Heritage of the Sikhs*. Delhi, 1983

M.G.S.

AMRITA SHER-GIL (1913-1941), colourful and innovative painter of modern India, was born on 30 January 1913 in Budapest, Hungary. Her father, Umrāo Siṅgh Sher-Gil, scholar and savant, learned in Sanskrit as well as in Persian, came of an old Sikh family of the village of Majīṭhā, in Amritsar district of the Punjab. Her mother, Marie Antoinette, was a Hungarian of noble descent with artistic leanings. She had some Jewish blood about which she was generally very discreet, and possessed a gregarious, gushing manner which could charm society snobs, but bewilder those close to her. She came out to the Punjab with Princess Bamba, who had through a public notice published in London sought a companion to travel with her to India, the land of her forbears. Princess Bamba was the daughter of the last Sikh king of the Punjab, Mahārājā Duleep Siṅgh, who after the occupation of his territory by the British and exile from the Punjab had been that time living in England. Marie Antoinette made the acquaintance of Umrāo Siṅgh in Shimlā and this acquaintance led to marriage. They travelled together to Budapest where their first child, Amrita, was born. To go by the census standards for determining the nationality of a child, Amrita was after her male parent a Punjabi Jaṭṭ. But her first visit to the Punjab came off only at the age of eight. World War I prevented her parents' return to India. In the Punjab, the family lived on the slopes of Summer Hill at Shimlā and in Sarayā, a village in the Gorakhpur district of Uttar Pradesh where her father held an estate.The scenic beauty of the hills and dales and of the Himalayan peaks not far away from their Summer Hill residence left a deep impact on Amrita's aesthetic sensibility. Upon the recommendation of the English teacher who had been hired to teach her art and music and who had soon recognized her unusual talent, she in 1924 went, accompanied by her mother, to Florence, Italy, to join the art school of Santa Anunciata. However, the daily religious routine, strict discipline and rigid curriculum there did not suit her temperament and she left the school after completing only one semester, returning to India with her mother.

In April 1929 she joined Grand Chaumiere, a well-known art school in Paris, where she studied for one semester, shifting thereafter to the Ecole Nationale des Beaux Arts. She made a very minute study of the human anatomy, perspective and various techniques of oil painting. The encouragement she received from her teacher, Lucien Simon, who admired her talent and frequently commended her progress, stimulated her creative energies. In Paris, she frequented art studios, art gallaries and art museums. She studied the original works of the great masters. The paintings of Paul Cezanne taught her the art of compact composition and the technique of modelling to represent the third dimension. Gauguin's Tahitian paintings, with their sensitive draughtsmanship and effective use of colour, especially his technique of using flat areas of pigments marking Tahitian sunshine, made a special appeal to her.

Graduating from the Ecole Nationale des Beaux Arts, Amrita left for India in November 1934 to find her own sunshine. But her romantic vision of her motherland — "voluptuous, colourful, sunny..." as she had imagined it to be - soon gave way to, again in her own words, "the vision of Winter in India — desolate, yet strangely beautiful — of endless tracks of luminous yellow-grey land, of dark-bodied, sad-faced, incredibly thin men and women who move silently, looking almost like silhouettes over which an indefinable melancholy reigns." To capture and interpret the weariness she saw on the faces of the vast numbers became the main concern of her creative vision.

In June 1938, she travelled to Hungary to marry her maternal cousin, Dr Victor Egan. After their honeymoon in Europe, the couple returned to India. Dr Egan took up employment with Amrita's uncle, Sundar Siṅgh Majīṭhīā, who owned a sugar factory at Sarayā. Dr Egan served there as a physician. Here at Sarayā, Amrita went through a new phase in her creative experience. She felt that "another period of transition is approaching, one of greater reflection, of more conscious painting, more observation and more stylization in the sense of nature." She blossoms forth into a jubilant mood and looks at her surroundings, at flora and fauna especially with fresh tenderness and excitement. Out of this period came paintings of landscapes and animals.

In September 1941, Amrita migrated to Lahore where her husband, Dr Egan, set up his own practice. Here she started work on a painting of buffaloes in a suburban setting which was never to be completed. In Lahore she fell a prey on 3 December 1941 to virulent bacillary dysentary and died two days later, not quite twenty-nine then.

Amrita Sher-Gil's career, tragically brief, remains a landmark in the history of the art of painting. She synthesized the technique of the West with the influence of Indian environment. The fact that Amrita Sher-Gil went to an art school in Paris and stayed there, ostensibly practising life drawing consistently for five years, shows that she made a conventional enough beginning. At an average art school in Western Europe drawing from the model and obvious construction are considered the most essential qualifications of an artist. A flower must look like a flower and figures reproduced the scale. The concrete object is exalted — and the feeling which this photographic and naturalistic representation is supposed to arouse is considered the supreme test. A painter who can draw men and women so that they look exactly like men and women generally wins the school medal or is hung in the academy.

It is easily conceivable how Amrita began to think of India, the India that had belonged to her child's world, romantically, almost as Gauguin had thought of the South Sea islands. And, obviously, she wanted to return and apply the technique she had learnt in the studios of Paris to India, to come and paint her dream-world with the 'objectivity' of Cezanne, who dominated her mind as he dominated the best part of the art world of Western Europe.

In Paris she practised drawing and sought to learn the lesson of Cezanne, that by painting still life pictures and landscapes, in which one had to concentrate on an object with definite structure, one is able to realize the objective nature of things in terms of paint and canvas. And she understood his emphasis on the intimate relation between form and colour in nature, on the necessity of design in colour, this to say of design not as a thing in itself but as a harmony of colour.

If Cezanne showed Amrita Sher-Gil the way to the organization of form, she took her initial cue for the organization of colour from Gauguin. But, as Mr Khaṇḍālāvālā has very pertinaciously pointed out, her affinity with Gauguin is superficial. For, actually, the broad planes of colour and the plastic effects which she tried to achieve in her canvases are owed to Cezanne's reduction of objects to their essential planes and to her own uncompromising quest for simplicity through her absorption of Western teachings as well as of the lessons of early Indian sculpture and medieval Indian painting.

The first few paintings on which Amrita worked in her studio in Shimlā show a sculpturesque technique, both in the folds of the dresses and the severity of planes. The still, immobile figures in *Hill Men* and *Hill Women,* thought almost static, are yet however essentially dramatic, because of the way in which they are related to each other in the composition. Already Amrita Sher-Gil is blending the skilled draughtsmanship she has learnt in Paris with a compassionate vision of the unhappy Indian people, with a strict avoidance of rhetoric or ornamentation, and she is gathering the uncontoured forms before her, through the organization of volume with colour, into a new kind of symmetry or balance. What seems like distortion or inadequate drawing in her pictures to some people is a coherence attained through inner feeling, a kind of metaphysical aim, the mastery of nature and its use by the artist to express deep emotion. And it is clear that few artists in contemporary India have handled colour with quite the passionate joy which Amrita Sher-Gil brought to it. And yet all these gay and bright colours are used to communicate the essential melancholy of this land and her inhabitants. In *Group of Three Girls* and *Child Wife* the colours are even brighter and the resultant sadness more poignant. For a fiery, almost searingly angry, imagination is at work, an elemental vision armed with a palette and a brush that are like fire and sword. And the curious thing is that it is precisely by eschewing obvious literary aims and concentrating on the organization of colour that Amrita has attained her imaginative aims.

The struggle to realize herself through paint dominated her and she remained an experimentalist throughout her life, waging an uncompromising war against complacence, and straining to achieve greater control over her medium. In 1936 she made pilgrimages to the shrines of Indian art. She went first to see the wall paintings of Ajantā and the nearby temple of Ellorā, hewn out of rock. Then she visited Travancore and Cochīn and saw the magnificent murals of the Mattancherī Palace. Her impressions of these places are characteristic. Though finding Ajantā "curiously subtle and fascinating" she thought the paintings "too involved compositionally and the details of jewellery in particular feebly painted, badly constructed." This reaction was natural from one who had made clear organization of form and colour her god. "Simply extraordinary," she exclaimed. "Dangerous stuff to take into the system unassimilated." But when she met good construction in the frescoes of the Mattancherī Palace after having seen the paintings in the Padmanābhapuram temple in Travancore, she wrote to Karl Khaṇḍālāvālā: "When I saw them I realized why I hadn't been colossally impressed by the ones at Travancore. I had a vague feeling that much more could be done with it than what had been done, that much greater possibilities lay in that material. And in Cochin I found that justification for that feeling. I have seldom seen such powerful drawing. It often surpasses Ajanta."

The charm and depth of the South worked on her, its rich, sensuous, intricate life with the bright colours of its flowers, the chiselled faces of its inhabitants and the grace of their garments captivated her. She wanted to stay and paint. She did actually settle down for a few days at Cape Comorin and executed the picture called *Fruit Vendors,* the first superb result of the pilgrimages to the

Deccan and the lower reaches of the Peninsula. For the new coherence of her draughtsmanship and brilliant colouring here seems to owe itself in part at least to Ajantā.

The harmony foreshadowed in the *Fruit Vendors* is more completely realized in three monumental pictures which she painted on her return to Shimlā, and which she called her South Indian trilogy, namely *The Bride's Toilet, The Brahmachārīs* and *South Indian Villagers Going to Market.* All the elements of her make-up have here combined to render possible three of the most vital canvases which she was ever to paint in her brief life. The plastic to which she was always reducing her figures flows with a linear rhythm, itself completely one with her newly mixed colours and her profound sense of irony, the pity in her. And her grasp of objective truth seems to have been compelled by an intense, almost convalescent, tenderness much like Dostoevsky's, and she seems near enough to achieving what Cezanne wanted to attain, in the manner of Poussin, poetic truth. As we gaze at *South Indian Villagers Going to Market* are we not meeting the very fatalism of India's malaise? Says Professor Dickinson, "Here is gathered no happiness, no laughter, but a brooding melancholy seems to beckon at us as we note those attenuated frames of old and young. Out of their eyes comes too that mute reproach to the god of seasons and unyielding crops." The sheer strain of working on the South Indian trilogy exhausted her. She had explored a new line of approach to her objectives in these pictures. So we find her now doing a series of small canvases, beginning with *Women in Red* and embracing *Siesta, The Story Teller, Ganesh Pūjā, Elephants Bathing in a Green Pool* and *Hill Scene,* before she left for Hungary in June 1938 to marry her cousin Dr Victor Egan.

In this phase of her development Amrita Sher-Gil was obviously influenced by the Basohlī paintings, which she knew well from Karl Khaṇḍālāvālā's collection and from the Lahore Museum, as well as by the Kāṅgṛā Kalam and the Mug͟hal miniatures. Colour is more intensely the hero of her work of this period than ever before. "I cannot control my appetite for colour," she said to her friend, "and I wonder if I ever will." About the particular way in which she used colour in these pictures she wrote: "I have tried, though it is very difficult, to give all the figures... the flat relief (I am avoiding volume) of card board figurines pasted into canvas. And also of obtaining my effects of colourless by play of light and shade, though they are all open-air things, than by the enamelled translucidity of the pate itself."

Although comparatively small, the canvases of this period are still in the mural tradition. And it is not surprising that she should choose to assimilate the intense colouring of Basohlī with the Kāṅgṛā designs, because the latter are mostly a reduced fresco style and not illustrative miniatures as Mug͟hal paintings generally are. But whatever the influences which she lived with and whatever environment she chose to paint in, whether Shimlā or Sarayā, Amrita Sher-Gil was always concerned to make a synthesis. During her visits abroad she painted some canvases in Hungary which, though in the European genre and not admitted by Mr Khaṇḍālāvālā in the Indian canon, are extremely interesting, because they reveal an unerring sense of visual relatedness in the midst of a phenomenon different from India and yet intimately connected both with Amrita's early childhood impressions and the preoccupation with paint which she derived from her Western inheritance.

The war broke out after her return to India in the summer of 1939. She painted very little in the atmosphere of uncertainty which prevailed, except *Resting,* which Mr Khaṇḍālāvālā rightly considers "one of her finest achievements for its sheer colour beauty," with its gaily clad females, each a gentle flower among the natural flowers. But when Amrita settled down in the village of Sarayā, where her husband was appointed medical officer at her uncle's sugar mill, she was conscious of a new phase in her work. "Another period of transition is approaching. One of greater reflection, of more conscious painting, more observation and more stylization in the sense of nature."

Elephant Promenade, The Swing, Horse and Groom, Ancient Story Teller, Woman Resting on a Charpoy, Haldī Grinders, and *Camels* show her experimenting with compositions more derivative from the Kāṅgṛā and Mug͟hal paintings than any of her previous work, but there is a new brightness, a new precision and a new simplicity here, without the atmosphere of a sad, elfin music, the hallmark of her tender sensibility.

When she returned from Paris in 1935, renaissance style of art fostered by the Bengal school held sway in India. Her own source of inspiration, medium and form had little in common with the Bengal school exponents of which depicted the gods and goddesses in water colour (wash method) in a strictly two-dimensional form, whereas Amrita interpreted contemporary life in oils using chiaroscuro, linear-aerial perspective, and other modelling derives to represent three-dimensional reality. Unlike the Bengal school which painted "Bhārat Mātā" (personification of Mother India) giving her an anthropomorphic form, she portrayed "Mother India" as an aged, forlorn woman with an anaemic son on her lap and a sickly daughter seated next to her. This is how Amrita pictured her country in British thraldom.

In the final analysis Amrita seems to have been concerned in her art with redressing the balance of certainty and restating basic truths about human nature, human folly, and human inadequacy, about the pain and pleasure of the creative act, and about suffering and the joy of being. She developed a unique style of painting, maintaining a mysterious harmony of idea, perception and visual image. She rejected verisimilitude and refused to reproduce a mirror-image of an actual scene and turned from an empirical to a conceptual method of representation. Her stylistic implications and colour harmonies introduced a new trend in Indian painting.

To quote Rudy von Leiden:

> Art in India was never the same after her comet-like appearance.There are only a few moments in the history of art which pin-point a new departure, a new direction. Such a moment in the history of modern Indian art was the appearance in the mid-thirties of Amrita Sher-Gil with whose paintings contemporary painting in India took shape and demonstrated the possibility of a contemporary style and expression that were, at the same time, of the soil and in direct continuation of the great national past.

BIBLIOGRAPHY

1. N. Iqbal Singh, *Amrita Sher-gil: A Biography*. Delhi, 1984
2. Khandalavala, Karl, *Amrita Sher-gil*. Bombay, 1944
3. Muggeridge, Malcolm, *Chronicles of Wasted Times: The Infernal Grove*. London, 1973
4. Wojtilla, Gyula, *Amrita Sher-gil and Hungary*. Delhi, 1981

M.R.A. & M.S.G.

AMRITDHĀRĪ (*amrit*, lit. nectar, commonly Sikh sanctified initiatory water + *dhārī* = practitioner) is one who has received baptismal vows of the K͟hālsā initiated by Gurū Gobind Siṅgh (30 March 1699) and abides by them and by the *pañj kakārī rahit*, distinctive insignia introduced by the Gurū on that day comprising five symbols each beginning with the Gurmukhī letter "ਕ" (*pronounced* "kakkā") or its Roman equivalent "k". These are *kes* (long unshorn hair and beard), *kaṅghā* (a comb to keep the hair tidy), *kirpān* (a sword), *kaṛā* (a steel bracelet worn about the wrist), and *kachh* (short breeches worn by soldiers).

See PĀHUL

BIBLIOGRAPHY

1. *Sikh Rahit Maryādā*, Amritsar, 1975
2. Kapur Singh, *Pārāśarapraśna*. Amritsar, 1989
3. Sher Singh, Giani, ed., *Thoughts on Forms and Symbols in Sikhism*. Lahore, 1927
4. Uberoi, J.P.S., "The Five Symbols of Sikhism," in *Sikhism*. Patiala, 1969
5. Nripinder Singh, *The Sikh Moral Tradition*. Delhi, 1990

P.S.S.

AMRIT RĀI, son of Chhail Rāi, a Bhaṭṭ of Lahore, and pupil of Chatar Dās, a noted poet, had completed his *Ras Ratnākar* and *Chitra Bilās* (the latter in 1679) before he came under the patronage of Gurū Gobind Siṅgh at Anandpur. What is left of his compositions while with the Gurū is his rendering in Hindi verse of a *parva* or part from the *Mahābhārata* and a stanza quoted by Bhāī Santokh Siṅgh, *Srī Gur Pratāp Sūraj Granth* (*q.v.*), *ritu* 5, *aṅsū* 26. In the latter stanza Amrit Rāi sings the fame of the Gurū as a bounteous patron and offers himself for service. The former, entitled *Sabhā Parab*, was completed on Baisākh *vadī* 2, 1753 Bk/ 8 April 1696. The only known Gurmukhī manuscript of this work is preserved in the private collection of the Mahārājā of Paṭiālā.

BIBLIOGRAPHY

1. Kāhn Siṅgh, Bhāī, *Gurushabad Ratnākar Mahān Kosh*. Patiala, 1974
2. Padam, Piārā Siṅgh, *Gurū Gobind Siṅgh Jī de Darbārī Ratan*. Patiala, 1976

P.S.P.

AMRIT SAṄSKĀR. *See* PĀHUL

AMRITSAR (31°-38'N, 74°-53'E), principal holy city of the Sikhs, is the headquarters of a district (Amritsar) in the Punjab. The foundation of the town was laid in 1577 by Gurū Rām Dās (1534-81) when he inauguarted the digging of the holy tank *Amrit-sar* (*amrit* = nectar, *sar* = pool) on a piece of land which, according to some sources, was purchased from the residents of the neighbouring village of Tuṅg during the time of Gurū Amar Dās (1479-1574) and, according to other sources, was a gift from the Mughal Emperor Akbar (1542-1605) to Gurū Amar Dās's daughter, Bībī Bhānī, married to (Gurū) Rām Dās. The habitation that grew around the sacred pool (*sarovar*) was initially called Rāmdāspur, or Chakk Rāmdās, or simply Chakk Gurū. Gurū Rām Dās encouraged people from various trades and professions to take up residence here. The town expanded further under his son and successor, Gurū Arjan (1563-1606), who completed and lined the tank and constructed in its middle the holy shrine, Harimandar, now famous as the Golden Temple and also had two more tanks, Santokhsar and Rāmsar, excavated near by. It was on the bank of Rāmsar that he carried out the compilation of the Ādī Granth (later Gurū Granth Sāhib). With the installation on 16 August 1604 of the Granth Sāhib in the Harimandar, the shrine and the *sarovar* Amritsar surrounding it together became the central attraction of the town and a site of pilgrimage for Sikhs from far and near. In time, the town itself came to be called Amritsar.

Gurū Hargobind (1595-1644) constructed near the pool and opposite the Harimandar, the Akāl Takht, lit. Throne Eternal, where he sat in state dispensing the secular business of the community. He also gave two more tanks, Kaulsar and Bibeksar, to the town. Gurū Hargobind constructed a fortress, Lohgaṛh (lit. steel fort) on the western outskirts of the town. He soon came into conflict with the Mughal authority and was involved in a succession of skirmishes in and around the town. He decided to leave Amritsar early in 1635 and shift to Kīratpur, a town in the Śivālik foothills founded at his bidding by his son, Bābā Gurdittā, a few years earlier. None of the later Gurūs resided at Amritsar which was controlled during the rest of the seventeenth century by Gurū Hargobind's cousin, Miharbān, and the latter's son, Harjī, who headed the schismatic Mīṇā sect. It was only after the creation of the Khālsā in 1699 that Gurū Gobind Siṅgh deputed Bhāī Manī Siṅgh with a few other Sikhs to go to Amritsar and resume control of the town and manage the holy shrines there on behalf of the Khālsā Panth.

During the eighteenth century, Amritsar, like the Sikh community as a whole, witnessed many vicissitudes of history. It suffered repeatedly desecration and destruction until it was finally liberated upon the establishment of sovereign authority of the Sikh *misls*, principalities, over the Punjab in 1765. The town was thereafter under the control of several *misl* chiefs although its surrounding district was held by Sardār Harī Siṅgh of the Bhaṅgī *misl*. Different *sardārs* or chiefs constructed their own *buṅgās* or residential houses around the principal *sarovar* and also their respective *kaṭrās* or wards encouraging traders and craftsmen to reside in them and over which each exercised exclusive control. The sacred shrines were however administered by a joint council comprising representatives of the chiefs who had made endowments in land for their maintenance. Even prior to the time of Sikh ascendancy, joint councils, known as *sarbatt khālsā* (lit. the entire Sikh Panth), to take crucial decisions on political matters had been held at Amritsar. Now again with all *misl* chiefs having their *buṅgās* there, it became the common capital of the Khālsā. Devotees from far and near, free to visit the holy city after six decades of the severest persecution, flocked to *Gurū kī Nagarī* (the Gurū's town). So did businessmen and tradesmen to take advantage of the increasing pilgrim and resident population. Trade, commerce and crafts flourished in different *kaṭrās* each having its own markets and manufactories. By the end of the eighteenth century, Amritsar had already become Punjab's major trading centre. Yet the town with its multiple command setup remained a confederated rather than a composite habitation until Mahārājā Raṇjīt Siṅgh (1780-1839) rose to power and consolidated the whole of the Punjab into one sovereign State.

Raṇjīt Siṅgh, chief of the Sukkarchakkīā *misl*, who first occupied, in 1799, Lahore, the traditional capital of the Punjab, and declared himself Mahārājā in 1801, extended his hegemony to Amritsar in 1805 when he took over from his traditional rivals, the Bhaṅgī chiefs, their fort with its mint striking the Nānakshāhī rupee, and the famous Zamzamā gun. The fort of the Rāmgaṛhīā *misl* was occupied in 1815 and with the possessions of Rāṇī Sadā Kaur of Kanhaiyā Misl and Fateh Siṅgh Āhlūvālīā in Amritsar during the early 1820's, Raṇjīt Siṅgh's occupation of Amritsar was complete. He then constructed a double wall and a moat around the city with twelve gates and their corresponding bridges over the moat. Already in 1809 he had constructed the Gobindgaṛh Fort outside Lāhaurī Gate complete with a formidable moat, three lines of defence and several bastions and emplacements for heavy guns. Amritsar thus had already become his second capital. The royal *toshākhānā* or treasury was kept in Gobindgaṛh Fort which was also used as the royal residence during the Mahārājā's frequent visits to the city before his palace in the city, Rām Bāgh, was completed in 1831. Several members of the nobility also raised palatial houses and beautiful gardens in and around the city. Raṇjīt Siṅgh devoutly provided liberal funds to have the dome and exterior of the holy Harimandar gold-plated and to have the interior ornamented with fine filigree and enamel work and with decorative murals and panels in marble inlaid with coloured stone. Sardār Desā Siṅgh Majīṭhīā (d. 1832), who had been appointed manager of the holy shrines in the city since its occupation by Raṇjīt Siṅgh, donated gold for gilding the top of Bābā Aṭal.

During Sikh rule, Amritsar grew into a leading industrial and commercial city. The most important industry was textiles, particularly shawl and fine cotton cloth called *sūsī*. The shawl-making industry received an impetus after a famine in Kashmīr in 1833, which led to the migration of a large number of skilled Kashmīrī weavers to the city. The raw material, *pashmīnā* wool, came from the trans-Himalayan regions of Ladā<u>kh</u>, Tibet and Central Asia. Other important industries included silk-weaving, carpet-making, brass and copper ware and ivory goods.

Amritsar continued to enjoy its precedence as the holiest city of the Sikhs as well as the most important commercial and industrial centre in the northwest India even after the annexation of the Punjab to the British empire in 1849. According to the first ever official census in the Punjab conducted in 1855, Amritsar had a population of 112,186 against 94,143 of Lahore. Its population increased by 30,000 during the next thirty years. In 1890, with its population of 152,000, it was the 13th largest city in India. It was connected by rail to Lahore in 1862 and to Delhi in 1870. Both circumstances provided further fillip to its industry, trade and commerce. For textiles and shawl-making, there were in 1883-84 nearly 4,000 looms in the city. As for commerce, here is a quotation from W.S. Caine, *Picturesque India* (1891):

> The *serai* at Amritsar is one of the most interesting sights in India.... It is a great open space, surrounded by small houses, in which are lodged the travelling merchants from Central Asia.... Here are white-skinned Kashmiris, stout Nepalese, sturdy little Baluchis, stately but filthy Afghans, Persians, Bokharans and Tartars, and even the ubiquitous Chinaman.... These people bring to Amritsar the raw material for the great staple manufacture of the city, the soft down, or under-wools of goats of the Great Tibet plateau and Kashmir, from which Kashmir shawls are woven.... Besides the shawls of home manufacture, Amritsar is the chief emporium for those of a similar kind made in Kashmir....

Amritsar made great strides in the field of education after annexation. According to the Settlement Report of 1852 for Amritsar *<u>Kh</u>ās* (i.e. the town proper), there were (besides the centres of Sikh religious learning in various *buṅgās* and *ḍerās*) 18 schools, 6 run by Muhammadan teachers and 12 by Brāhmaṇs, imparting instruction to 1,050 students. By 1882, there were in the city 132 *maktabs* and *madarsās*, 65 *pāṭhshālās*, 63 Gurmukhī schools and 24 Mahājanī schools with a total number of 4,860 pupils on their rolls. The first English school, the Zilā School Amritsar, was opened in 1851 under a European headmaster with an annual government grant of Rs 5,000. Christian missionaries opened other schools, the first of them in 1853. In 1870, the Christian Vernacular Education Society opened a Normal School for the training of teachers. It was a declaration in 1873 by four Sikh students of the Amritsar Mission School of their intention to embrace Christianity which led to the rise of a Sikh movement to promote rediscovery of the essentials of the teachings of the faith and education among the Sikh masses. It was at Amritsar that the first Srī Gurū Siṅgh Sabhā subscribing to these twin objectives was formed on 1 October 1873. The efforts of the Siṅgh Sabhā leaders culminated in the establishment in 1892 of the Sikhs' premier educational institution, the <u>Kh</u>ālsā College at Amritsar. At present the city claims a dozen colleges, including a medical college, as also the Gurū Nānak Dev University, established in 1969 in honour of quinquecentennial of Gurū Nānak Dev's birth. Besides, the Shiromaṇī Gurdwārā Parbandhak Committee, a statutory body representing the entire Sikh community, is running the Shahīd Sikh Missionary College here imparting instruction in Sikh religion and history.

In addition to incidents during the Kūkā uprise of the 1870's, what made Amritsar politically alive was the Jalliāṅvālā Bāgh massacre of 1919 (*q.v.*). The Indian National Congress held its annual session of 1919 in Amritsar. October 1920 saw the rise of the Akālī or the Gurdwārā reform movement when the Sikh *saṅgat* led by Akālī leaders, Kartār Siṅgh Jhabbar and Tejā Siṅgh Bhuchchar, occupied on behalf of the reformers the Akāl Takht, the *pujārīs* or officiants and the *sarbarāh*, i.e. manager, appointed by the government, fleeing the holy precincts. With the formation of the Shiromaṇī Gurdwārā Parbandhak Committee during the following month, Amritsar once again became the political headquarters of the Sikhs. Since then almost all *morchās* or agitations connected with the political struggle of the Panth have been launched and conducted from the Darbār Sāhib complex where the Shiromaṇī Gurdwārā Parbandhak Committee and its political counterpart, the Shiromaṇī Akālī Dal, have their main offices.

The growth of the city, population-wise, was irregular up to 1921. In fact, it was negative during the decades 1881-91 (-9.96%) and 1901-11 (-5.96%), the reason being the frequent epidemics and a decline in shawl trade caused by a change in fashions in Paris and in Europe as a whole. But the decades 1921-31 and 1931-41 saw a rapid increase (+65.30 and +47.64 per cent, respectively). The following decade again had a steep decline (-16.69%), this time owing to the partition of the Punjab, resulting in the emigration from the city of almost the entire Muslim population to what became Pakistan after the independence of India. The loss of Muslim population was scarcely compensated by immigrating Hindus and Sikhs who preferred the security of the interior to settling down in a disturbed frontier city which Amritsar had then become. With the restoration of normal conditions, however, the population began to increase. The number recorded during 1991 Census was 7,09,456 including persons living in the cantonment area. Although Amritsar was founded by the Sikh Gurūs and continued to be the most important sacred city of the Sikhs, Sikhs formed only a minority of its population. Before partition Sikhs in Amritsar were, according to the Census of 1931, only 12.09% against 49.98% Muslims and 36.94% Hindus. Even after the partition of 1947 with almost the entire Muslim population having emigrated, the Sikhs were 34.18% against Hindus 64.21% (last known figures of 1971 Census).

Population percentages notwithstanding, Amritsar still remains the holy city of the Sikhs dotted with Sikh shrines honouring the memory of Gurūs, martyrs and heroes. They are:

SRĪ HARIMANDAR SĀHIB. *See* SRĪ DARBĀR SĀHIB

AKĀL BUṄGĀ housing Srī Akāl Takht Sāhib. *See* AKĀL TAKHT

GURDWARA LĀCHĪ BER, a small, domed structure raised upon a marble-paved platform near the gateway to the Harimandar, is named after the *berī* (jujube) tree by its side which yields small (*lāchī* or cardamom-size) berries. According to tradition, Gurū Arjan used to sit under this tree and watch the digging of the *sarovar*, the sacred tank. Bhāī Sālho, a prominent Sikh of that time, also used to relax here after the day's labour at the tank. It is said that when Mahitāb Siṅgh Mīrāṅkoṭīā and Sukkhā Siṅgh arrived here to have the Harimandar liberated from the control of Masse Khān Raṅghaṛ, and chastised the desecrator of the holy shrine, they fastened their horses to this jujube tree before entering the building.

BER BĀBĀ BUḌḌHĀ JĪ, is an old jujube tree standing in the *parikramā* or circumambulatory terrace along the northern bank of the sacred pool. It is here that the celebrated Bābā Buḍḍhā, entrusted with the supervision of the digging of the tank, used to sit with his piles of digging tools and implements and other materials used for brick-lining the *sarovar* and later for the construction of the Harimandar. A marble platform now surrounds the tree trunk.

GURDWĀRĀ DUKH BHAÑJAṆĪ BERĪ stands on the eastern flank of the *sarovar* by the side of yet another jujube tree known as Dukh Bhañjaṇī (lit. eradicator of suffering) Berī. The place is associated with the legend of Bībī Rajanī whose leper husband is said to have been cured of his malady by having a dip in the old pond which had existed here since ancient times. Gurū Rām Dās, hearing the report of this miracle, decided to develop the reservoir into a proper bathing tank. He is himself said to have given the tree the name Dukh Bhañjaṇī. People have a strong faith that water in this portion of the tank will heal their ailments.

GURDWĀRĀ THAṚHĀ SĀHIB, situated in a narrow street called Bāzār Thaṛhā Sāhib, a little way north of the Akāl Takht, commemorates Gurū Tegh Bahādur's visit to Amritsar in 1664. Soon after assuming office as Gurū, he had come from Bakālā to pay homage at the Harimandar, but the priests in charge who belonged to the rival Mīṇā sect shut the doors of the holy shrine in his face. Gurū Tegh Bahādur then sat praying for some time at the spot now marked by Gurdwārā Thaṛhā (lit. platform) Sāhib and then went back towards the village of Vallā. The Gurdwārā is a two-storeyed domed structure. The Gurū Granth Sāhib is seated on the first floor. The ground floor which gives the look of a basement cellar has a platform and the stump of an old tree believed to be the one under which Gurū Tegh Bahādur had sat.

GURDWĀRĀ MAÑJĪ SĀHIB, adjacent to the eastern boundary of the compound housing the Harimandar and the *sarovar*, is situated in what was formerly known as Gurū kā Bāgh (the Gurū's garden). This was the place where Gurū Arjan used to hold the daily *dīvān*. A marbled platform marks the spot where the Gurū used to sit on a *mañjī* (cot) with the Sikhs squatting on the ground in front. The Gurū Granth Sāhib is seated in an adjoining room. A vast *dīvān* hall constructed in front of Mañjī Sāhib during recent decades now covers the whole of the former Gurū kā Bāgh.

GURDWĀRĀ GURŪ KE MAHAL, as the name signifies, marks the residential house of the Gurūs. It is situated west of the Akāl Takht across Gurū kā Bāzār street. Originally constructed as a modest hut by Gurū Rām Dās in 1573, it was enlarged and beautified by Gurū Arjan Dev and Gurū Hargobind. The old house has since been converted into a *gurdwārā* with the Gurū Granth Sāhib seated in a large rectangular hall. Besides the daily services, a special *dīvān* and Gurū kā Laṅgar are held on every Sunday following the first of a Bikramī month. The most important event of the year is the celebration of the birth anniversary of Gurū Tegh Bahādur who was born here on Baisākh *vadī* 5, 1678 Bk/1 April 1621.

GURDWĀRĀ BĀBĀ AṬAL SĀHIB, a 9-storey octagonal tower, over 45 metres high, standing close to the Kaulsar pool about 200 metres southeast of the Harimandar, marks the spot where Bābā Aṭal Rāi, 9-year-old son of Gurū Hargobind, passed away on 9 Assū 1685 Bk/ 13 September 1628. *See* AṬAL RĀI, BĀBĀ. A simple memorial in honour of Bābā Aṭal was raised on the site originally. The construction of the present edifice commenced after the Sikh *misls* had established their authority in the Punjab. The cornerstone was laid in 1770 and the first three storeys had been completed by 1784. The upper floors were raised by Mahārājā Raṇjīt Siṅgh during the 1820's. Sardār Desā Siṅgh Majīṭhīā contributed gold for gilding the dome at the top. The Gurū Granth Sāhib is seated in a small inner room on the ground floor. The first six storeys are larger than the upper ones which rise above the central sanctum. The doors on the ground floor, four in number, are decorated with embossed designs, on brass and silver sheets. Interior walls and the ceiling are covered with murals depicting scenes from the lives of Gurū Nānak, his two sons and nine successors, Gurū Gobind Siṅgh's four sons and Bābā Buḍḍhā.

In olden days, the surroundings of Bābā Aṭal Sāhib (as the building is popularly called) were used as a cremation ground and the area was dotted with *samādhs* (memorial shrines) raised for eminent *sardārs* (chiefs), saints (holy men), and warriors. The shrine was taken over by the Shiromaṇī Gurdwārā Parbandhak Committee in August 1921. During the process of widening the *parikramā*, most of the *samādhs* were demolished. Those surviving include the ones commemorating Jassā Siṅgh Āhlūvālīā and Nawāb Kapūr Siṅgh.

GURDWĀRĀ MĀĪ KAULĀṄ DĀ ASTHĀN is on the bank of the Kaulsar tank, both the tank as well as the shrine sharing the name Kaulāṅ. Kaulāṅ was, according to tradition, the daughter (slave-girl, according to some sources) of Rustam K͟hān, Qāzī of Muzaṅg, a suburb of Lahore. She was of a religious bent of mind from the very beginning and, as she grew up, she became acquainted with the teachings of the Gurūs and turned a devotee of Gurū Hargobind. Her father did not quite approve of this and subjected her to the harshest treatment to dissuade her from the path she seemed to be carving for herself. But she remained adamant and fled home to seek refuge with Gurū Hargobind at Amritsar. Gurdwārā Māī Kaulāṅ dā Asthān, as the name signifies, marks the site of the house where she lived. After a few years she shifted to Kartārpur, near Jalandhar, where she died in 1629. The tank Kaulsar was got excavated by Gurū Hargobind for Kaulāṅ's convenience. It was rain-fed and remained neglected until desilted, cleaned and renovated in 1872 and connected to the *haṅslī*, or water channel bringing waters of the River Rāvī to the Amritsar *sarovars*, in 1884.

GURDWĀRĀ RĀMSAR stands on the bank of the Rāmsar *sarovar*, near Chāṭīviṇḍ Gate, on the southeastern side of the walled city. After the completion of the Harimandar, Gurū Arjan undertook the compilation of Ādi Granth, the Holy Book, now revered as Gurū Granth Sāhib. For this task, he chose a secluded site. The spot selected was then a shady nook, one km away from the bustle of the town. To make the surroundings more agreeable, he had a tank dug which was named Rāmsar after Gurū Rām Dās. Here, Gurū Arjan composed his famous *Sukhmanī*, the Psalm of Peace, and with Bhāī Gurdās as his scribe compiled the Ādi Granth during 1603-04. The present Gurdwārā Rāmsar, a small marble-lined hall topped by a gilded, fluted lotus dome built in 1855, marks the site of the Gurū's labours.

GURDWĀRĀ BIBEKSAR stands on the eastern flank of the tank Bibeksar got dug by Gurū Hargobind in 1628 for the convenience of such pilgrims as would prefer seclusion to the hustle and bustle of the immediate environs of the main shrine. The Gurdwārā lies northeast of Rāmsar between Chāṭīviṇḍ and Sultānviṇḍ gates of the walled city. The Gurdwārā was raised by Mahārājā Raṇjīt Siṅgh in 1833. The building for Gurū kā Laṅgār and a well were added in 1905-06. The Gurdwārā was controlled by Nihaṅgs until its management statutorily passed to the Shiromaṇī Gurdwārā Parbandhak Committee in 1925.

GURDWĀRĀ ṬĀHLĪ SĀHIB is connected with yet another *sarovar* Santokhsar close to the Town Hall in the heart of the old city. Santokhsar, 148x110 metres and next only to Amrit *sarovar* in size, is said to be the first tank the digging of which was commenced by Bhāī Jeṭhā (later Gurū Rām Dās) in 1564 under the direction of Gurū Amar Dās. But before long Bhāī Jeṭhā was called back to Goindvāl, and Santokhsar remained half-dug until Gurū Arjan Dev completed it in 1588. It fell into neglect during the turbulent eighteenth century and was resurrected only in 1903 after the municipal committee of Amritsar had declared it a health hazard and threatened to fill it up. Although in 1824 it had been connected to a canal-fed channel, or *haṅslī,* to make it independent of the vagaries of rainfall, the channel had become choked with silt and the tank was turned into a receptacle for locality garbage. A complete desilting was carried out in 1919 through *kār-sevā* (voluntary free service) under Sant Shām Siṅgh and Sant Gurmukh Siṅgh. The Gurdwārā derives its name from a *ṭāhlī* tree, *Dalbergia sisoo,* of which only a stump now remains near the main gateway. It is believed that this was the tree under which Gurū Rām Dās and after him Gurū Arjan stood supervising the excavation of the tank. The Gurdwārā comprising a rectangular hall on the western side of Santokhsar *sarovar* is next to the Ṭāhlī Sāhib stump as one enters the walled compound enclosing the *sarovar* and the shrine.

GURDWĀRĀ CHAURASTĪ AṬĀRĪ, lit. a tall house at a road crossing (*chaurastā*, in Punjabi) is located by the side of a plaza at the end of Gurū kā Bāzār in the heart of the old city. It is dedicated to Gurū Hargobind who occasionally came here to rest. The plaza was the site of the initial encounter with an imperial force that attacked the Gurū in 1629. The original house was demolished under the orders of the British officials soon after the annexation of the Punjab, in order to widen the plaza. The present building, smaller in size, has the Gurū Granth Sāhib seated on the ground floor. Besides daily prayers, special congregations take place on the first and the fifth day of the light half of every lunar month.

GURDWĀRĀ LOHGAṚH SĀHIB, about one km to the northwest of Harimandar, marks the site of a fort of the same name (lit. fort of steel) constructed by Gurū Hargobind for the defence of the town. The main battle of Amritsar between the Gurū and an imperial force under Mukhlis Khān in May 1629 was fought here. The present Gurdwārā stands on the ruined mound of the fort, which was razed by Ahmad Shāh Durrānī during one of his invasions in the mid-eighteenth century. The nearby gate in the city wall constructed by Mahārājā Raṇjīt Siṅgh is also known as Lohgaṛh Gate.

GURDWĀRĀ PIPLĪ SĀHIB, about 1.5 km west of Amritsar railway station towards the Khālsā College, marks the spot where a large *saṅgat*, column of devotees, coming from Afghanistan and northwestern districts of the Punjab to take part in the excavation of the main Amritsar tank was welcomed by Gurū Arjan, who came forward personally to receive them and who subsequently made it into a resting place for *saṅgats* coming to Amritsar from that direction. The Gurdwārā is connected by a 150-metre link road to the main Sher Shāh Sūrī Mārg near Putlīghar. It came into prominence again in 1923 when crowds of volunteers for the *kār-sevā* or desilting operation of the Darbār Sāhib tank first assembled here and then proceeded to the work site in a procession on 17 June 1923. The Gurdwārā was reconstructed during the 1930's. Besides the daily services, a fair is held here on the occasion of Basant Pañchmī (January-February).

GURDWĀRĀ SHAHĪDGAÑJ BĀBĀ DĪP SIṄGH near the Chātīviṇḍ Gate of the walled city commemorates the martyrdom of Bābā Dīp Siṅgh (*q.v.*) of the Shahīd *misl*, who, coming from Damdamā Sāhib (Talvaṇḍī Sābo) in Baṭhiṇḍā district to liberate the Darbār Sāhib, which had been attacked and desecrated by the Afg͟hān invaders, was mortally wounded here on 11 November 1757. Jassā Siṅgh (d. 1803) of Rāmgaṛhīā *misl* raised a memorial platform on the site which was developed into a *gurdwārā* by Akālī Phūlā Siṅgh (d. 1823). It was managed for long by the descendants of Sardār Karam Siṅgh of Shahīd *misl*, and was handed over to the Shiromaṇī Gurdwārā Parbandhak Committee in 1924. The surrounding estate owned by the descendants of Jassā Siṅgh Rāmgaṛhīā was also donated later to the Gurdwārā Shahīdgañj.

GURDWĀRĀ SHAHĪDGAÑJ BĀBĀ GURBAK͟HSH SIṄGH, a small shrine standing in a narrow *bāzār* behind the Akāl Buṅgā, commemorates the saga of heroism of Bābā Gurbak͟hsh Siṅgh Nihaṅg and his twenty-nine comrades who faced a Durrānī horde in December 1764 and fell to the last man fighting in defence of the Harimandar.

DHARAMSĀLĀ BHĀĪ SĀLHO JĪ, near Gurdwārā Gurū ke Mahal, commemorates the name of Bhāī Sālho (d. 1628), a devout Sikh who served Gurū Rām Dās, Gurū Arjan, and Gurū Hargobind. Entrusted with the general administration of the nascent town, he was popularly called *kotwāl*, the police chief, of Amritsar. The Dharamsālā was his residence as well as his place of work. A nearby pond, called Bhāī Sālho's Ṭobhā (lit. pond), was filled up by the British in 1863. The Dharamsālā has since been converted into a *gurdwārā*, a two-storeyed building topped by a gilded dome with ancillary buildings such as Gurū kā Laṅgar and residential rooms for officiants.

GURDWĀRĀ DARSHANĪ DIOṚHĪ represents the gateway to Amritsar during its infancy built by Gurū Arjan. As one entered the new habitation through it, paths led to Gurū ke Mahal on the right and the Harimandar on the left with no houses in between to obstruct a glimpse (*darshan*, in Punjabi) of the two holy places. Hence the name Darshanī Dioṛhī (*dioṛhī* = portal or gateway). Converted into a small *gurdwārā*, it now stands amidst the crowded Bāzār Māī Sevāṅ, near its junction with Gurū kā Bāzār.

GURDWĀRĀ DAMDAMĀ SĀHIB, located between the railway line and the Sher Shāh Sūrī Mārg about 3 km east of Amritsar railway station, is dedicated to Gurū Teg͟h Bahādur who halted here for some time on his way from Amritsar to Vallā in 1664 (*See* Gurdwārā Thaṛhā Sāhib). *Damdamā* means a place for a brief halt. As the news that the Gurū had been denied entry into the Harimandar by the Mīṇā priests spread, the Amritsar *saṅgat*, mostly women, came out to see him. They went first to the Darbār Sāhib and, learning that the Gurū had already left, they with a view to atoning for the impudence and folly of the priests, followed him. They caught up with him at this spot and begged his forgiveness for what had happened and entreated him to return and visit the holy shrine with them. Gurū Teg͟h Bahādur declined their request to go back, adding that he had no complaint or rancour against anyone. He pronounced this blessing for the women: *māīāṅ rabb razāīāṅ* (Ever blessed by the Lord be the ladies). Construction of the present building of the Gurdwārā was started in the beginning of the twentieth century by Sant Siṅgh Kalīvāle, a trader in limestone.

Some other sacred spots in Amritsar are Har Kī Pauṛī, a flight of steps going down to the water level behind the Harimandar; Aṭhsaṭh Tīrath, a gilded kiosk constructed by Mahārājā Raṇjīt Siṅgh along the southern bank of the *sarovar*; and Thaṛhā Sāhib, a small shrine between Aṭhsaṭh Tīrath and Ber Bābā Buḍḍhā Jī commemorating Gurū Amar Dās and Gurū Arjan.

Besides spots and shrines sacred to the Sikhs, Amritsar has many other places of interest, the better known among them being the Durgiāṇā Mandir, a Hindu temple built during the 1930's on the model of the Golden Temple; Jalliāṅvālā Bāgh, the site of the tragedy of 13 April 1919; Gobindgaṛh Fort constructed by Mahārājā Raṇjīt Siṅgh; and Rām Bāgh gardens and palace where Mahārājā Raṇjīt Siṅgh used to put up during his frequent visits to the city.

BIBLIOGRAPHY

1. Giān Siṅgh, Giānī, *Twārīkh Srī Amritsar* [Reprint]. Amritsar, 1977
2. Ṭhākar Siṅgh, Giānī, *Srī Gurduāre Darshan*. Amritsar, 1923
3. Tārā Siṅgh, *Srī Gur Tīrath Saṅgrahi*. Amritsar, n.d.
4. Kirpāl Siṅgh, Giānī, "Srī Amritsar Shahir," in the *Gurdwārā Gazette*. November 1988
5. Pratāp Siṅgh, Giānī, *Amritsaru Sifatī dā Gharu*. Amritsar, 1977
6. Datta, V.N., *Amritsar Past and Present*. Amritsar, 1967
7. Madanjit Kaur, *The Golden Temple: Past and Present*. Amritsar, 1983
8. Patwant Singh, *The Golden Temple*. Delhi, 1988
9. Arshi, P.S., *Sikh Architecture in the Punjab*. Delhi, 1986

M.G.S.

AMRITSAR KHĀLSĀ DIWAN. *See* KHĀLSĀ DĪWĀN, AMRITSAR

AMRIT VELĀ, lit. ambrosial hour (*velā*=time or hour), the last quarter of night or predawn morning hours, is reckoned in Sikh spirituality as period of time most conducive to concentration and appropriate for meditation and practising *nām*, i.e. repetition of God's Name. Says Gurū Nānak in the *Japu*: *amrit velā sachu nāu vaḍiāī vīchāru* (early morning is the time for practising *nām*, God's Name synonymous with God Himself, and for contemplating His greatness —GG, 2). Gurū Aṅgad, Nānak II, says: *chauthai pahari sabāh kai surtiā upajai chāu/ tinā darīāvā siu dostī mani mukhi sachā nāu* (during fourth quarter of night, joy sprouts forth in the hearts of awakened ones; they go, befriend the rivers and brooks (for ablution) and have the True Name in their minds and on their lips —GG, 146). Shaikh Farīd, the Muslim saint, whose compositions are also included in the Sikh Scripture, is more forthright. Says he, "If you lose the last part of night to sleep, O Farid! count yourself as dead even as you live. (Remember that) if you have forgotten God, He has not forgotten thee (GG, 1383). Gurū Rām Dās, laying down the daily regimen for a Sikh accorded primacy to early-rising to contemplate God's Name, "Let him who calls himself a Sikh of the Gurū, rise early and meditate on God" (GG, 305). And, Gurū Arjan, Nānak V, says: "Rise early in the morning and repeat God's Name" (GG, 255). To quote Bhāī Gurdās: "The Gurū's Sikh rises early in the morning, performs ablutions at *amrit velā* and recites the Gurū's word" (*Vārāṅ*, 40:11)

Amrit velā in Sikhism is the prime hour not for its own sake, but because of its suitability for practising *nām*, i.e. for remembering God and contemplating His greatness. No special auspiciousness attaches to *amrit velā*. Every moment of one's life is meant for the remembrance of God. As Gurū Arjan says, "Blessed is the hour (*velā*) when one gets absorbed in contemplation of Him" (GG, 562).

BIBLIOGRAPHY

1. *Shabdārth Srī Gurū Granth Sāhib Jī*. Amritsar, 1964
2. Padam, Piārā Siṅgh, ed., *Gurū Granth Vichār-Kosh*. Patiala, 1969

M.G.S.

ANABHĪ, a Jain hierarch, who, according to *Purātan Janam Sākhī*, met Gurū Nānak during his journey to the South. Anabhī addressed the Gurū thus: "Eatest thou corn, old or new, consumest thou parched gram, and drinkest thou cold water without filtering to ensure absence of living organisms; yet thou art called a Gurū. What merit dost thou possess if thou art constantly killing living beings?" Gurū Nānak, according to *Purātan Janam Sākhī*, recited verses saying: "By the Master's grace is faith fulfilled," and not by "having the hair of one's head plucked, drinking befouled water and begging others for leftovers to eat." Anabhī, says the *Janam Sākhī*, took the precept and became a disciple.

BIBLIOGRAPHY

1. Vīr Siṅgh, Bhāī, *Srī Gurū Nānak Chamatkār*. Amritsar, 1928
2. Giān Siṅgh, Giānī, *Panth Prakāsh* [Reprint]. Patiala, 1970

Gn.S.

ANAHATA-ŚABDA figures variously in the Gurū Granth Sāhib as *anahada-sabad, anahada-tūrā, anahada-jhunkāra, anahada-bain, anahata-nāda, anahada-bāṇī* and *anahada-dhunī* and in the *Dasam Granth* as *anāhada-bāṇī* and *anāhada-bājā*. The word *anahata* is from the Sanskrit language. It occurs in Pāli and Prākrit texts as well. In the Sanskrit original, it implies unstruck; it stands for pure or immaculate in Pāli and for eternal in the Prākrit. The suffix words like *sabad* or *śabda, tūrā, jhuṇkāra, bāṇī* and *dhunī* stand for word, rhythm, sound or speech. Thus, *anahata-śabda* would mean the unstruck or pure or eternal sound. In a theistic system, *anahata-śabda* would signify an eternal voice symbolizing the reality of God. Indeed, Kabīr uses the word *anahata* as an epithet of God who is of the form of Light (*joti sarūpa anahata)*. This interpretation is paralleled in Gurū Nānak's *Japu* where he refers to God, the Creator, as the original, the pure, the beginningless and the eternal (*ādi anīlu anādi anāhati)*. The Gurūs have employed almost all the technical terms of Tantra and Haṭhayoga first used by the *siddhas, nāthas* and *yogīs*, but they have, at the same time, re-evaluated and reinterpreted these doctrines and practices. However, the former were neither theistic in outlook nor bhaktic in practice: their path was chiefly that of ascetic yogīs. On the other hand, Sikhism believes in the non-dual dynamic reality realizable through *bhakti* or loving devotion. Thus, the concept of *anahata-śabda* in Sikhism had to be understood in the light of the Sikh concept of Reality which cannot be realized through tāntric or *haṭhayoga* methods, but through *nām-simran*, i.e. constant remembrance of His Name—*hari kī kathā anāhad bānī* (GG, 483). In the Sikh ontological view, this mystic sound (*anahati-śabda*) has no meaning if it does not relate to the glory of God. The use of tāntric and haṭhayogic terminology has to be given a theistic and devotional content to understand it fully in the Sikh context. In Sikhism, the mystic sound in itself is not of much significance, but what matters is the source of this sound. Unlike the *haṭhayogīs* who believed that the source of this sound *(nāda* or *śabda)* is the *kuṇḍalinī* passing through the *suṣumnā*, the Sikh scripture declares that he who strikes the instrument and produces the sound is no other than God. It is the constant mindfulness of God (*nām simran*) which has to be made the life-breath (*prāṇa-pavana*) of the devotee; controlling his left and right nerves (*iḍā* and *piṅgalā*), he cultivates the central nerve (*suṣumnā*), and then starts the reverse process by turning the life-breath upwards. When this life-breath made by *nām-simran* passes in the reverse order through the *suṣumnā*, it pierces all the six plexuses on its upward march and it then settles in the void (*ulṭat pavan chakra khaṭu bhede surati sunn anarāgī* – GG, 333). The Gurūs are not concerned with the details of *nāḍīs, cakras,* and *kuṇḍalinī*; their central concern is to bear the eternal sound signalling the omnipresence of the Almighty. When this is achieved, by the grace of God (*gurprasādi*) the self realizes its innate nature spontaneously (*sahaja subhāi*), enjoys the innate bliss (*sahaja-sukha*), becomes free (*nirmala*) of all impurities, merges into the emptiness trance (*sunna-samādhi*) and attains supreme peace (*nirbāṇ pada*) which characterizes the fourth station (*chauthā pada*). It is not necessary to stress that the *anahata-śabda* heard by the released sages is not a physical sound to be heard with the physical ears. One has to 'kill' one's sinful existence and live an immaculate existence called *jīvan-mukti*; then alone can one hear the *anahada-bāṇī*.

BIBLIOGRAPHY

1. Eliade, Mircea, *Yoga, Immortality and Freedom*. Princeton, 1969
2. Bhattacharya, Haridas, *The Cultural History of India*. Calcutta, 1969
3. Jodh Singh, *The Religious Philosophy of Guru Nanak*. Varanasi, 1983
4. Chaturvedī, Parasūrām, *Uttarī Bhārat kī Sant Pramparā*. Allahabad, 1963

L.M.J.

ANAK SIṄGH, warrior son of Bhāī Manī Rām, resident of the village of 'Alīpur, district Multān (now in Pakistan), received baptismal rites at Anandpur at the time of the initiation of the Khālsā, on 30 March 1699, and took part in the battles of Nirmohgaṛh and Anandpur. As says *Gurū kīāṅ Sākhīāṅ*, he fell a martyr in the battle of Chamkaur fought on 7 December 1705.

BIBLIOGRAPHY

1. Padam, Piārā Siṅgh, and Giānī Garjā Siṅgh, eds., *Gurū kīāṅ Sākhīāṅ*. Patiala, 1986
2. Giān Siṅgh, Giānī, *Twārīkh Gurū Khālsā*. Patiala, 1970
3. Gupta, Hari Ram, *History of the Sikhs*, vol. I. Delhi, 1983

P.S.P.

ANAND (Skt. Anand, from *nand* meaning "to rejoice" or "to delight") denotes mystical experience, spiritual bliss or a state of consciousness such as that of a *jīvan mukta*, i.e. one released while still in body. Ānand in the Upaniṣadic texts is taken to be one of the three inherent attributes of *ātman* or Brahman, the other two being *sat* and *chit*. In the *Taittirīya Upaniṣad* (II. 1-5), it acquried this meaning of pure bliss. The self at the lowest or first stage of its evolution is defined as the *annamaya koṣa* (the matter) which evolves successively into *prāṇa* (life), *man* (mind or perceptual consciousness), *vijñāna* (self-consciousness) and *ānanda*, non-dual bliss.

In Sikh theology too, *anand* is one of the attributes of the Supreme Self; so it can be the state of the individual soul as well. Gurū Amar Dās's composition *Anandu*, in the measure Rāmkalī, gives an exposition of the experience of *anand*, of the union with the immaculate Hari attained through absorption in *nām*, i.e. repetition of Divine Name. Gurū Arjan attests that he has seen with his own eyes—*nain aloiā* — that the Supreme Self is *anand rūpu*, i.e. bliss itself is *anandamay*, full of bliss (GG, 387). Gurū Arjan further declares that the Lord of Nānak, the Supreme Being, who is the Cause of causes and is *antaryāmī* (the inner guide), experiences bliss—*anand karai* (GG, 387). Gurū Amar Dās prefaces his poem *Anandu* with the affirmation that the experience of *anand* comes only through meeting with the true Gurū and fully imbibing his instruction. He says that the longing for experiencing *anand* is inherent in men and is universal—*ānandu ānandu sabhu ko kahai* (GG, 917), but it actually falls to the lot of the very few, for it cannot be had without the grace of the Gurū which destroys sins, touches one's eye with the collyrium of true knowledge (*giān añjanu sāriā*), cuts asunder the knot of attachment (*mohu*) and bestows a sublime way of living, *sabadu savāriā*. These are essential conditions to experiencing *anand*. In the concluding stanza, Gurū Amar Dās says that *anand* is liberation from all suffering. It brings one complete fulfilment, and is realized by listening to the Divine word. Then all sorrow, sickness and pain end.

Anand is not an intermediate state in the journey of the individual self towards the Supreme Self, but the unitive one. The Gurū is the sole guide and remembrance of the Name is the sole discipline or *sādhnā*. Grace of the lord acts as the initial inspiration as well as the final arbiter.

Gurū Nānak, in *Japu*, has signified *anand* as the state of being *nihāl* or fulfilled; Gurū Arjan, in *Sukhmanī*, as the state of *sukh* or peace; Gurū Tegh Bahādur, in his *ślokas*, as the state of the *giānī*, the enlightened one who has achieved *sahaj* or equipoise and Gurū Gobind Siṅgh, in his verse, as the state of the heroic and dedicated one whose joy or *anand* is in philanthropic action and sacrifice. Gurū Nānak summing up the entire theme of the *Japu* says in the last stanza that the glance of grace of the Lord makes one *nihāl*, fulfilled or blessed.

BIBLIOGRAPHY

1. Kohli, Surindar Singh, *A Critical Study of Adi Granth*. Delhi, 1961
2. Tāran Siṅgh, *Sahij te Anandu*. Amritsar, n.d.
3. Caveeshar, Sardūl Siṅgh, *Sikh Dharam Darshan*. Patiala, 1969

T.S.

ANAND, BĀBĀ, was the second son of Bābā Mohrī and a grandson of Gurū Amar Dās. He received his name from the Gurū himself who also uttered a long hymn in Rāmkalī measure calling it *Anandu*. The hymn has since formed an important part of Sikh liturgy. Bābā Anand lived up to the time of the Sixth Gurū, Gurū Hargobind (1595-1644), who held him in high esteem. He once sent messengers, with a palanquin, to escort Bābā Anand to Kīratpur. The Gurū himself came out to receive him as he arrived. Offerings were heaped up before him by the Gurū as well as by the *saṅgat*. Bābā Anand, however, declined saying, "You are the Gurū—the same as Gurū Nānak and his successors. You alone are competent to receive offerings. I shall not touch them."

Bābā Anand returned to Goindvāl where he spent the rest of his days. The palanquin in which he travelled is still kept as a relic at Goindvāl.

BIBLIOGRAPHY

1. *Gurbilās Chhevīṅ Pātshāhī*. Patiala, 1970
2. Bhallā, Sarūp Dās, *Mahimā Prakāsh*. Patiala, 1971
3. Macauliffe, Max Arthur, *The Sikh Religion*. Oxford, 1909
4. Gupta, Hari Ram, *History of the Sikhs*, vol. I. Delhi, 1973

B.S.D.

ĀNANDGHANA, SVĀMĪ, an Udāsī *sādhū* known for the commentaries he wrote on some of the Sikh scriptural texts. Not much biographical detail is available about him, but references in his own works indicate that he was a disciple of Bābā Rām Dayāl, an Udāsī ascetic; also, that he was born into the family of Gurū Nānak, tenth in descent from him. Since his first *ṭīkā*, a commentary on the *Japu*, was completed in 1852 Bk/AD 1795, it may be presumed that he was born around the middle of the eighteenth century. He spent the early years of his life at Ḍerā Bābā Nānak where he was born. A wall-painting in a shrine there shows him sitting on a carpet, rosary in hand, facing his spiritual mentor, Rām Dayāl. At some stage he was sent for higher learning to Kāshī (Vārāṇasī) where he stayed for about ten years. At Kāshī, he frequently engaged in learned debate with the *paṇḍits,* trying to establish the supremacy of the Gurūs' word over other philosophical systems. He seems to have spent the last years of his life at Ḍerā Bābā Nānak. Of his works, a manuscript containing commentaries on *Japu, Āratī, Siddha Goṣṭi* and *Anand* is preserved in the Punjab State Archives, Paṭiālā, under No. M/691. The manuscript is divided into two parts—the first comprising 228 folios contains commentaries on *Japu* and *Āratī* and the second comprising 112 folios contains commentaries on *Siddha Goṣṭi* and *Anand.* Another manuscript copy of these four *ṭīkās* is also available in the Languages Department, Punjab, Paṭiālā. These four commentaries were, according to internal evidence, written at Kāshī between AD 1795 and 1802. Ānandghana's *ṭīkā* or commentary on *Āsā dī Vār,* references to which occur in his commentaries on *Siddha Goṣṭi* (1857 Bk/AD 1800) and *Anand* (1859 Bk/AD 1802), was held at the Dr Balbīr Siṅgh Sāhitya Kendra at Dehrā Dūn, and has recently been published (1990) by Punjabi University, Paṭiālā. The only known manuscript copy of his sixth commentary *Oaṅkār* was available at the Sikh Reference Library, Amritsar, until the collection perished in the Army attack on the Golden Temple premises in 1984.

Ānandghana's technique of writing commentary is that of a symposium. Wherever an important point is to be explained, he follows the question-answer format. He is well conversant with the tools of exposition, and writes with conviction. He is argumentative and at places prolix. The language used is old Hindi which is not exempt from the influence of his native Punjabi. Ānandghana's commentary on Gurū Nānak's *Japu* which he completed in Bk/1852/AD 1795 is considered to be his masterpiece and a representative work of the Udāsī school. It is available in two recensions—one exhaustive and the other abridged. Whereas the latter recension limits itself to an exposition of the text, the former contains considerable supplementary material on old Indian philosophical systems and religious practices in which context the commentator attempts to highlight the teaching of Gurū Nānak. He is however not chary of casting aspersions upon other commentators whom he declares to be "dunces". This led Bhāī Santokh Siṅgh, the Nirmalā scholar to write his own commentary on the *Japu* challenging the interpretations advanced by Ānandghana. He called his commentary *Garabgañjanī Ṭīkā (q.v.),* i.e. *ṭīkā* to humble the *garab* or pride (of Ānandghana). Whereas the interpretations of Ānandghana have a colouring peculiar to the Saguna school of Bhakti, Santokh Siṅgh in keeping with the Nirmalā tradition leans on the side of Vedānta.

BIBLIOGRAPHY

1. Nripinder Singh, *The Sikh Moral Tradition.* Delhi, 1990
2. Santokh Siṅgh, Bhāī, *Garabgañjanī Ṭīkā* [Reprint]. Delhi, 1961
3. Jaggi, R.S., ed., *Gurbāṇī Ṭīke: Ānandghana.* Patiala, 1970
4. — *Āsā dī Vār dā Ṭīkā.* Patiala, 1990

R.S.J.

ANAND KĀRAJ, lit. joyful ceremonial occasion or proceedings is the name given the Sikh marriage ceremony. For Sikhs married state is the norm and the ideal; through it, according to their belief, come the best opportunities for serving God's purpose and the well-being of humanity, and it affords the best means of fulfilment of individuality and attainment of bliss. Sikhism repudiates monkery, vows of celibacy, renunciation or the *sannyāsin* state. Unlike in the West, most marriages among Sikhs, as also in India as a whole, are arranged. It is regarded as a duty for the parents to arrange for and actively contribute towards the marriage of their offspring. *Prem Sumārag*, an eighteenth-century work on Sikh social code, lays down:

> When a girl attains maturity, it is incumbent upon her parents to look for a suitable match for her. It is neither desirable nor proper to marry a girl at tender age. The daughter of a Sikh should be given in marriage to a Sikh. If a man is a believer in Sikhism, is humble by nature, and earns his bread by honest means, with him matrimony may be contracted without a question and without consideration for wealth and riches. If he be a God-fearing man, the parents should marry their daughter to him upon God's faith. God willing, their daughter will have all happiness and her parents will reap great satisfaction... whatever arrangements the parents make for a marriage these should be well within their means. They should not imitate ostentatious people. This is incumbent upon both sides. One who conducts the ceremony of marriage should not accept any gratification for it.

Similarly, *Sikh Rahit Maryādā*, manual of Sikh conduct and custom issued by the Shiromaṇī Gurdwārā Parbandhak Committee, statutorily elected representative society of the Sikhs, prescribes marriage of a Sikh girl only to a Sikh male without consideration of caste or sub-caste. It prohibits child marriage, permits widow remarriage, and enjoins that a Sikh marriage must be performed under Anand marriage rites. The Anand Marriage Act, 1909, (*q.v.*) gives legal recognition and validates marriages solemnized following this ceremony. Section 2, the operative part of the Act, reads:

> All marriages which may be or may have been duly solemnised according to the Sikh Marriage ceremony called Anand shall be and shall be deemed to have been with effect from the date of the solemnisation of each respectively good and valid in law.

The history of Anand marriage ceremony is traced back to the time of Gurū Amar Dās (1479-1574), who composed the long 40-stanza hymn *Anandu*, in the Rāmkalī measure, suitable to be sung or recited on all occasions of religious import. His successor, Gurū Rām Dās, composed a four-stanza hymn, *Lāvāṅ*, which is recited and sung to solemnize nuptials. During the time of Mahārājā Raṇjīt Siṅgh and his successors, however, this ceremony fell into partial disuse under renewed Brāhmaṇical influence at court as well as in society. The Niraṅkārī reform movement of the mid-19th century made the practice of Anand ceremony a vital plank in its programme as did the later, more widely influential Siṅgh Sabhā. But there was opposition from the Ārya Samājīs and Brāhmaṇ priestly classes, the former anxious to prove that the Sikhs were but a sect of the Hindus and hence subject to Hindu Law, and the latter apprehensive of a reduction in their clientele and income. The Sikh form of wedding ceremonial eventually received legel sanction through the Anand Marriage Act which was adopted in 1909. The ceremony is now universally observed by the Sikhs.

According to *Sikh Rahit Maryādā*, a formal engagement or betrothal prior to marriage is not absolutely necessary, but if the parties so desire, the betrothal ceremony takes place usually at the boy's residence where a few near relations of the girl go with some gifts, sweets and fruit. The gifts may include a ring or *kaṛā* and *kirpān* for the prospective groom. They are handed over to him in the presence of relations, collaterals and friends assembled usually in *saṅgat* in the presence of Gurū Granth Sāhib. The eatables include a *chhuhārā* (dried date) of which the boy takes a bite signifying acceptance of the match as well as of the gifts. This ceremony concludes with *sirvārnā* (money waved around the head of the boy in offering, given away thereafter in charity) and *ardās* (liturgical supplicatory prayer).

Actual wedding takes place at the girl's residence. The date of the wedding is set by mutual consultation to suit both parties. Astrological or horoscopic considerations are discountenanced in Sikh calculations. Matters such as the strength of the *barāt* (the bridegroom's party), timing of arrival and departure, duration of stay, are also decided mutually so that the bride's parents may make suitable arrangements. Before setting out, the bridegroom may go to a *gurdwārā* to make obeisance and offer *ardās* before the Gurū Granth Sāhib. On arrival at the house of the girl's parents, the party is received by the girl's parents, relations and friends outside the house with the chanting of hymns of welcome and *ardās* followed by *milnī* or formal meeting of the two families, customarily restricted to the fathers (or guardians) and maternal uncles of the boy and the girl. *Barāt* is then escorted inside for refreshments after which *anand kāraj* takes place either in a *gurdwārā* or under a marquee in the presence of the Gurū Granth Sāhib. This purely religious part of the proceedings commences with *kīrtan*, singing of hymns, as the guests and hosts assemble in *saṅgat*. The couple to be wed sit facing the Gurū Granth Sāhib, the bride on the left of the bridegroom. Any Sikh chosen to conduct the ceremony will officiate. He will say a short opening *ardās* seeking felicity for the bridegroom and the bride, their respective parents or guardians only standing for this *ardās* with the rest of the *saṅgat* remaining seated. The choir will then sing a short hymn from the Gurū Granth Sāhib. Translated, the hymn would read:

> Call upon God for task thou wouldst have accomplished,
> He will bring the tasks to rights, so witnesseth the Gurū.
> In the company of the holy thou shalt rejoice and taste only nectar,
> Thou art the demolisher of fear, thou art compassionate, O' Lord,
> Nānak singeth the praises of the Incomputable Lord.
>
> (GG, 91)

The officiant may then give a sermon addressed especially to the couple-to-be explaining the significance of Sikh marriage and the duties and obligations of husband and wife towards each other and towards their families, community and society in general. Marriage in Sikhism, he tells the couple-to-be, is not merely a civil or social contract but a union of the souls and rests upon mutual love and loyalty, mutual understanding and adjustment. A verse from Gurū Amar Dās, Nānak III, is often quoted: "They are not husband and wife who but sit side by side with each other; only they are truly wedded who personify one single soul in two bodies" (GG,788).

After the sermon the girl's father places one end of a scarf, usually saffron or pink in colour, in the groom's hand, passing it over his shoulder and placing the other end in the bride's hand, signifying that he had entrusted her to his protection. The musicians then sing another short hymn:

> Praise and slander have I all ceased to relish, O Nānak,
> False, I count all other relationships,
> To the fold of Thy fabric am I now affianced.
>
> (GG, 963)

The Gurū Granth Sāhib is then opened at page 773 and the first stanza of the *Lāvāṅ* quartet is read from it. The same stanza is then sung by the choir while the couple slowly and reverentially circumambulate the Holy Book, Gurū Granth Sāhib, clockwise, the bridegroom leading and the bride following, both continuing to hold their ends of the scarf throughout. They bow together before the Gurū Granth Sāhib before rising up for the circumambulation and again before resuming their seats on completing it. This process is repeated for each of the remaining three stanzas. The ceremony is concluded with the customary singing of the first five and the concluding hymn of *Anandu* followed by *ardās*, in which the whole congregation joins; *vāk* or *hukam* (reading a verse from Gurū Granth Sāhib opened at random) is then received and *karāhprasād*, the Sikh sacrament, distributed.

Translated into English the *Lāvāṅ* quartet or the Sikh epithalamium would read:

1. By the first nuptial circuiting
The Lord sheweth ye His
Ordinance for the daily duties of wedded life:
The Scriptures are the Word of the Lord,
Learn righteousness, through them,
And the Lord will free ye from sin.
Hold fast to righteousness,
Contemplate the Name of the Lord,
Fixing it in your memory as the scriptures have prescribed.
Devote yourselves to the Perfect and True Gurū.
And all your sins shall depart.
Fortunate are those whose minds
Are imbued with the sweetness of His Name,
To them happiness comes without effort;
The slave Nānak proclaimeth
That in the first circling
The marriage rite hath begun.

2. By the second nuptial circumambulation
Ye are to understand that the Lord
Hath caused ye to meet the True Gurū,
The fear in your hearts has departed;
The filth of selfness in your minds is washed away,
By having the fear of God and by singing His praises
I stand before Him with reverence,
The Lord God is the soul of the universe!
There is naught that He doth not pervade.
Within us and without, there is One God only;
In the company of saints
Then are heard the songs of rejoicing.
The slave Nānak proclaimeth
That in the second circling
Divine Music is heard.

3. In the third roundabout
There is a longing for the Lord
And detachment from the world.
In the company of the saints,
By our great good fortune,
We encounter the Lord.
The Lord is found in His purity
Through His exaltation,
Through the singing of His hymns.
By great good fortune we have risen.
In the company of the saints
Wherein is told the story
Of the Ineffable Lord.
The Holy Name echoes in the heart:
Echoes and absorbs us.
We repeat the Name of the Lord,
Being blessed by a fortunate destiny
Written from of old on our foreheads.
The slave Nānak proclaimeth
That in the third circling
The love of God has been awakened in the heart.

4. In the fourth walk-around
The mind reaches to knowledge
of the Divine
And God is innerly grasped:
Through the Grace of the Gurū
We have attained with ease to the
Lord;
The sweetness of the Beloved
Pervades us, body and soul.
Dear and pleasing is the Lord to
us:
Night and day our minds are
fixed on Him.
By exalting the Lord
We have attained the Lord:
The fruit our hearts desired;
The Beloved has finished His
work.
The soul, the spouse, delighteth
in the Beloved's Name.
Felicitations fill our minds;
The Name rings in our hearts:
The Lord God is united with His
Holy Bride.
The heart of the Bride flowers
with His Name.
The slave Nānak proclaimeth
That in the fourth circling
We have found the Eternal Lord.
(GG, 773-74)

This is the religious part of the ceremony. Behind it and ahead lies a whole labyrinth of spectacular custom and rite. The dual sources of significance of Sikh marriage as an institution are: first, the doctrinal rules of the Sikh religious community, which are a few in number but universal in scope and intent; and second, the traditional usages or customs of the Punjabi ethno-linguistic community which are very many but confined to a particular social structure and associated with a particular territory or locality. The prescribed marriage ritual, the *anand kāraj*, is an expression of the basic principles of the faith. It was first given statutory recognition and thus officially and legally distinguished from the observances sanctioned under Hindu Customary Law, by the Anand Marriage Act of 1909. According to Sikh rules, religious endogamy is essential, but not endogamy within the caste or sub-caste group. Though customary rules of exogamy are held to prohibit the marriage of near consanguines, the precise position in this matter is difficult to determine and no ruling on this question is included in the Sikh code of conduct. Broadly speaking, the marriage of a person within his or her own *gotra* (sub-caste) is not permissible. There is a customarily sanctioned prejudice against a woman marrying her husband's younger brother. But all such prohibitions are of social rather than of religious nature.

Such practices as the tying of head-bands, rituals depicting ancestor-worship, pretended sulking or sadness, singing by professional dancing-girls, the drinking of alcohol, burning of so-called sacred fires and similar superstitions derived from old religious practices are completely contrary to Sikh belief.

In some parts *ṭhākā* is followed by another ceremony generally called *chunnī chaṛhauṇā* (the offering of the head scarf). In this ceremony the boy's parents send for the girl garments and gifts including a red thread *(lāl parāndī)* for plaiting the hair, a suite of clothes, some ornaments and cash. Before the marriage, a final engagement ceremony, known as *shagan, kuṛmāī* or *maṅgaṇī* takes place at the home of the boy's parents, when gifts are given by the girl's parents to the boy and to his close cognates. A *chhuhārā* (dried date) is offered to the boy by his would-be father-in-law or his representatives to eat for which reason the ceremony is called in some parts *chhuhārā lauṇā*. The *maṅgaṇī* can precede *anand kāraj* by months, even years, especially when the boy and the girl get engaged at a very young age.

A series of rites takes place separately in the home of the parents of the boy and the girl heralding nuptials. *Māīeṅ paiṇā* is the period of seclusion from kindred and outsiders observed by the boy and the girl for one to three days before the marriage. The bride and the groom refrain from bathing or changing their clothes. During this period of ritual seclusion, the girl is not to use ornaments or cosmetics; manual work or going out alone is also not permitted. Singing of songs by womenfolk starts a day, or sometimes several days, before the wedding ceremony at the homes of the girl's as well as of the boy's parents. Songs mostly from Punjabi folklore are sung to the accompaniment of a *ḍholak* or drum. The songs for the groom are called *ghoṛīāṅ* and those for the bride *suhāg*.

On the eve of the day of marriage, the bride and the groom take the ritual bath which is called *khāre chaṛhnā*, ascending the (bathing) basket. This is essentially a rite of purification following the state of seclusion. After the bath, both the boy and the girl put on new clothes specially prepared for the occasion. Generally these clothes are given by the respective *nānake*, that is, their maternal kin group. The *nānake* give gifts to the girl called *nānakī chhakk*. These may consist of ivory bangles, a nose ring, a suite of clothes, or a set of ornaments and some household utensils and articles. The gifts may include clothes for the bride's parents and siblings. Gifts from the maternal kin group are also given to the boy. These include clothes for the groom himself, for his parents and siblings and for his mother's brother.

Several ceremonies take place before the groom sets off for the bride's home with the wedding party. After the *ardās* is recited, the boy's sister ties around his head a circlet with a plume and gilded strings hanging in front of his face. This is the groom's crown or *sihrā*. *Sirvārnā* (offering of money over the head of the groom) is performed, and the money distributed among the poor. A sister of the groom, to the accompaniment of songs, braids the mare's reins with red thread (*maulī*); a brother's wife puts black antimony powder (*surmā*) in his eyes. Then, when all is ready, and the mare has been fed with barley and gram, the boy's sister seizes the reins of the mare and demands gift from her brother before allowing him to proceed. The groom gives some money to all his sisters; this is called *vāg phaṛāī* (holding of the reins). As the procession starts a younger brother or nephew of the groom, acting as best man (*sarvāhlā*) is seated behind him on the mare.

Before the groom departs with the bride, first the groom's party and then the bride's take lunch; the bride eats food provided by her parents-in-law and this is known as *sauhariāṅ dī roṭī*. As the bride is about to leave her home, her mother, female relatives and close friends come out to see her off. The band breaks into farewell songs. The bride and the groom leave together for the home of the latter's parents. The bride is usually accompanied by a younger brother, or traditionally, by the village barber's wife. This ceremony of the departure of the bride from her parents' home is known as *ḍolī*, a word denoting the litter which was formerly used as transport for the couple; nowadays a decorated car is usually provided for this purpose. As the car or carriage starts off, the father of the groom showers small coins over it, thus expressing his happiness over the successful conclusion of the ceremony. A basket of sweets (*bhājī*), to be distributed to the groom's kin and friends, is sent along with the bride.

The couple is ceremonially received at the entrance of the groom's family house. Then follows the ritual of uncovering the bride's face (*mūṅh vikhlāī*) in the presence of the female kin, friends and neighbours of the groom. The bride is fed with cooked *dāl* and rice (*khichaṛī*) signifying that she has become a member of her husband's household. She removes her veil and offers obeisance to the senior women kin who give her gifts of money after *sirvārnā* (revolving money around the head).

The custom of giving a reception by the groom's parents is becoming popular in urban society. The reception is held after the marriage ceremony. Close kin and friends of both families are invited. A day or two later the bride usually returns to her parental home. Only after the groom fetches her from there for the second time, may the marriage be consummated. This second trip is called *muklāvā*. On this occasion and on her subsequent visits to her parents' home, her parents give her gifts of clothes and ornaments. The word *dāj* denotes the gifts given at the time of the marriage to their daughter and to the groom's parents by the bride's parents. The gifts given to the bride by the groom's parents are called *varī*. Besides, giving the dowry, consisting of all the things that the bride will need to set up a household—clothes, ornaments, utensils, furniture and beddings—the bride's parents undertake expenses on the marriage ceremony, feasting, illuminations, etc. All this is not to be taken as constituting the Sikh marriage, but is the general practice in Punjabi society. Sikh reformers since the emergence of the Siṅgh Sabhā have been urging simple and inexpensive marriages strictly in accord with the spirit of the *anand* ceremony.

BIBLIOGRAPHY

1. *Sikh Rahit Maryādā*. Amritsar, 1975
2. Randhīr Siṅgh, ed., *Prem Sumārag Granth*. Jalandhar, 1965
3. Jogendra Singh, *Sikh Ceremonies*. Chandigarh, 1968
4. Teja Singh, *Sikhism: Its Ideals and Institutions*. Bombay, 1938
5. Cole, W. Owen, and Piara Singh Sambhi, *The Sikhs: Their Religious Beliefs and Practices*. Delhi, 1978

J.P.S.U., T.H. & N.Q.K.

ANAND MARRIAGE ACT was passed in 1909 by the Imperial (i.e. Governor-General's) Legislative Council to establish leg l "validity of the marriage ceremony common among the Sikhs called Anand." The origins of marriage by Anand ceremony go back to early Sikhism. The practice which somewhat lapsed during the time of Mahārājā Raṇjīt Siṅgh was sought to be revived as part of the religious reform initiated by the Niraṅkārī movement and followed up especially by the Siṅgh Sabhā. Anand marriages were readily reported in the Sikh Press towards the close of the 19th century. For instance, the *K͟hālsā Ak͟hbār* in its issue of 6 November 1886 reported the marriage of Bhāī Dalīp Siṅgh, son of Bhāī Raṇ Siṅgh of village Koṇḍī in the princely state of Paṭiālā by Anand ceremony. The same newspaper announced on 11 December 1886 Anand nuptials of Giān Siṅgh, son of Sūbahdār-Major Baghel Siṅgh, which took place at the village of Jaipurā. Again on 18 February 1888, the *K͟hālsā Ak͟hbār* reported the marriage of the daughter of Bhāī Sant Siṅgh, president, Siṅgh Sabhā, Lahore, performed in accordance with the Sikh ritual on 14 February 1888. At Siālkot, an early Anand marriage of modern times took place on 4 June 1903 (*K͟hālsā Ak͟hbār*,10 July 1903). Bhāī Mohan Siṅgh Vaid in his *Diary* recorded that he attended Anand Kāraj performed at the village of Kairoṅ on 7 June 1899. Presumably that was when Bhāī Nihāl Siṅgh Kairoṅ's daughter, sister of Partāp Siṅgh Kairoṅ, mighty latter-day political leader of the Punjab, was married. Early references to Anand marriages occur in old Sikh texts such as *Rahitnāmā Bhāī Dayā Siṅgh* and Giānī Giān Siṅgh, *Panth Prakāsh*.

The Anand ceremony was looked upon askance by Brāhmaṇical priests who administered the rites in the old Hindu fashion. They started caluminating the Sikh form. Sikhs wished to have their social laws accepted and codified and a beginning was made with their marriage rites.

The Anand Marriage Bill was introduced

in the Imperial Legislative Council in 1908 by Ṭikkā Ripudaman Siṅgh of the princely state of Nābhā. The House of Nābhā had always espoused simplification of wedding ceremonies and, as reported in *Khālsā Dharam Prachārak*, 13 July 1895, there was an order in force in Nābhā state laying down that no marriage party should exceed 11 guests. The Anand Marriage Bill had been drafted by a committee of the Chief Khālsā Dīwān. The Imperial Council referred the bill to a select committee. The bill received overwhelming support from the Sikh respondents. In 1909 Sundar Siṅgh Majīṭhīā replaced Ṭikkā Ripudaman Siṅgh of Nābhā state as a member of the Imperial Council. Moving the bill at a meeting of the Imperial Legislative Council held at the Viceregal Lodge, Shimlā, on Friday, 10 September 1909, Sundar Siṅgh Majīṭhīā commended the effort of Ṭikkā Ripudaman Siṅgh who had "laboured unremittingly" in behalf of the "useful measure." Elaborating, Sundar Siṅgh said the ceremony called Anand was initiated by the third Gurū of the Sikhs, Gurū Amar Dās (1479-1574), and his successor Gurū Rām Dās (1534-1581) was the author of the four hymns of *Lāvāṅ* which are included in the Gurū Granth Sāhib (Rāga Sūhī, pp. 773 -74) and which are recited to solemnize the Anand ceremony.

Sardār Sundar Siṅgh presented the report of the select committee. The bill was placed on the Statute Book on 22 October 1909.

The text of the Act reads:

5.The Anand Marriage Act 1909, Act No. VII of 1909. An Act to remove doubts as to the validity of the marriage ceremony among the Sikhs called 'Anand'.

1. Short title and extent	*The Act may be called the Anand Marriage Act 1909.*
2. Validity of Anand Marriages	*All marriages which may be or may have been duly solemnized according to the Sikh marriage ceremony called 'Anand' shall be and shall be deemed to have been with effect from the date of solemnization to each respectively, good and valid in law.*
3. Exemption of certain marriages from Act	*Nothing in this Act shall apply to (a) any marriage between persons not professing the Sikh religion or (b) any marriage which has been judicially declared to be null and void.*
4. Saving of marriage solemnized according to other ceremony	*Nothing in this Act shall affect the validity of any marriage duly solemnized according to any other marriage ceremony customary among the Sikhs.*
5. Non-validation of marriages	*Nothing in this Act shall be deemed to validate any marriage between persons who are related to each other in any degree of consanguinity or affinity which would, according to the customary law of Sikhs, render a marriage between them illegal.*

BIBLIOGRAPHY

1. Talwar, K.S., "The Anand Marriage Act," in *The*

Panjab Past and Present. Patiala, October 1968
2. Bajwa, Fauja Singh, *Kuka Movement.* Delhi, 1965
3. Soḍhī, Tejā Siṅgh, *Anand Prakās.* Amritsar, 1967

K.S.Tl.

ANANDPUR (31° - 13'N, 76° - 32'E), lit. City of Bliss, is situated on one of the lower spurs of the Śivālik range in Ropaṛ district of the Punjab. Connected to the rest of the country by rail and road, it lies 31 km north of Ropaṛ (Rūp Nagar) and 29 km south of Naṅgal Township. Being one of the supremely important pilgrimage centres of the Sikhs, it is reverently called Anandpur Sāhib. Ta<u>kh</u>t Srī Kesgaṛh Sāhib, one of the five *ta<u>kh</u>ts* (lit. thrones) or seats of highest religious authority for Sikhs, and several other holy shrines are located here. Having been the abode of the last two Gurūs of the Sikhs for two score years, the town was witness to many a momentous event of Sikh history.

The foundation of Anandpur was laid by Gurū Tegh Bahādur (1621-75), Nānak IX, on 19 June 1665, on a piece of land, covering the ruined mound of an older village, Mākhovāl, which the Gurū had earlier purchased for this purpose from the Rājpūt hill state of Kahlūr (Bilāspur). He named the new habitation Chakk Nānakī after his mother, and shifted here with his family from Kīratpur, 8 km south of it. But soon after, he set out on his extensive travels across the eastern parts. The development of Chakk Nānakī was thus interrupted till after his return in 1672. The small habitation then grew into a flourishing town frequented by devotees from the Punjab and elsewhere. In May 1675, a group of Brāhmaṇs from Kashmīr came to the Gurū with their tale of woe. The burden of their submission was the religious persecution and forcible conversion which were the order of the day in Kashmīr under its Mughal governor. Gurū Tegh Bahādur resolved to go to Delhi, the Imperial capital, to have their grievance remedied, or to lay down his life in the cause of religious freedom. Naming his young son, Gobind Dās (Later, Siṅgh), hardly nine years of age, his spiritual successor, he set out on the journey, preaching the holy word in towns and villages he passed through. In Delhi, he was taken into custody, tortured and executed publicly under the orders of Emperor Auraṅgzīb in the Chāndnī Chowk on 11 November 1675.

Back at Chakk Nānakī, the young successor, Gurū Gobind Siṅgh (1666-1708), received and cremated with exemplary courage and composure the severed head of his father, brought at great personal risk by a daring Sikh, Bhāī Jaitā. As he grew up, Gurū Gobind Siṅgh assumed a soldierly style which aroused the envy of the local ruler, Rājā Bhīm Chand of Kahlūr. To avoid an early conflict, Gurū Gobind Siṅgh, accepting an invitation from the chief of another hill state, Sirmūr, to visit him, left Chakk Nānakī in 1685 to stay at Pāoṇṭā on the bank of the Yamunā. After the battle of Bhaṅgāṇī (18 September 1688) fought against the combined force of Rājpūt hill monarchs, he returned to Chakk Nānakī, which he now renamed Anandpur after one of a ring of forts (Anandgaṛh) which he, apprehending further trouble from the hill rājās, now undertook to raise. The forts were Kesgaṛh, in the centre and Anandgaṛh, Lohgaṛh, Holgaṛh, Fatehgaṛh and Tārāgaṛh around it. Bhīm-Chand and his son, Ajmer Chand of Kahlūr, had not shed their chagrin over the defeat they had suffered at Bhaṅgāṇī at the hands of the Gurū, although the latter had helped them in the battle of Nadauṇ (1691) against a Mughal general sent against them by the governor of Jammū. They made an alliance with the Kaṭoch ruler of Kāṅgṛā and several other chiefs, attacking Anandpur more than once, but each time Gurū Gobind Siṅgh repulsed their onslaught.

On Baisākhī day, 30 March 1699, Gurū Gobind Siṅgh carried out the supreme task of his career converting the *saṅgat* into

Khālsā. Instructions had been sent out during the previous year to *saṅgats,* or Sikh communities, in various parts not to recognize any longer the *masands* as the Gurū's representatives and to come to Anandpur for the following Baisākhī festival in large numbers. They had also been asked to come, where practicable, mounted. On the appointed day a massive assembly took place in the Fort of Kesgaṛh at Anandpur. As all sat rapt in the morning service, Gurū Gobind Siṅgh, according to one of the earlier sources, Kuir Siṅgh, *Gurbilās Pātshāhī 10,* made a dramatic appearance, a naked sword in his hand, and asked if any one of the assembly would be willing to offer his head to him. The audience were benumbed to hear this strange demand. Gurū Gobind Siṅgh repeated his call twice. At the third call, one Dayā Rām, a Khatrī from Lahore, offered himself. The Gurū took him into an adjoining enclosure. After a while he returned, his sword dripping blood, and asked for another head. This time, Dharam Dās, a Jāṭ from Hastināpur, came forward and was led to the enclosure as had been his predecessor. Likewise, three other disciples, Mohkam Chand, a washerman from Dvārkā, Himmat, a water-carrier from Jagannāth, and Sāhib Chand, a barber from Bidar, in the South, offered themselves. The fear of the *saṅgat* turned to amazement and wonder when, soon after, the Gurū led the five back, all dressed alike in saffron-coloured gowns with neatly tied turbans on their heads and swords dangling by their sides. Gurū Gobind Siṅgh administered to the Five vows of baptism, giving them five palmsful of *amrit* or sweetened elixir sanctified by recitation over it of holy hymns and stirred with a steel *khaṇḍā,* double-edged sword, *and* introduced them to the *saṅgat* as his *pañj piāre,* Five Beloved. He announced that with the baptism of the Pañj Piāre he had inaugurated the Khālsā, a brotherhood of holy soldiers who would be distinguished by five symbols all beginning with the letter 'k', viz. *kes* (uncut hair), *kaṅghā* (comb), *kachchhā* (pair of shorts), *kaṛā* (steel bracelet) and *kirpān* (sword). The Khālsā were vowed to live up to the highest moral and ethical standards and to be ever ready to fight tyranny and injustice. They were to recognize no distinctions of caste, creed or status. The Gurū himself stood up before the Pañj Piāre and begged with folded hands to be admitted to their ranks. Several thousands followed on that and on subsequent days to receive the rites of initiation by the double-edged sword. Anandpur thus became the birthplace of the Khālsā. It is known commonly as *Khālse dī vāsī* (Home of the Khālsā).

The emergence of the Khālsā caused panic among the chiefs of the surrounding hill principalities and they planned together strategy to dislodge the Gurū from Anandpur. They sent to him emissaries who assured him on oath that they would forever cease troubling him and his Sikhs if only he would temporarily leave his citadel and move out of the town. At the same time, they secretly sought armed assistance from the Mughal *faujdār* of Sirhind in order to encircle Anandpur and force the Gurū out of the town. Gurū Gobind Siṅgh left Anandpur but, still suspicious of the rājās' intentions, encamped at the village of Hardo Namoh, 4 km south of Kīratpur, taking up a tactically viable defensive position. He was attacked by the hill chiefs from the north and by the Mughal contingents equipped with cannon from the south. These attacks, which according to Bhaṭṭ Vahīs took place on 7,12 and 13 October 1700, were repulsed and on 14 October, Gurū Gobind Siṅgh and his Sikhs broke the cordon and crossed the River Sutlej into Basohlī, a small chiefship friendly with the Gurū. This action is known as the battle of Nirmohgaṛh. As soon as the imperial troops withdrew, the Gurū reoccupied Anandpur. The hill chiefs then waited upon Emperor Auraṅgzīb and warning him of the new danger that the rise of the Khālsā spelt for his kingdom, entreated him to take some severe measures. Himself critically engaged in dealing with the Marāṭhā insurrection in the South, the emperor ordered the governor of Lahore and the *faujdār* of Sirhind to act in this behalf in concert with the hill chiefs. A combined force marched upon Anandpur and laid siege to the town in May 1705. The Gurū and his Sikhs withstood their repeated assaults for several months despite scarcity of provisions resulting from the prolonged blockade. The besiegers were eventually tired out and offered on solemn oath safe exit to the Gurū and the Sikhs if they evacuated Anandpur. Gurū Gobind Siṅgh along with his family and men left the town during the night of 5-6 December 1705.

Before departing, the Gurū directed one of his Sikhs, Gurbakhsh, an Udāsī by faith, to stay behind to look after the local *saṅgat* and the shrines, especially the one commemorating the site where Gurū Tegh Bahādur's head had been cremated. Years later, as the situation permitted, Gulāb Rāi and Shyām Siṅgh, sons of Gurū Gobind Siṅgh's first cousin, Dīp Chand, who had since the evacuation of Anandpur taken refuge with the friendly Rājā of Nāhan, came back. Gulāb Rāi purchased the town of Anandpur from the Rājā of Bilāspur and pretending to be a successor to Gurū Gobind Siṅgh established his own religious seat, remonstrances from Gurbakhsh Udāsī notwithstanding. All the four sons of Gulāb Rāi had predeceased him. His widow managed the affairs for some time, but soon died having bequeathed the *gaddī* to Soḍhī Surjan Siṅgh, a grandson of Shyām Siṅgh. After the conquest of the Punjab by the Sikhs, several rulers and chiefs made rich endowments to the shrines which continued to be managed by the local Soḍhī family until the rise of the Gurdwārā reform or the Akālī movement in the early 1920's. The shrines at Anandpur were occupied by the Akālīs on 12 January 1923; they were formally handed over to the Shiromaṇī Gurdwārā Parbandhak Committee by the local Soḍhīs on 15 March 1923. The historic shrines are now managed by the Shiromaṇī Gurdwārā Parbandhak Committee, Amritsar, through a manager appointed by it. The Jathedār of Takht Srī Kesgaṛh Sāhib is an ex-officio member of the Shiromaṇī Committee. The shrines:

TAKHT SRĪ KESGAṚH SĀHIB is the principal shrine at Anandpur. Resplendent in its white marble glory, the shrine stands on a hillock and marks the site of the Kesgaṛh Fort where the historic Baisākhī congregation of 1699 had taken place. The present complex was constructed during 1936-44 under the supervision of Sant Harī Siṅgh Kahārpurī. Being on a slope, the complex has two levels protected by retaining walls on the sides. On the lower level, approached by a flight of steps is the imposing two-storeyed gateway, offices, and a 30-metre square courtyard. The level on which stands the main building is 2.5 metres higher than the courtyard. The 16-metre square hall with a balcony in front contains within it the sanctum, a 5.5-metre square room in which some old weapons preserved as sacred relics from the time of Gurū Gobind Siṅgh are displayed on a low platform. The Gurū Granth Sāhib is seated under a canopy outside the sanctum, above which rises a fluted lotus dome topped by a tall ornamental pinnacle of gilded metal, and a gilded *khaṇḍā* as a finial. On the roof, corners of the hall and the balcony are adorned with domed kiosks. Gurū kā Laṅgar is on the lower level behind the central building. The lower slopes of the Kesgaṛh hill are covered with rows of residential rooms for staff and pilgrims. This complex is collectively known as Dashmesh Nivās. A 55-metre square *dīvān* hall, about 150 metres east of the central building, was added during the 1980's to cater for large congregations on festival occasions. A *sarovar* or bathing tank, 80-metre square, in a walled compound is situated at ground level to the west of the Takht Sāhib and close to the Ropaṛ-Naṅgal road. The relics placed in the inner sanctum of Takht Srī Kesgaṛh Sāhib include a *khaṇḍā*, a *kaṭār* (dagger), a *saif* (double-edged straight tapering sword), a muzzle-loading musket, a spear known as *karpā barchhā*, and a *nāganī* (a kind of spear with a twisted and pointed blade). Another set of weapons also believed to have once belonged to Gurū Gobind Siṅgh, which had been taken away by the British to England after the occupation of the Punjab in 1849 and which had been brought back from there at the time of the celebration of the 300th birth anniversary of Gurū Gobind Siṅgh in 1966-67 are now on display here.

GURDWĀRĀ QILĀ ANANDGAṚH SĀHIB is situated on another spur, about 800 metres south-east of Takht Srī Kesgaṛh Sāhib. It is a newly constructed building though marks of the old, original structure are also still traceable. The present building complex was raised during the 1970's by Sant Sevā Siṅgh (d. 1982) whose successors are now managing and further developing it. Earlier, during the 1930's, Kartār Siṅgh Kalāsvālīā had got a fort-like building constructed which is still intact on top of the hillock. The present Gurdwārā, separated from this building by a spacious terrace paved with slabs of streaked marble, is a 15-metre square hall with an 8x3 metre porch in front. The 6-metre square sanctum within the hall has above it a lotus dome topped with a gilded pinnacle and *khaṇḍa* as a finial. The entire wall surface has a facing of streaked marble. This building was completed in 1970. The water level of an old *bāolī*, a stepped well 4-metre in diametre, is approached through a covered passage. The *bāolī* has 135 marbled steps. At the lower levels on the eastern flank of the main building are a spacious hall for Gurū kā Laṅgar constructed in 1972, and 300 rooms for pilgrims and administrators.

GURDWĀRĀ QILĀ FATEHGAṚH SĀHIB, situated on the northern outskirts of the town of Anandpur, marks the site of another fortress bearing this name. The present building was constructed during the late 1980's under the supervision of the successors of Sant Sevā Siṅgh of Qilā Anandpur. The Gurdwārā is a two-storeyed domed building. In front of it is an old well which once served the needs of Fatehgaṛh Fort.

GURDWĀRĀ QILĀ LOHGAṚH SĀHIB, one and a half kilometre southwest of Takht Srī Kesgaṛh Sāhib, marks the site of the fort of that name constructed by Gurū Gobind Siṅgh to protect the riverside flank. It was here that Bhāī Bachittar Siṅgh faced and turned back a drunken elephant which the hill chiefs, during their siege of Anandpur in 1700, had sent to batter down the gate of this fort. The present building, octagonal in shape and three-storeyed high with a dome on top, was constructed during the late 1980's.

GURDWĀRĀ HOLGAṚH SĀHIB stands on the site of Holgaṛh Fort, one and a half km north-west of the town across the Charan Gaṅgā rivulet. It was here that Gurū Gobind Siṅgh introduced in the spring of 1701, the celebration of *holā* on the day following the Hindu festival of colour-throwing, *holī*. Unlike the playful sprinkling of colours as is done during *holī*, the Gurū made *holā* an occasion for Sikhs to demonstrate skills-at-arms in simulated battle. Holā or Holā Mahallā, became thereafter an annual tourney of warlike sports in Anandpur as long as the Gurū stayed there. The observance of Holā Mahallā was revived after the Sikhs had established their rule in Punjab. It is now the biggest festival of Anandpur. The *mahallā* or the march on this occasion starting from the Takht Sāhib on the concluding day of the week-long festival ends at Holgaṛh, where sports like fencing, coit-throwing and tent-pegging are held.

The present building, a three-storeyed octagonal, domed edifice, was constructed under the supervision of Sant Sevā Siṅgh and was completed in 1970. The sanctum is in the middle of the marbled ground floor.

GURDWĀRĀ MĀTĀ JĪTO JĪ, built within a half-acre enclosure just outside Agampurā village, about 2 km northwest of Anandpur marks the site where the body of Mātā Jīto Jī, wife of Gurū Gobind Siṅgh, was cremated in December 1700. The present three-storeyed domed building was completed in 1972. The 4-metre square sanctum marked off by four pillars is in the middle of the square hall on the ground floor. The fluted lotus dome on top of the building has a gold-plated pinnacle and a gilded *khaṇḍā* as finial.

GURDWĀRĀ MAÑJĪ SĀHIB also called Damālgaṛh located close to the precincts of Takht Srī Kesgaṛh Sāhib is dedicated to Gurū Gobind Siṅgh's sons who used this place for learning and practising martial skills. The double-storey domed building of the shrine stands in the middle of a 20-metre square marble-paved compound. Its 3-metre-square sanctum is in the middle of a 15-metre square hall on the ground floor.

GURDWĀRĀ SĪS GAÑJ SĀHIB within the town is sacred to Gurū Tegh Bahādur whose head was cremated here in November 1675. A memorial shrine in the form of a platform whithin a small room was got constructed over the ashes by Gurū Gobind Siṅgh himself. At the time of the evacuation of Anandpur in December 1705, Gurū Gobind Siṅgh especially entrusted it to the care of Gurbakhsh Udāsī. The renovation and enlargement of the monument were carried out under the supervision of Bābā Sevā Siṅgh of Anandgaṛh during the early 1970's. The original pavement in the front compound with old Nānakshāhī bricks arranged in geometrical patterns is still intact. The two-storey building with a pinnacled dome provides a 4.5-metre wide covered circumambulatory passage supported on exquisitively designed marble columns around the inner sanctum where the Gurū Granth Sāhib is seated.

AKĀL BUṄGĀ opposite Gurdwārā Sīs Gañj within the same compound is a small shrine housed in an old building said to have been built by a *pujārī*, priest, Mān Siṅgh in 1889. It comprises a pentagonal room on either side of a masonry pedestal on which the Gurū Granth Sāhib is seated behind glass panels. The pedestal marks the spot sitting where during the obsequies of his father, Gurū Gobind Siṅgh delivered a sermon to his followers.

GURDWĀRĀ DAMDAMĀ SĀHIB stands, along with Thaṛā Sāhib and Bhorā Sāhib in the same compound, close to Sīs Gañj, formerly called Gurū ke Mahal, i.e. residential quarters of Gurū Tegh Bahādur. Damdamā Sāhib marks the site where the Gurū used to sit while receiving and addressing visiting *saṅgats*. The ceremony of installing Gurū Gobind Siṅgh as Gurū was performed here. The present domed octagonal building was constructed during the early decades of the 20th century.

THAṚĀ SĀHIB, an half-a-metre high and 5-metre square marble-paved platform stands in the open space in front of Damdamā Sāhib. It was here that Gurū Tegh Bahādur received the group of Kashmīrī Paṇḍits who called on him in 1675.

GURDWĀRĀ BHORĀ SĀHIB, a three-storeyed domed building close to Damdamā Sāhib, was a part of Gurū ke Mahal. Here in a *bhorā* (basement) Gurū Tegh Bahādur used to retire for solitary meditation. A 1.5-metre square and half a metre high platform in the middle of the present basement marks the site of the original *bhorā*. The Holy Book is now seated on a platform on the ground floor. Extension of this Gurdwārā involving blocks for Gurū kā Laṅgar and residential accommodation is in progress.

BIBLIOGRAPHY

1. Trilochan Singh, *Guru Tegh Bahadur: Prophet and Martyr*. Delhi, 1967
2. Harbans Singh, *Guru Tegh Bahadur*. Delhi, 1982
3. Anand, Balwant Singh, *Guru Tegh Bahadur: A Biography*. Delhi, 1979
4. Fauja Singh, and G.S. Talib, *Guru Tegh Bahadur—Martyr and Teacher*. Patiala, 1975
5. Macauliffe, M.A., *The Sikh Religion*. Oxford, 1909
6. Kuir Siṅgh, *Gurbilās Pātshāhī 10*. Patiala, 1968
7. Santokh Siṅgh, *Srī Gur Pratāp Sūraj Granth*. Amritsar, 1926-37
8. Ṭhākar Siṅgh, Giānī, *Srī Gurduāre Darshan*. Amritsar, 1923
9. Tārā Siṅgh, *Srī Gur Tīrath Saṅgrahi*. Amritsar, n.d.

M.G.S.

ANANDPUR DĪ VĀR is a versified account in Punjabi, by one Rām Siṅgh, of a battle fought in 1812 between Soḍhī Surjan Siṅgh of Anandpur and Rājā Mahā Chand of Kahlūr. Soḍhī Surjan Siṅgh was a lineal descendant of Sūraj Mall, a son of Gurū Hargobind. His father, Nāhar Siṅgh, who was a brave and influential person, had established an independent state by force of arms. Surjan Siṅgh, too, was a man of prowess, and was increasing his area of influence. Mahā Chand, the chief of the neighbouring state of Kahlūr, was jealous of the growing power of Surjan Siṅgh whom he considered no more than a vassal of his. He sent him word demanding land revenue from him. The Soḍhī refused saying that he was an autonomous ruler in his territory. Rājā Mahā Chand led a force against him and a fierce battle ensued. The poem describes the action in some detail. Surjan Siṅgh received help from Sardār Hukmā Siṅgh, about whose identity no exact information is supplied by the poet. The invading troops were defeated and they fled leaving a large number of dead on the field. According to the poet, Bhāī Sukkhā Siṅgh, author of *Gurbilās Dasvīṅ Pātshāhī* and Bhāī Māhṇā Siṅgh, the Jathedār of Srī Kesgaṛh Sāhib, took part in this battle. From the minute details of the combat and of the feats displayed by some of the contestants, the poet seems to have been an eye-witness to the whole campaign.

BIBLIOGRAPHY

Ashok, Shamsher Siṅgh, ed., *Prachīn Jaṅg Nāme*. Amritsar, 1950

P.S.P.

ANANDPUR SĀHIB RESOLUTION, a frequently invoked document of modern Sikhism pronouncing its religious rule as well as its political goal. After having enjoyed power under chief ministers, Gurnām Siṅgh and Parkāsh Siṅgh Bādal in the Punjab, newly demarcated in 1966, Sikhs as represented by their premier political party, the Shiromaṇī Akālī Dal, were able to capture only one seat at the elections to Indian Parliament (1971) from among the 13 which were Punjab's portion. In the Punjab Assembly elections which took place in March 1972 their tally was a mere 24 seats out of a total of 117, and the Punjab Government passed into the hands of the Congress Party, with Giānī Zail Siṅgh (later, President of India) as chief minister. This electoral debacle led to self-introspection on the part of the Shiromaṇī Akālī Dal which appointed on 11 December 1972 a sub-committee to reflect upon the situation and to proclaim afresh the programme and policies of the Dal. The 12-member committee consisted of Surjīt Siṅgh Barnālā, Gurcharan Siṅgh Ṭauhṛā, Jīwan Siṅgh Umrānaṅgal, Gurmeet Siṅgh, Dr Bhagat Siṅgh, Balwant Siṅgh, Giān Siṅgh Rāṛewālā, Amar Siṅgh Ambālavī, Prem Siṅgh Lālpurā, Jaswinder Siṅgh Brāṛ, Bhāg Siṅgh, and Major-General Gurba<u>kh</u>sh Siṅgh of Badhaṇī. The first meeting of the sub-committee took place at Amritsar. The venue then shifted to Chaṇḍīgaṛh where the committee completed its task in ten successive meetings. Counsel was available to the subcommittee of the celebrated Sikh intellectual and thinker, Sirdār Kapūr Siṅgh, whose impress the draft emerging finally from its deliberations carried. The document was adopted unanimously by the working committee of the Shiromaṇī Akālī Dal at a meeting held at Anandpur Sāhib, town sacred to Gurū Gobind Siṅgh, also reverenced by Sikhs as the birthplace of the K͟hālsā. Since it was adopted at Anandpur Sāhib (October 16-17, 1973) the resolution came to be known as the Anandpur Sāhib Resolution. It was endorsed in the form of a succession of resolutions at the 18th All-India Akālī Conference of the Shiromaṇī Akālī Dal at Ludhiāṇā on 28-29 October 1978. An English version of the resolution is quoted below:

> Whereas, the Sikhs of India are a historically recognized political nation ever since the inauguration of the K͟hālsā in AD 1699, and
>
> Whereas, this status of the Sikh nation had been internationally recognized and accepted by the major powers of Europe and Asia, viz. France, England, Italy, Russia, China, Persia (now Iran), Afghanistan, Nepal, and the Company Bahādur, Fort William, Calcutta, till the middle of the 19th century, and again by the outgoing British as well as by the Hindu-dominated Congress and the Muslim League of India in the middle of the 20th century, and
>
> Whereas, the brute majority in India, in 1950, imposed a constitutional arrangement in India which denudes the Sikhs of their political identity and cultural popularity, thus liquidating the Sikhs politically and exposing them to spiritual death and cultural decay leading inevitably to their submergence and dissolution into the saltish sea waters of incoherent Hinduism, and
>
> Whereas, the Sikhs have been thus shackled and enslaved in unethical and cynical repudiation of solemn and binding commitments and public promises earlier made to the Sikhs, while the Sikh representatives in the Indian Constituent Assembly, in 1950, refused to affix their signatures to the official copy of the Indian Constitutional Act thus promulgated, the Shiromaṇī Akālī Dal in the name and on behalf of the Sikhs proclaims that the Sikhs are determined, by all legitimate means, to extricate and free themselves from this degrading and deathdealing situation so as to ensure firmly their honourable survival and salvage their inherent dignity within India and their birthright to influence meaningfully the mainstream of world history. The Sikhs therefore demand, firstly, that an autonomous region in the north of India should be set up forthwith wherein the Sikh interests are constitutionally recognized as the fundamental State policy. Secondly, that this autonomous region includes the present Punjab, Karnāl and Ambālā districts of Haryāṇā, inclusive of Kāṅgṛā district of Himāchal Pradesh, Chaṇḍīgaṛh, Pinjore, Kālkā, Dalhousie, Nālāgaṛh Desh, Sirsā, Gūhlā and Ratīā areas and Gaṅgānāgar district of Rājasthān, thus bringing main contiguous Sikh population and Sikh habitats within this autonomous Sikh region as an integral part of the Union of India, and, thirdly, this Sikh autonomous region may be declared as entitled to frame its own internal constitutions on the basis of having all powers to and for itself except Foreign Relations, Defence, Currency and General Communications which will remain

subjects within the jurisdiction of the Federal Indian Government.

"MAY THE RIDER OF THE BLUE HORSE HELP US."

A. BASIC POSTULATES

1. The Shiromaṇī Akālī Dal is the very embodiment of the hopes and aspirations of the Sikhs and as such is fully entitled to its representation. The basic postulates of this organization are human co-existence, human welfare and the ultimate unity of all human beings with the Lord.
2. These postulates are based upon the three great principles of Srī Gurū Nānak Dev Jī, namely *Nām Japo, Kirat Karo,* and *Vaṇḍ Chhako,* i.e. meditation on God's Name, honest labour, and sharing the fruits of this labour with the needy.

B. PURPOSES

The Shiromaṇī Akālī Dal shall ever strive to achieve the following aims:

1. Propagation of Sikhism, its ethical values and code of conduct to combat atheism.
2. Preservation and keeping alive the concept of distinct and sovereign identity of the Panth and building up of appropriate conditions in which the national sentiments and aspirations of the Sikh Panth will find full expression, satisfaction and facilities for growth.
3. Eradication of poverty and starvation through increased production and more equitable distribution of wealth as also the establishment of a just social order *sans* exploitation of any kind.
4. Vacation of discrimination on the basis of caste, creed or any other ground in keeping with the basic principles of Sikhism.
5. Removal of disease and ill health, checking the use of intoxicants and provision of full facilities for the growth of physical well-being so as to prepare and enthuse the Sikh Nation for the national defence.

For the achievement of the aforesaid purposes, the Shiromaṇī Akālī Dal owned it as its primary duty to inculcate among the Sikhs religious fervour and a sense of pride in their great socio-spiritual heritage through the following measures:

1. Reiteration of the concept of unicity of God, meditation on His Name, recitation of *gurbāṇī,* inculcation of faith in the ten holy Sikh Gurūs as well as in Gurū Granth Sāhib and other appropriate measures for such a purpose.
2. Grooming at the Sikh Missionary College the Sikh youth with inherent potential to become accomplished preachers, *rāgīs, ḍhāḍīs* and poets so that the propagation of Sikhism, its tenets and traditions and its basic religious values could be taken up more effectively and vigorously.
3. Baptising the Sikhs on a mass scale with particular emphasis on schools and colleges wherein the teachers as well as the taught shall be enthused through regular study circles.
4. Revival of the religious institution of *dasvandh* among the Sikhs.
5. Generating a feeling of respect for Sikh intellectuals including writers and preachers, who also would be enthused to improve upon their accomplishments.

   Streamlining the administration of the *gurdwārās* by giving better training to their workers. Appropriate steps would also be taken to maintain *gurdwārā* buildings in proper condition. The representatives of the party in the Shiromaṇī Gurdwārā Parbandhak Committee would be directed to pull their weight towards these ends.
6. Making suitable arrangements for error-free publication of *gurbāṇī,* promoting research in the ancient and modern Sikh history, translating holy *gurbāṇī* into other languages and producing first-rate literature on Sikhism.
7. Taking appropriate measures for the enactment of an All-India Gurdwārās Act with a view to improving the administra-

tion of the *gurdwārās* throughout the country and to reintegrate the traditional preaching sects of Sikhism like Udāsīs and Nirmalās, without in any way encroaching upon the properties of their *maṭhs*.

8. Taking necessary steps to bring the Sikh *gurdwārās* all over the world under a single system of administration with a view to running them according to the basic Sikh forms and to pool their resources for the propagation of Sikhism on a wider and more impressive scale.
9. Striving for free access to all those holy Sikh shrines, including Nankāṇā Sāhib, from which the Sikh Panth has been separated, for their pilgrimage and proper upkeep.

POLITICAL GOAL

The political goal of the Panth, without any doubt, is enshrined in the Commandments of the Tenth Lord, in the pages of Sikh history and in the very heart of the Khālsā Panth, the ultimate aim of which is the pre-eminence of the Khālsā (*KHĀLSĀ JĪ KE BOL BĀLE*).

The fundamental policy of the Shiromaṇī Akālī Dal is to seek the realization of this birthright of the Khālsā through the creation of a geographical entity and a constitutional set-up of its own.

For the attainment of this aim—

1. The Shiromaṇī Akālī Dal is determined to strive by all possible means to
   - (a) Have all those Punjabi-speaking areas, deliberately kept out of Punjab, such as Dalhousie in Gurdāspur district, Chaṇḍīgaṛh, Pinjore, Kālkā and Ambālā Sadar, etc. in Ambālā district, the entire Ūnā *tahsīl* of Hoshiārpur district, Shāhābād and Gūhlā blocks of Karnāl district, Ṭohāṇā sub-*tahsīl*, Ratīā block and Sirsā *tahsīl* of Hissār district and six *tahsīls* of Gaṅgānagar district in Rājasthān, merged with Punjab to constitute a single administrative unit wherein the interests of Sikhs and Sikhism are specifically protected.
   - (b) In this new Punjab (as in all other states) the Centre's interference would be restricted to Defence, Foreign Relations, Currency and Communications, all other departments being in the jurisdiction of Punjab (and other states) which would be fully entitled to frame their own Constitution. For the aforesaid departments of the Centre, Punjab (and other states) would contribute in proportion to their respective representation in Parliament.
   - (c) The Sikhs and other minorities living outside Punjab should be adequately protected against any kind of discrimination against them.
2. The Shiromaṇī Akālī Dal would also endeavour to have the Indian Constitution recast on real Federal principles with equal representation at the Centre for all the States.
3. The Shiromaṇī Akālī Dal strongly denounces the Foreign policy of India as framed by the Congress Party. It is worthless and highly detrimental to the interests of the country, its people and mankind at large. Shiromaṇī Akālī Dal shall extend its support only to such policies as are based upon the principles of peace and national interest. It strongly advocates a policy of peace with all neighbouring countries, particularly those which have within their borders Sikh population and Sikh shrines. The Akālī Dal is of the firm view that the foreign policy of India should in no case be one of playing second fiddle to any other country.
4. The Shiromaṇī Akālī Dal shall firmly resist any discrimination against any Sikh (or even other) employees of the Centre or State government [on the basis of his caste or creed]. It shall also endeavour to

maintain the traditional position of the Sikhs in all the wings of the Defence services and needs of the Sikh army personnel shall be adequately taken care of by the Panth. The Shiromaṇī Akālī Dal shall also ensure that *kirpān* is accepted as an integral part of the uniform of the Sikhs in the Army.

5. It shall be the primary obligation of the Shiromaṇī Akālī Dal to help rehabilitate ex-servicemen of the Defence forces in the civil life, and for such a purpose it would extend them every help to enable them to organize themselves and raise their voice in an effective way to gain adequate safeguards and concessions for an honourable and dignified life.
6. The Shiromaṇī Akālī Dal is of the firm opinion that all those persons, including women, who have not been convicted of any criminal offence by a court of law should have the right to possess any type of small arms like revolvers, guns, pistols, rifles, carbines, etc., without any license, the only obligation being their registration.
7. The Shiromaṇī Akālī Dal seeks ban on the sale of liquor and all other kinds of intoxicants, and shall press for a ban on the consumption of intoxicants and smoking in public places.

Apart from defining the basic postulates and principles of policies and its ultimate goal, the open session of the General House of the Shiromaṇī Akālī Dal, held at Ludhiāṇā, also traced the outlines of the long-term socio-economic and cultural aims and objectives of the Party, for the attainment of which it adopted twelve sub-resolutions. A closer analysis of these sub-resolutions shows that while the core of the basic resolutions passed by its working committee at Anandpur Sāhib in 1973, namely the attainment of special Constitutional state for the Sikhs to ensure their growth in accordance with their own socio-spiritual traditions and tenets was fully endorsed by the General House of the Shiromaṇī Akālī Dal, the scope of the greater autonomy to the state of Punjab for the aforesaid purpose was widened to include all the states. Thus, the shape and scope of the Anandpur Sāhib resolution as it finally emerged out of the Ludhiāṇā meet of the Shiromaṇī Akālī Dal envisages:

1. The attainment of pre-eminence of the Khālsā through special constitutional safeguards and powers for the Sikhs.
2. Greater autonomy to all the states by recasting the Centre-State relations on the basis of limited powers for the Centre.

Resolutions adopted, in the light of the Anandpur Sāhib Resolution, at the open session of the 18th All India Akālī Conference held at Ludhiāṇā on October 28-29, 1978, under the presidentship of Jathedār Jagdev Siṅgh Talvaṇḍī are as under:

Resolution No. 1

Moved by Sardār Gurcharan Siṅgh Ṭauhṛā, President, Shiromaṇī Gurdwārā Parbandhak Committee, and endorsed by Sardār Parkāsh Siṅgh Bādal, Chief Minister, Punjab.

The Shiromaṇī Akālī Dal realizes that India is a federal and republican geographical entity of different languages, religions and cultures. To safeguard the fundamental rights of the religious and linguistic minorities, to fulfil the demands of the democratic traditions and to pave the way for economic progress, it has become imperative that the Indian constitutional infrastructure should be given a real federal shape by redefining the Central and State relations and rights on the lines of the aforesaid principles and objectives.

The concept of total revolution given by Lok Nāik Jaya Parkāsh Narāiṇ is also based upon the progressive decentralization of powers. The climax of the process of centralization of powers of the states through repeated amendments of the Constitution during the Congress regime came before the countrymen in the form of the Emergency (1975), when all fundamental rights of all citizens were usurped. It was then that the programme of decentralization of powers ever advocated by Shiromaṇī Akālī Dal was openly accepted and adopted by other political parties including Janatā Party, C.P.I. (M), D.M.K., etc.

Shiromaṇī Akālī Dal has ever stood firm on this principle and that is why after a very careful consideration it unanimously adopted a resolution to this effect first at the All-India Akālī Conference, Baṭālā, then at Anandpur Sāhib which has endorsed the principle of State autonomy in keeping with the concept of federalism.

As such, the Shiromaṇī Akālī Dal emphatically urges upon the Janatā Government to take cognizance of the different linguistic and cultural sections, religious minorities as also the voice of millions of people and recast the constitutional structure of the country on real and meaningful federal principles to obviate the possibility of any danger to the unity and integrity of the country and, further, to enable the states to play a useful role for the progress and prosperity of the Indian people in their respective areas by a meaningful exercise of their powers.

Resolution No. 2

This momentous meeting of the Shiromaṇī Akālī Dal calls upon the Government of India to examine carefully the long tale of the excesses, wrongs, illegal actions committed [against the Sikhs] by the previous Congress Government, more particularly during the Emergency, and try to find an early solution to the following problems:

(a) Chaṇḍīgaṛh originally raised as a Capital for Punjab should be handed over to Punjab.
(b) The long-standing demand of the Shiromaṇī Akālī Dal for the merger in Punjab of the Punjabi-speaking areas, to be identified by linguistic experts with village as a unit, should be conceded.
(c) The control of headworks should continue to be vested in Punjab and, if need be, the Reorganization Act should be amended.
(d) The arbitrary and unjust Award given by Mrs Indira Gandhi during the Emergency on the distribution of Rāvī-Beās waters should be revised on the universally accepted norms and principles, and justice be done to Punjab.
(e) Keeping in view the special aptiude and martial qualities of the Sikhs, the present ratio of their strength in the Army should be maintained.
(f) The excesses being committed on the settlers in the Tarāī region of the Uttar Pradesh in the name of Land Reforms should be vacated by making suitable amendments in the ceiling law on the Central guidelines.

Resolution No. 3

(Economic Policy Resolution)

The chief sources of inspiration of the economic policies and programme of the Shiromaṇī Akālī Dal are the secular, democratic and socialistic concepts of Gurū Nānak and Gurū Gobind Siṅgh. Our economic programme is based on three basic principles:

(a) Dignity of labour.
(b) An economic and social structure which provides for the uplift of the poor and depressed sections of society.
(c) Unabated opposition to concentration of economic and political power in the hands of the capitalists.

While drafting its economic policies and programme, the Shiromaṇī Akālī Dal in its historic Anandpur Sāhib Resolution has laid particular stress on the need to break the monopolistic hold of the capitalists foisted on the Indian economy by 30 years of Congress rule in India. This capitalist hold enabled the Central government to assume all powers in its hands after the manner of Mughal imperialism. This was bound to thwart the economic progress of the states and injure the social and economic interests of the people. The Shiromaṇī Akālī Dal once again reiterates the Sikh way of life by resolving to fulfil the holy words of Gurū Nānak Dev:

"He alone realizes the true path who labours honestly and shares with others the fruits of that labour."

This way of life is based upon three basic principles:

(i) Doing honest labour.
(ii) Sharing with others the fruits of this labour, and
(iii) Meditation on the Lord's Name.

The Shiromaṇī Akālī Dal calls upon the Central and the State governments to eradicate unemployment during the next ten years. While pursuing this aim, special emphasis should be laid on ameliorating the lot of the weaker sections, scheduled and depressed classes, workers, landless and poor farmers and urban poor. Minimum wages should be fixed for all of them.

The Shiromaṇī Akālī Dal urges upon the Punjab government to draw up such an economic plan for the state as would turn it into the leading state during the next ten years by raising per capita income to Rs. 3,000 and by generating an economic growth rate of 7% per annum as against 4% at the national level.

The Shiromaṇī Akālī Dal gives first priority to the redrafting of the taxation structure in such a way that the burden of taxation is shifted from the poor to the richer classes and an equitable distribution of national income ensured.

The main plank of the economic programme of the Shiromaṇī Akālī Dal is to enable the economically weaker sections of the society to share the fruits of national income.

The Shiromaṇī Akālī Dal calls upon the Central government to make an international airport at Amritsar which should also enjoy the facilities of a dry port. Similarly, a Stock Exchange should be opened at Ludhiāṇā to accelerate the process of industrialization and economic growth in the State. The Shiromaṇī Akālī Dal also desires that suitable amendments should be made in the Foreign Exchange rules for free exchange of foreign currencies and thereby removing the difficulties being faced by the Indian emigrants.

The Shiromaṇī Akālī Dal emphatically urges upon the Indian government to bring about parity between the prices of the agricultural produce and that of the industrial raw materials so that the discrimination against such states as lack these materials may be removed.

The Shiromaṇī Akālī Dal demands that the exploitation of the producers of cash crops like cotton, sugarcane, oil seeds, etc., at the hands of traders should be stopped forthwith and for this purpose arrangements be made for purchase by government of these crops at remunerative prices. Besides, effective steps should be taken by government for the purchase of cotton through the Cotton Corporation.

The Shiromaṇī Akālī Dal strongly feels that the most pressing national problem is the need to ameliorate the lot of millions of exploited persons belonging to the scheduled classes. For such a purpose the Shiromaṇī Akālī Dal calls upon the Central and State governments to earmark special funds. Besides, the state governments should allot sufficient funds in their respective budgets for giving free residential plots both in the urban and rural areas to the Scheduled Castes.

The Shiromaṇī Akālī Dal also calls for the rapid diversification of farming. The shortcomings in the Land Reforms Laws should be removed, rapid industrialization of the State ensured, credit facilities for the medium industries expanded and unemployment allowance given to those who are unemployed. For remunerative farming, perceptible reduction should be made in the prices of farm machinery like tractors, tubewells, as also of the inputs.

Resolution No. 4

This huge gathering of the Shiromaṇī Akālī Dal regrets the discrimination to which the Punjabi language is being subjected in the adjoining States of Himāchal, Haryāṇā, Jammū and Kashmīr, Delhi, etc. It is its firm demand that in accordance with the Nehrū Language Formula, the neighbouring States of Punjab should give 'second' - language status to Punjabi because fairly large sections of their respective populations are Punjabi-speaking.

Resolution No. 5

The meeting regrets that against the 'claims' of the refugees who had migrated to Jammū and Kashmīr as a result of the partition of the country, no compensation had been provided to them even after such a long time and these unfortunate refugees have been rotting in the camps ever since then.

This Akālī Dal session, therefore, forcefully demands that their claims should be settled soon and immediate steps should be taken to rehabilitate them even if it involves an amendment to section 370 of the Constitution.

Resolution No. 6

The 18th session of the All-India Akālī Conference takes strong exception to the discrimination to which the minorities in other states are being subjected and the way in which their interests are being ignored.

As such, it demands that injustice against the Sikhs in other states should be vacated and proper representation should be given them in government service, local bodies and state legislatures, through nominations, if need be.

Resolution No. 7

The 18th session of the All-India Akālī Conference notes with satisfaction that mechanization of farming in the country has led to increase in the farm yield and as a result the country is heading towards self-sufficiency in foodgrain.

However, the session feels that poor farmers are unable to take to mechanization because of the enormity of the cost involved.

As such, the Shiromaṇī Akālī Dal urges upon the Government of India to abolish the excise duty on tractors, so that with the decrease in their prices, the smaller farmers may also be able to avail themselves of farm machinery and contribute to increase in agricultural produce of the country.

Resolution No. 8

This conference of the Shiromaṇī Akālī Dal appeals to the Central and State governments to pay particular attention to the poor and labouring classes and demands that besides making suitable amendments in the Minimum Wages Act, suitable legal steps be taken to improve the economic lot of the labouring class, to enable it to lead a respectable life and play a useful role in the rapid industrialization of the country.

Resolution No. 9

This session seeks permission from the Government of India to instal a broadcasting station at the Golden Temple, Amritsar, for the relay of Gurbāṇī Kīrtan for the spiritual satisfaction of those Sikhs who are living in foreign lands.

The session wishes to make it clear that the entire cost of the proposed broadcasting project would be borne by the Khālsā Panth and its over-all control shall vest with the Indian Government. It is hoped that the Government would have no hesitation in conceding this demand after due consideration.

Resolution No. 10

This mammoth gathering of the Shiromaṇī Akālī Dal strongly urges upon the Government of India to make necessary amendments in the following enactments for the benefit of the agricultural classes who have toiled hard for the sake of larger national interests:

1. Hindu Succession Act be suitably amended to enable a woman to get rights of inheritance in the properties of her father-in-law instead of the father's.
2. The agricultural lands of the farmers should be completely exempted from the Wealth Tax and the Estate Duty.

Resolution No. 11

This vast gathering of the Shiromaṇī Akālī Dal strongly impresses upon the Government of India that keeping in view the economic backwardness of the scheduled and non-scheduled castes, provisions proportionate to their population should be made in the budget for utilization for their welfare. A special ministry should be created at the Centre as a practical measure to render justice to them on the basis of reservation.

The session also calls upon the government that in keeping with the settlement already made, no discrimination should be made between the Sikh and Hindu Harijans in any part of the country.

Resolution No. 12

The Congress government is called upon to vacate the gross injustice, discrimination done to Punjab in the distribution of Rāvī-Beās waters. The Central government must also give approval for the immediate establishment of six sugar and four textile mills in Punjab so that the State may be able to implement its agro-industrial policy.

BIBLIOGRAPHY

1. Gurmit Singh, *History of Sikh Struggles*, vol. I. Delhi, 1989
2. Gopal Singh, *A History of the Sikh People*. Delhi, 1979

M.A.S.

ANAND SIṄGH, RĀI (d. 1827), *vakīl* or agent of the Sikh kingdom, belonged to the famed Bhaṇḍārī family of Baṭālā founded by Bhāg Mall, a wealthy adventurer. In 1809, Anand Siṅgh was appointed an agent of the Sikh Darbār at Ludhiāṇā, the British military station and political agency. He was later sent as the Darbār's envoy to the British resident at Delhi. He had a good knowledge of Persian and English and accompanied Sir Charles Metcalfe on the successful expedition against Bharatpur undertaken by Lord Combermere in January 1826, receiving on his return from Mahārājā Raṇjīt Siṅgh the title of Rāi with a robe of honour.

Rāi Anand Siṅgh died in 1827.

BIBLIOGRAPHY

1. Sūrī, Sohan Lāl, *'Umdāt-ut-Twārīkh*. Lahore, 1885-89
2. Griffin, Lepel, and C.F. Massy, *Chiefs and Families of Note in the Punjab*. Lahore, 1909
3. Ahluwalia, M.L., ed., *Select Documents Relating to Maharaja Ranjit Singh's Negotiations with the British Envoy Charles Theophilus Metcalfe 1808-1809*. Delhi, 1982

B.S.N.

ANANDU, noncanonically spelt *Anand*, by Gurū Amar Dās, is like Gurū Nānak's *Japu*, one of the more familiar texts in the Gurū Granth Sāhib. Set in the Rāmkalī musical measure and comprising forty stanzas, *Anand* is recited liturgically, especially in its shortened form, at the conclusion of all congregational services and at prayers offered at weddings and other ceremonies to seek God's grace and solace and to rejoice on happy occasions in the favours granted by Him. The Sikh marriage ceremony itself has come to be called *anand*, which term has also been used in the legislative enactment governing the custom. Tradition recounts that Gurū Amar Dās had just finished the recording of this composition when the news of the birth of a grandson (son of Mohrī, the younger of his two sons), was communicated to him. The child was named Anand after the title of the composition he had just completed. In Sanskrit, and so in Punjabi, the word *anand* means bliss. In the *Taittirīya Upaniṣad,* it has been used for Brahman Itself. The term there also denotes a *rasa* or emotion. Gurū Amar Dās's composition centres upon the experience of *anand* (bliss, supreme beatitude) resulting from the individual soul's merging with the Supreme Soul which is attained through constant remembrance of God under the direction of the Gurū. Herein, *anand* is a positive spiritual state of inner poise and equanimity wherein one is freed from all *dukkha* (suffering), *roga* (malady), and *santāpu* (anxiety) and one realizes the ultimate goal of union with the Lord.

A synoptic summary of the contents of the poem, stanza-wise, may go as under: (1) Anand is attained by the grace of the Gurū who has bestowed upon me enlightenment, equanimity, harmony and God-realization; (2) God has banished suffering, giving me the sense of fulfilment; (3) He bestows upon men all gifts including the gift of the Name; (4) the Name sustains life, banishes desires, gives peace, tranquillity and happiness; (5) it drives away the five lusts and cancels death; (6) the gift of the Name follows and it can come from Him alone; (7) the Gurū is the source of *anand,* for his teaching gives detachment and discrimination and banishes sin; (8) without the Gurū's guidance one gropes in the darkness of ignorance; (9) the Gurū leads the seeker to the company of the holy saints where the Immaculate One is meditated upon; (10) thus the mind gets detached from illusory *māyā,* the enchanter; (11) it surrenders itself to God, the Eternal Reality; (12) God, Creator, is beyond comprehension; (13) even the angels and *ṛṣis* are the seekers of the nectar of His Name which banishes ego and sin; (14) the *bhaktas* tread the path of non-ego and non-desire; (15) men do what God wills, some by His grace take to meditating on the Name; (16) they on whom is His grace listen to the Gurū's word; (17) they become pure by meditating on the Name, liberating their companions as well; (18) doubt and ignorance are dispelled by meditating on the Name alone and not by any ritual practices; one remains in impurity as long as doubt persists; (19) an impure mind can never win liberation; (20) they who practise what the Gurū teaches are pure inside and outside; (21) a disciple has to surrender completely to the Gurū by shaking off his ego and placing full faith in him; (22) none can achieve liberation without the Gurū's aid; (23) he has to concentrate on the True Gurū's word and this is possible by His grace only; (24) all other learning is of little avail; (25) the Gurū's *śabda* is a pure diamond which one receives through His grace alone; (26) the Gurū breaks the bondage of *māyā* and thus frees the spirit; (27) the Smṛtis and Śāstras cannot pierce *māyā;* (28) the Gurū teaches concentration on the Name which is one's protector and sustainer; (29) *māyā* charms one away from concentration; (30) *māyā* is worthless whereas the Name is priceless; (31) those who concentrate on the Name build up real capital; (32) the taste of the Name is sweetest and it eliminates all desire; (33) the Name is the divine spark within the bodily frame; (34) its realization gives bliss and annuls sorrow and suffering; (35) blessed is the man who is devoted to the Gurū and God; (36) blessed are the eyes which see God everywhere; (37) blessed are the ears which hear the nectar-sweet Name; (38) blessed is the realization of the state wherein one sees God in all His vastness; (39) of highest value is the Truth which abides in the pure hearts; and (40) with the realization comes *anand* or bliss which banishes suffering, maladies and anxities.

BIBLIOGRAPHY

1. Tāran Siṅgh, *Sahij te Anandu.* Amritsar, n.d.
2. Kohli, Surindar Singh, *A Critical Study of Adi Granth.* Delhi, 1961
3. Talib, Gurbachan Singh, *Bani of Guru Amar Das.* Delhi. 1979
4. Macauliffe, M. A., *The Sikh Religion.* Oxford, 1909

T.S.

ANANTĀ, BHAĪ, son of Bhāī Kuko, a Vadhāvan Khatrī, was a devoted Sikh of the time of Gurū Hargobind (1595-1644). According to Bhāī Santokh Siṅgh, *Srī Gur Pratāp Sūraj Granth,* he once earned the Gurū's displeasure for wantonly hitting a crow which became lame as a result of the injury. He was, however, repentant and was pardoned through Bhāī Bidhī Chand's intercession. Bhāī Anantā laid down his life fighting for the Gurū in the battle of Amritsar (1629).

BIBLIOGRAPHY

Santokh Siṅgh, Bhāī, *Srī Gur Pratāp Sūraj Granth.* Amritsar 1926-37

M.G.S.

ANANTĪ, MĀTĀ, wife of Bābā Gurdittā and mother of Gurū Har Raī, Nānak VII. She was popularly known as Mātā Nattī. Some chroniclers have also used for her the names of Nihāl Kaur and Bassī.

See NATTĪ, MĀTĀ

BIBLIOGRAPHY

Santokh Siṅgh, Bhāī, *Srī Gur Pratāp Sūraj Granth.* Amritsar, 1926-37

M.G.S.

ANANTNĀG (33° - 44'N, 75° -13'E), a district town on the southern edge of the Kashmīr valley, is named after a nearby spring which is regarded as sacred by the Hindus. The town claims a historical Sikh shrine commemorating the visit of Gurū Nānak (1469-1539), who passed through here on his way to Maṭṭan in 1517. The present building of Gurdwārā Gurū Nānak in the southern part of the town was constructed in 1950, and a second storey was added to it in 1970. The *dīvān* hall, with the sanctum along the middle of the rear wall, is in the central portion of the first floor. The Gurdwārā is affiliated to the Jammū and Kashmīr Gurdwārā Parbandhak Board and is managed by its district commitee for Anantnāg.

Gn.S.

ANĀRKALĪ, the oldest Mug͟hal tomb in Lahore, was built between 1605 and 1615 by Emperor Jahāṅgīr for his former favourite dancing girl Anārkalī. The tomb was surrounded by extensive gardens enclosed within a high protective wall, and several buildings and palaces were erected in the gardens by Mug͟hal princes and nobles. In 1799, Mahārājā Raṇjīt Siṅgh put up his headquarters there while besieging Lahore. Subsequently, he offered Anārkālī to his eldest son, the heir apparent Kharak Siṅgh.

In 1822, Raṇjīt Siṅgh gave this monument to his French generals, Allard and Ventura, as their personal residence and headquarters of the Fauj-i-K͟hās. The generals soon built a new, classical-style residence between Anārkalī's tomb and a Mug͟hal palace which has since disappeared. This new residence was embellished with paintings and mirrors inserted in golden frames, descriptions of which have been left by numerous travellers (Jacquemont, Hugel, Barr, Von Orlich, etc.) The headquarters of Fauj-i-K͟hās was in a part of this new building. In another wing were the private apartments of General Allard and Bannou Pān Deī, while General Ventura established his flourishing harem in the tomb itself.

Outside the garden, towards the east, was the *champ de manoeuvre* (operational headquarters) of the Fauj-i-K͟hās, and further east were the French Lines, or cantonments, of the troops under Allard and Ventura. It was the most comfortable and modern building of Lahore during the 1830's and 1840's. South of the *champ de manoeuvre* and the French lines was the small *bārādarī* of Allard and his wife, profusely decorated by Punjabi artists; that was the "country" seat of the Allard family. It is in this latter garden that Allard and his wife buried two of their children, and in the same tomb Allard himself was buried in 1839.

In 1846 Henry Lawrence, the British Resident, moved into the house of Allard and Ventura in Anārkalī—hence its present name: the Residence. Lord Dalhousie, the British Governor-General of India, however, refused Ventura's demand to be paid the price of the building. It occupies today a section of the Punjab Government Secretariat, and the tomb of Anārkalī has been transformed into the Punjab Records Office with a small, but interesting museum and library organized by H.L.O. Garrett by the 1930's.

J.M.L.

ANDREWS, CHARLES FREER (1871-1940), Anglican missionary, scholar and educationist, was born to John Edwin Andrews on 12 February 1871 in Newcastle-on-Tyne in Great Britain. His father was a minister of the Evangelical Anglican Church. Andrews grew up in an intense and emotional religious environment. A nearly fatal attack of rheumatic fever in childhood drew him to his mother with an intense affection and her love created in his mind the first conscious thoughts of God and Christ, and by the time he entered Cambridge, at the age of 19, he had already had "a wonderful conversion of my heart to God."

In 1893, Andrews graduated first class in Classics and Theology from Pembroke College, Cambridge. In 1895 he was confirmed in the Church of England, and for the next six years he worked in responsible positions in Cambridge. In 1903, he was accepted by the Society for the Propagation of the Gospel in Foreign Parts for missionary work in India with the Cambridge Brotherhood at Delhi. He arrived in India on 20 March 1904 to teach at St Stephen's College. After teaching at St Stephen's for 10 years, he moved to Tagore's Santiniketan, then a nursery of India's national aspirations. What Andrews saw of the manner of the British government in India shocked his Christian conscience.

Early during his stay in India, the Rev. C.F. Andrews formed an admiration for Sikh character and values. According to Daniel C'Connor, *The Testimony of C.F. Andrews,* he wrote: "Some of the most cherished days in all my religious experiences of the East have been spent among the Sikhs, dwelling among them in their homes, listening to their own religious songs and sharing life with them. I can say with conviction that these words, daily repeated by their lips, have sunk in their souls. It would be difficult to find a more generous or forgiving people, and a nation that bore less malice and hatred in its heart." There were several occasions when Andrews showed his solidarity with the Sikh people and interceded on their behalf when he found that they had been wronged.

After the Jalliāṅvālā Bāgh massacre (1919), Andrews was put under military arrest by the British to prevent him from going to the Punjab, yet he wrote extensively condemning the brutal incident. To suppress public reaction against it, the British administration let loose a reign of terror in the Punjab. All civil rights were suspended and public flogging and torture of innocent people became the order of the day. In September 1919 Andrews came to the Punjab to collect evidence to be placed before the Commission of Enquiry. He felt deeply hurt and chagrined to witness what the British authority was doing. "Andrews would go to the village gurdwara and listen to the account of the indignities and inhuman treatment to which the rural masses were subjected. He would beg for their forgiveness for the wrong which his fellow countrymen were doing. This overwhelmed the people. They would cry out and embrace Andrews." In this manner he went from one *gurdwārā* to another on his mission of atonement and healing.

Andrews had been closely following the Sikh struggle for religious autonomy and justice, which, by this time, had turned into a mass movement. He had been regularly going to the Golden Temple and other places to attend worship and Sikh rallies in order to show his solidarity with the Sikh cause. He wrote in *The Tribune* his account of what he had seen at the Gurū kā Bāgh *morchā*. The issue was the right of the Sikhs to cut firewood from the Bāgh for the requirements of the *laṅgar* (community kitchen). A fixed number of Sikh volunteers would daily go to the Bāgh to cut wood and the police would mercilessly beat them, often unconscious.

Andrews wrote, "... There were some hundred present seated on an open piece of ground watching what was going on in front, their faces strained with agony... There was not a cry raised from the spectators but the lips of very many of them were moving in prayer...

"...There were four Akālī Sikhs with their black turbans facing a band of about a dozen policemen, including two English officers... Their hands were placed together in prayer and it was clear they were praying. Then without the slightest provocation on their part, an Englishman lunged forward the head of his *lāṭhī*... the staff struck the Akālī Sikh...

"The blow which I saw was sufficient to fell the Akālī Sikh and send him to ground. He rolled over, and slowly got up once more, and faced the same punishment over again...

"The brutality and inhumanity of the whole scene was indescribably increased by the fact that the men who were hit were praying to God and had already taken a vow that they would remain silent and peaceful in word and deed...

"There was something far greater in this event than a mere dispute about land and property... A new heroism, learnt through suffering, has risen in the land. A new lesson in moral warfare has been taught in the world.

"I saw no act, no look of defiance. It was a true martyrdom to them as they went forward, a true act of faith, a true deed of devotion to God. They remembered their gurus how they had suffered, and they rejoiced to add their own sufferings to the treasury of their wonderful faith.

"...Many of them, old soldiers, who had fought in France, said to me afterwards in the hospital: This was a new kind of battle; we have not fought like this before."

In April 1929 Andrews went to Vancouver (Canada). For many years he had been advocating citizenship rights for Sikhs who had settled in Canada and now he came in personal contact with them. He was given a rousing welcome by the Sikh community there and was taken into *gurdwārās*. Andrews continued his effort to secure citizenship rights for them.

The Rev. C.F. Andrews died in Calcutta on 5 April 1940.

BIBLIOGRAPHY

1. Chaturvedi, Benarsidas, and Marjorie Sykes, *Charles Freer Andrews: A Narrative*. London, 1949
2. O'Connor, Daniel, *The Testamony of C.F. Andrews*. Madras, 1974
3. Bose, Somendranath, ed., *Oppression in the Punjab and C.F. Andrews*. 1970
4. Sykes, Marjorie, ed., *C.F. Andrews: Representative Writings*. Delhi, 1973
5. Roy Chaudhry, P.C., *C.F. Andrews: His Life and Times*. Bombay, 1971
6. Mohinder Singh, *The Akali Movement*. Delhi, 1978
7. Harbans Singh, *The Heritage of the Sikhs*. Delhi, 1983

C.O.M.

AṄGAD DEV, GURŪ, (1504-1552), the second of the ten Gurūs or prophet-teachers of the Sikh faith was born Lahiṇā on Baisākh *vadī* 1, Sammat 1561 Bikramī, corresponding with 31 March 1504. His father, Bhāī Pherū, was a Trehaṇ Khatrī and a trader of humble means, whose ancestral home was located near the village of Matte dī Sarāi, now known as Sarāi Nāṅgā, 16 km from Muktsar, in present-day district of Farīdkoṭ in the Punjab. His mother's name is variously given as Sabhirāī, Rāmo, Dayā Kaur and Mansā Devī.

In Māgh 1576 Bk/January 1520, he was married to Khīvī, daughter of Devī Chand, a Marvāh Khatrī from the village of Saṅghar, near Khaḍūr, in Amritsar district. Two sons, Dāsū and Dātū, and a daughter, Amaro, were born to the couple. According to some writers Gurū Aṅgad had two daughters, Amaro and Anokhī.

Lahiṇā became a disciple of Gurū Nānak in his late twenties. There are two main versions concerning the manner in which he was converted to the teachings of Gurū Nānak. The *janam sākhīs* of the *Purātan* tradition describe Lahiṇā as the *pujārī* of Khaḍūr. With only one exception, the inhabitants of Khaḍūr were all worshippers of the goddess Durgā and Lahiṇā accordingly served as a *pujārī* of the Devī cult. The one exception was a Sikh who regularly chanted Gurū Nānak's hymns. On one occasion, Lahiṇā overheard him singing a *śabda* and upon asking who had composed it he was told that it was by Gurū Nānak. Further converse with the Sikh convinced Lahiṇā of the truth of the Gurū's words and, casting aside the trappings of Durgā-worship, he too became a Sikh. No initial meeting with Gurū Nānak is described in this account. The next *Purātan* anecdote assumes that Lahiṇā is already in his company at Kartārpur. The other version, to be found in the *Ādi Sākhīāṅ (q.v.)*, the *B40 Janam Sākhī (q.v.)* and the *Miharbān Janam Sākhī (q.v.)*, opens with Lahiṇā living in the village of Harīke, near Matte dī Sarāi. In common with other inhabitants of the village, Lahiṇā made an annual pilgrimage to a "shrine of Durgā" which the *Mahimā Prakāsh Kavitā* later identifies as Jvālāmukhī. On one such pilgrimage, the party happened to pass by Kartārpur and, hearing that it was the abode of the renowned Gurū Nānak, they decided to visit the village in order to receive his *darshan*. While they were in his presence, Gurū Nānak briefly conversed with Lahiṇā who was instantly converted. In spite of the protests by the pilgrim party which he was leading, he announced that the purpose of the pilgrimage had been fulfilled in Kartārpur and that he would proceed no further. For the remainder of his master's lifetime, he resided partly in Kartārpur and partly in Khaḍūr.

Gurū Nānak bestowed the name Aṅgad on him to signify that the disciple had become as much a part of him as his own limbs (*aṅg*). Aṅgad devoted himself wholeheartedly to the Gurū's word and to deeds of service. He cleaned the utensils and swung the fan. The *janam sākhīs* and the *Mahimā Prakāsh* lay insistent stress on the patient, unquestioning loyalty of Aṅgad the disciple, distinguishing him in this respect not merely from Gurū Nānak's sons but also from other reputable disciples whose endurance proves to have limits. This quality of Aṅgad's character is repeatedly affirmed through a series of anecdotes, each seeking to express a limitless faith and boundless humility. These stories, explicitly or by implication, point forward to Aṅgad's succession as Gurū. Because he surpasses all others in loyal obedience, he is the disciple chosen to lead the Panth at the death of its first Master.

Two anecdotes from the *janam sākhīs* will serve to illustrate this aspect of Gurū Aṅgad's character. Aṅgad once visited Gurū Nānak out in the fields and was there commanded to carry a bundle of wet paddy back to the house. Notwithstanding the fact that he was wearing new clothes, Aṅgad unhesitatingly seized the sodden bundle and placed it on his head. By the time he reached the house, slime oozing from the paddy had ruined his clothing. When Gurū Nānak's wife protested at such apparently thoughtless treatment, he replied that far from being drenched with mud he had in fact been baptized with saffron. The slime was, in other words, the insignia of his unquestioning obedience and so of his fitness for the succession. The second anecdote recounts the incident which is said to have clinched the succession issue. In order to test the loyalty of his followers, Gurū Nānak once escorted them to a jungle where he made silver and gold coins appear before them. Many of his Sikhs immediately disqualified themselves by seizing all they could grasp. Further on most of those who remained eliminated themselves by picking up jewels which had similarly appeared on the ground before them. Only two Sikhs now remained, one of them being Aṅgad. Gurū Nānak led them to a funeral pyre and commanded them both to eat the corpse which lay on it concealed beneath a shroud. The second Sikh fled but Aṅgad, obedient to the end, lifted the shroud to do his master's bidding. Under it he discovered no corpse but Gurū Nānak himself. The test had been miraculously contrived and Aṅgad alone had passed it. Needless to say the truth of this anecdote lies not in the series of miracles which it related but in the supreme loyalty and obedience which it so vividly depicts.

Bypassing his own sons, Gurū Nānak nominated Aṅgad his successor on Hāṛ *vadī* 13, 1596 Bk/13 June 1539.

The installation on *gurgaddī* took place a few days before the death of Gurū Nānak on Assū *vadī* 10, 1596 Bk/7 September 1539. Gurū Nānak had made Aṅgad more than his successor. He had made him equal with himself. He transferred his own light to him. Aṅgad became Nānak, Nānak II.

Gurū Aṅgad now shifted to Khaḍūr from where he continued his work. Like his predecessor, he taught people the virtues of piety and dedicated service. The musician Balvaṇḍ, who composed in praise of the Gurū a portion of the panegyric popularly known as *Ṭikke dī Vār*, declares that Gurū Aṅgad was celebrated for his practice of meditation, austerities and abstinence (*japu tapu sañjamu*). Other anecdotes are on record testifying to these qualities, as also those of humility, wisdom and generosity. His regular daily programme consisted of the following activities. During the last watch of the night, he would rise, bathe and then meditate until daybreak. Then the musicians sang Gurū Nānak's *Āsā kī Vār*. Gurū Aṅgad was always present. Afterwards, he attended to sick persons. Such persons, particularly lepers, came from all parts to be healed by the Gurū. Later he preached and expounded Gurū Nānak's hymns. At mealtime, all sat together without distinctions of caste or creed to eat from the community kitchen. The Gurū's wife looked after the *laṅgar*. The Gurū and his family ate a simple meal which he earned by twisting *muñj*, reed fibre, into string. The afternoon was for children's instruction. Gurū Aṅgad himself taught them Gurmukhī letters. In the evening there would be more *kīrtan* followed by instruction from the Gurū. Khaḍūr became the centre of the Sikh faith as Kartārpur had been in Gurū Nānak's time. Sikhs came from far and near to seek instruction and renew their faith. According to Sikh tradition, Emperor Humāyūṅ came to Khaḍūr and sought Gurū Aṅgad's blessing.

Two varieties of memorials bear visible witness to the life and teachings of Gurū Aṅgad. The first consists of *gurdwārās* commemorating particular episodes in his life and these are almost all clustered in or near Khaḍūr. The main one, now named Darbār Sāhib, stands within the town at the place occupied by Gurū Aṅgad's residence and *darbār*. On the northern outskirts of the town is Mall Akhāṛā, marking the spot where the Gurū used to give instruction in wrestling. Further out in the same direction, Tapiāṇā Sāhib designates the place where the Gurū is said to have performed austerities (*tap*). This *gurdwārā* stands besides a tank, opposite the *samādh* of Bhāī Bālā. A short distance to the southwest of Khaḍūr, in the village of Khān Rajādā, stands a *gurdwārā* commemorating a specific episode in the life of Gurū Aṅgad. According to tradition, there once arrived in Khaḍūr a yogī who managed to persuade the local cultivators that a current drought would remain unbroken until they had evicted Gurū Aṅgad. The Gurū agreed to go and, leaving Khaḍūr, he moved to a *theh* (site of a ruined village), known at the time as Khān Rajādā. The drought persisted, however, and did so until (Gurū) Amar Dās intervened. Following his instructions, the cultivators tied a rope to the yogī's feet and pulled him round the village. Wherever they dragged him, rain fell in torrents. The humiliated charlatan was then permitted to depart and Gurū Aṅgad returned to his rightful place. There is another *gurdwārā* associated with Gurū Aṅgad in village Bharovāl, southwest of Khaḍūr, between Khān Rajādā and Khaḍūr Sāhib. In addition to these five commemorative *gurdwārās* in the Khaḍūr area there is one in Sarāi Nāṅgā, the village formerly known as *Matte dī Sarāi*, the birthplace of Gurū Aṅgad.

The second kind of memorial is provided by the small collection of compositions by Gurū Aṅgad preserved in the Gurū Granth Sāhib. Amongst the Gurū Granth Sāhib collections of works by the first five Gurūs, this is the smallest, comprising sixty-three *ślokas* scattered through *vārs* which are primarily the work of the first, third and fourth Gurūs. Fifteen of his *ślokas* have been incorporated in *Vār Āsā*, twelve in *Vār Mājh*, eleven in *Vār Sūhī*, nine in *Vār Sāraṅg*, and the remaining sixteen in the *vārs* of Sirī Rāga (2), Soraṭh (1), Rāmkalī (7), Mārū (1) and Malār (5).

Gurū Aṅgad was an inspired poet. The *ślokas*, in chaste Punjabi, faithfully reflect the teachings embodied in the works of Gurū Nānak. In them we find the same stress upon the perils of worldly concerns and self-centred attitudes, and the same insistence that regular meditation on the divine Name (*nām*) provides the only sufficient means of escape. Man is the creature of his self-centred *haumai*. God, however, is gracious and proffers in the Divine Name a means of liberation accessible to all who pursue a life of disciplined meditation and virtuous living. Early morning is the time for meditation and virtue is the necessary supplement during the remainder of the day. Two doctrines receive particular emphasis in these *ślokas*. One is the total authority of God. This imposes upon all who seek liberation an inescapable obligation to know and observe the Divine Will (*hukam*). The second prominent doctrine concerns the means of recognizing the Divine Will. It is, Gurū Aṅgad insists, by the grace of Gurū that man may know the way of liberation. Only those who turn to the Gurū may have both, the hope and the assurance of finding it. The style in which this message finds expression is simple, direct, and effective. Pungency is the quality which distinguishes the *ślokas* of Gurū Aṅgad, an unadorned vigour which communicates his message in terms easily understood by any member of his following. Using the same simple style, the Gurū gives pithy expression to refined doctrine as well as to homely wisdom.

Gurū Aṅgad passed away at Khaḍūr on Chet *sudī* 4, 1609 Bk/29 March 1552, passing on succession to Gurū Amar Dās who became Nanak III.

BIBLIOGRAPHY

1. Bhallā, Sarūp Dās, *Mahimā Prakāsh*. Patiala, 1971
2. Vīr Siṅgh, Bhāī ed., *Purātan Janam Sākhī*. Amritsar, 1982

3. Piār Siṅgh, ed., *Ādi Sākhīāṅ*. Ludhiana, 1989
4. Santokh Siṅgh, Bhāī, *Srī Gur Pratāp Sūraj Granth*. Amritsar, 1926-37
5. Satibīr Siṅgh, *Kudaratī Nūr*. Jalandhar, 1981
6. Macauliffe, Max Arthur, *The Sikh Religion*. Oxford, 1909

W.H.M.

ANGLO-SIKH RELATIONS need to be traced to the transformation of the British East India Company, a commercial organization, into a political power in India . Victory at Plassey (23 June 1757) brought Bengal under the *de facto* control of the British, and that at Buxar (22 October 1764) made Oudh a British protectorate. By August 1765, the grant of the *dīwānī* rights to the Company by the Mug̱hal Emperor Shāh 'Ālam made them the virtual rulers of Bengal, Bihār and Oṛissā. Robert Clive (1725-74), the victor of Plassey and governor of Bengal during 1765-67, watched with interest the repeated invasions of India by Ahmad Shāh Durrānī and rejoiced at his final repulse at the hands of the Sikhs in 1766-67. Expressing his happiness over Ahmad Shāh's failure to advance towards the Indian heartland, he wrote to Nawāb Wazīr of Oudh on 19 February 1767, "... extremely glad to know that the Shāh's progress has been impeded by the Sikhs... As long as he does not defeat the Sikhs or come to terms with them, he cannot penetrate into India. And neither of these events seems probable since the Sikhs have adopted such effective tactics, and since they hate the Shah on account of his destruction of the Chak [Gurū Chakk, i.e. Amritsar]." At the same time, in another despatch to Shāh Walī K̲hān, Ahmad Shāh's prime minister, Clive offered congratulations on the Shāh's victory over the Sikhs for whom he uses such epithets as "perfidious" and "tyrannous."

Since the fall of Sirhind to them in January 1764, the Sikhs had extended their area of operations to Gaṅgā-Yamunā Doāb and Ruhīlkhaṇḍ bordering on the territories of the Nawāb of Oudh. Jhaṇḍā Siṅgh Bhaṅgī (d. 1775), a powerful Sikh *sardār*, in a letter dated 19 August 1771 addressed to General Robert Barker (1729-89) sought friendly relations with the British. Warren Hastings (1732-1818), governor of Bengal since 1772 and made governor-general in 1773, was however deeply perturbed at the increasing power of the Sikhs. He wanted to know all about them. At his request Major Antoine Louis Henri Polier (1741-95), a Swiss Engineer in the company's military service but then employed by Emperor Shāh 'Ālam II, submitted to him, in 1776, a detailed account of the Sikhs. This paper was never published, but it was quoted by George Forster (d. 1792), a civil servant of the company who under Warren Hastings' order journeyed through the Punjab, Kashmīr and Afghanistan disguised as a Turkish traveller and wrote *A Journey from Bengal to England*, published in 1798. Two articles on Sikh history by Polier also appeared in the *Asiatic Annual Register* for 1800 and 1802.

Meanwhile, the Sikhs audaciously continued their raids into the Doāb and Ruhīlkhaṇḍ. The latter territory had been conquered by the Nawāb of Oudh with British help in 1774, and thus formed part of the British protectorate. In December 1778, the entry of the Sikhs into Ruhīlkhaṇḍ was resisted by British troops who, by their superior discipline and training as well as by their artillery, were able to force the Sikhs to retire. In January 1783, Sardār Beghel Siṅgh (d. 1802), at the head of a large force, approached Anūpshahr on the western bank of the Gaṅgā and was contemplating to cross the river into Ruhīlkhaṇḍ when the force of the Nawāb of Oudh appeared on the opposite bank. Some British battalions also arrived on the scene. The Sikhs retreated, changed direction and plundered, during Feburary 1783, the southern districts of the Doāb up to Shikohābād and Farruk̲hābād, pillaging Āgrā on their way back. In the following month they raided the northern parts of Delhi itself. Warren Hastings directed Major James Browne, the British Agent at the Mughal court, to organize a confederacy against the Sikhs consisting of the Emperor Shāh 'Ālam, the Marāṭhās, the Ruhīlās and the Nawāb of Oudh, and also to collect more information about the Sikhs. Browne's attempt to form a confederacy failed but he did get in touch with several Sikh *sardārs* including Baghel Siṅgh's *vakīl*, Lakhpat Rāi, and compiled an account under the title *History of the Origin and Progress of the Sicks* [sic] for the information of the governor-general. It was later published, in 1788, in the *Indian Tracts* series.

In response to Browne's overtures leading Sikh *sardārs* expressed their willingness to form a friendly alliance with the British, but the latter were too apprehensive of their power. In January 1784, a body of 30,000 Sikh horse and foot crossed the Yamunā. The British government was alarmed and strengthened their garrisons at Bareilly and Fatehgaṛh. James Browne informed Warren Hastings about the threatening attitude of the Sikhs, but said that Karam Siṅgh, the leader of the expedition, had, out of regard for British friendship, persuaded the other Sikh *sardārs* not to cross the Gaṅgā into the territories of the Nawāb of Oudh, an ally of the English. Warren Hastings prepared, in December 1784, his own plan to checkmate the Sikh influence at Delhi. According to it Jahāṅdār Shāh, the rebel son of the Emperor Shāh 'Ālam, was to be instigated to organize opposition to the Sikhs at the imperial court while the Emperor was to receive military help from the British and the Nawāb of Oudh. This plan, however, also failed partly because Mahādjī Scindīā, the Marāṭhā chief, would not allow a passage to British troops to reach Delhi through his trans-Yamunā territory. On 30 March 1785, Ambājī Iṅgle, one of Scindīā's generals, made a provisional treaty of peace and friendship with the Sikhs. But during April 1785, Sikhs' emissaries waited upon British commanders at Farrukhābād and Lucknow offering to form an alliance with them against the Marāṭhās. Nothing came out of either set of parleys.

Warren Hastings left India on 1 February 1785. John Macpherson, the acting governor-general, deputed on 19 June 1786 George Forster, who had already travelled through the Sikh territories, to establish contacts with the Sikhs and collect intelligence about their future designs. The new governor-general, Lord Cornwallis (September 1786 to October 1793), favoured a policy of caution and persuasion in dealing with the Sikhs and instructed the British Resident at Lucknow to please the Sikh *vakīl* or agent posted there. At the same time he cautioned the Nawāb of Oudh to ensure stricter vigilance at Anūpshahr and Dārānagar ferries and assured him of British reinforcements as and when needed.

In December 1790, a Sikh band of 300 men attacked Longcroft, an Englishman in indigo business, at village Jalaulī in 'Alīgaṛh district, but retired as their leader was killed by the villagers. Soon after, Bhaṅgā Siṅgh of Thānesar assuming the leadership advanced on Anūpshahr where he collected *rākhī* and captured, on 3 January 1791, the local British commander, Lieutenant-Colonel Robert Stuart, whom he brought to Thānesar and demanded 2,00,000 rupees as ransom for his release. Many Englishmen offered to collect this amount but Lord Cornwallis did not agree. Ultimately a sum of Rs 60,000 was paid through Begam Samrū and the Colonel was set free on 24 October 1791.

With their conquest of Delhi on 11 September 1803, the British had established their supremacy in the region. Meanwhile, Mahārājā Raṇjīt Siṅgh had emerged as the ruler of the Sikhs, overpowering the *misl* chiefs. The Sikh raids into the Doāb and the region north of Delhi came to an end. The cis-Sutlej Sikh chiefs accepted the suzerainty of the British who now entered into direct relationship with the Sikh monarch, Raṇjīt Siṅgh.

BIBLIOGRAPHY

1. Hasrat, B.J., *Anglo-Sikh Relations*. Hoshiarpur, 1968
2. Bal, S.S., *British Policy Towards the Panjab 1844-49*. Calcutta, 1971
3. Sarkar, Jadunath, *Fall of the Mughal Empire*. Calcutta, 1932
4. Harbans Singh, *The Heritage of the Sikhs*. Delhi, 1983

H.R.G.

ANGLO-SIKH TREATY (1806) followed Jasvant Rāo Holkar's crossing over into the Punjab in 1805 after he was defeated at Fatehgaṛh and Ḍīg in December 1804 by the British. Accompanied by his Ruhīlā ally, Amīr Khān, and a Marāṭhā force estimated at 15,000, Holkar arrived at Paṭiālā, but on hearing the news that the British general, Lake, was in hot pursuit, both the refugees fled northwards, entered the Jalandhar Doāb, and ultimately reached Amritsar. Raṇjīt Siṅgh, then camping near Multān, hastened to Amritsar to meet Holkar. He was hospitable and sympathetic towards the Marāṭhā chief, but was shrewd enough not to espouse a forlorn cause and come into conflict with the British, especially when he was far from securely established on the throne. Through diplomatic negotiation, he brought about reconciliation between Holkar and the British commander-in-chief. A treaty of friendship and amity was entered into by (Sardār) Raṇjīt Siṅgh along with Sardār Fateh Siṅgh Āhlūvālīā of Kapūrthalā with the East India Company on 1 January 1806 whereby it was agreed that, as long as these Sikh chiefs had no friendly connections with enemies of the British or committed no act of hostility, the British armies would never enter into the territories of the said chieftains, nor would the British government form any plan for the seizure or sequestration of their possessions or property.

The Anglo-Sikh treaty of 1806 brought the Sikh chief into direct contact with the British government. Raṇjīt Siṅgh's reluctance to precipitate a clash with the British saved the infant State of Lahore from being overrun by Lake's armies. The Mahārājā not only kept the Punjab from becoming a theatre of war between two foreign armies, but also saved the Marāṭhā chief from utter ruin and had his territories beyond Delhi restored to him.

The text of the treaty:

> Treaty of Friendship and Amity between the Honorable East India Company and the Sirdars Runjeet Sing and Futteh Sing—1806
>
> Sirdar Runjeet Sing and Sirdar Futteh Sing have consented to the following Articles of Agreement concluded by Lieutenant-Colonel John Malcolm, under the special authority of the Right Honorable Lord Lake, himself duly authorized by the Honorable Sir George Hilaro Barlow, Baronet, Governor General, and Sirdar Futteh Sing, as principal on the part of himself and plenipotentiary on the part of Runjeet Sing.
>
> Article 1. Sirdar Runjeet Sing and Sirdar Futteh Sing Aloowalia hereby agree that they will cause Jeswunt Rao Holkar to remove with his army to the distance of 30 coss from Amritsar immediately, and will never hereafter hold any further connection with him, or aid or assist him with troops, or in any other manner whatever, and they further agree that they will not in any way molest such of Jeswunt Rao Holkar's followers or troops as are desirous of returning to their homes in the Deccan, but, on the contrary, will render them

every assistance in their power for carrying such intention into execution.

Article 2. The British Government hereby agrees that in case a pacification should not be effected between that Government and Jeswunt Rao Holkar, the British Army shall move from its present encampment on the banks of the River Beas as soon as Jeswunt Rao Holkar aforesaid shall have marched with his army to the distance of 30 coss from Amritsar; and that in any Treaty which may hereafter be concluded between the British Government and Jeswunt Rao Holkar, it shall be stipulated that, immediately after the conclusion of the said Treaty, Holkar shall evacuate the territories of the Sikhs and march towards his own, and that he shall in no way whatever injure or destroy such parts of the Sikh country as may lie in his route. The British Government further agrees that as long as the said Chieftains Runjeet Sing and Futteh Sing abstain from holding any friendly connection with the enemies of that Government, or from committing any act of hostility on their own parts against the said Government, the British Armies shall never enter the territories of the said Chieftains, nor will the British Government form any plans for the seizure or sequestration of their possessions or property.

Dated 1st January, 1806, corresponding with 10th Shawal, 1220 H.E.

Seal of Runjeet Sing Seal of Futteh Sing

BIBLIOGRAPHY

1. Sūrī, Sohan Lāl, *'Umdāt-ut-Twārīkh*. Lahore, 1885-89
2. Hasrat, B.J., *Anglo-Sikh Relations*. Hoshiarpur, 1968

B.J.H

ANGLO-SIKH TREATY (AMRITSAR, 1809).

Napoleon's victories in Europe had alarmed the British, who, fearing a French attack on the country through Afghanistan, decided to win the Sikhs over to their side and sent a young officer, Charles Theophilus Metcalfe, to Mahārājā Raṇjīt Siṅgh's court with an offer of friendship. Metcalfe met the Mahārājā in his camp at Khem Karan, near Kasūr, on 12 September 1808, taking with him a large number of presents sent by the Governor-General of India. He told him how the English wished to have friendly relations with him and presented to him the draft of a treaty.

Raṇjīt Siṅgh did not credit the theory that the British had made the proposal to him because of the danger from Napoleon. On the other hand, he showed his willingness to co-operate with the British, provided the latter recognized his claim of paramountcy over all the Mājhā and Mālvā Sikhs. He suspected that the real object of the British was to put a seal on his southern boundary and draw a permanent line between his dominions and their own. He rejected Metcalfe's terms and made his own, seeking the British to recognize his authority over the Sikh country to the south of the Sutlej.

Metcalfe expressed his inability to make any changes in the draft of the treaty he had brought, but offered to forward Raṇjīt Siṅgh's proposal to the Governor-General. Raṇjīt Siṅgh suddenly struck camp and crossed the Sutlej. Metcalfe followed him from place to place, without being able to secure another interview with him for any serious discussions. Raṇjīt Siṅgh overran the territory on the left bank of the river, thus shrewdly imposing on his English guest the role of a witness to his cis-Sutlej acquisitions.

Raṇjīt Siṅgh's bold and skilful policy would have borne fruit, had not the situation in Europe changed. As the danger of Napoleon's attack lessened, the British became arrogant in their attitude. On his return to Lahore, Raṇjīt Siṅgh received a message from the Governor-General that the British had taken the Sikh chiefs south of the Sutlej under their protection. The British sent a force under the command of Colonel David Ochterlony who, passing through Būṛīā and Paṭiālā, came very close to the Sutlej and stationed himself at Ludhiāṇā. Raṇjīt Siṅgh also started making warlike preparations. Dīwān Mohkam Chand was asked to proceed with the troops and artillery from Kāngṛā to Phillaur, on the Sutlej. The guns were mounted on the Fort of Gobindgaṛh in Amritsar and powder and supplies laid in. The chiefs and nobles were asked to keep their soldiers in readiness. A large body of troops gathered in Lahore in a few days' time.

Meanwhile, Metcalfe, who had followed Raṇjīt Siṅgh to Lahore, presented a new treaty which was based on terms first offered by the British and the proposal made by Raṇjīt Siṅgh. The treaty in this form was acceptable to the Sikh ruler. Although it stopped him from extending his influence beyond the Sutlej, he was left master of the territories, south of the river, which were in his possession before Metcalfe's visit. The treaty was signed at Amritsar on 25 April 1809. It provided that the British government would count the Lahore Darbār among the most honourable powers and would in no way interfere with the Sikh ruler's dominions to the north of the Sutlej. Both governments pledged friendship to each other. Raṇjīt Siṅgh appointed Ba<u>kh</u>shī Nand Siṅgh Bhaṇḍārī to stay at Ludhiāṇā as his agent with the English. The English sent <u>Kh</u>ushwaqt Rāi to Lahore as their representative at the Sikh court.

Although the treaty of 1809 halted Raṇjīt Siṅgh's ambitions at the Sutlej and prevented the unification of the Mājhā and Mālvā Sikhs into a new commonwealth of the <u>Kh</u>ālsā, it gave the Sikh sovereign one clear advantage. Security on the southern frontier allowed him freely to consolidate his power in the Punjab, evolve a centralized system of government, build up a powerful army, and pursue unhampered his conquests in the north, northwest and southwest.

The text of the treaty:

Treaty with the Rajah of Lahore—1809

Whereas certain differences which had arisen between the British Government and the Rajah of Lahore have been happily and amicably adjusted, and both parties being anxious to maintain the relations of perfect amity and concord, the following Articles of treaty, which shall be binding on the heirs and successors of the two parties, have been concluded by Rajah Runjeet Sing on his own part, and by the agency of Charles Theophilus Metcalfe, Esquire, on the part of the British Government.

Article 1. Perpetual friendship shall subsist between the British Government and the State of Lahore. The latter shall be considered, with respect to the former, to be on the footing of the most favoured powers; and the British Government will have no concern with the territories and subjects of the Rajah to the northward of the Sutlej.

Article 2. The Rajah will never maintain in the territory occupied by him and his dependants, on the left bank of the River Sutlej, more troops than are necessary for the internal duties of that territory, nor commit or suffer any encroachments on the possessions or rights of the Chiefs in its vicinity.

Article 3. In the event of a violation of any of the preceding Articles, or of a departure from the rules of friendship on the part of either State, this Treaty shall be considered to be null and void.

Article 4. This Treaty, consisting of four Articles, having been settled and concluded at Amritsar, on the 25th day of April, 1809, Mr. Charles Theophilus Metcalfe has delivered to the Rajah of Lahore a copy of the same, in English and Persian, under his seal and signature, and the said Rajah has delivered another copy of the same, under his seal and signature; and Mr. Charles Theophilus Metcalfe engages to procure, within the space of two months, a copy of the same duly ratified by the Right Honourable the Governor-General in Council, on the receipt of which by the Rajah, the present Treaty shall be deemed complete and binding on both parties, and the copy of it now delivered to the Rajah shall be returned.

Seal and signature of	Signature and seal of
C.T. METCALFE	RAJAH RUNJEET SING

Company's Seal
MINTO (Sd)

Ratified by the Governor-General in Council on 30th May, 1809.

BIBLIOGRAPHY

1. Sūrī, Sohan Lāl, *'Umdāt-ut-Twārīkh*. Lahore, 1885-89
2. Harbans Singh, *Maharaja Ranjit Singh*. Delhi, 1980
3. Cunningham, Joseph Davey, *A History of the Sikhs*. London, 1849
4. Hasrat, B.J., *Anglo-Sikh Relations*. Hoshiarpur, 1968

B.J.H.

ANGLO-SIKH TREATY (1840). In 1832, a treaty was executed by Lord William Bentinck, the Governor-General of India, through Col. C.M. Wade, with the Lahore Darbār concerning navigation through the Sutlej and the Indus rivers within the Khālsā territory. Another treaty on the subject was subsequently executed in 1834, fixing a duty on every mercantile boat, independent of its freight and of the nature of its merchandise. A third treaty was executed on this subject on the arrival of George Russell Clerk, agent to the Governor-General, at the Sikh Darbār, in May 1839, adjusting the rate of duties on merchandise, according to quantity and kind. The treaty between the Sikh and British governments, signed in the time of Mahārājā Kharak Singh on 27 June 1840, provided for duties, on a fixed scale, proportionate to the measurements of boats, and not on the variety of commodities. The treaty provides a schedule of rates of duties on the mercantile boats, viz. on boats not exceeding 250 maunds of freight, 50 rupees; on boats exceeding 250 maunds but not exceeding 500 maunds, 100 rupees; and on all boats above 500 maunds, 150 rupees. Grain, wood and limestone were declared to be free of duty while duty was payable on every other commodity according to the measurement of the boat.

The text of the treaty:

Treaty with Maha Rajah Khurruk Singh—1840

(Signed by Maha Rajah Khurruk Singh)
Seal of
Maha Rajah Khurruk Singh

Formerly a Treaty was executed by the Right Honorable Lord William Cavendish Bentinck, the Governor-General of India, on the 14th of Poos, Sumbut 1889 (corresponding with AD 1832), through Colonel (then Captain) Wade, concerning the navigation of the Sutlej and the Scinde rivers in the Khalsa territory, in concurrence with the wishes of both the friendly and allied Governments. Another Treaty on the subject was subsequently executed through the same officer, in Sumbut 1891 (corresponding with AD 1834), fixing a duty on every mercantile boat, independent of the quantity of its freight, and the nature of its merchandize. A third Treaty was executed on this subject, in accordance with the wishes of both Governments, on the arrival of Mr. Clerk, Agent to the Governor-General, at the Durbar, in May 1839, adjusting the rate of duties on merchandize, according to quantity and kind, and although at the end of that document so much was specified as that the two high powers should after this never propose a rate below (less than) that specified, yet, notwithstanding after this, when that gentleman came to the Khalsa Durbar at Amritsur, in Jeth, Sumbut 1897 (corresponding with May 1840), he explained the difficulties and inconvenience which seemed to result to trade under the system proposed last year, in consequence of the obstruction to boats for the purpose of search and the ignorance of traders, and the difficulty of adjusting duties according to the different kinds of articles freighted in the boats, and proposed to revise that system by fixing a scale of duties proportionate to the measurement of boats, and not on the kind of commodities, if this arrangement should be approved of by both Governments. Having reported to his Government the circumstances of the case, he now drew up a Schedule of the rate of duties on the mercantile boats navigating the Rivers Scinde and Sutlej and forwarded it for the consideration of this friendly Durbar. The Khalsa Government, therefore, with due regard to the established alliance, having added a few sentences in accordance with the late Treaties, and agreeably to what is already well understood, has signed and sealed the Schedule, and it shall never be at all liable to any contradiction, difference, change or alteration, without the concurrence and concert of both Governments, in consideration of mutual advantages, upon condition it does not interfere with the established custom duties at Amritsur, Lahore, and other inland places, or the other rivers in the Khalsa territory.

Article1. Grain, wood and limestone will be free from duty.

Article 2. With exception to the above, every commodity to pay duty according to the measurement of the boat.

Article 3. Duty on a boat not exceeding two hundred and fifty maunds of freight, proceeding from the foot of the hills, Roopur or Loodiana, to Mithenkote or Rojan, or from Rojan or Mithenkote to the foot of the hills, Roopur or Loodiana will be Rs. 50

viz.,

From the foot of the hills to Ferozepore, or back	Rs. 20
From Ferozepore to Bhawulpore, or back	Rs.15
From Bhawulpore to Mithenkote or Rojan, or back	Rs.15
The whole trip, or down	Rs. 50

Duty on a boat above two hundred and fifty maunds, but not exceeding five hundred maunds, from the foot of the hills, Roopur or Loodiana, to Mithenkote or Rojan, or from Rojan or Mithenkote to the foot of the hills, Roopur or Loodiana will be Rs.100

viz.,

From the foot of the hills to Ferozepore, or back	Rs. 40

From Ferozepore to Bhawulpore, or back	Rs. 30
From Bhawulpore to Mithenkote or Rojan, or back	Rs. 30
The whole trip, up or down	Rs. 100
Duty on all boats above five hundred maunds will be	Rs. 150

viz.,

From the foot of the hills to Ferozepore, or back	Rs. 60
From Ferozepore to Bhawulpore, or back	Rs. 45
From Bhawulpore to Mithenkote or Rojan or back	Rs. 45
The whole trip, up or down	Rs. 150

Article 4. Boats to be classed 1,2,or 3, and the same to be written on the boat, and every boat to be registered.

Article 5. These duties on merchandize frequenting the Sutlej and Scinde, are not to interfere with the duties on the banks of other rivers, or with the established inland custom houses, throughout the Khalsa Territory, which will remain on their usual footing.

Dated 13th Assar, Sumbut 1897, corresponding with 27 June 1840

(True translation)

(Sd.) G. CLERK,

Agent to the Governor-General

Approved by the Governor-General, 10th August 1840

BIBLIOGRAPHY

1. Cunningham, Joseph Davey, *A History of the Sikhs*. London, 1849
2. Hasrat, B.J., *Anglo-Sikh Relations*. Hoshiarpur, 1968
3. Sūrī, Sohan Lāl, *'Umdāt-ut-Twārīkh*. Lahore, 1885-89

B.J.H.

ANGLO-SIKH TREATIES (LAHORE, 9 and 11 March 1846). After the end of the first Anglo-Sikh war, the British governor-general, Lord Hardinge, entered the Sikh capital on 20 February 1846, and on 9 March imposed upon the young Mahārājā Duleep Siṅgh, then aged seven and a half years, a treaty of peace. The preamble to the treaty accused the Lahore government and the Sikh army of having violated the terms of the treaty of 1809 by unprovoked aggression on British provinces. The territories of Mahārājā Duleep Siṅgh, situated on the left bank of the Sutlej, were confiscated and annexed. According to the terms of the treaty, the Mahārājā renounced for himself and his heirs all claims in connection with these territories. He ceded to the East India Company in perpetual sovereignty, "all his forts, territories and rights" in the Jalandhar Doāb — the territory both hilly and plain lying between the Sutlej and the Beās – and agreed to the payment of one and a half crores of rupees as indemnity for the expenses of the war. As the Lahore government was unable to pay this amount, additional hilly territory situated between the Beās and the Indus, including the provinces of Kashmīr and Hazārā, was taken over by the British. The Sikh army which the British dubbed in the treaty as "mutinous troops of the Lahore Army," was disbanded, and the strength of the new one to be organized was restricted to 25 battalions of infantry (20,000 men), and 12,000 cavalry. Under certain specific conditions, British troops were to have free passage through Lahore territories. All guns used in the war were to be surrendered to the British. Mahārājā Duleep Siṅgh also agreed never to take or retain in his service any British subject nor any European or American national without the consent of the British. The Lahore government were to recognize the independent sovereignty of Rājā Gulāb Siṅgh in his possessions, and in those which would be made over to him by the British government.

Additional articles supplementary to the treaty, added two days later (11 March 1846), provided (a) that at the solicitation of the

Darbār, a British force would remain in occupation of Lahore, in the fort as well as in the city, till the end of the year 1846, to protect the Mahārājā during the reorganization of the army, (b) that the British government shall respect the bona fide rights of *jāgīrdārs* in the Lahore territories, and (c) that the British government shall be at liberty to retain any part of the State property in the forts in the ceded territories, paying adequate compensation.

Texts of the treaties:

Treaty between the British Government and the State of Lahore—1846

Whereas the treaty of amity and concord, which was concluded between the British Government and the late Maharajah Runjeet Sing, the Ruler of Lahore, in 1809, was broken by the unprovoked aggression, on the British Provinces, of the Sikh Army, in December last; and whereas, on that occasion, by the Proclamation, dated 13th December, the territories then in the occupation of the Maharajah of Lahore, on the left or British bank of the River Sutlej, were confiscated and annexed to the British Provinces; and since that time hostile operations have been prosecuted by the two Governments; the one against the other, which have resulted in the occupation of Lahore by the British troops; and whereas it has been determined that, upon certain conditions, peace shall be re-established between the two Governments, the following treaty of peace between the Honorable English East India Company and Maharajah Dhuleep Sing Bahadoor, and his children, heirs and successors, has been concluded on the part of the Honorable Company by Frederick Currie, Esquire, and Brevet-Major Henry Montgomery Lawrence, by virtue of full powers to that effect vested in them by the Right Hon'ble Sir Henry Hardinge, G.C.B., one of her Britannic Majesty's Most Hon'ble Privy Council, Governor-General, appointed by the Hon'ble Company to direct and control all their affairs in the East Indies, and on the part of His Highness Maharajah Dhuleep Sing by Bhaee Ram Sing, Rajah Lal Sing, Sirdar Tej Sing, Sirdar Chuttur Sing Attareewalla, Sirdar Runjore Sing Majeethia, Dewan Deena Nath and Fakeer Nooroodden, vested with full powers and authority on the part of His Highness.

Article 1. There shall be prepetual peace and friendship between the British Government on the one part, and Maharajah Dhuleep Sing, his heirs and successors on the other.

Article 2. The Maharajah of Lahore renounces for himself, his heirs and successors, all claim to, or connection with the territories lying to the south of the River Sutlej, and engages never to have any concern with those territories or the inhabitants thereof.

Article 3. The Maharajah cedes to the Hon'ble Company, in prepetual sovereignty, all his forts, territories and rights in the Doab or country, hill and plain, situated between the Rivers Beas and Sutlej.

Article 4. The British Government having demanded from the Lahore State, as indemnification for the expenses of the war, in addition to the cession of territory described in Article 3, payment of one and half crore of Rupees, and the Lahore Government being unable to pay the whole of this sum at this time, or to give security satisfactory to the British Government for its eventual payment, the Maharajah cedes to the Honorable Company, in prepetual sovereignty, as equivalent for one crore of Rupees, all his forts, territories, rights and interests in the hill countries, which are situated between the Rivers Beas and Indus, including the Provinces of Cashmere and Hazarah.

Article 5. The Maharajah will pay to the British Government the sum of 60 lakhs of Rupees on or before the ratification of this Treaty.

Article 6. The Maharajah engages to disband the mutinous troops of the Lahore Army, taking from them their arms—and His Highness agrees to reorganize the Regular or Aeen Regiments of Infantry, upon the system, and according to the Regulations as to pay and allowances, observed in the time of the late Maharajah Runjeet Sing. The Maharajah further engages to pay up all arrears to the soldiers that are discharged, under the provisions of this Article.

Article 7. The Regular Army of the Lahore State shall henceforth be limited to 25 Battalions of Infantry, consisting of 800 bayonets each with twelve thousand Cavalry—this number at no time to be exceeded without the concurrence of the British Government. Should it be necessary at any time—for any special cause—that this force should be increased, the cause shall be fully explained to the British Government, and when the special necessity shall have passed, the regular troops shall be again reduced to the standard specified in the former Clause of this Article.

Article 8. The Maharajah will surrender to the British Government all the guns—thirty-six in number—which have been pointed against the British troops—and which, having been placed on the right Bank of the River Sutlej, were not captured at the battle of Subraon.

Article 9. The control of the Rivers Beas and Sutlej, with the continuations of the latter river, commonly called the Gharrah and the Punjnud, to the confluence of the Indus at Mithunkote—and the control of the Indus from Mithunkote to the borders of Beloochistan, shall, in respect to tolls and ferries, rest with the British Government. The provisions of this Article shall not interfere with the passage of boats belonging to the Lahore Government on the said rivers, for the purpose of traffic or the conveyance of passengers up and down their course. Regarding the ferries between the two countries respectively, at the several ghats of the said rivers, it is agreed that the British Government, after defraying all the expenses of management and establishments, shall account to the Lahore Government for one-half the net profits of the ferry collections. The provisions of this Article have no reference to the ferries on that part of the River Sutlej which forms the boundary of Bhawulpore and Lahore respectively.

Article 10. If the British Government should, at any time, desire to pass troops through the territories of His Highness the Maharajah, for the protection of the British territories, or those of their Allies, the British troops shall, on such special occasion, due notice being given, be allowed to pass through the Lahore territories. In such case the officers of the Lahore State will afford facilities in providing supplies and boats for the passage of rivers, and the British Government will pay the full price of all such provisions and boats, and will make fair compensation for all private property that may be damaged. The British Government will, moreover, observe all due consideration to the religious feelings of the inhabitants of those tracts through which the army may pass.

Article 11. The Maharajah engages never to take or to retain in his service any British subject—nor the subject of any European or American State—without the consent of the British Government.

Article 12. In consideration of the services rendered by Rajah Golab Sing of Jummoo, to the Lahore State, towards procuring the restoration of the relations of amity between the Lahore and British Governments, the Maharajah hereby agrees to recognize the Independent sovereignty of Rajah Golab Sing in such territories and districts in the hills as may be made over to the said Rajah Golab Sing, by separate Agreement between himself and the British Government, with the dependencies thereof, which may have been in the Rajah's possession since the time of the late Maharajah Khurruck Sing, and the British Government, in consideration of the good conduct of Rajah Golab Sing, also agrees to recognize his independence in such territories, and to admit him to the privileges of a separate Treaty with the British Government.

Article 13. In the event of any dispute or difference arising between the Lahore State and Rajah Golab Sing, the same shall be referred to the arbitration of the British Government, and by its decision the Maharajah engages to abide.

Article 14. The limits of the Lahore territories shall not be, at any time, changed without the concurrence of the British Government.

Article 15. The British Government will not exercise any interference in the internal administration of the Lahore State—but in all cases or questions which may be referred to the British Government, the Governor-General will give the aid of his advice and good offices for the furtherance of the interests of the Lahore Government.

Article 16. The subjects of either State shall, on visiting the territories of the other, be on the footing of the subjects of the most favoured nation.

This Treaty consisting of sixteen articles, has been this day settled by Frederick Currie, Esquire, and Brevet-Major Henry Montgomery Lawrence acting under the directions of the Right Hon'ble Sir Henry Hardinge, G.C.B., Governor-General, on the part of the British Government, and by Bhaee Ram Sing, Rajah Lal Sing, Sirdar Tej Sing, Sirdar Chuttur Sing Attareewalla, Sirdar Runjore Sing Majeethia, Dewan Deena Nath, and Faqueer Nooroodeen, on the part of the Maharajah Dhuleep Sing, and the said Treaty has been this day ratified by the seal of the Right Hon'ble Sir Henry Hardinge, G.C.B., Governor-General, and by that of His Highness Maharajah Dhuleep Sing.

Done at Lahore, this ninth day of March, in year of Our Lord one thousand eight hundred and forty-six, corresponding with the tenth day of

Rubbee-ool-awul, 1262 Hijree, and ratified on the same date.

(Sd.) H. Hardinge (L.S.)

(Sd.) Maharajah Dhuleep Sing (L.S.)
.. Bhaee Ram Sing (L.S.)
.. Rajah Lal Sing (L.S.)
.. Sirdar Tej Sing (L.S.)
.. Sirdar Chuttur Sing Attareewalla (L.S.)
.. Sirdar Runjore Sing Majeethia (L.S.)
.. Dewan Deena Nath (L.S.)
.. Faqueer Nooroodeen (L.S.)

ARTICLES OF AGREEMENT concluded between the BRITISH GOVERNMENT and the LAHORE DURBĀR on 11 March 1846

Whereas the Lahore Government has solicited the Governor-General to leave a British Force at Lahore, for the protection of the Maharajah's person and of the Capital, till the reorganization of the Lahore army, according to the provisions of Article 6 of the Treaty of Lahore, dated the 9th instant; and whereas the Governor-General has, on certain conditions, consented to the measure; and whereas it is expedient that certain matters concerning the territories ceded by Articles 3 and 4 of the aforesaid Treaty should be specifically determined, the following eight Articles of Agreement have this day been concluded between the aforementioned contracting parties.

Article 1. The British Government shall leave at Lahore, till the close of the current year, AD 1846, such force as shall seem to the Governor-General adequate for the purpose of protecting the person of the Maharajah and the inhabitants of the City of Lahore, during the reorganization of the Sikh Army, in accordance with the provisions of Article 6 of the Treaty of Lahore. That force to be withdrawn at any convenient time before the expiration of the year, if the object to be fulfilled shall, in the opinion of the Durbar, have been attained—but the force shall not be detained at Lahore beyond the expiration of the current year.

Article 2. The Lahore Government agrees that the force left at Lahore for the purpose specified in the foregoing Article shall be placed in full possession of the Fort and the City of Lahore, and that the Lahore troops shall be removed from within the City. The Lahore Government engages to furnish convenient quarters for the officers and men of the said force, and to pay to the British Government all the extra expenses in regard to the said force, which may be incurred by the British Government, in consequence of the troops being employed away from their own Cantonments and in a Foreign Territory.

Article 3. The Lahore Government engages to apply itself immediately and earnestly to the reorganization of its army according to the prescribed conditions, and to communicate fully with the British authorities left at Lahore, as to the progress of such reorganization, and as to the location of the troops.

Article 4. If the Lahore Government fails in the performance of the conditions of the foregoing Article, the British Government shall be at liberty to withdraw the force from Lahore at any time before the expiration of the period specified in Article 1.

Article 5. The British Government agrees to respect the *bona fide* rights of those jaghiredars, within the territories ceded by Articles 3 and 4 of the Treaty of Lahore, dated 9th instant, who were attached to the families of the late Maharajahs Runjeet Sing, Kurruk Sing and Shere Sing; and the British Government will maintain those jaghiredars in their *bona fide* possessions during their lives.

Article 6. The Lahore Government shall receive the assistance of the British Local Authorities in recovering the arrears of revenue justly due to the Lahore Government from the *kardars* and managers in the territories ceded by the provisions of Articles 3 and 4 of the Treaty of Lahore, to the close of the *khureef* harvest of the current year, *viz.* 1902 of the Sumbut Bikramajeet.

Article 7. The Lahore Government shall be at liberty to remove from the forts, in the territories specified in the foregoing Article, all treasure and State property, with the exception of guns. Should, however, the British Government desire to retain any part of the said property, they shall be at liberty to do so, paying for the same at a fair valuation, and the British officers shall give their assistance to the Lahore Government in disposing on the spot of such part of the aforesaid property as the Lahore Government may not wish to remove, and the British Officers may not desire to retain.

Article 8. Commissioners shall be immediately appointed by the two Governments to settle and lay down the boundary between the two States, as defined by Article 4 of the Treaty of Lahore, dated March 9th, 1846.

(Sd.) H. HARDINGE (L.S.)

(Sd.) Maharajah Dhuleep Sing (L.S.)
.. Bhaee Ram Sing (L.S.)
.. Rajah Lal Sing (L.S.)
.. Sirdar Tej Sing (L.S.)
.. Sirdar Chuttur Sing Attareewalla (L.S.)
.. Sirdar Runjore Sing Majeethia (L.S.)
.. Dewan Deena Nath (L.S.)
.. Faqueer Nooroddeen (L.S.)

BIBLIOGRAPHY

1. Sūrī, Sohan Lāl, *'Umdāt-ut-Twārīkh*. Lahore, 1885-89
2. Cunningham, Joseph Davey, *A History of the Sikhs*. London, 1849
3. Ganda Singh, *The British Occupation of the Panjab*. Amritsar, 1955
4. Hasrat, B. J., *Anglo-Sikh Relations*. Hoshiarpur, 1968
5. Harbans Singh, *The Heritage of the Sikhs*. Delhi, 1983

B.J.H.

ANGLO-SIKH TREATY (BHYROWĀL/ BHAROVĀL, December 1846), signed on 16 December 1846 between the East India Company and the minor Mahārājā Duleep Siṅgh, provided for a British-controlled regency till the Mahārājā came of age. Mahārāṇī Jind Kaur, who was acting as regent of her son, Duleep Siṅgh, had believed that, as stipulated in the treaty of Lahore (11 March 1846), the British force would leave Lahore. But she was soon disillusioned as the British, instead of quitting, started strengthening their authority over Lahore administration. Governor-General Henry Hardinge sent to Lahore his secretary, Frederick Currie, who isolating Mahārāṇī Jind Kaur, manipulated the leading *sardārs* and chiefs into requesting the British for a fresh treaty. This led to the signing of the Treaty of Bhyrowāl. By this agreement every article of the treaty of 9 March 1846 was reaffirmed except article 15, which precluded British interference in the internal administration of the State of Lahore. The regent (Mahārāṇī Jind Kaur) was pensioned off; a

British resident was to direct and control the administration of the State of Lahore with a new council of regency of eight members. A British force was to remain at Lahore for the protection of the Mahārājā and the cost for its maintenance (22 lakh rupees) was to be borne by the State of Lahore. The Governor-General could also disband and recruit Sikh armies and occupy any fort in the Punjab. The council of ministers was to hold office during the pleasure of the British resident. The treaty of Bhyrowāl effective during the minority of Mahārājā Duleep Siṅgh, was to terminate on 4 September 1854 when the Mahārājā would attain the age of sixteen.

The treaty of Bhyrowāl transformed the Sikh kingdom into a virtual British protectorate. The Darbār became a willing instrument subservient to the authority of the British resident, who was to superintend the internal and external affairs of the State in accordance with the instructions of the Government of India. This is how the new arrangement was described by John Marshman: "An officer of the company's artillery became, in effect, the successor of Ranjit Siṅgh."

The text of the treaty:

ARTICLES OF AGREEMENT concluded between the BRITISH GOVERNMENT and the LAHORE DURBĀR on 16 December 1846

Whereas the Lahore Durbar and the principal Chiefs and Sirdars of the State have in express terms communicated to the British Government their anxious desire that the Governor-General should give his aid and assistance to maintain the administration of the Lahore State during the minority of Maharajah Dulleep Sing, and have declared this measure to be indispensable for the maintenance of the Government; and whereas the Governor-General has, under certain conditions, consented to give the aid and assistance solicited, the following Articles of Agreement, in modification of the Articles of Agreement executed at Lahore on the 11th March last, have been concluded on the part of the British Government by Frederick Currie, Esquire, Secretary to Government of India, and Lieutenant-Colonel Henry Montgomery Lawrence, C.B., Agent to the Governor-General, North-West Frontier, by virtue of full powers to that effect vested in them by the Right Honorable Viscount Hardinge, G.C.B., Governor-General, and on the part of His Highness Maharajah Dulleep Sing, by Sirdar Tej Sing, Sirdar Shere Sing, Dewan Deena Nath, Fukeer Nooroodeen, Rai Kishen Chund, Sirdar Runjore Sing Majethea, Sirdar Utter Sing Kaleewalla, Bhaee Nidhan Sing, Sirdar Khan Singh Majethea, Sirdar Shumshere Sing, Sirdar Lall Sing Morarea, Sirdar Kehr Sing Sindhanwalla, Sirdar Urjun Sing Rungurnungalea, acting with the unanimous consent and concurrence of the Chiefs and Sirdars of the State assembled at Lahore.

Article 1. All and every part of the Treaty of peace between the British Government and the State of Lahore, bearing date the 9th day of March, 1846, except in so far as it may be temporarily modified in respect to Clause 15 of the said Treaty by this engagement, shall remain binding upon the two Governments.

Article 2. A British officer, with an efficient establishment of assistants, shall be appointed by the Governor-General to remain at Lahore, which officer shall have full authority to direct and control all matters in every

Department of the State.

Article 3. Every attention shall be paid in conducting the administration to the feelings of the people, to preserving the national institutions and customs, and to maintaining the just rights of all classes.

Article 4. Changes in the mode and details of administration shall not be made, except when found necessary for effecting the objects set forth in the foregoing Clause, and for securing the just dues of the Lahore Government. These details shall be conducted by Native officers as at present, who shall be appointed and superintended by a Council of Regency composed of leading Chiefs and Sirdars acting under the control and guidance of the British Resident.

Article 5. The following persons shall in the first instance constitute the Council of Regency, *viz.*, Sirdar Tej Sing, Sirdar Shere Sing Attareewalla, Dewan Deena Nath, Fukeer Nooroodeen, Sirdar Runjore Sing Majeethea, Bhaee Nidhan Sing, Sirdar Utter Sing Kaleewalla, Sirdar Shumshere Sing Sindhanwalla, and no change shall be made in the persons thus nominated, without the consent of the British Resident, acting under the orders of the Governor-General.

Article 6. The administration of the country shall be conducted by this Council of Regency in such manner as may be determined on by themselves in consultation with the British Resident, who shall have full authority to direct and control the duties of every department.

Article 7. A British Force of such strength and numbers and in such positions as the Governor-General may think fit, shall remain at Lahore for the protection of the Maharajah and the preservation of the peace of the country.

Article 8. The Governor-General shall be at liberty to occupy with British soldiers any fort or military post in the Lahore territories, the occupation of which may be deemed necessary by the British Government, for the security of the capital or for maintaining the peace of the country.

Article 9. The Lahore State shall pay to the British Government twenty-two lakhs of new Nanuck Shahee Rupees of full tale and weight per annum for the maintenance of this force, and to meet the expenses incurred by the British Government. Such sum to be paid by two instalments, or 13,20,000 in May or June, and 8,80,000 in November or December of each year.

Article 10. Inasmuch as it is fitting that Her Highness the Maharanee, the mother of Maharaja Dulleep Sing, should have a proper provision made for the maintenance of herself and dependants, the sum of one lakh and fifty thousand rupees shall be set apart annually for that purpose, and shall be at Her Highness' disposal.

Article 11. The provisions of this Engagement shall have effect during the minority of His Highness Maharajah Dulleep Sing, and shall cease and terminate on His Highness attaining the full age of sixteen years or, on the 4th September of the year 1854, but it shall be competent to the Governor-General to cause the arrangement to cease at any period prior to the coming of age of His Highness, at which the Governor-General and the Lahore Durbar may be satisfied that the interposition of the British Government is no longer necessary for maintaining the Government of His Highness the Maharajah.

This agreement, consisting of eleven articles, was settled and executed at Lahore by the Officers and Chiefs and Sirdars above named, on the 16th day of December, 1846.

(Sd.) F. CURRIE
H.M. LAWRENCE

(Sd.) Sirdar Tej Sing (L.S.)
,, Sirdar Shere Sing (L.S.)
,, Dewan Deena Nath (L.S.)
,, Fukeer Nooroodeen (L.S.)
,, Rai Kishen Chund (L.S.)
,, Sirdar Runjore Sing Majethea (L.S.)
,, Sirdar Utter Sing Kalewalla (L.S.)
,, Bhaee Nidhan Sing (L.S.)
,, Sirdar Khan Sing Majethea (L.S.)
,, Sirdar Shumshere Sing (L.S.)
,, Sirdar Lal Sing Morarea (L.S.)
,, Sirdar Kher Sing Sindhanwalla (L.S.)
,, Sirdar Urjan Sing Rungurnungalea (L.S.)

(Sd.) Hardinge (L.S.)
(Sd.) Dulleep Sing (L.S.)

Ratified by the Right Honorable the Governor-General, at Bhyrowal Ghat on the left bank of the Beas, twenty-sixth day of December, One Thousand Eight Hundred and Forty-Six.

(Sd.) F. CURRIE,
Secretary to the Government of India

BIBLIOGRAPHY

1. Hasrat, B. J., *Anglo-Sikh Relations.* Hoshiarpur, 1968
2. Cunningham, Joseph Davey, *A History of the Sikhs.* London, 1849
3. Ganda Singh, ed., *Private Correspondence Relating to the Anglo-Sikh Wars.* Amritsar, 1955

B.J.H.

ANGLO-SIKH WAR I, 1845-46, resulting in the partial subjugation of the Sikh kingdom, was the outcome of British expansionism and the near-anarchical conditions that overtook the Lahore court after the death of Mahārājā Raṇjīt Siṅgh in June 1839. The English, by then firmly installed in Fīrozpur on the Sikh frontier, about 70 km from Lahore, the Sikh capital, were watching the happenings across the border with more than a neighbour's interest. The disorder that prevailed there promised them a good opportunity for direct intervention.

Up to 1838, the British troops on the Sikh frontier had amounted to one regiment at Sabāthū in the hills and two at Ludhiāṇā, with six pieces of artillery, equalling in all about 2,500 men. The total rose to 8,000 during the time of Lord Auckland (1836-42) who increased the number of troops at Ludhiāṇā and created a new military post at Fīrozpur, which was actually part of Sikh dominions south of the Sutlej. British military preparations for a war with the Sikhs began seriously in 1843 when the new governor-general, Lord Ellenborough (1842-44), discussed with the Home government the possibilities of a military occupation of the Punjab. English and Indian infantry reinforcement began arriving at each of the frontier posts of Fīrozpur and Ludhiāṇā. Cavalry and artillery regiments moved up to Ambālā and Kasaulī. Works were in the process of erection around the magazine at Fīrozpur, and the fort at Ludhiāṇā began to be fortified. Plans for the construction of bridges over the rivers Mārkaṇḍā and Ghaggar were prepared, and a new road link to join Meerut and Ambālā was taken in hand. Exclusive of the newly constructed cantonments of Kasaulī and Shimlā, Ellenborough had been able to collect a force of 11,639 men and 48 guns at Ambālā, Ludhiāṇā and Fīrozpur. "Everywhere," wrote Lord Ellenborough, "we are trying to get things in order and especially to strengthen and equip the artillery with which the fight will be." Seventy boats of thirty-five tons each, with the necessary equipments to bridge the Sutlej at any point, were under construction; fifty-six pontoons were on their way from Bombay for use in Sindh, and two steamers were being constructed to ply on the River Sutlej. "In November 1845," he informed the Duke of Wellington, "the army will be equal to any operation. I should be sorry to have it called to the field sooner."

In July 1844, Lord Ellenborough was replaced by Lord Hardinge (1844-48), a Peninsula veteran, as governor-general of India. Hardinge further accelerated the process of strengthening the Sutlej frontier for a war with the Sikhs. The affable Colonel Richmond was replaced by the abrasive and belligerent Major George Broadfoot as the political agent on the Punjab frontier. Lord Gough, the commander-in-chief, established his headquarters at Ambālā. In October 1844, the British military force on the frontier was 17,000 infantry and 60 guns. Another 10,000 troops were to be ready by the end of November. Fīrozpur's garrison strength under the command of Sir John Littler was raised to 7,000; by January 1845, the total British force amounted to 20,000 men and 60 guns. "We can collect," Hardinge reported to the Home government, "33,000 infantry, 6,000 cavalry and 100 guns in six weeks." In March additional British and Indian regiments were quietly moved to Fīrozpur, Ludhiāṇā and Ambālā. Field batteries of 9-pounders with horses or bullocks to draw them, and 24 additional pieces of heavy ordnance were on their way to the frontier. In addition, 600 elephants to draw the battering train of 24-pounder batteries had reached Āgrā, and 7,000 camels between Kānpur and the Sutlej were to move up in the summer to Fīrozpur, which was to be the concentration point for a forward offensive movement.

Lord Hardinge, blamed unnecessarily by the Home government for inadequate military preparations for the first Sikh war, had, during the seventeen months between Ellenborough's departure and the commencement of hostilities with the Sikhs, increased the garrison strength at Fīrozpur from 4,596 men and 12 guns to 10,472 men and 24 guns; at Ambālā from 4,113 men and 24 guns to 12, 972 men and 32 guns; at Ludhiāṇā from 3,030 men and 12 guns to 7,235 men and 12 guns, and at Meerut from 5,573 men and 18 guns to 9,844 men and 24 guns. The relevant strength of the advanced armies, including those at the hill stations of Sabāthū and Kasaulī, was raised from 24,000 men and 66 guns to 45,500 men and 98 guns. These figures are based on official British papers, particularly Hardinge's private correspondence on Punjab affairs with his predecessor, Lord Ellenborough.

In addition to the concentration of troops on the border, an elaborate supply depot was set up by the British at Bassīāṅ, near Rāikoṭ, in Ludhiāṇā district. The Lahore Darbār's *vakīls* or representatives and newswriters in the cis-Sutlej region sent alarming reports of these large-scale British military movements across the border. The Sikhs were deeply wrought upon by these war preparations, especially by Broadfoot's acts of hostility. The rapid march in November 1845 of the governor-general towards the frontier and a report of Sir Charles Napier's speech in the *Delhi Gazette* saying that the British were going to war with the Sikhs filled Lahore with rumours of invasion. The Sikh ranks, alerted to the danger of a British offensive, started their own preparations. Yet the army *pañches* or regimental representatives, who had taken over the affairs of the Lahore forces into their own hands after the death of Wazīr Jawāhar Siṅgh, were at this time maintaining, according to George Campbell, a British civilian employed in the cis-Sutlej territory, *Memoirs of My Indian Career,* "wonderful order at Lahore...and almost puritanical discipline in the military republic."

However, the emergence of the army *pañchāyats* as a new centre of power greatly perturbed the British authority who termed it as "an unholy alliance between the republican army and the Darbar." In this process the Sikh army had indeed been transformed. It had now assumed the role of the Khālsā. It worked through elected regimental committees, declaring that Gurū Gobind Siṅgh's ideal of the Sikh commonwealth had been revived, with the Sarbatt Khālsā or the Sikh Panth as a whole assuming all executive, military and civil authority in the State. The British decried this as "the dangerous military democracy of the panchayat system," in which "the soldiers were in a state of successful mutiny."

When the British agent made a reference to the Lahore Darbār about military preparations in the Punjab, it replied that they were only defensive measures to counter the designs of the British. The Darbār, on the other hand, asked for the return of the treasure estimated at over seventeen lakh of rupees the Lahore grandee Suchet Siṅgh Ḍogrā had left buried in Fīrozpur, the restoration of the village of Mauṛāṅ granted by Mahārājā Raṇjīt Siṅgh to one of his generals, Hukam Siṅgh Malvaī, but subsequently resumed by the ruler of Nābhā with the active connivance of the British, and free passage for the Punjab armed constabulary—a right that had been acknowledged by the British on paper but more often than not denied in practice. The British government rejected the Darbār's claims and severed diplomatic relations with it. The armies under Hugh Gough and Lord Hardinge began proceeding towards Fīrozpur. To forestall their joining those at Fīrozpur, the Sikh army began to cross the Sutlej on 11 December 1845 near Harīke Pattaṇ into its own territory on the other side of the river. The crossing over the Sutlej by Sikhs was made a pretext by the British for opening hostilities and on 13 December Governor-General Lord Hardinge issued a proclamation announcing war on the Sikhs. The declaration charged the State of Lahore with violation of the treaty of friendship of 1809 and justified British preparations as merely precautionary measures for the protection of the Sutlej frontier. The British simultaneouly declared Sikh possessions on the left bank of the Sutlej forfeit.

Hesitation and indecision marred Sikh military operations. Having crossed the Sutlej with five divisions, each 8,000-12,000 strong, an obvious strategy for them would have been to move forward. They did in a bold sweeping movement first encircle Fīrozpur, then held by Sir John Littler with only 7,000 men, but withdrew without driving the advantage home and dispersed their armies in a wide semicircle from Harīke to Mudkī and thence to Ferozeshāh, 16 km southeast of Fīrozpur. The abandonment of Fīrozpur as a first target was the result of the treachery of the Sikh prime minister, Lāl Siṅgh, who was in treasonable communication with Captain Peter Nicholson, the assistant political agent of the British. He asked the latter's advice and was told not to attack Fīrozpur. This instruction he followed seducing the Sikhs with an ingenious excuse that, instead of falling upon an easy prey, the Khālsā should exalt their fame by captivity or the death of the Lāṭ Sāhib (the governor-general) himself. A division precipitately moved towards Ludhiāṇā also remained inactive long enough to lose the benefit of the initiative. The Khālsā army had crossed the Sutlej borne on a wave of popular enthusiasm; it was equally matched if not superior to the British force. Its soldiers had the will and determination to fight or die, but not its commanders. There was no unity among them, and each of them seemed to act as he thought best. Drift was the policy deliberately adopted by them.

On 18 December, the Sikhs came in touch with British army which arrived under Sir Hugh Gough, the commander-in-chief, from Ludhiāṇā. A battle took place at Mudkī, 32 km from Fīrozpur. Lāl Siṅgh, who headed the Sikh attack, deserted his army and fled the field when the Sikhs stood firm in their order, fighting in a resolute and determined manner. The leaderless Sikhs fought a grim hand-to-hand battle against the more numerous enemy led by the most experienced commanders in the world. The battle continued with unabated fury till midnight (and came thereafter to be known as "Midnight Mudki"). The Sikhs retired with a loss of 17 guns while the British suffered heavy casualities amounting to 872 killed and wounded, including Quartermaster-General Sir Robert Sale, Sir John McGaskill and Brigadier Boulton. Reinforcements were sent for from Ambālā, Meerut and Delhi. Lord Hardinge, unmindful of his superior position of governor-general, offered to become second-in-command to his commander-in-chief.

The second action was fought three days later, on 21 December at Ferozeshāh, 16 km both from Mudkī and Fīrozpur. The governor-general and the commander-in-chief, assisted by reinforcements led by General Littler from Fīrozpur, made an attack upon the Sikhs who were awaiting them behind strong entrenchments. The British—16,700 men and 69 guns—tried to overrun the Sikhs in one massive cavalry, infantry and artillery onslaught, but the assault was stubbornly resisted. Sikhs' batteries fired with rapidity and precision. There was confusion in the ranks of the English and their position became increasingly critical. The growing darkness of the frosty winter night reduced them to sore straits. The battle of Ferozeshāh is regarded as one of the most fiercely contested battles fought by the British in India. During that "night of horrors," the commander-in-chief acknowledged, "we were in a critical and perilous state." Counsels of retreat and surrender were raised and despair struck the British camp. In the words of General Sir Hope Grant, Sir Henry Hardinge thought it was all up and gave his sword—a present from the Duke of Wellington and which once belonged to Napoleon—and his Star of the Bath to his son, with directions to proceed to Fīrozpur, remarking that "if the day were lost, he must fall."

Lāl Siṅgh and Tej Siṅgh again came to the rescue of the English. The former suddenly deserted the Khālsā army during the night and the latter the next morning (22 December) which enabled the British to turn defeat into victory. The British loss was again heavy, 694 killed and 1,721 wounded. The number of casualities among officers was comparatively higher. The Sikhs lost about 2,000 men and 73 pieces of artillery.

A temporary cessation of hostilities followed the battle of Ferozeshāh. The English were not in a position to assume the offensive and waited for heavy guns and reinforcements to arrive from Delhi. Lāl Siṅgh and Tej Siṅgh allowed them the much-needed respite inasmuch as they kept the Sikhs from recrossing the Sutlej. To induce desertions, Lord Hardinge issued a proclamation on the Christmas day inviting all natives of Hindustān to quit the service of the Sikh State on pain of forfeiting their property and to claim protection from the British government. The deserters were also offered liberal rewards and pensions.

A Sikh *sardār*, Raṇjodh Siṅgh Majīṭhīā, crossed the Sutlej in force and was joined by Ajīt Siṅgh, of Lāḍvā, from the other side of the river. They marched towards Ludhiāṇā and burnt a portion of the cantonment. Sir Harry Smith (afterwards Governor of Cape Colony), who was sent to relieve Ludhīāṇā, marched eastwards from Fīrozpur, keeping a few miles away from the Sutlej. Raṇjodh Siṅgh Majīṭhīā harried Smith's column and, when Smith tried to make a detour at Baddovāl, attacked his rear with great vigour and captured his baggage train and stores (21 January). But Harry Smith retrieved his position a week later by inflicting a defeat on Raṇjodh Siṅgh Majīṭhīā and Ajīt Siṅgh, of Lāḍvā, (28 January).

The last battle of the campaign took place on 10 February. To check the enemy advance on Lahore, a large portion of the Sikh army was entrenched in a horse-shoe curve on the Sutlej near the village of Sabhrāoṅ, under the command of Tej Siṅgh while the cavalry battalions and the dreaded *ghoṛchaṛās* under Lāl Siṅgh were a little higher up the river. Entrenchments at Sabhrāoṅ were on the left bank of the Sutlej with a pontoon bridge connecting them with their base camp. Their big guns were placed behind high embankments and consequently immobilized for offensive action. The infantry was also posted behind earthworks and could not, therefore, be deployed to harass the opponents.

Early in February, the British received ample stores of ammunition from Delhi. Lāl Siṅgh had already passed on to the English officers the required clues for an effective assault. Gough and Hardinge now decided to make a frontal attack on Sabhrāoṅ and destory the Darbār army at one blow. A heavy mist hung over the battlefield, enveloping both contending armies. As the sun broke through the mist, the Sikhs found themselves encircled between two horse-shoes: facing them were the British and behind them was the Sutlej, now in spate. After a preliminary artillery duel, British cavalry made a feint to check on the exact location of the Sikh guns. The cannonade was resumed, and in two hours British guns put the Darbār artillery out of action. Then the British charged Sikh entrenchments from three sides.

Tej Siṅgh fled across the pontoon bridge as soon as the contest started and had it destroyed making reinforcement or return of Sikh soldiers impossible. Gulāb Siṅgh Ḍogrā stopped sending supplies and rations from Lahore. Lāl Siṅgh's *ghoṛchaṛās* did not put in their appearance at Sabhrāoṅ. In the midst of these treacheries, a Sikh warrior, Shām Siṅgh Aṭārīvālā, symbolizing the unflinching will of the K͟hālsā, vowed to fight unto the last and fall in battle rather than retire in defeat. He rallied the ranks depleted by desertions. His courage inspired the Sikhs to make a determined bid to save the day, but the odds were against them. Shām Siṅgh fell fighting in the foremost ranks along with his dauntless comrades. The British casualties at Sabhrāoṅ were 2,403 killed; the Sikhs lost 3,125 men in the action and all their guns were either captured or abandoned in the river. Captain J.D. Cunningham, who was present as an additional aide-de-camp to the governor-general, describes the last scene of the battle vividly in his *A History of the Sikhs*:

> ...although assailed on either side by squadrons of horse and battalions of foot, no Sikh offered to submit, and no disciple of Guru Gobind Singh asked for quarter. They everywhere showed a front to the victors, and stalked slowly and sullenly away, while many rushed singly forth to meet assured death by contending with a multitude. The victors looked with stolid wonderment upon the indomitable courage of the vanquished....

Lord Hugh Gough, the British commander-in-chief, under whose leadership the two Anglo-Sikh wars were fought, described Sabhrāoṅ as the Waterloo of India. Paying tribute to the gallantry of the Sikhs, he said:

> Policy precluded me publicly recording my sentiments on the splendid gallantry of our fallen foe, or to record

> the acts of heroism displayed, not only individually, but almost collectively, by the Sikh sardars and the army; and I declare were it not from a deep conviction that my country's good required the sacrifice, I could have wept to have witnessed the fearful slaughter of so devoted a body of men.

Lord Hardinge, who saw the action, wrote:

> Few escaped; none, it may be said, surrendered. The Sikhs met their fate with the resignation which distinguishes their race.

Two days after their victory at Sabhrāoṅ, British forces crossed the Sutlej and occupied Kasūr. The Lahore Darbār empowered Gulāb Siṅgh Ḍogrā, who had earlier come down to Lahore with regiments of hillmen, to negotiate a treaty of peace. The wily Gulāb Siṅgh first obtained assurances from the army *pañches* that they would agree to the terms he made and then tendered the submission of the Darbār to Lord Hardinge. The governor-general, realizing that the Sikhs were far from vanquished, forbore from immediate occupation of the country. By the terms imposed by the victorious British through the peace treaty of 9 March, the Lahore Darbār was compelled to give up Jalandhar Doāb, pay a war indemnity amounting to a million and a half sterling, reduce its army to 20, 000 infantry and 12,000 cavalry, hand over all the guns used in the war and relinquish control of both banks of the Sutlej to the British. A further condition was added two days later on 11 March: the posting of a British unit in Lahore till the end of the year on payment of expenses. The Darbār was unable to pay the full war indemnity and ceded in lieu thereof the hill territories between the Beās and the Indus. Kashmīr was sold to Gulāb Siṅgh Ḍogrā for 75 lakh rupees. A week later, on 16 March, another treaty was signed at Amritsar recognizing him as Mahārājā of Jammū and Kashmīr. Although Mahārāṇī Jind Kaur continued to act as the regent and Rājā Lāl Siṅgh as *wazīr* of the minor Mahārājā Duleep Siṅgh, effective power had passed into the hands of the British resident, Colonel Henry Lawrence.

B.J.H.

ANGLO-SIKH WAR II, 1848-49, which resulted in the abrogation of the Sikh kingdom of the Punjab, was virtually a campaign by the victors of the first Anglo-Sikh war (1945-46) and since then the *de facto* rulers of the State finally to overcome the resistance of some of the *sardārs* who chafed at the defeat in the earlier war which, they believed, had been lost owing to the treachery on the part of the commanders at the top and not to any lack of fighting strength of the Sikh army. It marked also the fulfilment of the imperialist ambition of the new governor-general, Lord Dalhousie (1848-56), to carry forward the British flag up to the natural boundary of India on the northwest. According to the peace settlement of March 1846, at the end of Anglo-Sikh war I, the British force in Lahore was to be withdrawn at the end of the year, but a severer treaty was imposed on the Sikhs before the expiry of that date. Sir Henry Hardinge, the then governor-general, had his Agent, Frederick Currie, persuade the Lahore Darbār to request the British for the continuance of the troops in Lahore. According to the treaty which was consequently signed at Bharovāl on 16 December 1846, Henry Lawrence was appointed Resident with "full authority to direct and control all matters in every department of the State." A Council of Regency, consisting of the nominees of the Resident and headed by Tej Siṅgh, was appointed. The power to make changes in its personnel vested in the Resident. Under another clause the British could maintain as many troops in the Punjab as they thought necessary for the preservation of peace and order. This treaty was to remain in operation until the minor Mahārājā Duleep Siṅgh attained the age of 16. By a proclamation issued in July 1847, the governor-general further enhanced the powers of the Resident.

On 23 October 1847, Sir Henry Hardinge wrote to Henry Lawrence:

> In all our measures taken during the minority we must bear in mind that by the treaty of Lahore, March 1846, the Punjab never was intended to be an independent State. By the clause I added the chief of the State can neither make war or peace, or exchange or sell an acre of territory or admit a European officer, or refuse us a thoroughfare through his territories, or, in fact, perform any act without our permission. In fact the native Prince is in fetters, and under our protection and must do our bidding.

In the words of British historian John Clark Marshman, "an officer of the Company's artillery became, in fact, the successor to Ranjit Singh." The Sikhs resented this gradual liquidation of their authority in the Punjab. The new government at Lahore became totally unpopular. The abolition of *jāgīrs* in the Jalandhar Doāb and changes introduced in the system of land revenue and its collection angered the landed classes. Mahārāṇī Jind Kaur, who was described by Lord Dalhousie as the only woman in the Punjab with manly understanding and in whom the British Resident foresaw a rallying point for the well-wishers of the Sikh dynasty, was kept under close surveillance. Henry Lawrence laid down that she could not receive in audience more than five or six *sardārs* in a month and that she remain in *purdah* like the ladies of the royal families of Nepal, Jodhpur and Jaipur.

In January 1848, Henry Lawrence took leave of absence and travelled back home with Lord Hardinge, who had completed his term in India. The former was replaced by Frederick Currie and the latter by the Earl of Dalhousie. The new regime confronted a rebellion in the Sikh province of Multān which it utilized as an excuse for the annexation of the Punjab. The British Resident at Lahore increased the levy payable by the Multān governor, Dīwān Mūl Rāj, who, finding himself unable to comply, resigned his office. Frederick Currie appointed General Kāhn Siṅgh Mān in his place and sent him to Multān along with two British officers, P.A. Vans Agnew and William Anderson, to take charge from Mūl Rāj. The party arrived at Multān on 18 April 1848, and the Dīwān vacated the Fort and made over the keys to the representatives of the Lahore Darbār. But his soldiers rebelled and the British officers were set upon in their camp and killed. This was the beginning of the Multān outbreak. Some soldiers of the Lahore escort deserted their officers and joined Mūl Rāj's army. Currie received the news at Lahore on 21 April, but delayed action. Lord Dalhousie allowed the Multān rebellion to spread for five months. The interval was utilized by the British further to provoke Sikh opinion. The Resident did his best to fan the flames of rebellion. Mahārāṇī Jind Kaur, then under detention in the Fort of Sheikhūpurā, was exiled from the Punjab. She was taken to Fīrozpur and thence to Banāras, in the British dominions. Her annual allowance, which according to the treaty of Bharovāl had been fixed at one and a half lakh of rupees, was reduced to twelve thousand. Her jewellery worth fifty thousand of rupees was forfeited; so was her cash amounting to a lakh and a half. The humiliating treatment of the Mahārāṇī caused deep resentment among the people of the Punjab. Even the Muslim ruler of Afghanistan, Amīr Dost Muhammad, protested to the British, saying that "such treatment is objectionable to all creeds."

Meanwhile, Lieutenant Herbert Edwardes, the Resident's Assistant at Bannū, having heard of the Multān revolt, began raising levies from among the Paṭhān mercenaries, and after summoning Van Cortlandt, the local Lahore commander, marched on Multān and called upon the rebels to submit. Although the British Resident approved of Edwardes' conduct, Lord Dalhousie was furious at the audacity of a "subaltern officer" to invest Multān without any authority and offer terms to Mūl Rāj. He was severely reprimanded and ordered not to extend his operations any further. However, Edwardes was not discouraged and ignoring these orders, he crossed the Indus on 14 June; four days later, he inflicted a crushing defeat on Mūl Rāj's forces at Kinerī. Edwardes' action turned Sikh national sentiment in favour of Mūl Rāj and there was restiveness among the troops. British forces began to be moved towards the frontier. The Lahore garrison was reinforced; likewise more regiments reached Ambālā and Fīrozpur. By June 1848, an army had been assembled at the frontier—11,740 men in the Bārī Doāb, 9,430 in the Jalandhar Doāb; in all 21,170 men ready to go into action against Multān to quell what was no more than a local rising. Meanwhile, Captain James Abbott, the Resident's assistant at Hazārā, suspecting that Sardār Chatar Siṅgh Aṭārīvālā, the governor of the province, had been hatching a conspiracy to lead a general Sikh uprising against the British, charged him with treason and cut off all communication with him and marched against him the Muslim peasantry and tribal mercenaries. Captain Nicholson who conducted an enquiry into Abbott's allegations, exonerated Chatar Siṅgh of the charge of treason, but offered him terms which amounted to his virtual dismissal and the confiscation of his *jāgīrs*. Chatar Siṅgh rejected these. Abbott's treatment of Chatar Siṅgh, a chief of eminence and position since Raṇjīt Siṅgh's time and whose daughter was betrothed to the young Mahārājā Duleep Siṅgh, was humiliating. Chatar Siṅgh's son Rājā Sher Siṅgh, who had steadfastly fought on the side of Herbert Edwardes against Dīwān Mūl Rāj, was greatly exercised, and he joined hands with the Dīwān's force on 14 September 1848.

Rājā Sher Siṅgh made a passionate appeal to his countrymen warning them of the fate that awaited the Punjab and inviting them to join his standard in a final bid to preserve their freedom. Many old soldiers of the Khālsā army responded to the call and left their homes to rally round Dīwān Mūl Rāj, Rājā Sher Siṅgh and Chatar Siṅgh. Lord Dalhousie received the news of Sher Siṅgh's action with unconcealed pleasure because it had brought matters to the crisis that he had for months been awaiting. At a public banquet on 5 October 1848 at Barrackpore (Calcutta), he announced:

> Unwarned by precedents, uninfluenced by example, the Sikh nation has called for war, and, on my word, Sirs, they shall have it with a vengeance....We are now not on the eve but in the midst of war with the Sikh nation and the kingdom of the Punjab....I have drawn the sword, and have thrown away the scabbard, both in relation to the war immediately before us, and to the stern policy which that war must precede and establish.

The Resident at Lahore found this position legally indefensible and practically untenable. He and his staff were there to superintend and aid the administration of the Sikh State and to look after the interests of the ruler, Mahārājā Duleep Siṅgh, during the period of his minority. The Lahore Darbār and the Mahārājā had supported the Resident in all his efforts to deal with the situation in Multān and Hazārā. Still the

British armies were marched without an open declaration of war towards the Punjab. Lord Hugh Gough, the commander-in-chief, left his headquarters at Shimlā towards the end of October and a huge army was assembled at Fīrozpur in the beginning of November. The army consisted of four columns. Lord Gough personally commanded 22 infantry divisions (14,419 men), a cavalry division (3,369 horse) and an artillery division with 66 guns, including ten 18-pounder batteries and six 8-inch howitzers drawn by elephants. In addition, there were 6 troops of horse artillery and 3 light and 2 heavy field batteries. Its total strength amounted to 24,404 men (6,396 Europeans). At Lahore, General Wheeler's Occupation Force of 10,000 men held firmly the capital of the Sikhs. In front of the citadel of Multān was the Ist Infantry Division under Major General Whish. The arrival of the Bombay column under Brigadier-General Henry Dundas had augmented its strength to over 21,000 men of all arms. In addition 5,300 men of the Lahore infantry were under British control at Multān. This brought the total regular force at the disposal of Major General Whish at Multān to 26,300 men. Besides, there were irregular Muslim levies and mercenaries raised by the British to fight the Sikhs. Taken in all these and other troops at Hazārā, Peshāwar, Bannū, Gobindgaṛh, Jalandhar and Hoshiārpur added up to the total of 1,04,666 men—61,366 of regular British army, 5,300 of the Lahore army and 38,000 irregular troops; 13,524 cavalry, 123 field and 22 heavy guns, all deployed at various points in the Punjab.

The numerical strength of the Sikhs was comparatively much smaller. Lord Gough's despatches enumerate the Sikh force at Rāmnagar and Chelīāṅvālā between 30,000 and 40,000 men and at Gujrāt 60,000 men and 60 guns, which figures are highly exaggerated. The powerful Khālsā army of Raṇjīt Siṅgh was broken up after its capitulation at Sabhrāoṅ in 1846. Its soldiers had been disbanded by the British, its generals discharged or won over, and its *jāgīrdārī* force reduced to starvation. A skeleton army of 25 battalions (20,000 men) and 12,000 horse permitted to the State under the treaty of March 1846 was a shadow force under British control and dispersed to far-flung districts for garrison duty. Lahore had a garrison strength of 6,500 men, Peshāwar of 3,000 men, Gobindgaṛh Fort 2,000 men, Hazārā 3,000 men, Bannū and Ṭoṅk 1,300 men, Attock 700 men, and Kohāṭ 500 men. The remaining 3,000 men of the entire force were at numerous small posts throughout the Punjab.

The contingents of the Lahore army which joined the rebels were those of Hazārā, Peshāwar, Ṭoṅk and Bannū, Kohāṭ, and Attock—9,400 men, inclusive of the force of Sher Siṅgh at Multān (900 infantry and 3,400 horse). Allowing that 3,000 men stationed at various isolated places throughout the Punjab could get through and join the rebels in the north, the regular Sikh force could scarcely have exceeded 13,000 men and 9,000 horse. Disbanded Sikh soldiers and the freelance who flocked round the banner did not exceed 10,000 men. The disbanded soldiery merely augmented the numerical strength of the Khālsā; it had few generals and fewer arms and no means of procurement of arms and supplies. The total strength thus could not have been more than 23,000 men and 12,000 horse.

Lord Gough crossed the Sutlej on 9 November and reached Lahore on 13 November. Moving rapidly into the Rachnā Doāb, he arrived at Rāmnagar on 22 November. Sher Singh's entire force was on the right bank of the River Chenāb. Brigadier-General Campbell with the 3rd Infantry Division (8,171 men) was ordered to move out to disperse the Sikh force in the vicinity of Rāmnagar; Brigadier-General Cureton in command of the cavalry accompanied Campbell's force. On arrival at Rāmnagar, Campbell found the Sikh force on the opposite side of the river. Cureton had numerous cavalry but no guns; he ordered the horse artillery under Colonel Lane to overtake the withdrawing Sikh troops through the sandy riverbed, but met with disaster. The Sikh artillery on the opposite bank opened up with disastrous effect, and Lane hastily withdrew the horse artillery leaving behind a heavy gun and two ammunition wagons, which the Sikhs captured. Suddenly, a column of the Sikh cavalry crossed the river under cover of artillery. The commander of the 14th Light Dragoons who led a squardon in support of Lane's horse artillery was shot dead. The charge failed and the British lost 90 officers and men including Brigadier-General Cureton and Lieutenant-Colonel Havelock, and 140 horse. The action at Rāmnagar was a victory for the Sikhs. Lord Dalhousie blamed both Campbell and Gough for the "sad affair" from which "there was no objective to be gained." Gough, on the other hand, claimed it as a victory. "The enemy," he announced in a General Order, "was signally overthrown on every occasion, and only saved from utter annihilation by their flight to the cover of their guns on the opposite bank."

For about a week after the British reverse, the two armies faced each other across the river. Lord Gough waited impatiently for the heavy guns to arrive. On 30 November, he detached a force under Major-General Thackwell across the river to take the Sikh army in the flank; another brigade of infantry under Brigadier Godby was ordered to ford the river 10 km from Rāmnagar to support Thackwell's force. Across the river, at the principal ford 3 km from Rāmnagar, Sher Siṅgh's entire force, now risen to 12,000 men and 28 guns, lay strongly entrenched. Thackwell's force moved about 30 km up the river to Wazīrābād and made the crossing, while Godby's brigade had crossed the river 25 km below. At midday on 3 December Thackwell arrived at Sadullāpur barely 6 km from the Sikh encampment. The Sikhs realized the imminent danger to their flanks and rear. The heavy Sikh artillery opened fire at Thackwell's position, while the Sikh cavalry barred the passage of Godby's force which failed to join up with his troops. At dusk, the entire Sikh army crossed over to the left bank of the river. Sher Siṅgh's action nullified the British manoeuvre; it also made it possible for Chatar Siṅgh's force to join him. The British General claimed a victory without a battle. He reported a meagre loss of 40 men at Sadullāpur, and claimed that the army under his command had upheld the tradition of valour. The Sikhs, he reported, were in full retreat, leaving behind some 60 boats which had been captured.

In British military and political circles in England, Lord Gough was severely castigated for lack of drive and initiative. Lord Dalhousie openly charged him with incompetency and blamed him for incomplete actions and enormous losses. Under the shadow of these adverse strictures, Lord Gough fought the battle of Chelīāṅvālā on 13 January 1849. The Sikh army 12,000 strong was drawn in battle array in the dense jungle in front, their heavy guns bearing upon Chelīāṅvālā, on the River Jehlum. British preparations for encampment were rudely interrupted by sharp Sikh artillery fire. Lord Gough hesitated, but instantly drew up the order of the battle. In the centre were placed heavy 18-pounders and 8-inch howitzers; Major-General Gilbert's 2nd Infantry Division (5,248 men) was placed on the right, flanked by Brigadier Pope's 2nd Cavalry Brigade and 14th Light Dragoons and horse artillery. To the left was Brigadier-General Campbell's 3rd Infantry Division (8,171 men) flanked by White's Ist Cavalry Brigade and 3 troops of horse artillery.

The British guns started firing upon the Sikh centre. The density of the jungle made it impossible to preserve order and formation and the British brigades and regiments got separated from one another. The ground proved unsuitable for cavalry action, and the artillery failed to provide cover. Sikhs fought with determination and their artillery took a heavy toll. The British infantrymen were mowed down by fire from Sikh musketry, and the successive onslaughts of the Sikh *ghoṛchaṛās* broke the British cavalry line. While Campbell's charge failed to dislodge the Sikhs, the K͟hālsā horsemen swept the field like lightning raising vociferous K͟hālsā war-cries.

In another direction, Brigadier Pennycuick's brigade moving in double time into the jungle, was routed by Sikh artillery. The brigade turned back to flee from the destructive fire of shot and shell leaving behind nearly half a regiment which faced total destruction. The most serious disaster befell Gilbert's division which halted in utter bewilderment when a large body of Sikhs surrounded the 2nd Infantry brigade. Gilbert's brigade had neither the cover of guns nor the support of cavalry. In the hand-to-hand fight, the brigade was repulsed and driven back with heavy loss. The battle lasted over three hours when Lord Gough ordered the whole army to retreat. British casualties in the action amounted to 2,446 men and 132 officers killed with four guns lost.

The British commander-in-chief claimed a victory, which claim the governor-general scornfully dubbed as "perhaps poetical." "We have gained a victory," he observed ruefully, "like that of the ancients; it is such a one that 'another such would ruin us.' " There was an outburst of popular indignation in England and Gough was squarely blamed for the defeat of the British. Military experts at home described him as a "superannuated general who could not mount his horse without assistance." It was decided to retire Lord Gough and replace him by Sir Charles Napier. In the meantime, however, Multān fell and Dīwān Mūl Rāj surrendered to Major-General Whish on 22 January 1849.

Lord Gough repaired his reputation in the battle of Gujrāt fought on 21 February 1849. The Sikh army had regrouped on the banks of the Jehlum. On 15 February, it arrived at Gujrāt where Chatar Siṅgh's force and an Afg͟hān contingent of 3,000 horse under Akram K͟hān encircled the town. On 13 February, Major-General Whish's Ist Division (13,400 men and 30 pieces of heavy artillery) joined the British force. The Bombay column (12,100 men and 3,000 cavalry) joined a few days later. Thus assured of an overwhelming superiority of men and heavy artillery, Lord Gough ordered the entire force forward and reaching a few days later Shādīvāl, a village 8 km from Gujrāt, he found himself face to face with the Sikhs.

The battle of Gujrāt must be reckoned as one of the most notable in the annals of British warfare in India. Never, perhaps, the British had amassed so many guns and men in any single battle. The British army now consisted of 56,636 men—four infantry divisions, 11,569 horse, 96 field-guns, and 67 siege-guns including ten 18-pounders and six 8-inch howitzers drawn by elephants. For this obvious reason the battle of Gujrāt has often been described as "the battle of guns."

On the morning of 21 February, the whole British army advanced with the precision of a parade movement. The Sikh guns opened fire, thus disclosing their positions and range. The British General brought the three divisions to a sudden halt and ordered the whole line of artillery to fire. The sustained cannonade of 100 guns, the fire of 18-pounders and 8-inch howitzers, which continued for two hours blunted Sikh artillery. When the British guns had spent up their fury, their infantry line advanced rapidly. The Sikh infantry positions were captured, and the Sikhs driven out of cover. The battle was over within a few hours. The advance of the whole British line completely overwhelmed the Sikhs and they fled the field in confusion. Their loss was estimated between 3,000 and 5,000 men and 53 guns; the British casualties were 96 killed and 700 wounded. "The Sikhs," commented Lord Dalhousie, "displayed the skill, courage and activity which belong to their race." With the decisive British victory at Gujrāt the hostilities ended on 11 March 1849. Sher Siṅgh and Chatar Siṅgh formally surrendered their swords to Major-General Gilbert near Rāwalpiṇḍī. They were followed on the 14th by the whole Sikh army. "Today is Raṇjīt Siṅgh dead," sighed the soldiers as they kissed their swords and laid them down on the ever-enlarging heap of steel.

Lord Dalhousie proclaimed annexation of the Punjab on 29 March 1849. His foreign secretary, Henry Meirs Elliot, arrived at Lahore to obtain the signatures of the members of the Council of Regency and of the minor king, Mahārājā Duleep Siṅgh. A darbār was held in the Lahore Fort and, with the British troops lined up on his right and his helpless sardārs on his left, the young Duleep Siṅgh affixed his signatures to the document which deprived him of his crown and kingdom.

BIBLIOGRAPHY

1. Ganda Singh, *Private Correspondence Relating to the Anglo-Sikh Wars.* Amritsar, 1955
2. ——,*The British Occupation of the Punjab.* Patiala, 1956
3. Cook, H.C.B., *The Sikh Wars 1845-49.* Delhi, 1975
4. Gough, Sir C. and A.D. Innes, *The Sikhs and the Sikh Wars.* London, 1897
5. Burton, R.G., *The First and the Second Sikh Wars.* Simla, 1911
6. Cunningham, Joseph Davey, *A History of the Sikhs from the Origin of the Nation to the Battles of the Sutlej.* London, 1849
7. Khushwant Singh, *A History of the Sikhs,* vol. 2. Princeton 1966
8. Harbans Singh, *The Heritage of the Sikhs.* Delhi, 1983
9. Nijjar, B.S., *Anglo-Sikh Wars.* Delhi, 1976
10. Hasrat, Bikrama Jit, *Anglo-Sikh Relations 1799-1849.* Hoshiarpur, 1968
11. ——, *The Punjab Papers.* Hoshiarpur, 1970
12. Gupta, Hari Ram, *Panjab on the Eve of First Sikh War.* Chandigarh, 1956

B.J.H

AŅĪ RĀI, author of *Jaṅgnāmā Gurū Gobind Siṅgh Jī,* was one of the numerous poets and scholars who enjoyed the patronage of Gurū Gobind Siṅgh (1666-1708). The *Jaṅgnāmā* is an account in verse of a battle on the banks of the River Sutlej in which an attack from the imperial troops was countered and repulsed by Sikhs under the personal command of Gurū Gobind Siṅgh. No date is given of the event, but a reference in the text to "Khālsā," inaugurated in 1699, and other details indicate that it was one of the last battles of Anandpur. A manuscript of the work is preserved in the private collection of the Mahārājā of Paṭiālā. The poem has been included by the Shiromaṇī Gurdwārā Parbandhak Committee in the collection *Prachīn Vārāṅ te Jaṅgnāme,* and by Bhāshā Vibhāg, Punjab, in *Pañch Nad.* The poet has tried several prosodic measures in the 70-stanza poem. The language used is *bhākhā,* or contemporary Hindi, except in the *pauṛīs* which are in chaste Punjabi.

BIBLIOGRAPHY

1. Padam, Piārā Siṅgh, *Gurū Gobind Siṅgh Jī de Darbārī Ratan.* Patiala, 1976
2. Kuir Siṅgh, *Gurbilās Pātshāhī 10.* Patiala, 1968

P.S.P.

AŅĪ RĀI, BĀBĀ (b.1618), son of Gurū Hargobind, was, according to *Gurbilās Chhevīṅ Pātshāhī,* born to Mātā Nānakī at Amritsar on 16 Maghar 1675 Bk/14 November 1618. The first to arrive to see the child's face was grandmother, Mātā Gaṅgā, and she was the most rejoiced of all the family. Gurū Hargobind, to quote the *Gurbilās* again, gave him the name Aṇī Rāi (*aṇī* , Skt. *anīk* = troops, army; *rāi* = *rājā* or chief), Lord of Armies. As he grew up, Aṇī Rāi remained absorbed within himself most of the time. He never married and lived the life of a recluse. All we learn from the biographer of Gurū Hargobind is that he carried the conch at the funeral of his stepmother (*Mātā* Marvāhī), his stepbrother, Sūraj Mal, giving his shoulder to the bier. Aṇī Rāi died at Kīratpur where a shrine honouring his memory still exists.

BIBLIOGRAPHY

1. *Gurbilās Chhevīṅ Pātshāhī*. Patiala, 1970
2. Giān Siṅgh, Giānī, Twārī*kh* *Gurū* *Kh*ālsā [Reprint]. Patiala, 1970
3. Macauliffe, M. A., *The Sikh Religion*. Oxford, 1909

Gn.S.

AÑJULĪĀ (Ṅ), by Gurū Arjan, is a short composition comprising two hymns entered in the Gurū Granth Sāhib under Mārū musical measure (GG, 1019). This word *añjulīā* (ṅ) is the plural form of Sanskrit *añjulī* which means the joining together of palms in supplication, reverence or salutation. The word *añjulīāṅ in* its plural sense has been used in the title perhaps because the composition comprises two hymns. It contains prayer to God seeking from Him the gift of *nām*, i.e meditation on His Name or constant remembrance or repetition of His Name. Everything in this world happens by His Will and those who are favoured by Him practise *nām* in holy company (*saṅgat*). The tragedy of man is that he seeks happiness in material life *sans* any spiritual reference. That is why he is ever in misery: when he has material possessions in plenty, he fears he might not lose them, and when he lacks these, he pines for them. In fact, this misery is owed neither to the excess of nor to the meagreness of material possessions, but to man's egoistic pursuits that guide his life in the world. Human life in this phenomenal world is transitory.

Añjulī is also the title of another of Gurū Arjan's hymns in measure Mārū (GG, 1007-08). The hymn rejects the ritual of *añjulī* as libation to the manes and teaches man willingly to accept God's *bhāṇā* or His Will. The word *añjulī* also occurs in a hymn by Gurū Rām Dās in measure Gauṛī (GG, 171) repeated in the *Sohilā* (GG, 12-13). One is adjured to offer *añjulī* or salutation to the Lord which counts as an act of virtue. Although the *Farīdkoṭ Ṭīkā* describes *añjulī* as a *chhand* or a prosodic form, it is employed in the Gurū Granth Sāhib generally as a synonym for salutation or supplication.

BIBLIOGRAPHY

1. *Shabdārth Srī Gurū Granth Sāhib Jī*, vol. III. Amritsar, 1964
2. *Ādi Srī Gurū Granth Sāhib Jī Saṭīk* (Farīdkoṭ Vālā Ṭīkā) [Reprint]. Patiala, 1970

D.S.

AÑJUMAN-I-PAÑJĀB, founded in Lahore on 21 January 1865 by the distinguished linguist, Dr Gottlieb Wilhelm Leitner, who became successively the first principal of the Government College at Lahore and the first registrar of the University of the Pañjāb, was a voluntary society which aimed at the development of "vernacular literature" and dissemination of popular knowledge through this medium. Its actual activities spanned a wide range of educational forums and social issues, including encouragement of Vedic and Unānī medicine, a *mushāirā* or poetical symposium, newspaper journalism, a free public library, a system of private primary schools, lecture series and publication of literary works in Indian languages. The Añjuman held meetings for the discussion of questions of literary, scientific and social interests, sent memorials to the government, established a public library and compiled a number of treatises and translations in Urdu, Hindi and Punjabi. It also started an Oriental school and was instrumental in the establishment of the Pañjāb University College, which was assigned to "promoting the diffusion of European science, as far as possible, through the medium of the vernacular languages of the Punjab, improving and extending vernacular literature generally, affording encouragement to the enlightened study of the Eastern classical languages and literature, and associating the learned and influential classes of the province with the officers of government in the promotion and supervision of popular education." On 14 October 1882, this college was converted into Pañjāb University which was the outcome primarily of the labours of the Añjuman.

The Añjuman had a membership of 244 in 1865—the year of its birth. Among its charter members were several Sikh "wards of the court," the surviving heirs of decimated Sikh nobility. Among the leading Sikh members of the Añjuman were Rājā Harbaṅs Siṅgh and his steward-adviser, Rāi Mūl Siṅgh. In papers read before the Añjuman they defended the right of Sikhs to study the Punjabi language written in Gurmukhī script. They later represented Sikh interests in the Senate of Pañjāb University College. They, however, encountered the hostility of the British officers of the Punjab Education Department who viewed Punjabi as little more than a rude dialect, without a redeeming literary tradition, and hence unworthy of admittance into the formal curriculum of Pañjāb University College. At this key juncture, it was the well-organized personal library of a Sikh scholar, Sardār Attar Siṅgh of Bhadauṛ, which turned the tide of argument on the floor of Pañjāb University College Senate in favour of those advocating Punjabi. Attar Siṅgh submitted a list of 389 works, written in Gurmukhī script, which he had been able to collect in his library. This proved that Punjabi possessed a written literature, although not one widely read or, in 1877, recently attended to by Sikh scholars.

Sardār (later Sir) Attar Siṅgh's impressive library won Punjabi studies admission at the Pañjāb University. Significantly, the first Gurmukhī instructor appointed to teach classes at the College was Bhāī Gurmukh Siṅgh, renowned in Sikh history as a vital figure in Siṅgh Sabhā renaissance. Supporting what he called "semi-secular" education, meaning the admission of religious training into government schools, G.W. Leitner actively sponsored the appointment of Bhāī Gurmukh Siṅgh to teach Gurmukhī and mathematics at the Pañjāb University College. Encouraging Sikh religionists, Leitner launched a Sikh "Bhāī Class" at Oriental College, Lahore, where Gurmukh Siṅgh taught the sons of traditional Sikh literati. This amalgam of Orientalist and Sikh studies led to the institution at the Pañjāb University College of Budhīmān examination in Gurmukhī. Attar Siṅgh became the first examiner. By 1883 a system of Gurmukhī examinations became standarized at Pañjāb University. Supported by Añjuman orientalists, the Siṅgh Sabhā delivered in 1880 a petition to the Senate of Pañjāb University College signed by prominent Sikhs, seeking that new schools they hoped to found be patronized by the Pañjāb University College and the college entrance examinations be held in Punjabi, as was then being done for Urdu and Hindi speakers. The same year the Siṅgh Sabhā joined hands with the Añjuman representing to Viceroy Ripon to raise the Pañjāb University College to University status. Just as a major portion of the Añjuman activities had shifted to the floor of the Pañjāb University College Senate after the creation of that Orientalist-inspired institution in 1870, Ripon's sanction in 1882 of a fully-empowered Pañjāb University witnessed the final decline of the Añjuman. Its principal objective, i.e. the creation of a university, had been realized. Moreover, increased competition between communities, Sikh, Hindu and Muslim, had made the cross-communally populated Añjuman an anachronism by the mid-1880's.

BIBLIOGRAPHY

1. Leitner, Gottlieb Wilhelm, *History of Indigenous Education in the Panjab since Annexation and in 1882* [Reprint]. Patiala, 1971
2. Harbans Singh, *The Heritage of the Sikhs*. Delhi, 1983
3. Perrill, Jeffrey, *Añjuman-i-Pañjāb* (unpublished Ph.D. thesis)

J.P.

ANNEXATION OF THE PUNJAB to British dominions in India in 1849 by Lord Dalhousie, the British governor-general, which finally put an end to the sovereignty of the Sikhs over northwestern India, was the sequel to a chain of events that had followed the death of Mahārājā Ranjīt Singh ten years earlier. Internal dissensions and treachery had caused the defeat of the Sikh army at the hands of the British in the first Anglo-Sikh war (1845-46). When on 16 December 1846, the Lahore Darbār was forced to sign the treaty of Bhyrowāl (Bharovāl), the kingdom of the Punjab was made a virtual British protectorate. The Regent was pensioned off; the British assumed the guardianship of the young Mahārājā Duleep Singh during his minority, and a British Resident was appointed to direct and control the entire civil and military administration of the State of Lahore with a council of ministers nominated by himself. For political, financial and military reasons, Lord Hardinge, the then Governor-General of India, had avoided annexation of the territory which was vaguely hinted at but not pressed upon him by Sir Robert Peel's government. The Whig opposition in British Parliament however strongly assailed the decision. Hardinge offered the plea that the arrangement of Bharovāl was in reality annexation, minus the disadvantages the direct acquisition would have entailed.

The Marquis of Dalhousie, the new governor-general, who arrived in India in January 1848 scarcely approved of Hardinge's "annexation without encumbrances." In April 1848 Dīwān Mūl Rāj's revolt at Multān opened the prospect of a fresh war in the Punjab. On the very day (4 May) Dalhousie received Resident Frederick Currie's report of the incident at Multān, he wrote to the Home government: "I shall feel it my duty as the servant of the Company and Crown to exact national reparation from the State of Lahore."

The Multān revolt in which two British officers, Vans Agnew and William Anderson, were murdered by Mūl Rāj's troops in their camp at the Īdgāh may, at the most, be described a local mutiny, which could have easily been suppressed by the despatch of a few British regiments.The whole incident was unpremeditated and Mūl Rāj had nothing to do with it. But Lord Hugh Gough, the British commander-in-chief, forbore from any immediate action with a view to letting the trouble spread. Lord Dalhousie accepted Gough's view of the situation, and pointed out to the Home government the advantages of temporary inaction, waiting meanwhile for a full-scale invasion of the Punjab.

Meanwhile, in England, no one was convinced that the Multān affair would become a national rising of the Sikhs in the Punjab, and eyebrows were raised at the resolution by Government of India to have " a grand hunt in the cold season." However nothing was done for full five months to quell the Multān revolt. In August, for the first time, Dalhousie signified to his friends in England that "the fight to annex the Punjab is beyond cavil." In the interval of British inactivity, a dramatic move made by Lieutenant Herbert Edwardes, the Resident's assistant at Bannū, shattered the deliberately created myth of the "invincibility" of Multān. He raised a crowd of Muslim levies and, crossing the Indus, took possession of the trans-Indus dependencies of Multān. On 18 June 1848, he inflicted a crushing defeat on Mūl Rāj's forces at Kinerī. Edwardes' action raised a storm at Fort William. In England, newspapers, which had begun commenting sarcastically at the "degeneration" of Gough's army which could act only in cold weather, hailed Edwardes' victory over Mūl Rāj. Dalhousie dubbed these "loud crowings" in England as "cock-a-hoop." He sharply reprimanded Frederick Currie for allowing Edwardes to march on Multān, and ordered him to keep his reckless subaltern *absolutely and utterly* away from Multān.

Edwardes' march on Multān with 14,500 Paṭhān and Balūch mercenaries with cries of *jihād* for the extermination of Sikh infidels had alerted the Sikhs. The K͟hālsā war cry began to be heard again; priests and prophets proclaimed Mūl Rāj as their leader to restore Sikh supremacy in the land of the five rivers. British troops moved from Ambālā to Fīrozpur and from Meerut to Ambālā; the fortress of Gobindgaṛh was taken possession of; "conspiracies" were unearthed and Mahārāṇī Jind Kaur was deported from the Punjab. The governor of Hazārā, Sardār Chatar Siṅgh Aṭārīvālā, was charged with leading a general rising of the Sikh nation against the British.

Lord Dalhousie had meantime prepared the case for the annexation of the Punjab. On 15 August 1848, he outlined his arguments in a private communication to the President of the Board of Control. Since the treaty of Bharovāl, he said, the British had given ample proof of their good faith by maintaining the Sikh Rāj. They had assumed the guardianship of the minor Mahārāja and had preserved the peace of the country by means of a British force, for which the Sikh Darbār had agreed to pay 22,00,000 rupees annually. A Council of Regency under the direct control of the British Resident had run their government, and had kept their army in a state of efficiency. On the other hand, the Lahore government, he added, had not given proof of its good faith. British debt had accumulated to 53,00,000 rupees, the Darbār had failed to punish the criminal who had murdered two British officers, and signs of a general conspiracy of the Sikhs for the expulsion of the British from the Punjab had become visible. "Even if the proof of a general conspiracy should fail, it is my opinion that, however contrary it may be to our past views and to our future wishes, the annexation of the Punjab is the most advantageous policy for us to pursue. The present policy of moderation has been carried on too far."

Lord Dalhousie's indictment of the Sikh people, however, surprised British statesmen conversant with Punjab political affairs. Lord John Russell's Cabinet was not much impressed with the vigour and vehemence of the governor-general's arguments. It agreed to putting down the rebellion, but was not willing to hold the minor Mahārājā and the Sikh Darbār responsible for the turn events had taken. Lord Dalhousie was reminded that, since the entire control of the civil and military administration of the Punjab was vested with the Government of India through the British Resident, it could not escape the responsibility. Although the British Cabinet was averse to the governor-general's drastic policy, both India Board and the Secret Committee were not so certain. " I can assure you on the part of the Government," wrote the President of the Board to the Governor-General, "that if you should feel yourself compelled by the urgency of the case to adopt that, or any other important change, without waiting for the sanction of the Home authorities, the most favourable construction would be put upon your proceedings." This meant endorsement of the policy of Lord Dalhousie, yet he eschewed henceforth all direct reference to annexation in his despatches to the Secret Committee.

In his private despatches to its president however he continued to emphasize that the insurrection in the Punjab was a general uprising of the Sikhs against British power, and that abolition of the Sikh dynasty had become essential to the security of India.

On 29 March 1849 after the second Anglo-Sikh war had ended, Dalhousie took the final step without any authority from the Home Government, declaring that the kingdom of the Punjab had ceased and that all the territories of Mahārājā Duleep Siṅgh had become part of the British dominions in India. The British Resident at Lahore, Sir Henry Lawrence, being strongly opposed to the annexation of the country, Lord Dalhousie selected his Foreign Secretary Henry M. Elliot as his agent for the final transaction.Under instructions from Dalhousie, Elliot saw the members of the Council of Regency privately, in the first instance, and made it clear to them on 28 March "that any reluctance on their part would be a great mistake, that the Maharaja as well as they themselves would be sufferers from it, that the decision of the Governor-General would in any case be carried out, the only difference being that if they with the Maharaja gave their formal assent, the advantageous position they then held would be guaranteed to them, while if they refused they would lose everything which the British Government chose to resume." With British troops in complete occupation of the Punjab, the members of the Regency Council had no choice but to sign the document which put an end to the independence of the Punjab. They then realized how the British Government had, throughout the past year, been acting in violation of the treaty of 16 December 1846 which provided for the protection of the Mahārājā and the preservation of the peace of the country during the minority of His Highness the Mahārājā Duleep Siṅgh up to his attaining majority on 4 September 1854. Sir Frederick Currie, the then Resident at Lahore, had proclaimed to the people of the Punjab on 18 November 1848, soon after the arrival of the British commander-in-chief with his army at Lahore, that British army "has entered the Lahore territories, not as an enemy to the constituted government, but to restore order and obedience." The Lahore Darbār had placed all the available troops and resources at the disposal of the British Resident for the suppression of the Multān rebellion and had been, throughout, under the impression that the British army had been called in "for the preservation of the peace of the country and to restore order and obedience," in fulfilment of the treaty of Bharovāl, 16 December 1846, and of the proclamation of 18 November 1848. They were completely disillusioned when they discovered that the British force had in fact entered the Punjab as an army of occupation. Early on the morning of 29 March 1849 a *darbār* was held in the palace inside the Fort and the Mahārājā was called upon to affix his signature to the document of terms drawn up by the British divesting him of his crown and kingdom. Immediately after the document had been signed, Elliot read out in the *darbār* the Proclamation issued by Lord Dalhousie to justify his policy and action. It was a most artful statement which, *inter alia*, said that whereas the British had faithfully kept their word and had scrupulously observed every obligation under the treaties made with the Sikhs, the latter had, on their part, grossly and faithlessly violated the agreements. The claim of Lord Dalhousie and his accusations against the Sikh government were not sustainable factually. There was severe criticism in both India and England of his action. Even the British Resident at Lahore, Sir Henry Lawrence, described the annexation of the Punjab and the deposition of young Mahārājā Duleep Siṅgh as unjust and impolitic. John Sullivan, a member of the Madrās Council, commenting on the whole transaction in his

Are We Bound by Our Treaties? said:

> This is perhaps the first instance on record in which a guardian has visited his own misdeeds upon his ward. The British Government was the self-constituted guardian of the Rajah [Mahārājā Duleep Siṅgh], and the regent of his kingdom; a rebellion was provoked by the agents of the guardian; it was acknowledged by the guardian to be a rebellion against the government of his ward, and the guardian punished that ward by confiscating his dominions and his diamonds to his use.

BIBLIOGRAPHY

1. Gough, Charles, and Arthur D. Innes, *Annexation of Punjab*[Reprint]. Delhi, 1984
2. Bell, Evans, *The Annexation of the Punjab & Maharaja Duleep Singh* [Reprint]. Ludhiana, 1969
3. Harbans Singh, *The Heritage of the Sikhs*. Delhi, 1983
4. Court, Henry, trans. and ed., *History of the Sikhs or Translation of the Sikhāṅ de Rāj dī Vithiā* [Reprint]. Patiala, 1970
5. Ganda Singh, *British Occupation of the Punjab*. Patiala, 1956
6. Khushwant Singh, *A History of the Sikhs*, vol. 2. Princeton, 1966

B.J.H

ANOKHĪ, BĪBĪ, born, according to Kesar Siṅgh Chhibbar, *Baṅsāvalīnāmā Dasāṅ Pātshāhīāṅ Kā*, in the Bikramī year 1592/AD 1535. She was the third child and the younger of the two daughters of Gurū Aṅgad and(Mātā) Khīvī.

M.G.S.

ANŪPDEĪ, MĀTĀ, mother of the fourth Gurū, Gurū Rām Dās (1534-81).

See HARDĀS, BĀBĀ

P.S.P.

ANŪP SIṄGH and Sarūp Siṅgh, grandsons of Dunī Chand a *masand* or parish leader during the time of Gurū Gobind Siṅgh, were residents of Majīṭhā, in present-day Amritsar district of the Punjab. They, according to Sarūp Siṅgh Kaushish, *Gurū kīāṅ Sākhīāṅ*, came to Anandpur to meet Gurū Gobind Siṅgh. They besought the Gurū to forgive their grandfather for having deserted him earlier. The Gurū granted their request.

BIBLIOGRAPHY

1. Padam, Piārā Siṅgh, and Giānī Garjā Siṅgh, eds., *Gurū kīāṅ Sākhīāṅ*. Patiala, 1986
2. Giān Siṅgh, Giānī, *Twārīkh Gurū Khālsā* [Reprint]. Patiala, 1970

Gn.S.

APOCRYPHAL COMPOSITIONS, known in Sikh vocabulary as *kachchī bāṇī* (unripe, rejected texts) or *vādhū bāṇī* (superfluous texts) are those writings, mostly in verse but prose not excluded,which have been attributed to the Gurūs, but which were not incorporated in the Gurū Granth Sāhib at the time of its compilation in 1603-04. Since the Sikh Scripture was compiled by one of the Gurūs and the text as approved by him has come down to us intact, compositions not included therein must be reckoned as extratextual and spurious. Moreover, the contents of the Gurū Granth Sāhib have been so arranged and numbered as to leave absolutely no scope for any extraction or interpolation. Still there are compositions which some attribute to the Gurūs. Most of them are attributed to Gurū Nānak, at least one *śabda* to Gurū Tegh Bahādur, and some to Gurū Gobind Siṅgh. "Nānak" was the *nom de plume* the Gurūs used for their compositions, and the custom was appropriated by some of the contemporary saints or religious poets. Some schismatists or those who had otherwise set themselves up as rivals to the growing faith adopted this pseudonym to benefit from its popularly accepted authority.

Apocryphal writings attributed to Gurū

Nānak fall into three categories, viz. (i) hymns addressed to the yogīs on the subject of true yoga; (ii) hymns addressed to the various Hindu sects on the ideal form of religion; and (iii) compositions generally called *nāmahs* (epistles or addresses) addressed to Muslims, expounding the true meaning of *sharā'* (Islamic laws) and the spirit of Islam. Writings falling in categories (i) and (ii) seem to have been collected in course of time, in one volume popularly called *Prāṇ Saṅglī*, the best-known among Sikh apocrypha on account of its spiritual insight, and closeness to Gurū Nanak's own diction and style. Besides *Prāṇ Saṅglī, Kakaṛ Vichār* and *Bihaṅgam Bāṇī* (guidance from birds about auspicious and inauspicious omens) are other apocryphal compositions attributed to Gurū Nanak, but which go against his teachings and have thus never been owned by the Sikhs. Verses by Bābā Miharbān (*q.v.*) and his successors which they composed using the *nom de plume* 'Nānak' under the title of Mahallā VI, VII and VIII are also apocryphal. Another category of the apocryphal literature comprises hymns written in Persianized Punjabi and addressed to the Muslim divines and kings. These compositions are available in Chapters LXXVII to LXXVIII of the *Prāṇ Saṅglī* also. Other compositions in this category are *Nasīhat Nāmah* or Epistle of Admonitions; *Hāzar Nāmah* or a discourse on the importance of being alert; *Pāk Nāmah* or an address on pure living; and *Karnī Nāmah* or an address on the importance of good conduct. The *śabda* attributed to Gurū Tegh Bahādur reads: *chit charan kamal kā āsrā chit charan kamal saṅg joṛīai/mana lochai buriāīāṅ guru sabadī ih mana hoṛīai/bāṅh jināh dī pakaṛīai sir dījai bāṅh nā chhoṛīai/gurū Tegh Bahādur boliā dhar paīai dharam nā chhoṛīai.* Among the apocryphal writings attributed to Gurū Gobind Siṅgh are *Sarbloh Granth* and *Prem Sumārag.*

Since Sikh Scripture was compiled by Gurū Arjan himself and its first copy was inscribed under his personal supervision and care and its contents were meticulously authenticated, arranged and numbered, the genuineness of the text is beyond question. As such, the apocryphal texts pose no serious problem. Compositions which do not form part of the acknowledged recension are therefore not genuine. It is only some portions of the *Dasam Granth*, the Book of the Tenth Master, which have been engaging the attention of scholars with regard to their authorship, but this work does not have scriptural status. As for Scripture, the Gurū Granth Sāhib, the original volume prepared by Gurū Arjan, is still extant, preserved in a descendant family at Kartārpur, in Jalandhar district of the Punjab.

T.S.

ĀRATĪ, from Sanskrit *ārātrik*, meaning the light or the vessel containing it which is waved before an idol, generally in the clockwise direction, accompanied by the chanting of *mantras.* This is also the name given the ceremony which for the Hindus is a mode of ritual worship to propitiate the deity. In the Sikh system, which totally rejects image-worship, there is no sanction for this form of worship. An incident in this regard is often summoned from the Janam Sākhīs, traditional accounts of Gurū Nānak's life. During his travels across Eastern India, Gurū Nānak accompanied by the ministrel, Mardānā, stopped near the temple of Jagannāth, Lord of the Earth, which is the title of Lord Viṣṇu, second god of the Hindu Triad. Gurū Nānak and Mardānā stopped near the shrine upon which sat centuries of history mute and immobilized. The notes from Mardānā's rebeck touched the devotees' hearts with fresh fervour. Several of them came to hear the Gurū's word. The temple priests felt angry and held the Gurū guilty for not making adoration to the deity within the sacred enclosure. The local chief whose name has been described as Krishanlāl one day visited the Guru and invited him to join the *āratī*, or the evening service of lights, in the temple. The Guru readily offered to go with him.

As dusk fell, the priests lighted the lamps and the sumptuous ritual for which the devotees had been waiting began. Twinkling lights fed by ghee were placed on a jewel-studded salver, amid flowers and incense, and worshipfully swung from side to side by the priests in front of the enshrined image to the accompaniment of the chanting of hymns, blowing of conches and the ringing of bells. The priests had a complaint as they concluded. The Guru had remained seated in his place and not participated in the ceremony. The Guru burst into a song:

The sky is the salver
And the sun and the moon the lamps.
The luminous stars on the heavens are
     the pearls.
Scented air from the sandal-clad hills is
     the incense,
The winds make the fan for Thee,
And the vast forests wreaths of flowers.
The unstruck music of creation is the
     trumpet.
Thus goes on the *āratī* (adoration) for
     Thee,
O Thou dispeller of doubt and fear!

Gurū Nānak taught the hearers how Nature's tribute to the Creator was superior to any ritualistic oblation offered before images.

In spite of such depreciation of the ritual, *āratī* was performed in some of the Sikh temples under Brāhmaṇical influence. But in the Sikh case the *āratī* was performed in front of the Gurū Granth Sāhib. Wherever the word *āratī* occurred in the Gurū Granth Sāhib, the hymn was pressed into service. For instance, there was a chain of *śabdas* culled from the compositions of Ravidās, Saiṇ, Kabīr and Dhannā. Ravidās's hymn

begins with the line, "Lord, Thy Name to me is the *āratī* and holy ablutions. All else is false show" (GG, 694). Says Saiṇ, "May I be a sacrifice unto the Lord: that for me is the *āratī* performed with lamps, ghee and incense" (GG, 695). Kabīr's hymn is in the same vein. It says, "Brothers! that is how the Immaculate Lord's *āratī* is made.... Let Divine essence be the oil, the Lord's Name the wick, and enlightened self the lamp. Lighting this lamp we invoke the Lord" (GG, 1350). Dhannā's hymn is simply a prayer for the common needs of life (GG, 695).

It is clear that these hymns reject the *āratī* ritual and lay down loving devotion shorn of all formal practices as the path of true worship. The reformists of the Siṅgh Sabhā school as well as those of the more strident Akālī school discarded the ritual waving of the lighted lamps placed in a tray before the Gurū Granth Sāhib. There could, however, be no objection to the singing of the *āratī* hymns occurring in the Gurū Granth Sāhib. The *Sikh Rahit Maryādā* or religious code of the Sikhs issued under the authority of the Shiromaṇī Gurdwārā Parbandhak Committee, a statutorily elected body representative of the entire Sikh community, lays down that *āratī* with incense and lighted lamps and ringing of bells is not permissible. Although *āratī* ritual is prohibited and no longer practised in Sikh places of worship, the continuous singing of the five Scriptural *āratī* hymns, often supplemented by some verses from the *Dasam Granth*, by the holy choir or by the entire *saṅgat* in unison, is still practised at places as part of the concluding ceremonies for an *akhaṇḍ pāṭh*, end-to-end unbroken reading of the Holy Book, or at the close of the evening service at a *gurdwārā*.

BIBLIOGRAPHY

1. *Sikh Rahit Maryādā.* Amritsar, 1975
2. Kohlī, Surindar Siṅgh, ed., *Janam Sākhī Bhāī Bālā.* Chandigarh, 1975

3. *Shabdārth Srī Gurū Graṅth Sāhib*. Amritsar, 1969

M.G.S.

ARDAMAN SIṄGH, BHĀYEE (1899-1976), of pious lineage was born on 20 September 1899 (father: Bhāyee Arjan Siṅgh; mother: Devinder Kaur) at Bāgaṛīāṅ, in present-day Saṅgrūr district of the Punjab. The family traces its descent from Bhāī Rūp Chand, a devout Sikh of the time of Gurū Hargobind (1595-1644) and has for the past several generations been a leading religious family among the Sikhs. For his schooling, Ardaman Siṅgh was not sent to a Chiefs College as was then customary for aristocratic families, but to the K͟hālsā School at Ludhiāṇā. He took his B.A. degree from K͟hālsā College, Amritsar, in 1918. He left off his law studies midway to lend his father a helping hand in his religious work. Ardaman Siṅgh studied music under famous musicologists of the day such as Mahant Gajjā Siṅgh, Bhāī Javālā Siṅgh and Bhāī Ghasīṭā, and the Sikh texts with his father, Bhāyee Arjan Siṅgh himself. In 1923 he was appointed an honorary magistrate in place of his father. He took out preaching trips to different parts of India to preach Sikh tenets and administer to seekers the vows of the K͟hālsā. He delivered lectures on different aspects of Sikhism at public meetings as well as at academic institutions. As it happened, his last lecture of a series, hosted by the Pañjāb University, Chaṇḍīgaṛh, was delivered on 23 December 1976, just two days before he died.

Besides lecturing and ministering religious rites and ceremonies on important occasions, Bhāyee Ardaman Siṅgh participated in Sikh activity in a variety of ways. He helped start the Sikh Academy of Religion and Culture, Paṭiālā, of which he was invited to be president. He was president of Gurmat Academy as well as of the Siṅgh Sabhā, Shimlā. He was closely associated with the Siṅgh Sabhā centenary celebrations. He was assigned (by the Siṅgh Sabhā Centenary Committee and the Shiromaṇī Gurdwārā Parbandhak Committee) to updating the *rahit maryādā* or the Sikh code of conduct. He could not complete the draft during his lifetime. He was a leading participant in the Dasam Granth Goṣṭī organized by Mān Siṅgh, editor of the Delhi weekly, *Mānsarovar*. The purpose of the Goṣṭī was to resolve the controversy about the authorship of certain compositions included in the *Dasam Granth*, or the Book of the Tenth Master (Gurū Gobind Siṅgh). Ardaman Siṅgh was strongly of the view that all the compositions in the *Dasam Granth* were not from the pen of Gurū Gobind Siṅgh.

Bhāyee Ardaman Siṅgh died on 25 December 1976 at Chaṇḍīgaṛh due to a cardiac obstruction, and was cremated the next day at his native village Bāgaṛīāṅ.

BIBLIOGRAPHY

1. Giān Siṅgh, Giānī, *Itihās Riyāsat Bāgaṛīāṅ*. Patiala, 1917
2. Caveeshar, Sardul Singh, *House of Bagrian*. Lahore, 1939
3. Griffin, Lepel and C.F. Massy, *Chiefs and Families of Note in the Punjab*. Lahore, 1940
4. *Golden Jubilee Book*. Amritsar, 1958

D.S.

ARDĀS, supplication and recollection, is the ritual prayer which Sikhs, individually or in congregation, recite morning and evening and in fact whenever they perform a religious service and at the beginning and conclusion of family, public or religious functions. The word *ardās* seems to have been derived from Persian *'arzdāsht*, meaning a petition, a memorial or an address to a superior authority. The Sikh *ardās* is rendered to God Almighty in a supplicatory mood standing in front of the Gurū Granth Sāhib or, where the Gurū Granth Sāhib is not present, standing in a similarly reverential posture. *Ardās* is not inscribed in the Gurū Granth Sāhib. It is an evolute of the community's heart in prayer over the centuries. Whenever, in history, the community in distress or in a mood of thanks-giving verbalized its supplications to God and wherever a congregation, in harmony with the entire community (as also with all mankind) has assembled prayerfully, apt expressions of its spiritual mood became incorporated into the *ardās.*

Broadly, the *ardās* consists of three parts. As the audience rise for *ardās,* the officiant leading the prayer usually begins by reciting a *pauṛī* or stanza from the *Sukhmanī: tū ṭhākuru tum pahi ardāsi...* Thou art the Lord-Master; to Thee our *ardās* (supplication) is addressed... Then will follow recitation *verbatim* of the prelude to Gurū Gobind Siṅgh's composition *Vār Srī Bhagautī Jī Kī.* This 41-word stanza invokes the Timeless One and the first Nine Gurūs. The first addition that the Panth made was to extend this invocation to include the name of Gurū Gobind Siṅgh himself and the Gurū Granth Sāhib, "body visible of the Gurūs" after him. The second part is a recital of Sikhs' deeds of dedication and sacrifice. The *ardās* thus encapsulates Sikh history, but transcending the time-and-space setting. The third part comprises words improvised to suit any given occasion. After the initial invocation, the *ardās* goes on to recount and reflect upon the memorable acts of the community's martyrs and heroes—men of unswerving resolution and unrelenting fortitude, who upheld their faith with their sacred hair unto their last breath. In this respect, history has been continually contributing to *ardās* with the result that, along with the martyrs of the Gurū period and of the periods of persecution following, it recalls those of the Gurdwārā reform movement of the 1920's and those who laid down their lives for the sake of their faith at the time of the partition of the country in 1947.

When early in the eighteenth century Sikhs were outlawed by royal edict and when they faced violent death wherever sighted, they in their places of refuge in jungles and deserts praying collectively or severally sought God's protection for the entire K͟hālsā wheresoever they be. The words have become a permanent part of the *ardās.* The prayer for the privilege of a dip in the sacred pool at Amritsar as well as for the preservation of the Panth's choirs, banners and mansions, likewise, has historical echoes. The Sikhs' entry into the precincts of the holy Harimandar and the tank had been banned by the ruling authority in mid-eighteenth century. Heavy armed posts were set up around the shrine and any Sikh pilgrims trying to come in to pay homage or make ablutions in the holy waters were hunted down. The line in *ardās* alludes to that historical situation and bears witness to the Sikhs' deep attachment to their places of worship.

Ārdās is, thus, the epitome of Sikh history and enshrines in its text the community's aspirations at various periods of its history and enables the devotees to unite in a brotherhood of faith over the centuries, transcending time. These aspirations are couched in expressions coined by minds saturated in faith. After recounting the deeds of faith and sacrifice over the expanse of time, the congregation recounts Sikh places of worship over the expanse of space. Thereafter, prayer is made for and on behalf of the whole community, seeking the Lord's protection and grace for the entire K͟hālsā, ending with a supplication for universal weal. Then it asks for the specific boons of holy discipleship, a life of restraint, discrimination and faith and a firm and confident attitude of mind inspired by the holy Name.

The focus shifts from the community life to the life of the individual believer and the quality of his life. Gifts like the virtues of humility and wisdom are besought, as well as purity of understanding to discern the Divine Will. Protection is sought against such evils as lust, wrath, greed, attachment and pride. Fellowship is craved with persons of faith and purity. Words of thanksgivings or words seeking God's blessing are finally added, depending upon what the occasion is. *Ardās* always concludes with a prayer for the welfare and prosperity for all mankind.

The whole assembly stands with folded hands to say *ardās* facing the Gurū Granth Sāhib when it is present. In the absence of the Gurū Granth Sāhib, it can be facing in any direction. Usually, a supplicatory *śabda* (hymn) is recited upon rising for *ardās*. Anyone from among the assembly can lead *ardās*

At prescribed intervals during *ardās*, the entire *saṅgat* associates itself with the leader repeating at his instance, 'Vāhigurū'. As the *ardās* concludes, the whole congregation kneels down and then rises again and utters in unison, '*Vāhigurū jī kā Khālsā Vāhigurū jī kī Fateh*' – The Khālsā belongs to the Lord to whom too belongs the Victory. This is followed by the slogan '*Bole so Nihāl*' – he who pronounces these words shall be fulfilled, to which the whole assembly responds by shouting, '*Sat Srī Akāl*' – True is the Timeless Lord.

Although, in its structure *ardās* is essentially a congregational prayer, it is equally the prayer for the individual. It is non-isolationalistic in character, not being for the individual alone, nor even only for the congregation. It is for the entire *panth*. It gives the individual a sense of unity with the community as well as with mankind at large.

Ardās has evolved over a long period of time and in this process it has not only absorbed several facets of the history of the community, but has also acquired a literary excellence. It is an exceedingly fine piece of prose in which there is a continuous flow of words and ideas carefully chosen. This aids the participants to attune themselves to the spiritual atmosphere it generates.

Below is given the *ardās* (English version) recited at the World Conference on Religion and Peace held at Kyoto, Japan, in October 1970. With the exception of the para concerning the particular purpose for which the *ardās* is performed, the remaining portions are generally the same for all occasions.

The Text of Ardās

Unto The One Supreme God Who by the grace of Satgurū is realized.

Remember, first, God the Almighty: think then of Gurū Nānak: of Aṅgad Gurū and Amar Dās, and Rām Dās. May their protection be ever with us!

Remember Arjan, Hargobind, and the holy Har Rāi.

Let us think of the holy Har Krishan whose sight annuls all sorrow.

Let us remember Tegh Bahādur, and all the nine treasures, will come flowing in.

May He protect us everywhere!

May the Tenth King, the holy Gurū Gobind Siṅgh, the lord of hosts, master of the hawk, and protector of faith, help us everywhere!

Turn your thoughts, O Khālsā, to the Gurū Granth Sāhib, the visible body of the Gurūs, and their word, and say, *Vāhigurū*, Glory be to God!!

The five Loved Ones, the Gurū's four sons, the Forty saved and other holy and heroic men, saints and martyrs: remember their selfless and heroic deeds, and say, *Vāhigurū*, Glory be to God!

Those, men and women, who laid down their lives in the cause of faith, who suffered themselves to be cut up limb by limb, and had their scalps scraped off, were broken on the wheel, were sawn or flayed alive and yet uttered not a moan from their lips, and remained steadfast in their Sikh faith to the last hair of their sacred tresses (*keś*) and to their last breath: think of their sweet resignation, and say, *Vāhigurū*, Glory be to God!

Those who, to purge the places of worship of corruption longstanding, suffered themselves to be ruthlessly beaten or imprisoned, to be shot, cut up, or burnt alive, but did not make any resistance nor uttered a word of complaint: think of their patient faith and fortitude, and say, *Vāhigurū*, Glory be to God!

Think of all the Gurdwārās, the places of divine remembrance, the thrones of religoius authority, and other places hallowed by the touch of the Gurūs' feet, and say *Vāhigurū*, Glory be to God!

The whole Khālsā offer their prayer,

Let the whole Khālsā bring to their minds the Name of the Wonderful Lord:

And as they think of Him, may they rejoice in His blessing!

May they bring peace and comfort to the whole world.

May God's protection and grace extend to all the Khālsā wheresoever they be.

May charity, justice, and faith flourish.

May the Khālsā be forever in the ascendant.

May the Sikh choirs, banners, mansions of the Khālsā be eternally blessed.

May the kingdom of justice prevail!

May the believers be united in love.

May the hearts of the believers be humble, high their wisdom, and may they be guided in their wisdom by the Lord. O Khālsā, say *Vāhigurū*, Glory be to God!

Save us, O Father, from lust, wrath, greed, attachment, and pride; and keep us attached always to Thy feet.

Grant to Thy Sikhs the gift of faith, the gift of Thy Name, the gift of trust in Thee, and the gift of recitation and comprehension of Thy holy word.

Give us light, give us understanding so that we may know Thy Will. Forgive us our sins. Bring us into the fellowship of only those in whose company we may remember Thy Name.

We make this prayer in Thy presence, Lord!

"Entrust unto the Lord what thou wishest to be accomplished.

"The Lord will bring all matters to fulfilment: know this as truth evidenced by the Lord Himself."

O true Master, Loved Father, here in this city of Kyoto, in Japan, had assembled representatives of world religions—men of faith who believe in Thee. This conclave is now concluding its week-long deliberations in behalf of world peace. Lord, give the members of this Conference Thy blessing and Thy guidance. Grant unto them the power and ability constantly to endeavour and pursue the goal they have set themselves. Extend Thy blessing and Thy grace to Thy servants and bless their humble efforts. This Conference has concluded its sessions without obstruction. This is by Thy own favour!

May this prayer be accepted at Thy door!

May God's name, may the human spirit forever triumph, Nānak!

And in Thy Will may peace and prosperity come to one and all...

Blessed is he who utters His name.

TheTimeless is the Eternal Reality

BIBLIOGRAPHY

1. Kapur Singh, *Pārāśarapraśna* [Reprint]. Amritsar, 1989

2. Teja Singh, trans. and annot., *Sikh Prayer*.
3. Harbans Singh, in *Religion in the Struggle for World Community*. Tokyo, 1980
4. Nripinder Singh, *The Sikh Moral Tradition*. Delhi, 1990
5. Cole, W. Owen, and Piara Singh Sambhi, *The Sikhs: Their Religious Beliefs and Practices* Delhi, 1978

J.S.N.

ARGOUD, BENOIT, a Frenchman, who joined Mahārājā Raṇjīt Siṅgh's infantry in November 1836 as an instructor. He was of a quarrelsome nature and readily picked rows with his colleagues and subordinates. Dismissed from service in April 1837, he proceeded to Afghanistan, but failed to get any employment there. Returning to Peshāwar in 1838 and thence proceeding to Calcutta, he applied for repatriation to France. The application being rejected, he, helped by some French merchants, returned to Kābul (1839). Disappointed here again, he returned to Peshāwar and took up service in General Court's brigade. He left service in 1843 and returned to France.

BIBILIOGRAPHY

Grey, C., *European Adventurers of Northern India*. Patiala, 1970

Gl.S.

ARJAN DEV, GURŪ (1563-1606), fifth in the line of ten Gurūs or prophet-teachers of the Sikh faith, was born on Baisākh *vadī* 7, 1620 Bk/15 April 1563 at Goindvāl, in present-day Amritsar district, to Bhāī Jeṭhā who later occupied the seat of Gurūship as Gurū Rām Dās, fourth in succession from Gurū Nānak, and his wife, Bībī (lady) Bhānī, daughter of Gurū Amar Dās, the Third Gurū. The youngest son of his parents, (Gurū) Arjan Dev was of a deeply religious temperament and his father's favourite. This excited the jealousy of his eldest brother, Prithī Chand. Once Gurū Rām Dās had an invitation to attend at Lahore the wedding of a relation. The Gurū, unable to go himself, wanted one of his sons to represent him at the ceremony. Prithī Chand, the eldest son, avoided going and made excuses. The second son, Mahādev, had little interest in worldly affairs. Arjan Dev willingly offered to do the Gurū's bidding. He was sent to Lahore with instructions to remain there and preach Gurū Nānak's word until sent for. Arjan Dev stayed on in Lahore where he established a Sikh *saṅgat*. From Lahore, he wrote to his father letters in verse, pregnant with spiritual overtones, giving vent to the pangs of his heart. Gurū Rām Dās recalled him to Amritsar, and judging him fit to inherit Gurū Nānak's mantle pronounced him his successor.

Gurū Arjan entered upon the spiritual office on the death of Gurū Rām Dās on 1 September 1581. Under his fostering care the Sikh faith acquired a strong scriptural, doctrinal and organizational base, and became potentially the force for a cultural and social revolution in the Punjab. Its religious and social ideals received telling affirmation in practice. It added to its orbit more concrete and permanent symbols and its administration became more cohesive. By encouraging agriculture and trade and by the introduction of a system of tithe-collection for the common use of the community, a stable economic base was secured. Gurū Arjan gave Sikhism its Scripture, the Granth Sāhib, and its main place of worship, the Harimandar, the Golden Temple of modern day. He taught, by example, humility and sacrifice, and was the first martyr of the Sikh faith. The work of the first four Gurūs was preparatory. It assumed a more definitive form in the hands of Gurū Arjan. Later Gurūs substantiated the principles manifested in his life. Gurū Arjan thus marked a central point in the evolution of the Sikh tradition.

Gurū Arjan remained in the central Punjab throughout his spiritual reign. Recorded history speaks of his movements between Goindvāl, Lahore, Amritsar, Tarn Tāran and Kartārpur, near Jalandhar. His policy seems to have been one of consolidation and development. Despite the many forms of opposition which he had to face, Gurū Arjan consolidated the community by his hymns, leadership and institutional reforms.

The first task that Gurū Arjan undertook was the completion of the Amritsar pool. Sikhs came from distant places to join in the work of digging. The Gurū also started extending the town. He had the Harimandar built in the middle of the holy tank and, according to Ghulām Muhayy ud-Dīn alias Būṭe Shāh (*Twārīkh-i-Punjab*), and Giānī Giān Siṅgh (*Twārīkh Gurū Khālsā*, Urdu), had the cornerstone of the building laid by the famous Muslim Sūfī Mīāṅ Mīr (1550-1635). Ghulām Muhayy ud-Dīn states that Shāh Mīāṅ Mīr came to Amritsar at Gurū Arjan's request, and "with his own blessed hand put four bricks, one on each side, and another one in the middle of the tank." As against the generality of the temples in India with their single east-facing entrance, the new shrine was given four doors, one in each direction, symbolizing the catholicity of outlook to be preached from within it. Each door could also be taken to stand for one of the four castes which should be equally welcome to enter and receive spiritual sustenance. At the temple, Gurū Arjan, in keeping with the tradition of his predecessors, maintained a community kitchen which was open to all castes and creeds. Inside the temple, the chanting of hymns would go on for most hours of day and night. Around the temple developed markets to which the Gurū invited traders from different regions to settle and open their business. Rest houses for pilgrims were also built and soon a city had grown up with the Harimandar as its focus. In addition Gurū Arjan completed the construction of Santokhsar and Rāmsar *sarovars* started by his predecessor. The precincts of the peaceful and picturesque latter pool provided the quiet retreat where over a considerable period the Gurū remained occupied in giving shape to the Sikh Scripture, the Granth Sāhib.

Gurū Arjan undertook a tour of the Punjab to spread the holy word. From Amritsar, he proceeded on a journey through the Mājhā territory. Coming upon the site of the present shrine of Tarn Tāran (The Holy Raft across the Sinful Waters of Worldliness), 24 km south of Amritsar, he felt much attracted by the beauty of its natural surroundings. He acquired the land from the owners, the residents of the village of Khārā, and constructed a tank as well as a sanctuary which became pilgrim spots for Sikhs. Especially drawn towards Tarn Tāran were the lepers who were treated here by the Gurū with much loving care. As he moved from village to village, Gurū Arjan helped people sink wells and undertake several other works of public weal, especially to alleviate the hardship caused by the famine which then gripped the Punjab. The city of Lahore even today has a *baolī*, or well with steps going down to water level, built by Gurū Arjan. Another town raised by the Gurū was Kartārpur, in the Jalandhar Doāb between the rivers Beās and Sutlej. He also rebuilt a ruined village, Ruhelā, on the right bank of the River Beās, and renamed it Srī Gobindpur or Srī Hargobindpur after his son (Gurū) Hargobind.

Many more people were drawn into the Sikh fold in consequence of Gurū Arjan's travels. The Gurū's fame spread far and wide bringing to him devotees from all over the Punjab, from the eastern parts then called Hindustān and from far-off lands such as Kābul and Central Asia. This growing following was kept united by an efficient cadre of local leaders, called *masands* who looked after the *saṅgats*, Sikh centres, in far-flung parts of the country. They collected from the disciples *dasvandh* or one-tenth of their income which they were enjoined to give away for communal sharing, and led the Sikhs to the Gurū's presence periodically. The Gurū's assemblies had something of the appearance of a theocratic court. The Sikhs had coined a special title for him – Sachchā Pādshāh, i.e. the True King, as distinguished from the secular monarch. Offerings continued to pour in which in the tradition of the Gurū's household would be spent on feeding the poor and on works of public beneficence – the Gurū and his family living in a state of self-imposed poverty in the way of the service of God.

A son, Hargobind, was born to Gurū Arjan and his wife, Mātā Gaṅgā, in 1595. At the birth of his only child, there were rejoicings in the Gurū's household which are reflected in his hymns of thanksgiving preserved in the Gurū Granth Sāhib.

A most significant undertaking of Gurū Arjan's career which was brought to completion towards the close of his short life was the compilation of the Ādi (Primal) Granth, codifying the compositions of the Gurūs into an authorized volume. According to Sarūp Dās Bhallā, *Mahimā Prakāsh*, he set to work with the announcement: "As the Panth (community) has been revealed unto the world, so must there be the Granth (book), too." The *bāṇī,* Gurus' inspired utterance, had always been the object of highest reverence for the Sikhs as well as for the Gurūs themselves. It was equated with the Gurū himself.

"The *bāṇī* is the Gurū and the Gurū *bāṇī*" (GG, 982). By accumulating the canon, Gurū Arjan wished to affix the seal on the sacred word and preserve it for posterity. It was also to be the perennial fountain of inspiration and the means of self-perpetuation for the community.

Gurū Arjan had his father's hymns with him. He persuaded Bābā Mohan, Gurū Amar Dās's son and his maternal uncle, to lend him the *pothīs* or collections of the compositions of the first three Gurūs and of some saints and sūfīs he had in his possession. In addition, he sent out emissaries in every direction in search of the Gurūs' compositions. The making of the Granth involved sustained labour and rigorous intellectual discipline. Selections had to be made from a vast mass of material. What was genuine had to be sifted from what was counterfeit. Then the selected material had to be assigned to appropriate musical measures, edited and recast where necessary, and transcribed in a minutely laid-out order. Gurū Arjan accomplished the task with extraordinary exactness. He arranged the hymns in thirty different *rāgas* or musical patterns. A precise method was followed in setting down the compositions. First, came *śabdas* by the Gurūs in the order of their succession. Then came *aṣṭpadīs* and other poetic forms in a set order and the *vārs*.

The compositions of the Gurūs in each *rāga* were followed by those of the *bhaktas* in the same format. Gurmukhī was the script used for transcription. A genius unique in spiritual insight and not unconcerned with methodological design had created a scripture with an exalted mystical tone and a high degree of organization. It was large in size – nearly 6,000 hymns containing compositions of the first five Gurūs (Gurū Arjan's own contribution being the largest) and fifteen saints of different faiths and castes, including the Muslim sūfī, Shai<u>kh</u> Farīd, Ravidās, a shoemaker, and Saiṇ, a barber.

Gurū Arjan's vast learning in the religious literature of medieval India and the varied philosophies current at the popular and academic levels, besides his accomplishment in music and his knowledge of languages ranging from the Sanskrit of Jayadeva (Jaidev) through the neo-classical tradition in Hindi poetry then developing into the various dialects spread over the great expanse of northern and central India and Mahārāshṭra is visible from his editing and evaluative work in putting together this authoritative collection. The completion of the Ādi Granth was celebrated with much jubilation. In thanksgiving, *kaṛāhprasād* was distributed in huge quantities among the Sikhs who had come in large numbers to see the Holy Book. The Granth was ceremonially installed in the centre of the inner sanctuary of the Harimandar on Bhādoṅ *sudī* 1,1661 Bk/16 August 1604. The revered Bhāī Buḍḍhā who was chosen to take charge of the Granth opened it with reverence to receive from it the divine command or lesson as Gurū Arjan stood in attendance behind. The following hymn was read as God's own word for the occasion:

> He Himself hath succoured His saints
> in their work;
> He Himself hath come to see their task
> fulfilled,
> Blessed is the earth, blessed the tank;
> Blessed is the tank with *amrit* filled.
> *Amrit* overfloweth the tank: He hath
> the task completed.

The Granth Sāhib, containing hymns of Gurūs and of Hindu and Muslim saints, was a puzzle for people of orthodox views. Complaints were carried to the Mughal emperor that the book was derogatory to Islam and other religions. The emperor, who was then encamped at Baṭālā in the Punjab asked to see Gurū Arjan who sent Bhāī Buḍḍhā and Bhāī Gurdās, two revered Sikhs, with the Granth. The book was opened at random and read from the spot pointed out by Akbar. The hymn was in praise of God. So were the others, read out subsequently. Akbar was pleased and made an offering of fifty-one gold *mohars* to the Granth Sāhib. He presented Bhāī Buḍḍhā and Bhāī Gurdās with robes of honour and gave a third one for the Gurū. Akbar had himself visited Gurū Arjan earlier, at Goindvāl, in November 1598 and besought him for spiritual guidance. At the Gurū's instance, the Emperor remitted 10 to 12 per cent of the land revenue in the Punjab.

Gurū Arjan was an unusually gifted and prolific poet. Over one-third of the Ādi Granth consists of his own utterances. They comprise more than two thousand verses. These are in part philosophical, enshrining his vision of the Absolute, the unattributed and the transcendental Brahman as also of God the Beloved. The deeper secrets of the self, the immortal divine spark lodged in the tenement of the flesh and of the immutable moral law regulating the individual life no less than the universe, find repeated expression in his compositions. Alternating with these is his poetry of divine love, of the holy passion for the eternal which is the true yoga-pursuit in joining the finite person to the infinite. In this devotional passion all humanity, without distinction of caste or status, is viewed as one and equally worthy to touch the feet of the Lord. The Gurū's lines are resplendent with bejewelled phrases and his hymns full of haunting melody. The essential message of his hymns is meditation on *nām*. Deep feelings of universal compassion find expression in his compositions binding the entire universe in a mystical union of love, in a sanctum of experience where nothing so gross as hate and egoism enters. His famous *Sukhmanī (q.v.)*, the Psalm of Peace, which has been commented upon many times and rendered into several Indian and foreign languages, is a symmetrical structure of twenty-four cantos, each of eight five-couplet stanzas, preceded by a *śloka* or key-couplet expressing the motif of the entire canto following. In this composition Gurū Arjan expatiated on the concept of Brahmgiānī (the enlightened soul). According to him, this enlightenment can be attained only through meditation on *nām*, the Lord's Name, and through the Gurū's grace. In depicting the attributes of the Brahmgiānī, he has compared him to a lotus flower which immersed in mud and water is yet pure and beautiful. Without ill will or enmity towards anyone, he is forever courageous and calm.

Gurū Arjan's compositions are in two strains from the point of view of the choice of vocabulary. In portions which are mainly philosophical in content, the character of the language is close to Brajī Hindi. In those portions where the main inspiration is devotional or touching the human personality with compassion and that peace which no pain, sorrow or encounter with evil may disturb, he uses the western Punjabi idiom which before him had been employed in similar contexts by Gurū Nānak. In a few of his hymns he has employed the current terminology of popular Islam in order to emphasize tolerance and inter-religious goodwill. A few of his compositions, like Gurū Nānak's before him, are couched in the Prākrit idiom called Sahaskritī or Gāthā. Gurū Arjan's many-sided learning is witnessed in his own compositions as well in the editing of the Holy Volume and his commentary on the work of the *bhaktas* whose compositions he included in Ādi Granth.

In the time of Gurū Arjan the Sikh faith gained a large number of adherents. On the testimony of a contemporary Persian source, the *Dabistān-i-Mazāhib*, "During the time of each Mahal (Gurū) the Sikhs increased till in the reign of Gurū Arjan Mall they became numerous and there were not many cities in the inhabited countries where some Sikhs were not to be found."

Gurū Arjan's martyrdom, pregnant with far-reaching consequences in the history of Sikhism and of the Punjab, occurred on Jeṭh *sudī* 4,1663 Bk/30 May 1606 after a period of imprisonment and torture. The scene of the Gurū's torture was a platform outside the Fort of Lahore near the River Rāvī. In the eighteenth century a shrine, Ḍehrā Sāhib, was erected on the spot where every year the day is marked by a vast concourse of pilgrims coming from all over the Sikh world.

There are conflicting accounts of the circumstances leading to Gurū Arjan's death. A Sikh tradition places the responsibility on a Hindu Khatrī official, Chandū, whose pride had been hurt when the Gurū refused to accept his daughter as a wife for his son, Hargobind. However, although Chandū took his opportunity to add to the Gurū's suffering, it is hardly likely that he had the influence to cause it. The real cause was the attitude of the Emperor himself. Jahāṅgīr who succeeded Akbar on the throne of Delhi in 1605 was not as liberal and tolerant as his father. In his early years on the throne, he depended more on the orthodox section among his courtiers. This coterie was under the influence of Shaikh Ahmad of Sirhind (1569-1624), leader of the Naqshbandī order of the Sūfīs. The Sikhs were the first to bear the brunt of Jahāṅgīr's malice. Jahāṅgīr felt especially alarmed at the growing influence of Gurū Arjan. As he wrote in his *Tuzk:* "So many of the simple-minded Hindus, nay, many foolish Muslims too had been fascinated by the Gurū's ways and teaching. For many years the thought had been presenting itself to my mind that either I should put an end to this false traffic, or that he be brought into the fold of Islam."

Within a few months of Jahāṅgīr's succession, his son, Khusrau, rebelled against his father and, on his way to Lahore, met Gurū Arjan at Goindvāl and sought his blessing. According to the *Mahimā Prakāsh*, the Prince partook of the hospitality of the Gurū kā Laṅgar and resumed his journey the following morning. Nevertheless after the rebellion had been suppressed and Khusrau apprehended, Jahāṅgīr wreaked terrible vengeance on the people he suspected of having helped his son. Gurū Arjan was heavily fined and on his refusal to pay the fine was arrested. To quote again from Jahāṅgīr's memoirs: " I fully knew of his heresies, and I ordered that he should be brought into my presence, that his property be confiscated and that he should be put to death with torture."

The Gurū was taken to Lahore. For several days he was subjected to extreme physical torment. He was seated on red-hot iron plates and burning sand was poured over him. He was made to take a dip in boiling water. Mīāṅ Mīr, the Gurū's Muslim friend, came to see him and offered to intercede on his behalf. But the Gurū forbade him and enjoined him to find peace in God's Will. The Gurū was then taken to the Rāvī. A dip in the river's cold water was more than the blistered body could bear. Wrapped in meditation, the Gurū peacefully passed away. As a contemporary Jesuit document—a letter written from Lahore on 25 September 1606 by Father Zerome Xavier– says, "In that way their good Pope died, overwhelmed by the sufferings, torments, and dishonours." The man who derived the most satisfaction from the execution of Gurū Arjan Dev was Shaikh Ahmad Sirhindī Mujaddid-i-alf-i-Sānī. In his letter, as quoted in the *Maktūbāt-i-Imām-i-Rabbānī*, he expressed jubilation over "the execution of the accursed *kāfir* of Goindvāl."

Gurū Arjan's martyrdom marked the fulfilment of Gurū Nānak's religious and ethical injunctions. Personal piety must have a core of moral strength. A virtuous soul must be a courageous soul. Willingness to suffer trial for one's convictions was a religious imperative. Gurū Arjan's life exemplified this principle.

Of Gurū Arjan's personality and death, his kinsman and contemporary, the revered Sikh savant Bhāī Gurdās wrote in his *Vārāṅ*, XXIV. 23 :

> As fishes are at one with the waves of the river,
> So was the Gurū, immersed in the River that is the Lord:
> As the moth merges itself at sight into the flame,
> So was the Gurū's light merged with the Divine Light.
> In the extremest hours of suffering he was aware of nothing but the Divine Word,
> Like the deer who hears no sound but the ringing of the hunter's bell.
> Like the humming-bee who is wrapped inside the lotus,
> He passed the night of his life as in a casket of bliss;
> Never did he forget to utter the Lord's word, even as the *chātrik* fails never to utter its cry;
> To the man of God joy is the fruit of devotion and meditation with equanimity in holy company.
> May I be a sacrifice unto this Gurū Arjan.

Gurū Arjan was succeeded on the spiritual throne by his son, Hargobind.

BIBLIOGRAPHY

1. Ganda Singh, *Gurū Arjan's Martyrdom Reinterpreted*. Patiala, 1969
2. Macauliffe, Max Arthur, *The Sikh Religion*. Oxford, 1909
3. Gunindar Kaur, *The Guru Granth Sahib: Its Physics and Metaphysics*. Delhi, 1981
4. Teja Singh, *Psalm of Peace*. Bombay, 1937
5. Jodh Siṅgh, Bhāī, *Srī Kartārpurī Bīṛ de Darshan*. Patiala, 1968
6. Satibīr Siṅgh, *Partakh Hari*. Jalandhar, 1977
7. Sūrī, Kartār Siṅgh, *Gurū Arjan Dev te Sant Dādū Diāl*. Chandigarh, 1969

G.S.T.

ARJAN SIṄGH (d. 1859), a military commander in Sikh times, was born the son of Jamīat Siṅgh of Raṅghaṛ Naṅgal, in Gurdāspur district. In 1845, on the eve of the first Anglo-Sikh war, he was given the command of four infantry regiments, one regiment of cavalry, and a troop of horse artillery, with which force he served at the battle of Sabhrāoṅ. In 1846, he took part in the Kaṣhmīr expedition and in August 1847 received a Persian title of honour on the recommendation of Major Henry Lawrence, the British Resident at Lahore. In 1848, he accompanied Rājā Sher Siṅgh Aṭārīvālā to Multān, and became an ally in his rebellion. His followers, hearing this, rebelled too and defended the fort of Raṅghaṛ Naṅgal successfully against two companies of the Lahore troops. After the annexation of the Punjab by the British, the estates of Arjan Siṅgh were confiscated.

Arjan Siṅgh died in 1859.

BIBLIOGRAPHY

1. Griffin, Lepel, and C.F. Massy, *Chiefs and Families of Note in the Punjab*. Lahore, 1909
2. Cunningham, Joseph Davey, *A History of the Sikhs*. London, 1849
3. Gupta, Hari Ram, *Panjab on the Eve of First Sikh War*. Chandigarh, 1956

S.S.B.

ARJAN SIṄGH, BHĀĪ (*c.* 1906-1924), born to Kishan Siṅgh of the village of Kamālīā, now in Sāhīvāl district of Pakistan, was a zealous worker in the cause of Sikh Gurdwārā reform. As a young boy he was deeply affected by events at Nankāṇā Sāhib in 1921 (*See* NANKĀṆĀ SAHIB MASSACRE). Closing down his business he joined the Akālī ranks. He participated in the Gurū kā Bāgh and Jaito agitations: he officiated as one of the Pañj Piāre when the *jathā* left for Jaito on Baisākh 1, 1981, Bk/12 April 1924. His health deteriorated while he was in police custody and he died on 26 November 1924.

Bhāī Arjan Siṅgh was tall and handsome and led a pious life. He used to compose verses, and one of his poems, "Naukarshāhī nūṅ Chailañj" or Challenge to Bureaucracy, was included in an anthology entitled *Shahīdī Khūn*. A *gurdwārā*, a boarding house and a library were erected at Kamālīā to honour his memory.

G.S.G.

ARJAN SIṄGH, BHĀYEE (1875-1946), of Bāgarīāṅ, titled chief much honoured in Sikh piety, was a descendant of Bhāī Rūp Chand, a devoted disciple of Gurū Hargobind, who had bestowed on him the title 'Bhāī' (also written as Bhāyee) or holy brother. Rūp Chand belonged to the village of Vaḍḍā Ghar, in Amritsar district, but upon receiving Gurū Hargobind's blessing he founded (1631) a village in the Mālvā region of the Punjab which he named Bhāī Rūpā. Rūp Chand's sons, Bhāī Param Siṅgh and Bhāī Dharam Siṅgh, received the rites of Khālsā baptism at the hands of Gurū Gobind Siṅgh. They accompanied the Gurū to Nānded in the South. Param Siṅgh is said to have died there while Dharam Siṅgh was sent back to the Punjab by the Gurū with many gifts, including a *guṭkā* or breviary and a sword which are still preserved by the descendants as sacred relics.

Born in 1875 the son of Bhāī Kishan Siṅgh at Bāgaṛīāṅ, a village now in Saṅgrūr district, to which the family had shifted, Arjan Siṅgh had his early education under his uncle Bhāī Narāiṇ Siṅgh who was a reputed man of letters and who taught him several modern Indian and classical languages. Arjan Siṅgh succeeded to his estate when he was very young. Besides his position as a landed aristocrat, he was acknowledged by the Sikh ruling chiefs of Paṭiālā, Nābhā, Jīnd, Farīdkoṭ, Kapūrthalā and Kalsīā as a religious mentor—a status the Bhāīs of Bāgaṛīāṅ had always enjoyed in view of the family having been blessed by the Gurūs themselves. They presided over the religious and social ceremonies in the Sikh princely families. Bhāī Arjan Siṅgh himself administered the rites of initiation to Mahārājā Bhūpinder Siṅgh of Paṭiālā and Mahārājā Ripudaman Siṅgh of Nābhā, and installed the latter on the throne after the death in 1911 of his father, Mahārājā Sir Hīrā Siṅgh.

Bhāī Arjan Siṅgh was widely respected in the Sikh community. He was chosen to be the first president of the Chief Khālsā Dīwān established on 30 October 1902, serving in that capacity for nearly 15 years. In 1934, he presided over the Sarab Hind Sikh Samparadāi Conference at Bhaiṇī Sāhib and in 1938 over the 27th Sikh Educational Conference at Amritsar. He was awarded by the British government the title of Sardār Bahādur in 1916, and, in June 1919, the Order of the British Empire was conferred upon him. He also served as president of the Khālsā Pratinidh Dīwān, Ludhiāṇā, and as a member of the Amritsar Khālsā College Managing Committee as well as of the Shiromaṇī Gurdwārā Parbandhak Committee.

Bhāī Arjan Siṅgh died at Bāgaṛīāṅ on 8 November 1946.

BIBLIOGRAPHY

1. Giān Siṅgh, Giānī, *Itihās Riyāsat Bāgaṛīāṅ*. Patiala, 1917
2. Caveeshar, Sardul Siṅgh, *House of Bagrian*. Lahore, 1939
3. Griffin, Lepel and C.F. Massy, *Chiefs and Families of Note in the Punjab*. Lahore, 1940

S.S.A.

ARJAN SIṄGH CHĀHAL, SARDĀR BAHĀDUR (1839-1908), was only seven when his father, Javālā Siṅgh, died in 1846 in the prime of his life. Arjan Siṅgh belonged to the village of Chāhal in Amritsar district. He held large *jāgīrs* in Tarn Tāran *tahsīl* and in Lyallpur district. He was an honorary magistrate and civil judge, an assistant collector and sub-registrar of his district, president of the Local Board of Tarn Tāran, a Fellow of the Pañjāb University, and a member of the Aitchison College Committee.

He received the title of Sardār Bahādur in 1894 and was made a Companion of the Indian Empire in 1906. He was manager of the Darbār Sāhib, Amritsar, for over seven years until he resigned in 1896. He was appointed president of the 11-member lighting committee set up in 1896 for the installation of electricity in the Golden Temple.

Arjan Siṅgh died in January 1908 at the age of 69.

BIBLIOGRAPHY

1. Griffin, Lepel, and C. F. Massy, *Chiefs and Families of Note in the Punjab*. Lahore, 1909
2. Harbans Singh, *The Heritage of the Sikhs*. Delhi, 1983

S.S.B.

ARJAN SIṄGH GAṚGAJJ (1905-1963), revolutionary and journalist, was born the son of Sundar Siṅgh Rāmgaṛhīā, an artisan of Tarn Tāran, in Amritsar district of the Punjab, in 1905. In 1919, when he was studying in class VI, young Arjan Siṅgh was expelled from school for refusing to salute the Union Jack, imperial standard of the British rulers. Undaunted, he plunged into the Akālī agitation launched in 1920. He left home soon after and took up residence in the office of the Gaṛgajj (lit. thunderous) Akālī Dīwān established by Jathedār Tejā Siṅgh Bhuchchar. This earned him the epithet "Gaṛgajj". Arjan Siṅgh was arrested in April 1922 on a charge of publicly reciting a seditious poem and sent to jail for six months—the youngest Akālī prisoner. Again in 1923, after the Shiromaṇi Akālī Dal as well as the Shiromaṇī Gurdwārā Parbandhak Committee had been outlawed in the wake of the Nābhā agitation, Arjan Siṅgh was taken into custody and awarded one-year imprisonment, but was not released until September 1926, when orders banning the Akālī Dal were withdrawn. From the Akālī Dal, he went across to Naujawān Bhārat Sabhā, an organization of young socialist revolutionaries. He became a member of the editorial staff of the *Kirtī*, a professedly leftist magazine founded in February 1926 by Santokh Siṅgh, a Ghadr revolutionary. He was imprisoned for his anti-government writings in 1929 and, again, in 1930. Speech-making was banned for him in 1931, and in 1932 he was interned in the town of Tarn Tāran. After briefly serving as sub-editor of the *Babar Sher* and chief editor of the *Cartoon*, he joined the *Akālī* as a sub-editor in 1935. He suffered imprisonment for his political convictions even after Independence and worked on newspapers such as *Jaṅg-i-Āzādī* and *Nawāṅ Zamānā*. His three published works, all in Punjabi, are *Do Pair Ghaṭṭ Turnā, Shahīd de Bol* and *Merā Āpṇā Āp*.

Arjan Singh Gaṛgajj died on 10 March 1963.

BIBLIOGRAPHY

1. Pratāp Siṅgh, Giānī, *Gurdwārā Sudhār arthāt Akālī Lahir*. Amritsar, 1975
2. Josh, Sohan Siṅgh, *Akālī Morchiāṅ dā Itihās*. Delhi, 1972

J.S.A.

ARJAN SIṄGH NALVĀ (d. 1848), a minor *jāgīrdār* in Sikh times, was youngest of the four sons of the famous general, Harī Siṅgh Nalvā. He was a favourite of Kaṅvar Nau Nihāl Siṅgh, Mahārājā Raṇjīt Siṅgh's grandson. In July 1840, it was reported that Arjan Siṅgh had killed one of his servants whose widow had burnt herself as a *satī*. Nau Nihāl Siṅgh became very angry and imposed upon him a fine of Rs 10,000. In October 1848, on the eve of second Anglo-Sikh war, he joined hands with the Sikh army fighting against the British and shut himself up in his fortified house at Gujrāṅwālā. A body of troops sent by Brigadier Campbell and a squadron of Skinner's Horse surrounded the house, but he escaped.

Arjan Siṅgh died soon after. His grandson, Naraiṇ Siṅgh, who was honoured by the British with the title of Sardār Bahādur, died in March 1934.

BIBLIOGRAPHY

1. Griffin, Lepel, and C.F. Massy, *Chiefs and Families of Note in the Punjab*. Lahore, 1909
2. Gaṇda Siṅgh, *The Panjab in 1839-40*. Patiala, 1952
3. Sohan Lāl Sūrī, *'Umdāt-ut-Twārīkh*. Lahore, 1885-89

J.R.G.

ARJAN SIṄGH THĀPĀ was the son of the Gurkhā general, Amar Siṅgh Thāpā, who had advanced his conquests up to Kāṅgṛā in the early years of the nineteenth century. Mahārājā Raṇjīt Siṅgh expelled him from the Kāṅgṛā hills, but the Gurkhās had fought so bravely that he decided to raise a Gurkhā regiment. Arjan Siṅgh recruited Gurkhās for the army of the Mahārājā who gave him the rank of a captain in that regiment.

BIBLIOGRAPHY

1. Sūrī, Sohan Lāl, *'Umdāt-ut-Twārīkh*. Lahore, 1885-89
2. Bhagat Singh, *Maharaja Ranjit Singh and His Times*. Delhi, 1990
3. Khushwant Singh, *Ranjit Singh: Maharajah of the Punjab 1780-1839*. Bombay, 1962

H.R.G.

ARMY OF MAHĀRĀJĀ RAṆJĪT SIṄGH, a formidable military machine that helped the Mahārājā carve out an extensive kingdom and maintain it amid hostile and ambitious neighbours, was itself the creation of his own genius. His inheritance was but a scanty force which, in the manner of the Sikh *misldārī* days, comprised almost solely horsemen, without any regular training or organization. Everyone brought his own horse and whatever weapon he could afford or acquire. What held these troopers together was their personal loyalty to the leader. The tactics followed were those of the guerilla warfare. The system had stood the Khālsā in good stead during the turbulent and anarchic eighteenth century, but was unsuited to the needs of the changed times and to Raṇjīt Siṅgh's ambition to establish a secure rule. Early in his career, he had watched how the British troops with their systematic training and their discipline, had vanquished Indian forces vastly superior in numbers. He had also realized how crucial in warfare was a well-drilled infantry as well as artillery. In 1802, soon after his occupation of Amritsar, he engaged some deserters from the army of the East India Company to train his own platoons of infantry. He even sent some of his own men to Ludhiāṇā to study the British methods of training and tactics. As Sikhs generally looked down upon infantry service, he recruited Pūrbīās, as soldiers of fortune from Gangetic plain were called, Punjabi Muslims and Afg̲hāns and, later, Gurkhās as well. These troops were soon tested during the short campaign against Ahmad K̲hān Siāl of Jhaṅg and the *zamīndārs* of Uchch during the winter of 1803-04. Their success and the fact that the Mahārājā himself regularly saw them train made the infantry an enviable service and Sikhs too started joining its ranks in large numbers. Raṇjīt Siṅgh gave equal importance to artillery which had, till his time, been limited to the use of *zambūraks* or swivels only. He increased the number of guns. The casting of guns of larger calibre as well as the manufacture of ammunition was undertaken on a large scale. The reorganization and training of cavalry, however, waited until the induction into Sikh service of European officers.

The arrival of Jean Baptiste Ventura and Jean Francois Allard, two veterans of the Napoleonic Wars, at Lahore in 1822, was the starting-point. Raṇjīt Siṅgh gave them employment after considerable initial hesitation and elaborate verification. He charged them with the raising of a special corps of regular army, the Fauj-i-K̲hās or Fauj-i-Ā'īn. General Ventura trained battalions of infantry and General Allard trained the cavalry. Artillery, its training and command and ordnance were under Punjabi generals, Ilāhī Bak̲hsh and Lahiṇā Siṅgh Majīṭhīā, until the arrival of a French officer, General Claude Auguste Court in 1827 and the American Colonel Alexander Gardner in 1832. Lahiṇā Siṅgh Majīṭhīā continued to head the armament workshops, and Dr John Martin Honigberger, a Hungarian physician, was entrusted with the mixing of gunpowder.

There was a rapid increase in the strength of the army during the years following 1822, as the following figures compiled by Professor Sītā Rām Kohlī from the records of the Sikh government show:

Year	Infantry	Cavalry	
		Regular	Irregular
1819	7,748	750	3,577
1823	11,681	1650	7,300
1828	15,825	4315	7,200
1838	26,617	4090	10,795

	Artillery		
Year	Guns	Swivels	Personnel
1819	22	190	834
1823	Figures not available		
1828	130	280	3,778
1838	188	280	4,535

The above table does not include the *jāgīrdārī fauj* or feudal levees for which no figures are available. This force consisted almost entirely of horsemen which the *jāgīrdārs* had to maintain and produce in time of need or at the annual general reviews, normally held at the time of Dussehrā in October. There were, besides, the king's bodyguards, *Fauj-i-Qilājāt* or garrison infantry to guard important forts, and a 4000-strong crack brigade of Akālīs or Nihaṅgs.

Infantry thus became the central force, with cavalry and artillery as supporting arms. It was organized into battalions of about 900 men each. A battalion, commanded by a *kumedān* or commandant, assisted by an adjutant and a major, was the standard administrative and manoeuvring unit. Its administrative staff included, besides the usual camp-followers and tradesmen, a *munshī* or clerk, a *mutsaddī* or accountant, and a *granthī* or priest and scripture-reader. A battalion had eight companies of 100 men each, further divided into sections of 25 men each. Similarly, regular cavalry was organized in *risālās,* regiments, sub-divided into *turps* or troops, and artillery into *ḍerās* and batteries. Artillery was further classified according to its mode of traction, which was generally determined by the size of the guns. In 1804, this arm had been bifurcated into *topkhānā kalāṅ*, heavy artillery and *topkhānā khurd*, light artillery. *Zambūraks* or swivels, usually carried on camels, were attached to infantry units. Horse-drawn artillery was introduced in 1810. During the same year, a special artillery corps, known as *topkhānā-i-khās* or *topkhānā-i-mubārak*, was formed as the royal reserve under Ghaus Muhammad Khān, popularly known as Mīāṅ Ghausā. In 1827, General Court reorganized the artillery into three wings. *Topkhānā jinsī*, literally personal artillery (reserve), was a mixed corps with batteries of *gāvī*, bullock-driven, *aspī*, horse-driven, *fīlī*, elephant-driven, guns and the *hobobs* or howitzers. *Topkhānā aspī* or horse-driven artillery consisted of batteries for attachment to divisions of irregular army. *Zambūraks* or camel-swivels and *ghubārās* or mortars were organized into *ḍerās* or camps sub-divided into batteries. Batteries were subdivided into sections of two guns each, with provision for even a single gun functioning as a sub-unit.

The entire field army was divided into *fauj-i-ā'īn* or regular army, *fauj-i-beqavā'id* or irregular army and *jāgīrdārī fauj* or feudal levees. Fauj-i-Ā'īn, with five infantry battalions under General Ventura, three cavalry regiments under General Allard and 34 guns under General Ilāhī Bakhsh, formed the hard core troops under the overall command of General Ventura. *Fauj-i-Beqavā'id* forming a larger bulk consisted of *ḍerās* of *ghoṛchaṛhās,* or irregular cavalry grouped into divisions, each under one of the many distinguished generals such as Harī Siṅgh Nalvā, Dīwān Mohkam Chand, Misr Dīvān Chand, Fateh Siṅgh Āhlūvālīā, and Fateh Siṅgh Kālīāṅvālā. Each *ḍerā* comprised several smaller groups, *misls,* composed of members of a clan or their close relations commanded by heads of respective clans known as *misldārs. Ḍerās* of *jāgīrdārī fauj*, or feudal levees, were similarly organized forming part of one or the other division. Artillery formed a single central corps from which attachments were made to the divisions, depending upon the requirements of a particular campaign. Nominal overall command of a particular expedition was vested in one of the princes royal. Raṇjīt Siṅgh himself was the supreme commander. He also led some expeditions personally. The crack brigade of Akālīs under their famous leader, Phūlā Siṅgh, was virtually an autonomous formation pressed into service when needed by the Mahārājā through his personal influence and tact.

Standard deployment at the commencement of a battle was guns in the centre and slightly forward of the rest of the force, infantry a little behind and also covering the flanks of artillery, and cavalry on the extreme flanks. The battle usually commenced with artillery barrage.

Regular troops wore distinctive uniforms prescribed for each arm. Cavalrymen were dressed in red jackets (French grey for lancers), long blue trousers with a red stripe, and crimson turbans. Woollen jackets were used during winter. The regiments were armed with varying combinations of weapons --- sword/sabres and carbines and matchlocks or lances. Infantry was clad in scarlet jacket/coat, white trousers with black belts and pouches. Different regiments were distinguished by the colour of their headdress — white, red, green or yellow. The Gurkhās had green jackets and black caps. *Postīns* or fur-coats, or padded jackets were used during winter.

The gunners wore white trousers and

black waist-coats with cross-belts. Officers were not bound by rules of uniform. They used gaudy dresses of bright-coloured silks each dressing differently. The *ghoṛchaṛhās* or the irregular cavalry had no uniform laid down for them; yet they turned out remarkably well, as testified by Baron Hugel, a Prussian noble, who visited Mahārājā Raṇjīt Siṅgh in 1836 and inspected a cavalry parade. " I never beheld," he wrote of a troop of *ghoṛchaṛhās*, "a finer nor a more remarkably striking body of men. Each one was dressed differently, and yet so much in the same fashion that they all looked in perfect keeping."

Recruitment to the army was on a purely voluntary basis. There was no class composition on the basis of religion or nationality, nor was there a prescribed age limit for enrolment or retirement. Physical fitness and loyalty to the State were the essential conditions. However, the clannish basis of the *misls* in the Fauj-i-Beqavā'id ensured solidarity in the lower rungs of military administration. Similarly, bravery in the field and efficiency in the performance of duty were the only considerations for promotion and reward, which were also extended to the sons of those who died in action. A well-defined system of reward and punishment was enforced to maintain discipline and morale. The system of *faslī* or six-monthly payment, or payment through *jāgīrs* was later replaced by regular monthly payment in cash. Rates of pay ranged between Rs 400-500 for a general, Rs 17-25 for an infantry soldier and Rs 22-26 for a horseman per month, including, in the last case, maintenance of a horse and accoutrements. European officers enjoyed much higher salaries. Ventura and Allard were, for instance, each paid Rs 25,000 per annum, in addition to certain *jāgīrs*. There was no provision for retirement benefits, but allowances were sometimes sanctioned from out of the *dharamārth* or religious charities fund to those permanently disabled on active service or to the dependants of those killed in action. Distinguished service in peace or war was also recognized through the award of civil and military titles, bestowal of *khill'ats* or robes of honour and grant of *jāgīrs* or landed estates.

There were three grades of *khill'at* marked by the number, variety and quality of the garments, ornaments and weapons comprising each of them. Military titles were high-sounding Persian expressions, which the recipients and their bards and ushers could use before their names, such as *Hizbar-i-Jaṅg* (the lion of battle), *Zafar Jaṅg Bahādur* (victorious, brave in war) *Samsam ud-daulah* (sharp sword of the State), *Shujā' ud-daulah* (valour of the State), *Tahavur-panāh* (asylum of bravery), and so on. The titles of *Rājā* and *Dīwān*, sparingly bestowed, were essentially for distinguished service on the civil side. For military officers, the title of Sardār was considered one of considerable distinction. Towards the end of his reign or, to be more exact, on the occasion of the marriage of Kaṅvar Nau Nihāl Siṅgh in March 1837, Raṇjīt Siṅgh instituted an Order of Merit named *Kaukab-i-Iqbāl-i-Pañjāb* (Star of the Prosperity of the Punjab). It was a gold medal, 2.25 inches across with five large and five small pointed branches issuing outwards alternately from a roundish centre bearing a likeness of the Mahārājā in bust on one side, and his name on the other. It was meant to be worn round the neck suspended on a gold and scarlet riband passing through a ring on top of the semi-globular head of the star. The *kaukab* was of three different classes representing the three grades of the Order, distinguished by the size and quality of the inset precious stones. Star of the first class, meant to be awarded only to members of the royal family and very few distinguished chiefs and nobles for their proven devotion and fidelity to the person of Mahārājā and his House, was ornamented with a single large diamond. The Order of the second grade was bestowed upon loyal courtiers, governors of provinces, generals and ambassadors in recognition of political services. It had a diamond (of smaller size) and an emerald on it. The Order of the third grade, having a single emerald, was awarded to military officers of the rank of colonel, major or captain for bravery, resourcefulness, alertness and faithfulness; to civil servants for distinguished administrative ability and honesty; and to others enjoying greater confidence of the sovereign. Bestowal of the *kaukabs* was accompanied by appropriate *khill'ats* and titles for the awardees.

BIBLIOGRAPHY

1. Bajwa, Fauja Singh, *Military System of the Sikhs*. Delhi, 1964
2. Balwant Singh, *The Army of Maharaja Ranjit Singh*. Lahore, 1932
3. Ganda Singh and Teja Singh, ed., *Maharaja Ranjit Singh: First Death Centenary Memorial Volume*. Amritsar, 1939
4. Cunningham, Joseph Davey, *A History of the Sikhs from the Origin of the Nation to the Battles of the Sutlej*. London, 1849
5. Osborne, W. G., *The Court and Camp of Runjeet Sing*. London, 1840
6. Khushwant Singh, *A History of the Sikhs*, 2 vols. Princeton, 1963 and 1966
7. Harbans Singh, *Maharaja Ranjit Singh*. Delhi, 1980

Gl.S.

ARŪṚ SIṄGH, Mahārājā Duleep Siṅgh's personal attendant and confidant, belonged to the village of Kohālī, in Amritsar district. He was one of the five Sikhs who administered *pāhul* or Sikh initiatory rites to Mahārājā Duleep Siṅgh at Aden on 25 May 1886. From Aden, Arūṛ Siṅgh accompanied the Mahārājā to Europe. In 1887, Arūṛ Siṅgh was sent by the Mahārājā to India as his accredited ambassador. He carried with him five letters from Duleep Siṅgh, one of them addressed to the princes of India and another to the King of Oudh. At Pondicherry, he stayed with Ṭhākur Siṅgh Sandhāṅvālīā. As he reached Calcutta in pursuit of his mission, he was betrayed by a professed supporter of the Mahārājā and arrested. He was sent to the Chunār Fort where he was detained for three years. In government reports, Arūṛ Siṅgh was described as a Europeanized Sikh whose hospitality requirements in jail ran to "some ice, brandy, claret and Vichy water." He was released from prison on 15 December 1890, with permission to return to England if he so wished.

BIBLIOGRAPHY

1. Ganda Singh, ed., *History of the Freedom Movement in the Punjab*, vol. III (*Maharaja Duleep Singh Correspondence*). Patiala, 1977
2. Harbans Singh, *The Heritage of the Sikhs*. Delhi, 1983

S.S.B.

ARŪṚ SIṄGH (1890-1917), also known as Doctor Rūr Siṅgh, described in British government records as "a dangerous man," was born the son of Arjan Siṅgh in 1890 at Saṅgvāl, a village in Jalandhar district of the Punjab. Working as a compounder in a veterinary hospital at Jalandhar, he came under the influence of Bantā Siṅgh of his own village who was a member of the Ghadr revolutionary party. Arūṛ Siṅgh resigned from the hospital and became a Ghadr activist. In collaboration with Bantā Siṅgh, he tampered with the railway lines and cut telephone wires near Sūrānasī railway station. He learnt bomb-making from Javand Siṅgh, of Naṅgal Kalāṅ. Soon warrants for Arūṛ Siṅgh's arrest were issued. He worked underground for two and a half years, exhorting the people to rise against the alien government. During this period, he killed one government informer and seven policemen. On 2 November 1916, he went to meet a friend of his in Lahore Jail, where he was immediately recognized and apprehended. Tried in the

Lahore Conspiracy Case III (1916), he was, on 4 January 1917, sentenced to death with forfeiture of property, and was hanged shortly thereafter. During his trial he refused to defend himself; rather he openly confessed to his revolutionary activity.

BIBLIOGRAPHY

1. Jagjīt Siṅgh, *G͟hadar Pārṭī Lahir*. Delhi, 1979
2. Puri, Harish K., *G͟hadar Movement*. Amritsar, 1983

G.S.D.

ARŪṚ SIṄGH, BHĀĪ (1872-1921), one of the Nankāṇā Sāhib martyrs, was born in November 1872 at Thothīāṅ village in Amritsar district, the son of Bhāī Nihāl Siṅgh and Māī Jīo. His education was limited to reading and writing the Gurmukhī script which he learnt in the village *gurdwārā*. He grew up into a tall young man and enlisted in 126th Balūch Battalion in British times but having been on active service only for three years came back as a reservist. He was recalled for active service at the outbreak of the First Great War in 1914. After his final retirement at the end of the war he started taking interest in the matter of reforming the management of the *gurdwārās,* then engaging the attention of the Sikh Panth. He received afresh the K͟hālsā *pāhul* at the instance of Bhāī Mūl Siṅgh Garmūlā. He joined the reformers' column led by Bhāī Lachhmaṇ Siṅgh massacred at Nankāṇā Sāhib on 20 February 1921.

See NANKĀṆĀ SĀHIB MASSACRE

BIBLIOGRAPHY

Shamsher, Gurbak͟hsh Siṅgh, *Shahīdī Jīvan*. Nankana Sahib, 1938

G.S.G.

ARŪṚ SIṄGH, SARDĀR BAHĀDUR SIR (1865-1926), *sarbarāh* (manager) of the principal Sikh shrines at Amritsar and Tarn Tāran from 1907 to 1920, much maligned for his role during the popular movement for reform in the managment of Sikh shrines, came of a well-known Shergil family of Naushahrā in Amritsar district, also called Naushahrā Naṅglī, to distinguish it from another village sharing the same name, Naushahrā Pannūāṅ, in the same district. His grandfather, Jassā Siṅgh, had been for two years in charge of the Golden Temple under Lahiṇā Siṅgh Majīṭhīā. Arūṛ Siṅgh was hardly four years old when his father, Harnām Siṅgh, a deputy superintendent of police, died in 1868. Brought up under a court of wards and educated at Government High School, Amritsar, Arūṛ Siṅgh came into full possession of his family estate in 1885. In 1888, he was made an honorary magistrate class II, with powers over 133 villages of Kathū Naṅgal police circle. In 1907 he was made magistrate class I and a provincial *darbārī* (courtier), and was also appointed by government *sarbarāh* in spite of the reformers' demand that the right to appoint the *sarbarāh* should vest in the Sikh community itself. It was bruited about that Arūṛ Siṅgh had set apart for certain British officers valuable presents from the *toshāk͟hānā* (treasury) of the Darbār Sāhib. An agitation was set afoot against him on this account. However, it came to nothing; likewise, later complaints laid against him of mismanagement and corruption in the *gurdwārās* under his charge were rejected.

Things came to a head when Arūṛ Siṅgh and the priests of Srī Darbār Sāhib publicly honoured General Dyer, responsible for Jalliāṅvālā Bāg͟h massacre in 1919. Demand for his removal as *sarbarāh* gathered momentum day by day. Ultimately, Arūṛ Siṅgh bowed to the popular will. He not only resigned the office of *sarbarāh* but also tendered at a meeting at Jalliāṅvālā Bāg͟h sometime during August 1920 a public apology for his acts of omission and commission relating to the management of the shrines under his charge. The government, however, in view of his loyal services, conferred on him a knighthood on the New Year Day of 1921. He had already been awarded a C. I. E. (Companion of the Indian Empire) in 1913; he now became Sardār Sir Arūṛ Siṅgh, K.C.I.E. (Knight Companion of the Indian Empire).

Arūṛ Siṅgh died in 1926.

BIBLIOGRAPHY

1. Griffin, Lepel, and C.F. Massy, *Chiefs and Families of Note in the Punjab.* Lahore, 1940
2. Mohinder Singh, *The Akali Movement.* Delhi, 1978
3. Dyer, R.E.H., *Disturbances in the Punjab.* London, 1920
4. Pratāp Siṅgh, Giānī, *Gurdwārā Sudhār arthāt Akālī Lahir.* Amritsar, 1975
5. Josh, Sohan Siṅgh, *Akālī Morchiāṅ dā Itihās.* Delhi, 1972

I.J.K.

ARZ UL-ALFĀZ, lit. breadth or scope *(arz)* of words (*alfāz*) or petition, request or address (*arz*) in words (*alfāz*), is a versified composition in Persian by Bhāī Nand Lāl Goyā, a noted poet and devout follower of Gurū Gobind Siṅgh. Bhāī Nand Lāl in between his periods of service at the imperial courts of Auraṅgzīb and Prince Mu'azzam (later, Emperor Bahādur Shāh) had the honour of enjoying the patronage of Gurū Gobind Siṅgh at Anandpur. *Arz* is a long poem of 1,346 couplets of much literary as well as spiritual import. That the poet intended the title to mean "breadth or scope of words" is clear from the introductory couplets:

> Thousands are praises and thanksgivings owed to the court of that Holy and Fearless Judge, who blessed the composition of these words with completion and illuminated the thoughts enshrined therein like the Sun. (1,2)
>
> Each word has many meanings found in old and new lexicons. These are the disciplines spread by scholars of intellect and vision. (3,4)
>
> Which are the kinds of "k" and "y", which are particles and prepositions, which the nouns related to "t"? Such words of spiritual, mathematical and physical content are given in this (book) with discriminative care. (5,6)
>
> Which are the six kinds of knowledge and two kinds of wisdom from either of which there grow three names for each? Then there are plural words and plurals of plurals; for the purpose of this work they are free from extraneous consideration. (7,8)
>
> Description of this kind is a virtuous task, because every task and capability to perform it is from Him. Therefore, it is proper to commence this book in the name of God, the Creator of the universe. (9,10)

After these introductory couplets begins the laudation of the Almighty panegyrizing His many attributes. The book ends with verbal annotations and interpretations.

BIBLIOGRAPHY

Gaṇḍā Siṅgh, ed., *Bhāī Nand Lāl Granthāvalī.* Malacca (Malaya), 1968

D. S.

ĀSĀ, one of the thirty-one *rāgas* or musical measures into which compositions comprising the Sikh holy book, Gurū Granth Sāhib, except the *Japu,* are cast and in which they are meant to be recited and sung. This *rāga* is important in the Sikh system of music, and is said to have developed from the tune of a folk ballad *Ṭuṇḍe Asrāje dī Vār* prescribed as the musical key for singing the Sikh morning liturgy, *Āsā kī Vār.* Āsāvarī and Āsā Kāfī are two subsidiaries of Āsā employed in the

Gurū Granth Sāhib. According to old texts, the tune Āsā is appropriately sung during the second part of the night; however, in the Sikh tradition it is sung both early morning and in the evening. Also, more appropriately, it is assigned to the cold season and is meant to evoke a calm mystical mood. Although in the concluding section of the Gurū Granth Sāhib called *Rāgamālā (q.v.)*, it is described as a *rāginī*, feminine subsidiary of the parent *rāga* Megh, it is employed in the main text as a full-fledged *rāga*. By its structure and mood, it lends itself very well to rendering devotional songs and hymns. *Komal nishād* and *Komal gandhār*, made as *vivādī*, are employed in the movements of this *rāga*. Āsā is a crooked *rāgā* in that approaches to certain notes have to be made from a set position. The melodic structure of the *rāga* is as under:

Thāṭ = Bilāval
Jāti = Auṛav, Sampūraṇ
Āroh = Sa Re Ma Pa Dha Ne, Pa Dha Ṡa
Avaroh = Ṡa Ne Dha Pa Ma Ga — Re Ga Sa
Pakaṛ = Sa Re Ma Pa Dha Pa, Ma Ga Re, Ga Re Ga Sa

Besides the Gurūs - Gurū Nānak, Gurū Amar Dās, Gurū Rām Dās, Gurū Arjan, and Gurū Tegh Bahādur -- Kabīr, Nāmdev, Ravidās, Dhannā, and Farīd have composed hymns in this musical measure contained in the Gurū Granth Sāhib.

BIBLIOGRAPHY

1. Charan Siṅgh, *Srī Gurū Granth Bāṇī Beurā*. Amritsar, 1860
2. Sundar Siṅgh, Bhāī, *Gurmat Saṅgīt*. Amritsar, n.d.

D.S.

ĀSĀ KĪ VĀR, as recorded in the index to the Gurū Granth Sāhib, but commonly designated *Āsā dī Vār*, lit. an ode *(vār)* in the musical measure Āsā, is a composition by Gurū Nānak sung by musicians at Sikh congregations as part of the early-morning service. Āsā is the *rāga* of pre-dawn hours and the custom of reciting the hymn at morning time is traced to the days of Gurū Nānak himself. It is said that Bhāī Lahiṇa (later, Gurū Aṅgad) was the first to sing it in the presence of Gurū Nānak. The *Vār* then comprised twenty-four *pauṛīs* or stanzas by Gurū Nānak and some *ślokas* which were also of his composition as indicated in the title given it by Gurū Arjan when entering the composition in the Holy Book (*salok bhī mahalle pahile ke likhe)*, the *ślokas* were also composed by the First Guru, Gurū Nānak. In its present form, it carries twenty-four stanzas with a total of fifty-nine *ślokas*, 45 by Gurū Nānak and 14 by Gurū Aṅgad. At the time of recitation, the choir will prefix each of the stanzas by a quatrain from the series by Gurū Rām Dās entered separately under Rāga Āsā, collectively known as *chhakkās*, or sextettes from the groups of six quatrains each counting as a unit. They will also punctuate the singing with illustrative hymns from Gurū Granth Sāhib and with passages from Bhāī Gurdās and Bhāī Nand Lāl whose compositions constitute approved texts. According to the musical direction recorded by Gurū Arjan at the beginning of the *Vār*, it is meant to be recited in the tune of an old folk ballad which had as its hero a prince by the name of Asrājā, called Ṭuṇḍā Asrāj because of a maimed hand (*ṭuṇḍā*).

From passage to passage, the *Vār* touches upon several different themes, but one central point of emphasis is the state of man, and how he may liberate himself from the bondage of self and prepare himself for union with the Divine. The text is also strewn with telling social comment. The ills of contemporary life–its inequalities and artificialities — are sharply noticed. There are lines alluding to the moral decay that had set in, and showing how cant, hypocrisy and superstition passed under the name of religion and how people had begun aping the dress and language of their foreign masters.

The *Vār* opens with the praise of the Gurū, the spiritual preceptor, who brings light into the world. "Were a hundred of moons to rise and a thousand suns, the light so created will be but utter darkness without the Gurū." In this *śloka* Gurū Aṅgad is saying how vital the Gurū's instruction is for the individual. God, says Gurū Nānak, is the creator of all that exists and in His creation He manifested His name. He, the Beneficent One, is the source of mercy and grace (1). They who attach themselves to His Name are the winners in life; the rest remain losers (2).

One will find by His grace alone the true Gurū who puts him in the path of righteousness and helps him rid himself of his ego (3). The Gurū will reveal to him the truth. Without the aid of the Gurū, no one has comprehended the Reality. The Gurū helps one to overcome one's attachment to what is unreal and leads one to liberation everlasting (6). They who cherish the true Lord turn not their feet towards sin. Their path is paved with good deeds and they practise righteousness. They sing praises of the Supreme Being and rejoice in His grace (7). All the formal acts of piety and all the austerities performed at holy places will be of little avail. They alone will please the Lord who give Him their loving devotion. God's own minstrel, Nānak, seeks the company of those who remain absorbed in Him (9).

In the world beyond neither caste nor power will prevail. They alone will receive honour there who are by the Lord favoured. Sweetness and humility are the essence of all virtue. Rejecting the sacred thread of the high-born, Gurū Nānak tells the Brāhmaṇ that he had little use for the ceremonial cord which got soiled and broke. What he would rather have was a cord made of the cotton of compassion, spun into the thread of contentment, twisted with truth and knitted with continence. He who submits to the Lord's will is approved and is received at the divine portal. Commenting upon the hypocrisy prevalent in contemporary society, he says that Brāhmaṇs wear their traditional apparels and plant the saffron mark on their foreheads, yet they eat the grain they receive from those they call unclean. Inside their homes they worship their idols, and outside they read books of the Muslims and take to their ways. Those wearing the sacred thread round their neck carry in their hand the butcher's knife.

The woman who has given birth to a child is not impure as the custom decrees. Impure is the mind which is filled with covetousness, impure is the tongue which utters falsehood, impure are the eyes which look at another's woman; impure is the ear which hears slander. The impurity of impurities is to become attached to anyone/anything other than Him. Why call woman evil of whom great men are born?

Do not stigmatize anyone as evil. That is the essence of all knowledge. Nor should one argue with a fool (19). He who carries a harsh tongue, his mind and body are both impaired. In the true Lord's court will he be discarded. Remember always the Lord by cherishing whom one lives ever in comfort (21). How just are they who sow poison and hope to distil nectar from it ? Infinite, unlimited is the Lord. He Himself is the doer and He Himself causes things to be done. Before whom else may one lay one's appeal (23)? Beyond enumerating are the excellences of the Supreme Being. He is the Creator, the Beneficent One, the Sustainer of all. One but does what one is assigned to.

BIBLIOGRAPHY

1. Tejā Siṅgh, *Āsā dī Vār*. Amritsar, 1968
2. Vohrā, Āshā Nand, *Āsā kī Vār*. Rohtak, 1969
3. Kohlī, Surindar Siṅgh, *Gurū Nānak : Jīvan, Darshan ate Kāvi-Kalā*. Chandigarh, 1969
4. Vīr Siṅgh, Bhāī, *Santhyā Srī Gurū Granth Sāhib*.

Amritsar, 1975

5. Sāhib Siṅgh, *Saṭīk Āsā dī Vār*. Amritsar, 1978
6. Sher Siṅgh, Giānī, *Ṭikā Āsā dī Vār* (3 parts). Rāwalpiṇḍī, 1910-20

D.S.

ĀSĀVARĪ. *See* ĀSĀ

ASCETICISM, derived from the Greek word *askesis*, connotes the 'training' or 'exercise' of the body and the mind. Asceticism or ascetic practices belong to the domain of religious culture, and fasts, pilgrimages, ablutions, purificatory rituals, vigils, abstinence from certain foods and drinks, primitive and strange dress, nudity, uncut hair, tonsure, shaving the head, circumcision, cave-dwelling, silence, meditation, vegetarianism, celibacy, virginity, inflicting pain upon oneself by whips and chains, mutilation, begging alms, owning no wealth or possessions, forbearance and patience, equanimity or impartiality towards friends and foes, eradication of desires and passions, treating the body as something evil or treating human life as a means of achieving ultimate release or union with God – all these are subsumed under ascetic practices.

The history of Indian religiousness presents the ultimate in the development of the theory and practice of asceticism. Evidence of the existence of ascetic practices in India has come down to us from the most ancient period of known history; archaeology and literature have documented its growth as a pan-Indian religious phenomenon; all the systems of religious thought that have ever appeared on the soil of India have been influenced in varying degrees by the philosophy and terminology of asceticism. Ancient Indian literature abounds in ascetic terminology and there are numerous terms which refer to ascetics or to diverse ascetic practices. *Muni, yati, bhikṣu, yogin, śramaṇa, tapasvin, tapas, muṇḍaka, parivrājaka, dhyānin, sannyāsin, tyāgin, vairāgin, atīta, udāsina, avadhūta, digambara*, etc. are terms frequently used in Indian religious tradition.

Non-theistic systems such as Jainism, Buddhism and Sāṅkhya-Yoga provide instances of ascetic culture in its classical form. All these Śramaṇic systems of faith are predominantly ascetic though their philosophical theories place varying degrees of emphasis on bodily *askesis*. Forms of asceticism differ in Jainism and Buddhism, the former being an extreme instance of it. Asceticism is the heart of Jaina *caritra* or *ācāra* which, along with *jñāna* and *darśana*, constitutes the way to *mokṣa*.

In the Buddhist form of asceticism, there is no metaphysical dualism of God and the world, or of soul and the body. Phenomenal existence is viewed as characterized by suffering, impermanence and not-self. The aim of ascetic culture is to go beyond this sphere of conditioned phenomena. The keynote of Buddhist ascetic culture is moderation; self-mortification is rejected altogether; *tapas* is a form of excess which increases *dukkha*. The aim of ascetic effort is to secure freedom from suffering; this ascetic effort is to be made within the framework of the Middle Way.

Among all schools of Indian ascetics the *gurū* or preceptor is held in the highest esteem. No one becomes an ascetic without receiving formal initiation (*dīkṣā*) or ordination (*pravargyā*) at the hands of a recognized teacher who is himself an ascetic of standing. Practice of various kinds of physical postures (*āsanas*), meditation, study of Scriptures, devotional worship, discussion on subjects of religious and philosophical importance, going on pilgrimage to holy places, giving instruction to the laity, accepting gifts of dress materials and food-stuff, and radiating good will and a sense of religiousness and piety, are the usual facets of the life of Indian ascetics. Ascetic way of life, in any religion is the way of self-mortification. Injury to others is however disallowed. But

Sikhism which of course emphasizes the importance of non-violence never lets this dogma to humiliate man as a man and accepts the use of force as the last resort. Says Gurū Gobind Siṅgh in the *Zafarnāmah : chū kār az hamah hīlte dar guzasht/halāl astu burdan ba shamshīr dast* (22). Sikhism denies the efficacy of all that is external or merely ritualistic. Ritualism which may be held to be a strong pillar of asceticism has been held as entirely alien to true religion.

Sikhism which may be described as *pravṛtti mārga* (way of active activity) over against *nivṛtti mārga* (way of passive activity or renunciation) enjoins man to be of the world, but not worldly. Non-responsible life under the pretext of ascetic garb is rejected by the Gurūs and so is renunciation which takes one away to solitary or itinerant life totally devoid of social engagement. Says Gurū Nānak: "He who sings songs about God without understanding them; who converts his house into a mosque in order to satisfy his hunger; who being unemployed has his ears pierced (so that he can beg); who becomes a *faqīr* and abandons his caste; who is called a *gurū* or *pīr* but goes around begging — never fall at the feet of such a person. He who eats what he has earned by his own labour and yet gives some (to others) – Nānak, it is he who knows the true way" (GG, 1245). Here one may find the rejection of asceticism and affirmation of disciplined worldliness. A very significant body of the fundamental teachings of the Gurūs commends non-attachment, but not asceticism or monasticism.

The necessity of controlling the mind and subduing one's egoity is repeatedly taught. All the virtues such as contentment (*santokh*), patience (*dhīraja*), mercy (*dayā*), service (*sevā*), liberality (*dāna*), cleanliness (*snāna*), forgiveness *(kṣamā)*, humility *(namratā)*, non-attachment (*vairāgya*), and renunciation (*tiāga*), are fundamental constituents of the Sikh religion and ethics. On the other hand, all the major vices or evils that overpower human beings and ruin their religious life, such as anger (*krodha*), egoism (*ahaṅkāra*), avarice (*lobha*), lust (*kāma*), infatuation (*moha*), sinful acts (*pāpa*), pride (*mān*), doubt (*duvidhā*), ownership (*mamatā*), hatred (*vair*), and hostility (*virodh*) are condemned. Man is exhorted to eradicate them but certainly not through ascetic self-mortification. *Sahaj* is attained through tension-free, ethical living, grounded in spirituality.

In Sikhism all forms of asceticism are disapproved and external or physical austerities, devoid of devotion to God, are declared futile. An ascetic sage who is liberated from all evil passions is called *avadhūta* in Indian sacred literature. Gurū Nānak reorientates the concept of *avadhūta* in purely spiritual terms as against its formularies. The sign of an *avadhūta* is that "in the midst of aspirations he dwells bereft of aspirations" *suṇi māchhindrā audhū nīsāṇī/āsā māhi nirāsu valāe/nihachaū Nānak karate pāe"* (GG, 877). An ascetic is defined again as "one who burns up his egoity, and whose alms consist in enduring hardships of life and in purifying his mind and soul. He who only washes his body is a hypocrite" (GG, 952).

BIBLIOGRAPHY

1. Hall, T.C., "Asceticism," in *Encyclopaedia of Religion and Ethics*. Ed. James Hastings. Edinburgh, 1969
2. Eliade, Mircea, *Yoga, Immortality and Freedom*. Princeton, 1969
3. Chakraborty, Haripada, *Asceticism in Ancient India*. Calcutta, 1973
4. Sher Singh, *The Philosophy of Sikhism*. Lahore, 1944
5. Nripinder Singh, *The Sikh Moral Tradition*. Delhi, 1990

L.M.J.

ĀS KAUR, daughter of Gurdās Siṅgh, was married to Rājā Sāhib Siṅgh (1773-1813) of Paṭiālā in 1792 and, in 1798, she bore him a son and heir who was named Karam Siṅgh. She was a woman of great ability and her wise administration of the Paṭiālā state during part of her husband's reign and during the minority of her son won the admiration of the neighbouring chiefs and was warmly praised by the British government. In 1821, she retired to her estate at Sanaur, about 7 km south of Paṭiālā, where she spent the last years of her life.

BIBLIOGRAPHY

Griffin, Lepel, *The Rajas of the Punjab*. Delhi, 1983

S.S.B.

ĀSMĀN KHĀN or ASMĀN KHĀN (d. 1635), a Paṭhān who sacrilegiously appropriated the robe of honour, a sword and a horse bestowed by Gurū Hargobind on his father-in-law, Pāindā Khān, and poached a hawk belonging to the Gurū's eldest son, Bābā Gurdittā. When questioned, Pāindā Khān defended his son-in-law and denied the charges levelled against him. However, Bhāī Bidhī Chand, at the bidding of Gurū Hargobind, recovered the articles from Āsmān Khān's possession. Both Pāindā Khān and Āsmān Khān rose against the Gurū, and enlisted the support of the Mughal *faujdār* of Jalandhar. A clash occurred at Kartārpur during the last week of April 1635. Āsmān Khān was killed in this battle with an arrow from Bābā Gurdittā's bow.

BIBLIOGRAPHY

1. *Gurbilās Chhevīṅ Pātshāhī*. Patiala, 1970
2. Gupta, Hari Ram, *History of the Sikhs*, vol. I. Delhi, 1973

B.S.

ASRĀR-I-SAMADĪ, a Persian chronicle by an anonymous writer who is now identified as Munshī Jot Prakāsh attached to the court of Nawāb 'Abd us-Samad Khān, the governor of Lahore from 1713 to 1726. Written around 1728, the work, which the author claims to be an eye-witness account of the events described, deals with the military expeditions of the Nawāb. The only two extant manuscripts of the work, written in *nastā'līq* hand, are lying at the Pañjāb University Library, Lahore. The author describes himself as a *munshī* at the court of Nawāb 'Abd us-Samad Khān, and states that he belonged to Kalānaur, now in Gurdāspur district of the Punjab, the beauty of the landscape of which he sketches in ecstatic terms. The work was edited by Muhammad Shujā' ud-Dīn and Dr Mohammad Bashīr Husain and published at Lahore in 1965.

Besides the preface, wherein the author sings glory of the Lord Almighty in elegant and florid Persian, the work has seven short chapters describing the Nawāb's victories in a series of battles. In the first chapter occurs an account of the stubborn resistance offered by Bandā Siṅgh and his Sikhs from inside the fortress of Gurdās-Naṅgal. The author showers unreserved praise on the Sikhs for the exemplary courage they displayed in battle and during the fierce siege they faced. He records how they thwarted capture of the fortress either by assault or by rash entry. The Nawāb promised safe conduct to the besieged Sikhs on condition that they evacuate, but he broke his word and Bandā Siṅgh and his companions were seized and despatched to Delhi where they were put to death with the harshest torments. The remaining chapters deal with the rebellion of Īsā Khān Mañjh of Chaklā Sirhind, the revolt of the Afghāns of Kasūr, the Nawāb's Kashmīr campaign, his transfer to Multān and his expeditions to Jammū and Kāṅgṛā.

The work throws light on the policy of Nawāb 'Abd us-Samad Khān and his son Zakarīyā Khān and is singularly free from any personal prejudice on the part of the author. It castigates the erring and tyrannical *faujdārs* who persecuted the people and rack-rented the peasantry. The author's appreciation of the Sikhs' spirit of heroic courage and fortitude is expressed equally strongly. A Punjabi translation of the book was brought out by Punjabi University, Paṭiālā, in 1972.

BIBLIOGRAPHY

1. Janak Siṅgh, trans., *Asrār-i-Samadī*. Patiala, 1972
2. M. Shujā' ud-Dīn, ed., *Asrār-i-Samadī*. Lahore, 1965

Gb.S.

AṢṬPADĪ, from Sanskrit *aṣṭapada, aṣṭāpad* or *aṣṭāpadī*, is a poetic composition comprising *aṣṭ* or eight *padās* or stanzas. No specific rhyme-scheme, measure or burden is prescribed for it, but all the eight stanzas must be in the same metre and measure. Lines in each stanza are generally rhymed.

In Sikh Scripture, the Gurū Granth Sāhib, there are *aṣṭpadīs* composed in different musical measures (*rāgas*) and metres. For instance,Gurū Nānak has written *aṣṭpadīs* in *rāgas* Gauṛī and Mārū; those under measure Gauṛī are in Chaupaī metre and those under Mārū in Nishānī metre. All the twenty-four *aṣṭpadīs* which constitute Gurū Arjan's *Sukhmanī* are in Chaupaī metre and Gauṛī *rāga*. Although each of the eight stanzas in an *aṣṭpadī* of *Sukhmanī* comprises ten verses, the number of verses in a stanza elsewhere in the Scripture is restricted from two to four lines.

BIBLIOGRAPHY

1. Kāhn Siṅgh, Bhāī, *Guruchhand Divākar*. Patiala, 1970
2. Charan Siṅgh, *Srī Gurū Granth Bāṇī Beurā*. Amritsar, 1860
3. Kohlī, Surindar Siṅgh, ed., *Pañjābī Sāhitt Kosh*. Chandigarh, 1972

M.G.S.

AṬAL RĀI, BĀBĀ (1619-1628), son of Gurū Hargobind (1595-1644), was born to Mātā Nānakī at Amritsar on 23 October 1619. He died at the tender age of nine years. The circumstances of his death, as narrated in *Gurbilās Chhevīṅ Pātshāhī*, were most extraordinary. Aṭal Rāi had a playmate, Mohan, who was the son of a local businessman, Suinī Shāh. One day as they played with ball and sticks far into the evening, the forfeit was upon Mohan. During the night Mohan was bitten by a snake and he died. When he did not turn up for play the following morning, Aṭal Rāi went to his home to find the members of his family wailing and lamenting. Bābā Aṭal Rāi innocently walked up to where Mohan was lying under a sheet spread over him, and spoke: "Why do you sleep so soundly, dear friend? It is not time for sleep: and, remember, you owe us the forfeit." Saying these words, he touched the boy with his stick. The boy stood up. The story that Aṭal Rāi had raised a dead body swept through the town. Gurū Hargobind was not pleased when he heard this. "*Karāmāt qahar hai* — miracle-making is violence. None should attempt to intervene in the Will of the Lord," he told his son. Aṭal Rāi took the admonition to heart. Making a respectful bow, he quietly retired from the Gurū's presence. After ablutions in the sacred pool of Amritsar and having recited the *Japu* on the bank of Kaulsar, he lay down on the ground with the stick underneath his head and went to his eternal repose. This happened on 13 September 1628. A 9-storey octagonal edifice in Amritsar commemorating the 9-year-old Sāhibzādā (Gurū's son) is also popularly known as Bābā Aṭal after him.

BIBLIOGRAPHY

1. *Gurbilās Chhevīṅ Pātshāhī*. Patiala, 1970
2. Santokh Siṅgh, Bhāī, *Srī Gur Pratāp Sūraj Granth*. Amritsar, 1926-37
3. Giān Siṅgh, Giānī, *Twārīkh Gurū Khālsā* [Reprint].Patiala, 1970
4. Macauliffe, M. A., *The Sikh Religion*. Oxford, 1909

Gn.S.

'ATĀ MUHAMMAD KHĀN BĀRAKZAĪ, son of Paindā Khān Bārakzaī, became the governor of Kashmīr in 1809. When Shāh Shujā', the king of Afghanistan, was dethroned, he fled towards the Punjab. At Attock he was captured by the governor, Jahāṅdād Khān, who sent him to Kashmīr to be handed over to his brother 'Atā Muhammad Khān. Kashmīr was coveted by Fateh Khān, the Kābul Wazīr, as well as by Raṇjīt Siṅgh. Both set up a joint expedition and their armies defeated 'Atā Muhammad Khān who was replaced by Fateh Khān's real brother, 'Azīm Khān, as governor of Kashmīr. Raṇjīt Siṅgh's prize was Shāh Shujā' who was freed from 'Atā Muhammad Khān's custody by the Mahārājā's men and brought to Lahore as his guest. From him the Mahārājā secured the celebrated diamond, Koh-i-Nūr.

BIBLIOGRAPHY

1. Sūrī, Sohan Lāl, *'Umdāt-ut-Twārīkh*. Lahore, 1885-89
2. Griffin, Lepel, *Ranjit Singh*. Delhi, 1957
3. Harbans Singh, *Maharaja Ranjit Singh*. Delhi, 1980

H.R.G.

ATAR SIṄGH, one of the twenty-two Kūkā *sūbās*, i.e. governors or deputies, appointed in different parts to espouse Kūkā or Nāmdhārī patriotism and reform during the latter part of the nineteenth century, belonged to Ludhiāṇā district. He was born in 1832 the son of Buddh Siṅgh. He sold all his property and, accompanied by his two daughters, took to the preaching of Kūkā tenets. In March 1875, he was arrested for having participated in a banned assembly of Kūkās and for having used seditious language against the British government.

BIBLIOGRAPHY

1. Fauja Singh, *Kuka Movement*. Delhi, 1965
2. Gaṇḍā Siṅgh, *Kūkiāṅ dī Vithiā*. Amritsar, 1944

M.L.A.

ATAR SIṄGH AṬĀRĪVĀLĀ (d. 1897), son of Chatar Siṅgh Aṭārīvālā, governor of Hazārā. He joined his father during the latter's revolt against the British in 1848-49 and was, after the annexation of the Punjab, confined within the limits of his village, along with his father and brother, Rājā Sher Siṅgh. With his father and brother, he was removed to Allāhābād in January 1850, and thence to Calcutta. In January 1854, he was released from confinement. Atar Siṅgh chose Rāe Bareilly in the then North West Province for his residence and gradually severed his connection with the Punjab. He died in 1897, leaving behind a son, Prem Siṅgh.

BIBLIOGRAPHY

1. Sūrī, Sohan Lāl, *'Umdāt-ut-Twārīkh*. Lahore, 1885-89.
2. Gaṇḍā Siṅgh, *Sardār Shām Siṅgh Aṭārīvālā*. Amritsar, 1942
3. Griffin, Lepel, and C.F. Massy, *Chiefs and Families of Note in the Punjab*. Lahore, 1909

G.S.

ATAR SIṄGH ATLEVĀLE, SANT (d. 1937), Sikh holy man and preacher, born in early fifties of the nineteenth century, was the eldest son of Bhāī Kishan Siṅgh and Māī Naraiṇī, a devoted couple of Mīrpur, in Jammū and Kashmīr state. Atar Siṅgh, originally known as Harī Siṅgh, was adopted by his childless uncle, Mehar Siṅgh, who had migrated to the village of Joṛe, in Khārīāṅ *tahsīl* of district Gujrāt, now in Pakistan. Harī Siṅgh thus moved to Joṛe and joined the business of his foster-father. His work frequently took him to Rāwalpiṇḍī where he began to attend congregations at the Niraṅkārī Darbār established by Bābā Dayāl (1783-1855) and then headed by Bhāī Sāhib Rattā (d. 1911) whose follower he became. The Niraṅkārīs were a reformist sect aiming at purifying the prevalent Sikh usage garbled in the rising tide of conservatism during the days of Sikh rule in the Punjab. The Niraṅkārīs popularized Anand ceremony, i.e. marriage by Sikh rites in the presence of the Gurū Granth Sāhib. Harī Siṅgh fled his own marriage in 1875 when he discovered that it would be solemnized not by Anand rites but in accordance with the old Brāhmaṇical custom. He quietly slipped away from the bride's village, Barnālī, and made his way to Srī Hazūr Sāhib at Nāndeḍ, in the South. From Nāndeḍ he returned to Damdamā Sāhib, in Baṭhiṇḍā district, where he devoted himself to the study of Sikh theology. Later, he changed his name to Atar Siṅgh and established a *ḍerā* or preaching centre at Atlā Kalāṅ, near Mānsā (29° - 59'N, 75° - 24'E), in Baṭhiṇḍā district, where students were trained in scripture-reading and in *kīrtan* or Sikh devotional music. He soon came to be known as Sant Atar Siṅgh Atlevāle. It was only years later that the members of his family learnt about his whereabouts. Harī Siṅgh had made Atlā Kalāṅ his permanent abode, though he started visiting Rāwalpiṇḍī to attend ceremonies marking the death anniversary of Bābā Dayāl.

Sant Atar Siṅgh Atlevāle died on 18 June 1937. He was succeeded as head of the *ḍerā* at Atlā Kalāṅ by his pupil, Sant Lakkhā Siṅgh, later, *jathedār* of Ta<u>kh</u>t Damdamā Sāhib, Talvaṇḍī Sābo.

M.S.N.

ATAR SIṄGH KĀLIĀṄVĀLĀ (d. 1851), soldier and feudatory chief in Sikh times, was son of Dal Siṅgh Nahernā, a military commander under Mahārājā Raṇjīt Siṅgh. Atar Siṅgh's ancestors belonged to the village of Kaṛiāl, in Sheikhūpurā district, now in Pakistan. His great-great-grandfather, Sāhib Siṅgh, had been given a *jāgīr* by Chaṛhat Siṅgh Sukkarchakkīā. Sāhib Siṅgh's son, Hakūmat Siṅgh, and grandson, Kaur Siṅgh, served the Sukkarchakkīās. Kaur Siṅgh's son, Dal Siṅgh, served with honour in the Kasūr, Multān, Kashmīr and Ḍerā Ismā'īl <u>Kh</u>ān campaigns. His son, Atar Siṅgh, was sent in 1834 to Peshāwar under the command of Prince Nau Nihāl Siṅgh. While there, Dīwān Hākim Rāi, who was chamberlain to the Prince and a great favourite, won over some of the *sardārs* under the command of Atar Siṅgh to his camp. On this Atar Siṅgh left the army without permission and came to Lahore to complain to Mahārājā Raṇjīt Siṅgh, who ordered him to re-join his regiment, then in Bannū. Upon Atar Siṅgh's refusal to do so, the Mahārājā confiscated all his *jāgīrs* which were later partially restored by Mahārājā Khaṛak Siṅgh. Mahārājā Sher Siṅgh, on the return to Lahore of Atar Siṅgh after consigning Mahārājā Khaṛak Siṅgh's and Prince Nau Nihāl Siṅgh's ashes to the River Gaṅgā, gave him in Piṇḍī Gheb and Mīrovāl *jāgīrs* valued at over a lakh of rupees, subject to the service of two hundred horse. Atar Siṅgh was made Adālatī (chief justice) of Lahore and the surrounding districts, and received command of the Piṇḍīvālā irregular cavalry which had been first raised by Milkhā Siṅgh Piṇḍīvālā. He took part in the first Anglo-Sikh war. After the treaty of Bharovāl, he was appointed a member of the Council of Regency formed in December 1846 which position he retained till the annexation of the Punjab (1849).

Atar Siṅgh died in December 1851.

BIBLIOGRAPHY

1. Sūrī, Sohan Lāl, *'Umdāt-ut-Twārī<u>kh</u>*. Lahore, 1885-89
2. Griffin, Lepel, and C.F. Massy, *Chiefs and Families of Note in the Punjab*. Lahore, 1909
3. Gupta, Hari Ram, *Panjab on the Eve of First Sikh War*. Chandigarh, 1956
4. Khushwant Singh, *Fall of the Kingdom of the Punjab*. Delhi, 1971

J.R.G.

ATAR SIṄGH MAJĪṬHĪĀ (d. 1843), commander and civilian officer under Mahārājā Raṇjīt Siṅgh. He was the adopted son of Uttam Siṅgh Majīṭhīā, and, in 1809, was appointed governor of Rāwalpiṇḍī and its dependencies. He held an estate worth Rs. 28,000 at Sayyid Kasrāṅ.

BIBLIOGRAPHY

1. Griffin, Lepel, and C.F. Massy, *Chiefs and Families of Note in the Punjab.* Lahore, 1909
2. Sūrī, Sohan Lāl, *'Umdāt-ut-Twārīkh*. Lahore, 1885-89

B.J.H.

ATAR SIṄGH SANDHĀṄVĀLĪĀ (d. 1844), son of Amīr Siṅgh, was a collateral of Mahārājā Raṇjīt Siṅgh. After the direct descendants of the Mahārājā, he, as the eldest of the Sandhāṅvālīā family, stood close to the throne. A daring soldier, Atar Siṅgh was a calculating and shrewd courtier. He took part in several trans-Indus campaigns in Peshāwar and Hazārā. After the death of General Harī Siṅgh Nalvā, he was considered to be the "champion of the Khālsā." He carried the titles "Ujjal Dīdār [of immaculate appearance], Nirmal Buddh [of clear intelligence], Sardār-i-bā-Waqār [the Sardār with prestige], Kāsir-ul-Iqtadār [eagle of power], Sarwar-i-Garoh-i-Nāmdār [leader of the renowned group], 'Ālī Tabā' [of exalted nature], Shujā'-ud-Daulā [valour of the State], Sardār Atar Siṅgh Shamsher-i-Jaṅg Bahādur [the valiant sword of battle]." But he was fickle-minded and ambitious. At Raṇjīt Siṅgh's death he refused to swear fealty either to Khaṛak Siṅgh or Nau Nihāl Siṅgh, and became an active partisan of the Ḍogrā faction at the court. Soon afterwards he changed sides and joined Kaṅvar Nau Nihāl Siṅgh's party against the Ḍogrā minister, Dhiān Siṅgh, and went to Ludhiāṇā to find in the British territory a possible substitute for the Wazīr. When both Khaṛak Siṅgh and Nau Nihāl Siṅgh died in November 1840, he endeavoured to raise a group which would check Ḍogrā dominance at the Darbār, and, at the same time, prevent the succession of Sher Siṅgh. The Sandhāṅvālīās became staunch supporters of Rāṇī Chand Kaur, and Atar Siṅgh Sandhāṅvālīā, who had led a force against Sher Siṅgh when he stormed the Lahore Fort in January 1841, had to flee when the Fort fell. Later feeling insecure in the Punjab, he took asylum in British territory at Thānesar along with his nephew, Ajīt Siṅgh. Both of them kept up an attitude of open hostility towards Mahārājā Sher Siṅgh who had since succeeded to the throne. They solicited British interference in favour of Rāṇī Chand Kaur, and wrote letters to the officers of the Khālsā army inciting them to rise against their sovereign. A mild flutter was caused at Fort William when Atar Siṅgh hobnobbed with Dost Muhammad Khān, the deposed Amīr of Afghanistan at Ludhiāṇā, to what purpose nobody could tell. However when, as a result of British mediation, a reconciliation was brought about between the Sandhāṅvālīās and Mahārājā Sher Siṅgh, they were pardoned and allowed to return to Lahore. But Atar Siṅgh refused to come back to the Punjab, and continued to conspire against the Mahārājā. When in September 1843, Mahārājā Sher Siṅgh was treacherously assassinated by Ajīt Siṅgh Sandhāṅvālīā and Lahiṇā Siṅgh Sandhāṅvālīā, Atar Siṅgh was at Ūnā. On hearing of the retribution which soon overtook both the Sandhāṅvālīā *sardārs,* he hastily fled to Thānesar before a column of troops sent by Hīrā Siṅgh could capture him.

Atar Siṅgh lived in exile at Thānesar along with the few remnants of the Sandhāṅvālīā family who had escaped destruction in 1843 — his son Kehar Siṅgh, and a nephew Raṇjodh Siṅgh, a brother of Ajīt Siṅgh. He nursed enmity against Hīrā Siṅgh and kept in touch with the disaffected elements in the Punjab. When in May 1844, Kaṅvar Pashaurā Siṅgh and Kaṅvar Kashmīrā Siṅgh revolted, he raised a small force and joined them at Nauraṅgābād after crossing the Sutlej, near Harīke. The Lahore Darbār protested to the British at Ludhiāṇā for allowing the rebels passage through their territory. A Sikh force 20,000 strong under Mīāṅ Lābh Siṅgh and General Gulāb Siṅgh crossed the Sutlej and surrounded the *ḍerā* of Bhāī Bīr Siṅgh Nauraṅgābādī. However, the Lahore commanders, respecting the sanctity of Bhāī Bīr Siṅgh, repaired to his camp to bring about an amicable settlement. As negotiations were in progress, Atar Siṅgh flew into a rage and fatally stabbed General Gulāb Siṅgh with his dagger. The attendants of the General instantly fell upon Atar Siṅgh and hacked him to pieces. This was in May 1844.

BIBLIOGRAPHY

1. Griffin, Lepel, and C.F. Massy, *Chiefs and Families of Note in the Punjab.* Lahore, 1909
2. Harbans Singh, *The Heritage of the Sikhs.* Delhi, 1983
3. Smyth, G. Carmichael, *A History of the Reigning Family of Lahore.* Delhi, 1982
4. Sūrī, Sohan Lāl, *'Umdāt-ut-Twārīkh.* Lahore, 1885-89

B.J.H.

ATAR SIṅGH, SANT (1866-1927), of Mastūāṇā, the most charismatic figure in latter-day Sikh piety, was born on 13 March 1866 in the village of Chīmā, in Saṅgrūr district of the Punjab. His father, Karam Siṅgh, was a farmer of modest means and could not afford to send him to a school in town. So Atar Siṅgh was apprenticed to Bhāī Buṭā Siṅgh, head of the Nirmalā *ḍerā* or monastery of Bhāī Rām Siṅgh, in his own village. He acquired proficiency in the Sikh religious texts and also read philosophical treatises such as the *Vichār Sāgar.* Side by side with his progress in Sikh learning, he developed a deeply religious cast of mind. While tending his cattle, he would become absorbed in reciting hymns from the Gurū Granth Sāhib.

At the age of seventeen, Atar Siṅgh enlisted as a gunner in the Artillery, later getting himself transferred to the 54th Sikh Battalion stationed at Kohāṭ. There he received Sikh initiation in the cantonment *gurdwārā* and continued his study of the Scripture under the guidance of its *granthī,* Bhāī Jodh Siṅgh. He was still in the army when he took a vow not to marry.

This was a stimulating period of time in the Punjab. English education and Christian missionary activity had created a new ferment. The Ārya Samāj was the Hindu response to the situation and the Siṅgh Sabhā represented the Sikh reaction. Atar Siṅgh became involved in the Siṅgh Sabhā's dual concerns of restoring the purity of Sikh belief and custom and rejuvenating Sikh society and of promoting Western education among the Sikhs. In the first instance, he went on a pilgrimage to Srī Hazūr Sāhib at Nāndeḍ, sacred to Gurū Gobind Siṅgh. In 1888, Atar Siṅgh was placed in the reserve list and, in 1891, he got his name finally struck off the rolls of the army to devote himself solely to preaching the holy message of the Gurūs. He toured extensively in Jammū and Kashmīr, Sindh and the North-West Frontier Province. In the Poṭhohār region, many Sikhs and Hindus received *pāhul* at his hands. Master Tārā Siṅgh, who later became famous as a political leader, and Bhāī Jodh Siṅgh, eminent theologian and educationist, were administered the rites of Khālsā baptism by him at Ḍerā Khālsā. In Jammū and Kashmīr, he visited Srīnagar, Mīrpur and other towns which had Sikh populations. At Peshāwar, in the North-West Frontier Province, he was received with honour not only by the Hindus and the Sikhs, but also by the Paṭhāns. Sant Kalyāṇ Siṅgh of Peshāwar became a devotee. In Sindh, he visited Sakkhar, Hyderābād and Karāchī. In 1902, he established his main centre in the Mālvā region, at Gursāgar Mastūāṇā, near Saṅgrūr. By his extensive tours and his melodious and resonant recitations of the Gurūs' *bāṇī* before vast audiences, he created a new religious fervour in the Sikh community. Many were impressed by his gentle and spiritual manner and were drawn into the fold of Sikhism. To receive baptism at his hands was considered especially meritorious. New *gurdwārās* sprang at in several places in the wake of Sant Atar Siṅgh's visit.

After 1920, Sant Atar Siṅgh focussed his attention on the area around Damdamā Sāhib where Gurū Gobind Siṅgh had sojourned in 1706 before proceeding to the South. At Damdamā Sāhib, he raised a magnificent *buṅgā* and turned it into a major centre for the propagation of Sikhism. He sent abroad four Sikh young men — Tejā Siṅgh, Amar Siṅgh, Dharmānant Siṅgh and Harī Siṅgh Basrā — for the twin purposes of receiving higher education and spreading the Gurūs' message. Tejā Siṅgh set up in London the K͟hālsā Jathā of the British Isles, and later went to the United States of America. He took his Master's degree at Harvard University and lectured on Sikhism widely in America and Canada, besides espousing the cause of Punjabi immigrants. Dharmānant Siṅgh received his Ph.D. degree from London University specializing in Platonic studies.

The K͟hālsā College Committee, Amritsar, requested Sant Atar Siṅgh to represent it at the Delhi Darbār in 1911. However, he went to Delhi as a guest of the Mahārājā of Jīnd. He was a distinguished participant in the ceremonial procession taken out from Paṭiālā House in Delhi in which, apart from the people in general, the chiefs of Paṭiālā and Jīnd participated. As he rode on an elegantly caparisoned elephant, he looked the very picture of holiness. He was naturally the centre of attention, overshadowing the princes. The sacred hymn he was reciting on that occasion of extraordinary display of imperial power and panoply contrasted the infirmity of worldly rulers with the omnipotence of the God Almighty. The opening lines ran:

> None of the sovereigns equals Hari the Almighty;
> All these worldly rulers last but a bare few days.
> False are the claims they set up. (GG, 856)

Equally with preaching the Word of the Gurūs, Sant Atar Siṅgh concerned himself with the promotion of modern education among Sikhs. He associated himself actively with the Sikh Educational Conference and participated in its annual sessions, presiding over that of 1915 at Fīrozpur. He helped found several institutions such as K͟hālsā High School, Lyallpur, K͟hālsā High School, Chakvāl, Missionary College, Gujrāṅwālā, Gurū Nānak K͟hālsā College, Gujrāṅwālā, Mālvā K͟hālsā High School, Ludhiāṇā, and Akāl College, Mastuāṇā. In 1914, he went to Banāras at the invitation of Paṇḍit Madan Mohan Mālavīya to participate in the ceremonies for laying the foundation of the Sanskrit College. Mahārājā Ripudaman Siṅgh of Nābhā, who was an admirer of Sant Atar Siṅgh took him to Vārāṇasī in his own saloon. Under the tent near the site of the college, Sant Atar Siṅgh performed a series of five *akhaṇḍ pāṭhs,* or continuous, uninterrupted readings of the Gurū Granth Sāhib, Mahārājā Ripudaman Siṅgh saying the Rahrāsi every evening. As these recitations of the Gurū Granth Sāhib were concluded, Mahārājā Gaṅgā Siṅgh of Bīkāner offered concrete in a silver plate and Santjī laid the foundation of the building by applying it to the eleven bricks of gold supplied by the Rājā of Kāshī. After the ceremonies were over, Sant Atar Siṅgh remained in Vārāṇasī for a week as the guest of the Rājā who treated him with deep reverence.

Sant Atar Siṅgh shared the Sikh community's wider social and religious concerns. He supported the Gurdwārā reform movement, and took part in the *dīvān* held at Nankāṇā Sāhib by the Shiromaṇī Gurdwārā Parbandhak Committee in honour of the Nankāṇā Sāhib martyrs in 1921. He was invited to attend the Bhog ceremonies at the conclusion of the Akālī *morchā* at

Jaito. In a report prepared in 1911 by the intelligence department of the Government of India, Sant Atar Siṅgh was described as the inspiration behind the Tatt Khālsā movement among the Sikhs. It was to this school of reformist Sikhs that the origins of the Akālī movement can be traced.

On 31 January 1927, Sant Atar Siṅgh passed away at Saṅgrūr. His body was cremated at Mastuāṇā where now a handsome monument in the form of a *gurdwārā* perpetuates his memory.

BIBLIOGRAPHY

1. Tejā Siṅgh, *Jīvan Kathā Gurmukh Piāre Sant Atar Siṅgh Jī Mahārāj*. Patiala, 1970
2. Khālsā, Bhāī Amar Siṅgh, *Sant Atar Singh Jī Mahārāj*. Lucknow, 1967
3. Balwant Siṅgh, Giānī, *Agam Agādh Purakh Shrīmān Pūjya Sant Atar Siṅgh Jī Mahārāj Mastūāṇe vāliāṅ dā Sampūran Jīvan Charittar*. Mastuana, 1983

S.S.G.

ATAR SIṄGH, SANT (1867-1927), of Gurdwārā Reṛū Sāhib at Rāmpur, in Ludhiāṇā district in the Punjab, was born in March 1867 at the village of Lopoṅ, now in Farīdkoṭ district. He was the son of Lāl Siṅgh, the village headman. Atar Siṅgh was married in 1885 to Bishan Kaur of Ṭoḍarpur, a village near Samrālā. A son, Indar Siṅgh, was born to them in 1887. On 8 June 1887, Atar Siṅgh enlisted in the 36th Sikh Battalion (present 2nd Battalion of the Sikh Regiment). While in the army, he received the vows of the Khālsā. He was promoted sergeant on 16 June 1896. Once, while his battalion was in the Peshāwar region, he along with several of his comrades went to see Sant Karam Siṅgh of Hotī-Mardān, who was then widely known for his piety. Atar Siṅgh, a devout Sikh, instantly fell under the saint's spell, and determined to lead a life of *sevā* (service) and *simran* (meditation). Once, while on leave from his regiment, he visited Rāmpur where he found the old historical shrine, Reṛū Sāhib, commemorating Gurū Gobind Siṅgh's brief halt under a *reṛū* tree (*Mimosa leucophloea*) during his journey from Māchhīvāṛā towards the Mālvā country in December 1705, in a dilapidated state and determined to have it rebuilt. During his next leave, in 1901, he with the help of the local *saṅgat* reconstructed Mañjī Sāhib, the inner sanctum. He spent his leave periods expanding the building and, after his retirement on 18 October 1907, he settled permanently at Rāmpur. He developed Gurū kā Laṅgar, and initiated monthly congregations on full-moon days. He also opened a school where young boys, especially the poor and the blind, were imparted instruction in scripture-reading and *kīrtan* or hymn-singing with a view to training them as preachers of Sikhism.

Sant Atar Siṅgh died at Gurdwārā Reṛū Sāhib on 21 January 1927. He was succeeded by Sant Bhagvān Siṅgh who kept the Reṛū Sāhib legend alive. Sant Bhagvān Siṅgh continued to manage the Gurdwārā until his death in 1975.

BIBLIOGRAPHY

1. Āzād, Sohan Siṅgh, *Jīvan Gāthā Sant Atar Siṅgh*. Ludhiana, 1971
2. Mehar Siṅgh, Giānī, *Amar Kathā*.

Bh. K.S.

ATĪ AKHAṆḌ PĀṬH (*atī* = extreme, arduous, of superlative degree; *akhaṇḍ* = nonstop, without a break; *pāṭh* = reading of the Holy Volume) means an unbroken *pāṭh* of the Gurū Granth Sāhib by a single reader in one continuous sitting without once getting up or interrupting the reading in any manner. This type of *pāṭh* has been undertaken only rarely, for a *pāṭhī* or reader, with such bodily stamina and discipline and with such fluency and speed is not easy to come by. This *pāṭh* has to be performed in about nine *pahars*, or twenty-seven hours. One instance cited in the modern period is that of Bābā Nārāyaṇ Siṅgh (1841-1916), father of the celebrated scholar, Bhāī Kāhn Siṅgh, of Nābhā, who is said to have performed this feat more than once in his lifetime.

BIBLIOGRAPHY

Kāhn Siṅgh, Bhāī, *Gurushabad Ratanākar Mahān Kosh*. Patiala, 1974

T.S.

ĀTMĀ, Sanskrit *ātman*, originally meant 'breath'. Later the term came to connote 'soul' or 'principle of life'. The different systems of Indian philosophy gave it further semantic shades. *Nyāya-Viśeṣaka* considered *ātmā* a substance and endowed it with qualities of cognition, pleasure, pain, desire, aversion and effort. Sāṅkhya recognized it as an object of inference. *Bhaṭṭa-Mimāṅsā* held it as the object of internal perception (*manaspratyakṣa*). *Prabhākara-Mimāṅsā* considered it to be the knowing ego revealed in the very act of knowledge and held it to be the subject and not the object of perception. The Upaniṣads regarded it as the object of higher intuition and equated it with Brahman, the Impersonal Absolute. Śaṅkara's *advaita* Vedānta held it to be pure consciousness above the distinction of subject and object, knowable by an immediate intuitive consciousness. Rāmānuja, however, rejected Śaṅkara's concept of *ātmā* as pure consciousness and considered it to be nothing but the knower or ego.

The Sikh concept is nearest to the Upaniṣadic-Advaitic viewpoint. In Sikh lore, *ātmā* is considered to be of the nature of pure resplendent consciousness : *man tūṅ joti sarūpu hai āpṇā mūlu pachhāṇu* — O my Self ! you are of the nature of light; do recognize your origin (GG, 441). 'Light' here signifies consciousness. The Self (*ātmā*) is conscious while the non-self is the object of consciousness. Though itself not an object of consciousness, *ātmā* is apprehended by unmediated intuition. "As the Self realizes, enlightenment grows without effort" (GG, 87). In fact, consciousness is directed outwards to objects, inwards to *ātmā*. *Ātmā* is pure consciousness without any content. Thus the contentless consciousness within is *ātmā*.

Ātmā is not different from *Param-ātmā*, the Cosmic Consciousness, but is only a fraction thereof. Kabīr designated it as *Rām kī aṅs* (a fraction of Rām). It is the subtlest, purest essence of life: *nirmal joti nirantari jātī*—purest light constantly seen inside (GG, 1039). It remains unperturbed—*ātmā aḍolu na ḍolaī* (GG, 87) — through life's vicissitudes, pleasures and pains. Uninterrupted tranquillity is its hallmark.

In its corporeal attire, it passes through cycles of transmigration. Through Divine Grace, it can merge back into the Cosmic Soul (*Paramātmā*) and escape the throes of birth and death again and again.

It is equated with Brahman : *ātam mahi pārbrahmu lahante* — they discover Pārbrahma in *ātmā* (GG, 276). The individual soul and the Cosmic Soul are indistinguishable one from the other: *ātmā parātmā eko karai* — (he) reckons the personal soul and Cosmic Soul as one (GG, 661). The *ātmā* is Divine, the Divine is ātmā: *ātam deu deu hai ātamu* (GG, 1325). *Ātmā* is also equated with the Creator: *ātam pasārā karaṇhārā prabh binā nahī jāṇīai.* The Self is the creator of the entire universe, beyond it reckon naught (GG, 846). It is also equated with the immanent God: *ātam Rāmu raviā sabh antari* — the immanent Self pervades everything (GG, 916).

The experiential realization of this identification is the *summum bonum* of Sikh mysticism. *Ātam dhiān* (self-absorption) is the operational mode for such an attainment and *ātam giān* (self-knowledge) is its apprehension.

The empirical ego (*haumai*) is only an object of consciousness. There must be a witness of the empirical ego, otherwise there can be no unity of apperception in our knowledge of the external objects and that of the empirical ego. *Ātmā*, in fact, is such witness. However, *ātmā* itself is not an object of knowledge; it is the presupposition of all knowledge—the knowledge of objects as well as that of the empirical ego. *Ātmā* is thus the transcendental Self as distinguished from the empirical ego. Intuitive apprehension of this is *ātam giān* and its actual experience is *ātam daras*, vision of the Self. Such experiential absorption in the Self is attended with the highest aesthetic pleasure, *ātam ras or ātam raṅg*—aesthetic, because it is based on an experience of ultimate beauty.

BIBLIOGRAPHY

1. Sher Singh, *The Philosophy of Sikhism*. Lahore, 1944
2. Avtar Singh, *Ethics of the Sikhs*. Patiala, 1970
3. Jodh Siṅgh, Bhāī, *Gurmati Nirṇāya*. Lahore, 1932
4. Nripinder Singh, *The Sikh Moral Tradition*. Delhi, 1990

J.S.N.

ĀTMĀ SIṄGH, also remembered as Ātmā Rām, was a *faqīr* of Shujā'bād, near Multān, who received the Sikh rites under the influence of Bābā K͟hudā Siṅgh. Before his initiation into the Sikh faith, he lived in a *dharamsālā* at Shujā'bād which received a grant of Rs 100 from the government. This grant reached him every six months, but he used to disburse it, both cash and kind, to the needy within a day or two, and himself subsisted on alms for the remaining period until the next grant was received. He was well familiar with musical measures or *rāgas*, and Bābā K͟hudā Siṅgh called him Aṭh (eight) Rāgā Siṅgh. He knew the entire 1430-page scripture by heart, and could recite the whole of it within 16 *pahars* or 48 hours. Once he performed the feat in the presence of Bābā Sāhib Siṅgh Bedī of Ūnā. Around 1900 Bk/AD 1843, he came to Bābā Bīr Siṅgh at Nauraṅgābād. In 1902 Bk/AD 1845 he shifted to Amritsar which became his last resting place.

BIBLIOGRAPHY

Sher Siṅgh, *Srī Bir Mrigesh Gur Bilās Dev Tru.*

D.S.

ĀTMĀ SIṄGH, BHĀĪ (1881-1921), one of the Nankāṇā Sāhib martyrs, was the son of Bhāī Hīrā Siṅgh, a Mazhabī Sikh of village Mustrābād in Gurdāspur district. The family later shifted to village Dhārovāli in Sheik͟hūpurā district where Ātmā Siṅgh came in contact with Bhāī Lachhmaṇ Siṅgh, an active Akālī reformist, and learnt reading and writing in Gurmukhī script and also received the rites of K͟hālsā initiation. He married and raised a family of five children—three sons and two daughters. Bhāī Ātmā Siṅgh enlisted at the outbreak of the First Great War in 1914 and served in the 32nd Punjab Battalion. On release from the army in 1918, he cultivated closer association with Bhāī Lachhmaṇ Siṅgh and started taking active interest in the Gurdwārā reform movement. He took part in the Dhārovālī conference on 1-3 October 1920 and later in the liberation of Gurdwārā Kharā Saudā. He was one of the members of the *jathā* led by Bhāī Lachhmaṇ Siṅgh Dhārovālī which entered Gurdwārā Janam Asthān at Nankāṇā Sāhib on 20 February 1921 and fell a martyr in the wholesale slaughter launched by the hired assassins of Mahant Naraiṇ Dās, the hereditary custodian of the shrine.

See NANKĀṆĀ SĀHIB MASSACRE

BIBLIOGRAPHY

Shamsher, Gurbak͟hsh Siṅgh, *Shahīdī Jīvan*. Nankana Sahib, 1938

G.S.G.

ATTAR SIṄGH, SARDĀR SIR (1833-1896), scholar nobleman, was a collateral of the rulers of Paṭiālā, and belonged to the village of Bhadauṛ, in present-day Saṅgrūr district of the Punjab. He was born in 1833, the son of Khaṛak Siṅgh. From the very beginning, he had a bent for learning and gained proficiency in Urdu, Persian, Punjabi and English. For study of Sanskrit, he went to Vārāṇasī. For his mastery in Sanskrit learning he was honoured by the British with the title of Mahāmahopādhyāya. He was equally at ease in the world of Arabic-Persian learning for which he earned the title of Shamas ul-'Ulemā. Succeeding to the family estates in 1858, Attar Siṅgh set up a library for himself and a school for the children at Bhadauṛ. In 1878, he moved to Ludhiāṇā, shifting his library from Bhadauṛ to that city as well. In pursuance of his will, this library was after his death transferred to the Pañjāb Public Library at Lahore. For his scholarly tastes and for his work in the cause of education, he was appointed a member of the senate of the Pañjāb University College, Lahore, in 1870. Already in 1869 he had been elected a member of Añjuman-i-Punjab, an educational and literary society started under the presidentship of Dr G.W. Leitner. Of the Añjuman, he was vice-president in 1880. He was elected a member of Asiatic Society of Bengal in 1869. The British authorities often consulted him on matters relating to Sikh affairs, faith and literature. A strong loyalist in sympathy, Attar Siṅgh helped the British especially at the time of the uprising of the Kūkās or Nāmdhārīs and maintained voluntary surveillance in keeping the government informed about their activities. For the benefit of the British government, he also translated into English in 1873 *Sau Sākhī* (lit. A Hundred Stories), an apocryphal text ascribed by some to Gurū Gobind Siṅgh, which was popularized towards the end of the nineteenth century by Kūkās who read some of its verses as predictory of their own triumph and prosperity and of Mahārājā Duleep Siṅgh, the deposed king of the Punjab.

When in 1873 Trumpp expressed his inability to translate the *Dasam Granth*, Attar Siṅgh at the request of the government prepared abstracts of certain texts from it, such as *Jāp Sāhib, Akāl Ustati, Bachitra Nāṭak, Zafarnāmah* and the *Hakāyāt* section in Persian and Punjabi which he supplied to the Government of India and to Dr Trumpp in March 1874. He also translated into English Rahitnāmās of Prahlād Siṅgh and Bhāī Nand Lāl for the benefit of the government. In January 1876, he published his English translation of *Mālvā Des Raṭan dī Sākhī Pothī*, popularly known as *Sākhī Pothī*, under the title *The Travels of Guru Teg Bahadur and Guru Gobind Singh*. He was a member of the Bengal Philharmonical Society and also served on the Committee of Management of the Aitchison Chiefs' College, Lahore. In recognition of his literary and political services he was awarded by the British the title of Fāzil ul-Fuzalā (lit. excelling the excellent learned men) in 1877, and C.I.E. (Companion of the Indian Empire) in 1880. In 1887, on the occasion of the Queen Victoria's Jubilee Celebrations, the newly-instituted title of Mahāmahopādhyāya was conferred on him in recognition of his eminent services in the promotion of Oriental learning. In 1888, he was admitted to Knighthood. Attar Siṅgh was consulted on the question of official permission to Mahārājā Duleep Siṅgh to visit India. He opposed the proposal and his advice was one of the factors which led to the refusal for the deposed Mahārājā to visit the Punjab.

Sardār Attar Siṅgh's services in the cause of Siṅgh Sabhā movement are as noteworthy as his loyalty to the British. He was founder president of Srī Gurū Siṅgh Sabhā, Ludhiāṇā, established in 1884. He also took a leading part in the establishment of the Khālsā Dīwān at Lahore of which he became patron-in-chief. In 1886 he had been nominated a member of the General Committee of the Darbār Sāhib (Golden Temple) at Amritsar. In 1890, he was made vice-president and trustee of the Khālsā College Establishment Committee and later vice-president of the Khālsā College Council. Attar Siṅgh made a signal contribution to the history of the development of Punjabi when he had the language included in the academic programme at the Oriental College at Lahore. To counteract the argument of the opponents that there was no mentionable literature in Punjabi, he produced a formidable list of books and manuscripts in Punjabi from his personal collection which clinched the issue. He brought to the notice of scholars, especially Dr Leitner, an old inscription at Haṭhūr, a village in Ludhiāṇā district. This inscription proved how far back the roots of Punjabi language and its script went.

Sardār Sir Attar Siṅgh died at Ludhiāṇā on 10 June 1896.

BIBLIOGRAPHY

1. Griffin, Lepel, and C.F. Massy, *Chiefs and Families of Note in the Punjab*. Lahore, 1909
2. *Punjab States Gazetteers, Phulkian States*. Lahore, 1904
3. *Silver Jubilee Book*. Amritsar, 1937

Nz.S.

AUCKLAND, GEORGE EDEN, EARL OF (1784-1849), Governor-General of India, son of William Eden, First Baron of Auckland, was born at Eden Farm, near Beckenham, in Kent, in August 1784. He was educated at Christ Church, Oxford, and was called to the bar at Lincoln's Inn in 1809. From 1810-13, he represented Woodstock in Parliament. He served as President of the Board of Trade from 1830-34. In 1834, he became the First Lord of Admiralty under Lord Melbourne, who sent him out in April 1836 to India as governor-general.

Auckland's policy towards the Sikhs was dominated by the prevalent fear of Russian invasion. While keeping up friendly relations with the Sikh sovereign, Mahārājā Raṇjīt Siṅgh, he sought by various measures to contain his influence. The penetration of Russian influence into Persia and Afghanistan was a reality, but the possibility of a Russian advance to India and its ultimate threat to British possessions in India were purely imaginary. Yet the despatches of MacNeil and Ellis from Tehran and persistent whispers from the Persian Gulf residency kept the myth alive. The British authority in India overlooked the fact that between the wild mountains of the Hindukush and the River Sutlej lived a strong and well-knit race in friendly alliance with the British and fanatically averse to any foreign intrusion. The British decided to resuscitate Saddozaī power in Afghanistan. The scheme aimed at the overthrow of Dost Muhammad K͟hān Bārakzaī and the installation on the throne at Kābul of ex-king Shāh Shujā' with the help of Sikh arms and British resources. This led up to Sir William Macnaghten's mission to Lahore and the signing of the Tripartite Treaty in June 1838 between Shāh Shujā', Mahārājā Raṇjīt Siṅgh and the British government. Towards the close of November 1838, the British armies assembled at Fīrozpur. This was the celebrated "Army of the Indus," as Lord Auckland called it. Further eclat was given to the opening of this campaign by a meeting which had meanwhile been arranged between the governor-general and Mahārājā Raṇjīt Siṅgh and which took place at Fīrozpur on 30 November 1838. The Mahārajā had been recovering from a serious illness, yet he displayed his wonted high spirits and acuteness of mind on the occasion. Auckland realized that any major military intervention by Sikhs in Afghanistan affairs would lead to their establishing influence at Kābul. So they were excluded from any positive role beyond the K͟haibar.

After the first Afg͟hān war, which resulted in a disaster, Auckland was recalled in February 1842. In 1846, Lord John Russel appointed him First Lord of Admiralty. He died on 1 January 1849.

BIBLIOGRAPHY

1. Hasrat, B.J., *Anglo-Sikh Relations*. Hoshiarpur, 1968

2. Majumdar, R.C., ed., *The History and Culture of the Indian People*, vol. IX. Bombay, 1963
3. Gupta, Hari Ram, *Panjab on the Eve of First Sikh War*. Chandigarh, 1956
4. Smith, Vincent A., *The Oxford History of India*. Oxford, 1958

B.J.H.

AUCKLAND PAPERS, comprising private correspondence and letters of Lord Auckland, governor-general of India (1836-42), now available in the British Library and Museum, London, provide interesting side-lights on political affairs in the Punjab (1836-1841), Sindh and Afghanistan, and also furnish useful information on the military power of the Sikhs, and persons and politics at the court of Mahārājā Raṇjīt Siṅgh. Some of these letters were used by L.J.Trotter in his *Earl of Auckland* (Oxford, 1893), and quite a few of them were published in the *Journal and Correspondence of William Lord Auckland* (London, 1861-62).

Of a total of eight volumes, six deal essentially with events leading to the first Anglo-Afg͟hān war, the tripartite treaty among Raṇjīt Siṅgh, Shāh Shūja' and the British Government, and despatches of Wade and other British officers who accompanied a British auxiliary force through the Punjab, under the nominal command of Shāh Shujā's eldest son, Prince Taimūr, to Afghanistan (MS. Volumes No. 37689-94). The other two volumes contain Lord Auckland's private correspondence with Sir John Hobhouse, President of the Board of Control, revealing the rising tension between the Sikhs and the English, and tracing the course of events which ended in the disaster in Afghanistan. Detailed information is provided about the Russo-Persian threat to India and the measures taken to counteract it; Sikh designs on Sindh ; Sir Henry Fane's visit to Lahore; the Sikh-Afg͟hān disputes and the British attitude; Raṇjīt Siṅgh's war and peace aims; French influence at Lahore; Burnes' negotiations at Kābul and Raṇjīt Siṅgh's reactions; danger of Sikh-Afg͟hān conflict; various schemes for the subversion of Dost Muhammad's power and rehabilitation of Shāh Shujā' with Sikh help; Auckland-Raṇjīt Siṅgh meeting; Wade's transactions at Peshāwar; Clerk's reports from Lahore; death of Raṇjīt Siṅgh; Wade's recall from Ludhiāṇā; death of Kharak Siṅgh and Nau Nihāl Siṅgh; Sher Siṅgh's overtures and conditions of British support; and Macnaghten's accusations against the Sikhs.

BIBLIOGRAPHY

Hasrat, B.J., ed. and annot., *The Punjab Papers*. Hoshiarpur, 1970

B.J.H.

AURAṄGĀBĀD, (19° - 54'N, 75° - 20'E) is a district town in Mahārāshṭra. It is a railway station on the Manmāḍ-Kāchīgudā section of the South Central Railway, 114 km from Manmāḍ towards Nānded. The site was once the capital of the Yādavas of Devgirī or Deogīr in the 12th and 13th centuries; Auraṅgzīb established his headquarters here when he was appointed governor of the four Deccan provinces in AD 1636. When as emperor he came to the Deccan in 1681 (never to return to the north again), he first stayed at Auraṅgābād, later shifting to Ahmadnagar.

In 1706, Gurū Gobind Siṅgh had sent Bhāī Dayā Siṅgh and Bhāī Dharam Siṅgh as his emissaries to the Deccan with his letter, known as the *Zafarnāmah*, addressed to Emperor Auraṅgzīb. The Sikhs halted for a short while at Auraṅgābād, on their way to Ahmadnagar, where they found that it was almost impossible to see the emperor and deliver to him the letter personally as the Gurū had directed. Bhāī Dayā Siṅgh sent his colleague back to the Gurū with a letter seeking his advice. But before Bhāī Dharam Siṅgh could re-join him with further instructions from the Gurū, Bhāī Dayā Siṅgh had managed to have the letter delivered and had returned to Auraṅgābād. The two went back to the Gurū, then travelling in Rājasthan.

At Auraṅgābād, Bhāī Dayā Siṅgh had stayed with a Sikh whose house became a meeting-place for the Gurū's disciples. The place, located in Dhāmī Mohallā in the interior of the town, is now known as Gurdwārā Bhāī Dayā Siṅgh. The present building was constructed by the local *saṅgat* in the 1960's.

The *gurdwārā* is managed by a local committee. Sikh services are held morning and evening and important anniversaries and festivals are observed. The Gurdwārā *granthī* runs a class for young resident scholars in scripture-reading.

M.G.S.

AURAṄGZĪB, MUHĪ UD-DĪN MUHAMMAD 'ĀLAMGĪR (1618-1707), the last of the great Mughal emperors of India, ascended the throne of Delhi on 21 July 1658 after he had gained a decisive victory in the war of succession at Sāmūgaṛh, near Āgrā, on 29 May 1658. Auraṅgzīb's appointment in 1636 as viceroy of the Mughal provinces in the Deccan had first brought him into prominence. In 1645, he was transferred to Gujarāt. Between 1648 and 1652, he served as governor of Sindh and Multān. He was next entrusted with the task of recovering Qandahār, taken by the Persians in 1649. In 1653 he was appointed viceroy of the Deccan for the second time and for the next five years he was engaged in constant warfare with the independent states of Bījāpur and Golconḍā.

The first half of Auraṅgzīb's long reign was devoted to consolidating his power in northern India while the second half was spent in the fruitless attempt to conquer the Deccan. A pious man in his personal life, Auraṅgzīb was an orthodox Muslim. He had waded through a river of blood to reach the throne and had imprisoned his father and killed his own brothers. By his fanatical religious policy he wished to please the Muslim orthodoxy and win reprieve for the crimes he had committed to gain the crown. For the first ten years of his reign, he did not feel strong enough to take any drastic steps, but in 1669 he issued a rescript to all provincial governors "to destroy with a willing hand the schools and temples of the infidels and put an entire stop to their religious practices and teaching." Among the many repressive edicts issued against the non-Muslims was one prohibiting all Hindus with the exception of Rājpūts from riding *pālkīs*, elephants or thorough-bred horses and from carrying arms. Most stringent was the imposition, in 1679, of *jizyah*, a tax the non-Muslims had to pay for permission to live in an Islamic State.

The growing Sikh order had also to bear the brunt of Auraṅgzīb's policy of intolerance and religious persecution. The seventh Sikh Gurū, Har Rāi, was at Goindvāl when Dārā Shukoh, heir apparent to the Mughal throne, entered the Punjab fleeing in front of the army of his brother, Auraṅgzīb, after his defeat in the battle of Sāmūgaṛh. At Goindvāl, where he arrived in the last week of June 1658, he called on Gurū Har Rāi, who, as the tradition goes, had once cured him of a serious illness with some rare herbs. Highly coloured stories about Dārā Shukoh's meeting with Gurū Har Rāi were carried to Auraṅgzīb by his officials who reported to him that Gurū Har Rāi was a rebel and that he had helped the fugitive prince and further that the Sikh Scripture contained verses derogatory to Islam. Auraṅgzīb summoned the Gurū to Delhi. As recorded in Santokh Siṅgh, *Srī Gur Pratāp Sūraj Granth,* Gurū Har Rāi wondered why he had been called to Delhi: "I rule over no territory. I owe the king no taxes, nor do I want anything from him. There is no connection of teacher and disciple between us, either. Of what avail will this meeting be ?" Guru Har Rāi sent his elder son, Rām Rāi, to meet the emperor. Rām Rāi succeeded in winning the confidence of the Emperor, but overreached himself when, to please him, he deliberately misread one of the verses from the Gurū Granth Sāhib. Auraṅgzīb decided to keep Rām Rāi in Delhi in the belief that, with the future incumbent of the Gurūship in his power, he would become the arbiter of the destiny of the Sikh people. For garbling the sacred text, Gurū Har Rāi anathematized Rām Rāi and chose his second son, Har Krishan, as his successor. The investiture of Har Krishan did not please Auraṅgzīb who summoned the infant Gurū to Delhi, with the intention of arbitrating between his claims and those of his elder brother, Rām Rāi. Gurū Har Krishan arrived in Delhi and was put up at the house of Mirzā Rājā Jai Siṅgh of Amber. According to the *Gurū kīāṅ Sākhīāṅ,* Gurū Har Krishan visited the Emperor's court on 25 March 1664, but owing to Auraṅgzīb's insistence that he show a miracle to prove his holiness he resolved never to see his face again. A few days later, Gurū Har Krishan was stricken with smallpox and he died on 30 March 1664.

The responsibility of instructing the Sikh community and guiding its affairs now fell on Gurū Tegh Bahādur, Nānak IX. As recorded in *Bhaṭṭ Vahī Talauḍā,* a group of Kashmīrī *paṇḍits* waited on him at Anandpur on 25 May 1675 and complained how Iftikhār Khān, Auraṅgzīb's satrap in Kashmīr, had been making forcible conversions. Gurū Tegh Bahādur is said to have advised his visitors to go and tell the authority in Delhi that if he (Gurū Tegh Bahādur) was converted, they would all voluntarily accept Islam. Resolved to lay down his life to redeem freedom of belief, Gurū Tegh Bahādur set out for Delhi. Under the orders of the Emperor, he was taken into custody on 12 July 1675 at Malikpur Raṅghrāṅ, near Sirhind, and despatched to Delhi. He was put in chains and on his refusal to renounce his faith was beheaded in public in the Chāndnī Chowk of Delhi on 11 November 1675, after three of his devoted disciples — Bhāī Dayāl Dās, Bhāī Matī Dās and Bhāī Satī Dās — had been tortured to death before his eyes. His son, Gobind Rāi (later Gobind Siṅgh), now succeeded to the spiritual throne of Gurū Nānak. Aurangzīb was occupied with his campaigns in the South, but his feudal vassals, the hill chieftains, resented the Gurū's presence in their midst. They were especially averse to the way the four castes mingled in the Sikh order. They plotted in collusion with the local Mughal officers and led out armies against Gurū Gobind Siṅgh. After the battle of Nadauṇ, fought on 20 March 1691, in which the Mughal commander, Alif Khān was defeated, Auraṅgzīb ordered his *faujdārs* in the Punjab to restrain Gurū Gobind Siṅgh from holding assemblies of Sikhs and to demolish his hearth and home and banish him from the country if he departed ever so little from the ways of a *faqīr* and did not cease to have himself addressed as Sachchā Pādshāh, the True King. On 13 July 1696, he sent his eldest son, Mu'azzam, who later succeeded to the throne of Delhi as Emperor Bahādur Shāh, to settle affairs in the Punjab. Anandpur had been subject to constant raid and encroachment since 1700 but the fiercest onslaught made was in 1705 when the hill chiefs, aided by Mughal troops from Lahore and Sirhind, invested Gurū Gobind Siṅgh's citadel, eventually forcing him to evacuate it on 5-6 December 1705. Reaching Dīnā, a village in present-day Farīdkoṭ district of the Punjab, Gurū Gobind Siṅgh wrote to Auraṅgzīb a letter in Persian verse called *Zafarnāmah,* Epistle of Victory. It was a severe indictment of Auraṅgzīb, who was repeatedly upbraided for breach of faith in the attack made by his troops on the Sikhs after they had vacated Anandpur on solemn assurance of safe passage given them by him and his officers. The letter emphatically reiterated the sovereignty of morality in the affairs of State as much as in the conduct of individual human beings and regarded the means as important as the end. Absolute truthfulness was as much the duty of a sovereign as of any one of the ordinary citizens. Two of the Gurū's Sikhs, Dayā Siṅgh and Dharam Sīṅgh, were sent to deliver the *Zafarnāmah* to Auraṅgzīb, who was then camping in Ahmadnagar. According to *Ahkām-i-'Ālamgīrī*, the Emperor immediately sent through Muhammad Beg, a *gurzbardār* or mace-bearer, and Shaikh Yār Muhammad, a *mansabdār*, a *farmān* to Mun'im Khān, deputy governor of Lahore, asking him to make peace with Gurū Gobind Siṅgh. He also invited the Gurū for a personal meeting. The *Gurū kīāṅ Sākhīāṅ* confirms the invitation sent by Auraṅgzīb and mentions two *gurzbardārs* accompanying Bhāī Dayā Siṅgh and Bhāī Dharam Siṅgh back to the Punjab. But before the Gurū could see the Emperor, the latter died on 20 February 1707.

BIBLIOGRAPHY

1. Sarkar, Sir Jadunath, *A Short History of Aurangzib*. Calcutta, 1962
2. Majumdar, R.C., ed., *The History and Culture of the Indian People*, vol. VIII. Bombay, 1974
3. Jaffar, S.M., *The Mughal Empire*. Delhi, 1974
4. Gupta, Hari Ram, *History of the Sikhs*, vol. I, Delhi, 1973
6. Sharma, Sri Ram, *Religious Policy of the Mughal Emperors*. Bombay, 1962

S.R.S.

AVITABILE, PAOLO CRESCENZO MARTINO (1791-1850), a Neapolitan soldier of fortune who, starting life as a private gunner, succeeded in obtaining high ranks in two widely separated Asiatic armies of Persia and Punjab, was born at Agerola, Naples, Italy, on 25 October 1791. From 1807 onwards he successively served in the local militia and in Napoleon's army. In 1817, he resigned from the army and, roaming about various countries, reached Persia in 1820 and joined the Shāh's army. He attained the rank of colonel and received several decorations. He left the Shāh's service in 1824 and after a brief visit to Italy, he came back to join Claude Auguste Court, a French adventurer, to Lahore, reaching there in early 1827. He took up service under Mahārājā Raṇjīt Siṅgh. Being a gunner and an expert in gun-making, he was employed in the artillery and was also given charge of the Mahārājā's arsenal and foundries. He was one of the few Europeans at the Sikh court given civilian appointments as well. Avitabile was made administrator of Wazīrābād in 1829. He improved the town, kept it very clean and himself lived in dignified style in a palace. In 1834, he was sent to Peshāwar of which province he was made governor after Harī Siṅgh Nalvā's death in 1837. He remained at this post till mid-1843 when he returned to Lahore and resigned on 17 July 1843. He had proved a stern administrator and his rule of Peshāwar is often described as one of "gallows and gibbets." To curb the turbulent and lawless Afghān tribes, he resorted to summary punishments, collective fines and reprisals.

Avitabile was an accomplished linguist and could speak Italian, French, Persian and Hindustānī with equal facility. He had served in the armies of France, Persia, Afghanistan and Lahore and won laurels everywhere. He was a much-decorated soldier. He was awarded Chevalier of the Legion of Honour; the Order of Merit of San Ferdinand of Naples; the Durrani Order of Afghanistan; Grand Cordon of the Lion and the Sun; and the two Lions and Crown of Persia. He received the Auspicious Star of the Punjab medal from Mahārājā Raṇjīt Siṅgh. The Mahārājā also awarded him titles of Dilāwar Jaṅg Bahādur, Amānat Panāh and Aṃīn ud-Daulā.

Avitabile left the Sikh service after Mahārājā Sher Siṅgh's assassination. He sailed from Calcutta on 15 December 1843 landing at Naples on 18 February 1844. At home, he was confirmed a general and made a knight. He got married to his own niece in order to keep his vast riches within the family. The marriage being against the wishes of the girl, she is said to have poisoned the general, who died on 28 March 1850.

BIBLIOGRAPHY

1. Grey, C. *European Adventurers of Northern India, 1785-1849.* Patiala, 1970
2. Harbans Singh, *Maharaja Ranjit Singh.* Delhi, 1980

Gl.S.

AVTĀR SIṄGH VAHĪRĪĀ, polemicist and scholar of Sikh texts, was born on 12 June 1848 at Thohā K̲h̲ālsā, a village in Rāwalpiṇḍī district, now in Pakistan. As a small boy, he learnt to recite the Sikh psalms from his mother and maternal uncle, Prem Siṅgh. After he had learnt Gurmukhī in his own village, he went to school in Rāwalpiṇḍī. At the age of eight years, he took *pāhul* at the hands of Bābā Khem Siṅgh Bedī. Bābā Khem Siṅgh was to become the focus of his adult life and, in 1869, he took him as his mentor and dedicated his career to him. He shifted his business to Rāwalpiṇḍī to be close to his spiritual guide. When a Siṅgh Sabhā was formed at Rāwalpiṇḍī in the early 1880's, Avtār Siṅgh was among the first to join it. In 1883, there was a proposal sponsored by Bābā Khem Siṅgh Bedī in the K̲h̲ālsā Dīwān, Amritsar, that Siṅgh Sabhās be called Sikh Siṅgh Sabhās so that Sahajdhārī Sikhs could also be enlisted as members. The proposal met with opposition in the Dīwān, but was readily accepted by the Rāwalpiṇḍī Siṅgh Sabhā. Avtār Siṅgh became assistant secretary, and later secretary of this Sabhā. Serious dissensions had cropped up in the K̲h̲ālsā Dīwān over the question of giving a special pontifical status to Bābā Khem Siṅgh Bedī. A monthly magazine, *Srī Gurmat Prakāshak*, was launched from Rāwalpiṇḍī in Baisākh 1942 Bk/April-May 1885 by the partisans of Bābā Khem Siṅgh. Avtār Siṅgh was its manager-cum-editor. The opponents led by Bhāī Gurmukh Siṅgh, chief secretary of the K̲h̲ālsā Dīwān, Amritsar, set up a separate K̲h̲ālsā Dīwān at Lahore on 10-11 April 1886. At Amritsar Bhāī Gaṇeshā Siṅgh became the chief secretary in place of Bhāī Gurmukh Siṅgh. He was assisted by Avtār Siṅgh, who along with his journal *Srī Gurmat Prakāshak* shifted to Amritsar. The magazine was made a fortnightly in April 1887. Avtār Siṅgh drafted the new constitution for the K̲h̲ālsā Dīwān, Amritsar, which was approved on the Dīvālī day of 1887. His views on Sikh rites and ceremonies were too conservative even for the traditionalist K̲h̲ālsā Dīwān of Amritsar, and he had serious differences with its new chief secretary, Giānī Sardūl Siṅgh. Avtār Siṅgh and his supporters formed a separate association called Anin Sikhī dī Saṅgat Bhāīchārā, parallel to Sardūl Siṅgh's K̲h̲ālsā Sat Saṅgat Sabhā. In 1894, Avtār Siṅgh Vahīrīā brought out *K̲h̲ālsā Dharam Śāstra: Saṅskār Bhāg.* To secure the approval of the *tak̲h̲ts, gurdwārās* and of the leaders of the Panth, the work was subsequently enlarged and published in 1914 under the patronage of Ṭikkā Sāhib Soḍhī Rām Narāin Siṅgh Jī, as *K̲h̲ālsā Dharam Śāstra,* with a sub-title in English, *Sikhs' Religious National Law.*

In 1898, Avtār Siṅgh formed Chaldā Vahīr, a moving band of preachers, to tour villages and towns exhorting Sikhs to preserve the prevalent religious ceremonial and not to be 'misled' by the 'new-fangled' ideas of the Siṅgh Sabhā. The Vahīr which earned him the epithet Vahīrīā, leader of the marching column, lasted for two years. Thereafter Avtār Siṅgh returned to preaching his ideas through the printed word and produced his 8-volume *K̲h̲ālsā Sudhār Tarū* (the Tree of Sikh Reformation) and a series of other books and pamphlets. The death of Bābā Khem Siṅgh Bedī, on 10 April 1905, deprived him of his principal patron. It was a personal calamity for him as well as a loss to the Sikh Panth, which he lamented in the *Shok Pattar*, or statement of grief, published in 1905. He shifted his residence back to Rāwalpiṇḍī and spent the rest of his days in comparative oblivion. But he kept up with his writing. His *Gur Darshan Śāstra,* a work interpreting the teachings of the Gurū Granth Sāhib according to his own conservative views, was published in 1916.

BIBLIOGRAPHY

1. Jagjīt Singh, *Siṅgh Sabhā Lahir 1873-1902.* Lahore, 1974
2. Dhillon, Gurdarshan Singh, "Character and Impact of the Singh Sabha Movement on the History of the Punjab," unpublished Ph.D. thesis.
3. Nripinder Singh, *The Sikh Moral Tradition.* Delhi, 1990

Jg.S.

AYODHYĀ (26° - 45'N, 82° - 10'E), on the right bank of the River Saryū, also known as Ghāgharā, is sacred to the Hindus as the birthplace of Lord Rāma. This ancient town has Sikh shrines in memory of the First, the Ninth and the Tenth Gurūs. All three are located within 50 metres of each other near Brahmā's Tap Sthān (Brahmā Kuṇḍ) on Saryū bank, and are collectively called Gurdwārā Brahmakuṇḍ. The memorial commemorating Gurū Nānak's visit at the beginning of the sixteenth century consists of only a Sikh flag on a platform constructed in 1972. Gurū Tegh Bahādur visited Ayodhyā in 1670 while on his way back to the Punjab from the eastern parts. It is said that after offering obeisance at the then existing shrine of Gurū Nānak he sat near by in meditation continuously for 48 hours. Before he left, the Brāhmaṇ priest serving the shrine made a request for a keepsake, and the Gurū left his wooden sandals with him. The pair is still kept in Gurdwārā Gurū Gobind Siṅgh Jī. A platform was raised on the site in memory of Gurū Tegh Bahādur's visit. A room was constructed over it by the Sikh troops of Faizābād cantonment in 1975. The Gurū Granth Sāhib is ushered in only on the occasion of the chain of 51 Akhaṇḍ Pāṭhs held here commencing from Assū *sudī* 1 and concluding on Maghar *sudī* 5 to honour the martyrdom anniversary of Gurū Tegh Bahādur.

Gurū Gobind Siṅgh passed through Ayodhyā when, as a child, he was travelling from Paṭnā to Anandpur. A platform was raised to commemorate the visit. This, like the other two shrines, was looked after by Brāhmaṇ priests till about the middle of the nineteenth century when Bābā Gulāb Siṅgh, a Kashmīrī Sikh, came and occupied the site. The present building was constructed in 1899. It commands a panoramic view of a landscape sprawling beyond the lazily flowing Saryū River. The central domed room, octagonal in shape and with a marble floor, is called Siṅghāsan Sthān (Throne Room) Gurū Gobind Siṅgh Jī. The Gurū Granth Sāhib is seated in a rectangular room in front of it. The relics preserved in the Siṅghāsan Sthān include, in addition to the pair of sandals left by Gurū Tegh Bahādur, an all-steel arrow, a *kaṭār* (dagger), and a *chakra* (quoit). There are also two hand-written volumes—a copy of the Gurū Granth Sāhib transcribed in 1838 Bk/AD 1781 and a copy of the *Dasam Granth*.

BIBLIOGRAPHY

1. Ṭhākar Siṅgh, Giānī, *Srī Gurduāre Darshan.* Amritsar, 1923
2. Tārā Siṅgh, *Srī Gur Tīrath Saṅgrahi.* Amritsar, n.d.

M.G.S.

ĀZĀD HIND FAUJ, or Indian National Army (I.N.A.for short) as it was known to the English-speaking world, was a force raised from Indian prisoners of war during World War II (1939-45) to fight against the British. The hostilities had started with the German invasion of Poland on 1 September 1939. The United Kingdom declared war against Germany, and India, then ruled by the British, automatically joined in under the governor-general's proclamation of 3 September 1939. While the smaller Indian political parties such as the Muslim League, Hindu Mahā Sabhā and the Shiromaṇī Akālī Dal were prepared to support government's war effort, Indian National Congress refused to co-operate. A resolution passed by its Working Committee on 15 September 1939, and subsequently endorsed by the All India Congress Committee and the plenary session of the Congress, declared: "India's sympathy is entirely on the side of democracy and freedom, but India cannot associate herself with a war said to be for democratic freedom when that very freedom is denied to her ..." The resolution demanded that the British government pronounce in unequivocal terms their war aims and "in particular how those aims are going to apply to India and to be given effect to in the present." Congress-led ministeries in eight of the provinces resigned and the party planned a programme of individual *satyāgraha* or protest. In fact a group of left-wingers in the Congress had already formed a separate party, the Forward Block, under the leadership of Subhās Chandra Bose. This group wanted to take advantage of the situation and to intensify their struggle for independence. Subhās Chandra Bose was arrested on 2 July 1940. He went on an indefinite hunger strike on 29 November and was released on 5 December, but was kept under police surveillance in his ancestral house in Calcutta. Giving the police the slip on the night of 16-17 December, Subhās Chandra Bose reached Berlin on 28 March 1941 after a hazardous journey through north India, Kābul and Moscow. There he made contact with Germany's foreign minister, Joachim von Ribbentrop, who accepted his offer of raising Free India units from Indian prisoners of war. That disaffection against the British existed among Indian troops had been evidenced when a Sikh squadron had refused to embark at Bombay in August 1940, and when Sikh soldiers in some other regiments had refused to wear steel helmets. Subhās Chandra's call to Indian prisoners of war was well received and 1,200 men, mostly Sikhs, were recruited during the first six months for a training camp set up at Frankenburg. This camp was the precursor of the Āzād Hind Fauj. It was initially named Lashkar-i-Hind or Indian Legion and its strength in the West rose in due course to 4,500. The name of the political organization corresponding to the Indian Independence League in the East was the Free India Centre.

Japan's entry into the War on 8 December 1941 and her rapid conquest of Malaya and Singapore, with Thailand's capitulation into neutrality, radically changed the situation so far as India was concerned. Certain Indian nationalist sections such as the Socialist Party and Forward Bloc entertained hopes of liberating the country with Japan's help. Indians, mainly Sikhs, living in Malaya, Singapore and other countries of the region had set up two secret anti-British groups, led by Giānī Prītam Siṅgh and Swāmī Satyānanda Purī, respectively.

A Japanese officer, Major Fujiwara, head of the field intelligence section in the region, had, even before the declaration of war by Japan, contacted Giānī Prītam Siṅgh and reached an agreement of collaboration with him at Bangkok on 4 December 1941. Following the Japanese advance in North Malaya, Fujiwara and Prītam Siṅgh reached Alorstar on 14 December 1941. It was here that Captain Mohan Siṅgh, a straggler from the 14 Punjab Regiment overrun by the invaders, contacted them. He surrendered on the following day and was asked to restore order in the town. All Indian prisoners of war and stragglers were put under his charge. Kuala Lumpur fell on 11 January 1942 with 3,500 Indian prisoners of war and Singapore on 15 February 1942 with 85,000 troops of whom 45,000 were Indians. Mohan Siṅgh asked for volunteers who would form the

Āzād Hind Fauj to fight for freeing India from the British yoke. A large number, again mostly Sikhs, came forward. Mohan Siṅgh established his headquarters at Neeson in Singapore with Lt-Col. Nirañjan Siṅgh Gill as Chief of Staff, Lt-Col. J.K. Bhonsle as Adjutant and Quartermaster-General and Lt-Col. A.C. Chatterjee as Director of Medical Services. The Āzād Hind Fauj, however, was formally established on 1 September 1942 by which date 40,000 prisoners of war had signed a pledge to join it.

Meanwhile another organization, Indian Independence League, had materialized under the leadership of Rāsh Behārī Bose, veteran Indian revolutionary, who had escaped to Japan in June 1915 and become a Japanese citizen. He arranged two conferences of Indians in the East to discuss political issues. The Tokyo Conference, 28-30 March 1942, besides establishing the Indian Independence League, resolved to form an Indian National Army. The Bangkok Conference, 15-23 June 1942, formally inaugurated the Indian Independence League adopting the Congress tricolour as its flag. One of the 35 resolutions passed by it invited Subhās Chandra Bose to East Asia. Through another resolution Captain Mohan Siṅgh was appointed commander-in-chief of the Army of Liberation for India, i.e. the Indian National Army. The Indian Independence League, which undertook to supply men, materials and money to the Army, established a Council of Action, with Rāsh Behārī Bose as president and Mohan Siṅgh as one of the four members with charge of the military department. News of the Quit-India movement launched by the Congress Party in India in August 1942 afforded further encouragement, and the Āzād Hind Fauj was formally inaugurated on 1 September 1942.

Difficulties, however, arose soon after. Mohan Siṅgh (now General) was disillusioned regarding the intentions of the Japanese, who wanted to use the Indian National Army only as a pawn and a propaganda tool. He was also dissatisfied with the functioning of the Council of Action and the Indian Independence League, who failed to secure Japanese recognition and official proclamation regarding the existence of the Fauj. The other members of the Council of Action, on the other hand, were unhappy with Mohan Siṅgh for his arbitrariness in military matters. The crisis came on 8 December 1942 when the Japanese arrested Colonel Nirañjan Siṅgh Gill branding him to be a British agent, without informing General Mohan Siṅgh, whose protest was ignored and who was not even allowed to see Colonel Gill. On the same day the three civilian members of the Council of Action resigned. On 29 December 1942, General Mohan Siṅgh was removed from his command and was taken into custody by the Japanese military police. The Indian National Army was disarmed. Efforts to revive it were made by Rāsh Behārī Bose who appointed a committee of administration to manage its affairs.

Subhās Chandra Bose, popularly called Netājī (lit. respected leader), left Europe on 8 February 1943 and arrived at Tokyo on 13 June 1943. After discussing matters with the Japanese prime minister, General Tojo, he came to Singapore on 2 July 1943. Two days later Rāsh Behārī Bose handed over the leadership of the Indian Independence League to him. On 5 July 1943 Netājī revived the Āzād Hind Fauj, giving it the battle-cry "Chalo Delhi" ("March to Delhi") and the salutation "Jai Hind" ("Victory to India"). On 23 October 1943 he proclaimed the setting up of the Provisional Government of Āzād Hind, which was recognized within a few days by nine countries, including Japan, Italy and Germany. On 6 November 1943, the Japanese premier announced the handing over of the Andaman and Nicobar Islands to the Provisional Government. Netājī organized the Fauj into three brigades for taking part in Japan's offensive campaign on India's eastern borders. After initial hesitation of the Japanese field commander, Field Marshal Terauchi, to associate Indians with actual fighting, it was agreed to employ one brigade as a trial, attaching smaller Indian detachments to different units of the Japanese army as irregulars. Accordingly, a new brigade of three battalions was raised by selecting the best soldiers out of the other three. Commanded by General Shāh Nawāz Khān, its 1st Battalion operated on the Arākān front and had its first notable success in May 1944 when it captured the British post of Mowdok in the Indian territory, about 80 km to the east of Cox Bāzār, and holding it till September 1944 in the face of repeated counter-attacks by British forces. The other two battalions also gave a good account of themselves in Falam and Haka area. Meanwhile, Subhās Chandra Bose had brought forward his headquarters to Rangoon. The Japanese commanders, satisfied with the fighting skill and courage of the Āzād Hind Fauj soldiers, associated another Indian brigade in their operations in Imphāl and Kohīmā sectors. The British forces, however, not only withstood the offensive during the winter of 1944-45 but also launched a counter-attack. The Japanese and the Āzād Hind armies retreated fast. Rangoon was occupied by the British early in May 1945. On 16 May, Shāh Nawāz, Gurbakhsh Siṅgh Ḍhilloṅ and many other officers and men of the Āzād Hind Fauj surrendered at Pegū in Lower Burma whereafter the Āzād Hind Fauj ceased to exist.

The War ended with Japan's surrender on 14 August 1945. Subhās Chandra Bose died in an air-crash on 18 August 1945. Officers and men of the Indian National Army were brought back to India and were interrogated and divided into three categories: *white* or loyal in their allegiance to the British throughout; *grey* or those whose loyalty was doubtful; and *black* or those who admitted that they had joined the Āzād Hind Fauj. The white were reinstated with benefits of seniority and arrears of pay; the grey were kept under observation and were later graded into either white or black. The black were summarily dismissed and their arrears of pay and allowances were confiscated. Mohan Siṅgh and Nirañjan Siṅgh Gill were set free. Shāh Nawāz Khān, Gurbakhsh Siṅgh Ḍhilloṅ and Prem K. Sehgal were, as a test case, put on trial in open court in the Red Fort at Delhi. They were charged with treason and with waging war against the King. This aroused India-wide sympathy for them. The trial began on 5 November 1945. Eminent lawyers and public men such as Tej Bahādur Saprū, Bhūlābhāī Desāī and Jawāharlāl Nehrū defended the accused in court. There were riots in their favour in several places between 21 and 24 November. The court on 31 December 1945 sentenced all the three to transportation for life. The government, however, yielded to the outburst of popular sympathy and the British commander-in-chief, Sir Claude Auchinleck, quashed the sentence on review.

BIBLIOGRAPHY

1. Mohan Singh, General, *Soldiers' Contribution to Indian Independence*. Delhi, 1974
2. Bhattacharya, Vivek, *Awakened India*. Delhi, 1986
3. Durlabh Singh, *Formation and Growth of the I.N.A.* Lahore, 1946

G.S.M.

ĀZĀD PUNJAB scheme, signifying a major shift in the kinds of political strategies to be pursued by Sikh political leadership in their efforts to enhance the political influence of their community, was a crucial turning-point in the development of modern Sikh politics.

With the introduction of the Montagu-Chelmsford Reforms of 1919, politics became pre-eminently focussed on the legislature. Hindus, Sikhs, and Muslims all saw the legislative council as the principal political arena for gaining and maintaining communal advantages; and the communal allocation of seats in the council was the dominant political issue in the Punjab during the 1920's and much of the 1930's. Under the Reforms, Sikhs who comprised 13 per cent of the total poplulation of the Punjab, were allocated 18½ per cent of the seats; and Muslims, who comprised a majority of the population (55 per cent), 50 per cent of the seats. The allocations satisfied no one in the province; Muslims attacked the Reforms as understating their majority; Hindus and Sikhs argued that the Reforms gave Muslims an absolute majority and left the other communities ineffectual. Disenchantment with the Reforms was particularly felt among the Sikh leadership. Although Sikh legislative council members sometimes supported pro-agriculturalist legislation initiated by the Muslim-led Unionist Party, Sikh organizations and representations to various government commissions repeatedly called for greater representation in the council for the Sikh community. The Akālī Dal, by mid-1920's an increasingly powerful force in the community, was particularly outspoken on the issue. Concern for the 'representational' issue in the Sikh community accelerated after the British Government, in the Communal Award of 1932, 'froze' Sikh representation in the Punjab council at 19 per cent and further enhanced the Muslim majority in that legislature.

Ironically, the Communal Award seemed to initiate a process which saw a decreasing emphasis on council representation as a means of community defence. Muslims, for example, saw little benefit from their majority in the Punjab. They still were a minority in India as a whole. Sikhs simply refused to accept their consignment to permanent political subordination. Increasingly, adjustment of territorial boundaries to enhance a community's political influence was stressed. In the 1930's the notion of a separate territorial entity for their community began to gain ground among Muslims. In 1940, at its Lahore session, the Muslim League pushed forward a separatist territorial claim for the Indian Muslim community and demanded Pakistan as a separate sovereign State for Muslims.

Sikhs, too, began to echo this concern for territory as protection. As early as the Round Table Conference in 1931, Sikhs had raised the possibility of boundary redistribution being used as a means of resolving Punjab's communal problem. In a memorandum to the Round Table Conference, Sikh delegate, Ujjal Siṅgh, had stated that continued Muslim intransigence would force Sikhs to press for a territorial rearrangement of the province to consolidate the Sikh population and to create a province in which no single community would constitute a majority. Although this proposal had little initial following, the notion of territorial rearrangement acquired credibility as both the British Government and the Congress Party seemed to accept the idea in its general form. In 1942, the proposals of the Cripps Mission granted the principle of territorial sovereignty as a means of communal protection in so far as they gave provinces the right of non-accession to the proposed Indian Federation to be created at the end of World War II. At the same time, the Congress seemed to concede the principle in a Working Committee resolution which stated that it would be unthinkable to compel "the people of any territorial unit to remain in the Indian Union against their declared and established will."

The demand for a territorial rearrangement to enhance Sikh political influence was revived in 1943 by the Akālī Dal in the form of the Āzād Punjab scheme, which was the brain-child of Giānī Kartār Siṅgh. Like the earlier formulation, the scheme called for the detachment of Muslim majority districts from Punjab to create a new province, Āzād Punjab, in which the Sikh population was maximized and in which no single community, constituted a majority. The Akālī Dal president, Master Tārā Siṅgh, said that Āzād Punjab "shall comprise Ambala, Jullundur, Lahore divisions, and out of the Multan division, Lyallpur District, some portion of Montgomery and Multan districts." In this way, Sikhs, it was argued, would achieve the balance of power in the province and would gain the maximum benefit from their numbers. Territory became the key to preservation of the Sikh community. Hindus and Muslims, Master Tārā Siṅgh pointed out, could look to their co-religionists in other provinces where they constituted majorities, but Sikhs had no such alternative and required this form of protection until something better was proposed. As radical as the Āzād Punjab scheme was and despite its popularity in the Sikh community, it was quickly shuttled aside by events. As the possibility of the partition of the Punjab grew, the scheme became less and less meaningful. The spectre of Muslim domination was replaced by the fear that the Sikh community would be split between India and Pakistan. Territorial rearrangement took a still more radical twist as increasing numbers of Sikhs began to demand an independent Sikh State, a demand ultimately lost in the politics surrounding Partition. The quick demise of the Āzād Punjab scheme is not a true measure of its significance. As the first popular formulation of territorial rearrangement as a means of protection for the community, it set a pattern that continued to persist in Sikh politics for a long time.

BIBLIOGRAPHY

1. Brass, Paul R., *Language, Religion and Politics in North India*. Delhi, 1975
2. Nayar, Baldev Raj. *Minority Politics in the Punjab*. Princeton, 1966
3. Harbans Singh, *The Heritage of the Sikhs*. Delhi, 1983
4. Khushwant Singh, *A History of the Sikhs*, vol. 2. Princeton, 1966
5. Gulati, Kailash Chander, *The Akalis : Past and Present*. Delhi, 1974

G.A.H.

'AZĪM KHĀN, MUHAMMAD (d. 1823), was one of the sons of Paindā Khān and a brother of Fateh Khān, who appointed him governor of Kashmīr in April 1813. In 1814, Mahārājā Raṇjīt Siṅgh made an unsuccessful attempt to conquer Kashmīr. On the death of Fateh Khān in 1818, 'Azīm Khān hurried from Kashmīr to Kābul, and inflicted a crushing defeat on Prince Kāmrān, the assassin of Fateh Khān. He placed Ayūb Khān, a son of Taimūr Shāh, on the throne and himself became prime minister. In 1819, Raṇjīt Siṅgh conquered Kashmīr and, in 1822, he seized the city and province of Peshāwar from Yār Muhammad Khān, brother of 'Azīm Khān. 'Azīm Khān led an expedition to recover Peshāwar and launched a holy war against the Sikhs. The Afghān army stood near Nausherā on both sides of the Kābul river. Raṇjīt Siṅgh himself held command of the Sikh army. A fierce battle was fought on 14 March 1823. The Afghān host was defeated and 'Azīm Khān fled to Kābul. Peshāwar was left with Yār Muhammad Khān as governor of the Sikh kingdom. 'Azīm Khān died of grief shortly afterwards.

BIBLIOGRAPHY

1. Sūrī, Sohan Lāl, *'Umdāt-ut-Twārīkh*. Lahore, 1855-89
2. Khushwant Singh, *A History of the Sikhs*, vol. I. Princeton, 1963
3. Bhagat Singh, *Maharaja Ranjit Singh and His Times*. Delhi, 1990

S.S.B.

'AZĪZ UD-DĪN, FAQĪR (1780-1845), physician, diplomat, and foreign minister at the court of Mahārājā Raṇjīt Siṅgh, was the eldest son of Ghulām Mohy ud-Dīn, a leading physician of Lahore. Of his two brothers, Nūr ud-Dīn held charge of the city of Lahore and had been governor of Gujrāt, and Imām ud-Dīn was *qilahdār* (garrison commander) of the Fort of Gobindgaṛh. The family claims its descent from Ansārī Arab immigrants from Bukhārā, in Central Asia, who settled in Lahore as *hakīms* or physicians. *Hakīm* is the original title by which 'Azīz ud-Dīn was known, the prefix *Faqīr* appearing for the first time in the official British correspondence only after 1826. Faqīr, Persian for a mendicant or dervish, was adopted by 'Azīz ud-Dīn as a mark of simplicity and humility. In the court he was referred to as Faqīr Razā, mendicant by choice.

In 1799, when Raṇjīt Siṅgh occupied Lahore, 'Azīz ud-Dīn was undergoing apprenticeship under the principal Lahore physician, Hakīm Hākim Rāi. Summoned to treat the Mahārājā for an ophthalmic ailment, the latter deputed his pupil to attend on the patient. Raṇjīt Siṅgh, impressed by the intelligence and skill of the young man, soon appointed him his personal physician and assigned a *jāgīr* to him. He was also entrusted with drafting State papers in Persian. This brought him still closer to the Mahārājā who began to repose great confidence in him for his ability correctly to interpret his policy. Faqīr 'Azīz ud-Dīn's first major diplomatic assignment was to look after Charles Metcalfe, the British envoy, and to help in the Mahārājā's negotiations with him which culminated in the Treaty of Amritsar (1809). He held negotiations on behalf of the Sikh ruler with David Ochterlony in 1810. In 1813, he was deputed to settle the country and dependencies of Attock and negotiated the transfer to the Sikhs of the Fort, by the Afghān governor Jahāṅdād Khān, who accepted the offer of a *jāgīr*. Thereafter, throughout Raṇjīt Siṅgh's reign, Faqīr 'Azīz ud-Dīn remained almost solely responsible for the conduct of foreign relations of the Sikh kingdom. In 1815, he held parleys with the rājās of Maṇḍī and Rājaurī and with the Nawāb of Bahāwalpur. In 1823, he was sent to Peshāwar to realize tribute from Yār Muhammad Khān Bārakzaī. After the death of Rājā Sansār Chand of Kāṅgṛā in 1824, his son, Anirodh Chand, demurred to the payment of *nazrānā* to Raṇjīt Siṅgh. 'Azīz ud-Dīn met him at Nadauṇ and brought him round to pay homage to the Mahārājā and get his succession recognized. In 1827, he travelled to Shimlā with a goodwill mission to call on Lord Amherst, the British governor-general. In April 1831, a similar mission waited upon Lord William Bentinck. Faqīr 'Azīz ud-Dīn was again a member and, although Sardār Harī Siṅgh Nalvā was the leader, the latter had royal instruction to rely on the counsel and advice of Dīwān Motī Rām and "the resourceful Faqīr." During the famous Ropaṛ meeting between Raṇjīt Siṅgh and William Bentinck in October 1831, 'Azīz ud-Dīn, through Captain Wade and Prinsep, acted as an interpreter between the two chiefs. He conducted negotiations that led to the signing of the Tripartite Treaty of 1838 aimed at putting Shāh Shujā' on the throne of Kābul, and acted as the Mahārājā's interpreter during his meeting with Lord Auckland towards the end of 1838.

Faqīr 'Azīz ud-Dīn has been described as "the oracle of the Mahārājā" and as "his master's mouthpiece." He was learned in Arabic as well as in Persian and was "the most eloquent man of his day"— "as able with his pen as with his tongue." He was one of the Mahārājā's most polished and accomplished courtiers, with a very gentle and affable manner and with a very catholic outlook. The Mahārājā had complete trust in him and rewarded him with *jāgīrs* and honours.

'Azīz ud-Dīn continued in the service of the Sikh State after the death of Raṇjīt Siṅgh. He represented Mahārājā Kharak Siṅgh on a complimentary mission to Lord Auckland at Shimlā in December 1839, and waited upon Lord Ellenborough at Fīrozpur in December 1842, under Mahārājā Sher Siṅgh's instruction. He remained scrupulously aloof from factional intrigues which had overtaken Lahore after Raṇjīt Siṅgh's death. Saddened at the turn events had taken and by the death of two of his sons, he died in Lahore on 3 December 1845.

BIBLIOGRAPHY

1. Sūrī, Sohan Lāl, *'Umdāt-ut-Twārīkh*. Lahore, 1885-89
2. Waheeduddin, Faqir Syed, *The Real Ranjit Singh*. Delhi, 1976
3. Bhagat Singh, *Maharaja Ranjit Singh and His Times*. Delhi, 1990
4. Harbans Singh, *The Heritage of the Sikhs*. Delhi, 1983

F.S.A.

B

B40 JANAM SĀKHĪ derives its name from the number attached to the manuscript in the catalogue of the India Office Library, London (MS. *Panj B40*). It consists of a unique collection of *sākhīs* or anecdotes concerning the life of Gurū Nānak, and, although it shares common sources with the *Purātan* and *Ādi Sākhīāṅ* traditions, it constructs a different *sākhī* sequence and incorporates a substantial block of stories which are to be found in none of the other major traditions. This cluster of anecdotes was evidently drawn from the oral tradition of the compiler's own area and includes all the principal *janam sākhī* forms such as narrative anecdote, narrative discourse, didactic discourse, and heterodox discourse. Another feature of particular interest and value is the inclusion of fifty-seven illustrations. The manuscript is also distinguished by the unusually clear description which is provided of its origins. Two notes appended to the manuscript (folios 84b, 230b) relate that the *Janam Sākhī,* commissioned by a patron named Saṅgū Mall and written in the hand of Dayā Rām Abrol and illustrated by Ālam Chand, a mason, was completed on Bhādoṅ *sudī* 3, 1790 Bk/ 31 August 1733. The manuscript is said to be a copy of some other now non-extant manuscript which might have originally been written subsequent to Gurū Tegh Bahādur's martyrdom (1675). This assumption is based on the fact that the manuscript makes no reference to Gurū Gobind Siṅgh or to his founding the Khālsā (1699) and historically the latest event to be mentioned is Gurū Tegh Bahādur's martyrdom. The manuscript comprises 231 folios (with five folios numbering 15-18 and 23 missing) and has two apocryphal works entitled *Madīne dī Goṣṭi* and *Makke dī Goṣṭi* conjointly entered under the title *Makke Madīne dī Goṣṭi* after the table of contents which follow the text. Since the entry on *Goṣṭi* is in a different ink and three more sheets have been added to complete the text of this *Goṣṭi,* it clearly is a later interpolation. According to internal evidence, the manuscript may have been recorded in Gujrāṅwālā district or near about although there is no clear indication about its provenance. Nothing is known of the manuscript's history since its completion in AD 1733 till 1907, although there is evidence which possibly indicates that the manuscript or a copy of it, may have been used in preparing Bhāī Santokh Siṅgh's *Srī Gur Nānak Prakāsh.* In 1885, Professor Gurmukh Siṅgh of Oriental College, Lahore, referred briefly and cryptically to a "Lahore Janam Sākhī" which had been recorded in 1790 Bk and in 1913 Karam Siṅgh, historian, reported having once seen an illustrated Janam Sakhī bearing the same date "in the possession of a Muslim bookseller of Lahore." Both reports evidently refer to the *B40 Janam Sākhī* which had meanwhile found its way to London. There it was purchased in 1907 for 10 pounds by the India Office Library from its owner, Hāfiz 'Abd ur-Rahmān.

At first sight the *B40* manuscript appears to follow the *Purātan* tradition because its first eight *sākhīs* have been drawn from a source which presented its material in the chracteristically *Purātan* style; the source appears , in fact, to have been the same manuscript as the *Hāfizābād Janam Sākhī* compiler used when recording his *Purātan* collection. From *Sākhī* 9 onwards, however, the *B40* compiler chooses selectively from at least five different sources, four of them apparently in manuscript form and the fifth his local oral tradition. In addition to the manuscript which he shared with his *Purātan* analogue, he also shared a separate manuscript with the *Ādi Sākhīān* compiler. A *Miharbān* source provided him with a small cluster near the end of his work and through the manuscript he has scattered six discourses of the heterodox variety.

The narrative structure imposed by its compiler is, for the most part, a rudimentary one. It retains its consistency for as long as he remains with his first source (the first eight *sākhīs*), but little heed is paid thereafter to systematic order or chronology apart from the introduction of the death *sākhī* at the very end.

The manuscript written in Gurmukhī script, has been edited by Piār Siṅgh and published under the title *Janam Sākhī Srī Gurū Nānak Dev Jī* (Amritsar, 1974). An English translation by W.H. McLeod has also been issued as *The B40 Janam-Sakhi* (Amritsar, 1979).

BIBLIOGRAPHY

1. Piār Siṅgh, *Janam Sākhī Srī Gurū Nānak Dev Jī*. Amritsar, 1974
2. Kirpāl Siṅgh, *Janam Sākhī Pramparā*. Patiala, 1969
3. McLeod, W.H., *The B40 Janam-Sakhi*. Amritsar, 1979

W.H.M.

BĀBĀ, a Persian word meaning 'father' or 'grandfather', is used among Sikhs as a title of affection and reverence. In its original Persian context, Bābā is a title used for superiors of the Qalandar order of the Sūfīs, but as transferred to India its meaning extends to cover the old as well as any *faqīr* or *sannyāsī* of recognized piety. This was also one of Gurū Nānak's honorific titles during his lifetime. It assumed a hereditary character and all the physical descendants of the Gurūs were generally addressed by this title. Apart from them, the title was also applied to one who combined piety with the exercise of a secular authority. The founder of the Paṭiālā city and the progenitor of its royal house is commonly known as *Bābā* Ālā Siṅgh. One most revered name in Sikh history is that of the long-lived *Bābā* Buḍḍhā (1506-1631), a Sikh of Gurū Nānak's time, who anointed with his hands five succeeding Gurūs. Beyond the orthodox ranks of the Panth, the title is also applied to the leaders of sects which claim to exist within the community or to have strong links with it.

W.H.M.

BĀBĀ BAKĀLĀ (31°-34'N, 75°-16'E), a small town in Amritsar district of the Punjab, is sacred to Gurū Hargobind and Gurū Tegh Bahādur. The original name of the place was Bakālā. As Gurū Har Krishan lay on his death-bed in Delhi, he was asked by the *saṅgat* to name his successor. All that the Gurū could say at that time was 'Bābā Bakāle' meaning that (Gurū) Tegh Bahādur, who was the brother of his (Gurū Har Krishan's) grandfather (*bābā)* and who was living at Bakālā, was to be the next Gurū. Bakālā, thereafter, came to be called Bābā Bakālā. Earlier, Gurū Hargobind had also resided at Bakālā with his mother, Mātā Gaṅgā, who died at this place. Several shrines perpetuate their memory.

DARBĀR SĀHIB marks the site where Gurū Tegh Bahādur was anointed Gurū and where he used to preach to his Sikhs. It comprises a congregation hall, with a square sanctum in the middle of it. The dome on top of the sanctum has an ornamental pinnacle and a large umbrella-shaped finial.

GURDWĀRĀ BHORĀ SĀHIB, a nine-storyed octagonal edifice with a gilded dome topped by an ornamental pinnacle and umbrella-shaped finial, marks the basement room, *bhorā* in Punjabi, where Gurū Tegh Bahādur used to sit in meditation. After the death of Gurū Hargobind in 1644, his youngest son, Tegh Bahādur, and his mother, Nānakī, had shifted from Kīratpur to Bakālā, where they stayed until Tegh Bahādur was anointed and proclaimed Gurū in 1664. He spent this interval in voluntary solitude and religious contemplation. Even after his formal installation on 11 August 1664 as Gurū, he continued to live in seclusion and did nothing to counter the claims of the several pretenders to the gurūship who were confusing and misleading the common Sikhs, until Makkhan Shāh, a wealthy trader and a staunch follower of the Sikh faith, came to Bakālā, discovered Tegh Bahādur sitting here in the *bhorā,* deeply absorbed in meditation, to be the real Gurū. and publicly proclaimed the fact from the rooftop. Gurū Tegh Bahādur then actively took up the responsibility of instructing the Sikh community and guiding its affairs. He travelled extensively and made Kīratpur his headquarters, but the *bhorā* at Bakālā became, and has remained ever since, a sacred shrine for the Sikhs. The present building was completed in 1952.

GURDWĀRĀ CHHĀOṆĪ SĀHIB is situated in a grove of old banyan and *pīpal* trees. According to local tradition, Gurū Hargobind's soldiery had their camp here. The place is now occupied by the Nihaṅgs of the Taruṇā Dal, who stay here with their horses and cattle. The Gurū Granth Sāhib is seated in a simple, 6-metre square, room.

GURDWĀRĀ MAÑJĪ SĀHIB, a small glass-covered domed pavilion raised over a marble-lined platform to the north of Darbār Sāhib and in line with Bhorā Sāhib, is the spot where, according to local tradition, Gurū Tegh Bahādur was fired at and wounded by Shīhāṅ, the Masand, at the behest of Dhīr Mall, a nephew of the Gurū and one of the pretenders to the gurūship.

GURDWĀRĀ MĀTĀ GAṄGĀ JĪ, half a kilometre northeast of Darbār Sāhib, is dedicated to Gurū Hargobind's mother, Mātā Gaṅgā, who died at Bakālā on 15 Hāṛ 1685Bk/12 June 1628. Mātā Gaṅgā had desired that her dead body should not be cremated but be immersed in the River Beās. Accordingly, the hearse was prepared and the body taken out in a procession, with the *saṅgat* chanting hymns. After the immersion of the dead body, the hearse was brought back to Bakālā where a symbolic cremation was carried out and a *samādh* built. The present Gurdwārā Mātā Gaṅgājī was constructed during the 1960's by Bābā Bishan Siṅgh Nihaṅg of the Taruṇā Dal who continues to administer it. The building, in a walled compound, is a rectangular hall, with the 5-metre sqaure sanctum at the far end.

SHĪSH MAHAL MĀTĀ GAṄGĀ JĪ, close to Bhorā Sāhib, represents the house where Mātā Gaṅgā and, later, Mātā Nānakī lived. It is a single flat-roofed room, with glass panelled doors on three sides. The Gurū Granth Sāhib rests here for the night.

Gurdwārās Bhorā Sāhib, Darbār Sāhib, Mañjī Sāhib and Shīsh Mahal, situated close to one another, are managed by the Shiromaṇī Gurdwārā Parbandhak Committee through a local commitee. The others are under the control of the Nihaṅgs of the Taruṇā Dal who have recently established some more shrines dedicated to Gurū Hargobind.

BIBLIOGRAPHY

1. Tārā Siṅgh, *Srī Gur Tīrath Saṅgrahi*. Amritsar, n.d.
2. Ṭhākar Siṅgh, Giānī, *Srī Gurduāre Darshan*. Amritsar, 1923
3. Faujā Siṅgh, *Gurū Teg Bahādur: Yātrā Asthān,*

Pramparāvāṅ te Yād Chinn. Patiala, 1976
4. Randhir, G.S., *Sikh Shrines in India*. Delhi, 1990

Jg.S

BĀBAK (d. 1642), a Muslim *rabābī* or musician, kept Gurū Hargobind company and recited the sacred hymns at *dīvāns* morning and evening. The word *bābak*, from Persian, means faithful. As says the *Gurbilās Chhevīṅ Pātshāhī*, Bābak was, at the death of Sattā and Balvaṇḍ, who used to recite sacred hymns for the Gurū, asked to perform the obsequies for them under their (Muslim) rites. Bābak, it is said, dug the graves for the deceased on the bank of the River Rāvī and after the burial service, performed the *kīrtan* on the site where sat Gurū Hargobind. To quote the *Gurbilās* again, he took part in the battle of Amritsar in 1629 during which he assisted in the evacuation of the Gurū's family to Jhabāl. Going by the *Gurbilās* account, Gurū Hargobind, before he departed the world, asked Bābak to return to Amritsar. As bidden by the Gurū, Bābak retired to Amritsar where he died in 1642.

BIBLIOGRAPHY

1. *Gurbilās Chhevīn Pātshāhī*. Patiala, 1970
2. Giān Siṅgh, Giānī, *Twārī<u>kh</u> Gurū <u>Kh</u>ālsā*. Patiala, 1970
3. Macauliffe, M. A., *The Sikh Religion*. Oxford, 1909

B.S.

BĀBĀ NAUDH SIṄGH, whose full title, "The Redemption of Subhāgjī through the Grace of Bābā Naudh Siṅgh," pronounces the homiletic character of the book at the start, was first published in 1921. Comprising a wide variety of elements ranging from romance to polemics, sermon and theology, it seeks to present the Sikh way and vision of life through incident, example and argument. In a manner, the author, Bhāī Vīr Siṅgh, has only extended the form effected by him in his earlier romances, *Sundarī, Bijay Siṅgh* and *Satvant Kaur*. The aim here is to create memorable portraits of the ideal Sikh *homo* whose spirit never falters or wilts in the midst of life's miseries, confusions and terrors.

The story principally involves the strange and troubled experiences of Jamunā, a young Jain widow, who is decoyed into false positions, appellations and conversions in rapid succession before she is ushered into the Sikh faith. *En route*, she encounters avarice, lust and sin in pious garbs. Each new experience brings home to her men's depravity. Utterly appalled, she seeks refuge in death to avoid harrowing humiliations. But the providential plunge into a nearby stream becomes the very means of her rescue and redemption. A young Sikh saint meditating there saves her and, initiating her into the ordained faith, disappears as suddenly and mysteriously as he had materialized. Quite clearly, he is, in Bhāī Vīr Siṅgh's transparent symbology, an emblem of divinity in human form. Jamunā turned Ḍumelī turned <u>Gh</u>ulām Fātimā is now rechristened Subhāgjī or "the Fortunate one." The wheel of her trials and tribulations having come full circle, she is forever liberated from the aches and illusions of life. She has entered a commonwealth of shared views and visions. Her advent into Bābā Naudh Siṅgh's household reveals another set purpose. A simple life of prayer and piety, of service and sacrifice, we learn, is the *beau ideal* of Sikh ethics. And a rural homestead vibrating to the music of daily life is the happiest habitat for a psyche in quest. Even dissenters, scoffers and tempters of varying persuasions who happen to come to this village are soon won over by the homespun logic of Bābā Naudh Siṅgh, who is held up as a shining example of virtue in repose and confidence. Under the benign shadow of Bābā Naudh Siṅgh, Subhāgjī learns to live in an atmosphere of peace and bliss, unmindful of worldly temptations and distractions. Nightly, she recites tales of Sikh piety and glory to eager audiences. Bābā Naudh Siṅgh delivers long talks on all manner of vices and practices such as dirt and drunkenness, untouchability and idol-worship. A barrister and his wife, a doctor, a Brahmo Samāj preacher, turning up in the village, provide him opportunities for instruction in Sikh religion and morals. The daily *kathā* or scriptural commentary and historical narration serve to authenticate the Sikh tradition embodied in the lives of the Gurūs and of their disciples. To the extent Bhāī Vīr Siṅgh succeeds in creating symbolic archetypes of Sikh virtue and in painting a picture of pastoral country life, he managed to rouse the interest of his contemporaries. Viewed from today's perspective, we find *Bābā Naudh Siṅgh* a horizontal study in idealism. It represents a moment in Sikh consciousness around the turn of the present century.

BIBLIOGRAPHY

1. Harbans Singh, *Bhai Vir Singh*. Delhi, 1972
2. Talib, Gurbachan Singh, and Attar Singh, eds., *Bhai Vir Singh: Life, Time and Works*. Chandigarh, 1973
3. Guleria, J.S., *Bhai Vir Singh: A Literary Portrait*. Delhi, 1985
4. Kohlī, Surindar Siṅgh, and Harnām Siṅgh Shān, eds., *Bhāī Vīr Siṅgh: Jīvan, Samāṅ te Rachnā*. Chandigarh, 1973

D.S.M.

BABAR AKĀLĪ MOVEMENT, a radical outgrowth of the Akālī movement for the reform of Sikh places of worship during the early 1920's. The latter, aiming to have the shrines released from the control of priests who had become lax and effete over the generations, was peaceful in its character and strategy. In the course of the prolonged campaign, Akālīs true to their vows patiently suffered physical injury and violence at the hands of the priests as well as of government authority. The incidents at Tarn Tāran (January 1921) and Nankāṇā Sāhib (February 1921) in which many Sikhs lost their lives led to the emergence of a group which rejected non-violence and adopted violence as a creed. The members of this secret group called themselves Babar Akālīs—*babar* meaning lion. Their targets were the British officers and their Indian informers. They were strongly attached to their Sikh faith and shared an intense patriotic fervour.

At the time of the Sikh Educational Conference at Hoshiārpur from 19-21 March 1921, some radicals led by Master Motā Siṅgh and Kishan Siṅgh Gaṛgajj, a retired havildār major of the Indian army, held a secret meeting and made up a plan to avenge themselves upon those responsible for the killings at Nankāṇā Sāhib. Among those on their list were J.W. Bowring, the superintendent of police in the Intelligence department and C.M. King, the commissioner. However, those assigned to the task fell into the police net on 23 May 1921. Arrest warrants were issued against Master Motā Siṅgh and Kishan Siṅgh as well, but both of them went underground. In November 1921, Kishan Siṅgh formed a secret organization called Chakravartī Jathā and started working among the peasantry and soldiers inciting them against the foreign rulers. While Kishan Siṅgh and his band carried on their campaign in Jalandhar district with frequent incursions into the villages of Ambālā and Kapūrthalā state, Karam Siṅgh of Daulatpur organized a band of extremist Sikhs in Hoshiārpur on similar lines. In some of the villages in the district, *dīvāns* were convened daily by the sympathizers and helpers of the *jathā* of Karam Siṅgh, who was under warrants of arrest for delivering seditious speeches. Towards the end of August 1922, the two Chakravartī *jathās* resolved to merge together and rename their organization Babar Akālī Jathā. A committee was formed to work out a plan of action and collect arms and ammunition. Kishan Siṅgh was chosen *jathedār* or president, while Dalīp Siṅgh Daulatpur, Karam Siṅgh Jhīngaṇ and

Ude Siṅgh Rāmgaṛh Jhuggīāṅ were nominated members. A cyclostyled news-sheet called the *Babar Akālī Doābā* had already been launched. Contacts were sought to be established especially with soldiers serving in the army and students. The party's programme of violence centred on the word *sudhār* (reformation)—a euphemism for liquidation of *jholīchuks* (lit. robe-bearers, i.e. stooges and lackeys of the British).

The Babar Akālī Jathā had its own code. Persons with family encumbrances were advised not to join as full members, but to help only as sympathizers. The members were to recite regularly *gurbāṇī*, the Sikh prayers. They were not to indulge in personal vendetta against anyone. Likewise, they must not molest any woman nor lift any cash or goods other than those expressly permitted by the group. The total strength of the Jathā scarcely exceeded two hundred: the exact number was not known even to its members. The outer circle of the Jathā consisted of sympathizers who helped the active members with food and shelter. Some ran errands for the leaders carrying messages from one place to another, others arranged *dīvāns* in advance for itinerant speakers and distributed Babar Akālī leaflets. In order to evade the police and keep their activities secret, the Babar Akālī Jathā also evolved a secret code. The movement was very active from mid-1922 to the end of 1923. Several government officials and supporters were singled out and killed. Encounters with the police took place during which some rare feats of daring and self-sacrifice were performed by Babar Akālīs.

The government acted with firmness and alacrity. In April 1923, the Babar Akālī Jathā was declared an unlawful association under the Criminal Law Amendment Act of 1908. Units of cavalry and infantry were stationed at strategic points in the sensitive areas, with magistrates on duty with them. A joint force of military and special police was created to seize Babars sheltering themselves in the Śivālik hills. Every two weeks propaganda leaflets were dropped from aeroplanes with a view to strengthening the morale of the loyalist population. Punitive police-post tax was levied and disciplinary action was taken against civil and military pensioners harbouring or sympathizing with the Babar Akālīs. These measures helped in curbing the movement. The arrests and deaths in police encounters of its members depleted the Jathā's ranks. The movement virtually came to an end when Varyām Siṅgh Dhuggā was run down by the police in Lyallpur district in June 1924.

The trial of the arrested Babar Akālīs had already begun inside Lahore Central Jail on 15 August 1923. Sixty-two persons were challaned originally and the names of 36 more were added in January 1924. Of them two died during investigations and five were acquitted by the investigating magistrates; the remaining 91 were committed to the sessions in April 1924. Mr J.K.M. Tapp, appointed Additional Sessions Judge to try conspiracy cases, opened the proceedings on 2 June 1924. He was assisted by four assessors. Dīwān Bahādur Piṇḍī Dās was special public prosecutor. The prosecution produced 447 witnesses, 734 documents and 228 other exhibits to prove its case. The judgement was delivered on 28 February 1925. Of the 91 accused, two had died in jail during trial, 34 were acquitted, six including Jathedār Kishan Siṅgh Gaṛgajj were awarded death penalty and the remaining 49 were sentenced to varying terms of imprisonment. The government, not satisfied with the punishments awarded, filed a revision petition in the High Court. The High Court overruled the Sessions Court judgement on a few points, but let the death sentences remain unaltered. Babars so condemned were hanged on 27 February 1926. They were Kishan Siṅgh Gaṛgajj, Bābū Santā Siṅgh, Dalīp Siṅgh Dhāmīāṅ, Karam Siṅgh Mānko, Nand Siṅgh Ghuṛīāl and Dharam

Siṅgh Hayātpur. The Babar Akālī Jathā ceased to exist, but it had left a permanent mark on the history of the Sikhs and of the nationalist movement in India. The Naujawān and Kirtī Kisān movements in the Punjab owned their militant policy and tactics to the Babar insurrection.

BIBLIOGRAPHY

1. Sahni, Ruchi Ram, *Struggle for Reform in Sikh Shrines*. Ed. Ganda Singh. Amritsar, n.d.
2. Khushwant Singh, *A History of the Sikhs*, vol. 2. Princeton, 1966
3. Nijjar, B.S., *History of the Babbar Akalis*. Jalandhar, 1987
4. Sundar Singh, *Babbar Akālī Lahir*. Amritsar, 1970
5. Nijjhar, Milkhā Siṅgh, *Babar Akālī Lahir dā Itihās*. Delhi, 1986

G.S.Z.

BĀBARVĀṆĪ (Bābar's command or sway) is how the four hymns by Gurū Nānak alluding to the invasions by Bābar (1483-1530), the first Mughal emperor of India, are collectively known in Sikh literature. The name is derived from the use of the term in one of these hymns: "*Bābarvāṇī phiri gaī kuiru na roṭī khāi*—Bābar's command or sway has spread; even the princes go without food" (GG, 417). Three of these hymns are in Āsā measure at pages 360 and 417-18 of the standard recension of Gurū Granth Sāhib and the fourth is in Tilaṅg measure on pages 722-23.

Zahīr ud-Dīn Muhammad Bābar, driven out of his ancestral principality of Farghānā in Central Asia, occupied Kābul in 1504. Having failed in his repeated attempts to reconquer the lost territory and unable to expand his new possessions in the direction of Khurāsān in the west (which had once formed part of his grandfather's dominions), he turned his eyes towards India in the east. After an exploratory expedition undertaken as early as January-May 1505, he came down better equipped in 1519 when he advanced as far as Peshāwar. The following year he crossed the Indus and, conquering Siālkoṭ without resistance, marched on Saidpur (now Eminābād, 15 km southeast of Gujrāṅwālā in Pakistan) which suffered the worst fury of the invading host. The town was taken by assault, the garrison put to the sword and the inhabitants carried into captivity. During his next invasion in 1524, Bābar ransacked Lahore. His final invasion was launched during the winter of 1525-26 and he became master of Delhi after his victory at Pānīpat on 21 April 1526.

Gurū Nānak was an eye-witness to the havoc created during these invasions. Janam Sākhīs mention that he himself was taken captive at Saidpur. A line of his, outside of *Bābarvāṇī* hymns, indicates that he may have been present in Lahore when the city was given up to plunder. In six pithy words this line conveys, "For a *pahar* and a quarter, i.e. for nearly four hours, the city of Lahore remained subject to death and fury" (GG, 1412). The mention in one of the *Bābarvāṇī* hymns of the use of guns by the Mughals against the Afghān defence relying mainly upon their war-elephants may well be a reference to the historic battle of Pānīpat which sealed the fate of the Afghan king, Ibrāhīm Lodhī.

Bābarvāṇī hymns are not a narrative of historical events like Gurū Gobind Siṅgh's *Bachitra Nāṭak*, nor are they an indictment of Bābar as his *Zafarnāmah* was that of Auraṅgzīb. They are the outpourings of a compassionate soul touched by scenes of human misery and by the cruelty perpetrated by the invaders. The sufferings of the people are rendered here in accents of intense power and protest. The events are placed in the larger social and historical perspective. Decline in moral standards must lead to chaos. A corrupt political system must end in dissolution. Lure of power divides men and violence unresisted tends to flourish. It could not be wished away by magic or sorcery. Gurū Nānak reiterated his faith in the Almighty and in His justice. Yet so acute was his realization of the distress of the people that he could not resist making the complaint: "When there was such suffering, such killing, such shrieking in pain, didst not Thou, O God, feel pity? Creator, Thou art the same for all!" The people for him were the people as a whole, the Hindus and the Muslims, the high-caste and the low-caste, soldiers and civilians, men and women. These hymns are remarkable for their moral structure and poetical eloquence. Nowhere else in contemporary literature are the issues in medieval Indian situation comprehended with such clarity or presented in tones of greater urgency.

In spite of his destructive role Bābar is seen by Gurū Nānak to have been an unwitting instrument of the divine Will. Because the Lodhīs had violated God's laws, they had to pay the penalty. Bābar descended from Kābul as God's chosen agent, demonstrating the absolute authority of God and the retribution which must follow defiance of His laws. Gurū Nānak's commentary on the events which he actually witnessed thus becomes a part of the same universal message. God is absolute and no man may disobey His commands with impunity. Obey Him and receive freedom. Disobey him and the result must inevitably be retribution, a dire reckoning which brings suffering in this present life and continued transmigration in the hereafter.

The hymn rendered in free English verse reads :

Lord, Thou takest Khurāsān under Thy wing, but yielded India to the invader's wrath.
Yet thou takest no blame;
And sendest the Mughal as the messenger of death.
When there was such suffering, killing, such shrieking in pain,
Didst not Thou, O God, feel pity ?
Creator, Thou art the same for all !
If one tyrant attacketh another, it troubleth not the heart;
But when a lion falleth upon a herd of cattle,
The master will be questioned for not protecting it.
The miserable dogs (the corrupt rulers of India) have lost their priceless jewel;
No one will remember them after they are gone.
But mysterious are Thy ways,
Thou alone makest and Thou alone severest.
Whosoever arrogateth unto himself greatness tasting pleasure to satiety
Is in the eyes of the Lord but a puny worm for all the grains he eateth.
Saith Nānak: True achievement is his
Who dieth unto his self
And uttereth the holy Name.

In a touching 8-stanza poem, Gurū Nānak portrays the tragic plight of women, both Hindu and Muslim, who lost their husbands and suffered ignominy at the hands of the invaders:

They whose hair made them look fairer by far and who touched it lovingly with sacred vermilion,
Have had their heads shorn with scissors, and their throats choked with dust.
They who stirred not out of their private chambers are now denied shelter even on the roadside.

Praise, praise be unto Thee, O Lord!
We understand not Thy ways;
Everything is in Thy power and
Thou seest Thyself in diverse forms at Thy Will.
When they were married, their handsome bridegrooms added to their splendour;
They came seated in palanquins with

ıvory bangles asport on their arms;
They were awaited with ceremonial pitchers full of water and with fans arabesqued in glass.

Gifts of money were showered on them as they sat, and gifts of money showered as they stood:
They were given coconut and dates to eat, and they joyed on the bridal bed.
Halters are now around their necks, and broken are their strings of pearls.

Riches, youth and beauty they formerly relished have turned into their enemies;
Minions at the conqueror's behest drag them to dishonour.
The Lord, if it pleaseth Him, bestoweth greatness, and sendeth chastisement if He so desireth.
Had they contemplated in advance, they might have escaped punishment,
But the rulers had lost their sense in their fondness for levity and frivolity;
[now that] Bābar's sway hath spread; even the princes go without bread.

Some, the Muslims, miss the timings of *namāz*, others, the Hindus, of their *pūjā*;
Hindu ladies, without their ritually cleansed cooking-squares, go about without a vermilion mark on their foreheads;
They never remembered 'Rāma' heretofore, and are allowed to utter even 'Allah' no more.

Some, after the carnage, have returned home and are enquiring about the well-being of their kin;
Others, in whose destiny it was so recorded, sit wailing over their sufferings.
Saith Nānak: what He desireth shall happen; who is man Him to question?

In another hymn in the series, Gurū Nānak describes the desolation which followed Bābar's invasion ending in the battle of Pānīpat:

Where is that sport now, where those stables and steeds, and where are the drums and where the flutes?
Where are the sword-belts and where the chariots; and where are those scarlet uniforms?
Where are those finger-rings studded with mirrors; and where are those handsome faces?
This world is Thine, Thou art its Master, O Lord !
In one moment Thou settleth and in another unsettleth.
The lure of gold sunders brother from brother.

Where are those houses, those mansions and palaces; and where are those elegant-looking *serāis*?
Where are those snug couches and where those beautiful brides a sight of whom made one lose one's sleep?
Where is the chewing-leaf, where the leaf-sellers and where those who patronized them?
All have vanished like a shadow.

For this gold many were led astray; many suffered ignominy for it.
Without sinning one doth not gather it, and it doth not go with one in the end.
Whomsoever the Creator would confound, He first forfeiteth his virtue.
Countless *pīrs* tried their miraculous powers to halt the Mīr (Bābar) as they heard of his approach.
He burned ancient seats and houses strongly built and cast into dust

princes after severing their heads.

Yet no Mug͟hal became blind and no magic of the *pīrs* worked.
The Mug͟hals and the Paṭhāns were locked in battle, and they wielded their swords relentlessly,
They fired their guns; they attacked with their elephants.
They whose writ is torn in the Lord's court must perish, my brethren.

Of the wives of Hindus, of Turks, of Bhaṭṭīs and of Ṭhākur Rājpūts –
Some had their veils torn from head to foot, others lay heaped up in cemeteries;
How did they pass their nights whose husbands returned not home?

The fourth *Bābarvāṇī* hymn is probably addressed to Bhāī Lālo, one of Gurū Nānak's devotees living at Saidpur itself. It ends on a prophetic note, alluding perhaps to the rise of Sher K͟hān, an Afg͟hān of Sūr clan, who had already captured Bengal and Bihār, defeated Bābar's son and successor, Humāyūṅ, at Chausā on the Gaṅgā in June 1539 (during the lifetime of Gurū Nānak), and who finally drove the Mug͟hal king out of India in the following year. The hymn in Tilaṅg measure is, like the other three, an expression of Gurū Nānak's feeling of distress at the moral degradation of the people at the imposition by the mighty. It is a statement also of his belief in God's justice and in the ultimate victory of good over evil. In an English rendering:

As descendeth the Lord's word to me, so do I deliver it unto you, O Lālo:
[Bābar] leading a wedding-array of sin hath descended from Kābul and demandeth by force the bride, O Lālo.
Decency and righteousness have vanished, and falsehood struts abroad, O Lālo.
Gone are the days of Qāzīs and Brāhmaṇs, Satan now conducts the nuptials, O Lālo.
The Muslim women recite the Qur'ān and in distress remember their God, O Lālo.
Similar is the fate of Hindu women of castes high and low, O Lālo.
They sing paeans of blood, O Nānak, and by blood, not saffron, ointment is made, O Lālo.
In this city of corpses, Nānak proclaimeth God's praises, and uttereth this true saying:
The Lord who created men and put them to their tasks watcheth them from His seclusion.
True is that Lord, true His verdict, and true is the justice He dealeth.
As her body's vesture is torn to shreds, India shall remember my words.
In seventy-eight they come, in ninety-seven shall depart; another man of destiny shall arise.
Nānak pronounceth words of truth, Truth he uttereth; truth the time calls for.

The words "seventy-eight" and "ninety-seven" in the penultimate line are interpreted as 1578 and 1597 of the Indian calendar, corresponding respectively with 1521 and 1540 which are the dates of Bābar's invasion and Humāyūṅ's dethronement by Sher K͟hān/Shāh.

Sb.S.S

BĀBAR, ZAHĪR UD-DĪN MUHAMMAD (1483-1530), soldier of fortune, founder of the Mug͟hal dynasty in India, diarist and poet, descending in the fifth generation from Timūr, was born on 14 February 1483. In June 1494, he succeeded his father, 'Umar Shaik͟h, as ruler of Farg͟hānā, whose revenues supported no more than a few hundred cavalry. With this force of helmeted, mail-clad warriors, Bābar began his career of conquest. He joined in the family struggle for power, thrice winning and thrice losing Samarkand, alternately master of a kingdom or a wanderer through the hills. In 1504, he made himself master of Kābul and so came in touch with India whose wealth was a standing temptation. In 1517 and again in 1519, he swept down the Afghān plateau into the plains of India. He entered the Punjab in 1523 on the invitation of Daulat Khān Lodhī, the governor of the province, and 'Ālam Khān, an uncle of Ibrāhīm Lodhī, the Delhi Sultān. Uzbegh pressure from Balkh, however, compelled Bābar to return so that his final invasion was not begun until November 1525.

Even then his total force did not exceed 12,000 men, a tiny army with which to attempt the conquest of Ibrāhīm Lodhī's realm and the vast mass of Hindu India. The hostile armies came to grips on 21 April 1526 on the plain of Pānīpat. In the fiercely contested battle, Ibrāhīm Lodhī was killed and Bābar carried the day. As a result the kingdom of Delhi and Āgrā fell into Bābar's hands. But Bābar's victory at Pānipāt did not make him the ruler of India. Rāṇā Saṅgrām Siṅgh of Mevāṛ claimed Rājpūt supremacy over India, and advanced towards Āgrā with a large army. On 16 March 1527, Bābar defeated the Rājpūts at Khānvāh. Early next year he carried the fortress of Chanderī by storm and defeated Medinī Rāo. Finally, Bābar defeated the Afghān chiefs of Bihār and Bengal in 1529 at Ghāgrā, near the junction of that river with the Gaṅgā above Paṭnā.

The Sikh tradition strongly subscribes to a meeting in 1520 between Gurū Nānak and Bābar during the latter's invasion of Saidpur, now called Eminābād, in Gujrāṅwālā district of Pakistan. The town was taken by assault, the garrison put to the sword and the inhabitants carried into captivity. According to the *Purātan Janam Sākhī,* Gurū Nānak and Mardānā, also among the captives, were ordered to be taken to prison as slaves. The Gurū was given a load to carry and Mardānā a horse to lead. But Mīr Khān, says the *Janam Sākhī,* saw that the Gurū's bundle was carried without any support and Mardānā's horse followed him without the reins. He reported this to Sultān Bābar who remarked, "If there was such a holy man here, the town should not have been destroyed." The *Janam Sākhī* continues, "Bābar kissed his (Gurū Nānak's) feet. He said, 'On the face of this *faqīr* one sees God himself.' Then all the people, Hindus and Musalmāns, began to make their salutations. The king spoke again, 'O dervish, accept something'. The Gurū answered, 'I take nothing, but you must release all the prisoners of Saidpur and restore their property to them'. King Bābar ordered, 'Those who are in detention be released and their property be returned to them'. All the prisoners of Saidpur were set at liberty."

Though Bābar's *Tuzk,* or Memoirs, a work of high literary quality, gives many interesting details of the campaigns and the events he was involved in and also describes the Indian life and customs very minutely, there is no mention in these recollections that he met Gurū Nānak. Nevertheless, the possibility of such a meeting having taken place cannot be ruled out. There are references in Gurū Nānak's *bāṇī* to Bābar's invasions. An open tragedy like the one that struck Saidpur moved him profoundly and he described the sorrows of Indians—Hindus and Muslims alike—in words of intense power and suffering. Bābar's army, in the words of Gurū Nānak, was "the bridal procession of sin." In fact, Indian literature of that period records no more virile protest against the invading hordes than do Gurū Nānak's four hymns of *Bābarvāṇī* in the Gurū Granth Sāhib.

Bābar died on 26 December 1530 at Āgrā. Several years later his body was moved to its present grave in one of the gardens of Kābul.

BIBLIOGRAPHY

1. Beveridge, Annette Susannah, trans., *Babur-nama*. Delhi, 1989
2. Smith, Vincent A., *The Oxford History of India*. Oxford, 1958
3. Jaffar, S.M., *The Mughal Empire*. Delhi, 1974
4. Harbans Singh, *Guru Nanak and Origins of the Sikh Faith*. Bombay, 1969

S.R.S.

BACHAN SĀĪṄ LOKĀ KE, a book of morals in Punjabi prose belonging to the Sevāpanthī sect. There is no internal evidence to establish its date or authorship, but several of the *bachans* or sayings in this work are identical with those in Sahaj Rām's *Pothī Āsāvarīāṅ*. A manuscript copy of this work is preserved in the Central Public Library, Paṭiālā, under MS. No. 2142. In the text, man is adjured to overcome attachment and ever to remember God who is the Creator of all things, sentient and insentient, and watches over all. Poverty is a blessing; the riches are not accumulated without sin (16-17). A well-taught person who does not meditate on God is like a tree which does not bear fruit; one beautiful but faithless is like the bow sans arrows; the king who does not dispense justice is like a cloud without rain (18-19). Woman is a sword which destroys *dharma* (16). The five human jewels, truth, intellect, contentment, knowledge and generosity, are countered by five enemies, falsehood, anger, greed, arrogance, and resilement (25). Man must vanquish these enemies, for then alone can he break the cycle of birth and death and get united with the Supreme Being.

D.S.

BACHCHHOĀṆĀ, village 7 km northeast of Buḍhlāḍā Maṇḍī (29°-55'N, 75°-33'E), is sacred to Gurū Tegh Bahādur, who, according to *Sākhī Pothī*, came here from Barhe and stayed for seven days under a *pīpal* tree on the bank of a pond. The Gurū was accompanied by a large *saṅgat* and the Raṅghaṛ inhabitants of Bachchhoāṇā served them ample quantities of milk and curds. Gurū Tegh Bahādur expressed delight at the extensive green pastures around the village and blessed the villagers for their good milch cattle. Gurdwārā Pātshāhī IX, commemorating the Gurū's visit, comprises a sanctum, within a hall, with a verandah on three sides. The walled compound, entered through a high gateway, also encompasses Gurū kā Laṅgar as well as rooms for pilgrims. The Gurdwārā owns 50 acres of land and is administered by the Shiromaṇī Gurdwārā Parbandhak Committee, through a local committee.

BIBLIOGRAPHY

1. *Mālvā Desh Raṭan dī Sākhī Pothī*. Amritsar, 1968
2. Faujā Siṅgh, *Gurū Teg Bahādar : Yātrā Asthāṇ, Pramparāvāṅ te Yād Chinn*. Patiala, 1976

Jg.S.

BACHITRA NĀṬAK (*bachitra* = marvellous, wondrous + *nāṭak* = drama, play) is the name given a complex of compositions, commonly attributed to Gurū Gobind Siṅgh, the Tenth Gurū or prophet-teacher of the Sikh faith, assembled in his book, the *Dasam Granth*: hence, the name *dasam* (tenth) *granth* (book), i.e. Book of the Tenth Master to distinguish it from the earlier work, the *Ādi* (first, primary or original) Granth, now venerated as Srī Gurū Granth Sāhib. The most familiar section of compositions collectively called *Bachitra Nāṭak Granth* is the *Bachitra Nāṭak* itself, some of the others being *Chaṇḍī Chritra Ukti Bilās, Chaṇḍī Chritra, Vār Srī Bhagautī Jī Kī* (or Chaṇḍī dī Vār), *Giān Prabodh*, and *Chaubīs Autār*.

The composition of *Bachitra Nāṭak* may have begun in 1688, at Paoṇṭā during the first spurt of Gurū Gobind Siṅgh's literary activity. The date (Bk 1755/AD 1698) of completion of the section "*Rāmāvatār,*" as mentioned in that section, may also be that of the completion of the whole work. In any case, autobiographical *Bachitra Nāṭak* must have been completed before 1699, when Gurū Gobind Siṅgh inaugurated the K͟hālsā Panth, for the text does not refer to the event. The poem, however, contains a detailed description of the battle of Bhaṅgāṇī which took place in 1688, which lays down the other end of the date, i.e. the work was completed *after* 1688.

The *Bachitra Nāṭak* opens with an invocation to Bhagautī, i.e. sword embodying the divine principle of justice. In the second canto the poet says that limitless is the Divine Reality, fathomless its deeds. The poet then says that he would narrate his own story. The implication appears to be that the Divine has relevance for man only in its role in the human context. This seems to be the reason why the poet provides his story with a long preface (cantos 2-5) giving its mythical, legendary, historical and genealogical antecedents which link the action in heaven to that on the earth. He traces the lineage of his house, the Soḍhīs, to Lava, the son of Rāma, a scion of Raghū. The Soḍhīs were long in conflict with the descendants of Kuśa (Lava's brother). Eventually when the latter, overthrown, immersed themselves in the Vedas (hence called Vedīs/Bedīs), the Soḍhī king, in recognition of their profound learning, gave them his throne. The Bedī chief, in return, promised that the throne would be returned to the Soḍhīs during the Kali age. So after Gurū Nānak, a Bedī, had shown the way, the leadership in the person of Gurū Rām Dās passed to the Soḍhīs. All the Gurūs from Gurū Nānak to the tenth and last successor, Gurū Gobind Siṅgh, embodied the light of Nānak. The poet recalls their names pausing particularly to reflect upon the martyrdom of the Ninth Gurū, Gurū Teg͟h Bahādur, "who sacrificed his life to save the symbols of Hinduism, a deed unparalleled for heroism in the Kali age."

In the sixth canto, beginning with the words *ab mai apanī kathā bakhāno* (now I relate my own story), the narrative becomes more personal. The poet tells us how in a previous life he practised intense meditation and austerity on the mount Hem Kuṇṭ until his spirit merged with the Divine. Then, how despite his desire to stay absorbed in harmony at His feet, he was told by the Almighty to take birth in the Kali age to show the world the path of truth, to rid it of superstition, and to teach it to worship God alone. Gurū Gobind Siṅgh accepted the charge humbly: "Thy word shall prevail in the world, with Thy support." Without fear or malice, he would, he said, proclaim what God had told him. Lest people should start worshipping him instead of God, he warns them, "Those who call me God shall into the pit of Hell be cast. I am but the slave of the Supreme Being come to watch the world spectacle." Gurū Gobind Siṅgh adored none but God and attached no importance to any religious garb or practice except the constant remembrance of God's Name.

Cantos 7 to 13 treat of the poet's life as Gobind Rāi, name by which Gurū Gobind Siṅgh was earlier known. (Gobind Siṅgh was the name he assumed after he had himself admitted to the K͟hālsā Panth). Apparently, owing to the hostility of the neighbouring hill *rājās*, he moved to Paoṇṭā where he lived happily for some time. Then Fateh Shāh (the Rājā of Srīnagar) attacked him "without provocation." The rest of the autobiography is largely a description of the armed conflicts between the Gurū and his adversaries. He defeated Fateh Shāh, and his allies at Bhaṅgāṇī. At Nadauṇ he defeated Alif K͟hān, a Mug͟hal commander sent to exact tribute from the hill chiefs. The Gurū's former enemy, Bhīm Chand of Bilāspur, sought the Gurū's help in this action. Three expeditions sent by Dilāwar K͟hān were also put to rout. The first, under Dilāwar's son, turned back merely upon hearing the tumult of assault by the Gurū's forces. The second and third, under strong commanders Hussain and Jujhār Siṅgh, were distracted by other hill chiefs and ended in the death of these commanders. Gurū Gobind Siṅgh ends the story in canto 14 reaffirming his faith in God's cosmic play. "All-Time saveth His saints and punisheth those who renege on Him. He protecteth his saints from all harm .... He hath succoured me, His own slave."

Bachitra Nāṭak is a clear and strong statement of God's, and Gurū Gobind Siṅgh's role in history. That is what gives it central importance in the formation of Sikhism. Gurū Gobind Siṅgh confirmed the preceding Gurūs' teaching centring on the oneness and perfection of the Absolute. Such oneness also implied the essential perfection of creation as part of the Absolute. But creation is perfect only in relation to the Creator not in itself. To see it as self-sufficient is to distort reality and convert its goodness into evil. If human life is believed to be a separate and complete affair in itself, selfishness prevails and human existence is perverted. Men thus immersed in the world are eventually chastised by God as is illustrated in Gurū Nānak's treatment of Bābar's invasion of India. One very common way of being severed from the Divine is to attach meaning to the external forms of religion in themselves rather than as means of attaining the Divine.

Gurū Gobind Siṅgh conceived God as the embodiment of the fighting spirit. But as the evil is in man's perspective, it must be remedied in human terms; the visible action in God's war on evil must be performed by men of realization. The Gurū's proclamation of his gospel is but a readiness to fight in God's name and when he goes to battle, he does God's work. No wonder, he always wins. The *Bachitra Nāṭak* is an exultation over God's triumph acted out by noble souls on the world's stage and an expression of faith in future victories. It is a confident call to saints to put on arms in continuation and transformation of earlier Sikhism.

Consequently, *Bachitra Nāṭak* is largely a series of vivid battle scenes created with forceful imagination. Through a variety of generally quick and sinuous metres, apt descriptions and a profusion of appropriate similes and metaphors, mention of the entire paraphernalia of battle, diction reproducing its very sounds and sensations, and glimpses into the psychology of the warriors, the poet captures the verve of battle and quickens the readers' spirit. To reproduce an image, Mahant Kirpāl Dās rising in his stirrups and shouting *Sat Srī Akāl* smote Hayāt K͟hān's head with his wooden truncheon that his skull was crushed and "his brains, spilt forth as butter flowed from the Gopīs' pitchers broken by Krishna."

BIBLIOGRAPHY

1. Macauliffe, Max Arthur, *The Sikh Religion*, Oxford, 1909
2. Gopal Singh, *Thus Spake the Tenth Master*. Patiala, 1978
3. Ashta, Dharam Pal, *The Poetry of the Dasam Granth*. Delhi, 1959
4. Loehlin, C.H., *The Granth of Guru Gobind Singh and the Khalsa Brotherhood*. Lucknow, 1971
5. Jaggī, Ratan Siṅgh, *Dasam Granth Parichaya*. Delhi, 1990
6. Raṇdhīr Siṅgh, Bhāī, *Shabadārth Dasam Granth Sāhib*, vol. I. Paṭiala, 1973

S.S.D.

BACHITTAR SIṄGH, BHĀĪ (d. 1705), warrior and martyr, was the second son of Bhāī Manī Rām, a Parmār Rājpūt and devotee of the Gurūs. One of the five brothers presented by their father for service to Gurū Gobind Siṅgh (1666-1708), he joined the order of the K͟hālsā on the historic Baisākhī day, 30 March 1699, and shot into prominence during the first battle of Anandpur against the hill chieftains, when, on 1 September 1700, he was selected by Gurū Gobind Siṅgh to face a drunken elephant brought forth by them to batter down the gate of the Lohgaṛh Fort. As the elephant reached near the gate,

Bachittar Siṅgh, says the *Gurbilās Pātshāhī 10,* sallied forth on horseback and made a powerful thrust with his spear piercing the plate and injuring the animal in the forehead. The wounded elephant ran back creating havoc in the besiegers' ranks. Bachittar Siṅgh also took part in actions at Nirmohgaṛh and Basālī and in the last battle of Anandpur. On the fateful night of 5-6 December 1705, when Anandpur was evacuated, he was one of those who safely crossed the torrential Sarsā rivulet. At the head of a flanking guard watching pursuers from the direction of Ropaṛ, he had an encounter with a body of irregulars near Malikpur Raṅghṛāṅ in which he was seriously wounded. He was carried to Koṭlā Nihaṅg Khān where he died two days later (8 December 1705).

BIBLIOGRAPHY

1. Giān Siṅgh, Giānī, *Panth Prakāsh* [Reprint]. Patiala, 1970
2. Santokh Siṅgh, Bhāī, *Srī Gur Pratāp Sūraj Granth.* Amritsar, 1926-37
3. Garjā Siṅgh, Giānī, ed., *Shahīd Bilās.* Ludhiana, 1961
4. Kuir Siṅgh, *Gurbilās Pātshāhī 10.* Patiala, 1968

P.S.

BACHITTAR SIṄGH, BHĀĪ (d. 1921), was a *granthī* (officiant) at the *gurdwārā* in Chakk No. 85 Ḍallā Chandā Siṅghvālā in Sheikhūpurā, in the newly colonized irrigation district in western Punjab. Nothing is known about his parentage or the date and place of his birth. He had arrived at the village in the company of a *Nāṅgā sādhū* as a boy of 10 or 12 years and had stayed on in the local *gurdwārā*. He had learnt to read Gurmukhī and the holy text from the *granthī* whom he replaced after the latter had left. On the night of 19-20 February 1921, he was participating in an *akhaṇḍ pāṭh,* unbroken reading of the Gurū Granth Sāhib, in a neighbouring village, when a *jathā* of reformist Akālīs under the leadership of Bhāī Lachmaṇ Siṅgh passed that way. The *jathā* was proceeding to Nankāṇā Sāhib. Bachittar Siṅgh had another *granthī* replace him on the *akhaṇḍ pāṭh* roster and joined the *jathā* going to Nankāṇā Sāhib. At Nankāṇā Sāhib he, along with other members of the *jathā,* was showered with bullets by the *mahant's* men.

See NANKĀṆĀ SĀHIB MASSACRE

BIBLIOGRAPHY

Shamsher, Gurbakhsh Siṅgh, *Shahīdī Jīvan.* Nankana Sahib, 1938

G.S.G.

BACHITTAR SIṄGH MALVAĪ (d. 1840), eldest son of Dhannā Siṅgh Malvaī, joined the army of Raṇjīt Siṅgh about 1827, and served first at Bahāwalpur. When Peshāwar was occupied by the Sikhs in 1834, Bachittar Siṅgh was sent to Shabqadar, where a new cantonment had been laid out and a fort built by Chatar Siṅgh Aṭārīvālā. He was still there when, in April 1837, the Afghān army attacked the post and the fort of Jamrūd. In January 1839, Bachittar Siṅgh accompanied the Sikh forces escorting Shāhzādā Taimūr, son of Shāh Shujā', to Peshāwar. He died in 1840.

BIBLIOGRAPHY

1. Griffin, Lepel, and C.F. Massy, *Chiefs and Families of Note in the Punjab.* Lahore, 1909
2. Khushwant Singh, *Ranjit Singh : Maharajah of the Punjab 1780-1839.* Bombay, 1962

J.R.G.

BADALĪ, BHĀĪ, a Soḍhī Khatrī, and Seṭh Gopāl figure in the roster of prominent Sikhs of the time of Gurū Hargobind (1595-1644) in Bhāī Gurdās, *Vārāṅ* XI. 31. As they sought the Gurū's instruction he, records Bhāī Manī Siṅgh, *Sikhāṅ dī Bhagat Mālā,* impressed upon them the virtue of humility. Both Bhāī Badalī and Bhāī Gopāl embraced the precept and won renown as devout Sikhs.

BIBLIOGRAPHY

Manī Siṅgh, Bhāī, *Sikhāṅ dī Bhagat Mālā*. Amritsar, 1955

Gn.S.

BAḌḌHAL KOṬLĀ, village 4 km northwest of Kīratpur (31° - 11'N, 76° - 35'E) along Ropaṛ-Naṅgal road in Ropaṛ district of the Punjab, is sacred to Gurū Hargobind, who used to pass through here following the chase. He got a well dug here for the benefit of the villagers. The shrine established near the well formerly known simply as Khūh (lit. well) Sāhib or Jhiṛā (lit. thicket) Sāhib is now called Gurdwārā Miṭṭhāsar (lit. pool of sweet water) Jhiṛā Sāhib Pātshāhī Chhevīṅ. The present building constructed in 1945 comprises a square congregation hall, including the sanctum. The old well in front of the main building is still in use. The Gurdwārā is maintained by Nihaṅgs of the Buḍḍhā Dal.

BIBLIOGRAPHY

1. *Gurbilās Chhevīṅ Pātshāhī*. Patiala, 1970
2. Giān Siṅgh, Giānī, *Twārīkh Gurū Khālsā*. Patiala, 1970

Gn. S.

BAḌḌOṄ, village 10 km southeast of Māhilpur in Hoshiārpur district of the Punjab, has a historical shrine, Gurdwārā Bābā Ajīt Siṅgh, commemorating the visit in March 1703 of Sāhibzādā Ajīt Siṅgh (1687-1705), the eldest son of Gurū Gobind Siṅgh. Sāhibzādā Ajīt Siṅgh, on his way back from Bassī Kalāṅ where he had gone to rescue a young Brāhmaṇ bride from the clutches of the local Paṭhān chieftain, halted here to cremate one of his warriors, Bhāī Karam Siṅgh, who had been wounded in the skirmish at Bassī and had since succumbed to his injuries. The Gurdwārā constructed by the local *saṅgat* in 1928 on the site of the original shrine inside the village comprises a flat-roofed hall, with the sanctum marked off by two pillars at the far end, and a 3-metre wide verandah on three sides. It is affiliated to the Shiromaṇī Gurdwārā Parbandhak Committee and is maintained by the local *saṅgat*.

Gn. S.

BADRĪ NĀTH (d. 1871), son of Paṇḍit Gobind Rām who migrated from Kashmīr to the Punjab at the beginning of the nineteenth century, entered Mahārājā Raṇjīt Siṅgh's army as a soldier in 1821, rising to the rank of colonel in 1835. He saw plenty of fighting during his service career and took part in the campaigns of Swāt, Peshāwar, Hazārā and Bannū. For long he served on the frontier and was for six years in charge of the forts of Ḍerā Ismā'īl Khān and Ṭoṅk. He was with General Harī Siṅgh Nalvā in 1834 when the Sikhs took Peshāwar from the Bārakzaīs. In 1845, he was stationed in Hazārā with the Kaṭār Mukhī Regiment. In 1846, he accompanied Major Henry Lawrence to Kashmīr where Shaikh Imām ud-Dīn was in revolt, and the next year went with Lieut. Herbert Edwardes to Bannū. He took part in the siege of Multān in 1848. During the uprising of 1857, the Fort of Multān, the magazine and the treasury were entrusted to Badrī Nāth's corps and he was granted Order of British India for his services in suppressing the rebellion. He retired from service in 1861.

Badrī Nāth died in 1871.

BIBLIOGRAPHY

Griffin, Lepel, and C.F. Massy, *Chiefs and Families of Note in the Punjab*. Lahore, 1909

S.S.B.

BAGGĀ SIṄGH, BHĀĪ (1893-1921), was born during Assū 1950 Bk/September-October 1893, the son of Bhāī Gaṅgā Siṅgh and Māī Mallāṅ, a peasant couple of Chakk No. 38 Devā Siṅghvālā in Sheikhūpurā district, in the newly developed canal area in western Punjab by the British. He learnt reading and writing in Gurmukhī script from the village *granthī* and took the initiation of the Khālsā at the age of 18. He was of a lissom athletic build interested in village sports and was also a member of the village holy choir. He attended the Akālī congregation at Dhārovālī on 1-3 October 1920. Impressed by the fiery speeches of Akālī reformers there, he became a member of the Dhārovālī Akālī Jathā led by Bhāī Lachhmaṇ Siṅgh, and attained martyrdom in Gurdwārā Janam Asthān on 20 February 1921.

See NANKĀṆĀ SĀHIB MASSACRE

BIBLIOGRAPHY

Shamsher, Gurbakhsh Siṅgh, *Shahīdī Jīvan*. Nankana Sahib, 1938

G.S.G.

BĀGHAṚ SIṄGH, BHĀĪ, killed in 1740, was the youngest son of Bhāī Ālam Siṅgh Nachnā, of Duburjī village in Siālkoṭ district, a warrior in Gurū Gobind Siṅgh's retinue at Anandpur. His elder brothers, Mohar Siṅgh and Amolak Siṅgh, too, were soldiers and are believed to have died fighting along with their father in the battle of Chamkaur on 7 December 1705. As he grew up, Bāghaṛ Siṅgh also joined the ranks of the Khālsā. That was the time when Sikhs were forced under State persecution to leave their hearths and homes and find shelter in distant deserts and woods. Once when Bāghaṛ Siṅgh came home to visit his family, a government informer spied on him and had him arrested. He was, under the orders of the Mughal governor, Zakarīyā Khān, tortured, his body was stretched on a revolving wheel before he was beheaded at Lahore in 1740.

BIBLIOGRAPHY

1. Visākhā Siṅgh, Sant, *Mālvā Itihās*. Kishanpura, 1954
2. *Khālsā te Khālsā Advocate*. October 11, 1930

M.G.S.

BAGHDĀD (33° - 20'N, 44° - 30'E), capital of Iraq, situated on the banks of Dajalā (Tigris) River, has a historical shrine dedicated to Gurū Nānak, who visited here on his way back from Mecca and Madina early in the sixteenth century. Here he held discourses with some local Sūfī saints. A memorial platfoım was raised on the spot where the Gurū and his companion, Mardānā, the Muslim bard, had stopped. A few years later, a room was constructed there and a stone slab with an inscription in Ottoman Turkish was installed in it. Translated into English it would read :

Look what was wished by the Glorious Lord in His majesty—
That a new establishment be built for the saint Bābā Nānak. —
The Seven gave help and there came this chronogram:
The blest disciple performed a meritorious work.
May He then recompense it !

The year which is now read as 917 Hijrī was in earlier photographs of the inscription read as 927. It seems the figure "2" has since been mutilated and now reads more like the figure "1".

In the literature relating to the life of Gurū Nānak the tradition about his visit to Baghdād is strong and persistent. The earliest testimony is that of Bhāī Gurdās who was born twelve years after Gurū Nānak and lived through the times of the five of the succeeding Gurūs. He was, throughout, in close touch with them and with some of the disciples from the time of Gurū Nānak himself. In his *Vārāṅ*, I. 35, Bhāī Gurdās wrote about Gurū Nānak's visit to Baghdād and said:

ਫਿਰਿ ਬਾਬਾ ਗਿਆ ਬਗਦਾਦ ਨੋ,
ਬਾਹਰ ਜਾਇ ਕੀਆ ਅਸਥਾਨਾ ।

Translated into English the lines say, "The Bābā, i.e. the Gurū, journeyed on to Baghdād and made his seat outside the town." This writing dates to about 60 years after Gurū Nānak. It is by one who had direct access to Sikhs of Gurū Nānak's time and to the tradition coming down from him. The statement is clear and unambiguous and the words that the Gurū sat outside the town are specially meaningful in this context. The Janam Sakhīs also refer to his visit to Baghdād. Mention has been made of Gurū Nānak having met Shaikh Abdul Qādir Jilānī and Bahlūl Shāh. These references are obviously anachronistic. Maybe, Gurū Nānak met the disciples or descendants of these Sūfī saints. But the very fact that Baghdād and the names of the Sūfī saints are connected with the tradition, indicates that there was some firm basis for the story which became current soon after Gurū Nānak's passing away.

The inscription was first discovered by Sikh soldiers going to Iraq, then Mesopotamia, during World War I and has since been a topic of much spirited speculation and scholarly discussion.

BIBLIOGRAPHY

1. Ṭhākar Siṅgh, Giānī, *Srī Gurduāre Darshan*. Amritsar, 1923
2. Harbans Singh, *Guru Nanak and Origins of the Sikh Faith*. Bombay, 1969

M.G.S.

BAGHEL SIṄGH (d. 1802), who succeeded in 1765 Karoṛā Siṅgh as leader of the Karoṛsiṅghīā *misl* or chiefship, is celebrated in Sikh history as the vanquisher of Mughal Delhi. A Dhālīvāl Jaṭṭ, Baghel Siṅgh arose from the village of Jhabāl, in Amritsar district, to become a formidable force in the cis-Sutlej region. According to Syad Muhammad Latīf, he had under him 12,000 fighting men. As well as being a soldier, he was an adept in political negotiation and was able to win over many an adversary to his side. The Mughals, the Ruhīlās, the Marāṭhās and the English sought his friendship. In the wake of the decay of Mughal authority in the Punjab owing to Ahmad Shāh Durrānī's successive invasions during the latter half of the eighteenth century, the Sikhs began extending their influence. Baghel Siṅgh took possession of portions of the Jalandhar Doāb and established himself at Hariāṇā, near Hoshiārpur. Soon after the Sikh conquest of Sirhind in January 1764, he extended his arms towards Karnāl, occupying a number of villages including Chhalaudī which he later made his headquarters.

In February 1764, Sikhs in a body of 40,000 under the command of Baghel Siṅgh and other leading warriors crossed the Yamunā and captured Sahāranpur. They overran the territory of Najīb ud-Daulah, the Ruhīlā chief, realizing from him a tribute of eleven lakh of rupees. In April 1775, Baghel Siṅgh with two other *sardārs*, Rāi Siṅgh Bhaṅgī and Tārā Siṅgh Ghaibā, crossed the Yamunā to occupy that country, then ruled by Zābitā Khān, son and successor of Najīb ud-Daulah. Zābitā Khān in desperation offered Baghel Siṅgh large sums of money and proposed an alliance jointly to plunder the crown-lands. The combined forces of Sikhs and Ruhīlās looted villages around the present site of New Delhi. In March 1776, they defeated the imperial forces near Muzaffarnagar. The whole of the Yamunā-Gangetic Doāb was now at their mercy. When in the autumn of 1779, a large Mughal army under the command of Prince Farkhandā Bakht and Wazīr Abdul Ahad Khān led an expedition against the cis-Sutlej Sikhs, Baghel Siṅgh along with Rāi Siṅgh of Būṛīā and Bhaṅgā Siṅgh of Thānesar joined hands with the imperial forces at Karnāl and encircled Paṭiālā. Rājā Amar Siṅgh visited Baghel Siṅgh in his camp at the village of Lahal and made peace with him and had his son, Sāhib Siṅgh, receive the rites of Khālsā initiation at his hands. Meanwhile, Amar Siṅgh had invited trans-Sutlej Sikhs for help. Baghel Siṅgh outwitted his imperial allies who sought safety in flight suffering heavy losses. When in April 1781, Mirzā Shafī, a close relative of the Mughal prime minister, captured the Sikh military post at Indrī, 10 km south of Lāḍvā, Baghel Siṅgh retaliated by attacking Khalīl

Beg Khān of Shāhābād who surrendered with 300 horse, 800 foot and 2 pieces of cannon. When on 11 March 1783, Sikhs entered the Red Fort in Delhi and occupied the Dīwān-i-Ām, the Mughal emperor, Shāh Ālam II, made a settlement with them agreeing to allow Baghel Siṅgh to raise *gurdwārās* on Sikh historical sites in the city and realize six *ānnās* in a rupee (37.5%) of all the octroi duties in the capital. Baghel Siṅgh stayed in Sabzī Maṇḍī, with 4000 troops, and took charge of the police station in Chāndnī Chowk. He located seven sites connected with the lives of the Gurūs and had shrines raised thereon within the space of eight months, from April to November 1783. Gurdwārā Sīs Gañj marked the spot in the main Mughal street of Chāndnī Chowk where Gurū Tegh Bahādur had been executed under the fiat of the emperor and Gurdwārā Rikābgañj, near modern-day Parliament House, where the body was cremated. Baṅglā Sāhib and Bālā Sāhib commemorated the Eighth Gurū, Gurū Har Krishan. Three other *gurdwārās* built were at Majnū kā Ṭillā, Motī Bāgh and Telīvāṛā.

Baghel Siṅgh died probably in 1802, at Hariāṇā, in present-day Hoshiārpur district. A *samādh* enshrining the memory of one of the more picturesque *misl sardārs* still stands in the town.

BIBLIOGRAPHY

1. Giān Siṅgh, Giānī, *Panth Prakāsh* [Reprint]. Patiala, 1970
2. Bhaṅgū, Ratan Siṅgh, *Prāchīn Panth Prakāsh* [Reprint]. Amritsar, 1962
3. Sītal, Sohan Siṅgh, *Sikh Mislāṅ*. Ludhiana, 1952
4. Gupta, Hari Ram, *History of the Sikhs*, vol. III. Delhi, 1979
5. Harbans Singh, *The Heritage of the Sikhs*. Delhi, 1983

H.R.G.

BĀGH SIṄGH VIRK (d. 1806), a feudatory chief under Mahārājā Raṇjīt Siṅgh. His father Lāl Siṅgh, who had migrated from Jammū, held sway in the tract between Sheikhūpurā and Mirālīvālā as the Sikh *sardārs* started acquiring territory in the Punjab in the latter half of the eighteenth century. He was considered an influential chief in the vicinity of Lahore when Raṇjīt Siṅgh occupied the city in 1799. He accepted the Mahārājā's sovereignty and was appointed to command a unit of the army with a grant of *jāgīr* amounting to one and a half lakh of rupees, consisting of eighty-four villages, in the neighbourhood of Kaṛiāl Kalāṅ and Mirālīvālā. Bāgh Siṅgh died in 1806, his son, Jodh Siṅgh, succeeding him in the command he held. Jodh Siṅgh took part in several of Raṇjīt Siṅgh's military campaigns and was killed in action in Kashmīr in 1814.

BIBLIOGRAPHY

Griffin, Lepel, and C.F. Massy, *Chiefs and Families of Note in the Punjab*. Lahore, 1909

G.S.N.

BAHĀDURGAṚH, Fort, 9 km northeast of Paṭiālā (30° - 20'N, 76° - 26'E), marks the site of the old Saifābād Fort, the residence of Nawāb Saif ud-Dīn Mahmūd or Saif Khān. The Fort was acquired by Rājā Amar Siṅgh (1748-82) of Paṭiālā in 1774 and was reconstructed by Mahārājā Karam Siṅgh (1798-1845) in 1837. The latter renamed it Bahādurgaṛh after Gurū Tegh Bahādur who had visited the place more than once. Mahārājā Karam Siṅgh also raised two *gurdwārās*, one outside the Fort and the other inside it, both honouring the memory of Gurū Tegh Bahādur.

GURDWĀRĀ SRĪ GURŪ TEGH BAHĀDUR, BAHĀDURGAṚH, is about 200 metres north of the Fort. According to tradition, Gurū Tegh Bahādur, during one of his travels through the Mālvā region, stayed here at the request of Nawāb Saif Khān. The latter, a pious Muslim and an ardent admirer of Gurū Tegh Bahādur, had met the Gurū earlier also. Gurū

Tegh Bahādur arrived here on 16 Hāṛ 1732 Bk / 14 June 1675 and stayed in the Nawāb's garden, no longer extant but for a few banyan trees around a tank. Saif Khān requested him to prolong his sojourn here. The latter stayed on during the rainy season. On several occasions, the Nawāb took him inside his fort so that the ladies of his house could also benefit from the Gurū's *darshan* and discourse. The Gurū left on 17 Assū 1732 Bk/17 September 1675 to continue his travels.

The Gurdwārā is in the shape of a large *havelī* or fortress with an imposing three-storeyed gateway. The heavy wooden gate is set in a red stone frame under an ogee-shaped trefoil arch. The gate is flanked on either side by door-sized niches. The first floor has projecting windows, and at the top there are decorative pavilions. Octagonal turrets are built all along the outer wall at regular intervals. Inside the *havelī* there is a cemented court-yard with rooms all around it. The sanctum where the Gurū Granth Sāhib is seated stands on a high square base in the middle. It consists of a small room crowned with a pinnacled lotus-dome and surrounded by a marble-floored verandah. The interior walls and the ceiling are set in with reflecting glass pieces and have decorative filigree work in delicate designs. Painted in miniature fresco are the portraits of the Gurūs. The *dīvān* hall is at the back of the sanctum. To the north of the Gurdwārā is the 90-metre square *sarovar*. This Gurdwārā is managed by the Shiromaṇī Gurdwārā Parbandhak Committee.

GURDWĀRĀ SRĪ GURŪ TEGH BAHĀDUR, BAHĀDURGAṚH FORT, is a modern construction enclosing the historical shrine built by Mahārājā Karam Siṅgh of Paṭiālā. The original building, still intact, consists of a small room with a door on each of the four sides, radiating arches and a lotus dome. The entire interior surface is richly decorated with coloured motifs. The outer surface of the walls, however, has since been plastered and colour-washed to match the colour scheme of the enclosing hall. The hall has a flat roof supported by four square-shaped pillars. In front of it is a spacious platform with a small pool within it. The Gurdwārā is maintained by the police contingent housed in the Fort.

BIBLIOGRAPHY

1. *Mālvā Desh Raṭan dī Sākhī Pothī.* Amritsar, 1968
2. Ṭhākar Siṅgh, Giānī, *Srī Gurduāre Darshan.* Amritsar, 1923
3. Trilochan Singh, *Guru Tegh Bahadur: Prophet and Martyr.* Delhi, 1967

M.G.S.

BAHĀDUR SHĀH (1643-1712), Mughal emperor of India from 1707 to 1712. Born Muhammad Mu'azzam at Burhānpur in the Deccan on 14 October 1643, he was actively employed by his father, Auraṅgzīb, from 1663 onwards for subduing the kingdom of Bījāpur and the Qutb Shāhī dynasty of Golcoṇḍā in the south. In 1695 he was appointed *sūbahdār* of Āgrā and in 1699 governor of Kābul. Mu'azzam was at Kābul when news arrived of the death, on 20 February 1707, of Auraṅgzīb. The Emperor's death was a signal for the usual war of succession and, in Mu'azzam's absence, his younger brother, 'Āzam Shāh, assumed the throne. Mu'azzam came down from Kābul and won a decisive victory in the battle of Jājaū, near Āgrā, on 8 June 1707. He sat on the throne of Delhi, with the title of Bahādur Shāh.

Bahādur Shāh, who had the reputation of being liberal in his religious policy, had requested Gurū Gobind Siṅgh for help in the war of succession and the Gurū had sent a body of Sikhs to fight on his side in the battle of Jājaū to defend his right to the crown, he being the eldest of the surviving sons of Auraṅgzīb. When Bahādur Shāh was firmly in the royal seat, Gurū Gobind Siṅgh came to Āgrā on 23 July 1707 to pay him a formal visit. The Emperor expressed immense happiness at seeing the Gurū and thanked him for his visit and for the help he had given him in the battle. Bahādur Shāh presented the Gurū with a khill'at including a jewelled scarf, a *dhukhdhukhī,* and an aigrette or *kalghī*. The Gurū's attendant who waited outside the hall was called in to carry the dress of honour to his camp, contrary to the Mughal practice of the recipient having to put it on in the court. This meeting became the starting-point of parleys between Gurū Gobind Siṅgh and the Emperor on the question of the State's religious policy. But Bahādur Shāh had to leave suddenly for the Deccan to quell a rebellion by his brother, Kām Bakhsh. Gurū Gobind Siṅgh travelled south with him to continue the negotiations. Nawāb Wazīr Khān of Sirhind felt alarmed at the Emperor's conciliatory treatment of Gurū Gobind Siṅgh, and he charged two of his trusted men with murdering the Gurū before his increasing friendship with the Emperor resulted in any harm to himself. When one of these two Paṭhāns stabbed Gurū Gobind Siṅgh, Bahādur Shāh sent expert surgeons, including an Englishman, to attend on the Gurū and his injury was temporarily healed. The negotiations, however, remained inconclusive.

On his return in 1710 from the Deccan after a successful campaign against his brother, Kām Bakhsh, Bahādur Shāh found himself confronted with a Sikh rebellion under the banner of Bandā Siṅgh Bahādur who had occupied territory in parts of the Punjab. Bandā Siṅgh's increasing influence roused the ire of Bahādur Shāh, who ordered a general mobilization of all his forces in Delhi, Uttar Pradesh and Oudh, and called for volunteers for a *jihād* against the Sikhs. Prohibitary laws against the Sikhs were passed. Fearing that some Sikhs might not have smuggled themselves into the royal camp disguised as Hindus, Bahādur Shāh ordered all Hindus employed in the imperial offices to shave off their beards. His order, issued on 10 December 1710, was a general warrant for the *faujdārs* to kill the worshippers of Nānak i.e. Sikhs, wherever found (*Nānak prastāṅ rā har jā kih bayāband baqatl rasānand*). Bahādur Shāh, with a massive imperial force— sixty thousand horse and foot—stormed the Lohgaṛh fortress in the submontane region where Bandā Siṅgh had taken shelter but could not capture him. Bahādur Shāh reached Lahore in August 1711 where for the next six months his courtiers fed him on stories of Mughal victories over Bandā Siṅgh's "rabble." But as the days rolled by with Bandā Siṅgh still free, still defiant, the Emperor became melancholic and died on 27 February 1712.

BIBLIOGRAPHY

1. Sarkar, Jadunath, *Fall of the Mughal Empire.* Delhi, 1971
2. Irvine, W., *Later Mughals.* London, 1922
3. Khushwant Singh, *A History of the Sikhs,* vol. I. Princeton, 1963
4. Sharma, Sri Ram, *Religious Policy of the Mughal Emperors.* Bombay, 1962

S.R.S.

BAHĀDUR SIṄGH, who belonged to Nankū, an obscure village in Jalandhar district of the Punjab, was among the close associates of Bhāī Mahārāj Siṅgh, leader of the anti-British revolt of 1848-49. After the failure of the design to rescue Mahārājā Duleep Siṅgh from British hands, Bhāī Mahārāj Siṅgh planned a general uprising and sent out emissaries to prepare the people for it. It was at the persuasion of Bahādur Siṅgh who had been assigned to Jalandhar Doāb that Bhāī Mahārāj Siṅgh shifted his headquarters to the Doābā. He accompanied Bhāī Mahārāj Siṅgh during his tour of the area and was arrested along with him on the night of 28-29 December 1849.

BIBLIOGRAPHY

Ahluwalia, M.L., *Bhai Maharaj Singh.* Patiala, 1972

M.L.A.

BAHEṚ, village 5 km east of Bassī Paṭhānāṅ (30° - 42'N, 76° - 25'B) in Paṭiālā district, has a historical shrine dedicated to Gurū Tegh Bahādur who, according to local tradition, made a brief halt here on his way from Nandpur-Kalauṛ to Dādū Mājrā-Bhagṛānā. A monument existed here in the form of a platform until a regular shrine was built in recent years. The complex comprises a *dīvān* hall, a gateway, the Gurū kā Laṅgar and rooms for pilgrims. The main hall, with the sanctum in the middle of it, is topped over by a low dome. The Gurdwārā is managed by a village committee.

BIBLIOGRAPHY

Faujā Siṅgh, *Gurū Teg Bahādur: Yātrā Asthān, Paramparāvāṅ te Yād Chinn.* Patiala, 1976

M.G.S.

BAHILO, BHĀĪ (1553-1643), a Siddhū Jaṭṭ of the village of Phaphṛe, in present-day Baṭhiṇḍā district of the Punjab, and a prominent Sikh of his time. He was originally a follower of Sultān Sak͟hī Sarwar and a local priest of that semi-Muslim sect of Sultānīās or Sarwarīās. In 1583, he visited Amritsar at the invitation of Gurū Arjan. Bahilo was converted the moment he saw the Gurū. He cast away the symbols of his former faith and received the rites of initiation at the hands of Gurū Arjan. His devotion was now addressed to Akāl, the Timeless One. He dedicated the labour of his hands to the excavation of the holy tank and construction of the Harimandar, then in progress at Amritsar. He supervised the baking of bricks in a kiln and carried on his head basketfuls of earth dug from the site. However heavy the load upon his head, Bhāī Bahilo's eyes, says Bhāī Santokh Siṅgh, *Srī Gur Pratāp Sūraj Granth,* always remained fixed on the Gurū. Bhāī Bahilo's piety and self-abnegating service were lauded by the Gurū as well as by Sikhs.

Bhāī Bahilo's descendants continue to live in Phaphṛe. They are known as Bhāīke, i.e. of or belonging to the Bhāī. Even the village is commonly known as Bhāīke Phaphṛe. There are some relics—a few garments, a gold coin and a dagger —which the family claims to have been bestowed by Gurū Gobind Siṅgh upon one of their ancestors, Bhāī Des Rāj. Bhāī Bahilo was a considerable poet. At least eight old manuscripts containing verse attributed to him are still extant. Most of them are transcriptions made in 1850 by one Pañjāb Siṅgh, a descendant of Bhāī Bahilo.

BIBLIOGRAPHY

1. Santokh Siṅgh, Bhāī, *Srī Gur Pratāp Sūraj Granth.* Amritsar, 1926-37
2. Giān Siṅgh, Giānī, *Twārīk͟h Gurū K͟hālsā* [Reprint]. Patiala, 1970
3. Satibīr Siṅgh, *Partakhu Hari.* Jalandhar, 1982
4. Harbans Singh, *The Heritage of the Sikhs.* Delhi, 1983

T.S.

BAHILOL, BHĀĪ, a resident of Qādīviṇḍ, a village near Kasūr, now in Pakistan, was a devotee of Gurū Amar Dās. Once the Gurū visited Qādīviṇḍ at his request and, pleased at his devotion, promised him any boon he might ask of him. Bhāī Bahilol spoke humbly : "Nothing is permanent in this world, Lord ! Grant me therefore the only boon worth asking for, that is, I may always remember God's Name." The Gurū gave him his blessing. The memorial *gurdwārā* dedicated to Gurū Amar Dās and constructed on the land donated by Bhāī Bahilol was looked after by a line of Udāsī priests until the partition of the Punjab in 1947. The *samādh* of Bhāī Bahilol also existed near the *gurdwārā.*

BIBLIOGRAPHY

1. Santokh Siṅgh, Bhāī, *Srī Gur Pratāp Sūraj Granth.* Amritsar, 1926-37
2. Giān Siṅgh, Giānī, *Twārīk͟h Gurū K͟hālsā* [Reprint]. Patiala, 1970

B.S.D.

BAHIR JACHCHH or Bahir Jakkh, a village in Samāṇā *tahsīl* of Paṭiālā district, situated on the left bank of the Sarasvatī, a small stream sacred to the Hindus, commemorates the visit of Gurū Tegh Bahādur, who is believed to have stayed here with a devotee, Mallā, a carpenter by trade. A small mud hut marked the site until Mahārājā Karam Siṅgh, of Paṭiālā, in whose territory the village lay, had a proper *gurdwārā* constructed in 1840. This, too, has since been demolished and replaced by a bigger *gurdwārā* and a *sarovar*, holy bathing pool.

There is a story connected with the construction of the Mañjī Sāhib at Bahir Jachchh by Mahārājā Karam Siṅgh. It is said that once the Mahārājā, accompanied by the Mahārāṇī, went on a pilgrimage to Pehovā, which fell in the territory of Bhāī Ude Siṅgh of Kaithal. There arose a dispute over protocol between the Mahārāṇī and the Rāṇī of Bhāī Ude Siṅgh as to who should take her dip in the Sarasvatī first. The Rāṇī of Kaithal remarked sarcastically that, if the Mahārāṇī of Paṭiālā was so jealous of her superiority even at holy places of pilgrimage, she should find a holy place in her own territory. Mahārājā Karam Siṅgh, on his return to Paṭiālā, enquired from the *paṇḍits* whether there was not a comparable holy place within his dominions. The *paṇḍits* recommended Bahir Jachchh for its location on the holy Sarasvatī, for its connection with the story of the *Mahābhārata* and for Gurū Tegh Bahādur's visit to the place. The Mahārājā then got a *gurdwārā* and a temple built in the village.

The Gurdwārā, named after Gurū Tegh Bahādur but commonly called Gurdwārā Bahir Sāhib, is affiliated to the Shiromaṇī Gurdwārā Parbandhak Committee. The management for the present is in the hands of *sants* of Pehovā who are supervising its reconstruction.

BIBLIOGRAPHY

1. Ṭhākar Siṅgh, Giānī, *Srī Gurduāre Darshan*. Amritsar, 1923
2. Tārā Siṅgh, *Srī Gur Tīrath Saṅgrahi*. Amritsar, n.d.
3. Faujā Siṅgh, *Gurū Teg Bahādar : Yātrā Asthān, Pramparāvāṅ te Yād Chinn*. Patiala, 1976

M.G.S.

BAHIRṚVĀL, village in Chūṇīāṅ *tahsīl* (subdivision) of Lahore district of Pakistan, is sacred to Gurū Arjan (1563-1606), who once visited it during his travels in these parts. According to tradition, as the Gurū arrived here from Jambar in the north, he met a poor peasant, Hemā, at a well just outside the village and asked him for water to drink. Bhāī Hemā said, "The water of this well is brackish and not fit to drink. But I shall run to the village and fetch sweet water for you." "No, brother," said the Gurū, "You should not take the trouble. The water of this well would do." It is said that the water drawn from the well was found to be sweet. Hemā fell at the Gurū's feet and sought instruction.

Gurdwārā Pātshāhī V marked the site where the Gurū had sojourned. The building raised during the 1930's comprised a flat-roofed hall with a verandah in front, inside a walled compound entered through a high gateway. The Gurdwārā was administered by the Shiromaṇī Gurdwārā Parbandhak Committee, Amritsar, through a local committee. A largely-attended annual fair used to be held on the occasion of Poh *sudī* 7, the birth anniversary of Gurū Gobind Siṅgh, falling in December-January. The Gurdwārā was abandoned in the wake of migrations caused by the partition of the Punjab in 1947.

M.G.S.

BAHOṚĀ, BHĀĪ, a goldsmith, who once came to Goindvāl to see Gurū Arjan and seek his blessing. He confessed to the Gurū that he cheated his customers skimping their gold, and asked what other calling he should turn to. The Gurū said, "Do not cheat, do not steal and then every calling is blessed.

Earn your living by honest labour and share what you earn with others in God's name. Go back to your home, absorb yourself in God's praise and run a community kitchen for the needy." Bahoṛā became a devoted disciple, and is remembered in Sikh tradition with honour.

BIBLIOGRAPHY

1. Santokh Siṅgh, Bhāī, *Srī Gur Pratāp Sūraj Granth*. Amritsar, 1926-37
2. Bhallā, Sarūp Dās, *Mahimā Prakāsh*. Patiala, 1971

T.S.

BAHOṚŪ, BHĀĪ, a Khoslā Khatrī of Lahore, received initiation at the hands of Gurū Arjan. As Bhāī Bidhī Chand in Gurū Hargobind's time went to Lahore to rescue the second of the two horses belonging to Bhāī Karoṛī, a horse-dealer of Kābul, who was bringing the pair as an offering for the Gurū but which had been forcibly taken away by the *faujdār*, Qāsim Beg of Lahore, he stayed with Bhāī Bahoṛū. The latter, a cloth-merchant by profession, provided garments for Bhāī Bidhī Chand to disguise himself as an astrologer in order to beguile the *faujdār* and his servants, and recover the horse.

BIBLIOGRAPHY

1. Giān Siṅgh, Giānī, *Twārīkh Gurū Khālsā*. Patiala, 1970
2. *Gurbilās Chhevīṅ Pātshāhī*. Patiala, 1970

T.S.

BAHR UL-MAWWĀJ (lit. stormy or tempestuous sea), also known as *Akhbār us-Salātīn*, is a comprehensive work on Muslim history divided into nine parts and 49 sections fancifully called *bahr* (sea) and waves (*mauj*) respectively, and hence the title. Its last part divided into six sections deals with Indian Timurides (i.e. the Mughals), with an account of Nādir Shāh and the Durrānīs down to 1796. Sir Henry Miers Elliot (1808-53) found a copy of the manuscript in the Library of the Rājā of Banāras. Other copies condensed into three volumes are available in Oriental Public (Khudā Bakhsh) Library, Bāṅkīpur Paṭnā; Preussische Staatsbibliothek, Berlin; and British Library, London. The author, Muhammad 'Alī Ansārī (d. 1827), also wrote another book, *Tārīkh-i-Muzaffarī* which is at places a word-for-word copy of the last part of *Bahr ul-Mawwāj*, but with many details added to the earlier text. References relevant to the Punjab and to Sikh history include martyrdom of the sons of Gurū Gobind Siṅgh; practices of the Sikhs; Mughal campaign against Bandā Siṅgh Bahādur; struggle between the sons of Zakarīyā Khān; Vaḍḍā Ghallūghārā or the holocaust of 1762; Sikhs' relations with Zābitā Khān Ruhīlā ; and the unsuccessful expedition of 'Abdul Ahd Khān against the cis-Sutlej Sikh chiefs in 1779.

S.H.A.

BAIHBAL KALĀṄ or Bahibal Kalāṅ, village 12 km southeast of Koṭ Kapūrā (30° - 35'N, 74° - 49'E) in Farīdkoṭ district of the Punjab, claims a historical *gurdwārā* in memory of Gurū Gobind Siṅgh who halted here for a short while during his westward journey in December 1705. The shrine, built on the top of a small mound (*ṭibbī*, in Punjabi) north of the village is known as Gurdwārā Ṭibbī Sāhib. It has a marble-floored *dīvān* hall, with a domed sanctum in the middle. The Gurdwārā owns 60 acres of land and is controlled by Nihaṅgs belonging to the Buḍḍhā Dal.

BIBLIOGRAPHY

1. Fauja Singh, ed., *Travels of Guru Gobind Singh*. Patiala, 1968
2. Ṭhākar Siṅgh, Giānī, *Srī Gurduāre Darshan*. Amritsar, 1923
3. Tārā Siṅgh, *Srī Gur Tīrath Saṅgrahi*. Amritsar, n.d.
4. *Mālvā Desh Raṭan dī Sākhi Pothī*. Amritsar, 1968

M.G.S.

BAINTĀṄ SHER SIṄGH KĪĀṄ, by Nihāl Siṅgh, is a poem dealing with some gruesome events from the history of the Sikhs – murders in 1843 of the Sikh monarch Mahārājā Sher Siṅgh, his young son Partāp Siṅgh, and minister Dhiān Siṅgh Ḍogrā at the hands of Sandhāṅvālīā collaterals Ajīt Siṅgh and Lahiṇā Siṅgh, and of the latter at the hands of Dhiān Siṅgh's son, Hīrā Siṅgh, and his supporters. No biographical details about the poet are known, except that he was a witness to these tragic events. As he himself says in the text, he composed the poem, in the *baint* poetic measure, "at the time of the happenings" (34). These murders occurred on 15-16 September 1843, followed by Duleep Siṅgh's installation on the throne referred to in the poem (24). The poem does not mention any other event, not even the sequential murders of Hīrā Siṅgh and his confidant Paṇḍit Jallā which took place on 21 December 1844, leading to the presumption that it was composed immediately after Mahārājā Sher Siṅgh's assassination. According to the poet, the poem comprises thirty-four stanzas (but in fact it contains thirty-three), with a couplet each at the beginning and at the end: the poet seems to have counted the opening couplet among the stanzas: the concluding couplet barely records the date of the event (1 Assū, 1900 Bk/15 September 1843). All stanzas comprise eight lines each, except two (2 and 24) which have six lines apiece.

The poet traces Sher Siṅgh's unpopularity among the army to dismissal by him of some old soldiers a few among whom had been serving since the days of his grandfather. He gives the instance of a Nihaṅg, also recorded in Sohan Lāl Sūrī, *'Umdāt-ut-Twārīkh* (Daftar IV, Part III), who as a mark of protest gifted away his horse and spent the remaining years of his life like a recluse at the *samādh* of Haqīqat Rāi. Ajīt Siṅgh Sandhāṅvālīā treacherously kills Sher Siṅgh (8); Lahiṇā Siṅgh slays prince Partāp Siṅgh despite his pitiful pleadings (10). Both kill Ḍogrā Dhiān Siṅgh (13). Hīrā Siṅgh, the son of Dhiān Siṅgh, avenges the murder of his father by killing, with the support of the army, Ajīt Siṅgh (30) and Lahiṇā Siṅgh (31). The poet does not conceal his hatred of the Sandhāṅvālīās, but also gives them credit for their soldierly feats (26) when fighting against Hīrā Siṅgh Ḍogrā.

The poem does not possess many literary merits, but is significant being a contemporary account of these bloody events at the Lahore court.

D.S.

BAIRĀGĪS, or Vairāgīs, are a sect of Hindu ascetics, eschewing colour or passion and detached from all worldly allurements. Founded by Srī Anand, the 12th spiritual descendant of Rāmānand, the sect comprises a class of nomadic penitents, living a secluded life of extreme poverty, wearing minimum of clothing and living on begging. They cast ashes upon their long hair and rub their bodies over with these, too. The sect is divided into four different orders, viz. Rāmānandī, Viṣṇusvāmī, Nīmānandī and Mādhavachārya, of whom only Rāmānandī and Nīmānandī orders are found in the Punjab. The Rāmānandīs are, like Viṣṇusvāmīs, the devotees of Lord Rāma/Kṛṣṇa; they celebrate the 8th of Bhādoṅ as the date of incarnation of their deity, study and revere the *Bhāgavadgītā* as their scripture, and visit Vrindāvan, Dvārkā and Mathurā as places of pilgrimage. They, as a rule, abstain from flesh and drink, but lately some of them have begun to make an exception in the case of hemp. The Rāmānandīs among them have the trident marked, as their insignia, on their foreheads in white the central prong being sometimes in red also, whereas the Nīmānandīs wear all white, a two-pronged fork on their forehead, the shape signifying the figure of Nar Siṅgh, lit. man-lion, believed in Hindu mythology to be the incarnation of God who saved Bhakta Prahlād. They lived, for the most part, in monasteries and were for some time quite a respectable class of *faqīrs*, a few of them rising quite high in the social set-up as well. Baron Charles Hugel, the famous German traveller who visited northern India during the reign of Mahārājā Raṇjīt Siṅgh, mentions one Tāmū or Tāmū Shāh, who was the *wazīr*, i.e. minister, of the Rājā of Nandauṇ.

The Sikh texts espouse the householder's life rejecting renunciation, contain passages criticizing the life-style of the Bairāgīs. According to the Sikh point of view, a true Bairāgī is one who cultivates a sense of *bairāg*, i.e. detachment, towards the material world while still living the life of a common householder, adheres to high moral and ethical standards, and attunes himself completely to the Will of God, constantly meditating upon His name. "He who hath his mind fully in control call him alone a *bairāgī*," says Gurū Amar Dās, Nānak III (GG, 569).

BIBLIOGRAPHY

1. Crooke, W., *The Tribes and Castes of the North Western India*. Delhi, 1974
2. Rose, H.A., *A Glossary of the Tribes and Castes of the Punjab and North-West Frontier Province*. Patiala, 1970
3. Ghurye, G.S., *Indian Sadhus*. Bombay, 1964

B.S.N.

BAIRĀṚĪ. *See* SIKH DEVOTIONAL MUSIC

BAISĀKHĀ SIṄGH, DĪWĀN (d. 1844), soldier and administrator in the service of Mahārājā Raṇjīt Siṅgh, was the son of Dīwān Kāhn Siṅgh Chamiārīvālā. In 1831, he accompanied Kaṅvar Sher Siṅgh and General Ventura to Peshāwar to put down the tumult raised by Sayyid Ahmad Barelavī. When in 1832 Kaṅvar Sher Siṅgh was appointed governor of Kashmīr, Dīwān Baisākhā Siṅgh was attached to him as a special assistant. Owing to some complaints received against him, he was recalled to Lahore, tried for fraud, and fined 1,25,000 rupees. He regained the Darbār's favour in 1835 and was given an assignment which took him to Peshāwar. In 1844, he earned the displeasure of Rājā Hīrā Siṅgh, the prime minister, and fled Lahore to take refuge with Bhāī Bīr Siṅgh of Nauraṅgābād. He was captured by a force led by Mīāṅ Lābh Siṅgh and executed in May 1844.

BIBLIOGRAPHY

1. Griffin, Lepel, and C.F. Massy, *Chiefs and Families of Note in the Punjab*. Lahore, 1909
2. Sūrī, Sohan Lāl, *'Umdāt-ut-Twārīkh*, Lahore, 1885-89

G.S.Ch.

BAISĀKHĪ, a seasonal festival popular in the Punjab which takes place on the first day of the solar month of Baisākh (Sanskrit Vaiśākha, so called because according to astrological calculations, the moon at this time passes through *viśākhā nakṣatra* or constellation) of the Indian calendar. Traditionally, the festival was celebrated as the harbinger of happiness and plenty being closely connected with harvesting. To ward off malignant spirits ruinous to the harvest, a ritual dance preceded the festivities. In the central districts of Gujrāṅwālā, Siālkoṭ and Gurdāspur as also in parts of Jammū, the popular dance form was, and still is, *bhaṅgṛā*.

As some Sikh texts record, Gurū Nānak (1469-1539) was born during the month of Baisākh. According to Sarūp Dās Bhallā, *Mahimā Prakāsh*, Part 2, Gurū Amar Dās (1479-1574), at the suggestion of Sikhs led by Bhāī Pāro, started an annual congregational fair at Goindvāl on the occasion of Baisākhī. It became customary for distant *saṅgats* of Sikhs to assemble at the seat of the Gurūs on every Baisākhī (and Dīvālī) day. With the inauguration by Gurū Gobind Siṅgh of the Khālsā on 1 Baisākh 1756 Bk, Baisākhī became an important festival on the Sikh calendar. The date then corresponded with 30 March 1699, but owing to the adoption of Gregorian calendar by the British in 1752 and the difference between the Christian and the Bikramī years since then, Baisākhi now usually falls on 13 and sometimes on 14 April. The Sikhs everywhere celebrate Baisākhī enthusiastically as birthday anniversary of the K͟hālsā. *Akhaṇḍ pāṭhs* are recited followed by *kīrtan* and *ardās* in almost every *gurdwārā*. Community meals form part of the celebrations. At bigger centres congregational fairs, *amrit-prachār*, i.e. initiation ceremonies for inducting novitiates into the K͟hālsā fold, and contests in manly sports are held. Until the partition of the Punjab in 1947, the largest attended Baisākhī fairs were those of Pañjā Sāhib, in Aṭṭock district, and Eminābād, in Gujrāṅwālā (now both in Pakistan). The most important venues now are the Golden Temple, Amritsar, Tak͟ht Damdamā Sāhib at Talvaṇḍī Sābo, in Baṭhiṇḍā district, and Tak͟ht Kesgaṛh Sāhib, Anandpur Sāhib, in Ropaṛ district, all in the Punjab. It was at Kesgaṛh Fort that conversion of Sikhs into the K͟hālsā through the administration of *khaṇḍe dī pāhul*, or baptism of the double-edged sword, first took place on the Baisākhī day of 1699.

BIBLIOGRAPHY

1. Kapur Singh, *Pārāśarapraśna*. Amritsar, 1989
2. Cole, W. Owen, and Piara Singh Sambhi, *The Sikhs: Their Religious Beliefs and Practices*. Delhi, 1978

S.S.V.B.

BĀJAK, village 30 km southwest of Baṭhiṇḍā (30°-14'N, 74°-59'E), is sacred to Gurū Gobind Siṅgh, who visited it in 1706. The villagers turned out with pitchers full of milk to serve him as he arrived. However, Sukkhū and Buddhū, two *sādhūs* of the Divānā sect, came intent upon reprisal for the death of one of their group fatally wounded in an encounter with a Sikh. But as soon as their eyes fell on the Gurū, anger was gone out of their hearts. They, says the *Sākhī Pothī*, made obeisance before him and carried him in a palanquin for some distance as he departed. GURDWĀRĀ PĀTSHĀHĪ 10, commemorating Gurū Gobind Siṅgh's visit, is at the south-western edge of the village. In the middle of a walled compound, entered through a gateway with rooms on either side, is the 8-metre square *dīvān* hall in front of the flat-roofed sanctum. The 60-metre square *sarovar* is at the back in a separate compound. A local committee administers the Gurdwārā under the auspices of the Shiromaṇī Gurdwārā Parbandhak Committee. Besides the daily services, special congregations take place on every new-moon day and on all major Sikh anniversaries.

BIBLIOGRAPHY

1. Ṭhākar Siṅgh, Giānī, *Sri Gurduāre Darshan*. Amritsar, 1923
2. *Mālvā Desh Raṭan dī Sākhī Pothī*. Amritsar, 1968

M.G.S.

BĀJ SIṄGH (d. 1716), a Bal Jaṭṭ, was a native of Mīrpur Paṭṭī, a village in Amritsar district of the Punjab. A devoted Sikh, Bāj Siṅgh had received the rites of initiation at the hands of Gurū Gobind Siṅgh himself. He accompanied the Gurū to the Deccan in 1708 and was one of the five Sikhs sent by him to the Punjab with Bandā Siṅgh Bahādur. He took part in all of Bandā Siṅgh's major campaigns. For his fearlessness in battle, he came to be known as Bāj Bahādur (*bahādur*, lit. brave). In the battle of Sirhind fought at Chappar Chiṛī in May 1710, Bāj Siṅgh was in command of the right wing of Bandā Siṅgh's army. He faced Nawāb Wazīr K͟hān in the battle striking his horse down with a lance. As the battle was won, Bāj Siṅgh was named administrator of the town. Bāj Siṅgh was captured at Gurdās-Naṅgal in December 1715 and taken to Delhi where he was executed in June 1716 along with Bandā Siṅgh and his other companions.

BIBLIOGRAPHY

1. Bhaṅgū, Ratan Siṅgh, *Prāchīn Paṅth Prakāsh*. Amritsar, 1962
2. Giān Siṅgh, Giānī, *Twārīkh Gurū Khālsā*. Patiala, 1970
3. Ganda Singh, *Banda Singh Bahadur*. Amritsar, 1935

G.S.D.

BAKĀPUR DĪVĀN, a largely attended religious assembly (*dīvān*) of the Sikhs, held on 13-14 June 1903 at Bakāpur, a small village 3 km from Phillaur railway station in the Punjab, marked a high point in Siṅgh Sabhā resurgence. The occasion was the conversion to Sikhism of Maulawī Karīm Bakhsh, born a Muslim, and his family of four sons and a daughter. Some Hindus of that village as well as Sikhs from among the audience were also initiated on that day. The ceremony was marked by considerable fanfare. The sponsors were the Srī Gurū Siṅgh Sabhā, Bhasauṛ, which under the leadership of Bābū Tejā Siṅgh (1867-1933), then a sub-overseer in the irrigation department of Paṭiālā state, was very active in purifying Sikh ritual and establishing its autonomy. Assertion of self-identity was then the dominating impulse of the Sikh community as a whole. A sweeping religious fervour, a new sense of identity and unity, and a decisive breach with the recent past dominated by customs and practices contrary to the Gurūs' teaching were the characteristics of contemporary Sikhism. These were dramatically highlighted at the Bakāpur *dīvān*.

A Shuddhī Sabhā had been established by Dr Jai Siṅgh in Lahore on 17 April 1893 with the object of "reclaiming those Sikhs and Hindus who had apostatized themselves by contracting alliances with Muslim men or women." The Bhasauṛ Siṅgh Sabhā cavilled at the limited objective of the Shuddhī Sabhā and questioned its designation. From its very inception, the Bhasauṛ Siṅgh Sabhā had accepted for conversion Muslims and those from lower Hindu castes. At its first *dīvān* held in 1894, 13 Jaṭṭs, six Jhīvars (water-carriers), two barbers, one Khatrī and one Musalmān (Mīrāṅ Bakhsh of Tahsīl Gaṛhshaṅkar who became Nihāl Siṅgh) were initiated into the Sikh faith. As reported in the *Khālsā Akhbār*, 18 September 1896, Bābū Tejā Siṅgh himself published in the press a report of a subsequent year saying: "By the power of the Word revealed by the Ten Masters and in accord with Akālpurkh's wish, Srī Gurū Siṅgh Sabhā Bhasauṛ has administered the *gurmantra* and holy *amrit* to a Muslim woman and ushered her into Soḍhbaṅs (the Soḍhī clan or the family of Gurū Gobind Siṅgh). Her Sikh name is Kishan Kaur. A Sikh who had fallen by living with a Muslim woman has been baptized and renamed Ude Siṅgh."

The news about the Bakāpur family had reached Bhasauṛ through Bhāī Takht Siṅgh of Fīrozpur, a pioneer of women's education among Sikhs. This was corroborated by some other members of the Siṅgh Sabhā who supplied further details of Karīm Bakhsh's interest in Sikhism. The Sabhā decided to make its own investigations. Bhāī Kāhlā Siṅgh, a Sikh saint who made a secret visit to Bakāpur confirmed the story. This led the Sabhā to offer to convert the Bakāpur family at its annual *dīvān* of 1901, but it had to give up the plan owing to the outbreak of the plague epidemic. Karīm Bakhsh attended the large annual *dīvān* of the Sikhs at Bhasauṛ in 1902, but returned empty-handed owing to a controversy that had arisen.

The Bhasauṛ Siṅgh Sabhā sent its emissaries—Bhāī Tejā Siṅgh of Maiṅgaṇ, Sardār Bishan Siṅgh and Bhāī Takht Siṅgh—to visit Bakāpur by turns and assure Karīm Bakhsh that his heart's wish must be fulfilled. Finally, Bābū Tejā Siṅgh went himself. At Bakāpur, he learnt that Karīm Bakhsh's wife had passed away less than a week earlier and that the last rites had been performed strictly in accordance with the Sikh custom. There was the Gurū Granth Sāhib kept with true reverence in a room in the house and the Sikh *kīrtan* was performed daily.

On return, Bābū Tejā Siṅgh issued a public notice signifying that a *dīvān* of the K͟hālsā would be convened in the village of Bakāpur on 13-14 June 1903. The letter was sent on behalf of the Bhasauṛ Siṅgh Sabhā to all leading Sikh societies and individuals inviting them to participate in the proceedings. The letter included a note on the Bakāpur family and its zeal for the Sikh faith.

The invitation, widely circulated, evoked a warm response. On the appointed day, batches of Sikhs converged on Bakāpur from places such as Lahore, Amritsar, Gujrāṅwālā, Gujjark͟hān, Kaṭānī, Nāraṅgvāl and Ludhiāṇā. The elderly uncle of Sardār Sundar Siṅgh Majiṭhīā, Bābā Hīrā Siṅgh, led a *jathā* from the Amritsar K͟hālsā College. The group included Bhāī Jodh Siṅgh, distinguished Sikh theologian and educationist of modern times, who was then a student of the final B.A. class, Tārā Siṅgh, who had just joined college and who later became famous as a political leader of the Sikhs, and Mān Siṅgh, who rose to be the president of the judicial committee in the princely state of Farīdkoṭ. The youth were asked by Bābū Tejā Siṅgh to fetch water from the well and scrub the "premises clean of *musalmānī.*"

On the morning of the first day of the *dīvān*, Maulawī Karīm Bak͟hsh rose at 2 in the morning, made his ablutions and came to the site of the *dīvān*. He sat in a room rapt in meditation. The *Āsā kī Vār* was sung after which different *jathās* took turns at *kīrtan*, hymn-singing. They included the Siṅgh Sabhā of Gujjarvāl, Basant Siṅgh and Anūp Siṅgh of Nāraṅgvāl and the Youth League of Ludhiāṇā. For a while, a group of women led the *kīrtan*. Chanting of the sacred *śabdas* went on until it was time for Gurū kā Laṅgar, or community meal. The afternoon *dīvān* was addressed by Bābū Tejā Siṅgh, who explained the purpose of the convention and sought from the audience names of those who would wish to be initiated into the way of the K͟hālsā. The first one to volunteer was Basant Siṅgh, B.A., of the village of Nāraṅgvāl, in Ludhiāṇā district, who, after initiation, was named Raṇdhīr Siṅgh and who became famous as a revolutionary and, later, as a saintly personage of much sanctity among the Sikhs.

To conduct the initiation ceremonies the following day, the five Piyārās (or the Gurū's chosen ones) designated were Bhāī Tejā Siṅgh of Rāwalpiṇḍī, Bhāī Tak͟ht Siṅgh, Zindā Shahīd (Living Martyr), of Fīrozpur, Bhāī Basant Siṅgh of Bappiāṇā (Paṭiālā state), Bhāī Sohan Siṅgh of Gujjark͟hān and Bhāī Amar Siṅgh of Rājā Ghumān. Bhāī Jodh Siṅgh was named *granthī* for the ceremonies.

In all, 35 persons received the vows of the K͟hālsā the following morning (June 14). Maulawī Karīm Bak͟hsh, 43, was named Lakhbīr Siṅgh after initiation. His four sons Rukan Dīn, 15, Fateh Dīn, 12, G͟hulām Muhammad, 6, and K͟hair Dīn, 4, became Matāb Siṅgh, Kirpāl Siṅgh, Harnām Siṅgh and Gurbak͟hsh Siṅgh, respectively. His daughter Bībī Nūrāṅ, 9, was given the Sikh name of Varyām Kaur. Lakhbīr Siṅgh won wide esteem in the Sikh community as Sant Lakhbīr Siṅgh. His son, Matāb Siṅgh, founded a society called the K͟hālsā Barādarī and played a pioneer role in the Akālī movement, or the campaign for the reformation of the Sikh sacred places. Matāb Siṅgh's son, Gurcharan Siṅgh Sākhī, took his Bachelor's degree at the K͟hālsā College, Amrtisar, in 1941, and edited, among others, a Sikh religious journal until he died suddenly in the Golden Temple premises in 1973.

BIBLIOGRAPHY

1. Lāl Siṅgh, *Itihās Pañch K͟hālsā Dīvān Saṅbandhī Sūchnāvāṅ*. Ludhiana, 1967
2. *Vīr Sudhār Pattar : arthāt Srī Gurū Siṅgh Sabhā Bhasauṛ de aṭhme te naume sālāne dīvān dā siṭṭā.* Bhasauṛ, 1903

3. Jagjīt Siṅgh, *Siṅgh Sabhā Lahir*. Ludhiāṇā, 1974
4. Harbans Singh, "The Bakapur Diwan and Babu Teja Singh of Bhasaur," in *The Panjab Past and Present*. Patiala, October 1975

S.S.B.

BAKER, GEORGE, a Eurasian, who served as a drum-major in one of the battalions of Mahārājā Raṇjīt Siṅgh's army.

BIBLIOGRAPHY

Grey, C., *European Adventurers of Northern India*. Patiala, 1970

Gl.S.

BAKHSHĪSH SIṄGH, one of the Sikhs of Gurū Gobind Siṅgh's time who, as says Bhāī Santokh Siṅgh, *Srī Gur Pratāp Sūraj Granth*, received *amrit* or initiatory vows at the time of the creation of the Khālsā in 1699. He took part in the battles of Lohgaṛh and Nirmohgaṛh.

BIBLIOGRAPHY

Santokh Siṅgh, Bhāī, *Srī Gur Pratāp Sūraj Granth*. Amritsar, 1926-37

M.G.S.

BAKHT KAUR, MĀTĀ, also called Lakhmī or Lakkho, was the mother of Gurū Amar Dās (1479-1574). Mātā Lakkho is the name mentioned by Kesar Siṅgh Chibbar, *Baṅsāvalīnāmā Dasāṅ Pātshāhīāṅ Kā*. Born in a Duggal Khatrī family, she was married to Bābā Tej Bhān of Bāsarke Gillāṅ, a village 12 km southwest of Amritsar. Four sons were born to her, Gurū Amar Dās being the eldest. The other three were Īshar Dās, Khem Rāi and Mānak Chand.

BIBLIOGRAPHY

1. Chhibbar, Kesar Singh, *Baṅsāvalīṇāmā Dasāṅ Pātshāhīāṅ Kā*. Chandigarh, 1972
2. Giān Siṅgh, Giānī, *Twārīkh Gurū Khālsā* [Reprint]. Patiala, 1970
3. Macauliffe, Max Arthur, *The Sikh Religion*. Oxford, 1909

Hn.S.

BAKHT MALL and Tārā Chand, *masands* or accredited Sikh preachers in Kābul, once led the *saṅgat* of their area to the Punjab to wait on Gurū Hargobind (1595-1644). Among the offerings they brought were two pedigree horses of excelling beauty, named Gulbāgh and Dilbāgh. As they were passing through Lahore, the imperial governor seized the two horses for the royal stable. The *masands* along with the *saṅgat* caught up with Gurū Hargobind, then travelling across the Mālvā region, at Mahrāj and complained about the highhandedness of the Mughal authority. Bhāī Bidhī Chand retrieved the horses by stratagem. This led to a clash of arms occurring at Mahrāj on 16 December 1634.

See BIDHĪ CHAND, BHĀĪ

BIBLIOGRAPHY

1. *Gurbilās Chhevīṅ Pātshāhī*. Patiala, 1970
2. Bhallā, Sarūp Dās, *Mahimā Prakāsh*. Patiala, 1971
3. Giān Siṅgh, *Giānī, Twārīkh Gurū Khālsā*. Patiala, 1970
4. Macauliffe, Max Arthur, *The Sikh Religion*. Oxford, 1909

B.S.

BĀLĀ, BHĀĪ (1466-1544), who, according to popular belief, was a life-long companion of Gurū Nānak, was the son of Chandar Bhān, a Sandhū Jaṭṭ of Talvaṇḍī Rāi Bhoi, now Nankāṇā Sāhib in Pakistan. Three years senior in age to Gurū Nānak, he was his childhood playmate in Talvaṇḍī. From Talvaṇḍī, he accompanied Gurū Nānak to Sultānpur where he stayed with him a considerable period of time before returning to his village. According to *Bālā Janam Sākhī*, Bhāī Bālā at the instance of Rāi Bulār set out from Talvaṇḍī to join Gurū Nānak who had already left Sultānpur on his travels abroad and met him in Bhāī Lālo's home at Saidpur. After Gurū Nānak's passing away, Gurū Aṅgad, Nānak II, invited Bālā from his native Talvaṇḍī to come to Khaḍūr and narrate to him events from the First Gurū's life. Very graphic, if somewhat miraculous, is the version contained in an old text, the *Mahimā Prakāsh.* To quote: "Gurū Aṅgad one day spoke to Bhāī Buḍḍhā, 'Seek the disciple who accompanied the Master, Gurū Nānak, on his journeys far and wide, who heard his preaching and reflected on it, and who witnessed the many strange events that occurred; secure from him all the circumstances and have transcribed a volume which may please the hearts of those who should apply themselves to it.' Bālā Sandhū made his appearance." The anecdotes narrated by Bālā were recorded in Gurmukhī characters in Gurū Aṅgad's presence by another Sikh, Paiṛā Mokhā. The result was what is known as *Bhāī Bāle Vālī Janam Sākhī,* a hagiographical account of Gurū Nānak's life. Bhāī Bālā died in 1544 at Khaḍūr Sāhib. A memorial platform, within the precincts of Gurdwārā Tapiāṇā Sāhib, marks the site where his mortal remains were cremated.

Among modern researchers, the identity of Bhāī Bālā is as controversial as is the authenticity of the Janam Sākhī ascribed to him. Bhāī Bālā is mentioned neither by Bhāī Gurdās who has recorded the names of a number of Sikhs contemporary of Gurū Nānak, nor by the authors of *Purātan Janam Sākhī* and *Miharbān Janam Sākhī,* both older than *Bālā Janam Sākhī,* the oldest available manuscript of which is dated 1658. However, owing to the popularity the last-named Janam Sākhī has attained and the fact that the 19th-century chroniclers such as Bhāī Santokh Siṅgh and Giānī Giān Siṅgh have relied on it more than on any other, the name of Bhāī Bālā is firmly established in Sikh lore.

BIBLIOGRAPHY

1. Macauliffe, Max Arthur, *The Sikh Religion.* Oxford, 1909
2. McLeod, W.H., *Gurū Nānak and the Sikh Religion.* Oxford, 1968
3. Harbans Singh, *Guru Nanak and Origins of the Sikh Faith.* Bombay, 1969
4. Kirpāl Singh, *Janam Sākhī Pramparā.* Patiala, 1969

Gn. S.

BĀLĀ, BHĀĪ, whose name occurs in Bhāī Gurdās, *Vārāṅ,* XI. 19, embraced the Sikh faith in the time of Gurū Arjan. As reports Bhāī Manī Siṅgh, *Sikhāṅ dī Bhagat Mālā,* he and his companions Mūlā, Sujā, Chandū, Rām Dās Bhaṇḍārī and SāīṅDās received instruction at the hands of Gurū Arjan.

BIBLIOGRAPHY

1. Manī Siṅgh, Bhāī, *Sikhāṅ dī Bhagat Mālā.* Amritsar, 1955
2. Santokh Siṅgh, Bhāī, *Srī Gur Pratāp Sūraj Granth.* Amritsar, 1926-37

T.S.

BALĀCHAUR, a village about 11 km northeast of Jagādhrī (30° - 10'N, 77° - 18'E) in Ambālā district of Haryāṇā, claims a historical shrine known as Gurdwārā Āgampurā dedicated to Gurū Gobind Siṅgh. Gurū Gobind Siṅgh visited the place travelling from Kapāl Mochan in 1688. The old shrine, a 4.5 metre square room with a low conical dome over it, built in his honour, has recently been enclosed in a larger rectangular hall. The Gurū Granth Sāhib is installed in the inner sanctum. The Gurdwārā is managed by a local committee under the auspices of the Shiromaṇī Gurdwārā Parbandhak Committee.

BIBLIOGRAPHY

Fauja Singh, ed. *Travels of Guru Gobind Singh.* Patiala, 1968

Jg.S.

BĀLĀ JANAM SĀKHĪ. The Janam Sākhīs of the Bālā tradition owe both their name and their reputation to Bhāī Bālā, a Sandhū Jaṭṭ from Gurū Nānak's village of Talvaṇḍī. According to the tradition's own claims, Bālā was a near contemporary of Gurū Nānak who accompanied him during his period in Sultānpur and during the course of his extensive travels. If these claims are correct and if in fact the eponymous tradition records the authentic narrative of such a man, it must follow that the Bālā Janam Sākhīs provide an essentially trustworthy account of the early life of Gurū Nānak. For more than a hundred years, from the late eighteenth until the early twentieth century, this claim was scarcely challenged. During the course of the present century it has been vigorously assaulted, without being wholly demolished. To this day popular portraits of the Gurū, flanked by Mardānā the minstrel and Bālā the attendant, testify to a continuing acceptance of its claims.

The tradition's claims to eye-witness authenticity are set forth at the beginning of all Bālā Janam Sākhīs. The earliest extant version opens as follows:

> In the year Sammat fifteen hundred and eighty-two, S.1582 [AD 1525] on the fifth day of the bright half of the month of Vaisākh, Paiṛā Mokhā, a Khatrī of Sultānpur, wrote this book. Gurū Aṅgad commanded that it be written. Paiṛā recorded the dictation of Bālā, a Sandhū Jaṭṭ who had come from Talvaṇḍī, the village of Rāi Bhoi. He had come in search of Gurū Aṅgad. The recording of his narrative took two months and seventeen days to complete. All the facts and all the places visited by Gurū Nānakjī were faithfully and fluently described by Bhāī Bālā, with the result that Gurū Aṅgad was greatly pleased with him. Bhāī Bālā and Mardānā, the Bard, accompanied Bābā Nānak on his travels and Bhāī Bālā was with him during the period he spent at the commissariat (of Daulat Khān in Sultānpur).

The text then relates the circumstances which brought Bālā to Gurū Nānak's successor, Gurū Aṅgad, who was at that time residing in the village of Khaḍūr. Gurū Aṅgad who previously knew nothing of Bālā,was one day reflecting on the fact that he did not know the date of Gurū Nānak's birth. Bālā, having only recently discovered the identity and abode of Gurū Nānak's successor, conveniently arrived in Khaḍūr and agreed to bring the first Gurū's horoscope from Talvaṇḍī. When he returned after locating the vital document, Paiṛā Mokhā was deputed to transcribe it. The process of transcription immediately becomes one of dictation as the horoscope, having served its purpose, is forgotten and the writer takes up Bālā's narrative. There then follows the lengthy collection of anecdotes which constitutes the earliest version of the *Bālā Janam Sākhī* tradition.

Two conflicting theories have been advanced to explain the origin of the earliest of the extant Bālā Janam Sākhīs. Neither accepts outright the text's own claim to represent an authentic narrative of the early life and travels of Gurū Nānak. Such an interpretation is rendered insupportable by the inconsistencies and fantasies which it provides in abundance.

The first theory does, however, affirm a modified version of the Bālā claim. Within the earliest text there are to be found references which are plainly traceable to the seventeenth-century Hindālī sect. These seek to denigrate Gurū Nānak at the expense of Bābā Hindāl, father of the sect's founder. Early in the nineteenth century, Bhāī Santokh Siṅgh suggested that these references were to be explained on the grounds that the original Janam Sākhī authentically dictated by Bhāī Bālā had been mischievously corrupted by Hindālī interpolations. A version of this theory is still current. The profuse legendary material is, it affirms, the product of interpolation. Behind it there lies an original and essentially reliable Janam Sākhī which may be restored by stripping away the extraneous content.

This theory is difficult to sustain in that a mere pruning, however drastic, cannot reduce any of the Bālā texts to a consistent narrative. The second theory takes account of Janam Sākhī as a typical seventeenth-century product, a composite work incorporating the results of a lengthy period of oral growth and transmission. Other extant Janam Sākhīs demonstrate the same process. The Bālā tradition differs in its wealth of fantasy and in its attempt to establish authenticity by the contrived introduction of an eye-witness narrator. Its actual composition may have been the work of the Hindālīs; or a seventeenth-century text may have been interpolated by them in the manner suggested by Santokh Siṅgh. Hindāl interest of some kind is plainly evident in all early manuscripts of the Bālā tradition.

This leaves unsolved the problem of Bālā's identity. It may be safely affirmed that no person of this name could have been the constant companion of Gurū Nānak as none of the other early traditions refer to him. This omission is particularly noteworthy in the case of Bhāī Gurdās. It would, however, be going too far to deny his existence entirely. Bālā Sandhū may well have been a real person.

Although the second of the theories outlined above reduces the *Bālā* tradition to the level of other early Janam Sākhīs it does nothing to minimize the importance of the tradition in later Sikh history. *Bālā* primacy had been firmly established by the end of the eighteenth century and its hold upon nineteenth-century affections is clearly demonstrated by the degree to which such writers as Santokh Siṅgh, Sant Reṇ, and Bhāī Bahilo rely on it. When the introduction of printing produced a spectacular expansion of recorded Janam Sākhī materials, the growth was almost wholly monopolized by the *Bālā* tradition. Many of the most treasured of all Janam Sākhī anecdotes derive from *Bālā* sources and, if today one asks for a Janam Sākhī in a bookshop, the volume which is produced will almost certainly be the twentieth-century *Bālā* version.

Amongst the numerous extant manuscripts of this tradition, two principal recensions are to be found. Whereas the earlier terminates the narrative prior to Gurū Nānak's death, the latter has Gurū Aṅgad relate this episode for Bhāī Bālā's benefit. In order to do so, the latter compiler has borrowed a death narrative from the *Miharbān* tradition. The oldest of the extant *Bālā* manuscripts is the earliest of all Janam Sākhī manuscripts of whatever tradition. It bears the date 1715 Bk/AD 1658 and is in a private collection in Delhi. *Pañjābī Hatth-likhtāṅ dī Sūchī* lists twenty-two *Bālā* manuscripts in the Punjab. Three are located in London and individual items are to be found in various other places.

Four editions have appeared since the printing press was first used for Janam Sākhīs in 1871. An edition lithographed by Hāfiz Qutab Dīn of Lahore in 1871 generally follows the earlier of the manuscript versions. Thereafter, however, there is progressive and substantial augmenting of the text, culminating in the letter-press version which has been current for most of the twentieth century.

A critical analysis of the linguistic characteristics of *Bālā* and *Purātan* Janam Sākhīs reveals that the language of the latter is older than that of the *Bālā* Janam Sākhī. Auxiliary verb which is conspicuous by its absence in the Gurū Granth Sāhib and has very low frequency in *Purātan*, appears in *Bālā* on the pattern of modern Punjabi. Many of the case-inflexions regularly used in the *Purātan* have disappeared in *Bālā*. Case-inflexions were a characteristic of the old language, which have been gradually giving way to the postpositions. Again in the use of nasalization, the language of *Purātan* is akin to that of the Gurū Granth Sāhib. Many of the verbal and nominal forms which contain nasalized vowels in *Bālā* (just as in modern Punjabi) are oral in the Gurū Granth Sāhib as well as in *Purātan Janam Sākhī*. The *Purātan* uses the older forms of the adverbs of time and place, whereas the *Bālā* employs the modern forms of the same adverbs. In general idiom, too, the language of the *Purātan Janam Sākhī* is certainly older than the language of *Bālā Janam Sākhī*.

BIBLIOGRAPHY

1. Mcleod, W.H. *Early Sikh Tradition*. Oxford, 1980
2. Kirpāl Siṅgh, *Janam Sākhī Pramparā*. Patiala, 1969
3. Kohlī, Surindar Siṅgh, ed. *Janamsākhī Bhāī Bālā*. Chandigarh, 1975

W.H.M.

BĀLĀ JHIṅGAṆ, a learned Brāhmaṇ who was known for his skill in debate and discourse. Accompanied by another learned Brāhmaṇ, Kishnā, of the same Jhiṅgaṇ subcaste, he visited Guru Arjan. Both confessed to the Gurū that despite their knowledge of the sacred texts and despite their ability to sway their audiences with their erudition, they had obtained little spiritual advantage. The Gurū, as says Bhāī Manī Siṅgh, *Sikhāṅ dī Bhagat Mālā*, advised them to address their preachings to themselves and act on those preachings. They fell at the Gurū's feet and took to his teaching. They became ardent preachers of the Sikh faith.

BIBLIOGRAPHY

Manī Siṅgh, Bhāī, *Sikhāṅ dī Bhagat Mālā*. Amritsar, 1955

T.S.

BĀLAK SIṅGH, BĀBĀ (1785-1862), mentor of Bābā Rām Siṅgh, acknowledged to be the forerunner of the Nāmdhārī movement, was born in 1841 Bk/AD 1785 to Diāl Siṅgh and Mātā Bhāg Bharī, in an Aroṛā family of village Chhoī in Attock district, in Rāwalpiṇḍī division, now in Pakistan. Bālak Siṅgh took from a young age to the family business of providing supplies to the garrison in the fort at Hazro, close to his native village. He was married to Māī Totī. No more biographical information is available about him except that he was a man of religious disposition and while at Hazro he was deeply influenced by Bhagat Jawāhar Mall. He soon attracted followers from among the inhabitants of Hazro and from among the garrison in the fort. Bābā Rām Siṅgh (*q.v.*), who succeeded him as head of the sect, was one of the garrison here. His study of Sikh history and letters made him well aware of the rot that was at the time corroding Sikh society. He took upon himself to lead a campaign against the evil and corruption of the tenet that had set in. His religious and social ideas were shaped by the teaching of Bābā Bālak Siṅgh, though the political edge his movement eventually acquired can only be traced to the advanced precept of Bhāī Mahārāj Siṅgh (d. 1856).

The religious and ethical code of conduct preached by Bābā Bālak Siṅgh for his followers included constant meditation on the Transcendental Reality; bathing at least thrice daily; not to use a leather bucket for drinking water; performing marriage rites according to the Anand ceremony; offering as sacrament *kaṛāhprasād* worth one and a quarter rupee every month; and not to eat food cooked by anyone outside of the Sikh faith. Giving of dowry, meat-eating and use of alcohol were totally prohibited. Honest labour and truth-telling were the virtues prized most.

Bābā Bālak Siṅgh built at Hazro a place where his followers used to meet regularly. It was here that Bābā Rām Siṅgh, who had earlier moved southwards with the garrison, came to meet his spiritual mentor around 1860 and sought permission to instruct the people in his doctrine. Prominent among his other disciples were Bhāī Kāhn Siṅgh, a son of his brother Mannā Siṅgh, and Bhāī Lāl Siṅgh. The former is said to have occupied the *gaddī* at Hazro and the latter preached in the Amritsar area.

Bābā Bālak Siṅgh died at Hazro on Saturday, Maghar *sudī* 15, 1919 Bk/6 December 1862.

BIBLIOGRAPHY

1. Vahimī, Taran Siṅgh, *Jass Jīvan*. Rampur (Hissar), 1971
2. Gaṇḍā Siṅgh, *Kūkiāṅ dī Vithiā*. Amritsar, 1944
3. Fauja Singh, *Kuka Movement*. Delhi, 1965
4. Jolly, Surjit Kaur, *Sikh Revivalist Movements*. Delhi, 1988

D.S.

BĀLĀ MARVĀHĀ, a devoted Sikh of the time of Gurū Arjan. He served diligently as the Harimandar at Amritsar was under construction. Once, as says Bhāī Manī Siṅgh, *Sikhāṅ dī Bhagat Mālā*, Bhāī Bālā, along with Bhāī Hamzā Jajjā, Bhāī Nānoṅ Ohrī and Bhāī Sūrī Chaudharī, went up to the Gurū and begged him to explain the greatness and significance of Amritsar. The Gurū said that Amritsar would remain of utmost sanctity for the Sikhs.

BIBLIOGRAPHY

Manī Siṅgh, Bhāī, *Sikhāṅ dī Bhagat Mālā*. Amritsar, 1955

T.S.

BALBĪR SIṄGH, RĀJĀ (1869-1906), born on 30 August 1869, the son of Rājā Bikram Siṅgh, ascended the throne of Farīdkoṭ state on 16 December 1898. He ruled for barely eight years, yet his reign was marked by new buildings such as the Victoria Memorial Clock Tower and the Rāj Mahal he constructed and the gardens he had laid out in Farīdkoṭ. He also did much to develop and promote the breeding of horses and cattle in the state. The first three of the four volumes of the monumental *Faridkoṭ Ṭīkā*, a full-scale commentary in Punjabi on the Gurū Granth Sāhib prepared by a synod of Sikh scholars appointed by his father Rājā Bikram Siṅgh, were published during his time.

Rājā Balbīr Siṅgh died in February 1906 and the succession passed on to his adopted son, Brijinder Siṅgh.

BIBLIOGRAPHY

1. Griffin, Lepel, *The Rajas of the Punjab*. Delhi, 1977
2. Ganda Singh, *The Patiala and the East Panjab States Union : Historical Background*. Patiala, 1951
3. Harbaṅs Siṅgh, *Farīdkoṭ Itihās Bāre*. Faridkot, 1947

S.S.B.

BALDEV SIṄGH (1902-1961), industrialist, politician and the first Defence Minister of India at Independence was born on 11 July 1902, of a Sikh family of Chokar Jaṭṭs at the village of Ḍummṇā, in Ropaṛ district of the Punjab. His father, Inder Siṅgh, who started life as a government official in the Central Provinces (now Madhya Pradesh), later became a contractor and ultimately rose to be a steel magnate at Jamshedpur, in Bihār. Baldev Siṅgh, after his education at Ambālā and then at K͟hālsā College, Amritsar, joined his father's firm as a director. Returning to the Punjab during the mid-1930's, he made his debut in politics when he became a candidate in the first elections to the provincial assembly under the Government of India Act, 1935, held in early 1937. The family's philanthropic work in the district, especially in the field of education, earned him popular support and he won as a candidate of the Panthic (Akālī) Party, a combination of Akālī and Nationalist Sikhs. He along with Master Tārā Siṅgh, Sir Jogendra Siṅgh and Sardār Ujjal Siṅgh was chosen to represent the Sikh community before the Cripps Mission which came out to India in the spring of 1942 on behalf of the British War Cabinet with proposals for the country's political future. In June 1942, there was an understanding between Sir Sikandar Hayāt K͟hān, Premier of the Punjab, and the Akālīs, who were invited to join the coalition government headed by him. As a result of what came to be known as the Sikandar-Baldev Pact, Baldev Siṅgh was sworn in as Development Minister on 26 June 1942. He retained his position in the Punjab cabinet until, after the death of Sir Sikandar in December 1942, a new ministry was formed under Malik Khizar Hayāt Khān Ṭiwāṇā. When a British Cabinet Mission visited India in 1946 to negotiate with Indian leaders about the future constitution of the country, Baldev Siṅgh was chosen a member of the delegation to present to it the Sikh viewpoint. He also met the Mission separately to seek special protection for the Sikhs. He favoured a united India with safeguards for the minorities, but, if partition of the country as insisted on by the Muslim League became inevitable, he wanted redemarcation of the boundaries of the Punjab, slicing off the Muslim-dominated divisions of Rāwalpiṇḍī and Multān to secure the Sikhs the balance of power in the remaining Punjab.

On 16 May 1946, the Cabinet Mission put forward a plan which, retaining the semblance of a central structure, conceded substantially the Muslim claim for autonomy, without any special safeguards for Sikhs. The Sikhs rejected the scheme at an assembly held at Amritsar on 9 and 10 June 1946 and set up a representative body called the Panthic Pratinidhi Board to resist its implementation. Baldev Siṅgh was one of the members of the Board. On Jawāharlāl Nehrū's appeal, the Panthic Board, at their meeting on 14 August 1946, while reiterating that the Cabinet Mission scheme was unjust to Sikhs, retracted their boycott of it. Baldev Siṅgh joined the Cabinet headed by Jawāharlāl Nehrū as the Sikhs' nominee on 2 September 1946. He took over the defence portfolio which had, throughout the British rule, been held by the British Commander-in-Chief, who had been, in order of precedence, next only to the Viceroy and Governor-General of India. The Indian Army (as also the Navy and the Air Force) had been organized and trained as a colonial force controlled, except at the bottom rungs, by British officers. That position had now to change. The Commander-in-Chief had to be under an Indian civilian minister of defence. Baldev Siṅgh brought about the change with tact and firmness. In a radio broadcast on 9 October 1946, he enunciated the policy of the Interim National Government in these words : "We aim at building up, in a truly national way, a National Army, which will be the pride of this great land of ours. It is indeed our right to have our armed forces completely Indianised. Nobody disputes that right. Indianisation of the armed forces will now be speeded up at an accelerated pace, compatible with efficiency, and our only concern will be to maintain and better the excellence of the standard you yourselves have built up." Referring to British officers he said, "We have at present many British officers who have served the Army loyally and faithfully. It is nobody's desire that in achieving our objective we be unjust to them. They and others before them have contributed greatly in fashioning the steel that is the envy of others. I have every hope that their help and co-operation in the great task of Indianisation will be available now, as in the past. We shall value their talent and their co-operation as ever before."

Independence accompanied by partition of the country into India and Pakistan brought in its wake the second biggest task for the Defence Minister, viz. the division of personnel, equipment and military installations between the two countries, and provision of escorting convoys of refugees from and to Pakistan. New challenges came with the Pakistan-aided invasion of Kashmīr and police actions in Jūnāgaṛh and Hyderābād. Baldev Siṅgh was not only a member of the Congress government, but was also a leading representative of his community which brought in its train further responsibilities. He failed to get the realization of past promises and assurances given by the Congress regarding constitutional guarantees for the protection of the rights of the Sikhs as a minority community. In the first general election held under the Constitution in 1952, he was elected to Indian Parliament (Lok Sabhā) on Congress nomination (without opposition from the Akālīs), but was not included in the Cabinet by Prime Minister, Jawāharlāl Nehrū. He was re-elected to Parliament in 1957. His health began to deteriorate and after a prolonged illness he died in Delhi on 29 June 1961. His body was flown to his native village where he was cremated with full military honours.

BIBLIOGRAPHY

1. Khushwant Singh, *A History of the Sikhs*, vol. 2. Princeton, 1966
2. Gopal Singh, *A History of the Sikh People (1469-1978)*. Delhi, 1979

K.S.

BALH. *See* BHAṬṬ BĀṆĪ

BALLŪ, son of Mūlā, was the grandfather of Bhāī Manī Rām of 'Alīpur, in Multān district, whose five sons were distinguished warriors in the retinue of Gurū Gobind Siṅgh (1666-1708). According to *Bhaṭṭ Vahī Multānī Sindhī*, Ballū himself was a retainer of Gurū Hargobind (1595-1644). He died fighting for the Gurū in the battle of Amritsar fought on 14 April 1634.

BIBLIOGRAPHY

Padam, Piārā Siṅgh, and Giānī Garjā Siṅgh, eds., *Gurū kīāṅ Sākhīāṅ*. Patiala, 1986

Gn.S.

BALLŪ, BHĀĪ, a barber who embraced the Sikh faith at the hands of Gurū Aṅgad came into prominence in the time of Gurū Amar Dās. When Gurū Amar Dās, after being consecrated Gurū by Gurū Aṅgad, retired to Goindvāl and shut himself in a room to meditate in seclusion, Bhāī Ballū, at the instance of *saṅgat*, anxious for a sight of the Gurū, persuaded him to come out of his solitude. Ballū accompanied the Gurū during visits to Kurukshetra and Haridvār. According to Sarūp Dās Bhallā, *Mahimā Prakāsh*, when Gurū Amar Dās composed the famous hymn, *Anandu*, on the occasion of the birth of his grandson, Anand, Bhāī Ballū sang it at his command to the beat of a drum. He also joined hands with Bhāī Pāro in inaugurating, with the Gurū's approval, an annual fair at Goindvāl to celebrate Baisākhī. Lastly, when Emperor Akbar met Gurū Amar Dās and wanted to make an endowment for Gurū kā Laṅgar, an offer politely turned down by the Gurū, it was at Bhāī Ballū's suggestion that the emperor made a gift of some land to the Gurū's daughter, Bībī Bhānī. It was on this site that the holy city of Amritsar was laid out by the third Gurū's successor, Gurū Rām Dās, Nānak IV.

BIBLIOGRAPHY

1. Bhallā, Sarūp Dās, *Mahimā Prakāsh*. Patiala, 1971
2. Giān Siṅgh, Giānī, *Twārī<u>kh</u> Gurū <u>Kh</u>ālsā*. Patiala, 1970
3. Macauliffe, Max Arthur, *The Sikh Religion*. Oxford, 1909

B.S.D.

BĀLŪ HASNĀ (1564-1660), Sikh preacher and the first head of a *dhūāṅ* or branch of the Udāsī sect, was born the son of Paṇḍit Hardatt and Māī Prabhā of Srīnagar (Kashmīr) on 13 November 1564. His original name was Bālū. Accompanying his elder brother, Ālū, better known as Bhāī Almast, he came to Amritsar in 1604, to receive instruction from Gurū Arjan. He devoted himself to the service of the Gurū. Of Gurū Hargobind he was a constant companion. Even when the Gurū went out for the chase, Bālū would trot along on foot with him.

Happy-go-lucky by temperament, he always bore a smile on his face so that the Gurū gave him the appellation of Hasnā, lit. the laughing one. At the instance of Gurū Hargobind, Bhāī Bālū Hasnā joined Bābā Gurdittā, the Gurū's eldest son and the spiritual successor of Bābā Srī Chand, founder of the Udāsī sect. Bābā Gurdittā deputed him to preach the tenets of Sikhism in the Poṭhohār region (northwestern Punjab) to which task he dedicated the remaining years of his life.

Bālū Hasnā passed away at Peshāwar on 2 December 1660. His disciples carried on his work in western and southern Punjab, North-West Frontier Province and Sindh. Two of them, Bhāī Lāl Dās Daryāī and Bhāī Jādo Rāi, both Punjabi poets of merit, are said to have accompanied Gurū Gobind Siṅgh to the South. Bhāī Lāl Dās took the baptism of the Khālsā and was renamed Prahilād Siṅgh. One of the *rahitnāmās* or the Sikh codes of conduct is ascribed to him. Another of the followers of Bhāī Bālū Hasnā, Ūdho Dās, served Mātā Pañjāb Kaur, the widow of Bābā Rām Rāi, at Dehrā Dūn, and succeeded to the *gaddī* or seat after her death in April 1741. He constructed at Dehrā Dūn a *samādh* or mausoleum commemorating Bhāī Bālū Hasnā.

BIBLIOGRAPHY

1. Raṇdhīr Siṅgh, Bhāī, *Udāsī Sikhāṅ dī Vithīā*. Amritsar, 1959
2. *Gurbilās Chhevīṅ Pātshāhī*. Patiala, 1970

P.S.P.

BALVAṆḌ, RĀI, a *rabābī* or rebeck-player in the time of Gurū Arjan and co-composer with Sattā, said to be his brother, of a *Vār* included in the Gurū Granth Sāhib in the Rāmkalī musical measure. He was by birth a *mirāsī*, Muslim minstrel and genealogist, and sang the sacred hymns to the accompaniment of rebeck like Bhāī Mardānā used to do during the time of Gurū Nānak. Not much authentic biographical information is available about him except that he and his brother, Sattā, were contemporaries with Gurū Arjan (1563-1606) for whom they recited *śabda-kīrtan*. According to another tradition, they started their career under Gurū Aṅgad sometime after he succeeded Gurū Nānak on the latter's demise in 1539 and continued to serve the Gurūs until the time of Gurū Arjan.

Story is recorded that Balvaṇḍ had become so proud of his art that he once refused Bābā Buḍḍhā's request for the recital of a *śabda*. He was reprimanded by the Gurū and was told that he (the Gurū) was within every Sikh and refusing a Sikh to recite a hymn meant refusal to the Gurū himself. On another occasion, Balvaṇḍ is said to have requested Gurū Arjan to let him and Sattā have all the offerings of the Baisākhī day of that year so as to enable them to meet the expenses of a marriage in the family. The Gurū agreed. But the offerings on that day fell far short of their expectations. They asked the Gurū for more which he refused. Under the mistaken notion of their indispensability, both Sattā and Balvaṇḍ left the Gurū, imagining that once they stopped reciting the hymns his following would dwindle. Gurū Arjan sent for them, but they refused to return. When the Gurū himself called on them, they spoke rudely of the House of Gurū Nānak. Now discarded by the Gurū, they found themselves alienated from the Sikhs. They suffered both mental anguish and fell sick with leprosy. A Sikh, named Laddhā, petitioned the Gurū on their behalf and secured them forgiveness. Back in the presence of the Gurū, they were cured of the disease. They then composed a *Vār*, popularly known as *Ṭikke dī Vār*, in praise of the Gurūs. They perceived all the Gurūs as sharing the same spirit, the same one light.

Both Balvaṇḍ and Sattā are said to have passed away at Lahore in the time of Gurū Hargobind (1595-1644) and were buried on the bank of the River Rāvī. Bābak (d. 1692), Gurū Hargobind's Muslim *rabābī* performed their last rites.

BIBLIOGRAPHY

1. Bhallā, Sarūp Dās, *Mahimā Prakāsh*. Patiala, 1970
2. Santokh Siṅgh, Bhāī, *Srī Gur Pratāp Sūraj Granth*. Amritsar, 1926-37
3. Vīr Siṅgh, Bhāī, *Srī Aṣṭ Gur Chamatkār*. Amritsar, 1952

F.S.

BALVANT SIṄGH CANADIAN (1882-1917), a prominent figure in the G͟hadr movement, was born on 14 September 1882 at K͟hurdpur, a village in Jalandhar district of the Punjab. His father, Budh Siṅgh, lived in easy circumstances. For his education, Balvant Siṅgh was sent to the middle school at Ādampur. But he left off midway after an early marriage. As he grew up, he joined the army as a soldier. While serving at Mardān, he, under the influence of Sant Karam Siṅgh, became a devout Sikh. He was promoted a lance *nāik*, but he resigned from the army in 1905. In April 1906, he migrated to Canada. He played a leading part in establishing the first *gurdwārā* at Vancouver which was opened in a rented house on 22 July 1906. When the new building of the *gurdwārā* was inaugurated, on 19 January 1908, Balvant Siṅgh was appointed *granthī*, i.e. minister. In 1908-09, the Canadian government mooted the idea of transfering all Indian settlers of British Columbia, over 90 per cent of whom were Sikhs, to Honduras, a British colony in the tropical Central America. Bhāī Balvant Siṅgh visited the United States for consultations with Sikh settlers there. He and Sant Tejā Siṅgh, one of the leaders of the Sikhs in the Western Hemisphere, advised the immigrants to refuse to move to Honduras. On the formation of the Hindustān Association, in 1909, Balvant Siṅgh was nominated its treasurer. The Association campaigned against the restrictive immigration laws enforced by the Canadian government with a view to refusing entry to the families of Indian settlers. Early in 1911, Bhāī Balvant Siṅgh and Bhāī Bhāg Siṅgh Bhikkhīviṇḍ returned to India to take out their families as a test case against these laws. While in India, they toured the country, describing to the people the hardships of Indian immigrants in Canada.

The Canadian immigration rules required that to be eligible for fresh entry into that country, an Indian must travel on a direct passage from India to a Canadian port, but the shipping companies, for fear of displeasure of the government, would refuse to issue direct tickets to Canada. Balvant Siṅgh and Bhāg Siṅgh met with similar treatment. From Calcutta, they complained by wire to the Viceroy of India, but to no purpose. The two families then proceeded to Hong Kong, but failed to obtain direct tickets for Vancouver there as well. Ultimately, they took passage in a ship that was going to San Francisco via Vancouver. But it was only after a hard contest that the Canadian government permitted their wives to land in January 1912 "as an act of grace, without establishing a precedent." The struggle against the restriction continued. On 22 February 1913, in a joint meeting of the K͟hālsā Dīwān Society and the United India League, it was decided to send a deputation, comprising Balvant Siṅgh, Naraiṇ Siṅgh and Nand Siṅgh, to London to seek the intervention of the British government. The deputation met an under-secretary in the colonial office on 14 May 1913, but nothing came out of the interview, and all three members sailed for India on 28 May. They addressed a public meeting held in Bradlaugh Hall, Lahore, on 18 August 1913, waited on Sir Michael O' Dwyer, Lieut-Governor of the Punjab, and presented a memorandum to the Viceroy on 20 December 1913. As Sir Michael recorded in his *India as I Knew It*, "They were really advance agents — though we did not know this at the time – -of the Ghadr Party."

During his return voyage to Canada, Bhāī Balvant Siṅgh met, on 19 April 1914 at the Japanese port of Mugi, the famous *Komagata Maru,* ready with its Indian passengers to set sail for the Canadian shore. He assisted Bābā Gurdit Siṅgh, who had hired the ship from a Japanese company, in raising funds to pay off part of the liability. He is also said to have exhorted the passengers "to rise against the British, if their entry to Canada was prevented," and travelled with them up to Kobe from where he took another ship for Vancouver, where he reached before the arrival of the *Komagata Maru* on 22 May 1914. Balvant Siṅgh was nominated a member of the Shore Committee set up by immigrants to organize relief for *Komagata Maru* passengers who were not allowed to land by the Canadian government. The ship was in the end forced to return on 23 July 1914. This infuriated the Indians in Canada, who now began forming contacts with the Ghadr party, based in the United States of America. The Canadian authorities, on the other hand, resorted to more stringent measures. Bhāī Balvant Siṅgh was arrested along with one Mevā Siṅgh Lopoke and two others on charge of importing arms from the United States. Belā Siṅgh, a police stooge, opened fire in the *gurdwārā* at Vancouver on 5 September 1914, as the *saṅgat* had assembled for a *bhog* ceremony, killing two and injuring four persons. In the eyes of the immigrants, the real culprit was William Hopkins, a former sergeant in British Indian police, who had been employed by the Canadian government as immigration inspector in British Columbia because of his knowledge of Hindi and Punjabi. Mevā Siṅgh, on 21 October 1914, killed Hopkins in the corridor of the court house, where the latter was waiting to appear as a defence witness for Belā Siṅgh. The police tried to implicate Bhāī Balvant Siṅgh also in this case and took him into custody, but he was let off after two months for want of any evidence against him. However, he was forced to leave Canada with his family. From Shanghai, he sent his family to India. He himself stayed back to preach revolution among the Indian community. In July 1915, he went to Thailand to join a group of Ghadrites who had arrived from the United States to work up a rising in Burma. But he fell sick and had to be admitted to hospital, from where he was arrested. He was brought to the Punjab and tried in the third (second supplementary) Lahore conspiracy case. In the court judgement, delivered on 4 January 1917, he was awarded death penalty, with forfeiture of property. He was hanged in Central Jail at Lahore on 30 March 1917.

BIBLIOGRAPHY

1. Jagjīt Siṅgh, *Ghadar Pārtī Lahir.* Delhi, 1979
2. Jas, Jasvant Siṅgh, *Bābā Gurdit Siṅgh.* Jalandhar, 1970
3. Deol, G.S., *The Role of the Ghadr Party in National Movement.* Delhi, 1969

G.S.D.

BAMBELĪ (also referred to locally as Dugg-Bambelī because of its proximity to another village called Dugg), 12 km north of Phagwāṛā (31° - 14'N, 75° - 46'E) in the Punjab, is sacred to Gurū Har Rāi who visited here during one of his journeys between Kartārpur and Kīratpur. Gurdwārā Chauntā Sāhib Pātshāhī VII, near the confluence of two *chos* or seasonal streams to the northwest of the village, marks the site where the Gurū had halted and sat on a platform of earthwork (*chauntā* in the local dialect of Punjabi). The Gurdwārā building, constructed during recent years, comprises a large hall with a square sanctum in the middle. The shrine is affiliated to the Shiromaṇī Gurdwārā Parbandhak Committee, but is administered by Sant Harbaṅs Siṅgh of Ḍumelī, who raised the present building. Two Sikh penants close to the Gurdwārā mark the spots where four Babar

Akālīs brought to bay by British police fell fighting in a prolonged encounter on 1 September 1923.

BIBLIOGRAPHY

1. Tārā Siṅgh, *Srī Gur Tīrath Saṅgrahi.* Amritsar, n.d.
2. Ṭhākar Siṅgh, *Srī Gurduāre Darshan.* Amritsar, 1923

M.G.S.

BAMBĪHĀ, village 36 km southwest of Baṭhiṇḍā, has a historical shrine dedicated to Gurū Gobind Siṅgh, who, according to Bhāī Santokh Siṅgh, *Srī Gur Pratāp Sūraj Granth,* halted here for nine days during his journey from Muktsar to Talvaṇḍī Sābo in 1706. Gurdwārā Pātshāhī Dasvīṅ is situated on the eastern edge of the village and is flanked by the village pond, a part of which has been enclosed and is being developed into a *sarovar* or sacred tank. The present building, constructed in the 1970's, has a *dīvān* hall with the sanctum at the far end. The Gurdwārā is managed by a Nihaṅg Sikh of the Buḍḍhā Dal.

BIBLIOGRAPHY

1. Ṭhākar Siṅgh, Giānī, *Srī Gurduāre Darshan.* Amritsar, 1923
2. Tārā Siṅgh, *Srī Gur Tīrath Saṅgrahi.* Amritsar, n.d.
3. Fauja Singh, ed., *Travels of Guru Gobind Singh.* Patiala, 1968

M.G.S.

BANĀRASĪ DĀS, alias Banārasī Bābū, who professed to be a Kūkā Sikh, was originally a resident of Allāhābād. Widely travelled, he had been to England in 1885-86 where he had met the deposed Mahārājā Duleep Siṅgh. On his return from England he went to Nepal, the favoured resort of the Kūkās espousing Mahārājā Duleep Siṅgh's cause. Banārasī Dās preached insurrection against the British. He declared that Duleep Siṅgh had joined hands with the Russians and would invade India via Kashmīr. He wielded considerable influence among the Hindus who venerated him as a person of sanctity. In 1886, he came to the Punjab and was arrested and charged with sedition. He was released on 16 February 1887 as a result of the amnesty granted on the occasion of the golden jubilee of Queen Victoria. Thereafter he roamed about places such as Calcutta, Paṭnā and Muzaffarpur spreading sedition against the British and rousing pro-Duleep Siṅgh sentiments.

BIBLIOGRAPHY

Ganda Singh, ed., *History of the Freedom Movement in the Panjab. (Maharaja Duleep Singh Correspondence),* vol. III. Patiala, 1972

K.S.T.

BANĀRASĪ, MĀTĀ, grandmother of Gurū Nānak and mother of Bābā Kālū or Kaliāṇ Rāi, was the wife of Shiv Rām, resident of Talvaṇḍī Rāi Bhoi Kī, now called Nankāṇā Sāhib. She was the mother of two sons, Kālū and Lālū.

See SHIV RĀM, BĀBĀ

BIBLIOGRAPHY

1. Kohlī, Surindar Siṅgh, ed., *Janamsākhī Bhāī Bālā.* Chandigarh, 1975
2. McLeod, W.H., tr., *The B40 Janam-Sākhī.* Amritsar, 1980
3. Vīr Siṅgh, Bhāī, ed., *Purātan Janam Sākhī.* Amritsar, 1982

Gn.S.

BANDAĪ, name given to the followers of the Sikh hero, Bandā Siṅgh Bahādur (1670-1716), who regarded him not only as a military leader but also as Gurū next to Gurū Gobind Siṅgh in spiritual succession. They were opposed and ultimately expelled in 1721 by the mainstream of the Sikhs, the Tatt K͟hālsā. A small number of Bandaī Sikhs still survive. They reverence the Gurū Granth Sāhib as their Scripture and most of them also undergo the K͟hālsā initiatory rites, but Bandā Siṅgh Bahādur is for them their eleventh Gurū against the common Sikh belief of the spiritual line having ended with Gurū Gobind Siṅgh, the Tenth Master.

BIBLIOGRAPHY

1. Giān Siṅgh, Giānī, *Twārīkh Gurū Khālsā.* Patiala, 1970
2. Cunningham, Joseph Davey, *A History of the Sikhs.* London, 1849
3. Ganda Singh, *Life of Banda Singh Bahadur.* Amritsar, 1935
4. Nripinder Singh, *The Sikh Moral Tradition.* Delhi, 1990

Sd.S.

BANDĀ SIṄGH BAHĀDUR (1670-1716), eighteenth-century Sikh warrior who for the first time seized territory for the Khālsā and paved the way for the ulimate conquest of the Punjab by them, was born Lachhmaṇ Dev on 27 October 1670 at Rājaurī in the Puñchh district of Kashmīr. According to Hākim Rāi, *Ahwāl-i-Lachhmaṇ Dās urf Bandā Sāhib,* his father Rām Dev, a ploughman, came of the Soḍhī sub-caste. Lachhmaṇ Dev had a very tender heart and the sight of a dying doe during one of the hunting excursions proved a turning-point in his life. So strong was his sense of penitence that he left his home to become an ascetic. He was then fifteen years of age. He first received instruction from a mendicant, Jānakī Prasād. At the shrine of Rām Thamman, near Kasūr, he joined Bairāgī Rām Dās and was given the name of Mādho Dās. Roaming about the country for some years, he settled down in the Pañchvaṭī woods, near Nāsik. He learnt yoga from Yogī Aughaṛ Nāth and, after his death, left Nāsik and established a *maṭh* (monastery) of his own at Nāndeḍ on the left bank of the River Godāvarī. Here he had an encounter with Gurū Gobind Siṅgh who happened to visit his hermitary on 3 September 1708, at the end of which he, as the chronicler records, fell at his feet, pronouncing himself to be his *bandā* or slave. Gurū Gobind Siṅgh escorted him to his own camp, administered to him the vows of the Khālsā and gave him the name of Bandā Siṅgh, from the word *bandā* he had used for himself when proclaiming his allegiance to the Gurū. Blessed by Gurū Gobind Siṅgh who bestowed upon him a drum, a banner and five arrows as emblems of authority, and accompanied by five Sikhs — Binod Siṅgh, Kāhan Siṅgh, Bāj Siṅgh, Dayā Siṅgh and Rām Siṅgh, he set out towards the north determined to chastise the tyrannical Mughal *faujdār* of Sirhind. As he reached the Punjab, Sikhs began to rally round his standard, amongst the first to join him being Bhāī Fateh Siṅgh, a descendant of Bhāī Bhagatū, Karam Siṅgh and Dharam Siṅgh of Bhāī Rūpā and Ālī Siṅgh, Mālī Siṅgh and other Sikhs of Salaudī. Rām Siṅgh and Tilok Siṅgh, the ancestors of Phūlkīāṅ rulers, provided material help. On 26 November 1709, Bandā Siṅgh attacked Samāṇā, the native town of Jalāl ud-Dīn, the executioner of Gurū Tegh Bahādur, and of the two executioners who had volunteered to behead Gurū Gobind Siṅgh's two young sons, at Sirhind. After the sack of Samāṇā, Bandā Siṅgh occupied Ghuṛhām, Ṭhaskā, Shāhābād and Mustafābād. The town of Kapūrī, whose *faujdār,* Qadam ud-Dīn, was notorious for his debaucheries and persecution of Hindus and Sikhs, was razed to the ground. Next came the turn of Saḍhaurā, whose chief, 'Usmān Khān, had not only oppressed the Hindus but had also tortured to death the Muslim saint, Sayyid Buddhū Shāh, for having helped Gurū Gobind Siṅgh in the battle of Bhaṅgāṇī. Bandā Siṅgh took this long circuitous route awaiting Sikhs from the Doābā and Mājhā areas to join his force before he attacked Sirhind where two of Gurū Gobind Siṅgh's sons had met with a cruel fate at the hands of Wazīr Khān, the Mughal satrap. Wazīr Khān was killed in the battle of Chappar Chiṛī on 12 May 1710, and on 14 May the city of Sirhind was captured and given over to plunder. Bāj Siṅgh, one of Bandā Siṅgh's companions, was appointed governor of Sirhind. Bandā Siṅgh was now the virtual master of territories between the Yamunā and the Sutlej, yielding an annual revenue of thirty-six lacs of rupees. He made the old Fort of Mukhlisgaṛh, in the safety of the Himalayas, his headquarters, renaming it Lohgaṛh. He assumed the style of royalty and introduced a new calendar dating from his capture of Sirhind. He had new coins struck in the name of Gurū Nānak-Gurū Gobind Siṅgh. Besides the names of the Gurūs, the inscription of his seal contained the word *deg* (the kettle in Gurū kā Laṅgar signifying charity) and *tegh* (the sword of the Khālsā signifying victory). Bandā Siṅgh's rule, though short-lived, had a far-reaching impact on the history of the Punjab. With it began the decay of the Mughal authority and the demolition of the feudal system of society it had created. Bandā Siṅgh abolished the Zamīndārī system and made the tillers masters of the land by conferring upon them proprietory rights. He was liberal in his treatment of Hindus and Muslims many of whom joined the Sikh faith and took up arms under him.

In the summer of 1710, Bandā Siṅgh crossed the Yamunā and seized Sahāranpur. On his arrival at Nanautā on 11 July 1710, crowds of Gujjars, who called themselves Nānakpanthīs swelled his ranks, but he had to return to the Punjab, without making any further conquest in the Gangetic valley. In the Punjab, he took Baṭālā and Kalānaur, marched towards Lahore, while a contingent proceeded to occupy the city and *parganah* of Paṭhānkoṭ. Seized with terror, Sayyid Aslam, the governor of Lahore, shut himself up in the Fort. Cries of *jihād* or religious war against the Sikhs proved of little avail and Bandā Siṅgh inflicted a crushing defeat upon the gathered host at the village of Bhīlovāl. Except for the city of Lahore, the whole of Mājhā and Riāṛkī had fallen into his hands. On 3 October 1710, he occupied Rāhoṅ in the Jalandhar Doāb.

Bandā Siṅgh's increasing influence roused the ire of the Mughal emperor Bahādur Shāh, who came northwards from the Deccan, and commanded the governors of Delhi and Oudh and other Mughal officers to punish the Sikhs. The order he issued on 10 December 1710 was a general warrant for the *faujdārs* to kill the worshippers of Nānak, i.e. Sikhs, wherever found *(Nānak-prastāṅ rā har jā kih ba-yāband ba-qatl rasānand)*. Even in face of this edict for wholesale destruction of the Sikhs, Bandā Siṅgh maintained towards the Muslims generally an attitude of tolerance. A report submitted to Emperor Bahādur Shāh stated that as many as five thousand Muslims of the neighbourhood of Kalānaur and Baṭālā had joined Bandā Siṅgh and that they were allowed the fullest liberty to shout their religious call, *azān*, and recite *khutbā* and *namāz*, in the army of the Sikhs and that they were properly looked after and fed.

In 1710, a massive imperial force drove the Sikhs from Sirhind and other places to take shelter in the Fort of Lohgaṛh in the submontane region. Here Bandā Siṅgh was closely invested by sixty thousand horse and foot. For want of provisions, the Sikhs were reduced to rigorous straits but on the night of 10 December 1710, Bandā Siṅgh made a desperate bid to escape and hacked his way out of the imperial cordon.

Bandā Siṅgh was far from vanquished and, within a fortnight of his escape from Lohgaṛh, he began to send out *hukamnāmās* exhorting the people to carry on the fight. He ransacked the submountainous state of Bilāspur; Maṇḍī, Kullū and Chambā submitted to his authority of their own accord. In June 1711, as he descended towards the plains he was engaged in an action at Bahrāmpur near Jammū, in which the Mughal troops were worsted. Bandā Siṅgh was, however, forced in the end again to retreat into the hills.

After the death, on 28 February 1712, of Emperor Bahādur Shāh, the war of succession for the imperial throne and the disturbed state of affairs in Delhi brought Bandā Siṅgh some respite, but Farruk̲h̲-Sīyar who ascended the throne of Delhi in 1713 accelerated the campaign against the Sikhs. They were hounded out of the plains where Bandā Siṅgh had reoccupied Saḍhaurā and Lohgaṛh. Their main column, led by Bandā Siṅgh, was subjected to a most stringent siege at the village of Gurdās-Naṅgal, about six kilometres from Gurdāspur. The supplies having run out, the Sikhs suffered great hardship and lived on animal flesh which they had to eat raw owing to lack of firewood. To quote the Muslim diarist of the time, K̲h̲āfī K̲h̲ān, "Many died of dysentary and privation....When all the grass was gone, they gathered leaves from the trees. When these were consumed, they stripped the bark and broke off the small shoots, dried them, ground them and used them instead of flour, thus keeping body and soul together. They collected the bones of animals and used them in the same way. Some assert that they saw a few of the Sikhs cut flesh from their own thighs, roast it, and eat it."

For eight long months, the garrison resisted the siege under these gruesome conditions. The royal armies at last broke through and captured Bandā Siṅgh and his famishing companions on 7 December 1715. They were at first taken to and paraded in the streets of Lahore and then sent to Delhi where they arrived on 27 February 1716. The cavalcade to the imperial capital was a grisly sight. Besides 740 prisoners in heavy chains, it comprised seven hundred cartloads of the heads of the Sikhs with another 2,000 stuck upon pikes. By Farruk̲h̲-Sīyar's order Bandā Siṅgh and some two dozen leading Sikhs were imprisoned in the Fort, while the remaining 694 were made over to the kotwāl, Sarbrāh K̲h̲ān, to be executed at the Kotwālī

Chabūtrā at the rate of a hundred a day. Then Bandā Siṅgh Bahādur and his remaining companions were taken to the tomb of K̲h̲wājā Qutb ud-Dīn Bak̲h̲tiyār Kākī, near the Qutb Mīnār. There he was offered the choice between Islam and death. Upon his refusal to renounce his faith, his four-year-old son, Ajai Siṅgh, was hacked to pieces before his eyes. He himself was subjected to the harshest torments. His eyes were pulled out and hands and feet chopped off. His flesh was torn with red-hot pincers and finally his body was cut up limb by limb. This occurred on 9 June 1716.

BIBLIOGRAPHY

1. Bhaṅgū, Ratan Siṅgh, *Prāchīn Panth Prakāsh*. Amritsar, 1962
2. Giān Siṅgh, Giānī, *Panth Prakāsh* [Reprint]. Patiala, 1970
3. Ganda Singh, *Life of Banda Singh Bahadur*. Amritsar, 1935
4. Bhagat Singh, *Sikh Polity in the Eighteenth and Nineteenth Centuries*. Delhi, 1978
5. Irvine, W., *Later Mughals*. London, 1922
6. Surman, John, and Edward Stephenson, "Massacre of the Sikhs at Delhi in 1716" in *Early European Accounts of the Sikhs*, edited by Ganda Singh [Reprint]. Calcutta, 1962

G.S.

BANDĪ BĪR (Warrior Bound), a poem in Bengali by Rabindranath Tagore, based primarily on McGregor's *History of the Sikhs* and Cunningham's *A History of the Sikhs* was composed by him in October-November 1899. The poem celebrates the heroism of the Sikh warrior Bandā Siṅgh Bahādur (1670-1716). The opening stanzas tell how Gurū Gobind Siṅgh's message had turned the Sikhs into a self-respecting and fearless people. The rest of the poem is devoted to panegyrizing the resolute resistance put up by Bandā Siṅgh Bahādur and his men against Mug̲h̲al oppression and to describing how bravely he met his end after he had been arrested at Gurdās-Naṅgal along with his companions. Before being executed with the cruellest torments, Bandā Siṅgh was, says the poet, ordered by the Qāzī to kill his own son holding him in his hands. The poem was a source of inspiration to several other Bengali writers as well as to Bengali militant youth engaged in the struggle for India's independence.

H.B.

BĀṆĪ, Sanskrit *vāṇī* (meaning sound, voice, music; speech, language, diction; praise, laudation), refers in the specifically Sikh context to the sacred compositions of the Gurūs and of the holy saints and sūfīs as incorporated in the Scripture, the Gurū Granth Sāhib. Compositions of Gurū Gobind Siṅgh comprising the *Dasam Granth* are also referred to as Bāṇī. For Sikhs, Bāṇī or the compound Gurbāṇī (Guru's *bāṇī*) is the revealed word. Revelation is defined as the way God discloses and communicates Himself to humanity. There are different views on how he does this. The Hindu belief is that God occasionally becomes incarnate as an *avatār* and thus communicates Himself through his word and action while living on this earth. For the Muslims the revelation consists in actual words in the form of direct messages conveyed from God through an angel, Gabriel, to the Prophet. Another belief is that God communicates not the form but the content of the words, i.e. knowledge, to man. A related view is that, as a result of the mystic unity they achieve with the Universal Self, certain individuals under Divine inspiration arrive at truths which they impart to the world. The Gurūs did not subscribe to the incarnation theory — "The tongue be burnt that says that the Lord ever takes birth" (GG, 1136), nor did they acknowledge the existence of angels or intermediaries between God and man. They were nevertheless conscious of their divine mission and described the knowledge and wisdom contained in their hymns as God-given. "As the Lord's word comes to me, O Lālo, so do I deliver it," says Gurū Nānak (GG, 722). Gurū Arjan: "I myself know not what to speak; all I speak is what the Lord commandeth" (GG, 763). It is in this sense that Bāṇī is revelation for the Sikhs. It is for them God's Word mediated through the Gurūs or Word on which the Gurūs had put their seal. The Bāṇī echoes the Divine Truth; it is the voice of God — "the Lord's own word," as said Gurū Nānak; or the Formless Lord Himself, as said Gurū Amar Dās:

vāhu vāhu bāṇī niraṅkār hai
tisu jevaḍu avaru na koi (GG, 515)
Hail, hail, the word of the Gurū,
Which is the Formless Lord Himself;
There is none other, nothing else
To be reckoned equal to it.

Being Word Divine, Bāṇī is sacred and the object of utmost veneration. That the Bāṇī was reverenced by the Gurūs themselves even before it was compiled into the Holy Book is attested by an anecdote in *Gurbilās Chhevīṅ Pātshāhī*. While returning from Goindvāl after the obsequies of his father, Gurū Arjan took with him some *pothīs* or books containing the Bāṇī of the first four Gurūs. The Sikhs carried the *pothīs*, wrapped in a piece of cloth, in a palanquin on their shoulders. The Gurū and other Sikhs walked along barefoot while the Gurū's horse trailed behind bareback. When the Sikhs suggested that the Gurū ride as usual, he replied, "These *[pothīs]* represent the four Gurūs, their light. It would be disrespectful [on my part to ride in their presence]. It is but meet that I walk barefoot." "The Bāṇī is Gurū and the Gurū is Bāṇī...." sang Gurū Rām Dās (GG, 982). Gurū Nānak, the founder, had himself declared, "*śabda*, i.e. word or *bāṇī*, is Gurū, the unfathomable spiritual guide; crazed would be the world without the *śabda*" (GG, 635). "Śabda-Gurū enables one to swim across the ocean of existence and to perceive the One as present everywhere" (GG, 944). Thus it is that the Bāṇī of the Gurū commands a Sikh's reverence.

The content of the Bāṇī is God's name, God's praise and the clue to God-realization. God is described both as immanent and transcendent. He is the creator of all things, yet He does not remain apart from His creation. He responds to the love of His creatures. *Hukam* or the Divine Law is the fundamental principle of God's activity. Man's duty is to seek an understanding of His *hukam* and to live his life wholly in accord with it. God is the source of grace *(nadar)* and it behoves man to make himself worthy of His grace. The Bāṇī, which is Gurū in essence, brings this enlightenment to men. It shows the way. Listening to, reciting and becoming absorbed in Bāṇī engenders merit and helps one to overcome *haumai*, i.e. finite ego or self-love which hinders understanding and realization. In proclaiming the supreme holiness and majesty of God, the Bāṇī has few parallels in literature. It contains one of the most intimate and magnificent expressions of faith in the Transcendent. It is an earnestly given testament about God's existence and a sterling statement of a deeply experienced vision of Him. The Bāṇī is all in the spiritual key. It is poetry of pure devotion, love and compassion. It is lyrical rather than philosophical, moral rather than cerebral. It prescribes no social code, yet it is the basis of Sikh practice as well as of the Sikh belief. It is the source of authority, the ultimate guide to the spiritual and moral path pointed by the Gurūs.

The form of the Bāṇī is as sublime as is its content. It is a superb body of verse in a variety of metre and rhythm, arranged under thirty-one different musical measures. Besides its ardent lyricism and abounding imagination, it displays a subtle aesthetic sensitivity. The aptness of its image and simile is especially noteworthy. Its musicality is engaging. The language is mainly Punjabi in its simple spoken idiom. The down-to-earth, sinewy presence of its vocabulary and the eloquence of its symbolism drawn from everyday life give it a virile tone. The Bāṇī constitutes the springhead of Punjabi literary tradition and the creative energy the latter acquired from it informed its subsequent growth and continues to be a vital influence to this day.

BIBLIOGRAPHY

1. Shackle, C., *A Gurū Nānak Glossary*. London, 1981
2. Kirpāl Siṅgh, *Janam Sākhī Pramparā*. Patiala, 1969
3. Kāhn Siṅgh, Bhāī, *Gurmat Mārtaṇḍ*. Amritsar, 1983

P.S.S.

BANĪ BADARPUR is the name popularly given to what are in fact two separate villages Banī and Badarpur, 6 km from Lāḍvā (29°-59'N, 77°-3'E) in Kurukshetra district of Haryāṇā. Gurū Tegh Bahādur visited this place twice. On his first visit, he came from Kurukshetra, via Muniārpur and Ḍuḍhī. He gave a bagful of money (*badrā*, in old Punjabi) to the headman, Rām Bakhsh, for the construction of a well for use by the villagers. The latter, however, misappropriated the amount. On his second visit, the Gurū had the well dug under his own supervision. Platforms were constructed on sites sanctified by the Gurū on the two occasions. Over the one, situated between the two villages, the construction of a shrine known as Gurdwārā Gurū Tegh Bahādur was started by Sardār Baghel Siṅgh of Chhalaudī, a minor Sikh principality about 3 km from Banī Badarpur. It was completed by his widow. A platform also existed inside Badarpur village. A room over it has been constructed recently.

BIBLIOGRAPHY

1. Tārā Siṅgh, *Srī Gur Tīrath Saṅgrahi*. Amritsar, n.d.
2. Ṭhākar Siṅgh, Giānī, *Srī Gurduāre Darshan*. Amritsar, 1923
3. Faujā Siṅgh, *Gurū Teg Bahādur: Yātrā Asthān*,

Pramparāvāṅ te Yād Chinn. Patiala, 1976

M.G.S.

BĀṆĪ BHAGATĀṄ SAṬĪK (*saṭīk* = exegesis or commentary) by Paṇḍit Tārā Siṅgh Narotam (*q.v.*) is an exposition of the *bāṇī* or hymns of the *bhaktas* or saints (here the word implies contributors to the Gurū Granth Sāhib other than the Gurūs). The work was, according to inner evidence, completed in 1939 Bk/AD 1882 and the scribe was one Sundar Siṅgh. It was published in AD 1907 by Rāi Sāhib Munshī Gulāb Siṅgh and Sons, Lahore. The book is divided into two parts— the first part (pp. 386) covering the compositions of the *bhaktas* included in Sikh Scripture up to Rāga Gūjarī and the second (pp. 522) covering the rest of them. The book opens with an Introduction in which the author states that *bhakta bāṇī*, as included in the Gurū Granth Sāhib, was composed by Gurū Arjan himself on behalf of the different saints and sūfīs.

Tārā Siṅgh Narotam's exposition is very detailed, even prolix. For instance, the exegesis of a *śabda* by Kabīr in Rāga Gauṛī runs into 15 pages (pp. 39-53), the author quoting in the process profusely from old Hindu scriptures. His interpretations are coloured by his Vedantic training and background.

BIBLIOGRAPHY

Shergill, Surinder Siṅgh, *Paṇḍat Tārā Siṅgh Narotam: Jīvan te Rachanā*. Patiala, 1985

D.S.

BĀṆĪ BIRDH PRATĀP is a collection of religious and devotional poetry in a mixture of Braj and Punjabi, written in Gurmukhī script by Bābā Rām Dās, a Dīvānā *sādhū*. The volume is preserved with reverence due to a religious scripture in the *ḍerā* or monastery of the Dīvānā sect established by Bābā Rām Dās himself when he arrived in 1800 Bk/AD 1743 at the head of a group of *sādhūs* and settled on the eastern outskirts of the town of Paṭiālā. According to the Dīvānā tradition, Rām Dās blessed Mahārājā Sāhib Siṅgh that a very lucky son will be born to him, and accordingly when a son was born to him in 1855 Bk/AD 1798, the Mahārājā named him Karam (*karam* = luck or fortune) Siṅgh, and donated to the *ḍerā* 500 *bighās* of land further eastwards of the town. The work, completed on Chet *sudī* 12, 1859 Bk/23 April 1802, was published in 1981 by the then custodian of the *ḍerā*. The volume contains hymns under different musical measures such as Sirī, Gūjarī, Kedārā, Tilaṅg, Bilāval, Rāmkalī, Prabhātī, Gauṛī, Jaijāvantī, Dhanāsarī and Bhairau. Poetical metres used include couplets, triplets, octets, etc. The volume begins with verses eulogizing the *gurū* whom the author identifies with God Himself (p. 45). The author pays homage to the Ten Gurūs of the Sikh faith whom he regards one in spirit sharing the same spiritual light (pp. 40-43). There are verses on themes such as the importance of repeating the Divine Name, truthful living and devotion to the *gurū*. The volume also contains *līlās* of Bālmīk and Draupadī as well as hymns lauding gods and goddesses from Hindu mythology and the *bhaktas*. It concludes with the *Rāgamālā* reproduced from Sikh Scripture, the Gurū Granth Sāhib.

D.S.

BĀṆĪ PRAKĀSH or *Srī Gurū Bāṇī Prakāsh* is a dictionary of the Gurū Granth Sāhib compiled by Soḍhī Tejā Siṅgh. According to the author, he started working on it in December 1928, and got it printed in 1932 at the Phulwāṛī Press, Lahore. The original version of the dictionary, according to the author, was based on the *Farīdkoṭ Ṭīkā* of Gurū Granth Sāhib, but subsequently he incorporated into it a considerable amount of more material from further study of exegetical and lexical works in the field of Sikh learning.

The *Bāṇī Prakāsh* is not a dictionary containing vocables arranged in alphabetical, or some other order; rather, it provides explanation of difficult words and phrases on a given page of Sikh scripture, the Gurū Granth Sāhib. Selections of words and phrases have been liberally made and in places very simple words have been chosen for explanation. As could expectably happen in a page-wise dictionary, repetitions abound.

The author has evolved his own technique of arranging entries. The relevant page of the Scripture is printed in bold figures on the top and then entries from that page are placed in run-on style. The portion of first line of the *śabda* (hymn) from which succeeding entries are taken is followed by the word/phrase entries in bold print with the connotation recorded in smaller type, after the mathematical symbol (=). The connotations recorded are, generally, in line with the Siṅgh Sabhā school of thought and the language used is simple, unadorned Punjabi.

The author is not fully conversant with the grammar of old Punjabi which was synthetic to some extent, and many nouns had case-endings attached to them. The significance of these case-endings has not been understood and the lexical entries, in many cases, have been recorded without these inflexions, resulting in the loss of clarity.

An index of the initial line of each *śabda* (hymn), arranged in alphabetical order is given in the beginning. At the end there is a short glossary of theological and mythological terms, requiring detailed exposition and explanation. Additional information has been provided wherever necessary in the form of footnotes.

The dictionary, short and handy, is fairly exhaustive. In spite of certain obvious shortcomings, the work has its utility. It certainly is helpful to the reader who finds all the important terms occurring in the page he is reading collected and explained at one place.

Hk.S.

BANNO, BHĀĪ (1558-1645), a prominent Sikh contemporary of Gurū Arjan and Gurū Hargobind, was the son of Bhāī Bishan Dev of village Māṅgaṭ, also called Khārā-Māṅgaṭ, Khārā being its older name, in Phālīā *tahsīl* of Gujrāt district (now in Pakistan). He was born on Saturday, Baisākh *sudī* 13, 1615 Bk/ 30 April 1558. Banno grew up with a deeply religious disposition. He turned a Sikh and rendered diligent service during the construction of Harimandar at Amritsar under Gurū Arjan. On the completion of the compilation of (Gurū) Granth Sāhib in 1604, Gurū Arjan deputed Bhāī Banno to carry the holy volume to Lahore for binding. The latter, with the Gurū's permission first carried it to his village and then brought it back to Lahore. During his journey to and from his village he prepared his own copy of the Holy Book. He got both the copies bound and brought them to the Gurū, who installed the original copy (Ādi Bīṛ) in the Harimandar and returned the other copy to Bhāī Banno. This recension came to be known as Bhāī Banno Vālī Bīṛ or Khāre Vālī Bīṛ, because the Bhāī had installed it in his own house at Khārā-Māṅgaṭ. *See* SRĪ GURŪ GRANTH SĀHIB.

Bhāī Banno continued to preach Sikh tenets in the northwestern parts of the Punjab till his death in Māgh 1701 Bk/January 1645.

BIBLIOGRAPHY

1. Bhallā, Sarūp Dās, *Mahimā Prakāsh*. Patiala, 1971
2. Bal, Rājinder Siṅgh, *Bhāī Banno Darpan*. Jalandhar, 1989
3. *Bhāī Banno Sāhib*. Kanpur, n.d.
4. *Gurbilās Chhevīṅ Pātshāhī*. Patiala, 1970

M.G.S.

BAṄSĀVALĪNĀMĀ DASĀṄ PĀTSHĀHĪĀṄ KĀ is a poeticized account of the lives of the Gurūs by Kesar Siṅgh Chhibbar. The term *baṅsāvalīnāmā* means a genealogy. Another term used in the text is "kursīnāmā" which is Persian for "genealogy." But, strictly speaking, this work is not a genealogical table. It is a rapid account, in rather incipient Punjabi verse, of the ten Gurūs and of Bandā Siṅgh Bahādur and some other Sikhs. Description of historical events and mythological elements occasionally overlap in this work. Its peculiar feature is the wealth of chronological detail it contains about the lives of the Gurūs and the members of their families. But the reliability of the dates recorded by the author is not established.

The author, Kesar Siṅgh Chhibbar, came of a family who had served the Gurūs as *dīwāns* or ministers. His grandfather, Dharam Chand, was in charge of the treasury of Gurū Gobind Siṅgh. Dharam Chand's father, Dargāh Mall, had been *dīwān* to Gurū Tegh Bahādur, the Ninth Gurū, and his two predecessors. Dharam Chand's son, Gurbakhsh Siṅgh, served Gurū Gobind Siṅgh. Kesar Siṅgh was Gurbakhsh Siṅgh's son. Too young at the time of Gurū Gobind Siṅgh's passing away, he did have the privilege of the company of some eminent Sikhs of his day, notably scholar and martyr Bhāī Manī Siṅgh. For many years he lived at Amritsar and also attended upon Mātā Sundarī, widow of Gurū Gobind Siṅgh, in Delhi. As he records himself, he wrote the *Baṅsāvalīnāmā* in a *dharamsālā* in Jammū and completed it in 1826 Bk/AD 1769.

The book, comprising 2,564 stanzas, is divided into fourteen chapters. The first ten deal with the Ten Gurūs. There is a chapter each on Bandā Siṅgh Bahādur, Jīt (Ajīt) Siṅgh, adopted son of Mātā Sundarī, and Mātā Sāhib Devāṅ. The last chapter of the book alludes to the state of the Sikhs in the early decades of the eighteenth century, persecution they suffered at the hands of the ruling authority and their will to survival. A point especially stressed is about the bestowal of Gurūship on the Holy Book by Gurū Gobind Siṅgh before he passed away. Kesar Siṅgh says, "At this time the Gurū Granth Sāhib is our Gurū (i.e. prophet-teacher)... Recognize him alone as the Gurū's true Sikh who accepts as eternally true the word enshrined in the Granth. He who abides by the word in the Granth, he alone will be the follower approved." He also mentions some other prescriptions for the Sikhs in the manner of Rahitnāmās or manuals of Sikh code. But some of his assertions are not in conformity with Sikh belief and teachings. For example, he accepts the Gurūs as incarnations of Viṣṇu. The Gurūs acknowledged no deity besides God, nor did they support the theory of incarnation. Again, the author has tried to prove the superiority of the Brāhmaṇs even among the Sikhs which may be due to his own Brāhmaṇ ancestry. In any case, this is contrary to the principles of Sikhism which rejects caste.

Till recently this Sikh chronicle was available only in manuscript. It was edited by Dr Rattan Siṅgh Jaggī and published in 1972, in the *Parakh*, a research journal of the Pañjāb University, Chaṇḍīgaṛh. The text used was a manuscript in a private collection at Baṭālā. No date is mentioned on the manuscript, but it could be about 150 years old. A manuscript is also preserved in the Khālsā College Library at Amritsar; there was as well one in the Sikh Reference Library at Amritsar until it perished in the Army attack on the Golden Temple complex in 1984.

R.S.J.

BANTĀ SIṄGH (1890-1915), a Ghadr revolutionary, was born the son of Būṭā Siṅgh in 1890 at Saṅgvāl, in Jalandhar district of the Punjab. He passed his matriculation examination from the local D.A.-V. High School and left for abroad, first travelling to China and then onwards to America. In 1914, he returned home from America fired with revolutionary fervour. He established a school and a *pañchāyat* in his village and undertook a tour of the district distributing Ghadr literature among the people and exhorting them to join in the rising to expel the British from India and engage in sabotage, tampering with railway lines and cutting telephone wires.

As he once went to Lahore to procure firearms, he was detected by two policemen who tried to catch him, but he escaped. He attended a meeting of a G͟hadr group on 2 May 1915 when it was planned to attack the magazine at Kapūrthalā to seize firearms. Two groups were organized to attack the guard posted at the Vallā bridge, near Mānāṅvālā railway station in Amritsar district, one of which was to be led by Bantā Siṅgh. He attacked the guard on the night of 11-12 June 1915 and captured six service rifles and 200 cartridges. The government announced a prize of two squares of land and two thousand rupees in cash for anyone catching him. Lured by this, Bantā Siṅgh's close relative, Partāp Siṅgh of the village of Jauṛā in Hoshiārpur district, had him arrested on 25 June 1915. He was tried in the Central Jail, Lahore, under martial law along with four others in the Vallā railway bridge case, and was sentenced to death. He was hanged on 12 August 1915.

BIBLIOGRAPHY

1. Deol, G.S., *The Role of the Ghadr Party in National Movement*. Delhi, 1969
2. Jagjīt Siṅgh, *G͟hadar Pārṭī Lahir*. Delhi, 1979
3. Saiṅsarā, Gurcharan Siṅgh, *G͟hadar Pārṭī dā Itihās*. Jalandhar, 1969

G.S.D.

BANTĀ SIṄGH, BHĀĪ (1894-1921), one of the Nankāṇā Sāhib martyrs, was the son of Bhāī Bholā Siṅgh Ḍhilloṅ and Māī Bhāg Kaur of village Biheṛā, in Hoshiarpur district. He was born on 25 October 1894. As a youth, he had engaged in wrestling and gone out hunting. He had also learnt to read and write Punjabi in the Gurmukhī script. He excelled at performing *kīrtan*, singing the holy hymns. He enlisted in 28th Punjabi Battalion in May 1911 and served with his unit in Ceylon (now Sri Lanka) during 1913-15. In 1915, the Battalion moved to Mesopotemia (now Iraq) to take part in the First Great War. Bantā Siṅgh was wounded in his right arm on 13 January 1916 and was retired on medical grounds in August 1916.

Back in his village, he took to his ancestral occupation of farming. He was visiting Chakk No. 91 Dhannūāṇā in the newly colonized canal district of Sheik͟hūpurā to see a relation. There he found some volunteers preparing to join Bhāī Lachhmaṇ Siṅgh Dhārovālī's *jathā* on its way to Gurdwārā Janam Asthān at Nankāṇā Sāhib. Bantā Siṅgh at once decided to accompany them. Inside the shrine, he was done to death, along with other members of the *jathā* at the bidding of the custodian, Mahant Naraiṇ Dās, on the morning of 20 February 1921.

See NANKĀṆĀ SĀHIB MASSACRE

BIBLIOGRAPHY

Shamsher, Gurbak͟hsh Siṅgh, *Shahīdī Jīvan*. Nankana Sahib, 1938

G.S.G.

BANTĀ SIṄGH DHĀMĪĀṄ (1900-1923), Babar revolutionary, was born in 1900 at the village of Dhāmīāṅ Kalāṅ, in Jalandhar district. He went to the village primary school, and joined the army serving in the 55th Sikh Battalion for about three years. While in the army he came in contact with Babar Akālīs, whose creed of violence appealed to him. After his meeting with Jathedār Kishan Siṅgh Gaṛgajj and Bābū Santā Siṅgh on 16 February 1923, he resigned from the army and became a member of the action group of the Babar Akālī Jathā. He was party to the Jamsher railway station dacoity (3 March 1923), to the murder of Būṭā *lambaṛdār* of Naṅgal Shāmāṅ (11 March), and of Javālā Siṅgh, a notorious money-lender of Koṭlī Bāvādās (13 November), and in the second murderous attempt on the lives of Kābul

Siṅgh and his father-in-law, Lābh Siṅgh, who had got Kishan Siṅgh Gaṛgajj arrested on 26 February 1923.

On 12 December 1923 Jagat Siṅgh, of Muṇḍer village, in Jalandhar district, connived with the police for trapping Bantā Siṅgh, Varyām Siṅgh Dhuggā and Javālā Siṅgh of Fatehpur Koṭhī in a *chaubārā* (room on the first floor) in his village. The police operations were personally supervised by W. W. Jacob, the deputy commissioner of Jalandhar, upon whose orders the *chaubārā* was at last set afire. While trying to escape from the smouldering *chaubārā*, both Bantā Siṅgh and Javālā Siṅgh were killed, but their third companion, Varyām Siṅgh, succeeded in making good his escape.

BIBLIOGRAPHY

1. Nijjar, B.S., *History of the Babbar Akalis.* Jalandhar, 1987
2. Sundar Siṅgh, *Babbar Akālī Lahir.* Amritsar, 1970
3. Nijjhar, Milkhā Siṅgh, *Babar Akālī Lahir dā Itihās.* Delhi, 1986

K.M.

BANVĀLĪ, BHĀĪ, and his brother Paras Rām, Brāhmaṇs by birth, were devotees of Gurū Hargobind. They were professional physicians and, as says Bhāī Manī Siṅgh, *Sikhāṅ dī Bhagat Mālā,* they treated Sikhs and holymen free of charge, and went travelling preaching the word of the Gurū. Once they asked the Gurū why attendance at holy congregation (*sādh saṅgat*) was given primacy when only *śabda* (the Holy Word) was efficacious enough to save all. Gurū Hargobind answered: "It is in *saṅgat* alone that seekers meet *gurmukhs,* i.e. the enlightened ones, and receive from them prescriptions for a holy life."

BIBLIOGRAPHY

1. Manī Siṅgh, Bhāī, *Sikhāṅ dī Bhagat Mālā.* Amritsar, 1955
2. Santokh Siṅgh, Bhāī, *Srī Gur Pratāp Sūraj Granth.* Amritsar, 1926-37

Gn.S.

BĀOLĪ or *bāvalī* is a masonry well with steps leading down to water level. This is perhaps the oldest type of well introduced when man had discovered the eixstence of sub-soil water and also the means to reach it, but had not yet invented mechanical devices to draw water out of it. Before masonry art was developed, *baōlīs* must have been only shallow pits with a sloping path down to the water, vertical walls and dented steps confined only to rocky regions. Gradually as the arts of brick-making and masonry developed, *bāolīs* began to be constructed in the plains and, although subsequently use of pulleys and, still later, of the Persian wheel was introduced to bring water up to the surface of the earth, the vogue of *bāolīs* continued up to comparatively more recent times.

During early Sikhism, successive Gurūs raised several villages and towns across the Punjab, with ponds and *bāolīs,* especially in areas where water was scarce.

In the Sikh system the importance of daily morning bath (*snāna*) is stressed equally with *nām* (meditation on God's name) and *dān* (charity). A historically famous *bāolī* which is today an important pilgrim site for the Sikhs was built by Gurū Amar Dās (1479-1574) at Goindvāl, town he had himself founded.

M.G.S.

BĀRAH MĀHĀ or BĀRAH MĀSĀ, in Hindi, is a form of folk poetry in which the emotions and yearnings of the human heart are expressed in terms of the changing moods of Nature over the twelve months of the year. In this form of poetry, the mood of Nature in each particular month (of the Indian calendar) depicts the inner agony of the human heart which in most cases happens to be a woman separated from her spouse or lover.

In other words, the separated woman finds her own agony reflected in the different faces of Nature. The tradition of Bārah Māhā poetry is traceable to classical epochs. In Sanskrit, the Bārah Māhā had the form of *shaḍ ṛtu varṇan*, i.e. description of the six seasons (*shaḍ* = six; *ṛtu* = season; *varṇan* = description), the most well-known example being Kālidāsa's *Ṛtu Saṅhār*. The mode was commonly employed to depict the moods of the love-stricken woman in separation, and it became an established vogue in medieval Indian poetry. Modern languages of northern India claim several distinguished models. In Hindi, the first instance of this poetic form occurs in Malik Muhammad Jāyasī's *Padmāvat*. In Punjabi, Gurū Nānak's *Bārah Māhā* in the measure Tukhārī is not only the oldest composition belonging to this *genre* but also the first in which the theme of love-poetry has been transformed into that of spiritual import. He made the human soul the protagonist which suffers in the cesspool of transmigration as a result of its separation from the Supreme Soul. This is followed by Gurū Arjan's *Bārāh Māhā*. Later some Sūfī poets such as 'Ālī Haider, Bulleh Shāh, Hāsham and Shāh Murād also wrote *bārah māhās*. Hāfiz Barkhurdār was the first poet in the Punjabi romantic tradition to compose a *bārah māhā* as an independent work. In the eighteenth and nineteenth centuries, there were a number of *bārah māhās* and *sīharfīs* written in Punjabi. Poetry in this class can be broadly divided into various types – religious, farmers' narrative (included in an epic poem), *virahā* (separation) and 'trial of chastity' variety. Gurū Arjan's *Bārah Māhā* falls in the *virahā* category, depicting through the twelve months the pangs of the bride, i.e. the human soul separated from her Divine Essence.

BĀRAH MĀHĀ MĀÑJH is Gurū Arjan's calendar poem in the measure Mājh included in the Gurū Granth Sāhib (GG, 133-36). The opening verse of the composition presents the binary theme of the poem: the factual situation of the human soul's separation from the Divine Soul (*kirati karam ke vīchhuṛe* – bound by our deeds are we parted from Thee), and its quest for union with Him (*kari kirpā melahu rām* – by Thy grace grant union, O' Lord). Torn asunder from her Immutable Origin, she suffers; for instance: *āsāṛu tapandā tisu lagai hari nāhu na jinnā pāsi* – the month of Āsāṛ burns for her who does not have her Divine Husband close to her. These individuals are tortured by duality: they see themselves apart from the Eternal One. Thus they remain victims to Yama, the god of death, and keep migrating from one birth to another. This existing tragedy is attributed to *karma*, past deeds, which are referred to as *malu* or filth which accumulates through successive births. But time passages. One month passes into the next. The Bikaramī year begins with Chet and ends with Phagaṇ (Phalguṇa) only to begin again with Chet (Chaitra). As one sows so shall one reap. With good deeds then, the chasm can be bridged. Time – these very twelve months– offers opportunities to unite with the Timeless One. But two conditions apply – first, initiative on the part of the individual in the form of an intense longing (8), keeping company of the holy (2,6,12), reciting the Divine Name (4, 6,8,10), singing the praises of the Infinite (13) and realizing that He is indeed with the self (2); and second, the favour, the grace of the Lord Divine. Throughout the composition we hear Gurū Arjan beseech Him for His mercy, His benevolent glance (*nadar*). Once united, ultimate libreration is achieved and one is freed from the cycle of birth and death. Through the months, months are transcended. Time takes one into the state of Timeless everlasting bliss.

Excluding the opening stanza which serves as a prologue and the concluding one which serves as epilogue, each of the intervening stanzas commences with the name of the month, beginning with Chet. By cherishing the Lord in the month of Chet one attains bliss abundant. Baisākh, the month following Chet, becomes gladsome only if one meets the Lord's devotees who help him end his duality (3). Āsāṛ is scorching for those separated from the Spouse (5) and Sāvaṇ is blessed for such of the united wives as cherish in their hearts the Name Divine (6). However, man's own forgetfulness of God is the cause of all his suffering. All duality and pangs end as one by excelling good fortune attains union with the Lord (9). In the month of Māgh, man must 'bathe' in the dust of the feet of the holy and remember His name, for thus alone can he wash off the dirt of past deeds (12). The poem concludes with the statement that for him upon whom rests the Lord's grace, all months and days and all timings are auspicious (14). It is this Divine *nadar* or benevolent glance coupled with the individual's own initiative which helps him break the cycle of transmigration and win acceptance at the Lord's portal.

The *Bārah Māhā* has its philosophical structure. It artistically celebrates the existence of the Singular Reality and reiterates that there is none other besides Him: *Prabh binu avaru na koi* (3); *prabh tudhu binu dūjā ko nahī* (5); *prabh viṇu dūjā ko nahī* (8). This adumbrates the basic tenet of the Sikh faith. The poem also poses the Sikh paradox that while He is in everything and is everywhere: *Jali thali mahiali pūriā raviā vichi vaṇā* – He pervades waters, the earth and the spaces and He is in the woods and glades (2), He is utterly unfathomable and unknowable – *agam agāhu* (11). Thus fully Immanent as well as Transcendent is He. The Sikh understanding of the world is here affirmed as a "separation" in which there is no essential gap between the Creator and His creation, but because of the illusionary vision, the human ego, the self is seen as apart from its ontological core. The soteriological goal thus is the "unity" which rather than being a physical merging is fundamentally a realization of That One within. Furthermore, in keeping with the Sikh metaphysical postulate, God is compassionate and merciful, and He will by His grace (*nadar*) end some day all duality and suffering. In fact, so caring is the Lord Master that "He will draw you unto Himself by the arm for union everlasting – *karu gahi līnī pārbrahmi bahuṛi na vichhuṛīāhu* (11). The concluding verses recall towards the phenomenal world. One must participate in life, discarding hesitation. All beginnings will be made auspicious for him were he to have trust in the Divine favour. Optimism is the keynote of this poem of *virahā* or the pang of separation. The philosophical ideals of the Sikh faith have thus been mirrored most poetically in the *Bārah Māhā*. The reader is struck immediately by the enthralling rhythm of the composition. Both assonance and consonance have been employed to telling effect. The lines in the different stanzas run in rhyme. For instance, in the opening passage, "*ām*" is repeated throughout; in the second, "*ṇā*"; in the last "*re*". Gurū Arjan's *Bārah Māhā* is recited ceremonially at Sikh congregations or by individuals at their homes on the first day of each of the Indian solar months. This is a way of announcing the beginning of the new month and invoking Divine blessing.

BĀRAH MĀHĀ TUKHĀRĪ, Gurū Nānak's twelve-month hymn in Rāga Tukhārī in the Gurū Granth Sāhib, stands out in Sikh literature for its poetic splendour and philosophical import. The movement of the twelve months, including the lunar and solar days, and the effect of their transition upon beings of diverse species – those born from the egg (*aṇḍaj*), those born from the foetus (*jeraj*), those born from the sweat (*setaj*), and those born from the earth (*utbhuj*)– have been poignantly and picturesquely portrayed in this poem. Herein, time and space – universal as well as particular – have been richly fused in the person of a young bride ardently searching for her Divine Bridegroom through the cameos of the changing reality of the twelve months.

The Indian calendar begins with the month of Chet or Chaitra (mid-March to mid-April). It is a month of splendour. Flowers in the woods are in bloom, the bumblebee hums rapturously, the koel sings on the mango tree, the bee hovers around the bush fully in blossom. Chet is springtime when Nature is at its glorious best and the air is saturated with joy. Every creature seems to have someone to celebrate the season's beauty with – the bumblebee its blossoms, the wood its flowers, the koel its mango tree.... But,

piru ghari nahī āvai dhan kiu sukhu pāvai
birahi birodh tanu chhījai
The Groom hasn't returned home;
then how will the bride be comforted?
She shrivels away in pangs of separation.
(GG, 1108)

The young woman, then, is the only one who stands isolated. She is the one who does not have her Groom by her side. The beauty and lusciousness of springtime sharpen her sense of deprivation. Whereas everything in Nature is blooming, she in separation is withering away. Paradoxical though it may sound, this state of contrast with the surroundings presents the picture of an organic structure to which she belongs and of which she indeed is the centre. But unfortunately she cannot participate in the reigning beauty of the season, for her Groom is not with her. Perhaps because of her separation and forlornness, she becomes all the more aware of the togetherness and rapture of everyone and everything around her and who all seem to her to fit into a perfectly integrated joyous "system."

Following Chet is the month of Vaisākh (mid-April to mid-May) when the tree boughs get clothed in fresh leaf. The bride "sees" *(dhan dekhai)* the newness in verdure and begs the Groom to come home. Since this is the month of harvest, the farmers negotiate business deals. Commerce enters the bride's vocabulary too : "... *tudhu binu aḍhu na molo kīmati kauṇ kare tudhu bhāvāṅ* ... — without you I am not worth a dime, but if you are with me, I become priceless" (GG, 1108). She then wishes that someone, somehow, would see her Beloved and help her to see Him – *dekhi dikhāvai ḍholo.* Nature, commerce, fellow human beings, spiritual quest become synthesized in the bride's world view.

In the month of Jeṭh "Why should the Groom be forgotten ? — *prītamu kiu bisarai*" (GG, 1108) sings the bride. In the heat of Jeṭh, the earth burns like a furnace. This external heat drives all beings to inwardness. In search of the cool, all creatures are on the lookout for the farthest interior. The bride too – like St. Teresa — moves into her Interior Castle, contemplating upon the Divine Groom and His virtues. The geographical locale is in harmony with her psychological state.

In the scorching month of Āsāṛ, the sun blazes in the skies. Its fire sucks the sap of the earth. The earth roasts and suffers. Even the crickets wail. But the chariot of the sun marches on. The bride seeks shade – *chhāiā dhan tākai.* Here the bride is a full participant in the cosmic scene: she shares the suffering of the earth, of the cricket. The great earth and the tiny cricket are representatives of the entirety of creation. All suffer. Their search for the cool shade is quintessentially reflected in the bride's search for *chhāiā* (shade).

After the blazing heat of Āsāṛ comes the month of Sāvaṇ bringing welcome rainshowers. The earth is cooled and quenched, but not the bride, for her Groom is still in the far-off land– *pir pardesi sidhāe.* She lies alone on the bed. Along with the pain of solitude is the fear: the lightning amid the monsoon clouds terrifies her. Nature around her does not soothe the pain of her heart. She addresses her mother: "*maraṇu bhaiā dukhu māe* – O' mother, it is death for me" (GG, 1108). Having lost her sleep and appetite, the bride in the month of Sāvaṇ lives a death-like life. The integration of polarities – life and death, lightning in the skies and the bed on which she, alone, tosses and turns in darkness – is accomplished in the person of the bride.

Bhādoṅ is the month of opulence : both land and river are in flood. During the entire dark night it rains. Birds and animals feel invigorated. They shriek as if they cannot contain the fullness within: peacocks sing, the frogs croak, the *papīhā* cries forth, "*priu priu*– Love O' my Love." Overflowing with life, the snakes sneak out to bite; the mosquitoes swarm out to sting. And the pools overflow with water. The pulsating animate and inanimate worlds are co-ordinated into a vivid pattern. Juxtaposed to this bursting forth of Nature is the bride's desolation. She yearningly contemplates the fullness, the energy, the joy surrounding her. Standing in the centre of it all, she exclaims, "*binu hari kiu sukhu pāīai* – where, where is comfort for one without the Groom ?"

The bride's actualization of Asuni (Asūj), the seventh month, is, in fact, a realization of her own self. The cosmic time and space mirror her situation. Because she is beguiled by a sense of duality, she stands forsaken by her singular Groom and remains in separation. On the ground, "*kukah kāh si phule* – the country-shrubs bearing white flowers are in bloom" (GG, 1109). These white flowers represent her own white hair; the bride is greying. Furthermore, the coming season frightens her: "*āgai ghām pichhai ruti jāḍā dekhi chalat manu ḍole* – gone is the summer and cold winter is soon to come; this makes my heart tremble" (GG, 1109). What the bride realizes at this seasonal juncture is the loss of her youth and the setting in of old age, and she becomes apprehensive. But she also sees in this autumn month some green boughs which instil optimism in her. The possibility of meeting with her Groom again strikes her. "*sahaji pakai so mīṭhā* – that alone is ripe-sweet which ripens slowly in its own sweet time" (GG, 1109), the bride tells herself.

In the month of Kattak or Kārtik, the days begin to get shorter. Lamps are lit earlier in the evenings. The lamp becomes in the poem a symbol rich in nuance. It represents the refined emotional and intellectual faculties of the bride which will eventually lead her to apprehend the Divine. The traditional lamp or *dīpak* is a tiny clay bowl, pointed at one end, with a cotton wick and filled with oil. But only that lamp shines steadily which is lighted by the match of knowledge – *dīpaku sahaji balai tati jalāiā*, and whose oil is *rasa*, the aesthetic essence of love – *dīpak rasa telo* (GG, 1109). Simultaneously, the lamp is essential to seeing, to recognizing. The powers of eyesight and insight coalesce in it. Suggesting coalition of knowledge (kindling match) and love (oil) in the bride's psychological condition, the *dipak* connects her physical with "cosmic" time, with the evenings of the month of Kattak. In this state she feels she is closer to achieving her goal– union with the Groom.

In the month of Maghar, the bride listens to the praise of her Divine Groom through song, music, and poetry, and her sorrow departs – "*gīt nād kavit kavai suṇī rām nāmi dukhu bhāgai*" (GG, 1109). Here can be discerned the effect of aesthetics upon the human mind: music/sound which travels in external atmosphere penetrates into the very being of the bride. Thereby, her sorrow (*dukhu*), literally vanishes away (*bhāgai*). Vividly comes through the passage the picture of the bride sitting amidst other women and men, listening to song, music and poetry. She is part of a symphonic gathering, the congregation or *saṅgat* in Sikh terminology – in the Tolstoyan sense, a community created by art. We thus see in the month of Maghar the bride as a participant within a community which cherished the recital of the Divine Name.

The description of the month of Poh or Pokh begins with the line:

pokhi tukhāru paṛai vaṇu triṇu rasu sokhai

In Pokh the snow falls, sapping the *rasa* from woods and grass. (GG, 1109)

And it ends with:

nānak raṅgi ravai rasi rasīā hari siu prīti saneho

Says Nānak, the bride who is in love with her Groom has the *rasa* of the charming Beloved to savour. (GG, 1109)

The contrast between the opening and the final line of the hymn is conspicuous : the cold white frost covering the earth sapping sway *rasa* of all vegetation is juxtaposed to the bride who, in her love for the charming Groom, would be savouring its *rasa*. Perhaps it is the panorama of the starkly white frost which ignites in the bride's imagination that warm and vibrant phantasy. Also, in the month of Pokh, the bride discerns herself to be related with all other creatures:

aṇḍaj jeraj setaj utbhuj ghaṭi ghaṭi joti samāṇī.
darsanu dehu daiāpati dāte gati pāvau mati deho.

(GG, 1109)

The one light (*jyoti*) permeates (*samāṇī*) all hearts (*ghaṭi ghaṭi*), be they egg-born (*aṇḍaj*), foetus-born (*jeraj*), sweat-born (*setaj*), or earth-born (*utbhuj*). Through the singular *elan vital* the bride perceives the unity of the universe. From within this linked circle, she, in a lovely alliteration of the "*d*"–"*d*'s" creating a circle of their own, ardently implores her Compassionate Groom (*daiāpati dāte*) to bestow upon her a vision of Himself (*darsanu dehu*).

In Māgh, the month of pilgrimage, the bride realizes that the pilgrim seat is within herself. The sacredness of all holy places and of all time would be hers, if her beauteous Groom was pleased with her:

prītam guṇ aṅke suṇi prabh baṅke tudhu bhāvā sari nāvā
Gaṅg jamun tah beṇī saṅgam sāt samund samāvā
puṅn dān pūjā parmesur jugi jugi eko jātā
nānak māghi mahārasu hari japi aṭhsaṭhi tīrath nātā

This would be my bath in the Gaṅgā, the Yamunā and confluence with the Sarasvatī and in the Seven oceans as well.

All charity and worship for me is the recognition that, throughout the *yugas*, there is but One Singular Groom.

Says Nānak, in the month of Māgh, to taste the great essence of the meditation upon the Beloved is alone worth bath in the sixty-eight holy rivers. (GG, 1109)

The pilgrim seat is within and not anywhere without. The sacredness of all holy places and of all time, the merit of bathing at the Gaṅga and the Yamunā and at their confluence with the Sarasvatī as well as in the seven oceans, of all charity and worship would be the bride's if she were to win the Groom's favour. The Sikh view that external ritual is empty and unnecessary is here artistically established. Also, time is not chopped up: "*yugas*" are, in the literal sense, "yoked together" by the knowledge that the Singular Beloved pervades time past, present, and future.

Finally, in the month of Phalgun, the bride effaces herself – "*āpu gavāiā.*" With the ego gone, her desires are ended – "*man mohu chukāiā.*" Paradoxically, with the "integrator" of time and space gone, what remains is the integration itself. Continuous bliss is experienced. All duality vanishes. Even night and day are conjoined, for what is experienced continuously is utter ecstasy: *"andinu rahasu bhaiā."* (GG, 1109).

The twelve months thus are very important, for it is within them that the "interaction of timeless with time" takes place: the young bride remains in quest of envisioning her Timeless Beloved within her historical context. One discerns here the foundations for the positive approach to life and living in the Sikh faith. In the final passage of the *Bārah Māhā*, Gurū Nānak esteems all the twelve months, the six seasons, the lunar and the solar days, the hours, the minutes, the seconds as *"bhale"* – blessed. Gurū Arjan in his composition *Bārāh Māhā*, in Rāga Mājh, reiterates this affirmative view of the phenomenal world in identical terminology. According to Nānak I, it is sometimes now, somewhere here, that the Singular Being pervading all time and space is instantaneously found:

be das māh rutī thitī vār bhale
gharī mūrat pal sāche āe sahaji mile.
(GG, 1109)

BIBLIOGRAPHY

1. Zbavitel, D., *The Development of the Baramosi in the Bengali Literature.* Archiv Orientalni 29, 1961
2. Vaudeville, Charlotte, *Barahmasa in India Literature.* Delhi, 1986
3. Gunindar Kaur, *Guru Granth Sahib : Its Physics and Metaphysics.* Delhi, 1981
4. Padam, Piārā Siṅgh, *Pañjābī Bārā Māhe.* Patiala, 1959
5. Gurmukh Siṅgh, *Bārah Māhā.* Ludhiana, 1986

G.K.

BĀRĀMŪLĀ (34° - 13'N, 74° - 23'E), a district town 52 km northwest of Srīnagar in Kashmīr is situated at the mouth of the gorge by which River Jehlum leaves the Kashmīr valley after passing through Wular Lake. Gurū Hargobind, Nānak VI, stayed at Bārāmūlā for a few days during his visit to the valley in 1621. A memorial platform was later constructed on the site by devotees. A *gurdwārā*, originally named Koṭ Tīrath but now known as Gurdwārā Chhevīṅ Pātshāhī, was established during the reign of Mahārājā Raṇjīt Siṅgh. Its building was badly damaged by an earthquake in 1885. The present building, a marble-floored domed hall was constructed about 1905. A new double-storeyed hall was erected later under the supervision of Bābā Harbaṅs Siṅgh Kār Sevāvāle. The Gurdwārā is managed by the Jammū and Kashmīr Gurdwārā Prabandhak Board through its Bārāmūlā district committee, which also has the responsibility of running an educational institution, Gurū Nānak Model School.

BIBLIOGRAPHY

1. *Gurbilās Chhevīṅ Pātshāhī.* Patiala, 1970
2. Giān Siṅgh, Giānī, *Twārīkh Gurū Khālsā.* Patiala, 1970

Gn.S.

BĀRĀ SIṄGH, BHĀĪ (1903-1921), one of the Nankāṇā Sāhib martyrs, was the son of Bhāī Pālā Siṅgh and Māī Mān Kaur of Baṇḍālā village in Amritsar district. Some time after his birth on 8 Kattak 1960 Bk/23 October 1903, the family migrated to Chakk No. 71 Baṇḍālā Bachan Siṅghvālā in the newly developed canal district of Lyallpur, now Faislābād in Pakistan. Bārā Siṅgh received his preliminary education in the village *gurdwārā* and joined, at the age of 13, Khālsā Prachārak Vidyālā at Tarn Tāran, where besides scripture-reading and study of Sikh lore he attained proficiency in *kīrtan* (Sikh music). He was deeply affected by the incident, at Tarn Tāran, of 26 January 1921 in which the priests of Darbār Sāhib Tarn Tāran treacherously attacked a band of Akālī reformers led by the Jathedār of Srī Akāl Takht who had come for a negotiated settlement with them. Several Akālīs were seriously wounded and two of them succumbed to the injuries later. The young and sensitive Bārā Siṅgh, disgusted with the acts of the priests within the precincts of the holy shrine, left off his studies and went home. He found the atmosphere in the village charged with commotion at the outrage. Already in that part of the country there had been a lot of resentment at the mismanagement of Gurdwārā Janam Asthān at Nankāṇā Sāhib in general and the unsavoury personal reputation of its *mahant*, or custodian, Naraiṇ Dās. The happenings at Tarn Tāran quickened the tempo of the Akālīs' agitation for the removal of the *mahant* . Two of the six brothers of Bārā Siṅgh – Prītam Siṅgh and Sammā Siṅgh — had already registered themselves as volunteers in the *jathā* of Bhāī Lachhmaṇ Siṅgh of Dhārovālī, a local Akālī leader. It so happened that when an urgent call came on 19 February 1921 for them to report for active duty, Prītam Siṅgh was away visiting some relatives. Bārā Siṅgh at once decided to take his place and immediately left with Sammā Siṅgh for Dhārovālī. Both were brutally done to death along with the rest of the *jathā* after their entry into Gurdwārā Janam Asthān on the morning of 20 February 1921.

See NANKĀṆĀ SĀHIB MASSACRE

BIBLIOGRAPHY

Shamsher, Gurbakhsh Siṅgh, *Shahīdī Jīvan*. Nankana Sahib, 1938

G.S.G.

BĀRAṬH, a village 8 km southwest of Paṭhānkoṭ (32° - 15'N, 75° - 32'E) in Gurdāspur district of the Punjab, has a historical shrine, Gurdwārā Tap Asthān Bābā Srī Chand Jī, popularly called Gurdwārā Bāraṭh Sāhib. Bābā Srī Chand, the elder son of Gurū Nānak, chose for himself the life of a recluse. After Gurū Nānak's passing away, he left Kartārpur and spending sometime at the village of Pakkhoke, established a hermitage at Bāraṭh which became the centre of the Udāsī sect he had founded. Gurūs held him in high esteem for his spiritual eminence. Gurū Arjan and, after him, Gurū Hargobind travelled to Bāraṭh especially to meet him. According to local tradition, Gurū Arjan sought Bābā Srī Chand's blessing for the completion of the tank at Tarn Tāran. During Gurū Hargobind's visit, Bābā Srī Chand nominated Bābā Gurdittā, the Gurū's eldest son, his successor as head of the Udāsī sect.

The shrine at Bāraṭh was maintained by Udasī priests until the Gurdwārā reform movement of 1920's when it passed into the control of the Shiromaṇī Gurdwārā Parbandhak Committee. Construction of the present complex commenced in 1968. It comprises the old domed room, with a tall brass pinnacle, on top of a mound, since renovated and extended by a circumambulatory verandah, a vast fenced compound on an elevated surface, and a row of rooms for pilgrims and the Gurū kā Laṅgar. An octagonal pillar of mosaic concrete, in front of a square flat-roofed room, is dedicated to the Fifth Gurū. It is known as Thamm Sāhib Srī Gurū Arjan Dev Jī. The old Bāolī Sāhib, since converted into a small circular tank, is in a separate compound about 50 metres away from the main shrine. A small pond and a few trees, to the southeast of the Gurdwārā, represent the old garden where Gurū Hargobind is believed to have encamped at the time of his visit to Bāraṭh.

The Gurdwārā owns 60 acres of arable land and is administered by a manager appointed by the Shiromaṇī Gurdwārā Parbandhak Committee and assisted by a local committee. The Tap Asthān, where the Gurū Granth Sāhib is now seated, is visited by a large number of devotees, especially on *amāvasyā*, the last day of the dark half of the lunar month, when religious *dīvāns* and community meals take place. The most important function of the year is a two-day fair held in mid-April to celebrate Baisākhī.

BIBLIOGRAPHY

1. Tārā Siṅgh, *Srī Gur Tīrath Saṅgrahi.* Amritsar, n.d.
2. Ṭhākar Siṅgh, Giānī, *Srī Gurduāre Darshan.* Amritsar, 1923
3. Raṇdhīr Siṅgh, Bhāī, *Udāsī Sikkhāṅ dī Vithiā.* Amritsar, 1959

M.G.S.

BARELAVĪ, SAYYID AHMAD (1786-1831), leader of the militant Wahābī movement in India for the purification and rehabilitation of Islam, was born at Rāe Barelī, in present-day Uttar Pradesh, on 29 November 1786, in a Sayyid family. At school, he took more interest in sports than in studies. He attained proficiency in wrestling, swimming and archery and developed a robust physique. During 1803-04, when 18 years of age, he set out for Lucknow with seven companions in search of employment. For seven months, he lived on the hospitality of a local aristocrat who knew the family, but got no employment. He then went to Delhi where he became a disciple of Shāh Abdul Azīz, son of Shāh Walīullah (1702-63) of the Naqshbandī order, who became the moving spirit for the reform and renovation of Islam in India. About 1808, he returned to Rāe Barelī and got married. He left for Delhi again in 1811 and, after a short stay there, proceeded to Central India to join Amīr K͟hān Ruhīlā, an ambitious Afg͟hān adventurer connected with the notorious predatory Piṇḍārīs. Amīr K͟hān was later elevated Nawāb of Ṭoṅk by the British. He stayed with Amīr K͟hān for about six years, and returned to Delhi in 1818. There he turned a religious zealot and began to preach and make disciples. He toured various districts of Uttar Pradesh, his following constantly increasing. In 1822, he visited Mecca and, on return to India the following year, proclaimed himself a reformer (*mujtahid*), preaching Wahābī doctrines.

Sayyid Ahmad gathered around himself a motley crowd of followers, religious enthusiasts, *mullahs,* mercenaries, and all those willing to wage war in the cause of Islam. Fearful of fomenting trouble in the British territory, he, in 1826, crossed over to Afg͟hān-Sikh borders. Among his supporters were the Nawāb of Ṭoṅk and the Tālpurian Amīrs of Sindh. He reached Qandahār and fording the River Kābul, entered the turbulent Yūsafzaī hills. From the barren Yūsafzaī hills, he raised the cry of holy war (*jihād)* against the "infidel Sikhs" who, he proclaimed, had usurped all Afg͟hān territories in India. In a manifesto issued in December 1826, he charged Sikhs with having committed atrocities on Muslims. To their total annihilation he pledged himself.

On 21 December 1826, Sayyid Ahmad crossed the Sikh frontier and fell upon Akoṛā, near Attock, but the garrison under Buddh Siṅgh Sandhāṅvālīā repulsed him. Sayyid Ahmad hastily retired, having lost a large number of his men. Early in 1827, about 80,000 Yūsafzaīs and 20,000 Durrānī troops, with 8 guns, swelled the ranks of the Sayyid's *mujāhidīn.* The host then advanced towards Buddh Siṅgh's new camp at Shaidū, a few kilometres south of Akoṛā. The *mujāhidīn* had some initial success in forcing the Sikh advance posts back to their camp, but ultimately the Sikhs won the day, though Buddh Siṅgh himself was killed in the battle.

Sayyid Ahmad continued inciting the Afg͟hān tribes against the Sikhs. In 1829, his men invaded Peshāwar whose tributary governor, Yār Muhammad K͟hān, was fatally wounded, but the arrival of a force under Kaṅvar Sher Siṅgh and General Ventura saved the situation for the Sikhs. Sayyid Ahmad fled towards Hazārā, but continued his campaign of calumny against the Sikhs. In 1830, a Sikh force commanded by Harī Siṅgh Nalvā and General Ventura drove him across the River Indus, but soon after he fell upon Peshāwar, defeated its new governor, Sultān Muhammad K͟hān Bārakzaī, and occupied the town. The jubilant Afghān tribes hailed him as the *Khalīfāt ul-Musalmīn,* i.e. the Caliph of the Muslims. He installed himself as the ruler of Peshāwar and struck coins in his name with high-sounding inscriptions.

His rule was, however, short-lived. The innovations he introduced in the agrarian system and in the administration of justice in accordance with his fanatical doctrines aroused the opposition of the Sunnī *mullahs.* Further, he imposed a tithe on the peasants. The Afghān *jirgās* denounced him as an impostor and the *mullahs* clamoured for his expulsion from among their midst. Sayyid Ahmad hastily surrendered Peshāwar to Sultān Muhammad Khān Bārakzaī, the Sikh tributary, and fled across the Indus.

In May 1831, a strong Sikh force under Prince Sher Siṅgh overtook him, and in a short action at Bālākoṭ, on 6 May 1831, he was slain along with his few adherents. Mahārājā Raṇjīt Siṅgh ordered celebration of the event with illuminations and discharge of guns throughout the kingdom.

BIBLIOGRAPHY

1. Sūrī, Sohan Lāl, *'Umdāt-ut-Twārīkh*. Lahore, 1885-89
2. Ahmad, Mohiuddin, *Saiyid Ahmad Shahid*. Lucknow, 1975
3. Hasrat, B.J., *Life and Times of Ranjit Singh*. Nabha, 1977
4. Khushwant Singh, *A History of the Sikhs,* vol. I. Princeton, 1963

S.S.B.

BARGĀṚĪ, village 15 km southeast of Koṭ Kapūrā (30° - 35'N, 74° - 49'E) in Farīdkoṭ district of the Punjab, is sacred to Gurū Gobind Siṅgh who visited it in December 1705 on his way from Dīnā to Koṭ Kapūrā. A shrine was established later on the site on the northern edge of the village where the Gurū had halted. Bargāṛī gained prominence in 1924 during the Jaito campaign when the first Shahīdī Jathā or band of Sikh volunteers, determined to reach Gurdwārā Gaṅgsar or meet martyrs' death, made, in its march from Amritsar, its last overnight halt at this village. The villagers served the *jathā* as well as the large crowd that had gathered around it during its long journey with great devotion and zeal.

Gurdwārā Pātshāhī Dasvīṅ, inside a walled compound entered through a gateway, preserves the old sanctum, a 5-metre square room, to which a 10-metre square hall has been added in recent years. The Gurdwārā is endowed with 20 acres of land and is managed by the Shiromaṇī Gurdwārā Parbandhak Committee through a local committee. Besides the daily services, special *dīvāns* take place on the first of every Bikramī month, and all major anniversaries on the Sikh calendar are observed. The occasion marked by special fervour is the annual festival of Baisākhī, birthday of the Khālsā.

BIBLIOGRAPHY

1. Tārā Siṅgh, *Srī Gur Tīrath Saṅgrahi*, Amritsar, n.d.
2. Ṭhākar Siṅgh, Giānī, *Srī Gurduāre Darshan*. Amritsar, 1923
3. *Mālvā Desh Raṭan dī Sākhī Pothī*. Amritsar, 1968

M.G.S.

BAṚH, a town in Paṭnā district of Bihār, 56 km east of old Paṭnā city (25° -37'N, 85° - 10'E), is sacred to Gurū Tegh Bahādur who stayed here during his tour of the eastern districts in 1666. It has one Suthrāshāhī Saṅgat and two Udāsī Saṅgats existing of old. Gurū Tegh Bahādur stayed at what is known as Baṛī (larger) Saṅgat, situated in Chūnā Khārī Mohallā. It was spread over a one-acre compound and had a prayer hall with the Gurū Granth Sāhib seated in the centre. But the building was completely destroyed in the 1934 earthquake, with the exception of an old well which is still in use. The priests never had the resources to rebuild it, though they continue to be in possession of the open site. They claim to belong to Nānak Panthī Udāsīn Mat, but do not observe celibacy. They live with their families in a couple of rooms in one corner, and follow mundane professions for their livelihood. However, a hand-written copy of the Gurū Granth Sāhib and an old Janam Sākhī are kept by them reverently wrapped in coverlets.

A small *gurdwārā* has been established in Baṛh in recent years by Takht Harimandar Sāhib, Paṭnā, for half a dozen families of native Bihārī Sikhs. It is located in Balīpur Mohallā, Pīpal Tāl, near Tirāhā Chowk.

BIBLIOGRAPHY

1. Tārā Siṅgh, *Srī Gur Tīrath Saṅgrahi.* Amritsar, n.d.
2. Ṭhākar Siṅgh, Giānī, *Srī Gurduāre Darshan.* Amritsar, 1923
3. Faujā Siṅgh, *Gurū Teg Bahādur : Yātrā Asthān, Pramparāvāṅ te Yād Chinn.* Patiala, 1976

M.G.S.

BARHE, village 6 km southwest of Buḍhlāḍā Manḍī (29° -55'N, 75° - 33'E) in Baṭhinḍā district of the Punjab, is sacred to Gurū Tegh Bahādur, who, according to the *Sākhī Pothī*, spent a rainy season here, while travelling through the Mālvā country. Gurdwārā Srī Gurū Tegh Bahādur Sāhib commemorating the visit is on the northwestern outskirts of the village, near a big pond a part of which has been converted into a *sarovar*. An extensive complex has developed around the old Mañjī Sāhib, a domed room with a square platform within it, near an old *vaṇ* tree. The Gurū Granth Sāhib is seated in a separate hall. There is a separate larger pavilion for holding special congregations on festival days. An annual fair is held on Nimāṇī Ekādashī or Nirjalā Ekādashī falling on the 11th of the brighter half of the lunar month of Jeṭh (May-June). The Gurdwārā owns 65 acres of land and is administered by the Shiromaṇī Gurdwārā Parbandhak Committee through a manager who is assisted by a local committee.

BIBLIOGRAPHY

1. *Mālvā Desh Raṭan dī Sākhī Pothī.* Amritsar, 1968
2. Tārā Siṅgh, *Srī Gur Tīrath Saṅgrahi.* Amritsar, n.d.
3. Ṭhākar Siṅgh, Giānī, *Srī Gurduāre Darshan.* Amritsar, 1923
4. Faujā Siṅgh, *Gurū Teg Bahādur : Yātrā Asthān, Pramparāvāṅ te Yād Chinn.* Patiala, 1976

M.G.S.

BARLOW (d. 1845) an Englishman, while serving with 44th Foot, was taken prisoner by the Afghāns during the British retreat from Afghanistan in 1841. In 1843, he escaped from prison, came to Lahore and entered the service of the Sikh Darbār. Barlow fought against the British in the first Anglo-Sikh war. He was killed in action at Ferozeshāh on 21 December 1845.

BIBLIOGRAPHY

Grey, C., *European Adventurers of Northern India.* Patiala, 1970

Gl.S.

BĀRNĀ, village in Kurukshetra district of Haryāṇā, about 20 km southwest of Kurukshetra (29° - 58'N, 76° - 50'E), is sacred to Gurū Tegh Bahādur who once stopped here while journeying from Kaithal to Kurukshetra. Local tradition recalls the story of a peasant who waited upon him and to survey whose land a revenue official arrived in the village the same day. The Sikh asked the Gurū's permission to go and have his land measured. The Gurū advised him to wait and rely on God. The surveyor measured the land thrice but was puzzled to note that it measured much less than what he had estimated. He therefore sent for the Sikh and asked him how much land he owned. The Sikh answered, "Sir, my land measures 125 *bīghās.*" The officer disclosed that he had measured the land thrice, but found it each time to be no more than twenty-five *bīghās.* The Sikh replied that this must be the Gurū's own miracle. The officer begged to see the Gurū. He became a disciple.

Local tradition also describes the Gurū's visit to Bārnā as having occurred in response to the prayers of a childless lady who wished to present him with a garment she had stitched out of home-spun cloth. Arriving in the village the Gurū received the garment from her and appreciated her dedication. The woman was later blessed with a child. She and her husband, Bhāī Suddhā, built a low platform on the spot where Gurū Tegh Bahādur had sat in their house. A *gurdwārā* was built over this memorial by Bhāī Ude Siṅgh (d. 1843), the ruler of Kaithal.

BIBLIOGRAPHY

1. Ṭhākar Siṅgh, Giānī, *Srī Gurduāre Darshan.* Amritsar, 1923
2. Tārā Siṅgh, *Srī Gur Tīrath Saṅgrahi.* Amritsar, n.d.
3. Faujā Siṅgh, *Gurū Teg Bahādur : Yātrā Asthān, Pramparāvāṅ te Yād Chinn.* Patiala, 1976

M.G.S.

BASĀLĪ, village about 20 km southwest of Kīratpur (31°-11'N, 76°-35'E) in Ropaṛ district of the Punjab, has a historical shrine, Gurdwārā Gurū Chauṅkī Jhiṛā Sāhib, dedicated to Gurū Gobind Siṅgh who after the battle of Nirmohgaṛh in October 1700 stayed here for several days at the invitation of the chief of Basālī. The original shrine inside the *havelī* or fortified house of the chief is no longer in existence. The present complex of the Gurdwārā, south of the village, was raised in 1982. It has two separate three-storeyed domed structures and a flat-roofed hall. The Gurū Granth Sāhib is seated in one of the domed buildings, and the other contains a relic, a *chauṅkī* or low wooden seat, believed to be the one on which Gurū Gobind Siṅgh used to sit for meditation or while preaching. The Gurdwārā is maintained by the local *saṅgat,* i.e. Sikh community.

BIBLIOGRAPHY

1. Tārā Siṅgh, *Srī Gur Tīrath Saṅgrahi.* Amritsar, n.d.
2. Ṭhākar Siṅgh, *Srī Gurduāre Darshan.* Amritsar, 1923

Gn.S.

BASANT, a musical measure used in the Gurū Granth Sāhib. It is a *rāga* of the season of Basant (Skt. *vasant*) or spring, and during that season can be sung any time of day or night. Otherwise, it is reserved for the night between 9 p.m. and midnight. It is a very popular and melodious measure tracing its origin to the eighth century. In the *Rāgamālā,* as included in the Sikh scripture, it is recorded as a son (*putra*) of Hiṇḍol which is also a *rāga* of spring. The only variant of Basant employed in the Gurū Granth Sāhib is Basant Hiṇḍol: the latter is not very popular and is used in no other *granth.* Basant is performed in slow tempo, and this gentle melody depicts quiet joy. The descending scale is usually found at the beginning of a composition with the ascending form following later.

Ascending : Sa Ga M̍a Dha Ṡa
Descending : R̍e Ne Dha Pa — M̍a Ga M̍a Ga Re Sa
Vādīs : *tar saptak* Ṡa and *madhya saptak* Pa
Pakaṛ : Sa Ma Ga, Ma Dha S̍a — R̍e Ne Dha Pa — M̍a Ga M̍a Ga Re Sa

If Basant melodies do not begin on upper Sa, they will move quickly to it, and then slowly descending on the high *vādī.* Descending *vādīs* are characterized by Ma/ *tivra* - Ga in alternate fast and slow sequence. Sometimes a glide comes between Ne and Dha *Komal.* In ascending patterns, Re *Komal* and Pa are avoided.

In the Gurū Granth Sāhib, Gurū Nānak, Gurū Amar Dās, Gurū Rām Dās, Gurū Arjan and Gurū Tegh Bahādur, besides Kabīr, Rāmānand, Nāmdev and Ravidās, have composed hymns in the Basant measure.

BIBLIOGRAPHY

1. Charan Siṅgh, *Srī Gurū Granth Baṇī Beurā.* Amritsar, 1860
2. Giān Siṅgh, *Gurbāṇī Saṅgīt.* Amritsar, 1972
3. Avtār Siṅgh, Bhāī, and Bhāī Gurcharan Siṅgh, *Gurbāṇī Saṅgīt Prāchīn Rīt Ratnāvalī.* Patiala, 1979
4. Srīvāstava, Harishchandra, *Rāg-Parichaya* (Part IV). Allahabad, 1968

D.S.

BASANT KĪ VĀR, by Gurū Arjan, is the shortest of the twenty-two *vārs*, i.e. holy poems composed in the style or tone of odes (*vārs*, in Punjabi) or heroic ballads included in the Gurū Granth Sāhib. Basant, Punjabi for spring, from which musical measure the *Vār* derives its title is, like Malhār (the *rāga* of the rainy season), an ancient seasonal *rāga*-the *rāga* of springtime.

Basant kī Vār comprises three *pauṛīs* or stanzas only, each *pauṛī* consisting of five lines. Like the *Vār* of Balvaṇḍ and Sattā and unlike any other *vār* in the Gurū Granth Sāhib, this *Vār* does not have any *ślokas* added to the *pauṛīs.* The *Vār* addresses itself to the theme of the Gurū's grace which alone will enable man to overcome his ego or selfhood and, thus, attain, communion with the Creator. Springtime is the period of newness when vegetation stirs to life and nature comes to bloom in all its beauty and splendour. As the Gurū's grace occurs, man sheds the winter-born leaves of ego, lust, greed, attachment and anger and blossoms into *nām*, joy in the constant remembrance of God. If Basant, i.e. spring, is the season of union, this *Vār* impresses upon man to submit himself to the true Gurū to achieve union with the Divine. Men who meditate on the Name and surrender themselves to the Will of the Lord are *gurmukhs.* They are holy, turned towards the Gurū (*gur=gurū, mukh*=face, i.e. face turned towards the Gurū). They alone overcome the five vices, companions of *manmukhs,* the self-willed. Such men succumb not to grief, nor are they beguiled by pleasures. They are freed from the cycle of birth and death. Transmigration thus annulled, the self merges in the Creator.

BIBLIOGRAPHY

Bishan Siṅgh, Giānī, *Bāī Vārāṅ Saṭīk.* Amritsar, n.d.

Hn.S.

BASANT SIṄGH, BHĀĪ (d. 1900), one of the founder-members of Srī Gurū Siṅgh Sabhā, Lahore, established on 2 November 1879, worked as its accountant and later became its vice-president. Differences between Bhāī Basant Siṅgh and other leaders of the K͟hālsa Dīwān, Lahore, originating in the expulsion in April 1886 of Bāvā Nihāl Siṅgh and Dīwān Būṭā Siṅgh in April 1886 for their advocacy of the restoration of Mahārājā Duleep Siṅgh to the throne of the Punjab, came to a head when, on 31 October 1887, the Nānak Panth Prakāsh Sabhā, celebrating its seventh anniversary at Gurdwārā Janam Asthān, Lahore, displayed a garlanded portrait of the Mahārājā by the side of the Gurū Granth Sāhib. Bhāī Jawāhir Siṅgh, secretary of Srī Gurū Siṅgh Sabhā, took exception to what he said was an act of sacrilege as well as an act against the pro-government policy of the K͟hālsa Dīwān of Lahore. He particularly criticized Bhāī Basant Siṅgh, who also bore an office in the Nānak Panth Prakāsh Sabhā. Bhāī Basant Siṅgh retaliated a few months later by passing strictures against Bhāī Jawāhir Siṅgh in the audit report (AD 1888) on the accounts of the Srī Gurū Siṅgh Sabhā of which he was the secretary. He and his colleagues were charged with misusing the Sabhā funds spent on defending Giānī Ditt Siṅgh, editor of the *K͟hālsā Ak͟hbār*, facing a defamation suit in a civil court for publishing in his newspaper a portion of his *Svapan Nāṭak* ("Dream Play"), a thinly-veiled satire on the leading figures of the Amritsar Khālsā Dīwān.

In September 1888, Bhāī Basant Siṅgh, who was vice-president of the Srī Gurū Siṅgh Sabhā, Lahore, and Bhāī Sant Siṅgh who was its president, broke away from it and formed a parallel association named Srī Gurū Hitkārnī Siṅgh Sabhā. The new Sabhā enjoyed the backing of Dīwān Būṭā Siṅgh, the proprietor of the paper and press named *Āftāb-i-Punjab*, and Mehar Siṅgh Chāwlā, a rich merchant of Lahore who also became secretary of the Hitkārnī Sabhā, with Sant Siṅgh as president and Basant Siṅgh as vice-president. The Khālsā Dīwān of Amritsar also supported it for its own factional reasons. Bhāī Basant Siṅgh supported the Shuddhī or proselytization movement started by Dr Jai Siṅgh although the Amritsar Khālsā Dīwān was opposed to it, but on the question of the location of the proposed Khālsā College, he sided with it preferring Amritsar to Lahore which was the choice of the Lahore Khālsā Dīwān as the seat for the new college. Again, unlike the Srī Gurū Siṅgh Sabhā and the Khālsā Dīwān of Lahore, he applauded the enterprise of Rājā Bikram Siṅgh of Farīdkoṭ to have a commentary on the Gurū Granth Sāhib prepared by a synod of scholars. He in fact joined the Amritsar Khālsā Dīwān deputation that called on the ailing Rājā on 10 February 1894 at Farīdkoṭ to ask after his health and offer their good wishes for his recovery. But in 1895, Bhāī Basant Siṅgh joined hands with Bhāī Mayyā Siṅgh, secretary of the Lahore Siṅgh Sabhā, and merged his Hitkārnī Sabhā with that body of which he once again became an active member. He also took over editorship of the *Khālsā Gazette* on which he continued to work until his death in Lahore on 13 August 1900.

BIBLIOGRAPHY

1. Pratāp Siṅgh, Giānī, *Gurdwārā Sudhār arthāt Akālī Lahir* [Reprint]. Amritsar, 1975
2. Jagjīt Siṅgh, *Siṅgh Sabhā Lahir*. Ludhiana, 1974

Jg.S.

BASANT SIṄGH, PAṆḌIT (1868-1941), eminent Nirmalā scholar which status is betokened by the prefix *Paṇḍit* (meaning a man of surpassing learning) added to his name, was born on 26 June 1868, the son of Bhāī Kālā Siṅgh of a Jaṭṭ Sikh family of Ḍhiṅgarīāṅ village, 3 km north of Ādampur in Jalandhar district of the Punjab. Having served his apprenticeship with the head of the village *ḍerā* or monastery, Basant Siṅgh left home at the age of 16 and went to Nirmal Pañchāyatī Akhāṛā, premier institution of the Nirmalās, at Kankhal, near Haridvār in Uttar Pradesh, where he learnt Sanskrit and studied classical religious literature under Paṇḍit Dīvān Siṅgh. Two other centres of learning where he studied were Amritsar and Vārāṇasī. Ordained a missionary *sādhū* of the Nirmalā sect, he joined the *ḍerā* at Ṭhīkarīvālā, in present-day Saṅgrūr district of the Punjab. After the death of Paṇḍit Dīvān Siṅgh in 1893, Basant Siṅgh became the head of the Ṭhīkarīvālā Ḍerā at the comparatively young age of 25. Among his students at the seminary was the well-known Paṇḍit Kartār Siṅgh of Dākhā. He also wrote commentaries on Gurū Granth Sāhib and the *Dasam Granth* which have remained unpublished. In 1901, he was appointed to impart religious instruction to the young Mahārājā of Paṭiālā, Bhūpinder Siṅgh. He continued to hold that position of royal tutor for a long time and taught many a young prince of the family, including its future ruler, Yādavinder Siṅgh. After his retirement from the state service he raised several new buildings for Nirmalā monasteries, among them the Ṭhīkarīvālā Ḍerā, Sukdev Kuṭī at Kankhal and Nirmal Anand Bhavan Nivās at Rishīkesh.

Paṇḍit Basant Siṅgh died at Kankhal on 28 June 1941.

BIBLIOGRAPHY

1. Gaṇeshā Siṅgh, Mahant, *Nirmal Bhūśan arthāt Itihās Nirmal Bhekh*. Amritsar, n.d.
2. Prītam Siṅgh, ed., *Nirmal Sampradāi*. Amritsar, n.d.

3. "Paṇḍit Basant Siṅgh Number" of the weekly *Nirmal Pattar.* 26 June 1943

G.B.S.

BĀSARKE GILLĀṄ, village 12 km southwest of Amritsar (31° -38'N, 74° - 52'E) on the Chheharṭā-Jhabāl link road, is sacred to Gurū Amar Dās, Nānak III, who was born here on 5 May 1479. There are three historical shrines in the village.

GURDWĀRĀ JANAM ASTHĀN, a small shrine privately managed, is situated on the site of the old village Bāsarke, now extinct, to the north of the present habitation. It marks the ancestral house and birthplace of Gurū Amar Dās.

GURDWĀRĀ SANNH SĀHIB, the premier shrine here, is also outside the village, 200 metres to the northeast of it. It marks the room where, according to tradition, Gurū Amar Dās coming from Goindvāl had shut himself, because Dātū, the son of Gurū Aṅgad, had objected to his succeeding his father as Gurū. Before the Gurū sat down in solitary meditation, he had hung a notice at its locked door saying that anyone who opened the door would earn his displeasure. When Bābā Buḍḍhā, leading a *saṅgat* anxious to see the Gurū, came and saw the notice, he entered through a *sannh*, lit. hole in the wall as made by burglars, from the rear, and, apologizing for the act, entreated the Gurū not to hide himself from the *saṅgat,* his followers and devotees. Gurū Amar Dās, amused at Bābā Buḍḍhā's stratagem, returned with him to Goindvāl. The room with the wall broken through was preserved as such by Sikhs as a consecrated place of pilgrimage. Sardār Lahiṇā Siṅgh Majīṭhīā (d. 1854) converted it into a proper *gurdwārā.* The present complex spreading over six acres including a congregation hall with its pinnacled dome over the sanctum, *sarovar,* Gurū kā Laṅgar, residential accommodation and parks, was constructed by Bābā Kharak Siṅgh Sevāvāle during the 1950's. The Gurdwārā is managed by the Shiromaṇī Gurdwārā Parbandhak Committee. An annual fair is held on the full-moon day of Bhādoṅ (September) to mark the death anniversary of Gurū Amar Dās.

SAMĀDH BĪBĪ AMARO DĪ, near the village pond north of the village, is a memorial to Bībī Amaro, daughter of Gurū Aṅgad who was married to Gurū Amar Dās's nephew. It was through her that Gurū Amar Dās became acquainted with the sayings of the Gurūs which led him to the presence of Gurū Aṅgad at Khaḍūr.

BIBLIOGRAPHY

1. Tārā Siṅgh, *Srī Gur Tīrath Saṅgrahi.* Amritsar, n.d.
2. Ṭhākar Siṅgh, Giānī, *Srī Gurduāre Darshan.* Amritsar, 1923

Gn.S.

BASĀVĀ SIṄGH, a resident of the village of Sūjovāl in Gurdāspur district of the Punjab, was a close associate of Bhāī Mahārāj Siṅgh, who led a revolt against the British in 1848-49. Basāvā Siṅgh was included in the delegation sent with letters to Bhāī Kishan Siṅgh, Bhāī Nihāl Siṅgh and Amīr Dost Muhammad Khān of Kābul to seek support for a fresh uprising after the defeat of the Sikhs in the second Anglo-Sikh war. He returned with a reply from the Amīr and re-joined Bhāī Mahārāj Siṅgh at Kurālā Kalāṅ, in Hoshiārpur district. He however was not present when Bhāī Mahārāj Siṅgh was arrested along with his companions on 28-29 December 1849.

BIBLIOGRAPHY

Ahluwalia, M.L., *Maharaj Singh.* Patiala, 1972

M.L.A.

BASĀWAN, SHAIKH, a ranked Muslim officer at Mahārājā Raṇjīt Siṅgh's court, started his career as an assistant to Misr Belī Rām, who had entered the Mahārājā's service in 1809 and who in 1816 had become superintendent of the *toshā<u>kh</u>ānā* or treasury. Basāwan by dint of hard work gradually rose in rank and status and had been made a colonel of the <u>Kh</u>ālsā army by 1838 when under the Tripartite Treaty he was given command of the Muslim contingent (6,146 men and 140 pieces of artillery) to escort Shahzādā Taimūr to Kābul across the <u>Kh</u>aibar. Shai<u>kh</u> Basāwan accomplished the task efficiently, occupying 'Alī Masjid on 29 July 1839 and reaching Kābul in time to participate in the victory parade there on behalf of the <u>Kh</u>ālsā army. Lord Auckland, the British Governor-General of India, expressed "high satisfaction" with the conduct of Colonel Shai<u>kh</u> Basāwan, to whom he sent a sword "in testimony of his gallantry and determination."

BIBLIOGRAPHY

1. Sūrī, Sohan Lāl, *'Umdāt-ut-Twārī<u>kh</u>*. Lahore, 1885-89
2. Khushwant Singh, *A History of the Sikhs,* Princeton, 1963, 1966

H.D.

BASSĪ KALĀṄ, pronounced Basī Kalāṅ, village 12 km southeast of Hoshiārpur (31°-32'N, 75°-55'E) claims a historical shrine called Gurdwārā Bābā Ajīt Siṅgh after the eldest son of Gurū Gobind Siṅgh, who, at his father's bidding, came here on 7 March 1703 at the head of 100 horsemen and rescued a Brāhmaṇ's bride forcibly taken away by the village chief, Jabbār <u>Kh</u>ān. The lady was restored to her husband and Jabbār <u>Kh</u>ān suitably punished. A simple mud hut that existed here as a memorial was replaced in 1980 by the present building, a 4-metre square room with a circumambulatory verandah around it, by Sant Javālā Siṅgh, who still manages it.

Gn.S.

BAṬĀLĀ (31° - 49'N, 75° - 12'E), an old town in Gurdāspur district of the Punjab, is sacred to Gurū Nānak, who was married here, according to local tradition, on Bhādoṅ *sudī* 7, 1544 Bk/24 September 1487, to Sulakkhaṇī, daughter of Mūl Chand, of the village of Pakkhoke, on the River Rāvī, but resident at Baṭālā as caretaker of the lands and property owned by an affluent landlord, Ajittā Randhāvā. Two historical shrines in Baṭālā commemorate the event. A third one is dedicated to Gurū Hargobind's eldest son, Bābā Gurdittā, who was also married at Baṭālā.

GURDWĀRĀ ḌEHRĀ SĀHIB, also known as Viāh Asthān Srī Gurū Nānak Dev Jī, marks the house where Bhāī Mūl Chand lived and where the nuptials were performed. It is situated along a narrow lane called Galī Ḍehrā Sāhib between Ṭibbā Bāzār and Baṛā Bāzār. In his later days, Mūl Chand shifted back to his native village, Pakkhoke Randhāve, and his house in Baṭālā became a holy shrine for the Sikhs. *Srī Gur Pratāp Sūraj Granth* mentions that Gurū Hargobind, at the time of the wedding of his son, Bābā Gurdittā, visited this house. It continued to be in private possession until taken over by the Shiromaṇī Gurdwārā Parbandhak Committee in 1921-22. A civil suit filed by the original occupants ended in the early forties by an agreement, out of court, under which the plaintiff, Mahant Harbaṅs Siṅgh, surrendered his right of ownership on receipt of appropriate compensation for the property attached to the Gurdwārā.

The building, constructed by Mahārājā Sher Siṅgh (1807-43), is a 5-metre square domed room with a verandah on three sides, and ancillary accommodation around a marble-paved courtyard. This Gurdwārā is managed by a local committee under the auspices of the Shiromaṇī Gurdwārā Parbandhak Committee. It owns about 40 acres of agricultural land and some urban property. The major event of the year is the fair held in August-September to mark Gurū Nānak's wedding day. A procession taken out from this Gurdwārā returns to it after visiting all other prominent *gurdwārās* of Baṭālā.

GURDWĀRĀ KANDH SĀHIB derives its name from *kachchī kandh*, i.e. mud wall, which, according to local tradition, stood on this site at the time of Gurū Nānak's marriage. It is said that as the wedding party arrived and stopped a little distance short of Bhāī Mūl Chand's house, waiting for formal reception by the host, Gurū Nānak sat down close to the wall. An old lady living near by, pointing to the dilapidated state of the wall, told him to move away from the spot lest the crumbling wall should fall on him. Gurū Nānak assured her that there was no cause for alarm, for the wall would stay intact for a long time. The wall so consecrated by the Gurū became an object of veneration for the devotees who also constructed a memorial platform near it. A symbolic mud wall, neatly plastered, 3 x 5 x 1.5 feet approximately, encased in glass, next to the Gurū Granth Sāhib at the ground floor, now represents the original wall. The shrine was maintained in a private house by a line of resident priests until it was acquired during the 1950's by the Sevā Committee Gurdwārā Kandh Sāhib. The foundation of the present building was laid on 17 December 1956. Standing in a marble-paved compound about 2 metres above the street level, it consists of a 10 metre square hall, with a square sanctum in the middle. The room at the second floor level is used for continuous readings of the Gurū Granth Sāhib. Above it and over the sanctum is a room with a dome covered with white glazed tiles and decorated with a tall gold-plated pinnacle and umbrella-shaped finial. Arched copings decorate the top room and decorative pinnacled domes surround the central dome, while square domed kiosks at the corners adorn the top. The verandah to the left, as one enters, has wall paintings depicting scenes from the life of Gurū Nānak. Gurū kā Laṅgar is across the street, opposite the main entrance.

The Gurdwārā is administered by the Sevā Committee Gurdwārā Kandh Sāhib. Largely-attended congregations take place on every full-moon day. All major anniversaries on the Sikh calendar are observed, but the most important function of the year is the fair held to mark the marriage anniversary of Gurū Nānak on the seventh day of the light half of the lunar month of Bhādoṅ (August-September).

GURDWĀRĀ SATKARTĀRĪĀṄ marks the site where the wedding party of Bābā Gurdittā is believed to have halted. The shrine is affiliated to the Shiromaṇī Gurdwārā Parbandhak Committee and is managed by the local committee of Gurdwārā Ḍehrā Sāhib. The Gurdwārā is a high-ceilinged hall, with a two-storeyed sanctum in the middle and a gallery at first floor level. Above the sanctum are two storeys of square pavilions topped by a dome. The Gurū Granth Sahib is temporarily seated in an old small room near by.

BIBLIOGRAPHY

1. Ṭhākar Siṅgh, Giānī, *Srī Gurduāre Darshan*. Amritsar, 1923
2. Tārā Siṅgh, *Srī Gur Tīrath Saṅgrahi*. Amritsar, n.d.
3. Santokh Siṅgh, Bhāī, *Srī Gur Pratāp Sūraj Granth*. Amritsar, 1926-37
4. Vīr Siṅgh, Bhāī, ed., *Purātan Janam Sākhī*. Amritsar, 1982

J.C.B.W.

BAṬHIṆḌĀ (30° - 14'N, 74° - 59'E), an old town in the Punjab, was called Vikramgaṛh during the pre-Muhammadan period. Tradition ascribes its foundation to Bhāṭī Rāo, a Rājpūt chief who also founded Bhaṭner, present Hanūmāngaṛh, in Rājasthān. The two towns together commanding the area between Hissār and Bīkāner known as Bhaṭiāṇā, land of the Bhaṭṭīs, also commanded the Delhi-Multān route used by early Muslim invaders. The early Muslim historians refer to Baṭhiṇḍā as Tabar-i-Hind (lit. axe of India). Its great Fort with 36 bastions and turrets rising up to 118 feet above the ground level of the surrounding country, is said to have been constructed by Rājā Vinay Pāl. In 1754, the combined forces of Bhāī Gurbakhsh Siṅgh of the house of Bhāī Bhagatū and Ālā Siṅgh, founder of the Paṭiālā family, conquered Baṭhiṇḍā. During the time of Rājā Amar Siṅgh of Paṭiālā (1748-82), who occupied it in 1771, it became part of Paṭiālā state. Mahārājā Karam Siṅgh of Paṭiālā (1798-1845) named the town Gobindgaṛh after Gurū Gobind Siṅgh, though the old name, Baṭhiṇḍā remained in common use. According to Bhāī Santokh Siṅgh, *Srī Gur Pratāp Sūraj Granth,* Gurū Gobind Siṅgh, during his stay at Talvaṇḍī Sābo visited Baṭhiṇḍā in 1706 to survey the strategic importance of the Fort. He was told that the Fort had long been deserted, for a demon resided there. The Gurū entered the Fort with his Sikhs and the legend has since prevailed that he exiled the demon. Two shrines were established later—one inside the Fort where Gurū Gobind Siṅgh had put up, and the other outside it where the Sikhs were encamped.

GURDWĀRĀ SĀHIB PĀTSHĀHĪ 10, QILĀ MUBĀRAK, inside the Fort, a 5-metre square domed sanctum, was constructed by Mahārājā Karam Siṅgh of Paṭiālā. Its interior is decorated with intricate designs in stucco, paint and inset work.

GURDWĀRĀ GOBIND NAGAR PĀTSHĀHĪ 10, in the Hājī Ratan locality adjacent to the Muslim shrine of Hājī Ratan, was reconstructed during the 1970's. The main building is a mosaic-floored hall, with a square marbled sanctum marked off by arches in *pīpal*-leaf design topped by multi-coloured friezes. Above the sanctum are two storeys of square pavilions with a lotus dome on top. Both these Gurdwārās are managed by the Shiromaṇī Gurdwārā Parbandhak Committee through a local committee. Recitation and *kīrtan* of *gurbāṇī* takes place morning and evening and all major Sikh anniversaries are marked by special *dīvāns.*

BIBLIOGRAPHY

1. Tārā Siṅgh, *Srī Gur Tīrath Saṅgrahi.* Amritsar, n.d.
2. Ṭhākar Siṅgh, Giānī, *Srī Gurduāre Darshan.* Amritsar, 1923
3. *Mālvā Desh Raṭan dī Sākhī Pothī.* Amritsar, 1968

M.G.S.

BĀTHŪ, village in Ūnā district of Himāchal Pradesh and 15 km west of Naṅgal along the Naṅgal-Gaṛhshaṅkar road, has a historical shrine, Gurdwārā Gurplāh Pātshāhī Dasmī, commemorating the visit of Gurū Gobind Siṅgh in 1700. Gurū Gobind Siṅgh arrived here from Bibhaur and reposed for some time under a *plāh* tree (*Butia fondosa*) and, according to local tradition, held a discourse with Gurū Nānak's direct descendant, Bābā Kalādhārī, then living at Ūnā. The single-room shrine situated on the bank of the rivulet Soāṅ (pronounced Suāṅ) 200 metres east of the village is said to have existed since the time of Mahārājā Ranjīt Siṅgh (1780-1839) and is now under the control of the Shiromaṇī Gurdwārā Parbandhak Committee.

Gn.S.

BAṬṬHĀ, BHĀĪ, was a *masand* or local leader heading the Sikh congregation at Paṭṭan Shaikh Farīd, better known as Pākpaṭṭan, in Montgomery (now Sāhīvāl) district of Pakistan, during the time of Gurū Har Krishan and Gurū Tegh Bahādur. As is evident from a number of *hukamnāmās* or edicts issued by the Gurūs to the *saṅgat* of Pākpaṭṭan, Bhāī Baṭṭhā was a prominent Sikh of his time.

BIBLIOGRAPHY

Padam, Piārā Siṅgh, and Giānī Garjā Siṅgh, eds., *Gurū kīān Sākhīāṅ*. Patiala, 1986

P.S.P.

BATTICE, an Italian, who joined the Sikh service in 1843. He was employed in the ordnance factory at Lahore for manufacturing gunpowder and saltpetre. In 1844, the army Pañchāyats removed him from the service, along with some other European officers. He died at Lahore soon afterwards.

BIBLIOGRAPHY

Grey, C., *European Adventurers of Northern India* [Reprint]. Patiala, 1970

Gl.S.

BAUṚĀṄ KALĀṄ, commonly called Rāmgaṛh-Bauṛāṅ, a village 5 km southwest of Nābhā (30° - 22'N, 76° - 9'E), in Paṭiālā district, is known for Gurdwārā Bāolī Sāhib, situated on the boundary of Rāmgaṛh and Bauṛāṅ, commemorating the visit of Gurū Tegh Bahādur. The *bāolī* which lends its name to the shrine was constructed in 1869 by the widow of Rājā Bharpūr Siṅgh of Nābhā (1840-63). The Gurdwārā building constructed by Mahārājā Hīrā Siṅgh (1843-1911) was replaced by a new one raised in 1972. The present complex has as its central building a well-ventilated, flat-roofed hall, with a wide verandah in front. The Gurdwārā is administered by the Shiromaṇī Gurdwārā Parbandhak Committee through a local committee.

M.G.S.

BĀVAN AKHARĪ, a poem constructed upon 52 (*bāvan*) letters (*akhar*) of the alphabet. In this form of poetry each verse begins serially with a letter of the alphabet. The origin of the *genre* is traced to ancient Sanskrit literature. Since the Devanāgarī alphabet, employed in Sanskrit, comprises fifty-two (*bāvan*, in Hindi) letters (33 consonants, 16 vowels and 3 compounds), such compositions came to be called *bāvan akharī* or *bāvan akṣarī*. Notwithstanding this nomenclature, no such composition consists exactly of fifty-two stanzas as few stanzas will open with a vowel, and the compounds are generally left out of this scheme of poetry. Sometimes a letter is used to begin more than one stanza. There are two compositions by this title included in the Gurū Granth Sāhib, both of them under *rāga* Gauṛī. One of them is by Gurū Arjan which is also perhaps the earliest in this style in Punjabi literature. The one by Kabīr, which is the other such composition recorded in the Gurū Granth Sāhib, dates chronologically prior to Gurū Arjan's, but Kabīr's language is Sādh Bhākhā inscribed in the Gurū Granth Sāhib in Gurmukhī characters.

BĀVAN AKHARĪ, by Gurū Arjan, comprises fifty-five *pauṛīs* or stanzas of eight lines each, preceded by *ślokas* all of which are couplets except the one preceding the last stanza which is of four lines. Besides, there is an additional couplet following the first *pauṛī* and a nine-line-long *śloka* at the very beginning of the composition which is repeated at the end as well. Since all letters, especially the vowels and conjuncts, of Devanāgrī cannot be used in the Gurmukhī script, this *Bāvan Akharī* does not follow either the order or pronunciation of Devanāgrī and even the number of stanzas is more than fifty-two. Only twenty-nine consonants in Gurmukhī (*k* to *v)* conform to those in the Devanāgrī script and stanzas 17-46 begin with these consonants, with *m* figuring twice. The following stanza (47) begins with a *ṛ*, the consonant that follows *v* in Gurmukhī is redundant in Devanāgrī. The opening sixteen and the last eight stanzas do not follow the order or pronunciation of Devanāgrī or even of

Gurmukhī; a few syllables open more than one stanza and a few which are redundant in Gurmukhī are missing.

The central theme of the composition is summed up in the couplet under *rahāu* or 'pause' which reads : "Extend Thy grace to the helpless one, Merciful Lord ! May my mind in humility adore the dust of the feet of Thy saints !!" "It is His grace one must seek. Through His grace one meets the true Gurū who will show the path to liberation." The opening *śloka*, which is also repeated at the end of the hymn, stresses the importance of the Gurū who is likened to mother, friend, brother – even God. He washes off one's sins and helps one swim across the worldly ocean. God is self-existent. He is the subtle essence as well as the form (1). He is the Giver and dispenses largesse to all, yet His treasures never fail (34). Words can comprehend and describe everything, but not Him (54). This human body has been attained after transmigrating through numerous lower births. This is now man's opportunity, and he must make the most of it. Now he can have the cycle of birth and death rescinded (30). The purpose of human life is to realize God, but man gets entangled in the world and becomes oblivious of Him (6). Yet man need not resort to the forests in search of Him, for He dwells within him (30). He must abandon his ego. Abstinence and physical mortification do not bring enlightenment. The only way to realization is to become worthy of His grace (52). His grace is attained through the aid of the Gurū who brings purity to the life of the devotee and puts him on the path. *Satsaṅg*, or company of the holy, is of crucial value. The mind gets detached from *māyā* and is stilled only if one meditates on the Divine Name. The last stanza is an invocation to God seeking the gift of His Name.

BĀVAN AKHARĪ by Kabīr is one of his longer compositions, comprising 45 stanzas, included in the Gurū Granth Sāhib. The first five stanzas of this composition are introductory and the sixth begins with *oaṅkār*, a word which itself begins with the opening vowel of the Sanskrit alphabet. Of the following thirty-nine stanzas, thirty-six are built around the consonants mostly in their Punjabi form, with certain consonants having been repeated.

Communion with the Supreme Being and the path leading to it form the principal theme of the poem. The letters, says Kabīr, expressing the spiritual bliss of communion with the Supreme Reality are not the fifty-two letters which are used in relation to mundane affairs: spiritual experience falls outside their realm.

Within the spiritual state, all dilemmas are dissipated and one finally realizes God as pervasive Reality like the banyan tree in the tiny seed (3). Once the lotus of the heart blooms with the rays of supreme knowledge, it never withers away in the illusive moonlight of *māyā* (7). The spiritual bliss of a person whose heart is illuminated by the Supreme Light is ineffable. For such spiritual achievement, man needs guidance of the Gurū, i.e. spiritual preceptor. A true follower of the Gurū remains uninvolved in worldly affairs, and revels in the love of the Divine (9). Kabīr affirms the unicity and eternity and pervasive nature of God. One who is detached from this world can alone realize the Divine Essence. There is the thick veil of *māyā* (delusion) over our eyes, which prevents us from perceiving the Ultimate Truth. One who discards evil, overcomes attachment, achieves serenity of mind and is emancipated from delusion.

The language of Kabīr's *Bāvan Akharī* is Sādhukaṛī, with an admixture of Bhojpurī, Persian and Sanskrit words in their then current and popular form. The poem makes use of imagery commonly found in other compositions of the Guru Granth Sāhib : "wife" for the self, "husband" for God, "temple" for the worldly abode, "lotus" for heart and "sun-rays" for the illumination of mind.

R.S.J.
Mm.S.

BAVAÑJĀ KAVĪ, lit. fifty-two poets, is how the galaxy of poets and scholars who attended on Gurū Gobind Siṅgh (1666-1708) is popularly designated. Gurū Gobind Siṅgh, Nānak X, prophet and soldier, was an accomplished poet and also a great patron of letters. According to Sarūp Dās Bhallā, *Mahimā Prakāsh,* he sent out Sikhs to different parts of the country to invite and bring to him scholars of repute. His instruction was: "Let them bring with them works pertaining to the fields they specialize in." When they came, "the True Gurū bestowed great respect and honour upon them and provided for them without discrimination." Although traditionally mentioned to be 52, the number of scholars who came and stayed with the Gurū at one time or the other was even larger. Bhāī Santokh Siṅgh, *Srī Gur Pratāp Sūraj Granth,* mentions 52 poets and Bhāī Sukkhā Siṅgh, *Gurbilās,* 36 *lekhaks* (writers or scribes). Besides, there were *bhaṭṭs* who often recited their own poetical compositions. Several poets like Paṇḍit Sukhdev, Brind, 'Ālim, Kuṅvaresh, Kāṅshī Rām and Nand Lāl Goyā, who had earlier been at the Mughal court, came to spend the rest of their lives at the feet of the Gurū. These men were assigned by Gurū Gobind Siṅgh to the task of rendering of Hindi, Sanskrit and Persian classics into Bhākhā written in Gurmukhī script. The work appears to have been taken in hand quite early in his career, probably in 1678 and spread over the next two decades and more, including four very productive years at Pāoṇṭā Sāhib (1685-88), until the Gurū, foreseeing the impending conflicts that were to engulf Anandpur, relieved the poets, scholars and scribes. Classics such as *Chāṇakya-nīti, Pañchtantra, Hitopadeśa, Upaniṣads* and parts of *Mahābhārata* were translated into Braj and Punjabi and works and manuals on martial arts such as rearing, training and employment of hawks, horses, elephants, camels and dogs were prepared. A few Hindi classics were transliterated into Gurmukhī. According to Bhāī Santokh Siṅgh, *Srī Gur Pratāp Sūraj Granth,* the entire work was collected into a single anthology called *Vidyā Sar* or *Vidyā Sāgar,* lit. ocean of knowledge. The poet even mentions the weight of the whole mass of manuscripts-- nine maunds or approximately 350 kilograms. Whatever the quantity of the material, the entire treasure was lost consequent upon the evacuation of Anandpur in December 1705, most of it in the flooded Sarsā stream. Only small fragments and copies of some of the manuscripts already prepared and carried out of Anandpur by the authors themselves or by others survived. The names of poets and scholars which have come down to us through these fragments or through other works such as *Sau Sākhī, Mahimā Prakāsh, Gurbilās Dasvīṅ Pātshāhī, Srī Gur Pratāp Sūraj Granth, Gurpad Prem Prakāsh* and *Twārīkh Gurū Khālsā* are listed below:

1. Āḍhā
2. 'Ālim
3. Allū
4. Amrit Rāi
5. Aṇī Rāi
6. Āsā Siṅgh
7. Ballū Bhaṭṭ
8. Bhagatū
9. Bhoj Rāj
10. Bidhī Chand
11. Bihārī
12. Brahm Bhaṭṭ
13. Brij Lāl
14. Brikkhā
15. Buland
16. Chand (Chandan)
17. Chandra Sain Saināpati
18. Desū Bhaṭṭ
19. Devī Dās

20. Dhannā Siṅgh
21. Dharam Siṅgh
22. Dhyān Siṅgh
23. Girdhārī Lāl
24. Guṇīā
25. Gurdās Guṇī
26. Gurdās Siṅgh
27. Haṅs Rām
28. Harī Dās
29. Hīr Bhaṭṭ
30. Husain 'Alī
31. Īshar Dās
32. Jādo Rāi
33. Jamāl
34. Kallū
35. Kāshī Rām
36. Kesho Bhaṭṭ
37. Khān Chand
38. Kuṅvaresh
39. Lakkhan Rāi
40. Lāl Khiālī
41. Madan Girī
42. Maddū Siṅgh
43. Madhū
44. Mālā Siṅgh
45. Mall Bhaṭṭ
46. Mān Dās Vairāgī
47. Maṅgal
48. Mathrā Dās
49. Mīr Chhabīlā
50. Mīr Mushkī
51. Nand Lāl Goyā
52. Nand Lāl, Paṇḍit
53. Nand Rām
54. Nand Siṅgh
55. Nan Vairāgī
56. Narbud Bhaṭṭ
57. Nihāl Chand
58. Nihchal Faqīr
59. Phat Mall
60. Piṇḍī Lāl
61. Prahilād Rāi
62. Rām Dās
63. Raghunāth, Paṇḍit
64. Raushan Siṅgh
65. Rāval
66. Shārdā
67. Shyām
68. Sudāmā
69. Sukhīā
70. Sukhīā Siṅgh
71. Sundar
72. Ṭahikan
73. Tansukh
74. Ṭhākar
75. Ude Rāi
76. Vallabh

BIBLIOGRAPHY

1. Bhallā, Sarūp Dās, *Mahimā Prakāsh*. Patiala, 1971
2. Sukkhā Siṅgh, *Gurbilās Dasvīṅ Pātshāhī*. Lahore, 1912
3. Santokh Siṅgh, Bhāī, *Srī Gur Pratāp Sūraj Granth*. Amritsar, 1926-37
4. Giān Siṅgh, Giānī, *Twārīkh Gurū Khālsā*. Patiala, 1970
5. Vidiārthī, Devindar Siṅgh, *Srī Gurū Gobind Siṅgh Abhinandan*. Amritsar, 1983
6. Padam, Piārā Siṅgh, *Srī Gurū Gobind Siṅgh Jī de Darbārī Ratan*. Patiala, 1976
7. Macauliffe, M.A., *The Sikh Religion*. Oxford, 1909

P.S.P.

BAZĪDPUR, village 7 km southeast of Firozpur Cantonment (31° - 55'N, 74° - 36'E) along the Fīrozpur-Ludhiāṇā highway, is sacred to Gurū Gobind Siṅgh (1666-1708), who passed through here in 1706 after the battle of Muktsar. Gurdwārā Gurūsar, formerly known as Tittarsar after a legendary partridge (*tittar*, in Punjabi), marks the site where Gurū Gobind Siṅgh had encamped, and was first constructed in the form of a small Mañjī Sāhib by Bishan Siṅgh Āhlūvālīā, an official under Mahārājā Raṇjīt Siṅgh (1780-1839). It was later developed by members of the ruling house of Farīdkoṭ. Further renovation and additions have been made in recent decades. The complex now has the domed sanctum, a capacious pavilion as *dīvān asthān*, or congregation hall, and the *sarovar* in one compound, and Gurū kā Laṅgar and residential accommodation in another one adjoining it.

BIBLIOGRAPHY

1. Tārā Siṅgh, *Srī Gur Tīrath Sangrahi.* Amritsar, n.d.
2. Ṭhākar Siṅgh, Giānī, *Srī Gurduāre Darshan.* Amritsar, 1923
3. *Mālvā Desh Raṭan dī Sākhī Pothī.* Amritsar, 1968

M.G.S.

BĀZĪGARS or acrobats, a counterpart of *naṭs* outside the Punjab, are a nomadic people travelling from one place to the other, using camels and donkeys as pack animals. Earlier they had been an occupational group performing *bāzī*, i.e. acrobatic feats, in the form of various types of jumps and other bodily exploits and tricks for the entertainment of the villagers for which they were rewarded by their patrons both in cash and kind. In modern times, however, most of them have turned into farm labourers and several groups of them have settled down on the outskirts of villages where they find work. The Indian Constitution recognizes them as a Scheduled Tribe and they enjoy advantages and facilities reserved for this category of people. Within their own tribe, they acknowledge the authority of their Rājā or King, and Rāṇī, the Queen, who are highly revered.

Bāzīgars do not belong to any one ethnic or religious group. The majority of them are either Hindus or Muslims. In the Punjab some of them have embraced the Sikh faith, especially since the days of the Siṅgh Sabhā reform. According to the 1891 census, out of 18,137 Bāzīgars in the Punjab, 1,211 were Sikhs; in 1911, out of a total of 36,354, the number of Sikhs rose to 4,724. The main shrine of the Bāzīgars is at Sāidāṅvālā, in Fīrozpur district, at which they worship and where they make offerings of liquor and where many of their marriages are solemnized.

BIBLIOGRAPHY

1. Rose, H.A., comp., *A Glossary of the Tribes and Castes of the Punjab and North-West Frontier Province.* Patiala, 1970
2. Juergensmeyer, Mark, *Religious Rebels in the Punjab.* Delhi, 1988
3. Sher, Sher Singh, *The Sansis of Punjab.* Delhi, 1965
4. —, *The Sikligars of Punjab.* Delhi, 1966

P.S.J.

BECHINT SIṄGH, BHĀĪ (1872-1921), one of the Nankāṇā Sāhib martyrs, was the son of Bhāī Sundar Siṅgh and Māī Sāhib Kaur, a peasant couple of the village of Pharālā in Jalandhar district. The family migrated to Chakk No. 258 Pharālā in the newly colonized district of Lyallpur in 1892. In 1907, while returning from Haridvār after immersing in the River Gaṅgā the ashes of his deceased wife, Bechint Siṅgh stayed for a couple of months at Amritsar where he came in contact with a holy man, Sant Kirpāl Siṅgh, at whose hands he took the *pāhul* of the Khālsā. He brought the Sant to his village where he lodged the latter in a room specially built for him on his farm. The Sant had the villagers raise a *gurdwārā* in the village. Bechint Siṅgh became a zealous Sikh and especially went to Mastūāṇā, near Saṅgrūr, to participate in *kār-sevā* in progress there under Sant Atar Siṅgh for raising a *gurdwārā*. He also volunteered to join the *jathā* or band of Sikhs who had offered to go to Delhi to rebuild one of the walls of Gurdwārā Rikābgañj demolished by the British or face death. He attended the Akālī *dīvān* at Dhārōvālī on 1-3 October 1920 and accompanied the *jathā* which proceeded straight from that meeting to Siālkoṭ, for the liberation of Gurdwārā Bābe dī Ber. On 19 February 1921, Bechint Siṅgh with his cousin Ghanaīyā Siṅgh was at Chakk No. 91, district Sheikhūpurā for a condolence call when the *jathā* of Bhāī Lachhmaṇ Siṅgh was passing by on their way to Nankāṇā Sāhib. Both joined the *jathā* and attained martyrdom at Nankāṇā Sāhib on 20 February 1921.

See NANKĀṆĀ SĀHIB MASSACRE

BIBLIOGRAPHY

Shamsher, Gurbakhsh Siṅgh, *Shahīdī Jīvan*. Nankana Sahib, 1938

G.S.G.

BEDĀVĀ, lit. disclaimer (*be*=without + *dāvā* = claim). The term came to be used by Sikh chroniclers in reference to an episode relating to the last days of Gurū Gobind Siṅgh's battle at Anandpur during the winter of 1705. As, in consequence of the protracted siege of Anandpur, hardships of the besieged Sikh garrison increased, a few of the Sikhs wavered in their resolution and asked the Gurū's permission to leave the Fort. The Gurū told them that they could go if they were prepared to disown him. A few of them, it is said, recorded a statement disowning him and left. This statement came to be termed as *bedāvā*. As Sikhs who had deserted Gurū Gobind Siṅgh reached their homes, their womenfolk charged them with pusillanimity, and chided them for betraying their Gurū in the hour of need. They offered to go and take to arms if the men would not re-join the Gurū. One of the ladies, Māī (mother) Bhāgo, of the village of Jhabāl in fact donned a warrior's dress and weapons and exhorted them to follow her if they had still any sense of honour left. The men became remorseful. They were preparing to return to the Gurū when news spread in the countryside of the evacuation of Anandpur. When they learnt that Gurū Gobind Siṅgh had himself survived the holocaust and was re-organizing the Khālsā somewhere in the Mālvā region, they, at once set out in search of him, Māī Bhāgo still with them. They caught up with the Gurū just when he faced a strong force led by the Mughal *faujdār* of Sirhind, Wazīr Khān, in hot pursuit of him. They challenged the invading host at Khidrāṇā, now Muktsar, but at that time a small pond, the only water reservoir in that vast desert. They fell fighting almost to a man, but forced the enemy to retreat. *See* MUKTSAR and CHĀLĪ MUKTE.

As quiet prevailed over the battlefield at sunset, Gurū Gobind Siṅgh came down from the high ground from where he had been raining arrows on the enemy to find all the Sikhṣ lying dead except one, Mahāṅ Siṅgh, at his last gasp. The Gurū sat beside him and, placing his head on his lap, asked him for his last wish. Mahāṅ Siṅgh's only desire was that the Gurū should annul the *bedāvā* he and his companions had written at Anandpur. As if the Gurū had anticipated the return of the truants, he had kept that deed of renouncement with him throughout those troublous days and months since leaving Anandpur. He now pulled out of his pocket the *bedāvā* and tore it up to the immense satisfaction of Bhāī Mahāṅ Siṅgh, who then died in peace.

BIBLIOGRAPHY

1. Kuir Siṅgh, *Gurbilās Pātshāhī 10*. Patiala, 1968
2. Santokh Siṅgh, Bhāī, *Srī Gur Pratāp Sūraj Granth*. Amritsar, 1926-37
3. Macauliffe, Max Arthur, *The Sikh Religion*. Oxford, 1909

M.G.S.

BEDĪ, a sub-caste of the Khatrīs, Prākritized form of the Sanskrit *kṣtriya* which is one of the four caste groups into which the Hindu society is divided. The Khatrīs are mainly Hindus though there is among them a Sikh element which is small in number but important historically. There are no Muhammadans in the caste because a Khatrī after conversion into Islam ceases to be a Khatrī and becomes a Khojā. The Khatrīs are further divided into four sub-groups—Bāhrī, Khukhrain, Buñjāhī and Sarīn. Bāhrīs have twelve castes, Khukhrain eight, Buñjāhī fifty-two and Sarīns twenty. In Sikhism, the Bedī caste became pre-eminent because of the birth into it of Gurū Nānak, founder of the faith. Although the caste acquired sacred character which is enjoyed not only by the descendants of Gurū Nānak but by all those born into this caste group, yet this inherited sanctity has not altered the social status of the people within the caste. A legend narrated in *Bachitra Nāṭak* by Gurū Gobind Siṅgh refers to the Paurāṇic division of the Kṣatriyas into three branches—Solar, Lunar and Agnī-kula (Fire race). According to this tradition, the Bedīs belong to the Solar race and are descendants of Kuśa, the twin brother of Lava and son of Lord Rāma. Owing to a misunderstanding, the descendants of Kuśa and Lava fought amongst themselves. In this fight, the descendants of Kuśa were defeated and they rehabilitated themselves at Kāshī (Vārāṇasī) where they studied the Vedas and thus came to be called Vedīs: in Punjabi 'v' often turns phonetically into a 'b'. Vedīs became Bedīs.

Bedīs are mostly concentrated in Ḍerā Bābā Nānak, in Gurdāspur district, in the Punjab. Among Sikhs, the Bedī lineage continued after Gurū Nāṇak through his younger son Bābā Lakhmī Dās. Lakhmī Dās's son Dharam Dās settled down at Ḍerā Bābā Nānak. Two other important centres of Bedīs in the Punjab were at Ūnā, Hoshiārpur district, and Kallar, Rāwalpindī district. Two of the charismatic personalities of later period in the line were Sāhib Siṅgh Bedī (1756-1834), a contemporary of Mahārājā Raṇjīt Siṅgh and Bābā Sir Khem Siṅgh Bedī (1832-1905), one of the founders of the Siṅgh Sabhā movement in the seventies of the twentieth century.

BIBLIOGRAPHY

1. Rose, H.A., *A Glossary of the Castes and Tribes of the Punjab and North-West Province.* Patiala, 1970
2. Nārā, Īshar Siṅgh, *Rājā Jogī arthāt Jīvan Itihās Srī Bābā Sāhib Siṅgh jī Bedī.* Delhi, n.d.
3. Sobhā Rām, Bhāī, *Gur-bilās Bābā Sāhib Siṅgh Bedī.* Patiala, 1988

S.S.V.B.

BEERWAH (pronounced Bīrvāh), a sub-divisional town in Badgām district of Jammū and Kashmīr, 35 km southwest of Srīnagar (34° - 5'N, 74° - 50'E), claims a historical Sikh shrine, Gurdwārā Srī Gurū Nānak Charan Asthān Dūkhnivāran, commemorating the visit of Gurū Nānak to these parts in the early years of the sixteenth century. The old building was washed away by floods in 1948. Only a single small room served as the *gurdwārā* until the present double-storeyed building was constructed in 1975. Situated on the bank of the rivulet Sukhnālā, south of the town, the shrine has a *dīvān* hall on the first floor, with the sanctum in the middle. A separate room to the east of the main building serves as Gurū kā Laṅgar. The Gurdwārā is managed by the Jammū and Kashmīr Gurdwārā Prabandhak Board through its Badgām district committee.

Gn.S.

BEGĀ, BHĀĪ, or Bhāī Vegā, a Pāsī Khatrī of the village of Ḍallā, now in Kapūrthalā district of the Punjab. His name appears among pious and devoted Sikhs of the time of Gurū Amar Dās in Bhāī Gurdās, *Vārāṅ*, XI. 16. He was among the Sikhs who waited upon the Gurū when he visited Ḍallā and received initiation at his hands.

See KHĀNŪ, BHĀĪ

BIBLIOGRAPHY

1. Manī Siṅgh, Bhāī, *Sikhāṅ dī Bhagat Mālā.* Amritsar, 1955
2. Santokh Siṅgh, Bhāī, *Srī Gur Pratāp Sūraj Granth.* Amritsar, 1926-37

B.S.D.

BELĀ, pronounced *bellā*, means, in Punjabi usage, a jungle of tall grasses, reeds and assorted shrubbery along the banks of rivers and streams. The word also received a different connotation when an Udāsī saint and preacher, Banakhaṇḍī, established in AD 1818 a preaching centre on an Island in the River Indus near Sakkhar in Sindh (now in Pakistan) and named it Shrī Sādhubelā Tīrath.

This created a new vogue and several other Udāsī centres adopted the name Sādhū Belā although they were nowhere near a river. Similarly, a Sikh *ḍerā* (habitation with a *gurdwārā)* established by a group of Sikh revolutionaries during 1927-33 was christened Siṅgh Belā. It was located about 12 km north of Bābā Bakālā along the Beās-Baṭālā road in Amritsar district. An innocent-looking place of worship, Siṅgh Belā functioned as the secret headquarters of the revolutionary group who planned and executed (on 8 December 1933) the retaliatory murder of a traitor, Belā Siṅgh, who had earlier shot dead, at the instance of a Canadian Immigration Officer, Bhāī Bhāg Siṅgh Granthī and another Sikh, Bhāī Batan Siṅgh, during a funeral service in a *gurdwārā* in Canada in 1914.

BIBLIOGRAPHY

1. Amar Siṅgh Tegh, *G̲h̲addār dā Katal.* Rajpura, 1966
2. Jagjīt Siṅgh, *G̲h̲adar Pārṭī Lahir.* Delhi, 1979
3. Saiṅsarā , Gurcharan Siṅgh, *G̲h̲adar Pārṭī dā Itihās.* Jalandhar, 1969

M.G.S.

BELĀ SIṄGH, BHĀĪ (1865-1921), son of Bhāī Mayyā and Māī Rājī, a Saiṇī Sikh couple, was born at Kartārpur in Jalandhar district. The family originally belonged to Farīdkoṭ state, from where Belā Siṅgh's grandfather, Bhāī Sobhā, had migrated to Kartārpur where he served in Gurū kā Laṅgar run by local *mahants,* who in recognition of his services had allotted some agricultural land to him. Belā Siṅgh was the first in the family to receive the K̲h̲ālsā- *pāhul.* He engaged himself in agriculture but also continued to serve in Gurū kā Laṅgar. For some reason the *mahants,* towards the end of the century, resumed the land granted to the family. Belā Siṅgh with his wife and two sons migrated to Chakk No. 10 Thothīāṅ in the newly developed irrigation district of Sheik̲h̲ūpurā in western Punjab where he earned his living by ploughing land taken on annual rent basis. At the outset of the Gurdwārā reform movement, Belā Siṅgh with some other Sikhs of Thothīāṅ joined the *jatha* of Bhāī Lachmaṇ Siṅgh Dhārovālī which was massacred on 20 February 1921 at Gurdwārā Janam Asthān Nankāṇā Sahib.

See NANKĀṆĀ SĀHIB MASSACRE

BIBLIOGRAPHY

Shamsher, Gurbak̲h̲sh Siṅgh, *Shahīdī Jīvan.* Nankana Sahib, 1938

G.S.G.

BELĪ RĀM (d. 1843), head of the royal *toshāk̲h̲ānā* at Lahore, was the second of the five sons of Misr Dīvān Chand, a general in Mahārājā Raṇjīt Siṅgh's army. He joined the Mahārājā's treasury in 1809 and within seven years rose to occupy the highest position in it. Besides, he received numerous *jāgīrs,* including that of Raṅghaṛ Naṅgal worth 30,000 rupees a year. Belī Rām maintained strict discipline. He annoyed Rājā Dhiān Siṅgh, the prime minister, by declining him to show a rare piece of jewellery in the *toshāk̲h̲ānā,* royal treasury, without the Mahārājā's permission. When during his last illness, the Mahārājā, on the astrologers' suggestion, desired the famous Koh-i-Nūr diamond to be sent to the Jagannāth Purī temple, Belī Rām refused to accede to the royal wishes declaring that the diamond was not the property of the Mahārājā but that of the State. He made an enemy of Kaṅvar Nau Nihāl Siṅgh by disallowing him entry into the *toshāk̲h̲ānā* without a written order from the Mahārājā. In January 1840, Nau Nihāl Siṅgh fined Misr Belī Rām 5,00,000 rupees and imprisoned him along with his five brothers. When Mahārājā Sher Siṅgh ascended the throne, Misr Belī Rām and his brothers were restored to their old positions. When Hīrā Siṅgh Ḍogrā became the prime minister after the assassination of Mahārājā Sher Siṅgh, he had Misr Belī Rām and his brothers arrested. Belī Rām was handed over to Shaikh Imām ud-Dīn, who kept him in chains in his stables, before strangling him to death on 17 September 1843. Belī Rām had three sons, Rām Dās and Ṭhākur Dās born to his Brāhmaṇ wife, and Khurram Rāi to his Muslim wife. Rām Dās escaped to Fīrozpur, and others to Ludhiāṇā. They returned to Lahore after Hīrā Siṅgh's death on 21 December 1844. After annexation, Rām Dās got from the British a pension of 2,000 rupees per mensem. Belī Rām's wives Gulāb Devī and Misrāṇī Begam received a pension of 1,387 rupees each.

BIBLIOGRAPHY

1. Sūrī, Sohan Lāl, *'Umdāt-ut-Twārīkh*. Lahore, 1885-89
2. Bhagat Singh, *Maharaja Ranjit Singh and His Times*. Delhi, 1990
3. Chopra, B.R ., *Kingdom of the Punjab*. Hoshiarpur, 1969

H.R.G.

BENET, a Frenchma n, was one of the European physicians at the court of Mahārājā Raṇjīt Siṅgh. He arrived at Lahore in 1838, and was given employment as a personal physician to the Mahārājā and surgeon-general to the Khālsā army on a monthly salary of Rs 1,000. After the Mahārājā's death, Benet left Lahore. He shifted to Ludhiāṇā and started practice as a physician. He had some trouble with the British there and was forced to return to his native France.

BIBLIOGRAPHY

Grey, C., *European Adventurers of Northern India*. Patiala, 1970

Gl.S.

BENGAL AND INDIA SECRET LETTERS, also known as Letters received from India and Bengal or merely Secret Letters to the Secret Committee, preserved at the India Office Library, London. This correspondence is arranged in two series: the first covers the period 1778-1859 and the second 1817-1857. Relevant Enclosures to Secret Letters on the events and matters of India policy, from 1778 to 1859, are huge in bulk – over 20,000 bound volumes. Some of these Secret Letters have been printed in the Blue Books, presented to British Parliament, viz. Shāh Zamān's apprehended invasion of India-1806-XV (11); Afghanistan - 1839-XI, XXV (30); Sind - 1843 - XXXIV; and the Sikh Wars-1846, XXI.

The letters of 1804 throw light on the transactions of Lake and Ochterlony in the cis-Sutlej region, and those of 1805 on Holkar's intrusion into the Punjab. As the British interest increased in the affairs of the Sikhs, the Secret Letters became more detailed, especially about Shāh Zamān's invasion of the Punjab and the first British mission to the Sikh court (1798); the Metcalfe Mission to Lahore (1808); the imagined Sikh-Marāṭhā intrigues (1810); and the warlike preparations of Raṇjīt Siṅgh. The Enclosures to this correspondence include important documents such as Metcalfe's Minute on the British policy towards the Sikh-Scindia tangle (1830); Trevelyan's report on the Indus Navigation Scheme (1831), and the Ropaṛ meeting between Lord William Bentinck and Mahārājā Raṇjīt Siṅgh (1831). Secret Letters of later period deal with Auckland's policy towards Afghanistan and the Sikhs (1838), Punjab affairs and the Sikh co-operation during the first Anglo-Afghān war (1841-42). A number of letters written during the years 1842-44 describe the uncertain political state in Lahore. Events leading to the Anglo-Sikh war of 1845-46, and the details of military operations at Mudkī, Baddovāl, 'Alīwāl and Sabhrāoṅ are given (1846). They also give an account of Lāl Siṅgh's administration and the rebellion in Kashmīr which led to the treaty of Bharovāl. A full account of the uprisings at Multān and Hazārā and particulars of the military operations against Multān, besides the actions at Cheliāṅvālā and Gujrāt are also provided (1848 and 1849).

B.J.H.

BENGAL SECRET AND POLITICAL CONSULTATIONS (1800-1834), a manuscript series of Indian records at the India Office Library, London. This series contains, in full, correspondence and despatches on the early British relations with the Sikhs. Among the more important documents are despatches of the Resident at Delhi concerning the cis-Sutlej region and Lord Lake's correspondence with the Mālvā Sikh chiefs (1804); correspondence relating to Holkar's intrusion into the Punjab, cis-Sutlej Sikhs, and general principles of British policy in the trans-Yamunā region (1805); correspondence concerning Holkar and Raṇjīt Siṅgh and the Anglo-Sikh treaty of 1806; correspondence relating to Raṇjit Siṅgh's Mālvā expeditions; cis-Sutlej Sikh mission to Delhi; Raṇjit Siṅgh-Minto correspondence; Metcalfe's despatches from Lahore; Treaty of Amritsar (1809); and despatches of Edmonstone, Ochterlony and Seton (1807-09). The correspondence on Sikh affairs after 1809 fades out in this series, but opens up again in 1831 and contains all relevant correspondence and despatches regarding the Anglo-Sikh relations till 1834 when this series was discontinued to be replaced by another named India Secret Proceedings.

B.J.H.

BEṆĪ, BHAGAT is one of the fifteen saints and sūfīs some of whose compositions have been incorporated in the Gurū Granth Sāhib. Very little is known about his personal life except that he spent most of his time in prayer and contemplation. Nābhājī's *Bhagatmāl,* which includes him in its roster of well-known *bhaktas* or devotees, narrates a popular anecdote about how Beṇī absorbed in meditation often neglected the household needs and how the Deity himself intervened and physically appeared to help him. Bhāī Gurdās (*Vārāṅ*, X. 14) has referred to Beṇī's single-pointed meditation in solitude enriched by moments of spiritual edification.

Beṇī's three hymns in the Gurū Granth Sāhib are marked by an intense spiritual longing. They also indicate the various paths tried by him in his quest, his practical experience of life and his mastery of religious lore of diverse traditions. His five-stanza *śabda* in Srī Rāga, in terse and elliptical form, traces the gradual spiritual degeneration of man from the time of his birth to the end. It so closely resembles Gurū Nānak's *Pahire* hymns in the same *rāga* that Gurū Arjan, when compiling the Holy Book, recorded the instruction that Beṇī's hymn be sung in the same tune as *Pahire.* In his hymn in Rāga Rāmkalī, Beṇī, using allegorical expressions of the *yogīs,* dwells upon the gradual process leading to the highest spiritual knowledge which is also the ultimate bliss. This hymn, too, has close similarity with several of Gurū Nānak's verses in the same measure. It reveals Beṇī's knowledge of the practices and terminology of *haṭhayoga* as well as his rejection of them in favour of the cultivation of the Divine Name. In the hymn in Rāga Prabhātī, Beṇī censures in the general tone of the Gurūs' *baṇī* the hypocrisy of the Brāhmaṇ who practises outward piety while harbouring evil in the heart. He adds in conclusion that without the true Gurū's instruction way to liberation will not be found.

BIBLIOGRAPHY

1. Kohli, Surindar Singh, *A Critical Study of Adi Granth.* Delhi, 1961
2. Tāran Siṅgh, *Srī Gurū Granth Sāhib Jī dā Sāhitik Itihās.* Amritsar, n.d.
3. Sāhib Siṅgh, *Saṭīk Bhagat-Bāṇī,* part I. Amritsar, 1979
4. Gurdit Siṅgh, Giānī, *Itihās Srī Gurū Granth Sāhib (Bhagat Bāṇī Bhāg).* Delhi, 1990

T.S.

BEṆĪ, PAṆḌIT, a learned Brāhmaṇ of

Chūnīāṅ, in present-day Lahore district of Pakistan, was a devoted Sikh of the time of Gurū Amar Dās. As he first visited Goindvāl, he came loaded with books to demonstrate his learning. Gurū Amar Dās spoke to him gently: "Mere learning begetteth pride. What aideth one is humility, love and devotion." Paṇḍit Beṇī, as says Sarūp Dās Bhallā, *Mahimā Prakāsh,* had no desire left to show his skill in arguing. He bowed at the Gurū's feet and became a disciple. Gurū Amar Dās, says the chronicler, uttered impromptu a hymn in the Malār measure, addressed to Bhāī Beṇī.

BIBLIOGRAPHY

1. Bhallā, Sarūp Dās, *Mahimā Prakāsh*. Patiala, 1971
2. Ranjit Singh, *Guru Amar Das Ji*. Amritsar, 1980

B.S.D.

BENTINCK, LORD WILLIAM CAVENDISH (1774-1839), Governor-General of India, son of William Henry, third duke of Portland, was born on 14 September 1774. In 1803, he was appointed governor of Madrās, but recalled in 1807 in consequence of the sepoy mutiny at Vellore. In 1827, Bentinck succeeded Lord Amherst as Governor-General of India in which capacity he served till 1835.

Lord William Bentinck's policy towards the Sikh kingdom was dictated by the steady growth of a supposed Russo-Persian threat to India's northwestern frontier. In face of it, the Government of India adopted certain extraordinary measures. In 1830, Alexander Burnes travelled up the River Indus to deliver to Mahārājā Raṇjīt Siṅgh the gift of a team of cart-horses from the King of England to cross with the breeds in the Punjab. His real object in resorting to this riparian mode of journey was to survey the River Indus and its navigavibility and to assess the political and military resources of the *amīrs* of Sindh. Burnes' mission was the first step in Lord William Bentinck's policy of counterpoising the Sikh advance southwards in the event of a Russian invasion. Out of Burnes' *Memorandum on the Indus* and deputy secretary Trevelyan's *Report on the Navigation of the Indus* was born the Indus navigation scheme, which in reality aimed at the establishment of British influence in Sindh and the prevention of Sikh advance southwards. Bentinck's scheme ostensibly aimed at the opening of the navigation of the Indus to the commerce of India and Europe. The river flowed 150 miles in Sindh, and from its junction with the Punjab rivers northwards of Pañjnad, it lay within the territories of Raṇjīt Siṅgh and his tributary, Bahāwalpur. Consequently it was thought essential to enter into agreements with Raṇjīt Siṅgh, the Dāūdpotās of Bahāwalpur, and the Tālpurian *amīrs* of Sindh. The scheme, after a short spurt of commercial activity, was given up. Yet, Bentinck's recourse to "material utilitarianism" did confer the desired political advantages on the British—the establishment of British political connections with the states and the chiefs of the Indus to the disadvantage of the Sikhs.

Lord William Bentinck's meeting with Mahārājā Raṇjit Siṅgh at Ropaṛ in October 1831 had likewise a political purpose. It was meant to be a camouflage to cover British negotiations with the *amīrs* of Sindh and to forestall the Sikh advance on Shikārpur and Sindh. The Ropaṛ meeting is memorable for the display of unparalleled oriental pageantry on both sides, yet its apparent affability was deceptive. Raṇjīt Siṅgh felt uneasy and expressed a desire to open negotiations with the British government on the subject of his relations with Sindh. He even hinted at a joint Anglo-Sikh enterprise in Sindh, but the Governor-General remained reticent. Three days earlier, Henry Pottinger had proceeded to the court of the *amīrs* to negotiate a defensive and offensive alliance with them. To lull the apprehensions of the Mahārājā, Bentinck gave him a vague written assurance for the continuance of "eternal friendly relations" with the Sikh State.

BIBLIOGRAPHY

1. Cunningham, Joseph Davey, *A History of the Sikhs*. London, 1849
2. Gupta, Hari Ram, *Panjab on the Eve of First Sikh War*. Chandigarh, 1975
3. Harbans Singh, *Maharaja Ranjit Singh*. Delhi, 1980
4. Buckland, C.E., *Dictionary of Indian Biography*. *London, 1906*

B.J.H.

BHADAUṚ, a small town 25 km northwest of Barnālā (30°-22'N, 75°-32'E) in Saṅgrūr district of the Punjab, is sacred to Gurū Gobind Siṅgh, who came here from Dīnā in December 1705 following the chase. The area was then an uninhabited jungle land, and it was only after the village of Bhadauṛ was founded by Bābā Ālā Siṅgh, eighteenth-century Sikh warrior and noble, that a shrine commemorating the Gurū's visit was established here. Local tradition had also preserved the memory of Gurū Hargobind having passed through this place so that the shrine was designated as Gurdwārā Sāhib Pātshāhī Chhemī Ate Dasmī (Andrūnī Qilā), i.e. the holy *gurdwārā* dedicated to the Sixth and the Tenth Gurūs, located inside the fort. Only a few traces remain of the fort and there are now two different historical shrines in the town.

GURDWĀRĀ SĀHIB ANDRŪNĪ PĀTSHĀHĪ 10 marking the site of the original shrine inside the town is a small building, the sanctum with a hall in front. A sword and a dagger, believed to have come down from Gurū Gobind Siṅgh, are kept here as sacred relics. The hilt of the sword has the Gurmukhī inscription: Srī Akāl Sahāi Pātshāhī 10. Its blade too has some numerals and legends inscribed on one side and a round seal in Persian on the other.

GURDWĀRĀ SĀHIB BAIRŪNĪ PĀTSHĀHĪ 6, half a kilometre west of the town, was known as Samādh Bhāī Charan Dās, until it was acquired by the Shiromaṇī Gurdwārā Parbandhak Committee during the 1970's and converted into a *gurdwārā* dedicated to the Sixth Gurū. The Gurū Granth Sāhib is now seated in the old *samādh* in the centre of what was once a *havelī* or a high-walled house entered through a high gateway which is still intact. An annual religious fair is held here on the occasion of Baisākhī.

BIBLIOGRAPHY

1. *Mālvā Desh Raṭan dī Sākhī Pothī*. Amritsar, 1968
2. Ṭhākar Siṅgh, Giānī, *Srī Gurduāre Darshan*. Amritsar, 1923
3. Tārā Siṅgh, *Srī Gur Tīrath Saṅgrahi*. Amritsar, n.d.
4. Grewal, J.S., and S.S. Bal, *Guru Gobind Singh*. Chandigarh, 1967
5. Harbans Singh, *Guru Gobind Singh*. Chandigarh, 1966

M.G.S.

BHĀDRĀ (29°-10'N, 75°-15'E) in Gaṅgānagar district in Rājasthān, was, according to Sikh chronicles, visited by Gurū Gobind Siṅgh in 1706. There is however no historical shrine there. There are very few Punjabi Sikhs in the town but a number of Sindhī families, who though shaven are followers of the Sikh faith, settled here after 1947. Sikhs of Punjabi and Sindhī origin have a small Pañchāyatī Gurdwārā in Sindhī Mohallā.

Notwithstanding what the chronicles say, the general belief among the Sikhs of this area is that the Gurū went from Nohar to Sāhvā (Suhevā) by the direct shorter route through the village of Sūrpur. This tradition is supported by Bhāī Kāhn Siṅgh, the author of *Gurushabad Ratnākar Mahān Kosh*. Possibly the Gurū visited Bhādrā during his stay either at Nohar or at Sāhvā (Suhevā)

BIBLIOGRAPHY

1. Kuir Siṅgh, *Gurbilās Pātshāhī 10*. Patiala, 1968
2. Ṭhākar Siṅgh, *Srī Gurduāre Darshan*. Amritsar, 1923
3. Tārā Siṅgh, *Srī Gur Tīrath Saṅgrahi*. Amritsar, n.d.

4. Fauja Siṅgh, ed., *Travels of Guru Gobind Singh*. Patiala, 1968

M.G.S.

BHĀGALPUR (25°-14'N, 86°-58'E), a district town in Bihār situated on the right bank of the River Gaṅgā, was visited by Gurū Tegh Bahādur in 1666. Baṛī Saṅgat on Būṛhānāth Ghāṭ, where he stayed, is now represented by a small shrine, constructed in a by-lane in 1974. It is called Gurdwārā Baṛī Saṅgat Srī Gurū Tegh Bahādur Jī Chaukī Sāhib. It contains a stone slab (*chaukī*) which, it is believed, was used by the Gurū to sit on for his bath. Every month, on *amāvasyā* (the last day of the dark half of the lunar month), the Gurū Granth Sāhib is brought here from Gurdwārā Srī Gurū Siṅgh Sabhā and Sikhs congregate for a *dīvān*. An old hand-written copy of the Gurū Granth Sāhib acquired from the former *mahant* of Baṛī Saṅgat is now kept in Gurdwārā Srī Gurū Siṅgh Sabhā, Bhāgalpur.

BIBLIOGRAPHY

1. Ṭhākar Siṅgh *Giānī, Srī Gurduāre Darshan*. Amritsar, 1923
2. Tārā Siṅgh, *Srī Gur Tīrath Saṅgrahi*. Amritsar, n.d.
3. Faujā Siṅgh, *Gurū Teg Bahādar: Yātrā Asthān, Pramparāvāṅ te Yād Chinn*. Patiala, 1976

M.G.S.

BHAGATĀ, BHĀĪ, an Ohrī Khatrī, figures in Bhāī Gurdās's roster of the principal disciples of Gurū Nānak, *Vārāṅ,* XI. 14. To quote Bhāī Manī Siṅgh, *Sikhāṅ dī Bhagat Mālā,* Bhāī Bhagatā, accompanied by Bhāī Jāpū Vaṅsī, presented himself before the Gurū and said, "Holy Sir, we are illiterate and can neither read nor write. How shall we be saved!" "By shunning the ways of the *manmukh,*" said Gurū Nānak. "Pray, unfold to us the ways of a *manmukh*." The Gurū replied, "Recognize a *manmukh* by his four traits, viz. envy, pride, backbiting and aversion to good counsel. These you must avoid, and you must share with your brethren food earned by the labour of your hands." Bhāī Bhagatā and Bhāī Jāpū, continues the *Bhagat Mālā,* practised the precept and attained liberation.

BIBLIOGRAPHY

1. Manī Siṅgh, Bhāī, *Sikhāṅ dī Bhagat Mālā*. Amritsar, 1955
2. Santokh Siṅgh, Bhāī, *Srī Gur Pratāp Sūraj Granth*. Amritsar, 1926-37
3. *Giān Siṅgh, Giānī,* Twārīkh Gurū Khālsā. Patiala, 1970

Gn.S.

BHAGAT (BHAKTA) BĀṆĪ. The Sikh Holy Book, Srī Gurū Granth Sāhib, comprises writings coming from two sources – the sayings of the Gurūs and those of the Bhagats (Bhaktas). The term *Bhagat* here broadly covers, besides some of the saints of medieval India whose compositions occur in the Gurū Granth Sāhib, those outside of the Gurū line whose compositions were entered in the holy book by Gurū Arjan (1563-1606) who compiled the Granth. All these contributors are in common parlance collectively called Bhagats. Under this rubric *bhagat* is included Shaikh Farīd, the Sūfī. Sometimes, the Bhaṭṭs, i.e. bards, who kept the Gurūs company and who recited panegyrics in their honour, Sattā and Balvaṇḍ who sang *kīrtan* or devotional songs in their presence, and Mardānā, Gurū Nānak's life-long Muslim companion who kept him company during his extensive travels, are loosely lumped with them. Strictly speaking, the *bhagat* contributors to the Gurū Granth Sāhib are: Kabīr, Trilochan, Beṇī, Ravidās, Nāmdev, Dhannā, Jaideva, Bhīkhan, Saiṇu, Pīpā, Sadhanā, Rāmānand, Parmānand, Sūr Dās and Shaikh Farīd, the Sūfī.

These two streams mingle together completely and no distinctions are ever made among the writings emanating from them. They all, the writings of the Gurūs as well as those of the Bhagats, constitute one single text. On any point of precept and doctrine both will have equal validity. Both enjoy equal esteem and reverence. In fact, the notion of "two" does not exist. Both signal one single metaphysical truth. The Sikhs have believed through the centuries that they embody one single moral and spiritual maxim.

That they are the product of the same inspiration is also borne out by the way the incorporation of Bhagat Bāṇī into the Sikh writ is comprehended by subsequent Sikh authorities. Tārā Siṅgh Narotam (1822-1891) makes an unnatural deduction. According to his *Granth Srī Gurmat Nirṇaya Sāgar*, Gurū Arjan composed the entire Bhagat Bāṇī keeping in mind "the thoughts of each individual Bhagat." This was a way of saying that those writings were like the Gurūs' very own. And for that reason no less binding on Sikhs than those by the Gurūs. The author of *Gurbilās Pātshāhī Chhevīṅ* had said that the *bhaktas* had their compositions recorded themselves. They—their souls—appeared in person and Bhāī Gurdās, who was writing, saw them with his own eyes. This was the account also given by the author of *Srī Gur Pratāp Sūraj Granth*, a very influential text of the mid-ninteenth century. This was another way of stressing the identity of the message communicated.

The title *Bhagtāṅ kī Bāṇī* appears in the Gurū Granth Sāhib for the first time on page 323 to designate the compositions of Kabīr, Nāmdev and Ravidās in Rāgu Gauṛī. Before that Kabīr's hymns in Rāgu Sirī appear under the title Sirī Rāgū Kabīr Jī Kā (GG, 91). Likewise, for the verses of Bhagat Trilochan, the title used is Sirī Rāgu Trilochan Kā (GG, 92) and for those of Beṇī, Sirī Rāga Bāṇī Bhagat Beṇī Jeo Kī (GG, 93). A verse of Ravidās appears at the end of the page. Generally, throughout the text the compositions of the Bhagats have been credited individually by their names and those of the Gurūs individually by the number in their order of succession – for instance, Mahalā (*mahallā* = Gurū-person) I will register the writings of the First Gurū, Gurū Nānak, Mahalā II, the writings of the Second Gurū, Gurū Aṅgad and so on until Mahalā V which means the Fifth Gurū, Gurū Arjan who compiled the Holy Book. The only other Gurū whose compositions figure in the Gurū Granth Sāhib is Gurū Tegh Bahādur, Nānak IX.

How did this corpus designated Bhagat Bāṇī enter the Holy Book? Bhāī Gurdās in his *Vārāṅ*, I.32, suggests that Gurū Nānak during his travels carried under his arm a book, which evidently comprised his own writings. It might have also contained his record of some of the hymns of the saint poets whom he met during his extensive travels across the country or who had preceded him. According to the *Purātan Janam Sākhī* he handed over such a manuscript to Gurū Aṅgad as he passed on the spiritual office to him. Two of the collections of hymns or *pothīs* prior to Gurū Granth Sāhib are still extant. They are in the possession of the descendants of Gurū Amar Dās, Nānak III. Besides the compositions of the Gurūs, these *pothīs* contain compositions of some of the saints as well—among them Kabīr, Nāmdev, Ravidās and Bhīkhan. Gurū Arjan had access to these *pothīs* and presumably to some other materials as well accumulating over the years. Among them may well have been some writings of the Bhagats as well.

Views differ on whether Gurū Arjan included the sayings of the Bhagats exactly as received or whether he used his discretion in choosing his contributors and in bringing their contributions to conform, in general at least, to the tenets of Sikhism. One thing is certain. Bhagats in the Gurū Granth Sāhib are represented by their hymns, lauding Nirguna Brahm, i.e. God without attributes. Worshippers of Sarguna Brahm, of His Rāma and Kṛṣṇa incarnations, were excluded. Vaiṣṇava *bhaktas* such as Chaitanya and Mīrā Bāī are examples. At places in the text, the

Gurū commented upon, even contradicted, the sayings of the Bhagats and both versions appear in the text. The purpose of such comments was to bring the sayings of the Bhagats in harmony with the Sikh teaching, which was uncompromisingly monotheistic, with a strong belief in a formless deity and which rejected caste and formal ritualism.

Gurū Arjan had the hymns transcribed with extraordinary exactness. He arranged the hymns in thirty different *rāgas* or musical patterns. A precise method was followed in setting down the compositions. First came *śabdas* by the Gurūs in the order of their succession. Then came *aṣṭpadīs, chhants* and *vārs* in a set order. The compositions of the Gurūs in each *rāga* were followed by those of the Bhagats in the same format. A very subtle system of numbering the hymns was evolved. Gurmukhī was the script used for the transcription.

From among the Bhagats, Kabīr's contribution is the largest. Besides two long compositions, *Bāvan Akharī* and *Thitīṅ*, 296 of his hymns in different *rāgas* and 239 *ślokas* are included in the Gurū Granth Sāhib, whereas Dhannā has only two hymns, one in Rāga Āsā and the other in Dhanāsarī; Saiṇu has only one hymn and there is only one line and a hymn from Sūr Dās.

Kabīr (1440-1518), according to a modern Sikh scholar and researcher 1398-1518, was born, near Vārāṇasī, to a poor Muslim couple. With a deep urge for a life of devotion from the very beginning, Kabīr became a major figure in medieval Indian *bhakti*. Besides loving devotion which is his principal theme, his verses in the Gurū Granth Sāhib contain a trenchant criticism of caste, idolatry and empty ritualism.

The main thrust of the compositions of Farīd (1173-1266) is that man, overcoming worldly temptation, remain attached to God, the creator of all. Fear of death and the need to live according to the Islamic code figure in his verse, but special stress is laid on following the universally accepted humanitarian values.

Nāmdev (1270-1350), a washerman of Mahārāshṭra, has 60 of his hymns recorded in the Gurū Granth Sāhib in seventeen different *rāgas*. They represent the work of his later years, for in his younger years he tended more towards idolatry.

Ravidās, as we learn from his own verses, belonged to a family of shoe-makers, but he enjoyed considerable esteem among the people of Vārāṇasī where he lived. Forty of his hymns figure in the Gurū Granth Sāhib, in sixteen different *rāgas*. He has dealt in his verses with the themes of the Godhead, Nature, Soul, *nām*, Gurū, transmigration and liberation. According to him, realization of the divine is possible only through loving devotion, all else being mere pretension.

The contribution of remaining eleven Bhagats is numerically very small—18 hymns and one line in all. Their hymns, too, generally celebrate unicity and love of God. They reject ritualism and formalism, and lay stress on the remembrance of God's Name, which does not mean mere mechanical repetition of any attributive name of God, but implies the continuous feeling and realization of His presence at every place and in every being.

BIBLIOGRAPHY

1. *Gurbilās Pātshāhī Chhevin.* Patiala, 1970
2. Bhallā, Sarūp Dās, *Mahimā Prakāsh.* Patiala, 1971
3. Santokh Siṅgh, Bhāī, *Srī Gur Pratāp Sūraj Granth.* Amritsar, 1926-37
4. Gurdit Siṅgh, Giānī, *Itihās Srī Gurū Granth Sāhib (Bhagat Bāṇī Bhāg).* Chandigarh, 1990
5. Sāhib Siṅgh, *Bhagat Bāṇī Saṭīk.* Amritsar, 1959-60
6. Jodh Siṅgh, Bhāī, *Bhagat Kabīr Jī—Jīvanī te Sikhiā.* Patiala, 1971
7. Chaturvedī, Parshū Rām, *Uttarī Bhārat kī Sant-Prampārā.* Allahabad, 1964
8. Macauliffe, M.A. *The Sikh Religion.* Oxford, 1909
9. Kohli, Surindar Singh, *A Critical Study of Adi Granth.* Delhi, 1961

Hn.S.

BHAGAT BHAGVĀN, recipient of one of the *bakhshishs* or seats of the Udāsī sect, was a contemporary of Gurū Har Rāi (1630-61). His original name was Bhagvān Gir. Little is known about his early life except that, according to Udāsī sources, he was born in a Brāhmaṇ family at Bodh Gayā and that he was a Sannyāsī *sādhū* roving in search of spiritual solace. Having heard about Gurū Nānak, Bhagvān Gir came to Kīratpur to meet his living successor, Gurū Har Rāi, who initiated him a Sikh, renamed him Bhagat Bhagvān and bestowed upon him what is known in Udāsī parlance a *bakhshish*, i.e. blessing or authority to establish preaching centres for the spread of Sikhism. Bhagat Bhagvān preached in the eastern provinces and set up Udāsī *ḍerās* or monasteries at several places. His disciples and successors spread the teaching of Gurū Nānak widely in northern India, from Bihār to Sindh.

BIBLIOGRAPHY

1. Raṇdhīr Siṅgh, Bhāī, *Udāsī Sikkhāṅ dī Vithiā*. Amritsar, 1959
2. Ashok, Shamsher Siṅgh, *Pañjāb dīāṅ Lahirāṅ*. Patiala, 1974

B.S.

BHAGAT MĀL, sub-titled *Sākhī Bhāī Gurdās Jī kī Vār Yārvīṅ Sikhāṅ dī Bhagatmālā*, is an anonymous manuscript (Kirpāl Siṅgh, *A Catalogue of Punjabi and Urdu Manuscripts*, attributes it to one Kirpā Rām, though in the work itself no reference to this name exists) held in the Khālsā College, Amritsar, under MS. No. 2300, bound with several other works all of which are written in the same hand. The manuscript comprises 83 folios and is undated. The opening page of the full volume, however, carries the date 1896 Bk/AD 1839 which may be the year of its transcription. *Bhagat Māl* is a parallel work to the more famous *Bhagatmālā* by Bhāī Manī Siṅgh and is, like the latter, meant to be an elaboration of Bhāī Gurdās's eleventh *Vār*, listing the more prominent of the Sikhs of Gurū Nānak's time. All the 30 stanzas of the *Vār* are reproduced each with explanation under the heading *tisdā vīchār* (explanation of that). First 12 stanzas contain no names: they are devoted to elaborating the theory of Sikhism and the characteristics of an ideal Sikh and his mode of living. From the 13th stanza onward (f. 260), the names of various Sikhs are given. Under "explanation,'' a question is put forward by a Sikh pertaining to the principles and practices of the Sikh faith such as *sevā*, selfless, voluntary service, charity, control of mind, remembrance of God, home life, lust, and anger. Occasionally, some questions relate to philosophical issues as well, for instance, whether God is transcendent or immanent. At places incidents from the Rāmāyaṇa and the Mahābhārata as well as hymns from the Gurū Granth Sāhib are quoted to illustrate a point. Some contemporary events from Sikh history such as the construction of the temple and the tank at Amritsar and the compilation of the Ādi Granth are also referred to. At folio 325, Bhāī Nand Lāl is quoted as saying that the Gurū bestowed all honour on the Khālsā adding that Sahajdhārīs were also accepted along with Keśādhārīs.

S.S.Am.

BHAGAT RĀM, BAKHSHĪ (1799-1865), son of Baisākhī Rām, a small money-changer in the city of Lahore, joined the service of Mahārājā Raṇjīt Siṅgh in 1818 at the age of nineteen as a writer in the treasury office under Misr Belī Rām, the chief *toshākhānīā* or keeper of the State treasury. In 1824, he was appointed assistant writer of the accounts of the privy purse. In 1831, he was deputed to accompany Kaṅvar Sher Siṅgh to the hills of Jalandhar Doāb to collect revenue from the defaulting states of Maṇḍī, Suket and Kullū. He came back to Lahore in 1832 and was appointed paymaster of fifty battalions of infantry, eight regiments of cavlary and twenty batteries of artillery. For his services to the State, he was granted in 1841 a *jāgīr* at Ajnālā by Mahārājā Sher Siṅgh. After the assassination of Mahārājā Sher Siṅgh, he became leader of a section of the Mutsaddī party, the other section being under the influence of Dīwān Dīnā Nāth. After the murder of Rājā Hīrā Siṅgh on 21 December 1844, Bakhshī Bhagat Rām's name was considered for appointment as one of the members of the council which was to carry on the government of the country, but the proposal fell through. He was sent to Jammū with the expedition against Rājā Gulāb Siṅgh in March 1845. Mahārājā Duleep Siṅgh granted him an additional *jāgīr* at Dātārpur, in the Jalandhar Doāb. Bhagat Rām lost this *jāgīr* when the Doāb was ceded to the British by the treaty of Lahore, 9 March 1846, but received one in lieu of it in Amritsar district.

Bhagat Rām died at Lahore in 1865, leaving behind one son, Jamīat Rāi.

BIBLIOGRAPHY

1. Sūrī, Sohan Lāl, *'Umdāt-ut-Twārīkh*. Lahore, 1885-89
2. Griffin, Lepel aad C.F. Massy, *Chiefs and Families of Note in the Punjab*. Lahore, 1909
3. Bhagat Singh, *Maharaja Ranjit Singh and His Times*. Delhi, 1990
4. Khushwant Singh, *Ranjit Singh: Maharaja of the Punjab* 1780-1839. Bombay, 1962

J.S.K.

BHAGAT RATNĀVALĪ, also known as *Sikhāṅ dī Bhagatmāl* or *Sikhāṅ dī Bhagatmālā* or *Bhagatāvalī* is a *ṭīkā* or exposition, in Punjabi prose, of a *Vār* (no.11) from Bhāī Gurdās's *Vārāṅ*. The *Vār* contains a roster of the names of some of the Sikhs of the time of the first six Gurūs, Gurū Nānak to Gurū Hargobind, without giving any details about how they got initiated into the Sikh faith or about their careers. The *Bhagat Ratnāvalī*, attributed to Bhāī Manī Siṅgh (*q.v.*), attempts to supply these. The name of Bhāī Manī Siṅgh occurs at several places in the text in the third person which makes it doubtful if he is the author. The anecdotes given are meant to have been those related by Gurū Gobind Siṅgh to Bhāī Manī Siṅgh. It is likely that they were recorded by another Sikh who heard Manī Siṅgh narrate these at a congregation. The work may be dated between AD 1706 (the year Gurū Gobind Siṅgh left Punjab for the South: it is said that Manī Siṅgh started relating the anecdotes after the Gurū's departure) and AD 1737 (the year of Bābā Kalādhārī's death to whom belonged a manuscript copy of the work).

However, some manuscripts contain, following the exposition of Bhāī Gurdās's *Vār*, anecdotes about some of the Sikhs connected with the last four Gurūs. Whereas the first part of the work ends with the words: "*Ṭīkā vār yārvīṅ dī pūrī hoī*– here ends the exposition of the eleventh *Vār*," the second part concludes with "*Sākhīāṅ pūrīāṅ hoīāṅ* – anecdotes end here." The language and style in both the parts is identical. The current printed version, edited by Bhāī Vīr Siṅgh, comprises only the first part. The general format is that of a Sikh – more often than not it is a group of Sikhs – visiting the Gurū and raising questions, he has had in his mind. The Gurū answers the questions and the Sikh bows at his feet convinced. Sikh teaching is in this manner rehearsed. For the dialogue form the book adopts, it has also been described as a *goṣṭi*.

Bb. S.N.

BHAGAT SIṄGH (1907-1931), revolutionary and martyr, was born on 27 September 1907 at the village of Baṅgā, Lyallpur district (now in Pakistan) the second son of Kishan Siṅgh and Vidyā Vatī. Bhagat Siṅgh was imbued from childhood with the family's spirit of patriotism. At the time of his birth, his father was in jail for his connection with the Canal Colonization Bill agitation, in which his brother, Ajīt Siṅgh (Bhagat Siṅgh's uncle), took a leading part. Through his father, who was a sympathizer and supporter of the Ghadr campaign of 1914-15, Bhagat Siṅgh became an admirer of the leaders of the movement. The execution of Kartār Siṅgh Sarābhā made a deep impression on the mind of the young man who vowed to dedicate his life to the country.

Having passed the fifth class from his village school, Bhagat Siṅgh joined Dayānand Anglo-Vedic School in Lahore. In response to the call of Mahātmā Gāndhī and other nationalist leaders, to boycott government-aided institutions, he left his school and enrolled in the National College at Lahore. He was successful in passing a special examination preparatory to entering college. He was reading for his B.A. examination when his parents planned to have him married. He vehemently rejected the suggestion and said that, if his marriage was to take place in "slave-India, my bride shall be only death." Rather than allow his father to proceed any further with the proposal, Bhagat Siṅgh left home and went to Kānpur where he took up a job in the Pratāp Press. In his spare time, he studied revolutionary literature. He joined the Hindustān Republican Association, a radical group, later known as the Hindustān Socialist Republican Association. When Bhagat Siṅgh was assured that he would not be compelled to marry and violate his vows sworn to his motherland, he returned to his home in Lahore. This was in 1925 when a *morchā* had been going on at Jaito to protest against the deposition by the British of Mahārājā Ripudaman Siṅgh of Nābhā because of his sympathy with the Akālī agitation. A warrant for the arrest of Bhagat Siṅgh was issued because he had accorded a welcome to one of the *jathās*, but he managed to elude the police and spent five months under the assumed name of Balvant Siṅgh in Delhi, where he worked in a daily paper *Vīr Arjun*.

As Akālī activity subsided, Bhagat Siṅgh returned to Lahore. He established contact with the Kirtī Kisān Party and started contributing regularly to its magazine, the *Kirtī*. He also remained in touch with the Hindustān Socialist Republican Association. In March 1926 was formed the Naujawān Bhārat Sabhā. Bhagat Siṅgh, one of the principal organizers became its secretary.

As the Simon Commission arrived at Lahore on 30 October 1928, an all-parties procession, headed by Lālā Lājpat Rāi, marched towards the railway station to make a protest. Intercepting the procession, police made a *lāṭhī* charge and Lālā Lājpat Rāi received injuries. He died a fortnight later. Although the British saw no connection between the *lāṭhī* charge and Lālā Lājpat Rāi's death, Bhagat Siṅgh and his associates did. They plotted the assassination of Mr Scott, the Superintendent of Police, believed to have been responsible for the *lāṭhī* blows given Lālā Lājpat Rāi, but instead J.P. Saunders, an Assistant Superintendent of Police, became the actual victim owing to mistake in identification. Bhagat Siṅgh and Rājgurū had done the actual shooting. They and those who had served as lookouts escaped through the D.A.-V. College grounds. The next day a leaflet was circulated by the Hindustān Socialist Republican Association announcing that the death of Lālā Lājpat Rāi had been avenged.

Bhagat Siṅgh escaped to Calcutta disguised as a wealthy personage. He remained quiet for several months, but became active again when Public Safety Bill and the Trade Disputes Bill were being debated in Delhi. As his group resolved to explode a bomb to express disapproval of the bill, Bhagat Siṅgh and B.K. Dutt volunteered to carry out the plan. They were seated in the gallery of the Central Assembly Hall awaiting the reading of the proclamation that would enact the bills. When the announcement was made, Bhagat Siṅgh jumped up and threw a relatively harmless bomb behind one of the members' benches. There was an explosion, followed by still another from a second bomb. No one was seriously injured. Bhagat Siṅgh and Dutt began shouting revolutionary slogans and threw leaflets explaining their intent of making "the deaf hear" with the loud noise of explosion. Both were promptly taken into custody. As the trial proceeded, a statement, written in its entirety by Bhagat Siṅgh, was read in defence of the two accused. Bhagat Siṅgh said that "force used for a legitimate cause has its moral justification." He and B.K. Dutt were found guilty and sentenced to transportation for life. After the sentence had been pronounced in the Assembly Bomb case, Bhagat Siṅgh was bound over for trial in the Saunders Murder case, approvers having identified his role in the killing. While awaiting trial in the Lahore Jail, Bhagat Siṅgh started a hunger-strike in behalf of political prisoners. The fast was continued even after the hearing of the case began on 10 July 1929, and was subsequently joined by many others. It was not until after the death of one of these, J.N. Das, on 13 September 1929, that facilities were promised to the prisoners and the hunger-strike abandoned.

At the time of trial, Bhagat Siṅgh offered no defence, but utilized the occasion to propagate his ideal of freedom. He and his fellow accused kept delaying the proceedings by refusing to appear before the court, by ignoring what was going on, or by disrupting the work by shouting revolutionary slogans. He heard with defiant courage the death-sentence pronounced on 7 October 1930. In the same spirit, he kissed the hangman's noose on 23 March 1931, shouting for the last time his favourite cry, "Down with British imperialism." His body was secretly cremated at Husainīvālā by police and the remains thrown into the River Sutlej. The next day, however, his comrades collected the bodily remains from the cremation site and a procession was taken out in Lahore. Mourning for him was spontaneous and widespread and homage was paid to him for his sterling character and sacrifice.

In 1950, after Independence, the land where Bhagat Siṅgh and his companions were cremated was procured from Pakistan and a memorial built. In March 1961, a Shahīdī Melā was held there. Every year, on 23 March, the martyr's memory is similarly honoured. The old memorial, destroyed in the 1971 Indo-Pak war, has been rebuilt. Bhagat Siṅgh is remembered by the endearing title of Shahīd-i-Āzam, the greatest of martyrs.

Paying his tribute to him at a meeting of the Central Sikh League at Amritsar on 8 April 1931, Subhās Chandra Bose said, "Bhagat Singh who set an example of character and patriotism by sacrificing himself for the sake of the country's freedom, was from the Sikh community. Today, he is known to be a brave Sikh hero throughout the world. The Sikh community has to produce thousands of Bhagat Singhs for the cause of the country."

BIBLIOGRAPHY

1. Deol, G.S., *Shaheed Bhagat Singh: A Biography.* Patiala, n.d.
2. Fauja Singh, ed., *Who's Who: Punjab Freedom Fighters*, vol. I. Patiala, 1972
3. Josh, Sohan Siṅgh, *Bhagat Siṅgh Nāl Meriāṅ Mulākātāṅ te Chār Hor Muḍhle Inqlābī.* Delhi, 1977
4. Mān Siṅgh, *Azādī dī Shamāh de Sikh Parvāne.* Delhi, 1973
5. Nāhar Siṅgh, Giānī, *Azādī diāṅ Lahirāṅ.* Ludhiana, 1960

E.C.B.

BHAGATŪ, BHĀĪ (d. 1652), a devoted Sikh who served the Fifth, Sixth and the Seventh Gurūs, was the son of Ādam (Uddam in some chronicles), a Siddhū Brāṛ of Mālvā country. Sikh chronicles record that Ādam, without a son for a long time and despaired of prayers at the feet of different holy men, Muslim as well as Hindu, was advised by a Sikh to go to Gurū Rām Dās. Ādam reached Amritsar and dedicated himself to the service of the Gurū and the *saṅgat*. The Gurū was pleased by his humility and sincerity. Ādam received his blessing and had a son born to him. Bhagatū, as the son was named, grew to be a saintly person with a firm faith in the Gurū. He made frequent visits to Amritsar where he stopped for long intervals rendering diligent service as construction of the Harimandar was in progress under the guidance of Gurū Arjan. He was at Kīratpur in 1644 when Gurū Har Rāi succeeded Gurū Hargobind on Gurū Nānak's throne. He later retired to his village, but continued to visit the Gurū, especially on Baisākhī and Dīvālī. During one of these visits, Gurū Har Rāi said to him, "You are fairly old now; it is time you were married." The Gurū was referring metaphorically to death, alluding to Shaikh Farīd's line in the Gurū Granth Sāhib :

> The soul is the bride, Death the bridegroom;
> He will wed her and take her away.
> (GG, 1377)

But the simple-minded Bhāī Bhagatū, taking the remarks literally, was greatly perplexed. He had two grown-up sons from his wife, now long deceased, and remarriage at his age would in any case be ridiculous. He went home without giving a reply, but the Gurū's words continued to ring in his ears. He was still ruminating over the "strange" suggestion when he made his next visit to Gurū Har Rāi, at Kartārpur, in present-day Jalandhar district. The Gurū asked Bhāī Bhagatū why he looked so preoccupied. As Bhāī Bhagatū shyly and haltingly revealed his problem, Gurū Har Rāi smiled at his naivette and told him that he had merely meant to comment on his age. Bhāī Bhagatū now feeling relieved, stayed on in the service of the Gurū until he died shortly after the next Baisākhī festival in April 1652. Gurū Har Rāi personally performed his last rites, and praised his simplicity and devotion.

Bhāī Bhagatū's elder son, Gaurā, through his enterprising spirit and prowess, became a minor chief at the village of Viñjhū, near Baṭhiṇḍa. One of his descendants, Bhāī Desū Siṅgh, founded the Sikh state of Kaithal in the eighteenth century. A *gurdwārā*, Bhāīāṇā Bhagatū, named after the celebrated Bhāī is located near village Gobindpurā, about 11 km northeast of Baṭhiṇḍā (30°-14'N, 74°-58'E). An annual fair is held there on the occasion of Baisākhī.

BIBLIOGRAPHY

1. Santokh Siṅgh, Bhāī, *Srī Gur Pratāp Sūraj Granth*. Amritsar, 1926-37
2. Giān Siṅgh, Giānī, *Twārīkh Gurū Khālsā*. Patiala, 1970

T.S.

BHAGATŪ, BHĀĪ, a Chhurā Khatrī of Burhānpur who, according to Bhāī Gurdās, *Vārāṅ*, XI. 30, received instruction at the hands of Gurū Hargobind.

See BHAGVĀN DĀS, BHĀĪ

BIBLIOGRAPHY

Manī Siṅgh, Bhāī, *Sikhāṅ dī Bhagat Mālā. Amritsar, 1955*

B.S.

BHAGAUTĪ or Bhavānī (Skt. Bhagavatī, consort of Viṣṇu, or the goddess Durgā) has had in Sikh usage a chequered semantic history. In early Sikhism, especially in the compositions comprising the Gurū Granth Sāhib, the word means a *bhakta* or devotee of God. "*So bhagautī jo bhagvantai jāṇai*; he alone is a true devotee who knoweth the Lord" (GG, 88). In Bhāī Gurdās, *bhagautī* has been used as an equivalent of sword. "*Nāu bhagautī lohu ghaṛāiā* – iron (a lowly metal) when properly wrought becomes a (powerful) sword" (*Vārāṅ*, XXV. 6). It is in the compositions of Gurū Gobind Siṅgh contained in the *Dasam Granth* that the term began to assume connotations of wider significance. Reference may here be made especially to three poems by Gurū Gobind Siṅgh – *Chaṇḍī Chritra Ukti Bilās* and *Chaṇḍī Chritra* both in Braj and *Vār Srī Bhagautī Jī Kī,* popularly called *Chaṇḍī dī Vār* in Punjabi – describing the exploits of the Hindu goddess (*Bhagavatī)* Chaṇḍī or Durgā. Each of these compositions is a free translation of "Sapt Sati" (lit. seven hundred), meaning the epic comprising 700 *ślokas,* chapter xiv, sub-sections 81-94, of the classical *Mārkaṇḍeya Purāṇa* which describes the battle between the goddess and demons whom she vanquished to reinstall Indra, the king of gods, on his throne. The heroic odes in fact are among many pieces of Paurāṇic (mythological) literature that Gurū Gobind Siṅgh translated or got translated for the avowed purpose of instilling martial spirit among his Sikhs.

The title of *Vār Srī Bhagautī Jī Kī,* which has also been appropriated into Sikh *ardās* or supplicatory prayer, along with the first stanza runs as follows :

Ik oṅkār srī vāhigurū jī kī fateh
God is one – To Him belongs the victory
Srī bhagautī jī sahāe

May Srī Bhagautī Jī be always on our side
Vār Srī Bhagautī Jī Kī Pātshāhī 10
The ode of Srī Bhagautī as sung by the Tenth Master.

The opening line of the Ode reads:

Pritham bhagautī simari kai gur nānak laīṅ dhiāi:

First call up Bhagautī in your mind, then meditate on Gurū Nānak.

Here, the primacy accorded Srī Bhagautī Jī is obvious. This leads to the question why.

Bhagautī is, it appears, a multifaceted archetypal symbol employed by Gurū Gobind Siṅgh to fulfil a multiplicity of functions simultaneously. He perhaps wanted to complement the exclusive masculinity of the Divine image. Until then, God had in Sikhism as in other major traditions by and large a masculine connotation. He had been called *Purakh* implying masculinity. Although, at times, He had been addressed as *mātā* (mother) as well as *pitā* (father), almost all the names employed for him in Sikh Scripture, the Gurū Granth Sāhib – Rām, Govind, Hari, Shiv, Allah, etc. – were only masculine names. To widen the conception Gurū Gobind Siṅgh may have chosen Bhagautī, a name with a clear faminine implication. It is significant that in the entire Hindu pantheon the warrior Bhagavatī, or Durgā, is the only goddess without a male spouse, thus symbolizing female independence, strength and valour. This derives further support from Gurū Gobind Siṅgh's autobiographical *Bachitra Nāṭak* wherein he designated God by a composite name *Mahākāl-Kālikā* (Mahākāl which is masculine is juxtaposed to Kālikā which is feminine). More specifically, what is really meant by Bhagautī (or its synonym *Bhavānī*) is made clear in the following verse of Gurū Gobind Siṅgh:

Soi bhavānī nām kahāī
Jin sagrī eh srishṭi upāī

The One who created this universe entire,
Came to be known as Bhavānī

– *Chaubīs Autār*

Notwithstanding the fact that names of the deities from many diverse sources occur in the Sikh text, here they mix naturally shedding, after acculturation in the new religious and theological environs, their original nuances and proclaiming one and one identity alone, i.e. God the Singular Being. All other meanings and shades are subsumed into One Indivisible entity. The names Hari (originally Viṣṇu), Keshav (also an epithet of

Viṣṇu – one with long hair), Dāmodar (Kṛṣṇa who had a rope tied around his belly), Murlī Manohar (also Kṛṣṇa, master of the melodious flute), Raghupati (Rāma, the Lord of Raghu dynasty), etc., all came to signify in the Sikh vortex the unitary Godhead. The same applied to *Bhagautī*.

Says Gurū Gobind Siṅgh in the second stanza of this poem, *Vār Srī Bhagautī Jī Kī*, the following about Bhagautī:

> *Taihī durgā sāji kai daitā dā nāsu karāiā:*
> It was you who created Durgā to destroy the demons.

The line establishes beyond ambiguity the contextual meaning of *bhagautī*. Durga could not be presumed to have created Durgā. She like all other gods and goddesses was indeed created by God Almighty.

The nomenclature seems to have been employed to smoothen the gender distinctions when referring to God.

The second archetypal significance of Bhagautī is linked to its other lexical meaning 'sword' as exemplified by Bhāī Gurdās. *Bhagautī* where prefixed with the honorific *srī* (lit. fortunate, graceful) signifies the 'Divine Sword' – the Power that brings about the evolution and devolution of the Universe.

In this kaleidoscopic universe, its Creator is immanent not in any static way. He is in all times and at all places dynamically protecting the good and destroying the evil (*Sant ubāran, dushṭ upāran*). "Everywhere through the great perplexed universe, we can see the flashing of 'His Sword' ! ... and that must mean His nature uttering itself in His Own form of forces (Phillip Brooks). That Srī Bhagautī, the Divine Sword, symbolizes Divine Power is further borne out in the Ode itself when about Bhagautī it is said:

> *Khaṇḍā prithmai sāji kai jin sabh sasāru upāiā*
> *Brahmā bisan mahes sāji kudratī dā khelu rachāi baṇāiā*
> *Sindh parbat medanī binu thammā gagani rahāiā*
> Creating first the Power of Destruction, who brought forth the whole universe,
> Who raised the trinity of the gods, and spread the game of nature,
> The Ocean, the mountains, the earth and the firmanent without support who shaped ...

The invocation to the Almighty through His image as the 'Divine Sword' as employed by Gurū Gobind Siṅgh purported again to instill the heroic spirit among his Sikhs, for:

> *Jehā sevai teho hovai*
> You become like the one you adore.
> (GG, 549)

Here a question arises: What is the special significance of remembering God with the name of a weapon? God is Pure Existence (*sat*), Absolute Essence (*nām*). Existence-Essence (sat-nām) is His primordial, archetypal, designation (GG, 1083). Whatsoever else is said to designate Him can only be symbolic. Though God is infinite, these symbols can only be finite. While the infinite includes the finite, it also transcends it. That is why every such symbol is not only affirmed by the symbolized but also negated at the same time. In the Sikh mystic lore, the prime symbol employed for God is the Word (*nām*). However, the other, even more structured symbol that Gurū Gobind Siṅgh introduced is 'the Sword' (Bhagautī). One might here ask: can a fragment of the finite symbolize infinite? The answer can be given in the affirmative for God being Pure Existence is immanent in everything that exists. Hence symbolization of God through a finite symbol 'Sword' is not only possible, but also, in a sense, true because it serves to symbolize Divine Power. Every mystic symbol is bipolar. On the one end it is in contact with the Infinite, at the other in contact with the finite. That is how it succeeds in fulfilling the symbolic function. *Bhagautī* is one such symbol as it is in its symbolic meaning of Divine Power, in contact with the Infinite, and in its concrete form, as a weapon, in contact with the finite. Gurū Gobind Siṅgh has consecrated not only the sword, but in fact a whole spectrum of weaponry:

As kripān khaṇḍo kharag tupak tabar aru tīr
Saif sarohī saihthī, yahai hamārai pīr:

The sword, the sabre, the scimitar, the axe, the musket, the shaft.
The rapier, the dagger, the spear: these indeed are our saints.

Remembering God through such heroic symbols was the exclusive style of Gurū Gobind Siṅgh.

Already in *gurbāṇī,* the theistic symbol of the Nigam (Vedic) tradition had been monotheized. Gurū Gobind Siṅgh chose to monotheize even the theistic symbols of the Āgam (Brāhmaṇic) tradition. Thus his was a process of the integration of the two great mystical traditions of India.

Finally, the word *bhagautī* stands for God or His devotee on the one hand (signifying *pīrī*), for the sword on the other (signifying *mīrī*). This integration of *pīrī* and *mīrī* in *Bhagautī* encapsulates another major dimension of Sikh thought.

J.S.N.
G.B.S.

BHĀGBHARĪ, MĀĪ (d. 1614), of a Brāhmaṇ family of Srīnagar, was converted to the Sikh faith by Bhāī Mādho Soḍhī, sent by Gurū Arjan to preach in Kashmīr. As she grew old, she wished to have a glimpse of the Gurū before she died. Gurū Hargobind then occupied the spiritual throne of Gurū Nānak. Māī Bhāgbharī had stitched a role of homespun fabric which she longed to present to the Gurū personally, but she was too old to travel to distant Amritsar. As says *Gurbilās Chhevīṅ Pātshāhī*, Gurū Hargobind did visit Kashmīr and, reaching Srīnagar, he went straight to Māī Bhāgbharī's house in Hāthī Gate area. Bhāgbharī and her son, Sevā Dās, served the Gurū with devotion. The former was specially rejoiced to have this chance of making to the Gurū the offering of the robe she had so lovingly prepared. Her cherished wish having been fulfilled, she died a contented person soon afterwards.

BIBLIOGRAPHY

1. *Gurbilās Chhevīṅ Pātshāhī.* Patiala, 1970
2. Giān Siṅgh, Giānī, *Twārīkh Gurū Khālsā.* Patiala, 1970

B.S.

BHĀGĪ BĀNDAR, village 3 km north of Talvaṇḍī Sābo (29°- 59'N, 75°- 5'E), in Baṭhiṇḍā district of the Punjab, claims a historical shrine, Gurdwārā Jaṇḍsar, sacred to Gurū Gobind Siṅgh, who visited the site during his stay at Talvaṇḍī Sābo. According to local tradition, the *jaṇḍ* tree (*Prosopis spicigera*) and the old well in the Gurdwārā compound have existed since before the time of the Gurū's visit. The present complex replacing the old shrine was raised in 1985. The Gurdwārā is maintained by the local community.

BIBLIOGRAPHY

1. *Mālvā Desh Raṭan dī Sākhī Pothī.* Amritsar, 1968
2. Ṭhākar Siṅgh, Giānī, *Srī Gurduāre Darshan.* Amritsar, 1923
3. Tārā Siṅgh, *Sri Gur Tīrath Saṅgrahi.* Amritsar, n.d.
4. Fauja Singh, ed., *Travels of Guru Gobind Singh.* Patiala, 1968

Gn. S.

BHĀGĪRATH or Bhagīrath, of Malsīāṅ, an old village in present-day Jalandhar district of the Punjab, who is recorded as being one of the early disciples of Gurū Nānak, was according to Bhāī Gurdās, *Vārāṅ*, XI. 14, known as a worshipper of the Goddess Kālī. As the Janam Sākhīs report, Bhāgīrath had served *faqīrs* and *sādhūs* and worshipped many gods and goddesses in quest of spiritual consolation. One night, it is stated, he went to sleep adoring the stone-idol in his room when he had a dream. A voice spoke to him that all his wanderings would cease if he were only to make a trip to Sultānpur, not far from his village, and meet Gurū Nānak who was a chosen one and had not till then fully revealed himself. Bhāgīrath, it is said, followed the direction and sought out Gurū Nānak, at the evening prayer in his home at Sultānpur. He became a disciple and remained there spending his time praying and singing hymns with the *saṅgat*, the holy fellowship. His is one of the fewest names from among Sikhs of Gurū Nānak's Sultānpur days mentioned in the Janam Sākhīs. From Sultānpur he was once sent on an errand by Gurū Nānak to Lahore to make purchases for the wedding of Bhāī Mardānā's daughter. According to Sarūp Dās Bhallā, *Mahimā Prakāsh*, Bhāgīrath re-joined Gurū Nānak and remained in attendance at Kartārpur where the Gurū had settled down at the end of his extensive travels lasting about 20 years.

BIBLIOGRAPHY

1. Bhallā, Sarūp Dās, *Mahimā Prakāsh*. Patiala, 1971
2. Kohlī, Surindar Singh, ed., *Janamsākhī Bhāī Bālā*. Chandigarh, 1975
3. Vīr Siṅgh, Bhāī, ed., *Purātan Janam Sākhī*. Amritsar, 1982
4. Trilochan Singh, *Guru Nanak*. Delhi, 1969

Gn.S.

BHAGĪRATH, BHĀĪ, whose name occurs in the roster of leading Sikhs in Bhāī Gurdās, *Vārāṅ*, XI. 18, was a Soinī Khatrī. He entered the Sikh faith in the time of Gurū Arjan. From the Gurū himself he received enlightenment and learnt to distinguish a true *gurmukh* (one with face turned towards the Gurū) from a *manmukh* (an ego-ridden one).

See BHULLĀ, BHĀĪ

BIBLIOGRAPHY

1. Manī Siṅgh, Bhāī, *Sikhāṅ dī Bhagat Mālā*. Amritsar, 1955
2. Satibīr Siṅgh, *Partakh Hari*. Jalandhar, 1982

T.S.

BHĀGO, MĀĪ, the sole survivor of the battle of Khidrāṇā, i.e. Muktsar (29 December 1705), was a descendant of Pero Shāh, the younger brother of Bhāī Laṅgāh, a Ḍhilloṅ Jaṭṭ who had converted a Sikh during the time of Gurū Arjan. Born at her ancestral village of Jhabāl in present-day Amritsar district of the Punjab, she was married to Nidhān Siṅgh Vaṛāich of Paṭṭī. A staunch Sikh by birth and upbringing, she was distressed to hear in 1705 that some of the Sikhs of her neighbourhood who had gone to Anandpur to fight for Gurū Gobind Siṅgh had deserted him under adverse conditions. She rallied the deserters persuading them to meet the Gurū and apologize to him. She set off along with them and some other Sikhs to seek out the Gurū, then travelling across the Mālvā region. Māī Bhāgo and the men she was leading stopped near the *ḍhāb* or pool of Khidrāṇā where an imperial army in pursuit of Gurū Gobind Siṅgh had almost overtaken him. They challenged the pursuing host and fought furiously forcing it to retreat. Gurū Gobind Siṅgh, who had supported them with a shower of arrows from a nearby high ground, found all the men except one, Mahāṅ Siṅgh, killed when he visited the battlefield. Mahāṅ Siṅgh, who had been seriously wounded, also died as the Gurū took him into his lap. Gurū Gobind Siṅgh blessed those forty dead as the Forty Liberated Ones. He took into his care Māī Bhāgo who had also suffered injury in the battle. She thereafter stayed on with Gurū Gobind Siṅgh as one of his bodyguard, in male attire. After the death of Gurū Gobind Siṅgh at Nānded in 1708, she retired further south. She settled down at Jinvāṛā, 11 km from Bidar in Karnāṭaka where, immersed in meditation, she lived to attain a ripe old age. Her hut in Jinvāṛā has now been converted into Gurdwārā Tap Asthān Māī Bhāgo. At Nānded, too, a hall within the compound of Takht Sachkhaṇḍ Srī Hazūr Sāhib marking the site of her residence is known as Buṅgā Māī Bhāgo.

BIBLIOGRAPHY

1. Kuir Siṅgh, *Gurbilās Pātshāhī 10.* Patiala, 1968
2. Santokh Siṅgh, Bhāī, *Srī Gur Pratāp Sūraj Granth.* Amritsar, 1926-37
3. Padam, Piārā Siṅgh, and Giānī Garjā Siṅgh, eds., *Gurū kīāṅ Sākhīāṅ.* Patiala, 1986
4. Harbans Singh, *Guru Gobind Singh.* Chandigarh, 1966

P.S.P.

BHĀGO, MALIK, was, according to Sikh chroniclers, the Hindu steward of the Muslim chief of Saidpur, present-day town of Eminābād, now in Gujrāṅwālā district of Pakistan, during the days of Gurū Nānak. The tradition relates that once while Gurū Nānak was staying with Bhāī Lālo, a poor carpenter, in the town, Malik Bhāgo gave a feast to which Gurū Nānak, along with other holy men and dignitaries, was invited. As the Gurū declined the invitation, the Malik had him summoned to his presence and asked the reason for his refusal. Gurū Nānak took into one hand a quantity of Malik Bhāgo's rich food and in the other a piece of Lālo's coarse bread. He then squeezed both. From Lālo's bread trickled milk, and from Malik Bhāgo's blood. The moral was clear. The rich man's wealth had been selfishly amassed at the cost of others and his charities were thus tainted, whereas Bhāī Lālo's simple bread earned by honest labour was holy.

See LĀLO, BHĀĪ

BIBLIOGRAPHY

1. Kohlī, Surindar Siṅgh, *Janamsākhī Bhāī Bālā.* Chandigarh, 1975
2. Kirpāl Siṅgh, *Janam Sākhī Pramparā.* Patiala, 1969

S.S.B.

BHAGṚĀṆĀ, village 20 km from Rājpura (30° - 28'N, 76° - 37'E), in Paṭiālā district, is celebrated for its Gurdwārā Nauviṅ Pātshāhī. Some old accounts assign this shrine to the neighbouring village of Dādū Mājrā, but it falls now within the revenue limits of Bhagṛāṇā. Gurū Tegh Bahādur halted here in the course of one of his journeys through this region. Two Sikhs, Bhāī Amarū and Bhāī Diālā, served him with devotion. The original memorial set up here was replaced with a Mañjī Sāhib and some ancillary buildings by Mahārājā Karam Siṅgh of Paṭiālā (1798-1845) who also allotted some land for its maintenance.

The 7-metre square domed Mañjī Sāhib is built on a high plinth. Inside it is seated the Gurū Granth Sāhib. The Gurdwārā is managed by the Shiromaṇī Gurdwārā Parbandhak Committee through a local committee.

BIBLIOGRAPHY

1. Tārā Siṅgh, *Srī Gur Tīrath Saṅgrahi.* Amritsar, n.d.
2. Ṭhākar Siṅgh, Giānī, *Srī Gurduāre Darshan.* Amritsar, 1923
3. Faujā Siṅgh, *Gurū Teg Bahādur : Yātrā Asthān, Pramparāvān te Yād Chinn.* Patiala, 1976

M.G.S.

BHĀG SIṄGH, also referred to in government records as Bāj Siṅgh, was an associate of Bhāī Mahārāj Siṅgh, leader of the anti-British revolt in the Punjab in 1848-49. Originally a disciple of Bhāī Bīr Siṅgh of Nauraṅgābād, he survived the attack on his *ḍerā* on 7 May 1844 and went on a pilgrimage to Nānded. On his return to the Punjab, he joined Bhāī Mahārāj Siṅgh at Amritsar shortly before the latter went underground in June 1847 to escape arrest by the British in connection with the Premā conspiracy case. Bhāg Siṅgh escaped towards Kāṅgṛā and re-joined Bhāī Mahārāj Siṅgh before the beginning of the second Anglo-Sikh war in 1848. After the battle of Chelīāṅvālā he made a trip to Peshāwar, re-joining his leader at Dev Baṭālā, in the Jammū area. He was one of a delegation carrying letters from Bhāī Mahārāj Siṅgh to Bhāī Nihāl Siṅgh and Bhāī Kishan Siṅgh, who had a large following in the North-West Frontier region, and to Sultān Muhammad Khān, brother of Dost Muhammad Khān, the Amīr of Kābul. He reported back with their replies at Kurālā Kalāṅ, in Hoshiārpur district. From here he was sent to take charge of the group's camels in Jammū. After the arrest of Bhāī Mahārāj Siṅgh, the police pursued Bhāg Siṅgh up to Jehlum but failed to capture him. Later on he accidentally fell into the hands of Major Lake at Peshāwar, and was tried and jailed.

BIBLIOGRAPHY

Ahluwalia, M.L., *Bhai Maharaj Singh*. Patiala, 1972

M.L.A.

BHĀG SIṄGH, BHĀĪ (1872-1914), one of the leaders of the Punjabi immigrants in Canada, was born at the village of Bhikhīviṇḍ, in Amritsar district. His father's name was Naraiṇ Siṅgh and mother's Mān Kaur. Bhāg Siṅgh joined the British Indian cavalry at the age of twenty, receiving a discharge certificate of meritorious service when he resigned. Thereafter he served in the municipal police at Hankow, China, for about three years, resigning from the service to go to Canada, where he settled in Vancouver. He was elected president of the Khālsā Dīwān Society of Vancouver. He and Balvant Siṅgh, of Khurdpur, became leaders of the Indian community in Canada and continued to campaign for its rights. Bhāg Siṅgh was once arrested by the immigration authorities but was released as the charges against him could not be substantiated. On 5 September 1914, Bhāī Bhāg Siṅgh was shot dead in the Gurdwārā, as he sat reciting the Gurū Granth Sāhib, by Belā Siṅgh, a tool in the hands of Inspector William Hopkinson of the Canadian immigration department, whose attitude towards Indians was very hostile and insulting. Bhāī Bhāg Siṅgh's murder was avenged by Mevā Siṅgh, of Lopoke, who killed Inspector Hopkinson at a hearing in the appellate court. A group of Sikh revolutionaries took the revenge on Belā Siṅgh, pursuing him back to the Punjab and killing him in his village.

BIBLIOGRAPHY

1. Jagjīt Siṅgh, *Ghadar Pārṭī Lahir*. Delhi, 1979
2. Sainsarā, Gurcharan Siṅgh, *Ghadar Pārtī dā Itihās*. Jalandhar, 1969

S.S.J.

BHĀG SIṄGH, BHĀĪ (1880-1921), one of the Nankāṇā Sāhib martyrs, was born in 1880, the son of Bhāī Amīr Siṅgh and Māī Nihāl Kaur of village Nizāmpur, in Amritsar district. The family later shifted to Chakk No. 38 Devā Siṅghvālā, in the newly developed canal colony of Sheikhūpurā. Bhāg Siṅgh's boyhood and early youth were spent as a common peasant until at the age of 26 when he enlisted in 124th Baloch Battalion. After ten years of service he retired on pension (two rupees per month). He joined the colours again during the First Great War (1914-18) but was wounded and discharged on medical grounds. He re-joined the army but came back home within six months, demobilized at the end of the war. Next, he stood among the ranks of the Akālī reformists falling a martyr in the Nankāṇā Sāhib massacre on 20 February 1921.

See NANKĀṆĀ SĀHIB MASSACRE

BIBLIOGRAPHY

Shamsher, Gurbakhsh Siṅgh, *Shahīdī Jīvan*. Nankana Sahib, 1938

G.S.G.

BHĀG SIṄGH CHANDRA UDAYA, an undated manuscript preserved in the Punjab State Archives, Paṭiālā, under accession No. M/773, deals with the life and achievements of Sardār Bhāg Siṅgh Āhlūvālīā (1745-1801), who succeeded Sardār Jassā Siṅgh Āhlūvālīā as ruler of Kapūrthalā state in 1783. Its author, Rām Sukh Rāo, was tutor to Bhāg Siṅgh's son and successor, Fateh Siṅgh Āhlūvālīā (1784-1836). The latter, after his accession in 1801, commissioned Ram Sukh Rāo to write biographies of Sardār Jassā Siṅgh and Sardār Bhāg Siṅgh. *Bhāg Siṅgh Chandra Udaya,* a biography of the latter, comprises 188 folios, size 22 x 16 cm, each page containing 16 lines. The first 107 folios cover events of the life of Jassā Siṅgh, and the rest deal with the rule of Bhāg Siṅgh ending with his death in 1801. The language of the manuscript is a mixture of Hindi, Sanskrit, Punjabi and Persian, but the script is Gurmukhī. Rām Sukh Rāo is also the author of a book devoted to the life of Jassā Siṅgh. That also is an unpublished manuscript under the title *Srī Jassā Siṅgh Binod,* preserved in the Punjab State Archives, Paṭiālā.

B.S.N.

BHĀG SIṄGH, RĀI (d. 1884) was son of Rāi Kishan Chand Bhaṇḍārī who worked as a *vakīl* or agent under the Sikh government. In the beginning of 1838 when Rāi Kishan Chand accompanied Colonel Wade to Peshāwar, Bhāg Siṅgh officiated in his place as agent at Ludhiāṇā, in the British territory. After the first Anglo-Sikh war (1845-46), Bhāg Siṅgh took over as agent of the Lahore Darbār with the Commissioner of trans-Sutlej states; in 1848 he was awarded the title of Rāi and a dress of honour. Rāi Bhāg Siṅgh also received a *jāgīr* worth rupees 2,500. The *jāgīr* was resumed when the Punjab was annexed by the British in 1849. Rāi Bhāg Siṅgh was employed a *tahsīldār* by the British government for some time. He was a provincial Darbārī and remained an honorary magistrate of Baṭālā for 17 years. He was also the first president of the Baṭālā municipality. He refused appointment as extra assistant commissioner offered to him by Sir John Lawrence, then the Lt- Governor of the Punjab. Rāi Bhāg Siṅgh died in 1884 at Baṭālā, leaving behind him a son named Kāṅshi Rām.

BIBLIOGRAPHY

Griffin, Lepel, and C.F. Massy, *Chiefs and Families of Note in the Punjab.* Lahore, 1909

G.S.N.

BHĀG SIṄGH, RĀJĀ (1760-1819), born on 23 September 1760, succeeded his father, Gajpat Siṅgh, to the *gaddī* of Jīnd state in 1789. He was a man of extraordinary vigour, intelligence and diplomatic astuteness. Like his father, he was also a close ally of Paṭiālā and joined hands with Bībī Sāhib Kaur's troops in 1794 against the Marāṭhās. He was mainly responsible for checking the advance of George Thomas towards Sikh territories and later on of General Perron of the Marāṭhā service. He maintained friendly relations with the British and accompanied Lord Lake to the River Beās in pursuit of Jasvaṅt Rāo Holkar. He was deputed by the British General to persuade his nephew, Mahārājā Raṇjīt Siṅgh, not to espouse the hopeless Marāṭhā cause. Bhāg Siṅgh's mediation in behalf of the British helped pave the way for the first Anglo-Sikh treaty of 1806. He gained in territory both from the British and Mahārajā Raṇjīt Siṅgh. Ludhiāṇā, later acquired by the British for establishing a poltical agency, once belonged to him.

Rājā Bhāg Siṅgh died in 1819 and was succeeded by his son, Fateh Siṅgh.

BIBLIOGRAPHY

1. Griffin, Lepel, *The Rajas of the Punjab.* Delhi, 1977
2. Harbans Singh, *The Heritage of the Sikhs.* Delhi, 1983

S.S.B.

BHĀG SIṄGH, SANT (1766-1839), of Kurī, a holy man widely respected in his time, was born the son of Bhāī Haṅs Rāi in 1766 at Qādirābād, a village in Gujrāt district (now in Pakistan), where his grandfather, Gurbakhsh Siṅgh, said to have been in the retinue of Gurū Gobind Siṅgh, settled after the Gurū's passing away at Nānded, in the Deccan. Bhāg Siṅgh learnt to read Gurmukhī letters and the Gurū Granth Sāhib at the village *gurdwārā*. As he grew up, he made a pilgrimage to Nānded. Returning to the north, he visited Ūnā, now in Himāchal Pradesh, where he became a disciple of Bābā Sāhib Siṅgh Bedī, a descendant of Gurū Nānak in direct line. After a few years, he, at the bidding of Bābā Sāhib Siṅgh, went to preach in the Poṭhohār region. He established himself at Kurī, a village on the bank of a small stream, Gumrāh, 8 km from Rāwalpiṇḍī. Such was his repute for piety that Mahārājā Ranjīt Siṅgh once came to visit him and seek his blessing. Bābā Bīr Siṅgh of Nauraṅgābād, who himself emerged as a figure of great sanctity in Sikh times, also sought advice from him. Sant Bhāg Siṅgh died on 20 January 1839.

BIBLIOGRAPHY

1. Sher Siṅgh, *Srī Bīr Mirgesh Gur Bilās Dev Tarū.*
2. Gaṇeshā Siṅgh, Mahant, *Nirmal Bhūśan arthāt Itihās Nirmal Bhekh.* Amritsar, n.d.
3. Sobhā Rām, *Gur-bilās Bābā Sāhib Siṅgh Bedī,* ed. Gurmukh Siṅgh. Patiala, 1988

S.S.Am.

BHAGTĀ or Bhagtā Bhāī Kā, village 20 km east to Jaito (30° - 26'N, 74° - 53'E) in Farīdkoṭ district of the Punjab, was founded during the latter half of the seventeenth century by Bhāī Bhagtā, grandson of Bhāī Bahilo (1553-1643) a leading Sikh of the time of Gurū Arjan. As Gurū Gobind Siṅgh visited the village in December 1705, the five sons of the founder – Gurdās, Tārā, Bhārā, Mohrā and Bhagtā–served him with devotion. Bhāī Santokh Siṅgh, *Srī Gur Prātap Sūraj Granth,* records a popular legend according to which Bhāī Bhagtā had a well sunk with the help of spirits which were still held in captivity by his sons. Gurū Gobind Siṅgh, says Bhāī Santokh Siṅgh, instructed them not to meddle with the supernatural and to set the spirits free. An old well in a corner of the compound of the historical Gurdwārā Pātshāhī 10 at the northern end of the village is still known as Bhūtāṅvālā Khūh or the well of the spirits. The old shrine is a small domed room with a platform in the middle of it. The new Gurdwārā building on a high plinth is a 15-metre square hall with the sanctum at one end and a verandah on three sides. A suite of rooms for the *granthī* and four rooms in a row for pilgrims and travellers complete the complex which is entered through a high gateway. The Gurdwārā, endowed with agricultural lands, is managed by the Shiromaṇī Gurdwārā Parbandhak Committee through a local committee. Besides the daily services, special *dīvāns* take place on the first of every Bikramī month, and on all major Sikh anniversaries. The largest-attended is the annual celebration on the 1st of Māgh (mid-January).

BIBLIOGRAPHY

Santokh Siṅgh, Bhāī, *Srī Gur Pratāp Sūraj Granth.* Amritsar, 1926-37

M.G.S.

BHĀGŪ, village in Baṭhiṇḍā district of the Punjab, is sacred to Gurū Gobind Siṅgh, who stopped here overnight on his way from Bhuchcho to Baṭhiṇḍā in 1706. Gurdwārā Dasvīṅ Pātshāhī marks the site where the Gurū had encamped. The old shrine, a small domed room, was replaced during the early 1980's by a larger hall, with the square sanctum at the far end. The Gurdwārā is managed by the village *saṅgat.*

BIBLIOGRAPHY

1. Tārā Siṅgh, *Srī Gur Tīrath Saṅgrahi.* Amritsar, n.d.

2. Ṭhākar Siṅgh, *Srī Gurduāre Darshan*. Amritsar, 1923
3. *Mālvā Desh Raṭan dī Sākhī Pothī*. Amritsar, 1968

M.G.S.

BHĀGŪ, BHĀĪ, of the village of Ḍallā, now in Kapūrthalā district of the Punjab, was a devoted Sikh of the time of Gurū Amar Dās. Bhāī Gurdās in one of his couplets praises him as "a devotee who to the Lord's love is dedicated.''

See SAHĀRŪ, BHĀĪ

BIBLIOGRAPHY

Manī Siṅgh, Bhāī, *Sikhaṅ dī Bhagat Mālā*. Amritsar, 1955

B.S.D.

BHAGVĀNĀ, BHĀĪ, along with Bhāī Laṭkan Ghūrā, Bhāī Gurdittā and Bhāī Kaṭārā, the jeweller, once came to see Gurū Arjan and asked for a *mantra,* or sacred formula. The Gurū, as says Bhāī Manī Siṅgh, *Sikhāṅ dī Bhagat Mālā*, told them that any name for God would save, but they might repeat and meditate upon the word *Vāhigurū* revealed by Gurū Nānak as a means of liberation. Bhāī Bhagvānā and his companions were pleased to be so instructed.

BIBLIOGRAPHY

Manī Siṅgh, Bhāī, *Sikhāṅ dī Bhagat Mālā*. Amritsar, 1955

T.S.

BHAGVĀN DĀS, BHĀĪ, a devoted Sikh of Burhānpur (21° - 18'N, 76° - 14'E), on the bank of the River Tāptī, once travelled to Amritsar along with Bhāī Bodalā, Bhāī Malak Kaṭārū, Bhāī Prithī Mall, Bhāī Bhagatū, Bhāī Ḍallū, Bhāī Sundar Dās and Bhāī Svāmī Dās to seek instruction from Gurū Hargobind. The Gurū, says Bhāī Manī Siṅgh, *Sikhāṅ dī Bhagat Mālā*, told them to construct a *dharamsāl* in their town where they should gather morning and evening for prayer and to raise charities for the needy. He taught them to overcome their *haumai,* i.e. egoity, and to learn to be humble. Bhāī Bhagvān Dās and his companions followed the Gurū's instructions and established a *saṅgat* at Burhānpur to which Bhāī Gurdās refers in his *Vārāṅ,* XI. 30.

BIBLIOGRAPHY

1. Manī Siṅgh, Bhāī, *Sikhāṅ dī Bhagat Mālā*. Amritsar, 1955
2. Santokh Siṅgh, Bhāī, *Srī Gur Pratāp Sūraj Granth*. Amritsar, 1926-37

B.S.

BHAGVĀN SIṄGH, BHĀĪ (1881-1921), one of the Nankāṇā Sāhib martyrs, was son of Bhāī Lahiṇā Siṅgh and Māī Tābo of village Nizāmpur, in Amritsar district. He lost his mother at the age of three. On the opening of the Lower Chenāb Canal Colony during the last decade of the 19th century, the family—father and son—migrated to Chakk No. 38 Devā Siṅghvālā in Sheikhūpurā district where young Bhagvān Siṅgh assisted his father carrying errands. When he grew up, he went abroad to China in search of fortune, but came back after three years, and received the rites of Khālsā initiation at Srī Akāl Takht Sāhib. He attended the Akālī conference at Dhārovālī on 1-3 October 1920 and joined Bhāī Lachhmaṇ Siṅgh's *jathā* of Akālī reformists. He shared the *jathā's* fate at Nankāṇā Sāhib on 20 February 1921.

See NANKĀṆĀ SĀHIB MASSACRE

BIBLIOGRAPHY

Shamsher, Gurbakhsh Siṅgh, *Shahīdī Jīvan*. Nankana Sahib, 1938

G.S.G.

BHAGVĀN SIṄGH LAUṄGOVĀLĪĀ (d. 1944), patriot, Akālī activist and one of the founders of the Prajā Maṇḍal, a platform meant to provide voice to the people of Indian states ruled by Indian princes during

British times to ventilate their grievances and protest against the oppression, misrule and extravagances of the autocrats who presided over their destinies, was born in Burma where his father Rūṛ Siṅgh was a soldier in the army. The only child of his parents, he was named Indar Siṅgh. The family originally belonged to the village of Lauṅgovāl in the present Saṅgrūr district of the Punjab. As he grew up, Bhagvān Siṅgh, then Indar Siṅgh, also joined the army and served in World War I. Under the influence of Ghadr radicalism, he deserted the army and went over to Nepal, disguised as a *sādhū*. It was during this phase of his life that he changed his name from Indar Siṅgh to Bhagvān Siṅgh. After remaining underground for 4-5 years, he came to India where he was apprehended by police. As he stepped out to freedom, he was drawn into the Gurdwārā reform movement, participating in *dīvāns* and activities connected with the liberation of the Sikh shrines from the control of the degenerate *mahants* or clergy. On 24 May 1922, he was convicted and sentenced to two years' rigorous imprisonment and a fine of Rs 1,000 for a "seditious" speech delivered at Sherpur (Paṭiālā state). Another "seditious" speech delivered at an Akālī gathering in his own native village, Lauṅgovāl, landed him in jail for a three-year sentence. All his property was confiscated by the princely ruler of Paṭiālā state. Bhagvān Siṅgh was released along with other Akālī prisoners after the Punjab Legislative Council passed the Sikh Gurdwārā laws in 1925. But almost immediately he plunged into the agitation for release from Paṭiālā jail of the veteran Akālī leader, Sevā Siṅgh Ṭhīkrīvālā. In open defiance of the orders of the district magistrate, Sunām, he led a *jathā* of agitators from his village to join a protest rally on 11 July 1926. In 1928, a largely-attended *dīvān* was held at Ṭhīkrīvālā in protest against the continued detention of Sevā Siṅgh. Speaking at the *dīvān*, Bhagvān Siṅgh denounced the British government as vehemently as he did the princely rulers of the states. The Paṭiālā police arrested a large number of Akālī workers who had attended the *dīvān*, but Bhagvān Siṅgh dodged the police and escaped into the (British) Punjab territory, thereafter operating mostly from outside the orbit of the princely states. Akālī leaders Master Tārā Siṅgh and Bābā Khaṛak Siṅgh were his new allies now.

Bhagvān Siṅgh represented the states' people at the All-India States Subjects Conference held at Calcutta in 1928. In December 1929, the first regular session of the Punjab Riyāstī Prajā Maṇḍal was held at Lahore where Bhagvān Siṅgh was elected general secretary of the Maṇḍal. Another detention and court trial earned him totally a sentence of 22 years. He was released from jail as a result of the Tārā Siṅgh-Bhūpinder Siṅgh Pact of 1935 concluded between the Akālī leader and Mahārājā Bhūpinder Siṅgh of Paṭiālā after the death in jail of Sevā Siṅgh. Against this pact Bhagvān Siṅgh along with five of his leading colleagues from the Riyāstī Prajā Maṇḍal undertook a fast unto death on 20 January 1936 in front of the Akāl Takht at Amritsar. The pact in fact signalled the exit of Bhagvān Siṅgh from the Akālī Dal and his gravitation towards the Communist Party.

Bhagvān Siṅgh married, late in his life, Dharam Kaur, widow of his cousin, who bore him two daughters and a son. He died on 16 September 1944 of phthisis of the lungs. His portrait occupies a place of honour among the galaxy of eminent Sikh leaders displayd in the Central Sikh Museum at the Golden Temple at Amritsar.

BIBLIOGRAPHY

1. Walia, Ramesh, *Praja Mandal Movement in East Punjab States.* Patiala, 1972
2. Fauja Singh, *Eminent Freedom Fighters of Punjab.* Patiala, 1972

Z.S.

BHAGVĀN SIṄGH, RĀJĀ (1842-1871), was

born at Nābhā on 30 November 1842, the younger son of Rājā Devinder Siṅgh. He ascended the throne of the princely state of Nābhā on 17 February 1864 after his elder brother, Rājā Bharpūr Siṅgh, had died issueless. Rājā Bhagvān Siṅgh too died childless on 31 May 1871 of tuberculosis at Nābhā.

BIBLIOGRAPHY

1. Griffin, Lepel, *The Rajas of the Punjab.* Delhi, 1977
2. Ganda Singh, *The Patiala and the East Panjab States Union*. Patiala, 1951

S.S.B.

BHAGVANT SIṄGH BAṄGESARĪ was, according to Sarūp Siṅgh Kaushish, *Gurū kīāṅ Sākhīāṅ*, the *nāik* or leader of a large *ṭāṇḍā* or trade caravan. In September-October 1708, he with his merchandise was passing through Nānded where he halted to pay homage to Gurū Gobind Siṅgh. As the Gurū deputed Bandā Siṅgh Bahādur with five of his Sikhs to come to the Punjab to chastise the persecutors, they travelled with Bhagvant Siṅgh's caravan.

BIBLIOGRAPHY

Padam, Piārā Siṅgh, and Giānī Garjā Siṅgh, eds., *Gurū kīāṅ Sākhīāṅ*. Patiala, 1986

Gn.S.

BHAGVANT SIṄGH HARĪJĪ, BHĀĪ (1892-1968), a lover of game, horticulturist and scholar, was born on 15 February 1892 to the erudition of his celebrated father, Bhāī Kāhn Siṅgh, of Nābhā, the creator of the immortal *Gurushabad Ratnākar Mahān Kosh*. Unobtrusively, and in his characteristically gentle and self-abnegating manner, Bhagvant Siṅgh carried the family learning into the second generation. His home provided the best education then available to a young man, though he did attend formally the Khālsā College at Amritsar, then the premier educational institution of the Sikhs. On 9 November 1915, he married Bībī Harnām Kaur, daughter of Jīvan Siṅgh, editor of the *Khālsā Sevak* of Amritsar, who was herself a poet of repute and who appreciated and sustained her husband's scholarly interests. Equally vital was Bhagvant Siṅgh's experience watching his father working on the *Mahān Kosh*, meeting with scholars in different fields who came to see him and listening to or joining the learned discussions that constantly went on in his father's study. This provided him with much valuable training in the art of lexicography.

"Harījī", as he was affectionately called by his friends and admirers, made *Dasam Granth,* Book of the Tenth Master, the focus of his study, and prepared a verse-index of it which was published posthumously by the Punjabi University, Paṭiālā. This is a work which enjoys high prestige in Sikh letters for its technical perfection and range of knowledge. Another of his books in the field of *Dasam Granth* scholarship, *Dasam Granth dā Bāṇī Beorā,* appeared in 1991 (publisher : Punjabi University, Paṭiālā). An earlier publication was *Vidhi Nikhedh* (a common man's book of do's and don'ts), August 1919.

Bhāī Bhagvant Siṅgh died on 9 October 1968 after a protracted illness.

R.K.

BHAGWĀN SIṄGH GYĀNEE (d. 1962), prominent Ghadr leader, was born the son of Sarmukh Siṅgh of the village of Vaṛiṅg, 15 km east of Tarn Tāran in Amritsar district of the Punjab. Their ancestors, Kashmīrī Brāhmaṇs, had migrated to the Punjab during the seventeenth century. Bhagwān Siṅgh learnt Urdu at the village school and then joined Gurmat Vidyālā, a missionary school at Gharjākh, in Gujrāṅwālā district, from where he passed the *gyānī* examination. He was employed as a teacher in the Gurmat Vidyālā, shifting after a short while to Khālsā School, Ḍaskā, in Siālkoṭ district, where he studied Vedānta under Sādhū Har Bilās. He delivered anti-government speeches during the agrarian unrest of 1907-08, and to escape prosecution left India sailing to Penang where he became a *granthī* or Scripture-reader in the *gurdwārā*, but his services were soon terminated owing to his radical views. Bhagwān Siṅgh next worked as a *granthī* at the Central Gurdwārā in Hong Kong. Here he was twice prosecuted in 1911-12 and, though he was acquitted on both occasions, he had to leave the colony. He reached Canada in April 1913 under the assumed name of Natthā Siṅgh, but was deported by the immigration authorities on the charge of having entered the country under a false name. He was put on a Japanese ship going to Hong Kong, but he managed to escape *en route* and entered Japan where a unit of the Ghadr Party had been established by Maulawī Barkatullah. Bhagwān Siṅgh and Barkatullah met the S.S.*Komagata Maru* on its outward journey at the end of April 1914 and addressed its inmates, setting sail soon thereafter for the United States and reaching Yugāntar Āshram, the Ghadr Party headquarters at San Francisco, on 23 May 1914. With the arrival of Bhagwān Siṅgh the control of the *gurdwārā* at Stockton passed from the hands of a moderate management to those of the revolutionaries. He addressed meetings and contributed patriotic and anti-British poems to the *Ghadr*. After the departure of Bābā Sohan Siṅgh Bhaknā for India on 21 July 1914, Bhagwān Siṅgh was elected president of the Ghadr Party. Besides guiding the work at party headquarters, he toured the Philippines, Japan, Shanghai (China) and Panama to enlist volunteers, establish branches and collect funds. In Manila (Philippines) in May 1915, his address was "B.S. Jakh, Post Box 1070."

British government had been bringing diplomatic pressure on the United States to check the Ghadr activity. The U.S. government acted swiftly after it had entered the war (World War I) and on 7 April 1917 took into custody Bhagwān Siṅgh and 18 others who were brought to trial at San Francisco. The charge against them was the violation of American Neutrality Law by conspiring to organize the movement in Thailand and Burma in order to weaken one of the allied governments and to send arms and ammunition to them. Bhagwān Siṅgh was sentenced to 18 months' imprisonment which he spent in the United States penitentiary at MacNeil Island. After his release, he and his comrades, who were in danger of being deported to India, applied for and were granted political asylum in the United States with the support of an organization known as Friends of Freedom for India. He edited the Punjabi monthly *Navāṅ Jug* (New Age) which was in a way a continuation of the *Ghadr*. Bhagwān Siṅgh Gyānee repatriated to India in 1958 on the invitation of Partāp Siṅgh Kairoṅ, then Chief Minister of the Punjab. He founded the Self-Culture Association of India, with headquarters at Saproon in the Himalayas. He travelled extensively addressing especially students at colleges and universities, his chosen themes being patriotism and national unity.

BIBLIOGRAPHY

1. Saiṅsarā, Gurcharan Siṅgh, *Ghadar Pārtī dā Itihās.* Jalandhar, 1969
2. Jagjīt Siṅgh, *Ghadar Pārṭī Lahir.* Delhi, 1979
3. Jas, Jaswant Siṅgh, *Bābā Sohan Siṅgh Bhaknā.* Jalandhar, n.d.
4. Khushwant Singh, *A History of the Sikhs,* vol. 2, Princeton, 1966

S.S.J.

BHĀĪ, of Indo-Āryan origin (Sanskrit *bhrātṛ*, Pālī *bhāyā*), means brother in its literal sense and is employed as an honorific as well as in the dominant familial sense and as a title of affection between equals. It has been used in the Gurū Granth Sāhib in the latter sense and there are several apostrophic examples none of which seems to imply any special rank or status. However, by the middle of the seventeenth century, it was being used as a title implying distinction: the earliest example is the *Bālā Janam Sākhī* (AD 1658) which refers to its putative author as *Bhāī* Bālā. The naturalness of its use in this particular context suggests that it must have developed the honorific connotation even earlier though it does not necessarily follow that these connotations were clearly apprehended in earlier usage. Mardānā and Gurdās may have received the title from their contemporaries without any deliberate intention to set them apart from ordinary Sikhs. It seems likely that the term, originally used in an egalitarian sense, progressively absorbed connotations of spiritual eminence from the reputations of those to whom it was characteristically attached. During the time of the later Gurūs and into the eighteenth century, the title came to be used for those in the community who occupied positions of leadership.

Generically, the term has naturalized among Sahajdhārī Sikhs (*q.v.*). Since the days of *Bhāī* Nand Lāl, of holy memory, who was a contemporary of Gurū Gobind Siṅgh, the term has been appropriated by them as a whole. Among modern exemplars may be cited the names of *Bhāī* Rām Lāl Rāhī who presided the Sahajdhārī Conference in the 1960's, and *Bhāī* Harbans Lāl, a U.S. pharmacologist.

Bhāī was in common use especially for the more devout of the Sikhs and *saṅgat* leaders such as Bhāī Lālo, Bhāī Bhagatū and Bhāī Bidhī Chand. It remained in active use until the time of Gurū Gobind Siṅgh. Pañj Piāre whom he initiated at the time of the inauguration of the K͟hālsā are to this day remembered in the daily *ardās* by the title of *Bhāī*. *Bhāī* gave way to more picturesque *sardār* (chief) as Sikhs started occupying territory. Under Nirankārī, Nāmdhārī and Siṅgh Sabhā reform *Bhāī* went through a revival, men like Jodh Siṅgh deliberatively choosing it in preference to other prevalent titles.

Modern usage, however, differs in two major respects: first, it applies the title much more rarely in its honorific sense, thereby enhancing its status when used and this process of contraction has tended to eliminate those whose authority is essentially administrative, restricting the title to the few who earn substantial reputations for piety or religious learning. Vīr Siṅgh, Kāhn Siṅgh Nābhā, and Raṇdhīr Siṅgh are notable twentieth-century recipients. No formal investiture is involved in such cases. It is conferred simply through repeated usage and thus reflects a general opinion rather than any conscious decision.

The term has meanwhile developed a different sense, one which denotes a range of vocational roles. Any person employed as manager, musician, or instructor in a *gurdwārā* is today commonly designated *bhāī*. The development is easily traced to and represents an entirely natural process. Distinguished disciples Mardānā and Manī Siṅgh were associated respectively with religious music and *gurdwārā* superintendence, and it is scarcely surprising that their modern successors should inherit their title without necessarily sharing their distinction. The result has been the emergence of a dual meaning in the case of 'Bhāī', with the divergence between the two continuing to grow wider. As the honorific title becomes increasingly rare, the vocational usage has gained popular currency today.

More recently, especially since the mid-eighties of the twentieth century, the term, *bhāī* has been avidly embraced by activist Sikh youth and, besides recovering the old comradely connotation, it has acquired a decided political edge. Among those who set the vogue was *Bhāī* Amrīk Siṅgh, president of the Sikh Students Federation, who fell a martyr during the Army attack on the Golden Temple premises in 1984.

W.H.M.

BHAIṆĪ BĀGHĀ, an old village 10 km north of the district town of Mānsā (29° - 59'N, 75° - 23'E) in the Punjab, has a historical shrine, Gurdwārā Rakābsar Pātshāhī Nauvīṅ. It is said that as Gurū Tegh Bahādur was proceeding from Khiālā towards Dikkh, a strap of the saddle stirrup, *rakāb* in Punjabi, broke. He stopped to get the stirrup mended by the village cobbler. A memorial in the shape of a platform was raised to mark the spot where the Gurū had alighted and sat. Later, a room was built by the side of the platform and the Gurū Granth Sāhib installed in it. The present building, constructed in the 1970's, replaced both. Standing in a corner of a 2-acre enclosure, it comprises a domed sanctum inside a square hall. The Gurdwārā owns seven acres of land. The Shiromaṇī Gurdwārā Parbandhak Committee has acquired the legal right to administer it, but the village *saṅgat* (Sikh community) continues to manage it through a five-member committee.

BIBLIOGRAPHY

1. *Mālvā Desh Ratan Dī Sākhī Pothī*. Amritsar, 1968
2. Ṭhākar Siṅgh, Giānī, *Srī Gurduāre Darshan*. Amritsar, 1923
3. Tārā Siṅgh, *Srī Gur Tīrath Saṅgrahi*. Amritsar, n.d.

Gn.S.

BHĀĪ PHERŪ, GURDWĀRĀ (also called Gurdwārā Saṅgat Sāhib), named after its founder, the well-known Udāsī Sikh preacher Bhāī Pherū (1640-1706), is located at Mīeṅ kī Mauṛ, in Chūnīāṅ *tahsīl* of Lahore district in Pakistan. During Sikh times, large endowments in land extending to about 2,750 acres were inscribed to the shrine which was administered by a line of priests belonging to Saṅgat Sāhib Ke sect of Udāsī Sikhs. As a campaign for bringing the Sikh places of worship under the management of a central body, the Shiromaṇī Gurdwārā Parbandhak Committee, formed in 1920, negotiations were opened with the *mahant* or custodian for the transfer of the Bhāī Pherū Gurdwārā and the landed property attached to it. The Mahant, Kishan Dās, agreed in consideration of a monthly pension of Rs 400 and free rations for life. The Shiromaṇī Committee took possession of the Gurdwārā on 28 December 1922. But later the Mahant, repudiating the agreement, filed with the police a complaint of trespass against the manager, Jagat Siṅgh, and other staff appointed by the Shiromaṇī Committee. The police, on 7 December 1923, arrested Jagat Siṅgh and ten other Sikhs. Thirty-four more arrests were made on 2 January 1924. This led the Shiromaṇī Committee to launch a *morchā*. Bands of Akālī volunteers started courting arrest daily from 5 January 1924 onwards. The *morchā* was pledged to non-violence and every day volunteers offered themselves for arrest. This went on for a period of 21 months. On 20 September 1925 there occurred an incident of violence at which the Shiromaṇī Committee called off the agitation. On 9 July 1925 the Punjab Government adopted the Sikh Gurdwaras Act providing for the transfer of control of Sikh shrines and their properties to the Shiromaṇī Gurdwārā Parbandhak Committee, but the matter of the Bhāī Pherū Gurdwārā and its properties was then before a court of law. The case was ultimately decided in favour of the reformers on 19 June 1931 enabling the Shiromaṇī Gurdwārā Parbandhak Committee to take over possession of the shrine and the lands. The Gurdwārā was abandoned at the time of mass migrations in the wake of the partition of the Punjab in 1947. Since then it is supposed to be maintained by the Pakistan Waqf Board.

BIBLIOGRAPHY

1. Raṇdhīr Siṅgh, Bhāī, *Udāsī Sikkhāṅ dī Vithīā*. Amritsar, 1959
2. Ashok, Shamsher Siṅgh, *Sharomaṇī Committee dā Pañjāh Sālā Itihās*. Amritsar, 1982

3. Josh, Sohan Siṅgh, *Akālī Morchiāṅ dā Itihās.* Delhi, 1972
4. Pratāp Siṅgh, Giānī, *Gurdwārā Sudhār arthāt Akālī Lahir* [Reprint]. Amritsar, 1975
5. Mohinder Singh, *The Akali Movement.* Delhi, 1978

M.G.S.

BHĀĪ PHERŪ MORCHĀ, one of a series of campaigns in the Sikhs' agitation in the 1920's for the reformation of their holy places. Gurdwārā Saṅgat Sāhib, located in Mīeṅ ke Mauṛ in Lahore district, about 15 km from Chhāṅgā Māṅgā railway station, dedicated to the memory of Bhāī Pherū (1640-1706), a *masand* or parish leader in the time of Gurū Har Rāi who was honoured for his devotion by Gurū Gobind Siṅgh with the titles of Sachchī Dāhṛī (True Bearded) and Saṅgat Sāhib, was an important shrine, with 2,750 acres of land attached to it, and was being managed by Mahant Kishan Dās. After the Shiromaṇī Gurdwārā Parbandhak Committee, a representative society of the Sikhs, had taken over management of some of the major shrines and *mahants* or priests had started voluntarily handing over *gurdwārās* under their control, Mahant Kishan Dās, on 28 December 1922, transferred Gurdwārā Bhāī Pherū to the Committee. He later went back on the agreement he had signed and petitioned the government to have the shrine and the lands restored to him. On 7 December 1923 the police arrested the manager, Jagat Siṅgh, and eleven other representatives of the Shiromaṇī Gurdwārā Parbandhak Committee. The possession of the shrine and the estate was restored to the Mahant and his tenants. However, the decision of the deputy commissioner of Lahore on the Gurdwārā lands went in favour of the Shiromaṇī Committee and, as its representatives arrived to take charge of these, Mahant Kishan Dās and his tenant Pālā Rām, brother of Mahant Naraiṇ Dās, of Srī Nankāṇā Sāhib, lodged a complaint with police that the Akālīs were forcibly taking possession of his property. Police arrested 34 Akālīs on 2 January 1924. The government revised its earlier decision given in favour of the Shiromaṇī Gurdwārā Parbandhak Committee and passed fresh orders declaring Pālā Rām to be temporarily in possession of the land. Akālīs launched a *morchā* in protest even as the *morchā* at Jaito was still continuing. *Jathās* or batches of Akālī volunteers started marching to Bhāī Pherū from different parts of the district. On 5 January 1924, the Shiromaṇī Gurdwārā Parbandhak Committee took the campaign into its own hands. By 10 September 1925, the number of arrests had reached 6,372. An unsavoury incident, however, led the local organizer, Arjan Siṅgh, to suspend the *morchā* on 20 September 1925. The Gurdwārā and the lands attached to it came under the Committee's control after the Sikh Gurdwaras Act of 1925 was passed by the Punjab Legislative Council, and the court case too was decided in the Committee's favour in June 1931.

BIBLIOGRAPHY

1. Josh, Sohan Siṅgh, *Akālī Morchiāṅ dā Itihās.* Delhi, 1972
2. Pratāp Siṅgh, Giānī, *Gurdwārā Sudhār arthāt Akālī Lahir.* Amritsar, 1975
3. Mohinder Singh, *The Akali Movement.* Delhi, 1978
4. Sahni, Ruchi Ram, *Struggle for Reform in Sikh Shrines.* Ed. Ganda Singh. Amritsar, n.d.

Gl.S.

BHAIROṄ. *See* SIKH DEVOTIONAL MUSIC

BHAIROṄ, BHĀĪ, a devout Sikh of the time of Gurū Hargobind (1595-1644). Bhāī Bhairoṅ's name occurs along with those of Sādh, Devā, Jhaṇḍā and Bidhīā in a contemporary Persian work, *Dabistān-i-Mazāhib.* The author narrates an interesting anecdote to illustrate the Sikhs' belief in the One Unincarnated Supreme Being.

BIBLIOGRAPHY

Ardistānī, Maubid Zulfiqār, *Dabistān-i-Mazāhib* (tr. into English by David Shea and Anthony Troyer). London, 1843

Gn.S.

BHĀĪ RŪPĀ, village 18 km north of Rāmpurā Phūl (30° - 16'N, 75° - 14'E) in Baṭhiṇḍā district of the Punjab, celebrates the name of a prominent Sikh, Bhāī Rūpā (Rūp Chand, 1614-1709), who laid the foundation of it in 1631 at the instance of Gurū Hargobind. Next to Bhāī Rūpā's house was built a *gurdwārā* in Gurū Hargobind's honour. The present Gurdwārā Sāhib Pātshāhī Chhevīṅ, a two-storeyed domed building, marks that site inside the village. Gurū kā Laṅgar is across a narrow lane. In the same direction is the pavilion raised recently to accommodate larger *dīvāns*. The Gurdwārā, though affiliated to the Shiromaṇī Gurdwārā Parbandhak Committee, is managed by the descendants of Bhāī Rūpā.

Close to the Gurdwārā, in a private house belonging to one of the descendants of Bhāī Rūpā, is preserved an old *rath* or chariot. It is said to have been brought from Ḍerā Rām Rāi at Dehrā Dūn by Bhāī Giān Chand, a grandson of Bhāī Rūpā. According to local tradition, it once belonged to Gurū Arjan and was used by his successors, Gurū Hargobind and Gurū Har Rāi.

M.G.S.

BHAKTI AND SIKHISM. The word *bhakti* is derived from Skt. *bhaj*, meaning to serve, honour, revere, love and adore. In the religious idiom, it is attachment or fervent devotion to God and is defined as "that particular affection which is generated by the knowledge of the attributes of the Adorable One."

The concept is traceable to the Vedas where its intimations are audible in the hymns addressed to deities such as Varuṇa, Savitra and Ushā. However, the word *bhakti* does not occur there. The word occurs for the first time in the Upaniṣads where it appears with the co-doctrines of grace and self-surrender (*prapatti*) (e.g.*Śvetāśvatar*, I,V. 23). The *Bhagavadgītā* attempts to expound *bhakti* in a systematic manner and puts *bhakti mārga* in juxtaposition with *karma mārga* and *jñāna mārga* as one of the three means of attaining liberation. The *Nārdīya Sūtra* , however, decrees that "*bhakti* is superior even to *karma, jñāna* and *yoga.*"

Bhakti took strong roots in South India where generations of Ālvār (Vaiṣṇavite) and Nāyanār (Śaivite) saints had sung their devotional lyrics and founded their respective schools of *bhakti* between AD 200-900. It came to north India much later. "The Dravid country is the birthplace of *bhakti* school; *bhakti* became young in Karnataka, it grew old in Maharashtra and Gujrat, but when it arrived in Vrindavana, it became young again." Munshī Rām Sharmā : *Bhakti kā Vikās.* p. 353.

In the north, the cult was essentially Vaiṣṇava-based, but instead of being focussed on Viṣṇu, it chose to focus itself on Viṣṇu's human incarnations, Rāma and Kṛṣṇa, the respective *avatārs* or deities central to the two epics Rāmāyaṇa and Mahābhārata. For *bhakti* now Viṣṇu's incarnations (Rāma and Kṛṣṇa) were the direct objects of devotion. Adoration of the devotees was focussed on them in association with their respective consorts : Sītā with Rāma; and Rukminī, his wedded wife, or Rādhā, his Gopikā companion, with Kṛṣṇa. Images of these deities and their consorts installed in temples were worshipped. The path of *bhakti* was not directly accessible to the lower castes; for them the path of *prapatti* (unquestioned self-surrender) was prescribed. Singing of *bhajans* and dancing formed an important part of this worship. The dancers were *deva-dāsīs* (female slaves of the deity) inside the temple, but *nagar-badhūs* (public wives) outside. Apart from being overwhelmingly ritualistic, the worship tended to be intensely emotional, frenzied and even erotic.

An important influence in north Indian *bhakti* was Rāmānand whose many disciples including Kabīr, Ravidās, Pīpā, Sadhanā and Saiṇu radicalized the Bhakti movement. Kabīr, out of them, was the most eloquent and outspoken. Besides *bhakti*, other influences which shaped him were Sufism and Buddhism. He repudiated *avatārvād*, social ideology of caste, ritualistic formalism and idol-worship, all of which were integral parts of traditional Vaiṣṇavite *bhakti*. Kabīr even questioned the authority of the Vedas and Purāṇas.

Sikhism undoubtedly accepted some of the aspects of radicalized *bhakti*, and admitted some of its practices into its own ordained set. It did lay down spiritual love as the way to the deity, but the deity to be worshipped was neither Śiva nor Viṣṇu nor even any of their incarnations, nor any of the gods or goddesses of the Hindu pantheon. It was the One and the Only God, the Lord of Universes who was at once transcendent (*nirguṇa*) and immanent (*saguṇa*). Although immanent in His Creation He was yet apart from it, being its Creator. Since He inhered in the world that He had created, the world could not be considered unreal or illusory (*mithyā* or *māyā*). It was real and sacred ("the abode of the True One"). It is therefore blasphemous to renounce it in quest of God. "He that is immanent in the Universe resides also within yourself. Seek, and ye shall find" (GG, 695). Renunciation of the world as a spiritual pursuit thus stood totally rejected. Celebacy was no longer countenanced, either. Full participation in life in a spirit of 'detachment' was prescribed instead. "Of all the religious rules and observances *grihasthya* (the homestead) is supreme. It is from here that all else is blessed" (GG, 587). Gurū is paramount in *bhakti* as well as in Sikhism.

The ideal that Bhakti laid down for man was to achieve personal release (*moksha* or *mukti*). In Sikhism the ideal was stated in these terms : "I long not for a kingdom or for *mukti* but only for the lotus feet of the Lord" (GG, 534). In the Sikh faith the highest ideal is to be able cheerfully to accept the will of God (*razā, bhāṇā*) and live one's life in its dynamic mould, to be ready to give oneself to carrying out what ought to happen. This concept of Divine Will (*hukam*) as well as the injunction to accept it cheerfully is peculiar to Sikhism. Also, whereas the ultimate aim of *bhakti* is for the individual to attain personal liberation, the Sikh ideal is well-being of all (*sarbatt kā bhalā*).

The modes of worship in Bhakti cults included not only *bhajan* (adoration) and *kīrtan* (singing the praises of the deity), but also Yogic *upāsanā* (literally, to sit beside, to meditate), Vedic sacrifices, Brāhmaṇical ritualism and Tāntric practices. Of these, Sikhism retains only *bhajan* and *kīrtan* and disclaims the rest. It categorically rejects sacrificial rites. The only sacrifice it approves of is self-sacrifice for the sake of righteousness. Sikhism strongly censures idol-worship. Instead, *śabda* (the Divine Word) is determined to be the focus of all adoration. However, as in *bhakti*, *nām* (Logos) is both the object and means of adoration of God.

Thus, *bhakti* has been radically transformed and redefined in Sikhism. Sikhism is in fact much wider than *bhakti* both in its conceptual gamut as well as in practice. For the Bhakti cults, *bhakti* is the be-all and end-all of everything; for Sikhism two other crucially important ends are ethical living and spiritual liberation. The cultivation of moral qualities, in Sikhism, is the requisite precondition for *bhakti*. "Without morality *bhakti* is not practicable" (GG, 4). Moral discipline is considered a vehicle for attaining nearness to God. "It is by our deeds that we become closer to God or become distant from Him'' (GG, 6).

While the *bhagats'* sole stress was on *bhakti* or loving devotion, the Gurūs also wanted to inculcate along with love and faith the spirit of fearlessness and valour among the Sikhs. A Sikh was to "overcome all fear by cherishing the Fearless Lord" (GG, 293). "He must not terrorize anyone, nor must he submit to anyone's fear" (GG, 1427). He was "to be subservient to none but the True Lord" (GG, 473). He was not to be a quietist ascetic but a valiant saint ready to "battle in open field" (GG, 931) to destroy the tyrants. In their scheme of ethical dynamism the Gurūs gave priority to zeal for freedom.

Sikhs were not only given *nām* (Logos) as the symbol of the Formless One (which they shared with the *bhaktas*) but were also given *kirpān* (sword) as the symbol of the Fearless One. Sikhism, thus addressed itself to dual ideals, the other-worldly (*pīrī*) as well as this-worldly (*mīrī*).

Since Fatherhood of God was the basic Sikh tenet, brotherhood of man *ipso facto* became its social corrolary. No one was to be reckoned low or high – "Reckon the entire mankind as One" (*Akāl Ustati,* 15.85) was the Gurū's precept. Most of the *bhakti* cults also decried inequality, and especially condemned caste-distinctions, giving the right of worship to the low caste. However, service continued to be a menial pursuit, and manual labour was looked upon as the job of the lowly. The Gurūs went further than just proclaiming the equality of man. They established dignity of labour, by making social service (*sevā*) as an important vehicle of spiritual advancement. "The hands and feet sans *sevā* are condemnable; actions other than *sevā* are fruitless" (Bhāī Gurdās, *Vārāṅ,* XXVII. 10). Begging is taboo for the Sikhs. While *bhaktas* could live on alms and public charity, not so a Sikh. He is ordained to earn his living by the honest labour of his hands (*kirt*) and share his earnings with others. It rehearsed in the fifteenth century the ideology of fraternity, equality and liberty. Devotion was defined as a positive phenomenon. Full-faced participation in life was recommended. In the time and space setting, *bhakti* and Sikhism lie close to each other which has led some to describe Sikhism as an offshoot of *bhakti*.

Like the *bhaktas* and the Sūfīs, Gurū Nānak, founder of Sikhism, proclaimed the love of God and, through it, communion with Him as the primary aim of man. More like the former, he repudiated caste and the importance of ritualism, and, in common with the latter, emphasized submission to God's will as the ultimate means to realization. Agreeably to the atmosphere created by Bhakti and Sufism, he rejoiced in singing praises of the Almighty and indicated the way to reconciliation between the Hindus and the Muslims. He brought to these general tendencies the force and urgency of a deeply inspired and forward-looking faith. He added elements which were characteristically his own and which empowered current trends with wholly new possibilities of fulfilment. Life in all of its different aspects was the subject of Gurū Nānak's attention. Integral to his intuition was an awareness of the ills and errors of society and his concern to remedy these. This was in contrast to the attitude of escape implicit in Bhakti and Sūfism. Gurū Nānak did not admit, like many of their protagonists, the possibility of man ever attaining, in his mystical progress, equality with Divinity. He also did not share the Bhaktas' belief in incarnation or the Sūfīs' insistence on bodily mortification and frenzied singing and dancing to bring about spiritual illumination. The faith begins with the revelation brought to light by Gurū Nānak. To understand Sikhism fully the study of the totality of its tenet and of what impact it made on history will be very vital. In this perspective, the precept he preached is definitively the starting-point of Sikhism and not *bhakti* or any other cult.

BIBLIOGRAPHY

1. Taran Singh, ed., *Guru Nanak and Indian Religious Thought.* Patiala, 1970

2. Sher Singh, *The Philosophy of Sikhism*. Lahore, 1944
3. Schomer, Karine, and W.H. Mcleod, eds., *The Sants : Studies in a Devotional Tradition of India*. Delhi, 1987
4. Ishar Singh, *The Philosophy of Guru Nanak*. Delhi, 1969
5. Jodh Singh, *The Religious Philosophy of Guru Nanak*. Varanasi, 1983
6. Hīrā, Bhagat Siṅgh, *Gurmatt Vichārdhārā*. Delhi, 1969
7. Chaturvedī, Parshu Rām, *Uttarī Bhārat Kī Sant - Promparā*. Allahabad, 1964

J.S.N.

BHALĀN, village near the confluence of Soāṅ rivulet with the River Sutlej 14 km south of Naṅgal in Ropaṛ district of the Punjab, is sacred to Gurū Gobind Siṅgh, who arrived here following Khānzādā Rustam Khān in the winter of 1693-94. As Gurū Gobind Siṅgh himself relates in his *Bachitra Nāṭak*, the Khānzādā had planned to surprise the Sikhs with a night attack, but finding the defendants alert he beat a hasty retreat. "Ravaging Barvā village (on his way back)," records Gurū Gobind Siṅgh, "he made a halt at Bhalān." The shrine rebuilt by the local *saṅgat* in 1960 is called Gurdwārā Dashmeshgaṛh (lit. Fort of the Tenth Master). It is a small square sanctum with a circumambulatory verandah around it. The Gurdwārā is managed by a committee of the local Sikhs.

BIBLIOGRAPHY

1. *Bachitra Nāṭak*
2. Kuir Siṅgh, *Gurbilās Pātshāhī 10*. Patiala, 1968
3. Ṭhākar Siṅgh, *Srī Gurduāre Darshan*. Amritsar, 1923
4. Tārā Siṅgh, *Srī Gur Tīrath Saṅgrahi*. Amritsar, n.d.

Gn.S.

BHĀLENDRA SIṄGH, RĀJĀ (1919-1992), distinguished cricketer and India's longest-lasting sports executive, was born on 19 August 1919, the son of Lieutenant-General Mahārājā Sir Bhūpinder Siṅgh, the glamorous princely ruler of the state of Paṭiālā in Southern Punjab. Brought up in the lap of luxury, Bhālendra Siṅgh shot up into a tall, handsome and lissom young man, with remarkable prowess in several branches of athletics. When his elder brother Yādavinder Siṅgh, the heir apparent of Paṭiālā state, was getting ready to don colours for India against Lord Tennyson's team (1937-38), Bhālendra Siṅgh was playing cricket for Southern Punjab, a formidable outfit, which claimed among its members famous cricketers of the day, such as Nissār, Amīr Alāhī and L. Amar Nāth who later rose to be India's Test captain.

Bhālendra Siṅgh was educated at the Aitchison College, Lahore, where, besides cricket, he distinguished himself in riding, polo and tennis. The Mahārājā of Paṭiālā had ace cricketers such as Col Mistry and Frank Tarrant, the Australian, to train his children. He also had famous Sikh scholars, notably Paṇḍit Rām Basant Siṅgh, to teach them the religious canon of their faith. Bhālendra Siṅgh was exceptionally well prepared to excel in study as well as in sports. He worked as hard as he played. He proved first-rate in athletics, tennis, swimming, shooting and angling. Very rarely in the history of the College had any one prince displayed such notable proficiency in so many diverse fields of sportsmanship. Bhālendra Siṅgh succeeded in doing all this without any detriment to his academic work. He was not greatly interested in *shikār* or gun-dogs – two activities to which his father was passionately attached. His own interests were finally divided between cricket and tennis. Another of his major interests was Indian classical music. A favourite hobby was cooking and he also turned out a book of recipes. He spent a time at Cambridge University where he continued to play first-grade cricket, excelling as a slow bowler. Slow-bowling had always been his forte.

After India's Independence, Bhālendra

Siṅgh held important positions in national sports. He was for many an year associated with the Amateur Athletic Federation of India, the Swimming Federation of India and the Indian Hockey Federation. In 1947, he became a life member of the International Olympic Committee and in 1959 he was elected president of Indian Olympic Association which office he continued to hold until 1975. He had another term in that office, 1980 to 1984. He was the architect of the Asian Games movement and was the moving figure behind the Asiad held in New Delhi during 1982. At the opening ceremonies of the Games he shared the podium with the President of India, Giānī Zail Siṅgh. Rājā Bhālendra Siṅgh had occupied with outstanding efficiency some high-ranking positions in the civil administration of Paṭiālā state. He had been working in the Home and Education departments of Paṭiālā and East Punjab States Union (PEPSU) as secretary until its amalgamation with the Punjab. Rājā Bhālendra Siṅgh was known for his exceptionally genteel and refined manner. His finesse and urbanity of speech were unmatched.

Rājā Bhālendra Siṅgh died in Delhi on 16 April 1992.

R.S.Q.E.

BHALH, BHAṬṬ. *See* Bhaṭṭ Bāṇī

BHALLĀ, a sub-division of Khatrī (Prākrit form *kṣtriya*) caste, one of the four castes into which the Hindu society is divided. Khatrīs are further divided into four subgroups, i.e. Bāhrī, Khukhrain, Buñjāhī and Sarīn; the Bhallās belong to the Sarīn subgroup. According to a legend, once 'Alā ud-Dīn Khiljī, the Muslim ruler of India (d. 1316), attempted to impose widow remarriage upon the Khatrī class. The Khatrīs of western region of the Punjab sent a deputation of fifty-two persons, each representing a sub-group of the Khatrīs, to plead their case at the Emperor's court. These memorialists who were against widow remarriage came to be known as Bavañjaī or Buñjāhī from the number *bavañjā* or 52, comprising the deputation. Those living in the eastern part of the Punjab or Bārī Doāb did not sign that memorandum and obeyed the royal dictum on widow remarriage. They came to be known as followers of *sharā'īn* (Muslim law) which subsequently got abbreviated into Sarīn. According to another view, *sarīn* is corruption of *śreṇī* or line or a guild of traders. The Baṛā, or elder, Sarīn group which Bhallās belong to comprises ten or, according to others, thirteen sections with whom they intermarry. Generally, they do not give their daughters outside their group, but take wives from Chhoṭā, or junior Sarīn group, which comprises 108 sections. The Bhallās trace their origin to a pious man, who being philanthropic and kind-hearted, was known as Bhalā, lit. a good person. It might be his name or an honorific. His descendants came to be known as Bhalās or Bhallās. This caste acquired sacred character among the Sikhs when the gurūship was conferred upon Gurū Amar Dās, the third in line from Gurū Nānak, who was born in a Bhallā Khatrī family and whose descendants are reverently called Bhallā-Bāvās.

BIBLIOGRAPHY

1. Rose, H.A., *A Glossary of the Tribes and Castes of the Punjab and North-West Frontier Province.* Patiala, 1970
2. Vaṇjārā Bedī, Sohinder Siṅgh, *Pañjābī Lokdhārā Vishav Kosh*, vol. II. Delhi, 1978

S.S.V.B.

BHĀṆĀ, lit. liking, pleasure, will, wish or approval, is one of the key-concepts in Sikh thought. In Sikhism, it refers specifically to God's will and pleasure. *Razā* , an Arabic term popular in the context of various schools of Sūfī thought, also appears frequently in the Sikh texts to express the concept of *bhāṇā*. According to this concept, the Divine Will is at the base of the entire cosmic existence. It was His *bhāṇā*, His sweet will which was instrumental in the world's coming into being: "Whenever He pleases He creates the expanse (of the world of time and space) and whenever He desires He (again) becomes the Formless One (all by Himself)" (GG, 294). All our actions, our pain and pleasure, our worship, penance and self-discipline, metempsychosis and liberation, heaven and hell, are subject to *bhāṇā* (GG, 963).

Bhāṇā or *razā*, the Divine Will, expresses itself through *hukam*, the Divine Law of nature. *Bhāṇā* and *hukam* are closely related and are often used synonymously. In the very first stanza of *Japu*, Gurū Nānak uses *hukam* and *razā* as a compound term. There is, however, a subtle difference between the two concepts. *Hukam* is the Divine Law while *bhāṇā* is the Divine Will. The latter is the source of and sanction behind the former; "*hukam* is that which you desire" (GG, 17). *Hukam* is the medium and instrument of the expression and operation of *bhāṇā*. The basic idea implicit in *hukam* is its imperative and unimpeachable nature to which man must submit, but such submission is again subject to His *bhāṇā*. "When He desires He makes man to submit to *hukam*" (GG, 337): "In His Will, the Lord makes man submit to His command" (GG, 1093).

The inexorable *hukam* having its source in *bhāṇā*, it follows that the latter is equally, even more, inescapable and inevitable subject only to itself in the form of *nadar* (*q.v.*). It therefore becomes the duty of man to submit to the Divine Will willingly and gracefully. Submission to *razā* is thus inherent in the concept of *bhāṇā*. *Bhāṇā* in the Sikh tradition yields primarily the meaning of Divine Will itself, though taking equal cognizance of the other meaning, viz. the attitude of submission on man's part to the Will Divine. The latter itself arises out of God's Will or Grace. In this sense, i.e. *bhāṇā* as attitude of submission of itself, is defined in *gurbāṇī* as a great gift. As says Gurū Arjan, "The truth is that there is no gift as great as *bhāṇā* (submission to the Lords' Will)" (GG, 1093); says Gurū Amar Dās, "On whomsoever Thou bestoweth *bhāṇā*, to him Thy Will is pleasing" (GG, 1064).

The Divine Will in the sense of inexorable ordinance or law of nature is intimately related to the problem of determinism versus free will. If nothing happens or can happen without the Divine Will, there would be no place for ethics and moral responsibility of man for his actions, good or bad, whereas the Sikh precept keeps reminding man to make the choice: to become acceptable at His portal or remain recalcitrant. Making a choice is a volitional act and pursuing it involves freedom of action. Thus Sikhism positing active participation in life does recognize freedom of action, but "within the contingencies of his finitude.'' In this context, the Sikh is required correctly to understand what pleases God, what is His pleasure (*bhāṇā*). Concentrated attention to and meditation upon the Gurū's word helps him in such understanding. Guided by his understanding of *bhāṇā*, the Sikh is not only free to act but is required to participate, "to battle oṅ in open field with his mind fully in control" (GG, 931). He is supposed to quell his *haumai* (I-ness), to dedicate his actions to the Lord's Will and to surrender himself to His *razā* as regards the outcome of his actions.

BIBLIOGRAPHY

1. Balbir Singh, *Foundations of Indian Philosophy.* Delhi, 1971
2. Nripinder Singh, *The Sikh Moral Tradition.* Delhi, 1990
3. Jodh Siṅgh, *Gurmat Nirṇaya.* Lahore, 1932

W.S.

BHĀNĀ, BHĀĪ (1536-1644), the youngest son of Bābā Buḍḍhā, was born in the village of

Katthū Naṅgal, in Amritsar district of the Punjab. Bābā Buḍḍhā, blessed by Gurū Nānak himself, was the most revered Sikh of his day. In his lifetime, he had had the privilege of anointing with his hands five successive Gurūs, Gurū Aṅgad to Gurū Hargobind. Upon his death in 1631, Bhāī Bhānā succeeded him in that position of honour in Gurū Hargobind's household. He was then in his ninety-fifth year. Such was his reputation for piety that he was commonly called Brahm-Giānī, i.e. one possessing divine knowledge and experience. He was married at the age of 18 and had three sons—Jalāl, Sarvaṇ and Dāsū. Dāsū died young and Jalāl outlived his father only by two months. Bhāī Bhānā founded two habitations near his village, one called Talvaṇḍī Bhānā after his own name and the other Jhaṇḍā Ramdās named after his grandson but now called simply Ramdās.

Bhāī Bhānā had the honour of performing the last rites of Gurū Hargobind and of anointing Gurū Har Rāi in March 1644 as his successor. He himself died the same year at Jhaṇḍā Ramdās where his *samādh* still exists by the side of his father's. His elder son, Jalāl, who succeeded him, did not live long. Bhāī Sarvaṇ, the younger son of Bhāī Bhānā, then waited upon the Gurū.

BIBLIOGRAPHY

1. *Gurbilās Chhevīṅ Pātshāhī.* Patiala, 1970
2. Giān Singh, Giānī, *Twārīkh Gurū Khālsā.* Patiala, 1970

M.G.S.

BHĀNĀ, BHĀĪ, of Sultānpur Lodhī, now in Kapūrthālā district of the Punjab, was a devoted Sikh of the time of Gurū Arjan. He once travelled with the *saṅgat* of his town to Amritsar and received the Gurū's blessing.

See ĀKUL, BHĀĪ, and BHIKHĀ, BHAṬṬ

BIBLIOGRAPHY

1. Manī Siṅgh, Bhāī, *Sikhāṅ dī Bhagat Mālā.* Amritsar, 1955
2. Santokh Siṅgh, Bhāī, *Srī Gur Pratāp Sūraj Granth.* Amritsar, 1926-37

T.S.

BHĀNĀ, BHĀĪ, resident of Prayāg (Allāhābād), is listed by Bhāī Gurdās, *Vārāṅ*, XI. 31, among leading Sikhs of the time of Gurū Hargobind (1595-1644). As recorded in Bhāī Manī Siṅgh, *Sikhāṅ dī Bhagat Mālā*, he asked the Gurū to indicate the way to release. The Gurū said, "Meditate always on Vāhigurū and make honest work your daily habit."

BIBLIOGRAPHY

1. Manī Siṅgh, Bhāī, *Sikhāṅ dī Bhagat Mālā.* Amritsar, 1955
2. Santokh Singh, Bhāī, *Srī Gur Pratāp Sūraj Granth.* Amritsar, 1926-37

Gn.S.

BHĀNĀ MALLAṆ, BHĀĪ, and Bhāī Rekh Rāo, store-keepers of the Mughal governor at Kābul, were pious and devoted Sikhs of the time of Gurū Arjan. Whatever they earned, they spent on feeding the needy Sikhs and others. Jealous of their generous hospitality, someone complained to the governor charging them with dishonesty. It was said that they used short weights and misappropriated the provisions in the stores. Bhāī Manī Siṅgh, *Sikhāṅ dī Bhagat Mālā,* records that the weights were in fact short, though Bhāī Bhānā and Bhāī Rekh Rāo did not know. Both were honest men and had deep faith in the Gurū. They made an *ardās,* supplicating the Gurū that their honour be vindicated. It is said that Gurū Arjan was on that day in a congregation at Amritsar. A Sikh made an offering of five pice. The Gurū took up the coins and, weighing them on his palm, began shifting them from one hand to the other and back again. The *saṅgat* was perplexed. Offerings, precious as well as humble, had always been made to the Gurū, but he had hardly ever touched them. Soon, however,

Guru Arjan dropped the coins and smiled. Asked by the Sikhs to reveal the mystery, the Gurū said that he was countervailing the weights of his innocent Sikhs in trouble. Meanwhile, the weights of Bhāī Bhānā's store had been tested and found to be correct.

Bhāī Kāhn Siṅgh Nābhā, *Gurushabad Ratnākar Mahān Kosh* and Bhāī Santokh Siṅgh, *Srī Gur Pratāp Sūraj Granth,* also mention this anecdote, but in reference to one Bhāī Kaṭārā and not to Bhāī Bhānā Mallaṇ and Bhāī Rekh Rāo.

BIBLIOGRAPHY

1. Manī Siṅgh, Bhāī, *Sikhāṅ dī Bhagat Mālā.* Amritsar, 1955
2. Santokh Siṅgh, Bhāī, *Srī Gur Pratāp Sūraj Granth.* Amritsar, 1926-37

T.S.

BHAṆḌĀRĀ from *bhaṇḍār* (Skt. *bhāṇḍāra* = *bhāṇḍā,* vessel, implement, + *āgāra,* house, meaning store-house, depository, treasure-house) has been used in this literal sense in Gurū Granth Sāhib, the Holy Book of the Sikhs. In extended connotation the term stands for a feast given especially for *yogīs* and *sannyāsins,* or to invoke divine favour for a private or public cause. Bhaṇḍārā in current usage means any feast under religious auspices by individuals or institutions open to laymen as well as to devotees. In this sense it would be like *gurū kā laṅgar,* a typically Sikh institution, except that the latter is not aimed at any specific object, nor is it restricted in duration. As an adjunct of the *gurdwārā* the *laṅgar* is always open for pilgrims, wayfarers and the needy. Periodically on festive occasions *sādhūs* of Udāsī, Nirmalā and other denominations hold their ritual *bhaṇḍārās* at famous places of pilgrimage with great fanfare. Bhaṇḍārās fall into two varieties —*pakkā* and *kachchā.* The former comprises rich viands with most of the eatables fried in ghee while the latter offers a simpler fare, closer to the workaday repast.

M.G.S.

BHAṆḌĀRĀ SIṄGH, a shopkeeper of Sirhind, was a devotee of Gurū Gobind Siṅgh. According to Bhāī Santokh Siṅgh, *Srī Gur Pratāp Sūraj Granth,* he received the vows of the Khālsā on the historic Baisākhī day of 1699.

BIBLIOGRAPHY

Santokh Siṅgh, Bhāī, *Srī Gur Pratāp Sūraj Granth.* Amritsar, 1926-37

P.S.P.

BHAṆḌĀRĪ PAPERS, a large collection of sundry papers, letters and documents preserved in the Punjab State Archives, Paṭiālā, and named after the collector, Rāi Indarjīt Siṅgh Bhaṇḍārī of Baṭālā. Little is known about the life of Indarjīt Siṅgh beyond a conjecture based upon some of the letters in the collection itself that he was a descendant or a relation of one of the Sikh kingdom's *vakīls* or agents at Ludhiāṇā, namely Rāi Kishan Chand, Rāi Rām Diāl, and Rāi Gobind Dās.

Bhaṇḍārī collection is a huge miscellany of 4103 items, mostly letters in Persian exchanged between the Sikh government at Lahore or its agents and the officers of the British agency at Ludhiāṇā. They also contain some MSS., records of court cases, revenue and civil, documents such as promissory notes, mortgages, registered deeds, family papers, land grants and a vast variety of administrative notes. There is very little that sheds new light on important political events. Yet the documents in the collection may be useful in making a general assessment of relations between the Lahore Darbār and the East India Company and understanding the approach and attitude of both the powers to matters diplomatic and administrative. For example, a letter written by George Russell Clerk, the British political agent at Ludhiāṇā, to Rāi Kishan Chand on 24 December 1838 about the programme of Shāh Shujā's artillery moving from Kasūr to

Fīrozpur shows that the fugitive king was allowed to keep a private force of his own during his stay at Lahore. A proclamation from the Governor-General's Council at Calcutta, dated 2 June 1829, forbids the offering of *nazars* or presents to British officers. There are letters to show strained relations between Mahārājā Raṇjīt Siṅgh and Sārdār Fateh Siṅgh Āhlūvālīā as a result of which the latter approached the British, promising allegiance to them if his claims to cis-Sutlej areas given him by the Mahārājā were upheld. Some letters concerning the British campaign in Afghanistan contain complaints to the Dārbār against Rājā Gulāb Siṅgh for not giving them his full support.

B.J.H.

BHAṄGĀṆĪ, a small village on the right bank of the River Yamunā about 11 km from Pāoṇṭā (30°-25'N, 70°-40'E) in Sirmūr district of Himāchal Pradesh was the scene of a battle between the hill *rājās* and Gurū Gobind Siṅgh. The chiefs taking exception to Gurū Gobind Siṅgh's teaching equalizing all castes and feeling jealous of his growing influence, marched against him, led by Rājā Fateh Chand of Srīnagar (Gaṛhvāl). Forestalling the attack on Pāoṇṭā, Gurū Gobind Siṅgh advanced towards Bhaṅgāṇī with his Sikhs. The *rājās,* reinforced by a few hundred Paṭhāns who had deserted the Gurū's camp, were confident of their strength and had imprudently collected their force in the open ground on the river bed. The Gurū established his base in a grove and kept his forward troops on a higher ground, and selected for himself a vantage point from where to direct the action. The battle fought on 18 September 1688 ended in favour of the Sikhs. Two shrines exist at Bhaṅgāṇī commemorating this battle.

GURDWĀRĀ TĪRGAṚHĪ stands on the mound where the Gurū had stood to control the battle. The present building at Gurdwārā Tīr Gaṛhī consists of a square hall with a verandah on all four sides.

GURDWĀRĀ BHAṄGĀṆĪ SĀHIB marks the site where the Gurū had kept his munitions and provisions. The Gurdwārā was reconstructed in late 1970's by Sant Sevā Siṅgh of Anandpur. Adjacent to the Gurdwārā is a well sunk in 1936-37 by Bābā Indar Siṅgh, a disciple of Bābā Karam Siṅgh of Hotī. Both these *gurdwārās* are managed by a local committee.

BIBLIOGRAPHY

1. Kuir Singh, *Gurbilās Pātshāhī 10.* Patiala, 1968
2. Ṭhākar Siṅgh, Giānī, *Srī Gurduāre Darshan.* Amritsar, 1923
3. Tārā Siṅgh, *Srī Gur Tīrath Saṅgrahi.* Amritsar, n.d.
4. Harbans Singh, *Guru Gobind Singh.* Chandigarh, 1966

M.G.S.

BHAṄGARNĀTH, was a Gorakhpanthī *yogī* whom, according to the *Bālā Janam Sākhī,* Gurū Nānak met in one of the mountain resorts of the *siddhas* or adepts who through austerities and penances had attained occult powers. Bhāī Gurdās, *Vārāṅ,* I. 39-41, places this meeting in Achal Vaṭālā (Baṭālā), now in Gurdāspur district of the Punjab, where Gurū Nānak is said to have arrived from Kartārpur on the occasion of the Śivarātrī fair. In the discourse that ensued, Bhaṅgarnāth chided the Gurū for having discarded the garb of a recluse [referring to the way he clad himself for his journeys through different parts] and for re-entering the life of a householder. Gurū Nānak, as Bhāī Gurdās reports, said, "How will they be approved who renounce worldly life and yet go to beg at the doors of the householders?"

BIBLIOGRAPHY

1. Kohlī, Surindar Siṅgh, ed., *Janamsākhī Bhāī Bālā.* Chandigarh, 1975
2. Jodh Singh, *Religious Philosophy of Guru Nanak.* Delhi, 1982

3. Trilochan Singh, *Guru Nanak*. Delhi, 1969

Gn.S.

BHAṄGĀ SIṄGH (d. 1815), a prominent *sardār* of the Karoṛsiṅghīā chiefship, seized in January 1764, after the fall of Sirhind, the *parganah* of Pehovā along the bed of the River Sarasvatī, 22 km west of Thānesar. Later he captured Thānesar leaving Pehovā in the possession of his brother, Bhāg Siṅgh. Bhaṅgā Siṅgh and Bhāg Siṅgh commanded a force of 750 horse and 250 foot. In 1779, Bhaṅgā Siṅgh aligned himself with the Mughal chief, Abdul Ahd Khān, to recover his territory from Rājā Amar Siṅgh of Patiālā. In January 1786, Bhaṅgā Siṅgh along with other Sikh chiefs entered the Gaṅgā Doāb at the head of 5,000 horse and ravaged Meerut, Hāpuṛ and Gaṛh Mukteshvar. In April 1789, Mahādjī Scindīā, regent of the Mughal empire, confirmed Bhaṅgā Siṅgh's right to *rākhī* or cess levied for protection in some of the areas under his influence. In January 1791, Bhaṅgā Siṅgh advanced up to Anūpshahar, a British cantonment on the Gaṅga under the charge of Lt-Col Robert Stuart. He captured the Colonel and brought him to Thānesar where he was confined for nine months in the fort before his release in October 1791 at the intercession of Lord Cornwallis, the British governor-general, and some Sikh and Mughal chiefs and on payment of sixty thousand rupees as ransom. In 1795 Bhaṅgā Siṅgh captured Karnāl and in 1799 he helped Rājā Bhāg Siṅgh of Jīnd against the attack of the Irish adventurer, George Thomas. Bhaṅgā Siṅgh joined hands with Lord Lake in attacking Delhi in September 1803 and was granted some additional territory. In 1806 he accompanied Mahārājā Raṇjīt Siṅgh on his return journey from Thānesar to the Sutlej and received from him a village in *jāgīr* in Talvaṇḍī *parganah* between Mogā and Fīrozpur.

Sir Lepel Griffin has described Bhaṅgā Siṅgh as a man "of a most savage and untameable character," and as "the fiercest and most feared of all the cis-Sutlej chiefs." Bhaṅgā Siṅgh died in 1815 and was survived by his son, Fateh Siṅgh, and daughter, Karam Kaur, married to Mahārājā Karam Siṅgh of Paṭiālā, and wife, Hassāṅ. Fateh Siṅgh died in 1819 without issue, and one half of his territory was confiscated by the British while the other half remained with his mother, Hassāṅ, who signed herself as Bhaṅgā Siṅgh in her correspondence with the British.

BIBLIOGRAPHY

1. Griffin, Lepel, *The Rajas of the Punjab*. Delhi, 1977
2. Gupta, Hari Ram, *History of the Sikhs*, vol. III. Delhi, 1980

S.S.B.

BHAṄGĪĀṄ DĪ TOP, or the gun belonging to the Bhaṅgī *misl*, known as *Zamzamā*, is a massive, heavy-weight gun, 80-pounder, 14 ft. 4½ inches in length, with bore aperture 9½ inches, cast in Lahore in copper and brass by Shāh Ṅazīr at the orders of Shāh Walī Khān, the *wazīr* of Ahmad Shāh Durrānī. In English literature, it has been immortalized by Rudyard Kipling as Kim's gun. It is perhaps the largest specimen of Indian cannon-casting, and is celebrated in Sikh historical annals more as a marvel of ordnance than for its efficiency in the battlefield. Yet for its effectiveness it has been called "a fire-raining dragon" and "a gun terrible as a dragon and huge as a mountain."

The casting of this gun cost the Durrānī invader almost nothing. A *jizyah* or capitation cess was imposed on the Hindu and Sikh families of Lahore in 1760 by Shāh Walī Khān requiring them each to contribute a copper or brass vessel for the manufacture of a cannon. Afghān and Indian ordnance manufacturers set to work, under the supervision of Shāh Nazīr, on casting the metal thus collected into a cannon, which according to the local chronicles of Lahore was completed before 1761. The gun was used in the third battle of Pānīpat in 1761.

Being too cumbersome to move, Ahmad Shāh left it with Khwājā Ubaid, the governor of Lahore. In 1762, the Bhaṅgī chief, Harī Siṅgh, attacked Lahore and took possession of the cannon. It then came to be known as Bhaṅgīāṅ dī Top. It remained in the possession of the Bhaṅgī Sardārs, Lahiṇā Siṅgh and Gujjar Siṅgh till 1764, when the Sukkarchakkīā chief, Chaṛhat Siṅgh, who had assisted the Bhaṅgīs in the capture of Lahore, claimed it as his share of the spoils. Chaṛhat Siṅgh had it carted to Gujrāṅwālā with the help of 2,000 soldiers. Soon afterwards, the Chaṭṭhās of Ahmadnagar wrested the cannon from the Sukkarchakkīā Sardār. A feud arose over its possession between the two Chaṭṭhā brothers, Ahmad Khān and Pīr Muhammad Khān. In the ensuing battle between the claimants two sons of Ahmad Khān and one son of Pīr Muhammad Khān were killed. Gujjar Siṅgh Bhaṅgī, who had helped Pīr Muhammad Khan against his brother, took the cannon to Gurjāt. In 1772, the Chaṭṭhās recovered it and removed it to Rasūlnagar. It was captured by Jhaṇḍā Siṅgh in 1773 and carried to Amritsar. In 1802, when Mahārājā Raṇjīt Siṅgh occupied Amritsar, the cannon fell into his hands.

Contemporary chroniclers of Raṇjīt Siṅgh's reign, particularly Sohan Lāl Sūrī and Būṭe Shāh, record that the Bhaṅgīs used the Zamzamā in the battle of Dīnānagar which they fought against the joint forces of the Kanhaiyās and the Rāmgaṛhīās. Raṇjīt Siṅgh employed it in his campaigns of Ḍaskā, Kasūr, Sujānpur, Wazīrābād and Multān. To Multān it was transported in a specially built carriage during the siege of the citadel in 1810, but it failed to discharge. In April 1818, it was again taken to Multān with reinforcements under Jamādār Khushāl Siṅgh, but its shells proved ineffective against the thick walls of the fortress. In these operations, the cannon was severely damaged and it had to be brought back to Lahore, unfit for any further use. It was placed outside Delhī Gate, Lahore, where it remained until 1860. When in 1864, Maulawī Nūr Ahmad Chishtī compiled the *Tahqīqāt-i-Chishtī*, he found it standing in the Bārādarī of the garden of Wazīr Khān, behind the Lahore Museum. During the years following the British occupation of the Punjab, many a legend grew around this massive relic of the Sikhs' victory over the Afghāns. In 1870, it found a new asylum at the entrance of the Lahore Museum, then located in the Tollinton Market. When the present building of the museum was constructed it was removed further west and placed opposite the University Hall. Repaired in 1977, the cannon now rests opposite the Institute of Chemical Engineering and Technology of the Pañjāb University at Lahore.

The cannon bears two Persian inscriptions. The front one reads: "By the order of the Emperor [Ahmad Shāh], Dur-i-Durrān, Shāh Walī Khān wazīr made the gun named Zamzamā or the Taker of Strongholds." The longer versified inscription at the back eulogizes its bulk and invincibility. "A destroyer even of the strongholds of the heaven." The following verses at the end of the inscription contain a chronogram:

From reason I enquire of the year of its manufacture;
Struck with terror it replied,
"Wert thou be willing to surrender thine life,
I wouldst unfold unto thee the secret."
I agreed, and it said, "What a cannon!
'Tis a mighty fire-dispensing dragon!"

BIBLIOGRAPHY

1. Sūrī, Sohan Lāl, *'Umdāt-ut-Twārīkh*. Lahore, 1885-89
2. Hasrat, B.J., *Life and Times of Ranjit Singh*. Nabha, 1977
3. Khushwant Singh, *Ranjit Singh Maharajah of the Punjab*. Bombay, 1962

4. Muhayy ud-dīn, Ghulām (alias Būṭe Shāh), *Twārīkh-i-Pañjāb* (MS. in the Dr Ganda Singh Collection of the Punjabi University, Patiala).

S.S.B.

BHAṄGĪ MISL. *See* MISLS

BHĀNĪ, BĪBĪ (1535-1598), daughter of Gurū Amar Dās, consort of Gurū Rām Dās and mother of Gurū Arjan Dev, was born to Mātā Mansā Devī on 21 Māgh 1591 Bk/19 January 1535 at Bāsarke Gillāṅ, a village near Amritsar. She was married on 18 February 1554 to Bhāī Jeṭhā (later Gurū Rām Dās), a Soḍhī Khatrī belonging to Lahore, then in Goindvāl rendering voluntary service in the construction of the Bāolī Sāhib. After marriage, the couple remained in Goindvāl serving the Gurū. From Goindvāl Bhāī Jeṭhā was deputed by the Gurū to go and establish a habitation (present-day Amritsar) on a piece of land gifted, according to one version, by Emperor Akbar to Bībī Bhānī at the time of his visit to Gurū Amar Dās. Three sons, Prithī Chand (1558), Mahādev (1560) and (Gurū) Arjan Dev (1563) were born to her. A popular anecdote mentioned in old chronicles describes how devotedly Bībī Bhānī served her father. One morning, it is said, as Gurū Amar Dās was absorbed in meditation, Bībī Bhānī noticed that one of the legs of the low wooden seat on which the Gurū sat was about to give way. She at once put forward her hand to support the stool. As the Gurū ended his devotions, he discovered how her hand was bleeding from the injury it had sustained. He blessed her saying that her progeny would inherit the gurūship. Bībī Bhānī died at Goindvāl on 9 April 1598.

BIBLIOGRAPHY

1. Bhallā, Sarūp Dās, *Mahimā Prakāsh*. Patiala, 1971
2. Chhibbar, Kesar Siṅgh, *Baṅsāvalīnāmā Dasāṅ Pātshāhīāṅ Kā*. Chandigarh, 1972
3. Giān Siṅgh, Giānī, *Twārīkh Gurū Khālsā*. Patiala, 1970

Hn.S.

BHĀNO KHEṚĪ, a village in Ambālā district of Haryāṇā, is sacred to Gurū Gobind Siṅgh. Being escorted as a small child from Paṭnā to Anandpur, in 1670-71, he made a fairly long halt at Lakhnaur. As he was playing with his friends one day, the ball *(gend)* hit by him landed near Bhāno Kheṛī and he came here to collect it. Hence the name of the Gurdwārā Gend Sāhib Pātshāhi Dasvīṅ—which now stands outside the village to the northeast. The Gurdwārā consists of a single domed room surrounded by a covered passage for circumambulation. It is managed by the Shiromaṇī Gurdwārā Parbandhak Committee through a local committee.

BIBLIOGRAPHY

1. Tārā Siṅgh, *Srī Gur Tīrath Saṅgrahi*. Amritsar, n.d.
2. Ṭhākar Siṅgh, *Srī Gurduāre Darshan*. Amritsar, 1923

Jg.S.

BHĀN SIṄGH (d. 1917), a Ghadr activist, was the son of Sāvaṇ Siṅgh, of the village of Sunet, in Ludhiāṇā district of the Punjab. As a young man, Bhān Siṅgh migrated to Shanghai and then moved to America where he started taking interest in Ghadr activity. He was among those who returned to India to make Ghadr or armed revolution in the country. Travelling by the *Tosa Maru* he reached Calcutta on 19 October 1914, but was arrested and interned in Montgomery jail. After preliminary interrogation, he was released from custody at the end of November 1914 to be interned in his village to prevent him from taking part in any revolutionary activity. He was rearrested in Feburary 1915. Tried in the first Lahore conspiracy case, he was sentenced to transportation for life and forfeiture of property.

Bhān Siṅgh died in 1917 in the Cellular Jail in the Aṇḍamans as a result of police torture.

BIBLIOGRAPHY

1. Saiṅsarā, Gurcharan Siṅgh, *Ghadar Pārṭī dā Itihās*

Jalandhar, 1969
2. Jagjīt Siṅgh, *G̲hadar Pārṭī Lahir*. Delhi, 1979

S.S.J.

BHĀNŪ, BHĀĪ, a Sikh of Gurū Arjan's time, earned the sobriquet of Bhagat (devotee) for his piety and devotion. Gurū Arjan appointed him to preach Gurū Nānak's word at Muzaṅg, in Lahore. By his *kīrtan* and exposition of the holy texts, Bhāī Bhānū, as says Bhāī Manī Siṅgh, *Sikhāṅ dī Bhagat Mālā*, converted many to the Sikh way of life.

See KISNĀ, BHĀĪ

BIBLIOGRAPHY

1. Manī Siṅgh, Bhāī, *Sikhāṅ dī Bhagat Mālā*. Amritsar, 1955
2. Santokh Siṅgh, Bhāī, *Srī Gur Pratāp Sūraj Granth*. Amritsar, 1926-37

T.S.

BHĀNŪ, BHĀĪ, Bhāī Jaṭṭu, Bhāī Nihālū and Bhāī Tīrathā, all Chaḍḍhā Khatrīs, were devoted Sikhs. Once they presented themselves before Gurū Arjan to have a doubt resolved. They made obeisance to the Gurū and said, "Lord, in one of your hymns there is a line: 'He alone kills and He alone saves; there is nothing in man's power.' Yet another hymn says: 'In this field of action, as thou sowest, so shalt thou reapest.' Which of the two precepts shall apply? Because, if He performs or gets performed all actions, how are we answerable for them? And, if we have to suffer the consequences of our actions, we must have the freedom to act with discretion." The Gurū, as says Bhāī Manī Siṅgh, *Sikhāṅ dī Bhagat Mālā*, replied: "Some merit liberation through action, some through worship, some through knowledge. For the first category, the precept is, 'Action is a field wherein you shall reap what you sow.' For the worshipper the advice is, 'He Himself is the Destroyer and He alone the Sustainer.' And for the man of intellect, 'God, the Only Being, abideth in each body, and prevaileth throughout space." "As for you, Sikhs," concluded Gurū Arjan, "Your merit is *bhagatī* or the path of devotion. You should, therefore, always repeat the Name and serve others." Bhāī Bhānū and his companions were, as says Bhāī Santokh Siṅgh, rid of their doubt.

BIBLIOGRAPHY

1. Manī Siṅgh, Bhāī, *Sikhāṅ dī Bhagat Mālā*. Amritsar, 1955
2. Santokh Siṅgh, Bhāī, *Srī Gur Pratāp Sūraj Granth*. Amritsar, 1926-37

T.S.

BHĀNŪ, BHĀĪ, a Bahil Khatrī of Rājmahal in the present Santhāl Parganah of Bihār, was a devout Sikh of the time of Gurū Hargobind. According to Bhāī Manī Siṅgh, *Sikhāṅ dī Bhagat Mālā*, Bhāī Bhānū once asked Gurū Hargobind, "O true king! Different religious books prescribe different paths to be followed such as austerities, pilgrimages, sacrifices, fasting, rituals, knowledge and meditation. Which is the best way to attaining the goal?" The Gurū replied, "Cultivate God's Name with humility, and you will obtain liberation."

Bhāī Bhānū combined with his saintly genius a rare skill in arms. He was commander of the Sikh force in the battle of Amritsar against Muk̲h̲lis K̲h̲ān in May 1629. He engaged Shamas K̲h̲ān, leading the Mug̲h̲al vanguard, in single combat, and felled him with a single blow. At this the enemy charged at him from all sides. Bhāī Bhānū fought back heroically and met a martyr's death.

BIBLIOGRAPHY

1. *Gurbilās Chhevīn Pātshāhī*. Patiala, 1970
2. Manī Siṅgh, Bhāī, *Sikhān dī Bhagat Mālā*. Amritsar, 1955
3. Macauliffe, Max Arthur, *The Sikh Religion*. Oxford, 1909

B.S.

BHARATGAṚH, an old village 18 km north of Ropaṛ (30°-58'N, 76°-31'E) in the Punjab, is sacred to Gurū Tegh Bahādur. Gurū Tegh Bahādur passed through this village travelling in July 1675 from Anandpur to Delhi resolved to make the supreme sacrifice to uphold the freedom of faith. His first halt was at Kīratpur where he spent a day meeting relations and making offerings at the holy shrines. The next halt was at Bharatgaṛh, a distance of about 10 km from Kīratpur. A platform was established here to commemorate his visit. The present *gurdwārā* was constructed in 1932. It is situated along the main street and consists of a flat-roofed rectangular hall with a verandah on the eastern side. The shrine is managed by a committee of the local Sikhs.

BIBLIOGRAPHY

Faujā Siṅgh, *Gurū Teg Bahādur: Yātrā Asthān, Pramparavāṅ te Yād Chinn*. Patiala, 1976

Jg.S.

BHAROĀṆĀ or Bhairoāṇā, a small village 16 km southwest of Sultānpur Lodhī (31°-13'N, 75°-12'E) in the Punjab, is the place where at the close of the fifteenth century lived Bhāī Phirandā, a pious-minded musician who also manufactured the stringed instrument called *rabāb* or rebeck. Gurū Nānak, before setting out from Sultānpur Lodhī on his extensive travels to deliver his message, sent Bhāī Mardānā to buy a *rabāb* from Phirandā. Phirandā produced the instrument but, on learning as to who had ordered it, refused to accept any money for it. A memorial shrine was constructed where Bhāī Phirandā had lived, which became the centre of an annual fair held on the tenth of the dark half of the lunar month of Assū (September-October). A handsome *gurdwārā,* named Gurdwārā Rabābsar Sāhib, has since been raised by the followers of Sant Gurmukh Siṅgh. It comprises a high-ceilinged hall, with a square sanctum in the centre where the Gurū Granth Sāhib is seated. The building is topped by a gold-plated pinnacle and an umbrella-shaped finial. Domed kiosks adorn the hall-corners. The old fair remains the principal annual festival.

BIBLIOGRAPHY

Santokh Siṅgh, Bhāī, *Srī Gur Pratāp Sūraj Granth*. Amritsar, 1926-37

M.G.S.

BHAROVĀL, village 15 km east of Tarn Tāran (31°-27'N, 74°-56'E) along the Tarn Tāran-Goindvāl road, is sacred to Gurū Aṅgad (1504-52), who stayed here awhile on his way back from Khān Chhāprī to Khaḍūr Sāhib. The commemorative shrine formerly known as Gurūāṇā is now called Gurdwārā Gurū Aṅgad Sāhib. The present complex, reconstructed during the 1980's, includes a marble-floored, rectangular *dīvān* hall, with the sanctum at the far end and a verandah around it. Above the sanctum is a domed square room with a gold-plated pinnacle on top. A rectangular *sarovar,* holy tank, 36x24 metres, is to the north of the hall. Two separate Nishān Sāhibs, Sikh standards, one at each corner, fly atop high flagpoles in front. Gurū kā Laṅgar is in an adjacent compound. The Gurdwārā is maintained by the local *saṅgat,* Sikh community.

BIBLIOGRAPHY

Ṭhākar Siṅgh, Giānī, *Srī Gurduāre Darshan*. Amritsar, 1923

Jg.S.

BHARPŪR SIṄGH, RĀJĀ (1840-1863), born on 4 October 1840, replaced his father, Rājā Devinder Siṅgh, on the throne of Nābhā state in January 1847 after he was removed by the British. During his minority, the state affairs were managed by his grandmother, Rāṇī Chand Kaur. An enlightened ruler, Rājā Bharpūr Siṅgh was a devout Sikh. He had a good knowledge of Persian, English, Punjabi and Hindi and wrote his orders with his own hand. Rājā Bharpūr Siṅgh helped the British during the mutiny of 1857 and was rewarded with the grant of the divisions of Bāval and Kāṇṭī with permission, later on, to purchase a portion of Jhajjar territory. Like other Phūlkīāṅ chiefs, he was granted the right of adoption, the power of life and death over his subjects and the promise of non-interference by the British in the internal affairs of his state. In September 1863, he was nominated a member of the Viceroy's Council but shortly thereafter he died childless at Nābhā on 9 November 1863.

BIBLIOGRAPHY

1. Griffin, Lepel, *The Rajas of the Punjab*. Delhi, 1977
2. Ganda Singh, *The Patiala and the East Panjab States Union: Historical Background*. Patiala, 1951

S.S.B.

BHĀRŪ, BHĀĪ, a devoted Sikh of the time of Gurū Rām Dās mentioned by Bhāī Gurdās in his *Vārāṅ*, XI. 17.

See PADĀRATH, BHĀĪ

BIBLIOGRAPHY

Manī Siṅgh, Bhāī, *Sikhāṅ dī Bhagat Mālā*. Amritsar, 1955

Gr.S.

BHASAUṚ SIṄGH SABHĀ, or to give its full name Srī Gurū Siṅgh Sabhā, Bhasauṛ, was established in 1893 – twenty years after the first Siṅgh Sabhā came into existence in Amritsar – at the village of Bhasauṛ in the then princely state of Paṭiālā. The Siṅgh Sabhā, a powerful reform movement among the Sikhs, was as much an urban phenomenon as it was rural. While there were very strong Siṅgh Sabhās in cities such as Rāwalpiṇḍī, Lahore, Shimlā and Fīrozpur, Siṅgh Sabhās flourished in small villages like Baḍbar and Bāgaṛīāṅ as well. Most dynamic of them all was the Siṅgh Sabhā located in the village of Bhasauṛ. Bhāī Basāvā Siṅgh, known as a *virakat* or recluse, was named the first president of the Bhasauṛ Siṅgh Sabhā and Bābū Tejā Siṅgh, then a sub-overseer in the irrigation department of Paṭiālā state, its secretary. They made a very good team. Basāvā Siṅgh was widely reputed for his piety and Bābū Tejā Siṅgh, a well-educated person, became the ideologue and source of much of the dynamite that came from Bhasauṛ. He brought to the Siṅgh Sabhā renaissance a new verve and thrust. He was a puritan of the extremist kind and a fundamentalist in the interpretation of Sikh principles and tradition, and challenged much of the prevalent Sikh usage.

The Bhasauṛ Siṅgh Sabhā was, from the very beginning, forthright in the rejection of caste and Brāhmaṇīcal customs which had infiltrated into Sikhism. It openly advocated the acceptance back into the fold of those who had been led into forsaking the Sikh faith, and it willingly converted those from other faiths, who volunteered for initiation. As the records say, at the very first annual *dīvān* of the Bhasauṛ Siṅgh Sabhā held in 1894, thirteen Jaṭṭs, six Jhīvars (water-carriers), two barbers, one Khatrī and one Musalmān (Mīrāṅ Bakhsh of Tahsīl Gaṛhshaṅkar who became Nihāl Siṅgh) were initiated into the Sikh faith. Bābū Tejā Siṅgh himself published in the press a report of a subsequent year saying, "By the power of the Word revealed by the Ten Masters and in accord with Akālpurkh's wish, the Srī Gurū Siṅgh Sabhā, Bhasauṛ, had administered the *gurmantra* and holy *amrit* to a Muslim woman and ushered her into Soḍhbaṅs (the family of Gurū Gobind Siṅgh who came of the Soḍhī clan; *baṅs* = family, line or clan). Her Sikh name is Kishan Kaur. A Sikh who had fallen by living with a Muslim woman had been baptized and renamed Ude Siṅgh." At the *dīvān* convened in the village of Bakāpur near Phillaur on 13-14 June 1903 by the Bhasauṛ Siṅgh Sabhā, 35 persons including

Maulawī Karīm Ba<u>kh</u>sh and his family of four sons and a daughter received the rites of *amrit*.

The Bhasauṛ Siṅgh Sabhā set up Pañch <u>Kh</u>ālsā Dīwān or <u>Kh</u>ālsā Parliament at Bhasauṛ under sanction of a Sikh synod held at Damdamā Sāhib on 13 April 1907. In 1909, a girls school called <u>Kh</u>ālsā Bhujhaṅgaṇ School was opened at Bhasaur. The Siṅgh Sabhā, Bhasauṛ, decreed that Sikh women tie turbans round their heads in the style of men. Rolling up, pressing or dyeing of beards was outlawed. It was stated that though the custom of splitting and rolling up the beards was not unknown in the <u>Kh</u>ālsā armies, it became firmly established only during British rule after an incident in 1868 in 15th Sikh Regiment when a Muslim Havildār's rifle got entangled in the flowing beard of a Sikh Havildār, Īshar Siṅgh, lined up next to him.

Against all evidence and authority, the Sikh term for God, "Vāhigurū", was replaced by "Vāhugur.'' The word "kaṛāhprashād" for Sikh sacrament was substituted by "Mahāprashād". The Sikh code prepared by the Chief <u>Kh</u>ālsā Dīwān was repudiated, use of the Sikh calendar beginning from the birth of Gurū Nānak (AD 1469), and introduction of titles and honorifics such as Kirpān Bahādur, Kakār Bahādur, Dāhṛā Bahādur, Vidayā Ratan, Hitkārī and Bīr Jaṅg were propagated. A motion adopted by the Pañch <u>Kh</u>ālsā Dīwān disclaimed the Sahajdhārī sect of the Sikhs. Likewise, it was proclaimed un-Sikh to install the Farīdkoṭ Ṭīkā by the side of Gurū Granth Sāhib. By a resolution of the Pañch <u>Kh</u>ālsā Dīwān (1928), the Chief Khālsā Dīwān of Amritsar was declared to be a body of men unfirm of conviction and Bhāī Vīr Siṅgh, the widely revered Sikh savant and scholar, was laid under penalty for what was called "his secret propagation of the cult of personal deification." At the annual *dīvān* of 1921, exception had been taken to Sikhs seeking advice of non-Sikh leaders in their religious matters. The instance was cited of the Akālīs being in touch with Mahātmā Gāndhī at the time of the Nankāṇā Sāhib *morchā*.

In his literalist zeal, Bābū Tejā Siṅgh, the all-powerful man at the helm of affairs of the Bhasauṛ Siṅgh Sabhā, started garbling the Sikh canon. He changed the traditional Sikh *ardās* or daily prayer of supplication. He jettisoned the preamble most of which is derived from Gurū Gobind Siṅgh's composition called *Chaṇḍī dī Vār*. He advocated expunging of *Rāgamālā* from the Gurū Granth Sāhib as well as the compositions of the saints and *bhaktas*, especially those of the Bhaṭṭs. Tejā Siṅgh printed courses of reading for his school comprising the *bāṇī* contained in the Gurū Granth Sāhib, but he deleted from it the *Savaiyyās* by Bhaṭṭs and he added some of Gurū Gobind Siṅgh's compositions. He also had copies of the Gurū Granth Sāhib printed without the *Rāgamālā*. This led to widespread protest in the Sikh community. Tejā Siṅgh was excommunicated on 9 August 1928 by an edict of Srī Akāl Ta<u>kh</u>t Sāhib, Amritsar, the highest seat of Sikh ecclesiastical authority. Tejā Siṅgh now ceased to be the force he used to be and with the decline in his popularity set in the downfall of the Bhasauṛ Siṅgh Sabhā.

BIBLIOGRAPHY

1. Lāl Siṅgh, *Itihās Pañch <u>Kh</u>ālsā Dīwān Sañbandhī Sūchnāvāṅ*. Ludhiana, 1967
2. *Vīr Sudhār Pattar arthāt Srī Gurū Siṅgh Sabhā Bhasauṛ de aṭhme te naume salāne dīvān dā siṭṭā*. Bhasaur, 1903
3. Harbans Singh, "The Bakapur Diwan and Babu Teja Siṅgh of Bhasauṛ," in *The Panjab Past and Present*. Patiala, October 1975

S.S.B.

BHĀṬṚĀS (the term *bhāṭṛā* appears to be a diminutive of the Sanskrit *bhaṭṭa*, a bard), an endogamous and tightly-knit group among the Sikhs with peddling and fortune-telling as their principal occupations. More than one story is current about their origin. However, the Bhāṭrās themselves trace it to Bābā Chaṅgā Rāi of Saṅglādīp (Ceylon), who was admitted as a disciple by Gurū Nānak during his journey to the South. His name figures in the old text *Haqīqat Rāh Mukām Rāje Shivanābh Kī*. Chaṅgā Rāi, himself a devout Sikh with a substantial following, added the suffix "Bhāṭrā" to his name. His followers came to be known as Bhāṭrās. Chaṅgā Bhāṭrā established Sikh *saṅgats* in many parts. Since Bhāṭrās were mostly itinerant missionaries, they did not take to settled life. Having no time to learn and practise skilled occupations, they were eventually drawn into the peddling profession. Their mobility led to the scattering of the community in several parts of the country and beyond. They are concentrated now mainly in Paṭiālā, Amritsar, Hoshiārpur, Gurdāspur and Bhaṭhiṇḍā districts of the Punjab and in some cities outside the state such as Delhi and Calcutta. Several migrated to the United Kingdom where they retailed from door to door clothes, jewellery and other articles. Their success lay in their spirit of enterprise, price manipulation and extension of credit. They were the first to get a *gurdwārā* registered in 1953 in Manchester, and many of the total number of Sikh *gurdwārās* in England are Bhāṭrā *gurdwārās*. With a view to retaining their identity and forging a common platform for the community, a Bhāṭrā conference convened in 1943 set up an All-India Bhāṭrā Union. The community in the Punjab comprises both Hindu Bhāṭrās and Sikh Bhāṭrās though the former are numerically much fewer than the latter.

BIBLIOGRAPHY

1. Rose, H.A., *A Glossary of the Castes and Tribes of the Punjab and the North-West Frontier Province*. Patiala, 1970
2. Mrigind, Makhaṇ Siṅgh, *Itihāsak-Tribaiṇī*. Patiala, 1977

B.S.N.

BHAṬṬ BĀṆĪ, recorded under the title *Savaiyye*, is the name popularly given to the compositions of the Bhaṭṭs as included in the Gurū Granth Sāhib (pp. 1389-1409). Bhaṭṭs were bards or panegyrists who recited poetry lauding the grandeur of a ruler or the gallantry of a warrior. Bhaṭṭ was also used as an epithet for a learned Brāhmaṇ. In the Sikh tradition, Bhaṭṭs are poets with the personal experience and vision of the spirituality of the Gurūs whom they celebrate in their verse. According to Bhāī Santokh Siṅgh, *Srī Gur Pratāp Sūraj Granth*, "They were the Vedas incarnate" (p. 2121). The Bhaṭṭs are said to have originally lived on the bank of the River Sarasvatī which is also the name of the Indian mythological goddess of knowledge. They were thus called Sārasvat, i.e. the learned Brāhmaṇs. Those living on the other side of the Sarasvatī were called Gauṛ. They showed little interest in learning and contended themselves with alms given them by their patrons whose *baṅsāvalīnāmās* or genealogies they recorded in their scrolls called *vahīs*. They are still found on the bank of the Sarasvatī in the Talauḍā (Jīnd), Bhādsoṅ (Lāḍvā) and Karsindhū (Safīdoṅ) villages in Haryāṇā. Some of these families shifted over to Sultānpur Lodhī, now in Kapūrthalā district of the Punjab, and settled there. Bhikhā and Ṭoḍā of these families embraced the Sikh faith during the time of Gurū Amar Dās. Bhāī Gurdās also gives in his *Vārāṅ*, XI. 21, a brief account of these Bhaṭṭs. What was the number of Bhaṭṭs whose compositions are included is a question not yet firmly answered. According to a tradition, Kalh, a leading Bhaṭṭ poet, took it upon himself to note down some of the verse of the Bhaṭṭs from the *vahīs* and passed it on to Gurū Arjan at the time of the compilation of the Holy Book. As for the number of Bhaṭṭ contributors to the Gurū Granth Sāhib, Sāhib Siṅgh, Tejā Siṅgh, Tāran Siṅgh and other modern scholars count 11 of them, whereas Santokh Siṅgh *(Srī Gur Pratāp Sūraj Granth)*,

Bhāī Vīr Siṅgh (*Gurū Granth Kosh*) and some others among the traditional scholars count 17, and Paṇḍit Kartār Siṅgh Dākhā puts the figure at 19. This variation in numbers is owed to the fact that the Bhaṭṭs used to sing in chorus and sometimes the chorus sung by a group went in the name of the leader and at other times individually in the names of the members of the group.

From among the 17 Bhaṭṭs whose compositions figure in the Gurū Granth Sāhib, Bhikhā, son of Rayyā, was a resident of Sultānpur Lodhī and had been a follower of Gurū Amar Dās. Of the total 123 *savaiyye* in the Gurū Granth Sāhib two are of his composition, both in praise of Gurū Amar Dās. Of the remaining sixteen Bhaṭṭ contributors, four are his sons; Kalh, also called Kalsahār or Kal Ṭhākur, who is reckoned to be the most learned of all the Bhaṭṭs, has 53 *savaiyye,* 10 in praise of Gurū Nānak, 9 each in praise of Gurū Aṅgad and Gurū Amar Dās, 13 in praise of Gurū Rām Dās and 12 in praise of Gurū Arjan; Jālap who had migrated to Goindvāl with his father has four *savaiyye,* to his name all of which are in praise of Gurū Amar Dās; Kīrat (d. 1634) has eight *savaiyye* four each in praise of Gurū Amar Dās and Gurū Rām Dās; and Mathurā 12, all in praise of Gurū Rām Dās. Salh who has three *savaiyye* extolling the pre-eminence of Gurū Amar Dās (1) and Gurū Rām Dās (2), and Bhalh who has one *savaiyya* in praise of Gurū Amar Dās were the sons of Sekhā, a brother of Rayyā. Balh who has five *savaiyye* stressing the spiritual oneness of the Gurūs was the son of Tokhā, another brother of Rayyā. Haribaṅs, the eldest son of Gokhā, a brother of Rayyā, has two *savaiyye* both in praise of Gurū Arjan. Nalh has five *savaiyye* all in praise of Gurū Rām Dās. Dās, also spelt as Dāsu or Dāsi, has composed ten *savaiyye* including one written conjointly with Sevak who, in addition to this one, has four *savaiyye* of his own. Parmānand's five *savaiyye* are in praise of Gurū Rām Dās, Ṭal's single one in praise of Gurū Aṅgad. Jalan has two *savaiyye,* both in praise of Gurū Rām Dās, Jalh one in praise of Gurū Amar Dās and Gayand five which glorify Gurū Rām Dās. Of the total 123, ten each pay homage to Gurū Nānak and Gurū Angad, 22 to Gurū Amar Dās, 60 to Gurū Rām Dās and 21 to Gurū Arjan.

The main purpose of these *savaiyyās* is to acclaim the Gurūs, not as individuals but as the revelation they embodied. The Bhaṭṭs see the Gurūs as one light, as one spirit passing from one body to the other. Bhaṭṭ Kīrat, for instance: "Just as (Gurū) Aṅgad was ever the part of Gurū Nānak's being so is Gurū Rām Dās of (Gurū) Amar Dās's" (GG, 1405). Again, Bhaṭṭ Kalh: "From Gurū Nānak was Aṅgad; from Aṅgad, Amar Dās received the sublime rank. From Gurū Rām Dās descended Gurū Arjan, the great devotee of God" (GG, 1407). This concept of all the Gurūs being one light, one voice has informed all along the Sikh belief and development and constitutes today a fundamental principle of the faith.

BIBLIOGRAPHY

1. Tāran Siṅgh, *Srī Gurū Granth Sāhib Jī dā Sāhitik Itihās.* Amritsar, n.d.
2. Sāhib Siṅgh, *Bhaṭṭāṅ de Savaiyye Saṭīk.* Amritsar, 1972
3. Gurdit Siṅgh, Giānī, *Itihās Srī Gurū Granth Sāhib.* Delhi, 1990
4. Kohli, Ṣurindar Singh, *A Critical Study of Adi Granth.* Delhi, 1961

Gr.S.

BHAṬṬŪ, BHĀĪ, a learned Tivārī Brāhmaṇ, is listed by Bhāī Gurdās, *Vārāṅ,* XI. 19, among the devoted Sikhs of the time of Gurū Arjan. As records Bhāī Manī Siṅgh, *Sikhāṅ dī Bhagat Mālā,* he once accompanied by Bhāī Phirnā Sūd, Bhāī Bholū and Bhāī Jaṭṭū, visited the Gurū and supplicated thus : "O support of the supportless, we have recently returned after a dip in the Ganges. The *paṇḍits* there said that all incarnations, gods, sages and saints had their preceptors. Who, they asked, was Gurū Nānak's ? We had no answer to their question. May we be enlightened, Lord ?" Gurū Arjan made a simple answer, "Gurū Nānak had no earthly *gurū*. He spoke what God made him to speak." Bhāī Bhaṭṭū and his companions were rid of their doubt. Bhāī Bhaṭṭū was appointed to preach the Sikh faith.

BIBLIOGRAPHY

1. Manī Siṅgh, Bhāī, *Sikhāṅ dī Bhagat Mālā*. Amritsar, 1955
2. Santokh Siṅgh, Bhāī, *Srī Gur Pratāp Sūraj Granth*. Amritsar, 1926-37

T.S.

BHAṬṬ-VAHĪS, scrolls or records maintained by Bhaṭṭs, hereditary bards and genealogists. According to Nesfield as quoted in W. Crooke, *The Tribes and Castes of the North Western India*, 1896, Bhaṭṭs are an "offshoot from those secularised Brahmans who frequented the courts of princes and the camps of warriors, recited their praises in public, and kept records of their genealogies." These bards constantly attended upon or visited their patron families reciting panegyrics to them and receiving customary rewards. They also collected information about births, deaths and marriages in the families and recorded it in their scrolls. These scrolls containing information going back to several past centuries formed the valued part of the bards' hereditary possessions.

A group of Bhaṭṭs was introduced to Gurū Arjan, Nānak V, by Bhaṭṭ Bhikhā who had himself become a Sikh in the time of Gurū Amar Dās. According to Bhāī Gurdās, *Vārāṅ*, XI. 21, and Bhāī Manī Siṅgh, *Sikhāṅ dī Bhagat Mālā*, he had once visited Gurū Arjan with the *saṅgat* of Sultānpur Lodhī. Some of the Bhaṭṭs who came into the Sikh fold composed hymns in honour of the Gurūs which were entered in the Gurū Granth Sāhib by Gurū Arjan. These Bhaṭṭs and their successors too maintained their *vahīs* in which they recorded information concerning the Gurūs, their families and some of the eminent Sikhs. These old *vahīs* are still preserved in the descendant families, now scattered mostly in Haryāṇā state. Their script is *bhaṭṭāksharī*, a kind of family code like *laṇḍe* or *mahājanī*. During the late 1950's, a researcher, Giānī Garjā Siṅgh, obtained Gurmukhī transcripts of some of the entries pertaining to the Gurū period, from Gurū Hargobind (1595-1644) to Gurū Gobind Siṅgh (1666-1708) through Bhaṭṭ Mān Siṅgh of Karsindhū village, in Jīnd district. Some of these were published as footnotes to *Shahīd Bilās Bhāī Manī Siṅgh*, edited by Giānī Garjā Siṅgh and published by Punjabi Sāhitya Akādemī, Ludhiāṇā, in 1961. The rest are still in manuscript form lying in the Department of Punjab Historical Studies, Punjabi University, Paṭiālā. These extracts provide valuable information regarding dates, places and events of the period.

As contemporary evidence, Bhaṭṭ-Vahīs have to be used with caution however, for they are not diaries of the eye-witnesses. It was customary for the Bhaṭṭs to visit their hereditary patrons usually twice a year at harvest time to sing their praises and receive rewards or customary donations as well as to collect information for record in their *vahīs*. These records are, therefore, based on information gathered generally after the occurrence of events and, possibly, sometimes received at second hand. This may not apply to entries regarding the Gurūs which were recorded by Bhaṭṭs who generally remained in attendance. For instance, an entry about the conferment of gurūship upon the Gurū Granth Sāhib in 1708 is by Bhaṭṭ Narbud Siṅgh (son of Keso Siṅgh and grandson of Bhaṭṭ Kīrat whose hymns are included in the Holy Book) who had accompanied Gurū Gobind Siṅgh to Nāndeḍ. On the whole, these Bhaṭṭ - Vahīs are a mine of information of historical and sociological value

G.G.S.

BHĀŪ MOKAL, BHĀĪ, a Mokal Khatrī, was a devoted Sikh of Gurū Arjan's time. He was one of the *saṅgat* who once waited on the Gurū and complained how some people were composing verses using Nānak as a pseudonym. According to Bhāī Manī Siṅgh, *Sikhāṅ dī Bhagat Mālā,* this led to the authentication by Gurū Arjan of the genuine *bāṇī,* inspired utterance, in the form of the Ādī Granth.

See GOPĪ MAHITĀ, BHĀĪ

BIBLIOGRAPHY

1. Manī Siṅgh, Bhāī, *Sikhāṅ dī Bhagat Mālā.* Amritsar, 1955
2. Santokh Siṅgh, Bhāī, *Srī Gur Pratāp Sūraj Granth.* Amritsar, 1926-37

T.S.

BHAVĀNĪ. *See* BHAGAUTĪ

BHAVĀNĪ DĀS, DĪWĀN (1770-1834), was the son of Dīwān Ṭhākur Dās, revenue and finance minister of the Afghān king, Ahmad Shāh Durrānī. Bhavānī Dās succeeded to the position after the death of his father and served successively Shāh Zamān, Shāh Mahmūd and Shāh Shujā' until 1808 when Mahārājā Ranjīt Siṅgh having heard of his reputation, invited him to Lahore to take charge of the State's finances. At Lahore, Bhavānī Dās set up 12 departments called *daftars* to deal with all civil and military accounts. In the districts of different *sūbahs* treasuries were established to maintain regular accounts of income and expenditure. In the newly-conquered territories, settlement officers were appointed to regulate revenue and finance. On occasions, Diwān Bhavānī Dās also performed diplomatic and military duties. He was one of the Mahārājā's counsellors at the negotiations with the British envoy, Charles T. Metcalfe. In 1809, he was sent to Jammū in command of a Sikh force, which conquered and annexed the city. In 1813, he reduced Harīpur state in the Kāṅgrā hills; in 1816, he annexed the Rāmgaṛhīā estates to the Lahore kingdom. Twice, in 1816 and 1817, he commanded a division of the Lahore army in the Multān expeditions. He also took part in the expeditions to Peshāwar and the Yūsafzaī country.

Dīwān Bhavānī Dās suffered a temporary eclipse in his career when he was accused of misappropriation of State revenues, and was expelled from Lahore to the hills of Kāṅgṛā. He was, however, soon recalled from Kāṅgṛā and reinstated in his position as the charges against him could not be proved.

He remained in the service of the Mahārājā till his death in 1834.

BIBLIOGRAPHY

1. Sūrī, Sohan Lāl, *'Umdāt-ut-Twārīkh.* Lahore, 1885-89
2. Griffin, Lepel, and C.F. Massy, *Chiefs and Families of Note in the Punjab.* Lahore, 1909
3. Garrett, H.L.O., and G.L. Chopra, eds., *Events at the Court of Ranjit Singh.* Delhi, 1986
4. Bhagat Singh, *Maharaja Ranjit Singh and His Times.* Delhi, 1990
5. Latif, Syad Muhammad, *History of the Panjab,* Delhi, 1964

H.R.G.

BHAVĀNĪGAṚH (30° - 14'N, 76° - 3'E), also called Ḍhoḍe locally, is a market town 36 km west of Paṭiālā. Gurū Tegh Bahādur arrived here from Ālo Harakh in the course of a journey through the Mālvā region. His devotees constructed a platform around two *pīpal* trees under which the Gurū had sat. A *gurdwārā,* called Gurdwārā Srī Gurū Tegh Bahādur Sāhib Jī Pātshāhī Nauvīṅ, was constructed by the local *saṅgat* in 1916. It is situated on the eastern outskirts of the town, next to Srī Gurū Tegh Bahādur College. It consists of a rectangular hall in front of the domed sanctum. The hall has a wide verandah on three sides with cubicles at the corners. The Gurdwārā is managed by the Shiromaṇī Gurdwārā Parbandhak Committee through a local committee.

BIBLIOGRAPHY

Faujā Siṅgh, *Gurū Teg Bahādur : Yātrā Asthān, Pramparāvāṅ te Yād Chinn.* Patiala, 1976

M.G.S.

BHEṚĀ SRĪ GOBIND SIṄGH JĪ KĀ, also known as *Vār Bheṛe kī Pātshāhī Das,* is an anonymous account, in Punjabi verse, of the battles of Anandgaṛh, Nirmohgaṛh and Chamkaur (1762 Bk/AD 1705). *Bheṛā* from *bheṛ* in Punjabi means a head-on clash between two rival forces. A manuscript of this work was discovered in Bābā Bīr Siṅgh's *ḍerā* at Nauraṅgābād, near Amritsar, and has since been published in an anthology, entitled *Prāchīn Vārāṅ te Jaṅgnāme,* brought out by the Shiromaṇī Gurdwārā Parbandhak Committee in 1950. The *Bheṛā* comprises twenty-four cantos of unequal length written in the poetic metre Nishānī, with each canto preceded by a *śloka.*

The *Bheṛā* opens in the traditional style with a hymn to the Deity. The hymn is followed by a verbal duel between Kalh and Nārad, the former urging the latter to incite some tumult. The poem then describes the battles which took place at Anandpur and Chamkaur. The immediate cause of the conflict is given as Gurū Gobind Siṅgh's refusal to pay the *nā'lbandī* tax imposed on him by the Rājā of Kahlūr within whose territory fell Anandpur. The poem provides vivid descriptions of battle-scenes which, from the details given, might be from the pen of an eye-witness. In the encounter against the attacking force which had besieged the Anandgaṛh Fort, near present-day Gurdwārā Srī Kesgaṛh Sāhib, Sikhs such as Jīvan Siṅgh Raṅghreṭā, Lāl Siṅgh Peshāvarīā, Bachittar Siṅgh, Ude Siṅgh and one called Halīm Khān fought with valour. Among the heroes of Chamkaur mentioned by name are Bhāī Sant Siṅgh and the two sons of Gurū Gobind Siṅgh, Ajīt Siṅgh and Jujhār Siṅgh. The poet erroneously includes the name of the third son Zorāwar Siṅgh as well. The last canto takes the narration from the battle of Chamkaur to Gurū Gobind Siṅgh's departure for the South, his meeting with the Mughal emperor and despatch of Bandā Siṅgh Bahādur to the Punjab, to chastise Nawāb Wazīr Khān of Sirhind.

J.S.S.

BHIKHĀ (pronounced as Bhikkhā), BHAṬṬ, a Brāhmaṇ bard of Sultānpur Lodhī in present-day Kapūrthalā district of the Punjab, became a Sikh receiving the rites of initiation at the hands of Gurū Amar Dās. He lived up to the time of Gurū Arjan to whom he introduced sixteen other Brāhmaṇ minstrels from his community. They sang in his presence praises to God and the Gurūs. Some of their compositions were included by Gurū Arjan in the Gurū Granth Sāhib. One of the two stanzas by Bhikhā recounts his wanderings in search of a true saint ending with his ultimate success by the grace of God. "Lord," sang the bard, "hath caused me to meet the Gurū; as thou willest for me so must I receive O God !"

BIBLIOGRAPHY

1. Macauliffe, Max Arthur, *The Sikh Religion.* Oxford, 1909
2. Manī Siṅgh, Bhāī, *Sikhāṅ dī Bhagat Mālā.* Amritsar, 1955
3. Santokh Siṅgh, Bhāī, *Srī Gur Pratāp Sūraj Granth.* Amritsar, 1926-37

T.S.

BHĪKHAN (1480-1573), a medieval Indian saint two of whose hymns are included in the Gurū Granth Sāhib. There are in fact two saints of that time sharing the same name—Bhakta Bhīkhan and Bhīkhan the Sūfī. Bhakta Bhīkhan was a devotee in the tradition of Ravidās and Dhannā. His hymns in the Gurū Granth Sāhib reflect his dedication to the Name of Hari (God) which he describes as "cure for all ills of the world."

BIBLIOGRAPHY

1. Sāhib Siṅgh, *Saṭīk Bhagat-Bāṇī*. Amritsar, 1979
2. Pratāp Siṅgh, Giānī, *Bhagat Darshan*. Amritsar, n.d.

T.S.

BHĪKHAN KHĀN (d. 1688) was a Paṭhān who had served in the Mughal army before joining Gurū Gobind Siṅgh at Pāoṇṭā Sāhib on the recommendation of Pīr Buddhū Shāh of Saḍhaurā. He had one hundred soldiers under his command, but he crossed over to the hill *rājās* on the eve of the battle of Bhaṅgāṇī (AD 1688). According to Bhāī Santokh Siṅgh, *Srī Gur Pratāp Sūraj Granth*, Bhīkhan Khān told the Paṭhāns in the employ of Gurū Gobind Siṅgh that the Gurū was mainly dependant on them and that the rest of his army was only a miscellaneous rabble who would run away when they heard the first shot fired. He suggested that they could save their lives by taking the side of the hillmen. They would fight in the rear of the hill armies and would obtain from the hill chiefs permission to plunder the Gurū's wealth. The Paṭhāns applauded Bhīkhan Khān's advice and joined the hill *rājās* against Gurū Gobind Siṅgh. When Buddhū Shāh learnt how the Paṭhān soldiers had reneged, he came forward with his four sons and seven hundred disciples to assist the Gurū. Gurū Gobind Siṅgh says in his *Bachitra Nāṭak* that as he saw Shāh Saṅgrām (Saṅgo Shāh), a cousin of his, fall in the battle of Bhaṅgāṇī, he took up his bow and arrows. With the first arrow, he struck a Khān who fell to the ground. He then drew out another one and aimed at Bhīkhan Khān, hitting him in the face. Leaving his horse, the bleeding Khān fled, but was killed by another arrow from the Gurū's bow.

BIBLIOGRAPHY

1. *Bachitra Nāṭak*
2. Santokh Siṅgh, Bhāī, *Srī Gur Pratāp Sūraj Granth*. Amritsar, 1926-37
3. Suri, V.S., and Gurcharan Singh, *Pir Budhu Shah*. Chandigarh, 1971
4. Harbans Singh, *Guru Gobind Singh*. Chandigarh, 1966

B.S.

BHĪKHAN SHĀH or SHĀH BHĪKH, PĪR, a seventeenth-century Sūfī saint, was born the son of Sayyid Muhammad Yūsaf of Siāṇā Sayyidāṅ, a village 5 km from Pehovā, now in Kurukshetra district of Haryāṇā. For a time, he lived at Ghuṛām in present-day Paṭiālā district of the Punjab and finally settled at Ṭhaskā, again in Kurukshetra district. He was the disciple of Abul Mu'ālī Shāh, a Sūfī divine residing at Ambhiṭā, near Sahāranpur in Uttar Pradesh, and soon became a *pīr* or saint of much repute and piety in his own right. According to tradition preserved in Bhāī Santokh Siṅgh, *Srī Gur Pratāp Sūraj Granth*, Pīr Bhīkhan Shāh, as he learnt through intuition of the birth of Gurū Gobind Siṅgh (1666-1708) at Paṭnā, made obeisance that day to the east instead of to the west. At this his disciples demurred, for no Muslim should make such respectful gestures except towards the Kā'bā. The Pīr explained that in a city in the east, the Beneficent Lord had revealed Himself through a new-born babe, to whom it was that he had bowed and to no ordinary mortal. Bhīkhan Shāh with his disciples then travelled all the way to Paṭnā to have a glimpse of the infant Gobind Rāi, barely three months old. Desiring to know what would be his attitude to the two major religious peoples of India, he placed two small pots in front of the child, one representing in his own mind Hindus and the other Muslims. As the child covered both the pots simultaneously with his tiny hands, Bhīkhan Shāh felt happy concluding that the new seer would treat both Hindus and Muslims alike and show equal respect to both. Sikh chronicles record another meet ing between (Gurū) Gobind Siṅgh and Pīr Bhīkhan Shāh which took place in 1672 when the latter went to see him at Lakhnaur, near Ambālā, where he was halting for some time on his way from Paṭnā to Kīratpur.

BIBLIOGRAPHY

1. Sukhā Siṅgh, *Gurbilās Dasvīṅ Pātshāhī.* Lahore, 1912
2. Santokh Siṅgh, Bhāī, *Srī Gur Pratāp Sūraj Granth.* Amritsar, 1926-37
3. Giān Siṅgh, Giānī, *Twārīkh Gurū Khālsā.* Patiala, 1970

P.S.P.

BHIKHĀRĪ, BHĀĪ, Bhābṛā by caste, was a devoted Sikh of the time of Gurū Arjan. He lived in the town of Gujrāt. Bhāī Gurdās, *Vārāṅ*, XI. 30, lists him among prominent Sikhs of the time. He plied an honest trade, helped needy Sikhs and other holy men and recited the sacred word. Once, as says Bhāī Manī Siṅgh, *Sikhān dī Bhagat Mālā,* a Sikh waited on Gurū Hargobind, Gurū Arjan's successor, and begged to be shown a model Sikh. The latter directed him to Bhāī Bhikhārī. As the Sikh reached Gujrāt, he found Bhāī Bhikhārī's household bustling with activity owing to preparations for the marriage of his son. But Bhāī Bhikhārī sat calm and unexcited, mending an old mat. The Sikh introduced himself and was warmly received by his host. Amid the festivity in the house, the Sikh was puzzled to see in one small room a bier, a shroud, and other funeral articles. Questioned about these, Bhāī Bhikhārī told his guest that he would know. The nuptials took place as arranged and Bhāī Bhikhārī distributed charity to mark the happy event. At night, as says *Sikhāṅ dī Bhagat Mālā*, the bridegroom had pain in the stomach. No treatment availed and the young man died within hours. Wailing broke out in the house, but Bhāī Bhikhārī remained serene and undisturbed. He cremated his son next day, using the bier and shroud the guest had seen in the house and spread out the mended mat for the mourners. He entreated everyone to accept the Will of God and not to lament. The visitor bowed his head in reverence to Bhāī Bhikhārī and took his leave. He related the episode to Gurū Hargobind and the *saṅgat*, who praised Bhāī Bhikhārī for his faith and piety.

BIBLIOGRAPHY

1. *Gurbilās Chhevīṅ Pātshāhī.* Patiala, 1970
2. Manī Siṅgh, Bhāī, *Sikhāṅ dī Bhagat Mālā.* Amritsar, 1955
3. Santokh Siṅgh, Bhāī, *Srī Gur Pratāp Sūraj Granth.* Amritsar, 1926-37

T.S.

BHĪKHĪ, popularly pronounced Bhikkhī (30° - 3'N, 75° - 33'E), an old town along the Sunām-Baṭhiṇḍā road in Baṭhiṇḍā district of the Punjab, is sacred to Gurū Tegh Bahādur, who halted here for several days during one of his travels through the Mālvā region. Desū, the local chief, who had been a follower of Sultān Sakhī Sarwar, became a Sikh and served the Gurū with devotion. Gurū Tegh Bahādur gave him five arrows to be kept as a memento. It is said that after the Gurū had left Bhīkhī, Desū's wife displeased at her husband's conversion, broke and burnt the arrows. According to local tradition, this brought a curse on Desū's house with the result that his son and grandson suffered assassination at the hands of his enemies and his direct line came to an end.

A memorial to Gurū Tegh Bahādur had been raised by his devotees at Bhīkhī. Mahārājā Karam Siṅgh (1798-1845) of Paṭiālā built a proper shrine and made land endowment for its maintenance. It is now designated Gurdwārā Sāhib Pātshāhī 9 and is located on the northern outskirts of the town near a pond. The present building, in a one-acre walled compound, consists of a square sanctum, under a four-cornered dome, and a rectangular hall, built on a high plinth.

The Gurdwārā owns 112 acres of land and is managed by the Shiromaṇī Gurdwārā Parbandhak Committee through a local committee. Besides the daily worship, special congregations occur on the first of each Bikramī month and on major anniversaries and festivals.

BIBLIOGRAPHY

1. *Mālvā Desh Raṭan dī Sākhī Pothi.* Amritsar, 1968
2. Tārā Siṅgh, *Srī Gur Tīrath Saṅgrahi.* Amritsar, n.d.
3. Ṭhākar Siṅgh, Giānī, *Srī Gurduāre Darshan.* Amritsar, 1923
4. Faujā Siṅgh, *Gurū Teg Bahādur : Yātrā Asthān, Pramparāvāṅ te Yād Chinn.* Patiala, 1976

M.G.S.

BHĪM CHAND, ruler of Kahlūr (Bilāspur), a princely state in the Śivāliks, from 1665-92. The family claimed descent from Chandel Rājpūts of Bundelkhaṇḍ. Bhīm Chand's father, Dīp Chand, was a tributary of the Mughals and he was allowed to exercise nominal authority over twenty-two states in the hills including Kulū, Kāṅgṛā, Maṇḍī, Suket and Chambā.

Till the accession of Bhīm Chand to the *gaddī* in 1665, the rulers of Kahlūr had maintained amicable relations with the Gurūs. In 1635, Gurū Hargobind had retired to Kīratpur, a town founded by his son, Bābā Gurdittā, on the base of the Kahlūr mount. Kīratpur remained thereafter the seat of the Gurūs until Gurū Tegh Bahādur founded, in 1665, Chakk Nānakī, later renamed Anandpur. His son, Gurū Gobind Siṅgh, continued to live there. However, Bhīm Chand became jealous of Gurū Gobind Siṅgh's growing popularity and of the royal style he maintained. Acceding to the solicitation of the friendly ruler of Sirmūr, Gurū Gobind Siṅgh departed to visit him in his capital Nāhan and establishing within his territory a habitation of his own called Pāoṇṭā, took up residence there. Rājā Bhīm Chand's envy was not assuaged. He, along with some other hill monarchs returning from the Himalayan state of Srīnagar (Gaṛhvāl) after the marriage of his son Ajmer Chand, attacked Gurū Gobind Siṅgh. The Gurū met the attacking host at Bhaṅgāṇī, 11 km northeast of Pāoṇṭā. In the battle that took place on 18 September 1688, the hill chiefs were worsted, and Bhīm Chand took to flight. Gurū Gobind Siṅgh returned to Anandpur later in 1688 and Bhīm Chand made his peace with him. The Gurū in fact went to his aid in his battle against the Mughal commander, Alif Khān, fought at Nadauṇ, on 20 March 1691.

Rājā Bhīm Chand abdicated in favour of his son, Ajmer Chand, in 1692. According to the *Gurū kīāṅ Sākhīāṅ,* he died on 16 Assū, 1749 Bk/16 September 1692.

BIBLIOGRAPHY

1. Teja Singh and Ganda Singh, *A Short History of the Sikhs.* Bombay, 1950
2. Hutchinson, J., and J. Ph. Vogel, *History of the Punjab Hill States.* Lahore, 1933
3. Macauliffe, Max Arthur, *The Sikh Religion.* Oxford, 1909
4. Harbans Singh, *Guru Gobind Singh.* Chandigarh, 1966
5. Sukhā Siṅgh, *Gurbilās Dasvīṅ Pātshāhī.* Lahore, 1912

K.S.T.

BHIRĀĪ, MĀĪ, spelt by some chroniclers also as Bharāī and Virāī, who belonged to Matte dī Sarāi, the birthplace of Gurū Aṅgad (1504-52), was married to Bhāī Mahimā, a Khahirā Jaṭṭ of Khaḍūr (Sāhib) in Amritsar district of the Punjab. She was like a sister to Bhāī Pherū Mall, the Gurū's father, who too had made Khaḍūr his home. According to Sarūp Dās Bhallā, *Mahimā Prakāsh,* after Aṅgad (formerly Lahiṇā) had been nominated by Gurū Nānak to be his spiritual successor at Kartārpur in 1539 and advised to return to Khaḍūr, the former instead of going back to his own home went to Māī Bhirāī's and stayed there for some time in seclusion, immersed in deep meditation. After the passing away of Gurū Nānak, the disciples, led by the venerable Bhāī Buḍḍhā, found him in the room in which he had locked himself and persuaded him to come out to assume charge of the *saṅgat.* A tall edifice, Gurdwārā Māī Bhirāī, now marks the site where the Māī's house once stood.

See KHAḌŪR SĀHIB

BIBLIOGRAPHY

1. Bhallā, Sarūp Dās, *Mahimā Prakāsh.* Patiala, 1971
2. Giān Siṅgh, Giānī, *Twārīkh Gurū Khālsā.* Patiala, 1970
3. Santokh Siṅgh, Bhāī, *Srī Gur Pratāp Sūraj Granth.* Amritsar, 1926-37
4. Macauliffe, Max Arthur, *The Sikh Religion.* Oxford, 1909

Gn.S.

BHIRĀĪ, MĀTĀ, the maternal grandmother of Gurū Nānak, was married to Rāmā of the village of Chāhal, near Lahore.

See RĀMĀ, BĀBĀ

BIBLIOGRAPHY

Santokh Siṅgh, Bhāī, *Srī Gur Pratāp Sūraj Granth.* Amritsar, 1926-37

Gn.S.

BHĪVĀ, BHĀĪ, and his brother, Rūp Chand, businessmen of Sirhind, were devout Sikhs of the time of Gurū Arjan. They lived honestly, celebrated the Sikh festivals, and entertained their brethren-in-faith on such occasions. Once a Mughal came to deposit with them gold *mohars* hid in a hollow piece of bamboo. They put away the bamboo-piece for safe custody, but forgot to make an entry of the deposit in their books. The Mughal returned after five years to claim the deposit. Bhīvā and Rūp Chand did not remember and, not finding any record of it in their books, they denied having ever received it. An altercation followed and the matter was taken before the *faujdār*, the local governor, who decided to make a trial. A trough of boiling hot oil was produced and both Bhīvā and the Mughal were ordered to dip their right hands in it if they still persisted in their respective claims. Both the contenders readily complied. Bhīvā's hand, as says Bhāī Manī Siṅgh, *Sikhāṅ dī Bhagat Mālā,* remained unscathed whereas the Mughal's was badly scalded. Bhīvā and his brother returned happily, acquitted of the blame. Yet, wondering why the Mughal had accepted to go through the ordeal so confidently, they carried out a thorough search of their house. They eventually found the bamboo filled with gold *mohars* lying in an obscure nook. Filled with remorse, they at once went to the Mughal, apologized to him and returned to him his money. As intrigued as he felt happy, he asked Bhāī Bhīvā, "But how was it that you came out of the ordeal unscathed?" Bhīvā replied, "Because I was honestly innocent to myself and had, moreover, prayed to my Gurū who protected my honour." Bhāī Bhīvā escorted the Mughal to the presence of Gurū Arjan. He bowed before him and became a disciple.

BIBLIOGRAPHY

1. Manī Siṅgh, Bhāī, *Sikhāṅ dī Bhagat Mālā.* Amritsar, 1955
2. Santokh Siṅgh, Bhāī, *Srī Gur Pratāp Sūraj Granth.* Amritsar, 1926-37

T.S.

BHOG (which by literal etymology, from Sanskrit, signifies "pleasure," "delight") is the name used in the Sikh tradition for the group of observances which accompany the reading of the concluding parts of Scripture, the Gurū Granth Sāhib. This conclusion may be reached as part of the normal and routine reading in the day-to-day lectionary of a major centre of worship with a staff of readers. But in the mind of the community the word is very deeply associated with a complete, end-to-end, reading of the Holy Book without interruption which is called *akhaṇḍ pāṭh.* This usually takes two twenty-four-hour days of non-stop reading by a relay of readers. This type of *pāṭh,* and hence the *bhog* which comes at its end, can be performed in conjunction with weddings, obsequies, anniversaries and other occasions when a family or a worshipping community may consider such a reading appropriate.

Similarly, a *bhog* takes place at the end of the slower reading (*sahaj pāṭh*) when, for instance, a family decides to read the entire book as continuously as circumstances permit. For such a reading no time-limit applies. Of course, the *bhog* comes at its end, and it must be recited entire in a single service, without a break.

Another variation on *pāṭh* is the *saptāhik pāṭh* in which case the reading of the Gurū Granth Sāhib is completed within one week (*saptāh*). The recital of the text is taken in parts and completed within the seven-day span. The *sahaj* or slow-reading *pāṭh* may continue for a longer time, even for months.

The verb form *bhog pauṇā* simply means to end or conclude. In Punjabi idiom it may mean to end or conclude an argument or discussion. *Bhog* especially stands for funeral service. In a derivative use of the term, sacramental *kaṛāhprasād* distributed at the end of any congregational service is also sometimes called *bhog.* Any occasion whether of joy or sorrow, wish fulfilment, or trial would usually prompt a Sikh householder to have a *pāṭh* of the holy book said, preferably by himself and/or jointly by members of the family. If however this is not possible, *pāṭhīs* or Scripture-readers will be invited or hired for the purpose. Date and time of *bhog* are notified in advance by word of mouth, through an announcement in *saṅgat* during routine service in the local *gurdwārā* (almost every Sikh hamlet has a *gurdwārā*), or through written letters to friends and relations. Coming into vogue is the custom of placing notices in newspaper.

In the case of *sādhāran* and *saptāhik pāṭhs,* the reader would have already completed the reading of the Holy Book except for the last five pages. While the *saṅgat* is gathering at the appointed time, the officiant will be preparing *kaṛāhprasād* in a steel cauldron over burning logs, coal or in an electric oven. When ready, it is respectfully lifted and carried overhead to the site of the congregation and placed on the right side of where the Holy Book rests. If a choir is on hand, some scriptural hymns appropriate to the occasion will be sung. The *granthī* (officiant) will then read from the Holy Book what may be called the inaugural hymn. Thereafter he will turn over reverently the pages of the Holy Volume to arrive at the unread portion. He will start reading slowly and in a singing tone the *ślokas* of Gurū Tegh Bahādur (couplets, 57 in number, popularly called *bhog de ślokas*), *Mundāvaṇī* and a *śloka* by Gurū Arjan. Then follows the last composition, *Rāgamālā.*

The *bhog* must in all cases include the reading of the end of the Holy Book. That is, the recitation of the last five pages, pages 1426 onwards. This begins with the reading of 57 *ślokas* by Gurū Tegh Bahādur and continues to the end of the Book. The music, cadences and imagery of these verses have a unique and exquisite beauty of their own.

After these *ślokas, Mundāvaṇī* by Gurū Arjan, is recited. This is a kind of seal to the Scripture. It reiterates the essentials of the teaching of the Book — *sat* (truth), *santokh* (contentment; rejoicing in one's lot), *vīchār* (wisdom) and the remembrance of the Holy Name (*nām*). It is essentially a word to all humankind.

After the Granth reading has been completed, *ardās* is recited by the entire congregation. In it a special blessing is called for the purpose for which the *pāṭh* was held. *Ardās* has its own powerful associations which are now brought into *bhog.* These include the recalling to mind of past Sikh heroism, devotion and martyrdom and the marking present of the *Khālsā* in all its venerable might.

After *ardās*, the Hukam or command for the day is obtained by reading out the hymn offered by the text which is naturally interpreted in the context of the intention of the *pāṭh*, that is, as the word of the Gurū to those receiving it at that point with their purposes particularly in mind, be it a family event, a funeral, a wedding, or invocation for blessing on a new venture.

N.Q.K.

BHOLŪ, BHĀĪ, a Tivāṛī Brāhmaṇ, is mentioned in Bhāī Gurdās, *Vārāṅ* , XI. 19, as a devoted Sikh of the time of Gurū Arjan. The Gurū, as says Bhāī Manī Siṅgh, *Sikhāṅ dī Bhagat Mālā*, once explained to him that Gurū Nānak's *Gurū* was God himself, though he did bow before Gurū Aṅgad whom he had chosen for succession as *Gurū* after him.

See BHAṬṬŪ, BHĀĪ

BIBLIOGRAPHY

1. Manī Siṅgh, Bhāī, *Sikhāṅ dī Bhagat Mālā*. Amritsar, 1955
2. Santokh Siṅgh, Bhāī, *Srī Gur Pratāp Sūraj Granth*. Amritsar, 1926-37

T.S.

BHULLĀ, BHĀĪ, and Bhāī Kullā, both Jhañjhī Sunārs, accompanied by Bhagīrath, a Soinī Khatrī, presented themselves before Gurū Arjan and begged to be instructed in the pious way. The Gurū told them, always to act like *gurmukhs*, and not like *manmukhs*. The Gurū, according to *Sikhāṅ dī Bhagat Mālā*, explained: "*Gurmukhs* are those who, turning their back on ego, heed the Gurū's word, who do not forget a good turn done to them but always forget anything done by themselves for the good of others. Still excelling *gurmukhs* are those who, having given up all ego, are good to others habitually, unmindful of how the others treat them. A *gurmukh* finally is one who has attained *giān*, or true knowledge. He consciously acts for the weal of others, even of those who bear him ill will." "*Manmukhs*, on the contrary," continued the Gurū, "are those ego-ridden persons who forget the good turn done them, but do not ever forget the injury inflicted upon them. Worse are those with malice towards all, good or evil. The worst are they who return evil for goodness. They are immune to the teaching of the Gurū." Bhāī Bhullā and his companions, enlightened by the Gurū's precept, continued to serve the *saṅgat* with devotion.

BIBLIOGRAPHY

1. Manī Siṅgh, Bhāī, *Sikhāṅ dī Bhagat Mālā*. Amritsar, 1955
2. Santokh Siṅgh, Bhāī, *Srī Gur Pratāp Sūraj Granth*. Amritsar, 1926-37

T.S.

BHULLŪ, BHĀĪ, a Sekhaṛ Khatrī who turned a mendicant, once waited upon Gurū Arjan to seek instruction. He was accompanied by Bhāī Nāū, also a mendicant like him, Bhāī Jaṭṭū, a Bhīvā Khatrī, and Bhāī Mūlā. The Gurū said neither action nor the world be shunned. What was important was shunning evil and temptation, serving others and practising the sacred Word. Bhāī Bhullū and others, says Bhāī Manī Siṅgh, *Sikhāṅ dī Bhagat Mālā*, followed the Gurū's precept and were blessed.

BIBLIOGRAPHY

1. Manī Siṅgh, Bhāī, *Sikhāṅ dī Bhagat Mālā*. Amritsar, 1955
2. Santokh Siṅgh, Bhāī, *Srī Gur Pratāp Sūraj Granth*. Amritsar, 1926-37

T.S.

BHŪMĀ SIṄGH (d. 1746), a Ḍhilloṅ Jaṭṭ of the village of Huṅg near Badhṇī, in present-day Farīdkoṭ district of the Punjab, gathered power in men and money during Nādir Shāh's invasion of India in 1739. At the time of the death of Nawāb Zakarīyā K͟hān, the Mug͟hal governor of the Punjab, Bhūmā Siṅgh's *jathā* was one of 25 roving bands of the Sikhs. Bhūmā Siṅgh commanded a body of about 300 men. It is believed that the name of the band, Bhaṅgī, owed its origin to Bhūmā Siṅgh, who used to pound *bhaṅg* (hemp) for preparing a cooling drink for Sikhs gathered at Amritsar during the summer months.

Bhūmā Siṅgh lost his life fighting against the Mughals led by Dīwān Lakhpat Rāi in the Chhoṭā Ghallūghārā in 1746 near Kāhnūvān, in Gurdāspur district.

BIBLIOGRAPHY

1. Griffin, Lepel, and C.F. Massy, *Chiefs and Families of Note in the Punjab.* Lahore, 1909
2. Gupta, Hari Ram, *History of the Sikhs,* vol. IV. Delhi, 1982

S.S.B.

BHŪNDAṚ, village 7 km south of Rāmpurā Phūl (30° - 16'N, 75° - 14'E) in Baṭhiṇḍā district of the Punjab, claims a historical shrine, Gurdwārā Sāhib Chhevīṅ Pātshāhī, commemorating the visit of Gurū Hargobind in 1634. The Gurdwārā, situated on the northern edge of the village, comprises an old domed structure and a *dīvān* hall added during the late 1950's. The old shrine has only a square platform on which a few weapons are displayed. The Gurū Granth Sāhib is seated in the sanctum within the hall marked off by rectangular pillars with decorative pilasters and *pīpal*-leaf arches. The Gurdwārā is maintained by the village *saṅgat* or community.

BIBLIOGRAPHY

Gurbilās Chhevīṅ Pātshāhī. Patiala, 1970

M.G.S.

BHUṄGARNĪ, village near the right bank of the Jalandhar branch of the Bist Doāb canal, 20 km south of Hoshiārpur (31° - 32'N, 75° - 55'E), is sacred to Gurū Har Rāi, who stayed here in the course of his journey between Kīratpur and Kartārpur. A platform and a small shrine, established inside the village in honour of the Gurū's visit, was looked after for a long time by a line of Mirāsī (Muslim bards or heralds) priests until the local Sikh *saṅgat* took it over in the Siṅgh Sabhā days. Later, a new building was raised on the site (cornerstone laid on 19 March 1917). Now known as Gurdwārā Srī Gurū Har Rāi Sāhib Jī Pātshāhī VII, the shrine is managed by a local committee under the overall control of the Shiromaṇī Gurdwārā Parbandhak Committee. Besides the daily services, special *dīvāns* are held on the first of each Bikramī month. The major festival of the year is Baisākhī which is celebrated with special eclat as the birthday of the K͟hālsā.

BIBLIOGRAPHY

1. Tārā Siṅgh, *Srī Gur Tīrath Sangrahi.* Amritsar, n.d.
2. Ṭhākar Siṅgh, Giānī, *Srī Gurduāre Darshan.* Amritsar, 1923

M.G.S.

BHŪPĀL, also called Bhupālāṅ, a village 13 km north of Mānsā (29°- 59'N, 75° - 23'E) in Baṭhiṇḍa district of the Punjab, is sacred to Gurū Teg͟h Bahādur, who halted here for a night during his travels across the Mālvā region. The shrine built inside the village to commemorate the visit, called Gurdwārā Nauvīṅ Pātshāhī, comprises a flat-roofed hall with a vaulted ceiling. The Gurū Granth Sāhib is seated in it on a canopied platform. Besides daily worship, special gatherings take place to mark the birth anniversaries of Gurū Nānak and Gurū Gobind Siṅgh and the martyrdom anniversary of Gurū Teg͟h Bahādur.

BIBLIOGRAPHY

Faujā Siṅgh, *Gurū Teg Bahādur : Yātrā Asthān,*

Pramparāvāṅ te Yād Chinn. Patiala, 1976

Jg.S.

BHŪPĀL SIṄGH, a son of the Gurkhā general, Amar Siṅgh Thāpā, came to Lahore and took up service under Mahārājā Raṇjīt Siṅgh (1780-1839). He became an officer in a battalion in the Sikh army under General Ventura. In 1838, Bhūpāl Siṅgh returned to Nepal and was appointed to command a check-post on the Indo-Nepalese border. Two years later he was selected to lead an embassy to Lahore. He left Kāṭhmaṇḍū on 6 June 1840, but the mission returned without transacting much business owing to the death in Lahore of Kaṅvar Nau Nihāl Siṅgh.

BIBLIOGRAPHY

Sinha, N.K., *Ranjit Singh.* Calcutta, 1968

H.R.G.

BHŪPINDER SIṄGH, LIEUTENANT-GENERAL MAHĀRĀJĀ SIR (1891-1931), Knight Grand Commander of the Order of the Star of India, Knight Grand Commander of the Order of the Indian Empire, Knight of the Order of the British Empire, ruler of the Sikh state of Paṭiālā, was one of the most colourful and influential Indian princes of the interwar years. Tall, robust, dashingly handsome, he was to the British the personification of the Punjabi martial races, a veritable "flower of Oriental aristocracy." In his own eyes, and in the eyes of many of his co-religionists, he was the temporal leader of Sikhism. Ten times elected Chancellor of the Chamber of Princes during the 1920's and 1930's, he was for much of that period the guiding hand of the princely order in its campaign to unlock the shackles of paramountcy which bound the princes to do the bidding of the British rāj.

Born on 12 October 1891, Bhūpinder Siṅgh was only ten years old when the premature death of his father, Mahārājā Sir Rājinder Siṅgh, catapulted him into the public arena. For nine years the state was ruled by a Council of Regency headed by Sardār Bahādur Gurmukh Siṅgh while the young prince finished his schooling at the Aitchison College in Lahore. He started ruling in his own right in 1909, and was invested with full powers on 3 November 1910. However, the outbreak of war in 1914 was the first real turning-point in Bhūpinder Siṅgh's career. Prior to 1914 Paṭiālā had been just one of many medium-sized states, having no special claims to distinction. During the war, under Bhūpinder Siṅgh's leadership, the state established itself as favoured ally of the British by contributing lavishly in men, money and materials to the imperial cause, the Mahārājā himself taking a personal role in the war effort as honorary lieutenant-colonel of the Ist Ludhiāṇā Sikhs. These earned Bhūpinder Siṅgh a clutch of imperial decorations, a seat at the Imperial War Conference of 1918, an appointment as honorary aide-de-camp to the King-Emperor and, later, an appointment as an Indian delegate to the League of Nations. More importantly, the state's salute was raised permanently from 17 to 19 guns which placed Bhūpinder Siṅgh among the dozen top-ranking Indian rulers.

Riding high on British favour, Bhūpinder Siṅgh began to see himself as a future leader of the princely order and as a power-broker in Sikh affairs. In 1917, he adjudicated at the behest of the Chief Khālsā Dīwān in a dispute about a corpus of Sikh scriptures; in 1921 he got himself elected to the standing committee of the newly formed Chamber of Princes; and in 1923 he took part in the *kār-sevā* (cleansing of the tank by voluntary service) at the Golden Temple.

As Chancellor of the Chamber of Princes, Bhūpinder Siṅgh worked long and hard to transform the Chamber into an efficient forum for the maintenance of princely rights against the encroachments of paramountcy. His vigorous lobbying helped to secure the appointment, in 1927, of an Indian States

Committee headed by Sir Harcourt Butler, to investigate the princes' claims that paramountcy had infringed their treaty rights. And in 1929 and 1930 he arranged for the Standing Committee to negotiate personally with the Viceroy. These efforts were rewarded when, in October 1929, Lord Irwin announced that representatives of the princes would be invited to a Round Table Conference in London to map out, conjointly with delegates of British India, a new constitution for the sub-continent.

Mahārājā Bhūpinder Siṅgh was a great sportsman. In his youth he was a crack shot, a first-rate polo player, and a hard-hitting batsman, captaining the Indian cricket team on its 1911 tour of England. Later he developed an interest in dog-breeding, and in the 1930's was president of the All-India Gundog League and vice-president of the Indian Kennel Association. He was also a lavish patron of sport, endowing a gymnasium in London for use by Indian students and several cricket grounds in India. One of these, at Chail, the Paṭiālā summer residence, 7,000 feet up in the foothills of the Himalayas, remains the highest playing field in the world.

Bhūpinder Siṅgh beautified the city of Paṭiālā by endowing it with new palace buildings, gardens and metalled roads. He established a high court, numerous hospitals and schools and a beautiful secretariat. He was chancellor and chief patron of the Sikhs' premier educational institution – the K͟hālsā College at Amritsar.

As his power and prestige grew, Bhūpinder Siṅgh came under increasing criticism from jealous rivals and opponents of the princely order. Sapped by over-indulgence, he died at Paṭiālā, ostensibly from heart failure, on 22 March 1938.

BIBLIOGRAPHY

1. Panikkar, K.M., *An Autobiography.* Oxford (Delhi), 1979
2. Ganda Singh, *The Patiala and the East Panjab States Union: Historical Background.* Patiala, 1951
3. Ramusack, Barbara, *The Princes of India.* Ohio State University, 1978
4. —, "Maharajas and Gurdwaras : Patiala and the Sikh Community," in *People, Princes and Paramount Power: Society and Politics in the Indian Princely States.* Ed. Robin Jeffrey. Delhi, 1978

I.C.

BHŪP SIṄGH, SARDĀR, remembered as Rājā Bhūp Siṅgh in local lore, was the chief of the Sikh principality of Ropaṛ, during the earlier half of the nineteenth century. Little is known about his life except that in 1808-09 he, along with Devā Siṅgh, was in possession of Ropaṛ and its adjacent districts including K͟hizrābād and Mīāṅpur, a tract covering 115 villages with an estimated annual revenue of Rs 53,000. He was probably a grandson of Sardār Harī Siṅgh of Ḍallevālīā *misl*, who, according to Lepel. H. Griffin, *The Rājās of the Punjab,* had taken possession, around 1763, of a large territory including Ropaṛ, Siālbā, K͟hizrābād and Kurālī. In 1792, one year before he died, Harī Siṅgh divided his possessions between his two surviving sons, Chaṛhat Siṅgh and Devā Siṅgh, the former getting Ropaṛ and the latter Siālbā. Bhūp Siṅgh was the son and successor of Chaṛhat Siṅgh, who might have died during the former's minority. This explains the reference to Devā Siṅgh being the co-ruler at Ropaṛ in lists prepared in 1809 by Lieut-Colonel D. Ochterlony and Lieutenant F.S. White of the East India Company. According to these lists, Ropaṛ was under Mahārājā Raṇjīt Siṅgh. It came under British protection as a result of the treaty of Amritsar (25 April 1809), which limited Raṇjīt Siṅgh's authority mainly to territories north of the River Sutlej. The chief of Ropaṛ, Bhūp Siṅgh, was removed as prisoner and his whole estate was confiscated in 1846 in consequence of his opposing the British during the first Anglo-Sikh war.

Rājā Bhūp Siṅgh is remembered as a just

ruler and as a pious Sikh who constructed Gurdwārā Dehrā Bābā Gurdittā Jī at Kīratpur and Gurdwārā Gurūgaṛh Sāhib at Ropaṛ. At the latter Gurdwārā he had started a *laṅgar*, or free kitchen, which remained open round the clock, for which reason, the shrine is still known as Gurdwārā Sadā Varat (where *laṅgar* is open all the time to serve food to whoever comes).

BIBLIOGRAPHY

Griffin, Lepel, *The Rajas of the Punjab*. Delhi, 1977

M.G.S.

BHŪRĪĀ, BHĀĪ, a resident of Chūnīāṅ now in Pakistan, was a pious Sikh contemporary of Gurū Arjan (1563-1606). As the Gurū was once touring the Nakkā country, southwest of Lahore, succouring people then living through a severe famine, he according to Giānī Giān Siṅgh, *Twārikh Gurū Khālsā*, came to Chūṇīāṅ on his way from Jambar to Bahiṛvāl. Bhāī Bhūrīā received the Gurū and acquainted him with the hardship the residents were undergoing. The Gurū called on Chūhaṛ Mall, the local revenue collector, who was also a disciple. The latter left no stone unturned to provide relief.

BIBLIOGRAPHY

Giān Siṅgh, Giānī, *Twārīkh Gurū Khālsā*. Patiala, 1970

T.S.

BHYROWĀL, TREATY OF. *See* ANGLO-SIKH TREATY (BHYROWĀL)

BIANCHI, an Italian engineer, who arrived at Lahore in Sikh times. According to the Khālsā Darbār pay-rolls, he served the Sikh State and was employed in 1835 as a road engineer on a salary of 9 rupees per day. He constructed a road from General Ventura's house to the Fort in Lahore. He was entrusted with the task of building a circular road enclosing the city and the fort of Lahore. However, he could not accomplish the task owing to illness. He proceeded to Italy, but died on the way.

BIBLIOGRAPHY

Grey, C., *European Adventurers of Northern India* [Reprint]. Patiala, 1970

Gl.S.

BIBEK BĀRDHĪ, (*bibek* = discrimination or discipline, *bārdhī* = ocean; by implication, "guide to Sikh religious practice") is a collection of *rahitnāmās* or codes of conduct compiled in AD 1877 by Paṇḍit Bhagvān Siṅgh, a Brāhmaṇ who converted to Sikhism under the influence of Bābā Sumer Siṅgh, celebrated high priest of Takht Srī Paṭnā Sāhib. The work has never been published and the manuscript, believed to be written in the compiler's own hand, is preserved at the Dr Balbīr Siṅgh Sāhitya Kendra at Dehrā Dūn. The manuscript comprises 140 sheets, written on both sides, of plain hand-made paper of approximately foolscap size. Paper, obviously procured at different times, ranges in colour from off-white to light cream. Different pens and inks have been used, but the hand is throughout the same. The text begins with the compiler's invocation to the goddess Kālī, followed by a section stressing the importance of *bibek*, i.e. strict observance of the Sikh code of conduct. Bhagvān Siṅgh, then, proceeds to specify the code a Sikh is expected to follow. Like other writers of *rahitnāmās*, he lays down rules of conduct for a Sikh embracing personal, social and religious aspects of his life. To support his prescriptions, he puts forth copious illustrations and quotations from the Sikh sacred literature, though these are not always relevant and germane to the point sought to be upheld. A major part of the work consists of reproduction of several older *rahitnāmās* such as those of Bhāī Manī Siṅgh (d. 1737), Bhāī Nand Lāl, Bhāī Chaupā Siṅgh, Bhāī Prahlād Siṅgh, and Kavī Saināpati.

Among the lesser-known *rahitnāmās* are "Rahatmālā Rahatnāmā Aṭhārvāṅ Muktnāmā Jo Sūraj Prakāsh Ādko Meṅ Kahā Hai," "Bhāī Sukhā Siṅgh Anandpurīe Ke Gur Bilās Me Se Rahat Bachan Chhānṭe Haiṅ," "Mālve kī Sākhī Me Jo Rahatnāme Ke Bachan Haiṅ Dasam Gurū Krit," "Bibek Bodhnī Sapat Satī Yāne Bābā Sumer Siṅgh Jī Krit," and "Jo Muktsar Tīrath Me Gurū Ji Sabh Sikhoṅ Ko Sunāye." In all, the manuscript has, according to the author's own calculation, 2,555 *bachans* or sayings. In the index, appended to the manuscript the author has classified various *rahits* and worked out the total number of injunctions set down. The work is important insofar as it gathers in one volume many old *rahitnāmās* and authorities, but most of the compiler's own writing is under Brāhamaṇical influence and at several places he goes against the Sikh tenets. For his involvement with this *genre* of Sikh literature, he is also known as Bhagvān Siṅgh Rahitnāmīā. He is the author as well of a *rahitnāmā* called *Rahit Darpaṇ*.

BIBLIOGRAPHY

1. Padam, Piārā Siṅgh, *Rahitnāme*. Patiala, 1974
2. Kāhn Siṅgh, Bhāī, *Gurushabad Ratnākar Mahān Kosh*. Patiala, 1974
3. Nripinder Singh, *The Sikh Moral Tradition. Delhi, 1990*

K.S.T.

BIBHAUR, village close to Nayā Naṅgal in Ropaṛ district of the Punjab, is sacred to Gurū Gobind Siṅgh who resided here for some time in 1700-01 at the invitation of the Rāo (chief) of Bibhaur. The commemorative Sikh shrine here is called Gurdwārā Bibhaur Sāhib. The present complex was raised during the 1960's under the supervision of Sant Sevā Siṅgh of Anandpur. The *dīvān* hall, with the sanctum marked off by four huge pillars at the far end, stands on a marble-topped terrace. Above the sanctum is a domed room with a gold-plated pinnacle on top. Gurū kā Laṅgar is to the north of the main building. An imposing gateway was erected during the 1980's. The Gurdwārā is administered by the Shiromaṇi Gurdwārā Parbandhak Committee. Besides the observance of major Sikh anniversaries, a religious fair is held on 19-21 September every year.

BIBLIOGRAPHY

1. Tārā Siṅgh, *Srī Gur Tīrath Saṅgrahi*. Amritsar, n.d.
2. Ṭhākar Siṅgh, *Srī Gurduāre Darshan*. Amritsar, 1923

Gn.S.

BĪBĪPUR KHURD, locally called Bīpur, is a small village in Paṭiālā district, 8 km southeast of Ghuṛām (30° - 7'N, 76° - 28'E). It has a historical shrine, Gurdwārā Pātshāhī Nauvīṅ, sacred to Gurū Tegh Bahādur, who visited the site during one of his travels through Mālvā and Bāṅgar regions. The Gurdwārā, out in the fields, is a single rectangular room, with a 4-metre wide verandah in front, built in 1964. It is managed by a village committee. Special *dīvāns* take place on the first of every Bikramī month, and an annual festival is held on the occasion of Holā Mohallā, recalling the Festival of Procession at Anandpur Sāhib in the month of March.

BIBLIOGRAPHY

1. Tārā Siṅgh, *Srī Gur Tīrath Saṅgrahi*. Amritsar, n.d.
2. Ṭhākar Siṅgh, Giānī, *Srī Gurduāre Darshan*. Amritsar, 1923
3. Faujā Siṅgh, *Gurū Teg Bahādur : Yātrā Asthān, Pramparāvāṅ te Yād Chinn*. Patiala, 1976

M.G.S.

BIDAR (17° - 55'N, 77° - 32'E) is a district town in Karnāṭaka. It is a railway station on the Vikārābād-Pārlī-Vaijnāth section of the South Central Railway. It is also connected by road with Nāndeḍ.

GURDWĀRĀ SRĪ NĀNAK JHĪRĀ SĀHIB at Bidar

honours the memory of Gurū Nānak. At the time of Gurū Nānak's visit, Bidar was the capital of the Bahmanī kingdom. Since the establishment in the town of the great Madarsā by Mahmūd Gāwāṅ in 1471-72, it had been a famous centre of Arabic learning in the Deccan. Gurū Nānak stayed next to a monastery of Muslim ascetics on the outskirts of the town. These *faqīrs* and their head, Pīr Jalāl ud-Dīn, attracted by the holy *bāṇī* being sung to the accompaniment of Mardānā's rebeck, came and made obeisance to the Gurū. The monastery was built on a rock in an undulating barren tract, without any water in the vicinity. Tradition says that, at the supplication of Jalāl ud-Dīn, Gurū Nānak lifted a stone and from underneath it a fountain of clear sweet water gushed forth. The spring, called Amrit Kuṇḍ, the Pool of Nectar, is still in existence. The place came to be known as Nānak Jhīrā and was looked after by Muslim priests. Māī (mother) Bhāgo, who had gone to the Deccan following Gurū Gobind Siṅgh used to visit it frequently during her stay at Jinvāṛā. But it gained prominence as a place of pilgrimage after the control passed to the Sikhs in 1948, confirmed by a judicial verdict in 1950. The construction of the Gurdwārā was commenced under a managing committee, headed by Sardār Bishan Siṅgh of Hyderābād. The main building, called Srī Harimandir Sāhib, was completed in 1966, and the Gurū Granth Sāhib was installed in it on the occasion of Holā Mohallā festival. Several other buildings, including the 101-room Gurū Nānak Bishrām Ghar (residential block for pilgrims), Gurū Nānak Hospital, a museum, *laṅgar* and a bathing tank have since been added.

The central building, a three-storeyed structure, is a handsome model of the mixture of modern and medieval styles of architecture. The ground floor, consisting of several rooms occupying a plinth area of about 50-metre square, serves as a basement for the main *dīvān* hall on the first floor. The hall consists of several rectangular projections in symmetrical order around a 10-metre-square sanctum. The roof of a large refectory, constructed adjacent to the main building, is on level with the *dīvān* hall and provides additional space for larger gatherings on festivals and other special occasions. The original spring, Amrit Kuṇḍ, is now a canopied square-shaped pool. It supplies water to the bathing tank, 50 metres away.

The Gurdwārā is managed by a committee which includes members from Bidar as well as from other towns in the South, such as Hyderābād, Wāraṅgal and Bombay. Gurbāṇī recital and *kīrtan* are held morning and evening, and all major anniversaries are celebrated, the most prominent of them being the birthday of Gurū Nānak and Holā Mohallā. The Gurdwārā also runs a college for training engineers and a charity hospital and a primary school, named after Gurū Nānak. Offerings and donations are the only source of income.

BIBLIOGRAPHY

1. Tārā Siṅgh, *Srī Gur Tīrath Saṅgrahi.* Amritsar, n.d.
2. Ṭhākar Siṅgh, Giānī, *Srī Gurduāre Darshan.* Amritsar, 1923

M.G.S.

BIDHĪ CHAND, a Khatrī by birth, was a devoted Sikh of the time of Gurū Rām Dās. Bhāī Gurdās, in his *Vārāṅ,* XI. 17, describes him as a man "of clear intelligence and of thought undefiled.''

See MAHĀNAND, BHĀĪ

BIBLIOGRAPHY

1. Manī Siṅgh, Bhāī, *Sikhāṅ dī Bhagat Mālā.* Amritsar, 1955
2. Santokh Siṅgh, Bhāī, *Srī Gur Pratāp Sūraj Granth.* Amritsar, 1926-37

Gr.S.

BIDHĪ CHAND, BHĀĪ (d. 1640), warrior as

well as religious preacher of the time of Gurū Hargobind, was a Chhīnā Jaṭṭ of the village of Sūrsiṅgh, 34 km south of Amritsar (31° - 37'N, 74° - 52'E). His father's name was Vassan and his grandfather's Bhikkhī. His mother was from Sirhālī, another village in the same district. As a young man Bidhī Chand had fallen into bad company and taken to banditry. One day, a pious Sikh, Bhāī Adalī of the village of Chohlā, led him into Gurū Arjan's presence. Bidhī Chand wished no longer to return home and decided to dedicate the rest of his life to the service of the Gurū. He was one of the five Sikhs chosen to accompany Gurū Arjan on his journey to Lahore where he was martyred in 1606. Gurū Hargobind chose him to be one of the commanders of the armed force he had raised and he displayed as a soldier great feats of valour in battles with the imperial troops. His best-known exploit, however, was the recovery of two horses, Dilbāgh and Gulbāgh, from the stables of the governor of Lahore. The horses belonged to a Sikh who was bringing them from Kābul as an offering for Gurū Hargobind, but they were seized on the way by the Mughal satrap. The first horse Bidhī Chand recovered disguised as a hay-seller, and the second disguised as an astrologer.

Besides being a brave warrior, Bidhī Chand was well versed in Sikh lore and tenet. From Kīratpur, he was sent out by Gurū Hargobind on a preaching mission to the eastern provinces where a Muslim saint, Sundar Shāh of Devnagar, became so attached to him that, before he left for the Punjab, he secured his word that he would return and spend his last days with him. According to *Gurbilās Chhevīṅ Pātshāhī*, Bidhī Chand remembered his promise and, as he saw his end drawing near, he took his leave of Gurū Hargobind and went to Devnagar. The two friends spent three days reflecting together on the teaching of Gurū Nānak, whereafter, continues the *Gurbilās*, both died at the same time (14 August 1640). Sundar Shāh's disciples buried the one in accordance with Muslim rites and cremated the other in accordance with Sikh rites, and raised shrines in their honour. Some time later, Lāl Chand, a nephew of Bhāī Bidhī Chand, brought from the site of his shrine at Devnagar some earth over which he built a *samādh* in his ancestral village, Sursiṅgh.

BIBLIOGRAPHY

1. *Gurbilās Chhevīṅ Pātshāhī*. Patiala, 1970
2. Giān Siṅgh, Giānī, *Twārīkh Khālsā*. Patiala, 1970
3. Macauliffe, Max Arthur, *The Sikh Religion*. Oxford, 1909
4. Banerjee, Indubhusan, *Evolution of the Khalsa*. Calcutta, 1980

B.S.

BIHĀGṚĀ. *See* SIKH DEVOTIONAL MUSIC

BIHĀGṚE KĪ VĀR, by Gurū Rām Dās, is one of the twenty-two *vārs* included in the Gurū Granth Sāhib. The *Vār*, originally comprised *pauṛīs* which were prefaced with *ślokas*, or couplets, by Gurū Arjan at the time of the compilation of the Gurū Granth Sāhib. All the twenty-one *pauṛīs* are of the composition of Gurū Rām Dās. Of the forty-three *ślokas*, thirty-three are by Gurū Amar Dās, four by Gurū Nānak, two each by Gurū Rām Dās and Gurū Arjan, one by Kabīr and one by Mardānā. Each *pauṛī* is preceded by two *ślokas* except *pauṛī* 12 which has three *ślokas* prefixed to it. The musical measure Bihāgṛā to which the *Vār* has been set and from which it derives its title is a midnight melody of northern India. The *Vār* lauds the Supreme Being in His transcendental as well as immanent, attributive as well as unattributive aspects. God Himself pervades unmanifest and Himself becomes manifest; for thirty-six aeons He created pitch darkness and Himself abided in the void; no Vedas, Purāṇas and Śāstras then existed; the Transcendent Lord God was all by Himself; withdrawn from all He Himself sat assuming absolute trance (18). He Himself created this universe (7), and in this process of creation He was the efficient as well as the material cause. God Himself is the Lord, an attendant and a devotee (5). He Himself created this universe and then filled it with His bounties; the Formless Lord Himself manifests Himself in form (7). He Himself is the philosopher's stone, Himself the metal and Himself He transforms it into gold (10). Man is advised to meditate on the Name of the Lord who is all-powerful and unique in Himself. He should in the company of the holy remember Him (4). But only those on whom He bestows His grace meet the true Gurū and sing His praises (17) in the company of the holy. Thus, all their worldly appetites cease and they enjoy everlasting beatitude (4). One learns how to swim across the ocean of life only following the path shown by the Gurū, but one can obtain both the Gurū and the *śabda* of the Gurū through His grace alone. Those who live under His grace are never distracted by material considerations. The Gurū's guidance frees them from worldly entanglements and they remain attached ever to His feet.

BIBLIOGRAPHY

1. Bishan Siṅgh, Giānī, *Bāī Vārāṅ Saṭīk*. Amritsar, n.d.
2. Sāhib Siṅgh, *Srī Gurū Granth Sāhib Darpaṇ*, vol. IV. Jalandhar, 1963

K.S.D.

BIHAṄGAM, from Sanskrit *vihaṅg* which means a bird, is a term applied to wandering ascetics who lead a life of complete detachment. A Bihaṅgam is a celebate who lives in poverty renouncing all worldly ties and follows the path of holiness. In the Hindu tradition, he, abjuring religious dogma, worships Śiva, Rāma and other incarnations. Bihaṅgams, among Sikhs, are likewise holy men who do not marry and who shun worldly ambition and temptation. The object of their devotion is the One Supreme Being. They recite *gurbāṇī*, the Sikh canon, and devote themselves to *nām* and *sevā*. They do not form any separate sect; in fact, the most unworldly of the followers of different orders give themselves this name. For instance, several of the Nirmalā Sikhs take pride in calling themselves Bihaṅgams. They wear white and, instead of learned study of the holy texts which is customary with the Nirmalās, they occupy themselves with humbler deeds of service. Their most popular centre is at Mastūāṇā, near Saṅgrūr, in the Punjab. They interpret the word *bihaṅgam* as a construction from *haṅgatā*, Skt. *aham* = *ahantā*, meaning egoity or pride, a Bihaṅgam being one who discarding these takes to the path of humility.

BIBLIOGRAPHY

1. Rose, H.A., *A Glossary of the Tribes and Castes of the Punjab and North-West Frontier Province*. Patiala, 1970
2. *The Census Reports*.

B.S.N.

BIJAY BINOD, a chronicle in Punjabi verse of the turbulent period following the death in 1839 of Mahārājā Raṇjīt Siṅgh, the sovereign of the Punjab, written according to internal evidence in 1901 Bk/AD 1844. The only known manuscript of the work, still unpublished, is preserved in the private collection of Bhāī Haridhan Siṅgh of Bāgaṛīāṅ. The manuscript, which comprises 84 folios, with 495 stanzas, is dated 1921 Bk/AD 1864. The poetic metres used include Doharā, Soraṭhā, Bhujaṅg Prayāt and Kabitt. The work was undertaken by the poet, Gvāl, at the instance of Paṇḍit Jalhā, a close confidant of Hīrā Siṅgh Ḍogrā, prime minister to Raṇjīt Siṅgh's son, Mahārājā Duleep Siṅgh, and that explains much of his bias in favour of the Ḍogrās.

The work begins with verses eulogizing Raṇjīt Siṅgh who is deified as an incarnation of Lord Kṛṣṇa. Rājā Dhiān Siṅgh, the Ḍogrā minister, is presented as the incarnation of Arjuna (25). The author dwells at length on the qualities of Dhiān Siṅgh (26-36) and is at pains to establish that Dhiān Siṅgh and his son Hīrā Siṅgh were the real well-wishers of the Sikh state and personally loyal to the Mahārājā which was not true of the Sandhāṅvālīās, especially Atar Siṅgh, Lahiṇā Siṅgh and Ajīt Siṅgh. Ajīt Siṅgh Sandhāṅvālīā visits Calcutta to seek the help of the British against Mahārājā Sher Siṅgh (269-71), but, when he fails in his mission, he asks for royal forgiveness which he obtains through the intercession of Dhiān Siṅgh and Bedī Bikram Siṅgh. Dhiān Siṅgh is also stated to have secured, on Ajīt Siṅgh's request, the release of Lahiṇā Siṅgh Sandhāṅvālīā. The poet casts the Ḍogrās as the benefactors of the Sikh state and Sandhāṅvālīās as traitors. The work concludes with Hīrā Siṅgh's protestation of loyalty to the new king, Duleep Siṅgh. The poet's object obviously was to clear the Ḍogrās of the slur that had accrued to them because of their betrayal of the trust the Mahārājā had reposed in them. This has led to severe distortions of historical fact.

D.S.

BIJAI SIṄGH, by Bhāī Vīr Siṅgh, is a historical romance constructed around the heroic figure of Bijai Siṅgh, a fictitious character, through whose spiritual integrity it endeavours to delineate a whole people, its inspiration and way of life. First published in 1899, *Bijai Siṅgh* is the author's second novel and, like its predecessor *Sundarī* (*q.v.*), it is situated in the same 18th-century period of suffering and trial for the Sikhs. Bijai Siṅgh is in every sense an exemplary character. Born Rām Lāl in a Hindu Khatrī family of Lahore, he received the new name Bijai Siṅgh as, moved by the gallant deeds of the Sikhs, he, along with his wife and son, receives the initiatory rites and joins the ranks of the K͟hālsā. The family quits home to take refuge in a forest, but is spied upon and captured by a Mug͟hal troop. All efforts to convert Bijai Siṅgh to Islam and persuade his wife, Sushīl Kaur, to enter the Nawāb's harem fail. Bijai Siṅgh is released on the intercession of a Sūfī saint Sābir Shāh, and his wife and son, the six-year-old Varyām Siṅgh, sent to a detention camp. The Nawāb is still desirous of marrying Sushīl Kaur, but Murād Begam who, like her husband Mīr Mannū, is a historical character, protects her. After her husband's death in an action against the Sikhs, Murād Begam assumed power in Lahore.

Bijai Siṅgh joins the *jathā* or band of Sardār Karorā Siṅgh — that is a real name from Sikh history, but wounded in a battle, he again falls into captivity and is taken to Lahore. Here Murād Begam loses her heart to him and proposes marriage, exempting him from the condition of renouncing his faith and embracing Islam. He, however, spurns the offer. The Begam's intrigue to get rid of Sushīl Kaur by having her thrown into the rivers also fails. The Sikh spy Bijlā Siṅgh who happens to be around, picks her up as well as her son and brings them back to the camp of their leader, Karoṛā Siṅgh. While the mother and son regain health in the *jathā*, an attack is planned to get Bijai Siṅgh released. Although the plan succeeds, Bijai Siṅgh is wounded grievously. Back in the camp, he bleeds profusely and dies with the Gurū's name on his lips. Sushīl Kaur also breathes her last at the same moment. Their son, Varyām Siṅgh, is brought up by Karoṛā Siṅgh.

As the author himself proclaims in the preface, he wrote the novel with a view to resurrecting Sikh values and belief. The Sikh actors in the story are presented at their idealistic best. This makes plot as well as characterization somewhat tentative. Yet the novelist did succeed in his purpose of stirring the hearts of his readers. For them Bijai Siṅgh and Sushīl Kaur became real persons, embodying the Sikh virtues of faith, tenacity and sacrifice.

BIBLIOGRAPHY

1. Harbans Singh, *Bhai Vir Singh*. Delhi, 1972
2. Kohlī, Surindar Siṅgh, and Harnām Siṅgh Shān, eds., *Bhāī Vīr Siṅgh, Jīvan, Samāṅ te Rachnā*. Chandigarh, 1973

D.S.

BIKRAMĀ SIṄGH, KAṄVAR (1835-1887), one of the pioneers of the Siṅgh Sabhā movement, was born in 1835. He was the son of Rājā Nihāl Siṅgh of Kapūrthalā. As he grew up, he developed interest in classical learning and music. He received several honours and distinctions from the British government. During the 1857 uprising, he commanded a Kapūrthalā contingent of 300 men, horse and foot, and 2 guns to defend Hoshiārpur. He also assisted in the subjugation of Oudh at the head of a Kapūrthalā contingent. He was awarded the title of Sardār Bahādur and a large *jāgīr* in land, with a *khill'at*. He was an honorary magistrate at Jalandhar and in 1879 was appointed an honorary assistant commissioner and was decorated with the title of Companion of the Star of India (C.S.I.). He also served as president of the newly created Municipal Board of Jalandhar for a term.

Well versed in English, Persian, Sanskrit, and Punjabi, Kaṅvar Bikramā Siṅgh was a strong advocate of Western learning. He equally supported the cause of women's education. In 1882, he initiated the proposal for the establishment of a Khālsā college. He also felt concerned about the state of Sikh faith in his day and was one of the three original founders of the Siṅgh Sabhā established at Amritsar on 1 October 1873, the other two being Sardār Ṭhākur Siṅgh Sandhāṅvālīā and Bābā Khem Siṅgh. His more important, though indirect, contribution to the Siṅgh Sabhā movement was his patronage of the renowned Bhāī Gurmukh Siṅgh. Gurmukh Siṅgh was the promising son of one of his family servants whom he had brought up and educated with loving care. He now helped Bhāī Gurmukh Siṅgh with funds for setting up Khālsā Press at Lahore. This led to the launching in 1886 of the Punjabi weekly, *Khālsā Akhbār*, which played a major role in spreading Siṅgh Sabhā ideology. Kaṅvar Bikramā Siṅgh stood by Giānī Ditt Siṅgh and helped him financially when he became involved in a defamation case for the publication of his *Svapan Nāṭak* (*q.v.*), a satirical work which gave offence to the patrons of the Khālsā Dīwān of Amritsar. Kaṅvar Bikramā Siṅgh, as president of the Jalandhar Siṅgh Sabhā, always took the part of the Lahore Khālsā Dīwān. Besides the patronage, encouragement and active assistance he gave to scholars like Bhāī Gurmukh Siṅgh and Bhāī Ditt Siṅgh, he himself wrote a book, *Upmā Sār Granth*. Kaṅvar Bikramā Siṅgh died, after a short illness, on 8 May 1887.

BIBLIOGRAPHY

1. Jagīt Siṅgh, *Siṅgh Sabhā Lahir*. Ludhiana, 1974
2. Ganda Singh, ed., *The Singh Sabha and other Socio-Religious Movements in the Punjab*. Patiala, 1984
3. Harbans Singh, *The Heritage of the Sikhs*. Delhi, 1983

Gd.S.

BIKRAM SIṄGH BEDĪ, BĀBĀ (d.1863), was the third and youngest son of Sāhib Siṅgh Bedī of Ūnā, a lineal descendant of Gurū Nānak. On Sāhib Siṅgh's death in 1834, Bikram Siṅgh suceeded to his father's *jāgīrs* and position as preceptor to royal family of Lahore. After the deaths of Mahārājā Kharak Siṅgh and Prince Nau Nihāl Siṅgh, Bābā Bikram Siṅgh tried to bring about a reconciliation between Mahārājā Sher Siṅgh and his collateral Sandhāṅvālīā *sardārs*. Bābā Bikram Siṅgh felt irked when British troops were stationed at Lahore after the Anglo-Sikh war of 1845-46. He was a powerful *jāgīrdār* in the Jalandhar Doāb holding lands worth over two lakh of rupees comprising more than a dozen villages granted to him by Mahārājā Sher Siṅgh and Mahārājā Duleep Siṅgh, including the forts of Nūrpur, Gunāchaur and Dakkhṇī Sarāi. The British after the annexation of the Doāb in 1846 dispossessed him of arms, and reduced his *jāgīrs*. He, however, turned down the offer of a reduced pension and started organizing an armed opposition to the British in the hilly areas of the Śivāliks. Alarmed at his activities, Robert Cust, the deputy commissioner of Hoshiārpur, recommended to the commissioner of the Jalandhar Doāb, John Lawerence, that the Bābā be banished from the Punjab and sent to Haridvār. Bābā Bikram Siṅgh sent his emissaries to Dīwān Mūl Rāj of Multān and Sardār Chatar Siṅgh Aṭārīvalā, the governor of Hazārā, who had raised the banner of revolt against the British. In December 1848, he crossed the Beās at Srī Hargobindpur and joined forces with Rājā Sher Siṅgh Aṭārīvālā and fought the British in the battles of Chelīāṅvālā (13 January 1849) and Gujrāt (21 February 1849). He surrendered to the British along with the Aṭārīvālā *sardārs* at Rāwalpiṇḍī in March 1849. He was interned at Amritsar where he died in 1863.

BIBLIOGRAPHY

1. Griffin, Lepel, and C.F. Massy, *Chiefs and Families of Note in the Punjab*. Lahore, 1890
2. Kushwant Singh, *Ranjit Singh Maharajah of the Punjab*. Bombay, 1962
3. Sobhā Rām, *Gur-bilās Bābā Sāhib Siṅgh Bedī*. Ed. Gurmukh Singh. Patiala, 1988

J.S.K.

BIKRAM SIṄGH, RĀJĀ (1842-1898), born in January 1842, succeeded his father, Wazīr Siṅgh, to the throne of Farīdkoṭ state in 1874. A dominant figure in Farīdkoṭ history, Rājā Bikram Siṅgh modernized the state administration. He employed retired British officials of experience and in 1875 set up offices and courts on the British model and adopted British law. Schools and charitable hospitals were opened and *dharamsālās* and rest houses for travellers constructed. *Sadāvarats* or free kitchens were established at Farīdkoṭ, Thānesar and Amritsar. Sanskrit *pāṭhshālās*, or schools were started where free food was served to the students. In 1881, one-pice postal stamp was introduced in the state.

Rājā Bikarm Siṅgh had a religious bent of mind and was a leading figure in the Sikh renaissance at the turn of the 19th century. He was a patron of the Khālsā Dīwān, Amritsar, to which Siṅgh Sabhās then springing up in the Punjab were affiliated. Following the publication in 1877 of Ernest Trumpp's *The Ādi Granth,* not received favourably by the Sikhs, Rājā Bikram Siṅgh commissioned a full-scale commentary in Punjabi on the Holy Book. To this end, he appointed a distinguished synod of Sikh schoolmen of the period. The work which resulted from its labours is now famous as the *Farīdkoṭ Ṭīkā* and occupies an honoured place in the Sikh exegetical literature. At a public meeting of the Sikhs in Amritsar convened on 14 August 1897, Rājā Bikram Siṅgh announced in honour of Queen Victoria's Diamond Jubilee a donation of rupees one lakh for electricity to be brought to the premises of the Golden Temple and for a new building for the Gurū kā Laṅgar. He was among those Indian princes who were sympathetic to the cause of the deposed Mahārājā Duleep Siṅgh. He had holy shrines raised in memory of Sikh Gurūs and martyrs at Gurūsar, Lakkhī Jungle, Muktsar (Gurdwārā Shahīd Gañj) and Srīnagar. He was appointed a Fellow of the Pañjāb University to which he donated large sums of money.

Rājā Bikram Siṅgh died on 8 August 1898 and was succeeded by his son, Balbīr Siṅgh.

BIBLIOGRAPHY

1. Griffin, Lepel, *The Rajas of the Punjab*[Reprint]. Delhi, 1977

2. Harbans Singh, *Farīdkot Itihās Bāre*. Faridkot, 1947
3. Ganda Singh, *The Patiala and the East Panjab States Union: Historical Background*. Patiala, 1951

S.S.B.

BILĀSPUR, a small town 16 km from Jagādhrī (30°-10'N, 77°-18'E) in Ambālā district of Haryāṇā, is close to Kapāl Mochan, a well-known place of Hindu pilgrimage. Gurū Gobind Siṅgh is said to have sojourned at Kapāl Mochan for 52 days in 1688. During this period, he made a brief visit to Bilāspur. A small shrine now honours his memory. It is a single 12-cornered domed room, inside a quadrangle enclosed by a low wall. The shrine is administered by the Shiromaṇī Gurdwārā Parbandhak Committee through a local committee.

BIBLIOGRAPHY

1. Tārā Siṅgh, *Srī Gur Tīrath Saṅgrahi*. Amritsar, n.d.
2. Ṭhākar Siṅgh, *Srī Gurduāre Darshan*. Amritsar, 1923

Jg.S.

BILĀVAL. *See* SIKH DEVOTIONAL MUSIC

BILĀVAL KĪ VĀR, by Gurū Rām Dās, is one of his eight *vārs* in a corpus of twenty-two included in the Gurū Granth Sāhib. It occurs in Rāga Bilāval, and consists of thirteen *pauṛīs* or stanzas, each comprising five lines, with the exception of *pauṛī* 10 which is of six lines. To the *pauṛis* which are of Gurū Rām Dās's composition, *ślokas* were added by Gurū Arjan at the time of the compilation of the Holy Book. In its present form, each *pauṛī*, except *pauṛī* 7 which has three ślokas prefixed to it, is preceded by two *ślokas*. Of these twenty-seven *ślokas*, two are of the composition of Gurū Nānak, one of Gurū Rām Dās and the remaining of Gurū Amar Dās. Rāga Bilāval is the melody of bliss which, as the poem stresses, consists in contemplation on the Divine Name. This constant remembrance of God becomes possible only through the grace and guidance of the Gurū. He who takes refuge in the Gurū acquires the wealth of *nām* or Divine Name thereby attaining the state of *sahaj*, the highest state of spiritual progress in which ignorance and dualism are expelled. Such a person called a *gurmukh*, i.e. one turned towards the Gurū, is honoured everywhere and by all. By pursuing the teachings of the Gurū, he becomes a *jīvan-mukta*, i.e. one who has attained liberation while still living. The *Vār* reiterates some of the basic principles of Sikh thought. God has created this universe and sustains it. He is eternal and formless, self-existent and all-pervading, and yet transcendent. He cannot be conceived or explained in empirical terms. He is the Lord of the universe and His Will governs all. He through His grace releases men from the cycle of birth and death. The human soul partakes of the Divine, but man becomes ignorant of his true origin because of the influence of *māyā* and his *haumai* or egoity. Contemplation on His Name by following the Gurū's counsel is the only way to overcome *haumai*. He who has overcome his ego becomes permanently attuned to the Ultimate Reality. On the ethical plane, the poem denounces vices such as pride, slander, avarice and attachment. Truthfulness, humility and purity of thought are recognized as prized virtues.

BIBLIOGRAPHY

Bishan Siṅgh, Giānī, *Bāī Vārān Saṭīk*. Amritsar, n.d.

S.S.W.

BILGĀ, village 14 km west of Phillaur (31°-1'N, 75°-47'E) in the Punjab, is sacred to Gurū Arjan, who passed through it in June 1589 on his way to Mau where he got married. According to local tradition, Bilgā was then a small settlement of only a few huts. The Gurū changed his apparel here and gave away the discarded articles to the poor hut-dwellers who, it is said, preserved them as sacred relics. These are now exhibited in Gurdwārā Pañjvīṅ Pātshāhī located inside the village. They include a gown, a pair of trousers, a scarf, a handkerchief, a shawl, a purse, a small rosary and a low stool fitted with a brass sheet. The Gurdwārā, built on high ground, comprises a *dīvān* hall, with the sanctum at the far end where the Gurū Granth Sāhib is seated. Besides the relics, large-sized paintings depiciting scenes from Sikh history are also on display. The Gurdwārā is administered by the Shiromaṇī Gurdwārā Parbandhak Committee through a local committee. A largely-attended fair from 18 to 20 Hāṛ (early July) commemorates Guru Arjan's visit.

M.G.S.

BINOD SIṄGH, a Trehaṇ Khatrī in direct descent from Gurū Aṅgad, Nānak II, was a devoted disciple of Gurū Gobind Siṅgh and was among the few Sikhs who accompanied him to the South in 1708. He was chosen to be one of the five companions of Bandā Siṅgh (1670-1716) sent by the Gurū in 1708 from Nāndeḍ to the Punjab to chastise the persecutors of the Sikhs. Binod Siṅgh was Bandā Siṅgh's ally in the campaign he launched upon arrival in the Punjab. In the battle of Sirhind fought in May 1710, Binod Siṅgh commanded the left wing of Bandā Siṅgh's army. He was pitched against Sher Muhammad K͟hān of Mālerkoṭlā who was commander of Sūbahdār Wazīr K͟hān's right wing. After Bandā Siṅgh's conquest of the province of Sirhind, the frontier district of Karnāl, bordering on Delhi territory, was entrusted to Binod Siṅgh. Soon thereafter, in October 1710, Binod Siṅgh had to fight four battles – the first at Tarāoṛī, 12 km north of Karnāl, second at Amīn, 25 km north of Karnāl, third at Thānesar, 8 km farther north, and the fourth at Shāhābād, 22 km north of Thānesar.

In the schism in Bandā Siṅgh's ranks into Tatt K͟hālsā and Bandaī Sikhs in October 1714, Binod Siṅgh with his followers parted company with Bandā Siṅgh. He was, however, in two minds: he wanted to obey Mātā Sundari's command, and at the same time was unwilling to fight against Bandā Siṅgh. He remained at Amritsar. He was taken to Gurdās-Naṅgal in the Mug͟hal army to fight on their side. There he tried to retire without fighting. No sooner had Binod Siṅgh started moving away at the head of his men than he was attacked by the imperial forces on all sides. According to K͟hāfī K͟hān three to four thousand of his men were killed. Binod Siṅgh is believed to have lost his life in this massacre, too. That was in 1716.

BIBLIOGRAPHY

1. Ganda Singh, *Life of Banda Singh Bahadur*. Amritsar, 1935
2. Giān Siṅgh, Giānī, *Panth Prakāsh* [Reprint]. Patiala, 1970
3. Padam, Piārā Siṅgh, and Giānī Garjā Siṅgh, eds., *Gurū kīāṅ Sākhīāṅ*. Patiala, 1986

G.S.D.

BĪṚ, a term used for a recension or copy of the Gurū Granth Sāhib, is derived from Skt. verb *vīḍ* meaning "to make strong or firm, strengthen, fasten, or to be strong, firm or hard." The Punjabi verb *bīṛanā* which means "to fix, bind or fasten (something) firmly, or to lay (a gun)" is from the same root. Gurū Arjan having compiled the Holy Book deputed one of his leading disciples, Bhāī Banno, to go and get the volume bound in Lahore, perhaps because facilities for proper binding did not then exist at Amritsar. Bhāī Banno utilized the opportunity to have another copy transcribed and he got both volumes "fastened and bound." These bound copies came to be called the Ādi Bīṛ and Bhāī Bannovālī Bīṛ. Further copies made from these two recensions were also called *bīṛs*. For *bīṛs* (recensions) of Sikh Scripture, *see* SRĪ GURŪ GRANTH SĀHIB.

The word *bīṛ* in Punjabi is also used for reserved forest or village land set aside as common pasture.

M.G.S.

BĪṚ BĀBĀ BUḌḌHĀ JĪ, GURDWĀRĀ, in the revenue limits of the village of Ṭhaṭṭā, 20 km south of Amritsar, commemorates Bābā Buḍḍhā (1506-1631), the venerable Sikh of the time of Gurū Nānak who lived long enough to anoint five succeeding Gurūs. He spent many years looking after the *bīṛ*, lit. a reserved forest used for cattle-grazing, said to have been offered to Gurū Arjan by Chaudharī Laṅgāh of Paṭṭī out of his private lands. According to *Gurbilās Chhevīṅ Pātshāhī* it was here that Mātā Gaṅgā, the consort of Gurū Arjan, received from him on 21 Assū 1651 Bk/20 September 1594, the blessing for an illustrious son, the future Gurū Hargobind, Nānak VI. Gurdwārā Bīṛ Bābā Buḍḍhā Sāhib Jī, popularly known as simply Bīṛ Sāhib, is situated about 2 km north-west of Ṭhaṭṭā. The present complex was raised by Bābā Khaṛak Siṅgh, a follower of Sant Gurmukh Siṅgh Sevāvāle. The sanctum, where the Gurū Granth Sāhib is seated on a canopied seat of white marble, is a metre-high square platform at the far end of a rectangular hall constructed in 1951. The 70-metre square *sarovar* is to the north of this hall. A spacious *dīvān* hall was added in 1975. Gurū kā Laṅgar with a large dining hall and a two-storeyed residential block for pilgrims are in a separate compound. Besides, there is a K͟hālsā higher secondary school (established 1963) as well as a K͟hālsā college (established 1969), both named after Bābā Buḍḍhā. The Gurdwārā is managed by a local committee under the auspices of the Shiromaṇī Gurdwārā Parbandhak Committee. Besides the daily prayers and the celebration of important anniversaries on the Sikh calendar, largely-attended *dīvāns* take place on the first of each Bikramī month. The biggest function of the year is a religious fair held on 21st of Assū, corresponding with 6 October.

BIBLIOGRAPHY

1. *Gurbilās Chhevīṅ Pātshāhī*. Patiala, 1970
2. Satibīr Siṅgh, *Partakh Hari*. Jalandhar, 1977

Gn.S.

BĪR GURŪ, by Rabindranath Tagore, is a life-sketch in Bengali of Gurū Gobind Siṅgh (1666-1708), the last of the Ten Gurūs of the Sikh faith, emphasizing especially how he had prepared Sikhs to stand up to oppression and injustice. This is Tagore's first writing on Gurū Gobind Siṅgh published in 1885 in the Śrāban/July-August issue of the *Bālak*. The poet was then in his early twenties. Though no reference is made in the text to any earlier work on the Sikhs, Tagore (1861-1941) seems to have been familiar with the writings of Malcolm (*Sketch of the Sikhs)*, McGregor (*History of the Sikhs*) and Cunningham (*A History of the Sikhs*). According to him, Gurū Gobind Siṅgh spent the time between the martyrdom of his father, Gurū Teg͟h Bahādur (1675) and the creation of the K͟hālsā (1699) in seclusion along the banks of the Yamunā mastering different languages and literatures. His encounter with the armies of the hill *rājās* and troops of the Mug͟hal Emperor are described in some detail. Emperor Auraṅgzīb's invitation to the Gurū is said to have been the result of the alarm caused by the latter's victory in the battle of Muktsar (1705). The account of the Gurū's death at Nāndeḍ is based on McGregor's version which runs counter to historical facts.

H.B.

BIRK, village 10 km northeast of Jagrāoṅ (30°-47'N, 75°-28'E) in Ludhiāṇā district, is sacred to Gurū Hargobind who travelling in 1631 arrived here from Siddhvāṅ Kalāṅ. The Gurdwārā, called Mañjī Sāhib Chhevīṅ Pātshāhī, is outside the village to the south-west of it. The present complex raised in the 1970's, has a 15-metre square hall, with a pavilion of the same size in front. The Gurū Granth Sāhib is seated in a glass-panelled square room in the centre of the hall. A lotus dome covered with white and green glazed tile chips in mosaic pattern tops the three storeys of the square pavilions above the sanctum. The Gurū Granth Sāhib is also seated in the older building, a flat-roofed structure with a vaulted ceiling. The Gurdwārā is managed by a village committee. The biggest festival of the year comes off on 18 Sāvan, marking Gurū Hargobind's visit three and a half centuries ago.

BIBLIOGRAPHY

Gurbilās Chhevīṅ Pātshāhī. Patiala, 1970

Jg.S.

BĪR MRIGESH, full title *SRĪ BĪR MRIGESH GURBILĀS DEV TARŪ*, is a voluminous nineteenth-century work by Bhāī Sher Siṅgh, a disciple of Bābā Khudā Siṅgh (1786-1861), who completed it in 1911. In bold Gurmukhī typography, the book runs to 1912 pages, divided into two parts comprising 847 and 1065 pages, respectively. It contains accounts, in ample detail, of the lives of Bābā Sāhib Siṅgh Bedī, Bābā Bhāg Siṅgh of Kurī, Bābā Bīr Siṅgh of Nauraṅgābād and Bābā Khudā Siṅgh. The author refers to these luminaries as *gurū* and calls his book *gurbilās* (biography of the Gurūs). The phrase *Dev Tarū* added to title literally means godly tree and accordingly its sub-parts are called *skandhs* (branches). *Skandhs* are further sub-divided into *adhyāyas* (chapters). The first part called *Pūrvārdh*, lit. earlier half, contains two *skandhs* and 61 *adhyāyas* while Part II, Uttarārdh, lit. the latter half, has three *skandhs* and 84 *adhyāyas*. The author describes the four holy men as spiritual adepts of the highest rank, and revels in a detailed exposition of their views. The language the author uses is *sādhūkaṛī*, a dialect common among the *sādhūs*, and the style is anecdotal.

G.S.G.

BĪR SIṄGH, BĀBĀ (1768-1844), soldier-become-religious preacher and saint, was born in July 1768 at the village of Gaggobūā, in Amritsar district of the Punjab, the son of Sevā Siṅgh and Dharam Kaur. After the death of his father in one of the campaigns against the Afghān rulers of Multān, Bīr Siṅgh joined the Sikh army. He participated in Mahārājā Raṇjīt Siṅgh's campaigns for the capture of Kashmīr and Peshāwar. After several years of active service, he secured his dismissal from the army as he came under the influence of Bābā Bhāg Siṅgh, a Sikh saint belonging to Kurī, in Rāwalpiṇḍī district. Bīr Siṅgh took to preaching Gurū Nānak's word and soon attracted a considerable following in the Mājhā area. He set up his *ḍerā* in the village of Nauraṅgābād, near Tarn Tāran. The *ḍerā*, named Santpurā, became a popular pilgrim centre and it is said that about 4,500 visitors were fed in the *laṅgar* every day. Such was the influence Bābā Bīr Siṅgh had acquired that a volunteer army of 1,200 musket men and 3,000 horse attended upon him.

Bābā Bīr Siṅgh was a true well-wisher of the dynasty of Raṇjīt Siṅgh and was deeply grieved at the disaster which had overtaken it through the envy of the courtiers after the death of the Mahārājā in 1839. During that critical period, Sikh soldiers and peasantry began to turn to him for guidance. On 2 May 1844, Atar Siṅgh Sandhāṅvālīā, who had been in residence in British India for some time, crossed the Sutlej into Sikh territory and joined Bābā Bīr Siṅgh who was then camping near Harīke Pattan. Prince Kashmīrā Siṅgh and Prince Pashaurā Siṅgh and many Sikh *sardārs*, including Jawāhar Siṅgh Nalvā, son of the celebrated Sikh general Harī Siṅgh Nalvā, and Dīwān Baisākhā Siṅgh, had already taken asylum at Bīr Siṅgh's *ḍerā*. Bīr Siṅgh's camp had become the centre of Sikh revolt against Ḍogrā dominance over the Punjab. Perturbed at these developments, Hīrā Siṅgh, the Ḍogrā prime minister of the Sikh kingdom, sent a strong force comprising 20,000 men and 50 guns under the command of Mīāṅ Lābh Siṅgh to attack the citadel of

Bābā Bīr Siṅgh. The troops besieged the camp on 7 May 1844. Bābā Bīr Siṅgh forbade his Sikhs to fight back saying, "How can we attack our own brethren?" He was in meditation in the presence of the Holy Book, when he was killed with a shell from the besiegers. Prince Kashmīrā Siṅgh and Atar Siṅgh Sandhāṅvālīā also lost their lives in the heavy cannonade and, in the panic, hundreds of Bābā Bīr Siṅgh's followers were drowned in the river while trying to cross it. The troops, however, never forgave Hīrā Siṅgh for forcing them into an action which led to the death of a holy man. He tried to atone for what had happened by promising to build a *samādh* where Bābā Bīr Siṅgh had been cremated, and set aside land yielding Rs 5,000 annually for its maintenance, but his critics were far from assuaged. He had to pay for this onslaught on Nauraṅgābād with his own life before the year was out. General Court's battalion, which had played a leading part in the action, was boycotted when it reached the headquarters and was always referred to as *gurūmār* (killer of the *gurū* or holy man).

BIBLIOGRAPHY

1. Smyth, G. Carmichael, *A History of the Reigning Family of Lahore*. Patiala, 1970
2. Bhagat Singh, *Maharaja Ranjit Singh and His Times. Delhi, 1990*
3. *Ganda Singh, ed., The Panjab in 1839-40*. Amritsar, 1952
4. Sher Singh, *Srī Bīr Mrigesh Gur Bilās Dev Tarū*.

J.S.K.

BĪṚS OF THE GURŪ GRANTH SĀHIB. *See* SRĪ GURŪ GRANTH SĀHIB

BISHAMBHAR DĀS, a businessman of Ujjain, was a devoted Sikh of the time of Gurū Gobind Siṅgh (1666-1708).

See DHIĀN SIṄGH of Mājrī

P.S.P.

BISHAN DĀS, BHĀĪ, a devoted Sikh of the time of Gurū Rām Dās, Nānak IV. His name is included in the roster of prominent Sikhs in Bhāī Gurdās, *Vārāṅ*, XI. 17.

See PŪRO, BHĀĪ

BIBLIOGRAPHY

1. Gurdās, Bhāī, *Vārāṅ*.
2. Manī Siṅgh, Bhāī, *Sikhāṅ dī Bhagat Mālā*. Amritsar, 1955

Gr.S.

BISHAN KAUR, mother of Mātā Gujarī and wife of Lāl Chand, was a woman gifted with good looks and fortune. Both husband and wife were the devoted Sikhs of Gurū Hargobind. They were among the guests assembled to witness the nuptial ceremonies of Sūraj Mall, son of Gurū Hargobind. It was there that she, as says *Gurbilās Pātshāhī Chhevīṅ*, had had a glimpse of young Tegh Bahādur who later occupied the holy office as the ninth Gurū of the Sikhs. She felt charmed by the handsome face of the young man and was doubly pleased to learn that he was still unaffianced. She saw him as the prospective groom for her seven-year old daughter, Gujarī. She and her husband went to Gurū Hargobind who willingly accepted the proposal. The marriage of Mātā Gujarī and Gurū Tegh Bahādur was solemnized on 9 Phāgun 1689 Bk/4 February 1633.

BIBLIOGRAPHY

1. *Guṛbilās Pātshāhī Chhevīṅ*. Patiala, 1970
2. Trilochan Singh, *Guru Tegh Bahadur*. Delhi, 1967
3. Harbans Singh, *Guru Tegh Bahadur*. Delhi, 1982

M.G.S.

BISHAN SIṄGH, a general in the Sikh army, was the adopted son of Jamādār Khushāl Siṅgh, the royal chamberlain (*deoṛhīdār*). He received his education at the Ludhiāṇā Mission School across the Anglo-Sikh frontier. In 1848, when stationed at Piṇḍ Dādan Khān, Bishan Siṅgh was ordered to move his troops to assist Herbert Edwardes, the British resident's assistant at Bannū, who was then marching against Dīwān Mūl Rāj at Multān. A few months after, his troops revolted and joined the insurrectionists, but Bishan Siṅgh sided with the British and joined Lord Gough's camp. For this he was rewarded with a pension by the British government..

BIBLIOGRAPHY

1. Sūrī, Sohan Lāl, *'Umdāt-ut-Twārīkh*. Lahore, 1885-89
2. Griffin, Lepel, and C.F.Massy, *Chiefs and Families of Note in the Punjab*. Lahore, 1909
3. Chopra, B.R., *Kingdom of the Punjab*. Hoshiarpur, 1969
4. Edwardes, Herbert, *A Year on the Punjab Frontier in 1848-49*. London, 1851
5. Gulcharan Singh, *Ranjit Singh and His Generals*. Jalandhar, n.d.

Gl.S.

BISHAN SIṄGH(d. 1868) was like his father, Sultān Siṅgh, in the Ghoṛchaṛhā regiment of Mahārājā Raṇjīt Siṅgh. In Mahārājā Sher Siṅgh's time, he was placed in charge of the artillery park at Lahore. After the annexation of the Punjab by the British, Bishan Siṅgh joined the 2nd Punjab Irregular Cavalry raised in 1849, and received the rank of Risāldār. During the uprising of 1857, he marched to Delhi with a squadron commanded by Sir Dighton Macnaghten Probyn and served his new masters with distinction. General Probyn writes of him: "He must have been in fifty fights; a braver man I never saw. He knew not what fear was, and delighted in danger. He was conspicuous for his gallantry on many occasions." For his services, Bishan Siṅgh received the Order of Merit and was shortly afterwards appointed Risāldār-Major of his regiment.

Bishan Siṅgh died in 1868.

BIBLIOGRAPHY

1. Sūrī, Sohan Lāl, *'Umdāt-ut-Twārīkh*. Lahore, 1885-89
2. Griffin, Lepel, and C.F.Massy, *Chiefs and Families of Note in the Punjab*. Lahore, 1909

S.S.B.

BISHAN SIṄGH, GIĀNĪ (1875-1966), cleric and exegete, was a *granthī* or priest at the Khālsā College at Amritsar for 30 years. The Khālsā College was then a premier Sikh college excelling in research and publication in the field of Sikh studies. Four of the foremost Sikh scholars of this period, namely Bhāī Jodh Siṅgh, Professor Tejā Siṅgh, Bhāī Sāhib Siṅgh and Dr Gaṇḍā Siṅgh, were members of the college faculty and between them they brought about a major enlightenment in Sikh letters. Bhāī Bishan Siṅgh imbibed much of their passion for learning. He took turns with them at expounding the holy text at the daily morning service at the College Gurdwārā. He also put his hand to preparing a full-scale commentary of the Holy Granth which was completed in 1945.

Bishan Siṅgh was born around 1875, the son of Bhāī Bulākā Siṅgh of the village of Lakkhūvāl in Amritsar district of the Punjab. After learning barely to read and write Punjabi he left home to go to Lahore to study the Sikh classic *Srī Gur Pratāp Sūraj Granth* with Bhāī Hīrā Siṅgh, a noted scholar of the Sikh texts in those days. Apprenticeship with him earned Bishan Siṅgh proficiency in Braj Bhāshā as well as in Sikh history. He then shifted to Amritsar, where he remained under the tutelage of Giānī Jodh Siṅgh and Giānī Bakhshīsh Siṅgh. In one of his books Giānī Bishan Siṅgh has mentioned Giānī Sant Siṅgh of Kapūrthalā also as his *vidyādātā* (teacher). Under these scholars, he mastered the subtleties of Sikh philosophical thought.

At Amritsar, he obtained employment as *granthī* at the Khālsā Collge in 1909, retiring from the position in 1939-40, as he attained the age of sixty-five. As the College *granthī*, Bishan Siṅgh made very good use of his time making the most of the library facilities available and of his contacts with the learned faculty. He found himself in full agreement with the new exegetical trends, breaking away from the traditional pedantic, Vedāntic style. He started working on his own *ṭīkā* or annotation of the Gurū Granth Sāhib, the first volume of which was published in 1918 and the eighth and the final in 1945. He also produced a full-length *ṭīkā* of the voluminous *Dasam Granth*. Among his other textual commentaries are *Ṭīkā Bāī Vārāṅ, Ṭīkā Bhagat Bāṇī, Ṭīkā Sahaskritī Salok, Ṭīkā Vārāṅ Bhāī Gurdās* and *Ṭīkā Kabitt Savaiyye Bhāī Gurdās*. Before launching upon his exegetical works, Giānī Bishan Siṅgh had written small books with titles such as *Twārīkh Gurū kā Bāgh, Bandā Bahādur, Shahīd Khālsā, Sher Khālsā, Sūrbīr Khālsā* and *Mahārāj Khālsā*. Noted among his other works are *Sāruktāvalī Saṭīk, Sākhī Pramāṇ* and *Vichārmālā Saṭīk*.

Giānī Bishan Siṅgh's exposition of the sacred texts is marked by a simple and direct style of writing, unencumbered by loaded jargon or verbiage. He was always concise, even though at places his explanations lacked literary elegance and finish.

After his retirement from the Khālsā College, Giānī Bishan Siṅgh returned to his native village Lakkhūvāl, where he carried on with his scholarly pursuits with unabated zeal. He also taught beginners who came to seek his advice.

Giānī Bishan Siṅgh died in his village in 1966.

BIBLIOGRAPHY

1. Tāran Siṅgh, *Gurbāṇī dīāṅ Viākhiā Pranālīāṅ*. Patiala, 1980
2. Bishan Siṅgh, *Srī Gurū Granth Sāhib Saṭīk*. Amritsar, 1918-1945

S.S.Am.

BISHAN SIṄGH, SANT (1862-1949), much honoured in recent Sikh piety, was the son of Bhāī Atar Siṅgh of Kāñjhlā, a village 18 km northwest of Saṅgrūr (30°-14'N, 75°-50'E) in the Punjab. Born in March 1862, Bishan Siṅgh received instruction in reciting Scripture from Sant Jagat Siṅgh of his own village. As he grew up he enlisted in the army, but did not serve long. Back in his village after getting his discharge, he married and had a son, whose death at the age of 13 years proved a severe blow. He left home to seek spiritual solace at the feet of Sant Atar Siṅgh of Mastūāṇā, and served him at Gur Sāgar (Mastūāṇā) and Gurū Kāshī (Talvaṇḍī Sābo). In 1935, he became the head of the centre founded by Sant Atar Siṅgh after the death of Sant Gulāb Siṅgh (also originally from Kāñjhlā) who had held the office since the passing away in 1927 of the founder. Sant Bishan Siṅgh completed in 1936-37 the present building of the historical Gurdwārā Jhiṛā Sāhib at Kāñjhlā, whose foundation had been laid by Sant Atar Siṅgh himself as early as 1912. Sant Bishan Siṅgh died in 1949 at a place called Koṭhī Bālevāl. His death anniversary is observed with much religious fervour in the month of August every year.

BIBLIOGRAPHY

1. Visākhā Siṅgh, Sant, *Mālvā Itihās*. Kishanpura, 1954
2. Balwant Siṅgh, Giānī, *Agam Agādh Purakh Shrīmān Pūjya Sant Atar Siṅgh Jī Mahārāj Mastūāṇe Vāliāṅ dā Sampūran Jīvan Charittar*. Mastuana, 1983
3. Tejā Siṅgh, *Jīvan Kathā Gurmukh Piāre Sant Atar Siṅgh Jī Mahārāj*. Patiala, 1970

M.G.S.

BISHAN SIṄGH, SANT (d. 1973), holy saint most of whose life was spent in works of *sevā*, raising of buildings by labour volunteered by devotees, at different shrine sites, came of a well-to-do Sindhī family. Nothing is known about his early life except that his parents were Sahajdhārī Sikhs and that he was in government service when he came in 1940 to the Punjab on a pilgrimage visiting Sikh places of worship and saw Sant Gurmukh Siṅgh of Paṭiālā, then engaged in massive works of *sevā* reconstructing the shrines and sacred pools at Khaḍūr Sāhib and Goindvāl. Bishan Siṅgh was so impressed by the piousness, humility and devotion of Sant Gurmukh Siṅgh and of the large number of Sikhs volunteering their labour that he resigned his post in the government, gave away his personal belongings and joined the holy company. He worked day and night like others, digging and carrying loads on his head. This inspired spell was interrupted by the death on 30 November 1947 of Sant Gurmukh Siṅgh. In a state of shock Bishan Siṅgh retired to Srī Abchalnagar, sacred to Gurū Gobind Siṅgh, where he remained in solitary meditation for more than five years. Returning to the Punjab, he took to his task with his old zest. Among the works undertaken were the beautification of the Bāolī Sāhib at Goindvāl and completion of Gurdwārā Qatalgaṛh at Chamkaur Sāhib. The last major project he was associated with was the construction of a spacious *dīvān* or congregation hall, at Gurdwārā Mañjī Sāhib, within the precincts of the Darbār Sāhib at Amritsar. He was one of the Pañj Piāre who performed its foundation-laying ceremony on 13 November 1969, which marked the 500th birth anniversary of Gurū Nānak, but did not live to see it completed. He suffered an attack of paralysis in November 1972 and although, responding to treatment and recovering partially, he had resumed supervision of *sevā*, he died on 22 November 1973.

P.S.G.

BISHNŪ, BHĀĪ, an Aroṛā of Bībṛā *gotra*, was a Sikh of Guru Arjan's time. He dedicated his life to the service of the Gurū, who appointed him to serve the *saṅgat*, especially those coming from afar. Bishnū would get up early in the morning and would in winter lay hot water for the pilgrims' bath. He rejoiced in washing the feet of the Sikhs with his own hands. Bhāī Bishnū, says the *Sikhāṅ dī Bhagat Mālā*, attained liberation through service and dedication.

BIBLIOGRAPHY

1. Gurdās, Bhāī, *Vārāṅ*.
2. Manī Siṅgh, Bhāī, *Sikhāṅ dī Bhagat Mālā*. Amritsar, 1955

T.S.

BOARD OF ADMINISTRATION, a set of triumvirs appointed by Lord Dalhousie, the British governor-general to manage affairs in the Punjab after its annexation on 29 March 1849 to the dominions of the East India Company. The Board consisted of three members. Henry Lawrence, the British resident at Lahore, was named president and entrusted with matters connected with defence and relations with the *sardārs* while his brother, John Lawrence, was put in charge of land settlement. Charles Grenville Mansel, a covenanted civilian, was entrusted with the administration of justice. He was replaced by Robert Montgomery after an year. The Board, placed directly under the control of the governor-general, was made the final court of appeal with powers of life and death.

The two regions, the cis-Sutlej and the trans-Sutlej, were reunited under the Board and the Punjab, along with the trans-Indus territories, now comprised an area of about 73,000 square miles. Its population was roughly estimated at ten million. The Board split the entire region into seven effectively controllable divisions each under a commissioner with headquarters at Ambālā, Jalandhar, Lahore, Jehlum, Rāwalpiṇḍī, Leiah and Multān. These divisions were further divided into districts controlled by 29 deputy commissioners and 43 assistant commissioners. In 1850 the districts of Hazārā, Peshāwar and Kohāṭ were joined together to form the eighth division. In the five-tiered administration, the divisional commissioners were next to the Board. Below the commissioners were deputy commissioners, and then assistant commissioners and extra assistant commissioners. This last cadre was specially constituted to provide jobs for such of the local people as had filled offices of trust under the Sikh Darbār. The lowest-grade gazetted officer was the *tahsīldār*. These officers were paid handsomely, monthly salary of a commissioner being Rs 2,750 and of the deputy commissioners in the first grade Rs 1,500, in the second Rs 1,200 and in the third Rs 1,000. The commissioners and deputy commissioners exercised both executive and judicial powers. The former acted as superintendents of revenue and police and as the appellate authority in civil and criminal cases as sessions judges. The deputy commissioners were collectors of revenue and magistrates, and tried civil suits above the value of Rs 1,000.

The Board of Administration had to deal with a disgruntled aristocracy and with the masses who had a strong feeling of antipathy towards their conquerors. The Punjab's cities and villages were placarded with notices demanding the surrender of arms. In a short while, 1,19,796 arms—swords and matchlocks, a few pieces of cannon, rifles and other weapons—were recovered. All military grants of Sikh times were abolished. The Guides Corps, raised by Henry Lawrence as resident in 1846 and now expanded to include troops of horse as well as of infantry, was charged with maintaining peace in the Ḍerājāt and guarding the chain of fortresses which were built to prevent tribal incursions from the northwest. For internal security ten regiments, five cavalry and five infantry, were raised. Some of the Darbār's soldiers were absorbed into these regiments. A military police force consisting of 8,000 men, largely Punjabi Muslims, was recruited. A secret intelligence *khufiā* service consisting of informers and detectives was attached to the police to alert the government to the prevailing temper of the people. The old village watch-and-ward system was revived. Village watchmen—*chaukīdārs*—were expected to keep police informed of the movements of any strangers. Special precautions were taken in the Mājhā area where the rebel Sikh Bhāī Mahārāj Siṅgh and his associates were reported to be active.

Once the peace of the province was assured, the Board started on a programme of works of public weal. The Grand Trunk Road from Peshāwar to Delhi was reopened. The Haṅslī canal or Shāh Nahar, which supplied water to the temple-tanks in Amritsar and to the Shālāmār Gardens in Lahore was cleared, and work was started to extend it and to dig branch canals. Trees were planted on canal banks and alongside the roads. Rest houses were built to accommodate the officials on tour, and afforestation of barren lands was undertaken. Land-holders were encouraged to plant trees and coppice lands were exempted from taxation. One of the Board's major concerns was to win over the peasantry. New varieties of crops were introduced to improve agriculture and a variety of root crops began to be grown in the plains. The revenue system was reorganized. Rules governing inheritance of property were given legal sanction. Since the *tahsīldār* was the only official conversant with these rules and customs, he was entrusted with the necessary judicial powers. Village *pañchāyats* were allowed to function in less important matters affecting the rural community. In cities, town councils were constituted to advise and assist English magistrates on civil matters. Practices such as the killing of female infants and *satī* were forbidden.

The working of the Board was affected by the differences between Henry Lawrence and his brother, John. In their mutual disputes, Lord Dalhousie openly sided with the latter. The conflict came to a head when both brothers put in their resignation at the beginning of 1853. Governor-General Dalhousie abolished the Board on 4 February 1853, transferred Henry Lawrence to Rājpūtānā and appointed John Lawrence chief commissioner of the Punjab. This change was more a matter of form, for John Lawrence continued to be in power assisted by two "principal commissioners." Montgomery remained in charge of judiciary as well as of education, roads, police, local and municipal administration. George Edmonstone was appointed financial commissioner.

BIBLIOGRAPHY

1. *First Administration Report of the Panjab,* 1849-51
2. Smith, Vincent, A., *The Oxford History of India.*Oxford, 1958
3. Khushwant Singh, *A History of the Sikhs,* vol. 2. Princeton, 1966
4. Gough, Sir C., and A.D. Innes, *The Sikhs and the Sikh Wars.* London, 1897
5. Hasrat, B.J., *Anglo-Sikh Relations.* Hoshiarpur, 1968

H.R.G.

BODAL, village 4 km south of Dasūyā (31°-49'N, 75°-39'E) in Hoshiārpur district of the Punjab, is sacred to Gurū Hargobind (1595-1644) who once visited here during a hunting expedition and rested under a *garnā* tree (*Capparis horrida*) for some time. Bhāī Chūhaṛ, a Muslim bard of the village, entertained him by playing on his rebeck. The Gurū advised him to learn to perform *kīrtan*, i.e. the singing of sacred hymns. The tree about 200 metres southwest of the village under which Gurū Hargobind had sat came to be known as Garnā Sāhib. Gurdwārā Garnā Sāhib was first established during the time of Sardār Jodh Siṅgh (d. 1816), leader of the Rāmgaṛhīā *misl*, in whose territory Bodal then lay. Later, Bhāī Īshar Siṅgh Rāmgaṛhīā of Taqīpur, a village 6 km northeast of Bodal, constructed the present marble-floored octagonal domed room with the sanctum in the middle and a covered passage around it for circumambulation. The old *garnā* tree still stands close to it. Further additions to the building have been made during recent times. An imposing three-storeyed gateway came up in 1972; a spacious mosaic-floored *dīvān* hall was constructed in 1980; and a new dining hall was added to Gurū kā Laṅgar in 1984. The Gurdwārā is administered by the Shiromaṇī Gurdwārā Parbandhak Committee through a local committee. Besides the daily services and celebration of major Sikh anniversaries, a religious fair is held on the occasion of Baisākhī (mid-April) every year.

Gn.S.

BODALĀ, BHĀĪ, a Sikh of Burhānpur included by Bhāī Gurdās, *Vārāṅ*, XI. 30, in the roster of prominent Sikhs of the time of Gurū Hargobind.

See BHAGVĀN DĀS, BHĀĪ

BIBLIOGRAPHY

1. Gurdās, Bhāī, *Vārāṅ.*
2. Manī Siṅgh, Bhāī, *Sikhāṅ dī Bhagat Mālā.* Amritsar, 1955

B.S.

BOLE SO NIHĀL, SATI SRĪ AKĀL is the Sikh slogan or *jaikārā* (lit. shout of victory,triumph or exultation). It is divided in two parts or phrases. The first, *bole so nihāl* or *jo bole so nihāl,* is a statement meaning "whoever utters (the phrase following) shall be happy, shall be fulfilled," and the second part *sati srī akāl* (Eternal is the Holy/ Great Timeless Lord). This *jaikārā,* first popularized by Gurū Gobind Siṅgh, Nānak X, has become, besides being a popular mode of expressing ebullient religious fervour or a mood of joy and celebration, an integral part of Sikh liturgy and is shouted at the end of *ardās* or prayer, said in *saṅgat* or holy congregation. One of the Sikhs in the *saṅgat,* particularly the one leading *ardās,* shouts the first phrase, *jo bole so nihāl,* in response to which the entire congregation, including in most cases the leading Sikh himself utter in unison *sati srī akāl* in a long-drawn full-throated shout. The *jaikārā* or slogan aptly expresses the Sikh belief that all victory (*jaya* or *jai*) belongs to God, Vāhigurū, a belief that is also expressed in the Sikh salutation *Vāhigurū jī kā Khālsā, Vāhigurū jī kī Fateh* (Khālsā is of God and to God belongs the victory, or Hail the Gurū's Khālsā! Hail the Gurū's victory!!) In their hour of triumph, therefore, the Sikhs remember *sati srī akāl* instead of exulting in their own valour.

Traditionally, the slogan or war-cry expressing communal fervour and assent to or enthusiasm for a cause, *sat srī akāl* has been so used through the three-hundred-year-old history of the Sikh people, since the creation of the Khālsā. In a normal situation when two Sikhs meet, they exchange greetings pronouncing Sat Srī Akāl thus pointing out the glory of God to each other. Although as a salutation it is by now the established form of Sikh greeting, it does not have the sanction of history or orthodoxy. Vāhigurū jī kā Khālsā Vāhigurū jī kī Fateh, the other form of salutation, is generally used only by people punctilious in the observance of proper form. Those addressing a Sikh religious congregation will, as a rule, greet the audience with the salutation, Vāhigurū jī kā Khālsā Vāhigurū jī kī Fateh. Sat Srī Akāl shouted in unison responding to the call *jo bole so nihāl* (whoever so pronounces shall prosper) is a call to action, or expression of ecstatic joy or an invocation for Divine aid or succour. While *sat* or *sati* (Sanskrit *satya*) means 'true', 'good', 'abiding', 'real' and 'eternal', *srī* is an honorific denoting beauty, glory, grace or majesty. *Sati* has the sanction of Gurū Nānak's Mūl Mantra in the *Japu* where after Ik Oṅkār, it appears as a constituent of Satināmu (Reality Eternal). *Akāl* also occurs in Mūl Mantra in the phrase Akāl Mūrati (Form Eternal), descriptive of the Absolute.

Akāl as the Divine name appealed particularly to Gurū Gobind Siṅgh, as his philosophical vision of the cosmos and the human life centred around this concept. *Akāl* means 'Timeless' or 'Transcending Time.' Time being the consuming element, making for birth, decay and death, in Gurū Gobind Siṅgh's vision the most essential attribute lying at the core of human conception of the Divine is Its timeless quality. *Kāl* is Sanskrit for time and in common parlance stands for death—more precisely, the inevitable hour of death. Fear being fear of death basically, in Gurū Gobind Siṅgh's metaphysical thinking and moral philosophy, to make the Timeless the centre of one's faith is the way to banish fear and to make heroes of ordinary mortals. Consequently, the inevitability of death and the futility of fear are among the principal themes of Gurū Gobind Siṅgh's teaching. In his compositions there are several verbal formations from *kāl* (time) which express his vision. God is Sarab Kāl (Lord of All-Time), Akāl-Purakh (the Eternal Pervasive Reality) and has all the attributes arising from His quality of Timelessness. Gurū Gobind Siṅgh's principal composition of adoration is entitled *Akāl Ustati* (Laudation of the Timeless). In places, the Gurū has identified God with Time or All-Time, that is eternity. The opening line of one of his hymns reads: *keval kāl ī kartār* (the All-Time, i.e. the Eternal alone is the Creator). This by implication repudiates the claim of Brahmā, one aspect of the Hindu trinity or of other deities, to be the true creator.

Akāl occurs at four places in the *Vārāṅ* of Bhāī Gurdās. In each context it conveys the sense of God the Eternal, Timeless. By the time of Bhāī Gurdās, whose active life spanned the periods of Gurū Arjan and Gurū Hargobind, this term was familiar and well established in the Sikh tradition, and consequently when Gurū Gobind Siṅgh picked it out to make it the vehicle for expressing his deepest inspiration, he was only enriching a concept already a constituent of the philosophical milieu of the Sikh people.

As reported by the royal news-writer, when in 1699 the new initiation by *amrit* was introduced by Gurū Gobind Siṅgh, for days afterwards the whole atmosphere around Anandpur, the venue of the baptismal ceremonies, was resounding with cries of Akāl, Akāl. This referred to the shouts of Sat Srī Akāl incessantly raised by the converts to the Khālsā faith filled with new fervour. In subsequent times, after the Sikhs acquired political power in the Punjab, the seal of the Sikh chiefs would bear the inscription, *Akāl Sahāi* (Akāl be our Succourer). The most militant section of the Sikh crusaders, the Nihaṅgs were called Akālīs (followers of Akāl). During the early 1920's, when the Sikh people were fired with a new reformist and patriotic zeal, the party spearheading these programmes took to itself the name Akālī, which is politically still a viable term.

The Sikh form of greeting or salutation has its individual significance and character. It is different from the Islamic salutation in which blessings of peace are sought for each other (*salām 'alaikum, wa'alaikum salām*). It is distinct also from Indian greetings (*namaste* or *namaskār*) which aim at paying homage or respects to the person addressed. The Sikh greeting exchanged with folded hands on either side in mutual courtesy and respect is essentially an utterance of laudation to the Timeless and an expression of faith in human unity and dignity.

Over the years, the boundaries between the Sikh slogan and Sikh greeting have become interlocked. *Sat srī akāl* which is part of the Sikh slogan is now the general form of Sikh greeting. This has usurped the place of the more formal and proper salutation which also carries the sanction of Sikh theological postulates, i.e. *Vāhigurū jī kā Khālsā Vāhigurū jī kī Fateh.* The Sikh mode of salutation has gone through a long-drawn process of evolution. The earliest form of Sikh salutation was *Pairī Pauṇā*. In one of the life-accounts of Gurū Nānak known as *Ādi Sākhīāṅ*, the injunction is said to have come down from the Almighty Himself. One day, it is recorded, the Formless (Niraṅkār) called Bābā Nānak into His presence and said :

> Nānak, I am greatly pleased with you ... Listen Nānak. I do, hereby, ordain a separate Order of yours. In the Kaliyug I shall be known as the True Lord and you as the Preceptor Lord ... And, I bless you with a unique Order. The greeting of your order shall be *Pairī Pauṇā* (I bow at your feet), whereas the greeting of the Vaiṣṇavas shall be *Rām Kishan*, of the Sannyāsīs, *Om Namo Nārāyaṇāya,* of the Yogīs, *Ādeśa*, and of the Muhammdans, *Salām 'Alaikum.*
>
> But O Nānak, all those who come into your fold, shall greet one another with *Pairī Pauṇā*, the reply in each case being *Satgurū Ko Pairī Pauṇā*.

This quotation is from a seventeenth-century compilation. We have still an earlier testimony vouchsafing that in the early days of Sikhism, the Sikhs had, as their greeting, *Pairī Pauṇā* and the practice of touching each other's feet. Bhāī Gurdās, a contemporary of the Fifth and Sixth Gurūs, mentions the practice of *pairī pauṇā*, i.e. touching the feet, in very clear terms. He writes :

> (In the Court of Gurū Nānak)
> The Ruler and the pauper were equal.
> He brought into vogue the practice of bowing at each other's feet.
> What a wonderful feat the Beloved wrought !
> Lo, the head bows at the feet.
>
> ***
>
> Do not give up the practice of bowing at others' feet. For in the Kaliyug this is the path.
>
> ***
>
> A Sikh should adopt the practice of bowing at another's feet ; He should listen to the advice of the (other)

Gursikh, and ponder over what he says.

These examples can be multiplied and even supplemented with *sākhīs* (stories) from the *Purātan Janam Sākhī* and even from the Janam Sākhī of Gurū Nānak by Miharbān. Both these life-accounts contain numerous stories to show the prevalence of this form of greeting at an early stage of the evolution of the Sikh Panth.

In the *Bālā Janam Sākhī* occurs a different form of greeting. Instead of *Pairī Pauṇā* of the *Purātan* cycle and of the *Miharbān* tradition, we have here, *Kartār Kartār* (Creator! Creator!) meaning let us bow to the Lord, and *Sat Kartār* (Creator is True). This, we are told, was anterior to the former. Even Miharbān himself writes:

> At that time whosoever of the Sikhs came, he did not greet others with the word, *Pairī Pae Jī*, nor would the addressee say, *Satgurū Ko Pairī Pauṇā*. On the contrary, whosoever came, he would greet others saying, "Kartār, Kartār, O' Sikhs of the Gurū, Kartār, Kartār." All the Sikhs who came to Gurū Nānak, too greeted him saying, "Kartār, Kartār." The congregation was known as the Kartārīs.

Supporting evidence may be found in Gurū Nānak naming the town he raised on the bank of the River Rāvī, Kartārpur. Besides, we have the testimony of Zulfikār Ardistānī, author of the famous Persian work *Dabistān-i-Mazāhib*. He lived during the time of the Sixth Gurū. He has left us a graphic account of Nānak-panthīs or Sikhs of his time. He records in his book that the followers of Gurū Nānak were known as *Kartārīs*. This obviously refers to their practice of repeating *Kartār Kartār* on meeting each other.

So *Kartār Kartār* is the first form of greeting which became prevalent in Sikhism. It was, however, soon replaced with *Pairī Pauṇā*. It is recorded in *Ādi Sākhīāṅ* that when Bhāī Lahiṇā came from Gurū Nānak back to Mate dī Sarāi, Ta<u>kh</u>t Mall, a close associate of Bhāī Lahiṇā came to see him. Bhāī Lahiṇā, who had by now become Gurū Aṅgad, wanted to receive him with an embrace. But Ta<u>kh</u>t Mall avoided this saying, "You are back from a place of great reverence. I stand to gain by bowing at your feet (and not hugging)." This probably was the beginning of the new form of greeting. And, the practice spread. It touched its zenith at Amritsar, the town founded by Gurū Rām Dās. The Gurū had encouraged people from all castes, high and low, and from all classes, to come and settle in the new town. All of them greeted each other with *Pairī Pauṇā* and touched one another's feet. This practice continued for a long time ; and even today it is not unlikely that one would be greeted by an old citizen with the words *Pairī Pauṇā Jī, rāzī ho*" (I bow at your feet, Sir, how do you do ?).

The next vital change occurred when the Tenth Gurū created the <u>Kh</u>ālsā. Since Gurū Gobind Siṅgh wanted a complete transformation of Sikh society, he ordered the overhauling of two fundamental institutions of the Sikhs. The first was the substitution of *Khaṇḍe dī Pāhul* for *Charan Pāhul* and the second was the substitution of *Vāhigurū Jī Kā <u>Kh</u>ālsā Vāhigurū Jī Kī Fateh* for *Pairī Pauṇā*. Sarūp Dās Bhallā, *Mahimā Prakāsh,* describes the end of the custom of the *Charan Pāhul* graphically in the following verse:

> The Gurū collected the washings of his feet in a jar,
> Sealed its mouth with wax,
> And consigned it to the River Sutlej
> In its place he now ordained *Khaṇḍe dī Pāhul*

Thus, the practice of administering *Charan Pāhul* was discarded and along with it was discarded the former mode of greeting, *Pairī Pauṇā.* In its place the Panth was now given a new salutation, a new form of greeting, *Vāhiguru Jī Kā Khālsā Vāhigurū Jī Kī Fateh* (Khālsā belongs to God, and to Him alone belongs the Victory).

The proper salutation for the *Khālsā*—Vāhiguru Jī Kā Khālsā Vāhigurū Jī Kī Fateh — was made current among the Sikhs by command of Gurū Gobind Siṅgh at the time of manifestation of the Khālsā in 1699. *Vāhigurū* (also spelt *Vāhgurū*) is expressive of wonder or ecstasy at Divine infinitude or glory. Vāhigurū has become the most characteristic name for God in the Sikh creed, like Allah in Islam. It occurs in the Gurū Granth Sāhib (Savaiyyās by Bhaṭṭ Gayand, p. 1402) repeated ecstatically as a *mantra.* In the compositions of Gurū Arjan (GG, 376), it is used in the inverted form as Gur Vāhu. Bhāī Gurdās in his *Vārāṅ* has used it as being synonymous with the absolute, the Creator in a number of places (I. 49, IV. 17, VI. 5, IX. 13, XI. 3 and 8, XII. 17, XIII. 2, XXIV. 1, XL. 22). This prolific use by one whose philosophical exposition of Sikh metaphysics and mysticism is the earliest on record indicates that by the time of Gurū Arjan (the Savaiyyās referred to above were also composed by poets, Bhaṭṭs, attending on him) Vāhigurū as the Sikh name for God was well established and had acquired the overtones which have since been associated with it as expression of the Sikh monotheistic affirmation of faith.

Because of this close and inalienable association, Gurū Gobind Siṅgh, at the time of introducing the new form of initiation with adjuration to the initiates to maintain a stern moral discipline and to cultivate qualities of crusaders and martyrs for the faith, administered the new faith in terms of the name of God which was held in the highest reverence in the tradition handed down to him. The new form of salutation, which annulled all the previous ones till then prevalent in Sikh society, was enunciation as Vāhigurū Jī Kā Khālsā Vāhigurū Jī Kī Fateh—the Khālsā is the Lord's own: to the Lord is the Victory. This two-fold affirmation was, in the first place, expression of a special relationship between God and those who dedicated their entire life to His service. Second, it was the expression of that faith in the ultimate triumph of the forces of goodness which, despite all apparent setbacks, trials and travail, is the just and essential end of the fight between good and evil in the world. This faith has been asserted over and over again by Gurū Nānak and his spiritual successors. After being administered *amrit* (water stirred with a two-edged dagger, sanctified by recitation of the Gurū's word and thus transmuted into the elixir of immortality), each initiate was adjured to raise the affirmation, Vāhigurū Jī Kā Khālsā Vāhigurū Jī Kī Fateh ! This was duly repeated, and the tradition continues till this day. Apart from being used as the affirmation of faith, this formula is also the orthodox approved Sikh form of salutation.

Two terms in this formula need elucidation. Khālsā is an Arabic word, meaning, literally, 'pure' and used in the administration terminology of the Muslim State system in India for lands or fiefs directly held by the sovereign and not farmed out to landlords on conditions of military service and of making over to the State a share of the produce. In the term *Khālsā*, both these meanings are discerned. In one of Gurū Hargobind's Hukamnāmās and in one of Gurū Tegh Bahādur's, *Khālsā* is used for the Gurū's devotees, with the implication particularly as 'the Gurū's Own !' As Gurū Gobind Siṅgh adopted the term and gave it centrality in the enunciation of the creed, the idea of purity perhaps came to acquire primacy. Khālsā occurs also in the Gurū Granth Sāhib (GG, 654), where it is used in the sense of 'pure', 'emancipated.' This term appealed to Gurū Gobind Siṅgh as being truly expressive of the vision of a noble, heroic race of men that he was creating.

Fateh, fatḥ in Arabic, literally means

opening or forcing the portal of a besieged fort, implying victory. It has been used in the *Qur'an* in the sense of victory, and one of the attributive names of God in the Muslim tradition is Fātih (lit. Opener, i.e. Vanquisher over all evil forces). While *jai, jaikār* have been used in the Sikh tradition for victory and are used thus even in the *Dasam Granth*, *jai* was dropped from the new Sikh tradition, though for shouts of victory the term *jaikārā* has become firmly established. *Fateh* was adopted as the current popular term for triumph or victory and made part of the Sikh affirmation and salutation. *Fateh* as *fatih* occurs once in the Gurū Granth Sāhib (GG, 258). "*Phāhe kāṭe miṭe gavan fatih bhaī mani jīt* – the noose of Yama hath been cleft, transmigration hath ceased and, with the conquest of the self, true victory hath been achieved." The implied meaning here is of a moral victory. *Jīt*, a word from Indian tradition, like *jaikārā* had got established also in Sikh tradition, and in the invocation Panth kī Jīt (Victory to the Panth) is repeated in the Sikh congregational prayer daily. Fateh nonetheless remains the prime Sikh term for victory, and has been repeated again and again in Sikh history, down from the Persian couplet put on Sikh coins (*Deg-o-Tegh-o-Fateh-e-nusrat bedaraṅg, yāft az Nānak Gurū Gobind Siṅgh)* to the common daily parlance of the Sikh people, wherein every success is designated as *fateh*.

BIBLIOGRAPHY

1. Piār Siṅgh, ed., *Ādi Sākhīāṅ*. Amritsar, 1983
2. Kirpāl Siṅgh, *Janam Sākhī Pramparā*. Patiala, 1969
3. Naraiṇ Siṅgh, *Vārāṅ Bhāī Gurdās Jī Saṭīk*. Amritsar, 1960
4. Kāhn Siṅgh, Bhāī, *Gurmat Mārtaṇḍ*. Amritsar, 1938
5. Gaṇḍā Siṅgh, *Hukamnāme*. Patiala, 1967
6. Kapur Singh, *Parāśarapraśna*. Amritsar, 1989
7. Macauliffe, M.A., *The Sikh Religion*. Oxford, 1909
8. Cole, W. Owen and Piara Singh Sambhi, *The Sikhs: Their Religious Beliefs and Practices*. Delhi, 1978

G.S.T.

BOTĀ SIṄGH (d. 1739), an eighteenth-century martyr of the Sikh faith, belonged to the village of Bhaṛāṇā in Amritsar district. In those days of dire persecution, he along with many fellow-Sikhs had sought the safety of wastes and jungles. At nightfall, he would come out of his hiding place and visit some human habitations in search of food. Occasionally he would come to Amritsar by night to have a dip in the holy tank, spending the day in the wilderness around Tarn Tāran. One day he was noticed by some people who thought he was a Sikh. But one of the party said that he was not a Sikh, for had he been one he would not conceal himself thus. The taunt cut Botā Siṅgh to the quick. Accompanied by his companion Garjā Siṅgh, a Raṅghreṭā Sikh, and with a bamboo club in his hand, he took up position on the grand trunk road, near Sarāi Nūr ud-Dīn, near Tarn Tāran. To announce his presence and proclaim the sovereignty of the Khālsā, he started collecting toll from the passersby. Finding everyone submitting tamely to his authority, he sent a communication to the provincial governor himself. The words of the letter, as preserved in Punjabi folklore, were:

Chiṭṭhī likhī Siṅgh Botā :
Hath hai soṭā,
Vich rāh khalotā
ĀNnā lāyā gaḍḍe nū,
Paisā lāyā khotā.
Ākho Bhābī Khāno nū,
Yoṅ ākhe Siṅgh Botā.

Botā Siṅgh writes this letter:
With a big club in hand,
On the road do I stand.
I levy an ānnā on a cart
And a pice on a donkey.

This, tell your sister, Khāno, who is my sister-in-law,
Is what Botā Siṅgh declares.
The wife of the Mughal governor is bur-

lesqued here using her popular name "Khāno." Botā Siṅgh calls her his *bhābī*, i.e. brother's wife with whom one could take liberties.

Zakarīyā Khān, the governor, sent a contingent of one hundred horse under Jalāl Dīn to arrest Botā Siṅgh alive and bring him to Lahore. Jalāl Dīn asked Botā Siṅgh and Garjā Siṅgh to surrender and accompany him to Lahore, promising to secure them the governor's pardon. Botā Siṅgh and his comrade spurned the offer and fell fighting valiantly against heavy odds. This happened in 1739.

BIBLIOGRAPHY

1. Bhagat Lakshman Singh, *Sikh Martyrs*. Madras, 1928
2. Chhibbar, Kesar Siṅgh, *Baṅsāvalīnāmā Dasāṅ Pātshāhīāṅ Kā*. Chandigarh, 1972
3. Bhaṅgū, Ratan Siṅgh, *Prāchīn Paṅth Prakāsh*. Amritsar, 1914

B.S.

BOYLE, a French national, who, deserting the First European Ligh Infantry, joined the Khālsā army in 1843. He was killed fighting against the British in the first Anglo-Sikh war (1845-46).

BIBLIOGRAPHY

Grey, C., *European Adventurers of Northern India* [Reprint]. Patiala, 1970

Gl.S.

BRAHAM GIĀN (Knowledge of the Divine), by a Sevāpanthī saint Gopāl Dās, is a treatise in Punjabi on theology. The work is unpublished and the only extant copy of the manuscript is preserved in the private collection of Dr Tarlochan Siṅgh Bedī at Paṭiālā. It contains 219 folios and was written presumably in the first half of the eighteenth century. Another incomplete copy of the manuscript existed under MS. No. 1700 in the Sikh Reference Library, Amritsar, until it perished in 1984 in the Army attack on the Golden Temple premises. The work can broadly be divided into two parts: the first defining the term *braham-giān* and setting forth the means of achieving this state of mind, and the second describing the state of mind of one who has attained *braham-giān*. In this sense, the work can also be called a free and detailed exposition of the eighth *pauṛī* or canto of Gurū Arjan's *Sukhmanī* (*q.v.*). To fortify his argument, the author has quoted profusely from numerous Persian, Sanskrit and Punjabi sources which include the works of the Gurūs and of several of the Bhaktas and Ṣūfīs, besides the *Bhagavadgītā* and the *Yoga Vaṣiṣṭha*. The excerpts and examples quoted in the original from Persian and Sanskrit works are written in red whereas their explanation in Punjabi (Gurmukhī characters) is in black ink. The issues like the nature of God, His creation and His relationship with that creation, and the role of Gurū and *saṅgat* in realizing the Divine are discussed in the light of Sikh tenets and explained with illustrations from Sūfī and Vedāntic texts. The language of the work is an admixture of Punjabi and Sādh Bhākhā, with a fair sprinkling of Braj, Persian and Sanskrit words. Western Punjabi vocabulary predominates which may be a clue to the locale to which the author belonged.

T.S.B.

BRĀHMAṆ MĀJRA, an old village, about 11 km southeast of Ropaṛ (30° - 58'N, 76° - 31'E), is sacred to Gurū Hagobind and Gurū Gobind Siṅgh. Gurdwārā Gurū Gaṛh Ṣāhib commemorates the visit of Gurū Gobind Siṅgh on 6 December 1705 when he, with his two elder sons and 40 Sikhs, was on his way from Koṭlā Nihaṅg Khān to Chamkaur. The Gurdwārā about 50 metres outside the village, constructed during the 1970's, consists of a square *dīvān* hall with a verandah in front. The sanctum within it is marked off by 16 square-shaped pillars. The one-acre walled compound also contains Gurū kā Laṅgar and rooms for the pilgrims.

The second shrine in the northern part of the village is called Gurdwārā Pātshāhī Chhevīṅ in memory of Gurū Hargobind who, it is believed, passed through here in 1638 on his way back from Kurukshetra. The Paṭhāns of Ropaṛ supported by Raṅghaṛs and Gujjars of the surrounding villages made an unprovoked attack on the Gurū to avenge an earlier defeat on 1 July 1635, when Rājā Himmat Chand Hinḍūrī, supported by 100 Sikhs under Bābā Gurdittā, had worsened the Paṭhāns in the battle of Naṅgal Gujjrāṅ. Now finding the Gurū with only a handful of his disciples, a rabble force blocked his way. The Gurū had to take shelter in Brāhmaṇ Mājrā village but the exemplary courage of the Sikhs and the Gurū's own skill in archery kept the multitude at a distance. Meanwhile, reinforcements arrived from Kīratpur and the assailants were driven away with heavy losses. The present Gurdwārā was constructed only in 1975 at the instance of Sant Kartār Siṅgh of Bhinḍrāṅ. It consists of a single square room in which the Gurū Granth Sāhib is installed.

Jg.S.

BRAHM DĀS, PAṆḌIT, described in the *Purātan Janam Sākhī* as a learned man of Kashmīr, is said to have been a resident of Bīj Bihāṛā, near Maṭan. Once Gurū Nānak journeying through the valley halted close to where he lived. As Brahm Dās, proud of his learning, heard of the arrival of a *faqīr*, holy man, he came in his accustomed manner with his packs of Purāṇas and other old texts amounting to "two camel-loads" and with a stone-idol suspended from his neck. No sooner had he uttered his greeting than he began questioning the Gurū on how he clad himself, what ritual he observed and what food he ate. The Gurū uttered this *śabda*:

> There is but one highway and there is but one entrance ;
> The Gurū is the ladder to reach one's native home ;
> Handsome is the Lord and in His Name lies all comfort.
> He created Himself and Himself He recognizeth.
> He created the sky and the earth,
> By making one the canopy for the other.
> Thus was His Word made manifest.
> He created the sun and the moon,
> And gave them His own light.
> He made night and day;
> Marvellous is His creation.
> His are the pilgrimages, His the holy converse,
> And his the festive ablutions.
> How can I describe Thee, O Lord,
> There is nothing to equal Thee.
> Thou occupiest Thy eternal throne;
> The rest but come and go.
>
> (GG, 1279)

Brahm Dās whose *forte* was disputation felt disarmed by the Gurū's words and manner. He asked him humbly this time how the Lord existed before creation. Another holy hymn burst forth from the Gurū's lips:

> Through aeons past reckoning,
> Utter darkness hung upon misty void.
> There were then no earths, nor firmaments;
> Pervasive infinitely was the Lord's Will alone;
> There was neither night nor day, neither sun nor moon;
> He alone was there
> Poised in perfect concentration.
> There was neither birth nor speech, neither air nor water ;
> There was neither creation nor destruction, neither coming nor going;
> There were neither the seven seas nor rivers overflowing with water.
> There were not the higher, middle or

neither regions, nor the hell or heaven, nor death the destroyer,
There was neither paradise nor purgatory,
neither birth nor death;
There was then no Brahmā, Viṣṇu, or Śiva ;
There was neither male nor female, neither caste nor reincarnation, neither pain nor pleasure.

* * *

There were neither Mullās, nor Qāzīs
neither sūfīs nor their disciples, nor the *hajj* pilgrims,
There were no mighty sovereigns, nor subjects for them to rule, no world of ego, no masters or slaves.

* * *

There were no Vedas, nor the books of the Semites,
There were no Smṛtis and no Śastras, and no reading of the scriptures by morning or evening.
The Unspeakable One was Himself the speaker, the Unknowable One had alone the knowledge of Himself.

* * *

When it pleased Him, He created the world;
Without support He Sustained the stars:

He created Brahmā, Viṣṇu snd Maheś:

He extended the love of *māyā*,
Communicating the enlightening Word to the chosen few.

"Then", says the *Purātan Janam Sākhī*, "Brahm Dās fell down at the Gurū's feet. He flung away the stone-image from his neck and became a disciple.

BIBLIOGRAPHY

1. Vīr Siṅgh, Bhāī, ed., *Purātan Janam Sākhī Srī Gurū Nānak Dev Jī*. Amritsar, 1971
2. Santokh Siṅgh, Bhāī, *Srī Gur Pratāp Sūraj Granth*. Amritsar, 1926-37
3. Macauliffe, Max Arthur, *The Sikh Religion*. Oxford, 1909

Gn.S.

BRAHMGIĀNĪ (Skt. *brahmajñānīn)*, lit. the knower of Brahman or one possessing the knowledge of Brahman. The knowledge (*giāna, jñāna*) of the Universal Spirit (Brahman) consists not in the mere recognition of His existence, but in a continuous consciousness about Him—His realization in the heart or rather the realization of a total identity of the individual soul (*ātman*) with that Universal Soul (Brahman), which makes the former transcend joy and sorrow and life and death. This total identity signifies, in essence, the oneness of the Universe with that Universal Soul and of the latter with the individual souls which a Brahmgiānī realizes as the Ultimate Reality. The concept of Brahman in Sikhism delineates the Universal Spirit in theistic terms as the Absolute, the Creator and the Ordainer of the Universe which is, as it were, His visible form. The concept of Brahmgiānī in Sikhism is elaborated in sublime poetry of Gurū Arjan, Nānak V, in his *Sukhmanī* (GG, 272-74). According to him Brahmgiānī is one who has realized, in his life, the One Supreme Spirit as well as his identity with the individual selves. Such a person has also been called *gurmukh, sādhū* or *sant*. The Brahmgiānī enjoys the highest spiritual status and he is accorded the highest veneration. The Brahmgiānī in *Sukhmanī* is postulated as being unattached (*nirlep*) like the lotus in water. He is endowed with Divine realization; he is deeply humane and compassionate. To all is he gracious casting an equal glance on all like the sun, and indifferent to praise or dispraise like the earth. He has humility and is ever anxious to do good to others. In a moment of exaltation, Gurū Arjan pronounces him the Supreme Being Himself– such is his merit, such his holiness: *"Nānak brahmgiānī āpi parmesur"* (GG, 273). He is compared to the earth to whom he who is digging it with the shovel and he who is plastering it with sandalwood are alike. Brahmgiānī is gracious, compassionate to all. From all bonds is he free. On God is solely his reliance and on Him are all his hopes centred. Ever is he awake in spirit. To all does he bring liberation by his counsel.

> Brahmgiānī is the creator of all, immortal, dying never.
> Brahmgiānī is the conferrer of the way of liberation, the perfect being, rewarder of deeds.
> Brahmgiānī is the succourer of the helpless;
> Brahmgiānī affords protection to all.
> All creation is Brahmgiānī's image;
> Brahmgiānī himself is the Supreme Being.
> Brahmgiānī alone is deserving of his high repute;
> Of all is Brahmgiānī the overlord, sayeth Nānak.
>
> (GG, 273-74)

Brahmgiānī looks on all beings equally and impartially—*brahmgiānī sadā samdarsī* (GG, 272). He showers the nectar of love and affection of all (GG, 373). An embodiment of compassion, he does good to others and helps those in distress. A model of piety and righteousness, he is the repository of all ethical virtues and a shunner of all vices and sins (GG, 272, 273). He is unaffected by the pleasures and enjoyments of the world just as the lotus-leaf remains untouched by water. He is fully in control of his mind and is pure and blemishless (GG, 272-73). He takes pleasure and pain, profit and loss alike. A Brahmgiānī leads others to the path of holiness and piety. He commands their spontaneous respect and reverence by virtue of his great glory and profund spiritual influence over them (GG, 273). He is a serene and sublime soul and an ideal human entity of ineffable greatness, who, in his supreme spiritual attainment, eminently commands the vision of the Universal Soul in himself and who has even been exalted by Gurū Arjan to the position of the Supreme Being, in the eighth *aṣṭpadī* or canto of *Sukhmanī*: "*Brahmgiānī pūran purakhu bidhātā ... Brahmgiānī āpi nirankāru* (GG, 273-74).

BIBLIOGRAPHY

1. Winternitz, M., *History of Indian Literature.* Tr. S. Ketkar. Calcutta, 1927
2. Sher Singh, *The Philosophy of Sikhism.* Lahore, 1944
3. Nripinder Singh, *The Sikh Moral Tradition.* Delhi, 1990
4. Jodh Siṅgh, Bhāī, *Gurmati Nirṇaya.* Lahore, 1932

D.K.G.

BRAHMO SAMĀJ. The expression "Brahmo Samāj" (correct transcription, "Brāhma Samāja") literally stands for a society of the worshippers of Brahman, the Supreme Reality, according to Hindu philosophy. It is the name of the Theistic Church founded by Rājā Rāmmohun Roy (1772-1833), in Calcutta on 20 August 1828. The history of the movement leading to the foundation of this "house of worship" is intimately bound up with that of the individual career of Rāmmohun Roy. Born in the village of Rādhānagar in the district of Hooghly, West Bengal, of wealthy and orthodox Brāhmaṇ (Vaiṣṇava) parents, he received in his boyhood the traditional education of the country and attained remarkable proficiency in Arabic, Persian and Sanskrit. Later in life he learnt English, Greek, Latin and Hebrew. A study of the Qur'ān and Islamic theology shook his faith in the popular idolatrous forms of Hindu worship and made him a lifelong admirer of the uncompromising monotheism of Islam. A profound acquaintance with the Upaniṣads, the *Brahmasūtra* and the *Gītā* and Indian philosophical literature in general, convinced him that the concept of the unity of the Godhead was the very essence of Hinduism. He had also deeply studied the philosophy of the Brāhmaṇical Tantras. He studied Mahāyāna Buddhism together with its later decadent phases, and he is said also to have mastered some Jaina scriptural texts. He had also a considerable familiarity, presumably due to his travels in upper India and stay at Banāras and Paṭnā as well as through his command over the Hindi language, with the literature of the medieval Indian *bhakti* movement. He drew inspiration from it and specifically claimed medieval saints like Kabīr, Dādū, and others as among the spiritual ancestors of his own monotheistic creed. His study of Indian and Islamic thought-movements was thus comprehensive and almost always firsthand.

Knowledge of a number of European languages enabled him to master both the spiritual and secular traditions of Western thought. By a cultivation of Christian scriptures he acquired a profound respect for the moral precepts of Jesus Christ. His secular studies included the literature of empirical philosophy from Bacon to Locke, the propaganda of free-thinking and illumination as represented by Hume, Voltaire, Volney, Thomas Paine and others, the philosophy of utilitarianism as propounded by Jeremy Bentham and James Mill and some forms of contemporary socialist thought and movement, particularly the school of Robert Owen. His extensive studies in philosophy and comparative religion thus prepared Rāmmohun Roy for the task to which he was to devote his life—the task of restoring Hinduism to its original norm of a monistic and monotheistic creed. He was however not a revivalist and was fully alive to the challenge that had arisen in the shape of the introduction of Western science and thought. He felt strongly the need of a new philosophy of life, which would, without sacrificing the genuine spiritual heritage of India, absorb and assimilate the spirit of modernism imported from the West. He warmly advocated the introduction of Western science and technology into the educational curriculum of India and became a pioneer of English education and enlightened journalism in this country. He fought the superstitions and prejudices that had gripped the contemporary Hindu community, raised his voice against the caste system and was chiefly instrumental in inducing the British government to abolish the rite of *satī* or burning widows alive. He laid the foundation of political agitation in India, appeared publicly as an advocate of the liberty of the press as well as the champion of the exploited Indian peasantry. In fact deeply religious as he was, he had conceived religion not as a narrow personal creed, but as an all-prevading elevating principle operating in every sphere of individual, social and national life.

The foundation of the Brahmo Samāj brought to a focal point this comprehensive scheme of religious, social, intellectual and political transformation of India as visualized and formulated by Rāmmohun Roy. The uncompromising monotheism of Islam, the doctrine of self-knowledge of the Upaniṣads, the moral teachings of Christ, the liberal social message of Buddhism and the deep and simple piety of the saints of the medieval Indian *bhakti* movement had helped to shape this universal outlook. The result was however not syncretism, but synthesis, Rāmmohun's emphasis being always on the unity of the fundamentals of the diverse faiths. The Brahmo Samāj was conceived by its founder not as the religious organization of a particular sect, but as a fellowship of worship which could be joined by anyone irrespective of his or her sectarian affiliation. The worship was made strictly monotheistic, no image, picture, symbol or any other created thing being allowed into the premises where it was conducted. The character of the service, though universal, was decidedly Hindu and at this stage it consisted of readings from the Vedas, exposition of the Upaniṣads and devotional music. The distinction of caste was not observed by the Hindus present, except in one respect. The Telegū Brāhmaṇs engaged to recite the Vedas could not be persuaded to admit non-Brāhmaṇ listeners to their presence and had to be placed within a separate enclosure. But the Upaniṣads were explained by the more liberal Bengali Brāhmaṇ *paṇḍits* to the general audience (including non-Brāhmaṇs, and sometimes non-Hindus) in violation of the orthodox rules of caste. In respect of religious music which he introduced into the Brahmo Samāj service, Rāmmohun had certainly been influenced by the practice of singing hymns as part of the Christian Church service. He however also drew inspiration from the examples of the followers of Gurū Nānak, Dādū and Kabīr as he had clearly indicated in his tract *Prārthanāpatra* (1823) and it is not difficult to see that Sikh *śabdas* had a large share in moulding Rāmmohun Roy's outlook in this regard. The creed of the Brahmo Samāj as conceived by Rāmmohun Roy was monotheism, its philosophy monism and its social ideal service to humanity. In his own interpretation of the Vedānta, Rāmmohun was a monist and he mainly followed Śaṅkara except on four points, viz. (a) he laid, consistently with his monistic or *advaita* position, a much greater emphasis on *upāsanā* (adoration and prayer); (b) he declared *Brahmajñāna* (knowledge of Brahman) and *mokṣa* (final liberation) to be within reach of the householder (*grihastha*); (c) he assigned a much more positive role than the conventional *advaitin* would be prepared to do to the doctrine of *māyā* as the creative power of Brahman; (d) he recognized the ideal of humanism and service as an adjunct to his *brahmavādā* (belief in Brahman) as absolute.

The Brahmo Samāj after remaining moribund for a few years following Rāmmohun's departure for England in 1830 and his premature death in 1833, was provided with a solid organizational framework by Debendranāth Tagore (1817-1905), eldest son of Dwārkānāth Tagore, Rāmmohun's trusted friend and collaborator. In 1839, Debendranāth established the Tattvabodhinī Sabhā the declared objective of which was "the extensive propagation of Brahmo Dharma." The Sabhā at once became the organizational wing of the infant Brahmo Samāj and on its platform assembled all sections of progressive elements in contemporary Bengal, including Paṇḍit Īsvarchandra Vidyāsāgar, philanthropist and social reformer, Akshay Kumār Datta, rationalist and one of the makers of Bengali prose, Rājendralāl Mitra, noted oriental scholar, Rājnārāyaṇ Bose, the saintly scholar and grandfather of Srī Aurobindo, Īsvarchandra Gupta, poet and journalist, and a number of brilliant young students of the Hindu College belonging to the group known as "Young Bengal." Rituals and ceremonies of the Church were now drawn up, the most prominent being the system of initiation and the form of divine service. On 21 December 1843, Debendranāth, along with twenty of his companions, was formally initiated into the new faith and the foundations of a sect of Brahmos were laid. A system of subscribed membership was started. Up to 1866, the year of the first schism in the history of the organization, Debendranāth remained the accredited leader of the Calcutta Brahmo Samāj which maintained and carried forward the best traditions of the days of Rāmmohun Roy. A remarkable change that occurred in Brahmoism during this epoch was the formal abandonment of the belief in the infallibility of scriptures. The basis of Brahmoism was declared to be "the human heart illumined by spiritual knowledge born of self-realization." The monotheistic creed of the

Samāj was however still regarded as the noblest and purest expression of Hinduism and the Hindu Śāstras (minus their polytheistic accretions) continued to be studied with respect. Less intellectual and more spiritual in his mental make-up than Rāmmohun Roy, Debendranāth laid a more pronounced emphasis on *bhakti* or devotion in his exposition of the Śāstras and ultimately veered round to qualified monism (Viśiṣṭādvaitavādā), a position which the Brahmo Samāj can be said to have retained till now. Under his inspiring leadership, the Samāj played a distinguished role on sponsoring social reforms such as widow marriage, spread of education, development of Bengali literature through its organ the *Tattvabodhinī Patrikā* and opposition to the efforts of Christian missionaries to villify Hinduism and to gain converts from the ranks of the Hindus. The Brahmo movement thus grew in extent and influence throughout Bengal and upper India and the Samāj became a great moral and spiritual force in the country. To the end of his long life, Debendranāth, called *maharṣī* (great sage) for the deep spirituality of his nature by his admiring fellow-believers, continued to enjoy the respect of all sections of his countrymen. In course of his spiritual quest, he found in the teachings of Gurū Nānak one abiding source of inspiration. He visited the Golden Temple of Amritsar more than once, joined the temple singers in the choric singing of hymns there, learnt the language of the Sikh Scripture and openly expressed his admiration of the democratic organization of Sikh places of worship and the Sikh mode of initiation. His autobiography, which is a charming account of the gradual unfolding of his spiritual life, is strewn with quotations from the Sikh Scripture, along with those from the Upaniṣads and Hāfiz.

The next phase of the Brahmo movement is dominated by the dynamic personality of Keshav Chandra Sen (1838-1884) who had joined the Samāj in 1857 and had become the right-hand man of Debendranāth Tagore. Differences arising from a conflict of two radically different temperaments, soon led to a parting of ways. Debendranāth was intensely national in his religious ideal drawing his inspiration mainly from the sublime doctrines of the Upaniṣads and he was always in favour of emphasizing the special relation that Brahmoism had with Hinduism of the Vedāntic form. In social questions too he was for a slow and cautious move forward always seeking, like Rāmmohun Roy before him, a harmony between an intended reform and the collective will of the people for whom it was meant. The character and personality of Keshav were however entirely moulded by Western culture and Christian influence and he was the advocate of a much more aggressive reform policy not hesitating to employ legislation as a weapon. In 1865, the progressives led by Keshav withdrew from the parent Church and, in the following year (11 November 1866), they established the Brahmo Samāj of India. The parent body came henceforth to be known as the Ādi Brahmo Samāj. The new wing proceeded to carry out its programme of spiritual and social reform with great sincerity and enthusiasm and achieved striking success within a short period. The whole of India now in a real sense became the field of activity of the Brahmo Samāj. The two Indian tours of Keshav in 1864 and 1867 had done much to foster the sense of spiritual and national unity among the Indians and his visit to England in 1870 carried the message of the Brahmo Samāj to Europe. The Samāj now adopted a much more radical and comprehensive scheme of social reform, including the programme of a complete abolition of caste-distinctions, promotion of female education and female emancipation, cheap newspaper, labour-welfare, etc. These activities found expression in the formation of the Indian Reform Association in 1870 and the enactment of the Civil Marriage Act of 1872. Doctrinally, a much greater emphasis now began to be laid, presumably due to Christian influence, on the sense of sin, the spirit of repentence and the efficacy of prayer. The universality of the theism of Keshav and his followers was much more pronounced than that of Debendranāth Tagore and the latter's compatriots. This found expression in the compilation of the *Śloka-Saṅgraha* (1866) which was a carefully compiled collection of extracts from the religious scriptures of various sects and in its revised editions covered Hindu, Buddhist, Jaina, Sikh, Jewish, Christian, Muhammadan, Parsee and Chinese sacred texts. Great religious systems of the world like Hinduism, Islam, Christianity, Buddhism, and Sikhism, were studied with reverence. The infusion of *bhakti* or devotional fervour into Brahmoism for which Keshav was indebted in some measure to the Vaiṣṇava followers of Chaitanya made it "a practical religious culture, sweet and soothing to the human heart." Finally, Keshav's doctrine of God in Conscience "developed the moral side of faith, by bringing human conduct within the domain of man's spirituality." The sympathetic and respectful attitude which he had displayed towards all faiths early in his career led to a rich synthesis of religions, which he proclaimed under the title of "New Dispensation" (Nava Vidhān) on 25 January 1880. The systematic study of the different religions of the world initiated since 1869 through Keshav's inspiration and direction had led saintly scholars of the Samāj like Gour Govinda Roy, Pratāp Chandra Mazoomdār, Aghor Nāth Gupta, Girīsh Chandra Sen and Mahendra Nāth Bāsu to enrich the store of human knowledge by their learned publications on Hinduism, Christianity, Buddhism, Islam and Sikhism. The last-named scholar is well known in Bengali literature for his *Nānak-Prakāsa,* part I (1885) and part II (1893), based on a comprehensive study of the Sikh Scripture in the original. It was Keshav who gave first public recognition to the spiritual genius of the contemporary saint, Rāmakrishna Paramahaṅsa; great spiritual fellowship had grown up between the two.

The second schism in Brahmo Samāj occurred when a band of Keshav's sincere and talented followers, including Paṇḍit Sivanāth Sāstrī, Ānanda Mohan Bose, Vijay Krishna Goswāmī, Durgāmohan Dās, Sivchandra Deb, Dvārkānāth Gāṅgūlī, Umesh Chandra Datta and others, left him to found the Sādhāraṇ Brahmo Samāj (15 May 1878) mainly on the following grounds: (i) their demand for the introduction of a democratic constitution in the Church was not conceded; (ii) they could not see eye to eye with Keshav on the question of *ādeśa* or Divine Command ; (iii) marriage of Keshav's daughter with the prince of the Cooch Behār state allegedly in violation of the provisions of the Marriage Act of 1872 which Keshav had himself done so much to get passed. Leaders of this new body made it their first objective to draw up a Trust Deed for their church and give the organization a democratic constitution based on universal adult franchise. They laid great emphasis on the ideas of freedom and democracy. In conformity with the democratic and constitutional ideals it was also affirmed that "nothing should pass as an act or deed or opinion of the *Samāj* until a majority of the members sanctioned it." There is really no important doctrinal difference between the second and third bodies of the Brahmo Samāj, apart from the fact that the Sādhāraṇ Brahmo Samāj does not lay the same emphasis on the theory of *ādeśa* or Divine Command when understood in a collective sense and on Keshav's ideal of the New Dispensation as is done by the Brahmo Samāj of India. The new body, however, laid renewed stress on the ideals of service and philanthropy that had been the characteristics of the movement since the days of Rāmmohun Roy and plunged whole-heartedly into a programme of social, educational and political reform. The concept of constitutional democracy is a distinct contribution of Sādhāraṇ Brahmo Samāj to modern Indian social polity. The anti-caste movement now took concrete shape all over India with the emergence of organizations like the Native Philanthropic Association for the regeneration of Pariahs in Southern India (1883) at Bangalore, the Depressed Classes Mission Society of India (1906) at Bombay, the All India Anti-Untouchability League (1907) at Puṇe and the Society for the Improvement of the Backward Classes (1913) at Calcutta.

From the ranks of men associated with the Sādhāraṇ Brahmo Samāj emerged nationalist leaders such as Ānanda Mohan Bose, Bepin Chandra Pāl, Chitta Rañjan Dās and J.M. Sengupta; revolutionaries such as Satyaendra Nāth Bose and Ullaskar Datta; and sponsors of labour welfare such as Dvārkānāth Gaṅgūlī, Rāmkumāı Vidyāratna and Sasīpada Banerjī. In the field of literature, philosophy and comparative religion too the members of the Samāj have left a permanent stamp. Special mention may be made in this context of the authoritative study of Gurū Nānak and the Sikh religion by Krishna Kumār Mitra, one of the leaders of the Samāj and of the Svadeshī movement, who studied the Sikh Scripture in the original in order to equip himself for the task. In fact the second schism in the history of the Brahmo Samāj "certainly indicated a forward look and an onward march which showed the life that was in the movement." The Sādhāraṇ Brahmo Samāj has proved to be the most powerful and active branch of the Brahmo Samāj in the country.

Numerically probably the smallest religious community in the world, the Brahmo Samāj has played a role of far-reaching importance in the history of modern India. It has not only sought to harmonize the conflicting religious trends of our day, but has also proceeded to meet the challenge thrown by a scientific and industrial age to the world of traditional spiritual values. The result has been a new spiritual philosophy which by its sheer dynamism has helped to transform the face of India.

BIBLIOGRAPHY

1. Sastri, Sivanath, *History of the Brahmo Samaj.* Calcutta, 1974
2. Farquhar, J.N., *Modern Religious Movements in India.* Delhi, 1977
3. Ganda Singh, ed., *The Singh Sabha and other Socio-Religious Movements in the Punjab.* Patiala, 1984

D.K.B.

BRIJINDAR SIṄGH, MAHĀRĀJĀ (1896-1918), son of Kaṅvar Gajindar Siṅgh, ascended the throne of Farīdkoṭ state in March 1906. He had his education at Aitchison College, Lahore. A council of regency headed by Sardār Bahādur Dyāl Siṅgh Mān was appointed during his minority to carry on the administration. Brijindar Siṅgh earned the title of Mahārājā by the help he gave the British during the First World War (1914-19). The last of the four volumes of the first-ever commentary on the Gurū Granth Sāhib prepared under the aegis of the royal house of Farīdkoṭ and popularly known as *Farīdkoṭ Ṭīkā* was published during his time. As the first edition of the work ran out, he ordered a reprint to be brought out.

Mahārājā Brijindar Siṅgh died on 22 December 1918. He was succeeded by his son, Harindar Siṅgh (1915-89).

BIBLIOGRAPHY

1. Griffin, Lepel, *The Rajas of the Punjab.* Delhi, 1977
2. Ganda Singh, *The Patiala and East Panjab States Union: Historical Background.* Patiala, 1951
3. Harbaṅs Siṅgh, *Farīdkoṭ Itihās Bāre.* Faridkot, 1947

S.S.B.

BRIJ RĀJ (d. 1833), a learned Paṇḍit came

to settle in Lahore in the latter half of the eighteenth century, was appointed by Mahārājā Raṇjīt Siṅgh to the position of *rājpurohit*, or royal priest, which office he held till his death in 1833. The Mahārājā and the court *sardārs* used to consult him on astrological matters. Paṇḍit Brij Rāj also held appointment as almoner in the Dharamārath department of Sarkār Khālsā. He had the village of Qilā Gujjar Siṅgh given him in *jāgīr* by the Mahārājā.

BIBLIOGRAPHY

1. Sūrī, Sohan Lāl, *'Umdāt-ut-Twārīkh*. Lahore, 1885-89
2. Griffin, Lepel, and C.F. Massy, *Chiefs and Families of Note in the Punjab*. Lahore, 1909

B.J.H.

BROADFOOT, GEORGE (1807-1845), joined service of the East India Company as a cadet in the Madrās Native Infantry in 1826. In May 1841, he went to Kābul in command of the escort which accompanied the families of Shāh Shujā' and Zamān Shāh. He took part in the first Afghān war and distinguished himself in the Khaibar operations under General Pollock. In 1844, he was appointed Agent to the Governor-General at the North-West Frontier Agency. The appointment was not liked by the Sikh Government. Major George Broadfoot was impulsive by nature and had a temperamental hostility towards the Sikhs. While leading a caravan of the royal Afghān families through the Punjab, he had annoyed the Sikh escort provided by the Lahore Government for the protection of the convoy. He incited the Muslim population to rise and rescue him and requisitioned a British brigade from Jalālābād to save him from what he called the violent intentions of the Sikhs. His distrust of the Sikh escort, however, proved imaginary, but his conduct had given offence to the Sikh Darbār.

Broadfoot had come to the Sikh frontier with the set policy of inciting antagonisms against the Lahore kingdom and bringing about a full-scale conflagration between the Sikhs and the British. He endeavoured to win over Mūl Rāj, the governor of Multān, to his side. He gave open encouragement to Gulāb Siṅgh, who had made numerous proposals to the British for the destruction of the Sikh army and offered to assist them in the occupation of the Punjab in return for his being recognized as an independent sovereign of Jammū and the neighbouring hills. In March 1845, Broadfoot challenged the right of the Sikh Government to administer its possessions to the south of the Sutlej. He arrested a party of Lahore officials, escorted by a cavalry force, proceeding to Koṭ Kapūrā to relieve State troops stationed there. He prepared a case for the seizure of Lahore lands on the left bank of the Sutlej, arguing that, if the river was the boundary between the Sikhs and the British, the former could not possess territories to the south of it. Soon afterwards took place the Anandpur Mākhovāl incident. The Colebrooke Award of 1828 had accepted Lahore supremacy over the town, which was managed by the Soḍhī priests, and the Sikh Darbār's right so established had never been challenged. A dispute having arisen among the Soḍhīs in the spring of 1845, Broadfoot took upon himself to settle it by force. The Sikh forces, however, upset Broadfoot's mediation and expelled both Lieutenant Cunningham and his assistant sent there by the British agent.

These provocative acts on the part of Major Broadfoot were among the chain of events which culminated in the first Anglo-Sikh war. What Broadfoot did was only in line with Lord Hardinge's policy, and had the approval of the Home Government. Hardinge's approbation was expressed in his cryptic comment: "Broadfoot is in his element on the frontier."

Major Broadfoot was killed in action on 21 December 1845 in the battle of Ferozeshāh.

BIBLIOGRAPHY

1. Gough, C., and A.D. Innes, *The Sikhs and the Sikh Wars*. London, 1897
2. Hasrat, B.J., *Anglo-Sikh Relations*. Hoshiarpur, 1968
3. Gupta, Hari Ram, *Panjab on the Eve of First Sikh War*. Chandigarh, 1956

B.J.H.

BROUGHTON PAPERS are official and private papers of Sir John Cam Hobhouse (Lord Broughton) in numerous bound volumes in the British Library. Lord Broughton, British administrator, who served as President of the Board of Control of the East India Company from 1835-41 and again from 1846-52, was responsible for the Home Government's major policy decisions on the Punjab and the Sikhs.

The relevant volumes in the Broughton Papers dealing with the Punjab and the Sikhs, in general, are:

(1) MS. vol. XIV containing papers concerning the British attitude towards the Russo-Persian menace in 1836-38, which led to the signing of the Tripartite treaty between the British government, Shāh Shujā' and Raṇjīt Siṅgh in 1838.

(2) MSS. vols. 36473-74 containing private correspondence of Lord Auckland with Sir John Hobhouse from 1835-41 throw fresh light on the British policy towards Afghanistan, Sindh and Lahore. The correspondence shows how Auckland was influenced by men like Macnaghten, Burnes and Wade to accept the scheme of resuscitating Saddozaī power in Afghanistan with Raṇjīt Siṅgh's help. Included in the correspondence is a report on the military strength of the Sikhs by Sir Henry Fane, the British commander-in-chief, who visited Lahore in March 1837 on the occasion of the marriage of the Mahārājā's grandson, Kaṅvar Nau Nihāl Siṅgh. The background to the Burnes' Mission to Kābul in September 1837, its ultimate failure, and Raṇjīt Siṅgh's suspicions that the British would appease the Afg͟hāns at the cost of the Sikhs are clear from the letters dated 5 August, 8 September and 9 October 1837. Schemes for the subversion of the authority of Dost Muhammad K͟hān, Auckland's decision in May 1838 to send a mission to the court of Raṇjīt Siṅgh and the signing of the Tripartite treaty, furnish fresh data not found in the public records of the period.

(3) MS. vol. 36475 containing Lord Hardinge's private correspondence with Sir John Hobhouse relates to the period from May 1846 to February 1848. This correspondence is of particular relevance to understanding Hardinge's "political experiment" in the Punjab. It reveals that his avoidance of annexation after the first Anglo-Sikh war was really motivated to destroy the Sikhs as a political and military power. Also fresh light is thrown on Lāl Siṅgh's administration and the Kashmīr revolt, which led to his expulsion from the Punjab. Hardinge's defence of his questionable deal with Gulāb Siṅgh regarding the sale of Kashmīr, which aroused vehement Whig criticism in England is found in his letter of 7 June 1846. Events leading to the second treaty of Lahore (December 1846), which transformed the kingdom of Raṇjīt Siṅgh into a British protectorate, are described with extraordinary candour.

(4) MSS. vols. 36476-77 include Lord Dalhousie's private correspondence with Sir John Hobhouse from 20 January 1848 to 3 March 1853. These volumes deal with the main events of Multān and Hazārā revolts, the details of the second Anglo-Sikh war and the annexation of the Punjab. Sundry letters of the years 1849-53 refer also to events connected with the life of Mahārājā Duleep Siṅgh after his deposition. This correspondence proves beyond any doubt that Dalhousie allowed the Multān revolt to spread for five months, refused any help to Herbert Edwardes to suppress the rebellion and, linking up the isolated Hazārā uprising in the

northwest with it, indicted the Sikhs for a conspiracy to overthrow British power in the Punjab. He had already ordered Lord Hugh Gough, the British commander-in-chief, in April 1848, to assemble a large army for a full-scale invasion of the Punjab. It is abundantly clear from these documents that the second Anglo-Sikh war was fought and precariously won without a formal declaration and the Punjab was annexed to the British empire without any positive directions from the government.

The correspondence concerning the Sikhs and the Punjab in the Broughton Papers has been published *vide* B.J. Hasrat (ed.), *The Punjab Papers,* Hoshiārpur, 1970.

BIBLIOGRAPHY

Hasrat, B.J., ed., *The Punjab Papers.* Hoshiarpur, 1970

B.J.H.

BROWN, JOHN, alias RICHARD POTTER, an Englishman, who, deserting the East Indian Company's service in the Bengal artillery, came to Lahore and joined the Sikh artillery in 1826. He was later promoted colonel and placed in charge of the artillery depot at Lahore. During the first Anglo-Sikh war, he acted as a British spy. Just before the battle of 'Alīwāl, he went to Ludhiāṇā and offered his services to his countrymen. He was told to continue serving with the Sikhs and be a secret agent of the British. He returned to Lahore and kept the British informed of the movements of the Sikh forces. During the battle of 'Alīwāl he is said to have intentionally elevated the Sikh guns. Later he was taken prisoner by the British. After the annexation of the Punjab, the British rewarded him by giving him a high-ranking job in the police department. In 1856, he became blind and was retired from service on pension.

BIBLIOGRAPHY

Grey, C., *European Adventurers of Northern India.* Patiala, 1970

Gl.S.

BUCHCHEKE, village 15 km southwest of Nankāṇā Sāhib in Sheikhūpurā district of Pakistan, had a historical shrine, Gurdwārā Pātshāhī V, dedicated to Gurū Arjan, who once came here from Nankāṇā Sāhib during his travels across this region. The Gurdwārā was looked after by Nirmalā Sikhs. A religious fair used to be held here on the first of Chet (mid-March) every year until 1947 when the Gurdwārā had to be abandoned in the wake of mass migrations caused by the partition of the Punjab.

M.G.S.

BUḌḌHĀ, BĀBĀ (1506-1631), a most venerated primal figure of early Sikhism, was born on 6 October 1506 at the village of Katthū Naṅgal, 18 km northeast of Amritsar (31° - 36'N, 74° - 50'E). Būṛā, as he was originally named, was the only son of Bhāī Sugghā, a Jaṭṭ of Randhāvā clan, and Māī Gaurāṅ, born into a Sandhū family. As a small boy, he was one day grazing cattle outside the village when Gurū Nānak happened to pass by. According to Bhāī Manī Siṅgh, *Sikhāṅ dī Bhagat Mālā,* Būṛā went up to him and, making obeisance with a bowl of milk as his offering, prayed to him in this manner: "O sustainer of the poor! I am fortunate to have had a sight of you today. Absolve me now from the circuit of birth and death." The Gurū said, "You are only a child yet. But you talk so wisely." "Once some soldiers set up camp by our village," replied Būṛā, "and they mowed down all our crops – ripe as well as unripe. Then it occurred to me that, when no one could check these indiscriminating soldiers, who would restrain Death from laying his hand upon us, young or old." At this Gurū Nānak pronounced the words : "You are not a child; you possess the wisdom of an old man." From that day, Būṛā, came to be known as Bhāī Buḍḍhā, *buḍḍhā* in Punjabi meaning an old man, and later, when advanced in years, as Bābā Buḍḍhā. Bhāī Buḍḍhā became a devoted disciple. His marriage at the age of seventeen at Achal, 6 km south of Baṭālā (31° - 49'N, 75°- 12'E), did not distract him from his chosen path and he spent more time at Kartārpur where Gurū Nānak had taken up his abode than at Katthū Naṅgal. Such was the eminence he had attained in Sikh piety that, at the time of installation of Bhāī Lahiṇā as Gurū Aṅgad, i.e. Nānak II, Gurū Nānak asked Bhāī Buḍḍhā to apply the ceremonial *tilak* on his forehead. Bhāī Buḍḍhā lived up to a ripe old age and had the unique honour of anointing all of the four following Gurūs. He continued to serve the Gurūs with complete dedication and remained an example of holy living for the growing body of disciples. He devoted himself zealously to tasks such as the digging of the *bāolī* at Goindvāl under the instruction of Gurū Amar Dās and the excavation of the sacred tank at Amritsar under Gurū Rām Dās and Gurū Arjan. The *berī* tree under which he used to sit supervising the excavation of the Amritsar pool still stands in the precincts of the Golden Temple. He subsequently retired to a *bīṛ* or forest, where he tended the livestock of the Gurū kā Laṅgar. What is left of that forest is still known, after him, as Bīṛ Bābā Buḍḍhā Sāhib. Gurū Arjan placed his young son, Hargobind, under Bhāī Buḍḍhā's instruction and training. When the *Ādi Granth* (Gurū Granth Sāhib) was installed in the Harimandar on 16 August 1604, Bhāī Buḍḍhā was appointed *granthī* by Gurū Arjan. He thus became the first high priest of the sacred shrine, now known as the Golden Temple. Following the martyrdom of Gurū Arjan on 30 May 1606, Gurū Hargobind raised opposite the Harimandar a platform called the Akāl Ta<u>kh</u>t, the Timeless Throne or the Throne of the Timeless, the construction of which was entrusted to Bābā Buḍḍhā and Bhāī Gurdās, no third person being allowed to take part in it. On this Ta<u>kh</u>t Bhāī Buḍḍhā performed, on 24 June 1606, the investiture ceremony at which Gurū Hargobind put on two swords, one on each side, symbolizing *mīrī* and *pīrī*, sovereignty and spiritual eminence, respectively.

Bābā Buḍḍhā passed his last days in meditation at Jhaṇḍā Ramdās, or simply called Ramdās, a village founded by his son, Bhāī Bhānā, where the family had since shifted from its native Katthū Naṅgal. As the end came, on 16 November 1631, Gurū Hargobiṅd was at his bedside. The Gurū, as says the *Gurbilās Chhevīṅ Pātshāhī*, gave his shoulder to the bier and performed the last rites. Bhāī Gurdās, further to quote the *Gurbilās*, started a reading of the *Ādi Granth* in memory of the deceased. The obsequies concluded with Bhāī Gurdās completing the recital and Gurū Hargobiṇd presenting a turban to Bhāī Buḍḍhā's son, Bhānā. Two shrines stand in Ramdās commemorating Bābā Buḍḍhā, Gurdwārā Tap Asthān Bābā Buḍḍhā Jī, where the family lived on the southern edge of the village, and Gurdwārā Samādhāṅ, where he was cremated.

BIBLIOGRAPHY

1. *Gurbilās Chhevīṅ Pātshāhī*. Patiala, 1970
2. Bhallā, Sarūp Dās, *Mahimā Prakāsh*. Patiala, 1971
3. Padam, Piārā Siṅgh, and Giānī Garjā Siṅgh, eds., *Gurū kīāṅ Sākhīāṅ*. Patiala, 1986

G.S.R.

BUḌḌHĀ DAL and Taruṇā Dal, names now appropriated by two sections of the Nihaṅg Sikhs, were the popular designations of the two divisions of Dal <u>Kh</u>ālsā, the confederated army of the Sikhs during the eighteenth century. With the execution of Bandā Siṅgh Bahādur in 1716, the Sikhs were deprived of a unified command. Moreover, losses suffered by the Sikhs during the anti-Bandā Siṅgh campaign around Gurdāspur and the relentless persecution that followed at the hands of 'Abd us-Samad <u>Kh</u>ān, governor of Lahore, made it impossible for Sikhs to continue large-scale combined operations. Hunted out of their homes, they scattered in small *jathās* or groups to find refuge in distant hills, forests and deserts, but they were far from vanquished. In 1726 the imperial government replaced 'Abd us-Samad K͟hān by his more energetic and disciplinarian son, K͟hān Bahādur Zakarīya K͟hān, but he too was unable to reduce the Sikhs to submission. He at last came to terms with them in 1733, offering them a *jāgīr* worth 1,00,000 rupees a year, the title of "Nawāb" for one of their leaders and their peaceful settlement at Amritsar and elsewhere in the Punjab. The Sikhs accepted the offer. Some went back to their old villages, but the bulk of the warriors among them, a few thousand in number and still grouped around their former leaders, concentrated in Amritsar under the command of Sardār Kapūr Siṅgh who, with Darbārā Siṅgh to assist him as his *dīwān,* made arrangements for their maintenance. Kapūr Siṅgh, finding it difficult to cater for such a large force centrally, particularly after Darbāra Siṅgh's death in 1734, divided the camp into two parts on the basis of age of the *jathedārs* or group leaders. The elders' camp comprising *jathās* of older leaders such as Shām Siṅgh, Gurbak͟hsh Siṅgh, Bāgh Siṅgh, Gurdiāl Siṅgh, Sukkhā Siṅgh and Kapūr Siṅgh himself came to be called Buḍḍhā (elderly) Dal, and the youths' camp Taruṇā (youthful) Dal.The latter was further sub-divided into five *jathās,* each with its own drum and banner. Buḍḍhā Dal too was similarly sub-divided after some time. Nawāb Kapūr Siṅgh remained in overall command of the two Dals jointly called Dal K͟hālsā. Men were free to join *jathās* of their choice. In old sources we come across only one reference to the strength of a *jathā.* That is in Ratan Siṅgh Bhaṅgū, *Prāchīn Panth Prakāsh,* which, referring to the fifth *jathā* of the Taruṇā Dal commanded by Bīr Siṅgh Raṅghreṭā, puts down its strength at 1300 horse. From this figure it may be surmised that the *jathās* broadly comprised 1,300 to 2,000 men each. It was generally agreed that Buḍḍhā Dal would remain at Amritsar and manage the shrines, leaving Taruṇā Dal free for operations in the country.

The entente with the Mug͟hals did not last long. Zakarīya K͟hān wanted the Sikhs to disperse and revert to civil life in villages or join the imperial army as regular soldiers. The governor eventually broke the compact and resumed his former policy of persecution through his *gashtī fauj* (roving army) and rewarding informers and private killers of Sikhs. While Taruṇā Dal crossed the Sutlej into the territory of Sirhind, Buḍḍhā Dal spread in the countryside of Mājhā (area of Bārī Doāb and Rachnā Doāb, especially the former). Its first clash with the *gashtī fauj* took place in 1736 near Chūnīāṅ, 50 km west of Kasūr. Both sides suffered heavy casualties. Buḍḍhā Dal crossed the Sutlej and, staying for some time at Barnālā, then the capital of Sardār Ālā Siṅgh, proceeded northwards again to celebrate Dīvālī (1736) at Amritsar. While camping at Bāsarke near Amritsar, they were surprised by a 7,000-strong force under Dīwān Lakhpat Rāi. The Dal retreated towards Chūnīāṅ and then to the Mālvā country, where it helped Ālā Siṅgh extend his territory southwards at the cost of Bhaṭṭī chiefs of that region. Infuriated by the martyrdom in 1737 of Bhāī Manī Siṅgh at the hands of Zakarīyā K͟hān, Sikhs prepared to converge again upon Lahore territory. Although Nādir Shāh's invasion in January-May 1739 had shaken the imperial government at Delhi to its very roots, Zakarīyā K͟hān in the Punjab was not deterred from his policy of repression against the Sikhs. The Buḍḍhā Dal was still in the desert region of Mālvā and Rājasthān when news was received of the desecration of the Harimandar by Masse K͟hān Raṅghaṛ, Kotwāl of Amritsar. Matāb Siṅgh and Sukkhā Siṅgh, members of the *jathā* of Sardār Shām Siṅgh, travelled incognito to Amritsar, killed Massā in broad daylight on 6 May 1740 and rejoined the *jathā* in their desert resort. The Buḍḍhā Dal and Taruṇā Dal soon returned to the Punjab and resorted to their usual hit-and-run tactics. They also resumed their gatherings at Amritsar on the occasion of Baisākhī and Dīvālī. Zakarīyā Khān thought it politic to ignore these assemblies. According to Khushwaqt Rāi, he did post Dīwān Lakhpat Rāi with a suitable contingent at Amritsar on these occasions, but his orders were not to pick a fight with the Sikhs. However, his campaign for general massacre of the Sikhs "wherever found" continued unabated till his death on 1 July 1745. Feeling the need for further dispersal, the Dal Khālsā, meeting at Amritsar on the following Dīvālī, 14 November 1745, divided itself into 25 *jathās* who, however, owed allegiance to Buḍḍhā Dal and Taruṇā Dal according to the affiliation of their leaders, and who often undertook joint operations. *Jathās* belonging to both Dals were involved in the bloody action known as Chhoṭā Ghallūghārā of April-May 1746 in which Sikh losses amounted to seven to eight thousand killed and captured. Taking advantage of the civil war which had broken out between the two sons of Zakarīyā Khān—Yahīyā Khān and Shāh Nawāz Khān—in November 1746, the *jathās* of the two Dals (their number had since gone up to 65) came out of their retreats and started converging on Amritsar whence they spread out again on their plundering raids in order to replenish their depleted stocks of stores, equipment and horses. Shāh Nawāz Khān, the victor in the civil war, on the advice of his Dīwān, Kauṛā Mall, and Ādīnā Beg, *faujdār* of Jalandhar, solicited peace with the Sikhs. The Sikhs at an assembly of the Sarbatt Khālsā at Amritsar on the occasion of Baisākhī, 30 March 1747, decided to build a fort near Amritsar which when completed came to be known as Rāmgaṛh or Rām Rauṇī.

The *jathās* harassed and plundered for a whole week (18-26 March) the columns of Ahmad Shāh Durrānī who, defeated in the battle of Mānūpur (16 March 1748), had recrossed the Sutlej and was on his way back to Afghanistan. Sardār Chaṛhat Siṅgh, grandfather of Mahārājā Raṇjīt Siṅgh, chased him up to the River Chenāb and returned with a rich booty. At a Sarbatt Khālsā conclave at Amritsar on Baisākhī, 29 March 1748, the entire force of 65 *jathās* was divided into eleven *misls* or divisions each under its own *sardār* or chief as follows : (1) Āhlūvālīā *misl* under Jassā Siṅgh Āhlūvālīā, (2) Siṅghpurīā (also called Faizullāpurīā) *misl* under Nawāb Kapūr Siṅgh, (3) Karoṛsiṅghīā *misl* under Karoṛā Siṅgh, (4) Nishānvālīā *misl* under Dasaundhā Siṅgh, (5) Shahīd *misl* under Dīp Siṅgh, (6) Ḍallevālīā *misl* under Gulāb Siṅgh, (7) Sukkarchakkīā *misl* under Chaṛhat Siṅgh, (8) Bhaṅgī *misl* under Harī Siṅgh, (9) Kanhaiyā *misl* under Jai Siṅgh, (10) Nakaī *misl* under Hīrā Siṅgh, and (11) Rāmgaṛhīā *misl* under Jassā Siṅgh Rāmgaṛhīa. The first six were under Buḍḍhā Dal and the latter five under Taruṇā Dal. Jassā Siṅgh Āhlūvālīā was chosen to be in joint command of the entire Dal Khālsā, while Nawāb Kapūr Siṅgh continued to be acknowledged as the supreme commander.

Taking advantage of the preoccupation of the Mughal governor, Mu'īn ul-Mulk, with Ahmad Shāh's second invasion (December 1749-February 1750), Buḍḍhā Dal under Nawāb Kapūr Siṅgh attacked and plundered Lahore itself, and the Mughal satrap had to permit his minister, Dīwān Kauṛā Mall, to enlist Sikhs' help in his expedition against Shāh Nawāz Khān who had risen in rebellion at Multān in September 1749. Jassā Siṅgh Āhlūvālīā with 10,000 men of the Buḍḍha Dal took part in the expedition. However, soon after the successful completion of the campaign, the Lahore governor renewed his policy of repression. The Buḍḍhā Dal retreated towards the Śivālik hills, while the Taruṇā Dal found refuge in the Mālvā and in Bīkāner. In October 1753, the Buḍḍhā Dal assembled in Amritsar to celebrate Dīvālī (26 October 1753). Mu'īn ul-Mulk died in an accident a week later.

Nawāb Kapūr Siṅgh, before his death at Amritsar on 7 October 1753, nominated Jassā Siṅgh Āhlūvālīā supreme commander of the Dal Khālsā. The appointment was ratified by Sarbatt Khālsā on Baisākhī, 10 April 1754. Mu'īn ul-Mulk's death had cleared the way for Sikh hegemony over vast areas in central and southern Punjab, from the Chenāb to the Yamunā. The Durrānīs' victory in the third battle of Pānīpat (January 1761) was a severe blow to the Mughal empire as well as to the Marāṭhās as rivals to the Sikhs in north-west India. The only contender left now was the Afghān invader, Ahmad Shāh Durrānī, who annexed the Punjab to his dominions and appointed his son, Taimūr, governor at Lahore in 1757. During 1753-64, the Sikhs replaced the strategy of plundering raids with the system of *rākhī*, literally protection, under which villages and minor chiefs accepting the protection of the Dal Khālsā paid to it a regular cess. The Taruṇā Dal was now spread over the Mājhā area, and the Buḍḍhā Dal operated in the Doābā and Mālvā regions. Both collaborated for operations against the Afghān invader, who took, on 5 February 1762, a heavy toll in what is known as Vaḍḍā Ghallūghārā (*q.v.*), the Great Holocaust, so called in comparison with a similar but lesser disaster of 1746.

With the conquest of Sirhind in January 1764 started the final phase of the development of the Dal Khālsā into a confederacy of sovereign political principalities called *misls*. The *misls* now occupied well-defined territories over which their Sardārs ruled independently while maintaining their former links as units of the Dal Khālsā. The *misls* of the Buḍḍhā Dal established themselves broadly as follows : Āhlūvālīā *misl* in Jagrāoṅ, Bharog and Fatehgaṛh (later in Kapūrthalā-Sultānpur Lodhī area in the Jalandhar Doāb); Siṅghpurīā in parts of Jalandhar Doāb and Chhat-Banūṛ-Bharatgaṛh areas south of the Sutlej; Karoṛsiṅghīā *misl* in a long strip south of the Sutlej extending from Samrālā in the west to Jagādhrī in the east; Nishānvālīā *misl* in area Sāhnevāl-Dorāhā-Māchhīvāṛā-Amloh, with pockets around Zīrā and Ambālā; Shahīd *misl* in area Shahzādpur-Kesarī in present-day Ambālā district, and territory around Rāṇīā and Talvaṇḍī Sābo; and Ḍallevālīā *misl* in *parganahs* of Dharamkoṭ and Tihāṛā to the south of the River Sutlej and Lohīāṅ and Shāhkoṭ to the north of it. Of these, Āhlūvālīā *misl* survived as the princely house of Kapūrthalā and a branch of Karoṛsiṅghīā *misl* as rulers of Kalsīā state. Others divided into several petty chieftainships were either taken over by Mahārājā Raṇjīt Siṅgh and the British East India Company or absorbed into the Phūlkīāṅ states of Paṭiālā, Nābhā and Jīnd.

Even after the consolidation of their territorial acquisitions, the *misls* of the Buḍḍhā Dal continued co-operating in joint operations in Ruhīlā and Mughal territories in the Gaṅgā-Yamunā Doāb and in the country north and west of Delhi. They collected *rākhī* from parts of the Doāb and their plundering raids extended up to Delhi itself and beyond. Instances of Buḍḍhā Dal's co-operation with the Taruṇā Dal, active in Bārī and Rachnā Doābs and further to the north and east, became far fewer. The two together defeated Ahmed Shāh Abdālī in a 7-day running battle in the Jalandhar Doāb in March 1765. Early in 1768, men from both the Dals were included in a 20,000-strong contingent engaged by Jawāhar Siṅgh, the Jāṭ ruler of Bharatpur, at Rs 7,00,000 a month, to fight against Rājā Mādho Siṅgh of Jaipur. The latter, however, retired without giving a fight, and the Sikhs came back to the Punjab receiving part of the contracted sum. The two Dals now entrenched in their respective spheres as separate *misls*, the terms Buḍḍhā Dal and Taruṇā Dal became redundant and went out of use.

BIBLIOGRAPHY

1. Cunningham, J.D., *A History of the Sikhs*. Delhi, 1972
2. Latif, Syad Muhammad, *History of the Panjab*. Delhi, 1964
3. Griffin, Lepel, *The Rajas of the Punjab*. Delhi, 1977
4. Narang, Gokul Chand, *Transformation of Sikhism*. Delhi, 1960
5. Teja Singh and Ganda Siṅgh, *A Short History of the Sikhs*. Bombay, 1950
6. Gupta, Hari Ram, *History of the Sikhs*, vol. II. Delhi, 1978
7. Bhaṅgū, Ratan Singh, *Prāchīn Panth Prakāsh*. Amritsar, 1962
8. Giān Siṅgh, Giānī, *Twārīkh Gurū Khālsā*. Patiala, 1970

Gl.S.

BUḌḌHĀ SIṄGH (d. 1718), great-great-grandfather of Mahārājā Raṇjīt Siṅgh, was the founder of the Sukkarchakkīā family. One of his ancestors, Bhārā Mall, who lived in the village of Sukkarchakk, in Gujrāṅwālā district, now in Pakistan, had been initiated into the Sikh faith by the Seventh Gurū, Gurū Har Rāi. Buḍḍhā Siṅgh received the rites of *amrit* at the hands of Gurū Gobind Siṅgh himself and fought in battles under him and under Bandā Siṅgh Bahādur. He constructed a big house at Sukkarchakk and acquired considerable influence in those turbulent times. He was elected the village *chaudharī* or chief. He was a daring horseman, and there were many legends current about his adventures on his favourite piebald mare called Desī. It is said that on the back of Desī, he swam across the Rāvī, Chenāb and Jehlum rivers as many as fifty times. The dauntless warrior had on his body scars of scores of wounds by sword, spear and gun. He died in 1718.

BIBLIOGRAPHY

1. Sūrī, Sohan Lāl, *'Umdāt-ut-Twārīkh*. Lahore, 1885-89
2. Griffin, Lepel, *Ranjit Singh*. Delhi, 1957
3. Harbans Singh, *Maharaja Ranjit Singh*. Delhi, 1980

J.S.K.

BUḌḌHĀ SIṄGH (b. 1891), a Ghadr revolutionary, was son of Īshar Siṅgh of the village of Sursiṅgh, now in Amritsar district. He served in the Mule Battery at Bareilly but deserted and went to Shanghai, where he became a night watchman. He returned to India to take part in the armed revolution planned by the Ghadr Party and arrived in Calcutta aboard the *S.S. Namsang* on 13 October 1914. Finding that deserters were being retaken by their regiments, Buḍḍhā Siṅgh went back to Bareilly and re-joined the Mule Battery. It was there that he was arrested and brought to Lahore to stand trial in the supplementary Lahore conspiracy case of 1915. He was 24 at that time and was sentenced to transportation for life and forfeiture of property on 30 March 1916. He died in the Aṇḍamans jail where prisoners were given the harshest treatment. Torture and beating were part of it.

BIBLIOGRAPHY

1. Saiṅsarā, Gurcharan Siṅgh, *Ghadar Pārṭī dā Itihās*. Jalandhar, 1969
2. Jagjīt Siṅgh, *Ghadar Pārṭī Lahir*. Delhi, 1979

S.S.J.

BUḌḌHĀ SIṄGH, BHĀĪ (d. 1774), a Brāṛ Jaṭṭ who had seen the stirring days of Gurū Gobind Siṅgh, took part in January 1764 in the joint attack of Sikh *sardārs* upon Sirhind. The town was seized from the Afghān governor, Zain Khān, who was killed in the action. Since none of the participating *sardārs* was willing to accept possession of the town of Sirhind accurst from its association with the execution of Gurū Gobind Siṅgh's two younger sons, it was assigned to Buḍḍhā Siṅgh by a unanimous vote. Along with the lands of Sirhind, Buḍḍhā Siṅgh got a camel-swivel and 150 matchlocks. Sirhind was, however, later purchased from him by Bābā Ālā

Siṅgh of Paṭiālā. Returning to his headquarters at Jhumbā, in Muktsar *tahsīl*, Buḍḍhā Siṅgh took possession of 28 villages around Abohar. After a fighting career lasting many years, Bhāī Buḍḍhā Siṅgh died in 1774 at Kaithal where his collateral, Bhāī Desū Siṅgh, had established his authority in 1767.

BIBLIOGRAPHY

1. Griffin, Lepel, and C.F.Massy, *Chiefs and Families of Note in the Punjab*. Lahore, 1909
2. Sītal, Sohan Siṅgh, *Sikh Misalāṅ*. Ludhiana, 1952

S.S.B.

BUDDHĪ or *buddhi* (from Sanskrit *budh*—to wake up, be awake, to perceive, learn) is the intellectual aspect of mind *(antahkaraṇa)* whose other aspects *man* and *haumai* are intertwined with it in close interrelationship. Its nearest English equivalent may be intellect.

Man (Sanskrit *manas*) as the receptacle of sense-impressions from sense-organs, organizes them into precepts, yet it has doubt or indetermination about them. *Buddhī* defines and ascertains them and brings about definite and determinate cognition. *Man* simply assimilates sense-impressions; *haumai* (or *ahaṅkāra*) self-appropriates the apperceived impressions, while *buddhī* determines their nature, categorizes them and welds them into concepts. Its function, then, is to bring about certainty and definitiveness in knowledge. Definitive apprehension might spur action. Thus it is *buddhī* which resolves to act and then guides the ensuing action.

A fundamental categorization of percepts as also of ensuing actions concerns their moral import. The deftness with which *buddhī* does that is variable. If it can exercise acute ethical discrimination, it is known as *bibek buddhī* (discriminative intellect). That can happen only if it has become God-centred. On the contrary, if it remains self-centred (*aham buddhī*), then it remains morally confounded and unable to discriminate.

Bibek buddhī in *gurbāṇī*, Gurū's utterance, has also been called *sār-buddhī* (the essential intellect), *tat buddhī* (the real intellect), *bimal* or *nirmal buddhī* (unclouded, clear intellect), *bal buddhī* (powerful intellect), *mati buddhī* (the counselling intellect) and *sudh buddhī* (pure intellect).

Aham buddhī has also been called *chapal buddhī* (the unstable intellect), *buddhi bikār* (foul intellect), *malīn buddhī* (turbid intellect), *nibal buddhī* (weak intellect), *durmat buddhī* (perverse intellect), and *phaṇin buddhī* (the deluding intellect).

This moral bipolarity of the functioning of intellect stands out in relief in *gurbānī*. In its decadent form, *buddhi* wastes itself in vain, egoistic pursuits : *kaunu karam merā kari kari marai*—for what reason does it die proclaiming mine ! mine ! ? (GG, 1159). However, when through evolution it ascends up the ethical scale (*buddhi-pragās)*, it flowers into *bibek buddhī* which is a divine attribute: *tū samrathu tū sarab mai tū hai buddhi bibek jīu* — You are omnipotent, you are all-pervasive, you are the discriminating intellect (GG, 761). However, if it begins to undergo the process of devolution (*visarjan*) down the moral scale, *buddhī* becomes delusional intellect *(phaṇin buddhī*).

Buddhī, also called *akal* (Arabic *'aql*) in *gurbāṇī*, is considered to be an instrument for serving the Divine purpose and acquiring merit: *akalī sāhibu seviai akalī pāiai mānu* – by wisdom is the Lord served; by intellect is honour attained (GG, 1245). By contrast, *buddhī* in its decadent form is not only infirm but also arrogant, which makes it despicable:

> Some are devoid of intellect, or sense,
> or comprehension
> And understand not a syllable.
> Such folk, saith Nānak, as fill themselves
> with pride,
> Without merit are asses pedigreed.
> (GG, 1246)

BIBLIOGRAPHY

1. Sher Singh, *The Philosophy of Sikhism.* Lahore, 1944
2. Avtar Singh, *Ethics of the Sikhs.* Patiala, 1970
3. Nripinder Singh, *The Sikh Moral Tradition.* Delhi, 1990
4. Jodh Siṅgh, *Gurmat Nirṇaya.* Lahore, 1932

J.S.N.

BUDDHO, BHĀĪ, a washerman of Sultānpur Lodhī, embraced Sikh faith in the time of Gurū Amar Dās. Over the years, he became reputed for his piety. He once visited Amritsar with the *saṅgat* of his town and received blessing from Gurū Arjan.

See ĀKUL, BHĀĪ, and BHIKHĀ, BHAṬṬ

BIBLIOGRAPHY

Manī Siṅgh, Bhāī, *Sikhāṅ dī Bhagat Mālā.* Amritsar, 1955

T.S.

BUDDH SIṄGH (d. 1816), son of Khushhāl Siṅgh, nephew of the leader of the Dal Khālsā, Nawāb Kapūr Siṅgh, succeeded his father as head of the Siṅghpurīa *misl.* He inherited territories in the Bārī Doāb, the Jalandhar Doāb and in the province of Sirhind. He built a fort at Jalandhar and reconstructed at a cost of a lakh of rupees the holy shrine and tank of Tarn Tāran demolished by Nūr ud-Dīn, the local Mughal chief. In 1814, Mahārājā Raṇjīt Siṅgh seized all the possessions of the Siṅghpurīās in the Bārī Doāb, including Kaṭrā Siṅghpurīāṅ in Amritsar, and Buddh Siṅgh's movable property consisting of elephants, horses and jewellery. A year or so later Buddh Siṅgh's possessions in the Jalandhar Doāb were also confiscated by the Mahārājā and Buddh Siṅgh shifted to his cis-Sutlej estates, establishing his headquarters at Manaulī. Buddh Siṅgh died in 1816 leaving behind seven sons. His territories were however gradually annexed by the British.

BIBLIOGRAPHY

1. Griffin, Lepel, and C.F. Massy, *Chiefs and Families of Note in the Punjab.* Lahore, 1909
2. Khushwant Singh, *A History of the Sikhs,* vol. I, Princeton, 1963
3. Gupta, Hari Ram, *History of the Sikhs,* vol. IV. Delhi, 1982

S.S.B.

BUDDH SIṄGH, BĀBĀ (1819-1906), to his followers 'Gurū' Harī Siṅgh, was the younger brother of Bābā Rām Siṅgh, founder of the Nāmdhārī or Kūkā movement. He was born on Assū *sudī* 3, 1876 Bk/22 September 1819, the son of Bhāi Jassā Siṅgh and Māī Sadā Kaur of Rilpur Rāīāṅ (now Bhaiṇī Sāhib) in Ludhiāṇā district. He lived the life of a householder in his native village till the time his elder brother, on the Baisākhī day of 1857, formally declared himself to be the initiator of the Nāmdhārī movement. Buddh Siṅgh was among the first batch of disciples to be initiated by Bābā Rām Siṅgh, and he undertook the responsibility of looking after the ever-increasing stream of devotees who flocked to Bhaiṇī Sāhib to have a glimpse of the new leader and to receive '*nām*' or initiation into the new sect. Bābā Rām Siṅgh had no male offspring. Therefore when he was seized by police on 18 January 1872 for transportation to Burma, Bābā Buddh Siṅgh took over the reins of the nascent community as its caretaker religious head. It was during 1874 that one Darbārā Siṅgh, a Kūkā devotee, met Bābā Rām Siṅgh at Rangoon and brought from there the latter's *hukamnāmā* or written order formally nominating Buddh Siṅgh as the successor his and renaming him Harī Siṅgh.

With the ruthless suppression by the British of the Nāmdhārīs, banishment of Bābā Rām Siṅgh, and posting of a police picket at Bhaiṇī Sāhib, the movements of Bābā Buddh Siṅgh (Harī Siṅgh) were restricted to the village itself. While this limited active religious preaching by him, he did not abandon the anti-British policies and programme of his predecessor. The boycott of British goods, courts and educational institutions by Kūkās continued and contacts with the rulers of Kashmīr and Nepal, already established, were maintained. These contacts had not been fruitful because the British were too powerful for these insignificant local states to be partners in any plot against them or to permit any anti-British activity within their territories. However, a new situation was developing across the northwestern borders of India of which Bābā Buddh Siṅgh decided to take full advantage. Europe's sleeping giant, Russia, had risen from a long slumber and was stretching its limbs to the West and the East. After her ambitions in the West had been frustrated by her defeat at the hands of the British in the Crimean War (1854-56), Russia diverted her attention to Central Asia. Bokhārā became a dependency of Russia in 1866, Samarkand was acquired in 1868, followed by Khīvā in 1873. A new province of Russian Turkistān bordering on Afghanistan was formed and a Russian base established at Tāshkent. British involvement in the second Anglo-Afghān war from 1878 onwards brought the British face to face with their strong rival, Russia. Bābā Buddh Siṅgh deputed Sūbā Gurcharan Siṅgh, a Kūkā preacher who knew Pashto and Persian, to contact the Russians. It is not known how many times and with what success Gurcharan Siṅgh visited the Russians, but a letter from a British spy, Gulāb Khān, confirms his return from Central Asia to Afghanistan on 1 May 1879, and his being honoured by the Russians during a subsequent visit on 1 October 1879. He was told on this latter occasion "to return to the Punjab and strengthen the friendship between the Russians and the Kūkās." A later statement of the spy mentions that "on 9 April 1880 Gurcharan Siṅgh sent another letter to Samarkand... This was from Bābā Rām Siṅgh, but in the handwriting of his younger brother (Bābā Buddh Siṅgh alias Harī Siṅgh)." Gulāb Khān, the spy, met Gurcharan Siṅgh at Peshāwar and won his confidence posing as a Russian secret agent and got from him two letters for Russian officers which he made over to the Commissioner of Peshāwar. Gurcharan Siṅgh, however, was not arrested there and was allowed to return to Bhaiṇī Sāhib, in India, and was ultimately apprehended at his native village Chakk Pirāṇā (or Chakk Rāmdās) in Siālkoṭ district. Gulāb Khān also met Bābā Buddh Siṅgh on 3 January 1881 and won the latter's full confidence. The detention of Gurcharan Siṅgh did not dampen the Bābā's enthusiasm for secret negotiations with the Russians. These continued through another Kūkā missionary, Sūbā Bishan Siṅgh. Upon the arrival of Mahārājā Duleep Siṅgh in Russia in 1887, Bishan Siṅgh met him and the two together made up plans to secure Russian support for invading the Punjab. The invasion, however, never took place, and Bābā Buddh Siṅgh's plans aborted.

From 1890 onwards, Bābā Buddh Siṅgh diverted his attention to preaching Nāmdhārī doctrines and consolidating the Kūkā movement in the Punjab. He died at Bhaiṇī Sāhib on Saturday, Jeṭh *vadī* 10, 1963 Bk/19 May 1906.

BIBLIOGRAPHY

1. Bajwa, Fauja Singh, *Kuka Movement.* Delhi, 1965
2. Vahimī, Taran Siṅgh, *Jass-Jīvan.* Rampur (Hissar), 1971

M.L.A.

BUDDH SIṄGH BĀVĀ, an associate of Ṭhākur Siṅgh Sandhāṅvālīā, who served as a link between him and his contacts in Puṇchh and Kashmīr. He was the son of Faujdār Siṅgh, a Khatrī of Baṭālā, in Gurdāspur district. He was first employed as a Sardār in Kashmīr irregular force and served in that capacity for seventeen years. In 1880, he took service with Rājā Motī Siṅgh of Puṇchh and stayed with him for two years. Leaving his family at Koṭhī in Jammū, Buddh Siṅgh then moved to Nepal where he was employed as a captain in Kālī Bahādur regiment. He met Ṭhākur Siṅgh Sandhāṅvālīā at Paṭnā while on leave from Nepal. Ṭhākur Siṅgh sought Buddh Siṅgh's assistance to further the cause of Mahārājā Duleep Siṅgh and to secure for himself entry into Nepal. Buddh Siṅgh was at Amritsar when Ṭhākur Siṅgh left for Pondicherry, where he became prime minister to Mahārājā Duleep Siṅgh's emigre government. He stayed at Ṭhākur Siṅgh's *havelī* from where he distributed Ṭhākur Siṅgh's letters and messages to his friends. Buddh Siṅgh was arrested in November 1887 and detained in the Chunār Fort. He was released in December 1890.

BIBLIOGRAPHY

1. Ganda Singh, ed., *History of the Freedom Movement in the Punjab (Maharaja Duleep Singh Correspondence)*. Patiala, 1977
2. Harbans Singh, *The Heritage of the Sikhs*. Delhi, 1983

K.S.T.

BUDDH SIṄGH, BHĀĪ (1903-1921), son of Bhāī Surjan Siṅgh and Māī Gaṅgā Kaur was born on 4 January 1903 at village Kartārpur in Siālkoṭ district. The family descended on the paternal side from Bhāī Ālam Siṅgh Nachanā, a prominent Sikh in Gurū Gobind Siṅgh's retinue. Young Buddh Siṅgh shared his elders' religious fervour and also received formal education up to the middle school standard. At the age of 15, he accompanied his parents on a pilgrimage to Sachkhaṇḍ Srī Hazūr Sāhib, Nāndeḍ, where he received the vows of the Khālsā and donned a Nihaṅg's uniform. He organized a *kīrtanī jathā* (choir) and began preaching the Gurū's teachings.

On 18 February 1921, Buddh Siṅgh went to Chakk No. 13 Nānakpurā, district Sheikhūpurā, where lived his mother's sister with her husband and their infant son. On 19 February 1921 the entire family including Buddh Siṅgh went to Nankāṇā Sāhib to offer homage and thanks-giving at different shrines in the town. They spent the night at Gurdwārā Pātshāhī Chhevīn. Early in the next morning, Buddh Siṅgh went out for a walk along the railway line and ran into the *jathā* of Bhāī Lachhmaṇ Siṅgh Dhārovālī bound for Gurdwārā Janam Asthān. Bhāī Buddh Siṅgh joined the *jathā* which was showered with bullets as they reached the shrine. Buddh Siṅgh fell a martyr along with others.

See NANKĀṆĀ SĀHIB MASSACRE

BIBLIOGRAPHY

Shamsher, Gurbakhsh Siṅgh, *Shahīdī Jīvan*. Nankana Sahib, 1938

G.S.G.

BUDDH SIṄGH MĀN (d. 1856), son of Mānā Siṅgh, entered the service of Mahārājā Raṇjīt Siṅgh in 1816 as a *khidmatgār* (attendant). He rose to the command of 30 horse, and was given a *jāgīr* worth 17,000 rupees. Later, he was promoted a colonel in General Court's brigade. According to British records, he commanded four regiments of infantry, one regiment of cavalry, and two troops of artillery. He remained on active duty during Mahārājā Sher Siṅgh's reign, but because of his relationship with Atar Siṅgh Sandhāṅvālīā, a confirmed opponent of the Mahārājā, he was reduced in rank.

Buddh Siṅgh was reinstated a general under Wazir Hīrā Siṅgh. He was put in command of General Court's force which had an important role to play during the disorderly conditions following the assassination of Mahārājā Sher Siṅgh and Wazīr Dhiān Siṅgh. Buddh Siṅgh's troops were sent in particular to quell the revolts of Kaṅvar Pashaurā Siṅgh and Kaṅvar Kashmīrā Siṅgh. He commanded a division of the Sikh army during the first Anglo-Sikh war. He continued in the service of the Lahore Darbār after the reorganization of the Sikh army under the treaty of

Lahore (1846). He served under Major John Nicholson in 1847 and later under Captain James Abbott. During the second Anglo-Sikh war, he remained with the British though the troops under his command had deserted him and joined Chatar Siṅgh Aṭārīvālā. He fought the Sikhs under the command of Major Nicholson at Margalla Pass, was wounded and taken prisoner. He secured his release after the battle of Gujrāt (21 February 1849). He died in 1856.

BIBLIOGRAPHY

1. Griffin, Lepel, and C.F. Massy, *Chiefs and Families of Note in the Punjab*. Lahore, 1909
2. Hotī, Prem Siṅgh, *Mahārājā Sher Siṅgh*. Ludhiana, 1951

B.J.H.

BUDDH SIṄGH SANDHĀṄVĀLĪĀ (d. 1827), soldier and *jāgīrdār* in the time of Mahārājā Raṇjīt Siṅgh, was son of Amīr Siṅgh Sandhāṅvālīā, his two brothers being the more famous Lahiṇā Siṅgh Sandhāṅvālīā and Atar Siṅgh Sandhāṅvālīā. Buddh Siṅgh entered the Mahārājā's service in 1811. The first independent command he held was at Bahāwalpur where he had been sent to collect tax arrears. In 1821, he captured the forts of Maujgaṛh and Jāmgaṛh and received *jāgīrs* in reward from the Mahārājā. Later, he was sent to the Jammū hills in command of two regiments of infantry and one of cavalry. He also commanded a Sikh force in the battle of Ṭīrī in 1823. Not long afterwards, he fell from favour and, to keep him away from Lahore, the Mahārājā gave him the Peshāwar command and sent him into the Yūsafzaī country against K͟halīfā Sayyid Ahmad, then preaching *jihād* against the Sikhs. Buddh Siṅgh fought against the K͟halīfā and inflicted on him such a crushing defeat that it took him two years to recover his forces sufficiently to go to battle again. After this victory Buddh Siṅgh returned to Lahore, where he was received with much honour. A few months later, at the close of 1827, he died of cholera. The Mahārājā wrote a letter to his family expressing his grief at his death and regretting that so brave a man should have died in bed like a common mortal.

BIBLIOGRAPHY

1. Sūrī, Sohan Lāl, *'Umdāt-ut-Twārīkh*. Lahore, 1885-89
2. Griffin, Lepel, *Ranjit Singh*. Delhi, 1957
3. Prinsep, Henry T., *Origin of the Sikh Power in the Punjab and Political Life of Maharaja Ranjit Singh*. Calcutta, 1834

B.J.H.

BUDDHŪ, BHĀĪ, a kiln-owner of Lahore, whose name occurs in Bhāī Gurdās, *Vārāṅ*, XI.25, among the prominent Sikhs of the time of Gurū Arjan, once waited upon the Gurū and begged to be instructed. The Gurū said, "Commence any task you may be launching on after an *ardās* or prayer in *saṅgat* seeking God's blessing, and distribution of *kaṛāhprasād*. Lay aside one-tenth of what you earn for the general weal." Bhāī Buddhū took the Gurū's precept and became a Sikh. Once, as the tradition goes, Bhāī Buddhū undertook a large brick-baking project, involving considerable investment. He invited all local Sikhs to a feast after which *ardās* was to be offered for the success of the enterprise. It so happened that a pious but poorly looking Sikh, Lakkhū by name, came late and was denied entry to the feast. He kept standing near the door. As *ardās* was being offered with the words, "May Buddhū's pile of bricks be perfectly baked," Bhāī Lakkhū cried: "May Buddhū's bricks remain half-baked!" Everyone was startled. Bhāī Buddhū was much concerned at the curse uttered by Lakkhū. He went to Gurū Arjan and begged him to cancel the curse. The Gurū said, "I cannot undo what my saintly Sikh has done. Your bricks will remain half-baked, but they will sell." That year was marked by heavy rains and bricks even of inferior quality were in great demand. The spot, about 1.5 km northeast of Lahore, where Bhāī Buddhū used to burn his bricks, is known to this day as Buddhū dā Āvā, or Buddhū's kiln.

BIBLIOGRAPHY

1. Manī Siṅgh, Bhāī, *Sikhāṅ dī Bhagat Mālā*. Amritsar, 1955
2. Bhallā, Sarūp Dās, *Mahimā Prakash*. Patiala, 1971
3. Santokh Siṅgh, Bhāī, *Sri Gur Pratāp Sūraj Granth*. Amritsar, 1926-37

T.S.

BUDDHŪ SHĀH, PĪR (1647-1704), a Muslim divine whose real name was Badr ud-Dīn and who was an admirer of Gurū Gobind Siṅgh, was born on 13 June 1647 in a prosperous Sayyid family of Saḍhaurā, in present-day Ambālā district of Haryāṇā. Because of his simplicity and silent nature during his early childhood he was given the nickname of Buddhū (lit. simpleton) which stuck to him permanently. He was married at the age of 18 to a pious lady, Nasīrāṅ, who was the sister of Said Khān, later a high-ranking officer in the Mughal army. It is not certain how Buddhū Shāh first became acquainted with Gurū Gobind Siṅgh, but it is recorded that he called on him in 1685 at Pāoṇṭā, on the bank of the Yamunā. At his recommendation, the Gurū engaged 500 Paṭhān soldiers under the command of four leaders, Kāle Khān, Bhīkhan Khān, Nijābat Khān and Hayāt Khān. In 1688, when Gurū Gobind Siṅgh was attacked by a combined force of the hill chiefs led by Rājā Fateh Shāh of Srīnagar (Gaṛhvāl), all the Paṭhāns with the exception of Kāle Khān deserted him and joined the hill monarch. The Gurū conveyed the news of the treachery to Pīr Buddhū Shāh, who immediately rushed to Bhaṅgāṇī, the battlefield, with 700 of his followers, including his brother and four sons. Many of the Pīr's disciples as well as two of his sons, Ashraf and Muhammad Shāh, and his brother, Bhūre Shāh, fell in the action. After the battle Gurū Gobind Siṅgh offered rich presents to the Pīr which the latter politely declined to accept. However he, as the tradition goes, begged the Gurū to bestow upon him the comb from his hair and the turban he was going to tie. The Gurū gave him the two articles and a small *kirpān* or sword which the Pīr and his descendants kept in the family as sacred heirlooms until Mahārājā Bharpūr Siṅgh of Nābhā (1840-63) acquired them in exchange for a *jāgīr* or land grant. The relics are still preserved in the family's palace at Nābhā (in the Punjab).

The Rājpūt chiefs defeated at Bhaṅgāṇī remained hostile towards Gurū Gobind Siṅgh, and wished to evict him from Anandpur to where he had returned. To solicit help from the imperial government, they sent to the emperor reports describing the Gurū as a dangerous rebel. Complaints also reached the authority against Pīr Buddhū Shāh who had rendered assistance to the Gurū. The *faujdār* of Sirhind, under whose jurisdiction the *parganah* of Saḍhaurā then fell, directed a local official, 'Usmān Khān, to chastise the Pīr. The latter marched on Saḍhaurā, arrested Buddhū Shāh and had him executed on 21 March 1704. Bandā Siṅgh Bahādur avenged the Pīr's execution in 1709 by storming Saḍhaurā and killing 'Usmān Khān. Pīr Buddhū Shāh's descendants migrated to Pakistan in 1947. Their ancestral house in Saḍhaurā has since been converted into a *gurdwārā* named after Pīr Buddhū Shāh.

BIBLIOGRAPHY

1. Sūrī, V.S., and Gurcharan Singh, *Pir Buddhu Shah*. Chandigarh, 1971
2. Harbans Singh, *Guru Gobind Singh*. Chandigarh, 1966
3. Macauliffe, Max Arthur, *The Sikh Religion*. Oxford, 1909
4. Khushwant Singh, *A History of the Sikhs*, vol. I, Princeton, 1963

Gch.S.

BUDHMOR, commonly called Budhmar, is a village in Paṭiālā district, 8 km southeast of Ghuṛām (30°-7'N, 76°-28'E). It is sacred to Gurū Tegh Bahādur, who visited it during one of his journeys through this region. A Mañjī Sāhib, constructed by Mahārājā Karam Siṅgh (1798-1845) of Paṭiālā, was located east of the village. It was replaced by a new building raised in 1980 by the followers of Sant Bābā Jīvan Siṅgh. It consists of a square *dīvān* hall with a domed sanctum, and other ancillary buildings. The shrine, known as Gurdwārā Mañjī Sāhib Pātshāhī Nauvīṅ, is affiliated to the Shiromaṇī Gurdwārā Parbandhak Committee and is administered by a local committee.

BIBLIOGRAPHY

1. Tārā Siṅgh, *Srī Gur Tīrath Saṅgrahi*. Amritsar, n.d.
2. Ṭhākar Siṅgh, Giānī, *Srī Gurduāre Darshan*. Amritsar, 1923
3. Faujā Siṅgh, *Gurū Teg Bahādur: Yātrā Asthān, Pramparāvāṅ te Yād Chinn*. Patiala, 1976

M.G.S.

BŪLĀ, BHĀĪ, mentioned by Bhāī Gurdās, *Vārāṅ*, XI. 15, as one of the devoted Sikhs of the time of Gurū Aṅgad.

See DĪPĀ, BHĀĪ

BIBLIOGRAPHY

1. Manī Siṅgh, Bhāī, *Sikhāṅ dī Bhagat Mālā*. Amritsar, 1955
2. Giān Siṅgh, Giānī, *Twārīkh Gurū Khālsā*. Patiala, 1970
3. Santokh Siṅgh, Bhāī, *Srī Gur Pratāp Sūraj Granth*. Amritsar, 1926-37

Gn.S.

BŪLĀ, BHĀĪ, figures in Bhāī Gurdās's roster of prominent Sikhs of the time of Gurū Rām Dās, *Vārāṅ*, XI. 17. Bhāī Gurdās describes him as Būlā the Dealer in Truth.

See DHARAM DĀS, BHĀĪ

BIBLIOGRAPHY

1. Manī Siṅgh, Bhāī, *Sikhāṅ dī Bhagat Mālā*. Amritsar, 1955
2. Santokh Siṅgh, Bhāī, *Srī Gur Pratāp Sūraj Granth*. Amritsar, 1926-37

M.G.S.

BŪLĀ DHĪR, BHĀĪ, whose name appears in the list of prominent Sikhs in Bhāī Gurdās, *Vārāṅ*, XI. 18, once came along with Bhāī Nihālū, Bhāī Tulsīā and Bhāī Chaṇḍīā, all Dhīr Khatrīs, to see Gurū Arjan. He brought with him one question: "Whose incarnation was Gurū Nānak?" The Gurū, as says Bhāī Santokh Siṅgh, *Srī Gur Pratāp Sūraj Granth*, explained: "Gurū Nānak was one with Brahman. He founded a unique faith. Discarding austerities, rituals and penances, he preached repetition of the True Name, and recommended charity, cleanliness and love. Give up vacillation, and concentrate your mind on the *bāṇī*." Būlā and his companions felt satisfied and all their doubts vanished.

BIBLIOGRAPHY

1. Manī Siṅgh, Bhāī, *Sikhāṅ dī Bhagat Mālā*. Amritsar, 1955
2. Santokh Siṅgh, Bhāī, *Srī Gur Pratāp Sūraj Granth*. Amritsar, 1926-37

T. S.

BULĀKĀ SIṄGH, an eighteenth-century Sikh musician who recited the holy hymns. He lived in the village of Ghuṛāṇī, in Ludhiāṇā district. He was once humiliated by the local anathematized group who were the followers of Bābā Rām Rāi. To avenge the insult, hero and warrior Bandā Siṅgh Bahādur sacked the village in 1710. Bulākā Siṅgh was appointed *thānedar* or police chief of the area.

BIBLIOGRAPHY

Bhaṅgū, Ratan Siṅgh, *Prāchīn Panth Prakāsh*. Amritsar, 1962

G.S.D.

BULĀKĪ DĀS was the *masand* or head of the

Sikh *saṅgat,* at Dhākā, now capital of Bangladesh, during the third quarter of the seventeenth century. Dhākā had been visited by Gurū Nānak at the beginning of the sixteenth century when a *saṅgat* had emerged in the town. During the time of Gurū Hargobind, a Sikh, Bhāī Mohan, had kept the Gurū's message alive there. Bhāī Natthā, third in succession to Almast, the Udāsī saint, who had been sent by Gurū Hargobind to preach in the eastern parts, had been deputed to supervise the *saṅgats* or Sikh fellowships or communities in Bengal. When Gurū Tegh Bahādur visited Bengal in 1666-67, Bulākī Dās was in charge of the Dhākā *saṅgat.* His old mother, a devout lady, had long wished to receive and behold the Gurū. She had a seat especially designed for him, and had also stitched garments of homespun cotton which she longed to present to him in person. Her heart's wish was fulfilled when upon reaching Dhākā Gurū Tegh Bahādur went straight to her house, and sat on the couch and received the offerings. Bulākī Dās and the *saṅgats* served Gurū Tegh Bahādur with devotion. Before he departed, the old lady had another request to make. She requested him to let a likeness of his to be painted. The Gurū acceded to her request. He told Bulākī Dās to have a *dharamsālā* raised in town. The *dharamsālā,* named Gurdwārā Saṅgat Ṭolā, still exists in a street named after it.

Later, in 1670, when he learnt that Gurū Tegh Bahādur had left for the Punjab asking his family to follow him, Bulākī Dās sent a gilded palanquin from Dhākā to Paṭnā for use by the young Gobind Rāi, later Gurū Gobind Siṅgh. Once he also travelled to Anandpur to pay homage to Gurū Tegh Bahādur. He lived to a ripe old age, and his name appears as one of the leading Sikhs of Dhākā in a letter *(hukamnāmā)* Gurū Gobind Siṅgh addressed to the *saṅgat* there in 1691, although he had by then been replaced as *masand* by Bhāī Hulās Chand.

BIBLIOGRAPHY

1. Gaṇḍā Siṅgh, ed., *Hukamnāme.* Patiala, 1967
2. Bhallā, Sarūp Dās, *Mahimā Prakāsh.* Patiala, 1971
3. Trilochan Singh, *Guru Tegh Bahadur.*Delhi, 1967
4. Harbans Singh, *Guru Tegh Bahadur.* Delhi, 1982

A.C.B.

BŪLĀ PĀNDHĀ, a learned Brāhmaṇ of Ḍallā in present-day Kapūrthalā district of the Punjab, called on Gurū Amar Dās as the latter once visited his village, and received the rites of initiation at his hands. One day Bhāī Būlā asked the Gurū how he might serve the *saṅgat,* for he could do little work physically. The Gūrū, in the words of Bhāī Manī Siṅgh, *Sikhāṅ dī Bhagat Mālā,* spoke: "Give discourses on the holy *bāṇī.* Besides, prepare copies of the *pothī,* breviary of hymns, for distribution among Sikhs. Do not ask for any payment for your labour, though you may accept what is voluntarily offered to you. This shall be your *sevā,* i.e. service." Bhāī Būlā adhered to the Gurū's direction and became a favourite Sikh of his. According to Giānī Giān Siṅgh, *Twārīkh Gurū Khālsā,* Bhāī Būlā was one of those who, led by Bhāī Jeṭhā (later Gurū Rām Dās), went to the Mughal court at Lahore in the time of Gurū Amar Dās when complaints had been laid before Emperor Akbar about the Gurū's teaching refuting the Hindus' traditional belief and practices. Bhāī Jeṭhā and his companions explained to the Emperor how Gurū Nānak's message was meant for all, making no distinction between the Hindu and the Muslim.

BIBLIOGRAPHY

1. Manī Singh, Bhāī, *Sikhāṅ dī Bhagat Mālā.* Amritsar, 1955
2. Giān Siṅgh, Giānī, *Twārīkh Gurū Khālsā.* Patiala, 1970

B.S.D.

BUṄGĀ, 5 km south of Kīratpur Sāhib (31°-10'N, 76°-35'E) in Ropaṛ district of the

Punjab, claims a historical shrine Gurdwārā Buṅgā Sāhib, also called Chubachchā Sāhib, dedicated to Gurū Har Rāi. Gurū Har Rāi, Nānak VII, complying with his predecessor's instruction, continued to maintain at Kīratpur a body of armed Sikhs, 2,200 strong. Buṅgā was the place where their horses were kept. At the back of the Gurdwārā, there is a row of rooms one of which has within it a square pit symbolizing the original *chubachchā* or trough where the horse feed was mixed. From this the shrine came to be called Chubachchā Sāhib.

The main building of the shrine stands on a high base, about 10 metres above the level of the canal bank. A double-storeyed gateway opens out on the main hall. At the eastern end of the hall is the sanctum, a square room with a circumambulatory passage around it. The Gurdwārā is managed by the Shiromaṇī Gurdwārā Parbandhak Committee through a local committee. Besides the morning and evening services, all the important religious anniversaries on the Sikh calendar are observed when largely-attended congregations take place.

BIBLIOGRAPHY

1. Tārā Siṅgh, *Srī Gur Tīrath Saṅgrahi*. Amritsar, n.d.
2. Ṭhākar Siṅgh, Giānī, *Srī Gurduāre Darshan*. Amritsar, 1923

Jg.S.

BUṄGĀS. The word *buṅga* is derived from the Persian *buṅgah* meaning a hospice, or a dwelling place. In the Sikh tradition, the word specifically refers to the dwelling places and mansions which grew up around the Harimandar at Amritsar and at other centres of Sikh pilgrimage. These were primarily the houses built by the conquering *sardārs* and chiefs in Sikh times or by Sikh schoolmen and sectaries. Amritsar housed the largest complex of such buildings. All of the Amritsar *buṅgās* have not survived, but a fairly comprehensive list of them can be compiled from references in old chronicles, including contemporary Persian sources. Ahmad Shāh Baṭālīā wrote in his Persian work *Twārīkh-i-Hind* AH 1233/AD 1817-18, that, around their place of worship amidst the *sarovar* at Amritsar, the Sikh *sardārs* had erected many mansions which they called *buṅgās*.

The English adventurer Major H.M.L. Lawrence, who is said to have attained the rank of colonel in the service of Mahārājā Ranjīt Siṅgh in May 1830, has recorded that there existed many *buṅgās* around the sacred tank at Amritsar. According to him, each *misl* had its own *buṅgā*, while some chiefs had built their personal *buṅgās* as well. The French scientist Victor Jacquemont and the British chronicler W.L. M' Gregor have also referred to these buildings though without using the word *buṅgā*.

Houses and hutments had existed around the holy tank at Amritsar since the time of Gurū Rām Dās who had begun the excavation. But the premises remained deserted during periods of persecution in the eighteenth century. The Afghān invader, Ahmad Shāh Durrānī, demolished the holy Harimandar and its surroundings more than once during his inroads into India. The Sikhs returned each time to rebuild these and when they established their authority in the Punjab with the twelve *misls* or chiefships dividing the country among themselves, Amritsar became their political capital as well. The *sardārs* reconstructed the temple, cleansed the tank and raised fortifications for the security of the town. Some of them built their *buṅgās* on the periphery of the sacred pool. Special importance was attached to the Akāl Takht, also called Takht Akāl Buṅgā, established by Gurū Hargobind himself in 1606 as the seat of highest religious authority for the Sikhs. At the Akāl Buṅgā, the Sarbatt Khālsā, i.e. the general body of the Sikhs, met from time to time, especially on the occasions of Baisākhī and Dīvālī, formulated policy and passed *gurmatās* or resolutions. It was at the

Ta<u>kh</u>t Akāl Buṅgā that *misls*, lit. files, of the territorial acquisitions of each of the *sardārs* were maintained.

The *buṅgās* could be broadly classified into three categories – (i) those belonging to the different ruling clans, (ii) those belonging to individual *sardārs* and chiefs, (iii) those belonging to different sects such as Udāsīs, Nirmalās, Sevāpanthīs and Akālīs. Some of these last-named were centres of Sikh education and learning. There were *buṅgās* which became famous as seats of eminent poets and scholars. Bhāī Kāhn Siṅgh of Nābhā lists in his *Guru Mahimā Ratnāvalī* names of a few men of letters who flourished in the *buṅgās*. For instance, Sant Nihāl Siṅgh II, a reputed poet was the *mahant*, or custodian, of Sohalāṅvālā Buṅgā. He was a pupil of Giānī Rām Siṅgh, and was the author of scholarly work *Kavīndra Prakāsh*. His disciple Nihāl Siṅgh, who succeeded him as the *mahant* of Buṅgā Sohalāṅvālā was himself a well-known scholar.

Bhāī Sant Siṅgh Giānī of Buṅgā Giānīāṅ was a renowned scholar and wrote a commentary in prose on Tulsī Dās's *Rāmacharita-Mānasa*. He enjoyed great esteem in the time of Maharājā Raṇjīt Siṅgh and was appointed head priest of the Harimandar.

Santokh Siṅgh, pen-name Tokh Harī, of Ghaṛiālvālā Buṅgā, was a famous poet of his time and composed *Guru Kabitva Māṇikya Mañjūshā*. Buddh Siṅgh, who has been referred to as a celebrated contemporary poet of Braj Bhāshā by Ganesh Dās Baḍherā in his Persian work *Chār-Bā<u>gh</u>-i-Pañjāb* and who translated *Pañch Tantra* from the Sanskrit, was associated with Shahīd Buṅgā. Ratan Siṅgh Bhaṅgū, the author of the *Prāchīn Panth Prakāsh*, composed his poeticized history of the Sikhs in the Buṅgā of Shyām Siṅgh of Karoṛsiṅghīā *misl*. The *buṅgās* belonging to the Nirmalās, Udāsīs, Sevāpanthīs, Giānīs and Granthīs also served as educational institutions. The Udāsī *buṅgās* belonging to Bābā Prītam Dās and Bhāī Vastī Rām were famous centres of learning. Two *buṅgās* were engaged in teaching Sanskrit. They were Buṅgā Hukam Siṅgh and Buṅgā Māikvāl. Hukam Siṅgh Buṅgā was run by Āgyā Rām. The Māikvāl Buṅgā had a *pāṭhshālā* attached to it presided over by Braj Lāl. Both the *buṅgās* were under the Udāsīs. Besides Sanskrit, they taught their pupils to read and write Gurmukhī. Some of the *buṅgās* were institutions of advanced studies and provided instruction in Vedānta, grammar and logic. One such *buṅgā* was that of the Malvaīs, which was built with the beneficence of the Sikh chiefs and *sardārs* of the Mālvā region. The Kapūrthalā Buṅgā served by Sant Chandā Siṅgh and Sant Dayā Siṅgh specialized in the interpretation of the Gurū Granth Sāhib. Giānī Sant Siṅgh and Parduman Siṅgh were also originally attached to this Buṅgā which claimed Mahāṅ Kavī Bhāī Santokh Siṅgh as its most distinguished alumnus. Another old pupil was Bhāī Rām Siṅgh, who ran a Gurmukhī *pāṭhshālā* and was for some time tutor to Kharak Siṅgh, the eldest son of Mahārājā Raṇjīt Siṅgh. The *buṅgās* of Rāgī Kāhn Siṅgh, Rāgī Chaṛhat Siṅgh and Rāgī Dhanpat Siṅgh trained pupils in Sikh music. The Āhlūvālīā Buṅgā was likewise an academy of music, with Rājā Fateh Siṅgh of Kapūrthalā as its chief patron. It excelled at instrumental music and was famous for its courses on Rabāb, Sāraṅgī, Mirdaṅg and Kachcchavā which were normally played in the Harimandar. The Buṅgā Siṅghpurīāṅ imparted training in Gurmukhī calligraphy for transcribing copies of the Gurū Granth Sāhib. Two of its inmates, Bhāī Lahora Siṅgh and Bhāī Harī Siṅgh, were especially known for their mastery of the art. The chief patron of the Buṅgā was Giānī Sant Siṅgh, himself a fine calligraphist. Some of the *ḍerās*, especially those belonging to Udāsīs, concentrated on indigenous medicine. Among these the Jalliāṅvālā Buṅgā was known for the treatment of skin diseases. Ghaṛiālvālā Buṅgā was concerned with announcing the time of the day at regular intervals, principally for services in the Harimandar.

Each *buṅgā* was managed by a supervisor called *buṅgaī*. He daily recited the Gurū Granth Sāhib and looked after the comfort of the pilgrims. For maintenance, the *buṅgās* depended on the sects or individual *sardārs* who had built them or who patronized them. Whenever Sikh chiefs visited the Harimandar to offer obeisance, they always left money and sweets to be distributed among the different *buṅgās*. The *sarbarāh* or manager of the Harimandar was in a position to issue instructions to the supervisors of the *buṅgās* about the management of their affairs, discipline, etc.

On the enactment of the Sikh Gurdwaras Act in 1925, the *buṅgās* and their properties were placed on the lists of the Shiromaṇī Committee. But the owners of the *buṅgās* challenged this in the Gurdwārā Tribunal. The Tribunal decided the case in their favour. An appeal against the decision of the Tribunal was lost in the Punjab High Court. In 1943, the Shiromaṇī Gurdwārā Parbandhak Committee decided to widen the *parikramā*, the circumambulatory terrace around the *sarovar*, for which many old *buṅgās* would have to be demolished. It therefore purchased the *buṅgās* which were not already the property of Darbār Sāhib and demolished those which fell within the *parikramā* - widening scheme. The actual work was, however, taken up and completed after the partition (Independence) of the country in 1947. Now all buildings adjoining the *parikramā*, with the exception of Buṅgā Akhāṛā Brahm Būṭā, are Gurdwārā property.

The names of the founders and owners of the *buṅgās*, the years of construction, details concerning the buildings, *jāgīrs* and properties attached and the names of the *buṅgaīs* are recorded in *Tarīkh-i-Amritsar ke Chand Mākhaz* and *Report Srī Darbār Sāhib*. The former lists 72 *buṅgās* and the latter 73. Below is given a list of 68 *buṅgās* and 12 *akhāṛās* as recorded by Giānī Giān Siṅgh in *Twārīkh Srī Amritsar*, written in 1946 Bk/AD 1889, first printed in AD 1923 and reprinted in 1977. Many of these buildings fell into disuse; most of the others were acquired by the Shiromaṇī Gurdwārā Parbandhak Committee and demolished to bring symmetry to the surroundings of the Harimandar.

Buṅgās on the western side of the Harimandar Sāhib:

1. Buṅgā Jalliāṅvālā
2. Buṅgā Shāhābādīāṅ
3. Buṅgā Majīṭhīāṅ
4. Buṅgā Siṅghpurīāṅ
5. Buṅgā Siṅghpurīāṅ, 2nd
6. Buṅgā Gaddovālīāṅ
7. Buṅgā Khushāl Siṅgh also known as Buṅgā Tīn Manzalā (three-storyed)
8. Buṅgā Kanhaiyā Sardārāṅ
9. Buṅgā Rājā Dhiān Siṅgh
10. Buṅgā Bārāṅdarīvālā
11. Akāl Buṅgā
12. Buṅga Jodh Siṅgh Chhāpāvālā
13. Buṅgā Bhāg Siṅgh Shahīd
14. Buṅgā Devā Siṅgh Shahīd
15. Buṅgā Rāgī Dhanpat Siṅgh
16. Buṅgā General Mīhāṅ Siṅgh
17. Buṅgā Bhāī Gurdās, Giānī
18. Buṅgā Abhai Siṅgh Hukamnāmīā
19. Buṅgā Nakaīāṅ (Nakaī Buṅgā)
20. Buṅgā Barkīvālīāṅ
21. Buṅgā Ghaṛiālvālā
22. Jhaṇḍā Buṅgā
23. Buṅgā Chamārīvalīāṅ
24. Buṅgā Khaḍūrīāṅ
25. Buṅgā Siālkoṭīāṅ
26. Buṅgā Gobind Dāsīāṅ
27. Buṅgā Chīchevālīāṅ
28. Buṅgā Sukkarchakkīāṅ

Buṅgās on northern side:

1. Ghaṇṭā Ghar (Clock Tower, which was erected, where earlier stood the

Buṅgā of Sardārs of Lāḍvā)
2. Buṅgā Soḍhīs of Anandpur/Buṅgā Soḍhīāṅ
3. Buṅgā Kāhn Siṅgh Nirmalā
4. Buṅgā Kāhn Siṅgh Rāgī
5. Buṅgā Nūrmahalīāṅ
6. Buṅgā Āhlūvālīāṅ
7. Buṅgā Malvaīāṅ/Malvaī Buṅgā
8. Buṅgā Bhāī Sāhibs of Kaithal
9. Buṅgā Jallevālīāṅ

Buṅgās on eastern side:

1. Buṅgā Akhāṛā Mahant Santokh Dās
2. Buṅgā Rām Siṅgh Giānī
3. Buṅgā Jassā Siṅgh Rāmgaṛhīā
4. Buṅgā Būṛīevālīāṅ
5. Buṅgā Jeṭhūvālīāṅ
6. Buṅgā Mazhabī Sikkhāṅ
7. Buṅgā Bhāī Vastī Rām
8. Buṅgā Javālā Siṅgh Bhaṛhāṇīāṅ
9. Buṅgā Sant Jogā Siṅgh Nirmalā
10. Buṅgā Ṭek Siṅghvālā

Buṅgās on southern side:

1. Buṅgā Sohalāṅvālīāṅ/Sohalāṅvālā
2. Buṅgā Buddh Siṅghvālā
3. Buṅgā Sohīāṅvālā
4. Shahīd Buṅgā
5. Buṅgā Kesgaṛhīāṅ
6. Buṅgā Anandpurīāṅ
7. Buṅgā Dasaundhā Siṅgh Sidhvāṅ
8. Buṅgā Jhabālīāṅ
9. Buṅgā Kālīāṅvāle Sardārāṅ
10. Buṅgā Tārā Siṅgh Kāhn Siṅgh Mān
11. Buṅgā Tārā Siṅgh G͟haibā
12. Buṅgā Bhaṅgā Siṅgh Thānesarī
13. Buṅgā Majjā Siṅgh Sāhnāvālīā
14. Buṅgā Baghel Siṅgh
15. Buṅgā Mīrāṅkoṭīāṅ
16. Buṅgā Shām Siṅgh Aṭārīvālā
17. Buṅgā Jassā Siṅgh Nirmalā
18. Buṅgā Lakkhā Siṅgh Nirmalā
19. Buṅgā Chaṛhat Siṅgh Rāgī
20. Buṅgā Jodh Siṅgh Sauṛīāṅvālā
21. Buṅgā Javālā Siṅgh Bhaṛhāṇīāṅ
22. Buṅgā Kabūlevālīāṅ

(This includes one Akhāṛā - Mahant Santokh Dās)

Akhāṛās of Amritsar:

1. Akhāṛā Santokh Dās , now known as Akhāṛā Brahm Būṭā (included in Buṅgās)
2. Akhāṛā Ghamaṇḍ Dās
3. Akhāṛā Chiṭṭā
4. Akhāṛā Ṭahil Dās
5. Akhāṛā Bālā Nand
6. Akhāṛā Mahant Prem Dās
7. Akhāṛā Saṅgalvālā
8. Akhāṛā Kāṅshīvālā, near Darwāzā Ghī Maṇḍī
9. Akhāṛā Kāṅshīvālā, near Darwāzā Sultānviṇḍ
10. Akhāṛā Prāg Dās
11. Akhāṛā Babeksar
12. Akhāṛā Samādhīāṅvālā

BIBLIOGRAPHY

1. Bhaṅgū, Ratan Siṅgh, *Prāchīn Panth Prakāsh*. Amritsar, 1914
2. Giān Siṅgh, Giānī, *Twārīk͟h Srī Amritsar*. Amritar, 1977
3. M'Gregor, W.L., *The History of the Sikhs* [Reprint]. Patiala, 1970
4. Forster, George, *A Journey from Bengal to England*. London, 1798
5. Ramgarhia, Sundar Singh, *The Annals of Ramgarhia Sardars*. Amritsar, 1902

M.K.

BURHĀNPUR (21°-18'N, 76°-14'E), a medieval walled town on the banks of the River Tāptī, is in East Nīmār (Khaṇḍwā) district of Madhya Pradesh. It is a railway station on the main Delhi-Iṭārsī-Bombay section of the Central Railway. There are two historical Sikh shrines in the town.

GURDWĀRĀ SAṄGAT RĀJGHĀṬ PĀTSHĀHĪ PAHILĪ, situated on the bank of the Tāptī, perpetuates the memory of the *saṅgat* established in the wake of Gurū Nānak's visit in the early sixteenth century. The Gurū is said to have stayed at Burhānpur with one Bhāī Bhagvān Dās, who became a Sikh and who lived up to the time of Gurū Hargobind. Bhāi Gurdās who, in his *Vārāṅ*, XI. 30, mentions the name of Bhāī Bhagvān Dās, also testifies to the existence of the flourishing Sikh *saṅgat* at Burhānpur. In later times, with the coming into prominence of Baṛī Saṅgat where Gurū Gobind Siṅgh stayed *en route* to Nānded̤, the Rājghāṭ site was neglected and became almost extinct. It was re-established by one Bhāī Sādhū Siṅgh in 1938. The present building, a modest single room, was opened for pilgrims on Kārtik Pūrṇimā 2014 Bk/7 November 1957.

GURDWĀRĀ BAṚĪ SAṄGAT. Gurū Gobind Siṅgh, while travelling to the Deccan in company with Emperor Bahādur Shāh I, arrived at Burhānpur on 13 May 1708 and stayed there till the crossing of the Tāptī between 11 and 14 June 1708 into the Deccan. He encamped outside the town, and the local Sikhs attended on him daily, and continued to assemble on the spot even after his departure. The site became the venue of the Burhānpur *saṅgat* or fellowship, and came to be designated Baṛī Saṅgat. After the sack of Mathurā by Ahmad Shāh Durrānī in 1757, Haṭhī Siṅgh, son of Ajīt Siṅgh, adopted son of Mātā Sundarī, settled at Burhānpur. Haṭhī Siṅgh died leaving no male heir, but the *saṅgat* continued under the guidance of Nirmalā and Udāsī priests. Some Sikh immigrants came to Burhānpur from the Punjab in the 1947 upheaval and they rebuilt the shrine. The present building complex consists of a *dīvān* hall, rooms for pilgrims, the Gurū kā Laṅgar and some farm houses. Two old *samādhīs*, or tombs, one of Haṭhī Siṅgh and the other of his spouse still exist at the back of the *dīvān* hall. A small room behind these *samādhīs*, called Nivās Asthān Pātshāhī 10, is inscribed to Gurū Gobind Siṅgh, who is believed to have stayed there at the time of his visit to Burhānpur.

In the Gurdwārā is kept an old handwritten copy of the Gurū Granth Sāhib with an inscription which is believed to be Gurū Gobind Siṅgh's autograph. Each page is decorated with exquisitely-wrought border in gold, red, green and blue colours and with floral designs.

BIBLIOGRAPHY

1. Tārā Siṅgh, *Srī Gur Tīrath Saṅgrahi*. Amritsar, n.d.
2. Ṭhākar Siṅgh, Giānī, *Srī Gurduāre Darshan*. Amritsar, 1923

M.G.S.

BŪṚĪĀ, an old town about 4 km east of Jagādhrī (30°-10'N, 77°-17'E), was the seat of a minor principality ruled by a scion of the Bhaṅgī *misl*. Gurū Tegh Bahādur is believed to have visited Buṛīā during one of his preaching journeys. The old Mañjī Sāhib built in his honour was replaced by the present Gurdwārā constructed in 1920 by Māī Hukam Kaur Ḍhilvāṅ Vālī, a lady of the ruling house. The main building stands on a metre-high octagonal platform. It has an inner sanctum, a domed room, with a circular base in which the Gurū Granth Sāhib is installed. The management of the Gurdwārā is in the hands of the erstwhile chiefs of Būṛīā.

BIBLIOGRAPHY

Faujā Siṅgh, *Gurū Teg Bahādur: Yātrā Asthān, Pramparāvāṅ te Yād Chinn*. Patiala, 1976

M.G.S.

BŪṚ MĀJRĀ, a small village about 8 km east of Chamkaur Sāhib (30°-53'N, 76°-25'E) in Ropaṛ district of the Punjab, claims a historical shrine, Gurdwārā Pātshāhī 10 located near an old well. It is said that Gurū Gobind Siṅgh, while proceeding to Chamkaur on 6 December 1705 after evacuating Anandpur Sāhib, halted here awhile. The well which has existed since then provided water for the travellers and their horses. The Gurdwārā commemorating the visit, comprises a *dīvān* hall with the sanctum for the Gurū Granth Sāhib in the centre. The management is in the hands of the Nihaṅgs.

BIBLIOGRAPHY

1. Tārā Siṅgh, *Sri Gur Tīrath Saṅgrahi*. Amritsar, n.d.
2. Ṭhākar Siṅgh, Giānī, Srī *Gurduāre Darshan*. Amritsar, 1923

Jg.S.

BURN, Lt-Col., who commanded British detachments at Deoband, now in Uttar Pradesh, led in 1804 an expedition against the cis-Sutlej Sikh chiefs, Gurdit Siṅgh of Lāḍvā and Karnāl, Sher Siṅgh of Būṛīā, Ṛāi Siṅgh of Jagādhrī, Jodh Siṅgh of Kalsīā and Mahtāb Siṅgh of Thānesar, who had fought against the British in alliance with the Marāṭhās in 1803. Burn's troops joined hands with those of Birch and Skinner, and defeated the Sikhs at Sahāranpur on 18 December 1804. The British commander-in-chief granted amnesty to all the Sikhs except Gurdit Siṅgh. Burn arrived at Karnāl, and secured from him the surrender of the town.

BIBLIOGRAPHY

Griffin, Lepel, *Rajas of the Punjab*. Lahore, 1870

B.J.H.

BURNES, SIR ALEXANDER (1805-1841), British traveller, explorer and writer, was born on 16 May 1805. He joined Bombay infantry in 1821. Upon his arrival in India, he devoted himself to the study of the local languages and was, while still an ensign, selected for the post of regimental interpreter. In 1829, he was transferred to the political department as assistant to the Political Resident in Cutch. In 1831, he was sent on a complimentary mission to Lahore, in charge of English horses, including a team of cart-horses, four mares and a stallion, sent by the King of England as presents for Mahārājā Raṇjīt Siṅgh. The real object of Burnes' mission was to survey the River Indus and assess the power and resources of the Amīrs of Sindh, then being threatened by the Mahārājā. He submitted to his government a geographical and military memoir on Sindh, which formed the basis of Lord William Bentinck's Indus navigation scheme, a political device cloaked under commercial garb which ultimately barred the advance of Sikh power towards Shikārpur and Sindh.

Burnes records in his writings observations on the Sikh State. He describes Mahārājā Raṇjīt Siṅgh's habits and government; his passion for horses, his troops and horse artillery, his dancing girls and the Koh-i-Nūr-diamond. In January 1832, Burnes visited Lahore again to solicit from the Mahārājā facilities of travel through the Punjab to Afghanistan, Central Asia and Balkh and Bokhārā. "I never quitted," he writes, "the presence of a native of Asia with such impressions as I left this man: without education and without a guide, he conducts the affairs of his kingdom with surprising energy and vigour, and yet wields his power with a moderation quite unprecedented in an eastern prince."

In 1837, Burnes was sent on another "commercial" mission to Kābul. His real aim was to wean Amīr Dost Muhammad Khān from Russian influence and to offer British mediation in his quarrel with the Sikhs. Dost Muhammad Khān readily agreed to Burnes' commercial proposals, but he pointed out that conflict with the Sikhs was an impediment to his participation in the Indus navigation scheme and suggested that the British government should assist him in recovering Peshāwar from Raṇjīt Siṅgh. Burnes gave him some vague assurance on behalf of the British, but Lord Auckland, the governor-, general, was not much impressed by his suggestion of placating the Amīr of Afghanistan at the cost of the Sikhs. Alexander Burnes was recalled from Kābul, but was sent to the Afg͟hān capital again in 1841 to succeed Sir William Macnaghten as British minister and envoy. He was assassinated by the Afg͟hān insurgents on 2 November 1841.

BIBLIOGRAPHY

1. Masson, Charles, *Narrative of Various Journeys in Baluchistan, Afghanistan and the Punjab*. London 1842
2. Shahamat Ali, *The Sikhs and Afghans*. Patiala, 1970

S.S.B.

BŪṚ SIṄGH (d. 1892), son of Ruldū Rām, appointed to do menial jobs first as an attendant in the household of Mahārājā Ranjīt Siṅgh's wife, Rāṇī Mahtāb Kaur, and then as a water-carrier in Kaṅvar Sher Siṅgh's, carried out some of the confidential errands he was assigned to with such great skill that he not only rose in rank but also had *jāgīrs* in Mukerīāṅ, and houses at Baṭālā and Lahore bestowed on him. For his assistance to the British on the occasion of General Pollock's advance on Kābul, he received a *jāgīr* near Peshāwar. His enemies took advantage of the murder in September 1843 of his master, Mahārājā Sher Siṅgh, to harm him. Prime Minister Hīrā Siṅgh, whom Būṛ Siṅgh had once abused in public, levied on him a fine of Rs 81,000—equal to the amount alleged to have been misappropriated by him. He resumed his *jāgīrs*, too, but his downfall was short-lived. On Hīrā Siṅgh's death in 1844, the power passed to Jawāhar Siṅgh and Rājā Lāl Siṅgh who speedily reinstated Būṛ Siṅgh and appointed him governor of Amritsar. Būṛ Siṅgh proved to be an able administrator. He was put in charge of Mahārāṇī Jind Kaur by Henry Lawrence, the Resident of Lahore, during her detention in the Fort of Sheik͟hūpurā while his brother, Suddh Siṅgh, was in attendance on Mahārājā Duleep Siṅgh at Lahore. After the annexation of the Punjab, Būṛ Siṅgh was made a sub-registrar for the cluster of villages around Mukerīāṅ where he resided. He was president of the Municipal Committee of Mukerīāṅ and for some time acted as an honorary magistrate. The Government of India conferred upon him the title of Sardār Bahādur in 1888.

Būr Siṅgh died at Mukerīāṅ in 1892.

BIBLIOGRAPHY

Griffin, Lepel, and C.F. Massy, *Chiefs and Families of Note in Punjab*. Lahore, 1909

S.S.B.

BŪṚ SIṄGH, BHĀĪ (1896-1921), son of Bhāī Mal Siṅgh Kamboj and Māī Ās Kaur, of Chakk No. 80 Mūlā Siṅghvālā, district Sheik͟hūpurā, was born on 10 Phāgun 1952 Bk/22 February 1896. His parents originally belonged to village Bahoṛū in Amritsar district and had settled in the newly developed canal colony in western Punjab, Chakk No. 80, only in 1892. Būṛ Siṅgh received elementary education in the village school and *gurdwārā*. He was present at Chūhaṛkāṇā on 30 December 1920 when Gurdwārā Sachchā Saudā was taken over from Udāsī *mahants* and brought under the management of the reformist Akālīs by K͟hālsā Dīwān Kharā Saudā Bār under the leadership of Jathedār Kartār Siṅgh Jhabbar. Būṛ Siṅgh took the K͟hālsā *pāhul* on the spot and became an Akālī activist. He joined the *jathā* of Bhāī Lachhmaṇ Siṅgh Dhārovālī and attained martyrdom at Nankāṇā Sāhib on 20 February 1921, which happened to be his 26th birthday.

See NANKĀṆĀ SĀHIB MASSACRE

BIBLIOGRAPHY

Shamsher, Gurbak͟hsh Siṅgh, *Shahīdī Jīvan*. Nankana Sahib, 1938

G.S.G.

BUTĀLĀ, a village 7 km northeast of Bābā Bakālā (31°-34'N, 75°-16'E) in Amritsar district of the Punjab, is sacred to Gurū Hargobind who, according to local tradition, visited here on 15 Phāgun 1665 Bk/10 February 1609. The inhabitants of Butālā, with the exception of an old lady and her son who followed the Sikh faith, were the worshippers of Sakhī Sarwar. One day, it is said, the son asked the mother, what offering they would have for the Gurū, should he, in answer to their prayers, come to them. They were very poor; the mother assured her son, "The Gurū accepts whatever is offered with devotion. The value does not count." From that moment, the son would always keep a rupee and a lump of jaggery tied in the corner, or *pallā*, of his waist-cloth so that he could make the offering even if he met the Gurū by chance out in the fields. The villagers started calling him by the name of Bhāī Pallā. One day, Gurū Hargobind, accompanied by his retinue of attendants, did come to Butālā. Pallā and his mother served him with devotion and received his benediction. They converted their house into a Sikh place of worship. Bhāī Pallā's descendants built the present Gurdwārā Pātshāhī VI in 1887. It comprises a square sanctum, with a varandah all around. The dome and pinnacle were erected in 1943. The adjoining pavilion for congregation and rooms for residence and Gurū kā Laṅgar were added later. The Gurdwārā is managed by a village committee. Besides the observance of important anniversaries on the Sikh calendar, an annual fair is held on the 15th of Phāgun, falling at the end of February.

BIBLIOGRAPHY

Ṭhākar Siṅgh, Giānī, Srī *Gurduāre Darshan*. Amritsar, 1923

M.G.S.

BŪṬĀ SIṄGH, DĪWĀN (b. 1826), journalist, printer and one of the last employees of the Sikh royal household, was born the son of Gurdiāl Siṅgh at Lahore in 1826. He was a man of wealth and influence, being the owner of a chain of printing presses. In his earlier career, he had served as *dīwān* or household minister to Mahārāṇī Jind Kaur in whose cause he had attempted to raise disturbances just before the second Anglo-Sikh war for which he was deported from the Punjab to Allāhābād where he was kept a political prisoner for seven years. In 1866, he set up *Āftāb-i-Punjab* press in Lahore and issued in Urdu a fortnightly law journal, *Anwār ul-Shams*. A branch of the press was opened at Ajmer where the Rājpūtānā government gazette used to be printed. In 1872, Būṭā Siṅgh founded the newspaper, *Āftāb-i-Punjāb* (Urdu), generally critical of the government's policy towards Mahārājā Duleep Siṅgh. Dīwān Būṭā Siṅgh was favourably disposed towards the Kūkā sect and applauded especially its pro-Duleep Siṅgh activity. He also served as a vice-president of the newly established Lahore Siṅgh Sabhā.

BIBLIOGRAPHY

1. Ganda Singh, ed., *History of the Freedom Movement in the Panjab (Maharaja Duleep Singh Correspondence)*. vol. III. Patiala, 1972
2. Gill, Avtar Singh, *Lahore Darbar and Rani Jindan*. Ludhiana, 1983
3. Jagjit Siṅgh, *Siṅgh Sabhā Lahir*. Ludhiana, 1974

K.S.T.

C

CAMPBELL, WILLIAM (d. 1866), a Scotsman, who came to Lahore in September 1828 and was employed in the Sikh cavalry and given command of a regiment of 1200 horse. He soon gained the favour of Mahārājā Raṇjīt Siṅgh, but was dismissed from the service in August 1829 on a charge of misbehaviour towards a woman, and sent across the River Sutlej under an escort. Later, he served the Afghān rulers. He died in Kābul in 1866.

BIBLIOGRAPHY

Grey, C., *European Adventurers of Northern India, 1785-1849* [Reprint]. Patiala, 1970

Gl.S.

CANORA (KANARA), FRANCIS JOHN (1799-1848), an Irishman, inscribed in Khālsā Darbār records variously as Kenny, Kennedy and Khora. Roaming across many countries, he reached Lahore in 1831, and joined Mahārājā Raṇjīt Siṅgh's artillery on a daily wage of Rs 3. Gradually, he rose to the rank of colonel, with a salary of Rs 350 per month. He continued to serve in the Sikh army after the first Anglo-Sikh war (1845-46). But his loyalty to the Lahore Darbār was suspect. In 1848, he was commanding an artillery battery at Hazārā and was under the overall command of Chatar Siṅgh Aṭārīvālā, the governor of Hazārā province. Chatar Siṅgh had raised the banner of revolt against the British on account of the extraordinary behaviour of Captain James Abbott, assistant to the British resident at Lahore, who had defied the governor's authority by raising Muslim levies to destroy the Sikh brigade stationed in the Fort. When James Abbott, accompanied by Muslim mercenaries, marched on Harīpur Hazārā with a view to expelling the governor, Chatar Siṅgh ordered Canora to move the cannon out of the Fort on the open ground outside. Canora, who was in secret communication with James Abbott, refused to do so. The Sardār charged two companies of infantry to arrest Canora for insubordination. Canora refused to surrender and was consequently shot down under the orders of Chatar Siṅgh.

BIBLIOGRAPHY

1. Grey, C., *European Adventurers of Northern India, 1785-1849* [Reprint]. Patiala, 1970
2. Gulcharan Singh, *Ranjit Singh and His Generals.* Jalandhar, n.d.

Gl.S.

CASTLE HILL, an 182-acre estate in Mussoorie, a hill city in the Himalayas, which was the summer residence for a short period of Mahārājā Duleep Siṅgh, the last Sikh sovereign of the Punjab who after the annexation of his dominions was exiled by the British to Fatehgaṛh, in present-day Uttar Pradesh. The entrance to the estate, in Laṇḍour Bazaar, is a fortress-like construction, with battlements for guards, an iron gateway and a reception room for visitors. The estate, originally known as Woodcraft and Greenmount, was the property of one G.B. Taylor before it was purchased by the government in 1853 for Mahārājā Duleep

Siṅgh. It came to be known as Castle Hill from Duleep Siṅgh's occupation of the 'castle' on the top of the hill as his residence. As Duleep Siṅgh arrived at the estate in the summer of 1852, he was, besides the train of servants, accompanied by his guardians, Dr and Mrs Login, the former officially designated as superintendent and agent to His Highness, his tutor, Walter Guise, and his nephew, Shāhzādā Sahdev Siṅgh, son of Mahārājā Sher Siṅgh and his Rājpūt queen, Rāṇī Dakno. The Mahārājā received here lessons in music and drawing and enjoyed outdoor activities such as cricket, hunting and hawking. He learnt especially to play the flute and raised a small band which performed at the Mall, in the city, in the evenings. He practised painting under the tutelage of the city's artist George Beechey. The summer of 1853 was again spent at Castle Hill, this time Prince Sahdev Siṅgh's mother, Rāṇī Dakno, also joining the party. In April 1854, Duleep Siṅgh left for England never to return to live in India again.

The estate now is the property of the Union government and houses the offices of the Survey of India.

Wm.S.

CENTRAL AKĀLĪ DAL. *See* AKĀLĪ DAL, CENTRAL

CENTRAL MĀJHĀ KHĀLSĀ DĪWĀN, also known as the Shiromaṇī Panth Milauṇī Jathā, was one of the several regional organizations that came into being on the eve of the Gurdwārā reform movement of the 1920's.

A Khālsā Dīwān in the Mājhā area had in fact been established as early as 1904, but it had merged with the Chief Khālsā Dīwān three years later. Upon its revival in 1918 as Central Mājhā Khālsā Dīwān, it concerned itself mainly with reforming the ceremonial in Sikh holy places, especially at Tarn Tāran and Amritsar. With its headquarters at Kīratangaṛh, near Amritsar, the Central Mājhā Khālsā Dīwān claimed a membership of over 1200 *amritdhārī* Sikhs from the central Mājhā districts of Lahore, Amritsar and Gurdāspur. The Dīwān had a collegiate executive of five persons, called Pañj Piāre, elected at a plenary meeting held during March every year. Leaders from outside central Mājhā such as Kartār Siṅgh Jhabbar from Sheikhupūrā *bār* area and Master Motā Siṅgh from the Doābā also lent their support and participated in the meetings of the Dīwān. Prominent among its own leaders were Jathedār Tejā Siṅgh Bhuchchar and the Jhabāl brothers, Amar Siṅgh, Sarmukh Siṅgh and Jaswant Siṅgh.

The *modus operandi* of the Dīwān was to hold religious congregations at different places on important Sikh anniversaries and other festivals and to provide services of *granthīs*, *rāgīs* and *prachāraks* for functions such as Akhaṇḍ Pāṭhs, initiation ceremonies and marriages, etc. A regular feature was the monthly *dīvān* on *amāvasyā*, the last day of the dark half of the lunar month, within the precincts of the Darbār Sāhib at Tarn Tāran. The refrain of the Dīwān speeches used to be criticism of the superstitious rites and ceremonies which had taken hold of the Sikh masses and of the malpractices in the administration of the shrines. The clerics in charge of the *gurdwārās* resented this reformist propaganda. Their persistent opposition forced the Central Mājhā Dīwān to change the venue of their monthly meeting in Tarn Tāran from the Darbār Sāhib to one of the nearby *buṅgās*.

At the annual meeting of the Dīwān held at the village of Bhuchchar in March 1919, Tejā Siṅgh Bhuchchar was elected Jathedār, with four others to assist him. A few days later, on 13 April 1919, occurred the Jalliāṅvālā Bāgh tragedy in the holy city of Amritsar which sent a wave of shock and anger across the entire country. The Sikhs had a further cause for offence when they learnt that Brigadier General Dyer who had ordered the Amritsar shooting had been received and honoured by the Sarbarāh, or manager and the priests of the Darbār Sāhib and that an address of welcome had been presented to the Lieut-Governor of the Punjab, Sir Michael O'Dwyer. A public agitation started against the Sarbarāh. The Central Mājhā Khālsā Dīwān took an active part in it and proposed social boycott of all those Sikhs who had been a party to the honour bestowed on General Dyer or to the address presented to the Lieut-Governor.

As the Gurdwārā reform movement got under way, the Central Mājhā Khālsā Dīwān was the first to swing into action. Its leaders, Jathedār Tejā Siṅgh Bhuchchar and Amar Siṅgh Jhabāl with a *jathā* of 25 reached Siālkoṭ and liberated Gurdwārā Bābe dī Ber on 5-6 October 1920. When Srī Akāl Takht was occupied by the reformists on 12 October the same year, the Central Mājhā Khālsā Dīwān offered to administer it, Tejā Singh Bhuchchar becoming its first Jathedār. Amar Siṅgh Jhabāl accompanied Kartār Siṅgh Jhabbar in November 1920 to liberate Gurdwārā Pañjā Sāhib at Hasan Abdāl. Towards the end of November 1920, Gurdwārā Bhāī Jogā Siṅgh at Peshāwar was taken over through the initiative of Tejā Siṅgh Bhuchchar.

The Central Mājhā Khālsā Dīwān lent full support to the Gurdwārā Rikābgañj agitation revived after the end of World War I. Sardūl Siṅgh Caveeshar asked, through the columns of the *Akālī,* for 100 volunteers for a *shahīdī jathā*, i.e. band of martyrs, to march to Delhi and reconstruct on 1 December 1920 the demolished wall of Gurdwārā Rikābgañj if the government failed to restore it by that date. The Jhabāl brothers endorsed the proposal, repeated the call at conventions held by the Central Mājhā Khālsā Dīwān and enrolled volunteers for the *jathā*. The government, however, had the wall rebuilt before the *jathā* intervened. When the Shiromaṇī Akālī Dal was formed, on 14 December 1920, to coordinate the work of regional Akālī groups, Sarmukh Siṅgh Jhabāl of the Central Mājhā Khālsā Dīwān was elected its first president.

The reform of the administration of Srī Darbār Sāhib at Tarn Tāran had since the days of the Khālsā Dīwān Mājhā (1904-07) been a live issue. On 26 January 1921, Jathedār Tejā Siṅgh Bhuchchar led a *jathā* of 40 volunteers to Tarn Tāran. Through the mediation of Bhāī Mohan Siṅgh Vaid negotiations began between the reformist Akālīs and the clerics in control of the shrine, but they remained inconclusive. The latter resorted to force and suddenly fell upon Bhuchchar's *jathā* in the evening with lethal weapons. Nineteen Akālīs were injured two of whom later died. Of these first two martyrs who died in the cause of Gurdwārā reform, Bhāī Hukam Siṅgh of Vasāūkoṭ, in Gurdāspur district, was a member of the Central Mājhā Khālsā Dīwān. The Darbār Sāhib at Tarn Tāran passed under Akālī management.

Then followed the massacre at Nankāṇā Sāhib (20 February 1921) and the transfer of the control of the *gurdwārās* there into the hands of the reformists. The Central Mājhā Khālsā Dīwān deputed its volunteers to assist the *gurdwārā* administration at Nankāṇā Sāhib for several months. It was there that in a meeting held in March 1921, the Mājhā Dīwān approved a motion affiliating itself to the Shiromaṇī Akālī Dal. It also passed a resolution of non-co-operation and called upon its members to withdraw their children from government schools. In spite of its affiliation to the Shiromaṇī Akālī Dal, the Central Mājhā Khālsā Dīwān maintained its autonomous entity. At its annual elections held in April 1921, Sarmukh Siṅgh Jhabāl, with four others, was chosen Jathedār. The members of the Dīwān continued to participate in the Akālī campaign for the release of Sikh shrines from the control of a corrupt priestly order. During the Gurū kā Bāgh

Morchā, the Dīwān sent a batch of 110 volunteers to face, under a vow of non-violent passive resistance, the police beating on 1 September 1922.

With the emergence of the Shiromaṇī Akālī Dal as a viable political party, the Central Mājhā K͟hālsā Dīwan, like other regional bodies, lost much of its relevance. Some members left it altogether, while others were absorbed in the district Akālī *jathās* which now formed constituent branches of the Shiromaṇī Akālī Dal. There are still some carrying on under the old banner, holding fast to their old schedule of monthly congregations at Tarn Tāran on the day of *amāvasyā*.

BIBLIOGRAPHY

1. Mohinder Singh, *The Akali Movement.* Delhi, 1978
2. Sahni, Ruchi Ram, *Struggle for Reform in Sikh Shrines.* Ed. Ganda Singh. Amritsar, n.d.
3. Pratāp Siṅgh, Giānī, *Gurdwārā Sudhār arthāt Akālī Lahir.* Amritsar, 1975
4. Josh, Sohan Siṅgh, *Akālī Morchiāṅ dā Itihās.* Delhi, 1972

Jg.S.

CENTRAL SIKH LEAGUE, political organization of the Sikhs which guided their affairs until the Shiromaṇī Akālī Dal emerged as a mass force. The inaugural session of the Central Sikh League was held at Amritsar on 29 December 1919, coinciding with the annual sessions of the Indian National Congress and the Muslim League. It was dominated by the educated Sikhs from the middle strata such as Sardūl Siṅgh Caveeshar, Harchand Siṅgh Lyāllpurī and Master Sundar Siṅgh Lyāllpurī. The first president was Sardār Bahādur Gajjaṇ Siṅgh representing moderate political opinion. But the leadership soon changed and Bābā Khaṛak Siṅgh, an ardent nationalist, was elected president for its second session at Lahore in October 1920.

The aims and objects of the Central Sikh League, according to its new constitution adopted on 22 July 1921, were the attainment of *svarāj*, i.e. political autonomy for the country, by legitimate, peaceful and constitutional means and the promotion of Panthic unity, the fostering of patriotism and public spirit among the Sikhs and the development and organization of their political, moral and economic resources. Membership was open to Sikhs who had attained the age of 21 years and the fee was four *ānnās* per month. The executive committee of the League consisted of 101 members, exclusive of ex officio members, 80 of whom were elected and 21 nominated. By August 1921, units of the Central Sikh League had been set up at Amritsar, Lahore, Gujrāṅwālā, Lyallpur, Siālkoṭ, Jehlum, Fīrozpur, Jalandhar and Hoshiārpur. The annual meeting of the League was held generally during the Dussehrā holidays.

In espousing Sikh interests, the Central Sikh League sought adequate representation for the community in the Punjab Legislative Council, removal of restrictions on the carrying by Sikhs of *kirpān*, one of their religious symbols, and reform of Sikh places of worship. The League maintained a close liaison with the Indian National Congress. At the second session of the Central Sikh League, Bābā Khaṛak Siṅgh, in his presidential address, exhorted the Sikhs to participate in national politics. At this session, the League passed a resolution supporting the non-cooperation movement of the Indian National Congress. Like the Congress and the Central K͟hilāfat Committee, the Sikh League also started enlisting volunteers to carry on the fight for *svarāj*. It issued a manifesto and asked for 10,000 Sikh volunteers to come forward and join the national movement. At the same time the League, with a view to stressing Sikh identity, insisted that the Congress include in the national flag it was designing a strip in yellow, the colour of the Sikhs.

The League supported the struggle for *gurdwārā* reform and appointed an enquiry committee to investigate the Nankāṇā tragedy in which about 150 reformist Sikhs were mercilessly butchered by the priest's hired killers. Similarly when the government took over the keys of the Golden Temple *toshā<u>kh</u>ānā*, the League called a series of protest meetings. When Ripudaman Siṅgh, the Mahārājā of Nābhā, relinquished in 1923 the *gaddī*, his royal seat, the Central Sikh League convened a special meeting to protest against what was described as undue pressure brought upon him by the British Government.

The Central Sikh League showed concern about the communal sentiment penetrating into Indian body politic. It favoured the complete abolition of communal representation in legislatures, but reiterated at the same time in its resolution of 10 October 1927 that, in case it was retained, the Sikhs must be given 30 per cent share in the Punjab legislative seats.

The Sikh League participated in the all-parties conference convened by the Congress in Delhi in February 1928 to work out a constitution which would be acceptable to various interests. It sent a delegation consisting of Bābā Khaṛak Siṅgh, Sardār Bahādur Mehtāb Siṅgh, Master Tārā Siṅgh, Giānī Sher Siṅgh, Amar Siṅgh Jhabāl and Maṅgal Siṅgh to take part in the conference. Maṅgal Siṅgh was appointed a member of the committee constituted under the chairmanship of Motīlāl Nehrū which prepared an exhaustive scheme which was published in August 1928 and came to be known as the Nehrū Report. The Report was however strongly opposed by the Central Sikh League, because, as Bābā Khaṛak Siṅgh said in his presidential address given extempore at the annual session of the Sikh League at Gujrāṅwālā on 22 October 1928, it had sinned against the self-respect and dignity of India by limiting the national objective to Dominion Status instead of demanding *pūrṇa (pūrṇa* = complete) *svarāj*, complete autonomy. The second point of criticism was that the Nehrū Report had laid the foundation of communalism by accepting separate electorates. The League advocated a system of joint electorate with plural constituencies adding that, if community-wise representation became inevitable, the Sikhs should have at least 30 per cent of the seats in the Punjab legislature and the same proportion of the representation from the Punjab to the Central legislature.

The temper against the Nehrū Report was so high that in the annual meeting of the Central Sikh League in October 1929, Bābā Khaṛak Siṅgh even proposed boycotting the forthcoming Congress session to be held in Lahore. But Master Tārā Siṅgh, the then president of the Central Sikh League, was not in favour of this. In the meantime, Mahātmā Gāndhī and other Congress leaders also urged the League not to dissociate itself from the Congress session. The problem was resolved when the Congress working committee at Lahore decided to drop the Nehrū Report. The Congress also adopted a motion assuring Sikhs and Muslims that no constitutional solution which did not satisfy them would be acceptable to it.

The Central Sikh League took part in the Civil Disobedience movement launched by Mahātmā Gāndhī on 6 March 1930. Master Tārā Siṅgh, while leading a batch of Akālī volunteers to help the Paṭhān *satyagrahīs* at Peshāwar, was taken into custody. The League like the Congress also boycotted the first Round Table Conference convened in London with the object of obtaining the views of Indians on the future constitutional reforms but, after the Gandhī–Irwin Pact signed on 5 March 1931, it agreed to participate in the second Round Table Conference. It also presented a memorandum listing 17 demands of the Sikhs to Mahātmā Gāndhī who was to represent the Congress at the Conference. These included the setting up of a national government in India, one-third share for the

Sikhs in the Punjab cabinet and public service commission, joint electorates without reservation of seats and transfer of Muslim areas to the Frontier Province to bring about communal balance in the Punjab, five per cent share for the Sikhs in the Indian upper and lower houses, inclusion of at least one Sikh in the Central cabinet, and adoption of Punjabi as the official language of the province.

In the scheme announced by the British government on 16 August 1932 which came to be known as the Communal Award, Sikhs were given only 18.85 per cent representation in the Punjab legislature. The Sikh League lodged a strong protest. What especially irked it was the statutory majority assured the Muslims in the Punjab by giving them 50.42 per cent seats. Anticipating the pronouncement, the Central Sikh League called a representative conclave of the Sikhs on 24 July 1932 at the *samādh* of Mahārājā Raṇjīt Siṅgh in Lahore at which a 16-member council of action was formed to oppose the British proposals. This council of action set up a new organization, the K͟hālsā Darbār, representing all sections of Sikh opinion, to lead the agitation against the Award. On 16 October 1933, a joint session of the Central Sikh League and the K͟hālsā Darbār was held whereafter the former ceased to be a separate organization. With this ended the short, but lively and chequered, career of the Central Sikh League.

BIBLIOGRAPHY

1. Tuteja, K.L., *Sikh Politics*. Kurukshetra, 1979
2. Gulati, K.C., *The Akalis : Past and Present*. Delhi, 1974
3. Teja Singh, *The Gurdwara Reform Movement and the Sikh Awakening*. Jalandhar, 1922
4. Nāhar Siṅgh, Giānī, *Azādī diāṅ Lahirāṅ*. Amritsar, 1960

K.L.T.

CHABBĀ, a village 10 km south of Amritsar (31° - 38'N, 74° - 52'E) along Amritsar-Tarn Tāran road, has a historical shrine called Gurdwārā Saṅgrāṇā Sāhib. The Gurdwārā itself is so named because, according to local tradition, one of the battles (*saṅgrām* in Hindi and Punjabi) of Amritsar between Gurū Hargobind (1595-1644) and the Mug͟hal troops was fought here. Another tradition connected with the place is that Sulakkhaṇī, a childless woman of the village, asked for and received a boon from Gurū Hargobind as a result of which she subsequently became the mother of seven sons. Local tradition also claims the place to have been consecrated by Gurū Arjan (1563-1606), who halted here for the night on his way to Amritsar along with *pothīs* or books containing the sacred hymns of his predecessors borrowed from Bābā Mohan of Goindvāl.

GURDWĀRĀ SANGRĀṆĀ SĀHIB is located within a walled compound entered through an imposing two-storeyed gateway. The central building is a hall with a square sanctum in the middle. Above the sanctum is a domed room topped by a gold-plated pinnacle. Gurū kā Laṅgar, community kitchen, is on the right of the central building and on the left side is an old well and the *sarovar*, holy tank. Adjoining the *sarovar* is the *dīvān* hall. The Gurdwārā is managed by the Shiromaṇī Gurdwārā Parbandhak Committee through a local committee.

BIBLIOGRAPHY

Tārā Siṅgh, *Srī Gur Tīrath Saṅgrahi*. Amritsar, n.d.

Gn.S.

CHĀHAL, 15 km southeast of Lahore, was the ancestral village of Mātā Triptā, mother of Gurū Nānak. This was the birthplace of Bībī Nānakī, Gurū Nānak's sister. Gurū Nānak visited the village on several occasions. Gurdwārā Ḍerā Chāhal, which marked the house of the Gurū's maternal grandfather, Rāmā, was under the management of the

Shiromaṇī Gurdwārā Parbandhak Committee, but had to be abandoned at the time of the partition of the Punjab in 1947.

BIBLIOGRAPHY

1. Tārā Siṅgh, *Srī Gur Tīrath Saṅgrahi.* Amritsar, n.d.
2. Ṭhākar Siṅgh, Giānī, *Srī Gurduāre Darshan.* Amritsar, 1923

M.G.S.

CHAIYĀ, BHĀĪ, son of Bulākī, who held charge of Ḍhākā as a *masand,* i.e. tithe-collector, was appointed to that office in Bihār province by Gurū Tegh Bahādur. In the time of Gurū Gobind Siṅgh, he was found guilty of misappropriating devotees' offerings and suffered punishment.

BIBLIOGRAPHY

1. Santokh Siṅgh, Bhāī, *Srī Gur Pratāp Sūraj Granth.* Amritsar, 1926-37
2. Giān Siṅgh, Giānī, *Twārīkh Gurū Khālsā.* Patiala, 1970
3. Macauliffe, Max Arthur, *The Sikh Religion.* Oxford, 1909

Gn.S.

CHAKAR, village 17 km south of Jagrāoṅ (30° - 47'N, 75° - 28'E), in Ludhiāṇā district, is sacred both to Gurū Hargobind and Gurū Gobind Siṅgh. Gurū Hargobind passed through here in the course of his tour of the Mālvā in 1631-32 and Gurū Gobind Siṅgh at the end of 1705 after the battle of Chamkaur. The Gurdwārā Gurū Sar Pātshāhī VI and X, an imposing structure, is situated at the north-western corner of the village. Constructed during the 1970's, it is a large square hall with a square sanctum at the far end. Above the sanctum are four storeys of square rooms, with decorative screens around them, topped by a ribbed lotus dome, an ornamental golden pinnacle and an umbrella-shaped finial. The walls and ceiling of the entrance porch as well as the main hall are coated with stucco and inset with reflecting glass pieces. The 35-metre square *sarovar* (holy tank) flanks the hall on the right as one enters the premises. Gurū kā Laṅgar (community kitchen) and lodgings are on the left. The Gurdwārā is managed by the Shiromaṇī Gurdwārā Parbandhak Committee through a village committee.

BIBLIOGRAPHY

1. Tārā Siṅgh, *Srī Gur Tīrath Saṅgrahi.* Amritsar, n.d.
2. Ṭhākar Siṅgh, Giānī, *Srī Gurduāre Darshan.* Amritsar, 1928

M.G.S.

CHAKK FATEH SIṄGHVĀLĀ, 3 km south of Bhuchcho Maṇḍī (30° - 13'N, 75° - 5'E) in Baṭhiṇḍā district of the Punjab, and one of the cluster of villages known as Bhāī ke Chakk because of the association of the family of Bhāī Bhagatū with them, was visited by Gurū Gobind Siṅgh, on his way from Talvaṇḍī Sābo to Baṭhiṇḍā. 18 Jeṭh 1763 Bk / 16 May 1706 is preserved in local tradition as the date of Gurū Gobind Siṅgh's arrival in the village where he put up for a week. The main shrine, Gurdwārā Srī Gurū Gobind Siṅgh Jī Sāhib, a 4-metre square domed sanctum on a high plinth, is on the eastern outskirts of the village, with a small *sarovar* or holy tank in the vicinity. For larger *dīvāns,* a more spacious Gurdwārā was raised, opposite the old shrine across a narrow lane, during the 1960's. Both shrines are managed by the Shiromaṇī Gurdwārā Parbandhak Committee through a local committee. The Gurdwārā in the interior of the village which is called Burj Sāhib is still part of a private house. It is a small circular mud-built room where a low cot and a few garments are shown as old relics. In another small square room through which the circular room is approached, the Gurū Granth Sāhib is seated. Devotees who gather to attend the fair at Gurdwārā Srī Gurū Gobind Siṅgh Jī Sāhib on the 18th of Jeṭh every year also visit this shrine.

BIBLIOGRAPHY

1. Tārā Siṅgh, *Srī Gur Tīrath Saṅgrahi.* Amritsar, n.d.
2. Ṭhākar Siṅgh, Giānī, *Srī Gurduāre Darshan.* Amritsar, 1928
3. *Mālvā Desh Raṭan dī Sākhī Pothī.* Amritsar, 1968

M.G.S.

CHAKK PREMĀ, village 6 km northeast of Phagwāṛā (31° - 14'N, 75° - 46'E) in Kapūrthalā district of the Punjab, has a historical shrine dedicated to Gurū Hargobind. It is known as Gurdwārā Jhaṇḍā Sāhib Chhevīṅ Pātshāhī. The old modest building has now been replaced by a spacious hall, with the sanctum in the middle. The Gurdwārā is managed by the village *saṅgat.* A major part of funds for the new building came in the form of donations from Sikhs settled abroad.

M.G.S.

CHĀLĪ MUKTE, lit. forty (*chālī*) liberated ones (*mukte*), is how a band of 40 brave Sikhs who laid down their lives fighting near the *ḍhāb* or lake of Khidrāṇā, also called Īsharsar, on 29 December 1705 against a Mughal force in chase of Gurū Gobind Siṅgh are remembered in Sikh history and daily in the Sikh *ardās* or supplicatory prayer offered individually or at gatherings at the end of all religious services. Gurū Gobind Siṅgh, who had watched the battle from a nearby mound praised the martyrs' valour and blessed them as Chālī Mukte, the Forty Immortals. After them Khidrāṇā became Muktsar – the Pool of Liberation. Etymologically, *muktā* from Sanskrit *mukt* means 'liberated, delivered, emancipated,' especially from the cycle of birth and death. *Mukti* (liberation, emancipation) in Sikhism is the highest spiritual goal of human existence, and *mukt* or *muktā* is the one who has achieved this state of final beatitude. *Muktā,* also means a pearl, and the word would thus signify a title or epithet of distinction. It was probably in this sense that the five Sikhs, who on 30 March 1699 received the vows of the Khālsā immediately after the first five Pañj Piāre (*q.v.*), were blessed with the title *muktā*, plural *mukte.*

The term Chālī Mukte is also used sometimes for the martyrs whom a huge army, in pursuit since the evacuation of Anandpur by Gurū Gobind Siṅgh during the night 5-6 December, caught up with and encircled at Chamkaur on 7 December, and who engaged the enemy in small sorties throughout the day with the result that the Gurū with three other survivors was able to escape during the following night. *See* CHAMKAUR SĀHIB.

While there is no unanimity over the names of the martyrs of Muktsar and Chamkaur Sāhib, the five Muktās who comprised the first batch of Sikhs to receive *amrit* at the hands of the Pañj Piāre are given in *Rahitnāmā* by Bhāī Dayā Siṅgh as Rām Siṅgh, Fateh Siṅgh, Devā Siṅgh, Ṭahil Siṅgh and Īsar Siṅgh. No other details of these five are available except that an old manuscript of Bhāī Prahlād Siṅgh's *Rahitnāmā* is said to contain a note associating Rām Siṅgh and Devā Siṅgh with the village of Bughiāṇā, Ṭahil Siṅgh and Īsar Siṅgh with Ḍall-Vāṅ and Fateh Siṅgh with Khurdpur Māṅgaṭ. According to Bhāī Chaupā Siṅgh, his *Rahitnāmā* or code of conduct was drafted by *muktās.* The text is said to have received Gurū Gobind Siṅgh's approval on 7 Jeṭh 1757 Bk / 5 May 1700. It appears that the title of *muktā* was bestowed subsequently also on persons other than the original five. The number of *muktās* is recorded variously in old Sikh texts. For instance, Kesar Siṅgh Chhibbar, *Baṅsāvalīnāmā Dasāṅ Pātshāhīāṅ Kā*, mentions 14, and Kuir Siṅgh, *Gurbilās Pātshāhī X,* 25. But *muktās* universally celebrated in the Sikh tradition are the forty martyrs of Muktsar who earned this title by sacrificing their lives for the Gurū and who redeemed their past apostasy of having disowned the Gurū and deserted him driven to desperation by the prolonged siege of

Anandpur by the hill chiefs and Mug̲h̲al forces by having their disclaimer torn by the Gurū.
See MUKTSAR

BIBLIOGRAPHY

1. Santokh Siṅgh, Bhāī, *Srī Gur Pratāp Sūraj Granth*. Amritsar, 1926-37
2. Padam, Piārā Siṅgh, *Darbārī Ratan*. Patiala, 1976
3. Chhibbar, Kesar Singh, *Bansāvalīnāmā Dasāṅ Pātshāhīāṅ Kā*. Chandigarh, 1972
4. Vīr Siṅgh, Bhāī, *Srī Kalg̲h̲īdhar Chamatkār*. Amritsar, 1963
5. Bhagat Lakshman Singh, *Sikh Martyrs*. Ludhiana, n.d.

P.S.P.

CHALITAR JOTĪ JOTI SAMĀVAṆE KE, one of a collection of seven unpublished Punjabi manuscripts held in the K̲h̲ālsā College at Amritsar under catalogue No. 1579E. Comprising a bare three folios (306-308), it is divided into two sections. The first part (ff. 306-307) entitled "Veṛyā Guriāī kā Likhiā," lit. details recorded of the gurūship, gives the duration for which each of the ten Gurūs occupied the holy seat, followed by a vague remark that 24 years and 3 months have elapsed since he passed away, implying thereby that the writing took place 24 years and 3 months after the death (in 1708) of the tenth and last of the Gurūs, Gurū Gobind Siṅgh, which takes the date of the compilation of the manuscript to 1732. The second part, ff. 307-08, records dates of the passing away of six of the Ten Gurūs, Gurū Nānak, Gurū Aṅgad Dev, Gurū Hargobind, Gurū Har Krishan, Gurū Teg̲h̲ Bahādur and Gurū Gobind Siṅgh. The author has also mentioned the day and time of Gurū Teg̲h̲ Bahādur's execution – Thursday, about 1 p.m. The dates given are generally reliable. The manuscript concludes with the statement that Gurū Gobind Siṅgh had passed on the office of Gurū to the K̲h̲ālsā.

S.S.Am.

CHAMKAUR SĀHIB (30° - 53'N, 76° - 25'E) in Ropaṛ district of the Punjab was the scene of two engagements which took place here between Gurū Gobind Siṅgh and the imperial troops in the opening years of the eighteenth century. There exist six shrines in the town commemorating the events of those fateful days.

GURDWĀRĀ DAMDAMĀ SĀHIB marks the spot where Gurū Gobind Siṅgh first alighted upon reaching Chamkaur late on 6 December 1705. The site was then a garden belonging to Rāi Jagat Siṅgh, the local landlord. The Gurū sent some of his disciples to request Rāi Jagat Siṅgh to let him take shelter in his *havelī*. Jagat Siṅgh, for fear of the rulers' wrath, refused, but his younger brother, Rūp Chand, asserting his right as a co-owner of the house, allowed Gurū Gobind Siṅgh to enter. According to some chroniclers, the names of the owners of the property were Budhī Chand and G̲h̲arībū. According to *Gurushabad Ratnākar Mahān Kosh*, Gurū Gobind Siṅgh had been here once before when he was on his way to Kurukshetra in 1702. A small *gurdwārā* was first constructed here around 1930 by Sardār Bahādur Dharam Siṅgh (1881-1933), a well-known philanthropist of Delhi. The present building was raised in 1963 by Sant Piārā Siṅgh of Jhāṛ Sāhib. It duplicates the design of the central building of the older Gurdwārā Qatalgaṛh Sāhib — a square sanctum on the ground floor within a square hall, and a domed room above the sanctum with decorative cupolas at the corners. The Gurdwārā is managed by the Shiromaṇī Gurdwārā Parbandhak Committee through a local committee, with offices located at Gurdwārā Qatalgaṛh Sāhib.

GURDWĀRĀ GAṚHĪ SĀHIB marks the site of the fortress-like double-storeyed house, with a high compound wall around it and only one entrance from the north, which was used by Gurū Gobind Siṅgh as a temporary citadel in the unequal battle on 7 December 1705.

On occupying the house during the night of 6-7 December, he had assigned 8 Sikhs each to guarding the four sides, while another two, Madan Siṅgh and Koṭhā Siṅgh, were posted at the entrance. Gurū Gobind Siṅgh, with his sons Ajīt Siṅgh and Jujhār Siṅgh and other disciples, took up position on the first floor of the house in the centre. The imperial army, now inflated with reinforcements from Ropaṛ, Sirhind and Mālerkoṭlā, arrived and surrounded the *gaṛhī*. The battle raged throughout the day. Successive efforts of the besiegers to storm the citadel were thwarted. As the ammunition and arrows in the fortress ran out, the Sikhs started coming out in small batches to engage the enemy in hand-to-hand fight. Two such successive sallies were led by the Sāhibzādās, Ajīt Siṅgh and Jujhār Siṅgh, 18 and 14 years old respectively, who like the other Sikhs fell fighting heroically. The valour displayed by the young sons of Gurū Gobind Siṅgh has been poignantly narrated by a modern Muslim poet Allahyār K͟hān Jogī who used to recite his Urdu poem entitled "Shahīdān-i-Wafā" from Sikh pulpits during the second and third decades of the twentieth century.

By nightfall, Gurū Gobind Siṅgh was left with only five Sikhs in the fortress. These five urged him to escape so that he could rally his followers again and continue the struggle against oppression. The Gurū agreed. He gave his own attire to Saṅgat Siṅgh who resembled him somewhat in features and physical stature, and, under cover of darkness, made good his way through the encircling host slackened by the fatigue of the day's battle. Dayā Siṅgh, Dharam Siṅgh and Mān Siṅgh also escaped leaving behind only two Sikhs, Saṅgat Siṅgh and Sant Siṅgh. Next morning as the attack was resumed, the imperial troops entered the *gaṛhī* without much resistance, and were surprised to find only two occupants who, determined to die rather than give in, gave battle till the last.

Upon the fall of Sirhind to the K͟hālsā in 1764 when this part of the country came under Sikh domination, the fortress at Chamkaur came to be preserved as a sacred monument. Mahārājā Karam Siṅgh of Paṭiālā had a *gurdwārā* constructed here. It was called Gaṛhī Sāhib ; also, Tilak Asthān (Anointment Site) in the belief that Gurū Gobind Siṅgh's act of obeying the five Sikhs with regard to his escape and giving his dress, turban and plume to Bhāī Saṅgat Siṅgh were symbolic of anointing the K͟hālsā as his successor to gurūship. The old Gurdwārā building has since been demolished and replaced by a four-storeyed structure. The sanctum is on the ground floor in the centre of a large *dīvān* hall. The building is topped by a lotus dome covered with chips of glazed tiles. There are decorative domed pavilions over the corners and walls of the main hall.

GURDWĀRĀ QATALGAṚH SĀHIB (SHAHĪD GAÑJ), west of Gaṛhī Sāhib, is the main shrine at Chamkaur Sāhib. This marks the site where the thickest hand-to-hand fight took place on 7 December 1705 between the Mug͟hal army and the Sikhs, including the Sāhibzādās, Ajīt Siṅgh and Jujhār Siṅgh, and three of the original five Piāre (the Five Beloved). A *gurdwārā* was constructed here by Sardār Hardiāl Siṅgh of Belā in 1831 but that building was replaced during the 1960's by a new complex raised under the supervision of Sant Piārā Siṅgh of Jhāṛ Sāhib and later of Sant Bishan Siṅgh of Amritsar. The main building called Mañjī Sāhib is an elegant three-storeyed domed structure standing upon a high base. The large *dīvān* hall contains an eight-metre square sanctum. Another vast hall close by is called Akāl Buṅgā. It was used for the daily congregations before Mañjī Sāhib was constructed. To the west of Akāl Buṅgā is an old Bāolī Sāhib still in use. The Gurū kā Laṅgar, community kitchen, is further north from Bāolī Sāhib and Akāl Buṅgā. The Gurdwārā also houses the offices of the local managing committee which administers all historical shrines at Chamkaur under the overall control of the Shiromaṇī Gurdwārā Parbandhak Committee. In addition to the daily services, largely attended assemblies take place on the first of each Bikramī month and on important anniversaries on Sikh calendar. A three-day fair called Shahīdī Joṛ Melā is held on 6, 7 and 8 Poh, usually corresponding with 20, 21 and 22 December, commemorating the martyrs of Chamkaur.

GURDWĀRĀ RAṆJĪT GAṚH is on the eastern outskirts of the town. As Gurū Gobind Siṅgh was returning from Kurukshetra to Anandpur early in 1703, it so happened that two imperial generals, Sayyid Beg and Alif Khān, were also moving with a body of troops towards Lahore. Rājā Ajmer Chand of Kahlūr, who bore hostility towards him, persuaded these generals by promises of money to attack him. A skirmish occurred on the site of the present Gurdwārā Raṇjītgaṛh. The Sikhs, though surprised by a superior force, fought tenaciously. Sayyid Beg, when he came face to face with the Gurū, was so affected by a sight of him that he immediately changed sides. Alif Khān, chagrined by his colleague's behaviour, attacked with redoubled vigour, but was repulsed. This happened on 16 Māgh 1759 Bk/15 January 1703. Gurdwārā Raṇjītgarh was built only recently to mark the scene of this battle.

GURDWĀRĀ SHAHĪD BURJ BHĀĪ JĪVAN SIṄGH is next to Gurdwārā Gaṛhī Sāhib and represents the site of the gate of the fortress used by Gurū Gobind Siṅgh as the bulwark of his defence in the unequal battle of 7 December 1705. The gate was guarded by Bhāī Madan Siṅgh and Bhāī Koṭhā Siṅgh, although the Gurdwārā came to be named after Bhāī Jīvan Siṅgh. Jīvan Siṅgh was the same Bhāī Jaitā who had brought Gurū Tegh Bahādur's head after his execution from Delhi to Kīratpur in 1675, and earned from Gurū Gobind Siṅgh the endearing title of 'Raṅghreṭe Gurū ke Beṭe.' Upon his initiation into the order of the Khālsā in 1699, he had received the name of Jīvan Siṅgh. According to the Bhaṭṭ Vahīs, he was killed in a rearguard action on the bank of the Sarsā. Gurdwārā Shahīd Burj, which commemorates his martyrdom, is a small shrine of old Sirhindī bricks to which a small hall has been added lately. The original shrine in which the Gurū Granth Sāhib is seated was built by Mazhabī Sikhs, the community to which Bhāī Jīvan Siṅgh originally belonged.

GURDWĀRĀ TĀṚĪ SĀHIB is situated on a low mound to the west of Gurdwārā Qatalgaṛh. When Gurū Gobind Siṅgh decided to leave the *Gaṛhī* at Chamkaur during the night of 7-8 December 1705, three Sikhs, Bhāī Dayā Siṅgh, Bhāī Dharam Siṅgh and Bhāī Mān Siṅgh, came out with him, too. They proceeded each in a different direction, agreeing to meet later at a common spot guided by the position of certain stars. Since he did not wish to leave unannounced, Gurū Gobind Siṅgh, upon reaching the mound where now stands Gurdwārā Tāṛī (literally, a clap) Sāhib, clapped and shouted: "Here goes the Pīr of Hind (the saint of India)!" From their different points the three Sikhs also raised shouts. This baffled the besieging host, and Gurū Gobind Siṅgh and the Sikhs were soon gone out of harm's way. The Gurdwārā on the mound marks the site from where Gurū Gobind Siṅgh had proclaimed his departure by hand-clapping.

BIBLIOGRAPHY

1. Tārā Siṅgh, *Srī Gur Tīrath Saṅgrahi*. Amritsar, n.d.
2. Ṭhākar Siṅgh, Giānī, *Srī Gurduāre Darshan*. Amritsar, 1923

M.G.S.

CHANAULĪ (also called Charnaulī), village 10 km west of Kīratpur (31° - 11'N, 76° - 35'E) along the Kīratpur-Nūrpur Bedī road, is sacred to Gurū Hargobind and Gurū Har Rāi both of whom visited it during their journeys to and from the Doābā region. The shrine in the village is known as Gurdwārā Gurū Har Rāi Sāhib Pātshāhī Satvīṅ. The present building was raised in 1977. The Gurdwārā is maintained by the local *saṅgat.*

Gn.S.

CHAND or CHANDĀ, a goldsmith by profession, was one of the poets and scholars who enjoyed the patronage of Gurū Gobind Siṅgh (*See* BAVAÑJĀ KAVĪ). He rendered "Udyoga Parva" of the *Mahābhārata* into Hindi verse. His work is preserved as a part of a *Mahābhārata* manuscript in the private collection of the Mahārājā of Paṭiālā. In one of the couplets at the beginning of his work, the poet says that he had already translated "Karṇa Parva" from the Sanskrit text, but no copy of this work is known to exist. Another short work of Chand is *Parīchhā,* preserved in manuscript (No. 135) in the Languages Department, Punjab, at Paṭiālā. Miscellaneous devotional stanzas by Chand have also been located in other manuscripts. A manuscript, *Triyā Charitra,* with Chand as the author's pseudonym, is also ascribed to this poet.

BIBLIOGRAPHY

Padam, Piārā Siṅgh, *Darbārī Ratan.* Patiala, 1976

P.S.P.

CHANDĀ SIṄGH (d. 1930), better known as Chandā Siṅgh Vakīl or lawyer, was born at Kāliāṅvālī, district Sirsā, in the present Haryāṇā state, in a Sikh farming family of moderate means. He was the eldest of the three sons of Diāl Siṅgh. An attack of smallpox in his childhood had deprived him of his eyesight, but this did not deter him from carving his way in life. He passed his primary classes from the village school and went to Amritsar for his middle school course. He took his Matriculation at Government High School, Delhi. He was gifted with a phenomenal memory and excelled at studies. Throughout his school career, he held a merit scholarship. He passed the qualifying examination in law from Lahore and started legal practice at Sirsā, where he soon made a name for himself as a lawyer.

In April 1889, Chandā Siṅgh was married to Ved Kaur daughter of Bhāī Uttam Siṅgh of the village of Būṛā Ḍallā, in Gurdāspur district. The marriage was a significant one at that period of time. It was solemnized strictly in accordance with the Sikh rites, for the bride's father was an enthusiastic member of the Siṅgh Sabhā. He had selected Chandā Siṅgh from among seven likely young men by casting lots in front of the Gurū Granth Sāhib. He cheerfully accepted the choice thus made even though the bridegroom was blind. Chandā Siṅgh was administered *amrit,* i.e. the vows of the K͟hālsā, before the nuptials.

Marriage into a Siṅgh Sabhā family brought Chandā Siṅgh into prominence in the Sikh community. He shifted from Sirsā to Fīrozpur, where he started taking active interest in the Siṅgh Sabhā. He was co-opted a member of the K͟hālsā Dīwān, Lahore. He and Giānī Ditt Siṅgh provided personal assistance to Dharam Siṅgh of Gharjākh, then working president of the K͟hālsā Dīwān. In 1890, he was appointed a member of the K͟hālsā College Establishment Committee and two years later he became a member of the working committee of the K͟hālsā Dīwān, Lahore, as well as of the K͟hālsā College Council. He also remained president of the Fīrozpur Siṅgh Sabhā for many years. He participated as a delegate in the annual session of the Indian National Congress at Lahore in December 1893, defying a resolution of the K͟hālsā Dīwān, Lahore, forbidding its members to attend the conference. Later, he figured prominently in two new Sikh societies – the Chief K͟hālsā Dīwān and the Sikh Educational Conference. During the Jaito campaign, he led out a *jathā* of Akālī volunteers from Fīrozpur and courted arrest.

Chandā Siṅgh died on 4 May 1930. He had no sons, and his only daughter had predeceased him. He bequeathed his house, land and property to Srī Gurū Siṅgh Sabhā, Fīrozpur. As willed by him, his house was converted into a *gurdwārā* which is now known as Gurdwārā Akālgaṛh.

BIBLIOGRAPHY

1. Jagjīt Siṅgh, *Singh Sabha Lahir.* Ludhiana, 1974
2. Dhillon, Gurdarshan Singh, "Character and Impact of the Singh Sabha Movement on the History of the Punjab." Ph.D. thesis submitted in1973 to the Punjabi University, Patiala.

Jg.S.

CHANDĀ SIṄGH, BHĀĪ (1885-1921) was born on 9 Sāvan 1942 Bk / 22 July 1885, the son of Bhāī Hukam Siṅgh and Māī Nand Kaur, a peasant couple of village Nizāmpur, in Amritsar district. The family shifted westward to Chakk No. 38 Nizāmpur Devā Siṅghvālā, in a newly colonized district. As he grew up, Chandā Siṅgh, was influenced by the current of Sikh reformation then sweeping the Punjab. When a call came for a *shahīdī jathā*, martyrs' column, to proceed to Delhi to rebuild the demolished wall of Gurdwārā Rikābgañj, Chandā Siṅgh registered himself as a volunteer. He also attended the Dhārovālī conference on 1-3 October 1920. As Bhāī Lachhmaṇ Siṅgh's *jathā* bound for Nankāṇā Sāhib was passing by his village on 19 February 1921, Bhāī Chandā Siṅgh along with his brother, Gaṅgā Siṅgh, joined it, and fell a martyr the following morning in Gurdwārā Janam Asthān.

See NANKĀṆĀ SĀHIB MASSACRE

BIBLIOGRAPHY

Shamsher, Gurbakhsh Singh. *Shahīdī Jīvan.* Nankana Sahib, 1938

G.S.G.

CHAṆḌĪĀ, BHĀĪ, a Dhīr Khatrī, was a devoted Sikh of the time of Gurū Arjan. He rendered dedicated service during the digging of the sacred pool and the construction of Harimandar at Amritsar. His name is included among the Gurū's devotees in Bhāī Manī Siṅgh, *Sikhāṅ dī Bhagat Mālā.*

See BŪLĀ DHĪR, BHĀĪ

BIBLIOGRAPHY

1. Manī Siṅgh, Bhāī, *Sikhāṅ dī Bhagat Mālā.* Amritsar, 1955
2. Santokh Siṅgh, Bhāī, *Srī Gur Pratāp Sūraj Granth.* Amritsar, 1926-37

T.S.

CHAṆḌĪ CHARITRA, title of two compositions by Gurū Gobind Siṅgh in his *Dasam Granth,* the Book of the Tenth Master, describing in Braj verse the exploits of goddess Chaṇḍī or Durgā. One of these compositions is known as *Chaṇḍī Charitra Ukti Bilās* whereas the second has no qualifying extension to its title except in the manuscript of the *Dasam Granth* preserved in the *toshākhānā* at Takht Srī Harimandar Sāhib at Paṭnā, which is designated *Chaṇḍī Charitra Trambī Mahātam.* The former work is divided into eight cantos, the last one being incomplete, and comprises 233 couplets and quatrains, employing seven different metres, with Savaiyyā and Doharā predominating. The latter, also of eight cantos, contains 262 couplets and quatrains, mostly employing Bhujaṅg-prayāt and Rasāval measures. In the former, the source of the story mentioned is *Satsaī* or *Durgā Saptaśatī* which is a portion of *Mārkaṇḍeya-purāṇa,* from chapters 81 to 94. There is no internal evidence to confirm the source of the story in the latter work, and although some attribute it to *Devī Bhāgavat Purāṇa (skandh* 5, chapters 2 to 35), a closer study of the two texts points towards one source, i.e. *Mārkaṇḍeya-purāṇa.* Both the works were composed at Anandpur Sāhib, sometime before AD 1698, the year when the *Bachitra Nāṭak* was completed. The concluding lines of the last canto of *Chaṇḍī Charitra Ukti Bilās* as included in the *Dasam Granth* manuscript preserved at Paṭnā, however, mention 1752 Bk / AD 1695 as the year of the composition of this work.

In these compositions, Chaṇḍī, the goddess of *Mārkaṇḍeya-purāṇa*, takes on a more dynamic character. Gurū Gobind Siṅgh reoriented the old story imparting to the exploits of Chaṇḍī a contemporary relevance. The *Chaṇḍī Charitra Ukti Bilās* describes, in a forceful style, the battles of goddess Chaṇḍī with a number of demon leaders, such as Kaiṭabha, Mahikhāsur (Mahiṣāsur), Dhūmra and Lochana. The valiant Chaṇḍī slays all of them and emerges victorious. The battle-scenes are portrayed with a wealth of poetic imagery. The last – incomplete – canto contains an invocation to God addressed as Śivā. The second *Chaṇḍī Charitra* treats of the same events and battles, though in minuter detail and in a somewhat different mode of expression. The main point of these works, along with their more popular Punjabi counterpart *Vār Srī Bhagautī Jī Kī*, commonly known as *Chaṇḍī dī Vār*, lies in their virile temper evoked by a succession of powerful and eloquent similes and by a dignified echoic music of the richest timbre. These poems were designed by Gurū Gobind Siṅgh to create among the people a spirit of chivalry and dignity.

BIBLIOGRAPHY

1. Ashta, Dharam Pal, *The Poetry of the Dasam Granth*. Delhi, 1959
2. Loehlin, C.H., *The Granth of Guru Gobind Singh and the Khalsa Brotherhood*. Lucknow, 1971
3. Jaggī, Ratan Siṅgh, *Dasam Granth Parichaya*. Delhi, 1990

R.S.J.

CHAṆḌĪ DĪ VĀR (the Ballad of goddess *Chaṇḍī*) or, to give it its exact title, *Vār Srī Bhagautī Jī Kī*, by Gurū Gobind Siṅgh and included in the *Dasam Granth*, is the story of the titantic contest between Chaṇḍī and other gods on the one hand and the demons on the other. The poem allegorizes the eternal conflict between good and evil. The source of the legend is "Devī māhātmya," a section of the *Mārkaṇḍeya-purāṇa*, and the narrative follows, in the main, the classical detail though the dominant interest lies in the character of Chaṇḍī which, through the creative genius of the poet, attains reality and firmness belying its mythical origin. The *Vār*, in Punjabi, is one of the trilogy of poems about Chaṇḍī in the *Dasam Granth*, the other two being in Braj.

Chaṇḍī, the eight-armed goddess, consort of Śiva, the god of destruction in the Hindu mythology, is also known by the name of Durgā or Bhagautī. This last name has multiple connotations: it stands for goddess Chaṇḍī as well as for the sword, which, according to Gurū Gobind Siṅgh, is the symbol of power (*śakti*) and ultimately of Akāl, the Timeless One Himself. Sikhism is strictly monotheistic and Gurū Gobind Siṅgh, like his nine spiritual predecessors, promoted belief in the One Formless God, excluding all incarnations and images. He chose the Pauranic story of Durgā's valorous fight against the demons for its martial import.

The *Vār* opens with an invocation to God symbolized as sword and then to the first nine Gurūs or preceptors of the Sikh faith. This part of the poem with the subsequent addition of invocation to the Tenth Gurū, Gurū Gobind Siṅgh, forms the opening section of the current Sikh ritual supplication, *Ardās*. The story begins with the demons overthrowing the gods and establishing their own sway where once the gods ruled. The Satyuga, the age of truth, is past and it is now the time of not-so-righteous Tretā. Great discords prevail in the world; Nārada – famous for his ability to stir up passions– is abroad. The gods in their helplessness turn to Mount Kailāsh where lives Durgā. Their leader, King Indra, supplicates the goddess for help : "Thy shelter we seek, Goddess Durgshāh!" Riding her demon-devouring lion, Durgā at once sets out to annihilate the evil-doers. A fierce battle ensues, and the heavens are torn by the beating of drums, blowing of shells and the piercing cries of war. The sun becomes invisible in the dazzling brilliance of shiny swords and spears. In the awesome confusion of battle, the warriors fall to the ground, in agony, like drunken madmen. Those pierced with spears lie motionless like olives on the branch of the tree. The fallen heroes look like so many domes and turrets struck down by lightning. The demons fight with dreadful determination and not one of them has been seen fleeing the field. Their womenfolk watch the bloody scene from their towers, amazed at the goddess's wondrous valour.

Durgā's sword seems dancing in her hand raining death on the dauntless foe. The demons, full of wrath, close in upon her roaring like the black clouds. The mighty Mahkhāsur comes in great fury, but Durgā smites him with such force that her sword, breaking the helmet to pieces and piercing through the body of the rider, the horse and the earth, rests on the horns of the bullock (who supports the earth). The Queen, upon her stately lion, tears through the battle-ranks of the demons demolishing them with her deathly sword. "Durgā, with God's grace, has won the day." Restoring to the gods their lost kingdom, she returns. But the troubles of the gods are not yet ended. The demons again rally under their chiefs, Śumbha and Niśumbha, and march upon the kingdom of Indra. The gods are again undone and are forced to seek Durgshāh's help. The goddess is ready for another battle.

Chanḍī – another name for Durgā in the poem – flashes upon the battle's dread array like lightning. Warlike heroes such as Lochana Dhūmra come forward to match the goddess's prowess, but they all fall to her fatal sword one by one. Śumbha sends out fresh armies to face the fight. The goddess meets them with an angry charge of arrows sending many a hero to eternal sleep. It is now the turn of another, Śraṇvat Bīj, who brings a mighty host of ironclad, vengeful soldiers. Durgā mounts the lion as she hears the fiendish din and, flourishing the mace of battle in her hand, leads her army on. But deathless is Śraṇvat Bīj. As the drops of his blood fall to the ground, hosts of demons arise from them to join the strife. Many more are born every instant than Durgā and the gods can destroy. The goddess, in a rage, remembers Kālī, who bursts forth from her forehead in a flame of fire. Durgā and Kālī both spread ruin in the enemy's ranks with their bloodwashed swords. At last, Śraṇvat Bīj is surrounded and "the swords around him look like a crowd of fair maidens eagerly gathered to see a newly arrived bridegroom." Kālī drinks the blood falling from Durgā's blows so that no drop touches the earth, thus preventing the birth of more demon-warriors.

Great is Śumbha's anguish when he learns of Śraṇvat Bij's death. The wrathful demons prepare for revenge. The firm earth trembles under the marching heroes like a vessel upon stormy seas. But resistless is Durgshāh on the field of battle. She cuts up the foemen like a hewer cuts the twigs. Those who were never tired of fighting have had more than their fill today. Mounting his fiery steed comes Niśumbha with a heavy bow he had specially sent for from Multān. But before he can take aim, a deadly blow from Durgshāh's sword bears him down. The same fate awaits Śumbha. Seeing their chiefs fall in this manner, the demons raise a loud howl of woe. They leave their horses and fly with weeds of grass in their months in token of surrender.

Durgshāh restores to Indra his crown. "Hail to Jagmāt – the Universal Mother," cry all the worlds.

Durgā emerges from this account triumphant, high-spirited and glorious. She is the symbol of divine power and justice. To the virtuous, she is a ready and kindly friend and protector.

In *Chaṇḍī dī Vār,* the different names used for the goddess are Durgshāh, Chaṇḍī, Devitā, Rāṇī, Bhavānī, Jagmāt and Māhā Māī— the Great Mother.

The chief point of *Chaṇḍī dī Vār* lies in its warlike temper which is evoked by a succession of powerful and eloquent similes and a dignified, echoic music of the richest timbre. The poem, though not the size of a true epic, has a remarkable breadth of sweep and intensity and a heightening rhythmical tempo with well-marked climactic patterns. On the reader's mind it makes a stirring and invigorating impact. Nihaṅgs, among Sikhs, especially include it in their daily devotion and derive much inspiration and spirit from reciting it.

BIBLIOGRAPHY

1. Loehlin, C.H., *The Granth of Guru Gobind Singh and the Khalsa Brotherhood.* Lucknow, 1971
2. Ashta, Dharam Pal, *The Poetry of the Dasam Granth.* Delhi, 1959
3. Nikky, Gunindar Kaur Singh, "Durga Recalled by the Tenth Guru," in *The Journal of Religious Studies,* vol. XVI, Nos. 1 & 2. Patiala, 1988
4. Harbans Singh, *Aspects of Punjabi Literature.* Firozpur, 1961
5. Jaggī, Ratan Siṅgh, *Dasam Granth Parichaya.* Delhi, 1990
6. Bedī, Kālā Siṅgh, ed., *Chaṇḍī dī Vār Saṭīk.* Delhi, 1965

Gbh.S.

CHAND KAUR, MAHĀRĀṆĪ (1802-1842), wife of Mahārājā Khaṛak Siṅgh, the eldest son of and successor to Mahārājā Raṇjīt Siṅgh, was born the daughter of Sardār Jaimal Siṅgh of the Kanhaiyā *misl* in 1802 at Fatehgaṛh, in present-day Gurdāspur district of the Punjab. She was married to Prince Khaṛak Siṅgh in February 1812 at the age of 10. After the death in most tragic circumstances of her husband, then Mahārājā of the Punjab, as well as of her son, Kaṅvar Nau Nihāl Siṅgh, in November 1840, she staked her claim to the throne of Lahore. She had won the support of the Sandhāṅvāliā collaterals – Atar Siṅgh, Lahiṇā Siṅgh and Ajīt Siṅgh, and of other influential courtiers such as Bhāī Rām Siṅgh, Bhāī Gobind Rām, Gulāb Siṅgh Ḍogrā and Jamādar Khushāl Siṅgh. She challenged Sher Siṅgh, the second son of Mahārājā Raṇjīt Siṅgh, on the grounds that her daughter-in-law, Kaṅvar Nau Nihāl Siṅgh's widow, Sāhib Kaur, was pregnant and that she would assume regency on behalf of the unborn legal successor to her husband's throne.

Chand Kaur's ambition was matched by her courageous spirit. She would, she declared, cast aside her veil and come out of the zenana, don a turban like a *sardār,* and like a monarch inspect the parade of the army troops. "Why should I not do as Queen Victoria does in England ?" Sher Siṅgh, winning support of a rival group at the court and of a section of the army, marched upon Lahore. A compromise was, however, arrived at between the two factions by which Chand Kaur became regent and Rājā Dhiān Siṅgh principal minister of the State. The truce, however, did not last long. Dhiān Siṅgh Ḍogrā, who wished Chand Kaur to adopt his son, Hīrā Siṅgh, as successor to the throne, became estranged when he saw little hope of his ambition being realized. In January 1841, he openly supported claims of Sher Siṅgh who was proclaimed by the army, also changing sides, sovereign of the Punjab. Chand Kaur was pensioned off with an annual *jāgīr* of 9,00,000 rupees, and her Sandhāṅvāliā supporters fled across the Sutlej into British territory. Chand Kaur retired gracefully to the segregation of her late son's palace inside the city of Lahore. Dhiān Siṅgh's elder brother, Gulāb Siṅgh, who looked after her property, had absconded from the Fort with cartloads of gold and silver. In July 1841,

Nau Nihāl Siṅgh's widow, Sāhib Kaur delivered a stillborn son. This ended whatever hopes Chand Kaur had of resurrecting her claims. But courtly intrigue had not ceased. Dhiān Siṅgh replaced the maidservants of the Dowager Mahārāṇī with hillwomen from his own country. The latter tried to kill her by poisoning her food and eventually finished her off on 11 June 1842, smashing her head with wooden pikes from the kitchen. Dhiān Siṅgh however had had their tongues cut off to prevent them divulging the plot. In the end, they were executed under his own orders.

BIBLIOGRAPHY

1. Surī, Sohan Lāl, *'Umdāt-ut-Twārīkh*. Lahore, 1885-89
2. Griffin, Lepel, and C.F. Massy, *Chiefs and Families of Note in the Punjab*. Lahore, 1890
3. Hasrat, B.J., *Life and Times of Ranjit Singh*. Hoshiarpur, 1977
4. Fauja Singh, ed., *Maharaja Kharak Singh*. Patiala, 1977

B.S.

CHAND KAUR, RĀṆĪ (d. 1840), daughter of Jai Siṅgh of the village of Chainpur in Amritsar district, was married to Mahārājā Raṇjīt Siṅgh in 1815 by the rite of *chādar andāzī*, i.e. covering the head with a piece of cloth (*chādar*=sheet or coverlet + *andāzī* = throwing around or enfolding or covering), a rite having sanction under customary law to facilitate marriage with a widow who is accepted into nuptials by unfurling a *chādar* or sheet of cloth over the head. No religious ceremony is required. Local gentry, kins and friends will be present. Covering the widow's head symbolizes that the man has vowed to take her under his care.

Rāṇī Chand Kaur died in 1840.

BIBLIOGRAPHY

1. Sūrī, Sohan Lāl, *'Umdāt-ut-Twārīkh*. Lahore, 1885-89
2. Ganda Singh, ed., *Maharaja Ranjit Singh* (First Death Centenary Volume). Amritsar, 1939

S.S.B.

CHANDO RĀṆĪ, MĀĪ, mother-in-law of Gurū Nānak, was married to Mūl Chand of Baṭālā.

See MŪL CHAND, BHĀĪ

BIBLIOGRAPHY

1. Manī Siṅgh, Bhāī, *Sikhāṅ dī Bhagat Mālā*. Amritsar, 1955
2. Santokh Siṅgh, Bhāī, *Srī Gur Pratāp Sūraj Granth*. Amritsar, 1926-37

Gn.S.

CHANDPUR, village connected by a 4-km stretch of link road to Ropaṛ-Naṅgal road near Koṭlā power house, is sacred to Gurū Har Rāi (1630-61), who came here on visits several times. Gurdwārā Gurū Har Rāi Sāhib marking the site of the Gurū's camp is also known as Gurdwārā Nīrā Sāhib (from *nīrā*, i.e. fodder for the Gurū's horses). The present three-storeyed domed building raised in 1950 has the sanctum on the ground floor. The Gurdwārā is affiliated to the Shiromaṇī Gurdwārā Parbandhak Committee, but is managed by the local *saṅgat*.

BIBLIOGRAPHY

Tārā Siṅgh, *Srī Gur Tīrath Saṅgrahi*. Amritsar, n.d.

Gn.S.

CHANDRA SAIN SAINĀPATI, commonly referred to as Saināpati and counted among the "fifty-two poets" of Gurū Gobind Siṅgh (1666-1708), was the son of Bāl Chand, an educated Mān Jaṭṭ of Lahore. His original name was Chandra Sain, Saināpati being the pseudonym he had taken. Chandra Sain, taught by one Devī Dās, joined the group of Gurū Gobind Siṅgh's poets, and rendered into Hindi verse *Chāṇakya Nīti*, the well-known Sanskrit treatise on statecraft and diplomacy. His *Srī Gur Sobhā*, a versified life-sketch of Gurū Gobind Siṅgh describing his major battles, the creation of the K͟hālsā, and events following the evacuation of Anandpur, is a work of much historical value. It was completed in 1711. The poet also lived for some time at Wazīrābād, in the present Gujrāṅwālā district of Pakistan, where he translated into Bhākhā verse a Sanskrit work on medicine, *Rām Binod,* earlier translated by a Hindi poet, Rām Chandra, in 1663 in mixed prose and verse. Sainăpati entitled his translation, made at the instance of his friend, Jagat Rāi, a Brāhmaṇ *vaid* or physician of Wazīrābād, *Sukh Sain Granth*. Besides these three works, a fragment containing two *kaṛakhās,* a prosodic form, describing the battles of Bhaṅgāṇī and Fatehgaṛh Fort (Anandpur), respectively, also survives.

BIBLIOGRAPHY

1. Gaṇḍā Siṅgh, ed., *Srī Gur Sobhā.* Patiala, 1980
2. Santokh Siṅgh, Bhāī, *Srī Gur Pratāp Sūraj Granth.* Amritsar, 1926-37
3. Giān Siṅgh, Giānī, *Twārīkh Gurū Khālsā.* Patiala, 1970
4. Padam, Piārā Siṅgh, *Darbārī Ratan.* Patiala, 1976

P.S.P.

CHANDŪ, BHĀĪ, a Chaujhar Khatrī, received initiation at the hands of Gurū Arjan. His name is included among the devotees in Bhāī Gurdās, *Vārāṅ*, XI. 19.

See SĀĪṄ DĀS, BHĀĪ

BIBLIOGRAPHY

1. Manī Siṅgh, Bhāī, *Sikhāṅ dī Bhagat Mālā.* Amritsar, 1912
2. Santokh Siṅgh, Bhāī, *Srī Gur Pratāp Sūraj Granth.* Amritsar, 1926-37

T.S.

CHANDŪ SHĀH, a wealthy banker and revenue official at the Mughal court at Lahore. He earned the annoyance of Sikhs by uttering disparaging words when his family priest proposed Gurū Arjan's son, Hargobind, for his daughter who was of marriageable age. Chandū Shāh accepted the suggestion but with reluctance and made the conceited remark that the Gurū's house was too low for his status and wealth. Report of what he had said reached the local *saṅgat,* who felt injured and sent request to Gurū Arjan to reject the proposal. The Gurū, honouring Sikhs' wishes, broke off the match. Chandū Shāh became a deadly foe of the Gurū and began to conspire against him. He got his chance when, after the death of the liberal-minded Akbar, his son, Jahāṅgīr, ascended the Mughal throne. Emperor Jahāṅgīr came to Lahore in April 1606 in pursuit of his rebel son, Khusrau. Chandū Shāh and other detractors of Sikhism slandered the Gurū before him. Gurū Arjan was arrested on the charge that he had received and blessed the rebel prince. The Emperor sentenced him to death with torture. Murtazā Khān, the governor of Lahore, was to carry out the sentence, but, according to Sikh chronicles, it was Chandū Shāh who took charge of the holy prisoner and had him done to death with the cruellest torments.

As time passed, Jahāṅgīr became reconciled to Gurū Arjan's successor, Gurū Hargobind. He had Chandū Shāh seized and delivered into the Gurū's custody. Dragged through the streets of Lahore by angry Sikhs who had witnessed the atrocities perpetrated by him, Chandū Shāh died a miserable death.

The final blow came ironically from the very person whom Chandū Shāh had employed to pour hot sand on Gurū Arjan's blistered body.

See GURDITTĀ BHAṬHIĀRĀ

BIBLIOGRAPHY

1. *Gurbilās Chhevīṅ Pātshāhī,* Patiala, 1970
2. Bhallā, Sarūp Dās, *Mahimā Prakāsh.* Patiala, 1971
3. Sāhib Siṅgh, *Jīvan-Britānt Srī Gurū Arjan Dev Jī.* Amritsar, 1979
4. Macauliffe, Max Arthur, The Sikh Religion. Oxford, 1909
5. Ganda Singh, *Guru Arjan's Martyrdom Reinterpreted.* Patiala, 1969

T.S.

CHAṄGĀ ,BHĀĪ, a Bhaṭṛā scion of Mādhav of Ceylon, became a devotee of Gurū Nānak. He converted the residence of Mādhav into a *dharamsālā* and started imparting instruction in the teachings of the Sikh faith. His name is mentioned in "Haqīqat Rāh Muqām," an apocryphal composition included in Bhāī Banno's *bīṛ*, i.e. a recension of the Gurū Granth Sāhib prepared by Bhāī Banno, a Sikh contemporary of Gurū Arjan.

BIBLIOGRAPHY

1. Kāhn Siṅgh, Bhāī, *Gurushabad Ratnākar Mahan Kosh*. Patiala, 1964
2. Mrigind, Makhaṇ Siṅgh, *Itihāsak-Tribaiṇī*. Patiala, 1977

Gn.S.

CHAṄGĀ, BHĀĪ, a Bahil Khatrī, was a devoted Sikh of the time of Gurū Arjan. Once he, along with Bhāī Phirnā and Bhāī Jeṭhā of the same clan, waited on Gurū Arjan. They had a question: "Some repeat the name of Rāma, others of Kṛṣṇa, some repeat Om, others Soham. We have been taught to meditate on Vāhigurū. Tell us, True King, which name is the most efficacious ?" The Gurū, says Bhāī Manī Siṅgh, *Sikhāṅ dī Bhagat Mālā,* replied, "Any boat would take one across a river, but one should stick to the boat one has boarded. All names of God lead to liberation. For Sikhs the name revealed by Gurū Nānak is Vāhigurū." Bhāī Chaṅgā and his companions concentrated on the name Vāhigurū and told others to do so.

BIBLIOGRAPHY

1. Manī Siṅgh, Bhāī, *Sikhāṅ dī Bhagat Mālā*. Amritsar, 1955
2. Santokh Siṅgh, Bhāī, *Srī Gur Pratāp Sūraj Granth*. Amritsar, 1926-37

T.S.

CHANNAṆ SIṄGH, SANT (1907-1972), elected president of the Shiromaṇī Gurdwārā Parbandhak Committee, successively from 1962 till his death in 1972, was born in 1907 to Tarlok Siṅgh and Prem Kaur, a peasant couple of modest means, belonging to the village of Mullāṅpur, in Ludhiāṇā district of the Punjab. As a small boy, he attended the Nirmalā monastery located in his village where he learnt to read and write Gurmukhī and made his early acquaintance with Sikh scriptural texts. In 1923, when batches of Sikh volunteers were marching through the countryside to Jaito, site of the Akālī agitation, Channaṇ Siṅgh, along with some other pupils of the Nirmalā *ḍerā,* persuaded one such *jathā* or band of volunteers to make a detour to his village, where he served them food with love and devotion. In 1928, when his elder sister's husband suddenly died, he migrated to her village, Chakk No. 18 Z, in Gaṅgānagar district of Rājasthān, to take care of her and her young children. Four years later, he joined the army as a sepoy. He was in Calcutta with his regiment when he fell sick and had to be hospitalized for some months. During this illness he decided to withdraw from worldly affairs, lead a celibate life and dedicate himself to religious pursuit. As he obtained his discharge from the army, he came in contact with Sant Fateh Siṅgh, who then (in 1933) barely 22, remained absorbed in meditation most of the time. This determined his life's calling. He began to assist Sant Fateh Siṅgh in his programme of religious and educational uplift of the Sikhs. From 1940 onwards, he was Sant Fateh Siṅgh's constant companion and helpmate in his campaign for opening Sikh schools and preaching the word of Gurū Nānak. This work was confined mainly to Gaṅgānagar district of Bīkāner state.

Sant Channaṇ Siṅgh's first introduction to politics was in 1949, when he led a *jathā* of 20 Sikhs from Gaṅgānagar to participate in the Akālī agitation against the Paṭiālā and East Punjab States Union (PEPSU) ministry. He was arrested and sentenced to eight months in prison. On release from jail, he took out another *jathā,* this time from

Ludhiāṇā district, and reached Paṭiālā, where he was again arrested and detained in jail till the end of the agitation. He served a brief term in jail in 1953 when he took part in the farmers' agitation in Gaṅgānagar against the increase in land revenue and a longer one in 1960 in the Akālī campaign for a Punjabi-speaking state. In 1950, he was unanimously elected Jathedār of the Akālī Dal of Gaṅgānagar, a position he retained until his election as president of the Shiromaṇī Gurdwārā Parbandhak Committee in 1962. During the period, he also served as president of Srī Gurū Siṅgh Sabhā of Gaṅgānagar and was a member of the working committee of the Shiromaṇī Akālī Dal, representing Gaṅgānagar. From 1958-60, he was vice-president of the Dal. He represented Gaṅgānagar district in the Shiromaṇī Gurdwārā Parbandhak Committee as well. In October 1962, he was elected president of the Shiromaṇī Gurdwārā Parbandhak Committee. He continued to hold this office until his death on 29 November 1972.

BIBLIOGRAPHY

1. Ghai, Charan Das, *God's Man: A Biography of Sant Fateh Singh*. Ludhiana, 1969
2. Sarhadi, Ajit Singh, *Punjabi Suba*. Delhi, 1970
3. Ashok, Shamsher Siṅgh, *Shiromaṇī Kameṭī dā Pañjāh Sālā Itihās*. Amritsar, 1982

Pk.S.

CHAPPAR CHIṚĪ (30° - 45'N, 76° - 40'E), Baṛī and Chhoṭī (senior and junior), are twin villages in Ropaṛ district, along Kharaṛ-Banūṛ road, now officially named Bandā Siṅgh Bahādur road. This area was the scene of a historic battle. Gurdwārā Bābā Bandā Bahādur is situated between the two villages by the side of the metalled link road joining them. The battle took place around here on 12 May 1710 between the Sikhs led by Bandā Siṅgh Bahādur and Wazīr K͟hān, the imperial *faujdār* of Sirhind. The latter was killed and the Mug͟hal army routed. The Sikhs occupied Sirhind on 14 May 1710. No memorial, however, existed to commemorate the historic event till the 1950's when the two villages jointly established a Gurdwārā. In the 1970's was added a new hall in which the Gurū Granth Sāhib is now seated. The old building is being used for a primary school. Another small room constructed recently is meant for Bābā Bandā Siṅgh Bahādur Library. The Gurdwārā is managed by a committee representing the two villages.

BIBLIOGRAPHY

1. Ganda Singh, *Life of Banda Singh Bahadur*. Amritsar, 1935
2. Harbans Singh, *The Heritage of the Sikhs*. Delhi, 1983

M.G.S.

CHARAN AMRIT. *See* PĀHUL

CHARAN SIṄGH, BHĀĪ (d. 1921), one of the Nankāṇā Sāhib martyrs, was the son of Bhāī Gokal Siṅgh and Māī Lachhmaṇ Kaur of Ḍiṅgā village, in Gujrāt district. He lost his mother during infancy. His old grandmother looked after him for about five years and was then sent to live with his maternal aunt in a village in Lyallpur district where a childless neighbour Bhāī Piārā Siṅgh adopted him as his son. He took the vows of the K͟hālsā at the age of 15. He adopted tattooing as a profession. On 18 February 1921, when he learnt that his adoptive father, Piārā Siṅgh, had left home to participate in the liberation of *gurdwārās* at Nankāṇā Sāhib, Charan Siṅgh, too, took a train and joined the Lyallpur *jathā* at Sāṅglā Hill railway junction. The *jathā* was attacked and massacred upon reaching Gurdwārā Janam Asthān at Nankāṇā Sāhib on the morning of 20 February 1921.

See NANKĀṆĀ SĀHIB MASSACRE

BIBLIOGRAPHY

Shamsher, Gurbak͟hsh Siṅgh, *Shahīdī Jīvan*. Nankana Sahib, 1938

G.S.G.

CHARAN SIṄGH, BHĀĪ (1902-1921), son of Bhāī Gurdit Siṅgh and Māī Sadā Kaur of the village of Koṭlā Santā Siṅgh in Sheikhūpurā district, now in Pakistan, was born on 12 Maghar 1959 Bk/26 November 1902. His original name was Karnail Siṅgh and he was renamed Charan Siṅgh when he received the vows of the Khālsā. He attended the village primary school. He had a musical voice and got up a *ḍhāḍī jathā* (band of preachers singing heroic ballads from Sikh history to the accompaniment of small tambourines called *ḍhaḍs* and a *sāraṅgī*, a stringed instrument). He himself played the *sāraṅgī*. He was present at the historic Dhārovālī conference (1-3 October 1920) and at the time of the liberation of Darbār Sāhib Tarn Tāran (27 January 1921). Charan Siṅgh was a member of Bhāī Lachhmaṇ Siṅgh Dhārovālī's *jathā* doing duty as a correspondent writing letters to volunteers summoning them to the liberation of Gurdwārā Janam Asthān at Nankāṇā Sāhib. He himself accompanied the *jathā* and fell a victim in the violence unleashed by the custodian Naraiṇ Dās and his men (20 February 1921).

See NANKĀṆĀ SĀHIB MASSACRE

BIBLIOGRAPHY

Shamsher, Gurbakhsh Siṅgh, *Shahīdī Jīvan*. Nankana Sahib, 1938

G.S.G.

CHARAN SIṄGH, DR (1853-1908), poet and musicologist, was born at Amritsar in 1853 (father: Kāhn Siṅgh ; mother Rūp Kaur) and was seventh in descent from Dīwān Kauṛā Mall, an influential eighteenth-century Sahajdhārī Sikh. Kāhn Siṅgh (1788-1878) who was of a retiring disposition had spent some years in the company of wandering ascetics before he was persuaded to give up the life of a recluse and become a householder. In addition to his practice of indigenous medicine, he collected and transcribed Sanskrit manuscripts and wrote verse in Braj thereby laying the foundations of the family's literary tradition. His son, Charan Siṅgh, studied Sanskrit, Braj, Persian and prosody, besides Ayurveda and Western medicine. A boyhood experience which must have left a deep impression on his mind was the preparation for his benefit of a copy of the Gurū Granth Sāhib in the hand of Suhel Siṅgh, his maternal uncle. Young Charan Siṅgh watched from day to day the large pages being inscribed in handsome Gurmukhī calligraphy. The completion of the work on Phāgun Vadī 5, 1918 Bk/25 February 1862 was marked by rejoicing and feasting and distribution of charity. He first practised Ayurvedic as well as Western medicine serving from 1 August 1872 to 12 November 1881 in government dispensaries. He resigned the appointment to set up as a private practitioner and to pursue his literary tastes. He was married in 1869 to Uttam Kaur, daughter of Giānī Hazārā Siṅgh (*q.v.*), a reputed man of letters. He had four sons of whom Bhāī Vīr Siṅgh (1872-1957), the celebrated Punjabi poet and savant, was the eldest and Dr Balbīr Siṅgh, scientist and scholar, the youngest.

Among his several works, Charan Siṅgh's *Aṭal Prakāsh* is a versified account of Bābā Aṭal Rāi's life, and the *Dasam Gur Charitra*, a vignette of Gurū Gobind Siṅgh. He translated Kālidāsa's *Abhijñāna Śakūntalam* into Punjabi and started working on two novels (*Jaṅg Maṛaulī* and *Shām Sundar*) which he left incomplete and which were published posthumously by the Khālsā Tract Society. His *Gurmat Saṅgīt Nirṇaya* is a work on the *rāgas* or musical measures employed in the Gurū Granth Sāhib. *Srī Gurū Granth Bāṇī Beorā* explains the titles of compositions comprising the Gurū Granth Sāhib, and furnishes information about the verse-forms and the *rāgas* or musical measures employed, with details of compositions in each *rāga* as well as of the individual contribution of each of the Gurūs and *bhaktas*. His *Gaṛgajj Bole* is a book on the Sikh martial *patois,* and *Srī Mahārāṇī Sharāb Kaur,* a book of didactic Punjabi prose. All his works have been published in one volume in the second part of *Shrī Charaṇhari Visthār.* Besides composing verse himself, Charan Siṅgh presided over a salon of local devotees of the Muse, and took active interest in the rising Siṅgh Sabhā movement.

He died at Amritsar on 13 November 1908.

BIBLIOGRAPHY

1. Balbīr Siṅgh, *Shrī Charaṇhari Visthār.* Amritsar, 1942
2. Harbans Singh, *Bhai Vir Singh.* Delhi, 1972

S.P.S.

CHĀR BĀGH-I-PAÑJĀB by Ganesh Dās Baḍherā, a history in Persian of the Punjab which, according to the author, then extended from the River Indus to the Sutlej. The work, completed in 1855, was published by Khālsā College, Amritsar, in 1965. The author served under the Lahore Darbār as a revenue official (*qānūngo*) of Gujrāt (now in Pakistan) where earlier his father Shiv Dayāl, had also served under Sardār Gulāb Siṅgh of the Bhaṅgī *misl.* Later he joined the service of Rājā Gulāb Siṅgh at Jammū where he compiled his *Rāj Darshanī,* a history of the Ḍogrā *rājās. Chār Bāgh-i-Pañjāb* was written after the annexation of the Punjab at the instance of the author's British patrons, specifically Sir Richard Temple (1826-1902), then secretary to the Punjab Government. It was in fact the updated version of his earlier work, *Chahār Gulshan-i-Pañjāb,* also called *Risālā Sāhib Numā.* Beginning in the traditional style with an account of the solar and lunar dynasties and referring briefly to the Greek invasion by Alexander the Great, *Chār Bāgh-i-Pañjāb* deals with the Punjab under the Muslims from the time of the Ghazanavids down to the Mughal Emperor Shāh Ālam II (1759-1806) and the invasions of Zamān Shāh, a grandson of Ahmad Shāh Durrānī. This is preceded by a sketchy account of early Sikhism based on traditional Sikh versions, with certain obvious discrepancies. For instance, the author states that Gurū Gobind Siṅgh conferred the title of Gurū on Bandā (Siṅgh) which is not correct. His account of the exploits of Bandā Siṅgh Bahādur and of his eventual execution is, however, graphic. Ganesh Dās is more reliable in treating of events closer to his own time. The period of turmoil in Sikh history, the rise of the *misls* particularly the Bhaṅgīs and the Sukkarchakkīās, and the emergence of Mahārājā Raṇjīt Siṅgh as the sovereign of the Punjab are described in considerable detail. So are the geographical and topographical features of the Sindh Sāgar Doāb and the revenue divisions, towns and villages, places of worship and prominent persons belonging to the kingdom of Raṇjīt Siṅgh. The work takes note of the court factions and intrigues which afflicted the Punjab after the death of the Mahārājā. It ends with an account of the two Anglo-Sikhs wars, leading to the occupation of the Punjab by the British. Ganesh Dās's occasional use of opprobrious terms for Sikhs is explainable by his eagerness to please his new masters.

BIBLIOGRAPHY

1. Latif, Syad Muhammad, *History of the Punjab.* Delhi, 1964
2. Sūrī, Sohan Lāl, *'Umdāt-ut-Twārikh.* Lahore, 1985-89
3. Ghulām Muhayy ud-dīn (alias Būṭe Shāh), *Twārīkh-i-Pañjāb* (MS. in the Dr Ganda Singh Collection of the Punjabi University Library, Patiala).
4. Baḍherā, Ganesh Dās, *Chār Bāgh-i-Punjab.* Ed. Kirpal Singh. Amritsar, 1965

S.H.A.

CHAṚHAT SIṄGH (d. 1770), grandfather of Mahārājā Raṇjīt Siṅgh, was the eldest of the four sons of Sardār Naudh Siṅgh. He took to arms while still very young and started taking part in the raids and expeditions led by his father. He also fought in the Sikhs' skirmishes with the Afghān invader Ahmad Shāh Durrānī. After the death of his father, he broke away from the Faizullāpurīā Misl and determined to acquire territory for himself. He left his ancestral village of Sukkarchakk and established his headquarters at Gujrāṅwālā, where he had gathered a considerable following within a short time. One of his constant companions was, Amīr Siṅgh, who was known in the area for his valour. In 1756, Chaṛhat Siṅgh married Desāṅ, the eldest daughter of Amīr Siṅgh. This united the resources of the two families and added considerably to the importance of the young Sukkarchakkīā chief.

Chaṛhat Siṅgh attached Eminābād, killing the *faujdār* and plundering the town. He next captured Wazīrābād. His most significant victory was at Siālkoṭ, where in August 1761 he besieged Ahmad Shāh Durrānī's general, Nūr ud-Dīn Bāmezaī. He pressed the Afghān general hard and forced him to flee the town. He had now to face *Khwājā* Ubaid Khān, the Afghān governor of Lahore, who marched upon Gujrāṅwālā to chastise him. The town was besieged, but Chaṛhat Siṅgh fought with courage and surprised the besiegers by his night sallies. In the meantime, other Sikh *sardārs,* under the leadership of Jassā Siṅgh Āhlūvālīā, came to his rescue. Ubaid Khān was forced to retreat, leaving behind siege guns, ammunition and stores. In the Vaḍḍā Ghallūghārā or Great Holocaust of 5 February 1762, when the Sikhs were involved in a pitched battle with Ahmad Shāh Durrānī, Chaṛhat Siṅgh fought with great skill and courage.

No sooner had Ahmad Shāh returned to Afghanistan than the Sikhs reappeared all over the Punjab. Chaṛhat Siṅgh and the Bhaṅgī *sardārs* sacked Kasūr in April 1763. In November 1763 he engaged at Sialkoṭ the Shāh's commander-in-chief, Jahān Khān, who had been especially sent to punish the Sikhs, and inflicted upon him a severe defeat. The Shāh who came out himself was forced to return home harassed by the pursuing Sikh bands.

Chaṛhat Siṅgh swept across Rachnā and Chaj Doābs and reached Ṛohtās. The Afghān commander of the fort, Sarfarāz Khān, offered stiff resistance, but was overcome near Aṭṭock. Chaṛhat Siṅgh defeated Sarbuland Khān, governor of Kashmīr, who was on his way to meet the Afghān ruler at Lahore. He followed these victories with the occupation of a large portion of Dhannī and Poṭhohār areas. He then took Piṇḍ Dādan Khān, and built a fort there. The Salt Range of Kheoṛā and Miāṇī was the next to fall to him.

Chaṛhat Siṅgh's rapid successes, especially in the Salt Range and Piṇḍ Dādan Khān, aroused the animosity of the Bhaṅgī *sardārs* who had always reckoned these areas within their sphere of influence. Their antagonism came into the open when Chaṛhat Siṅgh and the Bhaṅgī *sardārs* took up sides in the family dispute at Jammū. Its ruler, Raṇjīt Deo, wanted to pass on the succession to his younger son, but was opposed in this attempt by Brij Rāj Deo, the elder son, who managed to secure the active support of Chaṛhat Siṅgh and of the Kanhaiyās. Raṇjīt Deo enlisted the support of the Bhaṅgīs. The rival armies marched into Jammū in 1770. Chaṛhat Siṅgh was fatally wounded in the skirmishes that followed by the bursting of his own gun.

BIBLIOGRAPHY

1. Sūrī, Sohan Lāl, *'Umdat-ut-Twārīkh*. Lahore, 1885-89
2. Bhaṅgū, Ratan Siṅgh, *Prāchīn Panth Prakāsh*. Amritsar, 1962
3. Griffin, Lepel, *Ranjit Singh*. Oxford, 1905
4. Gupta, Hari Ram, *History of the Sikhs,* vol. IV. Delhi, 1982
5. Khushwant Singh, *Ranjit Singh, Maharajah of the Punjab*. London, 1962
6. Hasrat, B.J., *Life and Times of Ranjit Singh*. Nabha, 1977

7. Harbans Singh, *Maharaja Ranjit Singh*. Delhi, 1980

S.S.B.

CHAṚHAT SIṄGH, son of Jai Siṅgh, a Sandhū Jaṭṭ of Koṭ Sayyid Mahmūd, a small village near Amritsar, held a service *jāgīr* under Mahārājā Raṇjīt Siṅgh. His father had served as a trooper under Gulāb Siṅgh Bhaṅgī. Chaṛhat Siṅgh's sister Rūp Kaur married Mahārājā Raṇjīt Siṅgh in 1809. Chaṛhat Siṅgh and his brother Bhūp Siṅgh were assigned an area worth 30,000 rupees, subject to the service of 200 horse, which they held for 15 years when it was resumed. Chaṛhat Siṅgh was sanctioned a *jāgīr* in compensation to the value of 2,500 rupees free of service and was appointed commandant of an irregular regiment. In 1831, Chaṛhat Siṅgh suffered grievous injuries in the battle of Sayyid kī Sarāi fought by Prince Sher Siṅgh against Sayyid Ahmad Barelavī. In 1848, the family of Chaṛhat Siṅgh joined the revolt against the British who confiscated their *jāgīrs* after the occupation of the Punjab.

BIBLIOGRAPHY

1. Griffin, Lepel, and C.F. Massy, *Chiefs and Families of Note in the Punjab*. Lahore, 1890
2. Sūrī, Sohan Lāl, *'Umdāt-ut-Twārīkh'*. Lahore, 1885-89

G.S.N.

CHAṚHDĪ KALĀ, a subtly composite concept, commonly translated as "high morale" or "high spirit", signifies in the Sikh tradition, to which the usage is peculiar and native, a great deal more. It stands for a perennially blossoming, unwilting spirit, a perpetual state of certitude resting on unwavering belief in Divine justice. It is that everlasting spirit of bravery which makes light of all hardships and handicaps – a spirit that will prompt one who had nothing better to eat than a mouthful of gram to say that he was eating almonds, and spirit which would lead one to describe death as an expedition to the next world, a man with an empty stomach declaring himself to have gone mad with prosperity.

The word *kalā* of Sanskrit origin has several shades of meaning, a dominant one among which is 'energy.' *Chaṛhdī*, in Punjabi, is a verbal adjective meaning rising, ascending, soaring. So, *chaṛhdī kālā* would mean an intensely energized, ever-ascending state of the spirit of an individual or of a group. It is characterized by faith, confidence, cheerfulness, courage, fortitude, discipline and resolute willingness to uphold the cherished ideals and readiness to perform the assigned tasks even in face of the most daunting challenge.

Faith is reliance on God and confidence is reliance on the capacities He has endowed men with. These two engender in the individual a state of poise and aplomb. In *chaṛhdī kalā* there is also confidence in the ultimate victory of Truth over falsehood and of Good over evil.

Abiding cheerfulness (*sadā vigās*) is the hallmark of *chaṛhdī kalā*, which is essentially characterized by an unending flow of splendorous joy which washes away the debris of evil, depravity, brutality, knavery, and other infirmities. Cheerfulness is to morale, what compassion is to grace. It puts the heart in tune with the Lord's adoration. The Lord's praise is the keynote of *chaṛhdī kalā: "Nānak nām chaṛhdī kalā, tere bhāṇe sarbatt kā bhalā"* – May Thy Name be ever ascendant, O Nanak; may one and all prosper by Thy Grace," thus ends the prayer of the Sikhs, said at any time of day or night.

Courage is that state or quality of mind and spirit which enables one to face dangers with self-possession and resolution. It does not consist in overlooking danger, but in perceiving and overcoming it. It is resolute affirmation of an undaunted moral character. Such fearlessness is attained by contemplating on the Fearless One (*Nirbhau*). It dares seemingly the most impossible, and strives for it unfalteringly. Fortitude is the strength of mind that allows one to endure pain or adversity with unflinching courage. It consists in true patience and quiet endurance (*dhīraj*).

Discipline resulting from training that leads to controlled behaviour, mentally and morally, is also an essential constituent of *chaṛhdī kalā*. It tames the baseness of worldly passions, fortifies the heart with virtues, enlightens the mind with a discriminating intellect, and furnishes one with enjoyment from within.

Resolution is benevolent intention clothed with ideals for which one essentially finds a way or, else, makes one. 'Sacrificing oneself but flinching not' (*sir dījai kān na kījai*), spells the strength of its determination.

Perpetual readiness to act (*tiār-bar-tiār*) is another characteristic of *chaṛhdī kalā*. It is in action that a man of *chaṛhdī kalā* exists- not in pious resolution alone. He pursues the ideals he cherishes, makes no noise over a good deed, but proceeds on to another and yet another.

Kalā also means "fine art" or aesthetic pursuit. *Chaṛhdī kalā* thus also stands for aesthetic sublimity. The actions of one in *chaṛhdī kalā* are characterized by elegance and gracefulness. *Kalā* also connotes game. *Chaṛhdī kalā*, thereby, means playing a winning game according to the accepted rules of the game. One is confident of ultimate victory when one is playing on God's side and is not discouraged by temporary reverses. *Vāhigurū jī kā Kh̲ālsā* (the Kh̲ālsā belongs to God) has abiding faith in *Vāhigurū jī kī Fateh* (victory).

To sum up, *chaṛhdī kalā* is not just high morale, but also unwavering faith in Divine support, certainty of moral victory and sublimity of action. A buoyant endurance, an ever-smiling contentment, and sublime inspiration underlie its pursuit. Even in the most adverse of circumstances, its constancy does not wane.

Sikh history abounds in events exemplifying the spirit of *chaṛhdī kalā*. During the days of holocausts (*ghallūghārās* or public massacres), when Sikhs were being hounded out of their homes they chose to belittle their troubles and miseries and kept their faith and fighting spirit alive. They forged a whole new vocabulary (*siṅgh bole*) eulogizing their privations and ridiculing their misfortunes, and never giving in. They submitted to the Will of God with serene cheer. One of the most memorable proclamations of *chaṛhdī kalā* is by Gurū Gobind Siṅgh, who, during the most desolate of his days in a friendless forest sojourn, proclaimed:

> With Thee, O Lord, I'd prefer to sleep
> on bare ground,
> Accurst is living with those whom One
> loveth not.
>
> (*Khayāl : Shabad Hazāre*)

BIBLIOGRAPHY

Nekī, Jaswant Siṅgh, *Ardās : Darshan, Rūp te Abhiās*. Amritsar, 1989

J.S.N.

CHARPAṬ NĀTH, one of the *yogīs* whom, according to the *Miharbān Janam Sākhī*, Gurū Nānak met on Mount Sumer, was a Gorakhpanthī recluse. Gurū Nānak himself mentions his name twice in his compositions in the Gurū Granth Sāhib – in his *Sidh Gosṭi* and in another hymn in Rāga Rāmkalī. In the *Sidh Gosṭi* (lit. discourse or dialogue with the Siddhas), Charpaṭ is stated to have put this question to him: "How is one to go across the world described as an impassable ocean?" Answers the Gurū:

> As unaffected liveth the lotus in water,
> And the duck,
> So with the mind fixed on the Word,
> One swimmeth across the Ocean of
> Existence.
> He who liveth detached,

Enshrining the One Lord in his mind,
Who hopeth yet desireth not,
Canst see as well as show
The Unfathomable and the Unperceivable,
Of such a one will Nānak be a slave.
(GG, 938)

In the Nātha tradition, Charpaṭ, is known to have been a disciple of Gorakhnāth whose period falls somewhere in the 11th to 12th century. Gurū Nānak whose period is much later must have therefore met some contemporary incumbent of Charpaṭ's seat who also bore his name. Sixty-four *ślokas* attributed to Charpaṭ are included in the Hindi work *Nātha Siddhoṅ kī Bāṇiyāṅ* some of them relating to the preparation of elixir to prevent disease and infirmity. Charpaṭ is counted among Siddhas of the *rasāyaṇa* (alchemy) tradition.

BIBLIOGRAPHY

1. Dwivedī, Hazārī Prasād, *Nāth Sampradāya*. Varanasi, 1966
2. Malik, Kalyāṇī, *Siddhā Siddhānta Paddhti*. Pune, 1954
3. Jodh Singh, *The Religious Philosphy of Guru Nanak*. Varanasi, 1983

Gn.S.

CHĀR SĀHIBZĀDE, *(chār* = four + *sāhibzāde* = scions, young men of genteel birth) is a term endearingly used for the four sons of Gurū Gobind Siṅgh, Nānak X, all of whom died as martyrs while still very young. Their names are reverently preserved in Sikh memory and are recalled every time Sikh *ardās* or prayer of supplication is recited at a congregation or privately by an individual.

See AJĪT SIṄGH, SĀHIBZĀDĀ; FATEH SIṄGH, SĀHIBZĀDĀ; JUJHĀR SIṄGH, SĀHIBZĀDĀ; and ZORĀWAR SIṄGH, SĀHIBZĀDĀ

BIBLIOGRAPHY

Padam, Piārā Siṅgh, *Chār Sāhibzāde*. Patiala, 1970

S.S.B.

CHĀRYĀRĪ SOWĀRS was the name given to an irregular cavalry regiment in Sikh times. It owed its origin to four friends, or *Chār* (four) *Yār* (friends), who were seen together all the time. Their names were: Bhūp Siṅgh Siddhū, Jīt Siṅgh, Rām Siṅgh Saddozaī and Hardās Siṅgh Bāṇīā. They were all young men of the same age, very handsome, well built and always elegantly dressed. Mahārājā Raṇjīt Siṅgh became very fond of the foursome and employed them as soldiers. He was so impressed by their bearing that he gave them fine horses to ride and created a regiment named Chāryārī Sowārs after them. The force grew in strength under the patronage of the Mahārājā. It was placed under the command of Rājā Suchet Siṅgh, who was himself always splendidly turned out and who was known as the dandy of the Punjab. He was assigned a *ḍerā,* i.e. lodgings, near the Shālāmār Gardens at Lahore. *The K͟hālsā Darbār Records* as well as the *'Umdāt-ut-Twārīk͟h* includes it amongst the seventeen *ḍerās* of the *ghoṛchaṛās* of different sizes under the name of the Ḍerā Naulakkhā or the Ḍerā Chāryārī. The *ḍerā* consisted of a number of squadrons of varying strength. Each horseman wore a velvet coat, a shirt of mail and a steel helmet; the horses were bedecked with metal-capped peacock plumes. The recruitment was voluntary. The troops were seldom paid a salary, though provision was made for their food, uniform and equipment. The horses were their own, and they were under no feudal obligations.

The Chāryārī force was a fine body of horse, richly clad and mounted, strutting pompously on all ceremonial occasions during Raṇjīt Siṅgh's reign. After the death of the Mahārājā, it became involved in partisan feuds. It took the part of Rāṇī Chand Kaur when, in January 1841, Sher Siṅgh invested the Lahore Fort. Later, Sher Siṅgh won over the Chāryārī Sowārs, who, with Rājā Dhiān Siṅgh, joined his standard. But they deserted the Mahārājā to support his *mukhtiār* or attorney, Javālā Siṅgh, who had revolted against his master. The Chāryārī force sided with Rājā Hīrā Siṅgh in the fight with Atar Siṅgh Sandhāṅvālīā, who had taken shelter with Bhāī Bīr Siṅgh of Nauraṅgābād. On 18 December 1844, Rājā Hīrā Siṅgh discharged about five hundred men of the Chāryārī force. That was the end of this colourful and picturesque regiment.

BIBLIOGRAPHY

1. Sūrī, Sohan Lāl, *'Umdāt-ut-Twārīkh'*. Lahore, 1885-89
2. Giān Siṅgh, Giānī, *Panth Prakāsh*. Patiala, 1970
3. Griffin, Lepel, and C.F. Massy, *Chiefs and Families of Note in the Punjab*. Lahore, 1890

H.R.G.

CHATAR SIṄGH, a Brāṛ Jaṭṭ, was, according to Sarūp Siṅgh Kaushish, *Gurū kīāṅ Sākhīāṅ*, a Sikh spy who, during the siege of Anandpur by the hill *rājās* in September-October 1700, used to mix with the enemy and bring intelligence about their strength, dispositions and plans. It was he who carried to Gurū Gobind Siṅgh the news one evening how Rājā Kesarī Chand, one of the besieging chieftains, had planned to smash the gate of the Lohgaṛh Fort on the following morning with the help of a drunken war-elephant.

BIBLIOGRAPHY

Padam, Piārā Siṅgh, and Giānī Garjā Siṅgh, eds., *Gurū kīāṅ Sākhīāṅ*. Patiala, 1986

Gn.S.

CHATAR SIṄGH AṬĀRĪVĀLĀ (d. 1855), commander and provincial governor under minor Mahārājā Duleep Siṅgh, was the son of Jodh Siṅgh Aṭārīvālā. Jodh Siṅgh had joined the service of Mahārājā Raṇjīt Siṅgh in 1805 when he received large *jāgīrs* in the Poṭhohār country. On the death of his father in that year, Chatar Siṅgh succeeded to the *jāgīrs*, then amounting to over a lakh of rupees annually. He devoted most of his time to farming and kept generally aloof from state affairs during the reign of Mahārājā Raṇjīt Siṅgh. When after the assassination of his son, Mahārājā Sher Siṅgh, in September 1843, his daughter, Tej Kaur, was betrothed to Mahārājā Duleep Siṅgh, he came into prominence politically. He was appointed governor of Peshāwar in August 1846. In November 1847, the title of Rājā was recommended for him by the Council of Regency, but was at his request conferred upon his son Sher Siṅgh instead. Chatar Siṅgh was then transferred to Hazārā, where as the governor of the province he came into conflict with the overbearing Assistant British Resident, Captain James Abbott, his assistant and adviser for the demarcation of boundary between the Punjab and Kashmīr which had been given away by the British to the Ḍogrā Rājā Gulāb Siṅgh for his services to them during the first Anglo-Sikh war. Since the Multān outbreak in April 1848, James Abbott had been continually reporting to the Resident at Lahore that discontent prevailed among the Sikh troops stationed at Hazārā; in September 1848, he alleged that a conspiracy was being hatched by Chatar Siṅgh, its Sikh governor, to subvert British power in the Punjab. He charged him with high treason, and leading the local chiefs and large numbers of Muslim levies he had raised he marched on Harīpur to expel the Sikh governor. At this juncture, Commodore Canora, an artillery officer in the Fort, who was in secret communication with Captain Abbott, refused to move his battery, and was consequently shot down at Chatar Siṅgh's orders. Under the orders of the British Resident at Lahore this Hazārā incident was investigated by Captain Nicholson who in his enquiry report not only exonerated Chatar Siṅgh, but also justified the defensive measures he had taken to save the besieged capital of Hazārā from Abbott's Muhammadan mercenaries. Resident Frederick Currie, notwithstanding Nicholson's report, issued orders which amounted to Chatar Siṅgh's virtual dismissal and the confiscation of his *jāgīrs* which drove him to open defiance. The Hazārā revolt now escalated into hostilities between the British and the Sikhs. After their defeat at Gujrāt on 21 February 1849, Chatar Siṅgh and his sons, Rājā Sher Siṅgh and Avtār Siṅgh, were detained by the British in their village, Aṭārī, and then imprisoned at Allāhābād from where they were removed to Fort William at Calcutta to prevent them from establishing contact with the exiled Queen Mother, Mahārāṇī Jind Kaur. They were released in January 1854. Chatar Siṅgh died in Calcutta on 27 December 1855.

BIBLIOGRAPHY

1. Sūrī, Sohan Lāl, *'Umdāt-ut-Twārīkh*. Lahore, 1885-89
2. Griffin, Lepel, and C.F. Massy, *Chiefs and Families of Note in the Punjab*. Lahore, 1890
3. Hasrat, B.J., *Life and Times of Ranjit Singh*. Hoshiarpur, 1977

G.S.

CHATAR SIṄGH COLLECTION, comprising correspondence, papers, treaties, etc., particularly relating to transactions among the Ḍogrā chiefs of Jammū (Dhiān Siṅgh, Gulāb Siṅgh and Suchet Siṅgh) and between them and the Lahore Darbār, was put together by Ṭhākur Chatar Siṅgh of Dharamsālā and is now preserved in the Punjab State Archives, at Paṭiālā. These documents are mostly certified copies, very few of them being the original ones. The Handlist in the Archives (Nos. 490-551) enumerates sixty-two documents in this collection, beginning from 9 March 1846 and contains correspondence of O. St. John, the British Resident in Kashmīr (No. 497) ; Col. Nisbet (No. 498) ; H.S. Barnes (No. 500) ; and Sir Frederick Currie (No. 501) – all relating to Rājā Gulāb Siṅgh and Kashmīr. Copies of the treaty for the transfer of Kashmīr to Rājā Gulāb Siṅgh by Viscount Hardinge, dated 16 March 1846 (No. 491) and the Deed, dated 18 February 1859 (No. 494) also form part of the collection. So is the copy of the award of Punjab Board of Administration dividing territory between Rājā Jawāhar Siṅgh and Motī Siṅgh of Puṇchh (No. 493). Among the documents relating to the Ḍogrā family are the Deed of Agreement, dated 15 Maghar 1877 Bk, whereby Kishorā Siṅgh, Gulāb Siṅgh, Dhiān Siṅgh and Suchet Siṅgh received the grant of the *ta'aluqā* of Jammū made to them by Mahārājā Raṇjīt Siṅgh (No. 503) and the Deed of Affirmation (undated) by Mahārājā Khaṛak Siṅgh confirming all grants of estates, titles, etc. to Gulāb Siṅgh, Dhiān Siṅgh, and Suchet Siṅgh (No. 504). The collection also contains a copy of the Deed of Grant by Mahārājā Raṇjīt Siṅgh to Rājā Dhiān Siṅgh conferring on him the special title of *Rājā* and the state of Bhimbar, etc. (No. 507). There is a confirmation by Mahārājā Khaṛak Siṅgh of all grants and awards to Rājā Dhiān Siṅgh (No. 508). There is also a Deed of Grant by Mahārājā Raṇjīt Siṅgh to Hīrā Siṅgh, son of Dhiān Siṅgh (No. 509), followed by Mahārājā Raṇjīt Siṅgh's instructions as to the payments to be made to Hīrā Siṅgh.

The papers dealing with the Jammū chiefs contain the division of Rājā Suchet Siṅgh's property between Gulāb Siṅgh and Hīrā Siṅgh (No. 514-15); Gulāb Siṅgh's correspondence with Wazīr Jawāhar Siṅgh concerning disputes, adjustment of dues of money and jewellery (Nos. 516-23); Gulāb Siṅgh's letter to Jawāhar Siṅgh (dated 7 Chet 1902 Bk) claiming the title of Mahārājā as well as the hill territory from Jasroṭā to Hazārā (No. 526); *robakārs* of H.M. Lawrence to Jawāhar Siṅgh; *sanads* granted by Mahārājā Gulāb Siṅgh to various persons (Nos. 535-36 and 538); and a complaint of Jawāhar Siṅgh to the Chief Commissioner of the Punjab that he had suffered much at the hands of Mahārājā Gulāb Siṅgh (No. 541). Besides, the collection contains letters and *robakārs* from the Lt.- Governor of the Punjab to Rājā Amar Siṅgh of Puṇchh and other hill chiefs on diverse matters. Totally, these documents reveal how the hill chiefs looked up to the British for help and for the redress of their complaints against each other.

B.J.H.

CHAṬṬHIĀṄ DĪ VĀR is a Punjabi ballad describing the battle between Mahāṅ Siṅgh, father of Mahārājā Raṇjīt Siṅgh, and Ghulām Muhammad Chaṭṭhā, a Muslim chieftain of the Chaṭṭhā clan of the Jaṭṭs. The poet is some Pīr Muhammad, whose name appears in some verses of the poem. The *Vār* was first published in Persian script by Qāzī Fazal Haq, a teacher at Government College, Lahore. According to his statement, Pīr Muhammad, the poet, was a resident of Gujrāt district, and he composed this ballad in the early years of the British occupation of the Punjab. No evidence is available in the text to support this statement. Nevertheless, the details of the events provided, and the casual way in which the poet has introduced different personalities – as if everybody knew about them, indicate that he was an eye-witness to the happenings he has described.

The events of the strife are spread over a period of a few years but no dates are given. Ghulām Muhammad became the chief of the Chaṭṭhās, after the death of his father, Pīr Muhammad (not to be confused with the author of the poem), probably in 1785. His adversary, Mahāṅ Siṅgh, died in 1792. As such the events narrated in the *Vār* took place between 1785 and 1792.

The Sikh *sardārs* had occupied large portions of the Punjab by 1780, but some Muslim chiefs, who had created independent states for themselves in the wake of the downfall of Mughal authority, were holding out in certain areas. The Chaṭṭhās had their stronghold in the Wazīrābād and Hāfizābād *parganahs* where they were masters of 78 villages. They formed their own state under their leader, Nūr Muhammad, grandfather of Ghulām Muhammad, and had sufficiently strengthened their position by the time the latter became the chief. They had common boundary with Sardār Mahāṅ Siṅgh, and were always a source of trouble to the Sikh chieftain. Quite frequently they raided his territory and looted and plundered the villages. Mahāṅ Siṅgh was forced to retaliate. The Chaṭṭhās offered stubborn resistance to him from the fort of Manchar, which they were forced to evacuate after a long siege and considerable loss of life.

It is a lengthy *Vār*, with 91 *pauṛīs* (stanzas) available and published. But it remains incomplete, and nobody knows how many stanzas the poem originally contained. After the 91st stanza, one verse from 92nd stanza has been given in the text. The first verse is in praise of the Creator. Thereafter two full stanzas describe events from the lives of mythological and historical figures – prophets, kings, great men -- from Semitic traditions. The poet comes to the subject in the fourth stanza. His description of events is sketchy though he does not lack poetic fancy and imagination. He is at his best when depicting a battle scene.

Unlike most other Muslim poets he has no prejudice against words from Hindu or Sikh sources, nor is he excessively given to pedantic vocabulary of Perso-Arabic origin. He belonged to Gujrāt district and used the dialect of that region, which is a mixture of central Punjabi and Lahndī.

S.S.A.

CHATURBHUJ POTHĪ, which forms the third part of what is known as the Miharbān Janam Sākhī, is the work of Soḍhī Chaturbhuj, the youngest of the three sons of Soḍhī Miharbān (1581-1639), son of Gurū

Arjan's elder brother, Prithī Chand (1558-1618). The only known MS. of the *pothī* (book) preserved in the Sikh Historical Research Department of K͟hālsā College, Amritsar, forms part of a single work divided into three parts, *Sachkhaṇḍ Pothī* by Miharbān, *Pothī Harijī* by Miharbān's second son and successor, Harijī (d. 1696), and *Chaturbhuj Pothī*. The last one has its name recorded in the colophon as *Chatrabhoj Pothī*, the author's name is recorded as Chatar Bhoj, a variation on Chaturbhuj (lit. with four arms as Viṣṇu is usually shown in images). Chaturbhuj's *pothī* contains 74 *goṣṭis* or discourses and was completed in 1651. It has the same language, style and format as do the other two *pothīs* – the first by his father and the second by his brother. Each discourse in the *Pothī* commences with a general statement of the situation in which Gurū Nānak supposedly delivered it. Someone poses a question or expresses a doubt pertaining to some religious doctrine or practice, and Gurū Nānak proceeds to explain by quoting and expounding one of his hymns. The author, Chaturbhuj in this instance, rounds off the discourse with a *śloka*, usually a couplet, from Gurū Nānak's *bāṇī* or of his own composition. The *Pothī* is, as is the *Miharbān Janam Sākhī* as a whole, essentially exegetical rather than biographical, although the opening setting in each *goṣṭi* does contain references to some specific location and to the person or persons addressed. The primary concern, however, remains doctrinal – nature of God, *nām simran,* meditation on the Name, importance of the true Gurū, and so on. While Harijī chose for his exegesis the longer compositions of Gurū Nānak such as *Japu, Paṭṭī, Sidh Goṣṭi* and *Oaṅkār*, Chaturbhuj took up, besides *chaupadās* and *aṣṭpadīs* (4-stanza and 8-stanza hymns, respectively), *pauṛīs* from *Vārs* in Mājh and Malhār measures and *ślokas*.

G.N.R.

CHATURBHUJ, SOḌHĪ. *See CHATURBHUJ POTHĪ*

CHATUR DĀS KAPŪR, BHĀĪ, whose name appears in Bhāī Gurdās's roster of devotees of Gurū Arjan's time, *Vārāṅ*, XI. 20. Chatur Dās received initiation at the hands of the Gurū who taught him to be humble and, in humility, seek the company of holy men.

See GĀRŪ, BHĀĪ

BIBLIOGRAPHY

1. Manī Siṅgh, Bhāī, *Sikhāṅ dī Bhagat Mālā*. Amritsar, 1955
2. Santokh Siṅgh, Bhāī, *Srī Gur Pratāp Sūraj Granth*. Amritsar, 1926-37

T.S.

CHATUR DĀS, PAṆḌIT, a learned Brāhmaṇ of Vārāṇasī, who engaged Gurū Nānak in a discourse during his visit to the city. He was intrigued by the Gurū's apparel which was neither of a householder nor of a hermit. As relates the *Purātan Janam Sākhī,* he questioned him, "What faith do you profess? You carry no *sāligrām,* the devotee's stone, nor do you wear the necklace of *tulsī*. You carry no rosary, nor have you the mark of powdered *chandan*-wood on your forehead. What devotion have you attached yourself to?" Gurū Nānak in reply sang a hymn to the accompaniment of Mardānā's *rabāb* or rebeck:

> Let God's Name be the *sāligrām* thou adorest,
> Let good deeds be the basil-wreath round thy neck ;
> Make a raft of God's Name and seek His grace.
> Why waste thy time watering barren land,
> Or plastering walls built on sand ?
> Let good deeds be the string of vessels
> To draw water from the well,
> And yoke thy mind to the wheel.
> Distil the nectar and irrigate with it the land,

Then alone wilt thou be owned by the Gardener ...

Still proud of his learning, Chatur Dās said to Gurū Nānak, "I admit your devotion to God, but now that you have come to this city, stay awhile and take something of its merit. Here we teach all the fourteen sciences ..." Gurū Nānak said that for him only one word was of real account, adding that he reckoned him alone truly learned who engaged himself in the service of others. According to *Purātan Janam Sākhī*, Gurū Nānak here uttered all the fifty-four stanzas of his composition, *Oaṅkār,* in Rāmkalī Dakkhaṇī measure, which is preserved in the Gurū Granth Sāhib. In this long poem, he enunciated the nature of the True One and of His creation. A new understanding dawned upon Paṇḍit Chatur Dās. He fell at the Gurū's feet and became a disciple. A Sikh *saṅgat* or group of followers attached to the message of the Gurū grew up around him.

BIBLIOGRAPHY

1. Santokh Siṅgh, Bhāī, *Srī Gur Pratāp Sūraj Granth.* Amritsar, 1926-37
2. Vīr Siṅgh, Bhāī, ed., *Purātan Janam Sākhī.* Amritsar, 1971
3. Giān Siṅgh, Giānī, *Twārīkh Gurū Khālsā.* Patiala, 1970
4. Macauliffe, Max Arthur, *The Sikh Religion.* Oxford, 1909

Gn.S.

CHĀŪ, BHĀĪ, a Bammī Khatrī and a resident of Sultānpur Lodhī, embraced Sikhism during the time of Gurū Amar Dās. He was one of the *saṅgat* who, according to Bhāī Manī Siṅgh, *Sikhāṅ dī Bhagat Mālā,* went to see Gurū Arjan at Amritsar and received the holy precept.

See ĀKUL, BHĀĪ and BHIKHĀ, BHAṬṬ

BIBLIOGRAPHY

1. Manī Siṅgh, Bhāī, *Sikhāṅ dī Bhagat Mālā.* Amritsar, 1955
2. Santokh Siṅgh, Bhāī, *Srī Gur Pratāp Sūraj Granth.* Amritsar, 1926-37

T.S.

CHAUBĪS AUTĀR, a collection of twenty-four legendary tales of twenty-four incarnations of the god Viṣṇu, forms a part of *Bachitra Nāṭak,* in Gurū Gobind Siṅgh's *Dasam Granth.* The complete work contains a total of 4,371 verse-units of which 3,356 are accounted for by *Rāmāvtār* and *Krishnāvtār.* The shortest is *Baudh Avatār* comprising three quatrains, and the longest is *Krishnāvtār,* with 2,492 verse-units, mostly quatrains.

The introductory thirty-eight *chaupaīs* or quatrains refer to the Supreme Being as unborn, invisible but certainly immanent in all objects. Whenever evil predominates, saviours of the humanity or *avatārs* emerge by His *hukam,* i.e. order, to re-establish righteousness. They fulfil His will and purpose. Kāl Purash who creates them ultimately subsumes them all in himself. The poet asserts his monotheistic belief here and while enumerating the *avatārs* discountenances any possibility of their being accepted as the Supreme Being, i.e. Akāl Purakh. In the epilogue to one of the episodes in *Krishnāvtār* occurs a statement repudiating the worship of popular deities like Gaṇeśa, Kṛṣṇa and Viṣṇu (verses 434-40). The Supreme Being, called in the Gurū's authentic idiom, Mahākāl (the Supreme Lord of Time) is acknowledged as the Succourer to whom prayer is made to keep operative the defensive might (*tegh*) and dispensing of charity (*deg*). Thus is set forth the basic principle of the Sikh faith amid a long literary exercise.

The poet asserts that he, having descended from the martial Kṣatriyas, cannot think of adopting the attitude of a recluse towards the disturbed conditions of his time. The greater part of the tales of *Rāmāvtār* and *Krishnāvtār* are taken up with battle-scenes evoked through many alliterative devices with the clash and clang of arms constantly reproduced. At the close of *Krishnāvtār,* in a kind of postscript, is proclaimed the crusader's creed, which is ever "to remember God, to contemplate holy war; and, unmindful of the destruction of the perishable body, to embark the boat of noble repute." The poet has thus extracted the element of heroism from the prevalent stories without projecting the attitude of a worshipper, with the sole purpose of inspiring his followers with the resolve to fight for Dharma, i.e. to uphold righteousness. *Chaubīs Autār* does not appear to be the work of one period. It was a long project which was in execution for a decade or more. While *Krishnāvtār* is stated in verse 2,490-91 to have been composed in Samvat 1745/AD 1688 at Paonṭā when Gurū Gobind Siṅgh was residing there, *Rāmāvtar,* according to verses 860-61 was composed at Anandpur in Samvat 1755/AD 1698 near the temple of Naiṇādevī, close to the bank of the River Sutlej. Another component of the *Chaubīs Autār* is *Nihkalaṅkavtār* which is a sustained expression of appearance of Nihkalaṅk who would destroy evil and establish righteousness. An interesting phenomenon observable in *Krishnāvtār* is the sliding of the poet from Kṛṣna's mythical career into his own contemporary scene. Among the heroes mentioned some bear medieval Rājpūt names (Gaj Siṅgh, Dhan Siṅgh, Sūrat Siṅgh); some Muslim like Nāhar K͟hān, Tāhir K͟hān, and Sher K͟hān. In verse 1602 *malechh* which was the pejorative term used for Muslims is used. The name of the city of Delhi appears, which is an anachronism. Such anachronisms indicate how the poet's consciousness was touched by the turmoil in contemporary Mug͟hal times.

The texture of the language is neo-classical Braj. The poet has employed a variety of metres, and made them responsive to the passing moods or emotions and changing situations. The metres are alternately short and long in consonance with the increasing and lessening of the fury of battle. Blank verse in Punjabi has been inserted for the first time by the poet in the Sirkhaṇḍī metre (*Rāmāvtār,* verses 467-70). Punjabi words keep cropping up as in the heading of a *Krishnāvtār* episode *luk-mīchan* (hide and seek) and in referring to a king condemned to be incarnated as a lizard (*kirlā,* in Punjabi). At one place in *Rāmāvtār* (verse 657-68) Persian words are blended with Hindi to make *rek͟htā*: the language that was the precursor of modern Urdu. The range of vocabulary thus becomes vast and varied.

BIBLIOGRAPHY

1. Loehlin, C.H., *The Granth of Guru Gobind Singh and the Khalsa Brotherhood.* Lucknow, 1971
2. Ashta, Dharam Pal, *The Poetry of the Dasam Granth.* Delhi, 1959
3. Jaggī, Ratan Siṅgh, *Dasam Granth Parichaya.* Delhi, 1990

D.P.A.

CHAUṄKĪ or Chaukī, lit. quarter, a four-footed wooden platform upon which sat the holy choir to recite the sacred hymns in a *gurdwārā* or at a gathering of the devotees. The term *chauṅkī* also refers to a session of *kīrtan* or hymn-singing, the number of singers at such sessions commonly being four, nowadays usually three, playing different instruments. *Kīrtan* is a popular form of worship among Sikhs. At all major *gurdwārās* at least four *kīrtan chauṅkīs* are held. At the central shrine, in Amritsar, the Harimandar, *kīrtan* goes on all the time, from 2.45 a.m. to 9.45 p.m. Four major *chauṅkīs* or sittings are counted:

(a) *Āsā dī Vār dī chauṅkī* in the early morning;

(b) *Charan Kaṅval or Bilāval dī chauṅkī* in the forenoon commencing at about four hours after sunrise;

(c) *Rahrāsi dī chauṅkī* in the evening held immediately before the recitation of evening prayers of *Rahrāsi*; and

(d) *Kalyān dī chauṅkī*, later in the evening just preceding the recitation of the last prayer of the day, *Kīrtan Sohilā*.

These *chauṅkīs* take place in the presence of the Gurū Granth Sāhib, professional *rāgīs* or hymn-singers participating in them to the accompaniment of instruments, usually two harmoniums, a pair of *tablās* or drumlets and occasionally adding a pair of cymbals and/or *chimṭās* (tongs fitted with metallic discs).

But in the precincts of the Darbār Sāhib, Amritsar, some other *chauṅkīs* are led out by groups of devotees, chanting hymns as they walk, circumambulating the holy complex including the *sarovar*, the sacred tank, and the *sanctum sanctorum*. The column marching and reciting the hymns divides itself into two, one section leading and the other repeating the hymn verse by verse in a singing tune. The performance is called *chauṅkī chaṛhnī* (mounting or marching of the *chauṅkī*). These *chauṅkīs* are also four in number:

(a) The first and the oldest one is said to have been introduced by Bābā Buḍḍhā (d. 1635) during Gurū Hargobind's absence from Amritsar at the time of his internment by the Mug͟hal emperor, Jahāṅgīr, in the Fort at Gwālīor. It has a special procedure laid out for it and a special set of hymns assigned to it. After the conclusion of *Rahrāsi* prayer at the Akāl Tak͟ht those participating in the *chauṅkī* stand below the Akāl Tak͟ht; and officiant of the Tak͟ht hands to them a flag and a Srī Sāhib; one of the group says *ardās,* the initial supplication; the *chauṅkī* then commences its march, *parikramā* or circumambulation of the *sarovar* keeping the holy Harimandar on its right and singing hymns in groups; two torch-bearers walk, with the group, one in front and the other in the rear, with a herald alerting the pilgrims to the approaching procession; on completion of the *parikramā* the *chauṅkī* proceeds to the Harimandar across the causeway; as it approaches the sanctum, singing all the time, the *kīrtan* already being performed inside stops while the *chauṅkī* circumambulates the sanctum and performs *ardās* after which it returns to the Akāl Tak͟ht to deposit the flag and the sword before it disperses.

(b) In imitation of the above, Bhāī Ghanaiyā Siṅgh of the Aḍḍanshāhī sect introduced another *chauṅkī* in 1830. It has since split into two separate groups known as Chauṅkī Mahant Sobhā Siṅgh and Chauṅkī Mahant Dīnā Nāth. Both are mounted one after the other when the traditional *chauṅkī* of Bābā Buḍḍhā has completed its round. But the carrying of the banner and Srī Sāhib from the Akāl Tak͟ht is the privilege only of the old *chauṅkī*.

(c) A morning *chauṇkī* introduced by Bhāī Naraiṇ Siṅgh in 1905 is mounted immediately after the Gurū Granth Sāhib has arrived at the Harimandar at about 5 a.m.

(d) Another morning *chauṅkī* was introduced by Mahant Sant Siṅgh Kalīvāle in 1910. It is mounted after the conclusion of *Āsā dī Vār, ardās* and *hukam* in the Harimandar at about 6.45 a.m.

In addition to these daily *chauṅkīs,* based in Amritsar, there are other monthly and annual *chauṅkīs.* One of them is mounted from the Akāl Tak͟ht on the eve of the new-moon day. It travels throughout the night singing hymns all the way and arrives at Darbār Sāhib, Tarn Tāran, early in the morning. Another one mounted similarly on the eve of the full-moon day reaches Goindvāl the next morning. For return journey the devotees may use motor transport. Annual *chauṅkīs,* mounted on some *gurpurabs* or festivals in honour of the Gurūs, visit some historical *gurdwārās* in villages surrounding Amritsar such as Chheharṭā, Vallā, Verkā, Vaḍālī, Jhabāl, Bīṛ Bābā Buḍḍhā, and Bāsarke.

Smaller *gurdwārās* have their own schedules of taking out *chauṅkīs,* saying *śabdas,* usually as part of the evening service.

M.G.S.

CHAUPAĪ, or *KABYOBĀCH BENATĪ CHAUPAĪ (kabyobāch* = in the words of the poet; *benatī* = supplication; *chaupaī* = the name of the metre in which the poem has been composed), is a 25-stanza-long composition by Gurū Gobind Siṅgh occurring in the *Dasam Granth* at the end of the last of the tales in *Charitropākhayān. Chaupaī* is also recited as part of the *Rahrāsi (q.v.),* the evening prayer of the Sikhs and is included among the five bāṇīs or texts which are mandatorily chanted as *amrit* is being prepared for the Sikh baptismal ceremony. The composition, as the title suggests, is the Gurū's invocation, in *chaupaī* metre, to the Supreme Lord, seeking his blessing and protection. "O God, give me Thy hand and protect me, and all my desires shall be fulfilled: May my heart be ever attached to Thy feet ..." (1). "May the thirst for repeating Thy name abide with me ..." (3). God is described as all-pervading and all-powerful ; He is the Master of Power and the Lord of the Sword. "Beloved Lord, Protector of the saints, Friend of the poor, Destroyer of tyrants – Thou art Lord of the fourteen worlds (6)." It is such a Lord that Gurū Gobind Siṅgh calls on to provide relief to the oppressed and the aggrieved, and it is such a Lord that he seeks to cherish always. There are in the poem allusions to figures from Indian mythology and to Hindu gods Brahmā, Viṣṇu and Śiva who are all shown as subject to the Timeless Lord, their creator. "When the Creator projected his Being, creation of limitless variety came into existence; when He draws creation within Himself it ceases" (13). Also on cosmogony: "None can comprehend the extent of the cosmos and nobody knows how He first fashioned creation" (17). The poem concludes with some further invocatory verses: "O Thou with the sword on Thy banner, I seek Thy protection. Give me Thine own hand and save me. Be Thou everywhere my helper and save me from the designs of the malevolent" (25).

BIBLIOGRAPHY

1. Ashta, Dharam Pal, *The Poetry of the Dasam Granth.* Delhi, 1959
2. Loehlin, C.H., *The Granth of Guru Gobind Singh and the Khalsa Brotherhood.* Lucknow, 1971
3. Sāhib Siṅgh, *Saṭīk Jāpu Sāhib, Savaiyye, Chaupaī.* Amritsar, 1957

Gr.S.

CHAUPĀ SIṄGH (d. 1724), earlier name Chaupati Rāi, was a prominent Sikh in the retinue of Gurū Tegh Bahādur (1621-75) and then of Gurū Gobind Siṅgh (1666-1708). He was born in a Chhibbar (Brāhmaṇ) family of Kaṛiālā, a village in Jehlum district, now in Pakistan. His grandfather, Gautam, had accepted the Sikh faith and was followed in this allegiance by his two sons – Paiṛā and Prāgā. The former was Chaupati Rāi's father; in the lineage of the latter, known for his martial skill during the time of Gurū Hargobind (1595-1644), were Dargah Mall, Dharam Chand, Gurbakhsh Siṅgh and Kesar Siṅgh. Chaupati Rāi remained attached to the Gurūs' household from the time of Gurū Har Rāi to whose service he had been piously assigned by his parents. According to

Kesar Siṅgh Chhibbar, *Baṅsāvalīnāmā,* he accompanied Gurū Tegh Bahādur to Paṭnā where during the infancy and early childhood of (Gurū) Gobind Siṅgh he acted as his *khiḍāvā* or attendant. He also taught the child Gurmukhī and Ṭākrī letters. When Gurū Gobind Siṅgh inaugurated the Khālsā in 1699, Chaupati Rāi also received the initiatory rites and became Chaupā Siṅgh. Chaupā Siṅgh's title to permanent fame stems from the association of his name with a Sikh manual *Hazūrī Rahitnāmā*, popularly called *Rahitnāmā Chaupā Siṅgh.* The family tradition as recorded in the *Baṅsāvalīnāmā* affirms that Chaupā Siṅgh was selected by Gurū Gobind Siṅgh to produce the first *rahitnāmā,* code of conduct, and as he humbly pleaded insufficient competence for so weighty a responsibility, he was reassured by the promise that the Gurū himself would inspire and direct the words which he uttered. Further, that a copy was made in the hand of a Sikh, Sītal Siṅgh Bahrūpīā, and taken to the Gurū for his imprimatur. The colophon of the extant text is, however, vague about its authorship and some of the injunctions in it conflict with the accepted Sikh code. Chaupā Siṅgh remained with the Gurū until 1705 when at the time of evacuation of Anandpur he proceeded to Delhi in the entourage of the ladies of the Gurū's family. He remained in Delhi until his death by execution in 1724, except for a brief sojourn in Talvaṇḍī Sābo sometime in 1706 when with Mātā Sundarī and Mātā Sāhib Devāṅ he went there to see the Gurū. He was one of the band of the followers of Ajīt Siṅgh, adopted son of Mātā Sundarī, later discarded, which became involved in a public fracas resulting in the death of a Muslim *faqīr.* In consequence, sixty of them were arrested and executed on Māgh Sudī 4, 1780 Bk / 18 January 1724. Chaupā Siṅgh was one of them.

BIBLIOGRAPHY

1. McLeod, W.H., *The Chaupa Singh Rahitnama.* Dunedin, 1987
2. Chhibbar, Kesar Siṅgh, *Bansāvalīnāmā Dasāṅ Pātshāhīāṅ Kā.* Chandigarh, 1972

P.S.P.

CHAUTHĀPAD. *See* AMAR PAD

CHELLĀRĀM, BHĀĪ (1904-1964), a well-known Sahajdhāri Sikh of modern times who sang and preached *gurbāṇī,* the Gurū's inspired word, with a rare love and devotion, was born in a Sindhī family of Hyderābād (Sindh) on 3 May 1904, the son of Dr Ṭekchand Rāchūmal Mansukhānī and Chetībāī. Chellārām's parents died while he was still in his infancy and his only sister not long afterwards. Successive deaths in the family left him a lonely youth, with a rather pensive mind. He took his degree in Law and set up practice as a lawyer, but his heart was not in the profession. He joined civil service which left him ample time for the study of religious books. Sikh Scripture, the Gurū Granth Sāhib, took hold of his mind and he started reciting Sikh hymns in the Gurdwārā at Karāchī. He also taught children to recite *kīrtan,* i.e. hymn-singing. Soon a group of devotees formed around him dedicated to *nām-simran,* i.e. repetition of God's name. His growing popularity earned him the epithet of *dādā,* the equivalent of *bābā* in Punjabi (lit. grandfather), a term of respect for elderly or holy men. He was invited to perform *kīrtan* at Sikh *dīvāns* on special occasions in *gurdwārās* in the Punjab including those at Nankāṇā Sāhib and Amritsar. In 1938, Dādā Chellārām Āshram was established in Karāchī.

After the partition of the country in 1947, Dādā Chellārām joined service in the Ministry of Defence in New Delhi and continued to reside there. In 1958, he established a religious centre Nij Thāṅu (lit. His own place). It is an eclectic institution where recitations from the Bible, the Gītā, and the Qur'ān are made side by side with those from the Gurū Granth Sāhib. Another institution in Delhi which owes its origin to Dādā Chellārām is Nirguṇa Bālak Satsaṅg Maṇḍal. It has branches at Bombay, Puṇe and Saproon, near Solan in Himāchal Pradesh.

Dādā Chellārām died at Delhi on 7 March 1964.

L.C.

CHETO, or Chetū, was one of the *masands,* i.e. vicars and tithe-collectors, found guilty of misappropriating devotees' offerings and punished by Gurū Gobind Siṅgh, who finally abolished the system.

BIBLIOGRAPHY

1. Manī Siṅgh, Bhāī, *Sikhāṅ dī Bhagat Mālā.* Amritsar, 1955
2. Santokh Siṅgh, Bhāī, *Srī Gur Pratāp Sūraj Granth.* Amritsar, 1926-37

Gn.S.

CHETRĀMĪĀS, a cult of saint-worship incorporating elements from Christianity, Vaiṣṇavism and Sūfism founded by one Chet Rām (1835-94), an Aroṛā Hindu of the village of Sharakpur in present-day Sheikhūpurā district of Pakistan. Almost illiterate, Chet Rām was neither a saint nor a Sūfī. He was a camp-follower in the second Chinese war (1858-60), and on his discharge returned to India to settle down at Buchchoke where he got married and started dealing in opium and liquor. He came in contact with a Muslim Jalālī *faqīr*, named Mahbūb Shāh, a man with eclectic views who had a fascination for Christianity. Mahbūb Shāh died around the year 1865 at Buchchoke, and his tomb became a place of pilgrimage for the local populace. Chet Rām also had been a regular visitor to the tomb until one night he is said to have had a vision of Jesus Christ commanding him to build a church over the tomb. He composed a poem in Punjabi to recapture the glory of the vision he had had. At the church constructed at Mahbūb Shāh's tomb he unfolded his mission acknowledging the supremacy of Christ. Chet Rām attracted a small following and before his death, he named his daughter his successor and head of the sect. The daughter shifted the headquarters of the sect from Buchchoke to Lahore, near the Bādshāhī mosque, though the sanctuary at Buchchoke remained the main centre of the sect. Another disciple of some importance was one Munshī Natthā who expounded the doctrines of Chet Rām through his poetical compositions. The creed of the sect revolved around a vaguely-defined principle of trinity in which figured Allah, Parmeśvara and Khudā as creator, preserver and destroyer, respectively. The Bible was the sect's scripture but, since most of the adherents were illiterate, they hung it round their necks without understanding its contents. They carried a cross hung upon on a rod on which was inscribed the confession of their faith. The church service comprised recitation of the verses of Chet Rām with lamps lighted before the cross and the Bible. Two ethical principles stressed were philanthropy and fortitude in face of persecution. The novitiates had to undergo baptism, the monks among them having to tear off at the ceremony their clothes and cast dust upon their heads. The monks acted as missionaries and subsisted on alms. Never large in numbers, the sect had its adherents mainly in the districts of Fīrozpur, Amritsar, Gurdāspur and Montgomery. Many of them later converted to Sikhism.

BIBLIOGRAPHY

1. *The Census Reports,* 1891, 1901, and 1911.
2. Farquhar, J.N., *Modern Religious Movements.* Delhi, 1977
3. Rose, H.A., comp., *A Glossary of the Tribes and Castes of the Punjab and North-West Frontier Province.* Lahore, 1911-1919

F.S.

CHET SIṄGH, military commander, engineer and a *kārdār*, i.e. a revenue officer, under Mahārājā Raṇjīt Siṅgh. In 1831 he became engineer-in-charge for constructing a bridge over the River Sutlej for the Ropaṛ meeting between Mahārājā Ranjīt Siṅgh and Governor-General William Bentinck. He constructed another bridge at Harīke in 1837 to enable the British commander-in-chief to cross over the Sutlej for his visit to Lahore. Earlier in 1833 he was appointed *kārdār* of the cis-Sutlej estates of the Mahārājā. In 1835, he was deputed to Anandpur to settle the dispute between the local Soḍhī factions. Chet Siṅgh was on guard duty near the gate on the fateful evening (5 November 1840) when its archway fell upon Kaṅvar Nau Nihāl Siṅgh returning from the funeral of his father, Mahārājā Khaṛak Siṅgh. During the first Anglo-Sikh war, Chet Siṅgh commanded the Ropaṛ division along the western bank of the Sutlej. In the second Anglo-Sikh war, he fought in the battle of Rāmnagar (22 November 1848) when he was taken prisoner by the British.

BIBLIOGRAPHY

1. Sūrī, Sohan Lāl, *'Umdāt-ut-Twārīkh*. Lahore, 1885-89
2. Griffin, Lepel, *Ranjit Singh*. Delhi, 1957
3. Gupta, Hari Ram, *Panjab on the Eve of First Sikh War*. Chandigarh, 1956

Gl.S.

CHET SIṄGH BĀJVĀ (d. 1839), Mahārājā Khaṛak Siṅgh's distant relation and old tutor who wielded considerable influence at the Sikh court. The Ḍogrā minister, Dhiān Siṅgh, looked upon Chet Siṅgh as a potential rival to his position. The latter aligned himself with the Bhāīs and the Misrs at the court and sought the support of General Ventura and other Feringhee officers in open rivalry with the Ḍogrā faction. The Ḍogrās, on the other hand, won over Kaṅvar Nau Nihāl Siṅgh, the heir apparent, to their side. They spread rumours that Mahārājā Khaṛak Siṅgh and his favourite Chet Siṅgh had decided to disband the Khālsā army and place the kingdom of Ranjīt Siṅgh under British protection. Forged letters supposed to have been written by them to the British were produced in support of their contention. Nau Nihāl Siṅgh, determined to assume supreme authority in the State, urged his father to dismiss Chet Siṅgh. But Khaṛak Siṅgh would neither abjure authority in favour of his son nor would he agree to dispense with his favourite. Dhiān Siṅgh in concert with Kaṅvar Nau Nihāl Siṅgh plotted to finish off Chet Siṅgh. In the early hours of 9 October 1839, Dhiān Siṅgh and Nau Nihāl Siṅgh, accompanied by 15 other *sardārs* including Gulāb Siṅgh, Suchet Siṅgh, Misr Lāl Siṅgh and Atar Siṅgh Sandhāṅvālīā, entered the palace in the Fort and forced their way into the royal chambers where Mahārājā Khaṛak Siṅgh and Chet Siṅgh used to sleep. Chet Siṅgh hid himself in an interior gallery, but the glint of his shiny sword in the dark corner gave him away. Rājā Dhiān Siṅgh fell upon him and plunged his dagger into his heart. The assassination of Chet Siṅgh was the prologue to a long-drawn drama of intrigue and murder at the Sikh court.

BIBLIOGRAPHY

1. Sūrī, Sohan Lāl, *'Umdāt-ut-Twārīkh*. Lahore, 1885-89
2. Chopra, B.R., *Kingdom of the Punjab*. Hoshiarpur, 1969
3. Smyth, G. Carmichael, *A History of the Reigning Family of Lahore*. Patiala, 1970
4. Harbans Singh, *The Heritage of the Sikhs*. Delhi, 1983
5. Fauja Singh, ed., *Maharaja Kharak Singh*. Patiala, 1977

S.S.B.

CHET SIṄGH, BHĀĪ (1891-1921), son of Bhāī Javālā Siṅgh and Māī Rām Kaur, was born on 28 May 1891 at Buṇḍālā, in Amritsar district. In 1899 the family migrated westward to Chakk No. 64 Nihāleāṇā, in the newly colonized Lyallpur district. Chet Siṅgh studied up to the 5th standard in the village school. He grew up into a handsome, tall and fair-complexioned young man interested in manly sports. He took the vows of the Khālsā in early manhood and participated in the liberation of Gurdwārā Bhāī Jogā Siṅgh at Peshāwar (5 February 1921). Returning home, he learnt that his younger brother Kehar Siṅgh had registered himself with the *jathā* of Bhāī Lachhmaṇ Siṅgh Dhārovālī set to liberate Gurdwārā Janam Asthān at Nankāṇā Sāhib. Chet Siṅgh persuaded Kehar Siṅgh to stay back and went himself to take his place in the *jathā* which was massacred wholesale by the hirelings of the local custodian, Mahant Narain Dās, on 20 February 1921.

See NANKĀNĀ SĀHIB MASSACRE

BIBLIOGRAPHY

Shamsher, Gurbakhsh Siṅgh. *Shahīdī Jīvan*. Nankana Sahib, 1938

G.S.G.

CHHACHHRAULĪ, a small town about 12 km northeast of Jagādhrī (30° - 10'N, 77° - 18'E) in Ambālā district of Haryāṇā, was the capital of the princely state of Kalsīā. Gurū Gobind Siṅgh is believed to have visited Chhachhraulī during his sojourn at Kapāl Mochan in 1688. The site was brought to light only in 1920 by Sant Harnām Siṅgh of Mastūāṇā, and the building was erected by Rāṇī Raṇbīr Kaur of Kalsīā in 1924. The Gurdwārā, called Santokhpurā, is situated in a forest half a kilometre east of the town across Som Nadī, a tributary of the River Yamunā. It consists of a single flat-roofed room to which a verandah on three sides has been added recently. The management is in the hands of Siṅgh Sabhā Chhachhraulī, independent of the Shiromaṇī Gurdwārā Parbandhak Committee.

M.G.S.

CHHAJJŪ, BHĀĪ, a Bhallā Khatrī of Sultānpur Lodhī, whose name figures in Bhāī Gurdās, *Vārāṅ*, XI. 21, and who had embraced the Gurū's precept at the hands of Gurū Amar Dās. He once visited Amritsar with the *saṅgat* of Sultānpur and received instruction from Gurū Arjan.

See ĀKUL, BHĀĪ, and BHIKHĀ, BHAṬṬ

BIBLIOGRAPHY

1. Manī Siṅgh, Bhāī, *Sikhāṅ dī Bhagat Mālā*. Amritsar, 1955
2. Santokh Siṅgh, Bhāī, *Srī Gur Pratāp Sūraj Granth*. Amritsar, 1926-37

T.S.

CHHAJJŪ, BHĀĪ, a devoted Sikh of the time of Gurū Hargobind (1595-1644) who was also a brave warrior. He fought valiantly in the battle of Amritsar (1629). Bhāī Santokh Siṅgh, *Srī Gur Pratāp Sūraj Granth*, ranks him with warriors such as Mohrū, Bindhāvā, and Sujānā.

B.S.

CHHAJJŪ MALL (d. 1822), son of Keval Naraiṇ, belonged to a Brāhmaṇ family. He and his ancestors had been in the service of the emperors of Delhi. His father, who had shifted to Lahore in Sikh times, died young. Chhajjū Mall, entered the service of Sardār Jai Siṅgh of the Kanhaiyā *misl*. He received a command in the chief's force, and participated in most of the warfare against the neighbouring chiefs. He was present at the battle of Achal in 1783 when Gurbakhsh Siṅgh, the only son of Sardār Jai Siṅgh, was killed fighting against Jassā Siṅgh and Mahāṅ Siṅgh Sukkarchakkīā. After the battle, Chhajjū Mall was appointed *chaudharī* of Kaṭrā (quarter) Kanhaiyā in the town of Amritsar. On the death of Jai Siṅgh Kanhaiyā, he held the position courageously under the chief's daughter-in-law, Māī Sadā Kaur, defending the Kaṭrā against several successive assaults. He was able to reduce custom duties by more than half which attracted many merchants to come and settle in the Kaṭrā. Young Raṇjīt Siṅgh, after his marriage with the daughter of Māī Sadā Kaur, usually put up with Chhajjū Mall on his visits to Amritsar and received crucial assistance from him in getting possession of the city. Chhajjū Mall was entrusted with the collection of customs at Amritsar for some time and then moved to Kāngṛā where he served for three years before proceeding to Haridvār and Banāras on a pilgrimage. On his return in 1820, he received no public appointment.

Chhajjū Mall died in 1822.

BIBLIOGRAPHY

1. Griffin, Lepel, and C.F. Massy, *Chiefs and Families of Note in the Punjab*. Lahore, 1890
2. Sūrī, Sohan Lāl, *'Umdāt-ut-Twārīkh*. Lahore, 1885-89

S.S.B.

CHHATTIĀṆĀ, village 14 km north of Giddaṛbāhā (32° - 12'N, 74° - 39'E) in Farīdkoṭ district of the Punjab, claims an historical shrine, Gurdwārā Guptsar, sacred to Gurū Gobind Siṅgh who visited here after the battle of Muktsar (1706). Here warriors of the Brāṛ clan received payment for the services they had rendered to the Gurū. One who declined was Bhāī Dān Siṅgh. To quote an old chronicle, *Mālvā Desh Raṭan dī Sākhī Pothī,* "Bestow on me *sikkhī* (the Sikh faith), if you please; I have no other desire," begged he. The Gurū administered to him the rites of initiation. There was also a Muslim recluse, Ibrāhīm, who lived atop a sandy mound near by and was admitted to the Khālsā fold. He was renamed Ajmer Siṅgh after initiation.

Gurdwārā Guptsar, reconstructed during the 1970's, is a high-ceilinged hall with the sanctum at the far end. Above the sanctum are two storeys of square pavilions topped by a lotus dome with an electroplated pinnacle. To the east of the hall is the *sarovar* (holy tank) and to the south the Gurū kā Laṅgar (community kitchen) and a row of residential rooms. The Gurdwārā owns eight acres of farming land and is controlled by the Shiromaṇī Gurdwārā Parbandhak Committee.

BIBLIOGRAPHY

1. Tārā Siṅgh, *Srī Gur Tīrath Saṅgrahi.* Amritsar, n.d.
2. Ṭhākar Siṅgh, Giānī, *Srī Gurduāre Darshan*. Amritsar, 1928

M.G.S.

CHHEHARṬĀ SĀHIB, GURDWĀRĀ, 7 km west of Amritsar (31° - 38'N, 74° - 52'E), is named after a well got sunk by Gurū Arjan (1563-1606). The well was so wide that six Persian wheels installed around it could operate simultaneously. Hence its name Chhehartā, lit: having six (*chhe*) Persian wheels (*harṭ* or *halṭ*). The well is now covered up, but its water is pumped up to feed the main tank of the Gurdwārā. Now developed as an industrial township, Chheharṭā falls within the revenue limits of Vaḍālī Gurū, a village one km to the south, where Gurū Arjan had stayed during 1594-97. The Gurdwārā complex, set on a 6-acre walled compound, includes a *dīvān* hall, with a square sanctum in the middle enclosed by a brass palisade. Above the sanctum is a square room with a lotus dome topped by a gold-plated pinnacle. Two Nishān Sāhibs, Sikh flags, atop 25-metre tall flagposts, one on either side, stand in front of the hall. The Gurdwārā is managed by the Shiromaṇī Gurdwārā Parbandhak Committee through a local committee, which also controls other historical shrines of Vaḍālī Gurū. Congregations held on the fifth day of the light half of every lunar month attract large gatherings. The largest-attended is the fair held on this day in the month of Māgh (January-February) which marks the popular Basant Pañchamī festival.

BIBLIOGRAPHY

1. Tārā Siṅgh, *Srī Gur Tīrath Saṅgrahi.* Amritsar n.d.
2. Ṭhākar Siṅgh, Giānī, *Srī Gurduāre Darshan*. Amritsar, 1923

Gn.S.

CHHOṬĀ GHALLŪGHĀRĀ, lit. minor holocaust or carnage, as distinguished from Vaḍḍā Ghallūghārā (*q.v.*) or major massacre, is how Sikh chronicles refer to a bloody action during the severe campaign of persecution launched by the Mughal government at Lahore against the Sikhs in 1746. Early in that year, Jaspat Rāi, the *faujdār* of Eminābād, 55 km north of Lahore, was killed in an encounter with a roving band of Sikhs. Jaspat Rāi's brother, Lakhpat Rāi, who was a *dīwān* or revenue minister at Lahore, vowed revenge declaring that he would not put on his headdress nor claim himself to be a Khatrī, to which caste he belonged, until he had scourged the entire Sikh Panth out of existence. With the concurrence of the Mughal governor of Lahore, Yahīyā Khān, Lakhpat Rāi mobilized the Lahore troops, summoned reinforcements from Multān, Bahāwalpur and Jalandhar, alerted the feudal hill chiefs, and roused the general population for a *jihād* or crusade against the Sikhs. As an immediate first step, he had the Sikh inhabitants of Lahore rounded up and ordered their execution despite intercession on their behalf by a group of Hindu nobles headed by Dīwān Kauṛā Mall. He ignored the request even of his *gurū*, Sant Jagat Bhagat Gosāīṅ, that the killing should not be carried out on the appointed day which being an *amāvasyā*, the last day of the dark half of the lunar month, falling on a Monday was especially sacred to the Hindus. Execution took place as ordered on that very day, 13 Chet 1802 Bk / 10 March 1746. Lakhpat Rāi then set out at the head of a large force, mostly cavalry supported by cannon, in search of Sikhs who were reported to have concentrated in the swampy forest of Kāhnūvān, 15 km south of the present town of Gurdāspur. He surrounded the forest and started a systematic search for his prey. The Sikhs held out for some time striking back whenever they could but, heavily outnumbered and underequipped, they at last decided to make a final sally and escape to the hills in the northeast. They crossed the River Rāvī and made for the heights of Basohlī in the present Kaṭhūā district of Jammū and Kashmīr only to find that the Hindu hillmen in front were as hostile to them as the Muslim hordes following close upon their heels. Caught in this situation and bereft of provisions, they suffered heavy casualties in the area around Paṛol and Kaṭhūā. Yet making a last desperate bid, the survivors broke through the ring and succeeded in recrossing the Rāvī, though many were carried away in the torrent. With Lakhpat Rāi still close behind, they crossed the Beās and the Sutlej to find refuge in their old sanctuary, the Lakkhī Jungle, deep into the Mālvā region. An estimated 7,000 Sikhs were killed and 3,000 captured in the action fought on 1 and 2 May 1746. Lakhpat Rāi marched back in triumph to Lahore where he had the captives beheaded in batches in the Nakhās or site of the horse market outside the Delhi gate where, in later times, the Sikhs raised a memorial shrine known as the Shahīdgañj, lit. the treasure-house of martyrs. Lakhpat Rāi ordered Sikh places of worship to be destroyed and their holy books burnt. He even decreed that anyone uttering the word *gurū* should be put to death. Considering that the word *guṛ* meaning jaggery sounded like *gurū*, he ordered that jaggery should be called *roṛī*, lit. a lump, and not *guṛ*. The nightmarish episode of March-May 1746 came to be known among the Sikhs as Ghallūghārā, later Chhoṭā Ghallūghārā as compared to a still greater killing that befell them 16 years later, the Vaḍḍā Ghallūghārā of 5 February 1762.

Lakhpat Rāi's boast of a total annihilation of the Sikh people, however, was soon falsified. In about six months' time, the Sikhs were back on the scene converging upon Amritsar in small groups, and, on 30 March 1747, the Sarbatt Khālsā, congregation representative of the entire Panth, at Amritsar adopted a *gurmatā*, holy resolution, that a fort, named Rām Rauṇī be constructed by them at Amritsar as a permanent stronghold.

BIBLIOGRAPHY

1. Bhaṅgū, Ratan Siṅgh, *Prāchīn Panth Prakāsh*. Amritsar, 1914
2. Giān Siṅgh, Giānī, *Panth Prakāsh*. Patiala, 1970
3. Cunningham, Joseph Davey, *A History of the Sikhs*. London, 1849
4. Gupta, H.R., *History of the Sikhs*, vol. IV. Delhi, 1982

B.S.N.

CHHOṬĀ MĀRVĀ, a village about 6 km to the west of Bilāspur in Ambālā district of Haryāṇā, has a historical shrine known as Gurdwārā Golpur Sāhib dedicated to Gurū Gobind Siṅgh. While at Kapāl Mochan near Bilāspur in 1688, Gurū Gobind Siṅgh often went out on the chase. During one such excursion, his hawk named Gollā strayed and perched on the top of a tree in this village. Some Sikhs followed and tried to induce the hawk to return but the bird would not respond. Ultimately, the Gurū himself went and called the hawk using endearing names, "Gollā, Bhollā," and asking it not to turn away from his master. The hawk immediately came down and alighted on the Gurū's wrist. A small Mañjī Sāhib, a domed hut hardly three metres across, constructed in memory of Gurū Gobind Siṅgh's visit and named after his hawk, still exists in an orchard, half a kilometre northeast of the village. Inside is seated the Gurū Granth Sāhib. A square *dīvān* hall, with a wide verandah in the front, was added during the late 1970's. Birthday anniversary of Gurū Gobind Siṅgh is celebrated on a large scale. Devotees gather from the surrounding villages, there being very few Sikh families in Chhoṭā Mārvā itself.

M.G.S.

CHHOṬĀ MIRZĀPUR, a village in Mirzāpur district of Uttar Pradesh, 18 km south of Vārāṇasī (25° - 20'N, 82° - 58'E), is sacred to Gurū Gobind Siṅgh. He broke journey at Chhoṭā Mirzāpur while travelling as a child from Paṭnā, his birthplace, to the Punjab. A Sikh *saṅgat* developed here in course of time. The present Gurdwārā constructed recently on the site of an older one is, however, named Gurdwārā Srī Gurū Tegh Bahādur, Navamī Pātshāhī, perhaps because at the time of his visit, Gurū Gobind Siṅgh had not yet been anointed Gurū and the party travelling was only remembered as the family of the Ninth Gurū, Gurū Tegh Bahādur. Bhāī Mūsā Siṅgh, a native Sikh and head of the only Sikh family in the village, looks after the Gurdwārā.

BIBLIOGRAPHY

1. Tārā Siṅgh, *Srī Gur Tīrath Saṅgrahi*. Amritsar, n.d.
2. Ṭhākar Siṅgh, Giānī, *Srī Gurduāre Darshan*. Amritsar, 1928

M.G.S.

CHIEF KHĀLSĀ DĪWĀN. Until the emergence of more radical platforms such as the Sikh League (1919), Shiromaṇī Gurdwārā Parbandhak Committee (1920) and Shiromaṇī Akālī Dal (1920), the Chief Khālsā Dīwān, established on 30 October 1902, was the main council of the Sikhs, controlling their religious and educational affairs and raising its voice in behalf of their political rights. It has proved to be a durable setup and it still retains its initiative in education, though its role in the other spheres has progressively shrunken over the years. It was originally conceived as a central organization of the Sikhs to replace Khālsā Dīwān, Amritsar, and Khālsā Dīwān, Lahore, then torn by a conflict which was hampering the work of Siṅgh Sabhās affiliated to them.

A large public assembly held in the Malvaī Buṅgā, in the vicinity of the Golden Temple at Amritsar, on the Baisākhī day of 1901, constituted a committee to draw up the constitution of such a unitary body. The draft prepared was finally adopted on 21 September 1902. The opening session of the new society, designated Chief Khālsā Dīwān, was held in the Malvaī Buṅgā on the Dīvālī day, 30 October 1902, Bābū Tejā Siṅgh, of Bhasauṛ, saying the inaugural *ardās* or prayer. Bhāī Arjan Siṅgh, of Bagaṛīāṅ, was elected president, Sundar Siṅgh Majīṭhīā secretary and Soḍhī Sujān Siṅgh additional secretary. A total of twenty-nine Siṅgh Sabhās including those of Amritsar, Rāwalpīṇḍī, Āgrā, Bhasauṛ, Baḍbar, Multān, Dākhā and Kairoṅ affiliated themselves to the Dīwān, the number rising to 53 in an year's time. Enrichment of the cultural, educational, spiritual and intellectual life of the Sikhs, preaching the tenets of the Gurū Granth Sāhib, propagating Sikh history, and protecting the rights of the Sikhs by putting up memoranda and memorials to the government were among its main concerns. It especially aimed at opening schools and institutions for the spread of education among men and women, publishing books on Sikh history, sacred texts and doctrine, translating into Punjabi works from other languages and opening institutions of community welfare. Membership of the Dīwān was open to all *amritdhārī* Sikhs, i.e. those who had received the rites of Khālsā initiation and who could read and write Gurmukhī. Members were also expected to contribute for the common needs of the community the obligatory *dasvandh*, or one-tenth of their annual income. Any Siṅgh Sabhā or any other Sikh society sharing its ideology could have itself affiliated to the Dīwān.

The Chief Khālsā Dīwān theoretically incorporated the perspectives and decisions of five major committees. A general committee consisted of representatives from member institutions, members delegated by the *takhts* and the Sikh princely states and individuals who met fiscal and service criteria. That committee elected an executive committee that met monthly and conducted most of the regular business, referring critical matters to the broader body. The other three committees dealt with finances, advice (legal, administrative, religious) and life-members. In general, the Chief Khālsā Dīwān solicited public input on issues and spent considerable time discussing letters and differing opinions. It frequently circulated documents to Siṅgh Sabhās or published them in journals for public comment. For example, the Dīwān sent out a questionnaire about opening the Gurū Granth Sāhib in public meetings and decided on the basis of the replies received (over 1,600) that the correct thing to do was to open the Gurū Granth Sāhib in a room connected to the assembly but not in the public meeting hall.

To propagate the message of the Gurūs, the Chief Khālsā Dīwān recruited a cadre of preachers. The Delhi *darbār* of 1903 when the Duke of Connaught was visiting India as a representative of the British Crown was considered an appropriate occasion to initiate the programme and several religious *dīvāns* or congregations were convened in the city by the Dīwān to acquaint the people with the beliefs and practices of the Sikhs. An English translation of Gurū Nānak's *Japu* was distributed. Besides towns and cities in the Punjab, the Dīwān preachers made regular visits to adjacent provinces, notably North-West Frontier Province and Sindh. To train *rāgīs* (musicians who recited the sacred hymns), *granthīs* (Scripture-readers) and preachers, the Dīwān opened in 1906 a Khālsā Prachārak Vidyālayā at Tarn Tāran, near Amritsar. In 1903, it launched its weekly newspaper, the *Khalsa Advocate*.

Religious reform was one of the main objects of the Chief Khālsā Dīwān, and in pursuit of this aim it undertook to codify the Sikh ritual and rules of conduct. To this end, a committee was set up on 20 October 1910, consisting of Bhāī Tejā Siṅgh, of Bhasauṛ, Sant Gurbakhsh Siṅgh, of Paṭiālā, Bhāī Vīr Siṅgh, Bhāī Jodh Siṅgh, M.A., Bhāī Takht Siṅgh, Trilochan Siṅgh, M.A., and the Secretary of the Dīwān. The draft the committee prepared was circulated widely among the Siṅgh Sabhās and other Sikh societies as well as among prominent individuals. The process was repeated twice, and the code as finalized after prolonged deliberations was published in March 1915 under the title *Gurmat Prakāsh: Bhāg Saṅskār*. Historically, this was an important document, standing midway between the traditional *Rahitnāmās* and the *Sikh Rahit Maryādā* issued by the Shiromaṇī Gurdwārā Parbandhak Committee in 1950.

Linked with religious reform was the Chief Khālsā Dīwān's programme for the promotion of Punjabi language and literature. For this purpose it established a Punjabi Prāchārak sub-committee and assiduously sought to have Punjabi, in Gurmukhī script, accepted in government offices, especially in the postal and railways departments, for certain preliminary work. The Dīwān also opened libraries and Gurmukhī schools as well as night classes for adults. It established in 1908 a Khālsā Handbill Society to prepare lithographed posters in Punjabi for free distribution. Advancement of Punjabi was one of the main planks of the Sikh Educational Conference formed in 1908 at the instance of the Dīwān dignitaries such as Sundar Siṅgh Majīṭhīā and Harbaṅs Siṅgh Aṭārī who, travelling through Sindh preaching Gurū Nānak's word, had attended in December 1907 a session of the Muhammadan Educational Conference at Karāchī and returned with the idea of having a similar institution set up for Sikhs. Besides channelizing the Dīwān's work in behalf of Punjabi, the Sikh Educational Conference did much to promote Western-style education among Sikhs. Its annual sessions rotating from town to town were always occasions for considerable public fervour. They were largely attended and, besides discussion of the problems of Sikh education, they comprised religious sessions as well as competitions of Sikh *kīrtan* and poetry. The Conference still continues to be an active wing of the Chief Khālsā Dīwān.

To ensure for Sikhs their due share in government employment and in power then available to the Indian people, the Chief Khālsā Dīwān kept up pressure on the British authority through representations and memoranda. In 1913, one of its leaders, Sundar Siṅgh Majīṭhīā, presented Sikh demands and claims before the Royal Commission. Sundar Siṅgh had been nominated a member of the Imperial Council in 1909 replacing Ṭikkā Ripudaman Siṅgh, heir apparent of Nābhā state. There in the Council he piloted the Anand Marriage Bill introduced by his predecessor in 1908. This was a major step towards reforming Sikh ritual.

The Dīwān put up on 31 March 1911 a memorandum to the Viceroy, Lord Hardinge, then visiting the Punjab, seeking just representation for the Sikhs in the services and in Imperial and Provincial councils. In 1916 and 1917 the Dīwān's resolutions and public demonstrations gradually moved from requests to demands. A series of documents was sent to the government concerning Punjabi language, jobs, and commissions in the army.

As secretary of the Chief Khālsā Dīwān, Sundar Siṅgh Majīṭhīā sent a letter to the Punjab Government on 26 December 1916 reiterating the claims of the Sikh community for representation in government jobs and legislative bodies, which should be "adequate and effective and consistent with their position and importance." On 18 September 1918, the Chief Khālsā Dīwān called a representative conclave of the Sikhs to consider the Montagu-Chelmsford scheme of reform. In the memorandum prepared on behalf of the community, government was urged to carry out the assurances given the Sikhs. The publication of the Montagu-Chelmsford report was followed by the appointment of Franchise Committee to go into the question of the composition of the new legislatures in India. It had three Indian members, but none of them was a Sikh. When the Sikhs protested, Sundar Siṅgh Majīṭhīā was taken as a co-opted member for the Punjab, but their demand for one-third of the total number of non-official seats held by Indians in the Punjab, 7 out of 67 non-official seats in the Assembly of India and 4 seats in the Council of States for the Sikh community remained largely unfulfilled.

The political awakening among Indians in the early years of the twentieth century gave rise to certain mass movements. In the Punjab, the Chief Khālsā Dīwān came to be looked upon as moderate, pro-government and elitist over against the Shiromaṇī Gurdwārā Parbandhak Committee and the Shiromaṇī Akālī Dal which were more dynamic, anti-government and mass-based. They soon wrested from the Dīwān initiative in religious and political spheres. The Shiromaṇī Committee after the adoption of the Gurdwaras Act 1925 took over management of all the major historical Sikh shrines. The Shiromaṇī Akālī Dal has been over the years the premier political party of the Sikhs. The Chief Khālsā Dīwān thus had its area of influence and activity severely curtailed. It now restricts itself to expressing its opinion through resolutions and memoranda on religious and political issues facing the Sikh community.

In retrospect, the Chief Khālsā Dīwān may be seen to have made three key contributions to Sikh life. The first was institutionalizing the Siṅgh Sabhā view of Sikhism as a separate religion with distinct rituals and a tradition devoid of Hindu influence. The resulting consciousness affected the way Sikhs looked at each other and the world around them. Without that consciousness, the mobilization of Sikhs spread across the world would have been impossible. There would have been no drive for protecting Sikh rights nor assertion of community control over the *gurdwārās*.

Secondly, the Dīwān took existing but often disparate Sikh organizations and linked them together in an effective communication system. Efforts were focussed and information and ideas disseminated over time and distance. This enhanced the sense of Sikh identity and mission and opened up new paths of collaborative action and also conflict. The religious gatherings, conferences, district and provincial meetings, tracts and, most importantly, the journals and newspapers all were critical legacies from the Siṅgh Sabhā and Chief Khālsā Dīwān era. Without them, there would have been no dissemination of Sikh rituals, no sustained communication and exchange of ideas, no network that could be activated for legislation over *anand* marriage and no Akālī challenge to the community.

The final element was a strategy for dealing with internal division and survival as a minority community. Accommodation, negotiation and compromise were hallmarks of the Dīwān's policy. Sikhs could not be totally self-reliant. Some of the Chief Khālsā Dīwān leaders, such as Sundar Siṅgh Majīṭhīā, pursued collaborative arrangements in the widened legislature and attempted to help Sikh interests through alliances with other political groups and the British. The Chief Khālsā Dīwān, as an institution, however, resumed its familiar task of trying to buttress Sikhism through education, toleration and institution-building. The new representatives of the Sikhs, the Shiromaṇī Gurdwārā Parbandhak Committee and the Akālī Dal, now had to face the problems of disunity, political alternatives as a minority, and maintaining the contours of Sikh identity.

BIBLIOGRAPHY

1. Jagjīt Siṅgh, *Siṅgh Sabhā Lahir.* Ludhiana, 1974
2. Pratāp Siṅgh, Giānī, *Gurdwārā Sudhār arthāt Akālī Lahir.* Amritsar, 1975
3. Teja Singh, *Gurdwara Reform Movement and the*

Sikh Awakening. Jalandhar, 1922
4. Sahni, Ruchi Ram, *Struggle for Reform in Sikh Shrines.* Amritsar, 1965
5. Khushwant Singh, *A History of the Sikhs,* vol. 2. Princeton, 1966
6. Harbans Singh, *The Heritage of the Sikhs.* Delhi, 1983

D.S.

CHĪKĀ, an old village in Kaithal district of Haryāṇā, 26 km west of Pehovā (29° - 59'N, 76° - 35'E), is sacred to Gurū Hargobind and Gurū Tegh Bahādur. The former passed through Chīkā at the time of his visit to Kurukshetra in 1638. Gurū Tegh Bahādur arrived here from Samāṇā *en route* to Delhi, in 1675, and stayed here for two days with Bhāī Glaurā, the *masand* of the Bāṅgar area extending up to Hāṅsī and Hissār. A low platform in a room on the first floor of an old house in the northeastern part of the village commemorated the visits of the holy Gurūs. The place was taken over by the successors of Sant Gurmukh Siṅgh during late 1970's for reconstruction. The new Gurdwārā Chhevīṅ *ate* Nauvīṅ Pātshāhī has a large *dīvān* hall supported by twenty octagonal concrete pillars. Another complex in a compound close by comprises Gurū ka Laṅgar and rooms for pilgrims. The *gurdwārā* is affiliated to the Shiromaṇī Gurdwārā Parbandhak Committee.

BIBLIOGRAPHY

1. Tārā Siṅgh, *Srī Gur Tīrath Saṅgrahi.* Amritsar, n.d.
2. Ṭhākar Siṅgh, Giānī, *Srī Gurduāre Darshan.* Amritsar, 1928

M.G.S.

CHIRĀGH DĪN, FAQĪR (d. 1851), son of Faqīr Azīz ud-Dīn, foreign minister to Mahārājā Raṇjīt Siṅgh, was governor of Jasroṭā, a small principality in the Śivālik hills, and was shortly afterwards placed in attendance on Prince Kharak Siṅgh. In 1842, he succeeded his brother, Shāh Dīn, as the Sikh ruler's envoy (*vakīl*) at Fīrozpur and continued in the same position with the Council of Regency formed after the first Anglo-Sikh war under the treaty of Lahore of 16 December 1846. Chirāgh Dīn had five sons, the eldest of whom, Sirāj ud-Dīn, became the chief minister at Bahāwalpur where he met with a tragic end.

Chirāgh Dīn died at Lahore in 1851.

BIBLIOGRAPHY

1. Sūrī, Sohan Lāl, *'Umdāt-ut-Twārīkh.* Lahore, 1885-89
2. Griffin, Lepel, *Ranjit Singh.* Delhi, 1957
3. Waheed-ud-Din, Faqir Syed, *The Real Ranjit Singh.* Karachi, 1965

H.D.

CHITRA SAIN, a devotee of Gurū Hargobind, came to Kartārpur on the Baisākhī day to pay obeisance to the Gurū. He had come to present, as he had pledged in fulfilment of a wish, the Gurū with a horse, white hawk and the robes. The Gurū felt pleased with Chitra Sain, as says *Gurbilās Pātshāhī Chhevīṅ*, and blessed him. Of these gifts, the Gurū gave the hawk to Bābā Gurdittā and the robes to Paindā Khān, a devotee of the Gurū and a commander in his army, asking him to wear this dress while coming to the Gurū's presence.

BIBLIOGRAPHY

1. *Gurbilās Pātshāhī Chhevīṅ.* Patiala, 1970
2. Manī Siṅgh, Bhāī, *Sikhāṅ dī Bhagat Mālā.* Amritsar, 1955

D.S.

CHIṬṬĀ BĀZ, lit. white hawk, is traditionally the name given to one of Gurū Gobind Siṅgh's favourite falcons whom he would carry perched on his hand when going out for chase or falconry. This image of the Gurū – the white falcon resting upon his left hand – has survived in folklore and in portraiture, and he is known to this day as *chiṭṭiāṅ bājāṅvālā*, Master of the White Hawk.

M.G.S.

CHIṬṬĀGOṄG (22° - 21'N, 91° - 50'E), a major port town of Bangladesh, situated on the right bank of Karṇāphulī River, 20 km from its mouth, has a historic Sikh shrine, called Gurdwārā Sikh Temple, dedicated to Gurū Nānak, who is believed to have stayed here briefly in 1507-08. Local tradition connects this Gurdwārā with the story of the conversion by Gurū Nānak of Bhāī Jhaṇḍā Bāḍhī, Rājā Sudhar Sen and his nephew, Indra Sen. The story occurs briefly in the *B40 Janam-sākhī* and at some length in the *Bālā Janam Sākhī*. Gurdwārā Sikh Temple is situated in the middle of Chowk Bāzār. An old well adjoining it is still in use. There is some property in the name of the Gurdwārā donated to it by Bhāī Mohan Siṅgh, a Sikh who was Dīwān of Chiṭṭāgoṅg during the rule of Nawāb 'Alī Vardī Khān (d. 1756). The Gurdwārā was administered by a line of Udāsī priests until 1917 when the management was entrusted to a committee of local devotees under the chairmanship of the district judge of Chiṭṭāgoṅg. This arrangement still continues.

BIBLIOGRAPHY

1. Kohlī, Surindar Siṅgh, ed., *Janam Sākhī Bhāī Bālā*. Chandigarh, 1975
2. McLeod, W.H., ed., *The B40 Janam-Sakhi*. Amritsar, 1980

Bh.S.

CHOHLĀ, village 4.5 km southeast of Sirhālī Kalāṅ (31°- 16'N, 74°- 56'E) in Amritsar district of the Punjab, is sacred to Gurū Arjan (1563-1606). The village was called Bhaiṇī when the Gurū visited here. A housewife served him a delicious dish of *chohlā*, broken bread mixed with sugar and butter. Gurū Arjan was pleased and blessed her. He also uttered a hymn of thanks-giving with the refrain: "The Lord is our life and soul ; He cares for us everywhere in every respect." Its last line was: "God is our wealth, His Name is our food; this, O Nānak, is our *chohla*." The village thereupon came to be called Chohlā—Chohlā Sāhib for the devotees. There are three historical shrines in the village which, according to local tradition, was also visited by Gurū Hargobind (1595-1644).

GURDWĀRĀ CHOHLĀ SĀHIB at the western edge of the village marks the spot where Gurū Arjan sat and preached. The building comprises a marble-floored hall in front of the 3-storeyed sanctum where Gurū Granth Sāhib is seated on a canopied seat of white marble. Two Nishān Sāhibs, holy flags, fly, one at each corner, in front of the hall. A small *sarovar* has been added in recent decades. A nearby old well is believed to have existed since the time of Gurū Arjan's visit.

GURDWĀRĀ GURŪ KĪ KOṬHAṚĪ in the interior of the village marks the site of the house where Gurū Arjan and his wife, Matā Gaṅgā, had stayed. It is also known as Mātā Gaṅgā Jī dā Asthān. The present building, raised during the 1980's, comprises a square hall in front of the domed sanctum topped by a gold-plated pinnacle. Here, too, is an old well that local tradition connects with Gurū Arjan's time.

GURDWĀRĀ BĀBĀ ADALĪ, in the eastern part of the village, commemorates Bhāī Adalī, a pious Sikh contemporary of the fourth and the fifth Gurūs, Gurū Rām Dās and Gurū Arjan. It was he who brought the famous Bhāī Bidhī Chand (d. 1640) into the Sikh fold.

All these three Gurdwārās are affiliated to the Shiromaṇī Gurdwārā Parbandhak Committee. The administration is run by a local committee. Almost the entire village land, about 500 acres, is owned by the Gurdwārās as free grant since Mughal times.

BIBLIOGRAPHY

1. Tārā Siṅgh, *Srī Gur Tīrath Saṅgrahi*. Amritsar, n.d.

2. Ṭhākar Siṅgh, Giānī, *Srī Gurduāre Darshan*. Amritsar, 1923

Gn.S.

CHRITROPĀKHYĀN, a long composition comprising women's tales in verse, forms over one-third of the *Dasam Granth.* The work is generally ascribed to Gurū Gobind Siṅgh. A school of opinion, however, exists which asserts that *Chritropākhyān* and some other compositions included in the *Dasam Granth* are not by the Gurū but by poets in attendance on him. According to the date given in the last Chritra or narrative, this work was completed in 1753 Bk / AD 1696 on the bank of the River Sutlej, probably at Anandpur. The last tale in the series is numbered 405, but number 325 is somehow missing. The tales centre upon the theme of women's deceits and wiles, though there are some which describe the heroic and virtuous deeds of both men and women.

Tale one is a long introductory composition. It opens with an invocation to weapons, or to the God of weapons; then a number of Hindu mythical characters appear, and a terrific battle between the demons and the gods follows. Finally Chaṇḍī appears, riding on her tiger, and her enemies "fade away as stars before the rising sun." With a final prayer for help and forgiveness the introductory tale ends. In the last Tale 405 again the demons and gods battle. When Chaṇḍī is hard pressed, the Timeless One finishes off the demons by sending down diseases upon them.

Tale two tells how the wise adviser to Rājā Chitra Siṅgh related these tales of the wiles of women in order to save his handsome son Hanuvant from the false accusations of one of the younger *rāṇīs.* Some of these tales were taken from old Hindu books such as the *Mahābhārata,* the *Rāmāyaṇa,* the *Purāṇas,* the *Hitopadeśa,* the *Pañchatantra,* from Mughal family stories, from folktales of Rājpūtānā and the Punjab, and even from ancient Hebrew lore. The moral they aim at is that one should not become entangled in the intrigues of wily women by becoming a slave to lust, for trusting them is dangerous. This does not mean that it is wrong to trust one's own wife, or worthy women ; but that it is fatal to lose this world and the next by becoming enamoured of strange women and entrapped in their wiles. The theme of most of the tales, however, is that many women will stop at nothing – slander, arson, murder – to obtain their heart's desire; that men are helpless in their clutches; and that if men spurn them they have to reckon with the vilest and deadliest of enemies; but that, conversely, worthy women are the staunchest of allies, and think nothing of sacrificing their lives for their beloved.

In the *Dasam Granth* a title is given at the end of each tale. Thirty-two of a total of 404 Tales are thus labelled "Tales of Intrigue." The remaining 372 Tales are labelled as "The Wiles of Women." However, while most of these are about lustful, deceitful women, there are some 74 tales of the bravery and intelligence of women, such as Tale 102 where Rāṇī Kaikeyī drives Rājā Daśaratha into battle when his charioteer is killed; or Tale 137 where Draupadī rescues the unconscious Arjun and puts his enemies to flight. Men come in for at least a small share of being deceivers. In this mixture of tales of various sorts, there are ten "moral stories" of the folly of gambling, drinking, and opium-eating. There are also folktales; love stories of Kṛṣṇa and Rādhā; of Kṛṣṇa and Rukminī; of Auraṅgzīb's sister (Tale 278); and of Joseph and Zulaikhā, based on the Biblical story of Joseph and Potiphar's wife in Genesis.

The closing verses of Tale 405 have some lofty teaching about the Timeless Creator, His understanding love, and end with a plea for His continuing protection. Verses of gratitude for help in completing the composition form the final prayer of the author and close this strange mixture of the tales of intrigue, of women mostly, some worthy, many sinful, in which men are often pictured as the gullible tools of these enchantresses.

BIBLIOGRAPHY

1. Ashta, Dharam Pal, *The Poetry of the Dasam Granth.* Delhi, 1959
2. Loehlin, C.H., *The Granth of Guru Gobind Singh and the Khalsa Brotherhood.* Lucknow, 1971
3. Jaggī, Ratan Siṅgh, *Dasam Granth Parichaya.* Delhi, 1990

C.H.L.

CHŪHAṚ, BHĀĪ, Bhāī Sāīṅ, Bhāī Lālā, all Seṭhī Khatrīs, and Bhāī Nihālū were good musicians and had facility in expounding the holy hymns. Whenever they sang, discussed or discoursed on the sacred hymns, the *saṅgat,* records Bhāī Manī Siṅgh in his *Sikhāṅ dī Bhagat Mālā,* felt deeply impressed. Gurū Arjan appreciated their talent, too, and once spoke to them, "Good deeds are necessary along with a sweet voice. A preacher must match his word with action. Then alone will he be heeded. A tree in order to provide shade to others must first take root. One who does not practise what he preaches is wasting his breath."

BIBLIOGRAPHY

1. Manī Siṅgh, Bhāī, *Sikhāṅ dī Bhagat Mālā.* Amritsar, 1955
2. Santokh Siṅgh, Bhāī, *Srī Gur Pratāp Suraj Granth.* Amritsar, 1926-37

T.S.

CHŪHAṚ, BHĀĪ, a Chaujhaṛ Khatrī of Lucknow, once travelled to Amritsar to see Gurū Hargobind (1595-1644). He, according to Bhāī Manī Siṅgh, *Sikhāṅ dī Bhagat Mālā,* one day implored the Gurū: "Pray, instruct me, Lord, in what constitutes the root of the Sikh faith." "Humility is its root," spoke the Gurū, "service of humanity its branches, *saṅgat,* i.e. holy fellowship, its foliage and the fruit the understanding of the Word." Bhāī Chūhaṛ was known as a devoted Sikh who remained absorbed in repetition of the holy Name.

BIBLIOGRAPHY

1. Manī Siṅgh, Bhāī, *Sikhāṅ dī Bhagat Mālā.* Amritsar, 1955
2. Santokh Siṅgh, Bhāī, *Srī Gur Pratāp Sūraj Granth.* Amritsar, 1926-37

B.S.

CHŪHAṚ, CHAUDHARĪ and Purīā, both village headmen, attracted by Gurū Arjan's fame as a holy teacher, once visited him. They said, "O beneficent one, we have long desired to seek your precept. In our official capacity as village *chaudharīs,* we commit many wrongs and utter many falsehoods. Be pleased to tell us how we can be saved." The Gurū answered, "The remedy is simple; discard falsehood, anger and pride." At this Purīā argued, "But, Sir, as *chaudharīs* we have so often to tell lies." Gurū Arjan said, "Establish a *dharamsāl,* or place of religious congregation in your village ; attend it morning and evening; and get whatever falsehood you utter or wrongs you commit during the day recorded there in the evening. Record also your good deeds." Chūhaṛ and Purīā obeyed. They felt ashamed as they made their confessions to the *saṅgat* every evening. Gradually they got rid of their habit of lying. Listening to the Gurūs' hymns morning and evening they became pious and devoted Sikhs.

BIBLIOGRAPHY

1. Manī Siṅgh, Bhāī, *Sikhāṅ dī Bhagat Mālā.* Amritsar, 1955
2. Santokh Siṅgh, Bhāī, *Srī Gur Pratāp Sūraj Granth.* Amritsar, 1926-37

T.S.

CHŪHAṚ SIṄGH, owning allegiance to the Shahīd *misl,* was a close relation of the Bhaṅgī *sardār,* Rāi Siṅgh, the conqueror of Jagādhrī and Diālgaṛh. He received the Jaṛaulī area as his share of the spoils after the sack of Sirhind in January 1764. He retained ten villages for himself and made over the rest to his deputies. Returning to Amritsar, he held charge of the Shahīd Buṅgā for many years. He acquired considerable territory on either side of the River Rāvī, and was considered one of the most powerful *sardārs* of his day. He placed his younger son, Mohar Siṅgh, in charge of the village of Jaṛaulī, while Karam Siṅgh the elder, subsequently succeeded to the family estates north of the Sutlej. Karam Siṅgh died in 1808.

BIBLIOGRAPHY

1. Sītal, Sohan Siṅgh, *Sikh Misalāṅ*. Ludhiana, 1952
2. Griffin, Lepel, and C.F. Massy, *Chiefs and Families of Note in the Punjab*. Lahore, 1890

S.S.B.

CHŪHAṚVĀL, village 11 km west of Chamkaur Sāhib (30° - 53'N, 76° - 25'E), has a *gurdwārā* called Jhāṛ Sāhib, dedicated to Gurū Gobind Siṅgh, who quitting Chamkaur on the night of 7 December 1705, reached this spot. In a cluster of thorny bushes (Jhāṛ) here, he relaxed for a while before resuming his journey further west. A shrine was later established to mark the site. A land grant of 75 *bighās*, made to it by Mahārājā Raṇjīt Siṅgh, has been continued by successive governments. The old building has, however, been replaced by a new complex constructed during the fifties of the present century, under the supervision of Sant Piārā Siṅgh.

The central three-storeyed building is on a raised plinth and has a square hall on the ground floor, with the sanctum in the centre. The roof is decorated with domed pavilions at corners and at mid-points of the walls. There are halls on the first and second floors as well. The domes at different levels have ornamental gilded pinnacles. Further to the west is a small *sarovar*, i.e. holy tank. A row of rooms to the north houses the Khālsā girls college. Another component of the complex is a hall raised on the spot where Sant Piārā Siṅgh, who died on 7 August 1965, was cremated.

Gurdwārā Jhāṛ Sāhib is controlled by the Shiromaṇī Gurdwārā Parbandhak Committee through a managing committee functioning at Māchhīvāṛā.

BIBLIOGRAPHY

1. Tārā Siṅgh, *Srī Gur Tīrath Saṅgrahi*. Amritsar, n.d.
2. Ṭhākar Siṅgh, Giānī, *Srī Gurdūāre Darshan*. Amritsar, 1928

M.G.S.

CHUNG TONG, a small village on the bank of the River Teestā in Sikkim, 168 km north of the nearest railhead, Silīguṛī, has recently been discovered to have a connection with early Sikh history. Local tradition there refers to the visit of Gurū Nānak (1469-1539) to the place during his third *udāsī* or preaching tour. Although the Janam Sākhīs do not mention Tibet specifically, the mention of Gurū Nānak Rimpoche (lit. the great one) in Tibetan literature points to the Gurū's travel through Tibet, and it is likely that he passed through Chung Tong on his way back to India. According to tradition, there was a severe famine in the area when the Great One arrived there. He sat on a stone mount near the Teestā whereupon the imprints of his feet are still shown. The grateful villagers raised a Lhā-Khāṅg (shrine) in memory of Gurū Nānak, who it is said had prayed for them and presented them with a ripe crop of grain ready to be harvested. Along with other icons, a picture of the Gurū is placed in the shrine. People light butter lamps in front of it. They celebrate the birth anniversary of Gurū Nānak along with that of Gurū Padma Sambhava, the eighth-century teacher, who preached Buddhism in Tibet, Bhutan and Sikkim.

T.S.R.

CLERK, SIR GEORGE RUSSELL (1800-1889), diplomat, son of John Clerk, entered the service of the East India Company as a writer in 1817. After various appointments in Calcutta, Rājpūtānā and Delhi, he became political agent at Ambālā in 1831. He was appointed agent to the Governor-General at the North-West Frontier Agency in 1840. In this capacity, he shaped British policy towards the Sikhs during the days following the death of Mahārājā Raṇjīt Siṅgh. For almost a decade, as political agent at Ambālā, he had been responsible for British political relations with the cis-Sutlej states. Clerk possessed a legal mind, and his adjudications of territorial disputes among the cis-Sutlej Sikh chiefs became the basis of a new body of laws. Likewise, his contribution to the interpretation of the laws of succession and inheritance of the Sikhs was significant as is illustrated by his *Memorandum on the cis-Sutlej States.*

As political agent at Ludhiāṇā, Clerk attempted to restore friendly relations with the Sikh court after the acrimonious recall of his predecessor, Sir Claude Martine Wade. As his confidential reports reveal, he had an intimate knowledge of developments in Sikh politics. He visited Lahore frequently. But he started taking an overt interest in court factionalism. In October 1839, his encouragement to one of the rival parties led to the assassination by Dhiān Siṅgh of Mahārājā Khaṛak Siṅgh's favourite Chet Siṅgh. He encouraged Sher Siṅgh against Māī Chand Kaur in her claim to the throne, nodding significantly, at the same time, to the Jammū *rājās'* desire for succession to the State of Lahore.

In 1844, Clerk was appointed Lieutenant-Governor of North-West Frontier Province. From 1847 to 1848, he was Governor of Bombay. He was Under Secretary of the Board of Control (1856-58) and Under Secretary of State for India (1863-76). He died in London on 25 July 1889.

BIBLIOGRAPHY

1. Krishen, Indra, *An Historical Interpretation of the Correspondence of Sir George Russell Clerk.* Simla, 1952
2. Ganda Singh, *Private Correspondence Relating to the Anglo-Sikh Wars.* Amritsar, 1935
3. Hasrat, B.J., *Anglo-Sikh Relations.* Hoshiarpur, 1968

B.J.H.

COMMUNAL AWARD was an official statement of British government policy in respect of the composition of provincial legislatures as a further step in the transfer of responsibility to the Indian people. The Secretary of State for India presented the terms of the Award to Parliament as command paper 4147, and they were published on 16 August 1932 under the title Communal Decision. The terms of the Award defined the methods of selection and the relative strength of representation of various "communities" in the legislatures as they were expected to be formed under provisions of a new constitution for a federation of Princely Indian states and British Indian provinces, which was being devised at the time and which was given final shape later in the Government of India Act of 1935. In effect, the Award was a political settlement worked out for the people of British India by officials in London.

The provisions concerning representation which were set forth in the Award, and which led to its designation as "communal," carried forward the use of categories which had operated in Indian politics since the nineteenth century. When the rulers of British India began to respond positively to the claim that Indians should have an active role in governance, they created institutions which were designed to give representation to particular classes and special interests rather than to the population at large. Among those who were treated by the British as a class or a single interest group were each of the several "communities" composed of members of a particular religious tradition such as Muslims and, at a later stage, Sikhs and sections of Hindus. Under the regulations made to give effect to the Indian Councils Act of 1892, for example, British provincial executives were empowered to appoint to a minority of seats in their advisory councils non-officials who had been recommended by organizations such as municipal and district boards, universities and merchant associations. Although the Muslims were named at that stage among the classes and interests for which representation should be secured, only with the Minto-Morley reforms, embodied in the Indian Councils Act of 1909, were seats reserved in the provincial councils (except for those of Punjab and Burma) for Muslim representatives who were selected by direct election in separate electorates composed exclusively of members of the Muslim community. Communal electorates, therefore, date from this stage. This complex pattern of separate electorates, on non-communal as well as communal basis, was extended under the provisions of the Montagu-Chelmsford (or Montford) reforms contained in the Government of India Act of 1919. These reforms provided for enlarged and more powerful legislative councils in the provinces, added separate electorates for the Muslim community in the Punjab and in the Central Provinces where a council had been formed in 1914, and created additional electorates on the basis of religious community – most notably for the Sikhs in the Punjab.

The Montford reforms were subjected to a thorough examination in India and in Britain in the period from 1927 to 1932, with a view to assessing their effectiveness as a basis for Indian participation in responsible government and to framing a new constitution which would bring India closer to the status of a full dominion or a free nation. An official review of the reforms began in November 1927 when Parliament appointed Sir John Simon to chair an all-white Indian Statutory Commission. The Commission published its report in June 1930. Independent of the official inquiry, and in large measure in reaction to it, political leaders of India met in order to work out their own proposals for India's future. Under the chairmanship of Paṇḍit Motīlāl Nehrū, a broad coalition met as the All-Parties Conference in 1928 and recommended that India should become a dominion having a strong central government and a unitary electorate, with minority rights protected by reservation of seats in all legislative bodies except for those of the Punjab and Bengal. In the same year, an All-Parties Muslim Conference met in Delhi under the chairmanship of the Āgā K͟hān and resolved that India should become a federation of semi-autonomous states, which ought to be reconstituted into a framework designed to safeguard Muslim communal interest. The Sikhs rejected the report of the Nehrū conference. The Sikh League at its annual session, held at Gujrāṅwālā on 22 October 1928, passed by a large majority a resolution disapproving of the Report for limiting the national goal to the attainment of dominion status and demanding for the Sikhs 30 per cent share of the legislative seats in the Punjab, with adequate provisions for the protection of their rights in other provinces in case separate electorates were adopted.

In part, to offset the controversy generated by dissatisfaction in India over the appointees to the Statutory Commission and their work, and despite objections from Simon himself, Viceroy Irwin gained authorization to reaffirm the goal of dominion status for India and to announce that the British government would invite representatives from India to attend a conference where constitutional issues could be freely discussed. His announcement also indicated that the sphere of constitutional discussion would extend to include the prospect of a federation of the Princely states with British India. Irwin released it on 31 October 1929, and eventually three conferences took place in London between November 1930 and December 1932. A total of 89 delegates attended the first of these Round Table Conferences, 57 from British India and the remainder divided evenly between the Princely states and the Parliament, but the Indian National Congress, then engaged in civil disobedience, was not represented. The Sikhs were represented at it by Ujjal Siṅgh and Sampūran Siṅgh. Lacking representation from the Congress and preoccupied with problems of federation, the first conference adjourned in January 1931, without having made appreciable progress on the issue of communal representation.

The second Round Table Conference got off to an uncertain start in September 1931, with Mahātmā Gāndhī attending as the sole Congress delegate and the Princes demonstrating reluctance to enter a federation. The Sikhs were represented by the same two delegates, Ujjal Siṅgh and Sampūran Siṅgh. Of the enlarged membership of 114 at this conference, 51 were appointed to the Minorities Committee which was charged with the responsibility of formulating a recommendation concerning communal representation and procedures to protect the rights of minorities. Progress within the committee was made difficult by the tenacity with which Muslim delegates held to the demand for separate communal electorates. They claimed that seats in the legislatures of the Muslim majority provinces of the Punjab and Bengal should be based on the actual population ratios there, while seats in provinces in which Muslims were in a minority should be based on negotiated ratios weighted favourably towards Muslims in the manner of the Congress-Muslim League pact signed in Lucknow in 1916. Sikhs had not been party to that pact and did not favour perpetuation of the artificially high weightage in Muslim minority representation. Indeed, the Sikhs suffered the irony of being a minority of significant standing in the Punjab and of not having been accorded a strength of representation equivalent to that given Muslims in those provinces in which the latter were in a minority.

To prevent a deadlock, British officials sought to win co-operation from Muslim delegates. Already, at the end of the first conference, they had proposed that Sindh should be separated from Bombay as a governor's provinces; at the end of the second conference the Prime Minister declared that the North-West Frontier as well would be made a Governor's province. Elevation of these two Muslim majority regions to full provincial status was expected to have strong appeal for the delegates from that community. But the Muslim delegates were not reconciled. Of the other major interests present at the second conference, the Muslims were able to win the support of only the delegates of the so-called minor minorities–the Hindu depressed classes, the Anglo-Indians and a section of the Indian Christians – each of whom found it of advantage to conjoin their own claims with those of the Muslims. The Congress, the Hindu Mahāsabhā and the Sikhs remained opposed to the Muslim position. Negotiations within the committee broke down over the minor procedural question of whom to appoint to a sub-committee to assess the points at issue, but the actual matters at stake were major and the differences among the various interests represented at the conference were substantive.

Since the Muslims held to the position that unless their demands were satisfied they could not be a party to any new constitutional scheme, even one which would provide for Indian responsibility in the central government, an impasse occurred and the problem of finding agreement about representation in the provinces of British India, and in the Punjab and Bengal in particular, eluded solution. In his statement at the close of the second Round Table Conference on 1 December 1931, Prime Minister Ramsay MacDonald revealed that unless the spokesmen for the several Indian communities and interests could reach agreement among themselves, "His Majesty's Government would be compelled to apply a provisional scheme" which he acknowledged "will not be a satisfactory way of dealing with this problem," but which, he thought, would be preferable to no change at all. MacDonald's statement of promise and of warning was concretized some nine months later, after a final attempt to open the way to a negotiated settlement through a consultative committee but before the start of the third Round Table Conference, in the form of the Communal Award.

The Award was in the form of an arbital settlement of the conflicting claims of various interests in regard to the composition and method of election to the provincial legislatures. This involved not only the question of the method of providing representation to the religious communities but also of the relative strength to be accorded to each in relation to the other in every province, the method and relative strength of representation of non-communal special interests, and the size of the legislative bodies. Corresponding provisions for the Central Legislature were not taken up by the Award, for that matter depended on the outcome of discussions with the princes concerning whether the Indian states would join a federation and, if so, what percentages of seats should be assigned to the states and to the provinces of British India, respectively. The main consequence of the Award was the fragmentation of the Indian electorate still further.

The Award demarcated the following communal constituencies: general (composed of Hindus and other residual communal groups), Muslim, Sikh, Indian Christian, Anglo-Indian, European, depressed classes, (with electors voting also in the general constituency), and tribal or backward areas. Special seats were designated for women within the various communal categories to assure their representation in the provincial legislatures. The Award also preserved the following non-communal special constituencies : labour, commerce, landholders, and universities. Determination of the size of the electorate and the geographical extent of the communal constituencies was not complete at the time the Award was announced; so the government included a clause which would allow for slight variations in the final numbers of seats, except for the Muslim-majority provinces of Bengal and the Punjab. After a ten-year period the electoral arrangements established by the Award were to be subject to revision, with the assent of the communities affected.

In preparation for the Award, the British analysed the probable overall communal composition of each legislature from all constituencies. For example, in the Punjab the special constituency electorates were expected to return five Hindus, four Muslims, and one Sikh, thereby increasing the total number of seats held by Hindus to 48, those held by Sikhs to 33, and those held by Muslims to 90. Of 175 total seats in the Punjab legislature, Indian Christians would hold two and Anglo-Indians and Europeans one each. When compared with the figures for the population of the province, the anticipated composition of the Punjab legislature was to be as follows: with 23.2% of the population, Hindus would hold 27.4% of the legislative seats, with 56.5%, Muslims would hold 51.4% of the seats, and with 13%, Sikhs would hold 18.9% of the seats.

While Sikh leaders had anticipated that the Award would not fully meet their expectations regarding representation and safeguards for their community, they were stunned when the announcement actually came. They felt that the Muslims who had been granted relatively stronger representation in the Punjab legislature than had been recommended by the Simon Commission had been unduly favoured. Another point of resentment was the failure of the British government to take into account the 1.9% Sikh population increase documented by the 1931 census. Eight prominent Sikh leaders released on August 17 a statement to the press describing the Award as a repudiation of promises made to their community. They called for a unified response by Sikhs in peaceful opposition to the Award, and they urged that preparations be made for possible Sikh secession from the northern districts of the Punjab.

This initial Sikh response to the terms of the Communal Award was consistent with the position that had long been taken by leaders of the community. The earliest formal Sikh claim to representation in excess of the population ratio of the community was made in 1916 by Sardār Sundar Siṅgh Majīṭhīā in a private letter to the Chief Secretary to the Punjab Lieutenant-Governor. He foresaw that the British were likely to accept bilateral agreements between Hindus and Muslims concerning communal representation such as the 1916 Lucknow Pact which gave Muslims 50% of the communal seats in the Punjab. Recognizing the potentially disastrous implications for his own community, he warned that new reforms schemes were likely to fail if they did not recognize rightful Sikh claims to effective political representation. He cited as a model for the protection of Sikh interests the safeguards granted to Muslims under the Minto-Morley reforms and declared that, consistent with their position and importance, Sikhs would consider their just share to be one-third of all seats and appointments in the Punjab government and an adequate and fixed representation in the councils of the Viceroy and the Secretary of State for India. One further factor in favour of the claim put forth by Sundar Siṅgh Majīṭhīā was that, while by the 1911 census Sikhs were but 11.1% of the population of the Punjab, they comprised 24.1% of the electorate. Under the Montford reforms the government did create separate communal electorates in the Punjab for Sikhs, but the percentage of communal seats allocated to them was only 18.9.

Formation of the Simon Commission and the prospect of further reforms prompted Sikhs to organize mass meetings and demonstrations to press their claims for increased representation. As their primary goal, most Sikh leaders sought abolition of the system of communal electorates in favour of a system of reserved seats to protect the interests of minorities. Secondarily, they argued that, if communal electorates were perpetuated, weighted representation in excess of their community's numerical strength would be justified by several factors, i.e. comparisons with minority weightages in other provinces granted to Muslims, Anglo-Indians, and Europeans; contributions to military service; proportion of Punjab revenue paid; and the historical role of Sikh power in the Punjab.

In March 1931, following the failure of the Second Round Table Conference, the Central Sikh League adopted a resolution entitled "The Sikhs and the Future Constitution of India," which presented seventeen points of Sikh concern related to the proposed reforms. These seventeen points became the organizing focus for negotiations with other communities and with the government. They expressed opposition to a Muslim statutory majority in the Punjab whether through separate communal electorates or reservation of seats, demanded representation of 30% for the Sikh community in the Punjab legislature and administration, and required representation at the level of 33.3% in the Cabinet and in the Public Service Commission. Failing agreement on these terms, they proposed alteration of the boundaries of the province in order to transfer predominantly Muslim areas to the North-West Frontier. As a last resort, they resolved that the Punjab should be administered by the Central government until an agreement consistent with the seventeen points could be reached. Other points included provisions for Sikh participation in the army, services, and Central government; for Sikh representation in other provinces of British India; and for the support and use of Gurmukhī script.

During the summer of 1932, the community mobilized itself for protest against impending "communal rāj." An All-Parties Sikh Conference held at Mahārājā Ranjīt Siṅgh's *samādh* in Lahore on 24 July appointed and empowered a seventeen-member autonomous Council of Action to adopt necessary measures and to oppose the working of any constitution which failed to give Sikhs full protection or which did not provide for an effective balance of power for each of the principal communities in the Punjab. At the conference, political protest was linked to religious values. Members of the Council of Action made in the presence of the Gurū Granth Sāhib a vow that they would make "every possible sacrifice" in the fight against any form of communal majority. Sikh Rights Day was set for 31 July as a day of protest, to be preceded by the performance of Akhaṇḍ Pāṭhs. The day also served as the occasion for enlisting volunteers in the newly formed Akālī Shahīdī Dal. Widespread commitment to these principles from within the community and intransigence outside it prevented conventional negotiations from making any headway. In early August, Sir Jogendra Siṅgh convened sessions with Muslim leaders in Shimlā, but opposition to compromise as voiced by non-participating Council of Action spokesmen and the persistent rumours that Muslims would be given a clear majority in the Communal Award doomed these discussions.

After the Award was published, proving the rumours true, diverse strategies were proposed by Sikh leaders to protest its terms. While some called for total non-co-operation with the government and others optimistically appealed to Muslims to work towards a compromise which would recognize the legitimate demands of Sikhs, those realistically disposed advocated symbolic forms of protest and selective non-co-operation. The Council of Action planned the formation of a broadly representative organization to be called the Gurū Khālsā Darbār and announced 17 September to be observed as Panthic Day when all men should wear dark turbans and contribute to the Sikh Defence Fund. On 25 September, delegates from Sikh organizations throughout India convened an All-Sikh Conference at the Akāl Ta<u>kh</u>t in Amritsar. They resolved to establish a <u>Kh</u>ālsā Darbār composed of 250 members, of which 200 were to be elected popularly; further that all Sikh office-holders should prepare formal resignations and forward them to the new organization so that full non-co-operation could be launched if and when it were deemed necessary. Meanwhile, Sikh members of the Punjab Legislative Council had joined with Hindu members to vote for adjournment on 5 September, the first day of the Assembly. While they were denied a vote on procedural grounds, the Sikh members led a walk-out on 7 November. However, none of these measures nor any others succeeded in persuading the British to withdraw the Award or to recast its terms. It was left to the Poona Pact, an agreement among Hindus regarding the terms of depressed classes representation, to raise new hopes that the various communities together might devise their own settlement to replace the Communal Award. A Unity Conference was convened in Allāhabād in November, and the Council of Action, the Sikh League, and the <u>Kh</u>ālsā Darbār each sent delegates. They influenced the form of the agreement which was drafted at the conference. It incorporated safeguards for Sikhs in the Punjab in exchange for their acceptance of a majority of reserved seats for Muslims. But the agreement foundered on the question of working out terms relating to Bengal. For this reason, it did not receive official consideration as an alternative to the Award.

The experience of the Sikhs in relation to the Communal Award contributed to three developments within their community and province. First, the refusal of the government to accede in any respect to the demand for political safeguards against possible excesses under a communal majority meant that the era of Sikh collaboration with the government was on the wane. The strategy which had been effective in protecting Muslim interests produced few positive results for the Sikhs. Second, the crisis precipitated by the impasse in communal negotiations and announcement of the Award tended to contribute to the creation of new organizations within the Sikh community, and this process of rapid mobilization encouraged the formation of factions on the basis of strategy, ideology and style of leadership. Finally, the strength of Sikh opposition to a Muslim communal majority in the Punjab gave credibility to proposals for partitioning the province in order to form a separate Sikh-majority canton, district or province.

BIBLIOGRAPHY

1. Nayar, Baldev Raj, *Minority Politics in the Punjab*. Princeton, 1966
2. *Congress and the Problem of Minorities*. Allahabad, 1947
3. Chatterjee, Ramananda, "The Communal Award" in *The Modern Review*. September 1932
4. Gulati, K.C., *The Akalis : Past and Present*. Delhi, 1974
5. Khushwant Singh, *A History of the Sikhs*, vol. 2. Princeton, 1966
6. Harbans Singh, *The Heritage of the Sikhs*. Delhi, 1983

G.R.T.

CONSTITUTIONAL REFORMS OF 1919: SIKH DEPUTATION TO ENGLAND. In August 1917, the Secretary of State for India, Edwin Samuel Montagu, made the declaration that the aim of British policy was the introduction of responsible government in India. When Montagu visited India that autumn, Mahārājā Bhūpinder Siṅgh, ruler of Paṭiālā, met him on behalf of the Sikhs. A deputation of the Sikh leaders also waited upon the Viceroy, Lord Chelmsford, on 22 November 1917 and pressed their claim to one-third representation in the Punjab, especially in view of their services in World War I. The Montagu-Chelmsford report published in July 1918 proposed to extend to the Sikhs the system adopted in the case of Muslims in provinces where they were in a minority. To consider the report, the Chief K̲h̲ālsā Dīwān convened a representative conclave of the Sikhs at Amritsar on 18 September 1918. In the memorandum which they prepared on behalf of the community, government was urged to carry out the assurance given the Sikhs in the Montagu-Chelmsford report. The Montagu-Chelmsford proposals were debated in the joint committee of the Punjab Legislative Council. When Sir Fazl-i-Hussain, the Muslim leader, tried to push through a resolution that the Muslim proportion in the Punjab Legislative Council be based on the Lucknow Pact, Gajjan Siṅgh of Ludhiāṇā proposed that the words "subject to just claims of the Sikhs" be added to the resolution. The amendment was opposed by both Muslim and Hindu members and was lost. The publication of the Montagu-Chelmsford report was followed by the appointment of Franchise Committee under the chairmanship of Lord Southborough to go into the matter of the composition of the new legislatures. India was represented on the Committee by three members, but none of them was a Sikh. When the Sikhs protested, Sundar Siṅgh Majīṭhīā was taken as a co-opted member for the Punjab, but their demand for one-third of the total number of non-official seats held by Indians in the Punjab, 7 out of 67 non-official seats in the Assembly of India and 4 seats in the Council of States for the Sikh community remained largely unfulfilled. The Franchise Committee recommended 15 per cent Council seats for the Sikhs. In Bihār and Oṛīssā where they formed 10 per cent of the total population, the Muslims were given 25 per cent seats by the Franchise Committee. In the Punjab, where they constituted 11.8 per cent of the population and were otherwise an important factor in the life of the province Sikhs' share was fixed at a bare 15 per cent.

The Sikhs made representations to government. A deputation, consisting of Sewārām Siṅgh, a lawyer of the Chief Court of Lahore, Shivdev Siṅgh Uberoi, a senior member of the Chief Khālsā Dīwān, Sohan Siṅgh of Rāwalpiṇḍī and Ujjal Siṅgh, who later became the principal spokesman of the Sikhs on constitutional reforms, was sent to England. The deputation sailed from Bombay on 18 June 1919 and reached London on 11 July 1919. On arrival in London, they had interviews with Lord Selborne, Chairman, Joint Parliamentary Committee, Mr Montagu and others. The deputationists claimed seats for the Sikhs on the same principle as was being applied in the case of Muslims in Bihār and Oṛīssā. They demanded 33 per cent of Council seats in the Punjab and justified the demand on the grounds of their historical and economic position in the "province". The deputationists found the authorities in England quite receptive to their arguments and generally friendly to the claims of the Sikh community. Lord Selborne regretted that they did not have the benefit of these arguments while formulating their recommendations and promised to discuss the case again with his colleagues on the Joint Parliamentary Committee, but ultimately nothing tangible came forth and the deputationists returned disappointed.

BIBLIOGRAPHY

1. Gurmukh Nihal Singh, *Landmarks in Indian Constitutional and National Development*. Delhi, 1963
2. Mujeeb, M., *The Indian Muslims*. London, 1967
3. Nayar, Baldev Raj, *Minority Politics in the Punjab*. Princeton, 1966
4. Khushwant Singh, *A History of the Sikhs*, vol. 2. Princeton, 1966
5. Brass, Paul R., *Language, Religion and Politics in North India*. Delhi, 1975
6. Mohinder Singh, *The Akali Movement*. Delhi, 1978
7. Harbans Singh, *The Heritage of the Sikhs*. Delhi, 1983

K.S.T.

CORTLANDT, HENRY CHARLES VAN (1814-1888), son of Colonel Henry Clinton Van Cortlandt of the British army, by an Indian wife, was born at Meerut in 1814, and was educated in England. In 1832, he returned to India and joined Mahārājā Raṇjīt Siṅgh's army on a monthly salary of Rs 250, subsequently raised to Rs 800, with a monthly stipend of Rs 800 for his wife. Cortlandt participated in various campaigns including the battle of Jamrūd in which the famous general, Harī Siṅgh Nalvā, was killed. During the reign of Mahārājā Sher Siṅgh, Cortlandt's command was increased to two regiments and he was posted to Hazārā. He was recalled to Lahore upon the murder of Mahārājā Sher Siṅgh and his son, Partāp Siṅgh. While on leave in India in January 1845, he openly joined the British. During the first Anglo-Sikh war, he was sent to Fīrozpur as political agent in which capacity he witnessed the battles of Ferozeshāh and Sabhrāoṅ. On the conclusion of the war, he was reinstated in the Sikh army, promoted a general and made governor of Ḍerā Ismāīl Khān. In 1846, General Cortlandt accompanied the British, with the Sikh force under his command, to Kashmīr to quell the revolt instigated by Wazīr Lāl Siṅgh. During the Multān uprising (1848), he openly supported Lieut Herbert Edwardes. Similar was his role in the second Anglo-Sikh war. After the annexation of the Punjab, he was transferred to the British service as a civilian. He was made a Companion of the Bath for his services in the 1857 uprising. Cortlandt retired in March 1868 and proceeded to London where he died in 1888.

BIBLIOGRAPHY

1. Grey, C., *European Adventurers of Northern India, 1785-1849.* Patiala, 1970
2. Gulcharan Singh, *Ranjit Singh and His Generals.* Jalandhar, n.d.
3. Ganda Singh, *Private Correspondence Relating to the Anglo-Sikh Wars.* Amritsar, 1955

Gl.S.

COUNCIL OF REGENCY. To govern the State of the Punjab during the minority of Mahārājā Duleep Siṅgh, two successive councils of regency were set up at Lahore – the first functioning from 1844-46 and the second from 1846-49. After the assassination of Mahārājā Sher Siṅgh on 15 September 1843, Rājā Hīrā Siṅgh had won over the Khālsā army and established himself in the office of prime minister with the minor Duleep Siṅgh as the new sovereign. But his rule was short-lived, and he, along with his favourite and deputy, Paṇḍit Jallā, was killed by the Army on 21 December 1844. Mahārāṇī Jind Kaur, who had an active hand in overthrowing Hīrā Siṅgh, now cast off her veil and assumed full powers as regent in the name of her minor son, Duleep Siṅgh. To run the administration, she constituted a Council of Regency on 22 December 1844, composed of Jawāhar Siṅgh, Rājā Lāl Siṅgh, Bhāī Rām Siṅgh, Bakhshī Bhagat Rām, Dīwān Dīnā Nāth, Atar Siṅgh Kāliāṅvālā, Shām Siṅgh Aṭārīvālā, General Mahtāb Siṅgh Majīṭhīā, General Mevā Siṅgh Majīṭhīā and General Lāl Siṅgh Morāṅvālā. The composition of this Council represented a combination of elder statesmen of the Darbār and army generals. Mahārāṇī Jind Kaur acted with determination and courage in transacting public business. The Council nullified the enhanced taxes and burdens imposed by Rājā Hīrā Siṅgh, restored to the feudatory *sardārs jāgīrs* and fiefs resumed by him and enhanced the pay of the soldiery. It also quelled the revolts of Kaṅvar Kashmīrā Siṅgh and Kaṅvar Pashaurā Siṅgh and sent a force 35,000 strong to Jammū to crush the rebellious activities of Rājā Gulāb Siṅgh, who was brought to Lahore and arraigned on a charge of treachery against his sovereign.

After the first Anglo-Sikh war, under article 5 of the Agreement concluded between the British government and the Lahore Darbār at Bharovāl (16 December 1846), Henry Lawrence was appointed resident with "full authority to direct and control all matters in every department of the State" and a new eight-member Council of Regency was constituted, the members being Rājā Tej Siṅgh, Sher Siṅgh Aṭārīvālā, Dīwān Dīnā Nāth, Faqīr Nūr ud-Dīn, Raṇjodh Siṅgh Majīṭhīā, Bhāī Nidhān Siṅgh, Atar Siṅgh Kāliāṅvālā and Shamsher Siṅgh Sandhāṅvālīā. The Treaty of Bharovāl had changed the entire complexion of the Council of Regency. Its members could only hold office during the pleasure of the British resident. Mahārāṇī Jind Kaur was pensioned off, and the British government became the guardian of the minor Mahārājā of the Punjab. A British garrison was stationed at Lahore, and the entire civil and military administration of the country was vested in the British resident. The Council of Regency ceased to exist as a sovereign political body. It was more an instrument for subserving British interests as it did, for instance, in acquiescing in the removal of the Mahārāṇī from the capital in August 1847 and her final expulsion from the Punjab in June 1848; in forcing Dīwān Mūl Rāj to resign the governorship of Multān in December 1847; and in meekly accepting the blame of the Multān revolt under Resident Frederick Currie's pressure. In directing the course of events leading to the second Anglo-Sikh war, the Council of Regency had no voice at all. None of its members spoke to contradict British accusations that the whole Sikh nation was involved in a general resurrection to re-establish the Khālsā Rāj. The Council's last dismal act was the signing on behalf of the minor sovereign the Instrument of deposition and annexation of the Punjab to the British empire on 29 March 1849, which spelt the end of the dynasty of Raṇjīt Siṅgh.

BIBLIOGRAPHY

1. Cunningham, J.D., *A History of the Sikhs*. London, 1849
2. Khushwant Singh, *A History of the Sikhs*, vol. 2. Princeton, 1966
3. Hasrat, B.J., *Anglo-Sikh Relations*. Hoshiarpur, 1968

B.J.H.

COURT AND CAMP OF RUNJEET SING, THE, by W.G. Osborne, military secretary to Lord Auckland, Governor-General of India (1836-42), first published in 1840 in London, is a journal recording events in the Punjab of the period from 19 May to 13 July 1838 and the author's personal impressions. The author visited Lahore first as a member of Sir William H. Macnaghten's mission in May 1838, and then in December of the same year with the Governor-General during his meeting with Mahārājā Raṇjīt Siṅgh at Fīrozpur. The journal is preceded by an introduction about the origin and rise of the Sikh people and is followed by a few letters of the author to the Mahārājā and one from the Mahārājā to the author. The book is illustrated with sixteen beautiful lithographic portraitures drawn by the author himself.

Ostensibly the journal was written "to beguile the tedium of a camp life, and without the remotest intention of publication," but a careful study of the text would reveal that the purpose was to draw the attention of the English people to the state of affairs in the northwest frontier and to the possibility of annexing Punjab after the death of the ailing Raṇjīt Siṅgh. Osborne's account of the discipline and efficiency of the Sikh army carries the suggestion that it was inferior to the British army, though superior to the forces of other princes of India.

The book contains a vivid account of the person and character of Raṇjīt Siṅgh, his habits and idiosyncrasies, and his virtues and foibles. The Mahārājā was, observes Osborne, one of that order of men who seemed destined by nature to win their way to distinction and achieve greatness. Cool and calculating by nature, the Mahārājā kept a just proportion between his efforts and objectives. Unable to read and write, he was amply compensated for this deficiency by an accurate and retentive memory, an extraordinarily agile mind and fertile imagination. By sheer force of mind, personal energy and courage, he created a powerful nation. He was by temperament mild and merciful. He "had a natural shrewdness, sprightliness and vivacity, worthy of a more civilized and intellectual state." About men around Raṇjīt Siṅgh, Osborne has many interesting comments to make. Azīz ud-Dīn, he says, "is a fine-looking man, of about five and forty, not overclean in his person, but with a pleasant and good-humoured, though crafty-looking countenance, and his manners are so kind and unassuming that it is impossible not to like him." Comments likewise abound about Sher Siṅgh, Dhiān Siṅgh, Hīrā Siṅgh and others.

B.J.H.

COURT, CAROLINE FEZLĪ 'ĀZAMJOO (1821-1869), born as Fezlī 'Āzamjoo in Kashmīr on 13 June 1821, married Claude Auguste Court, a general in the Sikh army, by 1836. They had three children by the time they left the Punjab in 1843. On 25 June 1844, Fezlī and her children were baptized at Marseilles, and she was on the same day religiously married to General Court by the Bishop in the Cathedrale of Marseilles.

A fourth child was born in Marseilles in 1845.

Little else is known about Fezlī Āzamjoo's life at Marseilles. Her testament, however, states explicitly that she is grateful to her husband who left her in full possession of her dowry during her life. The same document provides a list of some Indian belongings she distributed to their children. A beautiful painting, oil on canvas (private collection), shows her in her residence at Lahore with her two elder children. Fezlī 'Āzamjoo died at Marseilles on 4 February 1869. One of her granddaughters, Valentina, married Theophile Allard, son of General Allard and Bannou Pān Deī.

J.M.L.

COURT, CLAUDE AUGUSTE (1793-1880), general in the Sikh army, honorary general of France, Chevalier of the Legion of Honour, recipient of the Auspicious Order of the Punjab, Fellow of the Royal Geographical Society of England, and Member of several continental scientific and learned societies, was born at Saint Cezaire, France, on 24 September 1793. In 1813, he joined the French army. After Napoleon's defeat at Waterloo in 1815 he was dismissed from service. He left France in 1818 for Baghdad and joined the Persian forces which were trained at Kermanshah by a handful of ex-officers of Napoleon's army including Ventura. While in Persia, he met another Neapolitan adventurer Avitabile and together they travelled on to Lahore reaching there in early 1827. Mahārājā Raṇjīt Siṅgh gave Court employment in the artillery befitting his talents and scientific attainments. Court was responsible for the training of artillerymen, the organization of batteries and the establishment of arsenals and magazines on European lines. The Mahārājā had his own foundries for casting guns and for the manufacture of shells. Court supervised these in collaboration with Sardār Lahiṇā Siṅgh Majīṭhīā. When Court produced the first shell at the Lahore foundry, the Mahārājā bestowed upon him an *inām* (prize) of Rs 30,000, and when he produced the fuse, he was rewarded with an *inām* of Rs 5,000.

Court received a salary of Rs 2,500 per month, besides a *jāgīr*. He took part in the expedition of Peshāwar (1834) and the battle of Jamrūd (1837). He was promoted general in 1836. He continued to serve the State after the death of Mahārājā Raṇjīt Siṅgh. During the struggle for succession after the death of Kaṅvar Nau Nihāl Siṅgh on 5 November 1840, Court along with Ventura sided with Sher Siṅgh who was installed as Mahārājā, with their help in investing the Fort of Lahore, on 20 January 1841. On 26 January, however, Court's regiments mutinied, accusing their general of being responsible for the reduction of the promised increment of Rs 4 per month to their salary to one rupee per month. The troops ransacked his residence and chased him and his family up to Anārkalī where Ventura's guards stopped them. Court then escaped to the British territory across the Sutlej where he stayed till Mahārājā Sher Siṅgh had negotiated his return to his regiments in April 1841. In January 1842, Court was sent with his brigade to Peshāwar where he and Avitabile with their regiments stormed the Khaibar Pass on 5-6 April 1842 to help the British General Pollock to cross over from Afghanistan. Court returned to Lahore in July or August 1843 and after Mahārājā Sher Siṅgh's assassination in September 1843, he fled to Fīrozpur, in British territory, and, ultimately securing his discharge from the Sikh army, proceeded with his Punjabi wife and the children to France in 1844. He purchased an estate in the countryside and a residence in the city of Paris where he lived until his death in 1880.

Court had antiquarian interests and contributed articles to the *Journal of the Asiastic Society of Bengal,* Calcutta, and later to the *Journal Asiatique* in Paris. He conducted several excavations at Manikyālā near Jehlum and later at Peshāwar collecting coins, artifacts and inscriptions. One of them, the *Manikyālā Inscription,* helped J. Prinsep to decipher the Kharoshṭī script, and is now preserved in the Lahore Museum. He also wrote his *Memoirs* covering his travels from 1818 to 1844, from Syria to Lahore. They present a minute description of the countries or provinces he visited, his interests extending from geology to archaeology. The last part of the book is devoted to the kingdom of Mahārājā Raṇjīt Siṅgh.

BIBLIOGRAPHY

1. Lafont, J.M., *La Présence francaise dans le Royaume Sikh du Penjab 1822-1849.* Paris, 1992
2. Grey, C., *European Adventurers of Northern India.* Lahore, 1929
3. Gulcharan Siṅgh, *Ranjit Siṅgh and His Generals.* Jalandhar, 1976

J.M.L.

CUNNINGHAM, JOSEPH DAVEY (1812-1851), the first British historian of the Sikhs (his *A History of the Sikhs* was published in London in 1849), was the eldest of the five sons of Allan Cunningham, a noted poet and playwright. Born at Lambeth on 9 June 1812, Joseph had his early education in private schools in London where he showed such a marked aptitude for mathematics that his father was advised to send him to Cambridge. But as the young boy was more keen on becoming a soldier, a cadetship in the East India Company's service was procured him through the good offices of Sir Walter Scott. He received his military training at Addiscombe and professional training in engineering at Chatham. Towards the end of 1832, he reached Delhi and joined the Corps of Sappers and Miners in the Bengal Army. In 1837, he was appointed assistant to Colonel (afterwards Sir) Claude Wade, the political agent at Ludhiāṇā and officer-in-charge of British relations with the Punjab and with the chiefs of Afghanistan. For the next eight years he held various appointments under Colonel Wade and his successors, and was, at the time of the outbreak of the first Anglo-Sikh war in 1845, political agent in the state of Bahāwalpur. He was summoned to the battlefront and attached first to the staff of Sir Charles Napier and then to that of Sir Hugh Gough. He was present, as political officer, with the division of Sir Harry Smith at the battles of Baddovāl and 'Alīwāl. At Sabhrāoṅ, he served as an additional aid-de-camp to the Governor-General, Sir Henry Hardinge. His services earned him a brevet and appointment as political agent to the state of Bhopāl. In 1849, appeared his *A History of the Sikhs* which he had written while at Bhopāl and which his brother had got published in London. His severe criticism, in the book, of Lord Hardinge's Punjab policy brought upon him the wrath of his superiors. He was removed from his political appointment and sent back to regimental duty. He took the disgrace to heart and, soon after his appointment to the Meerut division of Public Works, he died suddenly at Ambālā in 1851.

A History of the Sikhs from the Origin of the Nation to the Battles of the Sutlej, by Cunningham, is the first serious and sympathetic account of the Sikh people ever written of them by a foreigner. Cunningham explored the available materials with the meticulousness of a scholar. Besides official despatches and documents and the earlier English accounts, he went to the original sources and acquainted himself with the Sikh scriptures as well as with relevant manuscripts in Persian and Punjabi. The emphasis in Cunningham's *History* shifted from his predecessors' concern with the assessment of Sikhs' political and military strength or the description of the manner of their court to the identification of the ingredients of their moral and religious inspiration and of the driving force behind their rise from a religious sect to nationhood. The book is also significant for its account of the geography and economy of the Punjab and for its analysis of the social milieu in which Sikhism was born. Elaborate footnotes and appendices show the minuteness and range of Cunningham's learning.

Cunningham had aimed at achieving two objectives in writing his *History*. His main endeavour was "to give Sikhism its place in the general history of humanity, by showing its connection with the different creeds of India..." Secondly, he wished "to give some account of the connexion of the English with the Sikhs, and in part with the Afghans ..." His first four chapters, covering the history of the Sikhs from its beginning to 1764, traced the growth of "a nation" animated by a living faith. Their religious faith, he inferred, was the main motive force of their history. That was both because it had appeared at a time when the historical situation needed it the most and because of the "excellence" of Gurū Nānak's message. An important feature of Sikhism, in Cunningham's eyes, was its spirit of freedom and progress.

The last five chapters were a contemporary history of Cunningham's own times, based on the official and secret records of the government of the East India Company. A large part of these five chapters dealt with Raṇjīt Siṅgh's rise to power, his achievements and his relations with the British. Of these, the last chapter entitled "The War with the English," which detailed the immediate circumstances leading to the Anglo-Sikh war of 1845-46 was, however, a scathing criticism of Governor-General Lord Hardinge who, said Cunningham, had done nothing to prevent the earlier mistakes from continuing to add to the distrust of the Sikh army from feeling suspicious of British intentions, in which situation the war was an inevitability.

According to Cunningham's analysis, the British won the war they had precipitated but could have as well lost it. What really contributed to the success of the British was the treachery of the Lahore leaders who had instigated it. Rājā Lāl Siṅgh, Rājā Tej Siṅgh, the commander-in-chief and Rājā Gulāb Siṅgh had played a treacherous role and betrayed their own army in varying degree.

Besides having Cunningham dismissed from the political service, Hardinge who had taken grave umbrage at the publication of the book, prevailed upon J.W. Kaye, an acknowledged authority on Indian history, to write a detailed review of it. This review, published in *The Calcutta Review*, mostly attempted to rebut Cunningham's thesis. Kaye's review started a controversy which continued throughout the nineteenth century. Some looked upon the book as the outpourings of "the apologist of the Khalsa." But today Cunningham's *History* is commonly recognized as a standard, responsible work.

BIBLIOGRAPHY

1. Fauja Singh, ed., *Historians and Historiography of the Sikhs*. Delhi, 1978
2. Khurana, Gianeshwar, *British Historiography on the Sikh Power in Punjab*. Delhi, 1985
3. Darshan Singh, *Western Perspective on the Sikh Religion*. Delhi, 1991
4. Grewal, J.S., *From Guru Nanak to Maharaja Ranjit Singh: Essays in Sikh History*. Amritsar, 1972

S.S.Bl.

CURRIE, SIR FREDERICK (1799-1875), diplomat, son of Mark Currie, was born on 3 February 1799. He came out to India in 1820, and served in various capacities in the civil and judicial departments before being appointed a judge in the North-West Frontier Province. He became foreign secretary to Government of India at Fort William in 1842. During the first Sikh war (1845-46), he remained with Governor-General Lord Hardinge and was instrumental in arranging with the Sikhs the terms of the first treaty of

Lahore. He was an officiating member of the supreme council at Calcutta, 1847-48.

As foreign secretary, Sir Frederick Currie fell in with the designs of Governors-General Ellenborough and Hardinge on the Sikh kingdom. He supported Major George Broadfoot's action in 1845 which amounted to virtual seizure of Lahore possessions on the left bank of the Sutlej.

In March 1848, Currie was appointed Resident at Lahore. When in April 1848, the report of Multān uprising reached him, he hastily ordered a strong Sikh force to proceed to Multān. Governor-General Dalhousie rebuked him for despatching "an avowedly disloyal force" to Multān. Currie immediately countermanded the order. Following Lord Dalhousie's policy, he directed Herbert Edwardes, the Political Assistant at Bannū who had marched against Dīwān Mūl Rāj with his Lahore contingent to keep away from Multān, for the Dīwān's surrender would have rendered infructuous Lord Dalhousie's plan for an eventual full-scale campaign in the Punjab. Currie's inaction provoked much hostile criticism in Britain, but Dalhousie defended him in a long despatch to the Home Government.

Forestalling Lord Dalhousie's instructions, Currie expelled Mahārāṇī Jind Kaur from the Punjab. Since her removal to Sheikhūpurā in September 1847, the widow of Ranjīt Siṅgh had been kept under strict surveillance. She was considered to be a woman of great resolution and the British feared that she might sway the Sikh army against them. Currie implicated her in a fictitious plot, had her allowance reduced to one-third and, contrary to the advice of the Council, had her removed to Fīrozpur. She was soon after sent to Banāras.

Frederick Currie became a director of the East India Company in 1854 and its chairman in 1857. He died on 11 September 1875.

BIBLIOGRAPHY

1. Hasrat, B.J., *Anglo-Sikh Relations.* Hoshiarpur, 1968
2. Gupta, Hari Ram, *Panjab on the Eve of First Sikh War.* Chandigarh, 1975
3. Gough, C. and A.D. Innes, *The Sikhs and the Sikh Wars.* London, 1897
4. Ganda Singh, *Private Correspondence Relating to the Anglo-Sikh Wars.* Amritsar, 1955

B.J.H.

CUTTACK (20° - 30'N, 85° - 50'E), one of the principal towns of Oṛīssā, was visited by Gurū Nānak during his travels across the country. The local chief Rājā Pratāp Rudra Dev and many of his subjects received instruction at the hands of the Gurū. A commemorative shrine established later by Udāsī priests still exists near Kishtī Ghāṭ on the bank of the Mahānadī River.

M.G.S.

D

DABISTĀN-I-MAZĀHIB, a seventeenth-century work in Persian, is a unique study of different religious creeds and systems, including early Sikhism. It first attracted wide notice when it was translated into English by David Shea and Anthony Troyer and was published by Oriental Translation Fund of Great Britain and Ireland, London, in 1843. The section on Nānakpanthīs, i.e. Sikhs, was first translated into English by Sardār Umrāo Siṅgh Majīṭhīā, and into English and Punjabi by Dr Gaṇḍā Siṅgh. The latter's English translation was published in the *Journal of Indian History*, vol. XIX, part 2, August 1940. It reappeared in *Panjab Past and Present*, vol. I, part 1, April 1967. There has been a good deal of controversy about the authorship of *Dabistān-i-Mazāhib*. The writer himself has nowhere in the book mentioned his name, parentage or date of birth. Earlier, Mohsin-i-Fānī Kashmīrī was commonly known to be the author of the book, but the work is now attributed by scholars to an Iranian named Maubad Zulfiqār Ardastānī (1615 c. -70). Maubad was a general term for a member or leader of the priestly order of the Zoroastrians. Zulfiqār grew up under the care of Maubad Hushiyar, himself a disciple of Azhar Kaiwan (d. 1627), the high priest of the Zoroastrians, who had come from Iran to India in the time of Emperor Akbar (1542-1605) and made Paṭnā his second home. Zulfiqār was a religious-minded youth with a liberal outlook. He devoted himself to the comparative study of religions and travelled extensively to this end, visiting far-flung places such as Gujarāt, Hyderābād (1053-59 AH / AD 1643-49), Orīssā and Coromaṇḍal Coast (1061-63 AH / AD 1651-53). He also spent many years in Kashmīr and Lahore (1040-52 AH / AD 1631-42). Returning to Paṭnā, he settled down in the sector now known as Gulzārbāgh. There he started compiling from his notes the book which has become famous as *Dabistān-i-Mazāhib*. A manuscript of the work was discovered by Professor Syed Hasan 'Askarī in the city in the 1930's in the family of an Iranian Muslim who in his scribbles on the flyleaf (now lost) and in critical marginal notes on certain pages (still preserved) furnished valuable information about the author which was not available to Shea and Troyer.

The *Dabistān* (lit. school) is divided into 12 main sections dealing with Islām, Christianity, Judaism, Hinduism, Sūfīs, Kabīrpanthīs, Nānakpanthīs and different sects of Zoroastrianism. The account of Sikhism in this work, given under the title "Nānak Panthīāṅ," is the earliest from the pen of a non-Sikh contemporary writer. Despite certain errors of fact that have crept into it, it is impartial and sympathetic in tone. As the author tells us, he knew two of the Gurūs – Gurū Hargobind (1595-1644) and Gurū Har Rāi (1630-61) – personally and had met them at Kīratpur.

Nānakpanthīs, says the author, are known as Gurū-Sikhs. They have no faith in idols or temples containing idols. (Gurū) Nānak, a Bedī Khatrī, became famous during the reign of Emperor Bābar. He, like the Muhammadans, believed in the oneness of God, (but) he also believed in metempsychosis or transmigration of soul. He held the consumption of meat, pork and intoxicating drinks as forbidden. (However) after him meat-eating became common among his followers. Just as Nānak praised the Muhammadans so also he praised the incarnations and gods and goddesses of theHindus, but he knew them all as the creation of the Almighty Lord. Many legends and miracle stories about him had, continues the author, become current among his disciples. After Gurū Nānak, Aṅgad, a Trehaṇ Khatrī, Amar Dās, a Bhallā Khatrī, Rām Dās, a Soḍhī Khatrī, became Gurūs in that order. During the time of each Gurū, the Sikhs grew in number. In the reign of Gurū Arjan, successor of Gurū Rām Dās, "they had become so numerous that there were not many cities in the inhabited countries where some Sikhs were not to be found."

Again, in the words of *Dabistān-i-Mazāhib*, "The disciples of Gurū Nānak condemn idol worship. Their belief is that all their Gurūs are Nānaks. They did not read the *mantras* of the Hindus. They do not venerate their temples or idols, nor do they esteem their *avatāras*. They have no regard for the Sanskrit language which, according to the Hindus, is the speech of the angels." That the Sikhs believed all Gurūs to be of one light–one in spirit though different in body–is vividly perceived by the author. "The Sikhs say that when Gurū Nānak left the body, he descended (*halūl kard*) into Gurū Aṅgad ... who in turn similarly entered into the body of Gurū Amar Dās, ... and so on to Gurū Arjan Mall. They refer to each of them as *mahall* such as Gurū Nānak is Mahal I, Aṅgad Mahal II, and so on to Mahal V, Arjan Mall. They [the Sikhs] say that he who does not know Gurū Arjan Mall as Bāba Nānak is a *manmukh*, i.e. non-believer."

Zulfiqār Ardastānī then narrates certain anecdotes about the Gurūs and about some of the Sikhs. He alludes to the institutions of *masands* and tithes. He records that Gurū Hargobind "adopted the form of a soldier, girded sword against the practice of his father, kept servants and took to hunting .... He had to fight with the armies of Imperial agents and the servants of Shāh Jahāṅ .... In short, after the battle of Kartārpur he went to Phagwāṛā. As residence in places near Lahore was full of risk, he hastened from there to Kīratpur, which is in the hills of the Punjab .... Gurū Har Rāi is the grandson of Gurū Hargobind.... The Sikhs call Har Rāi the seventh *mahal*. He is very well known to the chronicler.... The Gurū kept 700 horses in his stable and had 300 horsemen and 60 gunners in his service."

BIBLIOGRAPHY

1. Shea, David, and Anthony Troyer, tr., *Dabistān-i-Mazāhib*. London, 1843
2. Ganda Singh, "Nanakpanthis" in *the Panjab Past and Present*, vol. I, part I. April 1967

S.H.A.

DĀDŪ DIĀL (1544-1603), ascetic and mystic, was in the line of the saints of medieval India. In his career and teaching he relived the Kabīr legend. He was born in AD 1544 in Ahmedābād in Gujarāt to a Muslim couple. He had little formal education and took to his father's profession of cotton-carding. At the age of eighteen he left home and wandered extensively all over northern India. He especially consorted with the Nāth yogīs whose influence left a permanent mark on him. At the age of twenty-five he renounced the world and migrated to Sāmbhar and spent the time wandering and preaching in the country around. He attracted a considerable number of followers who gave themselves the designation Brahma-sampradāya, later popularly designated as Dādū Panth. The core of his teaching was universal brotherhood and the worship of one God.

Dādū has left religious poetry amounting to five thousand verses. Another work called *Dādū Prakāsh* which is in Punjabi has recently been discovered by a modern scholar. Dādū laid great stress on *simran*, the contemplation of God's name. Caste, image-worship and pilgrimages were rejected. Towards the end of his life Dādū shifted to Nārāyaṇā, near Jaipur.

An anecdote is related in Sikh history. Journeying through these parts in the first decade of the seventeenth century, Gurū Gobind Siṅgh passed through Nārāyaṇā. He pitched his tents near the *Sant*'s shrine and to test the conviction of his Sikhs he saluted the sepulchre by lifting an arrow to his forehead. The Khālsā took exception to it, and demanded a fine. One of them, Mān Siṅgh, quoted the Gurū's own verse: *Gor maṛhī maṭ bhūl na mānai* (worship not even by mistake cemeteries or places of cremation). The Gurū immediately offered to pay. The fine was fixed at Rs 5,000, but a Sikh objected that it was too big a sum and proposed to reduce it to Rs 500. Another Sikh thought it too little and said the Gurū would not feel the loss of such a paltry amount. One of them said that he would not be satisfied with anything under five lakhs, but some of them argued that, though the Gurū could even pay that sum, the Khālsā would find it impossible to pay fines in proportion thereof. They at length asked the Gurū to pay Rs 125 which they spent on the purchase of a kitchen tent.

Dādū died in Nārāyaṇā in 1603.

BIBLIOGRAPHY

1. Sūrī, Kartār Siṅgh, *Gurū Arjan Dev te Sant Dādū Diāl*. Chandigarh, 1969
2. Bhaṇḍārkar, R.G., *Vaiṣṇavism, Śaivism and Minor Religious Systems*. Delhi, 1965
3. Hastings, James (ed.,), *Encyclopedia of Religion and Ethics*, vol. IV. New York, 1964
4. Oman, John Campbell, *The Mystics, Ascetics and Saints of India*. Delhi, 1973
5. Schomer, Karine and W.H. McLeod (eds.), *The Sants: Studies in a Devotional Tradition of India*. Delhi, 1987
6. Harbans Singh, *Guru Gobind Singh*. Delhi, 1979

Gn.S.

DAGGO, BHĀĪ, a rich landlord of Dhamtān, now in Jīnd district of Haryāṇā, was a *masand* having jurisdiction over the Bāṅgar region during the time of Gurū Tegh Bahādur. When the Gurū visited Dhamtān in 1665, Bhāī Daggo received him with exceeding joy and put him up in a new house he had constructed. The Gurū showered his blessings upon him: "For meeting me with presents, milk shall abound in thy house. Minister to the Sikhs and devotees, and remain with us during our stay in this place." Gurū Tegh Bahādur stayed at Dhamtān to celebrate the festival of Dīvālī. According to Sarūp Dās Bhallā, *Mahimā Prakāsh*, supported by evidence of the Bhaṭṭ Vahīs and an old Assamese journal *Pādshāh Burañjī*, the Gurū one day, while out on chase in a forest near Dhamtān, was arrested by an imperial officer, 'Ālam Khān Ruhīlā, and taken to Delhi. The Sikhs arrested along with him included Bhāī Daggo. They were, however, all released through the intercession of Kuṅvar Rām Siṅgh of Jaipur who stood surety for the Gurū. Bhāī Daggo thereupon came back to Dhamtān while Gurū Tegh Bahādur resumed his interrupted journey towards the eastern provinces. Ten years later, when Gurū Tegh Bahādur again passed through Dhamtān, Bhāī Daggo served him with devotion. According to Bhāī Santokh Siṅgh, *Srī Gur Pratāp Sūraj Granth*, the Gurū before leaving Dhamtān gave him funds for the construction of a public well and a *dharamsālā* for the travellers. Bhāī Daggo, it is said, became selfish and had the well dug in his own fields.

BIBLIOGRAPHY

1. Bhallā, Sarūp Dās, *Mahimā Prakāsh*. Patiala, 1971
2. Santokh Siṅgh, Bhāī, *Srī Gur Pratāp Sūraj Granth*. Amritsar, 1926-37
3. Macauliffe, M.A., *The Sikh Religion*. Oxford, 1909

P.S.P.

ḌAGRŪ, village 11 km west of Mogā (30° - 48'N, 75° - 10'E) in the Punjab, has a historical shrine, Gurdwārā Tambū Māl Sāhib Pātshāhī VII, dedicated to Gurū Har Rāi, who encamped here in the course of his journey through the Mālvā region, in the early 1650's. He is said to have stayed here for a considerable time during which he supervised the construction of shrines at Ḍaraulī Bhāī. The present building, constructed in 1968, comprises a hall with a high ceiling, with the sanctum in the centre where the Gurū Granth Sāhib is seated. The old *vaṇ* tree under which Gurū Har Rāi is believed to have held the daily services still stands, adjacent to the hall, to the north of it. The shrine is affiliated to the Shiromaṇī Gurdwārā Parbandhak Committee but is managed by a *granthī* supported by donations from the devotees.

M.G.S.

ḌAKHAṆE, title of sixty-nine *ślokas* by Gurū Arjan, incorporated in his *vār* in the measure Mārū, three each with its twenty-three *pauṛīs* or stanzas. The word *ḍakhṇe* (Skt. *dakṣiṇī*) means 'southern.' The language of these verses is a dialect of the southern Punjab, now in Pakistan, known as Multānī or Saraikī. *Ḍakhaṇe* is not the name of any language but of a style of song-verse of that region. Gurū Arjan, however, has complete mastery of the dialect of that region distant from his own central Punjab and these verses are remarkable for their poetic qualities.

The central theme of the *Ḍakhaṇe* is the intense longing of the human spirit for the all-pervading Supreme Spirit and they depict, first, the beauty of the Beloved; secondly, the intensity of longing for Him; thirdly, the helpfulness of the Gurū, the mediator between the seeker and the sought-after; and fourthly, some of the obstacles which bar union between the two.

The "woman" (devotee) addresses the all-pervading Spirit as 'my own good friend' (I); 'my good friend and true king' (II. 3); 'beloved dwelling with me' (IV. 1); 'my close friend who is fond of me and who is friend of all, never disappointing anyone' (VII.2); 'the hidden gem which I have found and which now shines on my forehead' (VII. 3); 'the One who is present in all and of whom none is bereft' (IX. 3); 'the colourful One' (XI. 1); 'the King of kings' (XII.1); 'the One whose light is reflected in all as is the moon in the water in the pitchers' (XIV.2); and implores Him to come and embrace her.

This is how "she" expresses the intensity of her longing: 'My eyes long for Thee' (I. 1); 'I am ready to give my head for Thy love' (I. 1); 'I am in love with Thee and with none else' (I. 2); 'do not separate me from Thee for a moment' (II. 1); 'my heart has been charmed by Thee' (II. 1); 'if Thou cometh to my courtyard, the entire earth will turn green for me' (III. 1); 'while embracing Thee, even the necklace I am wearing creates distance unbearable' (III. 3); 'I am longing ever to see how beautiful is Thy face' (VIII. 1); 'may I become a couch for the Beloved, my eyes spread on it as a sheet' (XII. 3); 'incomparable in beauty is the face of my Beloved' (XVII. 2); 'I have looked in all directions, searched everywhere, none is comparable to Him' (XVIII. 1).

'Those who take shelter with the *ustād* (teacher) are saved' (VI. 1); 'the saints whose deeds are for the well-being of others show the path' (XXI. 2); 'eyes which see the Loved One are different from the outward eyes' (XVI. 3); 'this is the opportunity and He must be realized here and now' (VII. 1). *Māyā* is compared to a wet stone of jaggery (*guṛ*) and men to flies which fall upon it and get caught (IX. 2). This is how man is beguiled from the path to union.

BIBLIOGRAPHY

1. *Shabadārth Srī Gurū Granth Sāhib,* vol. III. Amritsar, 1959
2. Sāhib Siṅgh, *Srī Gurū Granth Sāhib Darpaṇ,* vol.

VIII. Jalandhar, 1964

T.S.

DAKKHAṆĪ RĀI (d. 1815), a sixth-generation descendant of Bābā Prithī Chand, the elder brother of Gurū Arjan, who had founded an Udāsī *ḍerā* or preaching centre of the Udāsī sect at Gharāchoṅ, a village in present-day Saṅgrūr district of the Punjab. The rulers of Paṭiālā granted him two villages, Kapiāl and Baṭariāṇā, in freehold. Dakkhaṇī Rāi was a non-celibate Udāsī *sādhū*, and his descendants are still living at Gharāchoṅ. In Bāvā Brahmānand, *Gurū Udāsīn Matt Darpan,* Bābā Bishan Sarūp and Bābā Sarūp Dās are mentioned as the most respected and most active heads of this branch of Udāsīs. Bābā Sarūp Dās lived and preached for some time at Shikārpur in Sindh province, and at Amritsar from 1898 till his death there on 22 Assū 1979 Bk / 7 October 1922.

BIBLIOGRAPHY

1. Giān Siṅgh, Giānī, *Panth Prakāsh.* Patiala, 1970
2. Raṇdhīr Siṅgh, Bhāī, *Udāsī Sikhāṅ dī Vithiā.* Chandigarh, 1972
3. Brahmānand, Paṇḍīt, *Gurū Udāsīn Matt Darpan.* Sakhar (Sindh), 1923

M.G.S.

DAKKHAṆĪ SIKHS or Sikhs of the Deccan, a distinctive ethnic community scattered in parts of Āndhra Pradesh, Mahārāshṭra and Karnāṭaka, are the descendants of Punjabi Sikhs who went to the South during the eighteenth and the nineteenth centuries and permanently settled in what was then the princely state of Hyderābād. The first Punjabi Sikhs to travel to the South comprised the 300-strong contingent which arrived at Nāndeḍ in 1708 in the train of Gurū Gobind Siṅgh (1666-1708). The Gurū was assassinated and cremated at Nāndeḍ in October 1708. Many of his followers returned to the Punjab but some stayed back. Those who stayed on established a shrine at Nāndeḍ commemorating the Gurū and tilled the land around it for sustenance. They married local women willing to be converted to Sikhism and brought up their children and grandchildren as Sikhs. Nāndeḍ fell in the territory of Āsaf Jāh (d. 1748), a noble of the Mug͟hal court at Delhi, who became independent and founded the dynasty of the Nizāms of Hyderābād. Several Sikhs found employment in the irregular force of the Nizām. During the time of the third Nizām, Sikandar Jāh (1803-27), a Sikh force, 1200 strong, called Jamī'at Sikhāṅ was raised in 1810-11 on the recommendation of Rājā Chandū Lāl, a Punjabi Khatrī and influential dignitary at the Nizām's court. These men immigrated from the Punjab through arrangement made with Mahārājā Raṇjīt Siṅgh. Besides, some Punjabi Sikhs enlisted in the personal troops of Rājā Chandū Lāl and his brother, who was governor of Berār. Around 1830, Mahārājā Raṇjīt Siṅgh sent 150 men under a *sardār*, Chandā Siṅgh, for the construction of Gurdwārā Tak͟ht Sachkhaṇḍ Srī Hazūr Sāhib Abichalnagar at Nāndeḍ. Not all of them returned to their native land on the completion of the edifice. Further immigration took place during the time of the fourth Nizām, Nāsir ud-Daulā (1827-57). Most of them who settled in Hyderābād married local women, raised Sikh families, and built *gurdwārās* wherever they lived in sufficient numbers. Later generations usually intermarried within the nascent Sikh community, mostly concentrated in towns such as Hyderābād-Secunderābād, Nāndeḍ, Auraṅgābād, Nizāmābād, Karīmnagar and Waraṅgal. According to Captain A.H. Bingley, *Sikhs – A Handbook for Indian Army,* 1918, their total number, evidently based on the 1911 census, was 4,637.

The Dakkhaṇī Sikhs jealously preserved their religious and cultural identity, though they could not remain totally immune to local influence. To quote Captain Bingley again, "The Dekhani Sikh is distinguishable from his Punjabi *confrere* by his dress, which is still much the same as it was in the time of Govind Singh. They wear the *kachh* or short drawers, and their head dress is a small tightly tied *pag* such as the Sikhs of the Punjab now wear under the turban. As true Govindi Sikhs they are careful observers of the five *kakkas* and conform strictly to the ordinances of the tenth *Guru*."

Until the accession of Hyderābād state to India in 1948, the economic condition of the Dakkhaṇī Sikhs remained low and they were backward educationally, too. The situation has, however, improved considerably since. Among other factors, the influx of Sikhs uprooted from what became Pakistan in 1947, mostly belonging to trading class, deeply influenced the way of life of the Dakkhaṇī Sikhs. To-day there are among them flourishing businessmen, contractors, transporters, industrialists, educationists, lawyers and progressive farmers. Socially, they are no longer a diaspora struggling to preserve their identity in an alien land, but form an important element of the Sikh mainstream.

BIBLIOGRAPHY

Bingley, Capt. A.H., *Sikhs – A Handbook for Indian Army*. Calcutta, 1918

N.S.A.

DAKNO, RĀṆĪ, who came of a Rājpūt family of Kāṅgṛā district, was married to Mahārājā Sher Siṅgh in 1842. Reputed to be a most beautiful woman of her time, she was tall and slender, graceful and very fair, with a peculiarly gentle and winning expression of countenance. In the words of Lady Login, *Sir John Login and Duleep Singh*, "She might have passed for a living representation of the traditional conception of the Madonna, so often to be seen depicted by the old Italian masters." In 1843, she gave birth to a son who was named Sahdev Siṅgh. Both mother and son accompanied in November 1849 Mahārājā Duleep Siṅgh to Fatehgaṛh to which place he (the Mahārājā) had been exiled after being deprived of the throne of Lahore. Rāṇī Dakno and Sahdev Siṅgh died at Rāi Bareilly as prisoners of the British.

BIBLIOGRAPHY

1. Login, Lady, *Sir John Login and Duleep Singh* [Reprint]. Patiala, 1970
2. Ganda Singh, ed., *History of the Freedom Movement in the Punjab (Maharaja Duleep Singh Correspondence)*. Patiala, 1977

S.S.B.

DALHOUSIE, JAMES ANDREW BROUN RAMSAY, First Marquis of (1812-1860), Governor-General of India (1848-56), son of George (1770-1838), the ninth Earl in the peerage of Scotland, was born at Dalhousie Castle on 22 April 1812. He was educated at Harrow and at Christ Church, Oxford. He succeeded his father to the peerage in 1838 and became member of the House of Lords. In 1845, he became president of the Board of Trade. In 1846, he declined a post in the British cabinet under Sir Robert Peel. In 1847, however, he agreed to accept the office of Governor-General of India.

Lord Dalhousie arrived in India in January 1848. Soon thereafter incidents took place in Multān resulting in the revolt of the local Sikh governor, Mūl Rāj. This was merely a local affair which could have been easily put down by timely action, but Lord Dalhousie deliberately avoided intervention. The Dalhousie papers clearly indicate that immediate advance on Multān was neither perilous not impracticable. Yet the Governor-General delayed action for five months so that the trouble might spread, giving the British the excuse to come down on the Punjab with all their might and eventually annex it to their dominions.

Meanwhile, military preparations for a full-scale war in the Punjab and its final annexation were set afoot. The Governor-General began to call the Multān revolt a national rising of the Sikhs. "The die is cast", declared Dalhousie. In November 1848, Lord Gough invaded the Punjab. The main actions of this undeclared war were fought at Rāmnagar (22 November 1848), Chelīāṅvālā (13 January 1849) and Gujrāt (21 February 1849). On 29 March 1849, the kindgom of the Punjab was annexed to the British Crown. In England, public and private opinion was averse to annexation, and the British cabinet had directed the Governor-General to report the opinion of the Government of India. But Lord Dalhousie forestalled both the Secret Committee and the India Board by taking the step on his own responsibility.

Lord Dalhousie returned to England in 1856. He died on 19 December 1860.

BIBLIOGRAPHY

1. Gough, C., and A.D. Innes, *The Sikhs and the Sikh Wars.* London, 1897
2. Ganda Singh, ed., *Private Correspondence Relating to the Anglo-Sikh Wars.* Amritsar, 1955
3. Khushwant Singh, *A History of the Sikhs,* vol. 2. Princeton, 1966
4. Hasrat, B.J., *Anglo-Sikh Relations.* Hoshiarpur, 1968

B.J.H.

DALHOUSIE MUNIMENTS, a classified and catalogued collection of Lord Dalhousie's official, demi-official and private papers and diaries, preserved at the Scottish Record Office, Edinburgh. These are a part of the vast collection of Dalhousie papers which were deposited in the Scottish Record Office in 1951, and placed in the Gifts and Deposits series. These documents include Lord Dalhousie's private correspondence with Sir George Couper, known as Coulston House Papers, containing his frank opinions on various policy matters and events leading to the second Anglo-Sikh war resulting in the annexation of the Punjab; private correspondence on Punjab affairs with Abbott, Whish, Littler, the Lawrences and others; military minutes (1848-49); correspondence with the Board of Control ; letters from Sir Henry Lawrence, Lord Gough and Sir Frederick Currie: excerpts from Major Edwardes' diary concerning Multān; financial accounts of the Lahore Darbār; and paper relating to the return of troops engaged in the Punjab (1849). The Dalhousie Muniments deal mainly with the second Anglo-Sikh war (1849) and the annexation of the Punjab. These papers show how the minor Multān revolt in April 1848 was declared by Lord Dalhousie to be a major calamity, how immediate military operations were designedly postponed, and how a national reparation demanded from the State of Lahore. Immediately afterwards, "conspiracies" were unearthed, the Mahārāṇī of the Sikhs deported, and the Commander-in-Chief directed to organize a military preparation for a full-scale invasion of the Punjab.

BIBLIOGRAPHY

Hasrat, B.J., ed., *The Punjab Papers.* Hoshiarpur, 1970

B.J.H.

DALĪP SIṄGH (1894-1921), who fell a martyr at Nankāṇā Sāhib on the morning of 20 February 1921, was born to Karam Siṅgh and Har Kaur in January 1894 at the village of Sāhovāl, in Siālkoṭ district, now in Pakistan. Two of his three brothers having died young, Dalīp Siṅgh was brought up by his parents with extra attention and care. He was educated at Sāṅglā, Ḍaskā and Gujrāṅwālā. While at school, he developed a keen interest in Sikh history and *gurbāṇī,* utterances of the Gurūs, i.e. Sikh religious texts. He received the rites of Khālsā initiation, and lived a strict life. His fellow students called him 'Nihaṅg' for his orthodox ways. He passed the matriculation examination in 1908, and was married the same year. Instead of seeking government service, he took to farming combining with it social work in the district. At a *dīvān* in October 1920, when Punjab was seething with anti-British feeling following the passage of the Rowlatt Act and the Jalliāṅvālā Bāgh firing, Dalīp Siṅgh was much affected by the political temper of the speeches delivered. He discarded his old garments and wore *khādī* or homespun cotton never touching again dress made of imported cloth. This was in protest against the British rulers.

Dalīp Siṅgh was among those who fully endorsed the resolution of the Shiromaṇī Gurdwārā Parbandhak Committee to convene a *dīvān* at Nankāṇā Sāhib on 4-6 March 1921 to enter a protest against the control of the holy shrine by its *mahant* or chief priest, Naraiṇ Dās, who was charged with corruption and dissolute ways. On 18 February, while on his way to Amritsar to attend a meeting of the Shiromaṇī Gurdwārā Parbandhak Committee, he learnt from Tejā Siṅgh Samundrī and Master Tārā Siṅgh, that Jathedār Lachhmaṇ Siṅgh and Kartār Siṅgh Jhabbar, leaders of the Bār Khālsā Dīwān, had made a plan to occupy Gurdwārā Janam Asthān by surprise on 19-20 February when Naraiṇ Dās was scheduled to attend a Sanātan Sikh conference at Lahore. All of them disapproved of the plan and Dalīp Siṅgh, who was held in high esteem, was sent back to dissuade Lachhmaṇ Siṅgh, and his companions from marching towards Nankāṇā Sāhib. Dalīp Siṅgh met Kartār Siṅgh Jhabbar and his associates at Gurdwārā Kharā Saudā at Chūhaṛkāṇā and pleaded with them not to take any precipitate action. They yielded to his argument and it was decided that Lachhmaṇ Siṅgh, who at that time should have been on his way to Nankāṇā Sāhib, be stopped as well. A *hukamnāmā* or command on behalf of the Panth was drafted, ordering Lachhmaṇ Siṅgh to proceed no further. Six leading Sikhs, including Dalīp Siṅgh and Kartār Siṅgh Jhabbar, signed it, Dalīp Siṅgh undertaking to deliver it to Lachhmaṇ Siṅgh. He, along with a few companions, left Kharā Saudā at 9 p.m. The night was pitch dark and they were riding through uneven fields. At about midnight they reached Chandarkoṭ canal waterfall, the point where Lachhmaṇ Siṅgh's *jathā* was to meet Kartār Siṅgh Jhabbar's. No *jathā* came. Deploying Varyām Siṅgh to comb the surroundings, Dalīp Siṅgh, tired and worn out, came over to the factory of Uttam Siṅgh, near Nankāṇā Sāhib railway station, to rest for a while before resuming the search. In the meantime Varyām Siṅgh had succeeded in intercepting Lachhmaṇ Siṅgh and his *jathā*, who were taking a shorter route. He delivered the *hukamnāmā* to them, but failed to persuade them to stop. They argued that they had said their *ardās* and could not go back on their pledged word. They went forward singing the sacred hymns, and entered the precincts of the main shrine. Naraiṇ Dās and his men carrying firearms suddenly fell upon them and started an indiscriminate carnage.

Dalīp Siṅgh heard the sound of gunfire and ran towards Gurdwārā Janam Asthān, with Varyām Siṅgh following him. They found the main entrance gates bolted from inside. On the southern end they saw Mahant Naraīṇ Dās directing the bloody operations. Dalīp Siṅgh shouted and begged of him to stop the massacre of the innocents. But the Mahant, intent on murder, pressed the trigger of his pistol killing him and Varyām Siṅgh on the spot. The Mahant's men hacked their dead bodies with hatchets and hurled the pieces into a burning potter's kiln near by. Bhāī Dalīp Siṅgh met with his martyr's end on 20 February 1921.

See NANKĀṆĀ SĀHIB MASSACRE

BIBLIOGRAPHY

1. Shamsher, Gurbakhsh Siṅgh, *Shahīdī Jīvan*. Nankana Sahib, 1938
2. Pratāp Siṅgh, Giānī, *Gurdwārā Sudhār arthāt Akālī Lahir*. Amritsar, 1975
3. Josh, Sohan Siṅgh, *Akālī Morchiāṅ dā Itihās*. Delhi, 1972
4. Teja Singh, *Gurdwara Reform Movement and the Sikh Awakening*. Jalandhar, 1922

5. Mohinder Singh, *The Akali Movement.* Delhi, 1978

Rj.S.

DALĪP SIṄGH, Babar revolutionary, belonged to the village of Gosal, in Jalandhar district. His father's name was Īshar Siṅgh. Dalīp Siṅgh passed his matriculation examination and became a teacher in a primary school in Jalandhar. During his spare time, he toured the surrounding villages making patriotic speeches. He was drawn into the Akālī agitation for Gurdwārā reform, but he was too radical by temperament for its nonviolent strategy. He joined the secret Chakravartī group of Karam Siṅgh, of Daulatpur, and soon began to be counted among the leader's close associates. In March 1922, warrants for his arrest were issued for delivering speeches recommending to the people the creed of "reforming," i.e. liquidating the *jholīchuks* or loyalists of the British. In October 1922, he was elected secretary of the newly-formed Babar Akālī Jathā. He helped in the production of its secret literature, including the newssheet *Babar Akālī Doābā.*

Dalīp Siṅgh was arrested on 6 January 1923. During the course of his trial, he neither replied to any of the questions asked him nor signed his statement. For his seditious speeches he was sentenced, on 14 March 1923, to five years in jail. When the Babar Akālī conspiracy case trial began on 15 August 1923, he was tried afresh as one of the leaders of the movement and sentenced to transportation for life.

BIBLIOGRAPHY

1. Babbar, Sundar Siṅgh, *Itihās Babbar Akālī Lahir.* Amritsar, 1970
2. Nijjhar, Milkhā Siṅgh, *Babbar Akālī Lahir dā Itihās.* Delhi, 1986
3. Nijjar, B.S., *History of the Babbar Akalis.* Jalandhar, 1987

K.M.

DALĪP SIṄGH (1907-1926), the youngest of the Babar Akālī martyrs was born in 1907 at Dhāmīāṅ Kalāṅ, a village in Hoshiārpur district. Dalīp Siṅgh was barely 14, when a group of peaceful Akālī reformers was massacred in the Sikh shrine at Nankāṇā Sāhib by the men of the local *mahant* or custodian. Dalīp Siṅgh's young mind was filled with anger against the British who, he thought, were really responsible for the tragedy. He started attending the Babar Akālī *dīvāns* at which violence was preached. A meeting with one of the Babar leaders, Bābū Santā Siṅgh, led to his enlisting in the party in April 1923. He proved a determined and fearless worker, but was betrayed by one Javālā Siṅgh, pretending to be a sympathizer of the movement, and was arrested on 12 October 1923 at Mīāṅ Channū railway station, in Multān district. He was mercilessly tortured by police, yet he yielded no secret information to them. In the course of his trial in the sessions court, he refused to reply to any of the questions put to him. He however filed a written statement owning himself an active member of the Babar Akālī Jathā. The judge, J.K. Tapp, was inclined to be sympathetic because of his young age, but he had to record in his judgement : "This accused, young as he is, appears to have established a record for himself second only to that of Santa Singh accused, as to the offences in which he has been concerned in connection with this conspiracy. He is implicated in the murders of Buta Lambardar, Labh Singh Mistri, Hazara Singh of Bahibalpur, Ralla and Dittu of Kaulgarh, Ata Muhammad Patwari, in the 2nd and 3rd attempts on Labh Siṅgh of Dhada Fateh Singh, and in the murderous attack on Bishan Singh of Sandhara."

Dalīp Siṅgh was awarded the extreme penalty of the law and hanged on 27 February 1926, at that time not more than 19 years old.

BIBLIOGRAPHY

1. Ghosh, Kali Charan, *The Roll of Honour : Anecdotes*

of Indian Martyrs. Calcutta, 1965
2. Gurmukh Singh, Major, "Dalip Singh Dhamian," in *Child Heroes of Punjab.* Chandigarh, 1979
3. Nijjar, B.S., *History of the Babbar Akalis.* Jalandhar, 1987
4. Nijjhar, Milkhā Siṅgh, *Babbar Akālī Lahir dā Itihās.* Delhi, 1986
5. Babbar, Sundar Siṅgh, *Itihās Babbar Akālī Lahīr.* Amritsar, 1970

K.M.

DALĪP SIṄGH, SANT (1883-1948), son of Īshar Siṅgh and Har Kaur, was born in 1883 at the village of Lahrī, in Hoshiārpur district. He was hardly five years old, when his father died. He was brought up by his maternal grandfather, Nihāl Siṅgh, at his village Ḍumelī. He received his early education from a local Sikh priest, who also trained him in the singing of *gurbāṇī.*

Dalīp Siṅgh was a child with peculiar traits. He was fond of solitude. One day he went out and did not return home. He built for himself a cell (the site, now called Bābā Rāṇā) for meditation. He was then a youth of about twenty. He remained wrapped up in deep meditation for forty-eight days in his cell. As he refused to return home, the residents of the village built for him a cottage. He ground the grain into flour and did his own cooking, refusing to accept food even from his own mother. In his cottage, he started a small *laṅgar* (free kitchen) for the poor and needy. He was convinced that selfless service to fellow men was the essence of true religion and the highest worship of the Almighty. Whenever he came across a disabled, blind, dumb, lame, sick or orphaned child, he brought him to his cottage and looked after him. He brought up many such children and trained them for earning their livelihood. Sant Sarvan Siṅgh Ghandhārī, born blind, and Giānī Harbaṅs Siṅgh born a cripple, who are now running the *ḍerā* of Sant Bābā Dalīp Siṅgh, grew up under his care. The former was enabled to earn his Master's degree in Music (Classical and Instrumental) and the latter to qualify for practice in the indigenous system of medicine.

Bābā Dalīp Siṅgh combined with his saintly disposition a revolutionary urge. He gave shelter to the Babar Akālīs engaged in anti-government activities and provided them with food and money. He himself took part in the Akālī movement and led a *jathā* during the Jaito *morchā.* During the Hindu-Muslim riots in 1947, he saved the lives of many Muslims at great personal risk.

Sant Dalīp Siṅgh died in 1948. Apart from the *ḍerā* he founded, a Khālsā College at Ḍumelī commemorates his name.

G.S.P.

DALJĪT SIṄGH (d. 1937), one of the passengers on board the *S.S. Komagata Maru,* was born at the village of Kauṇī, now in Farīdkoṭ district. He passed his matriculation examination and became assistant editor on the *Pañjābī Bhaiṇ,* a journal sponsored by Sikh Kanyā Mahāvidyālaya, Fīrozpur, to promote the cause of women's education. At the age of 21, he left the Punjab to seek avenues for further education abroad. In Hong Kong, he met Bābā Gurdit Siṅgh, then negotiating the chartering of the *S.S. Komagata Maru* to take Indians to Canada after the country had passed new and stricter immigration laws. Daljīt Siṅgh became Bābā Gurdit Siṅgh's secretary and made the voyage with him to Vancouver where he carried on an extensive correspondence with the immigration authorities bent on expelling the ship from the harbour. In the melee at Budge Budge, near Calcutta, where the *Komagata Maru* passengers were fired upon, Bābā Gurdit Siṅgh and Daljīt Siṅgh were among those who escaped unhurt. Daljīt Siṅgh, avoiding arrest, went to Amritsar where he assumed the name of Rāi Siṅgh He came in contact with Master Tārā Siṅgh and joined the staff of the Shiromaṇī Gurdwārā Parbandhak Committee. He was arrested in the Akālī conspiracy case on the charge of having designs to establish Sikh *rāj* in the Punjab, and jailed for three years. He was released in September of 1926, along with Master Tārā Siṅgh, Gopāl Siṅgh Qaumī, Sohan Siṅgh Josh, and others. In the 1930's he served as manager of the Gurdwārā at Muktsar.

Daljīt Siṅgh, later Rāi Siṅgh, died on 8 December 1937.

BIBLIOGRAPHY

1. Josh, Sohan Singh, *Tragedy of Komagata Maru*. Delhi, 1975
2. Johnston, Hugh, *The Voyage of the Komagata Maru*. Oxford (Delhi), 1979

S.S.J.

DAL KHĀLSĀ is the term used to describe the militia which came into being during the turbulent period of the second half of the eighteenth century and which became a formidable fighting force of the Sikhs in the northwestern part of India. The first Khālsā army formed and led by the creator of the Khālsā, Gurū Gobind Siṅgh (1666-1708), had broken up at the time of the evacuation of Anandpur in December 1705. Another force, at one time 40,000 strong, raised by Bandā Siṅgh Bahādur (1670-1716) was scattered after the caputre and execution of its leader. The fierce persecution which overtook the Sikhs made the immediate re-formation of a similar force impossible, yet the Sikh warriors in small groups continued to challenge the State's might. Armed with whatever weapons they could lay their hands upon and living off the land, these highly mobile guerilla-bands or *jathās* remained active during the worst of times. It was not unusual however for the *jathās* to join together when the situation so demanded. Ratan Siṅgh Bhaṅgū, *Prachīn Panth Prakāsh,* records an early instance of the warrior bands of the Bārī Doāb (land between the Rivers Beās and Rāvī) being organized into four *tummans* or squadrons of 200 each, with specified area of operation and provision for mutual assistance in time of need. Moreover, it was customary for most *jathās* to congregate at Amritsar to celebrate Baisākhī and Dīvālī. Dīvān Darbārā Siṅgh (d. 1734), an elderly Sikh, acted on such occasions as the common leader of the entire congregation.

In 1733, Zakarīyā Khān, the Mughal governor of Lahore, having failed to suppress the Sikhs by force, planned to make terms with them and offered them a *jāgīr* or fief, the title of Nawāb to their leader and unhindered access to and residence at Amritsar. Kapūr Siṅgh, a senior and dedicated warrior, was accepted by Sikhs as their leader and invested with the title of Nawāb. Sikh soldiers grouped themselves around their leaders most of whom were stationed at Amritsar. In consideration of administrative convenience, Nawāb Kapūr Siṅgh divided the entire body of troops into two camps called Buḍḍhā Dal (the elderly group) and Taruṇā Dal (the younger group), respectively. Taruṇā Dal was further divided into five *jathās*, each with its own flag and drum. The compact with the government broke down in 1735 and, under pressure of renewed persecution, the Khālsā was again forced to split into smaller groups and seek shelter in hills and forests. Nādir Shāh's invasion in 1739 gave a severe blow to the crumbling Mughal empire, and this gave the Sikhs a chance to consolidate themselves. At their meeting on the occasion of Dīvālī following the death on 1 July 1745 of Zakarīyā Khān, they reorganized themselves into 25 groups of about 100 persons each. The number of *jathās* multiplied further and by March 1748 there were as many as 65 groups operating independently of each other, although they still acknowledged the pre-eminence of Nawāb Kapūr Siṅgh. By this time a new claimant to power had appeared on the scene. Ahmad Shāh Durrānī had launched his first invasion of India and occupied Lahore on 12

January 1748. On the Baisākhī day, 29 March 1748, when the Sikh *jathās* gathered at Amritsar, Nawāb Kapūr Siṅgh impressed upon them the need for solidarity. Through a *gurmatā* or resolution, the entire fighting force of the Khālsā was unified into a single body, called the Dal Khālsā, under the supreme command of Sardār Jassā Siṅgh Āhlūvālīā. The 65 bands were merged into 11 units, *misls,* each under a prominent leader and having a separate name and banner. The Dal Khālsā was a kind of loose confederacy, without any strict constitution. All *amritdhārī* Sikhs were considered members of the Dal Khālsā which was mainly a cavalry force. Anyone who was an active horseman and proficient in the use of arms could join any one of the eleven *misls,* having the option to change membership whenever desired. The *misls* were subject to the control of the Sarbatt Khālsā, the bi-annual assembly of the Panth at Amritsar. Akāl Takht was the symbol of the unity of the Dal Khālsā which was in a way the Sikh State in the making. The Dal, with its total estimated strength of 70,000, essentially consisted of cavalry; artillery and infantry elements were almost unknown to it.

The term Dal Khālsā, however, does not appear in any of the contemporary Indian chronicles before Browne. The title first appeared in James Browne's *India Tracts* published in 1788. He writes, "Since the Sicks [sic] became powerful and confederated for the purpose of conquest, they have called their confederacy *Khalsa Gee,* or the State, and their grand army *Dull Khalsa Gee,* or the Army of the State." Among the Indian writers, Sohan Lāl Sūrī, *'Umdat-ut-Twārīkh* refers to it thus: "They [the Sikh Sardārs] named their conquering armies as the Dal Khālsā Jīo."

The Dal Khālsā established its authority over most of the Punjab region in a short time. As early as 1749, the Mughal governor of the Punjab solicited its help in the suppression of a rebellion in Multān. In early 1758, the Dal Khālsā, in collaboration with the Marāṭhās, occupied Sirhind and Lahore. Within three months of the Vaḍḍā Ghallūghārā (*q.v.*) or the Greater Holocaust of 5 February 1762, the Dal Khālsā rose to defeat Ahmad Shāh's governor at Sirhind in April-May 1762 and the Shāh himself at Amritsar in October of the same year. Sirhind and its adjoining territories were occupied permanently in January 1764. The Khālsā thenceforward not only had the Punjab in their virtual possession, but also carried their victories right up to Delhi and beyond the Yamunā into the heart of the Gangetic Plain. Although they failed to sustain or consolidate their gains in that direction, they had liberated the Punjab from foreign rule inch by inch and had sealed forever the northwestern route for foreign invaders.

Themselves victims of the worst kind of religious tyranny, the leaders of the Dal Khālsā established a just and humane rule in the Punjab. After the initial period of predatory raids aimed at undermining the authority of the Mughal government, they established, like the *chauth* of the Marāṭhās, a system of *rākhī,* lit. protection, to protect the life and property of the people. *Rākhī* was a levy of a portion, usually one-fifth, of the revenue assessment of a territory as a fee for the guarantee of peace and protection. After the conquest of Sirhind in January 1764 when Sikh *sardārs* started occupying territory, the *misldārī* system came into operation. Peace that returned to the Punjab after half a century of turbulence resulted in increased prosperity of the people.

The removal from among its midst by death of the towering personality of Jassā Siṅgh Āhlūvālīā in 1783, virtually meant the end of the Dal Khālsā. Writing prophetically in the same year, a foreign observer, George Forster, *A Journey from Bengal to England,* records: "The discordant interests which agitate the Sicque [sic] nation, and the constitutional genius of the people, must incapacitate them, during the existence of these causes, from becoming a formidable offensive power .... Should any future cause call forth the combined efforts of the Sicques [sic] to maintain the existence of empire and religion, we may see some ambitious chief led on by his genius and success, and, absorbing the power of his associates, display, from the ruins of their commonwealth, the standard of monarchy ..." The observation became true seventeen years later when Mahārājā Raṇjīt Siṅgh occupied Lahore.

BIBLIOGRAPHY

1. Prinsep, Henry T., *Origin of the Sikh Power in the Punjab and Political Life of Maharaja Ranjit Singh.* Calcutta, 1834
2. Forster, George, *A Journey from Bengal to England.* London, 1798
3. Malcolm, John, *Sketch of the Sikhs* [Reprint]. Patiala, 1970
4. Ganda Singh, ed., *Early European Accounts of the Sikhs.* Calcutta, 1962
5. Gupta, Hari Ram, *History of the Sikhs,* vol. II. Delhi, 1978
6. Hasrat, B.J., *Life and Times of Ranjit Singh.* Hoshiarpur, 1977
7. Khushwant Singh, *A History of the Sikhs,* vol. I. Princeton, 1963
8. Harbans Singh, *The Heritage of the Sikhs.* Delhi, 1983
9. Bhaṅgū, Ratan Siṅgh, *Prāchīn Panth Prakāsh.* Amritsar, 1914
10. Giān Siṅgh, Giānī, *Panth Prakāsh*[Reprint]. Patiala, 1970

H.R.G.

ḌALLĀ, an old village, 6 km southeast of Sultānpur Lodhī (31° - 13'N, 75° - 12'E) in Kapūrthalā district of the Punjab, is one of the oldest centres of the Sikh faith. It had a flourishing *saṅgat* – a fact which has been noted by Bhāī Gurdās in one of his *Vārāṅ*. Prominent among the earliest devotees were Bhāī Pāro and Bhāī Lālū, contemporaries with Gurū Aṅgad and Gurū Amar Dās. According to Bhāī Manī Siṅgh, *Sikhāṅ dī Bhagat Mālā,* Gurū Amar Dās himself once visited Ḍallā. Gurū Arjan visited it in 1605 leading the marriage party of his son, Hargobind, who was married to (Mātā) Damodarī, of the family of Bhāī Pāro. There are a number of Gurdwārās raised in memory of the Gurūs and their Sikhs.

GURDWĀRĀ PRAKĀSH ASTHĀN BHĀĪ LĀLŪJĪ, most prominent of the local shrines, has a rectangular *dīvān* hall, in front of the sanctum. A high, domed tower stands at one end of the front verandah. The Gurū Granth Sāhib is also seated in Bhāī Lālū's *samādh,* a small domed structure, to the north of the hall.

GURDWĀRĀ JAÑJGHAR, an octagonal domed building, on a brick-paved platform in walled compound, marks the place where the marriage party accompanying (Gurū) Hargobind put up.

GURDWĀRĀ MĀTĀ DAMODARĪ JĪ, 100 metres to the west of the main building, marks the dwelling-house of the bride's parents where the nuptials were held on 15 February 1605. It is a small single-room shrine rectangular in shape, within a terraced compound. Opposite to the compound, across the village street, is an old *khūhī* or a narrow well called Khūhī Bhāī Pāro. A special congregation takes place in August every year.

GURDWĀRĀ BĀOLĪ SĀHIB, about 100 metres east of the village, is also a small rectangular room with a verandah in front. It stands next to the Bāolī, an open well with steps leading down to water level, which is said to have been constructed under the direction of Gurū Arjan.

All these shrines are managed by a village committee under the auspices of the Shiromaṇī Gurdwārā Parbandhak Committee. Thirty-two acres of land are assigned to them. A two-day religious fair is held in the month of Assū (September-October) at Gurdwārā Prakāsh Asthān Bhāī Lālū Jī. At Bāolī Sāhib is observed with special *dīvāns* the martyrdom day of Gurū Arjan (in May-June) and at Gurdwārā Mātā Damodarī Jī the anniversary of the marriage of Mātā Damodarī Jī.

BIBLIOGRAPHY

1. Manī Siṅgh, Bhāī, *Sikhāṅ dī Bhagat Mālā*. Amritsar, 1955
2. Tārā Siṅgh, *Srī Gur Tīrath Saṅgrahi*. Amritsar, n.d.
3. Ṭhākar Siṅgh, Giānī, *Srī Gurduāre Darshan*. Amritsar, 1923

M.G.S.

ḌALLĀ, BHĀĪ, a devout Sikh of the time of Gurū Arjan. Once he, accompanied by Bhāī Bhagīrath, Bhāī Jāpū and Bhāī Nivalā, waited upon Gurū Arjan and begged to be enlightened whether Gurū Nānak worshipped God in the *nirguṇa*, the unattributed, or *saguṇa*, the attributed form. The Gurū, as says Bhāī Manī Siṅgh, *Sikhāṅ dī Bhagat Mālā*, replied, "Gurū Nānak was the worshipper of the Name, *nām*, which covers both these attributes of God. You, too, should practise *nām* and seek refuge in the *saṅgat*." Bhāī Ḍallā and his companions were gratified to receive the Gurū's precept.

BIBLIOGRAPHY

1. Manī Siṅgh, Bhāī, *Sikhāṅ dī Bhagat Mālā*. Amritsar, 1955
2. Santokh Siṅgh, Bhāī, *Srī Gur Pratāp Sūraj Granth*. Amritsar, 1926-37

T.S.

ḌALLĀ, BHĀĪ (later Ḍall Siṅgh), a Siddhū Jaṭṭ and *chaudharī* or landlord of Talvaṇḍī Sābo, enthusiastically received Gurū Gobind Siṅgh when he arrived there with his entourage early in 1706, and attended diligently to the needs and comforts of the daily-growing *saṅgat*. According to Bhāī Santokh Siṅgh, *Srī Gur Pratāp Sūraj Granth*, Ḍallā maintained a private army of several hundred warriors of whom he was very proud. He more than once commiserated with Gurū Gobind Siṅgh on the events that had overtaken him, boastfully adding that had the Gurū called him for help he would have joined him with his bold warriors and that he (the Gurū) would have been saved much of the travail. Gurū Gobind Siṅgh every time dismissed the topic saying, "God's will must prevail. It is useless to brood over the past." Once as Ḍallā was repeating his boast, two artisans of Lahore came and presented the Gurū with two costly muzzle-loading guns. The Gurū asked Bhāī Ḍallā to provide a couple of his men as targets for him to test the range and striking power of the weapons. The strange demand stunned Ḍallā and put his men out of their wits, and none of them came forward. The Gurū thereupon invited two Raṅghreṭā Sikhs, father and son, who happened to be busy tying their turbans near by. They both came running, turbans in hand, each trying to be in front of the other in order to be the first to face the bullet. Bhāī Ḍallā, astonished at the Sikhs' spirit of sacrifice, was ashamed and learnt to be humble. He took the initiation of the K͟hālsā, receiving the name of Ḍall Siṅgh. A small domed shrine within the precincts of Tak͟ht Damdamā Sāhib at Talvaṇḍī Sābo honours Ḍall Siṅgh's memory to this day. A sword and shield and a few other articles claimed to have been bestowed upon him by Gurū Gobind Siṅgh are preserved in the descendant family as sacred relics.

BIBLIOGRAPHY

1. Santokh Siṅgh, Bhāī, *Srī Gur Pratāp Sūraj Granth*. Amritsar, 1926-37
2. Giān Siṅgh, Giānī, *Twārīk͟h Gurū K͟hālsā*. Patiala, 1970
3. Sukhā Siṅgh, Bhāī, *Gurbilās Dasviṅ Pātshāhī*. Lahore, 1912
4. Macauliffe, Max Arthur, *The Sikh Religion*. Oxford, 1909

P.S.P.

ḌALLEVĀLĪĀ MISL. *See* MISLS

ḌALLŪ, BHĀĪ, a Rihān K͟hatrī of Burhānpur, mentioned by Bhāī Gurdās, *Vārāṅ,* XI. 30, among prominent Sikhs of the time of Gurū Hargobind.

See BHAGVĀN DĀS, BHĀĪ

BIBLIOGRAPHY

1. Manī Siṅgh, Bhāī, *Sikhāṅ dī Bhagat Mālā.* Amritsar, 1955
2. Santokh Siṅgh, Bhāī, *Srī Gur Pratāp Sūraj Granth.* Amritsar, 1926-37

B.S.

DALPATI, son of Bhīm of the village of Maur in district Baṭhiṇḍā of the Punjab, served Gurū Gobind Siṅgh at Damdamā Sāhib (Talvaṇḍī Sābo) with a potful of curds and won his approbation. According to *Sākhī Pothī,* Gurū Gobind Siṅgh bestowed a robe of honour on him.

BIBLIOGRAPHY

1. Santokh Siṅgh, Bhāī, *Srī Gur Pratāp Sūraj Granth.* Amritsar, 1926-37
2. Giān Siṅgh, Giānī, *Twārīk͟h Gurū K͟hālsā.* Patiala, 1970
3. *Mālvā Desh Raṭan dī Sākhī Pothī.* Amritsar, 1968

P.S.P.

DAL SIṄGĀR, lit. ornament or embellishment (*siṅgār*) of the army (*dal*), was the name of one of Gurū Gobind Siṅgh's warhorses. According to Bhāī Santokh Siṅgh, *Srī Gur Pratāp Sūraj Granth,* one Kapūrā Jaṭṭ, "master of several villages in the jungle," (the reference probably is to Chaudharī Kapūrā Bairāṛ of Koṭ Kapūrā, founder of the Faridkoṭ family), had purchased this horse for Rs 1,100 and sent it to Gurū Gobind Siṅgh as a present. The Gurū assigned it to his personal stables and named it Dal Siṅgār.

BIBLIOGRAPHY

1. Santokh Siṅgh, Bhāī, *Srī Gur Pratāp Sūraj Granth.* Amritsar, 1926-37

2. Kāhn Siṅgh, Bhāī, *Gurushabad Ratnākar Mahān Kosh.* [Reprint]. Patiala, 1981

M.G.S.

DAL SIṄGH (d. 1845), son of Santokh Siṅgh, a follower of Kanhaiyā *misl* under Jai Siṅgh, and of village Talvaṇḍī in Gurdāspur district, fought in most of Mahārājā Raṇjīt Siṅgh's campaigns. He inherited Talvaṇḍī and some neighbouring villages. Dal Siṅgh was killed in the first Anglo-Sikh war in 1845 and his estates were resumed by the British.

BIBLIOGRAPHY

Griffin, Lepel and C.F. Massy, *Chiefs and Families of Note in the Punjab.* Lahore, 1909

S.S.B.

DAL SIṄGH, BHĀĪ (1885-1921), one of the Nankāṇā Sāhib martyrs, was born on 8 Assū 1942 Bk / 23 September 1885, the son of Bhāī Musaddā Siṅgh and Māī Gulābī, a Kamboj couple of Nizāmpur village in Amritsar district. The family later migrated to Chakk No. 38 Nizāmpur Devā Siṅghvālā in the newly developed canal district of Sheik͟hūpurā, now in Pakistan. Dal Siṅgh remained illiterate, but had committed to memory several of the religious and historical compositions. He also listened regularly to the local *granthī* reading from the *Akālī,* a newspaper floated by Akālī reformers in May 1920. He had already received the *pāhul* or vows of the K͟hālsā. He was one of the fifteen Sikhs of his village who joined Bhāī Lachhmaṇ Siṅgh Dhārovālī's *jathā* or batch of volunteers and laid down their lives for the liberation of Gurdwārā Janam Asthān, Nankāṇā Sāhib, on 20 February 1921.

See NANKĀṆĀ SĀHIB MASSACRE

BIBLIOGRAPHY

Shamsher, Gurbak͟hsh Siṅgh, *Shahīdī Jīvan.* Nankana Sahib, 1938

G.S.G.

DAMDAMĀ SĀHIB, also known as Tavwaṇḍī

Sābo (29° - 59'N, 75° - 5'E), a small town 28 km southeast of Baṭhiṇḍā in the Punjab, is sacred to the Sikhs as the seat of one of their five *takhts* or centres of highest religious authority. Damdamā Sāhib, place of repose where the Gurū had some respite after a period of continuous turmoil, was visited successively by Gurū Tegh Bahādur while travelling in these parts in the early 1670's, and Gurū Gobind Siṅgh who put up here for over nine months in 1706. Tradition also recounts a visit by Gurū Nānak during one of his journeys across the country. In the earlier half of the eighteenth century, the place became for the Sikhs a cantonment as well as a seat of learning. It gained renown especially under Bābā Dīp Siṅgh Shahīd (d. 1757). The Shiromaṇī Gurdwārā Parbandhak Committee approved, vide Resolution No. 32, dated 18 November 1966, Damdamā Sāhib as a *takht,* adjured the Khālsā to keep this *takht* in mind as they did in the past while saying their *ardās,* and recommended to the Punjab Government amendment to Gurdwara Act so that the *jathedār* of the *takht,* like those of the other four *takhts,* could be counted as an *ex officio* member of the Shiromaṇī Committee. Several shrines, *sarovars* and *buṅgās* survive as relics of its historical past.

GURDWĀRĀ MAÑJĪ SĀHIB SRĪ GURŪ TEGH BAHĀDUR PĀTSHĀHĪ NAUVĪṄ, also called Darbār Sāhib, is a flat-roofed rectangular room, marking the site where Gurū Tegh Bahādur is believed to have put up and preached. Daily gatherings for religious prayers, *kīrtan* and discourses take place here. Sacred relics including two swords, one muzzle-loading gun, a seal and an old copy of the Gurū Granth Sāhib are preserved here in a domed cubicle behind the sanctum. Another relic, a mirror, said to have been presented to Gurū Gobind Siṅgh by the *saṅgat* of Delhi, is displayed in the hall. Of the two swords, one is believed to have belonged to Gurū Gobind Siṅgh and the other, heavy and double-edged, to Bābā Dīp Siṅgh. The muzzle-loader is believed to be the one Gurū Gobind Siṅgh received as a present (*See* THAṚĀ SĀHIB below).

GURDWĀRĀ MAÑJĪ SĀHIB PĀTSHĀHĪ IX *ate* X is another shrine dedicated to Gurū Tegh Bahādur. About 100 metres to the west of Darbār Sāhib, it marks the spot where he used to sit supervising the digging of the tank, Gurūsar. Gurū Gobind Siṅgh also sanctified the site by a visit during his stay at Talvaṇḍī Sābo. The present building, constructed by the Sant Sevak Jathā, Buṅgā Mastūāṇā, is a marble-floored hall with a circular tower topped by a domed pavilion at each corner. The Gurū Granth Sāhib is seated on a canopied seat of white marble, tastefully carved, in a square sanctum marked off by marble-lined pillars. Above the sanctum are two storeys of square rooms overtopped by a lotus dome. The gold-plated pinnacle has an umbrella-shaped finial with a *khaṇḍā* on top.

GURŪSAR SAROVAR, a bathing tank, 130 x 90 metres, with a 10-metre wide marbled pavement around it, was got excavated originally by Gurū Tegh Bahādur. He is said to have inaugurated the work by digging the first few sods and carrying the earth in his *doshālā* or rug. Gurū Gobind Siṅgh is believed to have had the tank desilted and deepened. The lining and marble paving are works recently carried out.

GURDWĀRĀ NIVĀS ASTHĀN DAMDAMĀ SĀHIB PĀTSHĀHĪ X, a multi-storeyed octagonal tower, adjoining the Darbār Sāhib, marks the apartments of Gurū Gobind Siṅgh. According to *Sākhī Pothī,* when Gurū Tegh Bahādur arrived at Talvaṇḍī Sābo, he halted at the base of a huge ant-hill, which he saluted as he alighted. Questioned by the Sikhs accompanying him, he explained, "A grand temple, nine spears in height, with golden pinnacles will be erected on that spot by the great one who comes after me. Let my shrine be at the foot of his temple." The Gurū Granth Sāhib is now seated in a domed room at the top floor of the tower.

TAKHT SRĪ DAMDAMĀ SĀHIB, adjoining the Darbār Sāhib on the east, marks the site where Gurū Gobind Siṅgh during his stay here held his daily assemblies. Gurū Tegh Bahādur had called Talvaṇḍī Sābo Gurū kī Kāshī, predicting that "many scholars, philosophers, theologians, copyists with elegant hand, students and devotees will adorn the place." The prophecy came true when learned Sikhs poured in from far and near to be with Gurū Gobind Siṅgh. Among them was Bhāī Manī Siṅgh who came from Delhi escorting Mātā Sundarī and Mātā Sāhib Devāṅ, the Gurū's consorts separated from him after the evacuation of Anandpur. Gurū Gobind Siṅgh had Bhāī Manī Siṅgh prepare a fresh copy of the Gurū Granth Sāhib under his own supervision. The spot where this work was carried out is still shown the pilgrims. Copies continued to be prepared here from this recension. One such copy preserved here is believed to have been prepared by Bābā Dīp Siṅgh Shahīd himself. It contains 707 leaves excluding the list of contents spread over 29 leaves. It was from here that the Gurū issued his commands and letters to far-flung Sikh *saṅgats.* The place became in fact a centre of Sikh learning. This character it has maintained ever since as the home of what is known as Damdamī Ṭaksāl, or the Damdamā School of Learning.

The present building of the Takht Srī Damdamā Sāhib, constructed during the 1970's under the supervision of Sant Sevā Siṅgh of Srī Kesgaṛh, is a spacious high-ceilinged hall, with a pavilion, at either end. The *takht* (throne) proper is a 2 metre high square platform lined with white marble and marked off with marble-lined columns in the southern part of the hall. This is the sanctum sanctorum on which the Gurū Granth Sāhib is seated. After the evening service the Holy Book is carried to the old Mañjī Sāhib in a procession of hymn-singing devotees. The interior of the sanctum is decorated with reflecting glass pieces of varying colours set in geometrical and floral designs. Over the sanctum, above the hall roof, is a domed square room topped by a tall gold-plated pinnacle and an umbrella-shaped finial, with a *khaṇḍā* at the apex. Octagonal towers at the hall corners have also domed pavilions above them. All these domes are lined with glazed tiles in white, light yellow and light blue colours.

GURDWĀRĀ MĀTĀ SUNDARĪ JĪ *ate* MĀTĀ SĀHIB DEVĀṄ JĪ, to the southeast of the Takht Srī Damdamā Sāhib, marks the place where the holy ladies lived during their stay at Talvaṇḍī Sābo in 1706. The Gurdwārā comprises a square domed room with the Gurū Granth Sāhib seated on a platform in the middle of it.

GURDWĀRĀ LIKHANSAR is a square hall, including a domed sanctum within it, at the southeastern corner of the *sarovar,* holy tank. According to Bhāī Kuir Siṅgh, *Gurbilās Pātshāhī X,* there used to be a pool of water here in the days of Gurū Gobind Siṅgh, who sitting here sometimes would have reed-pens for the writers made and then throw them into the pool. Once, Bhāī Ḍallā, the local chief converted a disciple, entreated him to explain why he ordered thousands of pens to be cut and thrown away. To quote the *Sākhī Pothī,* the Gurū said: "Thousands of Sikhs will hereafter study the holy texts in this place and then pens will come into use. This is our Kāshī (seat of learning); those who study here will cast off their ignorance and rise to be authors, poets and commentators."

GURDWĀRĀ JAṆḌSAR, half a kilometre to the

northwest of Ta<u>kh</u>t Srī Damdamā Sāhib, marks the place referred to as Jaṇḍīāṇā in old chronicles. Here Gurū Gobind Siṅgh used to disburse largesse to his warriors. The Gurdwārā now comprises a domed sanctum, with a small *sarovar* adjacent to it.

ṬIBBĪ SĀHIB is an open space close to a pond known as Mahalsar. Here Gurū Gobind Siṅgh trained his Sikhs in mock battles.The site continues to be the venue for the traditional Holā Mahallā and Baisākhī.

NĀNAKSAR, an 80-metre square *sarovar* halfway between the Ta<u>kh</u>t Sāhib and Gurdwārā Jaṇḍsar, was till lately a natural pond called Nānaksar. It was so named in the belief that Gurū Nānak had stayed on the bank of it during his visit to Talvaṇḍī.

BURJ BĀBĀ DĪP SIṄGH, a 20-metre high tower with a dome at the top adjoining the northeast corner of the Ta<u>kh</u>t Sāhib, was constructed by Bābā Dīp Siṅgh of the Shahīd *misl*, who remained at Talvaṇḍī to look after the shrines after Gurū Gobind Siṅgh had left the place to resume his travels. He is also credited with the sinking of the well which still supplies drinking water to the complex.

SAMĀDH BHĀĪ ḌALL SIṄGH, a small domed shrine standing a bare 30 metres to the south of the Ta<u>kh</u>t Sāhib, marks the site where Chudharī Ḍallā, Ḍall Siṅgh after he had received the vows of the <u>Kh</u>ālsā at the hands of Gurū Gobind Siṅgh, was cremated.

THAṚĀ SĀHIB BHĀĪ BĪR SIṄGH *ate* DHĪR SIṄGH, a small room in the vicinity of Burj Bābā Dīp Siṅgh, has recently replaced a platform (*thaṛā*, in Punjabi) which marked the place where two Raṅghreṭā Sikhs, named, according to local tradition, Bīr Siṅgh and Dhīr Siṅgh, father and son respectively, offered themselves as targets for the Gurū to test a muzzle-loading gun presented to him by a Sikh. According to Bhāī Santokh Siṅgh, *Srī Gur Pratāp Sūraj Granth,* Chaudharī Ḍallā once boasted about the loyalty and courage of his soldiers. Gurū Gobind Siṅgh asked him to provide a couple of his men as targets so that he could test the range and striking power of the new weapon. The strange demand stunned Ḍallā and his men out of their wits, and none of them did in fact come forward. The Gurū thereupon called out the two Sikhs who were at that moment busy tying their turbans. They came running, turbans in hand, each trying to be in front of the other in order to be the first to face the bullet. Ḍallā, astonished at the Sikhs' spirit of sacrifice, learnt to be humble.

BUṄGĀ MASTŪĀṆĀ SĀHIB, established in 1923, by Sant Atar Siṅgh, is not a historical shrine as such but is a prestigious institution for training young scholars in the theory and practice of the Sikh faith. It is a vast complexcomprising dormitories, rows of cubicles, a dining hall, an agricultural farm and a magnificent *gurdwārā* with a large assembly hall.

All these shrines, other than Buṅgā Mastūāṇā Sāhib, are under the management of the Shiromaṇī Gurdwārā Parbandhak Committee, which took over control in 1963 from the family of the custodian, Captain Ranjīt Siṅgh of Shāhzādpur.

BIBLIOGRAPHY

1. Ṭārā Siṅgh, *Srī Gur Tīrath Saṅgrahi.* Amritsar, n.d.
2. Ṭhākar Siṅgh, Giānī, *Srī Gurduāre Darshan.* Amritsar, 1933
3. *Mālvā Desh Raṭan dī Sākhī Pothī.* Amritsar, 1968
4. Harbans Singh, *Guru Gobind Singh.* Chandigarh, 1966

M.G.S.

DĀMODAR, BHĀĪ, a pious Sikh of Sultānpur Lodhī. He visited Amritsar along with the *saṅgat* of that town to receive instruction at the hands of Gurū Arjan. His name figures among the devotees of the Gurū in Bhāī Gurdās, *Vārāṅ*, XI. 21.

See ĀKUL, BHĀĪ, and BHIKHĀ, BHAṬṬ

BIBLIOGRAPHY

1. Manī Siṅgh, Bhāī, *Sikhāṅ dī Bhagat Mālā*. Amritsar, 1955
2. Santokh Siṅgh, Bhāī, *Srī Gur Pratāp Sūraj Granth*. Amritsar, 1926-37

T.S.

DAMODARĪ, MĀTĀ (1597-1631), daughter of Narāiṇ Dās, a Julkā Khatrī of the village of Ḍallā, 6 km southeast of Sultānpur Lodhī in Kapūrthalā district of the Punjab, was married to Gurū Hargobind (1595-1644) on 15 February 1605. She gave birth to a son, Bābā Gurdittā (b. 1613), and a daughter, Bībī Vīro (b. 1615). She died at Ḍaraulī Bhāī now in Fạrīdkoṭ district on 13 July 1631. A small shrine on the outskirts of the village marks the site where the cremation took place.

BIBLIOGRAPHY

1. *Gurbilās Chhevīṅ Pātshāhī*. Patiala, 1970
2. Chhibbar, Kesar Siṅgh, *Baṅsāvalīnāmā Dasāṅ Pātshāhīāṅ Kā*. Chandigarh, 1972
3. Macauliffe, Max Arthur, *The Sikh Religion*. Oxford, 1909

Gn.S.

DĀN (Skt. *dāna* from the root *dā* 'to give') means the act of giving or that which is given either as charity or alms or as offering, fee or reward for spiritual instruction received or for religious rite or ritual performed. The latter, however, is more appropriately called *dakṣiṇā*. *Dān* (charity or alms-giving), according to the Brāhmaṇical code as well as the code of Manu, is a means of earning spiritual merit, and is thus a religious obligation and may not necessarily be the result of a feeling of compassion or pity, though the humanitarian motive cannot be completely excluded from the concept of *dān*. The mode of *dān* and the selection of person worthy of receiving it may, however, differ. For example, a Brāhmaṇ, according to Hindu tradition, retains preferential status as a fit recipient of *dān*. Next come wandering ascetics, and then ordinary beggars seeking alms. Orphans, widows and destitutes are also considered to be deserving of sympathy and help. According to Hindu texts, Kṣatrīyas and Vaiśyas are expressly forbidden to receive *dān*, while "all mendicants subsist through subsistence afforded by householders," and "for the Brahmachārīs (celibate students) not to beg alms is a sin," for it is their "special duty to beg alms for their teacher." On the other hand, most unworthy recipients of *dān* are the criminals, drunkards, gamblers and other evil-doers. There are unworthy donors too, such as prostitutes, gamblers and bandits.

Buddhism and Jainism laid great stress on compassion and liberality, but they rejected the claims of Brāhmaṇs as special recipients of alms. The *Jātaka* literature celebrates the virtue of giving; the Boddhisattva gives away everything – his wealth, clothes, food, his own body and even the religious merit he may have accumulated. But both Buddhist and Jain monks themselves depend for their subsistence on the alms and donations from the laity. The householders are therefore enjoined to give alms to the monks and to donate liberally for the upkeep of monasteries and other charitable institutions.

The word *dān* as well as the concept has been assimilated into the Sikh tradition. Though there exist no codified injunctions about it, the practice of *dān* is a significant feature of the Sikh way of life. The emphasis here is more on giving than on receiving. No fixed group or class of people is specified as favoured recipients of *dān*. Nor is any particular commodity out of material belongings considered especially sanctified for purposes of *dān*. However, whatever is given away in *dān* must have been earned by one's honest labour. Says Gurū Nānak: "He, O

Nānak, who himself lives by his honest labour and yet gives away something out of his hands, has alone found the (true) way" (GG, 1245). There are numerous other verses in the Gurū Granth Sāhib extolling the virtue of *dān*. Also from Gurū Nānak, "He alone realizes the truth who is truly instructed, who is compassionate towards all living beings and who dispenses *dān*" (GG, 468). A *gurmukh* or true devotee is advised to practise "*nām* (remembrance of the Divine Name), *dān* and *isnān* (holy bathing)" (GG, 942). Gurū Arjan, Nānak V : "Meditate on the Lord's Name, listen to the Lord's Name being recited and to all render *dān*" (GG, 135). For himself Gurū Nānak seeks the *dān* "of the dust from underneath the feet of the holy ones which, if obtained, to my forehead would I apply" (GG, 468). In the words of Gurū Arjan: "The most desirable boon to beg for is to beg of the *Gurū* love of singing the Lord's laudation" (GG, 1018). In his daily *ardās* or supplicatory prayer, the highest form of *dān* (*dānāṅ sir dān*) a Sikh seeks is the *nām-dān*, gift of God's Name.

Sikhism does not countenance renunciation of material goods, nor does it deprecate worldly callings. The popular aphorism *kirt karnī, nām japṇā, vaṇḍ chhakṇā* (to earn one's living by the labour of one's hands, to repeat the Name of God and to eat only after sharing with the others one's victuals) forms an essential part of its ethical code. Whereas *dān* of material goods is commended, one overriding implication is that what is given away has been acquired through honourable means. Another requisite is that *dān* must be given with a willing heart. It should be the result of a spontaneous urge for an humanitarian act. As Gurū Aṅgad, Nānak II, says, "Giving under compulsion earns no merit nor does it benefit anyone ; excellent is the deed, O Nānak, which is performed with pleasure" (GG, 787). Another shade especially stressed in the Sikh tradition is that *dān* be proffered in all humility and in an utterly selfless spirit. It should not create a sense of pride or ego in the mind of one who gives. Ego (*haumai*) vitiates the act of charity. Says Gurū Tegh Bahādur: "If one performing pilgrimages, observing fasts and giving *dān* nourishes in his mind a sense of pride, all such acts remain fruitless like the bathing of an elephant (who casts dust over his body after bath)" (GG, 1428). To dispense *dān*, one need not necessarily be affluent. A simple meal served by an humble labourer to a casual guest is more meritorious than a sumptuous feast given by a rich man to professional mendicants.

In the Sikh tradition, all *dān* or offering is in the name of the Gurū and, usually, through *golak* (treasure, or receptacle kept in a *gurdwārā* for the devotees' offerings) of the Gurū or the Panth representing the Gurū. The channels for *dān* to flow into the Gurū's treasury are by now well established. First, the dictum *gharīb kī rasnā, Gurū kī golak* (a destitute's tongue, i.e. mouth, is the Gurū's till) sets the general principle that the primary object of charity is to feed the needy. This is done through the systematized and organized institution known as Gurū kā Laṅgar. The second institutionalized channel for *dān* is *dasvandh* (lit. tithes) or one-tenth of his earning a Sikh is required to set apart for the welfare of the community. Contributions may be made at any recognized centre – the local *gurdwārā*, any historical shrine, an orphange, school, charitable hospital, and the like.

In the *ardās* or Sikhs' daily prayer are listed the categories of *dān* a Sikh supplicates for. The primary one is the *dān* or gift of the Holy Name. He prays, besides, for the *dān* of the ideal Sikh way of life, the *dān* of true Sikh conduct and discipline, the *dān* of unfaltering faith in Sikh principles, the *dān* of unflinching trust in the Gurū, the *dān* of company of pious Sikhs, the *dān* of pilgrimage to the Harimandar at Amritsar and other sacred places, and the *dān* of holy bath at Amritsar. The gifts that a Sikh supplicates for are for the whole community and not for himself alone. This sharing of blessing is part of the Sikh way of life.

BIBLIOGRAPHY

1. Sher Singh, *The Philosophy of Sikhism*. Lahore, 1944
2. Avtar Singh, *Ethics of the Sikhs*. Patiala, 1970
3. Nripinder Singh, *The Sikh Moral Tradition*. Delhi, 1990

T.S.

DĀNĪ, BĪBĪ, was the elder daughter of Gurū Amar Dās (1479-1574). Not much is known about her life except that she was married to Bhāī Rāmā and that the couple came to live at Goindvāl founded by Gurū Amar Dās.

BIBLIOGRAPHY

1. Santokh Siṅgh, Bhāī, *Srī Gur Pratāp Sūraj Granth*. Amritsar, 1926-37
2. Chhibar, Kesar Siṅgh, *Baṅsāvalīnāmā Dasāṅ Pātshāhīāṅ Kā*. Chandigarh, 1972
3. Macauliffe, Max Arthur, *The Sikh Religion*. Oxford, 1909

Hn.S.

DĀN SIṄGH, a Brār Jaṭṭ of the village of Mahimā Sarjā in present-day Baṭhiṇḍā district of the Punjab, joined along with his son the contingent of Brāṛs raised by Gurū Gobind Siṅgh after his escape from Chamkaur in December 1705. Dān Siṅgh by virtue of his devotion and daring soon won the Gurū's trust as well as the leadership of the Brāṛ force. The anonymous author of *Mālvā Des Raṭan dī Sākhī Pothī* states that he was appointed *asupālī (aśvapāl)* or keeper of horses. It was at his suggestion that Gurū Gobind Siṅgh chose a high ground near the *ḍhāb* or pool of Khidrāṇā (now known as Ṭibbī Sāhib near Muktsar), to defend himself against the pursuing host of the *faujdār* of Sirhind. When, during the Gurū's journey towards Talvaṇḍī Sābo, the Brāṛs became restive and demanded their arrears of pay from the Gurū, Dān Siṅgh tried to pacify them and advised them to be patient. As they remained adamant and sought immediate payment, the Gurū halted in the open near Chhateāṇā village and disbursed pay to all men who, according to the *Mālvā Desh Raṭan dī Sākhī Pothī*, numbered 500 cavalry and 900 foot. At the end, as the Guru asked Dān Siṅgh to come forward and receive his pay, he answered, "Be pleased to give me *sikkhī* (Sikh faith) instead, O True King! Of worldly possessions I have enough." The Gurū was pleased to hear this answer and remarked, "You have saved the honour of the faith for Mālvā as Mahāṅ Siṅgh (*See* CHĀLĪ MUKTE) saved it for Majhā." Dān Siṅgh received the vows of the Kẖālsā. Later, Gurū Gobind Siṅgh told him to ask for a boon, but the only wish Dān Siṅgh expressed was that the Gurū visit his village which was close at hand. The Gurū obliged him and blessed him as well as his co-villagers.

BIBLIOGRAPHY

1. Santokh Siṅgh, Bhāī, *Srī Gur Pratāp Sūraj Granth*. Amritsar, 1926-37
2. Bhallā, Sarūp Dās, *Mahimā Prakāsh*. Patiala, 1971
3. *Mālvā Desh Raṭan dī Sākhī Pothī*. Amritsar, 1968

P.S.P.

DĀRĀ SHUKOH, PRINCE (1615-1659), the eldest son of Prince Kẖurram (later Emperor Shāh Jahāṅ), was born on 30 March 1615 at Ajmer. Following the failure of his father's rebellion against his grandfather, Emperor Jahāṅgīr, Dārā and his brother, Auraṅgzīb, were sent to the Emperor as hostages. They arrived at Lahore in June 1626 and re-joined their father only after the latter's coronation on 4 February 1628. Educated under eminent Muslim scholars and trained in the affairs of State, Dārā was given his first military rank or *mansab* and assigned a *jāgīr* at the age of 18. He was appointed, at different times, *sūbahdār* of Allāhābad, Punjab, Gujarāt, Multān and Kābul. At Allāhābād he came in contact with the famous Chistī saint, Shāh Muhibullāh and, while in the Punjab, he developed particular attachment to the Qādirī saints, Miāṅ Mīr amd Mullā Shāh. According to Sikh chroniclers, he was also acquainted with Gurū Har Rāi (1630-61). Not very successful as a military commander or civil administrator, Dārā Shukoh was more interested in philosophical and literary pursuits. A predominant influence upon him was that of Upaniṣadic and Sūfī thought. Among his literary works is *Sirr-i-Akbar*, the great secret, which, completed in 1657, is a translation in Persian of 50 Upaniṣads. He possessed considerable knowledge of Sanskrit, and kept several Sanskrit scholars in his employ. Another work associated with him is *Mukālmah Bābā Lāl wa Dārā Shukoh*. Compiled by Munshī Chandra Bhān Brāhmaṇ, it records a dialogue between the prince and Bābā Lāl Dās, a Bairāgī *sādhū*. Popular with the commonalty for his liberal outlook, Dārā was also the most favoured son of his father. Highest honours were showered on him. He was granted the *mansab* of 60,000 *zāt* and 40,000 *sowār*, a command greater than even the combined commands of all his younger brothers. On 3 February 1655, he was given the title of Shāh-i-Buland Iqbāl and a seat on a gold throne by the side of the Emperor's throne. This excited the jealousy of the other princes who started conspiring against him. In September 1657, Shāh Jahāṅ fell ill with strangury. Despairing of his life, he made his last will appointing Dārā as the heir apparent. As the news reached the brothers – Shujā' in Bengal, Auraṅgzīb in the Deccan and Murād in Gujarāt – Auraṅgzīb, the ablest as also the most ruthless of the three, at once won over the pleasure-loving and indolent Murād to his side and made preparation to advance on the imperial capital. Auraṅgzīb marched from Burhānpur on 20 March 1657 and was joined by Murād and his army on 14 April. An imperial army sent to check the advance of the rebel princes was routed at Dharmat, near Ujjain, on 5 May. In a decisive battle fought on 29 May 1657 at Sāmūgaṛh near Āgrā, Dārā, who was personally in command, was defeated. He fled towards the Punjab. Auraṅgzīb sent a strong army in pursuit. According to Sarūp Dās Bhallā, *Mahimā Prakāsh*, Dārā, after crossing the River Beās, called on Gurū Har Rāi, then at Goindvāl. Gurū Har Rāi in order to delay the pursuers, deployed his warriors along the river and blocked the ferry for about six hours. Dārā's cause was, however, hopeless. He assembled an army of 20,000 men in Lahore, but fled to Multān on 18 August 1657, without giving a fight. Pursued from place to place through Sindh, Rājasthān, Gujarāt and Balūchistān, he was eventually captured and brought to Delhi, where he was put to death on the night of 30-31 August 1659.

BIBLIOGRAPHY

1. Bhallā, Sarūp Dās, *Mahimā Prakāsh*. Patiala, 1971
2. Khushwant Singh, *A History of the Sikhs*, vol. I. Princeton, 1963
3. Sharma, Sri Ram, *Religious Policy of the Mughal Emperors*. Bombay, 1962
4. Harbans Singh, *The Heritage of the Sikhs*. Delhi, 1983

K.A.N.

ḌARAULĪ BHĀĪ, Bhāī kī Ḍaraulī, or simply Ḍaraulī, village 14 km west of Mogā (30°-48'N, 75°-10'E), in Farīdkoṭ district is sacred to Gurū Hargobind who stayed here for fairly long periods on more than one occasion. His brother-in-law, Bhāī Sāīṅ Dās, the husband of Mātā Damodarī's elder sister, Māī Rāmoṅ, lived in Ḍaraulī. The couple were more than mere relations of the Gurū; they were his devoted disciples and felt honoured in rendering service to him. Bhāī Sāīṅ Dās had built a new house, but would not occupy it until the Gurū had come and stayed in it. Their heart's desire was fulfilled when Gurū Hargobind and his family arrived at Ḍaraulī in 1613. The Gurū's eldest son, Bābā Gurdittā, was born here on 15 November 1613. The second long stay of the Gurū at Ḍaraulī, in 1631, ended sadly. Mātā Damodarī, Māī Rāmoṅ, Bhāī Sāīṅ Dās and the Gurū's parents-in-law, Bhāī Naraiṇ Dās and Mātā Dayā Kaur, died one after the other within a few days. After performing the obsequies, Gurū Hargobind sent his own family to Kartārpur with Bābā Gurdittā, and himself went towards Bhāī Rūpā. The memory of the holy family was perpetuated in Ḍaraulī through the establishment of several shrines, now being controlled by the Shiromaṇī Gurdwārā Parbandhak Committee.

AṄGĪṬHĀ (SAMĀDH) MĀTĀ DAMODARĪ JĪ, a small shrine, marks the spot where Mātā Damodarī, her parents and her sister and her sister's husband were cremated.

GURDWĀRĀ DAMDAMĀ SĀHIB PĀTSHĀHĪ CHHEVĪṄ marks the site where Gurū Hargobind had set up camp and where he used to call religious assemblies. The present building, constructed in 1963, consists of a large marble-floored hall, with a square sanctum in the middle. There are two storeys of square rooms and a lotus dome above the sanctum. There are decorative domes and domed pavilions at the corners of the hall. The *sarovar*, holy tank, on a flank and lined with old-type bricks, is of much older construction.

JANAM ASTHĀN BĀBĀ GURDITTĀ JĪ is inside the village, in the midst of an extensive compound that was once the *havelī* of Bhāī Sāīṅ Dās. Constructed in 1970, the central building, in which the Gurū Granth Sāhib is placed, is a circular hall on a high plinth, with four storeys of square rooms rising above it topped by a lotus dome and a golden pinnacle.

GURŪ KĀ KHŪH is an old well believed to have been sunk under the orders of Gurū Hargobind himself.

The relics, preserved in a private house near Janam Asthān Bābā Gurdittā Jī, include a rosary with eight glass beads, a small scrubber, a huge wooden box, three letters and four garments. A volume of the Gurū Granth Sāhib known as Bhāī Nand Chand Vālī Bīṛ, is also preserved here. Bhāī Nand Chand was the *masand* of Ḍaraulī during Gurū Gobind Siṅgh's time. He was a reputed warrior who had fought bravely in the battle of Bhaṅgāṇī.

BIBLIOGRAPHY

1. *Gurbilās Pātshāhī Chhevīṅ*. Patiala, 1970
2. Tārā Siṅgh, *Srī Gur Tīrath Saṅgrahi*. Amritsar, n.d.
3. Ṭhākar Siṅgh, Giānī, *Srī Gurduāre Darshan*. Amritsar, 1923

M.G.S.

DARBĀR, a Perisan word meaning "a house, dwelling; court, area; court or levee of a prince; audience chamber," is commonly used in Punjabi to signify a royal, princely or any high-ranking officer's court (as distinguished from courts of justice) where dignitaries granted audience to the common people, listened to their grievances, or deliberated with their *darbārīs* (courtiers) on matters of public interest. In Sikhism the term came to have extended meaning as Gurū Nānak and his holy successors introduced terms such as *sachā pātisāhu*, True Emperor (GG, 17, 18, 463 *et al.*), *siri sāhā pātisāhu*, at the head of kings and emperors (GG, 1426) for God Almighty. Later, the Gurūs themselves came to be called *sachchā pātshāh*. The Gurū's court, therefore, also comes to be called *gur-darbār* or the *gurū's darbār*. In a hymn by Gurū Arjan addressed, according to tradition, to his father, Gurū Rām Dās, the Gurū's presence is referred to as *gur-darbār* (GG, 97). After Gurū Gobind Siṅgh had discontinued the institution of human *gurū* replacing it by *śabda-gurū* (the Word as

Gurū) and passed on the gurūship eternally to the Gurū Granth Sāhib, the Holy Book itself as well as its court, the *gurdwārā*, came to be popularly called Darbār or reverently, Srī Darbār Sāhib. This name is particularly given to the *gurdwārā* complexes at Amritsar and Tarn Tāran, as also officially to some other historical *gurdwārās* such as the principal shrine at Ḍerā Bābā Nānak and the shrine raised over the cremation site of Gurū Aṅgad at Khaḍūr Sāhib.

The Sikh usage of the term *darbār* for holy places has since spread to other communities so that Hindu devotees of Punjab, Himāchal Pradesh and Jammū region also refer to temples raised to their goddess as *Mātā dā Darbār,* the court of the Mother Goddess.

M.G.S.

DARBĀRĀ SIṄGH, BĀBĀ (1814-1870), second in the hierarchy of the Niraṅkārī sect, was the eldest of the three sons of Bābā Dayāl, the founder of the sect. He was born at Rāwalpiṇḍī on 1 Baisākh 1871 Bk / 11 April 1814 and succeeded to his father's seat on 30 January 1855. From among the creed of religious and social reform preached by his father, he gave his utmost attention to one item – marriage by Anand ceremony. He summoned an assembly of his followers and admirers at the Niraṅkārī Darbār at Rāwalpiṇḍī on 13 March 1855, and married a Sikh couple in the presence of Gurū Granth Sāhib, without inviting Brāhmaṇ priests and dispensing with the rite of circumambulations around a fire. This kind of simple ceremony had in fact been reintroduced by his father himself as far back as his (Bābā Dayāl's) own marriage in 1808. Bābā Darbārā Siṅgh aimed at demonstrating the Anand rite at a large gathering with a view to popularizing it. Bābā Dayāl's marriage, it is said, was solemnized by reciting the *Lāvāṅ* and *Anand* hymns from the Gurū Granth Sāhib as the couple sat reverently in front of it and by sealing the union with *ardās*. Bābā Darbārā Siṅgh had four circumambulations of the Gurū Granth Sāhib performed by the couple, each accompanied by melodious singing of a stanza from the four-part hymn, *Lāvāṅ,* by Gurū Rām Dās. He undertook an extensive tour of Dhannī-Poṭhohār and Chhachh areas in northwestern Punjab promoting this Anand form of conjugal rite and making many converts to the Niraṅkārī sect in the process. He is also said to have performed one such marriage at Amritsar on Monday, 15 April 1861, witnessed by a large congregation. In order to organize the expanding community he established several dioceses called *bīṛās,* and appointed diocesan heads known as *bīṛedārs.*

A significant contribution of Bābā Darbārā Siṅgh to standardizing the form of Sikh ceremonies was the preparation in 1856 of a *hukamnāmā*, setting forth a code of social conduct and giving detailed description of the rites of passage. To quote a few excerpts from the document:

> If a child is born, whether a son or a daughter, we sing the Gurū's hymns and offer the Gurū's *kaṛāhprasād* (the Sikh sacrament). Brother, there is no impurity (in child birth) as Gurū Nānak cautions in *Asā dī Vār* in the *śloka*: (the relevant *śloka* and the hymn follow) ....
>
> Then after forty days the mother comes to Darbār Sāhib along with the child. We then offer *kaṛāhprasād* in the name of the Gurū. The child is given a name from the Gurū Granth Sāhib ....
>
> When God brings the child to the age of understanding and when he is betrothed, we recite the following hymn of the Fifth Gurū in the measure Rāmkalī: (the hymn follows)....
>
> The Gurū's wedding hymns are chanted

as the marriage ceremony is performed. Sikh men and women recite the *Anand* by the Third Gurū in the measure Rāmkalī....

Brother, we do not display the dowry as this is prohibited by the Gurū.

And when, by the grace of the Formless One, a Sikh has completed his life, and the call comes, and the Sikh departs, we cover the body with a white shroud and, singing hymns, carry it for cremation or for releasing it into a flowing stream. We do not mourn... when we cremate a Sikh, we recite *Anand* and *Kīrtan Sohilā* and then distribute *kaṛāhprasād,* if we can afford to do so. After that we come before the Gurū Granth Sāhib, reciting hymns and inaugurate an end-to-end reading of the Gurū Granth Sāhib....

The *hukamnāmā* lays special emphasis upon cultivating the Divine Name, reciting the sacred hymns, and shunning of Brāhmaṇical rites and rituals. For instance, it says, "We should not seek advice from the Brāhmaṇs who in their pride spread superstition.... The Brāhmaṇ claims that it is disgraceful to eat at one's daughter's house, but he himself performs marriages for a fee.... Brother, all years, months and days created by the Gurū are auspicious. In the words of Gurū Gobind Siṅgh Jī, the Tenth Master, the Gurū's Sikh sets about his task remembering the Gurū's name, regardless of all ill omens... Moreover, brother, the opportunity for union (with God) comes only during this life. So let us repeat the Name now, no one will be able to do it later..." The various injunctions are supported by quotations from the Gurū Granth Sāhib.

Bābā Darbārā Siṅgh died at Rāwalpiṇḍī on 13 February 1870. He was succeeded by his younger brother, Bābā Ratan Chand, affectionately called Sāhib Rattā Jī.

BIBLIOGRAPHY

1. Webster, John C.B., *The Nirankari Sikhs.* Batala, 1979
2. Jolly, Surjit Kaur, *Sikh Revivalist Movements.* Delhi, 1988
3. Farquhar, J.N., *Modern Religious Movements in India.* Delhi, 1977
4. Harbans Singh, *The Heritage of the Sikhs.* Delhi, 1983

M.S.N.

DARBĀRĀ SIṄGH, BHĀĪ (d. 1921), still in his teens when he fell a martyr at Nankāṇā Sāhib in 1921, was the son of Bhāī Kehar Siṅgh and Bībī Ratan Kaur. His father was serving in the Indian army as a *havildār* (sergeant) and he was born at a cantonment station. His mother died when he was a bare three weeks old, and he was brought up by his grandmother. His father originally belonged to Jarg village, then in the princely state of Paṭiālā, but some time after his retirement in 1908 he migrated to Chakk No. 85 Ḍallā Chandā Siṅgh in a newly developed canal district. When on 19 February 1921, Bhāī Kehar Siṅgh prepared to join the *jathā* or batch of Akālī volunteers bound for Nankāṇā Sāhib, Darbārā Singh, too, much against the wishes of his father as well as against the entreaties of his old grandmother, joined it. Both father and son were hacked to pieces the following morning in the enclosed compound of Gurdwārā Janam Asthān.

See NANKĀṆĀ SĀHIB MASSACRE

BIBLIOGRAPHY

Shamsher, Gurbakhsh Siṅgh, *Shahīdī Jīvan.* Nankana Sahib, 1938

G.S.G.

DARBĀRĀ SIṄGH, DĪWĀN (d. 1734), originally from the mercantile community of Sirhind, became a Sikh receiving the initiatory rites on 30 March 1699, the day the Khālsā was created, and took part in the battles of Anandpur. During the period after Bandā Siṅgh he commanded much esteem as a veteran fighter and as *dīwān,* i.e. commissar in charge of rations and forage. In 1733 when Zakarīya Khān, governor of Lahore, decided to make it up with the Sikhs and sent his envoy, Subeg Siṅgh, with the offer of *nawāb*ship and a *jāgīr,* the Sikh assembly first decided to confer the mantle of *nawāb*ship upon Darbārā Siṅgh but he, according to Ratan Siṅgh Bhaṅgū, *Prāchīn Panth Prakāsh,* excused himself arguing that the Sikhs should not compromise their claim to sovereignty by accepting a title from the Mughal rulers. The *saṅgat,* however, overruling his objection, bestowed the title upon another leading Sikh, Kapūr Siṅgh. Darbārā Siṅgh Dīwān continued as controller of provisions till his death at Amritsar in 1734.

BIBLIOGRAPHY

1. Kuir Siṅgh, *Gurbilās Pātshāhī 10.* Patiala, 1968
2. Bhaṅgū, Ratan Siṅgh, *Prāchīn Panth Prakāsh.* Amritsar, 1914
3. Santokh Siṅgh, Bhāī, *Srī Gur Pratāp Sūraj Granth.* Amritsar, 1926-37

P.S.P.

DARGĀHĀ, BHĀĪ, a Bhaṇḍārī Khatrī, figures in Bhāī Gurdas's roster of prominent Sikhs of Gurū Hargobind's time, *Vārāṅ,* XI.28. According to Bhāī Manī Siṅgh, *Sikhāṅ dī Bhagat Mālā,* Bhāī Dargāhā once complained to the Gurū that some Sikhs when interpreting *gurbāṇī* fell into polemic. Gurū Hargobind said that while reasoning with a view to removing doubts and gaining or disseminating true knowledge was beneficial, Sikhs must shun pedantry born of *haumai* or pride.

BIBLIOGRAPHY

1. Manī Siṅgh, Bhāī, *Sikhāṅ dī Bhagat Mālā.* Amritsar, 1955
2. Santokh Siṅgh, Bhāī, *Srī Gur Pratāp Sūraj Granth.* Amritsar, 1926-37

B.S.

DARGĀHĀ SIṄGH, BHĀĪ (1713-1823), a Nirmalā saint, was born in 1713 the son of Bhāī Nigāhīā Siṅgh of the village of Lauṅgovāl, in present-day Saṅgrūr district of the Punjab. Nigāhīā Siṅgh was known to be the elder brother of Bhāī Manī Siṅgh, the martyr. For the *dīvālī* festival of 1725, Nigāhīā Siṅgh along with his seven sons went to Amritsar where the whole family received the initiatory rites of the Khālsā at the hands of Bhāī Manī Siṅgh. Three of the brothers remained in Amritsar, among them Dargāhā Siṅgh who showed marked aptitude for scholarly learning as well as for the martial arts. He gained proficiency in both fields, though he was more inclined towards religious pursuits. He left Amritsar and went to Kurukshetra where he became a disciple of Paṇḍit Mān Siṅgh, a noted Nirmalā scholar of the time. Later, he moved to Haridvār and settled at Kaṅkhal where he established his *ḍerā* or monastery on an extensive piece of land gifted by the Muslim chief of Jualāpur. He also built a shrine dedicated to Gurū Amar Dās (1479-1574) who had visited Haridvār several times. The *ḍerā* of Bhāī Dargāhā Siṅgh, patronized by Rājā Sāhib Siṅgh and Mahārājā Karam Siṅgh of Paṭiālā, developed into a prominent centre of the Nirmalā sect. Bhāī Dargāhā Siṅgh died there in 1823.

BIBLIOGRAPHY

1. Gaṇeshā Siṅgh, Mahant, *Nirmal Bhūshan arthāt Itihās Nirmal Bhekh.* Amritsar, n.d.
2. Jaggī, Rattan Siṅgh, *Bhāī Manī Siṅgh.* Patiala, 1983

B.S.V.

DARGĀH MALL, DĪWĀN (d. 1695), son of Dvārkā Dās Chhibbar, was, according to *Shahīd Bilās Bhāī Manī Siṅgh,* and *Gurū kīāṅ Sākhīāṅ,* a *dīwān* or minister in the time of Gurū Hargobind and his successors and managed, as such, their households. He was the great-grandfather of Kesar Siṅgh Chhibbar, the author of *Baṅsāvalīnāmā*. He was in attendance upon Gurū Har Rāi when summons arrived from Auraṅgzīb asking the Gurū to meet him in Delhi. The Gurū sent instead his son, Rām Rāi, to call on the emperor. Dīwān Dargāh Mall was deputed to escort him to the imperial capital. It was Dīwān Dargāh Mall who wrote to Gurū Har Rāi from Delhi informing him about Bābā Rām Rāi's arbitrary distortion, in Auraṅgzīb's court, of one of Gurū Nānak's hymns in the Gurū Granth Sāhib. He was also in the train of Gurū Har Rāi's successor, Gurū Har Krishan, who too had been summoned to Delhi by the emperor. After the sudden death of Gurū Har Krishan, Dīwān Dargāh Mall travelled with Mātā Sulakkhaṇī, the mother of the late Gurū, to Bakālā carrying the emblems of succession for the investiture of Gurū Tegh Bahādur.

As says *Baṅsāvalīnāmā*, Gurū Tegh Bahādur bestowed on Dargāh Mall a robe of honour and asked him to continue as *dīwān*, but the latter excused himself on the grounds of old age, and recommended to him his nephew, Matī Dās, for the position. He, however, did not leave the Gurū's presence. According to *Gurū kīāṅ Sākhīāṅ*, Dargāh Mall was among those who accompanied the Gurū on his journey through the eastern parts in 1665-70. He was present at the accession ceremony for Gurū Gobind Siṅgh on the eve of Gurū Tegh Bahādur's departure, in 1675, from Anandpur to make the supreme sacrifice. Dīwān Matī Dās and his brother Bhāī Satī Dās, also accompanied Gurū Tegh Bahādur to Delhi and embraced martyrdom on 11 November 1675. The duties of the *dīwān* of the holy household thus fell once again on the shoulders of Dargāh Mall. On the next Baisākhī day, 29 March 1676, however, he was finally relieved and his son, Dharam Chand, was appointed *dīwān* in his place.

Dargāh Mall continued to stay at Anandpur where he died on 10 February 1695.

BIBLIOGRAPHY

1. Chibbar, Kesar Siṅgh, *Bansāvalīnāmā Dasāṅ Pātshāhīāṅ Kā*. Chandigarh, 1972
2. Garjā Siṅgh, Giānī, ed., *Shahīd Bilās*. Ludhiana, 1961
3. Padam, Piārā Siṅgh, and Giānī Garjā Siṅgh, eds., *Gurū kīāṅ Sākhīāṅ*. Patiala, 1986
4. Trilochan Singh, *Guru Tegh Bahadur: Prophet and Martyr*. Delhi, 1967
5. Harbans Singh, *Guru Tegh Bahadur*. Delhi, 1982

A.C.B.

DĀROGĀ, from Persian *dāroghah*, lit. "head man of an office, prefect of a town or village, overseer, or superintendent of any department," is a term usually applied to a police officer in charge of a *thānā* (police station) exercising jurisdication over a police circle. The title, equivalent of *thānādār* or *thānedār* in the Punjab, is still used in some other Indian states to designate an inspector or sub-inspector of police in charge of a police station or, in official terminology, a station house officer, S.H.O. for short. During the medieval period, as even now, *dārogā*, as a government official responsible for maintaining law and order in the countryside, enjoyed wide powers of detention and arrest. His counterpart, in larger towns, or superior was *kotwāl*.

M.G.S.

DARSHAN SIṄGH PHERŪMĀN (1885-1969), political leader and martyr, was born at the village of Pherūmān, in present-day Amritsar district, on 1 August 1885. His father's name was Chandā Siṅgh and his mother's Rāj Kaur. After passing his high school examination, he joined in 1912 the Indian army as a sepoy. Two years later, he resigned from the army and set up as a contractor at Hissār. He was doing well as a contractor, when a taunt from his mother, who was deeply religious, led him to give up his business and plunge into the Akālī movement for the reform of Gurdwārā management. In 1921, he was arrested in the *morchā* launched by Sikhs for recovering from the British deputy commissioner of Amritsar keys of the Golden Temple treasury he had seized, and was imprisoned for one year. In December 1924, he led the 14th Shahīdī *jathā* to Jaito, and was jailed for ten months. He also took part in the non-cooperation movement launched by the Indian National Congress, serving a 14-month term in jail. In 1926, he visited Malaya where he was detained by the British on the basis of his political record in India. While in jail, he went on a fast in protest against the orders forbidding the wearing of *kachhā* or drawers, one of the five symbols of K͟hālsā discipline. He continued the fast for 21 days, ending it only when he had won his point.

Returning home, Darshan Siṅgh joined the Civil Disobedience movement and courted imprisonment thrice. He took part in the Quit India campaign during the Second World War. For a number of years, he was a member of the Shiromaṇī Gurdwārā Parbandhak Committee and its general secretary for two terms. He was elected a member of the Rājya Sabhā as a nominee of the Indian National Congress and retained his seat up to 1964. In 1959, he severed his connection with the Congress and joined the Swatantra Party of which he was one of the founders.

In August 1969, Darshan Siṅgh resolved to lay down his life to atone for what he termed as resilement on the part of some of the Sikh leaders from the solemn pledges they had taken at Srī Akāl Tak͟ht and to have their default in not being able to secure the inclusion of Chaṇḍīgaṛh and some other areas in the newly-demarcated Punjab redeemed. So determined, he went on a fast unto death inside the Central Jail at Amritsar on 15 August. He stuck to his vow and stubbornly refused to have any nourishment until his demand for the amalgamation with the Punjab of the Punjabi-speaking areas kept out of the new Punjab was conceded. On 27 October 1969, which was the 74th day of his fasting, he died. For the supreme sacrifice he thus made to rewrite the sanctity of a Sikh's plighted word, his name is honoured among the martyrs of the Sikh faith.

BIBLIOGRAPHY

1. Pratāp Siṅgh, Giānī, *Amar Shahīd Darshan Siṅgh Pherūmān*. Amritsar, n.d.
2. Fauja Singh, *Eminent Freedom Fighters of the Punjab*. Patiala, 1972
3. Sarhadi, Ajit Singh, *Punjabi Suba*. Delhi, 1970

Mb.S.

DĀSĀ, BHĀĪ, son of Bhāī Bālū and grandson of Bhāī Mūlā, of 'Alīpur Shamālī, district Multān, now in Pakistan. He was one of the devoted Sikhs of the time of Gurū Hargobind and was one of those who accompanied the Gurū as he was moving towards Jalandhar after leaving Amritsar. According to "Bhaṭṭ Vahī Multānī Sindhī," he fought bravely in the battle that took place on 1 Jeṭh 1692 Bk/ 29 April 1635 at Phagwāṛā between a Mug͟hal force and the Sikhs. Bhāī Dāsā was killed in this battle.

M.G.S.

DASAMDVĀR (Skt. *daśamadvārā*), lit. meaning 'tenth gate', is a concept in Sikhism which signifies the door to enlightenment and spiritual vision. *Dasamdvār* in the Haṭhayogic system is also known as *brahmrandhra, mokṣadvārā, mahāpatha* and *madhya mārga*, the terms frequently used in the esoteric literature of medieval India. It is term of religious physiology and its significance lies in its being a concept in the framework of soteriological ideology. Nine apertures (*nav-*

dvāras) opening towards outside the body serve the physical mechanism of human personality but when their energy, normally being wasted, is consciously channelized towards the self, the tenth gate or the *daśamdvār* opens inside the body and renders a hyper-physical service by taking the seeker beyond the bondage of embodied existence.

The human body is endowed with nine doors also called holes or streams. These nine are: two eyes, two ears, two nostrils, mouth, anus, and urethra. All these are vital organs of living organism called human being. The Pālī *Suttanipāta* (verse 199, in *Khuddak nikāya,* vol. I, p. 297) is perhaps one of the very first Indian texts which mentions the idea of nine 'holes' in the body. It is from a philosophically ascetic or Śramaṇic standpoint that the human body is described in this text as a mass of bones, sinews, flesh, etc. and as a bag for belly, intestines, liver, heart, bladder, lungs, kidneys, blood, bile, etc. "Ever from its nine streams (*navahi sotehi*) the unclean flows." *The Śvetāśvatara Upaniṣad* (III. 18) and the *Bhagavadgītā* (V. 13) refer to human body as "a city with nine gates" (*nava dvāra pure dehī*) in which the Self dwells, neither acting nor causing to act. The *Kaṭha Upaniṣad* (2.51), however, describes human abode of the Unborn One as "a city with eleven gates" (*puram-ekādaśa-dvāram*). Mystical and soteriological significance of *dasamdvār* is found in the writings of the *siddhas* and the *sants.* As a matter of fact the history of the idea of *dasamdvār* begins with the Buddhist Siddhas and we owe its popularity to Nātha yogīs. The term as well as the concept first appears in the works of Siddhas who flourished during the period between eighth and eleventh centuries. The Siddhas transmitted the theory of *dasamdvār* as a mystical spiritual gateway to Vaiṣṇava Sants and thence it came to the Sikh Gurūs. The process of transmission was direct and natural since the Sants (or *bhagats)* and Gurūs lived and taught in a society thoroughly acquainted with and influenced by the terms, concepts and precepts of the Siddhas. Although the concept of *dasamdvār* remained the same, its functional value in theistic theology and socio-devotional methodology of the Sikh Gurūs became decidedly different from its original one in the non-theistic ideology and esoteric-ascetic methodology of Buddhist Siddhas and Nātha yogīs.

In the Buddhist *caryāpadas* or hymns of spiritual practice, the *daśamadvāra* is also called *vairocana-dvāra,* the brilliant gate or the supreme gate. In the texts of the Nātha school such as the *Siddhasiddhānta paddhati* (II. 6), the mouth of *śaṅkhinī* is called the tenth gate (*śaṅkhinī-bibaram-daśam-dvāram*). *Śaṅkhinī* is the name of a curved duct *(baṅkā nāla)* through which nectar (*soma rasa, mahārasa* or *amrit*) passes downwards. This curved duct lies between the moon *(candra)* below the *sahasrāra-cakra* or thousand-petalled lotus plexus in the cerebrum region and the hollow in the palatal region. The *Gorakṣavijaya* describes *śaṅkhinī* as a double-mouthed *(dvi-mukhīā)* serpent (*sarpiṇī*), one mouth above, the other below. The life elixir called *amrit* or nectar pours down through the mouth of *śaṅkhinī.* This mouth called *daśamdvār* has to be shut up and the quintessence of life, *amrit* or *mahārasa* has to be conserved by the yogī. The *amrit* which pours down from the *daśamdvār* falls down in the fire of the sun *(sūrya)* where it is dried up by time (*kālāgni*). The yogī by closing the *daśamdvār* and preserving the *amrit* deceives Time (death) and by drinking it himself through cumbersome *khecarī-mudrā* he attains immortality. Some other *haṭhayogic* texts name *suṣumnā nāṛī* instead of *śaṅkhinī.* However all the texts agree that the *brahmrandhra* or the *daśamdvār* is the cavity on the roof of the palate and *khecarī mudrā* has to be performed for tasting the elixir or the *amrit* pouring down from it.

The notion of *daśamdvār,* written as *dasamduār,* occurs several times in the Gurū Granth Sāhib. Sikhism is a strictly monotheistic system of belief and it must be stated at the outset that according to Sikh view of the *daśamdvār,* the tenth door opens into the abode of God, the Creator – *dasam duārā agam apārā param purakh kī ghāṭī* (GG, 974), and again -- *nau ghar thāpe thāpaṇhārai dasvai vāsā alakh apārai* (GG, 1036). This fact distinguishes Sikhism from the non-theistic non-dualistic philosophy of the Siddhas. Second outstanding difference is that Sikhism is predominantly a devotional pathway, relying chiefly on the discipline of *bhakti,* i.e. loving devotion for the Divine; the Siddhas and Nāthas, on the other hand, practised Tantra or Haṭhayoga in which the disciplines of psychology and physiology were fused together. With these differences the notion of *dasamduār* in Sikhism employs the same terms and symbols as used by Siddhas and Nāthas.

The nine doors (*nau darvāje*) and the tenth door are often mentioned together to show their differences. The unstruck sound is heard at the tenth door when it is freed from the shackles of nine doors in the body – *nau darvāje dasvai muktā anahad sabadu vajāvaṇiā* (GG, 110). It is believed that the tenth door is closed by a hard diamond-like door (*bajar kapāṭ*) which is *haumai* (self-centredness). This hard and strong door is opened and the darkness of *haumai* is dispelled by the instruction of the Teacher (Gurū). In other words, the tenth door is the door of enlightenment and it opens only when the door consisting of *haumai* is broken. It is taken for granted in Sikhism that the tenth door is the supreme state of the mind. It is certainly not a physical door; it is that state of purified consciousness in which God is visible and all contacts with physical existence are cut off. It is called a being's own house (*nij-ghar*), that is to say, a being's real nature which is like light *(joti sarūp)*. One hears day and night the *anahad śabda* there when one dwells in one's own house through the tenth door – *nau dar ṭhāke dhāvatu rahāe, dasvai nijghari vāsā pāe* (GG, 124).

At few places in the Gurbāṇī, the term *dasamduār* has been used to denote ten organs – five sensory organs and five organs of action, i.e. *jñānendriyas* and *karmendriyas.* Says Gurū Nānak: "*Hukami sañjogī gaṛi das duār, pañch vasahi mili joti apār*" – in the fortress of the body created in his *hukam* are ten doors. In this fort five subtle elements of *śabda* (sound),, *sparśa* (touch), *rūpa* (sight), *rasa* (taste) and *gandha* (smell) abide having the infinite light of the Lord in them (GG, 152). The *amrit* which flows at the tenth door is the essence of Divine name (*nām ras*) according to the Gurū; it is not the physical elixir of immortality conceived by the Siddhas, nor is this *amrit* to be found by awakening *kuṇḍalinī* or by practising *khecarī mudrā*; it is to be found through the Teacher's instruction. When the Satgurū is encountered then one stops from running (after the nine doors) and obtains the tenth door. Here at this door the immortalizing food (*amrit bhojan*), the innate sound *(sahaj dhunī)* is produced -- *dhāvatu thammiā satiguri miliai dasvā duāru pāiā; tithai amrit bhojanu sahaj dhuni upajai jitu sabadi jagatu thammi rahāiā* (GG, 441).

This wholesome spot is not outside the physical frame. The second Gurū also refers to the fort (*koṭu*) with nine doors; the tenth door is hidden (*gupatu*); it is closed by a hard door which can be opened by the key of the Gurū's word (GG, 954). According to Gurū Amar Dās, Nānak III, he alone is released who conquers his mind and who keeps it free from defilement; arriving at the tenth door, and staying there he understands all the three spheres (GG, 490).

The importance of *dasamdvār* is of considerable theological interest. Here at the tenth door the *anahad śabda* (unstruck sound) is heard; here the divine drink of immortality trickles down; and here the devotee meets with the invisible and inaccessible transcendental Brahman who is described by the sages as unutterable (GG, 1002).

The devotional theology of Sikhism requires that the gateway of ultimate release can open only by God's will. The tenth door is closed with the adamantine hard door (*bajar kapāṭ*) which can be opened duly with the Gurū's word. Inside the front(i.e. the body) is the tenth door, the house in the cavity (*guphā ghar*); in this fort nine doors have been fixed according to Divine ordinance (*hukam*); in the tenth door the Invisible, Unwritten, Unlimited Person shows Himself – *bhītari koṭ guphā ghar jāī, nau ghar thāpe hukami rajāī; dasvai purakhu alekhu apārī āpe alakhu lakhāidā* (GG, 1033). This is the view expressed by the founder of Sikhism and he repeats it at another place also. He says that the Establisher has established nine houses (*nau ghar*) or nine doors in the city of this body; the Invisible and Infinite dwells at the tenth house or tenth door (GG, 1036). The nectar-like essence (*amrit ras*) is dripped by the Satgurū; it comes out appearing at the tenth door. The sounding of the unstruck sound announces, as it were, the manifestation of God at this door – *Amrit rasu satigurū chuāiā; dasavai duāri pragaṭu hoi āiā; taha anahad sabad vajahi dhuni bāṇī sahaje sahaji samāī he* (GG, 1069). The Siddhas, unlike the Sikh Gurūs, find the *amrit* by their own effort.

Occasionally the term *das duār* is used in *gurbāṇī* in the sense of sensory and motor organs of body which should be kept under control. For the most part, however, the Sikh Scripture stresses the need for realization of the *dasam duār*, apart from God's ordinance (*hukam*) and Teacher's compassion (*kirpā, prasād*) and the necessity of transcending the realm of three-strand nature (*triguṇa māyā*). Kabīr, for instance, says that the tenth door opens only when the trinity (*trikuṭī*) of *sattva, rajas* and *tamas* is left behind – *trikuṭī chhūṭai dasvā daru khūlhai tā manu khīvā bhāī* (GG, 1123).

BIBLIOGRAPHY

1. Sher Singh, *The Philosophy of Sikhism*. Lahore, 1944
2. Dasgupta, Sasibhusan, *Obscure Religious Cults*. Calcutta, 1962
3. *Haṭhyoga-Pradīpikā*. Adyar, 1972
4. Briggs, George Weston, *Gorakhnath and the Kanphata Yogis*. Delhi, 1973
5. Jodh Singh, *Religious Philosophy of Guru Nanak*. Varanasi, 1983

L.M.J.

DASAM GRANTH (lit. the Tenth Book, generally signifying the Book of the Tenth Gurū) is how the collection of compositions attributed to the Tenth Gurū, Gurū Gobind Siṅgh, is named to distinguish it from the earlier work, the *Ādi Granth*, the First or Primary Book, compiled by Gurū Arjan, the fifth in the spiritual line from Gurū Nānak and to which Gurū Gobind Siṅgh added the hymns of the Ninth Gurū, Gurū Tegh Bahādur, forbearing from adding any of his own. His own compositions were gathered into a separate volume. According to Kesar Siṅgh Chhibbar, *Baṅsāvalīnāmā Dasāṅ Pātshāhīāṅ Kā*, the two volumes sat in *gurdwārās* separately when in Sammat 1755 (AD 1698), Sikhs, says Chhibbar, proposed to Gurū Gobind Siṅgh that the two Granths be got bound together into one volume. But the Gurū spoke, "This one is Ādi Gurū Granth, the root book; that one is only for my diversion. Let this be kept in mind and let the two stay separate."

Earlier, too, Gurū Gobind Siṅgh had, when concluding the story of Lord Kṛṣṇa, versified by him, stated that the purpose of the composition was nothing but to acclaim the righteous war. Although the *Dasam Granth* is revered equally with the Gurū Granth Sāhib and in some *gurdwārās* is seated side by side with the latter, it does not enjoy the same status nor does it rank theologically as Shabad-Gurū as does the Ādi Granth. Even the authorship and authenticity of some of the writings in it are sometimes questioned. The volume was compiled at Amritsar by Bhāī Manī Siṅgh, one of his devoted followers, some two decades after the passing away of Gurū Gobind Siṅgh. What with the intrigues of the jealous hill *rājās* and the hostility of the Mughal satraps, those were perilous times. Gurū Gobind Siṅgh continued to patronize bards and poets who had gravitated to Anandpur and encouraged them to produce translations into *bhākhā* (vernacular) of martial episodes from the Purāṇas and other ancient texts. Many of the manuscripts from his own pen and from those of the poets were lost at the time of the final evacuation of Anandpur in December 1705. Manī Siṅgh spent years tracing and collecting whatever could be salvaged or whatever had been preserved by Sikhs who had retained copies of some of the texts in their possession. From this material came the first recension of the *Dasam Granth*. A second recension was prepared by Bābā Dīp Siṅgh, chief of the Shahīd clan at Damdamā Sāhib. The bulk of the contents of these recensions was common to both. Yet another recension was got up by Bhāī Sukkhā Siṅgh, an officiant at Takht Srī Paṭnā Sāhib. Several other recensions, copies and copies made from copies, appeared successively, not without some mutual textual variations.

During the Siṅgh Sabhā days, the Khālsā Dīwān, Amritsar, took up the question of verification and standardization of the text of the *Dasam Granth*. The work was entrusted to Gurmat Granth Prachārak Sabhā, established in March 1885. Bhāī Mannā Siṅgh, son of the secretary to the Sabhā, Bhāī Āgyā Siṅgh Hakīm, undertook to finance the project. Thirty-two copies of the *Granth* were collected from different places and brought to the Akāl Takht, where a group of eminent scholars pored over them, studying and discussing them threadbare between 8 Sāvaṇ 1952 Bk/ 5 July 1895 and 5 Phagaṇ 1952 Bk/ 17 February 1896. Among these scholars were Bhāī Mannā Siṅgh Hakīm, Bhāī Naraiṇ Siṅgh, Bhāī Ṭhākar Siṅgh, Bhāī Sant Siṅgh (son of Giānī Giān Siṅgh), Bhāī Bishan Siṅgh, Sant Gopāl Dās Udāsī, Mahant Amīr Siṅgh, *et al.* Opinions were invited from a wider circle by correspondence, and a complete report on the deliberations was published on 1 Kārtik 1954 Bk / 14 October 1897. The result was the recension now current. It was first published by Wazīr Hind Press, Amritsar, in October 1902.

A few of the compositions in the *Dasam Granth* bear the signature title, Srī Mukhvāk Pātshāhī X, literally, holy word from the mouth of the Tenth Sovereign, i.e. the Tenth Gurū, Gurū Gobind Siṅgh. Some compositions are preceded by simply, Pātshāhī X. Two or three, covering about 75 pages of the *Dasam Granth*, bear no signatures at all. In general, those with the full signature title are accepted as written or dictated by the Gurū himself, whereas those with the abbreviated title, or those with no title, may or may not be so accepted.

The *Jāpu*, the opening meditation in the *Dasam Granth*, is one of the morning prayers of the Sikhs and one of the hymns recited as part of the Sikh initation ceremony. It is a *stotra* or panegyric, a well-established poetic form used in devotional Sanskrit literature. The *Jāpu* consists of 199 stanzas in which ten different metres have been used. God is described by a variety of names which are all notable for their linguistic and poetic ingenuity. The *Jāpu* is placed at the head of the *Dasam Granth* as is the *Japu* at the head of the *Ādi Granth*. The *Jāpu* is all a hymn of laudation to the Lord who is remembered by many different names and attributes of Sanskrit, Arabic and Persian origin. Gurū Gobind Siṅgh has tried in the *Jāpu* the novel experiment of juxtaposing oriental and semitic terminology by using compound expressions derived from both sources; for examle: *ki sarabaṅ kalīmai; ki paramaṅ fahīmai* (*sarabaṅ kalīmai* = all eloquence, *paramaṅ fahīmai* = most wise). At places he used *a* and *an* which are Sanskrit prefixes denoting negative sense with Arabic and Persian words to a very telling effect; for example, *namastaṅ a-majabe* and *a-nrañj bāt* (*a* = without, *majabe* = religion; *amajabe* = without any religion; *an* = without, *rañj* = rancour; *anrañj* = without rancour). The *Jāpu* carries the signature title, Mukhvāk Pātshāhī X. The text may be taken as an example of the blending of Indian and Semitic linguistic cultures.

The *Akāl Ustati,* spelt "Ustat" in the original (Praises of the Timeless), occupying 28 pages in the *Dasam Granth* edition comprising 1428 pages, is a poem mixing *stotra* and didactic forms of verse. The real purpose of man, according to this poem, is to live and remember God. The poet becomes attuned to the Supreme Being as he utters the expression *tū hī* (Thou alone art, Thou alone existest). He repeats the expression 16 times (verses 69-70). The *Akāl Ustati* focusses upon the unity of all mankind, saying that the temple and mosque are the same. All mankind is one. It is but error to see it divided. Gurū Gobind Siṅgh commences this poem with an invocation to God, All-Steel, and ends it picturing Hindus and Muslims, in fact people the world over, as one, seeking the same God whose blessings they cherish.

The *Bachitra Nāṭak* (Play Marvellous) carries the signature Srī Mukhvāk Pātshāhī X. It consists of 14 cantos. The style is autobiographical. Gurū Gobind Siṅgh tells us how he was called into the world by the Almighty himself: "I cherish thee as my own son and charge thee to go out into the world, to extend faith." Says Gurū Gobind Siṅgh, "I assumed birth for the purpose of upholding *dharma,* saving the saints and destroying tyrants. The fierce battles between the armies of Lava and Kuśa are described in grim detail. Vultures and foul spirits abound. Gorgeously robed *houris* fly about the battlefield wheedling the warriors. Death on the battlefield is reckoned glorious.

Among the battles described is that of Bhaṅgāṇī (18 September 1688) in which Gurū Gobind Siṅgh himself took part. The poem contains many a personal allusion and allusions to participants on both sides. The opening invocation to the Creator and Saviour hailed as the Sword sets the mood for the battle scenes. Verses of war and worship intermingle and a picture emerges of an ideal warrior-saint. The text comprising 14 chapters is part of the larger *Bachitra Nāṭak Granth* which also includes the *Chaṇḍī Charitra,* I and II, *Chaubīs Autār, Brahmā Avatār* and *Rudra Avatār* . Some stories of the *avatārs* such as that of Kṛṣṇa are based on the "Dasam Skandh" of the *Bhāgavat Purāṇa,* whereas those of the *Chaṇḍī Charitra,* I and II, are based on *Mārkaṇḍaya-purāṇa. Chaṇḍī dī Vār* is the only long composition in Punjabi in the *Dasam Granth. Chaṇḍī Charitra,* I and II, and *Chaṇḍī dī Vār* describe battles between Durgā and the demons, allegorically the cosmic conflict between good and evil. The opening verses of the Punjabi *Vār* now form part of the *ardās* or daily supplicatory prayer of the Sikhs. The verses run as under:

> Meditate first on God and then turn your thoughts to Gurū Nānak.
> Aṅgad Gurū, Amar Dās, each with Rām Dās, be our protectors.
> Arjan and Hargobind, remember them and remember Srī Hari Rāī.
> Remember Srī Har Krishan whose very sight dispels all sorrow.
> Think of Gurū Tegh Bahādur;
> So will all the nine treasures throng thy door.
> May they, the Gurūs, be our guides, our protectors in all places.

Giān Prabodh (Consciousness of Knowledge), comprising 336 stanzas in all, is a mixture of praises of the Timeless and of pantheistic poetry, riddles, and stories from the *Mahābhārata*.

Shabad Pātshāhī X (Verses of the Tenth Sovereign) are ten in number and might be a part of a larger collection. The theme is laudation of the Creator Lord. Verses titled "*Khayāl*" (of the Tenth Sovereign) etch a picture of a true devotee. *Savaiyyās* are quatrains comprising 33 four-line stanzas. The text carries the signature Srī Mukhvāk Pātshāhī X. Truth is sifted from falsehood. "One in whose heart the light of the Perfect One shines is a true member of the *K͟hālsā*."

Sastra Nāṁ Mālā (The Necklace of the Names of Weapons) consists of 1318 verses, with "Pātshāhī X" appended at the beginning as the signature of the Tenth Master with their Paurāṇic background. It is a catalogue of weapons used in warfare of olden days. Weapons of war are praised as protectors and deliverers. Largest number of pages are reserved for *tupak,* a kind of firearm, reckoned to be the deadliest of weapons.

Chritropākhyān (Tales of Deceit) covering 7555 verses of Charit Kāvya is the largest composition in the *Dasam Granth*. "Patshahi X" is mentioned at the very beginning of the work as the signature title. The date of completing this compilation is given in the last verse as Sunday, *sudī aṣṭamī* of Bhādoṅ 1753 Bk / 24 August 1696. The 404 tales may be divided into categories such as tales of the bravery, devotion, or intelligence of women, 78 in number; of the deceitfulness and unscrupulousness of women, 269; of the deceitfulness of men 26. Tales come from foreign lands as well. Tale 201 comes originally from the story of Joseph and Potiphar's wife in the Bible, Genesis chapter 39. In the Qur'ān it is Yūsuf and Zulaik͟hā.

Zafarnāmah (The Letter of Victory), bearing the signature title Srī Mukhvāk Pātshāhī X, was sent to Emperor Auraṅgzīb from Dīnā in the southern Punjab in December 1705. It consists of 111 verses in Persian and is a homily on the sanctity of one's pledged word. The Emperor has been taxed with breaking faith, *Paimāṅshikan,* oath-breaker, referring obviously to the violation of the pledge of safe-conduct given the Gurū by the Emperor's generals at Anandpur.

Hikāyat comprises stories in the Persian language, written in Gurmukhī characters. They are placed at the end of *Dasam Granth* after the Persian *Zafarnāmah*. Several of these tales are Persian duplicates of some of the Braj tales. *Hikāyat* 4 is *Charitra* 52: *Hikāyat* 5 is *Charitra* 267; and 9 is *Charitra* 290.

Gurū Gobind Siṅgh's poetry is marked by a very vast range of metres he employed. There is much innovation and novelty he introduced in his prosodic schemes. In Indian classical prosody the time required to pronounce the syllables, according to their phonetic make-up, is designated into two forms: short (*laghu*) and long (*guru*) known by the signs I and S, respectively. In words comprising specific placement of consonants, long and short vowels enhance the intensity of their musical content and hence the flow and incision are elicited.

Poetry and metre have existed together all along. On account of different rhythms produced by different metres they have acquired different names. Metres in their present form have come down to us passing through many changes and varieties in Sanskrit, Prākrit, Apabhraṅśa and old Hindi languages with concomitant extensions. These are divided into *mātrik* (in which syllabic instants are counted) and *varṇik* (in which order and number of short and long vowels are taken into account). In earlier Sanskrit literature only *varṇik* metres were popular and at a later stage, due to the influence of Prākrit and Apabhraṅśa languages, poets of Sanskrit also turned to the use of *mātrik* metres.

The Hindi verse has recognized both the metrical categories, *mātrik* and *varṇik*, but to facilitate the development of poetry, Hindi poets have increasingly relaxed and modified certain conditions of *varṇik* metres like *kabitt* and *savaiyyā* to suit the flow of expression. Before the advent of devotional poetry in Hindi, Dohā, Sorṭhā, Tomar, Toṭak, Gāhā, Chhappaya, etc., were popular metres. Devotional poetry was mostly composed in *padas*. Other important metres were Dohā, Chaupaī, Tribhaṅgī, Jhūlanā, Toṭak, Nāgsvarūpinī (Nāgsarūpī), Basant, Tilkā, Kirīṭ, Māltī, Mālinī, Kabitt, Savaiyyā, Bhujaṅg-prayāt, etc.

Both kinds of metres (syllable or *varṇik* and syllabic instants or *mātrik*) are employed in the *Dasam Granth*, but *varṇik* metres have been used more frequently and with perfect ease. Apart from the above two main varieties of Indian origin, the *bait*, a metre of Persian poetry, has also been used. Secondly, out of a total number of about 150 metres used in the *Dasam Granth*, over one hundred metres have their origin in Sanskrit, Prākrit, Apabhraṅśa and old Hindi languages. The remaining metres, either new or traditional ones, appear under new names to suit the flow of narration. Gurū Gobind Siṅgh invented new metres which contribute a great deal to the realization of sentiments *(rasa)* in their sublimity. Keeping the contents in view, he gives many alternative names to some of the metres. In the *Dasam Granth*, the Chaupaī metre has been used to the maximum followed by Doharā and Savaiyyā.

In the *Dasam Granth* the battle scenes have been described through the metres Kabitt, Savaiyyā, Padhisṭakā and Bisnupadā. Savaiyyā hitherto had been generally used for sensuous love poetry, but Gurū Gobind Siṅgh used it with consummate artistry for heroic poetry. To capture the sounds as well as the swift movements on the battlefield he has used small metres like Padhisṭakā. Metres are changed frequently with a view to describing different types of combat. In this process the similes and metaphors are sometimes relegated to the background but where similes and metaphors dominate, the metres remain mostly unchanged. Through Bisnupadās, which are held to be highly musical, the battle scenes are portrayed with the help of onomatopoeic words. Gurū Gobind Siṅgh also introduced for the first time in his *Chaṇḍī dī Vār* blank verse in Punjabi poetry: the metre used was Sirkhiṇḍī. Following is a note on the different metres used in the *Dasam Granth*, with their prominent features and frequency of their usage in different compositions. Of them, the first ninety-seven are examples of metres regulated by syllables (*varṇik chhand*) and the rest are of those regulated by syllabic instant (*mātrik chhand*):

SYLLABLE (VARṆIK) METRES

1. *Achkaṛā* is of 12 syllables having four *ragaṇs* (SIS) in each line. It is a new name and alternative names for it are Sragviṇī, Kāminī Mohanā and Lakshmīdhārā. It has been used 12 times in the *Rudra Avatār* (Pāras Nāth).

2. *Ajā* is of 8 syllables having *yagaṇ* (ISS), *ragaṇ* (SIS), *laghu* (I) and *guru* (S) consecutively in each quarter. It is a new name and the alternative name for it is Añjan. It has been used thrice in the *Chaubīs Autār* (Nihkalaṅkī).

3. *Ajbā* is of 4 syllables having *magaṇ* (SSS) and *guru* (S) consecutively in each quarter. It is a new metre and alternative names for it are Akvā, Kanyā and Tīrṇā. It has been used 19 times in the *Chaubīs Autār* (Rāma) for the purpose of reproducing the sound of the actual action in the battlefield.

4. *Akrā* is of 5 syllables having *nagaṇ* (III) and *yagaṇ* (ISS) consecutively in each quarter. It is of Sanskrit origin and alternative names for it are Aṇakā, Anahad, Anubhav, Śaśivadnā, Chaṇḍrasā and

Madhurdhuni. It has been used 16 times in the *Chaubīs Autār* (Rāma).

5. *Akṛā* having one *sagaṇ* (IIS), two *jagaṇs* (ISI) consecutively in each quarter is a new name. It has been used eight times in the *Chaubīs Autār* (Rāma).

6. *Akvā* is of 4 syllables having *magaṇ* (SSS) and *guru* (S) consecutively in each quarter. It is a new metre and alternative names for it are Ajbā, Kanyā and Tīrṇā. It has been used six times in the *Chaubīs Autār* (Nihkalaṅkī) for the purpose of reproducing the sound of the actual action in the battlefield.

7. *Alkā* is of 12 syllables having *nagaṇ* (III), *yagaṇ* (ISS) *nagaṇ* (III) and *yagaṇ* (ISS) consecutively in each quarter. It is of Sanskrit origin and the alternative name for it is Kusam-vichitra or Kusam-bichitra. It has been used six times in the *Chaubīs Autār* (Rāma).

8. *Anād* is of 8 syllables having *magaṇ* (SSS) *yagaṇ* (ISS), *guru* (S) and *laghu* (I) consecutively and pause at 4 syllables in each quarter. It is also called Vāpī. It has been used eight times in the *Chaubīs Autār* (Rāma).

9. *Anant Tukā Bhujaṅg Prayāt*: An unrhymed 12 syllable metre with four *yagaṇs* is a new name and the alternative name for it is Bhujaṅg-Prayāt. It has been used eight times in the *Chaubīs Autār* (Rāma).

10. *Anhad* is of 6 syllables having *nagaṇ* (III) and *yagaṇ* (ISS) consecutively in each quarter. Alternative names for it are Akrā, Aṇakā, Anubhav, Śaśivadnā, Chaṇḍrasā and Madhurdhuni. It has been used four times in the *Chaubīs Autār (Nihkalaṅkī)*.

11. *Aṇakā* is of 6 syllables having nagaṇ (III) and *yagaṇ* (ISS) consecutively in each quarter. It is of Sanskrit origin and alternative names for it are Akrā, Anhad, Anubhav, Śaśivadnā, Chaṇḍrasā and Madhurdhuni. It has been used sixteen times in the *Chaubīs Autār* (Rāma).

12. *Anūp Narāj* is of 16 syllables having *jagaṇ* (ISI), *ragaṇ* (SIS), *jagaṇ* (ISI), *ragaṇ* (SIS), *jagaṇ* (ISI) and *guru* (S) consecutively in each quarter. It is of Sanskrit origin and alternative names for it are Narāj, Bichitra Narāj, Narāch and Bridhi. It has been used forty-seven times in the *Chaubīs Autār* (Rāma - 29; Nihkalaṅkī - 5) and *Rudra Avatār* (Datta - 13).

13. *Anubhav* is of 6 syllables having *nagaṇ* (III) and *yagaṇ* (ISS) consecutively in each quarter. Alternative names are: Akrā, Aṇakā, Anhad, Śaśivadnā, Chaṇḍrasā and Madhurdhuni. It has been used once in the *Chaubīs Autār* (Sūraj).

14. *Apūrab* or *Apūrav* is of 6 syllables having *ragaṇ* (SIS) and *tagaṇ* (SSI) consecutively in each quarter. It is of Sanskrit origin and alternative names for it are Arūpā and Krīṛā.It has been used 26 times in the *Chaubīs Autār* (Rāma).

15. *Aṛūhā* is of 10 syllables having *sagaṇ* (IIS), *jagaṇ* (ISI), and *guru* (S) consecutively in each quarter. Alternative names for it are Sañjutā, Saṅyuktā and Priyā. It has been used six times in the *Chaubīs Autār* (Rāma).

16. *Arūpā* is of 4 syllables having *yagaṇ* (ISS) and *guru* (S) consecutively in each quarter. Krīṛā is the alternative name given it. It has been used four times in the *Chaubīs Autār* (Rāma).

17. *Astā* is 12 syllables having four *sagaṇs* (IIS) in each quarter. It is of Sanskrit origin and alternative names given it are Kilakā, Tārak and Toṭak. It has been used five times in the *Chaubīs Autār* (Nihkalaṅkī).

18. *Astar* or *Astra* is of 12 syllables having four *yagaṇs* (ISS) in each quarter. It is of Sanskrit origin and alternative name for it is Bhujaṅg-prayāt. It has been used twice in the *Brahmā Avatār* (Māndhātā Rājā).

19. *Bachitra Pad* is of 8 syllables having two *bhagaṇs* (SII) and two *gurus* (S) consecutively in a quarter. It has been used twice in the *Rudra Avatār* (Datta).

20. *Bahir Tvīl Paschamī* is of five syllables having *sagaṇ* (IIS) and two *laghus* (I) consecutively in each quarter. Its formation is based on Pashto lyric and alternative name given it is Nāyak. It has been used 19 times in the *Giān Prabodh*.

21. *Bānturaṅgam* is of seven syllables having *magaṇ* (III), *ragaṇ* (SIS) and *guru* (S) consecutively in each quarter. It has been used four times in the *Chaubīs Autār* (*Nihkalaṅkī*).

22. *Belī Bindram* is of two kinds ; one is of eleven syllables having *nagaṇ* (III), two *sagaṇs* (IIS), *laghu* (I) and *guru* (S) consecutively in each quarter. The other is of ten syllables having *sagaṇ* (IIS), two *jagaṇs* (ISI) and *guru* (S) consecutively. It has been used fifteen times in the *Chaṇḍī Charitra II* (11) and *Chaubīs Autār* (Narsiṅgh - 2 and Sūraj - 2).

23. *Bhagvatī* or *Bhagautī* is of two kinds ; one is of six syllables having two *yagaṇs* (ISS) and the other is of 8 syllables having *jagaṇ* (ISI), *sagaṇ* (IIS), *laghu* (I) and *guru* (S) consecutively in each quarter. It is of Hindi origin and Bhavānī and Srī Bhagvatī are the other names given it. The first kind is also known as Somrājī or Śaṅkhanārī. It has been used 141 times in the *Jāpu* (41), *Chaubīs Autār* (Nihkalaṅkī - 17), and the *Rudrā Avatar* (Datta - 60; and Pāras Nāth - 23).

24. *Bhaṛthūā* is of six syllables having two *yagaṇs* (ISS) in each quarter. The alternative name given it is Śaṅkhanārī and it suits the description of destruction in war. It has been used twenty-five times in the *Chaubīs Autār* (Nihkalaṅkī).

25. *Bhavānī* is of two kinds : one is of six syllables having two *yagaṇs* (ISS), and the other is of eight syllables having *jagaṇ* (ISI), *sagaṇ* (IIS), *laghu* (I) and *guru* (S) consecutively in each quarter. The alternative name given it is Bhagautī. It has been used six times in *Chaubīs Autār* (Nihkalaṅkī). (See *Bhagvatī*)

26. *Bhujaṅg* is similar to Bhujaṅg-prayāt. It has been used 317 times (*Bachitra Nāṭak* (41), *Chaubīs Autār* (55) and *Pākhyān Charitra* (221).

27. *Bhujaṅg-prayāt* is of 12 syllables having four *yagaṇs* (ISS) in each quarter. It is of Sanskrit origin and alternative names for it are Bhujaṅg and Astar. It has been used 609 times (*Jāpu* (62), *Akāl Ustati* (30), *Bachitra Nāṭak* (72), *Chaṇḍī Charitra* II (70), *Giān Prabodh* (88), *Chaubīs Autār* (117), *Brahmā Avatār* (22), *Rudra Avatār* (Datta: 17 and Pāras Nāth: 65) and *Pākhyān Charitra* (66). In some of the old manuscript copies of the *Jāpu*, Aradh Bhujaṅg is found written in place of Bhujaṅg-prayāt.

28. *Bidhūp Narāj* is of 8 syllables having *jagaṇ* (ISI), ragaṇ (SIS) *laghu* (I) and *guru* (S) consecutively in a quarter. Alternative names for it are Aradh Narāj and Pramāṇikā. It has been used six times in the *Chaubīs Autār* (Nihkalaṅkī).

29. *Birāj* is of six syllables having two *ragaṇs* (SIS) in each quarter. It is of Hindi origin and alternative names for it are Vijohā and Vimohā. It has been used four times in the *Chaubīs Autār* (Rāma).

30. *Bisekh* or *Bisheshak* is of sixteen syllables

having five *bhagaṇs* (SII) and *guru* (S) consecutively in each quarter. Alternative names given it are Aśvgati, Manaharaṇ and Nīl. It has been used four times in the *Chaubīs Autār* (Nihkalaṅkī).

31. *Bridh Narāj*. See *Narāj Bridh*.

32. *Chāchari* is of two kinds – one is of four syllables having *jagaṇ* (ISI) and *guru* (S) and the other is of three syllables having one *yagaṇ* (ISS). Alternative names given it are Sudhī and Śaśī. It has been used 57 times in the *Jāpu* (32) and *Chaubīs Autār* (Rāma - 6; and Nihkalaṅkī - 19).

33. *Chāmar* is of 15 syllables having *ragaṇ* (SIS), *jagaṇ* (ISI), *ragaṇ* (SIS), *jagaṇ* (ISI), *ragaṇ* (SIS) consecutively in each quarter. It is of Sanskrit origin and alternative names for it are Somvallarī and Tūṇ. It has been used two times in the *Chaubīs Autār* (Nīhkalaṅkī).

34. *Chañchalā* is of 16 syllables having *ragaṇ* (SIS), *jagaṇ* (ISI), *ragaṇ* (SIS), *jagaṇ* (ISI) and *laghu* (I) consecutively in each quarter. Alternative names given it are Chitra, Birāj and Brahmrūpak. It has been used twice in the *Chaubīs Autār* (Nihkalaṅkī).

35. *Charpaṭ* is of five syllables having *bhagaṇ* (SII) and two *gurus* (S) or *sagaṇ* (IIS) and two *gurus* (S) consectively in each quarter. It is of Sanskrit origin and alternative names for it are Uchhāl, Haṅsak and Paṅkti. It has been used 27 times in the *Jāpu* and Rudra Avatār (Datta) 19.

36. *Dodhak* is of eleven syllables having three *bhagaṇs* (SII) and two *gurus* (S) in each quarter. It is of Sanskrit origin and alternative names for it are Bandhu, Modak and Sundarī. In *Chaubīs Autār* (Narsiṅgh) this metre has been used for Modak with four *bhagaṇs* (SII) in each quarter. It has been used 22 times, in the *Chaubīs Autār* (Narsiṅgh 3; Chand - 4; and Rāma - 10) and *Brahmā Avatār* (Māndhātā Rājā - 5).

37. *Ek Achharī* is of three types, i.e. Mahī with two syllables having *laghu* and *guru* (IS) in each quarter beginning with the same letters ; Mrigendra with three syllables in the formation of *jagaṇ* (ISI) in each quarter beginning with the same letter ; and Śaśi with three syllables in the formation of *yagaṇ* (ISS) in each quarter beginning with the same letter. Alternative names given it are Ekākharī and Śrī. It has been used eight times in the *Jāpu*.

38. *Haribolmanā* (six syllables with two *sagaṇs* (IIS), in each quarter) is also called Tilkā. It has been used 69 times, in the *Jāpu* (14), *Chaubīs Autār* (Nihkalaṅkī) (30) and *Brahmā Avatār* (Manu Rājā - 1, Prith Rājā - 24).

39. *Hohā* is of four syllables having *jagaṇ* (ISI) and *guru* (S) consecutively in each quarter. The alternative name for it is Sudhi. It has been used 14 times in the *Chaubīs Autār* (Rāma).

40. *Jhūlā* is of six syllables having two *yagaṇs* (ISS) in each quarter. Alternative names given it are Somrājī and Aradh Bhujaṅg. It has been used four times in the *Chaubīs Autār* (Rāma).

41. *Jhūlnā* (24 syllables having eight *yagaṇs* (ISS) in each quarter) is also known as Maṇidhar Savaiyyā. It has been freely used by the poets of medieval period and one kind of it is also included in *mātrik* metres. It has been used seven times in the composition *Chaubīs Autār* (Kṛṣṇa - 4 ; Rāma - 3).

42. *Kabitt* is of 31 syllables with pause at 8,8,8,7 and *guru* (S) at the end of each quarter. Its origin is not known though it is

profusely found in old Hindi and Punjabi poetry. Tulsīdās, Padmākar, Bhāī Gurdās and Hirdya Rām Bhallā were quite fond of using it in their works. Alternative names for it are Daṇḍak, Manaharaṇ and Ghanākṣarī. It rhymes and ends with a *guru*. It has been used 154 times in the *Dasam Granth – Akāl Ustati*: 44, *Chaṇḍī Charitra I*: 7, *Giān Prabodh*: 8, *Chaubīs Autār*: 69 (Kṛṣṇa: 58 and Rāma 11), *Brahmā Avatār* (Vyās): 1, and *Pākhyān Charitra*: 25.

43. *Kaṇṭh Abhūkhaṇ* is of eleven syllables having three *bhagaṇs* (SII) and two *gurus* (S) in each quarter. In Sanskrit it is called Dodhak. It has been used eight times in the *Chaubīs Autār* (Rāma).

44. *Kilkā* is of twelve syllables having four *sagaṇs* (IIS) in each quarter. Alternative names for it are Astā and Toṭak. It has been used twice in *Chaubīs Autār* (Nihkalaṅkī).

45. *Kripānkrit* is of seven syllables having *sagaṇ* (IIS), *nagaṇ* (III) and *laghu* (I) consecutively in each quarter. The alternative name for it is Madhubhār. It has been used 34 times in the composition *Chaubīs Autār* (Nihkalaṅkī) 12 and *Rudra Avatār* (Datta) 22.

46. *Kulak* or *Kulkā* is of two kinds ; one, *Kulak,* has six syllables in order of *bhagaṇ* (SII) and *jagaṇ* (ISI), and the other, *Kulkā,* has six syllables in order of *nagaṇ* (III) and *yagaṇ* (ISS) in each quarter. It is of Sanskrit origin and the alternative name for is *Śaśivadanā.* It has been used 23 times in the *Chaṇḍī Charitra II* (4), *Chaubīs Autār* (Nihkalaṅkī - 11), and *Rudra Avatār* (Datta - 8).

47. *Kumār-lalit* is of eight syllables having *jagaṇ* (ISI), *ragaṇ* (SIS), *laghu* (I) and *guru* (S) consecutively in each quarter. It is of Hindi origin and the alternative name for it is Mallikā. It has been used eight times in the *Chaubīs Autār* (Nihkalaṅkī).

48. *Kusam Bichitra,* also written as *Kusum Vichitra,* is of 12 syllables having *nagaṇ* (III), *yagaṇ* (ISS), *nagaṇ* (III) and *yagaṇ* (ISS) consecutively in each quarter. It is of Sanskrit origin and was adopted by Keshav in his works. It has been used eight times in *Chaubīs Autār* (Rāma).

49. *Madhurdhuni,* is also known by the names of Akrā, Aṇkā, Anhad, Anubhav, Śaśivadanā and Chaṇḍrasā, is of six syllables having *nagaṇ* (III) and *yagaṇ* (ISS) consecutively in a quarter. It has been used 18 times in the *Chaubīs Autār* (Rāma - 11, and Sūraj - 7).

50. *Māltī* is of twenty-three syllables having seven *bhagaṇs* (SII) and two *gurus* (S) consecutively in each quarter. It is of Sanskrit origin and is a kind of Savaīyyā. Alternative names given it are Indav, Bijai and Mattagyand. It has been used four times in the *Chaubīs Autār* (Nihkalaṅkī).

51. *Manohar* is of 23 syllables, having seven *bhagaṇs* (SII) and two *gurus* (S) consecutively in each quarter. It is of Hindi origin and is a kind of Savaīyyā. Alternative names given it are Bijai and Mattagyand. It has been used 24 times in the *Chaṇḍī Charitra II* (I) and *Chaubīs Autār* (Rāma - 23).

52. *Mathān* is of six syllables having two *tagaṇs* (SSI) in each quarter. It has been used nine times in the *Chaubīs Autār*. (Nihkalaṅkī).

53. *Medak* or *Toṭak* is of twelve syllables having four *sagaṇs* (IIS) in each quarter. It has been used five times in the *Brahmā Avatār* (Vyās).

54. *Nāgsarūpiṇī,* also called Pramāṇikā, is of eight syllables having *jagaṇ* (ISI), *ragaṇ* (SIS),

laghu (I) and *guru* (S) consecutively in each quarter. It is of Sanskrit origin and has been used 10 times in the *Chaubīs Autār* (Nihkalaṅkī - 6 ; and Rāma - 4).

55. *Nāgsarūpiṇī Aradh* is of Sanskrit origin and is of 4 syllables having *jagaṇ* (ISI) and *guru* (S) in each quarter. Alternative names given it are Sudhi and Narāj-laghu and it has been used five times in the *Chaubīs Autār* (Rāma).

56. *Narāj,* of Sanskrit origin and also called Narāch, Nāgrāj, Pañch Chāmar and Vichitra, is of 16 syllables having *jagaṇ* (ISI), *ragaṇ* (SIS), *jagaṇ* (ISI), *ragaṇ* (SIS), *jagaṇ* (ISI) and *guru* (S) consecutively in each quarter. It has been used 150 times in the *Akāl Ustati* (20), *Bachitra Nāṭak* (33), *Chaṇḍī Charitra II* (21), *Giān Prabodh* (37), *Brahmā Avatār* (8), *Rudra Avatār* (Pāras Nāth 30) and *Pākhyān Charitra* (1).

57. *Narāj Aradh* is of eight syllables having *jagaṇ* (ISI), *ragaṇ* (SIS), *laghu* (I) and *guru* (S) consecutively in each quarter. Alternative names for it are Nagsarūpiṇī and Pramāṇikā. It has been used 21 times, in the *Giān Prabodh* (12) and *Chaubīs Autār* (Sūraj - 4, Rāma - 5).

58. *Narāj Briddh,* also called Mahānarāch, is of 16 syllables having *jagaṇ* (ISI), *ragaṇ* (SIS), *jagaṇ* (ISI), *ragaṇ* (SIS), *jagaṇ* (ISI), and *guru* (S) consecutively in a quarter. It has been used 10 times, in the *Chaṇḍī Charitra II* (1) *Giān Prabodh* (5) and *Chaubīs Autār* (Rudra) (4).

59. *Narāj Laghu* is of 4 syllables having *jagaṇ* (ISI) and *guru* (S) consecutively in each quarter. Alternative names given it are Sudhī and Hohā. It has been used 20 times in the *Akāl Ustati.*

60. *Nav Nāmak,* also named Narhari, is of 8 syllables having two *nagaṇs* (III) and two *laghus* (I) consecutively in each quarter. It has been used six times in the *Chaubīs Autār* (Rāma).

61. *Nispāl* is of 15 syllables having *bhagaṇ* (SII), *jagaṇ* (ISI) *sagaṇ* (IIS), *nagaṇ* (III) and *ragaṇ* (SIS) consecutively in each quarter. It is also known by the names of Nispālikā and Niśipāl. It has been used four times in the *Chaubīs Autār.* (Nihkalaṅkī).

62. *Padhisṭakā* is of 12 syllables having four *sagaṇs* (IIS) in each quarter (*See* Saṅgīt Padhisṭakā). The alternative name for it is Toṭak, and it has been used twice in the *Chaubīs Autār* (Nihkalaṅkī)

63. *Pādhṛī Aradh,* also named Madhubhār, is of five syllables having two *gurus* (S) and *jagaṇ* (ISI) consecutively in each quarter. It has been used five times in the *Brahmā Avatār* (Vyās).

64. *Paṅkaj Bāṭikā,* of Sanskrit origin, is of 12 syllables having four *bhagaṇs* (SII) in each quarter. The alternative name given it is Modak. In the books of prosody its composition is different, i.e. *bhagaṇ* (SII), *nagaṇ* (III), two *jagaṇs* (ISI) and *laghu* (I). It has been used twice in the *Chaubīs Autār* (Nihkalaṅkī).

65. *Priyā,* of Sanskrit origin and also known as Aṛūhā and Saṅyut, is of ten syllables having *sagaṇ* (IIS), two *jagaṇs* (ISI) and *guru* (S) consecutively in each quarter. It has been used twice in the *Chaubīs Autār* (Nihkalaṅkī).

66. *Ramāṇ* is of six syllables having two *sagaṇs* (IIS) in each quarter. Alternative names for it are Ramāṇakā and Tilkā. It has been used four times in the *Chaubīs Autār* (Nihkalaṅkī).

67. *Rasāval* is of six syllables having two *yagaṇs*

(ISS) in each quarter. It has been used in the compositions titled *Jāpu* (8), *Bachitra Nāṭak* (90), *Chaṇḍī Charitra II* (69), *Giān Prabodh* (17), *Rudra Avatār* (17), and *Chaubīs Autār* (179) having been named as Aradh Bhujaṅg in the *Jāpu* and the *Bachitra Nāṭak*.

68. *Rāvaṇbād* is of six syllables having two *jagaṇs* (ISI) in each quarter. It has been used twice in the *Chaubīs Autār* (Nihkalaṅkī).

69. *Rekhtā* is of 31 syllables having pause at 8,8,8,7. This is not the name of a metre but is a metrical composition of mixed Persian and Hindi words. In *Chaṇḍī Charitra I,* Rekhtā is used only once for Kabitt (Manhar).

70. *Rūāmal* is of 17 syllables having *ragaṇ* (SIS), *sagaṇ* (IIS), two *jagaṇs* (ISI), *bhagaṇ* (SII), *guru* (S) and *laghu* (I) consecutively in each quarter, with pause at 10,7. Alternative names for it are Rūāl and Rūāmaṇ. It has been used 186 times in the *Jāpu* (8), *Akāl Ustati* (20), *Chaṇḍī Charitra II* (15), *Giān Prabodh* (30), *Chaubīs Autār* (26), *Brahmā Avatār* (25), *Rudra Avatār* (57), *Sastra Nām Mālā* (2) and *Pākhyān Charitra* (3).

71. *Ruṇjhuṇ* is of six syllables having *nagaṇ* (III) and *yagaṇ* (ISS) consecutively in each quarter. Alternative names for it are Akvā and Śaśivadnā. It has been used thrice in *Rudra Avatār.*

72. *Samānikā* is of eight syllables having *ragaṇ* (SIS), *jagaṇ* (ISI) and *guru* (S) consecutively in each quarter. The alternative name given it is *Pramāṇikā* (ISI, SIS, I, S). It has been used 12 times in the *Chaubīs Autār* (Rāma - 8 and Nihkalaṅkī - 4).

73. *Saṅgīt Bhujaṅg-prayāt* has been used 44 times in the *Chaṇḍī Charitra II* (7) and *Chaubīs Autār* (Rāma - 13 and Nihkalaṅkī - 24).

74. *Saṅgīt Narāj* has been used only once in the *Chaṇḍī Charitra II.*

75. *Saṅgīt Padhisṭakā* is of eleven syllables having *ragaṇ* (SIS), *jagaṇ* (ISI), *tagaṇ* (SSI), *guru* (S) and *laghu* (I) consecutively in each quarter. But in the *Nihkalaṅkī Avatār,* this name has been given to Toṭak (*See* Padhisṭakā). It has been used 8 times in *Chaubīs Autār* (Rāma).

76. *Sañjutā* or *Saṅyutā,* of Sanskrit origin, is of 10 syllables having *sagaṇ* (IIS), two *jagaṇs* (ISI) and *guru* (S) consecutively in each quarter. Alternative names given it are Sañjuktā, Arūhā and Priyā. It has been used six times in the *Brahmā Avatār.*

77. *Saṅkhnārī* is of six syllables having two *yagaṇs* (ISS) in each quarter. Its other alternative names are Somrājī and Aradh Bhujaṅg. In the *Dasam Granth* (*Jāpu*) it is given under the name of Aradh Bhujaṅg.

78. *Sarasvatī* is of 17 syllables having *ragaṇ* (SIS), *sagaṇ* (IIS), two *jagaṇs* (ISI), *bhagaṇ* (SII), *guru* (S), *laghu* (I) consecutively in each quarter, with pause at 8,9. It is of Prākrit and Apbhraṅśa origin and its other alternative names are Rūāmal, Rūāl and Rūālā. It has been used 8 times in the composition *Chaubīs Autār* (Rāma).

79. *Savaiyyā* is of 48 kinds out of which Madirā, Indav, Māltī, Ramaya, Kirīṭ, Drumilā, Manoj, Uṭaṅkaṇ, Surdhunī and Sarvagāmī are found in the *Dasam Granth.* Final alliteration of all the quartets is essential in a Savaiyyā. Its origin lies in the Braj. In the medieval Hindi poetry it has been usually chosen for sensuous love poetry due to its smoothness, but in the *Dasam Granth* it is applied for war poetry with unique success. It has been used for a total of 2252 times in

the *Dasam Granth,* the maximum use (1782 times) of it being in the "Kṛṣṇa Avatār" in the *Chaubīs Autār.*

80. *Savaiyyā Anant-tukā* is a kind of Savaiyyā with no final alliteration as is clear from its name. It has been used only once in the Chaubīs Autār (Rāma).

81. *Somrājī* is of 6 syllables having two *yagaṇs* (ISS) in each quarter. It is of Sanskrit origin and its other alternative names are Utbhuj, Aradh Bhujaṅg, Śaṅkhanārī and Jhūlā. In the *Dasam Granth* ("Nihkalaṅkī Avatār" in the *Chaubīs Autār),* this name has been given to four Bhujaṅg-prayāt metres.

82. *Sukhdā Bridh* is of eight syllables having *laghu* (I) in the beginning and *guru* (S) at the end of each quarter, with pause at 5,3. Its other alternative name is Sagaunā. It has been used four times in the *Chaubīs Autār* (Nihkalaṅkī).

83. *Sundarī* is a form of Savaiyyā comprising 25 syllables – eight *sagaṇs* (IIS) and one *guru* (S). In the "Rāmā Avatār" of the *Chaubīs Autār* it has been used eighteen times.

84. *Tārak* is of 12 syllables having four *sagaṇs* (IIS) in each quarter. Alternative names for it are Astā and Toṭak. It has been used 26 times in the *Dasam Granth – Chaubīs Autār* (Nihkalaṅkī - 24), Rudra Avatār (Datta - 2).

85. *Tārkā* is of 13 syllables having four *sagans* (IIS) and *guru* (S) consecutively in each quarter. Alternative names given it are Ugādh and Yaśodā. It is used 8 times in the *Chaubīs Autār* (Rāma).

86. *Tar Narāj* is of 7 syllables having *ragaṇ* (SIS), *jagaṇ* (ISI) and *guru* (S) consecutively in each quarter, but in the *Dasam Granth* we find it consisting of only two quarters (*charaṇs*) instead of four. The alternative name for it is Samānikā. It has been used eight times in the *Chaubīs Autār* (Nihkalaṅkī).

87. *Tilkā* is of 4 syllables having *magaṇ* (SSS) and *guru* (S) consecutively in each quarter. Alternative names for it are Akvā, Ajbā, and Kanyā. It has been used eight times in the *Chaubīs Autār* (Rāma).

88. *Tilkaṛīā* is of five syllables having *jagaṇ* (ISI) and two *gurus* (S) consecutively in each quarter. Alternative names for it are Ugādh and Yaśodā. A speciality of this metre is that herein sound conveys the sense. It has been used six times in *Chaubīs Autār* (Rāma).

89. *Toṭak* is of 12 syllables having four *sagaṇs* (IIS) in each quarter. It is of Sanskrit origin and its other alternative names are Astā, Kilkā and Tārak. It has been used 232 times in the compositions namely *Akāl Ustati* (20), *Bachitra Nāṭak* (6), *Chaṇḍī Charitras* (6), *Giān Prabodh* (15), *Chaubīs Autār* (101), *Brahmā Avatār* (3), *Rudra Avatār* (63), and *Pākhyān Charitra* (18).

90. *Trigatā* is of 4 syllables having *magaṇ* (SSS) and *guru* (S) in each quarter. The first letter of each line (*charaṇ*) is repeated thrice with a view to reproducing the sound of actual action. Alternative names for it are Akvā and Ajbā. It has been used 10 times in the *Chaubīs Autār* (Rāma).

91. *Triṇṇiṇ* is of six syllables having *nagaṇ* (III) and *yagaṇ* (ISS) consecutively in each quarter. The first word of each line (*charaṇ*) is *triṇṇiṇ* or similarly sounding word so that its repetition helps to produce the sound of actual fighting in the field. It has been used 8 times in the *Chaubīs Autār* (Rāma).

92. *Triṛkā* is of 6 syllables having *nagaṇ* (III) and *yagaṇ* (IIS) consecutively in each quarter. Alternative names are: Akvā and Śaśivadnā.

The sound of *mridaṅg* is reproduced through the use of alliteration of words. It has been used ten times in the *Chaubīs Autār* (Nihkalaṅkī).

93. *Uchhlā* is of 5 syllables having *bhagaṇ* (SII) and two *gurus* (S) consecutively in each quarter. Alternative names for it are Uchhāl, Haṅsak and Paṅkti. It has been used nine times in the *Brahmā Avatār*.

94. *Ugādh* is of 5 syllables having *jagaṇ* (ISI) and two *gurus* (S) consecutively in each quarter. It is of Sanskrit origin and is also called Tilkaṛīā and Yaśodhā. It has been used 13 times in the *Chaubīs Autār* (Rāma).

95. *Ugāthā* is of 10 syllables having *jagaṇ* (ISI) *tagaṇ* (SSI), *ragaṇ* (SIS) and *guru* (S) consecutively in each quarter with pause at 5,5. It is of Sanskrit origin. It has been used nine times in the *Chaubīs Autār* (Rāma).

96. *Uṭaṅkaṇ* is of 22 syllables having seven *ragaṇs* (SIS) and *guru* (S) consecutively in each quarter with pause at 12,10. It is of Sanskrit origin and the alternative name given it is Uṭaṅgaṇ. It is a kind of Savaiyyā. It has been used 10 times in the *Chaubīs Autār* (Rāma).

97. *Utbhuj,* also called *Udbhuj,* is of 6 syllables having two *yagaṇs* (ISS) in each quarter. Alternative names are: Arad, Bhujaṅg, Somrājī, Śaṅkhanārī, Jhūlā and Rasāval. It has been used four times in the *Chaubīs Autār.* (Nihkalaṅkī).

SYLLABIC INSTANT (*MĀTRIK*) METRES

98. *Abhīr* is of 11 syllabic instants having *jagaṇ* (ISI) at the end of each quarter. It is of Prākrit and Apbhraṅś origin and the alternative name for it is Ahīr. It has been used four times in the *Chaubīs Autār* (Nihkalaṅkī).

99. *Aṛill* is of 21 syllabic instants having pause at 11,10 with *ragaṇ* (SIS) at the end of each quarter and use of 'Ho' syllabic instant at the beginning of the fourth quarter, which is always in addition to the actual count. It is of Apbhraṅś origin and is an early form of Chaupaī. It is a popular metre of narrative Hindi poetry. It has been used 962 times in the *Bachitra Nāṭak* (1), *Sastra Nām Mālā* (253), *Pākhyān Charitra* (690) and *Chaubīs Autār* (18 : Kṛṣṇa 14, Sūraj -2, Rudra - 2).

100. *Aṛill Dūjā* is of 16 syllabic instants with *bhagaṇ* (SII) at the end of each quarter. It is of Apbhraṅś origin and alternative names for it are Ḍillā and Pādā Kulak. It has been used twice in the *Chaubīs Autār* (Nihkalaṅkī).

101. *Atimāltī* is of 16 syllabic instants having pause at 8,8, with two *gurus* (S) at the end of each quarter. It is of Sanskrit origin and the alternative name given it is Pādā Kulak. It has been used four times in the *Chaubīs Autār* (Nihkalaṅkī).

102. *Avatār* is of 23 syllabic instants having pause at 13,10 with *laghu* (I) and *guru* (S) consecutively at the end of each quarter. The alternative name for it is Mritgati. According to Bhāī Kāhn Siṅgh, only Aradh Avatār has been used in the *Dasam Granth,* but the scribe has erroneously put it under the heading of Doharā (See *Dohara*).

103. *Bahoṛā* is of 16 syllabic instants having pause at 8,8 with *jagaṇ* (ISI) at the end of each quarter. The alternative name for it is Pādharī. It has been used four times in the *Chaubīs Autār* (Rāma).

104. *Bahṛā* is of 21 syllabic instants having pause at 11,10 with *jagaṇ* (ISI) at the first pause and *ragaṇ* (SIS) at the second pause. The alternative name given it is Punhā. It has been used twice in *Chaubīs Autār* (Rāma).

105. *Bait* is of 18 syllabic instants having pause at 10,8 with *laghu* (I) at the end of each *charaṇ*. It is of Arabic and Persian origin and is popular in narrative Punjabi poetry. It has been used 863 times in the *Zafarnāmah* (111) and *Hikāyats* (752).

106. *Bishanpad* is of different syllabic instants in different kinds and alternative names for it are Śabda, Viṣṇupad and Bisanpad. It is of Hindi origin and was freely used by poets of Bhakti tradition. In the *Dasam Granth* it is found only in the *Chaubīs Autār*, (Kṛṣṇa - 5) and the *Rudra Avatār* (Pāras Nāth - 45).

107. *Charpaṭ Chhīgā* is of eight syllabic instants having six *mātrās* and *guru* (S) consecutively in each quarter. It is a kind of Charpaṭ and has been used for eight times in the *Chaubīs Autār* (Rāma).

108. *Chatuspadī* or *Chaturpadī* is of 30 syllabic instants having pause at 10,8,12 with *sagaṇ* (IIS) and *guru* (S) at the end of each quarter. Alternative names given it are Chavpaīyā and Chaupaīyā. It has been used four time in the *Chaubīs Autār* (Nihkalaṅkī).

109. *Chaupaī* is of 16 syllabic instants having *guru* (S) at the end of each quarter. It is of Apbhraṅś origin and alternative names for it are Rūp-Chaupaī, Jaykarī and Śaṅkhinī. This metre is known as of two kinds, namely Chaupaī and Chaupāī. The first kind is of 15 *mātrās* and the second is of 16 *mātrās*, but in the Sikh scriptures there is no such distinction and usually it is of 16 *mātrās*. It is a popular metre in Hindi narrative poetry. Tulsīdās's *Rāma-charita Mānasa* is in this metre. In early periods Paddharīā was preferred to Chaupaī. This metre has been used 5555 times in the *Dasam Granth – Akāl Ustati*, (10), *Bachitra Nāṭak* (162), *Chaṇḍī Charitra II* (20), *Giān Prabodh* (46), *Chaubīs Autār* (414), *Brahmā Avatār* (56), *Rudra Avatār* (79), *Sastra Nām Mālā* (344), and *Pākhyān Charitra* (4424).

110. *Chhand* can be used for all kinds of metres. It is of Hindi origin and the alternative name for it is Chhant. It has been used 29 times in the *Sastra Nām Mālā* (5) and *Pākhyān Charitra* (24).

111. *Chhand Vaḍḍā* is of 28 syllabic instants having pause at 16,12, and *ragaṇ* (SIS) at the end of each quarter. It is of Hindi origin and has been used once in the *Sastra Nām Mālā* in place of Harigītikā, vide Kāhn Siṅgh Nābha, *Gurushabad Ratnākar Mahān Kosh*, p. 498.

112. *Chaubolā* is a kind of Savaiyyā but is defined as Chaubolā because of the use of four different languages in it. It has been used thrice in the *Chaubīs Autār* (Rāma).

113. *Chhappai*, a combination of Ullālā and Rolā, is of six *charaṇs*. It is of Apbhraṅś origin and alternative names for it are Chhappā, Chhappaya, Khaṭpad and Śārdulvikrīṛit. In the *Dasam Granth* it has been used in various forms for 81 times in the *Jāpu* (I), *Bachitra Nāṭak* (I), *Giān Prabodh* (8), *Chaubīs Autār* (19), *Rudra Avatār* (47) and *Pākhyān Charitra* (5).

114. *Doharā*, of two *charaṇs* and 24 syllabic instants with pause at 13,11 and *guru laghu* (SI) at the end of each *charaṇ* is of Apbhraṅś origin and alternative names given it are *dohā* (in Apbhraṅś), *gāthā* (in Prākrit) and *śloka* (in Sanskrit). It is of many kinds and almost all the kinds have been used in the *Dasam Granth*. It is always preferred for shorter patterns of verse. Gorakh Nāth, Kabīr, Jayasī, Tulsīdās, Bihārī, *et al.* had expressed themselves through this metre. It has been used 3150 times in the *Dasam Granth: Akāl Ustati* (10), *Bachitra Nāṭak* (38), *Chaṇḍī Charitra I* (80), *Chaṇḍī Charitra II* (14), *Chaṇḍī dī Vār* (I), *Giān*

Prabodh (2), *Chaubīs Autār (454)*, *Brahmā Avatār* (I), *Rudra Avatār* (8), *Savaiyyā: Jo kicch lekh likhio bidhātā* (I), *Sastra Nām Mālā* (711), and *Pākhyān Charitra* (1830).

115. *Elā* is of 24 syllabic instants having pause at 11,13 with two *gurus* (S) at the end of each line. It is made of three *charaṇs* (lines) and is of Sanskrit origin. It is *viṣam mātrik* in the *Dasam Granth* but according to *Hindi Chhand Prakāsh* it is *varṇik* metre. It has been used four times in the *Chaubīs Autār* (Nihkalaṅkī).

116. *Gāhā Dūjā* is of 27 syllabic instants having two *charaṇs* with pause at 14,13 in each *charaṇ*. It is of Prākrit origin and other name given it is Gāthā. It is also said to be four *charaṇs* with 62 *mātrās* in all, but it has been given a new form in the *Dasam Granth*. It has been used four times in the *Chaubīs Autār* (Nihkalaṅkī).

117. *Ghattā* is generally of two *charaṇs* having 32 syllabic instants but in the *Dasam Granth* it is of three *charaṇs* – the first foot of 24 syllabic instants with pause at 11,13; the second of 16 syllabic instants with pause at 8,8, and the third of 32 syllabic instants with pause at 8,8,16 and having two *laghus* (I) at the end. It is a Viṣam metre and is of Prākrit and Apbhraṅś origin. It has been used twice in the *Chaubīs Autār* (Nihkalaṅkī).

118. *Gītmālatī* is of 28 syllabic instants with pause at 16,12 in each quarter. It has been used 16 times in the *Chaubīs Autār* (Rāma - 8; Nihkalaṅkī - 8).

119. *Haṅs* is of 15 syllabic instants having two *charaṇs* with pause at 7,8 and *guru* (S) and *laghu* (I) at the end of each *charaṇ*. It is of Sanskrit origin and has been used four times in the *Chaubīs Autār* (Nihkalaṅkī).

120. *Harigītā* is of 28 syllabic instants having pause at 16,12 with *ragaṇ* (SIS) at the end of each quarter. It is of Hindi origin and the alternative name given it is Harigītikā. It has been used twice in the *Chaubīs Autār* (Nihkalaṅkī).

121. *Hīr* is of 23 syllabic instants having pause at 6,6,11 with *guru* (S) in the beginning and *ragaṇ* (SIS) at the end of each quarter. It is of Prākrit and Apbhraṅś origin and the alternative name for it is Hīrak. It is also counted in Varṇik metres. It has been used twice in the *Chaubīs Autār* (Nihkalaṅkī).

122. *Kalas* is the name of a combined metre. In the *Dasam Granth* it is made of Chaupaī and Tribhaṅgī, in which the last *pad* of the first stanza is reproduced in the beginning of the following stanza. The Gurū has given the name Kalas in place of Chaupaī and named the second metre independently as *Tribhaṅgī*. Alternative names for it are Ullās and Hullās. It has been used 13 times in the *Giān Prabodh* (4), and *Chaubīs Autār* (Rāma - 9).

123. *Kuṇḍalīā* is of 24 syllabic instants and is a combination of Dohā and Rolā with pause at 13,11 in the two *charaṇs* of Dohā and pause at 11,13 in the four quarters of Rolā, but in the *Dasam Granth* only two *charaṇs* of Rolā are combined with Dohā and as such this metre is of four *charaṇs* instead of six. It is of Apbhraṅś origin and the alternative name for it is Kuṇḍarīā. It is commonly used in Hindi poetry. In the *Dasam Granth* it has been used five times in the *Chaubīs Autār* (Nihkalaṅkī).

124. *Mādho* is of 16 syllabic instants having two *gurus* (S) at the end of each quarter. It is a kind of Aṛill and the alternative name given it is Karīṛā. It has been used seven times in the *Chaubīs Autār* (Nihkalaṅkī).

125. *Madhubhār* is of 8 syllabic instants having *jagaṇ* (ISI) after four *mātrās*. It is of

Prākrit and Apbhrańś origin and alternative names for it are Chhabi and Mohanā. It has been used 97 times in the *Jāpu* (17), *Bachitra Nāṭak* (12), *Chaṇḍī Charitra - II* (8), *Chaubīs Autār* (Nihkalańkī - 11), *Brahmā Avatār* (34), and *Rudra Avatār* - 15.

126. *Makrā* is of 12 syllabic instants and has three kinds of rhymes. It has been used 14 times in the *Chaubīs Autār*.

127. *Mārahā* or *Mārāh* is of 29 syllabic instants having pause at 10,8,11 with two *gurus* (S) at the end of each quarter. Alternative names for it are Manharī, Marharī and Marhaṭā. It has been used twice in the *Chaubīs Autār* (Nihkalańkī).

128. *Mohan* is of 28 syllabic instants having pause at 16,12 with *ragaṇ* (SIS) at the end of each quarter. Alternative names given it are Mohanā and Madhubhār. It has been used four times in the *Chaubīs Autār* (Nihkalańkī). Another form of it, *Mohaṇā*, is a kind of Harigītikā which is of 8 syllabic instants having *jagaṇ* (ISI) at the end of each quarter.

129. *Mohaṇī* is of 16 syllabic instants having *sagaṇ* (IIS) in the beginning and *magaṇ* (SSS) at the end of each quarter. Its alternative name in the *Dasam Granth* is Modak. It has been used 52 times, in the *Chaubīs Autār* (Rāma - 8) *Brahmā Avatār* (Aj Rājā - 8) and *Rudrā Avatār* (36).

130. *Mritgat* is of 12 syllabic instants with *nagaṇ* (III) at the end of each quarter. It is of Sanskrit origin and alternative name for it is Amritgati. It has been used thrice in the *Chaubīs Autār* (Rāma).

131. *Navpadī* is of 16 syllabic instants having *bhagaṇ* (SII) at the end of each quarter. It is a type of Chaupaī and Aṛill and has been used four times in *Chaubīs Autār* (Nihkalańkī).

132. *Pad* is of different syllabic instants in different kinds. It is of Hindi origin and alternative names for it are Śabda, Viṣṇupada and Bishanpad. It was a favourite with the medieval Indian poets writing in the devotional mould. It is actually not a metre, but a poetic form as in the case of Pauṛī. Its first *charaṇ* is comparatively short. It has been used 55 times in the *Shabad Hazāre* (10) and *Rudra (Pāras Nāth) Avatār* (45).

133. *Pāddharī,* also written as *Pāddhaṛī,* is of 12 syllabic instants having *jagaṇ* (ISI) at the end of each quarter with pause at 8,8. It is of Apbhrańś origin and is taken, at times, to mean Chaupaī. It has been used 312 times in the *Akāl Ustati* (38), *Bachitra Nāṭak* (2), *Giān Prabodh* (16), *Chaubīs Autār* (92), *Brahmā Avatār* (40), and *Rudra Avatār* (124).

134. *Pāddhaṛī Aradh* is of eight syllabic instants having two *gurus* (S) and *jagaṇ* (ISI) consecutively in each quarter. It resembles Madhubhār. It has been used five times in the *Brahmā Avatār* (Vyās).

135. *Padmāvatī* is of 30 syllabic instants having *sagaṇ* (IIS) and *guru* (S) at the end of each quarter with pause at 10,8,12 and rhyming at the first and the second pause. It resembles Chaupaī and its other alternative names are Chaturpadī and Chavpaīyā. It has been used thrice in the *Chaubīs Autār* (Nihkalańkī).

136. *Pauṛī* is a Viṣam Chhand having no limitation of lines *(charaṇs)* but its last *charaṇ* is generally short. The alternative name for it is Nihshreṇī, and is usually of two kinds: one, Nishānī which rhymes at the end of each *charaṇ* and the other, Sirkhiṇḍī having only middle-rhyme without any rhyming at the end. This metre is usually sung by the court-bards or *ḍhāḍhīs* and is musical in character. It is more a form of poetry than a metre. It has been used 61 times in the *Chaṇḍī dī Vār*

(54) and *Chaubīs Autār* (7).

137. *Punhā* is of 21 syllabic instants having pause at 11,10. Some poets have stressed the use of *jagaṇ* (ISI) in the middle while others have emphasized *ragaṇ* (SIS) in the end. Alternative names given it are Harihāṅ, Chāndrāyan, Parihāṅ and Punhā. It is also considered a kind of Aṛill. It has been used twice in *Chaṇḍī Charitra I.*

138. *Sadd* is of 29 syllabic instants having pause at 17,12 with *yagaṇ* (ISS) at the end of each *charaṇ*. It has been used only once in the *Dasam Granth*.

139. *Saṅgīt Bahṛā*, which is different from Bahṛā metre used in the *Dasam Granth,* has been treated four times in the *Chaubīs Autār* (Rāma).

140. *Saṅgīt Chhappaya* has been used 17 times – 8 times in the *Chaubīs Autār* (Rāma) and 9 times in the *Rudra Avatār* (Pāras Nāth).

141. *Saṅgīt Madhubhār.* The *Saṅgīt* is prefixed to it as it contains the strains of musical instruments which increases the tempo of war. It has been used 9 times in the *Chaṇḍī Charitra II.*

142. *Saṅgīt Pāddhaṛī* (*See* Pāddharī) has been used twice in the *Brahmā Avatār* (Vyās).

143. *Sirkhiṇḍī* is of 21,22, or 23 syllabic instants having pause at 12,9 or 12,10 or 14,9 respectively. It is of Sanskrit origin and alternative names for it are Palvaṅgam and Srīkhaṇḍ. It has been used in the *Dasam Granth* generally under the name of Pauṛī (*See* Pauṛī).

144. *Soraṭhā* is of 24 syllabic instants and is an inverted form of Dohā (Doharā). It has two *charaṇs* with pause at 11,13. The first pause ends with *laghu* (I), whereas the second pause ends with *guru* (S). It is of Hindi origin and has been used 80 times in the *Chaṇḍī Charitra I* (7), *Chaṇḍī Charitra II* (I), *Chaubīs Autār* (44), *Sastra Nām Mālā* (2), and *Pakhyān Charitra* (26).

145. *Sukhdā* is of 8 syllabic instants having *guru* (S), *laghu* (I) consecutively at the end of each quarter. It has been used 8 times in the *Chaubīs Autār* (Rāma).

146. *Supriyā* is of 16 syllabic instants with *bhagaṇ* (SII) at the end of each quarter. Its other alternative name is Ḍillā and has been used 4 times in the *Chaubīs Autār* (Nihkalaṅkī).

147. *Tilokī* is of 16 syllabic instants having *guru* (S) after four and eight *mātrās* and also at the end of each quarter. The alternative name given it is Upchitrā, and it has been used twice in the *Chaubīs Autār* (Nihkalaṅkī).

148. *Tomar* is of 12 syllabic instants having *guru* (S) and *laghu* (I) at the end of each quarter. It is of Sanskrit origin and its other alternative name is Padhaṛikā. Bhāī Kāhn Siṅgh has defined it as *varṇik* metre also, having *sagaṇ* (IIS) and two *jagaṇs* (ISI) in each quarter. But this definition does not disturb the pattern of *mātrik* metre as it is treated in Hindi poetry. It has been used 204 times in the *Dasam Granth*: *Akāl Ustati* (20), *Giān Prabodh* (22), *Chaubīs Autār* (26), *Brahmā Avatar* (70), *Rudra Avatār* (60), and *Pākhyān Charitra* (6).

149. *Tribhaṅgī* is of 32 syllabic instants having pause at 10,8,8,6 with *guru* (S) at the end of each quarter. There are ordinarily three subordinate rhymes at each pause. It is of Sanskrit origin and poets of Prākrit and Apbhraṅś have also practised it. It has been used 41 times in the *Akāl Ustati* (20), *Bachitra Nāṭak* (2), *Giān Prabodh* (7), and *Chaubīs*

Autār (12).

150. *Vijaya,* also written as Bijai, is of 40 syllabic instants having pause at 10,10,10,10 with *ragaṇ* (SIS) at the end of each quarter. It is of Prākrit and Apbhraṅś origin and also falls under the category of *varṇik* metre. It has been used 19 times in the *Chaṇḍī Charitra II* (2), *Chaubīs Autār* (1) and *Pākhyān Charitra* (16).

BIBLIOGRAPHY

1. Ashta, Dharam Pal, *The Poetry of the Dasam Granth.* Delhi, 1959
2. Loehlin, C.H., *The Granth of Guru Gobind Singh and the Khalsa Brotherhood.* Lucknow, 1971
3. Sher Singh, *Social and Political Philosophy of Guru Gobind Singh.* Delhi, n.d.
4. Kohli, Surindar Singh, "Dasam Granth," in Mircea Elide, ed., *The Encyclopaedia of Religion,* vol. 4. New York, 1987
5. Gopal Singh, *Thus Spake the Tenth Master.* Patiala, 1978
6. Jaggi, Rattan Singh, *Dasam Granth Parichaya.* Delhi, 1990
7. ——, *Dasam Granth dā Kartritav.* Delhi, 1965
8. Padam, Piārā Siṅgh, *Dasam Granth Darshan.* Patiala, 1968
9. Mahīp Siṅgh, *Gurū Gobind Siṅgh Aur Unkī Hindī Kavitā.* Delhi, 1968
10. Bhārdwāj, Om Prakash, *Ramavtār Tathā Krishaṇavtār Kā Kāvya-Shāstrīya Adhyan.* Patiala, 1978

C.H.L.
R.S.J.

DASAUNDHĀ SIṄGH, a Ḍhilloṅ Jaṭṭ of Jhabal in Amritsar district, was half-brother of the celebrated Baghel Siṅgh, leader of the Karoṛsiṅghīā *misl.* He crossed the Beās in 1759, and seized some villages in the Jalandhar Doāb. The family retained possession of these under Mahārājā Raṇjīt Siṅgh, supplying in return a contingent of 26 horsemen.

BIBLIOGRAPHY

Griffin, Lepel, and C.F. Massy, *Chiefs and Families of Note in the Punjab.* Lahore, 1909

S.S.B.

DASAUNDHĀ SIṄGH (d. 1767), founder of the Nishānāvālī *misl,* was the son of Chaudharī Sāhib Rāi belonging to the village of Mansūr, in Fīrozpur district of the Punjab. He received *pāhul,* the K͟hālsā initiatory rites at the hands of Dīwān Darbārā Siṅgh, a prominent Sikh leader of the post-Bandā Siṅgh period. By 1734, Dasaundhā Siṅgh was a leading figure in the Taruṇā Dal. At the time of the formation of the Dal K͟hālsā in 1748, he was proclaimed the leader of the Nishānāvālī *misl.* The Nishānāvālī *misl,* kept as a reserve force at Amritsar, used to act as standard-bearers of the K͟hālsā army. Hence the name (*nishān* = flag or standard; *vālī* = owning or unfurling). In January 1764 after the conquest of Sirhind, Dasaundhā Siṅgh took possession of Siṅghāṅvālā in Fīrozpur district, Sāhnevāl, Sarāi Lashkarī K͟hān, Dorāhā, Amloh, Zīrā and Ambālā. At the last-named station, he established his headquarters. He was killed in May 1767 at Meerut in a sudden attack by Jahān K͟hān and Zābitā K͟hān and was succeeded to the headship of the *misl* by his younger brother, Saṅgat Siṅgh.

BIBLIOGRAPHY

1. Griffin, Lepel, and C.F. Massy, *Chiefs and Families of Note in the Punjab.* Lahore, 1909
2. Seetal, Sohan Singh, *The Sikh Misals and the Panjab.* Ludhiana, n.d.

S.S.B.

DASAUNDHĀ SIṄGH, BHĀĪ (1892-1921), one of the Nankāṇā Sāhib martyrs, was born on 28 August 1892, the son of Bhāī Hīrā Siṅgh and Māī Mān Kaur of village Harīpur, in Jalandhar district. The family later migrated to Chakk No. 91 Dhannuāṇā in the newly developed canal district of Lyallpur, now in Pakistan. Dasaundhā Siṅgh was married and was father of two children – a daughter and a son – when he enlisted in the *jathā* or column of Akālī volunteers led by Lachhmaṇ Siṅgh Dhārovālī, and attained martyrdom at Nankāṇā Sāhib on 20 February 1921.

See NANKĀṆĀ SĀHIB MASSACRE

BIBLIOGRAPHY

Shamsher, Gurbakhsh Singh, *Shahīdī Jīvan*. Nankana Sahib, 1938

G.S.G.

DĀS, BHAṬṬ. *See* BHAṬṬ BĀṆĪ

DAS GRANTHĪ, a *pothī*, i.e. a small book, containing selected *bāṇīs* or texts from the *Dasam Granth*. *Das*, meaning 'ten', here stands for 'tenth', or the Tenth Master's *granth* or book to distinguish it from the older *Ādi Granth*, i.e. the first or primary *granth* ; *granthī*, a small book (the suffix "ī" is generally added to a word in Punjabi to indicate its diminutive form; an exception is the word *granthī* when it stands for a *gurdwārā* officiant), *Das Granthī* thus being a small anthology comprising selections from the *Dasam Granth* of Gurū Gobind Siṅgh. Anthologies styled *Das Granthī* evidently began to be compiled with a view to making the writings of Gurū Gobind Siṅgh which constitute a voluminous *granth* accessible to beginners and lay readers. No standardized selections exist, but the *Das Granthī* in its current form issued under the seal of the Shiromaṇī Gurdwārā Parbandhak Committee contains eight texts namely, *Jāpu, Shabad Pātshāhī 10, Akāl Ustati, Bachitra Nāṭak, Chaṇḍī Charitra I, Chaṇḍī Charitra 2, Chaṇḍī dī Vār* and *Giān Prabodh*. *Das Granthī* is now available in several different recensions, but not without variations in selection.

A parallel compilation, *Pañj Granthī* is also in existence that contains selections of *bāṇīs* from the *Ādi Granth*. Selections differ in different editions, but the *bāṇīs* anthologized are usually more than five (*pañj*).

T.S.

DAS GUR KATHĀ, by Kaṅkaṇ, one of the poets in attendance on Gurū Gobind Siṅgh, is a versified account, in an admixture of Braj, Hindi and Punjabi, of the events of the lives of the Ten Gurūs. The only known manuscript of the work is present in the Pañjāb Public Library at Lahore, a copy of which was obtained for the library of the Khālsā College at Amritsar in 1956 and which was published with annotation in book-form, in 1967, by the Khālsā Samāchār, Amritsar. The colophon indicates the author's name, but not the year of composition which from internal evidence is reckoned to be around AD 1699. The work deals with events up to the creation of the Khālsā which took place during this year. The *Kathā* comprises 234 stanzas and is written in different poetical metres such as Dohā, Savaiyyā, Chaupaī, Pauṛī, Soraṭhā and Aṛill.

The poet attributes the popularity of Gurmukhī characters to Gurū Nānak who, according to him, communicated his message in a much easier language and form than those of the Vedas. Succession in Gurū Nānak's line was determined by qualities of humility and dedication and not by ties of blood. Gurū Nānak's spiritual successor was Gurū Aṅgad, his own devoted disciple. Especially detailed is the account of Gurū Hargobind, Nanak VI, comprising 84 stanzas. The poet hails him as one who combined the spiritual with the temporal and describes the battles he had to engage in. Among other details is the enumeration of Mughal provinces under Emperor Shāh Jahāṅ. The poet panegyrizes Gurū Tegh Bahādur's martyrdom which, as he says, he voluntarily embraced to uphold righteousness. The concluding twenty-one stanzas describe the cremation of Gurū Tegh Bahādur's severed head brought from Delhi to Anandpur by a disciple, Gurū Gobind Siṅgh's investiture as successor to Gurū Tegh Bahādur and creation of the Khālsā. Events are described with considerable embellishment, and no dates are given. Certain factual errors such as ascription to Gurū Gobind Siṅgh worship of the goddess Durgā have also crept into the work.

Kr.S.

DĀSŪ, BĀBĀ (b. 1524), eldest son of Gurū Aṅgad and Mātā Khīvī, was born on 9 Bhādoṅ 1581 Bk / 7 August 1524 at Khaḍūr Sāhib in present-day Amritsar district of the Punjab. He was ambitious to succeed his father in the spiritual line, but the latter, as records Kesar Siṅgh Chhibbar, *Baṅsāvalīnāmā*, spoke: "He [Amar Dās] is my brother and to him I am entrusting the responsibility .... Him I have reckoned as capable of bearing the burden." Dāsū kept quiet at the time, but, after the passing away of Gurū Aṅgad, as his duly anointed successor, Gurū Amar Dās shifted to Goindvāl, he proclaimed himself Gurū at Khaḍūr even against the remonstrances of his mother. Later he recanted and apologized to his mother who took him to Goindvāl. He made obeisance to Gurū Amar Dās whose true disciple he remained thereafter.

BIBLIOGRAPHY

1. Macauliffe, Max Arthur, *The Sikh Religion*. Oxford, 1909
2. Santokh Siṅgh, Bhāī, *Srī Gur Pratāp Sūraj Granth*. Amritsar, 1926-37
3. Chhibbar, Kesar Siṅgh, *Baṅsāvalīnāmā Dasāṅ Pātshāhīāṅ Kā*. Chandigarh, 1972
4. Vīr Siṅgh, Bhāī, *Srī Ashaṭgur Chamatkār*. Amritsar, 1971

M.G.S.

DASVANDH or Dasaundh, lit. a tenth part, refers to the practice among Sikhs of contributing in the name of the Gurū one-tenth of their earnings towards the common resources of the community. This is their religious obligation – a form of *sevā* or humble service so highly valued in the Sikh system. The concept of *dasvandh* was implicit in Gurū Nānak's own line: "*ghāli khāi kichhu hathhu dei, Nānak rāhu pachhāṇahi sei* – He alone, O Nānak, knoweth the way who eats out of what he earneth by his honest labour and yet shareth part of it with others" (GG, 1245). The idea of sharing and giving was nourished by the institutions of *saṅgat* (holy assembly) and *laṅgar* (community kitchen) the Gurū had established. In the time of Gurū Amar Dās, Nānak III, a formal structure for channelizing Sikh religious giving was evolved. He set up 22 *mañjīs* or districts in different parts of the country, each placed under the charge of a pious Sikh who, besides preaching Gurū Nānak's word, looked after the *saṅgats* within his/her jurisdiction and transmitted the disciple's offerings to the Gurū. As the digging of the sacred pool, *amrit-sar*, and erection in the middle of it of the shrine, Harimandar, began under Gurū Rām Dās entailing large amounts of expenditure, Sikhs were enjoined to set apart a minimum of ten per cent (*dasvandh*) of their income for the common pool, Gurū kī Golak (*q.v.*). *Masands*, i.e. ministers and tithe-collectors, were appointed to collect *kār bheṭ* (offerings) and *dasvandh* from Sikhs in the area they were assigned to, and pass these on to the Gurū.

Dasvandh has since become part of the Sikh way of life. The custom bears parallels to Christian tithes requiring members of the church to pay a tenth part of the annual produce of their land or its equivalent in money to support it and the clergy, and to Muslim *zakāt* requiring assignment of 2.5 per cent of one's annual wealth for the welfare of the destitute and the needy. Classical Indian society had no set procedure for regulating donations or charities, though references are traceable such as those in Parāśar Rishi's writings urging the householder to reserve 1/21 part of his income for Brāhmaṇs and 1/31 part for the gods. The Upaniṣads and the *Bhagavadgītā* commend "true alms" given with a sense of duty in a fit place and at a fit time to a deserving person from whom one expects nothing in return. *Dasvandh* is, however, to be distinguished from *dān* or charity. It essentially attends to the needs of the community and contributions are made specifically for the maintenance of its religious institutions such as *gurdwārās* and *gurū kā laṅgar* and projects of social welfare and uplift.

The custom of *dasvandh* was codified in documents called *rahitnāmās,* manuals of Sikh conduct, written during the lifetime of Gurū Gobind Siṅgh or soon after. For example, Bhāī Nand Lāl's *Tankhāhnāmā* records: "Hear ye, Nand Lāl, says Gobind Siṅgh, one who does not give *dasvandh* and, telling lies, misappropriates it, is not at all to be trusted." The tradition has been kept alive by chosen Sikhs who to this day scrupulously fulfil the injunction. The institution itself serves as a means for the individual to practice personal piety as well as to participate in the ongoing history of the community, the Gurū Panth.

BIBLIOGRAPHY

1. Sher Singh, *The Philosophy of Sikhism.* Lahore, 1944
2. Gopal Singh, *A History of the Sikh People.* Delhi, 1979
3. Avtar Singh, *Ethics of the Sikhs.* Patiala, 1970
4. Nripinder Singh, *The Sikh Moral Tradition.* Delhi, 1990
5. Cole, W. Owen and Piara Singh Sambhi, *The Sikhs: Their Religious Beliefs and Practices.* Delhi, 1978

W.S.

DĀTŪ, BĀBĀ (1537-1628), son of Gurū Aṅgad and Mātā Khīvī, was born in 1537 at Khaḍūr Sāhib in present-day Amritsar district of the Punjab. Like his elder brother, Dāsū, he too was not reconciled to Gurū Amar Dās succeeding his father as Gurū. But whereas Dāsū had soon realized his error and acknowledged Gurū Amar Dās as true inheritor of Gurū Nānak's spiritual legacy, Dātū remained hostile. He took to yogic practices to attain supernatural powers and thereby to create a following of his own. One day he went to Goindvāl and, as says Bhāī Santokh Siṅgh, *Srī Gur Pratāp Sūraj Granth,* he gave vent to his malice by administering Gurū Amar Dās a kick as he sat amid his disciples after the evening service. The *saṅgat* was stunned, but Gurū Amar Dās turned round, grasped Dātū's foot and caressing it said, "Pardon me, my Master's son ! Your tender foot may not have been hurt by my aged bones." Instead of being put to shame by the Gurū's humility, Dātū flew into a rage, called him a usurper and told him to quit Goindvāl. Gurū Amar Dās quietly left for his native Bāsarke. Next morning, Dātū and his men collected whatever they could lay their hands on. He had his eyes especially on Gurū Amar Dās's mare, but it would not let him mount it. In his effort to control it, he injured his leg. As he was returning to Khaḍūr, he was waylaid by robbers and deprived of the booty he was carrying. Dātū limped back to Khaḍūr empty-handed. Yet he was unrepentant and it was not until Gurū Arjan's time that he realized his error and made amends. Bābā Dātū lived up to a ripe old age. In September 1628, he visited Amritsar to condole with Gurū Hargobind on the passing away of his son, Aṭal Rāi, but died soon after his return to Khaḍūr.

BIBLIOGRAPHY

1. Bhāllā, Sarūp Dās, *Mahimā Prakāsh.* Patiala, 1971
2. Santokh Siṅgh, Bhāī, *Srī Gur Pratāp Sūraj Granth.* Amritsar, 1926-37
3. Vīr Siṅgh, Bhāī, *Srī Ashaṭgur Chamatkār.* Amritsar, 1971
4. Macauliffe, Max Arthur, *The Sikh Religion.* Oxford, 1909

M.G.S.

DĀŪ, BHĀĪ, a devoted Sikh of Gurū Hargobind (1595-1644), is listed by Bhāī Santokh Siṅgh, *Srī Gur Pratāp Sūraj Granth,* among warriors who fought in the battle of Amritsar (1629).

B.S.

DAUDHAR, village 22 km southeast of Mogā (30° - 48'N, 75° - 10'E) in Farīdkoṭ district, claims a historical shrine called Gurdwārā Pātshāhī Pahlī te Chhevīṅ (first and sixth), commemorating the visits of Gurū Nānak and Gurū Hargobind, Nānak VI. Situated on a sandy mound amidst cultivated fields about one kilometre to the northwest of the village, the Gurdwārā is referred to in the *Gurushabad Ratnākar Mahān Kosh* as Gobindgaṛh, but is locally known as simply Kuṭīā, i.e. a cottage. It originally celebrated the name of Gurū Hargobind who had halted here during one of his tours of the Mālvā, but, since the discovery, in 1914, of a copper plate and a seal during the diggings here, the name of Gurū Nānak has also been associated with it. The copper plate had on one side the inscription, *Nānak Tapā īhāṅ rame.* (Nānak, the ascetic, visited here), and on the other *Pahlī Pātshāhī Chhemī Āe,* (the First Lord (and) the Sixth came). The seal had a single word 'Nānak' on it. The plate and the seal are no longer there and were probably lost when the shrine was taken over from the Udāsī priests. The Gurdwārā, a small modest building, is now maintained by the village *saṅgat.*

M.G.S.

DAUDHAR ḌERĀ, a school for training Sikh musicians popularly known as Vaḍḍā Ḍerā, was established in 1859 by Sant Suddh Siṅgh (d. 1882) at Daudhar, village 22 km southeast of Mogā (30° - 48'N, 75° - 10'E), in Farīdkoṭ district of the Punjab. Suddh Siṅgh was a disciple of Ṭhākur Dīdār Siṅgh, a Nirmalā saint of Māṇūke, with whom he studied Sikh texts. According to local tradition, a chance meeting with a *bairāgī sādhū,* formerly a court musician to a chief in Uttar Pradesh from where he had migrated at the time of the uprising of 1857, led Suddh Siṅgh to invite him to his Ḍerā to teach classical music to the inmates. Mahant Vīr Siṅgh (d. 1902), who succeeded Suddh Siṅgh as head of the Ḍerā, was himself an accomplished musician. He and his equally talented disciple Khushāl Siṅgh trained their pupils in the subtleties of Sikh devotional music, instrumental as well as vocal. The instruments taught were *sarandā, sitār, tānpūrā, tāūs, tablā* and *ḍholakī* (drums); cymbals, *chimṭā khartāls* (concussion); and harmonium. The next *mahant* or head priest, Maṅgal Siṅgh (*c.* 1860-1937), himself an adept at playing *tablā,* not only continued instruction in devotional and classical music but also added to the curriculum lessons in recitation and interpretation of the Gurū Granth Sāhib, in Gurmukhī calligraphy and in classical Punjabi prosody. He admitted to the Ḍerā the blind, the crippled and the orphans, whose number during his time rose to about 150. Free board and lodging were provided for them. The Ḍerā set up branches at some other villages such as Badhnī Khurd, Maliāṇā, Buṭṭar and Jagrāoṅ. After the death on 28 July 1937 of Mahant Maṅgal Siṅgh the pace of activity slackened somewhat, and yet the daily routine of *kīrtan* in the morning, followed by *kathā* or discourse on *gurbāṇī,* and *chaukī* or a session of *kīrtan* in the evening continues, with the Gurū kā Laṅgar catering to the needs of the inmates, casual visitors and travellers. Special congregations mark important days on the Sikh calendar and the death anniversary of Mahant Maṅgal Siṅgh.

BIBLIOGRAPHY

Visākhā Singh, *Mālvā Itihās.* Kishanpura, 1954

Aj.S.

DAULAT KHĀN LODHĪ, NAWĀB, an Afghān noble, was, during the last quarter of the fifteenth century, governor of Jalandhar Doāb with Sultānpur, a town in present-day Kapūrthalā district, as his capital. One of his officials, Jai Rām, was married to Gurū Nānak's sister, Nānakī. Jai Rām secured young Nānak employment as keeper of the Nawāb's granaries and stores at Sultānpur. Nānak applied himself to his duties diligently, and impressed everyone with his gentleness and open-handed generosity. Yet there were some who felt jealous of his growing repute. Complaints were carried to the Nawāb that Nānak was squandering his stocks ; but checks made on two different occasions found the stores full and accounts correct. Some time later accusations were laid before the Nawāb about what was described as an heretical pronouncement made by Gurū Nānak. The reference was to the Gurū's pronouncement: "There is no Hindu and there is no Musalmān." The Nawāb dismissed the complaint saying that Nānak was a *faqīr* whose words they did not easily understand. On the insistence of the Qāzī, Gurū Nānak was summoned to the court. As reports *Purātan Janam Sākhī,* the Nawāb finally said, "Qāzī, Nānak hath arrived at the truth. Any further questioning will be futile." Likewise, Daulat Khān refused to intervene when Gurū Nānak's father-in-law, Mūl Chand, petitioned him to stop his son-in-law from leaving his home and family and launching upon his journeys abroad.

Nawāb Daulat Khān later became the governor of the entire Punjab with Lahore as his capital. He however fell out with Ibrāhīm Lodhī, the emperor of Delhi, and, conspiring with the latter's uncle, 'Ālam Khān, invited Babar, the ruler of Afghanistan, to attack India. As Babar led his armies into the country, Daulat Khān realized that he had come more like a conqueror and new master than like an ally, and turned against him, but he was no match for Babar and suffered a defeat at his hands. Babar stayed to establish his rule in India, whereas Daulat Khān died in obscurity.

BIBLIOGRAPHY

1. Vīr Singh, Bhāī, ed., *Purātan Janam Sākhī*. Amritsar, 1982
2. McLeod, W.H., *Early Sikh Tradition*. Oxford, 1980
3. Harbans Singh, *Guru Nanak and Origins of the Sikh Faith*. Bombay, 1969

Gn.S.

DAULAT RĀI, DĪWĀN, a civil administrator in Sikh times, was the son of Dīwān Lakkhī Mall, governor of Ḍerā Ismā'il Khān and Bannū. In 1844, Dīwān Lakkhī Mall died and Daulat Rāi was allowed to succeed him in his office by Wazīr Hīrā Siṅgh on payment of a *nazarānā* or tribute of 50,000 rupees. He also became the governor of Ṭoṅk wrested from Fateh Khān Ṭiwāṇā by Dīwān Lakkhī Mall a few months before his death. On the death of Wazīr Hīrā Siṅgh, Jawāhar Siṅgh became the prime minister. Fateh Khān Ṭīwāṇā, who was Jawāhar Siṅgh's supporter, was appointed governor of Ḍerā Ismā'il Khān and Bannū in place of Dīwān Daulat Rāi, but he earned unpopularity for his harsh treatment of the local *zamīndārs.* Dīwān Daulat Rāi was recalled as governor only to be removed soon afterwards by Sir Henry Lawrence, the British Resident at Lahore after the first Anglo-Sikh war (1845-46).

BIBLIOGRAPHY

1. Sūrī, Sohan Lāl, *'Umdāt-ut-Twārīkh*. Lahore, 1885-89
2. Latif, Syad Muhammad, *History of the Panjab*. Delhi, 1964
3. Griffin, Lepel, and C.F. Massy, *Chiefs and Families of Note in the Punjab*. Lahore, 1909

G.S.Ch.

DAULOVĀL,4 km north of Kīratpur (31° - 11'N, 76° - 35'E) in Ropaṛ district of the Punjab, is sacred to Gurū Har Rāi (1630-61), who used to encamp here during his visits in summer. According to local tradition, it was here that the Gurū received the royal summons to see the emperor at Delhi. Gurdwārā Pātshāhī Satvīṅ marks the site of the Gurū's camp. Its present building raised in 1965 is a square congregation hall, with a verandah around it. The Gurdwārā is managed by the local *saṅgat.*

BIBLIOGRAPHY

1. Tārā Siṅgh, *Srī Gur Tīrath Saṅgrahi.* Amritsar, n.d.
2. Ṭhākar Siṅgh, Giānī, *Srī Gurduāre Darshan.* Amritsar, 1923
3. Satibīr Siṅgh, *Nirbhau Nirvair.* Jalandhar, 1984

Gn.S.

DAULTĀṄ, a Muslim midwife of the village of Talvaṇḍī Rāi Bhoi, who attended the birth of Bābā Kālū's son who became renowned as Gurū Nānak. As the birth of a male child was announced, Bābā Kālū requested the family Paṇḍit, Hardiāl, to cast the child's horoscope. As Hardiāl worked out the stellar configuration, he was, says *Bālā Janam Sākhī,* much impressed and wished to know if the midwife had not seen any signs. Daultāṅ, who was sent for to speak with him, said that there were many children born under her care, but none so extraordinary as Kālū's son. She described his first cry as the laughter of a grown-up person and expressed her amazement at the portents she had witnessed.

BIBLIOGRAPHY

1. Vīr Siṅgh, Bhāī, ed., *Purātan Janam Sākhī,* Amritsar, 1982
2. Santokh Siṅgh, Bhāī, *Srī Gur Pratāp Sūraj Granth.* Amritsar, 1926-37
3. Kohlī, Surindar Siṅgh, ed., *Janam Sākhī Bhāī Bālā.* Chandigarh, 1975
4. Macauliffe, Max Arthur, *The Sikh Religion.* Oxford, 1909
5. Harbans Singh, *Guru Nanak and the Origins of the Sikh Faith.* Delhi, 1969

Gn.S.

DAYĀ (usually spelt *daiā* in Punjabi), from Skt. *day* meaning to sympathize with, to have pity on, stands for compassion, sympathy. It means 'suffering in the suffering of all beings.' It is deeper and more positive in sentiment than sympathy. *Dayā,* cognitively, observes alien pain; affectively, it gets touched by it and moves with affectional responses for the sufferer; and conatively, it moves one to act mercifully, pityingly, with kindness and forgiveness. *Dayā* is antithetical to *hiṅsā* (violence). One imbued with *dayā* "chooses to die himself rather than cause others to die," says Gurū Nānak (GG, 356).

Dayā is a divine quality and a moral virtue highly prized in all religious traditions. In the Sikh Scripture, *mahādaiāl* (super compassionate), *daiāpati* (lord of compassion), *daiāl dev* (merciful god), *karīmā, rahīmā* (the merciful one), etc., have been used as attributive names of God (GG, 249, 991, 1027, 727). In Sikh ethics, too, *dayā* is, *inter alia,* a basic moral requirement, a moral vow. "Keep your heart content and cherish compassion for all beings; this way alone can your holy vow be fulfilled" (GG, 299).

At the human level, one can comprehend feeling of another's anguish, but as a theological doctrine it is to risk allowing suffering in God's life. This has often caused much controversy in theological circles. God does not suffer in the sense of pain from evil as evil, but may suffer compassion (*dayā*) as bearing the pain of others to relieve them (of pain as also of evil). That is why at the time of Bābar's invasion of India, Gurū Nānak, when he witnessed the suffering of people, complained to God:

etī mār paī kurlāṇe taiṅ kī dardu nā āiā

So much agony were they put through
So much anguish did they suffer –
Were you not, O God, moved to compassion ? (GG, 360)

The Gurū, in the image of God, is also *daiāl purakh* (compassionate being) and *bakhasand* (forgiver) – GG, 681

Dayā is a virtue of the mind. In Indian thought, virtues are classified into (i) those of the body: *dāna* (charity), *paritrāṇa* (succouring those in distress), *paricharaṇa* (social service); (ii) those of speech: *satya* (veracity), *hitovachana* (beneficial speech), *priyavachana* (sweet speech), *svādhyāya* (reciting of Scriptures) and (iii) those of the mind which, besides *dayā,* also include *aparigraha* (unworldliness) and *śraddhā* (reverence and piety).

In Sikh thought *dayā* is considered the highest virtue:

aṭhsaṭhi tīrath sagal punn jīa daiā parvānu

> The merit of pilgrimages of holy places sixty-eight, and that of other virtues besides, equal not compassion to living beings. (GG, 136)

Dayā, in fact, is considered to be Truth in action:

sachu tā paru jāṇīai jā sikh sachī lei ;
daiā jāṇai jīa kī kichhu punnu dānu karei

> Truth dawns when truthful counsel is accepted,
> Seeking familiarity with compassion, one gives away virtuous charity. (GG, 468)

Dayā is, in reality, true action or action par excellence (*karṇī sār*) as are truth and contentment, the other two high virtues (GG, 51).

BIBLIOGRAPHY

1. Sher Singh, *The Philosophy of Sikhism*. Lahore, 1944
2. Nripinder Singh, *The Sikh Moral Tradition*. Delhi, 1990
3. Avtar Singh, *Ethics of the Sikhs*. Patiala, 1970

J.S.N.

DAYĀ CHAND, a devotee of Gurū Hargobind (1595-1644), who has been counted by Bhāī Santokh Siṅgh, *Srī Gur Pratāp Sūraj Granth,* among warriors who fell fighting for the Gurū in the battle of Amritsar (1629).

B.S.

DAYĀ KAUR, MĀTĀ, mother of Gurū Aṅgad Dev, was born and brought up at Matte dī Sarāi, a village now called Sarāi Nāṅgā, 15 km northeast of Muktsar in present-day Farīdkoṭ district of the Punjab. Two other names given her by chroniclers are Sabhrāī and Rāmo.

See PHERŪ MALL, BĀBĀ

BIBLIOGRAPHY

1. Santokh Siṅgh, Bhāī, *Srī Gur Pratāp Sūraj Granth*. Amritsar 1926-37
2. Giān Siṅgh, Giānī, *Twārīkh Gurū Khālsā*. Patiala, 1970
3. Macauliffe, Max Arthur, *The Sikh Religion*. Oxford, 1909

M.G.S.

DAYĀ KAUR, RĀṆĪ (d. 1823), widow of Gurbakhsh Siṅgh of the Nishānāvālī principality of the Sikhs who ruled over Ambālā, assumed control of the *misl* and the family estate upon her husband's death in 1786. She ruled over the territory remarkably well for nearly 37 years. Sir Lepel Griffin in his *The Rajas of the Punjab* says, "She was an excellent ruler and her estate was one of the best managed in the protected territory." In November 1808, Mahārājā Raṇjīt Siṅgh ejected Dayā Kaur from the city and seized all her property and possessions. He divided her country between Rājā Bhāg Siṅgh of Jīnd, his maternal uncle, and Bhāg Siṅgh's friend and ally, Bhāī Lāl Siṅgh of Kaithal. In 1809, the cis-Sutlej chiefs passed under British protection. Dayā Kaur appealed to Colonel David Ochterlony, agent to the Governor-General at the Ludhiāṇā Political Agency, who forced the chiefs of Jīnd and Kaithal to restore to Dayā Kaur territories which originally belonged to her.

Dayā Kaur died in 1823 and on her death her estates and property lapsed to the British government.

BIBLIOGRAPHY

Griffin, Lepel, *The Rajas of the Punjab* [Reprint]. Delhi, 1977

S.S.B.

DAYĀ KAUR, RĀṆĪ (d. 1843), widow of Sāhib Siṅgh Bhaṅgī of Gujrāt, was married, in 1811, to Mahārājā Raṅjīt Siṅgh by the rite of *chādar andāzī*, a rite having sanction under customary law to facilitate marriage with a widow who is accepted into nuptials by unfurling a *chādar* or sheet of cloth over her head. Princes Kashmīrā Siṅgh and Pashaurā Siṅgh were born to her.

Rāṇī Dayā Kaur died in 1843.

BIBLIOGRAPHY

1. Sūrī, Sohan Lāl, *'Umdāt-ut-Twārīkh*. Lahore, 1885-89
2. Griffin, Lepel, *Ranjit Singh*. Oxford, 1905
3. Khushwant Singh, *Ranjit Singh : Maharajah of the Punjab 1780-1839*. Bombay, 1962

S.S.B.

DAYĀL, BĀBĀ (1783-1855), founder of the Niraṅkārī sect of the Sikhs, was born at Peshāwar on Baisākh *sudī* 15, 1840 Bk / 17 May 1783. He was the only son of Rām Sahāi, a banker, and his wife Laḍikkī, daughter of Bhāī Vasākhā Siṅgh of Rohtās. He lost his father while he was still an infant. He learnt Gurmukhī from his mother and Persian and Pushto at a *maktab* (elementary school kept by a Muslim *maulawī*). His mother, a devout Sikh, nurtured him in the best traditions of the faith and took him out daily to make obeisance at the local Gurdwārā Bhāī Jogā Siṅgh. After the death of his mother in 1802, Dayāl migrated to Rāwalpiṇḍī where he opened a grocer's shop and also started preaching a message of simple living, commonly addressing congregations at Gurdwārā Peshaurīāṅ and Gurdwārā Bhāī Rām Siṅgh. A recurring theme he developed was criticism of the rituals and practices which, rejected by the Gurūs, were creeping into Sikh society. His main target was worship of the images against which he launched a vigorous campaign. He re-emphasized the Sikh belief in Niraṅkār, the Formless One. From this the movement which grew out of the protest he voiced with such sincere concern came to be known as Niraṅkārī. For solemnizing his own marriage in 1808 (bride : Mūl Devī, daughter of Charan Dās Kapūr of Bherā), Dayāl, refusing to invite the traditional Brāhmaṇ priest, had *Lāvāṅ* and *Anand* hymns recited from the Gurū Granth Sāhib. This is cited as the first instance of a wedding performed by *anand* ceremony in the modern period of Sikh history. The simple *anand* form of marrying rite became a cardinal point in the Niraṅkārī scheme of religious and social reform. Bābā Dayāl was averse to ostentation and cavilled at the rich style of the Sikh aristocracy of the day. He enjoined honest living, respect for parents and abstinence from liquor and drugs. Idolatrous worship and extravagant religious ceremonial were his principal rejections.

Although Bābā Dayāl's preaching was confined to the northwestern corner of the Punjab, its intimations spread to distant parts. It is said that the reigning Sikh monarch in Lahore, Raṇjīt Siṅgh, once visited him in Rāwalpiṇḍī in 1820. From across the Sikh frontier came emissaries of the American Presbytarian Mission at Ludhiāṇā "to ascertain the true nature of the movement." It struck the Mission that by overruling image worship and Brāhmaṇical ritual the reformer of Rāwalpiṇḍī was preparing ground favourable to the reception of the Gospel. Observations of the emissaries were published in the Annual Report of the Lodiana [Ludhiāṇā] Mission for 1953. This is how the Report described the sect forming around Bābā Dayāl's teaching:

> On investigation... it was found that the whole movement was the result of the efforts of an individual to establish a new *panth* (religious sect) of which he should be the instructor and guide. The sect has been in existence eight or nine years, but during the Sikh reign, fear kept them quiet; since the exten-

sion of the Company's Government over the country, they have become more bold, and with the assistance of our religious publications to furnish them with arguments against idolatry, they have attacked the faith of the Hindus most fiercely. They professedly reject idolatry, and all reverence and respect for whatever is held sacred by Sikhs or Hindus, except Nanak and his Granth.... The Hindus complain that they even give abuse to the cow. This climax of impiety could not be endured, and it was followed by some street disturbances, which brought the parties into the civil courts.. They are called Nirankaris, from their belief in God, as a spirit without bodily form. The next great fundamental principle of their religion is that salvation is to be obtained by meditation on God. They regard Nanak as their saviour, in as much as he taught them the way of salvation. Of their peculiar practices only two things are learned. First, they assemble every morning for worship, which consists of bowing the head to the ground before the Granth, making offerings, and in hearing the Granth read by one of their numbers, and explained also if their leader be present. Secondly, they do not burn their dead, because that would assimilate them to the Hindus; nor bury them, because that would make them too much like Christians and Musulmans, but throw them into the river.

For what were understood as his heterodox views, Bābā Dayāl was debarred from Gurdwārā Peshauriāṅ. He thereupon acquired, on 3 November 1851, a plot of land and erected a small room, thus laying the foundation of the Niraṅkārī Darbār which became the central religious seat of the new sect.

Babā Dayal died on 30 January 1855, and was succeeded by his eldest son, Darbārā Siṅgh (1814-70).

BIBLIOGRAPHY

1. Vahimī, Taran Siṅgh, *Jass Jīvan*. Rampur (Hissar), 1971
2. Gaṇḍā Siṅgh, *Kūkiāṅ dī Vithyā*. Amritsar, 1944
3. Jolly, Surjit Kaur, *Sikh Revivalist Movements*. Delhi, 1988
4. Farquhar, J.N., *Modern Religious Movements in India*. Delhi, 1977
5. Harbans Singh, *The Heritage of the Sikhs*. Delhi, 1983

M.S.N.

DAYĀ RĀM, Brāhmaṇ Sikh in the retinue of Gurū Gobind Siṅgh, was the son of Jātī Mall, popular as Jātī Malik (d. 1643) and grandson of Siṅghā, *prohits* or family priests of the Soḍhīs as well as fearless warriors in the service of Gurū Hargobind (1595-1644). Dayā Rām, too, was trained in the martial art. Gurū Gobind Siṅgh, in his autobiographical poem, *Bachitra Nāṭak*, praises Dayā Rām's part in the battle of Bhaṅgāṇī (1688) in these words: "Dayā Rām, the Brāhmaṇ, entered the field filled with fury and excelled in the just battle like Droṇāchārya (teacher and general in the epic *Mahābhārata*)."

BIBLIOGRAPHY

1. *Bachitra Nāṭak*
2. Santokh Siṅgh, Bhāī, *Srī Gur Pratāp Sūraj Granth*. Amritsar, 1926-37
3. Giān Siṅgh, Giānī, *Twārīkh Gurū Khālsā*. Patiala, 1970
4. Macauliffe, Max Arthur, *The Sikh Religion*. Oxford, 1909

P.S.P.

DAYĀ SIṄGH, BHĀĪ (1661-1708), one of the Pañj Piāre or the Five Beloved celebrated in the Sikh tradition, was the son of Bhāī Suddhā, a Sobtī Khatrī of Lahore, and Māī Diālī. His original name was Dayā Rām. Bhāī

Suddhā was a devout Sikh of Gurū Tegh Bahādur and had visited Anandpur more than once to seek his blessing. In 1677, he travelled to Anandpur along with his family including his young son, Dayā Rām, to make obeisance to Gurū Gobind Siṅgh, this time to settle there permanently. Dayā Rām, already well versed in Punjabi and Persian, engaged himself in the study of classics and *gurbāṇī*. He also received training in the use of weapons. In the historic *dīvān* in the Kesgaṛh Fort at Anandpur on 30 March 1699, he was the first to rise at the Gurū's call and offer his head, followed by four others in succession. These five were the first to be admitted to the fold of the Khālsā and they in turn administered the rites of initiation to Gurū Gobind Siṅgh who called them collectively Pañj Piāre. Dayā Rām after initiation became Dayā Siṅgh. Although the five enjoyed equal status as the Gurū's close confidants and constant attendants, Bhāī Dayā Siṅgh was always regarded as the first among equals. He took part in the battles of Anandpur, and was one of the three Sikhs who followed Gurū Gobind Siṅgh out of Chamkaur on the night of 7-8 December 1705, eluding the besieging hordes. He was Gurū Gobind Siṅgh's emissary sent from the village of Dīnā in the Punjab to deliver his letter which became famous as *Zafarnāmah*, the Letter of Victory, to Emperor Auraṅgzīb, then camping at Ahmadnagar. Bhāī Dayā Siṅgh, accompanied by Bhāī Dharam Siṅgh, another of the Pañj Piāre, reached Ahmadnagar via Auraṅgābād, but found that it was not possible to have access to the Emperor and deliver to him the letter personally as Gurū Gobind Siṅgh had directed. Dayā Siṅgh sent Dharam Siṅgh back to seek the Gurū's advice, but before the latter could re-join him with fresh instructions, he had managed to have the letter delivered, and had himself returned to Auraṅgābād. A shrine called Gurdwārā Bhāī Dāyā Siṅgh marks the place of his sojourn in Dhāmī Mahallā.

Bhāī Dayā Siṅgh and Bhāī Dharam Siṅgh returned and, according to Sikh tradition, they re-joined Guru Gobind Siṅgh at Kalāyat, a town 52 km southwest of Bīkāner (28° - 4'N, 73° - 21'E) in Rājasthān. Bhāī Dayā Siṅgh remained in attendance upon the Gurū and was with him at the time of his death at Nāndeḍ on 7 October 1708. He died at Nāndeḍ soon after and a joint memorial there for him and for Bhāī Dharam Siṅgh known as Aṅgiṭhā (lit. burning pyre) Bhāī Dayā Siṅgh *ate* Dharam Siṅgh marks the site of their cremation.

Bhāī Dayā Siṅgh was a learned man. One of the Rahitnāmās, manuals on Sikh conduct, is ascribed to him. The Nirmalās, a sect of Sikh schoolmen, claim him as one of their forebears. Their Ḍaraulī branch traces its origin to Bhāī Dayā Siṅgh through Bābā Dīp Siṅgh.

BIBLIOGRAPHY

1. Santokh Siṅgh, Bhāī, *Srī Gur Pratāp Sūraj Granth*. Amritsar, 1926-37
2. Kuir Siṅgh, *Gurbilās Pātshāhī 10*. Patiala, 1968
3. Chhibbar, Kesar Siṅgh, *Bansāvalīnāmā Dasāṅ Pātshāhīāṅ Kā*. Chandigarh, 1972
4. Macauliffe, Max Arthur, *The Sikh Religion*. Oxford, 1909
5. Khushwant Singh, *A History of the Sikhs*, vol. I. Princeton, 1963
6. Harbans Singh, *Guru Gobind Singh*. Chandigarh, 1966

S.S.A.

DEATH, the primordial mystery and one of the cardinal conditions of existence. Scientifically, death is defined as "the permanent cessation of the vital function in the bodies of animals and plants" or, simply, as the end of life caused by senescence or by stoppage of the means of sustenance to body cells. In Sikhism the universal fact of mortality is juxtaposed to immortality (*amarāpad)* as the ultimate objective (*paramārtha)* of life. As a biological reality death is the inevitable destiny of everyone. Even the divines and prophets have no immunity from it. Mortality reigns over the realms of the gods as well.

Death will inevitably strike
Even in the land of Lord Indra*
Nor is Brahmā's* domain free from it.
Likewise is Lord Śiva's* world decreed to come to naught.
**three gods of the Hindu pantheon*

(GG, 237)

We all entered this world "with death as our written fate" (GG, 876), says Gurū Nānak.

Death cannot be apprehended apart from life. Contemplating both together, one truly comprehends the phenomenon of life and death (*maraṇ jīvaṇ kī sojhī pāe*).

A significant term used for death is *kāl* which has a dual meaning. It connotes death as well as time. Both connotations interwine theologically. *Kāl* is often denoted as *jam kāl* (*jama* = *yama*, the Vedic God of Death). Day in and day out it gnaws at the fabric of life. But man remains ignorant and perceives it not.

That *kāl* is constantly nibbling at life brings home to one the ephemerality of existence and therefore the necessity of making the most of it. If life has been lived in accord with acceptable laws it will win approval.

Death is the privilege of men
Who live life positively.

(GG, 579)

Death is legitimated by the ends it serves - surmounting the throes of transmigration or sacrifice for an ideal or laying down of one's life in a righteous cause. Such a death carries one beyond the realm of Time into the realm of Eternity (*akāl*). Eternity does not signify extended Time, but the state beyond Time, and therefore beyond mortality. Participation in Eternity does not lie hereafter. It is the state of immortality (*amarāpad*) here in life which is liberation (*mukti*) from the throes of Time. That signifies the death of Death itself (*kāl kāle*).

To attain this state of immortality one need not necessarily pass through the portals of biological death. This state can be attained while one is still alive. To achieve this, however, one has to *die to oneself.*

This state is attainable by contemplating the Self by the grace of the Divine:

As by the Lord's favour one contemplates the self,
So one learns to die while still living.

(GG, 935)

Dying to oneself has several kindred nuances in Sikh theology. Spoken, not only in terms of decimation of *man* and even of egoity (*haumai*), this is also the connotation of dying in *śabda* (the Holy Word):

He who ceases in *śabda*
His death is blessed.

(GG, 1067)

Another type of "blessed" dying is through sacrifice. When he initiated the order of the Khālsā in 1699, Gurū Gobind Siṅgh invited Sikhs to offer him their own heads. Five volunteered in response to the call. The baptismal initiation ceremony fashioned after that event even now encapsulates its symbolic sacrifice. The initiate is required to die to his past *saṁskāras* and be born into the Gurū's family.

The kindred spirits who
Served their Lord while they lived
Kept Him in mind while departing,

(GG, 1000)

yearn for their departure to their 'real home' (*nij ghar*) where they have a tryst with their Divine Spouse. At that time they invoke the blessings of one and all:

Predestined is the hour of my nuptials*
Come ye, my friends, and anoint the

doorsteps.

*mystical term for death

Men are thus advised to meditate on Him who sends the call:

May the day of union for each arrive

(GG, 12)

Death, then, marks the day of union with the Divine. It is not an occasion for grief. Lamentation over death is forbidden the Sikhs. In his Rāmkalī *Sadd,* The Call, the poet in the Gurū Granth Sāhib records:

By his wish the holy Gurū(Gurū Amar Dās) his entire family to himself called, and said:
No one after me should cry,
Such that cry shall no way please me.

The Sikh bereavement ceremony consists of having the Holy Book, the Gurū Granth Sāhib, recited from end to end, praying for the departed soul and distributing the sacramental (*kaṛāhprasād).*
See BHOG

BIBLIOGRAPHY

1. *Sikh Rahit Maryādā.* Amritsar, 1975
2. Padam, Piārā Siṅgh, ed., *Gurū Granth Vichār-Kosh.* Patiala, 1969
3. Jodh Siṅgh, Bhāī, *Gurmati Nirṇaya.* Lahore, 1945
4. Sher Singh, *The Philosophy of Sikhism.* Lahore, 1944
5. Jogendra Singh, Sir, *Sikh Ceremonies.* Bombay, 1941
6. Cole, W. Owen and Piara Singh Sambhi, *The Sikhs: Their Religious Beliefs and Practices.* Delhi, 1978

J.S.N.

DECCAN KHĀLSĀ DĪWĀN, a philanthropic organization of the Sikhs, now non-existent, was formed in Bombay on the eve of Indian Independence (August 1947), with Partāp Siṅgh as president and Harī Siṅgh Shergill as general secretary. The Dīwān's main object was to provide help for the rehabilitation of persons uprooted from their homes in the north in the wake of intercommunal rioting. It also offered its services to protect the old Sikh residents of Nānded in Hyderābād state, who were numerically a very small group and who felt apprehensive about the safety of their historic shrine in the town and of their own lives in the deteriorating law and order situation in the state, then held to ransom by the fanatical Qāsim Rizvī. The Dīwān sent a *jathā,* i.e. a band of volunteers, to Nānded at that critical juncture. For resettling nearly 1,000 displaced families who happened to come to Bombay leaving their hearths and homes in what became the State of Pakistan, it secured use of some military barracks in Kolīwāḍā locality, built during World War II and had them renovated. The government later constructed pucca tenements which were rented out to the refugees, homeless immigrants. The colony is now known as Gurū Tegh Bahādur Nagar. Under the auspices of the Deccan Khālsā Dīwān was established the Gurū Nānak Vidyak Society which opened in July 1947 a high school. The Society is now running more than two dozen schools in different suburbs of Bombay. It also took up the cause of Punjabi and had an optional paper in the language introduced in high schools as well as in colleges within the jurisdiction of Bombay University.

Hr.S.

DE COURCY, an English adventurer who joined Mahārājā Raṇjīt Siṅgh's army in 1835 as a gunner. According to the Khālsā Darbār records, his monthly salary was Rs 350.

BIBLIOGRAPHY

Grey, C., *European Adventurers of Northern India, 1785-1849* [Reprint]. Patiala, 1970

Gl.S.

DE FACIEU, HENRI JOSEPH (d. 1893) son of Jean Alexis de Facieu, a colonel in the Sikh army, joined the Darbār's service in 1841. He commanded the Sher Regiment of

Dragoons in General Ventura's brigade. After Mahārājā Sher Siṅgh's death, he left Lahore for Fīrozpur eventually moving down to Allāhābād where he set up business. The business being ruined during the 1857 uprising, he left for Burma and joined the Burma army in which he rose to be a general. On Burma's annexation by the British in 1888, he retired and lived in Rangoon until his death in 1893.

BIBLIOGRAPHY

Grey, C. *European Adventurers of Northern India,* (1785-1849). Patiala, 1970

Gl.S.

DE FACIEU, JEAN ALEXIS (d. 1843), a Frenchman who had been a colonel in the French army. Securing his dismissal from the service, he came to India in 1840, and joined the Sikh army the following year as colonel of Cuirassiers. However, he left the service after the assassination of Mahārājā Sher Siṅgh and went to Fīrozpur, where he died in December 1843. He was buried by the British with full military honours.

BIBLIOGRAPHY

Grey, C., *European Adventurers of Northern India, 1785-1849.* Patiala, 1970

Gl.S.

DEG TEGH FATEH, a Sikh saying which literally means victory (*fateh*) to kettle (*deg*) and sword (*tegh*). All the three words have been taken from Persian which was the State language in the formative period of Sikhism. The word *deg,* i.e. a large-sized kettle or cauldron having a wide mouth, which in the Muslim Sūfī tradition signified charitable distribution of cooked food, also called *laṅgar,* has here acquired an expanded meaning. While retaining its literal meaning, it has come to stand in the Sikh tradition for the ideal of public welfare or general benevolence or munificence. Gurū Nānak in one of his hymns likens the Earth to a *deg* from which sustenance is received by all living beings (GG, 1190). Similarly, *tegh* has also acquired a wider connotation and has been used in the Sikh tradition as a symbol for chatisement of the evil and protection of the good. As Gurū Hargobind is said to have told a Mahārāshṭrian saint, Rām Dās, during their meeting at Srīnagar (Gaṛhvāl), the *tegh* is for *garīb kī rakhiā* (defence of the weak) and *jarvāṇe kī bhakkhiā* (destruction of the aggressor). Gurū Gobind Siṅgh identified the *tegh* or sword with the Lord Creator and thereby gave it a still deeper meaning. He addressed it as Bhagautī (goddess), Srī Khaṛag (Lord Sword), Jag Kāran (Creator of the World) and Srisṭi Ubāran (Saviour of the Creation), besides reiterating its role as protector of the good (*sukh santāṅ karṇaṅ*) and destroyer of the evil (*durmati darṇaṅ*). The two ideals of *deg* and *tegh* supplemented each other. In a supplicatory passage in his *Krishnāvtār* Gurū Gobind Siṅgh says: "*Deg teg jag mai doū chalai* – *deg* and *tegh* both prevail in the world." In *Charitropākhyān, deg* and *tegh* (charity and valour) constitute a composite virtue that was the characteristic of the heroes of yore (*Charitra* 200. 1; 272. 3; 307. 2).

When Sikhs passing through a period of fierce persecution established their power in the Punjab, this maxim was adopted as an ideal for the Khālsā State and imprinted on their seals, coins and banners. The term *fateh* added to *deg* and *tegh* was the expression of Sikhs' belief that the use of *tegh* (in the last resort, as permitted by Gurū Gobind Siṅgh), with the ideal of *deg* or charity steadfastly cherished, must lead to *fateh* or victory. Gurū Gobind Siṅgh had introduced the salutation "Vāhigurū jī kā Khālsā, Vāhigurū jī kī Fateh," ascribing victory to God. The Khālsā affirmed through this slogan that victory, a gift from God, followed the use of *tegh* in a righteous cause and adherence to the principle of magnanimity (*deg*) – *deg, tegh, fateh*. Bandā

Siṅgh who first occupied territory, had a Persian inscription on his seal which, rendered into English, read: "Kettle and Sword (symbols of charity and power) and Victory and Ready Patronage have been obtained through the grace of Gurū Nānak-Gobind Siṅgh." Here *teg͟h* (sword) is used as a symbol of victory over tyranny and *deg* (kettle) as a symbol of ready patronage (welfare) for the good. Both being gifts from the Gurūs constituted the governing principles of the polity of the new State. The same Persian inscription incorporating the Sikh ideal of Deg Teg͟h Fateh was reproduced on the coin introduced by Sardār Jassā Siṅgh Āhlūvālīā in 1765 after the K͟hālsā had gained a decisive victory over the Afg͟hāns. The practice continued during the time of Mahārājā Raṇjīt Siṅgh, the first Sikh sovereign of the Punjab as well as in some of the cis-Sutlej Sikh states which had accepted British suzerainty.

Over the centuries the principle of Deg Teg͟h Fateh has taken a firm root in Sikh psyche and tradition. The maxim has become part of the Sikh *ardās*, prayer which is recited at the end of all Sikh services. Every time when the *ardās* is offered, blessings of the Lord are invoked for the triumph of the ideal of *deg* and *teg͟h*. In the *ardās* Sikhs also recall their past heroes : "They who dwelt on His Name, ate only after sharing their victuals with others, maintained the *deg* and wielded the *teg͟h* and sacrificed their lives for the sake of *dharma*, remember them, K͟hālsā Jī and proclaim Vāhigurū ...."

BIBLIOGRAPHY

1. Teja Singh, *Sikhism : Its Ideals and Institutions*. Bombay, 1937
2. Sher Singh, *The Philosophy of Sikhism*. Lahore, 1944
3. Prakash Singh, *The Sikh Gurus and the Temple of Bread*. Amritsar, 1964
4. Nripinder Singh, *The Sikh Moral Tradition*. Delhi, 1990.
5. Harbans Singh, *Deg͟h Teg͟h Fateh*. Chandigarh, 1986

F.S.

ḌEHLOṆ, village in Ludhiāṇā district, 19 km from the city (30° - 54'N, 75° - 52'E), claims a historical shrine, Gurdwārā Damdamā Sāhib Pātshāhī Chhevīṅ. The Gurdwārā commemorates the visit of Gurū Hargobind, who halted here while on his way from Jagheṛā to Gujjarvāl. The building comprises a domed square hall, including the *prakāsh asthān*, site where the Gurū Granth Sāhib is installed during the day and a cubicle where the holy book is placed for the night. A verandah covers the hall on three sides. Rooms for the *laṅgar* and the *granthī* are close by. The Shiromaṇī Gurdwārā Parbandhak Committee manages the shrine through a local committee.

M.G.S.

DE LA FONT, CAPTAIN AUGUSTE, a Frenchman, who entered Mahārājā Raṇjīt Siṅgh's service in 1838. He was appointed an aide-de-camp to General Ventura. Later, he acted as a staff officer to Colonel C.M. Wade during his journey to Kābul. He took active part in the action at Fort 'Alī Masjid and was also helpful in maintaining peace between the Sikh contingent and Wade's "somewhat unruly" force. He left service in the Punjab in 1843 and returned to France. His younger brother (Christian name not known) also served in the Sikh army under Generals Avitabile and Ventura.

BIBLIOGRAPHY

Grey, C., *European Adventurers of Northern India, 1785-1849* [Reprint]. Patiala, 1970

Gl.S.

DE LA ROCHE, HENRI FRANCOIS STANISLAUS (d. 1842), a Frenchman born in Mauritius, served in the army of Begam Samrū. As the force was disbanded by the British after the Begam's death, he came to Lahore in 1838 and took up service under Mahārājā Raṇjīt Siṅgh as a cavalry officer on a salary of Rs 500 per month. Apart from army duties, he was occasionally deputed to settle boundary disputes on the Sikh frontier. After the death of Mahārājā Kharak Siṅgh he openly supported Sher Siṅgh's claim to the throne. At Christmas in Lahore in 1842, he fell off his horse in an intoxicated state and died. His widow, Fateh Bakhsh, built a tomb in his memory.

BIBLIOGRAPHY

Grey, C., *European Adventurers of Northern India, 1785 to 1849.* Patiala, 1970

Gl.S.

DELHI, also called Dillī (28° - 40'N, 77° - 13'E), the capital of India, is also connected with Sikh history. The first, sixth, eighth, ninth and tenth Gurūs visited it. Mātā Sundarī and Mātā Sāhib Devāṅ, consorts of Gurū Gobind Siṅgh, stayed here for a long time before and after the death of the Gurū. A Sikh *saṅgat* existed in what came to be known as Kūchā Dilvālī Siṅghāṅ in Old Delhi. After the downfall of the Mughal empire and the rise of Sikh power in the Punjab during the latter half of the eighteenth century, the confederated armies of the Dal Khālsā extended their area of operations right up to the walls of the metropolis, and in March 1783 they ransacked Malkā Gañj and Sabzī Maṇḍī and actually entered the Red Fort on 11 March 1783. The helpless Mughal emperor Shāh 'Ālam II sought mediation by Begam Samrū and came to terms with the Sikhs, who agreed to retire with their main force to the Punjab provided Sardār Baghel Siṅgh of Karoṛsiṅghīā *misl* was permitted to stay on in the capital with 4,000 men till the construction of *gurdwārās* on sites of historical importance to the Sikhs was completed. To meet the expenses, Baghel Siṅgh was authorized to charge six *ānnās* in a rupee (37.5 per cent) of all income from octroi duties in the capital. During his stay in the capital from March to December 1783, Baghel Siṅgh located seven sites and constructed *gurdwārās* upon them. Besides these seven, another historical shrine, Nānak Piāo, was already in existence on the outskirts of Delhi. Another, Damdamā Sāhib, dedicated to Gurū Gobind Siṅgh was established later. Like most other historical *gurdwārās*, these Delhi shrines had been administered severally by hereditary *mahant* families till the rise of the Gurdwārā reform movement in the Punjab during the early 1920's. The Shiromaṇī Gurdwārā Parbandhak Committee sent a deputation comprising Dān Siṅgh Vachhoā, Harbaṅs Siṅgh Sīstānī and Gurdit Siṅgh to negotiate with the *mahants* the transfer of *gurdwārās* to Panthic management. Mahant Harī Siṅgh, B.A., head priest of Gurdwārā Sīs Gañj Sāhib was the first to hand over the Gurdwārā and its property to the Shiromaṇī Gurdwārā Parbandhak Committee on 19 December 1922. The *mahants* of most other historical *gurdwārās* at Delhi followed suit. The committee appointed, on 19 March 1923, a managing committee comprising Raghbīr Siṅgh and Bahādur Siṅgh, an engineer, to take over the administration. Later, in March 1926, an 11-member committee, designated the Delhi Gurdwārā Parbandhak Committee was constituted. The members included among others, Rāi Bahādur Wasākhā Siṅgh, Jodh Siṅgh, Surinderpāl Siṅgh Advocate, Nānak Siṅgh, Beant Siṅgh and Āgyāpāl Siṅgh. Chañchal Siṅgh was appointed manager.

The partition of India, in 1947, brought about significant demographic changes in Delhi including the influx of a large number of Sikh immigrants from what then became Pakistan. The immigrants were mostly artisans, businessmen and industrialists. While attendance and the finances of the *gurdwārās* improved considerably, group rivalries and factionalism raised their hand, which affected the management of the *gurdwārās* and the functioning of the Delhi Gurdwārā Parbandhak Committee. In 1974, the Government of India entrusted the control of *gurdwārās* to the Delhi Sikh Gurdwārās Management Committee (D.S.G.M.C.), a statutory body set up under the Delhi Sikh Gurdwaras Act, 1971, and independent of the Shiromaṇī Gurdwārā Parbandhak Committee at Amritsar. The historical *gurdwārās* under the Committee's management include:

GURDWĀRĀ SĪS GAÑJ SĀHIB in Chāndnī Chowk area of Old Delhi about half a kilometre west of the main Delhi railway station marks the spot where Gurū Tegh Bahādur, Nānak IX, was beheaded on 11 November 1675 under the orders of the Mughal emperor Auraṅgzīb. *See* TEGH BAHĀDŪR, GURŪ. The site next to the city Kotwālī where Sardār Baghel Siṅgh had established his main post was at the time occupied by a mosque which the Sardār had to demolish before raising a *gurdwārā*. The *gurdwārā* was later demolished and replaced by a mosque. The case for the demolition of this mosque and its replacement by Gurdwārā Sīs Gañj was taken up with British government after the 1857 Mutiny by Rājā Sarūp Siṅgh, ruler of the princely state of Jīnd. The local Muslims opposed the proposal and took the case to courts. Mosques and *gurdwārās* appeared on the site alternately during the prolonged litigation. Ultimately, the present building of Gurdwārā Sīs Gañj was raised in 1930 in consequence of the verdict of the British Privy Council. The two-storeyed hall, with only a mezzanine forming the first floor, was barely adequate for the increasing number of devotees and visitors especially after immigration of 1947, and efforts were made to acquire the adjoining Kotwālī (police post) with a view to enlarging the sitting area. Half the Kotwālī precincts were acquired by the Delhi SikhGurdwārās Management Committee (D.S.G.M.C.) in 1971 at a cost of Rs 1,625,000. The other half was offered to the Committee by government in 1983. This led to a programme of large-scale renovation and development. However, the old domed building continues to house the sanctum-sanctorum. The Gurū Granth Sāhib is seated on a gilded palanquin on a raised platform, the basement below which represents the exact spot of execution. The trunk of the tree under which the execution took place is also preserved behind a glass screen. The additional buildings include Gurū kā Laṅgar and Gurū Tegh Bahādur Nivās, lodgings for pilgrims. The offices of the Delhi Sikh Gurdwārās Management Committee are also located in Gurdwārā Sīs Gañj Sāhib. The Committee publishes a Punjabi religious and literary monthly, the *Sīs Gañj*. While all important Sikh days on the annual calendar are observed at the Gurdwārā, special programmes are earmarked in honour of Gurū Tegh Bahādur's martyrdom.

GURDWĀRĀ RIKĀBGAÑJ SĀHIB on Paṇḍit Pant Mārg near Parliament House in New Delhi marks the place where the body of Gurū Tegh Bahādur was cremated. After the execution of the Gurū on 11 November 1675, his headless body and the severed head were left lying in the Chāndnī Chowk. The awe-struck people of Delhi did not dare to come forward and claim the Gurū's remains. It was only after nightfall that, while a Raṅghreṭā Sikh, Bhāī Jaitā, picked up the head and carried it post-haste to Anandpur, the body was carried by Bhāī Lakkhī Shāh Vañjārā and his son, Nigāhīā, to their house in the Rāisīnā village (now New Delhi). Still afraid of performing an open cremation, they set the house itself on fire and collecting the ashes of the Gurū's body in an urn buried them there. When, after the death of Auraṅgzīb in 1707, Gurū Gobind Siṅgh came to Delhi to meet Prince Mu'azzam, later emperor Bahādur Shāh-I, he with the help of local Sikhs located the site and raised a simple memorial thereon. Later a mosque came to be built on the site which Sardār Baghel Siṅgh had to demolish when he built Gurdwārā Rikābgañj in 1783. During the Mutiny (1857), the Muslims again demolished the Sikh shrine and rebuilt a mosque here. Sikhs took the matter to the law court which restored possession of the site to them, and they quickly rebuilt the *gurdwārā*. In 1914 another dispute arose, this time regarding the boundary wall of the Gurdwārā, a portion of which had been demolished by government for the purpose of straightening a road to the British Viceroy's mansion (now Rāshṭrapatī Bhavan). The Sikhs protested and would have launched an agitation to oppose the proposal. Meanwhile, World War I (1914-1918) broke out on which account the protest was held in abeyance. But as soon as the war ceased, the agitation was resumed. In the end the government yielded and the Gurdwārā wall was rebuilt at public expense. *See* GURDWĀRĀ RIKĀBGAÑJ AGITATION.

The construction of the present building of Gurdwārā Rikābgañj Sāhib was started in 1960 and was completed in 1967-68. It is an impressive white marble structure. The two-storeyed building on a high plinth comprises a high-ceilinged hall with a mezzanine at mid-height forming the first floor. It is topped by a pinnacled dome of the type of an inverted lotus, with kiosks adorning the roof corners. The basement below the hall marks the actual cremation site of Gurū Tegh Bahādur's headless body. The Gurdwārā has a vast campus. Besides, about two dozen staff quarters, a sub-office of the Delhi Sikh Gurdwārās Management Committee, offices of the Kendrī Srī Gurū Siṅgh Sabhā, a 65-metre square congregation hall completed in 1980 and Gurū ka Laṅgar are located on the premises. An institution for the training of young musicians in Sikh *kīrtan* is also functioning here. Sacred relics preserved in the Gurdwārā include two swords, a dagger and two *kaṭārs* (poniards) given by Gurū Gobind Siṅgh to Mātā Sāhib Devāṅ before her departure from Nāndeḍ in 1708.

GURDWĀRĀ NĀNAK PIĀO (lit. a water booth) situated along Sher Shāh Sūrī Mārg, near Azādpur, on the northern outskirts of Delhi commemorates Gurū Nānak's visit to the place during which he got a well dug and a booth set up to serve water to wayfarers. The present building of the Gurdwārā replacing the older shrine was constructed during the 1980's. It is a high-ceilinged hall with a mezzanine forming its first floor. The high dome above the hall is topped by a gilded pinnacle and an umbrella-shaped finial. The Gurū Granth Sāhib is seated in a marble palanquin in the middle of the hall. The 40-metre square marble-lined *sarovar* with colonnades on three sides was built in 1978. The old well is still in use. Two educational institutions– Gurū Tegh Bahādur Institute of Electronics and a branch of Gurū Har Krishan Public School – are also functioning on the campus. A flour mill installed here supplies wheat flour to all historical *gurdwārās* in Delhi for Gurū kā Laṅgar as well as for *karāhprasād*. Special congregations take place on the occasion of the death anniversary of Gurū Nānak which comes off in September-October.

GURDWĀRĀ MAJNŪ ṬILLĀ is situated on a mound (*ṭillā*) on the bank of the River Yamunā beyond Timārpur Colony on the outer Ring Road of Delhi.

According to chroniclers, a Muslim recluse lived here during the reign of Sultān Sikandar Lodhī (1488-1517). He used to ferry people across the river but was usually absorbed in prayer and penitence unmindful of his physical health and appearance. People had nicknamed him Majnū after a romantic hero of Persian folklore. Hence the name of the place Majnū kā Ṭillā (Majnū's mound) or Majnū Ṭillā.

Gurū Nānak during his visit to Delhi met and held discourse with Majnū upon whom he impressed the importance of selfless service of mankind which was far superior to austerities for self-purification. Gurū

Hargobind, Nānak VI, is also said to have halted for some time at Majnū Ṭillā on his way to Delhi summoned by Emperor Jahāṅgīr. Sardār Baghel Siṅgh established a *gurdwārā* here in 1783. Later Mahārājā Raṇjīt Siṅgh (1780-1839) had a small marble building constructed which still exists. It is a two-storeyed building comprising a hall with two cubicles at ground floor. Recently a new magnificent hall, 20-metre square, and lined with white marble slabs has been constructed close to the old building.

Old copies of Gurū Granth Sāhib from other *gurdwārās* in Delhi and the neighbouring states are kept in the mezzanine of the older shrine here till their periodical disposal by consigning them reverently to fire in a small kiln especially built for this purpose. Sunday *dīvāns* and community meals at Gurdwārā Majnū Ṭillā attract large gatherings of devotees. The most important celebration of the year, however, is Baisākhī, the birth anniversary of the Khālsā, when largely attended *dīvāns* take place.

GURDWĀRĀ BAṄGLĀ SĀHIB near the Gole Post Office about one kilometre from Connaught Place in New Delhi perpetuates the memory of Gurū Har Krishan, who stayed here in the bungalow (*baṅglā*) or mansion of Mirzā Rājā Jai Siṅgh during February-March 1664 when he came to Delhi summoned by Emperor Auraṅgzīb. Delhi was at that time in the grip of severe cholera and smallpox epidemics. The young Gurū started serving the sick and the destitute and, in the process, himself got smallpox infection.In order to save its spread to the inmates of Rājā Jai Siṅgh's household, the Gurū shifted to a place on the bank of the River Yamunā where he passed away on 30 March 1664. According to some chroniclers, Gurū Har Krishan breathed his last in Rājā Jai Siṅgh's house, now the site of Gurdwārā Baṅgla Sāhib, and was only taken to the bank of the Yamunā for cremation.

Rājā Jai Siṅgh dedicated the *havelī* or house where the Gurū had stayed to his memory. The Mughals demolished this shrine and built a mosque in its place sometime between 1753 and 1775. Sardār Jassā Siṅgh Rāmgaṛhīā razed this mosque during his attack on Delhi on 1 October 1778, and Sardār Baghel Siṅgh raised Gurdwārā Baṅglā Sāhib on the site in 1783. The present building was constructed by Sikhs of Delhi after the partition of 1947. It is a two- storeyed building on a high plinth and has an all-round gallery at mid-height of the rectangular domed hall. The Gurū Granth Sāhib is displayed in a wooden palanquin on the ground floor. Another single-storeyed hall, also rectangular in design, has since been constructed adjoining the main hall. The extensive Gurdwārā campus is flanked on the one side by the Gurū kā Laṅgar, community kitchen, and by a vast sheet of shimmering water, *sarovar*, the holy tank, on the other, and is entered through a high archway. The Gurdwārā is also served by a charitable hospital, a library and a museum named after Sardār Baghel Siṅgh. Besides the daily services, special *dīvāns* take place on the first of each Bikramī month and other special days on the annual Sikh calendar. The major annual celebration however is the birth anniversary of Gurū Har Krishan falling on Sāvan 10, occurring usually in July.

GURDWĀRĀ BĀLĀ SĀHIB, near Sunlight Colony, on the outer Ring Road of Delhi, marks the site where Gurū Har Krishan was cremated. The place was then right on the bank of the Yamunā which has, however, changed its course since. The Gurū, hardly eight years old at the time of his visit to Delhi, became popular among the residents of Delhi as Bālā Pīr (lit. young prophet). Hence the name of the Gurdwārā. Mātā Sundarī and Mātā Sāhib Devāṅ, consorts of Gurū Gobind Siṅgh, were also cremated at this site where a simple memorial shrine had existed when Sardār Baghel Siṅgh established a larger *gurdwārā* here in 1783. The present building of Gurdwārā Bālā Sāhib on an 18-acre estate was constructed in 1955. It comprises a flat-roofed hall, 30 x 25 metres. Its roof is supported by 18 columns. The Gurū Granth Sāhib is seated on a raised platform under a domed canopy of masonry. *Samādh* of Mātā Sāhib Devāṅ is also under the same roof, only a wooden partition separating it from the sanctum of Bālā Sāhib. It comprises the small kiosk with the Gurū Granth Sāhib seated inside it. It is called Aṅgīṭha Mātā Sāhib Kaur. Mātā Sundarī's *samādh* is in a separate room, 8-metre square with a verandah around it, flanking the main Gurdwārā Bālā Sāhib. The Gurū Granth Sāhib is seated here in a marble palanquin.

Besides the daily morning and evening services, larger *dīvāns* and community meals are held on the first of each Bikramī month and on every full-moon day. Most important of all is the death anniversary of Gurū Har Krishan which is observed on Chet *sudī* 14 occurring during March-April.

GURDWĀRĀ MĀTĀ SUNDARĪ, behind J.P. Hospital (formerly Irwin Hospital) near G͟hālib Urdu Academy in New Delhi, marks the residence of Mātā Sundarī and Mātā Sāhib Devāṅ from 1727 till their death. The holy mothers had at first been staying in a house in Kūchā Dilvālī Siṅghāṅ in Old Delhi. Following the execution of Ajīt Siṅgh Pālit (adopted son of Mātā Sundarī) in 1725, the ladies went to stay at Mathurā, but on return from there after two years they took up residence in a house which came to be called Havelī Mātā Sundarī Kī, now Gurdwārā Mātā Sundarījī. The Gurdwārā built during the 1970's is a two-storeyed flat-roofed structure with its facade decorated with projecting windows and kiosks on roof top. Besides the usual morning and evening services, special *dīvāns* are held on full-moon days. Still larger *dīvāns* take place in December every year to mark the death anniversaries of the four sons of Gurū Gobind Siṅgh.

GURDWĀRĀ MOTĪ BĀG͟H is situated on the Ring Road near Dhaulā Kūāṅ in New Delhi. It marks the site where Gurū Gobind Siṅgh on his arrival at Delhi in 1707 set up his camp. The *gurdwārā* here was first established by Sardār Baghel Siṅgh Karoṛsiṅghīā. While its double-storeyed old building is still preserved with the Gurū Granth Sāhib presiding it, a new complex was raised in 1980 with a 22-metre square high-ceiling domed hall and a mezzanine at mid-height. The Gurū Granth Sāhib is enshrined in it in a marble palanquin under a canopy. The entire wall surface, exterior as well as interior, is lined with slabs of white marble. The major festival of the year celebrates the first installation of the Gurū Granth Sāhib in the Harimandar at Amritsar (August).

GURDWĀRĀ DAMDAMĀ SĀHIB near Humāyūṅ's tomb on the outer Ring Road in New Delhi is where a meeting between Gurū Gobind Siṅgh and Prince Mu'azzam (later Emperor Bahādur Shāh) took place sometime in May-June 1707. The Gurū agreed to help the latter in his struggle for the throne against his younger brother, Prince 'Āzam. A *gurdwārā* was established later to mark the spot. Its present building constructed during 1977-84 is a 20-metre square high ceilinged, domed hall on a raised plinth with a mezzanine at mid-height forming the first floor. The entire wall surface is lined with marble slabs. The hall has three doors on each side making the building a *bārādarī* (lit. building with 12 doors). The inner design with arches supporting the mezzanine forming a covered passage under it, duplicates the design followed in the construction of Harimandar Sāhib at Amritsar. Domed kiosks adorn the roof corners. The most important celebration of the year is on the occasion of Holā Mohallā festival falling in March.

BIBLIOGRAPHY

1. Tārā Siṅgh, *Srī Gur Tīrath Saṅgrahi*. Amritsar, n.d.
2. Ṭhākar Siṅgh, Giānī, *Srī Gurduāre Darshan*. Amritsar, 1923
3. Kāhn Siṅgh, Bhāī, *Gurushabad Ratnākar Mahān Kosh* [Reprint]. Patiala, 1974
4. Trilochan Singh, *Historical Sikh Shrines in Delhi*. Delhi, 1972
5. Johar, S.S., *The Sikh Gurus and Their Shrines*. Delhi, 1976
6. Randhir, G.S., *Sikh Shrines in India*. Delhi, 1990

Hn.S

DELHI SIKH GURDWĀRĀS MANAGEMENT COMMITTEE was a by-product of the Akālī campaign for the reformation of the management of *gurdwārās* in the Punjab. To wrest control of the holy shrines from the hands of a corrupt and effete priestly order, the Sikhs had set up on 15 November 1920 a body called the Shiromaṇī Gurdwārā Parbandhak Committee (SGPC), Amritsar. In 1923, the SGPC took charge of all the historical *gurdwārās* in Delhi as well, and formed a committee of 11 members known as the Delhi Gurdwārā Parbandhak Committee (DGPC) to manage them. The SGPC, however, continued to exercise powers of control and supervision over the affairs of DGPC. With the influx into Delhi after the partition of India in 1947 of a large number of Sikh immigrants from West Punjab, the situation changed and the authority of DGPC began to be challenged. Attempts were made to dispossess the committee functioning under the auspices of the SGPC. Litigation and use of physical force from both sides were tried. In 1971, the Government of India entrusted the management, through an ordinance, to a five-member Gurdwārā Board. The ordinance was replaced by the Delhi Sikh Gurdwaras Act, 1971, passed by Parliament, providing for a committee to be elected by Sikh vote. Elections took place under the supervision of government authority and the new body called Delhi Sikh Gurdwārās Management Committee (DSGMC) came into existence in 1974. Under the provisions of the Act, the elections must take place every four years. The DSGMC controls nine historic and five other *gurdwārās* in Delhi. The historic shrines are Gurdwārā Sīs Gañj, Gurdwārā Rikābgañj, Gurdwārā Baṅglā Sāhib, Gurdwārā Mātā Sundarī, Gurdwārā Damdamā Sāhib, Gurdwārā Bālā Sāhib, Gurdwārā Motī Bāgh, Gurdwārā Majnū Ṭillā and Gurdwārā Nānak Piāo, and the others are Gurdwārā Karol Bāgh, Gurdwārā Daryā Gañj, Gurdwārā Pahāṛī Dhīraj, Gurdwārā Pīpal Mahādev, and Gurdwārā Dhakkā Dhīrpur. It also runs four degree colleges, eleven schools, a technical training institute (electronics) and a hospital.

The purpose of the 1971 Act, according to its preamble, is to provide for the proper management of the Sikh Gurdwārās and Gurdwārā property in Delhi and for matters connected therewith. The main aims and objects of the Delhi Sikh Gurdwārās Management Committee established under the Act are:

(a) To manage the historic and other *gurdwārās* of Delhi in such a way as to make them inspiring centres of the Sikh tradition, Sikh culture and Sikh religion;

(b) To spread education, especially the knowledge of Punjabi language in Gurmukhī script; to maintain free kitchen (*laṅgar*); to open free dispensaries and to perform other religious and charitable work;

(c) To render all help in the cause of the uplift and welfare of the Sikh community.

The Committee consists of 55 members, 46 of whom are elected by the Sikhs of Delhi and 9 are co-opted. Out of the nine co-opted members, two represent the Siṅgh Sabhās of

Delhi, one the SGPC (Amritsar), four the Ta<u>kh</u>ts at Amritsar, Anandpur, Paṭnā and Nānded̤, and two those Sikhs of Delhi who do not want to or cannot contest elections but whose services can be of value to the Committee. The term of the office of a member of the Committee is four years from the date on which the first meeting of the Committee is held. The Executive Board, which is elected by the Committee, consists of five office-bearers-president, senior vice-president, junior vice-president, general secretary and joint secretary — and ten members. To be elected a member of the Committee, one should have attained the age of twenty-five years, should be an *amritdhārī* or baptized Sikh, should not trim his beard or shave his *kes* (hair), should not take alcoholic drinks, and should be able to read and write Gurmukhī.

The sources of income of the DSGMC are *charhat* (offerings to the Gurū Granth Sāhib), *kaṛāhprasād* (sacramental offering), donations for *laṅgar* (free kitchen), *pāṭhs* (readings of Gurū Granth Sāhib), rent from property, and occasional individual donations. The principal sources of course are *charhat* and *prasād* which constitute nearly 80 per cent of the total income. Between 1956 and 1986, the income of the DSGMC increased from Rs 13 lakhs to about Rs 3.5 crores an year.

BIBLIOGRAPHY

1. Jitinder Kaur, *The Politics of Sikhs.* Delhi, 1986
2. *Bye-laws and Rules of the Gurdwara Prabandhak Committee, Delhi Province.* Delhi, 1942

J.K.

DE MEVIUS, BARON, also known as Frank Ernest Mevins, was a Prussian who came to the Punjab in March 1827 and was employed in the Sikh army in the rank of colonel. According to the <u>Kh</u>ālsā Darbār records, Mevius had to sign a pledge that he would, "during his period of service, abstain from eating beef, smoking or shaving, would domesticate himself in the country by marriage, would never quit the service without formal permission from the Maharajah, and would engage to fight any nation with whom the Maharajah declared war, even should it be his own." These were the usual conditions under which foreigners were admitted into Sikh service. Once Mevius was charged with using a whip against a Sikh soldier which led to a revolt in his command and he was compelled to take refuge in the Mahārājā's tent. Raṇjīt Siṅgh saved his life, but refused to retain him in service. He was given his discharge in 1830.

BIBLIOGRAPHY

Grey, C. *European Adventurers of Northern India.* Patiala, 1970

Gl.S.

DEPUIS or DE L'UST, a French soldier of fortune who came to Lahore in 1842, and was employed by the Sikh Darbār as a trainer of gunner recruits. Later, he was made commandant of a battalion, but, being found unfit for command, he was removed from service in 1844. He then proceeded to Shimlā where he opened a school for teaching French and dancing.

BIBLIOGRAPHY

Grey, C., *European Adventurers of Northern India, 1785 to 1849.* Patiala, 1970

Gl.S.

ḌERĀ, a word of Persian extraction, has several connotations. The original Persian word *ḍerāh* or *dirāh* means a tent, camp, abode, house or habitation. In current usage in rural Punjab, a farmhouse or a group of farmhouses built away from the village proper is called *ḍerā*. Even after such an habitation develops into a separate village or a town, it may continue to be called *ḍerā*, e.g. Ḍerā Bassī in Paṭiālā district of the Punjab, or

Ḍerā Ghāzī Khān and Ḍerā Ismā'īl Khān in Pakistan. Where colloquially used in place of Hindi *deharā*, the word will carry the connotation of a temple or memorial over a cremation site. The examples are Ḍerā Sāhib Gurdwārā at Lahore and Ḍerā Bābā Nānak, a town in Gurdāspur district of the Punjab.

In a different but not totally unrelated sense, *ḍerā* is apparently derived from the Persian *dair* meaning a monastery or convent. Monasteries, hermitages or seminaries set up by religious persons are almost invariably called *ḍerās*. They, too, are usually at some distance from the nearest village or town, and have an exclusively male population. For example, Daudhar Ḍerā. Among Sikhs, Nirmalās and Udāsīs have their *ḍerās* spread throughout the countryside. Although the Gurū Granth Sāhib is installed in most of them, their custodians prefer to call them *ḍerās* rather than *gurdwārās*.

In Sikh times, the word *ḍerā* was also used for army camps or cantonments to particularize regiments or armies commanded by different generals, such as Ḍerah Ghoṛchaṛhā Khās Shām Siṅgh Aṭārīvālā, Ḍerah Rāmgaṛhīāṅ, Ḍerah Naulakkhā and Ḍerah Imām ud-Dīn.

In the Gurū Granth Sāhib *ḍerā* is used to mean abode or living place, permanent rather than temporary (GG, 256), and also in the sense of a camp or citadel (GG, 628).

BIBLIOGRAPHY

1. Fauja Singh, *Military System of the Sikhs*. Delhi, 1964
2. Cunningham, J.D., *A History of the Sikhs*. London, 1849

M.G.S.

ḌERĀ BĀBĀ NĀNAK (30° - 2'N, 75° - 2'E), on the left bank of the River Rāvī in Gurdāspur district of the Punjab, is sacred to Gurū Nānak, who on the conclusion of one of his long travels arrived here and sat near a well owned by Ajittā Randhāvā, the *chaudharī* or headman of Pakkhoke Randhāve, village where the Gurū's family had been staying with his wife's parents. Around the spot where he had halted grew the town of Ḍerā Bābā Nānak. As the news of the Gurū's arrival spread, people from the surrounding villages started pouring in ever-increasing numbers to see him and receive his blessing. Bhāī Ajittā requested him to settle down permanently at or near Pakkhoke. This led to the foundation of a habitation across the Rāvī, which the Gurū named Kartārpur. On his death, on 7 September 1539, his ashes were buried near Kartārpur and a monument raised over them. But the monument was soon after washed away by a flood in the river. Gurū Nānak's elder son, Bābā Srī Chand, who was then staying at Pakkhoke, got the urn containing the ashes salvaged, reburied it close to Ajittā's well and raised over the spot a mud hut which came to be called Dehrā or *samādh* of Gurū Nānak. Later Bābā Dharam Dās, the son of Gurū Nānak's younger son, Lakhmī Dās, founded a new habitation around this Dehrā and named it Ḍerā Bābā Nānak. There are two historical *gurdwārās* in the town now.

GURDWĀRĀ DARBĀR SĀHIB, in the centre of the town, comprises three separate memorials. The well which originally belonged to Bhāī Ajittā Randhāvā still exists and is reverently called Sarjī Sāhib. Pilgrims take its water home in the belief that it possesses curative properties. The second memorial is the Kīrtan Asthān, a rectangular hall, which marks the site where Gurū Arjan had sat rapt in *kīrtan* when visiting Ḍerā Bābā Nānak for condolence on the death of Bābā Dharam Dās. The Gurū Granth Sāhib is seated in the hall. The central shrine, called Thaṛā Sāhib, marks the *thaṛā*, or platform, on which Gurū Nānak had sat when he first came to Ajittā's well and where, later, Bābā Srī Chand buried his father's ashes. The Gurū Granth Sāhib is seated here in a small square pavilion with a pinnacled lotus dome under an over-hanging gilded canopy. The whole pavilion is covered with gold-plated metal sheets with some of the hymns of Gurū Nānak embossed on them. The Thaṛā Sāhib is at one end of a recently constructed spacious hall, above which, over the sanctum, is a square domed room with an ornamental arched coping and domed kiosks at the corners. The entire exterior above the roof level of this room is covered with gold-plated metal sheets. The gold-work on top as well as on the sanctum was got executed in 1827 by Mahārājā Raṇjīt Siṅgh, who also made endowments in cash and land for the maintenance of the shrine.

The Gurdwārā is administered by the Shiromaṇī Gurdwārā Parbandhak Committee through a local committee. Special *dīvāns* take place on every *amāvasyā*, the last day of the dark half of the lunar month, and all major anniversaries, especially the one marking the death of Gurū Nānak, are observed. But the most important annual event is the fair celebrating the Baisākhī festival. A handwritten copy of the Gurū Granth Sāhib is preserved in this Gurdwārā. It has 1660 pages, each page having a handsomely illuminated border.

GURDWĀRĀ LAṄGAR MANDIR CHOLĀ SĀHIB, in the eastern part of the town, is connected with a relic — a *cholā*, or cloak, believed to have been presented to Gurū Nānak by a Muslim devotee at Bag͟hdād. The *cholā*, bearing some Qurā'nic verses and Arabic numerals, arranged in the form of charms embroidered on it, was procured from Bag͟hdād by Bābā Kābalī Mall, a descendant of Gurū Nānak, it is said. It was brought to Ḍerā Bābā Nānak on 20 Phāgun 1884 Bk / 1 March 1828. A special shrine was constructed where the Cholā Sāhib was kept and where it was put on display at the time of a fair held from 21 to 23 Phāgun, early March, every year. From the Gurū kā Laṅgar which serves the pilgrims, the shrine has come to be known as Gurdwārā Laṅgar Mandir Cholā Sāhib. It was under private management of the resident descendants of Gurū Nānak. As the Gurdwārā reform movement got under way, the Shiromaṇī Gurdwārā Parbandhak Committee claimed possession of the shrine, but the owners resisted. In the end, the control of the Gurdwārā passed to the Committee, but Cholā Sāhib, the relic, remained with the family. It is now displayed in a glass case in a private house, about 50 metres from the Gurdwārā, attended in rotation by three Bedī families living there.

Gurdwārā Laṅgar Mandir Cholā Sāhib is now administered by the local committee managing Gurdwārā Darbār Sāhib. The 3-day annual fair and Gurū kā Laṅgar are held as usual in the adjoining compound. The Gurdwārā compound also has within it the *samādh* of Bābā Kābalī Mall and an octagon-shaped old well. The local belief is that the water of this well cures women whose offspring die during infancy.

BIBLIOGRAPHY

1. Tārā Siṅgh, *Srī Gur Tīrath Saṅgrahi*. Amritsar, n.d.
2. Ṭhākar Siṅgh, Giānī, *Srī Gurduāre Darshan*. Amritsar, 1923

M.G.S.

ḌERĀ SĀHIB, GURDWĀRĀ, commonly pronounced Ḍehrā Sāhib is located in the revenue limits of Lohar village, 10 km east of Naushahrā Panvāṅ (31° - 20'N, 74° - 57'E), in Amritsar district of the Punjab. It marks the site of a village called Paṭṭheviṇḍ where Gurū Nānak's ancestors had lived. Gurū Nānak himself often visited the village. An old well within the Gurdwārā compound is said to be the one near which he had once stopped. The shrine was first established by Gurū Hargobind (1595-1644), who also had the nearby pond converted into a *sarovar* or holy tank. The construction of the present complex, including the renovation of the *sarovar*, was carried out by Sant Gurmukh Siṅgh Sevāvāle (1849-1947). Situated inside a high-walled enclosure, the Gurdwārā comprises a high-ceilinged *dīvān* hall with the domed sanctum at one end and a marbled terrace in front. It is administered by the Shiromaṇī Gurdwārā Parbandhak Committee through a local committee. Besides the celebration of major Sikh anniversaries, a three-day fair is held to mark the festival of Māghī, the first of the Bikramī month of Māgh (mid-January).

Gn.S.

DESĀṄ, MĀĪ, a childless woman from a Sandhū Jaṭṭ family of Paṭṭī in Amritsar district, once approached Gurū Hargobind praying for the boon of a child. The Gurū advised her to remain content with what God had willed for her, but, as she persisted in her request, he made a prayer for her. Māī Desāṅ, says *Gurbilās Chhevīṅ Pātshāhī,* had in course of time seven sons, whose descendants now inhabit the village of Chabbā, 8 km south of Amritsar. Gurdwārā Saṅgrāṇā Sāhib at Chabbā marks the spot where Māī Desāṅ is believed to have met the Gurū.

BIBLIOGRAPHY

1. *Gurbilās Chhevīṅ Pātshāhī.* Patiala, 1970
2. Santokh Siṅgh, Bhāī, *Srī Gur Pratāp Sūraj Granth.* Amritsar, 1926-37
3. Macauliffe, Max Arthur, *The Sikh Religion.* Oxford, 1909

B.S.

DESĀṄ, MĀĪ (d. 1778), daughter of Amīr Siṅgh of Gujrāṅwālā, was married to Chaṛhat Siṅgh Sukkarchakkīā in 1756. When her husband died in 1770, their eldest son, Mahāṅ Siṅgh, was barely ten years old. Māī Desāṅ took the control of the Sukkarchakkīā *misl* or chiefship into her own hands, and showed uncommon sagacity and courage in administering its affairs. She had the advantage of the advice of her brothers, Gurbakhsh Siṅgh and Dal Siṅgh, and of the support of Jai Siṅgh of the Kanhaiyā *misl.* One of the first tasks she undertook was the rebuilding of the fort at Gujrāṅwālā which had been destroyed by Ahmad Shāh Durrānī. She renamed the new fort Mahāṅ Siṅgh kī Gaṛhī. She brought further strength to the *misl* by securing influential matrimonial alliances for her children. She married off her daughter, Rāj Kaur, to Sāhib Siṅgh, of the Bhaṅgī *misl,* and her son, Mahāṅ Siṅgh, to the daughter of the Rājā of Jīnd. She died in 1778.

BIBLIOGRAPHY

1. Griffin, Lepel, *Ranjit Singh,* Oxford, 1905
2. Harbans Singh, *Maharaja Ranjit Singh.* Delhi, 1980
3. Sītal, Sohan Siṅgh, *Sikh Mislāṅ.* Ludhiana, 1952

J.S.K.

DESĀ SIṄGH MAJĪṬHĪĀ (1768-1832), an army general and civil administrator in Sikh times, was the son of Naudh Siṅgh, a feudal retainer under Amar Siṅgh Baggā of the Kanhaiyā *misl.* When Naudh Siṅgh died in 1788, Desā Siṅgh succeeded to the family estates. He served Buddh Siṅgh Baggā, successor of Amar Siṅgh Baggā, for a number of years before joining Raṇjīt Siṅgh's army. In 1804, Desā Siṅgh was made a commander of 400 *sowārs.* He served the Mahārājā in many of his early campaigns. In August 1809, he was appointed commandant of the Fort of Kāṅgṛā after Raṇjīt Siṅgh had occupied it driving away the Gurkhā general, Amar Siṅgh Thāpā. In 1811, he was charged with reducing the Fort of Koṭlā, half-way between Kāṅgṛā and Nūrpur. Soon after he was made the *nāzim* (administrator) of Kāṅgṛā and hill districts of Chambā, Nūrpur, Koṭlā, Shāhpur, Jasroṭā, Basohlī, Mankoṭ, Jasvān, Sībā, Guler, Maṇḍī, Suket, Kullu and Dātārpur. Desā Siṅgh who had made the hill region his home married a Kāṅgṛā girl to whom was born his son Raṇjodh Siṅgh.

Desā Siṅgh participated in the campaigns launched to capture Multān (1818), Kashmīr (1819) and Nausherā (1823). He commanded great influence at the Sikh court and was the recipient of several titles and *jāgīrs*. For a few years he served as the *nāzim* of Amritsar and its adjoining territories, with management of the Golden Temple as his special charge. He was often sent to receive and look after foreign dignitaries visiting the court. He established in the hill territories under his control a mild and humane administration. The Guler style of Sikh painting with the ten Sikh Gurūs and the Mahārājā and his courtiers as its main themes developed during his time.

Desā Siṅgh died in 1832, and was succeeded in all his estates and honours by his eldest son, Lahiṇā Siṅgh Majīṭhīā.

BIBLIOGRAPHY

1. Sūrī, Sohan Lāl, *'Umdāt-ut-Twārīkh*. Lahore, 1885-89
2. Griffin, Lepel and C.F. Massy, *Chiefs and Families of Note in the Punjab*. Lahore, 1909
3. Prinsep, Henry T., *Origins of the Sikh Power in the Punjab and Political Life of Maharaja Ranjit Singh*. Calcutta, 1834
4. Lawrence, H.M., *Adventures of an Officer in the Punjab in the Service of Ranjit Singh*. London, 1846
5. Hasrat, Bikrama Jit, *Life and Times of Ranjit Singh*. Nabha, 1977

B.J.H.

DESH BHAGAT PARIVĀR SAHĀIK COMMITTEE, originally named Sikh Desh Bhagat Parivār Sahāik Committee, to help the families of patriots, was set up in October 1920 under the chairmanship of Bābā Vasākhā Siṅgh, a Ghadr revolutionary who had been sentenced to transportation for life, but was released from the Cellular Jail, Andamans, on medical grounds in 1920. He reached his village, Dadehar in Amritsar district on 14 April 1920, and almost immediately started preparing lists of families of other patriots who had been with him in the Andamans. As his poor health did not allow him to travel, he contacted those families through his younger brother, Magghar Siṅgh, and communicated to them the news of their relatives in detention. He was deeply touched to hear stories of the hardships of these families, which had not only been deprived of their bread-earners, but also had their properties confiscated. He also gathered mailing addresses of many other families in similar straits.

In October 1920, the Central Sikh League held its second annual session in Bradlaugh Hall, Lahore. It had invited some released freedom fighters to the session in order to honour them. Bābā Vasākhā Siṅgh was one of them. From the pulpit of the Sikh League he made a fervent appeal, seeking help for the families in distress. At his suggestion, the League resolved to set up to this end Desh Bhagat Parivār Sahāik Committee. Bābā Vasākhā Siṅgh was unanimously chosen to be its chairman, an office he held throughout its life. The aims and objects of the Committee were:

1. To provide economic assistance to needy families of the patriots;
2. To look after the education and upbringing of their children;
3. To visit detained patriots to convey to them news of their families and to bring to the families news from them;
4. To create public opinion in order to press for release of political prisoners; and
5. To defend political prisoners in courts of law.

Bābā Vasākhā Siṅgh and other members of the committee made a tour collecting information about those detained in jails for their political views or activities and acquainting themselves with their problems which they brought to the notice of the people through their press statements and public speeches. The committee also raised a fund to aid the families of detainees. Bābā Vasākhā Siṅgh toured the entire country and also went abroad to Burma, Singapore, Hongkong, Shanghai and other places in South East Asia to collect donations. Donations also began to flow from western countries into the committee's office set up in a hired building near the Darbār Sāhib, in Amritsar.

Up to 1930, the committee's efforts were primarily directed to meetings with political prisoners and to providing financial assistance to their families. The second phase began when it started mounting pressure for the release of political prisoners who had already spent many long years in jails. By this time Bābā Vasākhā Siṅgh had also begun his work in the Kirtī-Kisān (workers and peasants) movement which the government distrusted because of its leftist leanings and involvement. The committee's sphere of activity extended to ensuring the welfare of the families of those taken prisoners in the Kirtī-Kisān campaign. On the outbreak of World War II the offices of the Desh Bhagat Parivār Sahāik Committee was raided by police and the records seized.

After independence in 1947, when most of the political prisoners were released by the new government, the committee remained dormant until 1952 when it was reactivated in Jalandhar to raise funds for a memorial in honour of the patriots. In 1955, the Desh Bhagat Parivār Sahāik Committee was amalgamated with the newly formed Desh Bhagat Yādgār Committee.

BIBLIOGRAPHY

Jas, Jaswant Siṅgh, *Bābā Visākhā Siṅgh*. Jalandhar, 1979

J.S.J.

DES RĀJ, BHĀĪ, a Khatrī Sikh of Amritsar, was entrusted with the supervision of the reconstruction of the Harimandar during the sixties and seventies of the eighteenth century. Nothing is known about his early life or family except that he originally came from Sursiṅgh village, 30 km southwest of Amritsar, from where he migrated to the town and flourished in business, with a reputation for honesty and truthfulness. When the Sikhs sacked Sirhind in January 1764 and allocated several hundred thousands rupees from the plunder for the restoration of Srī Harimandar Sāhib at Amritsar, demolished by Ahmad Shāh Durrānī two years earlier, they assigned Bhāī Des Rāj to undertake the reconstruction. The money was deposited with some bankers of repute at Amritsar from whom Bhāī Des Rāj was authorized to withdraw amounts as and when needed. He was also given a seal, *Gurū kī mohar* or the Gurū's seal by the Khālsā to raise more funds. The foundation of the holy sanctum was laid on 19 April 1764 by Jassā Siṅgh Āhlūvālīā, supreme commander of the Dal Khālsā. According to Giānī Giān Siṅgh, *Twārīkh Srī Amritsar,* the construction of the Harimandar, the approach bridge, the Darshanī Deoṛhī or gateway, and the clearance of the sacred tank filled by the debris in 1762 were completed by 1776. After the sack of Khurjā, a rich market-town in the present Bulandshahar district of Uttar Pradesh, by the Dal Khālsā in February 1783, one tenth of the plunder, amounting to 1,00,000 rupees, was also placed at the disposal of Bhāī Des Rāj, who now started having the *parikramā* or the circumambulatory terrace paved. This work, including the platform around the Dukhbhañjanī Berī and two large masonry screens for ladies' baths, was completed by 1784.

BIBLIOGRAPHY

1. Giān Siṅgh, Giānī, *Twārīkh Srī Amritsar* [Reprint]. Amritsar, 1977
2. Fauja Singh, ed., *The City of Amritsar — An Introduction*. Patiala, 1977
3. Madanjit Kaur, *The Golden Temple : Past and Present*. Amritsar, 1983
4. Arshi, P.S., *Sikh Architecture in Punjab*. Delhi, 1986

S.S. Am.

DESŪ, Jaṭṭ of Chahal clan, was a minor chief at Bhīkhī, in present-day Baṭhiṇḍā district, when Gurū Tegh Bahādur visited that village travelling through the Mālvā region in 1672-73. As he came to see him, the Gurū asked him why he carried a walking stick in his quiver. Desū replied that although he was a Hindu by birth, he was a follower of Sultān Sakhī Sarwar, and carried the stick as an emblem of that faith. According to *Mālvā Desh Raṭan dī Sākhī Pothī*, the Gurū gave Desū five arrows from his quiver and said that if he kept these with him he should prosper and want nothing. Desū discarded the Sultānī stick. Desū's wife broke and burnt the arrows given by the Gurū. This, it is said, brought a curse on his house and his son and grandson perished at the hands of his enemies and his direct line came to an end.

BIBLIOGRAPHY

1. *Mālvā Desh Raṭan dī Sākhī Pothī*. Amritsar, 1950
2. Santokh Siṅgh, Bhāī, *Srī Gur Pṛtāp Sūraj Granth*, Amritsar, 1926-37
3. Giān Siṅgh, Giānī, *Twārīkh Gurū Khālsā*. Patiala, 1970

M.G.S.

DESŪ SIṄGH, BHĀĪ (d. 1781), was the second of the five sons of Bhāī Gurbakhsh Siṅgh of the well-known Bhāī family, deriving its name from the celebrated Bhāī Bhagatū, contemporary of three successor Gurūs, Gurū Arjan, Gurū Hargobind and Gurū Har Rāi. According to Bhāī Santokh Siṅgh, *Garb Gañjanī Ṭīkā*, Desū Siṅgh was the fifth in the line of Bhāī Bhagatū's descendants. His father, Bhāī Gurbakhsh Siṅgh, was a close associate of Ālā Siṅgh of Paṭiālā and had carved for himself some territories around Sirhind and Kaithal besides his ancestral possessions in several villages around Bhuchcho, near Baṭhiṇḍā. After his death in 1764, his territories were divided among his sons. Desū Siṅgh collected a force, and, advancing from Bhuchcho, marched straight to Kaithal and defeating Bhīkh Bakhsh and Niāmat Khān, two brothers in possession of Kaithal, established himself there as an independent chief sometime between 1764 and 1768. He began further to extend his territories and seized the town of Thānesar with one of its two forts. This excited the jealousy of another Sikh chief, Mit Siṅgh, who seized the second fort at Thānesar, and after his death, his son, Bhaṅgā Siṅgh, evicted Desū Siṅgh's forces from that town.

Bhāī Desū Siṅgh also fell out with Rājā Amar Siṅgh, of Paṭiālā, in 1778, because he did not support the Rājā in his punitive action against Harī Siṅgh, of Siālbā, who had been friendly with the Kaithal chief. After dealing with the Siālbā chief, Rājā Amar Siṅgh sent a force against Kaithal, too, but an attack was averted by the intercession of some of the Bhāī brothers.

Bhāī Desū Siṅgh died at Kaithal in 1781.

BIBLIOGRAPHY

1. Griffin, Lepel, *The Rajas of the Punjab* [Reprint]. Patiala, 1970
2. Gupta, Hari Ram, *History of the Sikhs*, vol. II. Delhi, 1978
3. Santokh Siṅgh, Bhāī, *Garb Gañjanī Ṭīkā*. Lahore, 1910

S.S.B.

DEVĀ SIṄGH, BHĀĪ, and Bhāī Īshar Siṅgh were among the Five Muktās, who formed the first batch after the Pañj Piāre to receive baptism of the Khālsā on the Baisākhī day of AD 1699. According to *Rahitnāmā Hazūrī Bhāī Chaupā Siṅgh Chhibbar*, the draft of a *rahitnāmā* was prepared by these Muktās which later received Gurū Gobind Siṅgh's approval. Bhāī Devā Siṅgh and Bhāī Īshar Siṅgh fell fighting in the battle of Chamkaur (7 December 1705).

BIBLIOGRAPHY

1. Macauliffe, Max Arthur, *The Sikh Religion*. Oxford, 1909

2. Santokh Siṅgh, Bhāī, *Srī Gur Pratāp Sūraj Granth.* Amritsar, 1926-37
3. Giān Siṅgh, Giānī, *Twārīkh Gurū Khālsā.* Patiala, 1970

M.G.S.

DEVĀ SIṄGH NAROTAM, PAṆḌIT (d. 1924), Nirmālā scholar, was the son of Mahitāb Siṅgh of the village of Janetpurā, 13 km north of Jagrāoṅ (30° - 47'N, 75° - 28'E), in Ludhiāṇā district of the Punjab. He received his early lessons in the Sikh texts at the hands of Bhāī Gurdit Siṅgh and then left home to continue his studies under Sant Natthā Siṅgh of Gurdwārā Tapiāṇā Sāhib at Khaḍūr Sāhib, in Amritsar district, and later under Sant Māhṇā Siṅgh (d. 1890) at the Nirmalā *ḍerā* or monastery at Khaṇḍūr, near Mullāṅpur, in Ludhiāṇā district. He accompanied Sant Māhṇā Siṅgh to Bhāī Rūpā, a village 18 km north of Rāmpurā Phūl in Baṭhiṇḍā district, to join the Nirmalā monastery called Ḍerā Khūhāṅvālā. Here, Devā Siṅgh, already reputed enough as a scholar to be known as *paṇḍīt* (lit. learned scholar), was put by his mentor through a course of comparative study of *gurbāṇī* in the light of his knowledge of Sanskrit and Vedānta. Mahant Māhṇā Siṅgh, pleased with his progress, not only conferred on him the title of Narotam (lit. man *par excellence*) but also nominated him to succeed him as *mahant* or chief priest of the *ḍerā*. Paṇḍit Devā Siṅgh completed, in 1896, an exegesis of Gurū Granth Sāhib which was, however, never published and is preserved (in incomplete form) in a private collection in Ludhiāṇā. The work is in two parts – *Prayāy Bhagat Bāṇī Ke* and *Srī Gurū Granth Gūṛhārth Pradīp. Prayāy* means a convertible term or synonym. *Bhagat Bāṇī* refers to hymns of saints other than the Gurūs included in the Gurū Granth Sāhib. Only 78 sheets of the manuscript of *Prayāy Bhagat Bāṇī,* covering compositions in Sirī Rāga, Rāga Gauṛī and a part of Rāga Āsā survive. *Srī Gurū Granth Gūṛhārth Pradīp* (*gūṛhārth* = deeper meaning or signification; *pradīp* = a light or lamp), a more voluminous manuscript comprising 400 sheets, contains selected verses from the Gurū Granth Sāhib, with annotation and comment. The language of the two manuscripts is *sādh-bhāshā,* admixture of Hindi and Punjabi, popular among the writers of the time and the script used is Gurmukhī. Another work of Paṇḍit Devā Siṅgh, *Sidh Gosṭ Saṭīk,* a commentary on the long scriptual hymn, *Sidh Gosṭi,* was however published by Lālā Achhrū Mall of Fīrozpur in 1898.

Paṇḍit Devā Siṅgh Narotam died at Bhāī Rūpā in 1924.

BIBLIOGRAPHY

Gaṇeshā Siṅgh, Mahant, *Nirmal Bhūshaṇ arthāt Itihās Nirmal Bhekh.* Amritsar, n.d.

Gr.S.

DEVĀ SIṄGH, SARDĀR BAHĀDUR(d. 1872), son of Fateh Siṅgh and a great-grandson of Sāvan Siṅgh, cousin of Saṅgat Siṅgh, the leader of the Nishānāvālī *misl,* came of a Shergil Jaṭṭ family of Mansūrvāl, in Fīrozpur district. Devā Siṅgh joined service under Mahārājā Raṇjīt Siṅgh in 1816 at a very young age. After some time, he was put under Lahiṇā Siṅgh Majīṭhīā who made him commandant of the regiment of his brother, Gujjar Siṅgh. In 1834, he accompanied the young Sardār to Calcutta on a mission half complimentary, half political. In 1842, he was transferred to the Gurkhā regiment to serve in Hazārā. Under the Darbār he was posted at Ḍerā Ismā'īl Khān in command of the Sūrajmukhī regiment. At the time of the outbreak at Multān, he left with his regiment to join Herbert Edwardes and General Van Cortlandt with whom he served throughout the campaign and earned much distinction and fame.

In 1853, when the Punjab Military Police was formed, Devā Siṅgh was selected to raise and command the Seventh Police Battalion at Amritsar. He preserved order in the city and upheld the civil authority on the eve of the revolt of 1857. He also raised levies for service at Delhi and, during 1857-58, a considerable number of men were recruited and sent down country by him. For his services, Devā Siṅgh was granted the Star of the Order of British India with the title of Sardār Bahādur and a personal allowance of Rs 1,200 per annum. On the reorganization of the Punjab police and disarming of the old force, Devā Siṅgh retired from government service. He received a special retiring pension of Rs 3,000 per annum, and a grant of six hundred acres of waste land with proprietory rights. Devā Siṅgh died in 1872.

BIBLIOGRAPHY

1. Sūrī, Sohan Lāl, *'Umdāt-ut-Twārīkh*. Lahore, 1885-89
2. Griffin, Lepel and C.F. Massy, *Chiefs and Families of Note in the Punjab*. Lahore, 1909

S.S.B.

DEVĀ SIṄGH, SIR (1834-1890), a high-ranking Paṭiālā state administrator, was born in 1834 into an Aroṛā Sikh family, the son of Colonel Khushāl Siṅgh, a brave soldier who had once killed a tiger (*sher*, in Punjabi) near one of the city gates conferring upon it the name Sherāṅvālā which lasts to this day. Devā Siṅgh received the only formal education available at that time by attending a *maktab* or Persian school, and entered Paṭiālā state service at a very early age in 1846. In 1853, he was appointed assistant judicial minister and in 1855, a Risāldār in a cavalry unit. Mahārājā Narinder Siṅgh (1824-1862), who thought highly of his abilities elevated him in 1858 to the position of Sardār Sāhib Deoṛhī Mu'allā or royal chamberlain. He was made captain in the cavalry in 1860 and then Nāzim or deputy commissioner of Pinjore district which comrpised the hill areas of the state. In 1867, he was transferred to Mahendergaṛh district in the same capacity only to be recalled in 1873 to the capital to become the Dīwān or finance minister. He was appointed president of the Regency Council set up to administer the affairs of the state after the premature death of Mahārājā Mahinder Siṅgh (1852-1876). The two other members of the Council were K͟hān Sāhib Nāmdar K͟hān and Chaudharī Chaṛhat Rām. Devā Siṅgh was honoured with a knighthood and the title of K.C.S.I. He had a *gurdwārā* erected near the Paṭiālā railway station and donated money and lands for its maintenance. His son, Partāp Siṅgh, who also rose to be the finance minister of the state, founded in memory of his father an orphange which is still in existence.Devā Siṅgh was also a fellow of Pañjāb University, Lahore, and lent support to the campaign for the establishment of K͟hālsā College at Amritsar. He was very enthusiastic in espousing the cause of the K͟hālsā College Establishment Committee.

Sir Devā Siṅgh died on 6 January 1890.

Jn.S.

DEV GANDHĀRĪ. *See* SIKH DEVOTIONAL MUSIC

DEVĪ DĀS was, according to Bhāī Santokh Siṅgh, *Srī Gur Pratāp Sūraj Granth*, a devout Sikh of the time of Gurū Hargobind (1595-1644), trained in martial skills. He took part in the battle of Amritsar (1629) in which the Sikhs worsted the attacking Mug͟hal force led by Muk͟hlis K͟hān, the *faujdār* of Lahore.

BIBLIOGRAPHY

1. Santokh Siṅgh, Bhāī, *Srī Gur Pratāp Sūraj Granth*. Amritsar, 1926-37
2. Giān Siṅgh, Giānī, *Twārīk͟h Gurū K͟hālsā*. Patiala, 1970

B.S.

DEVĪ DĀS, DĪWĀN (1767?-1830), eldest son of Dīwān Ṭhākur Dās Khatrī of Peshāwar, was, like his father, in the service of the

Afghān rulers prior to joining the court of Mahārājā Raṇjīt Siṅgh. At the time of Shāh Zamān's last invasion of northern India (1798-99), the Mahārājā, who had heard about the reputation of Devī Dās, offered him the post of Dīwān at Lahore. Devī Dās entered the service of the Mahārājā in 1803 as the keeper of the royal seal, accountant-general and head of the secretariat (*mīr munshī*). Devī Dās found that the financial administration needed his immediate attention. The territories which fell to the Mahārājā's arms were generally farmed out to individuals who were always in arrears with their payments. Devī Dās settled the amount of the *deohṛī* fees in each district, and *kārdārs*, revenue officers, were made responsible for having them deposited into government treasuries through the *deohṛīdārs*. He also established a rudimentary Sarishtā'-i-Hazūr where records of all major financial transactions were kept; to it was attached a Naqal Daftar or copying office. All vouchers of expenditure and pay orders were scrutinized by him for approval and sanction by the Mahārājā.

As the *mīr munshī* of the Mahārājā, Devī Dās read out to him reports from various parts of the kingdom, and wrote out royal orders to the chiefs and *kārdārs*. He kept ready money for State expenditure and royal charities. In 1819, when Kashmīr was conquered, Devī Dās was sent there for the settlement of the country.

Devī Dās died at Lahore in 1830.

BIBLIOGRAPHY

1. Sūrī, Sohan Lāl, *'Umdāt-ut-Twārīkh*. Lahore, 1885-89
2. Griffin, Lepel and C.F. Massy, *Chiefs and Families of Note in the Punjab*. Lahore, 1909
3. Garrett, H.L.O. and G.L. Chopra, eds., *Events at the Court of Ranjit Singh 1810-1817*. Delhi, 1986
4. Hasrat, B.J., *Life and Times of Ranjit Singh*. Nabha, 1977

H.R.G.

DEVĪ DĀS, PAṆḌIT, one of the numerous poets and scholars who kept company with Gurū Gobind Siṅgh (*See* Bavañjā Kavī), was born in a Chhibbar Brāhmaṇ family who had been followers of the Gurūs. His father, Hardayāl, was the younger brother of Bhāī Gavāldās who, according to the Bhaṭṭ Vahīs, had accompanied Gurū Tegh Bahādur during his visit to the eastern provinces; and Bhāī Chaupā Siṅgh, author of one of the Rahitnāmās, was his grand-uncle. Chandra Sain Saināpati, another of Gurū Gobind Siṅgh's poets, in his *Sukh Sain Granth*, acknowledges Devī Dās to be his teacher. Manuscripts of three of Devī Dās's works — *Rājnītī, Siṅgh-Gaū kī Kathā* and *Lav Kus dī Vār* — survive. The first two are in Hindi, while the third is in Punjabi.

BIBLIOGRAPHY

1. Padam, Piārā Siṅgh, *Srī Gurū Gobind Singh Jī de Darbārī Ratan*. Patiala, 1976
2. — and Giānī Garjā Siṅgh, eds., *Gurū kīāṅ Sākhīāṅ*. Patiala, 1986

P.S.P.

DEVINDER SIṄGH, RĀJĀ (1822-1865), was born on 5 September 1822, the son of Rājā Jasvant Siṅgh of Nābhā. He ascended the throne of Nābhā on 5 October 1840 at the age of eighteen. During the first Anglo-Sikh war of 1845-46, Devinder Siṅgh whose sympathy was with the Lahore Darbār did not help the British for which reason nearly a quarter of his possessions were confiscated and he was removed from his state and sent to Mathurā. He was granted an annual pension of Rs 50,000, and in his place his minor son, Bharpūr Siṅgh, was installed on the *gaddī*. In December 1855, Rājā Devinder Siṅgh was shifted to Mahārājā Kharak Siṅgh's mansion in Lahore where he died ten years later, in November 1865.

BIBLIOGRAPHY

1. Griffin, Lepel, *The Rajas of the Punjab*. Delhi, 1977

2. Ganda Singh, *The Patiala and East Panjab States Union: Historical Background*. Patiala, 1951

S.S.B.

DEVNO DEVĪ, RĀṆĪ (d. 1839), daughter of a Chib Khatrī of Dev Baṭālā, in Jammū, was married to Mahārājā Raṇjīt Siṅgh. She immolated herself on the burning pyre of her husband on 28 June 1839.

BIBLIOGRAPHY

Teja Singh and Ganda Singh, eds., *Maharaja Ranjit Singh Centenary Volume*. Amritsar, 1939

S.S.B.

DEV SAMĀJ, a religious and social reform society, was founded on 16 February 1887 in Lahore by Paṇḍit Shiv Nārāyaṇ Agnihotrī (1850-1929). The story of the Dev Samāj is in essence the story of its founder. Paṇḍit Agnihotrī was born in the village of Akbarpur, in Uttar Pradesh, on 20 December 1850. At sixteen he went to Thomson College of Engineering at Roorkee. In November 1873, he moved to Lahore taking a position as drawing master at the Government College. Paṇḍit Agnihotrī, who had already begun seriously to question orthodox Hinduism through the influence of Munshī Kanhayālāl Alakhdhārī and his personal *gurū*, Paṇḍit Shiv Dayāl, soon joined the Lahore Brahmo Samāj. He was a dramatic and effective speaker, a prolific writer of tracts and pamphlets and a successful journalist. In all, he wrote nearly 300 books and pamphlets during his lifetime.

Initially Paṇḍit Agnihotrī accepted the rational, eclectic, and reformist ideology of the Brahmo Samāj. He wrote and spoke in favour of marriage reform, against the evils of child marriage, and supported vegetarianism. In 1877, he met Swāmī Dayānand and although they agreed on many of the values commonly shared, Dayānand and Agnihotrī clashed persistently. In the years that followed, Paṇḍit Agnihotrī defended Brahmo ideals in opposition to the new Ārya Samāj. Agnihotrī also defended Sikhism against attacks made by the Ārya Samāj in 1888-89.

Agnihotrī dedicated more and more of his energy to the Brahmo cause. He became a Brahmo missionary travelling extensively throughout the Punjab and, finally, on 20 December 1882, he took *sannyās* with the new name, Satyānand Agnihotrī. He decided to devote his entire life to religious pursuit and social service. Factional strife, competition for leadership, differences over beliefs and the resulting tensions began to impinge on Agnihotrī's commitment to the Brahmo Samāj. He found himself less and less comfortable within the Brahmo movement, and finally resigned from the Punjab Brahmo Samāj in 1886.

The founding of the Dev Samāj in 1887 provided Agnihotrī with a new opening. By the end of 1887, he and his new organization began to move away from the central ideology of the Brahmo Samāj. In place of the eclectic rationalism of the Brahmos based on a reinterpretation of traditional Hindu texts, the Dev Samāj made the 'Gurū' Paṇḍit Agnihotrī, and his own personal revelations the central principle. "Book revelations" whether Ārya, Brahmo, Christian, or Islamic were rejected; the 'gurū' became all. In 1892, Agnihotrī initiated a policy of dual worship, both of himself and of God. Three years later the worship of God ended, leaving only the 'Gurū' Paṇḍit Agnihotrī as the focus of worship and of all ideological innovation.

Although the Dev Samāj followed patterns of leadership and legitimization different from those of other reform movements within Punjabi Hinduism, its ideology remained similar. As with the Brahmos and Āryas, the Dev Samāj rejected contemporary Hinduism. Its rituals and deities were replaced by worship of the true 'gurū,' Dev Bhagvān Ātmā. All caste restrictions were rejected. Members of the Dev Samāj were expected to practise interdining and intercaste marriage. Paṇḍit Agnihotrī also sought to change the role of women through the elimination of child marriage; he set the approved age of marriage at twenty for boys and sixteen for girls. He discouraged excessive dowries, *pardah*, and the traditional mourning rites carried out by Punjabi women. Agnihotrī taught that widow marriage was acceptable and married a widow himself following the death of his first wife. The Dev Samāj maintained that women as well as men should be educated and, to further this end, it opened a co-educational school at Mogā on 29 October 1899. This later became the Dev Samāj High School, and in 1901 the Samāj opened a separate girls' school, the Dev Samāj Bālikā Vidyālayā. Over the years the Dev Samāj founded other schools and colleges in many parts of the Punjab.

Above all else, the Dev Samāj taught a strongly moral doctrine. Its members were urged to be completely honest in both their public and private lives. They should not lie, steal, cheat, accept bribes, or gamble. They should take neither liquor nor drugs and should practise strict vegetarianism. The Samāj members were divided into three classes, Sahāyaks, or sympathizers and Navajīvan Yāftās, those who had found a new life. The former joined the Dev Samāj, paid Rs 10 per year, and accepted the leadership of Paṇḍit Agnihotrī. The latter members were expected to follow the strict moral code of the Dev Samāj, to reject all "false" religious symbols and to donate one-tenth of their income to the Samāj. A third section of members included those who had taken a strict religious vow dedicating themselves to the pursuit of Dev Dharam.

The strict moral code of the Dev Dharam appealed to educated Punjabis, who came to make up the membership of the Samāj. Dev Samājīs were almost all educated, literate men and even a large percentage of their women were literate. Their position in society gave the movement far greater influence than sheer numbers would allow. The Samāj was always an elite organization even at its peak during the 1920's. Following the death of Paṇḍit Agnihotrī the movement declined, but did not disappear. Partition saw the loss of its properties in Lahore and as a result the centre of the movement shifted to the Mogā-Fīrozpur area where it still continues to adhere to the *Vigyān Mūlak Dharam,* the Science-Grounded Religion of Paṇḍit Shiv Nārāyaṇ Agnihotrī.

BIBLIOGRAPHY

1. Kanal, P.V., *Bhagwan Dev Atma*. Lahore, 1942
2. Farquhar, J.N., *Modern Religious Movements in India*. Delhi, 1977
3. Jones, Kenneth W., *Arya Dharm*. Delhi, 1976
4. Mittal, K.K., *Perspectives of the Philosophy of Devatma*. Delhi, 1983

K.W.J.

ḌHAḌḌE, village 10 km south of Rāmpurā Phūl (30° - 16'N, 75° - 14'E) in Baṭhiṇḍā district of the Punjab, claims a historical shrine, Gurdwārā Gurūsar Pātshāhī Nauvīṅ, commemorating the visit of Gurū Tegh Bahādur (1621-75), who halted here coming from Ḍikkh (*q.v.*). The Gurdwārā is half a kilometre away from the village to the south of it. Its present complex constructed in 1952 comprises a square *dīvān* hall, including the sanctum, and some ancillary buildings within a walled compound. The Gurdwārā is managed by a committee of the local *saṅgat.*

Gn.S.

ḌHĀḌĪ, one who sings *vārs* or ballads to the accompaniment of a musical instrument called *ḍhaḍ*, a drumlet held in the palm of one hand and played with the fingers of the other. A concomitant of *ḍhaḍ* is the *sāraṅgī*, a stringed instrument. *Ḍhāḍīs*, patronized by chiefs and princes, eulogized the deeds of valour of the members of the families they served or of popular folk heroes. In the *Dasam Granth* (Charitra 405), their origin is traced back to the mythological combat between Mahākāl and Suāsvīrya, the first ancestor of the *ḍhāḍīs* being born of the sweat of the former. Although the institution of *ḍhāḍī* dates back to time immorial and Gurū Nānak (1469-1539) has recorded himself in the Gurū Granth Sāhib as a *ḍhāḍī* singing praises of the Supreme Lord, yet history mentions Bakhshū (d. 1535) who was patronized first by Rājā Mān Siṅgh Tomar (1486-1516) of Gwālīor and after his death by the kings of Kāliñjar and Gujrāt, as the first *ḍhāḍī*. He is also credited with the invention of a new *rāga* which he named Bahādur Toṛī after the name of Sultān Bahādur of Gujrāt, who was his patron during the last years of his life. In the Sikh tradition, *ḍhāḍīs* have flourished since the days of Gurū Hargobind (1595-1644) who engaged some leading exponents of the art to recite heroic balladry at Sikh assemblies. The two names recorded in old chronicles are those of Abdullah and Natthā, of the village of Sursiṅgh, in present-day Amritsar district. Among the leading *ḍhāḍīs* of the time of Gurū Gobind Siṅgh are mentioned Mīr Chhabīlā Mushkī and Natth Mall. *Ḍhāḍīs* have continued to be popular and at larger Sikh *dīvāns*, especially honouring the memory of heroes and martyrs, they are listened to avidly as they render in ringing folk tunes their deeds of gallantry and sacrifice. Natth Mall, who also composed a *vār* entitled *Amar Nāmā*, originally in Persian and later translated into Punjabi by Dr Gaṇḍā Siṅgh, is said to have been in the train of Gurū Gobind Siṅgh at the time of his journey to the South.

BIBLIOGRAPHY

Gaṇḍā Siṅgh, trans., Nath Mall's *Amar Nāmā*. Amritsar, 1953

P.S.G.

ḌHĀKĀ (23° - 43'N, 90° - 24'E), an old city now capital of Bangladesh, situated on the north bank of Būṛhī Gaṅgā river, has shrines sacred to Gurū Nānak and Gurū Tegh Bahādur. Three such *gurdwārās* commemorating the visits of the Gurūs to the city existed until the partition of the country in 1947, but only two of them are now extant.

GURDWĀRĀ NĀNAKSHĀHĪ, situated in Ramnā locality behind the Public Library adjoining the Ḍhākā University campus, marks the spot where Gurū Nānak is believed to have preached at the time of his visit in 1507-08. A Sikh *saṅgat* grew up in the locality, then known as Shujā'atpur or Sujātpur. Bhāī Gurdās as well as Bhāī Manī Siṅgh has recorded one Bhāī Mohan of Ḍhākā having visited the Punjab in the time of Gurū Hargobind to seek his blessing. Sikh missionary centres were established by Gurū Hargobind in the eastern parts under the guidance of Bhāī Almast, one of the principal apostles of Bābā Gurdittā, Bābā Srī Chand's successor as head of the Udāsī sect. Bhāī Natthā was Almast's representative in eastern Bengal and Assam. *Masands* were also appointed by the Gurūs to guide and manage the *saṅgats*. Bulākī Dās was the *masand* at the time of Gurū Tegh Bahādur's visit in the late 1660's. Bhāī Natthā, who lived up to the time of Gurū Tegh Bahādur, is said to have constructed the Gurdwārā building, with a square sanctum, which still exists. It was repaired by Mahant Prem Dās in 1833. The decorative art work on the interior wall was still intact when a Sikh commission visited it in January 1972 after Bangladesh emerged as a soverign State. A tank and a well, also said to have been dug by Bhāī Natthā, however, no longer exist. In fact, a major portion of the land once belonging to the Gurdwārā has been lost to appropriation by Ḍhākā University and by some individuals.

GURDWĀRĀ SAṄGAT ṬOLĀ, a double-storeyed

building situated along 14 Sorees Dās Lane in the Baṅglā Bāzār and lending its name to the entire locality, is dedicated to Gurū Tegh Bahādur who stayed here in the house of a Sikh, Bhāī Bulākī Dās, in 1667-68. As says Bhāī Santokh Siṅgh, *Srī Gur Pratāp Sūraj Granth,* Bulākī Dās's old mother, who had long waited for a sight of the Gurū, felt very pleased to have her wish fulfilled as he came and accepted from her hands garments of homespun cotton she had stitched for him. The house in which Gurū Tegh Bahādur had put up was converted into a *dharamsālā* or *gurdwārā*. It was known to possess one of the oldest handwritten copies of the Gurū Granth Sāhib and a few *hukamnāmās* of Gurū Gobind Siṅgh. The Sikh commission that visited Ḍhākā in January 1972 attested to a copy of the Gurū Granth Sāhib autographed by Gurū Gobind Siṅgh, a portrait believed to be that of Gurū Tegh Bahādur and two *hukamnāmās* being still there.

GURŪ NĀNAK'S WELL (SIKHER MANDIR) or Sikhs' Temple in what was called Rayor Bāzār to the north of old Ḍhākā city, was another shrine commemorating the visit of Gurū Nānak.The well and the two-roomed *gurdwārā* with a vaulted roof was frequented by devotees of all faiths in the belief that the water of this well cured many diseases. But in 1960-61 the Pakistan government took over the entire area, levelled it up and sold it as habitation sites to develop what is now known as Dhān Maṇḍī Colony.

Another old shrine was the Suthrāshāhī Saṅgat in the Urdu Bāzār which for several decades before 1947 had been administered by the *mahants* of Gurdwārā Nānakshāhī. The site is untraceable now.

BIBLIOGRAPHY

1. Tārā Siṅgh, *Srī Gur Tīrath Saṅgrahi.* Amritsar, n.d.
2. Ṭhākar Siṅgh, Giānī, *Srī Gurduāre Darshan.* Amritsar, 1923

Bh.S.

ḌHAKAULĪ, a village in Paṭiālā district, 14 km east of Chaṇḍigaṛh (30° - 44'N, 76° - 46'E), is famous for Gurdwārā Bāolī Sāhib, dedicated to Gurū Gobind Siṅgh. According to local tradition, the Gurū, on his way back from Pāoṇṭā to Anandpur in November 1688 decided to encamp on this site. He was told by the villagers that the nearest source of water was the stream Sukhnā which was 2 km away. At this the Gurū pierced the ground with his spear and caused water to trickle forth and form a pool. A shrine was established later on the bank of this pool and the original spring was converted into a well. In 1979-80, the Gurdwārā was handed over by the Shiromaṇī Gurdwārā Parbandhak Committee to the followers of Sant Bābā Jīvan Siṅgh for reconstruction. Special *dīvāns* are held on *amāvasyā*, the last day of the dark half of every month, when pilgrims throng in large numbers.

BIBLIOGRAPHY

1. Tārā Siṅgh, *Srī Gur Tīrath Saṅgrahi.* Amritsar, n.d.
2. Ṭhākar Siṅgh, Giānī, *Srī Gurduāre Darshan.* Amritsar, 1923

M.G.S.

DHALEO, locally called Dhalevāṅ, village 6 km southeast of Bhīkhī (30° - 3'N, 75° - 33'E) in Baṭhiṇḍā district of the Punjab, is sacred to Gurū Tegh Bahādur who arrived here travelling from Bhīkhī during his sojourn in the Mālvā region. It is said that as Gurū Tegh Bahādur was riding towards Gaṇḍhūāṅ to see an old Sikh, Bhāī Mughlū, lying on his death-bed, he noticed a *jogī* in meditation on the bank of the pond at Dhaleo. The Gurū alighted here on his way back from Gaṇḍhūāṅ and held a discourse with the *jogī*, whose name was Tulsī Dās. The Gurū recited the following *śabda* to him:

> Why dost thou go to a forest in search of Him ?
> All-pervading yet ever detached,

He resideth inside thee.
As fragrance is in the flower, and reflection in the mirror,
So the Lord liveth everywhere;
Search for Him in thy heart, Brother.
Knowest the same Light within and without,
This is the knowledge imparted by the Gurū.
Without knowing the Self, says Nānak,
The crust of illusion is not erased (GG, 684).

Tulsī Dās, thus instructed and liberated, dedicated himself to preaching the Gurū's message. A memorial platform was raised later on the spot where the discourse had taken place. A proper shrine, called Gurdwārā Mañjī Sāhib Pātshāhī IX, was constructed in 1916 near the village pond on the northern outskirts of the village. The present building on a low mound consists of a domed sanctum with a rectangular hall, in front. The older building is now used as lodgings for the *granthī*, Scripture-reader or Gurdwārā custodian. Recently, traces of brick-lined steps leading down to the water level have been found in a corner of the pond, signifying the existence of an old *sarovar* which the village committee managing the Gurdwārā now proposes to renovate.

M.G.S.

DHAMOṬ (30° - 42'N, 76° - 2'E), village in Ludhiāṇā district, has a historical shrine sacred to Gurū Hargobind. The simple monument which commemorated the Gurū's visit, was replaced in 1917 by a large domed hall to which an imposing double-storeyed gateway was added in 1937. The construction of a still larger *dīvān* hall to replace the older one was inaugurated on 6 August 1977. The Gurdwārā is managed by the Shiromaṇī Gurdwārā Parbandhak Committee through a local committee.

M.G.S.

DHAMTĀN, a large village in Jīnd district of Haryāṇā, is sacred to Gurū Tegh Bahādur. He visited it first in 1665 in the course of his travels through Mālvā and Bāṅgar territories. Chaudharī Daggo, who was a cattle lifter and lived on plunder, came with pitchers full of milk, but the Gurū declined the offering saying that he would not take what was not honestly earned. Daggo asked forgiveness for his past misdeeds and promised to abide by the Gurū's teaching. Gurū Tegh Bahādur gave him funds to construct a well and a *dharamsālā* for the travellers. While at Dhamtān, Gurū Tegh Bahādur was pleased with the devoted service of his loyal Sikh, Bhāī Mīhāṅ. He bestowed on him a kettle, a drum and a flag, and appointed him to look after the *saṅgat* or community in that area. According to some chroniclers, Gurū Tegh Bahādur was first arrested near Dhamtān in 1665 and taken to Delhi where, however, he was released at the intervention of Kaṅvar Rām Siṅgh, son of Mirzā Rājā Jai Siṅgh, of Āmber (Jaipur), and allowed to continue his journey towards the east.

Dhamtān became the most important centre of Sikh faith in the Bāṅgar region. Later, when this area became part of Paṭiālā state, a large endowment was made for the shrine commemorating the visits of Gurū Tegh Bahādur. The present complex was constructed by Mahārājā Karam Siṅgh of Paṭiālā (1798-1845). The building is in the form of a large *havelī*. A high arched gateway with massive wooden doors leads to the outer compound from which another heavy gate opens into an inner courtyard. The sanctum representing the actual spot where Gurū Tegh Bahādur had put up is on the left. Constructed in the inner courtyard in the traditional style, the Mañjī Sāhib is a domed square room on a high plinth, the interior walls being decorated with floral designs in colour. The Gurū Granth Sāhib is seated on a high platform in the centre. The *havelī* is flanked by the village pond a part of which has been enclosed and converted into a bathing tank. The shrine is managed by the Shiromaṇī Gurdwārā Parbandhak Committee. Two important festivals celebrated are Holā and Dussehrā which are attended by a large number of devotees from the neighbouring villages and towns. Dhamtān itself has very few Sikh families.

BIBLIOGRAPHY

1. *Mālvā Desh Raṭan dī Sākhī Pothī*. Amritsar, 1968
2. Tārā Siṅgh, *Srī Gur Tīrath Saṅgrahi*. Amritsar, n.d.
3. Ṭhākar Siṅgh, Giānī, *Srī Gurduāre Darshan*. Amritsar, 1923

M.G.S.

DHANĀSARĪ. *See* SIKH DEVOTIONAL MUSIC

ḌHAṆḌ, village 15 km southwest of Amritsar (31° - 38'N, 74° - 52'E) along the Chhehartā-Jhabāl road, is sacred to Gurū Hargobind (1595-1644), who once came here to fulfil the wish of an old Sikh, Bhāī Laṅgāhā. Gurdwārā Pātshāhī Chhevīṅ commemorating the visit stands on the southern outskirts of the village. Its present building was constructed by Sant Gurmukh Siṅgh Sevāvāle in 1929. The Gurū Granth Sāhib is seated on a canopied seat of white marble in the double-storeyed sanctum in the middle of the *dīvān* hall. Two Nishān Sāhibs, flags, stand at the entrance of the hall, one on each side. The Gurdwārā is managed by the local *saṅgat*. Special *dīvāns* take place on no-moon days and an annual fair is held on *amāvasyā*, the last day of the dark half of the lunar month of Bhādoṅ (August-September).

Gn.S.

DHANNĀ, BHAGAT (b. 1415?), one of the medieval saints whose *bāṇī* has been incorporated in the Gurū Granth Sāhib, describes himself in a hymn, in Rāga Āsā, as an ignorant Jaṭṭ and explains how he was attracted to the worship of God by the examples of Nāmdev (a calico-printer), Kabīr (a weaver), Ravidās (a cobbler) and Saiṇ (a barber). Nābhādās, *Bhaktamāl,* includes Dhannā among the twelve disciples of Rāmānand (1299-1410), though it has been questioned if all the twelve did indeed live at the same time. Max Arthur Macauliffe fixes AD 1415 as the year of Dhannā's birth, but his name nowhere appears in the writings of Kabīr (*fl.* 15th century) or Ravidās (*fl.* 15th century). The earliest mention of him is in Mīrā Bāī (1498-1546), who in one of her songs proclaims how Dhannā grew corn without sowing seed.

Dhannā was born in the village of Dhūān, in Ṭoṅk district of Rājasthān. His father was a simple, godfearing farmer, who frequently entertained *sādhūs* in his house. Dhannā, as a child, was deeply impressed by these holy visitors and his mind turned to the pursuit of spiritual grace. Like his Brāhmaṇ neighbour, he started worshipping *ṭhākurs* or idols. He was later converted to *nirguṇa bhakti,* i.e. worship of the Formless One without attributes, as is evident from his hymns in the Gurū Granth Sāhib. "Loving devotion," says Dhannā in his *śabda* in Rāga Āsā, "is now fixed in my heart and thereby have I found solace and fulfilment. In whose heart is light divine manifested he alone recognizeth the Immaculate One." That the devotee does not deny himself the needs of the body is attested by another hymn in which Dhannā supplicates the Lord for "foodgrains produced by tilling the land seven times over," "a cow in milk as well as a buffalo," "a dutiful wife to look after the household." Totally, there are three hymns by Dhannā in the Gurū Granth Sāhib.

BIBLIOGRAPHY

1. Sāhib Siṅgh, *Bhagat-Bāṇī Saṭīk*, vol. I. Amritsar, 1979
2. *Gurū Granth Ratnāvalī*. Patiala, n.d.

Hr.B.

DHANNĀ SIṄGH (1888-1923), a Babar revolutionary, was born at the village of Bahibalpur, in Hoshiārpur district. His father, Indar Siṅgh, could barely afford to send him to the village primary school where Dhannā Siṅgh learnt to read and write in Punjabi and Urdu. Early in his youth he was converted to radical politics by Karam Siṅgh, of Daulatpur, leader of the Chakravartī Jathā, and helped organize the Jathā's major *dīvāns* at Māhalpur (March 1921) and at Kukkaṛ Muzārā (October 1921). The Chakravartī Jathās of Kishan Siṅgh Gaṛgajj and Karam Siṅgh merging together made up plans at a meeting at Jassovāl on 25 December 1922 to maim, plunder or murder informers and helpers of the British government. Dhannā Siṅgh was assigned to "liquidating" Arjan Siṅgh, a *paṭvārī*, who had caused the arrest of Master Motā Siṅgh in June 1922. He, along with Būṭā Siṅgh and Sādhā Siṅgh, of Paṇḍorī Nijjhrāṅ, made attempts on the life of Arjan Siṅgh. He was also involved in the murders of Būṭā, *lambardār* of Naṅgal Shāmāṅ, Hazārā Siṅgh of Bahibalpur and Lābh Siṅgh, a *mistrī* of Gaṛhshaṅkar, who had had Kishan Siṅgh Gaṛgajj arrested in February 1923. Dhannā Siṅgh himself fell victim to a ruse. Javālā Siṅgh, described as a "black sheep" of the Babar Akālīs, acting in collusion with a police sub-inspector, Gulzārā Siṅgh, lured Dhannā Siṅgh to Mannanhāṇā village, in Hoshiārpur, where Mr Horton, the British superintendent of police, and his party reached on the midnight of 25-26 October 1923. Dhannā Siṅgh was overpowered but, displaying remarkable presence of mind, he had his hand released with a sudden jerk and crashed into one of the officers holding him, simultaneously pulling out the safety pin of the bomb which he always carried hidden around his waist. Dhannā Siṅgh was torn to pieces by the explosion, but so were his captors. Two head constables and three constables died on the spot, sub-inspector Gulzārā Siṅgh and another constable died at Māhalpur on their way to hospital, and Mr Horton at Hoshiārpur.

BIBLIOGRAPHY

1. Babbar, Sundar Singh, *Itihās Babbar Akālī Lahir.* Amritsar, 1970
2. Nijjhar, Milkhā Siṅgh, *Babbar Akālī Lahir dā Itihās.* Delhi, 1986
3. Nijjar, B.S., *History of the Babbar Akalis.* Jalandhar, 1987
4. Mohan, Kamlesh, *Militant Nationalism in the Punjab 1919-1935.* Delhi, 1985

K.M.

DHANNĀ SIṄGH, BHĀĪ (d. 1935), an indefatigable Sikh pilgrim, was born about 1893, the son of Sundar Siṅgh, a Chahal Jaṭṭ of the village G͟hanaurī in Saṅgrūr district of the Punjab. His original name was Lāl Siṅgh. His father died when he was barely ten years old, and he and his younger brother were brought up in the Rajendra-Devā Yatīmk͟hānā, an orphange in the princely city of Paṭiālā. As he grew up, he trained as a driver and was employed in the state garage of Mahārājā Bhūpinder Siṅgh (1891-1938). Religious instruction had formed part of Lāl Siṅgh's education at the orphanage; the influence now of a senior colleague, Jīvā Siṅgh, a pious Sikh and a driver in the same garage, proved decisive. Lāl Siṅgh proceeded on a pilgrimage to Srī Abichalnagar Hazūr Sāhib at Nāndeḍ, sacred to Gurū Gobind Siṅgh. There he received the rites of K͟hālsā initiation, and was renamed Dhannā Siṅgh. During his stay at Srī Hazūr Sāhib, he was deeply impressed by the piety of Sant Nidhān Siṅgh (1882-1947). Dhannā Siṅgh obtained his release from state service and set out on a pilgrimage of Sikh shrines on a bicycle. He visited historical *gurdwārās* in Uttar Pradesh, Bihār, Bengal and Assam, returning to Paṭiālā after three years. Some of the information about the *gurdwārās* he had visited was published in the Sikh newspapers. Dhannā Siṅgh, thereafter, purchased a camera, learnt photography, and resumed his travels with a view to visiting Sikh shrines in other parts of India and taking photographs and preparing notes. The project as well as his life was, however, cut short by an accident. During his travels in the North-West Frontier Province in 1935, he stayed one night in a village, Hasokhel, near Mīr 'Alī, in Bannū district. It was a common practice for the people in that disturbed area to keep their weapons loaded at night. Next morning, on 2 March 1923, as the host was unloading his gun, it went off, killing Dhannā Siṅgh on the spot.

Dhannā Siṅgh's travel notes are said to be intact in the custody of one Sevā Siṅgh, son of the late Mistrī Gurbakhsh Siṅgh, of Paṭiālā.

M.G.S.

DHANNĀ SIṄGH MALVAĪ (1775-1843), soldier and *jāgīrdār* under Raṇjīt Siṅgh, belonged to the village of Mauṛ in Nābhā territory. Mall Siṅgh, Dhannā Siṅgh's father, who was the first in the family to be initiated a Sikh, left his village about 1760 and entered the service of Chaṛhat Siṅgh Sukkarchakkīā as a *sowār*. He was killed in a campaign in the northwest. His son, Dhannā Siṅgh, left Mauṛ in 1793 and took up service with Sāhib Siṅgh Bhaṅgī of Gujrāt. About the year 1800, he enlisted himself in the force of Fateh Siṅgh Kāliāṅvālā as a trooper, and soon rose in his favour, obtaining an independent command. He fought in the Kāliāṅvālā contingent in Piṇḍī Bhaṭṭīāṅ and Kasūr campaigns. On the death in 1807 of Fateh Siṅgh Kāliāṅvālā at Naraiṇgaṛh in Ambālā district, Dhannā Siṅgh entered the service of Mahārājā Raṇjīt Siṅgh. In 1810, he fought against Fateh Khān of Sāhīvāl, receiving a wound in the face. He was one of the agents sent by Raṇjīt Siṅgh to Wazīr Fateh Khān of Kābul to arrange an interview between the two which took place in December 1812 at Jehlum. In July 1813, he fought in the battle of Aṭṭock, when Fateh Khān Bārakzaī was defeated by Dīwān Mohkam Chand. He accompanied the detachment of Rām Diāl and Dal Siṅgh Nahernā in the first expedition against Kashmīr. He distinguished himself in the siege of Multān in 1818, the jewelled sword and shield of the defending Nawāb, Muzaffar Khān, falling into his hands. In 1819, he took part in the final Kashmīr expedition and in 1821 in the siege of Mankerā. He was present at the capture of Jahāṅgīrā Fort and at the battle of Ṭerī in 1823, and remained on duty for some time in the Peshāwar district under the command of Buddh Siṅgh Sandhāṅvālīā and Prince Kharak Siṅgh. In 1837, he took part in the battle of Jamrūd.

Dhannā Siṅgh enjoyed great esteem in the Mahārājā's court. There were few *sardārs* whose influence was greater or whose advice was better regarded. He was sent on some political embassies and was a member of the mission which called on Lord William Bentinck at Shimlā in April 1832. He was granted several *jāgīrs* by the Mahārājā who also secured him at his request his ancestral village, Mauṛ, in 1819. Dhannā Siṅgh died in May 1843. His sons, Bachittar Siṅgh (d. 1840) and Hukam Siṅgh (d. 1846), held prominent positions in the Lahore Darbār.

BIBLIOGRAPHY

1. Sūrī, Sohan Lāl, *'Umdāt-ut-Twārīkh*. Lahore, 1885-89
2. Griffin, Lepel and C.F. Massy, *Chiefs and Families of Note in the Punjab*. Lahore, 1909
3. Ganda Singh, *The Punjab in 1839-40* . Patiala, 1952
4. Khushwant Singh, *The Fall of the Kingdom of the Punjab*. Bombay, 1962
5. Chopra, G.L., *The Panjab as a Sovereign State*. Hoshiarpur, 1960

S.S.B.

DHANPAT RĀI, DĪWĀN (d. 1831), son of Rām Kumār, served Mahārājā Raṇjīt Siṅgh in various capacities. His grandfather Guṭū Mall, who belonged to Shāhpur district, was employed as *dīwān* to the Bhaṅgī *sardārs*, Gujjar Siṅgh and Sāhib Siṅgh, regulating the civil affairs of a large tract of land under those chiefs. Dhanpat Rāi's father, Rām Kumar, succeeded Guṭū Mall and held the office until 1810 when Mahārājā Raṇjīt Siṅgh occupied Sāhib Siṅgh's estates. Rām Kumār obtained places for Dhanpat Rāi and his other two sons in the Sikh government. Dhanpat Rāi was granted *jāgīrs* at Majīṭhā and Jagdeo which in the year 1814 were exchanged for the territory of Sodhrā belonging previously to Sāhib Siṅgh. Dhanpat Rāi was handed over the charge of the Mājhā area. He was afterwards appointed commander of Prince Khaṛak Siṅgh's force which post he held for more than a year. He rendered good service with his contingent at Multān, Mankerā, and Kashmīr and his *jāgīrs* were enhanced after each of these campaigns.

Dhanpat Rāi died in 1831.

BIBLIOGRAPHY

1. Sūrī, Sohan Lāl, *'Umdāt-ut-Twārīkh*. Lahore 1885-89
2. Griffin, Lepel and C.F. Massy, *Chiefs and Families of Note in the Punjab*. Lahore, 1909

S.S.B.

DHARAM ARTH BOARD, a body representing different sections of the Sikh community constituted in May 1949 by Mahārājā Yādavinder Siṅgh, Rājpramukh of the Paṭiālā and East Punjab States Union (PEPSU), to manage the major Sikh shrines within the new state which had come into being in consequence of the amalgamation of the eight princely territories in the Punjab. Before merger some of these states had their own boards or committees for the purpose. Paṭiālā state had, for instance, its Interim Gurdwārā Board formed on 8 November 1946; Kapūrthalā its General Gurdwārā Committee; and Jīnd its Gurdwārā Committee. The *gurdwārās* in the Punjab were controlled by the Shiromaṇī Gurdwārā Parbandhak Committee under the Gurdwaras Act of 1925, the jurisdiction of which statute did not extend to the princely states. After the formation of PEPSU, a notification (No. 2, dated 20 May 1949) was issued by Sardār Sāhib Deoḍhī Mu'allā, constituting the Dharam Arth Board for the state. The Board comprised twenty-five members to which number ten more were added through a later notification. At the first meeting of the 25-member committee convened in the Paṭiālā Secretariat on 27 June 1949, Jathedār Balwant Siṅgh Chanārthal, an Akālī leader, was unanimously elected president and a sub-committee was nominated to draft rules and regulations which were finally approved by the Board at its meeting on 26 August 1949. The Board had about two hundred *gurdwārās* under its control. Prominent among the twenty-five under its direct management were Gurdwārā Srī Dūkh Nivāran Sāhib at Paṭiālā, the shrines at Fatehgaṛh Sāhib, Gurdwārā Srī Ber Sāhib at Sultānpur Lodhī, Gurdwārā Srī Gurū Tegh Bahādur Sāhib at Jīnd, Gurdwārā Srī Gurū Tegh Bahādur Sāhib at Dhamtān and the *state gurdwārā* at Kapūrthalā. For *gurdwārās* not directly managed by the Board there were local committees under its supervision. Owing to acute factionalism that arose within its ranks the Dharam Arth Board was superseded under a government notification, dated 4 May 1954, by a 13-member Interim Gurdwārā Board, with Balwant Siṅgh Chanārthal as its president.

As PEPSU became part of the Punjab in 1956, the new state government by a notification dated 10 January 1958, allowed the Interim Gurdwārā Board to continue functioning until it was merged with the Shiromaṇī Gurdwārā Parbandhak Committee on 8 January 1959.

M.S.G.

DHARAM CHAND, son of Lakhmī Chand and grandson of Gurū Nānak. According to *Gurbilās Pātshāhī Chhevīṅ*, he received Gurū Hargobind when the latter, along with Bhāī

Gurdās and Bhāī Bhānā, went to Kartārpur which Gurū Nānak had made his dwelling place during the last years of his life. Dharam Chand received the Gurū and his entourage along with other persons of the Bedī clan, with honour. Gurū Hargobind made him an offering of a horse and five hundred gold mohars.

D.S.

DHARAM DĀS, BHĀĪ, one of the prominent Sikhs of the time of Gurū Rām Dās mentioned by Bhāī Gurdās in his *Vārāṅ*, XI. 17, was a Khoṭrā devotee from what is now Sāhīvāl district of Pakistan. He, accompanied by Bhāī Ḍūgar Dās Ṭakiār, Bhāī Dīpā, Bhāī Jeṭhā, Bhāī Tīrathā, Bhāī Saisārū and Bhāī Būlā, once waited upon Gurū Rām Dās to seek instruction. The Gurū, according to Bhāī Manī Siṅgh, *Sikhāṅ dī Bhagat Mālā*, spoke to them as follows: "Abandon pride; help the Sikh who comes to you; walk morning and evening to where the *saṅgat* congregates; raise a *dharamsālā* in your village; recite *gurbāṇī* and be truthful in word and deed." Bhāī Dharam Dās and his companions, says the chronicler, followed the Gurū's precept and attained spiritual enlightenment.

BIBLIOGRAPHY

Manī Siṅgh, Bhāī, *Sikhāṅ dī Bhagat Mālā*. Amritsar, 1955

Gr.S.

DHARAM DHUJĀ, lit. standard or banner of *dharma* or faith, is the popular name of Akhāṛā Nirmal Panth Gurū Gobind Siṅgh Jī, a seminary at Paṭiālā in the Punjab belonging to the Nirmalā sect of the Sikhs. Now affiliated to the Nirmal Pañchāitī Akhāṛā at Kankhal near Haridvār, Dharam Dhujā was the first permanent centre of the Nirmalās established in 1862 under the patronage of the rulers of Paṭiālā, Nābhā, Jīnd and Kalsīā.

See NIRMAL PAÑCHĀITĪ AKHĀṚĀ.

J.S.S.

DHARAMSĀLĀ or *dharamsāl* from Sanskrit *dharmaśālā*, lit. court of justice, tribunal, charitable asylum, religious asylum, stands in Punjabi for a place of worship or the village hospice. *Dharamsālā* as a Sikh institution is the precursor of *gurdwārā* (*q.v.*). According to *janam sākhīs*, accounts of the life of Gurū Nānak (1469-1539), the Gurū, wherever he went, enjoined his followers to build or set apart a place where they should meet regularly to sing praises of the Lord and to discuss matters of common concern. These places came to be called *dharamsālās* and the congregations assembling therein became *saṅgats*. *Dharamsālās* grew up in far-flung places in the wake of Gurū Nānak's extensive travels. In the time of the successive Gurūs, the main *dharamsālā* was the one which was the seat of the reigning Gurū. Gurū Arjan, Nānak V, said in one of his hymns preserved in the Gurū Granth Sāhib, "I have set up a true *dharamsāl*, I seek out the Gurū's Sikhs and bring them here; I wash their feet, wave the fan over them, and I bow at their feet ...." (GG, 73). The washing of feet and waving of fan underline the importance of *dharamsālā* as a place for practising *sevā* (service), a highly prized virtue in Sikhism. Similarly, bowing at the feet of the Sikhs emphasizes the virtue of humility in *saṅgat*. In another hymn, this one in honour of Bābā Mohan, the elder son of Gurū Amar Dās, held in high regard for his piety, Gurū Arjan extols Bābā Mohan's house as a *dharamsālā* for the saints who always gather there and sing praises of the Compassionate Lord (GG, 248). Besides providing opportunities for devotional worship and humble service, *dharamsālās* functioned as religious asylums providing food and shelter to travellers and the needy. Gurū Nānak had called this very earth as *dharamsāl*, the place for practising *dharma* or religion, which in the Gurū's vision was not only individual piety but also an active way of life.

After the installation of the Holy Book,

Gurū Granth Sāhib, in *dharamsālās* from the seventeenth century onward, they came to be called *gurduārās* or *gurdwārās*, portals of the Gurū, though the word *dharamsālā* is still current in popular speech.

BIBLIOGRAPHY

1. Cole, W. Owen and Piara Singh Sambhi, *The Sikhs: Their Religious Beliefs and Practices.* Delhi, 1978.
2. Harbans Singh, *Berkley Lectures on Sikhism.* Delhi, 1963
3. Kohli, Surindar Singh, *Sikh Ethics.* Delhi, 1974

M.G.S.

DHARAM SIṄGH, a cousin of the celebrated Tārā Siṅgh G͟haibā of the Ḍallevālīā Misl, participated in the campaigns of the K͟hālsā, fighting against Mug͟hals and Afg͟hāns in the second half of the eighteenth century. He figured in the conquest of Sirhind and partition of the territory by Sikhs in January 1764 when he occupied a cluster of villages and founded amid them his own Dharamsiṅghvālā.

BIBLIOGRAPHY

1. Seetal, Sohan Singh, *The Sikh Misls and the Punjab.* Ludhiana, n.d.
2. Griffin, Lepel and C.F. Massey, *Chiefs and Families of Note in the Punjab.* Lahore, 1909

S.S.B.

DHARAM SIṄGH, a Jaṭṭ Sikh of the village of Chiṭṭī, 15 km southwest of Jalandhar in the Punjab, was one of the associates of Bhāī Mahārāj Siṅgh (d. 1856), leader of anti-British revolt in the Punjab during 1848-49. Dharam Siṅgh assisted Bhāī Mahārāj Siṅgh by mobilizing help for him in the Doābā region during the latter half of 1849. He especially introduced two artillerymen of Kapūrthalā to Bhāī Mahārāj Siṅgh, in Hoshiārpur area. He was arrested along with Mahārāj Siṅgh on the night of 28-29 December 1849, but managed to escape. However, he was rearrested at Wazīrābād in Gujrāṅwālā district and was held in custody in Lahore jail.

BIBLIOGRAPHY

Ahluwalia, M.L., *Bhai Maharaj Singh.* Patiala, 1972

M.L.A.

DHARAM SIṄGH, BHĀĪ (1666-1708), one of the Pañj Piāre or the Five Beloved, the forerunners of K͟hālsā, came of farming stock. He was the son of Bhāī Sant Rām and Māī Sābho, of Hastināpur, an ancient town on the right bank of the Ganges, 35 km northeast of Meerut (29°N, 77° - 45'E). Dharam Dās, as he was originally named, was born around 1666. As a young man, he fell into the company of a Sikh who introduced him to the teachings of the Gurūs. He left home at the age of thirty in quest of further instruction. At the Sikh shrine of Nānak Piāū, dedicated to Gurū Nānak, he was advised to go to Gurū Gobind Siṅgh at Anandpur, where he arrived in 1698. A few months later came the historic Baisākhī congregation at which five Sikhs responding to five successive calls of Gurū Gobind Siṅgh offered one after the other to lay down their heads. Dharam Dās was one of those five. The Gurū blessed them and called them Pañj Piāre, the five beloved of him. They were anointed as the first five members of the brotherhood of the K͟hālsā inaugurated on that day. Gurū Gobind Siṅgh then begged them to administer to him the vows of initiation. Dharam Dās, who, after initiation, became Dharam Siṅgh, took part in the battles of Anandpur. He was in Gurū Gobind Siṅgh's train when Anandpur and thereafter Chamkaur were evacuated. He accompanied Bhāī Dayā Siṅgh to the South to deliver Gurū Gobind Siṅgh's letter, the *Zafarnāmah,* to Emperor Auraṅgzīb.

During the war of succession following the death of Auraṅgzīb on 20 February 1707, Gurū Gobind Siṅgh took the part of the rightful claimant to the imperial throne,

Prince Mua'zzam, and sent for his help Bhāī Dharam Siṅgh who with his small band of Sikhs fought in the battle of Jājaū (8 June 1707). He accompanied Gurū Gobind Siṅgh to Nāndeḍ and was with him at the time of his death on 7 October 1708. Dharam Siṅgh died at Nāndeḍ. A *gurdwārā* there preserves the memory jointly of Bhāī Dharam Siṅgh and Bhāī Dayā Siṅgh.

BIBLIOGRAPHY

1. Kuir Siṅgh, *Gurbilās Pātshāhī 10*. Patiala, 1968
2. Chhibbar, Kesar Siṅgh, *Bansāvalīnāmā Dasāṅ Pātshāhīāṅ Kā*. Chandigarh, 1972
3. Santokh Siṅgh, Bhāī, *Srī Gur Pratāp Sūraj Granth*. Amritsar 1926-37
4. Macauliffe, Max Arthur, *The Sikh Religion*. Oxford, 1909
5. Harbans Singh, *Guru Gobind Singh*. Chandigarh, 1966

S.S.A.

DHARAM SIṄGH, BHĀĪ (d. 1921) was the youngest of the four sons of Bhāī Sant Siṅgh and Māī Hukmī, of the village of Buṇḍālā, in Amritsar district. He was only four years old when the family migrated to Chakk No. 71 Buṇḍālā Bachan Siṅghvālā in the newly colonized district of Lyallpur. His education was limited to rudimentary knowledge of the Punjabi language which he could barely read in the Gurmukhī script. He was robustly built and enjoyed wrestling. He married and was the father of four, two sons and two daughters, at the advent of the Gurdwārā reform movement. Dharam Siṅgh and his elder brother, Ichchhar Siṅgh, offered themselves as volunteers for the liberation of Gurdwārā Janam Asthān at Nankāṇā Sāhib. Preparations for the marriage of their nephew were in hand when the call came. Both left at once and joined the Dhārovālī column which was massacred to a man by the hired assassins of Naraiṇ Dās, the Mahant, on 20 February 1921.

See NANKĀṆĀ SĀHIB MASSACRE

BIBLIOGRAPHY

Shamsher, Gurbakhsh Siṅgh, *Shahīdī Jīvan*. Nankana Sahib, 1938

G.S.G.

DHARAM SIṄGH, SARDĀR BAHĀDUR (1881-1933), Sikh philanthropist, was born at the village of Koprā, in Siālkoṭ district, now in Pakistan, on 18 January 1881. His father, Bhāī Natthā Rām, was a *sahajdhārī* Sikh who became Natthā Siṅgh after receiving the rites of *amrit*.

Dharam Siṅgh learned Gurmukhī characters at the village *dharamsālā* from Bāvā Narāyan Siṅgh. He had a religious bent of mind, and could read fluently the Gurū Granth Sāhib before he was 8 years of age. For his primary education, he joined the Mission School, Wazīrābād, later passing his matriculation from Khālsā High School, Gujrāṅwālā. In 1901, he qualified to be a sub-overseer from Thompson Engineering College, Roorkee, and got a job in Burma. In 1903, he was married to Sadā Kaur of Sodhrā. In 1905, he returned to the Punjab, and took over as a sub-overseer on the Upper Jehlum Canal. In the Punjab, he came under the influence of Sant Atar Siṅgh of Mastūāṇā. In 1912, he resigned his government post to become a contractor. He supplied red stone for New Delhi buildings, including the secretariat and the viceregal lodge. In 1928, he was given by the British Government the title of Sardār Sāhib, followed by Sardār Bahādur in 1930. True to his name, Dharam Siṅgh helped humanitarian causes and contributed to public charity. For promoting education among the Sikhs, he founded a trust called Gurū Nānak Vidyā Bhaṇḍār. The trust runs a school of Sikh studies at Gurdwārā Rikābgañj, New Delhi.

Sardār Dharam Siṅgh died in Vienna (Austria) on 19 June 1933.

BIBLIOGRAPHY

1. Dukhī, Munshā Siṅgh, *Jīvān Bhāī Sāhib Bhāī Mohan*

Siṅgh Jī Vaid. Tarn Taran, 1939
2. Vaid, Mohan Siṅgh, *Sajjan Vichhoṛā*. Tarn Taran, 1933

Jg.S.

DHĀRĀ SIṄGH (d. 1860) succeeded his father, Mehar Siṅgh, to the family estate situated in the Nakkā tract of land upon the latter's death in 1843. Dhārā Siṅgh joined Rājā Sher Siṅgh with his horsemen at Multān in 1848. He fought against the British in the battles of Rāmnagar (22 November 1848) and Gujrāt (21 February 1849). He died in 1860.

BIBLIOGRAPHY

Griffin, Lepel, and C.F. Massy, *Chiefs and Families of Note in the Punjab*. Lahore, 1909

S.S.B.

DHARMĀ, BHĀĪ, a devoted Sikh of the time of Gurū Arjan. He received instruction at the hands of the Gurū himself and learnt to repeat always the Name Vāhigurū. His name occurs in the roster of devotees recorded by Bhāī Gurdās, *Vārāṅ*, XI. 19.

See UDDĀ, BHĀĪ

BIBLIOGRAPHY

1. Manī Siṅgh, Bhāī, *Sikhāṅ dī Bhagat Mālā*. Amritsar, 1955
2. Santokh Siṅgh, Bhāī, *Srī Gur Pratāp Sūraj Granth*. Amritsar, 1926-37

T.S.

DHĀRO, BHĀĪ, a Sikh of Sultānpur Lodhī and a soldier by profession, went to Gurū Arjan in the *saṅgat* of his town. The Gurū gave them his blessing (*See* ĀKUL, BHĀĪ and BHIKHĀ, BHAṬṬ). According to Bhāī Manī Siṅgh, *Sikhāṅ dī Bhagat Mālā*, Gurū Arjan spoke to Bhāī Dhāro: "There are warriors who vanquish their foe, and there are those who reign victorious over their own minds. The triumphs of the former are sung by bards, but the glory of the latter is sung by saints."

BIBLIOGRAPHY

1. Manī Siṅgh, Bhāī, *Sikhāṅ dī Bhagat Mālā*. Amritsar, 1955
2. Santokh Siṅgh, Bhāī, *Srī Gur Pratāp Sūraj Granth*. Amritsar, 1926-37

T.S.

DHAULĀ, village 11 km southwest of Barnālā (30° - 23'N, 75° - 34'E) in Saṅgrūr district of the Punjab, has two historical shrines, both dedicated to Gurū Tegh Bahādur. According to tradition, Gurū Tegh Bahādur riding from Haḍiāyā to Dhaulā arrived at the boundary between the two villages when his horse suddenly stopped. No amount of coaxing or spurring could make him go forward and enter the fields of Dhaulā. The Gurū explained to the Sikhs in his train that the Dhālīvāls of Dhaulā were not yet ready to receive him. "They will come round in time," he remarked. He then turned west and arrived at the *ḍhāb*, or pond, of Sohīvāl where he made his ablutions.

GURDWĀRĀ AṚĪSAR, 2 km north of Dhaulā by a sandy cart track, marks the spot where the Gurū's horse had stubbornly stopped (*aṛī* in Punjabi means an act of stubbornness). The Gurdwārā comprises a 5-metre square sanctum and a suite of rooms for the *granthī*. It is affiliated to the Shiromaṇī Gurdwārā Parbandhak Committee and is administered by the manager of Gurdwārā Gurū Sar Pakkā at Haḍiāyā. Special *dīvāns* take place on the full-moon day every month.

GURDWĀRĀ SĀHIB PĀTSHĀHĪ NAUMĪ SOHĪVĀL, locally called Sohīāṇā Sāhib, stands on a low mound. It consists of a memorial platform on the first floor of a domed building. The Gurū Granth Sāhib is seated in a hall near by. The old *ḍhāb* has been lined and converted into a *sarovar*, holy tank. This Gurdwārā is also attached for administration to Gurdwārā Gurū Sar Pakkā at Haḍiāyā.

BIBLIOGRAPHY

Mālvā Desh Raṭan dī Sākhī Pothī. Amritsar, 1968

M.G.S.

DHAUṄKAL SIṄGH (d. 1844), a drill-nāik in the army of the East India Company who deserted the service of the British and joined the Sikh army about 1805. In 1807, Jamādar Khushāl Siṅgh, who had come to Lahore to seek his fortune and had eventually risen to the position of *ḍeohṛīdār* or chamberlain, was placed under Dhauṅkal Siṅgh. In 1828-29, when the Lahore army was reorganized, Dhauṅkal Siṅgh was given command of a regiment composed mainly of Pūrbīā deserters from the East India Company and a few Sikhs. Subsequently, he was promoted general who took an important part in the military administration of Mahārājā Ranjīt Siṅgh. As a regimental commander in the Sikh army, Dhauṅkal Siṅgh participated in various military campaigns — Kāṅgṛā (1809), Aṭṭock (1813), Multān (1818), Kashmīr (1819), and Ḍerā Ismā'īl Khān (1820). From 1830 to 1833, he was active in operations in the Peshāwar valley. Dhauṅkal Siṅgh's troops were stationed at Hazārā in 1844 when he was ordered to move to Muzaffarābād to reduce the rebels who had risen in support of Ghulām Mohī ud-Dīn, the governor of Kashmīr. He secured some initial success against the rebels, but eventually fell in the fighting.

BIBLIOGRAPHY

1. Sūrī, Sohan Lāl, *'Umdāt-ut-Twārīkh*. Lahore, 1885-89
2. Griffin, Lepel, and C.F. Massy, *Chiefs and Families of Note in the Punjab*. Lahore, 1909
3. Chopra, B.R., *Kingdom of the Punjab*. Hoshiarpur, 1969

Gl.S.

ḌHERĀ SIṄGH, BHĀĪ (1890-1921), was born on 29 August 1890, the son of Bhāī Jaimal Siṅgh and Māī Jīvan Kaur, a peasant couple of Paṇḍorī Nijjarāṅ, in Jalandhar district. On the opening of the Lower Chenāb Canal Colony in West Punjab, the family settled in Chakk No. 91 Dhannūāṇā in Lyallpur district. Ḍherā Siṅgh, though illiterate, was an anointed Siṅgh. He never married and led a simple life of honest hard labour until his martyrdom as a member of the *jathā* that was massacred in the walled compound of Gurdwārā Janam Asthān at Nankāṇā Sāhib on the morning of 20 February 1921.

See NANKĀṆĀ SĀHIB MASSACRE

BIBLIOGRAPHY

Shamsher, Gurbakhsh Singh, *Shahīdī Jīvan*. Nankana Sahib, 1938

G.S.G.

ḌHESĪ, BHĀĪ, and Bhāī Jodh, both Brāhmaṇs converted to Sikhism, once came to Gurū Arjan and complained, "O True King ! other Brāhmaṇs treat us as outcastes, for they tell us that by taking a Khatrī as a *gurū*, by discarding Sanskrit, the language of the gods, and singing hymns of *gurbāṇī* composed in the common dialect, and by the non-observance of fasts and other rituals and prayers, we are no longer fit to sit and dine with them. They are especially sore because in preference to the traditional places of pilgrimage like the Gaṅgā and Kāshī, we come to Amritsar. Pray, tell us how should we answer them." "Caste," said Gurū Arjan, "has no meaning. He alone is a true Brāhmaṇ who meditates on Brahman. You should concentrate on *śabda*, the Divine Word. Thereby will you attain true understanding." Bhāī Ḍhesī and Bhāī Jodh fell at the Gurū's feet.

BIBLIOGRAPHY

1. Manī Siṅgh, Bhāī, *Sikhāṅ dī Bhagat Mālā*. Amritsar, 1955
2. Santokh Siṅgh, Bhāī, *Srī Gur Pratāp Sūraj Granth*.

Amritsar, 1926-37

T.S.

DHIĀN SIṄGH (d. 1705), a devoted Sikh of the time of Gurū Gobind Siṅgh. He was one of the warriors who took part in the battle against Said K͟hān. He fell a martyr in the battle of Chamkaur (7 December 1705).

M.G.S.

DHIĀN SIṄGH, resident of the village of Mājrī near Chamkaur in present-day Ropaṛ district of the Punjab, was a devoted Sikh of the time of Gurū Gobind Siṅgh (1666-1708). According to *Gur Ratan Māl (Sau Sākhī)*, Bishambhar Dās, a shopkeeper and a Sikh devotee of Ujjain in Central India, once sent his son, Har Gopāl, to the Punjab with an offering of six hundred rupees to be made over to Gurū Gobind Siṅgh at Anandpur. Har Gopāl made the offering and the Gurū gave him some *kaṛāhprasād* or consecrated food to be delivered to his father along with his message blessing him. Har Gopāl, on his way back, stayed with Dhiān Siṅgh and expressed to the latter his doubt about the Gurū's justice in giving a handful of food and a word of blessing in return for six hundred rupees. Dhiān Siṅgh told him that if he considered the blessing a poor return on his money, he could sell it to him (Dhiān Siṅgh) at a profit. Har Gopāl agreed and Dhiān Siṅgh bought the blessing for six hundred and five rupees. Har Gopāl resumed his homeward journey and investing his money on the way added to it a large profit. But when he reached home and narrated his experience and his deal, his father chided him for his folly. Bishambhar Dās with his son came to Dhiān Siṅgh and expressing his regrets over his son's error, begged for his intercession in obtaining the Gurū's pardon. Dhiān Siṅgh took them to Anandpur where the Gurū graciously pardoned Har Gopāl and instructed them in the virtue of *ardās* or prayer and in the Sikh code of ethics.

BIBLIOGRAPHY

Nayyar, Gurbachan Siṅgh, ed., *Gur Ratan Māl arthāt Sau Sākhī*. Patiala, 1985

P.S.P.

DHIĀN SIṄGH, RĀJĀ (1796-1843), the second son of Mīāṅ Kishorā Siṅgh Ḍogrā and the middle one of the three brothers from Jammū serving Mahārājā Ranjīt Siṅgh, was born on 22 August 1796. He was presented before Ranjīt Siṅgh at Rohtās in 1812 by his elder brother, Gulāb Siṅgh, and was given employment as a trooper on a monthly salary of sixty rupees. Dhiān Siṅgh by his impressive bearing, polished manner and adroitness, steadily rose in the Mahārājā's favour and, in 1818, replaced Jamādār Khushāl Siṅgh as *ḍeoṛhīdār* or chamberlain to the royal household. In this capacity, he had ready access to the Mahārājā and became a man of influence at the court. He was at times assigned to military duties as well. He took part in the battle of Nausherā in March 1823. As Ranjīt Siṅgh, following the death on 30 April 1837 of Harī Siṅgh Nalvā, hastened towards the northwest frontier, Dhiān Siṅgh marched with his force in advance.

Dhiān Siṅgh received from the Mahārājā endless favours. He was granted a large number of *jāgīrs* in the hilly country of Jammū and created Rājā in 1822. On 20 June 1827, he was given the title of Rājā-i-Rājgān Rājā Kalāṅ Bahādur. He became the principal minister of the Mahārājā and the most powerful person in the kingdom after him. The highest distinction came on 21 June 1839 when Mahārājā Ranjīt Siṅgh proclaimed in the presence of the entire court and the army stationed in Lahore that he had granted full powers to Prince Khaṛak Siṅgh, the heir apparent, over all his dominions and troops, and that the Prince had chosen Rājā Kalāṅ Bahādur to be his Wazīr, principal minister or counsellor. The Mahārājā also conferred upon Dhiān Siṅgh the title of Nāib-us-

Salatnat-i-'Azamat, Khairkhwāh-i-Samīmī-i-Daulat-i-Sirkār-i-Kubrā, Wazīr-i-'Āzam, Dastūr-i-Mu'azzam, Mukhtār-i-Mulk.

On the morning of the funeral of the Mahārājā, 28 June 1839, Dhiān Siṅgh expressed his intention to immolate himself on the late monarch's pyre and had to be dissuaded by the queens and courtiers. Mahārājā Khaṛak Siṅgh himself begged him to continue to steer the State. Dhiān Siṅgh agreed that he would remain in the service of Khaṛak Siṅgh for one year and proceed thereafter on a pilgrimage to sacred places. But he soon found himself at the centre of courtly intrigue. He set afloat the remour that Khaṛak Siṅgh and his favourite, Chet Siṅgh, were soliciting British protection and were going to compromise the sovereignty of the Punjab. He summoned Prince Nau Nihāl Siṅgh from Peshāwar, and won over the Sandhāṅvālīā *sardārs* to join him in a plot to kill Chet Siṅgh. The scheme was carried out and Chet Siṅgh was assassinated on 9 October 1839 by Dhiān Siṅgh in the presence of the Mahārājā who was himself placed under restraint, Prince Nau Nihāl Siṅgh running the affairs of the State on his behalf. Death, however, removed from the scene Nau Nihāl Siṅgh returning from his father's cremation on 5 November 1840. Dhiān Siṅgh now chose to place Prince Sher Siṅgh on the throne. He concealed the fact of Nau Nihāl Siṅgh's death for three days, till Sher Siṅgh had arrived at Lahore at his summons. But his plans were upset by his rivals, the Sandhāṅvālīās, who decided to support Khaṛak Siṅgh's widow, Chand Kaur, as a regent for Nau Nihāl Siṅgh's child yet to be born. On 2 December 1840, Chand Kaur was proclaimed Mahārāṇī. Sher Siṅgh went back to his estate in Baṭālā the following day, and Dhiān Siṅgh retired to Jammū a few days later. This was, however, only a tactical withdrawal by the astute Rājā Kalāṅ. Even while on his way to Jammū, he wrote to army commanders at different levels and to other government officials to render obedience and assistance to Prince Sher Siṅgh upon his return to Lahore. Sher Siṅgh arrived at Lahore on 13 January 1841 and the bulk of the royal army then in Lahore went over to him. Rājā Dhiān Siṅgh returned from Jammū on 17 January. Sher Siṅgh was proclaimed Mahārājā of the Punjab on 18 January with Dhiān Siṅgh as his Wazīr. On 15 September 1843 the Sandhāṅvālīā Sardārs, Ajīt Siṅgh and Lahiṇā Siṅgh, assassinated Mahārājā Sher Siṅgh and Kaṅvar Partāp Siṅgh, the heir apparent, on the outskirts of Lahore. As they were returning to the Fort with the heads of Sher Siṅgh and Partāp Siṅgh hung on spikes, they were met on the way by Dhiān Siṅgh who was lured into the Fort. As he advanced his claim to be Wazīr to the succeeding Mahārājā, Ajīt Siṅgh fired a shot and killed him on the spot.

BIBLIOGRAPHY

1. Sūrī, Sohan Lāl, *'Umdāt-ut-Twārīkh*. Lahore, 1885-89
2. Griffin, Lepel, *Ranjit Singh*. Delhi, 1957
3. Khushwant Singh, *Ranjit Singh: Maharajah of the Punjab, 1780-1839*. Bombay, 1962
4. Osborne, W.G., *The Court and Camp of Runjeet Sing*. London, 1840
5. Hasrat, Bikrama Jit, *Life and Times of Ranjit Singh*. Nabha, 1977
6. Charak, Sukhdev Singh, *Gulabnama of Diwan Kirpa Ram*. Delhi, 1977

K.J.S.

ḌHILLĪ MAṆḌAL, BHĀĪ, was a devoted Sikh of the time of Gurū Arjan. Once, as says Bhāī Manī Siṅgh, *Sikhāṅ dī Bhagat Mālā,* he reported to the Gurū that he had come across verses using the pseudonym Nānak, but which did not seem genuine at all. Gurū Arjan, continues Bhāī Manī Siṅgh, undertook thereupon the task of preparing an authorized volume sifting the genuine from the counterfeit. Thus emerged the Holy Granth which was installed in the Harimandar at Amritsar in 1604.

See GOPĪ MAHITĀ, BHĀĪ

BIBLIOGRAPHY

1. Manī Siṅgh, Bhāī, *Sikhāṅ dī Bhagat Mālā*. Amritsar, 1955
2. Santokh Siṅgh, Bhāī, *Srī Gur Pratāp Sūraj Granth*. Amritsar, 1926-37

T.S.

ḌHILVĀṄ, a small village 5 km east of Barkī (31° - 28'N, 74° - 30'E) in Lahore district, is sacred to Gurū Hargobind, Nānak VI. Gurdwārā Pātshāhī VI on the eastern outskirts of the village marked the site where the Gurū stayed under a *pīpal* tree during his visit to the village. The shrine had to be abandoned at the time of mass migration of Sikhs from the area at the time of the partition of the Punjab in 1947.

M.G.S.

ḌHILVĀṄ, village 25 km from Barnālā (30° - 23'N, 75° - 34'E), is sacred to Gurū Tegh Bahādur, who, according to local tradition, stayed here for several months in the course of one of his journeys across the Mālvā country. Large numbers of people in the area were converted to his teaching. Gurdwārā Pātshāhī Nauvīṅ, commemorating his visit, is on the southeastern outskirts of the village. The building comprises Tap Asthān, seat of meditation, marking the site where Gurū Tegh Bahādur used to sit in contemplation, a *dīvān* hall and the Gurū kā Laṅgar. The Tap Asthān, a square domed room on a raised plinth, contains only a platform, reverently covered with a fabric length. The Gurū Granth Sāhib is seated under a canopy in the middle of the hall. The Gurdwārā owns 55 acres of land and is managed by the Shiromaṇī Gurdwārā Parbandhak Committee. Besides the daily services and major Sikh anniversaries, solar eclipses are marked by special celebrations.

BIBLIOGRAPHY

1. *Mālvā Desh Raṭan dī Sākhī Pothī*. Amritsar, 1968
2. Tārā Siṅgh, *Srī Gur Tīrath Saṅgrahi*. Amritsar, n.d.
3. Ṭhākar Siṅgh, Giānī, *Srī Gurduāre Darshan*. Amritsar, 1923

M.G.S.

ḌHILVĀṄ KALĀṄ, village 5 km southeast of Koṭ Kapūrā (30° - 35'N, 74° - 49'E) in Farīdkoṭ district of the Punjab, was the abode of Soḍhī Kaul, shortened from Kaulnaiṇ, a descendant of Gurū Arjan's elder brother, Prithī Chand, and thus a collateral relation of Gurū Gobind Siṅgh. According to Bhāī Santokh Siṅgh, *Srī Gur Pratāp Sūraj Granth,* Gurū Gobind Siṅgh, displeased at Chaudharī Kapūrā's refusal to assist him in warding off the pursuing army from Sirhind, left Koṭ Kapūrā and came to Ḍhilvāṅ Kalāṅ, where Soḍhī Kaul and his four sons received him with honour. Here, at the suggestion of Soḍhī Kaul, the Gurū discarded the blue attire he had put on at Māchhīvāṛā as a disguise. Gurdwārā Godāvarīsar, marking the site where Gurū Gobind Siṅgh had put up, is situated on a low mound about 250 metres northwest of the village. It is a small domed room where the Gurū Granth Sāhib is seated. Besides the daily services, special *dīvāns* take place on the first of each Bikramī month. Baisākhī is the major annual festival.

BIBLIOGRAPHY

1. Santokh Siṅgh, Bhāī, *Srī Gur Pratāp Sūraj Granth*. Amritsar, 1926-37
2. Tārā Siṅgh, *Srī Gur Tīrath Saṅgrahi*. Amritsar, n.d.
3. Ṭhākar Siṅgh, Giānī, *Srī Gurduāre Darshan*. Amritsar, 1923

M.G.S.

DHIṄGA, BHĀĪ, a barber by profession, became a follower of Gurū Nānak. He once came to Gurū Aṅgad, Nānak II (1502-52), and sought instruction. The latter advised him to emulate Saiṇ, famous saint who too was a barber by profession and who had gained spiritual enlightenment by his loving devotion to the Deity.

BIBLIOGRAPHY

1. Manī Siṅgh, Bhāī, *Sikhāṅ dī Bhagat Mālā*. Amritsar, 1955
2. Santokh Siṅgh, Bhāī, *Srī Gur Pratāp Sūraj Granth*. Amritsar, 1926-37
3. Macauliffe, Max Arthur, *The Sikh Religion*. Oxford, 1909

Gn.S.

DHIṄGAṚ, BHĀĪ, a carpenter, was a devoted Sikh of the time of Gurū Hargobind (1595-1644). According to Bhāī Manī Siṅgh, *Sikhāṅ dī Bhagat Mālā,* Bhāī Dhiṅgaṛ, along with Bhāī Maddū, a fellow worker in the craft, came to serve at the Gurū's feet. During the day they hewed wood for Gurū kā Laṅgar, community kitchen, and made cots and other articles for use by the disciples; in the *dīvān* they attentively listened to recitations and discourses; and early in the morning they drew water for Sikhs' ablutions. As it happened, they died the same day, with the word *Vāhigurū* upon their lips. Gurū Hargobind attended their cremation in person. The Gurū, says Bhāī Santokh Siṅgh, *Srī Gur Pratāp Sūraj Granth,* praised them for their humility and modesty in never showing off the true knowledge they had attained through realizing in practice the *gur-shabad,* i.e. the Gurū's word.

BIBLIOGRAPHY

1. Manī Siṅgh, Bhāī, *Sikhāṅ dī Bhagat Mālā*. Amritsar, 1955
2. Santokh Siṅgh, Bhāī, *Srī Gur Pratāp Sūraj Granth*. Amritsar, 1926-37

B.S.

DHĪRĀ, BHĀĪ, a devoted Sikh of the time of Gurū Hargobind, was a resident of Ujjain. He used to visit Amritsar twice a year, to make obeisance to the Gurū. Once, records Bhāī Manī Siṅgh, *Sikhāṅ dī Bhagat Mālā,* he begged Gurū Hargobind to enlighten him about the qualities of a true saint. Gurū Hargobind recalled Gurū Arjan's *śloka* (GG, 1357) which, defines a man of God as one who meditates upon the *mantra* of God's Name; for whom *dukh* and *sukh*, suffering and pleasure, are the same; who, purged of rancour, has compassion for all; who subsists on singing God's praise and is free from *māyā* or worldly attachment; who treats friend and foe alike and instructs both in the love of God; who is selfless and humble; and who does not lend his ear to slander of others. According to *Srī Gur Pratāp Sūraj Granth,* Bhāī Dhīrā, along with his brother, Hīrā, took part in the battle of Amritsar.

BIBLIOGRAPHY

1. Manī Siṅgh, Bhāī, *Sikhāṅ dī Bhagat Mālā*. Amritsar, 1955
2. Santokh Siṅgh, Bhāī, *Srī Gur Pratāp Sūraj Granth*. Amritsar, 1926-37

B.S.

DHĪR MALL (1627-1677), the elder son of Bābā Gurdittā and a grandson of Gurū Hargobind, was born at Kartārpur, now in Jalandhar district of the Punjab, on 10 January 1627. From his early years, he was prone to stubbornness which trait became stronger as he grew up. He stayed behind in Kartārpur when Gurū Hargobind moved along with the family to Kīratpur. At the death, in 1638, of his father, Bābā Gurdittā, he did not go to Kīratpur to attend the obsequies, nor did he part with the original volume of the *Ādi Granth* which had been left at Kartārpur at the time of Gurū Hargobind's migration to Kīratpur and which had to be recited as part of the rites. When Gurū Hargobind named Har Rāi, his (Dhīr Mall's) younger brother, as his successor in the spiritual line, he set himself as Gurū at Kartārpur and appointed his own *masands,* or ministers, to collect tithes. He made friends with Rām Rāi who had been anathematized by his father, Gurū Har Rāi, for garbling a line from the Holy Writ, and together they took complaints to the Mughal emperor, Auraṅgzīb, challenging especially the installation of Gurū Har Krishan as successor to Gurū Har Rāi. Gurū Har Krishan's sudden illness and death at Delhi in March 1664 gave Dhīr Mall another chance to stake his claim to the *gurgaddī*, i.e. the spiritual seat of the Gurūs. He installed himself at Bakālā as successor to Gurū Har Krishan and, when Gurū Tegh Bahādur was formally anointed Gurū, he turned an enemy. He conspired with one of his *masands*, Shīhāṅ, who one day fired at Gurū Tēgh Bahādur, but missed the target. His men attacked the Gurū's house and ransacked it unchecked. Makkhaṇ Shāh, one of Gurū Tegh Bahādur's followers, retaliated by pillaging Dhīr Mall but the Gurū had everything returned to him, including the old volume of the Holy Book and what had been plundered from his own home.

Dhīr Mall remained unrepentant and continued to attract followers who formed a sect of their own. A few months after the martyrdom of Gurū Tegh Bahādur, Dhīr Mall was also summoned to Delhi by Emperor Auraṅgzīb and was imprisoned in the Fort at Raṇthambhor, where he died on 16 November 1677. His descendants, the Soḍhīs of Kartārpur, are still in possession of the original copy of the Ādi Granth prepared under the direction of Gurū Arjan. The shrine at Kartārpur dedicated to the founder of the sect is known as Ḍerā Dhīr Mall.

BIBLIOGRAPHY

1. *Gurbilās Chhevīṅ Pātshāhī*. Patiala, 1970
2. Bhallā, Sarūp Dās, *Mahimā Prakāsh*. Patiala, 1971
3. Chhibbar, Kesar Siṅgh, *Baṅsāvalīnāmā Dasāṅ Patshāhīāṅ Kā*. Chandigarh, 1972
4. Santokh Siṅgh, Bhāī, *Srī Gur Pratāp Sūraj Granth*. Amritsar, 1926-37
5. Giān Siṅgh, Giānī, *Panth Prakāsh*. Patiala, 1970
6. Macauliffe, Max Arthur, *The Sikh Religion*. Oxford, 1909
7. Trilochan Singh, *Guru Tegh Bahadur*. Delhi, 1967
8. Harbans Singh, *Guru Tegh Bahadur*. Delhi, 1982

M.K.

DHŪĀṄ, Punjabi for smoke, is a term which is particularly used for seats of certain monkish orders where a fire is perennially kept alive. In the Sikh context it is employed for the four branches of Udāsī Sikhs established by Bābā Gurdittā (1613-38), on whom the headship of the sect was conferred by Bābā Srī Chand, traditionally considered founder of the sect. The *dhūāṅs* are generally known after their respective heads who were initially assigned to different regions in north India for preaching the tenets of Sikhism as laid down by Gurū Nānak. Later, however, each of the four branches spread and established their preaching centres all over the country. The four *dhūāṅs* were: (1) Dhūāṅ Bhāī Almast Jī Kā preaching in the eastern parts with headquarters at Nānak Matā and branches, among several other places, at Ḍhākā, Paṭnā and Purī; (2) Dhūāṅ Bhāī Bālū Hasnā Jī Kā in western Punjab and Kashmīr; (3) Dhūāṅ Bhāī Goind or Gondā Jī Kā in southern Punjab popularly called Mālvā region; and (4) Dhūāṅ Bhāī Phūl Jī Kā in Doābā, i.e. the tract between the Rivers Beās and Sutlej.

See UDĀSĪS; ALMAST, BHĀĪ; BĀLŪ HASNĀ; GOIND, BHĀĪ; and PHŪL, BHĀĪ

BIBLIOGRAPHY

1. Randhīr Siṅgh, *Udāsī Sikhāṅ dī Vithiā*. Chandigarh, 1912
2. *Gurbilās Pātshāhī Chhevīṅ*. Patiala, 1970
3. Macauliffe, M.A., *The Sikh Religion*. Oxford, 1909

M.G.S.

DHUBṚĪ (26° - 2'N, 89° - 55'E), on the right bank of the River Brahmputra, in Assam, is sacred to the memory of Gurū Nānak and of

Gurū Tegh Bahādur. Assam in Indian legend and history has been the land of black magic. Janam Sākhīs record how at the time of Gurū Nānak's visit, his constant companion and follower, Mardānā, fell into the clutches of a sorceress who transformed him into a ram, and how the Gurū not only rescued him but also reformed the woman practising witchcraft. Gurū Tegh Bahādur visited Dhubṛī in early March 1670. Rājā Rām Siṅgh of Āmber, who had been sent by Auraṅgzīb on a punitive expedition to Assam against the Ahom chief, Rājā Chakradhvaj, was with him. Gurū Tegh Bahādur put up at Dhubṛī at a spot overlooking the sprawling river and now marked by Gurdwārā Srī Gurū Tegh Bahādur Jī. He brought about peace between the warring armies, and, to celebrate the happy conclusion of a dreaded expedition, he, with the help of Rājā Rām Siṅgh's troops, had a high mound constructed, each soldier contributing five shieldfuls of earth. The small octagonal room with a circular sloping roof and a narrow circumambulatory passage, constructed on top of this mound in 1966, is called Thaṛā Sāhib or Damdamā Sāhib. The Gurū Granth Sāhib is installed inside the room. The main shrine, Gurdwārā Srī Gurū Tegh Bahādur Jī, close by, consists of a well-ventilated and fly-proofed square hall with wooden walls and a sloping roof of corrugated sheets. The local Gurdwārā Parbandhak Committee and the Sikh Pratinidhi Board, Eastern Zone, have planned to extend the building.

BIBLIOGRAPHY

1. Tārā Siṅgh, *Srī Gur Tīrath Saṅgrahi*. Amritsar, n.d.
2. Ṭhākar Siṅgh, Giānī, *Srī Gurduāre Darshan*. Amritsar, 1923

M.G.S.

DHUNĪ, from Skt. *dhvani* meaning sound, echo, noise, voice, tone, tune, thunder, stands in Punjabi generally for sound and tune. In the Gurū Granth Sāhib, the term appears in the sense of tune at the head of 9 of the 22 *vārs* (odes) under different *rāgas* or musical measures. Directions with regard to the tunes in which those *vārs* were meant to be sung were recorded by Gurū Arjan when compiling the Holy Book. The classical system of Indian music had well-established tunes and corresponding prosodic forms; but the *vār*, being basically a folk form, did not have any prescribed order. The Gurū laid down tunes at least for odes for which models existed. The *vārs*, with corresponding *dhunīs*, are:

1. Vār Mājh by Nānak I – Malak Murīd tathā Chandraharā Sohīā kī dhunī (GG, 137).
2. Gauṛī kī Vār by Nānak V – Rāi Kamāldī Mojdī kī Vār kī dhuni (GG, 318).
3. Āsā kī Vār by Nānak I – Ṭuṇḍe Asrājai kī dhunī (GG, 462).
4. Gūjarī kī Vār by Nānak III – Sikandar Birāhim kī Vār kī dhunī (GG, 508).
5. Vaḍahaṅs kī Vār by Nānak IV – Lalāṅ Bahalīmā kī dhuni (GG, 585).
6. Rāmkalī kī Vār by Nānak III – Jodhai Vīrai Pūrabāṇī kī dhunī (GG, 947).
7. Sāraṅg kī Vār by Nānak IV – Rāi Mahme Hasane kī dhuni (GG, 1237).
8. Vār Malār Kī by Nānak I – Rāṇe Kailās tathā Māl de kī dhuni (GG, 1278).
9. Kānaṛe kī Vār by Nānak IV – Mūse kī Vār kī dhunī (GG, 1312).

Some scholars following *Gurbilās Pātshāhī Chhevīṅ*, an eighteenth-century work, assert that these *dhunīs* were added in the Holy Book under the direction of Gurū Hargobind, Nānak VI. They support their assertion by stating that in the original recension of Gurū Granth Sāhib preserved at Kartārpur, near Jalandhar, directions as to *dhunīs* were written in a different pen above or in between the lines. But Bhāī Jodh Siṅgh who, along with Professor Tejā Siṅgh and Gaṅgā Siṅgh, minutely researched this rare manuscript in 1945, affirms that the *dhunīs* were recorded by Bhāī Gurdās who originally transcribed the sacred volume, there being no change of hand. Bhāī Jodh Siṅgh's finding is that a finer pen has been used by him in recording *dhunīs* above or in between the lines as he has done at places elsewhere to mark *mahalā* indicating authorship of the verses.

BIBLIOGRAPHY

1. *Gurbilās Pātshāhī Chhevīṅ*. Patiala, 1970
2. Jodh Siṅgh, Bhāī, *Srī Kartārpurī Bīṛ de Darshan*. Paṭiālā, 1968
3. Harbaṅs Siṅgh, Giānī, *Āsā dī Vār Nirṇaya*. Amritsar, 1974
4. Tejā Siṅgh, *Āsā dī Vār*. Amritsar, 1968

M.G.S.

DHŪPĪĀ, from Skt. *dhūpa* or incense, means incense-burner, i.e. a temple functionary whose duty it is to burn incense before the deity at appointed hours especially during the *āratī* ritual, which the priests perform swaying a tray carrying lighted lamps in front of the deity. Though the ritual as such is rejected in Sikhism, the burning of incense and use of flowers and perfumes in *gurdwārās* as freshener of air are not prohibited. Bigger shrines attracting large gatherings of devotees such as Srī Darbār Sāhib at Amritsar may have *dhūpīās* on their establishment, but generally the function of incense burning may be performed by any officiant or by any one from the *saṅgat*. The office of *dhūpīā* as a member of the former hereditary priesthood has increasingly lost its importance since the days of the Gurdwārā reform.

M.G.S.

DIĀL DĀS, son of Gaurā and grandson of the celebrated Bhāī Bhagatū, lived at Bhuchcho, now in Baṭhiṇḍā district of the Punjab, at the time of Gurū Gobind Siṅgh's journey through those parts in 1706. At the village of Bhāgū, Diāl Dās took the rites of *amrit* at the hands of Gurū Gobind Siṅgh and received the name of Diāl Siṅgh. Thereafter the Gurū and the Sikhs partook of the food he had brought for them. It so happened, says the *Sākhī Pothī*, that a few more Sikhs arrived after all the food had been consumed. Diāl Siṅgh sold his gold ring and bought fresh victuals for the new-comers.

BIBLIOGRAPHY

1. Santokh Siṅgh, Bhāī, *Srī Gur Pratāp Sūraj Granth*. Amritsar, 1926-37
2. *Mālvā Desh Raṭan dī Sākhī Pothī*. Amritsar, 1968
3. Padam, Piārā Siṅgh, and Giānī Garjā Siṅgh, eds., *Gurū kīāṅ Sākhīāṅ*. Patiala, 1986
4. Macauliffe, Max Arthur, *The Sikh Religion*. Oxford, 1909

P.S.P.

DIĀL DĀS, BHĀĪ or Bhāī Diālā (d. 1675), martyr to the Sikh faith, was, according to *Shahīd Bilās Bhāī Manī Siṅgh*, the son of Māī Dās and an elder brother of Bhāī Manī Rām. He was a prominent Sikh of his time and was in the train of Gurū Tegh Bahādur during his journey across the eastern parts in 1665-70. He was one of the Sikhs detained and later released by the Mughal rulers in 1665. As the Gurū proceeded further east from Paṭnā, Diāl Dās was left behind to look after the Gurū's family. Several epistles addressed by Gurū Tegh Bahādur to *saṅgats* in Vārāṇasī-Paṭnā area adjured them to abide by Bhāī Diāl Dās's directions. Bhāī Diāl Dās accompanied Gurū Tegh Bahādur when the latter left Anandpur on 11 July 1675 to court martyrdom. He was arrested along with Gurū Tegh Bahādur and was, on his refusal to abjure his faith, boiled to death in a heated cauldron of water on 11 November 1675.

BIBLIOGRAPHY

1. Giān Siṅgh, Giānī, *Panth Prakāsh* [Reprint]. Patiala, 1970
2. Garjā Siṅgh, Giānī, ed., *Shahīd Bilās*. Ludhiana, 1961
3. Padam, Piārā Siṅgh, and Giānī Garjā Siṅgh, eds., *Gurū kīāṅ Sākhīāṅ*. Patiala, 1986
4. Trilochan Singh, *Guru Tegh Bahadur*. Delhi, 1967

A.C.B.

DIĀLPURĀ BHĀĪ KĀ, village in Baṭhiṇḍā district of the Punjab, 38 km west of Barnālā, named after its founder, Bhāī Diāl Siṅgh, a grandson of Bhāī Rūpā (1614-1709), around the middle of the eighteenth century, claims a historical shrine, Gurdwārā Zafarnāmah Sāhib Pātshāhī X. According to local tradition, Gurū Gobind Siṅgh, during his stay at Dīnā in December 1705, retired during the day to a grove around a pool of water which stood at the site marked by the present *gurdwārā*. Here he composed the *Zafarnāmah* or the Letter of Victory, which he sent from Dīnā to Emperor Auraṅgzīb. The present building constructed by Sant Manī Siṅgh during the 1930's is a large-sized hall with a square sanctum in the middle of it, marked off by massive pillars and wide arches. The lotus dome above the sanctum has a tall pyramidal brass pinnacle. The old pool has been converted into a 40-metre square *sarovar*. The Gurdwārā is managed by Nihaṅgs of the Taruṇā Dal.

BIBLIOGRAPHY

1. Tārā Siṅgh, *Srī Gur Tīrath Saṅgrahi*. Amritsar, n.d.
2. Ṭhākar Siṅgh, Giānī, *Srī Gurduāre Darshan*. Amritsar, 1923

M.G.S.

DIĀL, RĀJĀ (d. 1691), of Bijhaṛvāl who allied himself with Alif Khān, the Mughal commander, despatched by Mīāṅ Khān, the viceroy of Jammū, to exact tribute from the hill chieftains. The hill princes sought Gurū Gobind Siṅgh's help and a battle took place on 20 March 1691 at Nadauṇ on the left bank of the River Beās, 32 km southeast of Kāṅgṛā. According to Bhāī Santokh Siṅgh, *Srī Gur Pratāp Sūraj Granth*, Rājā Diāl fell to a shot from Gurū Gobind Siṅgh.

BIBLIOGRAPHY

1. Santokh Siṅgh, Bhāī, *Srī Gur Pratāp Sūraj Granth*. Amritsar, 1926-37
2. Macauliffe, Max Arthur, *The Sikh Religion*. Oxford, 1909
3. Grewal, J.S., and S.S. Bal, *Guru Gobind Singh*. Chandigarh, 1967

K.S.T.

DIĀL SIṄGH, BHĀĪ (1860-1921) was the son of Bhāī Devā Siṅgh and Māī Rām Kaur of Ghasītpur village, in Amritsar district. He learnt to read the Gurū Granth Sāhib in the village *gurdwārā* and enlisted in an infantry battalion at Poonā in his early youth. He served for 20 years and had received a gallantry award before he retired on a monthly pension of Rs 4. Diāl Siṅgh had married but had no offspring. Shortly before the happenings at Nankāṇā Sāhib, he attended a *dīvān* (Sikh religious congregation) at Chakk No. 75 Lahuke where he took the initiatory vows of the Khālsā at the hands of Bhāī Naraiṇ Siṅgh, and offered himself as a volunteer for the *jathā* or band of Bhāī Lachhmaṇ Siṅgh of Dhārovālī. He fell a martyr at Nankāṇā Sāhib on 20 February 1921.

See NANKĀṆĀ SĀHIB MASSACRE

BIBLIOGRAPHY

Shamsher, Gurbakhsh Siṅgh, *Shahīdī Jīvan*. Nankana Sahib, 1938

G.S.G.

ḌIKKH, village 12 km to the north of Mauṛ Kalāṅ (30° - 4'N, 75° - 14'E) in Baṭhiṇḍā district of the Punjab, is sacred to Gurū Tegh Bahādur, who visited it during his travels in these parts. According to *Sākhī Pothī*, an humble Sikh entreated the Gurū to come and put up in his house. The Gurū accepted his invitation. He blessed his host who had served him with complete devotion. The Sikh, who was childless, had four sons thereafter. A memorial platform raised in honour of the Gurū, about 200 metres west of the village, was later buried under sand; but, as memory of the Gurū's visit survived, it was uncovered again and a single-room *gurdwārā* established on the site in 1917. The shrine, now known as Gurdwārā Sāhib Pātshāhī

Nauvīṅ, comprises a domed sanctum within a square hall with a verandah on three sides. In an adjacent compound on a lower level are the Gurū kā Laṅgar and rooms for pilgrims. The Gurdwārā owns 10 acres of land and is affiliated to the Shiromaṇī Gurdwārā Parbandhak Committee. Special congregations take place on full-moon days.

BIBLIOGRAPHY

1. Ṭhākar Siṅgh, Giānī, *Srī Gurduāre Darshan*. Amritsar, 1923
2. *Mālvā Desh Raṭan dī Sākhī Pothī*. Amritsar, 1968

M.G.S.

DILĀWAR KHĀN, a Mughal chief, who during the closing years of seventeenth century sent his son, referred to as Khānzādā in Gurū Gobind Siṅgh's *Bachitra Nāṭak*, as head of an imperial expedition to exact tribute from the Gurū. The young commander, marching with alacrity, reached the vicinity of Anandpur at midnight and intended to surprise the town. But the Gurū was alerted by his chamberlain, Ālam Chand, and the Sikhs, putting on their armour, rushed out to meet the invaders. The beating of the Raṇjīt Nagārā and the war-cries of the Sikhs echoed widely in the stillness of the dark winter's night, giving an exaggerated estimate of their numbers. The Mughal force was completely unnerved at the suddenness of the Sikhs' movement and beat a hasty retreat without giving battle. The Khān fled deserting the field. Dilāwar Khān fell into a rage on hearing of the disaster. He made attempts to retrieve the lost position by sending, first, his slave-general Husain Khān and, then Jujhār Siṅgh Hāḍā, a Rājpūt, against Gurū Gobind Siṅgh, but without success.

BIBLIOGRAPHY

1. Saināpati, Kavī, *Srī Gur Sobhā*. Patiala, 1967
2. Kuir Siṅgh, *Gurbilās Pātshāhī 10*. Patiala, 1968
3. Giān Siṅgh, Giānī, *Twārīkh Gurū Khālsā*. Patiala, 1970
4. Macauliffe, M.A., *The Sikh Religion*. Oxford, 1909
5. Harbans Singh, *Guru Gobind Singh*. Chandigarh, 1966

B.S.

DĪNĀ, village 15 km south of Nihālsiṅghvālā (30° - 35'N, 75° - 16'E) in present-day Farīdkoṭ district of the Punjab, is sacred to Gurū Gobind Siṅgh, who, after evacuating Anandpur in December 1705, came here and stayed a few days. Chaudharī Shamīr and Lakhmīr, grandsons of the local chief, Rāi Jodh, who had fought on the side of Gurū Hargobind in the battle of Mahrāj in December 1634, served the Gurū with devotion. A few hundred warriors from the surrounding districts joined Gurū Gobind Siṅgh here. According to tradition, it was from Dīnā that the Gurū despatched his famous letter in Persian, *Zafarnāmah,* lit. Letter of Victory, to Emperor Auraṅgzīb through Bhāī Dayā Siṅgh and Bhāī Dharam Siṅgh. The place mentioned in the *Zafarnāmah* is, however, Kāṅgaṛ, 2 km south of Dīnā. The commemorative shrine established here was named Gurdwārā Lohgaṛh Sāhib. The old building raised by Rājā Harindar Siṅgh of Farīdkoṭ in 1934 was replaced by the present complex constructed by the followers of Sant Gurmukh Siṅgh Kārsevāvāle during the 1980's. The sanctum at the far end of the *dīvān* hall has above it four storeys of rooms, with the dome at the top having a gilded pinnacle. The *sarovar*, holy tank, also constructed by the ruler of Farīdkoṭ, is to the west of the main building. The Gurdwārā is managed by the Shiromaṇī Gurdwārā Parbandhak Committee. Besides the daily services and observance of major Sikh anniversaries, a religious fair is held every year on the occasion of Māghī, the first of the Bikramī month of Māgh usually corresponding with 13-14 January.

BIBLIOGRAPHY

1. Tārā Siṅgh, *Srī Gur Tīrath Saṅgrahi*. Amritsar, n.d.

2. Ṭhākar Siṅgh, Giānī, *Srī Gurduāre Darshan*. Amritsar, 1923

Gn.S.

DĪNĀ NĀTH, DĪWĀN (1795-1857), civil administrator and counsellor of considerable influence at the Sikh court for well over three decades, was the son of a Kashmīrī Paṇḍit, Ba<u>kh</u>t Mall, who had migrated to Delhi during the oppressive rule of the Af<u>gh</u>ān governors of the valley. He was also closely related to Dīwān Gaṅgā Rām, head of the military accounts and keeper of the privy seal at Lahore. In 1815, at the instance of Dīwān Gaṅgā Rām, Mahārājā Raṇjīt Siṅgh invited Dīnā Nāth to Lahore and offered him the post of *mutsaddī*, or writer, in the department of military accounts. In 1826, when Dīwān Gaṅgā Rām died, Dīnā Nāth succeeded him as the head of military accounts department and keeper of the privy seal. In 1834, when Dīwān Bhavānī Dās passed away, the Mahārājā made him the head of the civil and finance office and conferred upon him, in 1838, the honorary title of Dīwān.

By his ability and political acumen, Dīnā Nāth rose to the highest position of power and influence in the affairs of the State. Lepel Griffin styles him the Talleyrand of the Punjab. Dīnā Nāth knew how to keep his ambition in check and was one man in Lahore who made no enemies at the court. In the turbulent days following Raṇjīt Siṅgh's death, he refused to take sides with Rāṇī Chand Kaur or Kaṅvar Sher Siṅgh. However, Sher Siṅgh upon his succession to the throne, reposed his full trust in him. Dīnā Nāth retained his position at the court during the *wazārats* of both Hīrā Siṅgh and Jawāhar Siṅgh as well as during the regency of Mahārāṇī Jind Kaur. After the Anglo-Sikh war of 1845-46, the British nominated him a member of the Council of Regency established in Lahore for the minor king, Duleep Siṅgh. In November 1847, the title of the Rājā of Kalānaur, with a *jāgīr* worth 20,000 rupees annually, was conferred upon him.

After the annexation of the Punjab in 1849, Dīnā Nāth served under the British who confirmed him in his *jāgīrs* worth about fifty thousand rupees annually.

Dīwān Dīnā Nāth died at Lahore in 1857.

BIBLIOGRAPHY

1. Sūrī, Sohan Lāl, *'Umdāt-ut-Twārīkh*. Lahore, 1885-89
2. Griffin, Lepel, and C.F. Massy, *Chiefs and Families of Note in the Punjab*. Lahore, 1909
3. Hasrat, B.J., *Life and Times of Ranjit Singh*. Hoshiarpur, 1977

H.R.G.

DĪNĀ NĀTH, PAṆḌIT (b. 1888), active supporter of and participant in the Sikh Gurdwārā reform movement 1920-25, was born in 1888, the son of Paṇḍit Bāl Krishan of Amritsar. In the wake of the agrarian protest in the Punjab in 1907, he joined the Indian National Congress. He was secretary of the Amritsar District Congress Committee when the Gurdwārā reform or Akālī movement got under way with the establishment in November 1920 of a representative Sikh body, the Shiromaṇī Gurdwārā Parbandhak Committee. Paṇḍit Dīnā Nāth was in sympathy with the movement and joined the Akālī agitation for the restoration of the keys of the *toshā<u>kh</u>ānā* or treasury of the Darbār Sāhib, which had been taken away by the British Deputy Commissioner on 7 November 1921. He was arrested on 26 November 1921 along with a group of Sikh leaders at Ajnālā, a sub-divisional town in Amritsar district, was charged with delivering seditious speeches in defiance of the ban on political meetings, and was sentenced to five months' rigorous imprisonment and a fine of 1,000 rupees or six months' additional imprisonment in default thereof. Similar punishments were awarded to other arrested leaders. This, however, led to further intensification of the agitation, and the government was eventually forced to surrender the keys to the Akālī leader, Bābā Khaṛak Siṅgh, on 17 January 1922. Of the 193 persons arrested, 150 were released but Paṇḍit Dīnā Nāth was one of those who were retained in custody. The Deputy Commissioner offered to set him free if he would put in an application in writing which he refused to do. Paṇḍit Dīnā Nāth was however released soon thereafter unconditionally along with other detainees.

BIBLIOGRAPHY

1. Josh, Sohan Siṅgh, *Akālī Morchiāṅ dā Itihās*. Delhi, 1972
2. Pratāp Siṅgh, Giānī, *Gurdwārā Sudhār arthāt Akālī Lahir*. Amritsar, 1975
3. Teja Singh, *Gurdwara Reform Movement and the Sikh Awakening*. Jalandhar, 1922
4. Mohinder Singh, *The Akali Movement*. Delhi, 1978

Aj.S.L

DIN-RAIṆ, lit. (*din* + *raiṇ*) day and night, is the title (*din-raiṇi)* of a single 4-stanza hymn by Gurū Arjan Dev in the Mājh measure (GG, 136-37). The composition evidently follows the prosodic vogue of inscribing verses to *kāl-krama* (process of time) embracing forms such as *bārāmāhā* (twelve months of the year), *thitī* (lunar-dates) and *vār* (days of the week). Otherwise, the contents of this hymn are in harmony with the tenor of the entire text, i.e. praise of, surrender to, and love of God, the Ultimate Reality. Writing in the first person and in conversational style mixed with soliloquy, Gurū Arjan expresses the soul's yearning for reunion with the Lord and, besides panegyrizing the Timeless, Merciful, True Creator. He also gives homage to those who day and night remember and serve Him.

dinu raiṇi ji prabh kauṅ sevade tin kai sad balihār —
I am a hundred times sacrifice unto those who serve the Lord day and night;

dinu raiṇi jisu na visarai so hariā hovai jantu—
He who does not forget Him during day or night remains evergreen;

sarab kaliāṇā titu dini hari parsī gur ke pāu—
The day during which one worships at the feet of God-gurū brings total liberation.

Besides using *din-raiṇ* as the title of this hymn, the term frequently appears in *gurbāṇī* impressing upon the devotees the need and significance of remembering the Name (*nām*) constantly during day and night. Other variations on the term are *raiṇī-dinasu, din-rāti, nisi-dinu, rāt-dinant* and plain *dinu ar rāti.*

M.G.S.

DĪPĀ, BHĀĪ, a Jaṭṭ of Deū clan, once came along with Bhāī Narāiṇ Dās and Bhāī Būlā to Gurū Aṅgad (1504-52) and begged to be instructed how they could have themselves released from the cycle of birth and death. The Gurū, according to Bhāī Manī Siṅgh, *Sikhāṅ dī Bhagat Mālā,* told them to follow the *bhakti mārga,* path of devotional love of God, to the exclusion of the paths of *bairāg* (renunciation), *yogā* (austerities) and *giān* (knowledge). *Bhaktī,* he explained, involved complete self-surrender to the Will of the Lord.

BIBLIOGRAPHY

1. Manī Siṅgh, Bhāī, *Sikhāṅ dī Bhagat Mālā*. Amritsar, 1955
2. Santokh Siṅgh, Bhāī, *Srī Gur Partāp Sūraj Granth*. Amritsar, 1926-37

Gn.S.

DĪPĀ, BHĀĪ, resident of the village of Ḍallā in present-day Kapūrthalā district of the Punjab, has been listed by Bhāī Gurdās,

Vārāṅ, XI. 16, amongst the leading Sikhs of the time of Gurū Amar Dās. He had received instruction at the hands of the Gurū himself.

See RĀMŪ, BHĀĪ

BIBLIOGRAPHY

1. Manī Siṅgh, Bhāī, *Sikhāṅ dī Bhagat Mālā*. Amritsar, 1955
2. Santokh Siṅgh, Bhāī, *Srī Gur Partāp Sūraj Granth*. Amritsar, 1926-37

B.S.D.

DĪPĀ, BHĀĪ, a prominent Sikh of the time of Gurū Rām Dās mentioned by Bhāī Gurdās in his *Vārāṅ*, XI. 17.

See DHARAM DĀS, BHĀĪ

BIBLIOGRAPHY

1. Manī Siṅgh, Bhāī, *Sikhāṅ dī Bhagat Mālā*. Amritsar, 1955
2. Santokh Siṅgh, Bhāī, *Srī Gur Pratāp Suraj Granth*. Amritsar, 1926-37
3. Macauliffe, Max Arthur, *The Sikh Religion*. Oxford, 1909

Gr.S.

DĪPĀ, BHĀĪ, was a devoted Sikh of Gurū Arjan's time (Bhāī Gurdās, *Vārāṅ*, XI. 22). He zealously served in the Gurū kā Laṅgar. He cooked food and served it to visiting Sikhs. He took the last turn and ate what was left over. He washed with warm water the feet of those who came from afar and kneaded their limbs to relieve them of fatigue. On cold winter nights he went round adjusting the quilts and coverlets of sleeping visitors. Upon his lips were always the Gurū's hymns. According to Bhāī Manī Siṅgh, *Sikhāṅ dī Bhagat Mālā*, Gurū Arjan pleased with his devotion, once said, "Dīpā is a *dīpak*, i.e. a lamp. As one lamp flame lights another, so would Bhāī Dīpā, having received true knowledge, diffuse it among those who come in contact with him." Bhāī Dīpā was appointed a *masand*, or area leader to spread the Gurū's message.

BIBLIOGRAPHY

1. Manī Siṅgh, Bhāī, *Sikhāṅ dī Bhagat Mālā*. Amritsar, 1955
2. Santokh Siṅgh, Bhāī, *Srī Gur Pratāp Sūraj Granth*. Amritsar, 1926-37

T.S.

DĪPĀLPUR (30° - 40'N, 73° - 32'E), *tahsīl* (sub-division) town of Montgomery (or Sāhīwāl) district of Pakistan, was, according to *Miharbān Janam Sākhī*, visited by Gurū Nānak (1469-1539) on his way back from Pākpaṭṭan to Talvaṇḍī. According to local tradition, the Gurū sat under a dead *pīpal* tree on the southeastern outskirts of the town. The tree foliated. Gurū Nānak is also said to have cured a leper named Nūrī or Nauraṅgā. The *pīpal* tree and the grave of Nauraṅgā still existed near the Gurdwārā Pahilī Pātshāhī, Dīpālpur, in 1947 when the shrine was abandoned following the partition of the Punjab.

In Dīpālpur were also preserved a cot and a wooden chest believed to have been mementos bestowed upon one Natthū Rām — the first one by Gurū Har Rāi and the second by Gurū Gobind Siṅgh. They were the proud possessions of his family which lived in Dīpālpur until 1947.

BIBLIOGRAPHY

Ṭhākar Siṅgh, Giānī, *Srī Gurduāre Darshan*. Amritsar, 1923

M.G.S.

DĪP SIṄGH SHAHĪD, BĀBĀ (1682-1757), founder of the Shahīd *misl* or principality as well as of the Damdamī Ṭaksāl or Damdamā school of Sikh learning, was born in 1682, the son of Bhāī Bhagatā and Māī Jiūṇī, a Sikh couple living in Pahūviṇḍ, a village 40 km southwest of Amritsar. He received the vows of the Khālsā at Anandpur where he stayed for some time to study the sacred texts under Bhāī Manī Siṅgh. He re-joined Gurū Gobind Siṅgh at Talvaṇḍī Sābo in 1706 and, after the latter's departure for the South, stayed on there to look after the sacred shrine, Damdamā Sāhib. He, at the head of a small group of warriors, joined Bandā Siṅgh Bahādur in his campaign against the Mug̱hal authority, but left him in 1714 when the Tatt K̲hālsā rose against him (Bandā Siṅgh). Retiring to Damdamā Sāhib at Talvaṇḍī Sābo with his band of warriors, he resumed his study and teaching of the Scripture and training in martial skills. In 1726, he had four copies of the Gurū Granth Sāhib made from the recension prepared earlier by Bhāī Manī Siṅgh under the supervision of Gurū Gobind Siṅgh during their stay at Damdamā Sāhib. In 1732, he went to the rescue of Sardār Ālā Siṅgh who had been besieged in Barnālā by Mañjh and Bhaṭṭī Rājpūts in collaboration with the *faujdār* of Jalandhar and the *nawāb* of Mālerkoṭlā. In 1733, when the Mug̱hal governor of Lahore sought peace with the Sikhs offering them a nawābship and a *jāgīr*, Dīp Siṅgh and his *jathā* or fighting band joined Nawāb Kapūr Siṅgh at Amritsar to form a joint Sikh force, the Dal K̲hālsā, which was soon divided for administrative convenience into Buḍḍhā Dal and Taruṇā Dal, the latter being further split into five *jathās*. Dīp Siṅgh, now reverently called *Bābā,* was given the command of one of these *jathās* which in 1748 were redesignated *misls.* It came to be known as Shahīd *misl* after its founder met with the death of a martyr (*shahīd*, in Punjabi). The *misls* soon established their authority over different regions under *rākhī* system which meant, like *chauth* of the Marāṭhās, collection of a portion of the revenue of the region for guaranteeing peace, protection and security. Shahīd *misl* had its sphere of influence south of the River Sutlej and Dīp Siṅgh's headquarters remained at Talvaṇḍī Sābo. The tower in which he lived still stands next to the Tak̲ht Srī Damdamā Sāhib and is known as Burj Bābā Dīp Siṅgh Shahīd.

During his fourth invasion of India in the winter of 1756-57, Ahmad Shāh Durrānī annexed the Punjab to the Afg̲hān dominions and appointed his son, Taimūr, viceroy at Lahore, with the veteran general, Jahān K̲hān, as his deputy. Jahān K̲hān invested Amritsar in May 1757, razed the Sikh fortress of Rām Rauṇī and filled up the sacred pool. As the news of this desecration reached Dīp Siṅgh, he set out with his *jathā* towards the Holy City. Many Sikhs joined him on the way so that when he arrived at Tarn Tāran he had at his command a force of 5,000 men. Jahān K̲hān's troops lay in wait for them near Gohlvaṛ village, 8 km ahead. They barred their way and a fierce action took place. Dīp Siṅgh suffered grave injury near Rāmsar, yet such was the firmness of his resolve to reach the holy precincts that he carried on the battle until he fell dead in the close vicinity of the Harimandar. This was on 11 November 1757. A legend grew that it was Bābā Dīp Siṅgh's headless body holding his severed head on his left hand and wielding his *khaṇḍā,* double-edged sword, with his right hand that had fought on until he had redeemed his pledge to liberate the holy shrine. Two shrines now commemorate the martyr, one on the circumambulatory terrace of the *sarovar* surrouding the Golden Temple where he finally fell and the other, Shahīdgañj Bābā Dīp Siṅgh Shahīd, near Gurdwārā Rāmsar, where his body was cremated.

BIBLIOGRAPHY

1. Bhaṅgū, Ratan Siṅgh, *Prāchīn Panth Prakāsh.* Amritsar, 1914
2. Giān Siṅgh, Giānī, *Panth Prakāsh* [Reprint]. Patiala, 1970
3. Ṭhākar Siṅgh, Giānī, *Shahīd Bilās Bābā Dīp Siṅgh Jī.* Amritsar, 1904
4. Cunningham, Joseph Davey, *A History of the Sikhs.* London, 1849

K.S.T.

DIṚHBĀ, an old town 30 km southeast of

Saṅgrūr (30° - 14'N, 75° - 50'E) in the Punjab, has a historical shrine commemorating the visit of Gurū Tegh Bahādur during the third quarter of the seventeenth century. It is known as Gurdwārā Sāhib Pātshāhī IX and is situated on the bank of a deep pond on the northwestern outskirts of the town where the Gurū is believed to have encamped. The sanctum is in the middle one of the three small cubicles built in a row. Over the sanctum there is a square pavilion. A hall was constructed facing the cubicles by Mahant Pākhar Siṅgh alias Kishan Siṅgh in 1955. More recent is the complex comprising the Gurū kā Laṅgar and rooms for pilgrims and a small *sarovar*, holy tank, dug in 1978. The Gurdwārā owns 7 acres of land and is administered by a village committee under the auspices of the Shiromaṇī Gurdwārā Parbandhak Committee.

M.G.S.

DITT SIṄGH, GIĀNĪ (1853-1901), scholar, poet and journalist, was an eminent Siṅgh Sabhā reformer and editor. He was born on 21 April 1853 at Kalauṛ, a village in Paṭiālā district of the Punjab. His ancestral village was Jhallīāṅ, near Chamkaur Sāhib, but his father, Dīvān Siṅgh, had migrated to his wife's village, Kalauṛ. Dīvān Siṅgh, a Ravidāsīā by caste and a weaver by trade, was a religious-minded person who had earned the title of Sant for his piety. Himself an admirer of the Gulābdāsī sect, he sent Ditt Siṅgh at the age of nine, to be educated under Sant Gurbakhsh Siṅgh at Ḍerā Gulābdāsīāṅ in the village of Tioṛ, near Kharaṛ in Ropaṛ district. Ditt Siṅgh studied Gurmukhī, prosody, Vedānta and *Nītī-Śāstra* at the Ḍerā, and learnt Urdu from Dayā Nand, a resident of Tioṛ. At the age of 16-17, he shifted to the main Gulābdāsī centre at Chaṭṭhiāṅvālā, near Kasūr, in Lahore district. Formally initiated into the sect of Sant Desā Siṅgh, he became a Gulābdāsī preacher. Not long afterwards, he came under the influence of Bhāī Jawāhir Siṅgh, formerly a follower of Gulābdāsī sect, who had joined the Ārya Samāj. Ditt Siṅgh also became an Ārya Samājist. He was introduced to Swāmī Dayā Nand, the founder of the Ārya Samāj, during the latter's visit to Lahore in 1877. Soon, however, he and his friend, Jawāhir Siṅgh, were drawn into the Sikh fold through Bhāī Gurmukh Siṅgh, then an active figure in the Siṅgh Sabhā movement. In 1886, Bhāī Gurmukh Siṅgh, following the establishment of the Lahore Khālsā Dīwān parallel to the one at Amritsar, floated a weekly newspaper, the *Khālsā Akhbār*. Though its first editor was Giānī Jhaṇḍā Siṅgh Farīdkoṭī, the principal contributor was Giānī Ditt Siṅgh, who soon took over editorship from him. He had passed the Gyānī examination the same year and had been appointed a teacher at the Oriental College. In his hands the *Khālsā Akhbār* became an efficient and powerful vehicle for the spread of Siṅgh Sabhā ideology. The Khālsā Dīwān Amritsar led by Bābā Khem Siṅgh Bedī and the ruler of Farīdkoṭ, Rājā Bikram Siṅgh, had Bhāī Gurmukh Siṅgh excommunicated, under the seal of the Golden Temple, in March 1887. On 16 April 1887, Giānī Ditt Siṅgh issued a special supplement of his *Khālsā Akhbār* in which appeared a part of his *Svapan Nāṭak* (*q.v.*), or Dream Play, a thinly-veiled satire, ridiculing the Amritsar leaders and their supporters. One of the victims of the burlesque, Bāvā Ude Siṅgh, filed a defamation suit against Giānī Ditt Siṅgh in a Lahore court. The latter was sentenced to pay a fine of Rs 5 but was on appeal acquitted by the sessions court on 30 April 1888. The case had dragged on for over a year, imposing severe financial hardship on the *Khālsā Akhbār*. It had already suffered a setback by the death in May 1887 of its chief patron, Kaṅvar Bikramā Siṅgh of Kapūrthalā. In 1889, it had to be closed down, along with the Khālsā Press. Bhāī Gurmukh Siṅgh, however, secured, through Bhāī Kāhn Siṅgh, help from the Mahārājā of Nābhā and the *Khālsā Akhbār* recommenced publication on 1 May 1893. Editorship was again entrusted to Ditt Siṅgh. Ditt Siṅgh also helped Bhagat Lakshman Siṅgh to launch from Lahore on 5 January 1899 the *Khālsā,* a weekly in English.

Giānī Ditt Siṅgh and his friend, Jawāhir Siṅgh, had not severed their connection with the Ārya Samāj even after their initiation into the Sikh faith. The final breach came on 25 November 1888 when, in a public meeting held on the eleventh anniversary of the Lahore Ārya Samāj, Paṇḍit Gurū Dutt of Government College, Lahore, and Lālā Murlī Dhar spoke disparagingly about the Sikh Gurūs. This hurt the feelings of Giānī Ditt Siṅgh and Jawāhir Siṅgh and they left the Ārya Samāj for good. They joined hands with Bhāī Gurmukh Siṅgh and threw themselves whole-heartedly into the Siṅgh Sabhā work.

Giānī Ditt Siṅgh wielded a powerful pen and was equally at home in prose as well as in verse. He wrote more than forty books and pamphlets on Sikh theology and history and on current polemics. Well-known among his works are: *Gurū Nānak Prabodh, Gurū Arjan Charittar, Dambh Bidāran, Durgā Prabodh, Panth Prabodh, Rāj Prabodh, Merā ate Sādhū Dayānand dā Sambād, Naqlī Sikh Prabodh* and *Panth Sudhār Binai Pattar.* He also published accounts of the martyrdoms of Tārā Siṅgh of Vāṅ, Subeg Siṅgh, Matāb Siṅgh Mīrāṅkoṭīā, Tārū Siṅgh and Botā Siṅgh.

Ditt Siṅgh's marriage took place in Lahore in 1880 according to Sikh rites. His wife, Bishan Kaur, shared his religious zeal and the couple had a happy married life. They had two children, a son, Baldev Siṅgh, born in 1886, and a daughter, Vidyāvant Kaur, born in 1890. Ditt Siṅgh was very fond of his daughter who was a highly precocious child. Her death on 17 June 1901 was a great blow to Ditt Siṅgh, who had already been under a strain owing to persistently heavy work since the death in 1898 of Bhāī Gurmukh Siṅgh. He still continued to work with patience and fortitude, but his health deteriorated rapidly and he fell seriously ill. A Muslim doctor, Rahīm Khān, treated him, but it was of no avail. Giānī Ditt Siṅgh died at Lahore on 6 September 1901. The loss was mourned widely by the Sikhs. A 15-member memorial committee was formed with Bhāī Sāhib Arjan Siṅgh Bāgaṛīāṅ as chairman. Notable memorials honouring his name were Giānī Ditt Siṅgh Khālsā Boarding House in Lahore and Bhāī Ditt Siṅgh Library opened at Sikh Kanyā Mahāvidyālā Fīrozpur by Bhāī Takht Siṅgh, one of his former students and a close friend.

BIBLIOGRAPHY

1. Amar Siṅgh, Giānī, *Siṅgh Sabhā Lahir de Ughe Sañchālak Giānī Ditt Siṅgh Jī.* Amritsar, 1902
2. Daljīt Siṅgh, *Siṅgh Sabhā de Moḍhī Giānī Ditt Siṅgh Jī.* Amritsar, 1951
3. Jagjīt Siṅgh, *Siṅgh Sabha Lahir.* Ludhiana, 1974
4. Harbans Singh, *The Heritage of the Sikhs.* Delhi, 1983
5. Jolly, Surjit Kaur, *Sikh Revivalist Movements.* Delhi, 1988
6. Chandar, Gurmukh Singh, *My Attempted Excommunication from the Sikh Temples and the Khalsa Community at Faridkot in 1887.* Lahore, 1898

Gds. S.

DĪVĀLĪ, festival of lights (from Sanskrit *dīpamālā* or *dīpāvalī* meaning row of lamps or nocturnal illumination), is observed all over India on *amāvasyā,* the last day of the dark half of the lunar month of Kārtika (October-November). Like other seasonal festivals, Dīvālī has been celebrated since time immemorial. In its earliest form, it was regarded as a means to ward off, expel or appease the malignant spirits of darkness and ill luck. The festival is usually linked with the return to Ayodhyā of Lord Rāma at the end of his fourteen-year exile. For the Hindus it is also an occasion for the worship of Lakṣmī, the goddess of good fortune, beauty and wealth.

Among the Sikhs, Dīvalī came to have special significance from the day the town of Amritsar was illuminated on the return to it of Gurū Hargobind (1595-1644) who had been held captive in the Fort at Gwālīor under the orders of the Mughal emperor, Jahāṅgīr (1570-1627). Henceforth Dīvālī, like Baisākhī, became a day of pilgrimage to the seat of the Gurūs. Bhāī Gurdās (d. 1636) in his *Vārāṅ*, XIX. 6, has drawn an image of "lamps lighted on the night of Dīvālī like the stars, big and small, twinkling in the firmament going out one by one bringing home to the *gurmukh*, one who has his face turned towards the Gurū, i.e. he who is attached to the Gurū, how transitory the world is."

During the turbulent eighteenth century, it was customary for the roaming warrior-bands of Sikhs to converge upon Amritsar braving all hazards to celebrate Dīvālī. It was for his endeavour to hold such a congregation at Amritsar that Bhāī Manī Siṅgh, a most widely revered Sikh of his time, was put to death under the imperial fiat. Amritsar still attracts vast numbers of Sikhs for the festival and although all *gurdwārās* and Sikh homes are generally illuminated on Dīvālī night, the best and the most expensive display of lights and fireworks takes place at the Darbār Sāhib (Golden Temple), Amritsar.

S.S.V.B.

DĪVĀN, in Persian, means royal court, conference, audience. Appearing as *dībān* or *dībāṇu* in Gurū Nānak's compositions, the word stands for both the divine court of justice and the law courts of the State. In the Sikh tradition, *dīvān* has come to mean the court of the Gurū or a congregation in the name of the Gurū. The Gurū was addressed by Sikhs as *Sachchā Pātishāh* or True King whose audience was given the name of *dīvān* or court. As the office of Gurū became vested in the Gurū Granth Sāhib, any assembly in the hall or court where the Sacred Volume was installed was called the *dīvān*. A gathering of devotees in the presence of the Gurū Granth Sāhib at which holy hymns are sung and the holy Name is meditated upon is a *dīvān*. Nowadays Sikh social and political gatherings and conferences, with Scripture presiding over them, are also designated *dīvāns*. The term nevertheless applies primarily to Sikh religious assemblies in *gurdwārās* or elsewhere.

At a Sikh *dīvān*, Gurū Granth Sāhib is seated on a high pedestal or throne. Sikhs enter reverentially with folded hands and kneel down touching the ground in front of it with their foreheads and making offerings, usually of money. They will, thereafter, greet the assembly, and, where the hall is spacious enough to permit this, circumambulate the Sacred Volume in token of allegiance to the Gurū before taking their seats on the ground among the *saṅgat*. Dispersal is in the same reverent style; the departing member will leave his seat, stand before the Gurū Granth Sāhib, with hands clasped, fall on his knees making a low bow and retreat respectfully, taking care not to turn his back towards the Holy Book.

In Sikh *gurdwārās* commonly two *dīvāns* take place daily — one in the morning and the second in the evening. In the morning, the service will begin with the induction and installation of the Gurū Granth Sāhib. After the *ardās* or supplicatory prayer, the Book will be opened to obtain from it what is called *hukam*, i.e. the Gurū's command or lesson for the day. This will be followed by *kīrtan* or chanting by a choir of musicians of holy hymns from the Gurū Granth Sāhib, if not of the entire composition entitled *Āsā kī Vār*. At larger *gurdwārās, kīrtan* will be preceded by the recitation of Gurū Arjan's *Sukhmanī* and of morning *nitnem*, i.e. texts comprising the daily regimen of Sikh prayers for that hour. Then there will take place *kathā* or exposition of the *hukam* of that morning or of any other hymn from the

Gurū Granth Sāhib, followed by a discourse or lecture on Sikh theology or history. Recitation of the six cantos by the whole assembly from Gurū Amar Dās's composition, the *Anand,* and of the last *śloka* of the *Japu, ardās,* proclamation of the *hukam* from the Gurū Granth Sāhib and distribution of *kaṛāhprasād* or communion will bring the *dīvān* to a conclusion. At the evening *dīvān,* besides *kīrtan,* two *bāṇīs* prescribed for the service, *Rahrāsi* and the *Kīrtan Sohilā* are recited. At the central shrine at Amritsar, the Harimandar, the *dīvān* remains in session continuously from early hours of the morning till late in the evening, with *kīrtan* being recited uninterruptedly. Special *dīvāns* are held to mark important anniversaries on the Sikh calendar and social events in families. The format allows for variations to suit the occasion, but one binding condition is that the congregation occurs in the presence of the Gurū Granth Sāhib.

T.S.

DĪVĀN CHAND, MISR (d. 1825), a general in Mahārājā Raṇjīt Siṅgh's army, was the son of a Brāhmaṇ shopkeeper of the village of Gondlāṅvālā, in Gujrāṅwālā district, now in Pakistan. He had come to the notice of Mahārājā Raṇjīt Siṅgh in 1812 during one of his tours and was appointed a clerk in the accounts section of the ordnance department. In 1814, when G͟haus K͟hān, head of this department, died, Raṇjīt Siṅgh appointed Dīvān Chand in his place. Between 1814 and 1825, Dīvān Chand was virtually the commander-in-chief of the armies that conquered Multān and Kashmīr. The city of Multān had been besieged for four months since February 1818 before it was finally conquered on 2 June 1818. In the final conquest of Kashmīr (1819) the main army was placed under Dīvān Chand while a supporting column under Prince Khaṛak Siṅgh marched behind him. Dīvān Chand destroyed the fort of Rājaurī. Jabbār K͟hān, the Afg͟hān governor of Kashmīr, opposed him at the inner entrance to the pass and seized two Sikh guns, but was forced to flee and Kashmīr became part of the Sikh kingdom. Dīvān Chand was honoured by the Mahārājā with the title of Nusrat Jaṅg, "Victor in War." Earlier, after the conquest of Multān, he had received the title of Zafar Jaṅg, "Conquerer in War." In 1820, Dīvān Chand captured Rāṇī Sadā Kaur's fort of Aṭalgaṛh, and took Mankerā in 1821. He also took part in the campaigns of Pakhlī, Ṭoṅk, Bannū and Nausherā.

Misr Dīvān Chand died of cholera at Lahore on 18 July 1825.

BIBLIOGRAPHY

1. Griffin, Lepel, *Ranjit Singh*. Delhi, 1957
2. Latif, Syad Muhammad, *History of the Panjab*. Delhi, 1964
3. Gulcharan Singh, *Ranjit Singh and His Generals*. Jalandhar, n.d.

H.R.G.

DĪVĀN SIṄGH, BHĀĪ (1888-1921), one of the Nankāṇā Sāhib martyrs, was born in 1888, the son of Bhāī Hīrā Siṅgh and Māī Pān Kaur of Paṇḍorī Nijjarāṅ, in Jalandhar district. The family later shifted to Chakk No. 91 Dhannūāṇā, in the newly colonized district of Lyallpur, now in Pakistan. Dīvān Siṅgh, an illiterate bachelor, made a name for himself in that area as a wrestler and as an intrepid fighter. As the Gurdwārā reform movement picked up momentum, he took the vows of the K͟hālsā and decided to join the *jathā* or band of Akālī volunteers marching towards Nankāṇā Sāhib. His companions doubted if he would remain peaceful and keep the vow of non-violence to which the *jathā* had committed itself, but Dīvān Siṅgh assured them that he would keep his word even in face of the gravest provocation. He was one of those who were burnt to death at Nankāṇā Sāhib by the hirelings of Mahant Naraiṇ Dās.

See NANKĀṆĀ SĀHIB MASSACRE

BIBLIOGRAPHY

Shamsher, Gurbakhsh Siṅgh, *Shahīdī Jīvan*. Nankana Sahib, 1938

G.S.G.

DĪVĀN SIṄGH, BHĀĪ (d. 1924), one of the martyrs of Jaito Morchā, was born around 1874, the son of Sāhib Siṅgh of the village of Mahingarvāl in Hoshiārpur district of the Punjab. As he grew up, he joined government service in the railways and was an assistant engineer when he resigned in protest against the deposition by the British of Mahārājā Ripudaman Siṅgh, ruler of the princely state of Nābhā, in July 1923, and became an activist in the Akālī movement for the reformation of the management of Sikh shrines. As the Shiromaṇī Gurdwārā Parbandhak Committee was outlawed by government in October 1923, Dīvān Siṅgh was appointed chairman of the district committee for the management of *gurdwārās* in Hoshiārpur district. When the Akālīs decided to lead 500-strong *shahīdī jathās,* bands of volunteers vowed to win martyrdom, to Jaito where a Sikh religious ceremony had been intruded upon by police in February 1924, Dīvān Siṅgh offered himself as a volunteer, but the Shiromaṇī Committee turned down his request. The first *shahīdī jathā* left Amritsar on 9 February 1924. Its progress on foot through the countryside caused much excitement. Dīvān Siṅgh could not restrain himself and he caught up with the Jathā at Bargāṛī, its last halting-point before reaching Jaito on 21 February 1924. He was marching in line with the standard-bearers ahead of the Jathā when the waiting contingent of the Nābhā State army opened fire on them. Dīvān Siṅgh was hit by a bullet in the head and died on the spot near Ṭibbī Sāhib, a sandy hillock, about a furlong short of the destination, Gurdwārā Gaṅgsar Sāhib.

BIBLIOGRAPHY

Akālī te Pradesī. Amritsar, 15 March 1924

G.S.G.

DĪVĀN SIṄGH MAFTOON (1890-1974) was in his day the most talked-about editor in Urdu journalism. Born in the Punjab he migrated to Delhi in the early twenties. His sole asset was a smattering of Urdu. Gradually, he grew in his command of the language and became known for his mastery of Urdu prose acclaimed for its lucidity and exactness. Through his felicity in Urdu prose, he naturalized himself in the *milieu* of Ghālib's Delhi. He achieved to a considerable degree its style and refinement. In his conversation, in his dress and in his tastes, he became a sovereign Delhi-ite. He had a natural genius in personal relationships. Among his lifelong friends and admirers was Josh Malīhābādī. The poet's description of Dīvān Siṅgh in his autobiography *Yādoṅ kī Bārāt* (Procession of Memories) is evidence of his esteem for him: "In eye contented, short of stature, of high courage, generous in hospitality, lion-hearted, friend of friends, the death of the enemy, prince-baiter, helper of the weak, worst of foes, best of friends."

Dīvān Siṅgh was born of a Sikh family of Hāfizābād in the Gujrāṅwālā district of West Punjab on 4 August 1890. His father, a physician in government service, died when he was still an infant. This imposed severe hardship on the family. Young Dīvān Siṅgh had to interrupt his studies when he was a student of the middle school and seek employment with a cloth-merchant. Even at that age, he was an avid reader of Urdu newspapers. He also contributed an occasional piece to the only Urdu daily of that time in northern India, the *Aam*.

A pamphlet (*Khūn-i-Shahādat kā Tāzā Qatrā Qaum kī Nazar)* he wrote about the excesses of Mahārājā Bhūpinder Siṅgh of Paṭiālā won him the favour and patronage of the Nābhā ruler, Mahārājā Ripudaman Siṅgh. With his support he launched from Delhi a weekly called the *Rayyat,* with Hassan Nizāmī as his collaborator. But the paper ran only for six months, and had to fold up owing to heavy losses. Dīvān Siṅgh took employment in the Nābhā court, but was dismissed from service with the deposition by the British of the Mahārājā on 9 July 1923.

Dīvān Siṅgh returned to Delhi to start another Urdu paper — the *Riyāsat.* The birth of the *Riyāsat* was a notable event in Urdu journalism. It was a real *putsch* so far as princely India was concerned. Dīvān Siṅgh threw open the columns of the *Riyāsat* to the grievances and complaints of the subjects of Indian states. He boldly took up the cause of the victims. The Indian princes began to feel vulnerable in the presence of the *Riyāsat.* Several were the cases brought up against it and its editor. The most famous was the suit started by the Nawāb of Bhopāl which lasted six years.

Apart from its political importance, the *Riyāsat* evolved a distinctive literary style. Dīvān Siṅgh's Urdu prose, smooth and direct, was utterly exempt from rhetoric. It was considered a model of chastity and correctness and won his paper instant audience. Many new writers began to copy it. Yet Dīvān Siṅgh was always modest about it. He used to say that no Punjabi could really master the subtle nuances of the Urdu idiom and, least of all, as he put it funnily, a Sikh.

The *Riyāsat,* as edited by Dīvān Siṅgh, was an experience for the people of that generation. Apart from leaders characterized by deep humanitarian concern and uncompromising nationalist views, he wrote two regular columns for his paper. These were "Nāqābil-i-Frāmosh" (Memories Unforgettable) and "*Jazbāt-i-Mashriq*" (Sentiments from the East). The former was a column of memoribilia rendered in brisk, captivating style, with a sting or moral at the end. The latter sampled a wide range of Indian folklore and poetry in several of the languages. These columns each yielded a fascinating book — *Nāqābil-i-Frāmosh* and *Jazbāt-i-Mashriq,* both permanent possessions of Urdu literature.

Nāqābil-i-Frāmosh is not a schematic autobiography, yet it is an intimate book of memoirs. Its prodigality of confidence is entrancing. In short, clipped epsiodes it unfolds the life of the author. It does not fail to capture its turmoil and irony, its fun and enjoyment. The outlook is throughout sane and robust. There is no attempt here either at self-pity or self-glorification. Nothing about the story seems manipulated — it reads naturally and unobtrusively. In parts, it has the excitement of a thriller, especially in the unravelling of courtly intrigue. It could thus be read also as documentation of princely India. Vast numbers of the author's friends and enemies tumble in and out of the narrative and they make a whole age come alive. Among friends whom Dīvān Siṅgh mentions with real affection are Bhāī Kāhn Siṅgh of Nābhā, Qāzī Sir Azīz ud-Dīn, prime minister, Datiā state, Mr K.C. Roy, managing director, Associated Press of India, Sir John Thompson, Political Secretary, Government of India, Sardūl Siṅgh Caveeshar, B.G. Horniman, Bhayyā Shaikh Ehsān ul-Haq, and Josh Malīhābādī. *Nāqābil-i-Frāmosh* has been translated into Hindi and published under the title of *Triveṇī.* An abbreviated paperback was also brought out in Punjabi.

Jazbāt-i-Mashriq reflects Dīvān Siṅgh's eclectic literary taste. Song and verse of delicate emotion have been gathered here mainly from Hindi, Braj and Avadhi and, occasionally, from Punjabi, Pushtu, Kashmiri, Bengali and, even, Persian and Arabic. These are reproduced in the original, in Persian characters, with Dīvān Siṅgh's Urdu rendering which is always lucid and evocative. The book seems to have given him immense satisfaction. For he wrote in the Preface "My religious belief is no secret from my friends and others who know me. Throughout my life I have neither declared my faith in God nor had ever the courage to deny Him. I do not believe in heaven or hell. But, from the endeavour I have made to serve literature through this book, I am mentally conviced and satisfied that, if God, heaven and hell exist, I have secured myself a niche in heaven by the publication of this book. The prophets and poets whose verses I have here collected must intercede on my behalf."

In his politics Dīvān Siṅgh was a rebel. On several occasions he came into clash with authority. He challenged the powerful men of his day and fought out valiantly. But he would never hit below the belt. He throughout remained severely critical of leaders in communal politics of all shades — Hindu, Muslim and Sikh. About Master Tārā Siṅgh's policies he wrote with extra acerbity and persiflage, perhaps because he knew him personally. But he recorded readily and sportingly his appreciation of many of his qualities.

BIBLIOGRAPHY

1. Maftoon, Dīwān Siṅgh, *Nāqābil-i-Framosh*. Delhi, 1957
2. ———, *Jazbāt-i-Mashiq*.
3. Malīhābādī, Josh, *Yādoṅ kī Bārāt*.

D.S.

DĪVĀN SIṄGH RĀMGAṚHĪĀ (d. 1834), soldier and *jāgīrdār* in Sikh times, was son of Tārā Siṅgh (d. 1759) and nephew of Jassā Siṅgh (d. 1800), the famous Rāmgaṛhīā Sardār. As a young man he built for himself a fort near Qādīāṅ and named it Ṭhākargaṛh. With a garrison of 1400 horsemen, he fixed his residence in it. When on the death in 1816 of his cousin, Jodh Siṅgh, there was a dispute about the family estate and Mahārājā Raṇjīt Siṅgh tried to intervene, he fled to Paṭiālā. He met with a friendly reception there, but was forced to leave the city. Eventually, he submitted to Mahārājā Raṇjīt Siṅgh and was granted a handsome *jāgīr*. He was sent in command of about 1,000 men to Bārāmūlā cantonment in Kashmīr, a difficult hill post on the road to Srīnagar. He remained on duty in Bārāmūlā cantonment until he died in 1834.

BIBLIOGRAPHY

1. Sūrī, Sohan Lāl, *'Umdāt-ut-Twārīkh*. Lahore, 1885-89
2. Griffin, Lepel and C.F. Massy, *Chiefs and Families of Note in the Punjab*. Lahore, 1909

J.R.G.

DOĀBĀ REGION of the Punjab lying between 30° - 57' to 32° -7' North latitudes and 75° - 4' to 76° - 30' East longitudes, and bounded by the Himalayas on the east, and by the Beās on the north and the west, and the Sutlej on the south, embracing the present districts of Jalandhar, Hoshiārpur and Kapūrthalā, is a distinct geographical region by virtue of its interfluvial character, its distinctive cultural identity and its recognition as such in geographical and historical literature. It is also known as Bist Doāb (from *bist* which is an abbreviation for the twin rivers Beās and Sutlej, and *doāb*, a Persian term meaning a land mass lying between two rivers) or Jalandhar Doāb (after the name of its principal town). With an area of 8,915 square kilometres, Doābā has 24 towns and 3,580 villages. With a population of well over four million, it is one of the densely populated regions of the Punjab. The upland plain covering about two-thirds of the total area and ranging in elevation from 270 to 300 metres above sea level, is by virtue of its alluvial soil the most fertile and thickly populated. It has therefore been the focus of main historical events, political acitivity and economic development. The low-lying flood plains along the two rivers, locally called *beṭ*, with profusion of wild grasses and scrubs are not suitable for regular and intensive cultivation and are therefore sparsely populated. The foothill plain ranging in elevation from 300 to 470 metres and lying along the Śivālik foothills is dissected by numerous seasonal streams called *chos*. This zone lies between the upland plain in the west and the economically backward and sparsely populated hilly tract known as *kaṇḍī* in the east.

Broadly speaking, the Doābā region is characterized by a continental sub-humid climate, with sharply varying winter and summer temperatures. Like the rest of the northwest India, it receives 80 per cent of its rainfall from the monsoons during July-September and the balance from cyclones during December-January. Natural vegetation of the region is of a dry-deciduous type. However, intensive cultivation necessitated by population pressure and paucity of arable land has resulted in clearance of entire upland plain for agriculture. Still *kikkar (Acacia arabica), berī (Zizyphus jujuba), shīsham (dabergia), ḍhak (Butea trondosa)* and mango trees are found scattered or in small groves. Grasses and scrubs like *sar (saccharum)* and *kans* (*Saccharum spontaneoum*) abound in *beṭ* areas. Commercial planting of eucalyptus is a recent development. The region hardly produces any minerals.

Doābā with its sturdy, hardworking population holds a place of pride in Sikh history. Gurū Nānak's connection with one of its ancient towns, Sultānpur Lodhī, the founding of Kartārpur by Gurū Arjan and the travels of the fifth, sixth, seventh and the ninth Gurūs through the length and breadth of the region resulted in the early spread of Sikhism in the area. Being on the old route from the northwest to Delhi, it had to bear the brunt of successive invasions. At the same time it, along with the districts of the central Punjab collectively known as Mājhā, was a recruiting and training ground for the Sikh warriors during the eighteenth century. At the close of the nineteenth century and at the beginning of the twentieth, Sikhs of the Doābā were among the first to migrate to Canada and the United States of America, where they were in the forefront of the Ghadr movement. The Babar Akālī movement of the 1920's was almost exclusively sustained by Doābā Sikhs. Land holdings being very small, emigration to countries of the western world still remains an attraction for the people.

BIBLIOGRAPHY

1. Singh, G.B., "Changing Patterns of Cropland Use in Bist Doab," unpublished Ph.D. thesis submitted to the University of Edinburgh.
2. Mehta, Swarnjit, "Patterns of Migration in the Bist Doab 1951-61," in *Panjab University Research Bulletin* (Arts), vol. IV, No. I. Chandigarh, 1973
3. Latif, Syad Muhammad, *History of the Panjab*. Delhi, 1964

S.M.

ḌOḌ, village 13 km northeast of Jaito (30° - 26'N, 74° - 53'E) in Farīdkoṭ district of the Punjab, is sacred to Gurū Gobind Siṅgh, who visited here during his journey westward from Dīnā in December 1705. According to local tradition, Gurū Hargobind had also been here during his travels through the Mālvā country. Gurdwārā Dhaulsar Pātshāhī Chehmī te Dasmī on the northwestern outskirts of the village is dedicated to Gurū Hargobind and Gurū Gobind Siṅgh. It comprises a flat-roofed hall with a verandah on three sides. Another shrine, Gurdwārā Har Sar Pātshāhī X, commemorating Gurū Gobind Siṅgh's visit, is inside the village, and comprises a high-ceilinged hall, with a square sanctum at the far end and a lotus dome overtopping the four-storeyed building. Both these Gurdwārās are administered by the Shiromaṇī Gurdwārā Parbandhak Committee through a local committee. A largely-attended religious fair is held on 17,18 and 19 Phāgun (early-March) every year.

BIBLIOGRAPHY

1. Tārā Siṅgh, *Srī Gur Tīrath Saṅgrahi*. Amritsar, n.d.
2. Ṭhākar Siṅgh, Giānī, *Srī Gurduāre Darshan*. Amritsar, 1923

M.G.S.

DODṚĀ, village 5 km southwest of Samāṇā (30° - 11'N, 76° - 11'E) in the Punjab, is sacred to Gurū Tegh Bahādur who visited it during one of his travels through the Mālvā region. A platform raised as a memorial to the Gurū's visit was replaced by the present Gurdwārā Pātshāhī IX in the beginning of the present century. Situated in a half-acre low-walled compound on the northern edge of the village, it consists of a domed sanctum, with a hall in front. An old *pīpal* tree, believed to be the one under which Gurū Tegh Bahādur had sat and delivered his message, still exists at the back of the hall. The Gurdwārā is maintained by the village *saṅgat.*

Gn.S.

DORĀHĀ (30° - 48'N, 76° - 2'E), an old village along the Grand Trunk Road 20 km east of Ludhiāṇā, claims an historical shrine, Gurdwārā Damdamā Sāhib Pātshāhī Chhevīṅ, sacred to Gurū Hargobind, Nānak VI. According to local tradition, Gurū Hargobind encamped here for a night travelling back from the Gwālīor Fort. The present complex, a rectangular flat-roofed hall with ancillary buildings inside a walled compound, was constructed in 1932. The Gurdwārā is managed by the local *saṅgat.*

M.G.S.

DOST MUHAMMAD KHĀN, AMĪR (1791-1863), ruler of Kābul and Qandāhār, was the son of Paindā Khān (executed 1799), the Bārakzaī chief. Dost Muhammad's first engagement with the Sikhs was at Attock, the Afghān citadel, which had fallen into the hands of the Sikhs in June 1813. In the conflict which lasted three months, Dost Muhammad Khān, who himself led the attack in the battle of Haidrū, 8 km from Attock, was badly mauled by the Sikh force commanded by Dīwān Mohkam Chand. As a result of the fighting among the members of the Durrānī and Bārakzaī families, Dost Muhammad finally established himself in 1823 in Kābul, Kashmīr having been lost to the Sikhs in 1819. In 1833, Shāh Shujā', the dethroned king of Afghanistan, attempted to regain his throne, but he was defeated by Dost Muhammad Khān at Qandāhār. In 1834, Mahārājā Raṇjīt Siṅgh annexed Peshāwar. Dost Muhammad Khān, resolved to recover the city, marched with an army to the Khaibar Pass in 1835, but, fearing that the Sikh army would cut off his rear, retired towards Kābul. Dost Muhammad led out another expedition in 1837, and a fierce engagement took place at Jamrūd in which the Sikh general, Harī Siṅgh Nalvā, was killed, but the fort of Jamrūd remained in the possession of the Sikhs. Soon afterwards, Dost Muhammad made overtures to the British soliciting their help for the recovery of Peshāwar. The British, however, decided to replace Shāh Shujā' on the Kābul throne. Dost Muhammad was defeated and exiled to Calcutta in November 1839. He was set free in November 1842, and re-established on the throne of Kābul. Dost Muhammad thereafter maintained cordial relations with the Sikhs and there was a regular exchange of embassies between the two governments. A representative of the Sikh kingdom was accredited to Kābul, while an agent of the Amīr was always present at Lahore. Dost Muhammad received the support of the Sikhs at the time of the treaty made at Peshāwar with the British governor-general, by which the independence of Afghanistan was recognized.

Dost Muhammad Khān died at Herāt on 9 June 1863.

BIBLIOGRAPHY

1. Sūrī, Sohan Lāl, *'Umdāt-ut-Twārīkh.* Lahore, 1885-89
2. Khushwant Singh, *A History of the Sikhs.* Princeton, 1963, 1966
3. Hasrat, Bikrama Jit, *Life and Times of Ranjit Singh.* Hoshiarpur, 1977

4. Bhagat Singh, *Maharaja Ranjit Singh and His Times*. Delhi, 1990

S.S.B.

DOTTENWEISS or DOTTERWICH, a short-statured, stoutly-built German who, in 1835, joined the army of Mahārājā Raṇjīt Siṅgh as a military tactician. He was found unequal to the appointment and was dismissed from the service soon afterwards.

BIBLIOGRAPHY

Grey, C., *European Adventurers of Northern India, 1785-1849*. Patiala, 1970

Gl.S.

DUBUIGNON, ROBERT WALTER, DE TALBOT (1809-1868), a French adventurer in the employ of Begam Samarū of Sardhānā, who came to Lahore to seek better prospects. He obtained employment in the Sikh court through the good offices of General Ventura, and was assigned to General Allard as aide-de-camp. He left the service after about a year to go into business, exporting goods from Kashmīr to France in exchange for French merchandise. He died at Ludhiāṇā in 1868.

BIBLIOGRAPHY

Grey, C., *European Adventurers of Northern India, 1785-1849*. Patiala, 1970

Gl.S.

ḌUḌḌHĪ, a village 7 km to the southwest of Lāḍvā (29° - 59'N, 77° - 3'E) in Kurukshetra district of Haryāṇā, has a historical shrine, Gurdwārā Ḍioṛhī Sāhib, dedicated to Gurū Tegh Bahādur. As he was travelling in those parts, the Gurū was invited by the inhabitants to visit their village. By this they wished to expiate a misdemeanour they had committed. Gurū Tegh Bahādur accepted their invitation and gave them his blessing. The villagers constructed a platform to commemorate his visit. A Mañjī Sāhib was raised on the site in 1923 by Sikhs from the neighbouring villages, there being no Sikh families in Ḍuḍḍhī itself. The marble-floored Mañjī Sāhib now stands within a spacious hall and has a domed pavilion above it. A lone *granthī*, custodian, looks after the shrine. Devotees from the neighbourhood gather in large numbers on the first of each Bikramī month when *kīrtan* and community meals take place. A largely attended annual fair is held on 20 Māgh (early February).

M.G.S.

DUDDŪṄ RĀM, a saintly person of Paṇḍorī, in present-day Amritsar district of the Punjab. He gave shelter in his *ḍerā* at Paṇḍorī to some Sikh women and children when the Sikhs were being hounded out in 1817 Bk / AD 1760 by the joint forces of the *sūbahs* of Sirhind, Multān and Lahore under the orders of Ahmad Shāh. A Nirañjanīā informed the Mughal scouts, who searched the *ḍerā*. As no Sikhs were apprehended inside the *ḍerā*, Duddūṅ Rām and his disciples were tortured, but they gave out nothing. The informer thought that the Sikh women and children had taken refuge in the adjoining sugarcane fields. As the Sikhs were captured, Duddūṅ Rām and some others went to Momin Khān, the Mughal chief, to request him to intercede on their behalf, but to no avail. Momin Khān took the captives to Paṭṭī where many other Sikh prisoners were being treated with much harshness.

D.S.

ḌŪGAR DĀS, BHĀĪ, Sarīn Khatrī of Takiār clan, received instruction from Gurū Rām Dās and became a devoted Sikh. "Takiār the virtuous" is how Bhāī Gurdās describes him in his *Vārāṅ*, XI. 17.

See DHARAM DĀS, BHĀĪ

BIBLIOGRAPHY

1. Manī Siṅgh, Bhāī, *Sikhāṅ dī Bhagat Mālā*. Amritsar, 1955

2. Santokh Siṅgh, Bhāī, *Srī Gur Pratāp Sūraj Granth*. Amritsar, 1926-37
3. Macauliffe, Max Arthur, *The Sikh Religion*. Oxford, 1909

Gr.S.

ḌUGGHRĪ, 5 km east of Chamkaur Sāhib (30° - 53'N, 76° - 25'E) in Ropaṛ district of the Punjab, is sacred to Gurū Tegh Bahādur and Gurū Gobind Siṅgh. Gurū Gobind Siṅgh passed through this village on his way to Chamkaur on 6 December 1705, after leaving Anandpur. It had also been visited by his predecessor, Gurū Tegh Bahādur. Gurdwārā Pātshāhī 9 and 10, commemorating successive visits by the Gurūs, was constructed by the villagers in the early 1930's near an old banyan tree. A new and bigger building for the Gurdwārā has been raised recently. The shrine is maintained and managed by the village *saṅgat* or community.

M.G.S.

DUKH BHAÑJAṆĪ BERĪ. *See* AMRITSAR

DŪLĀ SIṄGH (d. 1857), son of Khushāl Siṅgh, was a cavalry officer in the Sikh army. He was most of the time employed on the Afghān frontier, and received severe wounds in the expedition against Dost Muhammad Khān. This forced him to retire, on a *jāgīr*, from active service while still a young man.

Dūlā Siṅgh died in 1857 at his native village Kalāsvālā, in Siālkoṭ district, leaving behind six sons.

BIBLIOGRAPHY

Griffin, Lepel and C.F. Massy, *Chiefs and Families of Note in the Punjab*. Lahore, 1909

G.S.N.

DULEEP SIṄGH, MAHĀRĀJĀ (1838-1893), the last Sikh sovereign of the Punjab, was born at Lahore on 6 September 1838, the youngest son of Mahārājā Raṇjīt Siṅgh. On 18 September 1843, at the age of five, he was, after the murder of Mahārājā Sher Siṅgh, proclaimed Mahārājā of the Punjab with his mother, Mahārāṇī Jind Kaur, as his Regent. The country was in a state of disorder and the army had become all-powerful. Though little Duleep Siṅgh attended all the council meetings seated on the royal throne, the real authority had passed from the palace to the cantonment and the military *pañchāyats*. The English, who had been watching the happenings in the Sikh State with more than a neighbour's interest, were looking for an opportunity to strike and penetrate into the Punjab. Matters were brought to such a pass that war between them and the Sikhs became inevitable. Hostilities in fact broke out in December 1845. The British who emerged victorious forbore to annex the State, but occupied a rich piece of the country between the rivers Beās and Sutlej under the peace treaty concluded on 9 March 1846. More stringent terms were imposed under the Treaty of Bharovāl (16 December 1846), reducing the kingdom of the Punjab to a virtual British protectorate. The Regent was pensioned off ; the British government assumed the guardianship of the young Mahārājā Duleep Siṅgh during his minority ; and a British Resident was to direct and control the entire civil and military administration of the State of Lahore with a council of ministers which was to be nominated by him. After the second Anglo-Sikh war (1848-49), the ten-year-old Mahārājā whom, under the Treaty of Bharovāl the government was committed to protect and maintain until he attained maturity, was deprived of his crown and kingdom and the Punjab was annexed to the British dominions.

On 6 April 1849, soon after the annexation, the deposed Mahārājā Duleep Siṅgh was formally introduced to his new 'superintendent,' Dr John Login, a native of Orkney, Scotland, who had started his Indian career as a medical officer in the Bengal army. Duleep Siṅgh was removed from the Punjab to Fatehgaṛh, a small village in Farrukhābād district in the then North-West Province, where he arrived in February 1850. John Login took a great liking to the Mahārājā whom he treated like his own son. Walter Guise was named his tutor. On 8 March 1853, Duleep Siṅgh was quietly baptized a Christian at a private ceremony at Fatehgaṛh. The conversion was hailed as "the first instance of the accession of an Indian prince to the communion of the Church." On 19 April 1854, the Mahārājā and his party sailed for England where they reached in May 1854. In England Mahārājā Duleep Siṅgh lived in the first instance with the Login family and was presented to Queen Victoria who took very favourably to him. In January 1861, Duleep Siṅgh visited India, but was not permitted to come to the Punjab. He halted at Calcutta where his mother, Mahārāṇī Jind Kaur, then living in exile at Kāṭhmaṇḍū in Nepal, met him after 13 years. Duleep Siṅgh took her to England where she died after about two years later on 1 August 1863. In October the same year died the Mahārājā's most sincere and devoted guardian, Dr Sir John Login, on whom he had come to depend a great deal for negotiations with the British government for the settlement of his affairs.

Mahārājā Duleep Siṅgh made another trip to India in the spring of 1864, this time with his mother's ashes which, on being disallowed by the British to proceed to the Punjab, he consigned to the River Godāvarī. On his way back, the Mahārājā married at the British Consulate at Alexandria in Egypt, on 7 June 1864, Bamba Muller, daughter of a German merchant, Ludwig Muller, and Abysenian-Egyptian mother, Sofia. On his return to England, the Mahārājā and Mahārāṇī Bamba lived for the first few years at Elveden, a sporting estate, of which the Mahārājā had got possession in September 1864. Mahārājā Duleep Siṅgh and Mahārāṇī Bamba had six children, Victor Albert Jay Duleep Siṅgh, Fredrick Victor Duleep Siṅgh, Bamba Sofia Jindāṅ Duleep Siṅgh, Catherine Hilda Duleep Siṅgh, Sofia Alexandra Duleep Siṅgh and Albert Edward Alexander Duleep Siṅgh, born between the years 1866 and 1879.

The Mahārājā now lived in the extravagant style of Victorian English nobility. He loved art; he was an accomplished musician, was fond of the theatre, of hunting and of hawking. He came to be known as one of the best shots in Britain and entertained the greatest in the land, including the Prince of Wales. Living beyond his means, the Mahārājā incurred heavy debts. He sought from the India Office enhancement of his allowances. At the instance of his mother Mahārāṇī Jind Kaur, Malikā Muqaddisā (the holy queen mother) of the regency days, he claimed from the British lands which belonged to the family prior to the installation of his father as king of Lahore. Under her influence, Duleep Siṅgh was also gradually estranged from what had become his natural English style. The question of his private properties he pursued to the breaking-point. To prepare a detailed list of his ancestral estates, Duleep Siṅgh sent his solicitor, Mr Talbot of Farrer and Co., to India. He also invited his collateral Ṭhākur Siṅgh Sandhāṅvālīā to visit him in England. Reaching London in 1884, Ṭhākur Siṅgh stayed with the Mahārājā, then putting up at Holland Park. He daily read out from the holy Gurū Granth Sāhib to the Mahārājā and instructed him in the tenets of the Sikh faith. Ṭhākur Siṅgh had brought with him a document signed by the custodians of the Sikh Takhts (the highest ecclesiastical seats) in India confirming the prophecies about Duleep Siṅgh's restoration to the throne of the Punjab. These prophecies, attributed to Gurū Gobind Siṅgh himself, announced in crisp, aphoristic Punjabi: "He [Duleep Siṅgh] will drive his elephant throughout the world ... Dissensions will arise at Calcutta and quarrels will be in every home. Nothing will be known for 12 years. Then will rise the

Khālsā whom the people of four castes will like .... Fighting will take place near Delhi .... When Delhi remains 15 *kos* away, the King will cease. Duleep Siṅgh will sit on the throne and all people will pay him homage."

When in August 1885, Ṭhākur Siṅgh Sandhāṅvālīā returned to the Punjab, Duleep Siṅgh gave him Rs 1,000 for distribution of *kaṛāhprasād,* the Sikh ritual food, at the Golden Temple, Amritsar. The Mahārājā himself decided to return to his motherland and left England on 31 March 1886 to settle down quietly in Delhi. He invited Ṭhākur Siṅgh to meet him at Bombay and arrange for his reinitiation into Sikhism. As the government was reluctant to permit Ṭhākur Siṅgh to receive him, Duleep Siṅgh wrote to the Secretary of State:

> As my cousin, Sardar Thakur Singh Sandhanwalia, informs me that he fears permission will not be accorded him to go to Bombay by the Liutenant-Governor of Punjab, and as I particularly desire to be rebaptized into the faith of my ancestors by some relative of my own, may I therefore beg your Lordship kindly to request His Excellency by telegraph on my behalf or permit me to do so, that the Sardar be allowed to meet me on reaching India.

The news of Duleep Siṅgh's likely return sent a thrill of expectation across the Punjab. The government warily stopped him at Aden. This was the advice it had from one of its leading Sikh supporters Mahāmahopādhyāya Sardār Sir Attar Siṅgh of Bhadauṛ. Stung by this insult, Duleep Siṅgh resigned his allowance and forswore fealty to the British crown. One favour he sought was that the government continue payment of pound 500 each annually to the widows, respectively, of his superintendent, Login, and Comptroller, Oliphant. On 3 June 1886, he left for Paris. But before departing from Aden, he had, on 25 May 1886, received the rites of Sikh baptism from the Five Beloved (Pañj Piāre) — Ṭhākur Siṅgh of Wāgāh, another cousin of his (son of his mother's sister), Būṛ Siṅgh of village Kohālī in Amritsar district, Javand Siṅgh of Barkī in Lahore district, and two Sikhs brought for the ceremony from a transport ship which happened to touch at Aden.

The Punjab at this time was astir with rumour. Anticipation filled the air. Reports were studiously kept in circulation that Mahārājā Duleep Siṅgh would lead a Russian invasion into India and overthrow the British. A network of secret communication was established; Duleep Siṅgh's emissaries kept filtering into India in spite of government vigilance. The most important of them were Ghulām Rasūl, a wool merchant of Amritsar, who had lived for many years in the Sudan and Egypt, and Arūṛ Siṅgh of village Kohālī (Amritsar), a Europeanized Sikh. The Mahārājā's statements and proclamations — as from "the Sovereign of the Sikh nation and Implacable Foe of the British Government" — were smuggled into the country for distribution. The Kūkā Sikhs who had come into clash with the government in 1872 were the most enthusiastic in pro-Duleep Siṅgh activity.

The brain behind this entire movement for furthering the cause of Duleep Siṅgh was Ṭhākur Siṅgh Sandhāṅvālīā who had implanted the seeds of rebellion in the mind of the Mahārājā and who had finally persuaded him to renounce Christianity and rejoin the faith of his forefathers. From Pondicherry, where he had taken asylum to escape British authority, he masterminded the operations in behalf of Duleep Siṅgh. To win support for him, he visited secretly the Indian princely states and the Sikh shrines. He maintained an active liaison with people in distant places through a chain of servants, dependents and relations. Major Evans Bell's book *The Annexation of the Punjab and the Maharaja Duleep Singh,* exhibiting the illegality and immorality of British occupation of the Punjab, was widely circulated. Pondicherry had become the seat of Duleep Siṅgh's peripatetic government with Ṭhākur Siṅgh as his prime minister. Ṭhākur Siṅgh hoped that his sovereign master would one day land in Pondicherry. The latter had in fact written to *The Tribune* (3 July 1886) the following letter:

> Although the Indian Government suceeded in preventing me from reaching Bombay, yet they are not able to close all the roads that there are in India; for when I return I can either land at Goa or at Pondicherry ...

Mahārājā Duleep Siṅgh left Paris on 21 March 1887 for St. Petersburg (Russia) where he tried to seek the help of the Czar. Arūṛ Siṅgh who had been with Duleep Siṅgh in Russia brought from him secret missives including a circular letter for the ex-king of Oudh, Holkar, Scindia and the rulers of Paṭiālā, Nābhā, Farīdkoṭ, Jīnd and Kapūrthalā. The princes generally implicated in the cause of Duleep Siṅgh were Rājā Bikram Siṅgh of Farīdkoṭ, Rājā Hīrā Siṅgh of Nābhā, the Mahārājā of Kashmīr and Rājā Motī Siṅgh of Puṇchh. From Russia Duleep Siṅgh sent to Ṭhākur Siṅgh a seal and letter in token of his appointment to the office of prime minister.

> I appoint you my Prime Minister should Sri Satguru Ji one day replace me on the throne of the Punjab.

After Ṭhākur Siṅgh's sudden death on 18 August 1887, his son Gurbachan Siṅgh was invested by Duleep Siṅgh with the title of prime minister. But returning from Russia to Paris, Duleep Siṅgh had a stroke and remained bedridden for three years, the passion and grand designs of former day pathetically congealed in his heart. Drained financially and destitute of friends, he died in his humble hotel room in Paris on 22 October 1893. His body was taken to Elveden, England, by his son Prince Victor, where it was interred beside the graves of Prince Fredrick and Prince Edward. Thus was completed a life cycle drawn, as it were, to stated requirements of the tragedian, the poet, the philosopher.

BIBLIOGRAPHY

1. Alexander, Michael and Sushila Anand, *Queen Victoria's Maharaja Duleep Singh 1838-93*. Delhi, 1979
2. Login, Lady, *Sir John Login and Duleep Singh*. Patiala, 1970
3. Bell, Evans, *The Annexation of the Punjab and the Maharaja Duleep Singh*. London, 1882
4. Cunningham, Joseph Davey, *A History of the Sikhs*. London, 1849
5. Ganda Singh, *Private Correspondence Relating to the Anglo-Sikh Wars*. Amritsar, 1955
6. Ganda Siṅgh, ed., *History of the Freedom Movement in the Panjab (Maharaja Duleep Singh Correspondence)*. Patiala, 1972
7. Khushwant Singh, *A History of the Sikhs*. vol. II. Princeton, 1966
8. Sūrī, Sohan Lāl, *'Umdāt-ut-Twārīkh*. Lahore, 1885-89

P.M.W.

DULEY, village in Ludhiāṇā district, 17 km southwest from the city (30° - 54'N, 75° - 52'E), claims a historical shrine called Gurdwārā Phalāhī Sāhib Pātshāhī 10. Gurū Gobind Siṅgh halted here awhile under a *phalāhī* tree, while travelling from Ālamgīr to Jodhāṅ at the close of 1705. An imposing new *gurdwārā* building, a large rectangular hall, has been completed recently. There is a basement below the *prakāsh asthān* representing the site of the original building, and above it is a room topped by a high-domed pavilion. Four more double-storeyed domed pavilions surround the central pavilion. At each corner of the large hall is a 4-storeyed domed tower, octagonal in shape. For the pilgrims' ablutions, Dasmesh Ghāṭ was constructed in 1967 in commemoration of the 300th birth anniversary of Gurū Gobind

Siṅgh. Similarly, a dining hall with a verandah in front was added to the Guru kā Laṅgar building in 1969 while celebrating the 500th birth anniversary of Gurū Nānak. Besides the morning and evening religious services, there are classes in scripture-reading and devotional music held in the *gurdwārā*.

M.G.S.

ḌUMELĪ, village 18 km north of Phagwāṛā (31° - 14'N, 75° - 46'E) in the Punjab, is sacred to Gurū Hargobind who, according to local tradition, visited here on 11 Chet 1695 Bk / 9 March 1638. The shrine raised in his honour is named Gurdwārā Thamm Sāhib Pātshāhī VI after a wooden column (*thamm*, in Punjabi), which, preserved as a sacred relic, is believed to have been installed by the Gurū himself. The Gurdwārā, entered through a small gateway opening on a narrow lane inside the village, is a hall with a high, vaulted ceiling. The sanctum, a raised platform in the middle of the room, has the Thamm Sāhib draped in cloth in the centre with the Gurū Granth Sāhib seated on a *pālakī* (palanquin). The Gurdwārā is managed by the Shiromaṇī Gurdwārā Parbandhak Committee through a local committee. The major annual celebration is the birthday of Gurū Hargobind.

BIBLIOGRAPHY

1. Tārā Siṅgh, *Srī Gur Tīrath Saṅgrahi*. Amritsar, n.d.
2. Ṭhākar Siṅgh, Giānī, *Srī Gurduāre Darshan*. Amritsar, 1923

M.G.S.

DUNĪ CHAND is described in *Purātan Janam Sākhī* as a Dhuppaṛ Khatrī of Lahore who held in the *parganah* the revenue rank of *karoṛī* (lit. the holder of a *karoṛ* or ten million). He was performing *srāddha* or anniversary feast for his deceased father when he learnt that the holy saint Gurū Nānak had arrived in the city. He invited him to his house which displayed seven flags fastened upon the door-top. Asked what these flags signified, Dunī Chand proudly explained that they indicated the degree of his opulence, each flag denoting wealth worth a lac or a hundred thousand. The Gurū, continues the *Purātan Janam Sākhī*, gave him a needle and said, "Keep it as a deposit of mine. We shall take it from you in the next world." Puzzled to hear this strange request, Dunī Chand took the needle to his wife and told her what the Gurū had said. "What is to be done now?" he asked her. "Go and give the needle back to the Gurū," replied his wife. "Who can take anything with him from here to the hereafter?" Dunī Chand came and bowed at the Gurū's feet. He knew that his wealth would not go with him, nor would the victuals ritually offered to the Brāhmaṇs on the *srāddha* day avail his father. The Gurū, says the *Janam Sākhī*, spoke to him, "Give in the name of the Lord. Put food in the mouth of the needy. Thus wilt thou have something to go with thee."

BIBLIOGRAPHY

1. Vīr Siṅgh, Bhāī, ed., *Purātan Janam Sākhī*. Amritsar, 1971
2. Santokh Siṅgh, Bhāī, *Srī Gur Pratāp Sūraj Granth*. Amritsar, 1926-37
3. Harbans Siṅgh, *Guru Nanak and Origins of the Sikh Faith*. Bombay, 1969

Gn.S.

DUNĪ CHAND, grandson of the well-known Bhāī Sālho (d. 1628), a Dhālīvāl Jaṭṭ of Majīṭhā in Amritsar district in the Punjab, was a *masand* of the Gurū's nominee in the Mājhā area. A hefty man of immense bulk, Dunī Chand led out a band of 500 warriors to Anandpur in 1700 when the Rājpūt hill chiefs had laid siege to the town. One day it was reported to Gurū Gobind Siṅgh that the besiegers were planning to use a drugged elephant the following morning to force open the gate of the Lohgaṛh Fort. To quote Kuir Siṅgh, *Gur Bilās Pātshāhī X*, the Gurū said, "I too have an intoxicated elephant, Dunī Chand. When he goes forth like a lion, the enemy will quail before him." The prospect of facing a mad elephant however unnerved Dunī Chand, who decided to seek safety in desertion. As he along with a few of his companions was climbing down the wall of the fort, he fell and broke his leg. His men carried him back to his village where he soon died of snake-bite.

BIBLIOGRAPHY

1. Santokh Siṅgh, Bhāī, *Srī Gur Pratāp Sūraj Granth*. Amritsar, 1926-37
2. Kuir Siṅgh, *Gurbilās Pātshāhī 10*. Patiala, 1968
3. Giān Siṅgh, Giānī, *Panth Prakāsh*. Patiala, 1970

P.S.P.

DURGĀ, BHĀĪ, a devoted Sikh living in the time of Gurū Aṅgad and Gurū Amar Dās. His name occurs in Bhāī Gurdās, *Vārāṅ*, XI. 15.

See JĪVANDĀ, BHĀĪ

M.G.S.

DURGĀ, BHĀĪ, accompanied by Bhāī Paiṛā, once visited Gurū Arjan and begged to be instructed in the duty of a householder. The Gurū spoke: "Earn your living by the labour of your hands. Share with the needy from what you save. Feed the poor and clothe the naked. They receive God's bounty who give away in His name." Durgā and Paiṛā acted on the Gurū's instruction. They, as says Bhāī Manī Siṅgh, *Sikhāṅ dī Bhagat Mālā*, distributed in charity all they had, and yet they were never in want. They received more than they gave.

BIBLIOGRAPHY

1. Manī Siṅgh, Bhāī, *Sikhāṅ dī Bhagat Mālā*. Amritsar, 1955
2. Santokh Siṅgh, Bhāī, *Srī Gur Pratāp Sūraj Granth*. Amritsar, 1926-37

T.S.

DURGĀ, PAṆḌIT, or Durgo Bhambī, a Sārsvat Brāhmaṇ of Bhambī clan living in the village of Mihṛā or Maheṛā (location obscure), predicted great name and fame for (Gurū) Amar Dās when the latter even had not yet met Gurū Aṅgad. According to Sarūp Dās Bhallā, *Mahimā Prakāsh*, Amar Dās, at the time of one of his pilgrimages to Haridvār, halted at Mihṛā for rest in a house maintained by Durgā Paṇḍit for travellers. As he lay asleep, Durgā, who was an astrologer as well as a palmist, observed in one of his feet a lotus mark which is believed to be the sign of sovereignty or exceptional spiritual eminence. "He is a noble Kṣatriya," said Durgā to himself. "Let me receive from him a promise for a reward." As Amar Dās awoke, Durgā pronounced his prophecy. Amar Dās offered him money, but Durgā declined saying, "Not now. But do promise to give me what I ask for when my prediction is fulfilled." Amar Dās gave him his word. Years later, as Gurū Amar Dās sat on the seat of Gurū Nānak, Durgā Paṇḍit called on him. No sooner did he set his eyes on the Gurū than all thoughts of claiming the reward he had come to seek vanished from his mind. He begged instead to be initiated a disciple. In the Sikh hierarchy, Paṇḍit Durgā held, as recorded in an old inscription in Gurdwārā Havelī Sāhib at Goindvāl, charge of a *mañjī* or preaching district around his own village, Maheṛā.

BIBLIOGRAPHY

1. Santokh Siṅgh, Bhāī, *Srī Gur Pratāp Sūraj Granth*. Amritsar, 1926-37
2. Bhallā, Sarūp Dās, *Mahimā Prakāsh*. Patiala, 1971

B.S.D.

DURGĀPUR, village 2 km east of Nawāshahr in Jalandhar district of the Punjab, claims a historical shrine called Gurdwārā Pātshāhī Chhevīṅ, dedicated to Gurū Hargobind (1595-1644) who arrived here from Jindvāl in early 1635. According to local tradition, one Bhāī Mohan attended on the Gurū. A small *gurdwārā* was established here in 1863 with the support of Bābā Rām Siṅgh Nāmdhārī. The present building raised in 1950 comprises a mosaic-floored hall, with the sanctum at the far end, and verandah all around. Above the sanctum is a square room topped by a dome lined with pieces of glazed tiles. The Gurdwārā is managed by the Shiromaṇī Gurdwārā Parbandhak Committee through a local committee.

BIBLIOGRAPHY

1. Tārā Siṅgh, *Srī Gur Tīrath Saṅgrahi*. Amritsar, n.d.
2. Ṭhākar Siṅgh, Giānī, *Srī Gurduāre Darshan*. Amritsar, 1923

Gn.S.

ḌURLĪ JATHĀ was an impromptu band of Sikh volunteers active during the Jaito agitation, 1923-24, to force their way through in contrast to the Akālī *jathās* vowed to a non-violent and passive course. Ḍurlī is a meaningless word: whatever sense it possesses is communicated onomatopoetically. At Jaito, on 14 September 1923, an *akhaṇḍ pāth* (non-stop end-to-end recital of the Gurū Granth Sāhib) being said for the Sikh princely ruler of Nābhā state, Mahārājā Ripudaman Siṅgh, who had been deposed by the British, was interrupted which, according to the Sikh tradition, amounted to sacrilege, and the *saṅgat* had been held captive, no-one being allowed to go out or come in, not even to fetch food or rations for those inside. Jathedār Dullā Siṅgh and Suchchā Siṅgh of Roḍe village, in Mogā *tahsīl*, then in Fīrozpur district, organized a small band of desperadoes, naming it Ḍurlī Jathā, who collected the required rations and managed to smuggle these in through feint or force. When large-sized *shahīdī jathās* began to be sent to Jaito by the Shiromaṇī Gurdwārā Parbandhak Committee from Amritsar, the Ḍurlī Jathā also mobilized support and sustenance for them *en route*. When the first Shahīdī Jathā, sworn to non-violence, was fired at by government troops on 21 February 1924 resulting in 19 dead and 30 injured, the government in order to justify its action held fake enquiries by two magistrates, first by Lālā Amar Nāth and then by Balvant Siṅgh Nalvā, who gave the verdict that Ḍurlī Jathā personnel who had accompanied the Shahīdī Jathā were armed and it was they who fired the first shot forcing the troops to open fire. Twenty-two members of Ḍurlī Jathā including Jathedār Dullā Siṅgh, Suchchā Siṅgh and Māī Kishan Kaur were tried in the court of Lālā Amar Nāth, who had meanwhile been elevated to sessions judge, on 17 May 1924. They were sentenced to rigorous imprisonment for seven years each. The Ḍurlī Jathā, however, remained active until the Jaito *morchā* ended successfully for the Akālīs in August 1925.

BIBLIOGRAPHY

Pratāp Siṅgh, Giānī, *Gurdwārā Sudhār arthāt Akālī Lahir*. Amritsar, 1975

M.G.S.

DUSĀÑJH KHURD, village 3 km south of Baṅgā (31° - 11'N, 76°E) in Jalandhar district of the Punjab, has a historical shrine called Gurdwārā Gurū Har Rāi Sāhib Pātshāhī Satvīṅ (seventh) dedicated to the Seventh Gurū, Gurū Har Rāi. In 1940, the local *saṅgat* raised a new building on the site of the older shrine. The Gurū Granth Sāhib is seated on a high dais in the centre of the central hall, to which another hall was added later. Residential quarters and Gurū kā Laṅgar are on the left of the main building. The Gurdwārā is affiliated to the Shiromaṇī Gurdwārā Parbandhak Committee.

BIBLIOGRAPHY

1. Tārā Siṅgh, *Srī Gur Tīrath Saṅgrahi*. Amritsar, n.d.
2. Ṭhākar Siṅgh, Giānī, *Srī Gurduāre Darshan*. Amritsar, 1923
3. Satibīr Singh, *Nirbhau Nirvair*. Jalandhar, 1984

Gn.S.

DVĀRKĀ DĀS, BĀBĀ, great-grandson of

Gurū Amar Dās, lived in his ancestral town of Goindvāl, in Amritsar district. Gurū Har Rāi was his guest, when the Mughal prince, Dārā Shukoh, defeated in the battle of Sāmūgaṛh crossed the River Beās and called on him in June 1658. In 1664, when, after the death of Gurū Har Krishan at Delhi, Mātā Bassī, grandmother of the deceased Gurū, came to Bakālā with tokens of succession to be bestowed on Gurū Tegh Bahādur, she sent for Bābā Dvārkā Dās to be present at the ceremony which took place on 11 August 1664. Bābā Dvārkā Dās thereupon retired to his home at Goindvāl.

BIBLIOGRAPHY

1. Padam, Piārā Siṅgh, and Giānī Garjā Siṅgh, eds., *Gurū kīāṅ Sākhīāṅ*. Patiala, 1986
2. Bhallā, Sarūp Dās, *Mahimā Prakāsh*. Patiala, 1971
3. Harbans Singh, *Guru Tegh Bahadur*. Delhi, 1982

P.S.P.

DYĀL SIṄGH MAJĪṬHĪĀ, (1849-98), Sikh aristocrat and philanthropist, was the son of Lahiṇā Siṅgh Majīṭhīā and grandson of Desā Siṅgh Majīṭhīā, both of whom had served Mahārājā Raṇjīt Siṅgh with distinction in the first half of the nineteenth century. He was born in 1849 at Banāras. His extensive education came from a dual source — from the family's keen interest in science and religion as well as from English tutors appointed by the court of wards which became responsible for Dyāl Siṅgh's upbringing after Lahiṇā Siṅgh's death in Banāras in 1854.

Dyāl Siṅgh was among the first Sikhs exposed to the Western systems of thought. Thereafter he lived in two worlds — not one Eastern and the other Western, as one might assume — but rather one of solitary experience, searching after ideas through reading, and the other a whirl of Punjabi culture not without its Westernized elements, which spun round Dyāl Siṅgh daily as a prominent *raīs*, an urban entrepreneur, a patron of social reform and sponsor of political causes. Nevertheless, as Punjabi Sikhs faced the task of reconstructing self-respect and identity following the British occupation of the Punjab, Dyāl Siṅgh's youth caught the full force of exposure to Westernization which included study of the Bible, and a journey to England. All these were reflected in his education. Yet intellectual interests and alterations in lifestyle did not end in conversion to any new creed or in desertion of Sikhism. Rather it was orthodoxy of all kinds and devotion to any single dogma that Dyāl Siṅgh had left behind. Comparative theology became his passion. He knew the elements of Sikhism well, had a great reverence in his heart for the Sikh Gurūs, read with a Fīrozpur *paṇḍit* the *Bhagavad-gītā*, discussed (then rejected) the tenets of the Ārya Samāj with its founder Swāmī Dayānand, and refused to side with any faction of the Brahmo Samāj. He became and remained in essence his own man.

Dyāl Siṅgh cannot be termed a typical nineteenth-century *raīs*, aristocrat, of the Punjab, yet he did not seek to avoid the various traditional roles consequent upon such influence and wealth as were his. Rather, he intensified those roles and gave them modern currency.

The brief biographical notes left behind reporting his daily life indicate a mercantile sagacity, a particular attention to detail, an accumulation of urban property during a successful career as financer. During his younger years even more 'typical' activities occupied Dyāl Siṅgh, the nobleman. He demonstrated a "... keen interest in sports, [became] an expert at kite-flying, spent large sums of money holding wrestling contests, liberally patronized musicians, offered magnificent hospitality and arranged poetical symposiums ..."

Dyāl Siṅgh Majīṭhīā is remembered, however, as anything but a typical nobleman of his day. Rather, his name is linked with reform, institutions of higher education, the founding of the Punjab branch of the Indian National Congress and perhaps above all with the Hindu reformist society, the Brahmo Samāj. He often had been claimed by Brahmos as a Brahmo and certainly he became their saviour through patronage.

In other words, Dyāl Siṅgh became a grand patron of many causes. When issues or ideas of importance impressed him he gave support-money, to aid the fervent (but often penniless) students, journalists, reformers, teachers — Punjabis as well as Bengalis. He supported men of words and ideas who had set about trying to alter, establish and build institutions, belief-systems and socio-political reforms in a Punjab struggling to express itself to find its identity, while the law was dominated by the British whose rule was despotic though inclined to be benevolent. It would be a mistake to consider him as confined to a single creed, society or dogma.

Dyāl Siṅgh patronized a half century of causes and institutions. He served as a member of the managing committee of the Darbār Sāhib (Golden Temple), Amritsar, and he accepted to be president of the standing committee of the Indian National Congress. He sponsored a number of prominent social roles, but occupied the stations of an honoured patron and not an activist. His short book, *Nationalism* (1895) is filled with moderate admiration and protestations of loyalty to the order and progress which British rule brought to the Punjab — not with slogans for ending imperialism. This would be a job for the activists of the next century. But such a man could take exception and he did take exception to what he regarded as the excesses and omissions of British authority.

On 27 December 1893, the Indian National Congress met in Lahore for its ninth annual convention. As reception committee chairman, Dyāl Siṅgh was to speak first. He could not, however, speak for he was racked with pain. Nevertheless, he appeared on the platform and sat stiffly as another read his carefully chosen words. While the Sardār spoke of the literary influence of England, it would be premature in those times to voice the demand for sharing political power. His was the role of a man born to multiple privileges, taking up the task of reform and to initiate action in the educational and cultural spheres. In his address he said:

> We happily live under a constitution whose watchword is freedom, and whose main pillar is toleration. We look back complacently on our past history, and glory in it. Can we then in the midst of this national upheaval remain quiescent and indifferent?

He was a pioneer in those nation-building activities, like the spread of Western Education (viz. his founding of the Dyāl Siṅgh College and Dyāl Siṅgh Library) and the establishment, in 1881, of a daily paper in English, *The Tribune,* that built up the nationalist cause in the Punjab, as a matter of fact in northwestern India as a whole. In this respect, his is a significant role as one of the builders of modern Punjab.

Dyāl Siṅgh Majīṭhīā died on 9 September 1898.

BIBLIOGRAPHY

1. Griffin, Lepel, and C.F. Massy, *Chiefs and Families of Note in the Punjab.* Lahore, 1909
2. Nair, Lajpat Rai, and Prem Nath Kirpal, *Dyal Singh Majithia.* Lahore, 1935
3 Besant, Annie, *How India Wrought Freedom ?* Bombay, 1915

J.P.